The Oxford Handbook of Positive
Psychology and Disability

OXFORD LIBRARY OF PSYCHOLOGY

Editor in Chief PETER E. NATHAN

The Oxford Handbook of Positive Psychology and Disability

Edited by

Michael L. Wehmeyer

OXFORD
UNIVERSITY PRESS

OXFORD
UNIVERSITY PRESS

Oxford University Press is a department of the University of Oxford.
It furthers the University's objective of excellence in research, scholarship,
and education by publishing worldwide.

Oxford   New York
Auckland   Cape Town   Dar es Salaam   Hong Kong   Karachi
Kuala Lumpur   Madrid   Melbourne   Mexico City   Nairobi
New Delhi   Shanghai   Taipei   Toronto

With offices in
Argentina   Austria   Brazil   Chile   Czech Republic   France   Greece
Guatemala   Hungary   Italy   Japan   Poland   Portugal   Singapore
South Korea   Switzerland   Thailand   Turkey   Ukraine   Vietnam

Oxford is a registered trademark of Oxford University Press in the UK and certain other
countries.

Published in the United States of America by
Oxford University Press
198 Madison Avenue, New York, NY 10016

Library of Congress Cataloging-in-Publication Data
The Oxford handbook of positive psychology and disability / edited by Michael L. Wehmeyer.
    pages cm
ISBN-13: 978–0–19–539878–6

1. Positive psychology.   2. People with disabilities–Psychology.   I. Wehmeyer, Michael L.
BF204.6.O953 2013
155.9′16—dc23
2012050012

9 8 7 6 5 4 3
Printed in the United States of America
on acid-free paper

SHORT CONTENTS

OXFORD LIBRARY OF PSYCHOLOGY

The *Oxford Library of Psychology*, a landmark series of handbooks, is published by Oxford University Press, one of the world's oldest and most highly respected publishers, with a tradition of publishing significant books in psychology. The ambitious goal of the *Oxford Library of Psychology* is nothing less than to span a vibrant, wide-ranging field and, in so doing, to fill a clear market need.

Encompassing a comprehensive set of handbooks, organized hierarchically, the *Library* incorporates volumes at different levels, each designed to meet a distinct need. At one level are a set of handbooks designed broadly to survey the major subfields of psychology; at another are numerous handbooks that cover important current focal research and scholarly areas of psychology in depth and detail. Planned as a reflection of the dynamism of psychology, the *Library* will grow and expand as psychology itself develops, thereby highlighting significant new research that will impact on the field. Adding to its accessibility and ease of use, the *Library* will be published in print and, later on, electronically.

The *Library* surveys psychology's principal subfields with a set of handbooks that capture the current status and future prospects of those major subdisciplines. This initial set includes handbooks of social and personality psychology, clinical psychology, counseling psychology, school psychology, educational psychology, industrial and organizational psychology, cognitive psychology, cognitive neuroscience, methods and measurements, history, neuropsychology, personality assessment, developmental psychology, and more. Each handbook undertakes to review one of psychology's major subdisciplines with breadth, comprehensiveness, and exemplary scholarship. In addition to these broadly conceived volumes, the *Library* also includes a large number of handbooks designed to explore in depth more specialized areas of scholarship and research, such as stress, health and coping, anxiety and related disorders, cognitive development, or child and adolescent assessment. In contrast to the broad coverage of the subfield handbooks, each of these latter volumes focuses on an especially productive, more highly focused line of scholarship and research. Whether at the broadest or most specific level, however, all of the *Library* handbooks offer synthetic coverage that reviews and evaluates the relevant past and present research and anticipates research in the future. Each handbook in the *Library* includes introductory and concluding chapters written by its editor to provide a roadmap to the handbook's table of contents and to offer informed anticipations of significant future developments in that field.

An undertaking of this scope calls for handbook editors and chapter authors who are established scholars in the areas about which they write. Many of the nation's and world's most productive and best-respected psychologists have agreed to edit *Library* handbooks or write authoritative chapters in their areas of expertise.

For whom has the *Oxford Library of Psychology* been written? Because of its breadth, depth, and accessibility, the *Library* serves a diverse audience, including graduate students in psychology and their faculty mentors, scholars, researchers, and practitioners in psychology and related fields. Each will find in the *Library* the information they seek on the subfield or focal area of psychology in which they work or are interested.

Befitting its commitment to accessibility, each handbook includes a comprehensive index, as well as extensive references to help guide research. And because the *Library* was designed from its inception as an online as well as a print resource, its structure and contents will be readily and rationally searchable online. Further, once the *Library* is released online, the handbooks will be regularly and thoroughly updated.

In summary, the *Oxford Library of Psychology* will grow organically to provide a thoroughly informed perspective on the field of psychology, one that reflects both psychology's dynamism and its increasing interdisciplinarity. Once published electronically, the *Library* is also destined to become a uniquely valuable interactive tool, with extended search and browsing capabilities. As you begin to consult this handbook, we sincerely hope you will share our enthusiasm for the more than 500-year tradition of Oxford University Press for excellence, innovation, and quality, as exemplified by the *Oxford Library of Psychology.*

Peter E. Nathan
Editor-in-Chief
Oxford Library of Psychology

ABOUT THE EDITOR

Michael L. Wehmeyer

Michael L. Wehmeyer, Ph.D., is professor of special education; director, Kansas University Center on Developmental Disabilities; and senior scientist, Beach Center on Disability at the University of Kansas. His research and intervention efforts focus on promoting the self-determination of children, youth, and adults with and without disabilities. He is past president and a fellow of the American Association on Intellectual and Developmental Disabilities, a fellow of the American Psychological Association, a fellow and vice president of the Americas of the International Association for the Scientific Study of Intellectual and Developmental Disabilities, past president of CEC's Division on Career Development and Transition, and former editor-in-chief of *Remedial and Special Education*. He holds undergraduate and master's degrees in special education from the University of Tulsa, a master's degree in experimental psychology from the University of Sussex, in Brighton, England, and a Ph.D. in human development and communication sciences from the University of Texas at Dallas.

CONTRIBUTORS

Lena Almqvist
School of Education and Communication
Malardalen University
Jönköping, Sweden

Miguel Angel Verdugo Alonso
Institute on Community Integration
University of Salamanca
Salamanca, Spain

Bruce L. Baker
Department of Psychology
University of California, Los Angeles
Los Angeles, California

Brittany Beard
Department of Psychology
Moravian College
Bethlehem, Pennsylvania

Lauren D. Berkovitz
Department of Psychology
University of California, Los Angeles
Los Angeles, California

Jan Blacher
Graduate School of Education
University of California, Riverside
Riverside, California

Vicki Brooke
Rehabilitation Research and Training
  Center on Workplace Supports
Virginia Commonwealth University
Richmond, Virginia

Brenda Jo Brueggemann
Department of English
The Ohio State University
Columbus, Ohio

Cindy L. Buchanan
Anschutz Medical Campus
University of Colorado
Denver, Colorado

Wil H. E. Buntinx
Maastricht University
Maastricht, Netherlands

William D. Bursuck
Department of Specialized Education
  Services
University of North Carolina—Greensboro
Greensboro, North Carolina

Caya Chiu
University of Kansas
Lawrence, Kansas

Laura Corona
Center for Social Development and
  Education
University of Massachusetts–Boston
Boston, Massachusetts

Robert A. Cummins
School of Psychology
Deakin University
Burwood, Australia

Bonnie Doren
School of Education
University of Wisconsin–Madison
Madison, Wisconsin

Glen Dunlap
Department of Child and Family Studies
University of South Florida
Tampa, Florida
Center for Excellence in Disabilities
University of Nevada–Reno
Reno, Nevada

Dana S. Dunn
Department of Psychology
Moravian College
Bethlehem, Pennsylvania

Timothy R. Elliott
Department of Educational Psychology
Texas A&M University
College Station, Texas

Lea Ferrari
University of Padova
Padova, Italy

Sharon L. Field
College of Education
Wayne State University
Detroit, Michigan

William Gaventa
University of Medicine and
Dentistry
New Jersey–Robert Wood Johnson Medical
School
New Brunswick, New Jersey

Vivi Aya Gomez
University of Sabana
Chia, Colombia

Mats Granlund
School of Health Sciences
Malardalen University
Jönköping, Sweden

Lora Tuesday Heathfield
Department of Continuing Education
University of Utah
Salt Lake City, Utah

Tamar Heller
Department of Disability and Human
Development
University of Illinois at Chicago
Chicago, Illinois

Linda Hickson
Teachers College
Columbia University
New York, New York

Donald Jackson
Behavior Analysis Program
University of Nevada–Reno
Reno, Nevada

William R. Jenson
Department of Educational
Psychology
University of Utah
Salt Lake City, Utah

Joanne Kersh
Center for Social Development and
Education
University of Massachusetts–Boston
Boston, Massachusetts

Ishita Khemka
Teachers College
Columbia University
New York, New York

Donald Kincaid
Department of Child and Family
Studies
University of South Florida
Tampa, Florida

Kathleen Kyzar
Beach Center on Disability
University of Kansas
Lawrence, Kansas

Alissa Lastres
Department of Psychology
Moravian College
Bethlehem, Pennsylvania

Stephanie Lau
Virginia Commonwealth University
Richmond, Virginia

Todd D. Little
Center for Research Methods and Data
Analysis
Department of Psychology
University of Kansas
Lawrence, Kansas

Shane J. Lopez
Clifton Strengths Institute
Omaha, Nebraska

Holly Majszak
University of Utah
Salt Lake City, Utah

Chelsea Mitamura
Department of Psychology
University of Wisconsin–Madison
Madison, Wisconsin

Dennis E. Mithaug
Teachers College
Columbia University
New York, New York

Christopher Murray
College of Education
University of Oregon
Eugene, Oregon

Laura Nota
Faculty of Psychology
University of Padua
Padua, Italy

Daniel E. Olympia
Department of Educational Psychology
University of Utah
Salt Lake City, Utah

Virginia Ramos-Matias
University of Utah
Salt Lake City, Utah

Kevin L. Rand
Department of Psychology
Indiana University–Purdue University
Indianapolis, Indiana

Lillian R. Reuman
Vassar College
Poughkeepsie, New York

Jennifer L. Rowland
University of Texas Medical Branch
Galveston, Texas

Robert L. Schalock
Department of Psychology
Hastings College
Hastings, Nebraska

Dale H. Schunk
School of Education
University of North Carolina–Greensboro
Greensboro, North Carolina

Teresa Maria Sgaramella
Faculty of Psychology
University of Padua
Padua, Italy

Amanda M. Shea
Indiana University–Purdue University
Indianapolis, Indiana

Karrie A. Shogren
College of Education
University of Illinois at Urbana–Champaign
Champaign, Illinois

Gary Siperstein
Center for Social Development and
  Education
Department of Public Policy and Public
  Affairs
University of Massachusetts–Boston
Boston, Massachusetts

Salvatore Soresi
Faculty of Psychology
University of Padua
Padua, Italy

Jean Ann Summers
Beach Center on Disability
Schiefelbusch Institute for Life Span
  Studies
University of Kansas
Lawrence, Kansas

Pamela Targett
Virginia Commonwealth University
Richmond, Virginia

Marc J. Tassé
Nisonger Center
The Ohio State University
Columbus, Ohio

Monique Thacker
University of Utah
Salt Lake City, Utah

James R. Thompson
Department of Special Education
Illinois State University
Normal, Illinois

Michele M. Tugade
Department of Psychology
Vassar College
Poughkeepsie, New York

Ann Turnbull
School of Education
University of Kansas
Lawrence, Kansas

Gitendra Uswatte
Department of Psychology
University of Alabama at Birmingham
Birmingham, Alabama

Lieke van Heumen
Department of Disability and Human
  Development
University of Illinois at Chicago
Chicago, Illinois

Yuwadee Viriyangkura
Illinois State University
Normal, Illinois

Paul Wehman
Department of Physical Medicine and
  Rehabilitation
School of Education
Virginia Commonwealth University
Richmond, Virginia

Michael L. Wehmeyer
Kansas University Center on
  Developmental Disabilities
Beach Center on Disability
Department of Special Education
University of Kansas
Lawrence, Kansas

Jenny Wilder
   School of Education, Culture, and
      Communication
   Malardalen University
   Västerås, Sweden

Dianne Zager
   School of Education
   Pace University
   New York, New York

Nina Zuna
   Department of Special Education
   University of Texas at Austin
   Austin, Texas

CONTENTS

PART 1

Overarching Themes in Positive Psychology and Disability

Beyond Pathology: Positive Psychology and Disability

Michael L. Wehmeyer

Abstract

Historically, disability has not been conceptualized within the context of strengths and positive attributes. This chapter briefly recalls the history of how disability has been understood and the consequences of such understandings in the lives of people with disabilities. The chapter discusses the complexity inherent in the notion of disability and the seeming lack of homogeneity among and between people with disabilities, noting that the universal experiences of people with disabilities have been discrimination and marginalization. The potential for positive psychology to contribute to paradigmatic changes in the field with regard to how disability is understood is discussed.

Key Words: disability, people with disabilities, disability history, understanding disability

One theme repeated frequently in the chapters that comprise this volume on positive psychology and disability is the seeming incongruity between these two constructs. Put bluntly, across history, people with disabilities have not been viewed in the context of strengths and capacities. Shogren (Chapter 3) provides a historical analysis that clearly shows that, although progress has been made, the literature in the field of disability has not been strengths-focused, and the literature in the field of positive psychology has not addressed disability. So, why create a volume of the *Oxford Library of Psychology* on positive psychology and disability? Quite simply, the trends of the past decade have created an impetus to consider issues of disability through the lens of positive psychology, and it is intended that this volume provide a catalyst to accelerate that trend, both on the disability side and on the positive psychology side.

Buntinx and Shogren (Chapters 2 and 3), among other authors in this volume, articulate those changes in the way in which disability is understood that are driving a focus toward a strengths-based psychology for people with disabilities, and readers

are referred to the next two chapters for a thorough treatment of how "functional" models of disability—or person-environment fit models—are shifting the understanding of disability from an interiorized pathology to an exteriorized state best characterized by the fit between personal capacity and the demands of the environment or context. What may not be as evident to those readers of this volume who do not have a history in disability is exactly how older ways of understanding disability have affected the lives of people with disability. "What is past is prologue," Antonio says in Act II of Shakespeare's *The Tempest*. With the hope that this is not the case with regard to how people with disability are treated, it is important to understand what that past looked like for many people with disability so as to avoid repeating prior mistakes.

First, though, a note on "disability" and "people with disabilities." Any discussion about disability must acknowledge that, fundamentally, there is no such thing as a unitary "disability identity." Indeed, it is difficult to generalize almost anything as applying to the group referred to as "people with disabilities" due in part to the sheer number of people in this category and in part to the wide range of experiences associated with varying types of disability. According to census data, there are 54 million people with disabilities in the United States alone, a large and diverse group in and of itself, and, of course, there are many more millions of people with disabilities around the world. Some of these people are born with a disability, others experience injuries or are identified later in childhood or adolescence. Some disabilities are "hidden," known only to the people who have them and by those close to them, whereas others are openly discernible. Some disabilities impact cognitive development and performance; others do not. Not surprisingly, then, differences among and between people with disabilities are often as notable as differences between people with and without disabilities.

Some people with disability and some scholars in the field would question the utility of even talking about disability, sentiments that are discussed, in part, by Brueggemann (Chapter 19). And, whereas given the lack of homogeneity among "people with disabilities" makes creating a valid taxonomy under this term difficult, if not impossible, there is one universal among and between people with disabilities that, in our minds, justifies a volume on positive psychology and disability. That is, people with disabilities have experienced discrimination and marginalization as a function of their disability.

For purposes of this volume, we have drawn from literature pertaining to a variety of disabilities, with a section containing chapters that focus on specific disability populations (physical disability, cognitive and developmental disabilities, severe multiple disabilities, emotional and behavioral disabilities, and autism spectrum disorders). Although chapters in the application to disability section include literature pertaining to a wide array of disabilities, including traumatic brain injury and sensory disabilities, this volume is not intended to cover the field of rehabilitation psychology for the simple fact that findings in the area of rehabilitation and rehabilitation psychology would justify a volume unto itself. By and large, the focus of this volume is on people who have experienced lifelong disability, and does not as much concern people who have been injured later in life (spinal cord injury, traumatic brain injury, etc.). Again, to flesh out topic areas such as optimism, coping, and resilience, it was necessary to cast a broad net and include research from these rehabilitation areas. But this volume is not intended to provide a comprehensive synthesis of the literature in rehabilitation medicine, cognitive rehabilitation, and rehabilitation psychology.

Pathology and Discrimination: Disability in History

Disability has always been associated with "differentness" and, consequently, people with disabilities have, throughout time, been treated as such, sometime benignly, other times not. The Greek city-state of Sparta and Rome, for example, are frequently identified as practicing infanticide for newborns who were weak or disabled. People with intellectual impairments in the Middle Ages were portrayed as "village idiots," and people with physical disability or epilepsy were relegated to the role of beggars.

Beginning in the late 18th and through much of the 19th centuries, there emerged efforts to educate people with disabilities, almost all associated with segregating people with disabilities in institutions. Over time, these institutions lost their habilitative nature and become warehouses for isolating people with disabilities from society. Physicians and, eventually psychologists, in the early 20th century created the professional discipline of "disability services" and had the sole voice in decisions about how people were treated.

Perhaps the darkest period for people with disabilities since the Middle Ages was the first two decades of the 20th century; ironically, an era of progressivism and social reform in America. Of most importance was the emergence of the pseudoscience of eugenics and its application to social services. *Eugenics*, a term coined by the originator of the concept, Charles Darwin's half-cousin, Francis Galton, referred to the supposed study of hereditary improvement of the human race by controlled or selective breeding. By the first decade of the 20th century, the most rabid eugenicists were Americans. The agendas of men like Charles B. Davenport, Paul Popenoe, and Harry H. Laughlin focused on limiting immigration and curtailing opportunities for people who were seen as "poor genetic stock" to reproduce. Their tools were segregation and sterilization (Smith & Wehmeyer, 2012).

It was, in some ways, a "perfect storm" that resulted in gross human and civil rights violations of America's most vulnerable citizens. Contributing to the mix were the massive overcrowding of institutions; the growing sense of futility with regard to solving what seemed to some to be irresolvable social problems; the notion of science, in the form of genetics and eugenics, as providing answers to these social problems; unresolved class and racial issues festering in America since the Civil War; and the growing concern that the "unfit" were flooding the genetic stock of the population with poor genes. People with disabilities began to be portrayed as menaces to society and blamed for social problems like prostitution, poverty, crime, alcoholism, and moral decline. Stories about "degenerate" families who propagated generations of "unfit" people reinforced these beliefs, including 1877's *The Jukes* and Vineland psychologist Henry Herbert Goddard's 1912 book, *The Kallikak Family* (Smith & Wehmeyer, 2012). The general public heard their president and Spanish-American war hero, Theodore Roosevelt, bombastically talk about "race suicide," the idea that the purported watering down of the genetic stock, caused by "unfit" people reproducing at higher rates than the so-called "fit," would eventually lead to the downfall of America. Thus, the already burgeoning institutionalized population of people with disabilities exploded in the first decade of the 1900s as a first line of defense against these dire consequences, segregation, was implemented. Institutionalization was no longer about education or habilitation, but was mainly about "protecting" society (Smith & Wehmeyer, 2012).

In 1910, Goddard translated and began to use the Binet-Simon intelligence test on inmates at the Vineland Training School. It was such a success that he then implemented it with school children in the New York City public schools. At a 1910 meeting of the American Association for the Study of the Feebleminded (the new name for the superintendents' group), Goddard suggested a classification scheme for intellectual disability that included the levels of "idiot," "imbecile," and "moron," determined by mental age scores from the Binet-Simon. The latter category, moron, which Goddard defined as people testing with a mental age between 8 and 12 years, was a new category. The term "moron" was derived by Goddard from the Greek word for fool. Soon immigrants, the poor, and, particularly, those women of child-bearing age who were viewed as morally "loose," were being classified as morons and sentenced to institutions (Trent, 1994).

Eventually, though, eugenicists saw segregation as insufficient to address the problem (as, of course, they defined it). In 1907, Indiana became the first state in the nation to legalize involuntary sterilization, providing for the "prevention of the procreation of 'confirmed criminals, idiots, imbeciles, and rapists'" (Landman, 1932, p. 55). By the late 1920s, more than half the states had laws similar to Indiana's. Propelled by the 1927 U.S. Supreme Court ruling (*Buck v. Bell*) that involuntary sterilization was constitutional, it is estimated that 50,000 people who had been labeled "feebleminded" were involuntarily sterilized. Meanwhile, under pressure from eugenicists and the general public, the U.S. Immigration Offices added "imbeciles and feeble-minded persons" to its exclusion list (Gould, 1981; Trent, 1994; Wehmeyer, 2013).

The catalyst to change came in several forms. In the economic (and population) boom of the post-World War II 1950s, a growing parents' movement rejected the notion that their children would be better off in an institution. Advances in science and medicine changed the way disability was perceived and greatly increased the lifespans of people with disabilities. Influenced by the large number of veterans disabled in World War II, who spurred an emphasis on rehabilitation and training, and by the successful development of vaccines for diseases like polio, which gave hope to greater cures for disabling conditions, the earlier stereotypes of disability were replaced with more humane (although still in many ways debilitating) stereotypes. People with disabilities were viewed as objects to be fixed, cured, rehabilitated and, at the same time, pitied. They were seen as "victims" worthy of charity, thus precipitating the emergence of the poster child as a fund raising tool (Shapiro, 1993).

A combination of the passage of federal legislation prohibiting discrimination against people with disabilities in education, employment, and access to the community, combined with a civil rights movement by people with disabilities and their allies that focused on community inclusion and equal access has, over the past four decades, encouraged us to consider issues of disability through the lens of positive psychology. The historical view of disability as pathology has run its course, although it remains far too prevalent. The success of people with disabilities in all aspects of life, aided by civil protections and equal opportunities, has made pathology-based understandings of disabilities irrelevant or inaccurate. It is well past time to begin to consider disability using a strengths-based focus, and this volume provides, it is hoped, a step in that direction.

Beyond Pathology: Disability and Positive Psychology

This volume assembles chapters by leading scholars in the fields of disability and positive psychology to provide a comprehensive synthesis of the state of the combined field of positive psychology and disability. Chapters are organized into thematic sections, beginning with three chapters (including this chapter) providing information on overarching themes in positive psychology and disability. This is followed by a section highlighting the application of positive psychological constructs to disability. In some cases (quality of life, self-determination, adaptive behavior), a robust disability-related psychological literature is available from which to draw; in other cases (optimism, hope, problem solving), the psychological literature base is limited, but work in other disciplines is available as well as models under which to consider the construct's application to disability. In still other cases, we have turned to experts in disability outside the sphere of psychology because the psychological literature simply has not addressed certain issues pertaining to disability. Chapter 16 on forgiveness, gratitude, and spirituality, for example, is authored by a clergyman who has worked in the field of intellectual and developmental disabilities. Similarly, Chapter 19 on disability studies and disability culture is written by an expert in that field. These different perspectives are important, we believe, because no single field or discipline can adequately address the complexity of the lives of people with disabilities.

The third section addresses systemic issues in disability that impact positive psychology, again turning to disciplines beyond psychology (special education, rehabilitation sciences, family and disability policy) to address areas in which positive psychology can be applied. A fourth section highlights the knowledge base in positive psychology by disability type. There is, necessarily, much overlap in what is important to people across disability types, but equal knowledge or emphasis has not been accorded across such categories, so a disability-type section seemed justified. Finally, to challenge readers to think hard about the application of positive psychology to disability, the text closes with a thoughtful chapter by psychologist Robert Cummins on the limitations of positive psychology.

References

Gould, S. J. (1981). *The mismeasure of man.* New York: Norton.

Landman, J. H. (1932). *Human sterilization: The history of the sexual sterilization movement.* New York: MacMillan.

Shapiro, J. P. (1993). *No pity: People with disabilities forging a new civil rights movement.* New York: Random House.

Smith, J. D., & Wehmeyer, M. L. (2012). *Good blood, bad blood: Science, nature, and the myth of the Kallikaks.* Washington, DC: American Association on Intellectual and Developmental Disabilities.

Trent, J. W. (1994). *Inventing the feeble mind: A history of mental retardation in the United States.* Berkeley: University of California Press.

Wehmeyer, M. L. (2013). An *informal history of intellectual disability.* Baltimore: Paul H. Brookes.

Understanding Disability:
A Strengths-Based Approach

Wil H. E. Buntinx

Abstract

In the past 30 years, "disability" has moved from the area of pathology into the area of human functioning. New models of disability were developed, such as the International Classification of Functioning, Disability, and Health (WHO) and the conceptual framework of human functioning (AAIDD). Accordingly, the focus of professionals moved from diagnosing impairments and limitations to also assessing functional strengths and support needs and resources to enhance human functioning. At the individual level, the concept of quality of life provides a positive aid for aligning personal support goals with supports strategies in the context of individualized supports planning. At the societal level, the United Nations Convention on the Rights of Persons with Disabilities constitutes an overarching set of internationally accepted values to guiding positive disability policies. The chapter demonstrates the relationships between these concepts and models and points to parallel developments in psychology. Implications of the new strengths-based approach for professional practices are discussed.

Key Words: ICF, UN convention, quality of life, assessment, supports, ecological psychology, interdisciplinary intervention

The purpose of this chapter is to reflect on the background of a positive and strengths-based approach to disability and its implications for professional practice. It aims more at offering an overview of a number of related developments and less at in-depth descriptions of specific items and constructs; most of the concepts and constructs used in this chapter have been discussed in more depth elsewhere in this volume.

Psychology is, essentially, a discipline that studies behavior and related mental processes using scientific methodology. As such, psychology is neither positive nor negative. However, as human endeavors, both academic activities and the application of resulting evidence by professionals in practice take place within a cultural context of contemporary knowledge, values, and social axioms. So, which questions are asked, what purposes are served, and

what technology is used depend not only on the state of scientific knowledge of the discipline but are also determined by social context.

This is particularly true for "disability," a phenomenon that "exists at the intersection between the particular demands of a given impairment, society's interpretation of that impairment, and the larger political and economic context" (Braddock & Parish, 2002, p. 3). And, as for the psychology of disability, context is exactly what has changed significantly in the past 50 years.

In the 20th century, the psychology of disability and mental disorder gradually moved from psychoanalysis and behaviorism to ecological and humanistic psychology. Psychoanalysis, although it may inspire the study of social attitudes toward disability, does not specifically address the understanding of disability as such. Behaviorism introduced behavior therapy and behavior modification as powerful tools for changing individual behavior, which appeared very useful in the field of disability. The question, however, as to what behavioral changes should be made proved strongly related to environmental and personal conditions. For example, learning how to travel by bus or prepare meals would not be very useful for a person living in an institutional environment with no place to go and with food provided by the facility's central kitchen. Taking the environment into account not only offers a more complete understanding of present behavior but also offers a more realistic context for intervention in terms of opportunities and resources. Ecological psychology introduced a useful theoretical frame for both scientific study and professional practice. In the area of disability, Uri Bronfenbrenner's ecological theory on human development (Bronfenbrenner, 1979, 1999; Bronfenbrenner et al., 1994) added a fruitful perspective, but there is more to understanding disability than even ecological theory addresses. Even moving toward normalized community settings implies more than learning and applying skills and (re)arranging relations between person and environment: it also needs to take into account the perspective of the person and address his or her needs, goals, preferences, subjective experiences, and life perspectives. From the 1960s on, humanistic psychology called for a holistic approach to human existence and addressed the development of human potential in a broader, existential context. Motivation, life goals, and meaning became important "variables" in the understanding of behavior and the enhancing of human functioning (Aanstoos, Serlin, & Greening, 2000; Bugental, 1967; Sutich & Vitch, 1969). More recently, positive psychology enlarged the view because it intends to promote positive functioning in individuals, families, and communities by using psychological knowledge in a growth- and well-being–enhancing way. It focuses not only on positive human functioning and personal well-being but also on civic virtues, relationships, and even on social institutions that constitute the playing field of human existence (Peterson, 2006; Seligman & Csikszentmihalyi, 2000).

Understanding and successfully applying positive psychology in the disability field requires an extension of the perspective beyond psychology. In this chapter, this broader perspective will be described around three related developments with respect to new conceptual frames of disability, new perspectives of rights and quality of life (QOL), and new systems of supports. Then, implications for professional practice will be discussed.

Understanding Disability

The historical dynamics of defining and understanding disability have been documented in the literature (Braddock & Parish, 2002; Kanner, 1964; Stiker, 1997; Trent, 1995). From this literature, it is clear that disability has to do with impairments in physical and/or mental functions. But it is also clear that the identification of the impairment as such is hardly predictive of the functioning of the person as an individual and even less so as a member of society. In other words, how impairment interacts with a person's specific abilities and how society responds to people with an impairment is as relevant for understanding disability as is the understanding of the impairment as a functional defect. A pathological approach alone will, therefore, not lead to a full understanding of a person with a disability nor will it lead to successful interventions. Knowledge of social contexts and their responses is necessary to understand the effects of impairment on a person's functioning and to develop a professional approach to mitigating that person's impaired functioning. Hence, ecological models that take the role of behavior context and environment into account became potent factors in the development of the psychology of disability (Barker, 1965; Fuhrer, 1990; Landesman, Dossett, & Echols, 1996; Schalock & Begab, 1990). In social science, the ecological approach focuses on the congruence between people and environments. One of the features of the ecological approach is the organization of the environment into micro (face-to-face relationships), meso (settings), and macro (overarching cultural, attitudinal factors and systems) levels.

Such a complexity of perspectives, however, leads readily to Babel-like confusion in communication, a confusion that not only exists within or between different academic disciplines but also in the arena of social policy, where many different interests and stakeholders meet. So, both understanding and intervening in matters of disability benefit from models that clarify and organize the different perspectives. The need for such models grew in the last quarter of the 20th century, when it became clear that disability was not a problem of small and specific minorities; the number of persons with disabilities was increasing as a result of aging and longevity; increased social risk factors, such as becoming victim of accident; medical interventions that help patients survive with disability; and an increasing demand for equal rights, access to resources, and participation in society. It was clear that these models should be multidimensional and multidisciplinary.

World Health Organization Models of Disability

The *International Classification of Impairments, Disability and Handicap* (ICIDH, World Health Organization [WHO], 1980) was the first systematic attempt to combine different perspectives for looking at disability. The ICIDH defined three planes of experience in explaining disability as the consequences of a "disease" or pathological health condition. According to the ICIDH, a disease may manifest or express itself in:

1. Problems in body functions and/or anatomy, resulting in *impairment*
2. Related problems in the person's activities, resulting in *disability*
3. Problems in performing social roles in society, resulting in a *handicap* (WHO, 1980, p. 30)

These three perspectives coincide with the functional levels of the body, the individual, and the society. The ICIDH was a breakthrough in integrating the medical model with the psychological and social models of disability and in combining the individual perspective with the social perspective. For the first time, the ICIDH provided a conceptual model with clear definitions and an extensive classification system.

However, the ICIDH was criticized for conceptual as well as technical reasons (Fougeyrollas, 1998; Kraijer, 1993; Tarlov, 1993; WHO Collaborating Center, 1994; WHO, 1999). This criticism included:

1. The unidirectional and alleged causal nature of the disabling process, starting with a disease or health condition, leading toward impairment, which consequently leads to disability, and, finally, results in handicap.
2. The absence of the environment as a factor in the disabling process.
3. Weaknesses of application in problems of children and the elderly (the system is not sensitive to development).
4. The use of negative language ("impairment," "disability," "handicap") and hence stigmatizing effects.
5. The conception of disability as a separate phenomenon, without reference to the functioning of people without a disability. This could enhance categorization and conceptually separate persons with from persons without disabilities. Disability was seen as a class in its own and not as being on a continuum of human functioning.

This criticism, as well as feedback from the worldwide use of the ICIDH in research, provided input to a fundamental revision that started in 1993 and ended in November 2001 with the official release of the ICF; the *International Classification of Functioning, Disability, and Health* (WHO, 2001). This new conceptual model of human functioning comprises six components. The three core components of human functioning (similar to the ICIDH components worded differently) are distinguished from health conditions, and two contextual components are seen as influencing factors.

The ICF provides a multidimensional framework for the description of human functioning and disability in a more positive way. *Functioning* is used as an umbrella term for neutral or nonproblematic functional states, whereas *disability* is used as an umbrella term for problems in functioning. Disability is seen as part of human functioning and not as an independent phenomenon.

The ICF model takes into account the interacting domains of human functioning. Definitions and descriptions of these domains can be considered the grammar of a "language" that allows professionals from different disciplines to communicate in clear terms and to compile and organize information from different sources. The domains of the ICF model are defined as follows.

Body functions and structures. Body functions and structures comprise two major domains, defined as the physiological and psychological functions of body systems, respectively, such as the anatomical parts of the body (e.g., organs, limbs, and their components). *Impairments* are problems in body functions or structures, such as a significant deviation or loss. For example, in the context of intellectual disability, intellectual functions and cognitive functions are subdomains of body functions; intellectual disability would code: b117.

Activities. Activities refer to a person's execution of a task or action. Activities can be understood as referring to learned activities or skills. Difficulties a person may have in capacity and/or in the performance of activities are referred to as *activity limitations*.

Participation. Participation refers to a person's involvement in life situations. It denotes the degree of the person's involvement in the community. Problems that an individual may have in the manner or extent of involvement in life situations are called *participation restrictions*. Unlike the activity dimension, which is about individual performance and the presence of skills relevant to various aspects of life, the participation dimension is about the actual involvement of the person in real-life social settings. Participation restrictions are about disadvantages that limit the fulfillment of social roles considered normal (depending on age, sex, culture) for the individual. The term *participation restrictions* is congruent with the earlier term *handicap* in the ICIDH. *Health conditions* are disorders and diseases as listed in the WHO International Classification of Diseases (WHO, 1994). *Environmental factors* make up the physical, social, and attitudinal environment in which people live and conduct their lives. *Personal factors* occur in the background of a particular individual's life, such as gender, race, age, fitness, lifestyle, habits, social background, education, profession, and significant life events. The same model and definitions apply to the children and youth version of the ICF published in 2007.

The AAIDD Model of Human Functioning

In the field of intellectual disability, a breakthrough was realized in 1992 through its multidimensional conceptualization by the American Association on Intellectual and Developmental Disabilities (AAIDD)—at that time acting under the name American Association on Mental Retardation (AAMR). In the 9th edition of the AAIDD "manual on definition" (Luckasson et al., 1992), a very important shift was made through the adoption of a social-ecological approach to disability that took environmental considerations fully into account (even before the ICF included them). A second innovation of the 9th edition was its positive approach to the classification and description of the person's functioning by considering not only problems and weaknesses but also the person's strengths in different dimensions of functioning. This implied looking for possibilities and opportunities during the interdisciplinary assessment process, not just for difficulties and barriers. A third innovation was shifting the center of gravity from classifying defects and limitations to the determination of needed supports. Supports are not restricted to specialized and institutionalized programs but extend to the environmental context and include generic support resources in the community. These innovations accounted for a paradigm shift in the assessment of and intervention in disabilities.

The new paradigm was further developed in the manual's 10th edition (Luckasson et al., 2002) and finalized in the 11th edition, in 2010 (Schalock et al., 2010). The present AAIDD conceptual framework of

human functioning represents a positive view on disability that starts from a nonpathological concept of "human functioning" that allows identifying strengths and weaknesses in five functional dimensions. The most important addition to this model, compared with the ICF, is the central role of supports. Supports act precisely at the center of the person–environment interaction and can significantly affect the quality of a person's functioning. As a consequence, the role of professionals in disability can be redefined as facilitating the support process to enhance positive life experiences. Typical professional tasks in this process encompass the assessment of strengths and weaknesses in all dimensions of functioning and arriving at a description of the person's support needs. Next, the role of professionals is to facilitate the support process by contributing from their field's knowledge base (e.g., psychology, health and medical sciences, social work). Such a support contribution may focus either on the person (e.g., by offering specialized therapeutic or educational interventions), on the environment (e.g., by strengthening and enabling access to nonspecialized resources, such as family, friends, and informal and nonpaid supports, or to generic services, such as schools, housing services, employers, communities), or on more effectively delivering supports (Buntinx & Schalock, 2010).

Although the ICF and AAIDD models were developed independently, both stem from an ecological view of disability and their conceptualizations of dimensions are also related. In fact, both models can be translated into each other, which facilitates their use in interdisciplinary practice (Buntinx, 2006; Wehmeyer, Buntinx, Lachapelle, Luckasson, & Schalock, 2008).

The Perspective of Supports

Although a multidimensional view of human functioning would certainly help us arrive at a better understanding of disability, the question remains about how and to what end supports should be given in order to be effective. The ICF and AAIDD multidimensional frameworks of human functioning, although rooted in a positive perception of human functioning, are primarily tools for identifying problem areas in functioning. Knowing these problems, and even considering strengths, does not automatically result in supports. There are three reasons for this. First, these frameworks are professional and highly analytic constructs. The associated classifications do not exact reflect a person's experiences but are for use within professional or academic settings. Indeed, assuming that supports should simply try to reverse the assessed limitations and weaknesses would be naïve and ineffective as a guide for real-life support actions: positive personal functioning is not the reverse of disability. Second, the identification of impairment, activity limitation, participation restriction, or contextual barriers may not correspond easily with treatment or mitigating activities. Some limitations are beyond treatment or "repair," and limitations in activities and participation resulting from these conditions would still exist despite supports. Third, these frameworks do not take subjective experiences and personal life goals into consideration, and people seldom express their goals and ambitions in life in terms of the ICF. So, the notion of "supports" calls for an orientation or perspective that goes beyond disability. Thus, the language of supports should be different from the language of limitation classification.

Two developments at the end of the 20th century answered this problem. One was the introduction of the concept of *quality of life,* and the other is the human rights approach to disability. The first resulted in concepts and instruments that would help identify personal needs for supports, formulate personal goals, and set criteria for the evaluation of supports outcomes and a person's overall well-being. Quality of life is a concept at the individual, psychological level.

The second resulted in the clarification of human rights for persons with disabilities that eventually culminated in the United Nations (UN) Convention on the Rights of Persons with Disabilities (WHO, 2006). This international rights document addresses the social-political environment of human functioning as expressed in laws, regulations, and cultural norms that govern society.

Quality of Life

According to the World Health Organization (WHO), QOL is the "individuals' perception of their position in life in the context of the culture and value systems in which they live and in relation to their goals, expectations, standards and concerns. It is a broad ranging concept affected in a complex way by the person's physical health, psychological state, personal beliefs, social relationships and their relationship to salient features of their environment" (WHO, 1997, p. 1). The Quality of Life Research Unit of the University of Toronto defines it as "[t]he degree to which a person enjoys the important possibilities of his or her life" (Quality of Life Research Unit, 2012).

In the 1990s, considerable work was done in the field of disabilities and QOL by authors David Felce (1995, 1997), Roy Brown (1997), Robert Cummins

(1997), Robert Schalock (1990), and Schalock et al., 2002). The construct developed into multidimensional models that identify a number of life domains to cover human existence as a whole. Within these domains, specific indicators and measurement instruments can be operationalized. An essential feature of the construct of QOL is the acknowledgment of both subjective and objective criteria for evaluation. The subjective approach refers to a person's satisfaction with a domain or indicator and their relative importance for that person in his or her life. The objective approach refers to objective norms available in society. For example, a person can be perfectly satisfied with his or her health (subjective) but can suffer from high blood pressure or other health conditions or maintain an unhealthy lifestyle (objective); or, a person may be satisfied with his or her living situation in a run-down institutional building and see no reason to move (subjective), but institutional environments and large living groups in congregate settings are not considered positive environments by contemporary professional standards (objective). Objective norms can be found in legal and professional standards. Subjective norms can be obtained by simply asking the person about his or her life experiences or by using satisfaction inventory methods.

Three commonly used QOL domain frameworks are shown in Table 2.1. The concept of QOL serves as a reference frame for identifying support needs, both subjective and objective. Subjective support needs follow from the person's personal aspirations and goals in life. Objective support needs result from a professional appraisal of the person's present functioning, taking both his or her (dis)abilities and contextual circumstances into account.

The construct of QOL adds a powerful perspective to positive support practices in disability because it introduces positive values and offers a background for formulating positive goals. Although specific indicators may be sensitive to cultural and lifespan perspectives, they involve universally perceived aspects of personal well-being (Schalock et al., 2005; Schalock, Gardner, & Bradley, 2007). Quality of life is a sensitizing notion for identifying individual support needs, assessing support outcomes, and also for guiding the development of social policies (Schalock et al., 2012).

The United Nations Convention on the Rights of Persons with Disabilities

The UN Convention on the Rights of Persons with Disabilities (henceforth, the Convention) is the culmination of a history of applying human rights to

Table 2.1 Domains of Quality of Life According to Three Major Authors

Domains of Quality of Life according to Schalock et al. (2007), World Health Organization (WHO, 1997), and the Quality of Life (QOL) Research Unit (Toronto)

Schalock	WHO	QOL Research Unit
1. Personal development	1. Physical Health	1. Physical Being
2. Self-determination	2. Psychological	2. Psychological Being
3. Interpersonal relations	3. Level of Independence	3. Spiritual Being
4. Social inclusion	4. Social Relations	4. Physical Belonging
5. Rights	5. Environment	5. Social Belonging
6. Emotional well-being	6. Spirituality/Religion/Personal beliefs	6. Community Belonging
7. Physical well-being		7. Practical Becoming
8. Material well-being		8. Leisure Becoming
		9. Growth Becoming

the situations of persons with disabilities. Although the Universal Declaration of Human Rights, adopted by the UN General Assembly on December 10, 1948, addresses all humans without exception, the need was felt to more explicitly translate these rights to the situations of persons with disabilities. This led to the Declaration on the Rights of Mentally Retarded Persons (December 20, 1971) followed by the Declaration on the Rights of Disabled Persons (December 9, 1975). The awareness that rights do not automatically lead to a better life if people lack opportunities to actually exercise those rights led to the Standard Rules on the Equalization of Opportunities for Persons with Disabilities (December 20, 1993). This non-legally binding UN document described the conditions and target areas for community participation of persons with disabilities. Finally, the legally binding Convention was adopted (December 13, 2006), stating the terms and conditions with which states should comply to create conditions for full citizenship and participation for persons with disabilities. It is important to realize that this document was developed with significant input from persons with disabilities and their organizations. The Convention reaffirms that all people with disability must enjoy all human rights and fundamental freedoms. It clarifies and qualifies how all categories of rights apply to persons with disabilities. It identifies areas where adaptations have to be made for persons with disabilities to effectively exercise their rights and where protection of rights must be reinforced.

The importance of this Convention can hardly be overestimated. In terms of ecological psychology, the Convention is an instrument at the macrolevel. It represents the fundamental and universal values that states and their institutions need to observe in developing an equitable society. Professional support organizations for people with disabilities are part of society and are, in most cases, governed by national (health) policy. Therefore, people with disabilities are fully affected by the values and targets of the Convention. Thus, promoting social participation and inclusion, enhancing self-determination and development, and striving for equal opportunities for persons with disabilities cannot be considered local idealism or naïve enthusiasm on the part of organizations or individual professionals; it is simply their duty "under the law" to enhance the dignity, equality, and inclusion of their clients as equal citizens. Because the Convention represents universal values and targets, every individual professional and every organization in the field has a moral obligation to define its position against this backdrop.

Quality of Life and the Convention

It is important to realize that the fundamental values expressed in the QOL concept and in the Convention are identical. In that the conceptualization and operationalization of QOL is directed more at the level of individual supports, it is fitter for clinical use. The Convention is better fit to social-political applications at the societal level.

One can say that the Convention creates societal conditions for QOL to be effective at the individual level, but both share the same underlying values. Therefore, the QOL domains and the articles of the Convention can be aligned as shown in Table 2.2 (Schalock et al., 2012, p. 45).

Because the Convention is rooted in internationally accepted values, it is a strong binding force across sociopolitical, professional, and academic stakeholders in support processes at any level. This was emphasized at the 14th Congress of the International Association for the Scientific Study of Intellectual and Developmental Disabilities (IASSIDD) in Halifax by Klaus Lachwitz (2012), president of Inclusion International, and Michael Bach, vice-president of the Canadian Association for Community Living. In Bach's view, the scientific (and I would add as well the professionals') task is not to determine *if*, but *how*;

> Not *if* people with intellectual disabilities have a will and preference, but *how* to determine it even when its contours are occluded by our usual ways of seeing and knowing; not *if* people with even the most complex disabilities can live in the community,

but *how* that is to be made possible.... Not *if* people with intellectual disabilities benefit from being supported to exercise self-determination and making their own choices,... but *how* to enable others to respect and act upon the legal power they possess. It is only with such knowledge, founded on a law, science and ethics of inclusion, that we might nurture a new relationship between the state, society and people with intellectual disabilities. (Bach, 2012)

Supports System

Supports are defined as resources and strategies that aim to promote the development, education, interests, and personal well-being of a person and enhance individual functioning (Schalock et al., 2010; et al., 2002, 2009). The AAIDD framework of human functioning moves supports to the center of the professional's involvement with persons with disabilities. This involvement should focus on the identification of support needs and the development of an individualized support plan to enhance individual functioning. The supports system addresses three items: support needs, support resources, and support strategies.

Table 2.2 Relationships Among Quality of Life (QOL) Domains and United Nations Convention Articles

QOL Domains	Exemplary QOL Indicators and Applicable UN Convention (Art. 5–30)
Personal Development	Education status, personal skills, adaptive behavior *Art. 24*
Self-determination	Choices/decisions, autonomy, personal control, personal goals *Art. 14, 19, 21*
Interpersonal Relations	Social networks, friendships, social activities, relationships *Art. 23*
Social inclusion	Community integration/participation, community roles, supports *Art. 8, 9, 18, 20, 27, 29, 30*
Rights	Human (respect, dignity, equality) legal (legal access, due process, privacy) *Art. 5, 6, 7, 10, 11, 12, 13, 15, 22*
Emotional Well-Being	Safety and security, positive experiences, contentment, lack of stress) *Art. 16, 17*
Material Well-Being	Health and nutrition status, recreation, leisure *Art. 16, 25, 26*
Material Well-Being	Financial status, employment status, housing status, possessions *Art. 28*

Support needs. Support needs are defined as a psychological construct referring to the pattern and intensity of supports that are necessary for a person to participate in activities associated with normative human functioning (Thompson et al., 2009). Normative functioning is related to the construct of QOL. Therefore, support needs are rooted in both subjective and objective needs. Objective needs can be identified in a professional assessment process using professional or social standards. For example, when a person has a severe mobility limitation due to impairment in movement related body structures and/or functions (e.g., related to cerebral palsy or paralysis), this person will need support to go shopping or to more generally move around in the community. Subjective needs are related to the life goals, preferences, ambitions, and wants of the person or his or her actual dissatisfaction in specific QOL domains or indicators. Developing supports is therefore based on an assessment of both subjective and objective needs. Professional support process models currently include both (Buntinx et al., 2010; Thompson et al., 2009). For the assessment of support needs from the professional perspective, instruments such as the Supports Intensity Scale are available (Thompson et al., 2004).

Support resources. Traditionally, support resources in the disability field are seen as professional and specialized organizations such as institutions, sheltered workshops, day activity centers, or group homes. However, the need for supports does not necessarily mean that they should be delivered in a specialized or restricted setting.

The AAIDD conceptualization of support resources starts with the personal strengths and possibilities of the person with disabilities. This person always possesses relative strengths, as assessment using ICF and AAIDD frameworks should make clear. Even in the case of very severe and multiple disabilities, a positive approach may identify relative strengths in functioning that may be relevant to enhancing the person's QOL. The person can be pictured in the middle of a set of concentric circles. Surrounding the person are the three circles of family and friends, informal supports (such as colleagues at work, co-members of a club, fellow pupils at school), and generic services that are open to the public at large (such as shops, sports and cultural facilities, health services). These three circles are natural resources that are available in the general community environment. The use of public resources supposes that these are inclusive to persons with disabilities. In states and nations that ratified the Convention,

general obligations to inclusion exist. The fourth and last circle regards specialized services-based resources. These are supports provided by people and equipment that are not typically part of the person's natural environment, such as specially trained professionals like psychologists, teachers, therapists, nurses, direct support staff, or paid volunteers. These services usually are provided under some form of contract with the government and use public funding. In the past, support resources for persons with disabilities were mainly restricted to specialized services. In the case of institutions and other special or segregated facilities, this often resulted in the person being cut off from his or her natural support strengths. Family were merely "visitors" in the facility when they came to see their relative; contact with friends was hardly possible and not part of the facility's "treatment" policy. Specialized organizations offered alternatives for school, work, sports, or cultural activities, separated from the same functions and organizations in the community at large. In the last quarter of the 20th century, the tide turned, and persons with disabilities began to make more use of their natural support resources. However, to succeed, this movement supposes a change in the structures and culture of specialized services and in the attitudes of professionals. Although this might be seen by some politicians as a rationale for budget cuts, the primary reason for making use of natural resources is the common sense that people with disabilities are and want to be part of their community. Discovering, however, the support potential of a community may require facilitation, which may, in some cases, also require additional funding and professional facilitation. In addition to direct face-to-face contacts and personal assistance, supports also include the access to and use of technical aids, information and communication technology, social media, financial means, and information.

In the ecological conceptualization of disability, focusing on natural resources is closer to QOL thinking, and it is certainly closer to the implications of the Convention than is focusing on specialized services alone.

Support strategies. Strategies integrate goals with resources and support activities for an individual with disabilities in the context of an individualized support plan (ISP). Before developing an ISP, it is assumed that an assessment of functioning and support needs has been made. On the basis of the person's ambitions for the future, preferences, and wants, as well as based on information about the more objectified assessed support needs (e.g., through the use of the Supports Intensity Scale), personal goals can be selected and prioritized. This is the first step of the ISP. Next, for each goal, relevant support activities and resources are identified. Support activities can refer to development, teaching, education, befriending, assistance, coaching, or treatment (health and behavioral) activities. Support resources refer the natural and/or service-based resources discussed in the previous section. Finally, the person's goals and related support activities are placed within a timeframe, and support agreements and responsibilities are specified.

The ISP is placed within a systematic cycle, which involves monitoring progress and evaluating outcomes. The ISP should be developed with as full involvement of the person as possible and, eventually, with the participation of significant others or advocates. The ISP takes the form of an agreement between the person with disabilities and others with respect to supports delivery (both natural and specialized). In the strengths approach, individualized supports are typically created around the person and not around a professional service or funding stream.

In the past few decades, the emphasis of professional intervention moved away from developing "programs" for persons with common characteristics such as " type of impairment," "level of functioning," or "behavior problems" and toward developing strictly individualized strategies. The voice of the person and his or her self-determination in terms of personal dreams, goals, and a say in the way these would be pursued, are key to the supports process. This changes the role of the professional from "program designer" and "expert" to "partner" in developing and delivering individualized supports.

With respect to supports strategies that make use of the person's strengths and empower natural resources, a new range of strategies and methods is being developed. *Person-centered planning* has become an umbrella term for such strategies (Claes, Van Hove, Vandevelde, Van Loon, & Schalock, 2010). Methods associated with person-centered planning strategies include Planning Alternative Tomorrows with Hope (PATH), Making Action Plans (MAPS) (O'Brien & O'Brien, 2002; O'Brien, Pearpoint, & Kahn, 2010), and Active Support (Felce et al., 2000). Examples of methods that focus on the mobilization of support strengths in natural resources include *wraparound care* (Winters & Metz, 2009) and *family group conference* (Huntsman, 2006; Kyeong-Hwa & Turnbull, 2004; Lupton, 1998).

The participation of the person with disabilities in these methods is more than a physical presence at an ISP meeting; it supposes an active involvement in the process (Carnaby, 1997; Dowling, Manthorpe, & Cowley, 2007; Wehmeyer, 2002; Williams & Robinson, 2000). Self-determination in the support process leads to dynamic partnerships among persons with disability, their natural environment, and professionals.

Looking at support strategies in an ecological context focuses on aspects of the broader macrosystems, such as social and cultural attitudes toward disability and factors that affect the availability and accessibility of services. Moreover, funding systems and regulations (e.g., social security, health care system) strongly affect the provision of supports strategies. Thus, successful support strategies in practice are not just a matter of strategies at the individual level but will also depend on facilitating strengths and weaknesses on the level of services and society. The synergetic alignment of macro, meso, and micro strategies is therefore an important condition and remains, in many cases, a challenge.

Implications for Professional Practice

In recent decades, significant developments took place to change scientific and societal views on disability. What is considered good practice in disability is affected by these developments, as discussed in the previous sections. The implications of these developments for professional practice can be summarized as follows.

Understanding disability has definitely moved from describing impairments and limitations to understanding human functioning as a whole and understanding individual needs for support. Developing and delivering supports require an individualized process, organized around the person's desired life experiences and goals and taking into account assessed support needs. The direction of the support process points to the common denominator of QOL, a perspective that people with disabilities share with all other people in society and that has been incorporated in internationally recognized rights documents. Good practice implies that person-centered strategies should be observed.

The process as a whole can be aligned along the concepts of functional strengths and weaknesses, needs, goals, and perspective. Translated into good practice for clinical professionals, these concepts can be arranged in a four-phase approach (Buntinx & Schalock, 2010). First, assessment of a person's strengths and weaknesses in functioning along a multidimensional (i.e., interdisciplinary) path is necessary to identify relevant potentials, but also to discover relevant impairments, activity limitations, and participation restrictions together with associated health conditions (etiology) and contextual factors. It must be clear that emphasizing the importance of strengths and facilitators does by no means make diagnosis of health conditions, etiology, impairments, and limitations less important. On the contrary, failure to identify relevant pathology could result in serious health risks and ineffective supports. However, the strengths-based approach will not stop at identifying pathology, impairments, limitations, and barriers but will go beyond these to look for functional strengths. Second, assessment of a person's desired life experiences, ambitions, and wants, as well as an assessment of objectified support needs and needs intensities, is another aspect of the process. Third, the individualized supports planning process is directed toward linking personal goals with a range of related resources and action strategies. People involved in the delivery of supports should participate as closely as possible in the ISP planning process. The ISP should be monitored and evaluated in a systematic way.

Fourth, supports outcomes are evaluated in terms of QOL. The basic question here is if and how the person has benefited from support efforts and investments. From this evaluation, new support goals and strategies can be formulated.

Although this four-phase approach reflects an analytic view on disability from the professional's point of view, it does by no means imply a mechanical process. The elements as discussed in this chapter are the rational backbone of good practice that also requires communication and client-centered skills that allow for a flexible approach to real life. In the same way that a patient does not need to study functional analysis, behavior therapy, or medicine in order to participate in treatment, a person with disabilities does not need to learn the language of the ICF or ISP methodology. The professional, however, will need not to simply study the theory and methods of disability but will also need to become familiar with their application in practice, as part of his or her education.

In a strengths-based supports strategy, the person's own abilities and strengths are explicitly considered before calling in other resources. Thus, the empowerment of the person has a high priority; in addition, the strategy also emphasizes the empowerment of other nonspecialized or natural resources. For professionals in the field of disability, this means that they should not only apply their knowledge and competencies in direct face-to-face interventions with the person but also in empowering natural resources to playing a role in the overall provision of supports. For professionals who are used to dealing with persons with disability within the borders of their service or facility, this may mean a shift of focus. Instead of applying their professional skills and time in direct assistance, teaching, or treatment activities, they may need to learn how to involve and facilitate nonprofessionals to effectively support the person with disabilities (Carr et al., 2002). In these cases, the professional must undertake a mediating role in the support process. Hence, positive practice professionals and their organizations will not just need expertise with respect to impairments but also skills in communication, and with scouting and empowering environments.

Positive approaches to disability involve not only academic and clinical input. As demonstrated, part of the understanding of disability and, even more, a lot of intervention, presupposes the involvement of the community and societal environment as conditions for success. Therefore, positive practices in disability will always require a multipath approach that includes clinical, organizational, and social-political factors. The message here is that support of a person with disabilities is never a one-person affair. It will always require the involvement of a broad range of contextual stakeholders. As such, disability support is a community endeavor involving professionals and nonprofessionals alike. As argued in this chapter, tools are available to enhance a common language and concerted actions on the individual as well as the societal level. That is a positive factor. Improving these tools through research and putting them to work effectively to the benefit of people with disabilities is an academic and professional challenge. It may require not simply shifting working procedures for professional disciplines but also redesigning organizational structures, developing new disability policies and systems, and possibly changing societal attitudes as well.

References

Aanstoos, C., Serlin, I., & Greening, T. (2000). A history of Division 32 (Humanistic Psychology) of the American Psychological Association. In D. Dewsbury (Ed.), *Unification through division: Histories of the divisions of the American Psychological Association*, Vol. V. (pp. 23–24). Washington, DC: American Psychological Association.

Bach, M. (2012). *Towards an ontology of inclusion: Re-writing the law, science and ethics of intellectual disability* (Opening plenary session, IASSID World Congress, Halifax, July 9,

2012). Retrieved from http://www.cacl.ca/sites/default/files/uploads/docs/Bach%20-%20IASSID%20Congress%20-%20Opening%20Remarks.pdf on August 28, 2012.

Barker, R. G. (1965). Explorations in ecological psychology. *American Psychologist*, 20, 1–14.

Braddock, D., & Parish, S. L. (2002). An institutional history of disability. In Braddock D. (Ed.), *Disability at the dawn of the 21st. century and the state of the states* (pp. 3–61). Washington, DC: American Association on Mental Retardation.

Bronfenbrenner, U. (1979). *The ecology of human development. experiments by nature and design*. Cambridge: Harvard University Press.

Bronfenbrenner, U. (1999). Environments in developmental perspective: Theoretical and operational models. In S. L. Friedman & T. D. Wachs (Eds.), *Measuring environment across the life-span* (pp. 3–28). Washington, DC: American Psychological Association.

Bronfenbrenner, U., & Ceci S. J. (1994). Nature–nurture reconceptualization in developmental perspective: A bioecological model. *Psychological Review*, 101, 568–585.

Brown, R. I. (1997). *Quality of life for people with disabilities. Models, research and practice*. Cheltenham: Stanley Thornes.

Bugental, J. F. T. (1967). *Challenges of humanistic psychology*. New York: McGraw-Hill.

Buntinx W. H. E. (2006). The relationship between the WHO-ICF and the AAMR-2002 system. In Switzky H. & Greenspan S. (Eds.), *What is mental retardation? Ideas for an evolving disability in the 21st century* (pp. 303–323). Washington, DC: American Association on Mental Retardation.

Buntinx, W. H. E., & Schalock, R. L. (2010). Models of disability, quality of life, and individualized supports: Implications for professional practice in intellectual disability. *Journal of Policy and Practice in Intellectual Disabilities*, 7(4), 283–294.

Carr, E. G., Dunlap, G., Horner, R. H., Koegel, R. L., Turnbull, A. P., Sailor, W., et al. (2002). Positive behavior support: Evolution of an applied science. *Journal of Positive Behavior Interventions*, 4, 4–16.

Carnaby, S. (1997). 'What do you think?': A qualitative approach to evaluating individual planning services. *Journal of Intellectual Disability Research*, 41(3), pp. 225–231.

Claes, C., Van Hove, G., Vandevelde, S., Van Loon, J., & Schalock, R. L. (2010). Person-centered planning: analysis of research and effectiveness. *Intellectual and Developmental Disabilities*, 48(6), 432–453.

Cummins, R. A. (1997). Assessing quality of life. In R. I. Brown (Ed.), *Quality of life for people with disabilities: Models, research, and practice* (pp. 116–150). Cheltenham: Stanley Thornes.

Dowling, S., Manthorpe, J., & Cowley, S. (2007). Working on person-centered planning: from amber to green light? *Journal of Intellectual Disabilities*, 11, 65–82.

Felce, D. (1997). Defining and applying the concept of quality of life. *Journal of Intellectual Disability Research*, 14(2), 126–135.

Felce, D., Bowley, C., Baxter, H., Jones, E., Lowe, K., & Emerson, E. (2000). The effectiveness of staff support: Evaluating Active Support training using a conditional probability approach. *Research in Developmental Disabilities*, 21(4), 243–255.

Felce, D., & Perry, J. (1995). Quality of life: its definition and measurement. *Research in Developmental Disabilities*, 16(1), 51–74.

Fougeyrollas, P. (Ed.). (1998). ICIDH and environmental factors [Special Issue]. *International Network, 9*. Monograph Supplement.

Fuhrer, U. (1990). Bridging the ecological-psychological gap. Behavior settings as interfaces. *Environment and Behavior*, 22, 518–537.

Huntsman, L. (2006). *Family group conferencing in a child welfare context. A literature review*. Ashfield: Centre for Parenting & Research.

Kanner, L. (1964). *A history of the care and study of the mentally retarded*. Springfield, IL: Charles Thomas.

Kraijer D. W. (1993). *Use of the international classification of impairments, disabilities and handicaps (ICIDH) in the field of mental retardation*. Strasbourg: Council of Europe Press.

Kyeong-Hwa, K., & Turnbull, A. (2004). Transition to adulthood for students with severe intellectual disabilities: Shifting toward person-family interdependent planning. *Research and Practice for Persons with Severe Disabilities*, 29(1), 53–57

Lachwitz, K. (2012). *Linking local voices to global change*. Opening Speech at the IASSIDD World Congress in Halifax, July 8, 2012. Retrieved from http://www.inclusion-international.org/2012/07/23/opening-speech-by-klaus-lachwitz-at-the-2012-iassid-world-congress/ August 28, 2012.

Landesman, S., Dossett, E., & Echols, K. (1996). The social ecology of mental retardation. In J. W. Jacobson & J. A. Mulick (Eds.), *Manual of diagnosis and professional practice in mental retardation* (p. 55–65). Washington, DC: American Psychological Association.

Luckasson, R., Brothwick-Duffy, S., Buntinx, W., Coulter, D., Craig, P., Reeve, A., et al. (2002). *Mental retardation: Definition, classification and systems of supports*. Washington, DC: American Association on Mental Retardation.

Luckasson, R., Coulter, D. L., Polloway, E. A., Reiss, S., Schalock, R. L., Snell, M. E., et al. (1992). *Mental retardation: Definition, classification, and systems of supports* (9th ed.). Washington, DC: American Association on Mental Retardation.

Lupton, C. (1998). User empowerment or family self-reliance? The family group conference model. *British Journal of Social Work*, 28, 107–128.

O'Brien, C. L., & O'Brien, J. (2002). The origin of person-centered planning. In S. Holburn & P. Vietze (Eds.), *Person-centered planning: Research, practice, and future directions* (pp. 3–27). Baltimore, MD: Paul H. Brookes.

O'Brien, J., Pearpoint, J., & Kahn, L. (2010). *The PATH & MAPS Handbook. Person-centered ways to build community*. Toronto: Inclusion Press.

Peterson, C. (2006). *A primer in positive psychology*. Oxford: Oxford University Press.

Quality of Life Research Unit. (2012). *The quality of life model*. Retrieved from www.utoronto.ca/qol/ August 28, 2012.

Seligman, M. E. P., & Csikszentmihalyi, M. (2000). Positive psychology. An introduction. *American Psychologist*, 55(1), 5–14.

Schalock, R. L. (Ed.). (1997). *Quality of life. Applications to persons with disabilities*. Washington, DC: American Association on Mental Retardation.

Schalock, R. L., & Begab, M. J. (Eds.). (1990). *Quality of life. Perspective and issues*. Washington, DC: American Association on Mental Retardation.

Schalock, R. L., Borthwick-Duffy S. A., Bradley, V. J., Buntinx, W. H. E., Coulter, D. L., Craig, E. M., Gomez, S. C., et al. (2010). *Intellectual Disability: Definition, Classification, and Systems of Supports* (11th edition). Washington, DC: American Association on Intellectual and Developmental Disabilities.

Schalock, R. L., Gardner, J. F., & Bradley, V. J. (2007). *Quality of life for people with intellectual and other developmental disabilities. Applications across individuals, organizations, communities, and systems.* Washington, DC: American Association on Intellectual and Developmental Disabilities.

Schalock, R. L., & Kiernan, W. E. (1990). *Habilitation planning for adults with disabilities.* New York: Springer-Verlag.

Schalock, R., Luckasson, R., Bradley, V., Buntinx, W., Lachapelle, Y., et al. (2012). *User's guide to accompany the 11th edition of intellectual disability: Definition, classification, and systems of supports. applications for clinicians, educators, organizations providing supports, policymakers, family members and advocates, and health care professionals.* Washington, DC: American Association on Intellectual and Developmental Disabilities.

Schalock R. L., & Verdugo, M. A. (2012*).* A conceptual and measurement framework to guide policy development and systems. *Journal of Policy and Practice in Intellectual Disabilities, 9*(1), 70–79.

Schalock, R. L., Verdugo, M. A., Jerano, C., Wang, M., Wehmeyer, M., Xu, J., & Lachapelle, Y. (2005). A cross-cultural study of quality of life indicators. *American Journal on Mental Retardation, 110,* 298–311.

Schalock, R., & Verdugo Alonso, M. A. (2002). *Handbook of quality of life for human service practitioners.* Washington, DC: American Association on Mental Retardation.

Stiker, H. J. (1997). *A history of disability.* Ann Arbor: Michigan University Press.

Sutich, A. J., & Vich, M. A. (1969). *Readings in humanistic psychology.* New York: Free Press.

Tarlov, A. R. (1993). Persons with disabilities: Definition and conceptual framework. *Dolentium Hominum: Journal of the Pontifical Council for Pastoral Assistance to Health Care Workers, 22,* 40–43.

Thompson, J. R., Bradley, V., Buntinx, W. H. E., Schalock, R. L., Shogren, K. A., Snell, M., et al. (2009). Conceptualizing supports and the support needs of people with intellectual disabilities. *Intellectual and Developmental Disabilities, 47,* 135–146.

Thompson, J. R., Bryant, B. R., Campbell, E. M., Craig, E. M., Hughes, C. M., Rotholz, D. A., et al. (2004). *Supports intensity scale. Users manual.* Washington, DC: American Association on Mental Retardation.

Thompson, J. R., Hughes, C., Schalock, R. L., Silverman, W., Tasse, M. J., Bryant, B. R., Craig, E. M., & Campbell, E. M.

(2002). Integrating supports in assessment and planning. *Mental Retardation, 40*(5), 390–405.

Trent, J. W. (1995). *Inventing the feeble mind. A history of mental retardation in the United States.* Ewing: University of California Press.

United Nations (2006). *Convention on the Rights of Persons with Disabilities.* Retrieved from http://www.un.org/disabilities/default.asp?id=259 on May 11, 2013.

Wehmeyer, M. L. (2002). The influence of person-centered planning and self-determination. In S. Holburn & P. Vietze (Eds.), *Person-centered planning: Research, practice, and future directions* (pp. 55–69). Baltimore, MD: Paul H. Brookes.

Wehmeyer, M. L., Buntinx, W. H. E., Lachapelle, Y., Luckasson, R. A., & Schalock, R. L. (2008). The intellectual disability construct and its relation to human functioning. *Intellectual and Developmental Disabilities, 46*(4), 311–318.

World Health Organization (WHO). (1980). *International classification of impairments, disabilities, and handicaps. A manual of classification relating to the consequences of disease.* Geneva: Author.

World Health Organization (WHO). (1994). *International classification of diseases.* Geneva: Author.

World Health Organization (WHO) (Division of mental Health and Prevention of Substance Abuse). (1997). *WHOQOL. Measuring Quality of Life.* Geneva: Author.

World Health Organization (WHO). (1999). *International classification of functioning and disability (Beta-2 draft, full version).* Geneva: Author.

World Health Organization (WHO). (2001). *International classification of functioning, disability, and health (ICF).* Geneva: Author.

World Health Organization (WHO). (2006). *International classification of functioning, disability and health. Children & youth version.* Geneva: Author.

World Health Organization (WHO) Collaborating Center for the ICIDH. (1994). *A survey of criticism about the ICIDH.* Zoetermeer (Netherlands): WCC Dutch Classification and Terminology Committee for Health.

Williams, V., & Robinson, C. (2000). "Tick this, tick that": The views of people with learning disabilities on their assessments. *Journal of Intellectual Disabilities, 4,* 293–315.

Winters, N. C., & Metz, P. (2009). The wraparound approach in systems of care. *Psychiatric Clinics of North America, 32,* 135–151.

Positive Psychology and Disability: A Historical Analysis

Karrie A. Shogren

Abstract

The disability and psychology fields have undergone significant changes since the latter part of the 20th century. Within psychology, positive psychology has emerged as an alternate paradigm through which to understand the complete human condition. Within disability, person-environment fit and social-ecological models have influenced conceptualizations of disability. This chapter analyzes the historical trends in psychology and disability that have led to the emergence of these paradigms, analyzes the impacts that these shifts have had on literature in each field, and explores implications for future research, policy, and practice.

Key Words: positive psychology, social-ecological, disability, supports

Substantial changes have emerged within the fields of psychology and disability in recent decades. In psychology, an alternate paradigm—positive psychology—has grown into a flourishing subfield. In the disability field, there have been major shifts in our understanding of the construct of disability, including a movement away from a deficit-based or medical model of disability to a social-ecological model of human functioning. The purpose of this chapter is to analyze the historical trends in psychology and disability that have led to the emergence of these paradigms, analyze the impacts that these shifts have had on literature in each field, and explore implications for future research, policy, and practice.

Historical Trends
Positive Psychology

In 1998, while president of the American Psychological Association, Martin Seligman stated that "psychology has moved too far away from its original roots, which were to make the lives of all people more fulfilling and productive, and too much toward the important, but not all-important,

area of curing mental illness" (Seligman, 1999, p. 559). Seligman called for a "reoriented science that emphasizes the understanding and building of the most positive qualities of an individual" (Seligman, 1999, p. 559), which he called "positive psychology." Although other researchers (cf. Maslow, 1954) had called for greater attention to be paid to the positive within psychology, it was not until Seligman's call that "positive psychology" began to receive significant and organized attention from psychology scholars.

Seligman and Csikszentmihalyi (2000) elaborated, "before World War II, psychology had three distinct missions: curing mental illness, making the lives of all people more productive and fulfilling, and identifying and nurturing high talent" (p. 6) but a number of factors following the war led to the focus of psychology narrowing, with the greatest emphasis in the field placed on curing mental illness. Two highly influential factors included the founding of the Veterans Administration, which provided funding for treating mental illness, and the founding of the National Institute of Mental Health, which provided funding for researching mental illness.

These factors led to psychology adopting, in large part, a disease model of human functioning (Linley, Joseph, Harrington, & Wood, 2006). Although research that focused on making life productive and fulfilling and nurturing high talent continued, it was a minority in the field. Psychology primarily focused on the "dark side of human existence" (Snyder & McCullough, 2000, p. 151), where:

> Human beings were seen as passive foci: Stimuli came on and elicited "responses," or external "reinforcements" weakened or strengthened "responses," or conflicts from childhood pushed the human being around. Viewing the human being as essentially passive, psychologists treated mental illness within a theoretical framework of repairing damaged habits, damaged drives, damaged childhoods and damaged brains. (Seligman, 1998a, p. 2)

Seligman's call for positive psychology had a substantial impact on psychology. Although research on constructs associated with positive attributes and values had existed throughout the history of psychology, never before had a positive, strengths-based model of understanding human functioning, rather than a disease model, been described and systematically integrated into research and practice in the field. And, since Seligman's presidential address, there has been, as some researchers characterize it, an "explosion" of research on positive psychology (Yen, 2010).

In 2000, in a special issue of *American Psychologist*, Seligman and Csikszentmihalyi (2000) introduced positive psychology and presented 15 articles that described constructs that fit within the positive psychology paradigm. Since that time, dozens of general and specialized (e.g., social psychology, clinical psychology, humanistic psychology, behavioral psychology, school psychology) psychology journals have published special issues or special sections on positive psychology (Linley et al., 2006). In a recent review, Hart and Sasso (2011) found that more than 20,000 articles had been published in the area of positive psychology between 1998 and 2009, with a steady growth in the number of publications since Seligman gave his presidential address in 1998. In 2006, *The Journal of Positive Psychology* published its first issue and has continued to publish theory and research in positive psychology.

As with research, a number of scholarly books have been published that describe the science of positive psychology. *The Oxford Handbook of Positive Psychology* (Snyder & Lopez, 2002), now in its second edition (Lopez & Snyder, 2009), defines positive psychology and constructs included within its parameters. Specialized handbooks have been published, including the present text, as well as others on topics ranging from work and positive psychology (Linley, Harrington, & Garcea, 2009) to positive psychology in schools (Gilman, Huebner, & Furlong, 2009). Texts have been published on methods (Ong & van Dulmen, 2006) and assessment in positive psychology (Lopez & Snyder, 2003). Books have been published on positive psychology coaching (Biswas-Diener, 2010), flourishing (Keyes & Haidt, 2003), and authentic happiness (Seligman, 2003), just to name a few. *Character Strengths and Virtues: A Handbook and Classification* (Peterson & Seligman, 2004) was published as a definition and classification system for strengths and virtues, much like the *Diagnostic and Statistical Manual* defines and classifies mental disorders. Undergraduate textbooks in positive psychology have been developed (Baumgardner, 2008; Peterson, 2006; Snyder, Lopez, & Pedrotti, 2010), and courses are offered at universities all over the United States and Europe. In fact, at Harvard, positive psychology has been identified as one of the most popular undergraduate courses (Yen, 2010). The Clifton Strengths School (http://www.strengths.org/) was established to support strengths-based education and development. Gallup polls the hope, engagement, and well-being of youth grades 5–12 across the nation (http://www.gallupstudentpoll.com/home.aspx). Research centers on positive psychology have been funded, such as the Positive Psychology Center at the University of Pennsylvania (http://www.ppc.sas.upenn.edu/). A yearly Positive Psychology Summit has been held since 1999, bringing together scholars interested in positive psychology. Multiple foundations and federal agencies, including the Annenberg Foundation, the Templeton Foundation, the Gallup Foundation, and the U.S. Department of Education, have funded grants on positive psychology research (Seligman, Park, & Peterson, 2005). Positive psychology has received significant attention in the popular media; *Time* magazine has covered positive psychology (Wallis, 2005, 2009). Researchers have presented on daytime news programs (e.g., *Good Morning America*), and multiple lay websites and blogs have emerged. Clearly, since 1998, there has been a substantial increase and interest in positive psychology research.

Definitional Framework

Positive psychologists assert that positive psychology is not meant to supplant the disease model of human functioning but, instead, to create a new paradigmatic lens through which to view psychology (Snyder & Lopez, 2002). In early writings on positive psychology, Seligman (1998b) defined the mission of positive psychology as "to measure, understand and then build the human strengths and the civic virtues" (p. 2). People are viewed "as decision makers, with choices, preferences, and the possibility of becoming masterful, efficacious, or in malignant circumstances, helpless and hopeless" (Seligman & Csikszentmihalyi, 2000, p. 8). Seligman and Csikszentmihalyi (2000) characterized positive psychology as focusing on three "pillars": valued subjective experience, positive individual traits, and civic values and the institutions that support them.

However, as in any new field, the parameters of positive psychology are still being defined. Multiple definitions of positive psychology and the constructs included in its parameters exist (Hart & Sasso, 2011). Some definitions align with the three pillars offered by Seligman and Csikszentmihalyi (2000), others focus on a specific pillar, and still others focus on specific aspects of "the good life," such as happiness, fulfillment, and flourishing. The degree and manner in which positive psychology focuses on "problems" is also a matter of debate. Positive psychology has been criticized by researchers and the popular media alike for adopting a "Pollyanna" view, ignoring the negative issues in life (Lazarus, 2003) or focusing on "happiology" or a hedonic happiness that promotes passive, wishful thinking and coping only in those who are already living "the good life" (VanNuys, 2010a, 2010b). But, as Diener (2009) writes, "positive psychologists do not ignore the negative in life. However, they maintain that often one form of solution to problems, and in some cases the most effective one, is to build on the positive rather than directly work on the problem" (p. 10). Diener and others assert that positive psychology does not ignore problems; it simply searches for strengths-based approaches for addressing problems. But Diener also states that "we have for too long focused almost exclusively on the negative and on problems, and that positive aspects of humans are at least equally important, if not more so" (p. 10). Thus, an emerging consensus appears to be that positive psychology focuses on the positive in life—the things that make life good—but also explores ways to approach problems that emerge in life from a positive, strengths-based perspective.

Given the multiple frameworks forwarded in the literature for positive psychology, Hart and Sasso (2011) did a content analysis of definitions of positive psychology in the published literature (identified through PsycINFO searches), in course syllabi, and in undergraduate textbooks in the United States and Canada. Despite slight differences in the themes in the definitions across the sources and across countries, there was general consistency. They identified six themes across the 53 definitions of positive psychology forwarded in the published literature from PsycINFO: (a) virtues, character strengths, positive personality traits, abilities, and talents; (b) happiness, positive emotional well-being, fulfillment, and quality of life; (c) development processes associated with growth, fulfillment, actualization of potential, and the authentic self; (d) the good life or the life worth living; (e) thriving and flourishing, and (f) resilience or adaptive functioning/behavior. The first two themes dominated the literature, found in 40% and 34% of definitions, respectively, although the remaining themes were also frequently noted, ranging from 11% to 21% of the definitions. Hart and Sasso argue that the first five themes correspond to two of the pillars of positive psychology identified by Seligman and Csikszentmihalyi (2000) in their definition of positive psychology: positive subjective experiences and positive personal traits. However, Seligman and Csikszentmihalyi's third pillar—positive institutions—was not well represented in the definitions forwarded in the literature. Instead, another theme that was not clearly defined in the original framework emerged—resiliency under conditions of adversity. Notably, although research on the other themes steadily increased since Seligman's 1998 presidential address, research on resiliency showed a very large gain in publications in the 2000s, suggesting increased attention to this body of research in recent years (Hart & Sasso, 2011). This may correspond with researchers expanding the framework of positive psychology, as suggested by Diener (2009), to include both positive constructs and positive approaches/responses to problems or challenging situations.

Clearly, the diversity of research suggests, as do Hart and Sasso (2011), that positive psychology focuses on more than "the study of 'enjoyable feelings' and 'happy thinking' in fortunate people who are privileged to live in pleasant circumstances." It also has an increasing focus on "morphing of the experience of suffering, and...[transforming] the conditions that give rise to this suffering" to create a "subjective sense of meaning and a purpose and a style of virtuous living marked by a quest for authenticity" (p. 91).

Included constructs and approaches. As described previously, there are emerging themes that define the field of positive psychology; any construct or approach that focuses on "what makes life most worth living" (Snyder & Lopez, 2009, p. xxiii) and approaches this from a scientific perspective has the potential to be included in the positive psychology movement. And it is likely that the breadth and scope of included constructs will change over time. In the first special issue of *American Psychologist* (2000) devoted to positive psychology, a handful of constructs were identified that fit within the pillars of positive psychology. For example, articles were included on positive experiences: subjective well-being (Diener, 2000), optimal experience (Massimini & Delle Fave, 2000), optimism (Peterson, 2000), and happiness (Myers, 2000); and on positive traits: self-determination (Ryan & Deci, 2000), wisdom (Baltes & Staudinger, 2000), mature defenses (Vaillant, 2000), and exceptional performance (Lubinski & Benbow, 2000; Simonton, 2000). The first edition of *The Oxford Handbook of Positive Psychology* (Snyder & Lopez, 2002) included an even more diverse array of constructs that fit within the parameters of positive psychology. The second edition of the *Handbook* (Lopez & Snyder, 2009) includes 65 chapters on topics ranging from emotional intelligence (Salovey, Mayer, Caruso, & Yoo, 2009) to creativity (Simonton, 2009), love (Hendrick & Hendrick, 2009), humility (Tangney, 2009), and to happiness and positive growth after physical disability (Dunn, Uswatte, & Elliott, 2009). The *Handbook* even includes chapters on biological approaches to positive psychology, such as the role of neuropsychology in understanding positive affect (Isen, 2009) and the role of the heart in generating and sustaining positive emotions (McCraty & Rees, 2009). Given the newness of the positive psychology field, it is likely that there will be expansion and contraction of the constructs identified as key to prompting "the good life." Key future research directions may include exploring the relationships among various positive constructs and the degree to which diverse experiences and traits are associated with positive outcomes. Other key issues may include integrating research and practice, as well as integrating diverse lines of research across disciplines and subfields that contribute to understanding the good life (Lopez, 2009).

Paradigms of Disability

Within the disability field, a deficit-based model has also dominated modern (and historical) paradigms of disability. Commonly called the *medical* or *functional limitations model*, the focus here was on an "abnormality or deficiency…held to be central to

actions, experiences, and social identity. The underlying physical or biological defect is considered the primary causal source of an individual's enduring state of limitation in thinking and acting within the social world. An imperfection within the individual…results in actions or behaviors that fall significantly short of what one would want or expect" (Danforth, 2001, p. 349). The medical model of disability led to disability being viewed as a trait rather than a state of functioning (Luckasson et al., 1992), with a narrow focus on identifying, quantifying, and remediating the deficits experienced by the individual. For example, for persons with intellectual disability, the predominant focus throughout much of the 20th century was on quantifying intellectual functioning through IQ scores to identify the extent of the intellectual deficit and ascribe interventions to remediate the problem based on the level of intellectual functioning (Snell et al., 2009; Wehmeyer et al., 2008). And, if the deficit could not be remediated (or was perceived to be unremediable), people with disabilities were often placed in segregated institutions, schools, and classrooms. Several sources detail the impact of these deficit-based conceptualizations of intellectual disability in the late 19th and 20th century (Scheerenberger, 1983; Trent, 1994; Wehmeyer & Patton, 2000).

During the latter part of the 20th century, social and political movements within the disability field drew increased attention to the role of the environment in shaping the experiences of people with disabilities and began to shift conceptualizations of disability in the field. These social and political movements included the disability rights movement (Shapiro, 1993), which defined disability as a form of diversity and the barriers experienced by people with disabilities not as inherent to the individual but as a result of oppression and discrimination from a society that did not integrate and accommodate people who learned, moved, and interacted in diverse ways. The normalization (Nirje, 1969; Wolfensberger, 1972) and deinstitutionalization (Bradley, 1994) movements brought increased attention to the inherent rights of people with disabilities to live, learn, work, and play in typical environments. The self-advocacy and self-determination movements (Ward, 2005; Wehmeyer, Bersani, & Gagne, 2000) brought attention to the right of people with disabilities to be causal agents in their own lives. Principles and practices related to universal design (Connell et al., 1997) and universal design for learning (Rose & Meyer, 2002) highlighted how modifying environments to make them more physically and cognitively accessible could significantly change the experiences of people with disabilities.

These movements brought increased attention to the range of factors that impacted the functioning of people with disabilities—especially the influence of the environment. Whereas previous conceptualizations of disability placed exclusive focus on the physical or biological difference and remediating that difference, new conceptualizations of disability emphasized the person-environment interaction and incorporated a social-ecological model of human functioning (Bronfenbrenner, 1979; Shogren et al., 2009). This model of disability acknowledges that people with disabilities experience differences in functioning that can impact their functioning in a given environment. A functional limitation is defined as "the effect of specific impairments on the performance or performance capability of the person" (Luckasson et al., 1992, p. 10). However, a disability is the "expression of such a limitation in a social context" (Luckasson, 1992, p. 10). Disability is not the same as a functional impairment nor is it a trait inherent to a person; instead, disability is a state of functioning resulting from the interaction of functional limitations and environmental demands. Further, although people with disabilities do have functional limitations, it is also important to note that this conceptualization of disability recognizes that the functional limitations are only one aspect of a person's capabilities. In defining intellectual disability, for example, a key assumption in the application of the definition is that "within an individual, limitations often coexist with strengths" (Schalock et al., 2010, p. 1).

Thus, a new framework for understanding disability has emerged that recognizes that disability is influenced by a range of factors, internal and external to the individual. A functional limitation is simply one of many internal factors that influence the functioning of people with disabilities in the multiple environments in which they live, learn, work, and play. This model, which is referred to as a *social-ecological model* (Buntinx & Schalock, 2010; Schalock et al., 2010) or a *biopsychosocial approach* (World Health Organization, 2007), emphasizes the interaction between diverse personal capabilities and environmental demands and acknowledges the multidimensional nature of human functioning. It shifts the focus from remediating a limitation to identifying "mismatches" between personal capabilities and environmental demands as a means to identify supports needed to optimize functioning in valued contexts to promote subjective personal outcomes, including quality of life (Schalock et al., 2010).

Definitional Framework

Since the latter part of the 20th century, the social-ecological model of disability has received increased attention in the disability filed. The model emphasizes the interactive effects of personal capabilities (which can include both limitations and strengths in functioning) and the demands of the environment. Essentially, disability exists when there is a mismatch between a person's capacities and the demands of the environment. This social-ecological model has been integrated into the World Health Organization's *International Classification of Impairment, Disability and Health* (ICF; World Health Organization, 1980, 2001, 2007) since the 1980s, as well as into the American Association on Intellectual and Developmental Disabilities' (AAIDD) conceptual framework of human functioning since 1992 (Luckasson et al., 2002; Luckasson et al., 1992; Schalock et al., 2010). In these frameworks, disability is viewed as a universal human experience, something that anyone can experience if there are changes in personal capabilities or environmental demands. For example, the *International Classification of Functioning, Disability and Health* (ICF; World Health Organization, n.d.) states that "disability is not something that only happens to a minority of humanity. The ICF thus 'mainstreams' the experience of disability and recognises it as a universal human experience. By shifting the focus from cause to impact it places all health conditions on an equal footing" (World Health Organization, n.d.).

By focusing on the universality of disability and the interactive role of personal capabilities and environmental demands, the social-ecological model incorporates a multidimensional approach to human functioning. For example, the AAIDD conceptual framework of human functioning (Schalock et al., 2010) includes five dimensions: intellectual abilities, adaptive behavior, health, participation, and context. The ICF framework (World Health Organization, 2007) focuses on bodily functions and structures, activities and participation, and personal and environmental factors. Other sources more fully describe and compare these models (Buntinx & Schalock, 2010; Schalock et al., 2010; World Health Organization, 2001). However, a key emphasis in each framework is that each individual has a unique profile of strengths and functional limitations across the domains of human functioning.

The social-ecological approach significantly changes the way that we approach diagnosing, classifying, and supporting people with disabilities. Rather than view disability as a defect that resides within the person and that needs to be remediated, the social-ecological model emphasizes the importance of identifying mismatches between personal capacities and environmental demands and identifying the supports needed to address these mismatches. It: "(a) exemplifies the interaction between the person and their environment; (b) focuses on the role that individualized supports can play in enhancing individual functioning; and (c) allows for the pursuit and understanding of 'disability identity' whose principles include self-worth, subjective well-being, pride, common cause, policy alternatives, and engagement in political action" (Schalock, Luckasson et al., 2007, p. 117).

From a social-ecological perspective, the ultimate goal of identifying disability is to build systems of supports that promote optimal human functioning. The purpose of diagnosis and classification is to identify needed supports to enhance human functioning (Thompson et al., 2009). These supports may be instruction to promote new skill development, environmental modifications through universal design, natural supports, technology supports, or any other resources and strategies to "promote the development, education, interests, and personal well-being of an individual and that enhance human functioning" (Schalock et al., 2010, p. 175). Unlike the medical model, the focus is not on remediating the deficit (although this might happen). Instead, the focus is on identifying the demands of the environments where the individual lives, works, learns, and plays and identifying the supports that will lead to optimal functioning in those environments.

The social-ecological model also shifts the focus from the outcome of promoting "normal" or "typical" human functioning (which was, by and large, the goal of the medical model) to promoting personally defined quality-of-life outcomes referenced to individually valued environments. Quality of life has become a key indicator of personal outcomes in the disability field (Schalock, Gardner, & Bradley, 2007). In the disability field, quality of life is defined by three factors with eight associated domains: independence (associated with the domains of personal development, self-determination); social participation (interpersonal relations, social inclusion, rights); and well-being (emotional well-being, physical well-being, material well-being) (Schalock, Bonham, & Verdugo, 2008). Consistent with the

social-ecological model, quality of life is believed to be influenced by personal characteristics and environmental factors, and quality of life is assessed primarily through self-report measures of perceived well-being on indicators of each domain, although objective assessment through direct observation can also be incorporated into quality-of-life assessment, particularly for people with significant disabilities. A key aspect of assessing quality of life is to provide information on the subjective experiences of people with disabilities to provide a framework for quality improvement in supports and services (Schalock et al., 2008; Schalock et al., Verdugo, Jenaro, Wang, Wehmeyer, Xu et al., 2005).

Thus, under a social-ecological framework, the primary purpose of identifying functional limitations is to understand mismatches between personal capabilities and environmental demands so that a personalized system of support can be developed that will promote valued personal outcomes. The AAIDD (Schalock et al., 2010; Thompson et al., 2009) has developed a process for assessing, planning, monitoring, and evaluating individualized supports that begins with identifying desired life experiences and goals, moves on to assessing supports needed to achieve these desired life experiences and goals, and then developing, implementing, and evaluating a plan to make those outcomes occur. This process clarifies that the only purpose of identifying deficits or limitations experienced by an individual in a given environment is to develop a profile of needed supports to promote optimal human functioning. It also emphasizes the importance of building on strengths and capacities that an individual has to promote personally valued outcomes.

Parallel Directions

As described in the previous sections, both the disability and psychology fields have undergone significant changes in recent history. Although these changes mostly occurred independently of each other (i.e., there was limited overlap in the research and political agendas of leaders in the positive psychology and disability fields), there is conceptual overlap in the factors that contributed to the emergence of these new paradigms and the key concepts associated with each paradigm.

In both psychology and disability, until the latter part of the 20th century, a deficit model of human functioning dominated, with a narrow focus on identifying and describing problems in functioning (i.e., mental illness, functional limitations). Although some researchers studied positive aspects of functioning, research and practice were dominated by deficit-based models. Relatedly, there was a focus on remediating problems rather than promoting optimal human functioning. This led, at times, to narrow interventions that focused simply on curing a problem rather than on promoting optimal functioning and "the good life." Finally, rarely studied were the positive aspects of life (e.g., positive traits or experiences) or the optimal growth and development for people with and without disability.

In response to these issues, and because of the limited ability to work to promote quality of life or "the good life" when starting from a focus on deficits, both fields began to shift toward a more comprehensive framework of human functioning, attempting to understand "the *complete* human condition" (Gable & Haidt, 2005, p. 109). In positive psychology, this involved infusing more of a focus on positive experiences, traits, and institutions. In the disability field, this involved acknowledging the multidimensionality of human functioning, the presence of strengths and limitations within each individual, and the influence of the environment in shaping experiences and creating support needs. Both fields also began to focus on outcome variables that did not simply target the absence of mental illness or disability, but instead emphasized positive subjective experiences, including quality of life and subjective well-being. The ultimate goal of each area was to identify positive approaches to promoting optimal functioning for all individuals.

Intersection of Positive Psychology and Disability

Clearly, the emergence of positive psychology and the social-ecological model of disability were shaped by limitations of previous paradigms in the psychology and disability fields. Clear also is that there is significant overlap in the focus of positive psychology and the social-ecological model of disability—promoting positive experiences and the good life. However, there are differences. Psychology is a much broader field. Positive psychologists describe the importance of promoting the good life for all people and often emphasize the importance of including people who do not experience mental illness. Lopez and Gallagher (2009) write, "People not suffering from a mental disorder, more than 80% of the population on a given day, are trying to make sense of the work and use available information to make a good life. Positive psychology science and practice is accessible and . . . meets the daily needs of 'normal' people" (p. 4).

The disability field, by definition, focuses on people who experience disability or are at risk for disability, including people who experience mental illness. However, divisions between "normal" and "non-normal" are increasingly rejected in the disability field. Instead, a social-ecological perspective emphasizes that disability is a part of the continuum of human experience, something that anyone can experience or be impacted by in some way (e.g., family member, friend). Further, evidence-based practices created for people with disabilities can have applicability and relevance for all people (e.g., universal design and universal design for learning). People with disabilities may need more intensive supports to achieve optimal functioning, but no matter where a person falls on the continuum, everyone needs support to achieve optimal functioning, and the most useful way to provide this support may be to focus on building on strengths and promoting positive traits and experiences. From this perspective, it becomes about identifying positive, strengths-based approaches to promote the good life for all people, including those who experience disability. However, this framework has not yet been widely acknowledged within positive psychology, with a few notable exceptions (Dunn et al., 2009; Shogren, Lopez, Wehmeyer, Little, & Pressgrove, 2006)

In summary, within positive psychology and disability, an increased emphasis has been placed on recognizing the entire range of human functioning and supporting all people by using strengths-based approaches to achieve a good life. The focus in neither field is on fixing problems (although this can happen along the way to building a good life), but instead is on creating this good life using positive, proactive approaches that build on positive traits and experiences through the creation of positive institutions.

From medical → social model model

Effect on the Literature

In the previous sections, the historical trends in psychology and disability that led to the emergence of positive psychology and the social-ecological model of disability were analyzed and parallel directions and intersections identified. In this section, the effect that these two movements have had on the literature in the psychology and disability field is analyzed.

Effect on Psychology Literature

As briefly described in the previous section, researchers have begun to quantify the effect that positive psychology has had on scholarship in psychology. Hart and Sasso (2011), in a review of the positive psychology literature, found more than

20,000 articles published since Seligman's 1998 presidential address, with a steady increase in articles over time. Other researchers have investigated the permeation of positive psychology within specific subfields of psychology. For example, Lopez et al. (2006) examined the degree to which positive psychology constructs were represented in the published literature in four main counseling psychology journals. They found substantial increases in the number of articles in the counseling psychology literature that emphasized positive constructs over time. In the 1950s, only 16% of articles focused on positive constructs; by the 1970s, this percentage had increased to 23% of articles; by the 1990s, 34% of articles; and by the 2000s, 40% of articles. The most commonly studied positive constructs included values/ethics, self-efficacy, self-esteem, achievement, adjustment, coping, and empathy.

Schmidt and colleagues (2011) undertook a similar analysis in the subfield of health psychology and replicated the pattern of increases documented by Lopez et al. (2006). Schmidt et al. reviewed three primary health psychology journals and found that a 227% increase in the number of articles focused on constructs related to optimal human functioning between 1996–2000 and 2001–2005. The most frequently studied positive constructs included social support, coping, well-being, self-efficacy, quality of life, locus of control, positive affect, adjustment, treatment adherence, and self-esteem. Interestingly, a majority of articles (57%) that focused on positive constructs did so in populations that had some form of diagnosis (i.e., a medical disease, impairment, or disability). The remaining articles focused on promoting optimal health in individuals without diagnoses.

However, in a review in the subfield of school psychology, researchers found a slightly different pattern. Froh, Scott, Youssef, and Conte (2011) examined four guild journals in school psychology over a 50-year period. They found limited change over time in the degree to which the literature published in these journals focused on positive constructs and processes. For example, in the 1960s, 33% of articles had a positive focus; in the 1980s, 28%; in the 1990s, 25%; and in the 2000s, 27%. These numbers suggest that, unlike in the field of psychology as a whole and the subfields of counseling and health psychology, school psychology has not experienced a shift in the positive focus of the literature over the past 50 years. A quarter to a third of articles published over time in these guild journals have focused on positive constructs and processes.

The most frequently positive construct/process was achievement, distantly followed by adjustment and competency. Froh et al. suggest that this may result from the historic (and continued) emphasis in school psychology on psychoeducational problems and the process of diagnosing and remediating problems.

Thus, although within the field of psychology as a whole and within two specific subfields there has been a substantial impact of positive psychology on the literature, there appears to be variation across different subfields, perhaps influenced by the characteristics of those subfields.

Positive Psychology Constructs and Processes in the Disability Literature

Given the concurrent trends in psychology and disability emphasizing a positive, strengths-based perspective to understanding human functioning and the theoretical overlap just described, it is also important to explore the degree to which positive constructs and processes have permeated the disability literature. Shogren, Wehmeyer, Pressgrove, and Lopez (2006) reviewed the application of positive psychology constructs to research in the intellectual disability subfield between 1975 and 2004. We selected five top journals in the intellectual disability field: *American Journal of Intellectual and Developmental Disabilities (AJIDD), Education and Training in Autism and Developmental Disabilities (ETADD), Intellectual Disability (ID), Research and Practice for Persons with Severe Disabilities (RPSD),* and *Research in Developmental Disabilities (RIDD).* We reviewed one randomly selected issue of each journal from 1975 to 2004 (with the exception of RIDD, which was first published in 1980, and RPSD, which was first published in 1976), resulting in a total of 144 journals and 1,124 research articles or literature reviews/program descriptions. Each article was coded across multiple dimensions (see Shogren, Wehmeyer et al. [2006] for a full description of the methods) relevant to the adoption of a strengths perspective and the inclusion of positive psychology constructs in intellectual disability research. First, each article was reviewed to determine if it focused on human capacities of people with intellectual disability (not family members, other support providers, or systems). A human capacity was defined as "the ability to perform or produce or the innate potential for growth, development, or accomplishment (American Heritage Dictionary of the English Language, 2000)" (Shogren, Wehmeyer et al., 2006, p. 340). Articles that focused on human capacities in people with intellectual disability were coded to determine if they adopted a strengths perspective, a deficits perspective, a mixed, or a neutral perspective to understanding human capacity. A strengths perspective was defined as "locating and developing personal and social resources and adaptive tendencies so that the person can be assisted in making more effective use of them (Super, 1955, p. 5)," whereas a deficits perspective was coded when "articles focused on quantifying deficits in a given aptitude or ability and developing strategies to remediate this lack of aptitude or ability" (Shogren, Wehmeyer et al. 2006, p. 340). Articles that adopted a strengths or a mixed perspective were further coded to determine if they incorporated a construct associated with positive psychology.

Of articles that focused on a human capacity in people with intellectual disability, 35% of articles adopted a strengths perspective; however, this focus changed significantly over time, from a low of 22% of articles in 1975–1984 to a high of 50% of articles in 1995–2004. Of these articles, 15% included a construct associated with positive psychology as a primary focus over time, but, as has been found by other researchers (Lopez et al., 2006; Schmidt et al., 2011), this focus shifted over time. From 1975 to 1984, only 9% of articles focused on a positive psychology construct; from 1985 to 1995, 15% of articles had this focus; and from 1995 to 2004, 24% of articles. The most frequently cited positive psychology constructs included personal control (13% of articles), personal relationships (10%), and interpersonal skills (5%). Interestingly, happiness, one of the most frequent themes in positive psychology research and definitions, was only included in 1% of studies.

We also explored the degree to which articles focused on key dimensions of human functioning identified in the AAIDD conceptual framework of human functioning: intellectual abilities, adaptive behavior, participation, interaction and social roles, and health. Historically, articles focused on intellectual abilities were the most common, likely because of the focus on IQ testing and classification by levels of intelligence in the intellectual disability field. However, over time, the number of articles focused on the other dimensions increased significantly, suggesting more emphasis being placed on the multidimensionality of human experience for people with intellectual disability. These findings suggest that there has been a significant shift in the disability field, with more focus on a strengths-based perspective incorporating positive psychology constructs that focus on the multidimensionality of human experiences. This shift is consistent with the shift in the psychology field and the subfields of counseling psychology and health psychology toward a focus on positive constructs and processes.

Indications are that a greater emphasis continues to be placed on research focused on building on strengths and positive psychology constructs and processes in the disability field. Recently, authors have argued for the importance of positive psychology in rehabilitation psychology, a subfield of psychology that focuses on disability-related issues (Ehde, Frank, Rosenthal, & Caplan, 2010) and described how acquired disability can contribute to positive development (Dunn et al., 2009). The application of positive psychology has been explored for specific disability groups, including those that experience intellectual disability (Dykens, 2006; Shogren, Lopez et al., 2006), dual diagnoses of intellectual disability and mental illness (Baker & Blumberg, 2011), spinal cord injury (Catalano, Chan, Wilson, Chiu, & Muller, 2011; Smedema, Catalano, & Ebener, 2010), physical disability (Quale & Schanke, 2010), and stroke (Berges, Seale, & Ostir, 2011).

Inclusion of Disability Issues in the Positive Psychology Literature

It is also important, given the aforementioned intersections of positive psychology and a social-ecological model of disability, to understand the degree to which disability issues have permeated the positive psychology literature. To date, there has been no review of the infusion of disability issues in the broader field of positive psychology.

Review of The Journal of Positive Psychology. To provide initial insight into the degree to which disability issues have permeated the positive psychology literature, I reviewed abstracts of articles published in *The Journal of Positive Psychology* since its inception in 2006 (through volume 6, issue 2) to determine the extent to which articles focused on (a) the application of positive psychology constructs and processes to people with disabilities and (b) the degree to which people with disabilities were included in research on positive psychology constructs and processes relevant for all people (e.g., if people with disabilities mentioned as a subgroup or part of a sample included in research studies or reviews). Clearly, there are limitations in the interpretation of this cursory review. There are a number of specialized disability journals that researchers may gravitate to when publishing work specific to disability. Further, positive psychology research is also published in many other sources in the psychology field. Additionally, only abstracts were reviewed, so it is possible that further discussion of subpopulations was contained in the article. However, this review provides initial insight into the inclusion of disability issues in the leading positive psychology journal.

I found a limited, but promising, focus on disability issues within *The Journal of Positive Psychology*. Of the 162 articles published in *The Journal of Positive Psychology* from 2006 to 2011 (vol. 2), six abstracts (4% of articles) explicitly mentioned people with disabilities or people with health-related issues that could be associated with disability. Of the six articles, the majority focused on specific health-related conditions that may be associated with disability (e.g., asthma, chronic illness, and cancer). For example, Peterson, Park, and Seligman (2006) explored the relationship of character strengths to recovery from illness. They analyzed the relationship between adults with physical illness and psychological disorders and found associations between a history of these conditions and character strengths including beauty, curiosity, and love of learning. They also found that when people did not "recover" from their illnesses, they had decreased life satisfaction, and these researchers concluded that recovering from illness could benefit character.

Reynolds and Lim (2007) studied how art could promote positive well-being for women living with cancer, especially when this fit with their skills, personal values, and models of managing adversity. Berg and colleagues (2007) analyzed adherence to medical treatments in children with asthma and found that hope was a significant predictor of adherence. Pavot and Diener (2008) reviewed the literature on the Satisfaction with Life Scale (Diener, Emmons, Larson, & Griffin, 1985) and explored the application of the construct of life satisfaction to multiple populations, including those experiencing significant health concerns. Weis and Ash (2009) explored the influence of hopefulness on treatment outcomes for adolescents referred to psychotherapy and found that when youth and parents were hopeful about treatment, better outcomes resulted. Finally, Shogren, Lopez, Wehmeyer, Little, and Pressgrove (2006) examined the degree to which positive psychology constructs (hope, optimism, locus of control, and self-determination) predicted life satisfaction in adolescents with and without cognitive disabilities (e.g., learning disabilities, intellectual disability). They found that the same constructs were being measured in both groups, and that hope and optimism predicted life satisfaction in youth with and without cognitive disabilities. However, there were mean level differences across youth with and

without cognitive disabilities in self-determination, hope, and locus of control, but not in optimism and life satisfaction, suggesting the influence of personal capabilities and environmental demands.

These six articles demonstrate that there are researchers in the field of positive psychology who are interested in disability-related issues and who view disability issues as a part of positive psychology. Although articles that specifically mentioned disability or conditions that could be associated with disability were a minority in the field, this could be expected because of the vast range of issues encompassed within the field of positive psychology. However, it is important to note that the majority of the articles that highlighted issues related to disability published in *The Journal of Positive Psychology* focused on health-related conditions that may or may not lead to disability in different environmental contexts (e.g., cancer, asthma). Furthermore, several of the articles focused on the role of positive psychology constructs in "recovery" or "treatment" to remediate conditions (Peterson et al., 2006; Weis & Ash, 2009), rather than focusing on building a good life when living with a disability. Also of note is the fact that disability was rarely mentioned as a part of the range of the human experience in articles focused on other positive psychology constructs and processes for the general population.

Future Directions

As mentioned in the preceding sections, there have been parallels in the emergence of positive psychology and a social-ecological model in the disability field. However, with a few notable exceptions, there has been little discussion of the overlap of these two paradigms and how they might intersect to promote positive outcomes for all people, including those who experience disability. In analyzing the degree to which these paradigms have permeated research in the psychology and disability fields, it is clear that there has been a substantial impact. Furthermore, it appears that disability issues are receiving attention within the broader field of positive psychology. However, there are clearly more avenues for the mutual engagement of researchers in positive psychology and disability to promote the good life and optimal functioning for all people, including people with disabilities.

First, a vision articulated by positive psychologists is that positive psychology can "unify" psychology, creating a framework for researchers from various subfields to come together and study "the *complete* human condition" (Gable & Haidt, 2005, p. 109).

Clearly, disability issues fit within this unified mission. If positive psychologists accept disability as part of the universal human experience, then the impact of positive psychology constructs and processes for all people, including people with disabilities, can become part of this unified mission. Further, the social-ecological model and the frameworks derived from it focus on the multidimensional nature of human functioning, a perspective that would enhance the ability of positive psychology researchers to look at the multiple internal and external factors that influence optimal functioning in all people.

Second, although the disability field is moving toward a social-ecological model, with its emphasis on individualized, strengths-based interventions, there is still significant room for growth in the degree to which positive psychology constructs and processes are studied in relation to disability. Although positive constructs like quality of life (Schalock et al., 2002; Schalock, Verdugo, Jenaro, Wang, Wehmeyer, Jiancheng et al., 2005; Wang, Schalock, Verdugo, & Jenaro, 2010) and satisfaction with life (Pavot & Diener, 2008; Shogren, Lopez et al., 2006) have been researched in recent years with people with disabilities, other constructs that have received significant attention in positive psychology (e.g., happiness, flow, optimism) have not yet been extensively researched. However, researchers have started to explore ways to measure and promote happiness in people with disabilities, even in those with the most significant disabilities (Lancioni, Singh, O'Reilly, Oliva, & Basili, 2005; Lancioni et al., 2007) and have explored the application of happiness (Dykens, 2005) and hope (Lloyd & Hastings, 2009; Ogston, Mackintosh, & Myers, 2011) to parents and siblings of people with disabilities. Greater collaboration and unification of research among disability and positive psychology scholars could advance these efforts. Furthermore, given the focus on unification in positive psychology, rather than defining, assessing, and intervening to promote happiness and hope in people with disabilities and their families separately, integrating research across the range of human experience holds promise to enable an analysis of the complete human condition, for all people, not just a select few.

Third, one of the initial pillars of positive psychology introduced by Seligman and Csikszentmihalyi (2000) was *positive institutions*, which they defined as "institutions that move individuals toward better citizenship: responsibility, nurturance, altruism, civility, moderation, tolerance, and work ethic" (p. 5). Reviews of positive psychology research

(Hart & Sasso, 2011), however, have suggested that less research has been devoted to building positive institutions, with more emphasis being placed on positive traits and subjective experiences. The social-ecological model, however, brings increased focus to the role of the environment and the institutions within the environment. People with (and without) disabilities interact with many "institutions" to access the supports they need to promote optimal functioning. As well, a great deal of research has occurred within the disability field on ways to shift organizations that previously used a deficit model to become ones that focus on individualized supports and services to promote valued life outcomes (Bradley, 1994; Bradley & Moseley, 2007; Shogren et al., 2009). This work could inform efforts to reform multiple institutions within our society, ranging from education to health care, to long-term supports and services to create an environment supportive of valued outcomes for all citizens. This focus may also facilitate more change in those subfields of psychology, such as school psychology, that are strongly influenced by institutions (i.e., the education system), thus promoting better outcomes for all youth served by those institutions.

A greater infusion of disability within positive psychology also has the potential to bring greater attention to the role of supports in promoting optimal functioning for all individuals. The role of supports in addressing the mismatch between personal capabilities and environmental demands for people with disabilities was discussed earlier, but it is important to emphasize that the role of supports in enhancing human functioning is not specific to disability. All of us benefit when we have supports available to address mismatches between our capabilities and environmental demands, regardless of whether these mismatches define a "disability." People with disabilities simply have a greater need for support because of their functional limitations, but there is room for increased attention to the importance of understanding person-environment fit for all people and for building strengths-based approaches to addressing the mismatches that we all experience in certain environments. This may even help address emerging criticisms of positive psychology that suggest too limited a focus on the role of contextual factors (McNulty & Fincham, 2011).

Conclusion

In conclusion, the fields of disability and psychology have undergone significant changes. Both fields have moved from a deficit-driven perspective to focus more comprehensively on the complete human condition, including positive constructs and processes and strengths-based approaches to promoting optimal functioning and the good life. However, these changes have largely occurred in parallel, despite overlapping concepts. In fact, within positive psychology, the degree to which "adversity" or "disability" fits within its parameters has been questioned. And, within the disability field, although functional limitations are acknowledged as a defining feature of disability, more emphasis is being placed on viewing disability not as a pathology to be fixed but as a difference in functioning that is part of the continuum of human experience, something that anyone can experience with changes in personal capabilities or environmental demands. This perspective has the potential to open up a new perspective within positive psychology. Disability does not have to be viewed simply as a form of adversity or as an area within which to study resilience, but rather as one aspect of human functioning that can inform positive growth and development, particularly when strengths-based approaches aiming to build individualized supports that promote optimal human functioning are created within positive institutions and contexts.

References

Baker, D. J., & Blumberg, E. R. (2011). Positive psychology for persons with intellectual or developmental disabilities. In R. J. Fletcher (Ed.), *Psychotherapy for individuals with intellectual disability* (pp. 67–90). Kingston, NY: NADD.

Baltes, P. B., & Staudinger, U. M. (2000). Wisdom: A meta-heuristic (pragmatic) to orchestrate mind and virtue toward excellence. *American Psychologist, 55*(1), 122–136.

Baumgardner, S. C., M. (2008). *Positive psychology.* Englewood Cliffs, NJ: Prentice Hall.

Berg, C. J., Rapoff, M. A., Snyder, C. R., & Belmond, J. M. (2007). The relationship of children's hope to pediatric asthma treatment adherence. *The Journal of Positive Psychology, 2*(3), 176–184.

Berges, I.-M., Seale, G., & Ostir, G. V. (2011). Positive affect and pain ratings in persons with stroke. *Rehabilitation Psychology, 56*(1), 52–57.

Biswas-Diener, R. (2010). *Practicing positive psychology coaching: Assessment, diagnosis and intervention.* Hoboken, NJ: John Wiley & Sons.

Bradley, V. J. (1994). Evolution of a new service paradigm. In V. J. Bradley, J. W. Ashbaugh & B. C. Blaney (Eds.), *Creating individual supports for people with developmental disabilities: A mandate for change at many levels* (pp. 11–32). Baltimore: Brookes

Bradley, V. J., & Moseley, C. (2007). National core indicators: Ten years of collaborative performance measurement. *Intellectual and Developmental Disabilities, 45*, 354–358.

Bronfenbrenner, U. (1979). *The ecology of human development: Experiments by nature and design.* Cambridge: Harvard University Press.

Buntinx, W. H. E., & Schalock, R. L. (2010). Models of disability, quality of life, and individualized supports: Implications for professional practice in intellectual disability. *Journal of Policy and Practice in Intellectual Disabilities, 7*(4), 283–294.

Catalano, D., Chan, F., Wilson, L., Chiu, C.-Y., & Muller, V. R. (2011). The buffering effect of resilience on depression among individuals with spinal cord injury: A structural equation model. *Rehabilitation Psychology, 56*(3), 200–211.

Connell, B. R., Jones, M., Mace, R., Mueller, J., Mullick, A., Ostroff, E., et al. (1997). The principles of universal design. Retrieved January 2, 2011, from http://www.ncsu.edu/ncsu/design/cud/about_ud/udprinciplestext.htm

Danforth, S. (2001). A pragmatic evaluation of three models of disability in special education. *Journal of Development and Physical Disabilities, 13*(4), 343–359.

Diener, E. (2000). Subjective well-being: The science of happiness and a proposal for a national index. *American Psychologist, 55*(1), 34–43.

Diener, E. (2009). Positive psychology: Past, present, and future. In S. J. Lopez & C. R. Snyder (Eds.), *The Oxford handbook of positive psychology* (2nd ed., pp. 7–11). Oxford: Oxford University Press.

Diener, E., Emmons, R. A., Larson, R. W., & Griffin, S. (1985). The Satisfaction with Life scale. *Journal of Personality Assessment, 49,* 71–75.

Dunn, D. S., Uswatte, G., & Elliott, T. R. (2009). Happiness, resilience, and positive growth following physical disability: Issues for understanding, research, and therapeutic research. In S. J. Lopez & C. R. Snyder (Eds.), *The Oxford handbook of positive psychology* (2nd ed., pp. 651–664). Oxford: Oxford University Press.

Dykens, E. M. (2005). Happiness, well-being, and character strengths: Outcomes for families and siblings of persons with mental retardation. *Mental Retardation, 43*(5), 360–364.

Dykens, E. M. (2006). Toward a positive psychology of mental retardation. *American Journal of Orthopsychiatry, 76*(2), 185–193.

Ehde, D. M., Frank, R. G., Rosenthal, M., & Caplan, B. (2010). Application of positive psychology to rehabilitation psychology. In R. G. Frank, M. Rosenthal & B. Caplan (Eds.), *Handbook of rehabilitation psychology* (2nd ed., pp. 417–424). Washington, DC: American Psychological Association.

Froh, J. J., Scott, H. E., Youssef, A.-J., & Conte, V. (2011). Acknowledging and appreciating the full spectrum of the human condition: School psychology's (limited) focus on positive psychological functioning. *Psychology in the Schools, 48*(2), 110–123.

Gable, S., & Haidt, J. (2005). What (and why) is positive psychology? *Review of General Psychology, 9,* 103–110.

Gilman, R., Huebner, E. S., & Furlong, M. J. (Eds.). (2009). *Handbook of positive psychology in schools.* New York: Routledge.

Hart, K. E., & Sasso, T. (2011). Mapping the contours of contemporary positive psychology. *Canadian Psychology, 52*(2), 82–92.

Hendrick, C., & Hendrick, S. S. (2009). Love. In S. J. Lopez & C. R. Snyder (Eds.), *The Oxford handbook of positive psychology* (2nd ed., pp. 447–454). Oxford: Oxford University Press.

Isen, A. M. (2009). A role for neuropsychology in understanding the facilitating influence of positive affect on social behavior and cognitive processes. In S. J. Lopez & C. R. Snyder (Eds.), *The Oxford handbook of positive psychology* (2nd ed., pp. 503–518). Oxford: Oxford University Press.

Keyes, C. L. M., & Haidt, J. (Eds.). (2003). *Flourishing: Positive psychology and the life well-lived*. Washington, DC: American Psychological Association.

Lancioni, G. E., Singh, N. N., O'Reilly, M. F., Oliva, D., & Basili, G. (2005). An overview of research on increasing indices of happiness of people with severe/profound intellectual and multiple disabilities. *Disability and Rehabilitation: An International, Multidisciplinary Journal, 27*(3), 83–93. doi: 10.1080/09638280400007406

Lancioni, G. E., Singh, N. N., O'Reilly, M. F., Sigafoos, J., Didden, R., Oliva, D., et al. (2007). Effects of micro-switch-based programs on indices of happiness of students with multiple disabilities: A new research evaluation. *American Journal on Mental Retardation, 112*(3), 167–176. doi: 10.1352/0895-8017(2007)112[167:eompoi]2.0.co;2

Lazarus, R. S. (2003). Does the positive psychology movement have legs? *Psychological Inquiry, 14*, 93–109.

Linley, P. A., Harrington, S., & Garcea, N. (Eds.). (2009). *Handbook of positive psychology and work*. New York: Oxford University Press.

Linley, P. A., Joseph, S., Harrington, S., & Wood, A. M. (2006). Positive psychology: Past, present, and (possible) future. *The Journal of Positive Psychology, 1*(1), 3–16.

Lloyd, T. J., & Hastings, R. (2009). Hope as a psychological resilience factor in mothers and fathers of children with intellectual disabilities. *Journal of Intellectual Disability Research, 53*(12), 957–968. doi: 10.1111/j.1365-2788.2009.01206.x

Lopez, S. J. (2009). The future of positive psychology: Pursuing three big goals. In S. J. Lopez & C. R. Snyder (Eds.), *The Oxford handbook of positive psychology* (2nd ed., pp. 689–694). Oxford: Oxford University Press.

Lopez, S. J., & Gallagher, M. W. (2009). A case for positive psychology. In S. J. Lopez & C. R. Snyder (Eds.), *The Oxford handbook of positive psychology* (2nd ed., pp. 3–11). Oxford: Oxford University Press.

Lopez, S. J., Magyar-Moe, J. L., Petersen, S. E., Ryder, J. A., Krieshok, T. S., O'Byrne, K. K., et al. (2006). Counseling psychology's focus on positive aspects of human functioning. *Counseling Psychologist, 34*(2), 245–259.

Lopez, S. J., & Snyder, C. R. (Eds.). (2003). *Positive psychological assessment: A handbook of models and measures*. Washington, DC: American Psychological Association.

Lopez, S. J., & Snyder, C. R. (Eds.). (2009). *The Oxford handbook of positive psychology* (2nd ed.). Oxford: Oxford University Press.

Lubinski, D., & Benbow, C. P. (2000). States of excellence. *American Psychologist, 55*(1), 137–150.

Luckasson, R., Borthwick-Duffy, S., Buntinx, W. H. E., Coulter, D. L., Craig, E. P. M., Reeve, A., et al. (2002). *Mental retardation: Definition, classification, and systems of support* (10th ed.). Washington, DC: American Association on Mental Retardation.

Luckasson, R., Coulter, D. L., Polloway, E. A., Reiss, S., Schalock, R. L., Snell, M. E., et al. (1992). *Mental retardation: Definition, classification, and systems of supports* (9th ed.). Washington, DC: American Association on Mental Retardation.

Maslow, A. H. (1954). *Motivation and personality*. Oxford, England: Harpers.

Massimini, F., & Delle Fave, A. (2000). Individual development in a bio-cultural perspective. *American Psychologist, 55*(1), 24–33.

McCraty, R., & Rees, R. A. (2009). The central role of the heart in generating and sustaining positive emotions. In S. J. Lopez & C. R. Snyder (Eds.), *The Oxford handbook of positive psychology* (2nd ed., pp. 527–536). Oxford: Oxford University Press.

McNulty, J. K., & Fincham, F. D. (2011). Beyond positive psychology: Toward a contextual view of psychological processes and well-being. *American Psychologist, 67*, 101–110. doi: 10.1037/a0024572

Myers, D. G. (2000). The funds, friends, and faith of happy people. *American Psychologist, 55*(1), 56–67.

Nirje, B. (1969). The normalization principle and its human management implications. In R. B. Kugel & W. Wolfensberger (Eds.), *Changing residential patterns for the mentally retarded* (pp. 179–186). Washington, DC: President's Committee on Mental Retardation.

Ogston, P. L., Mackintosh, V. H., & Myers, B. J. (2011). Hope and worry in mothers of children with an autism spectrum disorder or down syndrome. *Research in Autism Spectrum Disorders, 5*(4), 1378–1384. doi: 10.1016/j.rasd.2011.01.020

Ong, A., & van Dulmen, M. H. M. (Eds.). (2006). *The Oxford handbook of methods in positive psychology*. Oxford: Oxford University Press.

Pavot, W., & Diener, E. (2008). The Satisfaction with Life Scale and the emerging construct of life satisfaction. *The Journal of Positive Psychology, 3*(2), 137–152.

Peterson, C. (2000). The future of optimism. *American Psychologist, 55*(1), 44–55.

Peterson, C. (2006). *A primer in positive psychology*. New York: Oxford University Press.

Peterson, C., Park, N., & Seligman, M. E. P. (2006). Greater strengths of character and recovery from illness. *The Journal of Positive Psychology, 1*(1), 17–26.

Peterson, C., & Seligman, M. E. P. (2004). *Character strengths and virtues: A classification and handbook*. New York: Oxford University Press/Washington, DC: American Psychological Association.

Quale, A. J., & Schanke, A.-K. (2010). Resilience in the face of coping with a severe physical injury: A study of trajectories of adjustment in a rehabilitation setting. *Rehabilitation Psychology, 55*(1), 12–22.

Reynolds, F., & Lim, K. H. (2007). Turning to art as a positive way of living with cancer: A qualitative study of personal motives and contextual influences. *The Journal of Positive Psychology, 2*(1), 66–75.

Rose, D., & Meyer, A. (2002). *Teaching every student in the digital age*. Alexandria, VA: ASCD.

Ryan, R. M., & Deci, E. L. (2000). Self-determination theory and the facilitation of intrinsic motivation, social development, and well-being. *American Psychologist, 55*(1), 68–78.

Salovey, P., Mayer, J. D., Caruso, D., & Yoo, S. H. (2009). The positive psychology of emotional intelligence. In S. J. Lopez & C. R. Snyder (Eds.), *The Oxford handbook of positive psychology* (2nd ed., pp. 237–248). Oxford: Oxford University Press.

Schalock, R. L., Bonham, G. S., & Verdugo, M. A. (2008). The conceptualization and measurement of quality of life: Implications for program planning and evaluation in the field of intellectual disabilities. *Evaluation and Program Planning 31*, 181–190.

Schalock, R. L., Borthwick-Duffy, S., Bradley, V., Buntix, W. H. E., Coulter, D. L., Craig, E. P. M., et al. (2010). *Intellectual disability: Definition, classification, and systems of support* (11th ed.). Washington, DC: American Association on Intellectual and Developmental Disabilities.

Schalock, R. L., Brown, I., Brown, R., Cummins, R. A., Felce, D., Matikka, L., et al. (2002). Conceptualization, measurement, and application of quality of life for persons with intellectual disabilities: Report of an international panel of experts. *Mental Retardation, 40*(6), 457–470. doi: 10.1352/0047-6765(2002)040<0457:cmaaoq>2.0.co;2

Schalock, R. L., Gardner, J. F., & Bradley, V. (2007). *Quality of life: Applications for people with intellectual and developmental disabilities*. Washington, DC: American Association on Intellectual and Developmental Disabilities.

Schalock, R. L., Luckasson, R. A., Shogren, K. A., with, Borthwick-Duffy, S., Bradley, V., et al. (2007). The renaming of *mental retardation*: Understanding the change to the term *intellectual disability*. *Intellectual and Developmental Disabilities, 45*, 116–124.

Schalock, R. L., Verdugo, M. A., Jenaro, C., Wang, M., Wehmeyer, M., Jiancheng, X., & Lachapelle, Y. (2005). Cross-cultural study of quality of life indicators. *American Journal on Mental Retardation, 110*(4), 298–311. doi: 10.1352/0895-8017(2005)110[298:csoqol]2.0.co;2

Schalock, R. L., Verdugo, M. A., Jenaro, C., Wang, M., Wehmeyer, M. L., Xu, J., & Lachapelle, Y. (2005). A cross-cultural study of quality of life indicators. *American Journal on Mental Retardation, 110*, 298–311.

Scheerenberger, R. C. (1983). *A history of mental retardation*. Baltimore: Brookes.

Schmidt, C. K., Raque-Bogdan, T. L., Piontkowsi, S., & Schaefer, K. L. (2011). Putting the positive in health psychology: A content analysis of three journals. *Journal of Health Psychology, 16*(4), 607–620.

Seligman, M. E. P. (1998a). Building human strength: Psychology's forgotten mission. *APA Monitor, 29*(1), 2.

Seligman, M. E. P. (1998b). What is the 'good life'? *APA Monitor, 29*(10), 2.

Seligman, M. E. P. (1999). The President's address. *American Psychologist, 54*(8), 559–562.

Seligman, M. E. P. (2003). *Authentic happiness: Using the new positive psychology to realize your potential for lasting fulfillment*. New York: Free Press.

Seligman, M. E. P., & Csikszentmihalyi, M. (2000). Positive psychology: An introduction. *American Psychologist, 55*(1), 5–14.

Seligman, M. E. P., Park, N., & Peterson, C. (2005). Positive psychology progress: Empirical validation of interventions. *American Psychologist, 60*(5), 410–421.

Shapiro, J. P. (1993). *No pity: People with disabilities forging a new civil rights movement*. New York: Three Rivers Press.

Shogren, K. A., Bradley, V., Gomez, S. C., Yeager, M. H., Schalock, R. L., et al., with Wehmeyer, M. L. (2009). Public policy and the enhancement of desired outcomes for persons with intellectual disability. *Intellectual and Developmental Disabilities, 47*(4), 307–319.

Shogren, K. A., Lopez, S. J., Wehmeyer, M. L., Little, T. D., & Pressgrove, C. L. (2006). The role of positive psychology constructs in predicting life satisfaction in adolescents with and without cognitive disabilities: An exploratory study. *The Journal of Positive Psychology, 1*, 37–52.

Shogren, K. A., Wehmeyer, M. L., Pressgrove, C. L., & Lopez, S. J. (2006). The application of positive psychology and self-determination to research in intellectual disability: A content analysis of 30 years of literature *Research and Practice for Persons with Severe Disabilities, 31*, 338–345.

Simonton, D. K. (2000). Creativity: Cognitive, personal, developmental, and social aspects. *American Psychologist, 55*(1), 151–158.

Simonton, D. K. (2009). Creativity. In S. J. Lopez & C. R. Snyder (Eds.), *The Oxford handbook of positive psychology* (2nd ed., pp. 261–269). Oxford: Oxford University Press.

Smedema, S. M., Catalano, D., & Ebener, D. J. (2010). The relationship of coping, self-worth, and subjective well-being: A structural equation model. *Rehabilitation Counseling Bulletin, 53*(3), 131–142. doi: 10.1177/0034355209358272

Snell, M. E., Luckasson, R. A., with, Borthwick-Duffy, S., Bradley, V., Buntix, W. H. E., et al. (2009). The characteristics and needs of people with intellectual disability who have higher IQs. *Intellectual and Developmental Disabilities, 47*(3), 220–233.

Snyder, C. R., & Lopez, S. J. (Eds.). (2002). *Handbook of positive psychology*. London: Oxford University Press.

Snyder, C. R., Lopez, S. J., & Pedrotti, J. T. (2010). *Positive psychology: The scientific and practical explorations of human strengths* (2nd ed.). Thousand Oaks, CA: Sage.

Snyder, C. R., & McCullough, M. E. (2000). A positive psychology field of dreams: "If you build it, they will come...." *Journal of Social and Clinical Psychology, 19*(1), 151–160.

Super, D. E. (1955). Transition: from vocational guidance to counseling psychology. *Journal of Counseling Psychology, 2*, 3–9.

Tangney, J. P. (2009). Humility. In S. J. Lopez & C. R. Snyder (Eds.), *The Oxford handbook of positive psychology* (2nd ed., pp. 483–490). Oxford: Oxford University Press.

Thompson, J. R., Bradley, V., Buntinx, W. H. E., Schalock, R. L., Shogren, K. A., Snell, M. E., et al. (2009). Conceptualizing supports and the support needs of people with intellectual disability. *Intellectual and Developmental Disabilities, 47*(2), 135–146.

Trent, J. W. (1994). *Inventing the feeble mind: A history of mental retardation in the United States*. Berkley, CA: University of California Press.

Vaillant, G. E. (2000). Adaptive mental mechanisms: Their role in a positive psychology. *American Psychologist, 55*(1), 89–98.

VanNuys, D. (2010a, November 15). Popping the happiness bubble: The backlash against positive psychology (Part 2). *Psychology Today*.

VanNuys, D. (2010b, November 3). Popping the happiness bubble: The backlash against positive psychology (Part 1). *Psychology Today*.

Wallis, C. (2005, January 17). The Science of Happiness. *Time, 165*(3), A2-A9.

Wallis, C. (2009). The Science of Happiness Turns 10: What Has It Taught? *Time*. Retrieved from http://www.time.com/time/health/article/0,8599,1908173,00.html

Wang, M., Schalock, R. L., Verdugo, M. A., & Jenaro, C. (2010). Examining the factor structure and hierarchical nature of the quality of life construct. *American Journal on Intellectual and Developmental Disabilities, 115*(3), 218–233. doi: 10.1352/1944-7558-115.3.218

Ward, M. J. (2005). An historical perspective of self-determination in special education: Accomplishments and challenges. *Research and Practice for Persons with Severe Disabilities, 30*, 108–112.

Wehmeyer, M. L., Bersani, H., Jr., & Gagne, R. (2000). Riding the third wave: Self-determination and self-advocacy in the 21st century. *Focus on Autism and Other Developmental Disabilities, 15*(2), 106–115.

Wehmeyer, M. L., Buntix, W. H. E., Lachapelle, Y., Luckasson, R. A., Schalock, R. L., Verdugo, M. A., et al. (2008). The intellectual disability construct and its relation to human functioning. *Intellectual and Developmental Disabilities, 46,* 311–318.

Wehmeyer, M. L., & Patton, J. R. (Eds.). (2000). *Mental retardation in the 21st century.* Austin, TX: Pro-ed.

Weis, R., & Ash, S. E. (2009). Changes in adolescent and parent hopefulness in psychotherapy: Effects on adolescent outcomes as evaluated by adolescents, parents, and therapists. *Journal of Positive Psychology, 4*(5), 356–364.

Wolfensberger, W. (1972). *Normalization: The principle of normalization in human services.* Toronto: National Institute on Mental Retardation.

World Health Organization. (1980). *The international classification of impairment, disability and handicap.* Geneva: Author.

World Health Organization. (2001). *International classification of functioning, disability, and health* Geneva: Author.

World Health Organization. (2007). *International classification of functioning, disability and health: Children and youth version.* Geneva: Author.

World Health Organization. (n.d.). International Classification of Functioning, Disability and Health (ICF) Retrieved September 2, 2011, from http://www.who.int/classifications/icf/en/

Yen, J. (2010). Authorizing happiness: Rhetorical demarcation of science and society is historical narratives of positive psychology. *Journal of Theoretical and Philosophical Psychology, 30,* 67–78.

PART 2

Application of Positive Psychological Constructs to Disability

The Impact of the Quality of Life Concept on the Field of Intellectual Disability

Robert L. Schalock *and* Miguel Angel Verdugo Alonso

Abstract

This chapter focuses on five significant impacts that the quality of life (QOL) concept has had on persons with intellectual and closely related developmental disabilities (IDD). The chapter begins with a discussion of paradigms and paradigmatic shifts and explores how the current IDD paradigm has altered the conceptual and service delivery framework that mediates the interaction between a scientist or practitioner and persons with IDD. The second section describes the five significant impacts the QOL concept has had on public and organization policies and practices toward persons with IDD. The chapter concludes by asking a simple question: "Has the QOL concept really made a difference?"

Key Words: continuous quality improvement, evidence-based practices, individualized supports, quality of life, redefined organizations

Over the past three decades, a significant paradigm shift has occurred in public policies and practices regarding people with intellectual and closely related developmental disabilities (IDD), one that parallels the paradigmatic shift in psychology toward positive psychology. The concept of quality of life (QOL) has been integral to this paradigm shift, along with the development of an ecological model of disability and the provision of individualized supports. The power of the QOL concept is that it integrates these two paradigm shifts and, in the process, has become a change agent in the redefinition of organizations and systems that provide services and supports to people with IDD.

This chapter focuses primarily on five significant effects that the concept of QOL has had on people with IDD. The chapter begins with a discussion of paradigms and paradigmatic shifts and how the current IDD paradigm has altered the conceptual and service delivery framework that mediates the interaction between a scientist or practitioner and persons with IDD. The second section describes five significant impacts that the QOL concept has had on public and organization policies and practices toward persons with IDD. These five effects of the QOL concept include fostering the provision of individualized supports, furthering the development of evidence-based practices, encouraging the evaluation of personal outcomes, providing a quality framework for continuous quality improvement, and becoming a major catalyst in the redefinition of organizations and systems providing services and supports to persons with IDD. The chapter concludes by asking a simple question: "Has the QOL concept really made a difference?"

Much of the material presented in this chapter is based on the collaborative work of the two authors and their colleagues who have focused over the past three decades on the conceptualization, measurement, application, and evaluation of the QOL construct as applied to persons with IDD.

Throughout the chapter, *individual-referenced QOL* is defined as:

> A multidimensional phenomenon composed of core domains influenced by personal characteristics and environmental factors. These core domains are the same for all people, although they may vary individually in relative value and importance. The assessment of quality of life domains is based on culturally sensitive indicators.

For the interested reader, parallel developments and the application of family-related QOL can be found in Brown, Schalock, and Brown (2009), Isaacs, Clark, Correia, and Flannery (2009), and Summers et al. (2005).

The QOL Concept and the Paradigm Shift in Public Policy and Practices

A paradigm can be defined as a constellation of beliefs and techniques that reflect an approach to an issue and provide a pattern or example. The notion of a paradigm and paradigm shift was first introduced by Kuhn (1970), in reference to a conceptual scheme that mediates the interaction between the scientist and the world. More recently, the notion of a paradigm shift has been discussed in reference to revolutions in the history and philosophy of science (Weinert, 2009).

A significant paradigm shift has occurred over the past three decades in how we view and interact with persons with IDD. The three phases of this paradigm shift in public policies and practices are:

• *Phase I (1960s and 1970s).* Doubts and difficulties (i.e., a "crisis") arose regarding the then-current paradigm, which was characterized by viewing disability as a defect in the person and segregating persons with IDD from the mainstream of life.
• *Phase II (1970s and early 1980s).* An "anomaly" occurred due to a persistent disagreement between the pre-1960s paradigm and personal observations of the lives of persons with IDD and invalid predictions regarding their potential. The anomaly was reinforced based on results of the civil rights and deinstitutionalization movements, the focus on adaptive behavior and the learning potential of persons with IDD, the beginning of the self-advocacy movement, and the successful integration of persons with IDD into more normalized inclusive education, residential, vocational, and community-based environments.
• *Phase III (mid 1980s to present).* As a result of phase II factors, there emerged in the mid-1980s a new IDD paradigm based on social and scientific developments involving the investigation of the lives and perspectives of persons with IDD. This paradigm is characterized by its emphasis and focus on an ecological (i.e., person × environment) conception of disability and the provision of individualized supports within community and inclusive environments. It is important to note that the QOL concept also emerged in the 1980s and was thus well positioned to provide an overarching principle that integrated the current (phase III) IDD paradigm and also provided a common language across key stakeholders, a vehicle to implement the paradigm shift in public policies and practices, and a basis for policy development and evaluation (Schalock, Gardner, & Bradley, 2007).

The Concept of Quality of Life, the Ecological Model of Disability, and an Individualized System of Supports
The Concept of Quality of Life

Over the past three decades, the QOL concept has evolved from a sensitizing notion to a social construct that guides program practices, outcomes evaluation, and continuous quality improvement. The issue that the concept addresses is the lives of persons and ensuring that citizens with IDD experience "the good life." To this end, the QOL concept reflects the following four principles: (a) QOL is composed of the same factors and relationships for all people, (b) QOL is experienced when a person's needs are met and when that person has the opportunity to pursue life enrichment in major life activity settings, (c) QOL has both subjective and objective components, and (d) QOL is a multidimensional construct, influenced by individual and environmental factors. These four principles are congruent with a number of postmaterialist values that are impacting people throughout the world. Chief among these values are the emergence of cultural modernization tenets related to equality, personal freedom, and self-fulfillment; an emphasis on relationships, spirituality, networking, and ecological sustainability; the power of communitarianism and social capital; and the rise of responsible individualism and taking responsibility for the design of our personal and social futures.

Over the past two decades, the authors have developed and validated cross-culturally a QOL conceptual and measurement framework that is summarized in Table 4.1. In the framework depicted in Table 4.1, indicators refer to QOL-related perceptions,

Table 4.1 Quality of Life Conceptual and Measurement Framework

Factor	Domain	Exemplary Indicators
Independence	Personal Development	Activities of daily living
	Self-Determination	Choices, decisions, personal goals
Social Participation	Interpersonal Relations	Social networks, friendships
	Social Inclusion	Community involvement
	Rights	Human and legal
Well-Being	Emotional Well-Being	Safety and security
	Physical Well-Being	Health and nutrition status
	Material Well-Being	Financial status, employment

behaviors, and conditions that operationally define each QOL domain. Furthermore, psychometrically robust and culturally sensitive indicators are used to assess either the person's perceived well-being ("self-report") or an objective indication of the person's life experiences and circumstances ("direct observation"). More details about the development and validation of this framework can be found in Schalock, Keith, Verdugo, and Gomez (2010b), Schalock, Verdugo, Jenaro, Wang, Wehmeyer, Xu, and Lachapelle (2005), and Wang, Schalock, Verdugo, and Jenaro (2010).

Table 4.2 Relationship Between Quality of Life (QOL) Domains and United Nations (UN) Convention Articles

Domains of QOL	Indicators	UN articles	Other related articles
Personal Development	– Education status – Personal skills – Adaptive behavior	**24**	27
Self-Determination	– Choices/Decisions – Autonomy-Personal control – Personal goals	**14, 19, 21**	9, 12
Interpersonal Relations	– Social networks – Friendships – Social activities – Relationships	**23**	30
Social Inclusion	– Community integration/participation – Community roles – Supports	**8, 9, 18, 20, 27, 29, 30**	19, 21, 24
Rights	– Human (respect, dignity, equality) and legal (legal access, due process)	**5, 6, 7, 10, 11, 12, 13, 15, 22**	14, 16, 18, 21
Emotional Well-Being	– Safety and security – Positive experiences –Contentment-Lack of stress	**16, 17**	23, 25
Physical Well-Being	– Health and nutrition status – Recreation – Leisure	**16, 25, 26**	17
Material Well-Being	– Financial status – Employment status – Housing status – Possessions	**28**	

The QOL conceptual and measurement framework presented in Table 4.1 can also be used to integrate international disability policies (Verdugo, Navas, Gomez, & Schalock, in press). For example, Table 4.2 shows the relationship among the eight QOL domains listed in Table 4.1 and corresponding articles in the United Nations Convention on the Rights of Persons with Disabilities (2006).

The application of the QOL concept emphasizes person-centered planning and individualized supports based on the principles of human potential, inclusion, equity, self-determination, and the rights of citizenship. In addition, its application enhances well-being within cultural contexts; provides a basis for a multidimensional approach to the provision of individualized services and supports; should be evidence-based and have a prominent place in education and training; and should be applied across environments, all levels of intellectual and adaptive behavior limitations, and all dimensions of human functioning (Brown et al., 2009; Claes, van Hove, van Loon, Vandevelde, & Schalock, 2010).

The Ecological Model of Disability

The basic tenet of the current ecological model of disability is that human functioning is determined by an interaction between the person's capability and the performance demands of his or her environment. As we discuss later in reference to supports, the purpose of an individualized system of supports is to reduce the discrepancy or mismatch between an individual's capability and the requirements of his or her environment.

Both the World Health Organization through its *International Classification of Function* (ICF; World Health Organization [WHO], 2001) and the American Association on Intellectual and Developmental Disabilities (AAIDD) through its conceptual framework for human functioning (Schalock et al., 2010a) stress that human functioning is determined by interactions among:

• Health condition, body functions and structures, activities, participation, and context (WHO, 2001).
• Intellectual abilities, adaptive behavior, health, participation, context, and the pattern and intensity of support provision (Schalock et al., 2010a).

In both models, context includes personal and environmental factors. Personal factors or characteristics include gender, age, race/ethnicity, motivation, lifestyles, habits, coping styles, social background, education levels, and individual psychological assets. Environmental factors include public policies, attitudes toward people with IDD, and opportunities for community living/access, employment, and inclusive education.

The QOL model summarized in Table 4.1 and the ecological model of disability just described can be compared on a number of variables, such as their conceptual basis, content, assessment focus, intended purposes, and role of the person. This comparison is found in Table 4.3 (Buntinx & Schalock, 2010). As shown clearly in these comparisons, the integrative role of the QOL concept is to provide a conceptual basis for service delivery (i.e., to enhance human functioning and personal outcomes) and a measurement framework for assessing personal, QOL-related outcomes. The different roles of the person in the two models should not be overlooked.

Table 4.3 Comparison of the Quality of Life (QOL) Concept and the Ecological Model of Disability

Primary Component	Model	
	ICF/AAIDD	Quality of Life
Conceptual basis	Human functioning dimensions Functional limitations	Personal well-being
Content	Components of functioning	QOL factors and domains
Assessment focus	Strengths and limitations in functioning; contextual factors	Objective status & subjective personal experiences
Intended purpose	Description, classification (ICF) diagnosis, classification, and system of supports (AAIDD)	Framework for services and supports, personal outcomes evaluation, and quality improvement
Role of person	Secondary ("object of assessment")	Primary ("participant")

An Individualized System of Supports

This paradigmatic component focuses on the provision of individualized supports that reduce the discrepancy between a person's competence and the performance demands of his or her environment. The purposes of an individualized system of supports are to promote the development, education, interests and personal well-being of a person; to enhance human functioning and an individual's QOL; and to bridge between the present state of functioning ("what is") to a desired state of functioning ("what could be"). A brief summary of the conceptual basis, content, and implementation process components of the supports paradigm are summarized in Table 4.4 (Schalock & Verdugo, in press; Thompson et al., 2009).

Since its introduction into the IDD field in the mid-1980s, the concept of supports has been expanded to include a "system of supports" that provides a structure for the organization and enhancement of human performance elements that are interdependent and cumulative. The major components of such a system are summarized in Table 4.5

Table 4.4 Major Components of the Supports Paradigm

Conceptual Basis:

- Support needs: the pattern and intensity of supports necessary for a person to participate in activities linked with normative human functioning
- Supports: resources and strategies that aim to promote the development, education, interests, and personal well-being of an individual and to enhance human functioning
- A system of supports: planned and integrated use of individualized support strategies and resources that encompass the multiple aspects of human performance in multiple settings

Content:

- Assessed support needs in major life activity areas and exceptional medical and behavioral support needs
- Provision of a system of supports (see Table 4.5)

Implementation Process:

- Identify desired life experiences and personal goals
- Assess the pattern and intensity of the person's support needs
- Develop and implement an Individual Support Plan
- Monitor progress
- Evaluate personal outcomes

(Schalock et al., 2010a, Schalock & Verdugo, in press; Thompson et al., 2009).

The material summarized in Tables 4.4 and 4.5 clearly identifies two integrative roles that the QOL concept plays in the development, implementation, and evaluation of a system of supports. These two integrative roles are to provide a conceptual framework to develop an Individual Support Plan around the supports needed to enhance QOL domains and a measurement framework to evaluate the impact of the respective system components on personal, QOL-related outcomes.

In summary, the QOL concept has integrated important components of both an ecological model of disability and an individualized system of supports. In reference to the ecological model of disability, the QOL concept has provided a conceptual basis for service/supports delivery and a measurement framework for assessing personal, QOL-related outcomes and using that information for continuous quality improvement. In reference to an individualized system of supports, the QOL concept has provided a conceptual framework to develop individual support plans and a measurement framework to evaluate the impact of specific support strategies on personal outcomes. Because of these significant integrative functions, the QOL concept has impacted the IDD field in five specific ways. Specifically, and as discussed in the following section, it has: (a) fostered the provision of individualized supports, (b) furthered the development of evidence-based practices, (c) encouraged the assessment and evaluation of personal outcomes,

Table 4.5 Components to a System of Supports

Component	Examples
Technology-based	Assistive technology, information technology
Prosthetics	Sensory-motor devices, environmental accommodation
Staff directed	Incentives, skills/knowledge, positive behavior supports
Professional services	IT, physical therapy, occupational therapy, speech, medical, psychological, psychiatric
Natural supports	Family, friends, colleagues, generic agencies
Policies	Public policies and laws and organization policies

(d) provided a quality framework for continuous quality improvement, and (e) been a major catalyst in the redefinition of organizations and systems providing services and supports to persons with IDD.

The Five Effects of the QOL Concept on the Field of Intellectual Disability
Fosters the Provision of Individualized Supports

Table 4.4 summarized the major aspects of the supports paradigm, including its conceptual basis, intent, content, and implementation process. In addition to that information, it is also important to stress that a system of supports:

• Integrates the three systems that impact human functioning: the individual (microsystem), the organization (the mesosystem), and the larger society and culture (macrosystem).
• Aligns the individualized supports provided to the individual's personal goals and assessed support needs.
• Provides a structure for the organization or system to enhance human performance elements and impact positively a person's QOL.

Table 4.6 provides a template that shows how exemplary individualized supports, including those components of a system of supports summarized in Table 4.5, can be aligned with each of the eight QOL domains/outcome categories listed in Table 4.1. This alignment enhances the individual's functioning in regard to the respective domain. Evidence of the effectiveness of one or more of these individualized supports on enhancing QOL-related personal outcomes can be found in Bonham, Basehart, Marchand, Kirchner, and Rumenap (2004), Felce and Emerson (2005), Gardner and Caran (2005), Schalock et al. (2007), and Walsh, Emerson, Lobb, Hatton, Bradley, Schalock, and Moseley (2010).

Furthers the Development of Evidence-Based Practices

The importance of evidence-based practices has emerged as the current IDD paradigm and has impacted intervention and rehabilitation strategies based on the concept of QOL, the ecological model of disability, and the provision of individualized supports. As discussed by Schalock, Verdugo, and Gomez (2011) and Schalock and Verdugo (2012), evidence-based practices are those that are based on current best evidence and used as a basis to guide clinical, managerial, and policy decisions. Furthermore, current best evidence is that which

Table 4.6 Exemplary Support Strategies Aligned with Personal Outcome Categories

Personal Outcome Category	Exemplary Individualized Supports
Personal Development	Functional skill training, assistive and information technology, augmentative communication system
Self-Determination	Choice making, personal goals, decision making, personal involvement in the ISP process
Interpersonal Relations	Family involvement, circle of friends, natural supports
Social Inclusion	Community activities, volunteer activities, varied community roles, environmental accommodation, natural supports
Rights	Public and organization policies and practices built on QOL-related values, statutory rights
Emotional Well-Being	Safe and secure environment, positive feedback, positive behavior supports, professional services, incentives, predictable environment, self-identity mechanisms
Physical Well-Being	Health care, mobility assistance, prosthetics, health promotion programs, proper nutrition/diets
Material Well-Being	Ownership, employment, transportation

is obtained from credible sources that used reliable and valid methods and is based on a clearly articulated and empirically supported theory or rationale.

Three standards regarding evidence are generally used in the field: (a) quality, which refers to the experimental/research design used; (b) robustness, which refers to the magnitude of the observed effects; and (c) relevance, which relates to the purpose to which the evidence will be used (Schalock et al., 2011). As discussed later, the QOL concept has significantly impacted the relevance standard used to evaluate any particular evidence-based practice.

Determining the relevance of the evidence requires three cognitive skills that are increasingly being recognized as the cognitive engine driving the process of knowledge development and use: analysis, evaluation, and interpretation (Schalock & Verdugo, 2012). Analysis involves examining the evidence and its component parts and reducing the complexity of the evidence into simpler or more basic components or elements. The focus of the analysis should be on determining the degree of alignment among the practices in question, the evidence indicators, and the evidence-gathering strategy used. Evaluation involves determining the precision, accuracy, and integrity of the evidence through careful appraisal of the results of the evidence-gathering strategy. Interpretation involves evaluating the evidence in light of the practices in question, the intended application purpose(s), and the intended effect(s). Such interpretation should be guided by the person's perception of benefit versus cost, field congruence models (e.g., United Nations, 2006), and clinical judgment (Schalock & Luckasson, 2005).

Guidelines for evaluating the relevance of the evidence are just emerging in the IDD field. The following three guidelines are based on our reading of the evidence-based literature as it relates to making QOL-related clinical, managerial, and policy decisions.

1. For those making clinical decisions, information regarding specific evidence-based practices should facilitate more accurate diagnoses, the development of more functional and useful classification systems, and the provision of a system of supports based on the person's assessed support needs and personal goals. Additionally, information regarding the specific evidence-based practice should also assist the person in making personal decisions that are consistent with his or her values and beliefs. Examples include involving the person in decisions regarding informed consent, placement options, and the selection of service/support providers; agreeing to a specific intervention, such as medication; and/ or respecting the person's opinions regarding the intensity and duration of individualized supports.

2. For those making managerial decisions, relevant evidence identifies those policies and practices that enhance a program's effectiveness in terms of personal outcomes.

3. For those making policy decisions, relevant evidence is that which (a) supports and enables organizations to be effective, efficient, and sustainable; (b) impacts public attitudes about persons with IDD; (c) enhances both short- and long-term outcomes for persons with IDD; and (d) changes education and training strategies to focus on the sensitizing and practical implications of implementing the concept of QOL as a service delivery framework, the requirements of shifting attitudes and behaviors associated with the ecological model of disability, and the components of a system of supports.

Encourages the Evaluation of Personal Outcomes

National and international disability policy is currently premised on a number of concepts and principles that are person-referenced (such as self-determination, inclusion, empowerment, individual and appropriate services, productivity and contribution, and family integrating and unity) and system-referenced (such as antidiscrimination, coordination and collaboration, and accountability) (Stowe, Turnbull & Sublet, 2006; Shogren & Turnbull, 2010). Over time, as our understanding of disability and human functioning has deepened and become more progressive, these evolving core principles have fostered public policy that promotes change based on various types of information (e.g., research, evaluation, quality assessment). They have also increased the need to generate outcome data that operationalize the core principles guiding public policy. Such data help to assess the effectiveness of public policies and practices, which creates a feedback loop that can be used for continuous quality improvement.

One of the major impacts of the QOL concept in the field of IDD has been to provide both a conceptual and measurement framework for the assessment of personal outcomes. This framework was presented in Table 4.1. Personal outcomes are generally defined as valued personal experiences and circumstances that follow as a result or consequence of some activity, intervention, or service and are measured on the basis of QOL-related domains and indicators.

Key to this impact of the QOL concept has been the development and implementation of a number of QOL assessment instruments that allow organizations and systems to use a common approach to outcomes evaluation. Examples include the *Ask Me! Survey* (United States; Bonham et al., 2004), the *GENCAT* (Spain and South America; Verdugo, Arias, Gomez, & Schalock, 2010), *The Personal Outcomes Scale* (Belgium, the Netherlands, Taiwan, Mainland China; van Loon, van Hove, Schalock, & Claes, 2010), and the *Personal Outcomes Index* (Canada; Edmonton PDD, 2011). Each of these instruments has been developed and validated based on the QOL conceptual and measurement model summarized in Table 4.1 and is based on the QOL measurement principles listed in Table 4.7 and discussed more fully in Brown et al. (2009), Claes et al. (2010), and Verdugo, Schalock, Keith, and Stancliffe (2005).

Table 4.7 Quality of Life (QOL) Measurement Principles

• What to measure: QOL-referenced domains and indicators that reflect culturally based valued personal experiences and circumstances

---

• Item selection criteria: domain-referenced indicators that:
  • Reflect what people want in their lives
  • Reflect life experiences and circumstances that service/support providers have some control over
  • Can be used in a performance-based reporting, monitoring, evaluation, and quality enhancement system

---

• How to measure: subjective appraisal (e.g., satisfaction, importance) and objective assessment (e.g., objective indicators of personal experiences and life circumstances)

• Who should be involved in item selection and the assessment process: individuals with IDD and persons who know the individual best

---

• Where to assess: the natural environment

• When to assess: depends on questions asked (generally every 1.5 to 2 years)

• Research methods used: multivariate designs and observational studies that focus on individual and environmental predictors of personal outcomes and methods that take into account the importance of personal choice

Once an organization or system has implemented a standardized approach to assessing QOL-related personal outcomes, information from the assessment can be used for multiple purposes. Again, the QOL concept has impacted the field by providing a multiple perspective for the use of personal outcomes data at the individual, organization, and system levels. Chief among these uses are:

• At the individual level:
  • Provide feedback regarding the individual's status on the eight QOL domains
  • Establish an expectation that change is possible
  • Confirm that the organization/system serving the person is committed to a holistic approach
  • Compare subjective versus objective assessment information
• At the organization level:
  • Share outcome data and change over time
  • Determine the predictors of personal outcomes

• Use information about outcomes and their significant predictors as a basis for continuous quality improvement that involve data tutorials, right-to-left thinking, and targeting the significant predictor variables
• At the systems level:
  • Provide empirical benchmarks of the agency over time, the agency versus the larger system, and the agency/system versus the community
  • Provide an approach to outcomes evaluation and the assessment of personal outcomes that is consistent across agencies receiving funding
  • Evaluate the degree to which services provided to individuals are contributing to personal outcomes
  • Provide an avenue through which to engage agencies in discussions about how to enhance personal outcomes

Provides a Quality Framework for Continuous Quality Improvement

Continuous quality improvement can be defined as using tacit knowledge (i.e., that which comes from experience) and explicit knowledge (i.e., empirically based information) to enhance an organization's effectiveness in terms of enhancing personal outcomes and efficiency in terms of enhancing organization outputs (Schalock & Verdugo, 2012). Continuous quality improvement is based on values (such as dignity, equality, self-determination, nondiscrimination, and inclusion) and a set of strategies that focus on changing organization policies, practices, training, and use of technology that enhance personal outcomes and organization outputs.

A detailed discussion of continuous quality improvement is beyond the scope of this chapter. The interested reader is referred to Keith and Bonham (2005), Schalock, Verdugo, Bonham, Fantova, and van Loon (2008), and Schalock and Verdugo (2012) for that discussion. The following two examples demonstrate how the QOL concept has provided a framework for continuous quality improvement.

Quality improvement learning sessions. This approach uses the organization's profile of personal outcomes to provide data tutorials (i.e., describe what the data/information really means); share personal outcomes data across agencies so they can learn from one another; introduce empirical evidence, such as that presented in the second example; and engage in creative planning based on common data, shared experiences, empirical research, and right-to-left thinking

Targeting the predictors of personal outcomes. Over the past decade, QOL researchers have begun to identify personal, organization, and systems-level factors that are statistically related to assessed QOL-related personal outcomes. A general summary of this research is presented in Table 4.8, which that is based on the work of Schalock et al. (2008) and Walsh et al. (2010). Once the predictors are identified, then that information can be integrated into the quality improvement learning sessions just described.

A Catalyst for Redefining an Organization or System

Anyone reading this chapter who is familiar with the IDD field is aware of the significant changes that have occurred over the past three decades in the IDD-related service delivery system. Part of this change has been driven by the emergence of a wide range of community living and employment alternatives and some part is due to political and economic issues. The authors have identified a number of additional catalysts that include 21st-century thinking styles (i.e., systems thinking, alignment, and synthesis), changed leadership styles (e.g., mentoring and directing, coaching and instructing,

Table 4.8 Factors Significantly Affecting Quality of Life (QOL)-Related Personal Outcomes

Person-Level Factors:

• Health status
• Intellectual functioning and adaptive behavior level
• Amount of self-determination

Organization-Level Factors:

• Staff support strategies (e.g., facilitative assistance including communication support, ensuring a sense of basic security)
• Support staff characteristics (e.g., teamwork, job satisfaction, staff turnover, job stress, organization management practices)
• Employment programs (including opportunities for volunteerism)
• Home-like community living alternatives

Systems-Level Factors:

• Participation opportunities (e.g., contact with family members, friends, and people in one's social networks)
• Normalized community living arrangements
• Availability of public transportation

inspiring and empowering, and collaborating and partnering), the movement toward horizontally structured organizations and work groups, and the reward that comes from creativity and being part of a learning culture (Schalock & Verdugo, 2012).

We also feel that a major catalyst for this change has been the QOL concept, with its associated values of dignity, equality, empowerment, self-determination, nondiscrimination, and inclusion. This impact is reflected in:

• Increased consumer involvement in participatory action research, as reflected in the key involvement of persons with IDD in focus groups to identify culturally sensitive QOL indicators and as surveyors of QOL-related personal outcomes.

• Increased consumer membership on high-performance teams that are involved in the assessment of support needs, Individual Support Plan development and implementation, information gathering and analysis, outcomes evaluation, and quality improvement.

• Redefined ID/DD organizations that are characterized by being community-based and horizontally structured; having support coordinators, evidence-based practitioners, and knowledge producers; and being focused on continuous quality improvement.

Conclusion: Has the QOL Concept Made a Difference?

The paradigm that emerges from a "scientific revolution" has certain qualities, such as appearing to resolve issues that the previous paradigm could not, attracting converts because it is attractive and hopeful, and being sufficiently open ended so it is testable. These qualities certainly apply to the current IDD paradigm that is characterized by its QOL framework, an ecological model of disability, and the provision of individualized supports. These qualities also provide one or more criteria by which the current IDD paradigm can be evaluated.

In this final section, we ask the question, "Has the QOL concept really made a difference in the lives of persons with IDD?" In answering that question, we cannot separate out the interactive and cumulative effects of the other two components of the current IDD paradigm. Certainly, the ecological model of disability has significantly changed mental models regarding the potential of persons with IDD and the power of one's environment to enhance both a person's functional level and QOL. Similarly, the supports component of the paradigm has significantly changed the specific interventions and habilitation strategies provided by both organizations and systems serving individuals with IDD. What we can say about the QOL concept is that, based on our experiences over the past 30 years, the concept has made five significant contributions both to the lives of persons with IDD and their families and to the organizations and systems providing services and supports. The five significant contributions are:

1. The QOL concept has provided a service delivery framework that is based on the values of dignity, equality, empowerment, self-determination, nondiscrimination, and inclusion.

2. The QOL concept has provided an outcomes evaluation framework that focuses on evaluating QOL-referenced personal outcomes associated with each of the eight QOL domains, determining the significant predictors of those outcomes, and using that information for continuous quality improvement.

3. The measurement of QOL-related personal outcomes has documented short-term increases in most of the QOL domains. However, there is significant work that still needs to be done since most organizations and systems are just now beginning to assess these outcomes, including embarking on longitudinal assessment studies evaluating the long-term impacts (such as social-economic position, health, and subjective well-being) of services and supports.

4. The measurement of QOL-related personal outcomes has allowed organizations and systems to use a *balanced scorecard* approach to evaluation that permits multiple datasets that are used in program evaluation and development. Two obvious components of such an approach are subjective versus objective outcomes and short- versus long-term effects.

5. The QOL concept has become an organization- and systems-level change agent based on the administrative principles of individualization, collaboration and coordination, capacity building in reference to evaluation capability, program options, cultural responsiveness, and accountability.

Future Directions

Despite these five significant contributions, there are still a number of significant challenges that researchers and practitioners need to address regarding the efficacy of the QOL concept. Chiefly, does it solve the problems associated with the previous paradigm? Does it enhance human functioning, inclusion, and equity? Does it reduce the discrepancy between the valued personal outcomes for persons with IDD and those persons without a disability? And, does it enhance an organization's effectiveness and efficiency, and hence the organization's sustainability?

Paradigms are never static. They continue to evolve and change, based largely on how well they solve the issues and problems addressed. The current IDD paradigm, with its QOL framework, its ecological model of disability, and its commitment to the provision of individualized supports, is definitely impacting organizations and systems throughout much of the world in their provision of services and supports to persons with IDD. To what degree this paradigm and its components truly make a difference in the lives of persons with IDD depends on many players and partnerships: policy makers are critical; service and support providers are essential; persons with IDD and their families are critical players; and transdisciplinary and cross-cultural research is a must.

References

Bonham, G. S., Basehart, S., Schalock, R. L., Marchand, C. B., Kirchner, N., & Rumenap, J. M. (2004). Consumer-based quality of life assessment: The Maryland Ask Me! Project. *Mental Retardation, 42*(5), 338–355.

Brown, R. I., Schalock, R. L., & Brown, I. (2009). Quality of life: Its application to persons with intellectual disabilities and their families—introduction and overview. *Journal of Policy and Practice in Intellectual Disabilities, 6*(1) 2–6.

Buntinx, W. H. E., & Schalock, R. L. (2010). Models of disability, quality of life, and individualized supports: Implications for professional practice in intellectual disability. *Journal of Policy and Practice in Intellectual Disabilities, 7*(4), 283–294.

Claes, C., van Hove, G., van Loon, J., Vandevelde, S., & Schalock, R. L. (2010). Quality of life measurement in the field of intellectual disability: Eight principles for assessing quality of life-related outcomes. *Social Indicators Research, 98*, 61–75.

Edmonton PDD. (2011). *My life: Personal Outcomes Index.* Edmonton, Alberta, Canada: Author.

Felce, D., & Emerson, E. (2005). Community living: Costs, outcomes, and economies of scale: Findings from UK research. In R. Stancliffe and K. Lakin (Eds.), *Costs and outcomes of community services for people with intellectual disabilities* (pp. 45–62). Baltimore, MD: Brookes Publishing Co.

Gardner, J. F., & Caran, D. (2005). Attainment of personal outcomes by people with developmental disabilities. *Mental Retardation, 43*(3), 157–174.

Isaacs, B., Clark, C., Correia, S., & Flannery, J. (2009). Using quality of life to evaluate outcomes and measure effectiveness. *Journal of Policy and Practice in Intellectual Disabilities, 6*(1), 52–61.

Keith, K. D., & Bonham, G. S. (2005). The use of quality of life data at the organization and systems level. *Journal of Intellectual Disability Research, 49*(10), 799–805.

Kuhn, T. S. (1970). *The structure of scientific revolutions.* Chicago: University of Chicago Press.

Schalock, R. L., Borthwick-Duffy, S., Bradley, V. J., Buntinx, W. H. E., Coulter, D. L., Craig, et al. (2010a). *Intellectual disability Definition, classification, and systems of supports.* Washington, DC: American Association on Intellectual and Developmental Disabilities.

Schalock, R. L., Gardner, J. F., & Bradley, V. J. (2007). *Quality of life for persons with intellectual and other developmental disabilities: Applications across individuals, organizations, communities, and systems* Washington, DC: American Association on Intellectual and Developmental Disabilities.

Schalock, R. L., Keith, K. D., Verdugo, M. A., & Gomez, L. E. (2010b). Quality of life model development and use in the field of intellectual disability. In R. Kober (Ed.), *Enhancing the quality of life for people with intellectual disabilities: From theory to practice* (pp. 8–18). New York: Springer.

Schalock, R. L., & Luckasson, R. (2005). *Clinical judgment.* Washington, DC: American Association on Mental Retardation.

Schalock, R. L., & Verdugo, M. A. (2012). *A leadership guide to redefining ID/DD organizations: Eight successful change strategies.* Baltimore, MD: Brookes Publishing Co.

Schalock, R. L., Verdugo, M. A., Bonham, G. S., Fantova, F., & van Loon, J. (2008). Enhancing personal outcomes: Organization strategies, guidelines, and examples. *Journal of Policy and Practice in Intellectual Disabilities, 5,* 276–285.

Schalock, R. L., Verdugo, M. A., & Gomez, L. E. (2011). Evidence-based practices in the field of intellectual and developmental disabilities. *Evaluation and Program Planning, 34*(3), 273–282.

Schalock, R. L., Verdugo, M. A., Jenaro, C., Wang, W., Wehmeyer, M., Xu, J., & Lachapelle, Y. (2005). Cross-cultural study of quality of life indicators. *American Journal on Mental Retardation, 110,* 298–311.

Shogren, K. A., & Turnbull, H. R. (2010). Public policy and outcomes for persons with intellectual disability: Extending and expanding the public policy framework of the 11th edition *of Intellectual disability: Definition, classification, and systems of supports. Intellectual and Developmental Disability, 48*(5), 375–386.

Stowe, M., Turnbull, H. E., & Sublet, C. (2006). The Supreme Court, "our town", and disability policy: Boardrooms and bedrooms, courtrooms, and cloakrooms. *Mental Retardation, 44,* 83–99.

Summers, J. A., Poston, D. J., Turnbull, A. P., Marquis, J., Hoffman, L., Mannan, H., et al. (2005). Conceptualizing and measuring family quality of life. *Journal of Intellectual Disability Research, 49*(10), 777–783.

Thompson, J. R., Bradley, V. J., Buntinx, W. H. E., Schalock, R. L., Shogren, K., Snell, M. E. et al. (2009). Conceptualizing supports and the support needs of people with intellectual disability. *Intellectual and Developmental Disabilities, 47,* 135–146.

United Nations. (2006). Convention on the rights of persons with disability. Retrieved August 20, 2010 from: www.un.org/disabilities/convention.

Van Loon, J., van Hove, G., Schalock, R. L., & Claes, C. (2010*). Personal Outcomes Scale: A Scale to Assess an Individual's Quality of Life.* Middleburg, The Netherlands: Stichting Arduin; Gent, Belgium: University of Gent.

Verdugo, M. A., Arias, B., Gomez, L. E., & Schalock, R. L. (2010). Development of an objective instrument to assess quality of life in social services reliably and validly in Spain. *International Journal of Clinical and Health Psychology, 10*(1), 105–123.

Verdugo, M. A., Navas, P., Gomez, L. E., & Schalock, R. L. (2012). The concept of quality of life and its role in enhancing human rights in the field of intellectual disability. *Journal of Intellectual Disability Research, 56,* 1036–1045.

Verdugo, M. A., Schalock, R. L., Keith, K. D, & Stancliffe, R. (2005). Quality of life and its measurement: Important principles and guidelines. *Journal of Intellectual Disability Research, 49,* 707–717.

Walsh, P. N., Emerson, E., Lobb, C., Hatton, C., Bradley, V., Schalock, R. L., & Moseley, C. (2010). Supported accommodation for people with intellectual disabilities and quality of life. *Journal of Policy and Practice in Intellectual Disabilities, 7,* 137–142.

Wang, M., Schalock, R. L., Verdugo, M. A., & Jenaro, C. (2010). Examining the factor structure and hierarchical nature of the quality of life construct. *American Journal on Intellectual and Developmental Disabilities. 115,* 218–233.

Weinert, F. (2009). Copernicus, Darwin, and Freud: *Revolutions in the history and philosophy of science.* West Sussex, UK: Blackwell Publishing.

World Health Organization (WHO) (2001). *International classification of functioning, disability, and health* (ICF). Geneva: Author.

Optimism Within the Context of Disability

Kevin L. Rand *and* Amanda M. Shea

Abstract

Optimism, embedded in self-regulation theory, offers multiple hypotheses for coping, goal attainment, and physical and psychological well-being. There is broad empirical support for the benefits of optimism in populations of people without disabilities. Although there is a dearth of research on the impact of optimism among people with disabilities and their caregivers, we review the literature that does exist, which suggests that optimism is an important predictor of adaptive coping, successful goal attainment, and overall well-being for people with disabilities and their caregivers. We propose future directions for understanding optimism in people with disabilities and their caregivers.

Key Words: optimism, disability, caregivers, self-regulation, coping, well-being, performance

"The optimist sees the rose and not its thorns; the pessimist stares at the thorns, oblivious of the rose."

—*Kahlil Gibran*

Introduction

Optimism is generally defined as the tendency to focus on the positive in life, including the expectation that good things will happen in the future. Moreover, conventional wisdom holds that being optimistic can function as a self-fulfilling prophecy and actually shape the outcome of future events. As an example, take the following insight attributed to Henry Ford: "Whether you think you can or you think you can't, you're right."

Although extreme positivity has been derided, consider Dr. Pangloss in Voltaire's *Candide* (1759), optimism is generally considered a virtue in Western culture. People who are more optimistic are thought to be happier, healthier, and more successful than their pessimistic counterparts. Over the past several decades, researchers have been examining the empirical evidence regarding optimism's role in human behavior and well-being. With some

notable exceptions, the scientific evidence about optimism is consistent with conventional wisdom. Moreover, the science of optimism has important implications for the well-being of people with disabilities and their families.

In this chapter, we will summarize the conceptualization of optimism put forth by Scheier and Carver (1985), who defined optimism as a generalized expectancy. That is, optimism is the general belief that good as opposed to bad things will happen in the future. Consistent with the lay definition of optimism, Scheier and Carver's optimism construct involves a positive view of the world. However, it is more specifically focused on expectations for the future. To understand the implications of this conceptualization and evaluate the empirical evidence related to it, it is necessary to briefly summarize the broader theory that gives rise to this particular definition of optimism: *self-regulation theory.*

Self-Regulation Theory

Self-regulation theory (Carver & Scheier, 1998) is a comprehensive model of human behavior that posits that all behaviors are organized around the pursuit of goals. Indeed, goals are what give meaning and structure to people's lives (Rasmussen, Wrosch, Scheier, & Carver, 2006). Goals are mental targets of desired states or conditions. People also have "anti-goals," which are conditions that are to be avoided, such as getting sick (Rasmussen et al., 2006). Furthermore, goals can be purposefully chosen (e.g., "I want to go to law school") or non-consciously adopted (Bargh & Chartrand, 1999). For example, most people don't consciously identify survival as a goal, but when they feel threatened, this goal becomes salient.

Another important characteristic of goals is that they vary in specificity and can be arranged hierarchically. More abstract goals are generally more important and subsume more concrete goals (Carver & Scheier, 1998). Indeed, lower-order goals often serve as means for achieving higher-order ones. For example, the specific goals of exercising and eating vegetables serve the more general goal of staying healthy. At the most abstract level, goals can be thought of as values or "being" goals, whereas the more specific goals can be thought of as "doing" goals (Rasmussen et al., 2006).

People attempt to control their behaviors (and their thoughts and feelings) to maximize the likelihood that goals will be achieved and that anti-goals will be avoided. In other words, people regulate themselves to attain their goals (hence the name of the theory). Differences in how people control themselves and the resulting effects on their goal pursuits are posited to account for many of the individual differences in psychological and physical well-being. For example, a particular subtype of depression, learned helplessness, is thought to be caused by experiencing insurmountable goal blockages (Abramson, Metalsky, & Alloy, 1989; Abramson, Seligman, & Teasdale, 1978). Similarly, research has shown that physical well-being is related to people's goal pursuits (Emmons, 1992).

According to self-regulation theory, two important elements are involved in people's efforts at controlling their goal-directed behaviors: values and expectancies (see expectancy-value theories of motivation; Atkinson, 1964; Feather, 1982). The *value* of a goal is its subjective importance within the context of a person's entire goal-scape. The more value ascribed to a goal, the more motivated a person is to strive for it. In contrast, if a goal is unimportant, a person will have little motivation to pursue it. An *expectancy* is the perceived likelihood that a goal can be achieved. Expectancy has been described as a sense of confidence or doubt that a particular goal pursuit will be successful (Carver & Scheier, 2002).

This confidence or doubt about goals is the essence of the optimism construct. People are more motivated to pursue goals that are likely to be attained and less motivated to pursue goals that are unlikely or impossible. When a person is optimistic that a goal will be achieved, s/he is willing to persist longer and endure more hardship in striving for that goal. This increased persistence, in turn, increases the chances that a particular goal will be achieved. In this way, expectancies can function as self-fulfilling prophecies. In other words, when someone expects a goal to be achievable, s/he works harder at reaching that goal, often bringing it to fruition.

As is the case with goals, expectancies vary from general to specific. Specific expectancies are usually proximal determinants of goal-directed behaviors. For example, if a student believes that she is likely to be able to complete her homework assignment one evening, she is more likely to begin and sustain efforts at completing her homework. Conversely, if a student doubts that the homework assignment can be completed, she is less likely to start her homework or to persist if she encounters difficulties.

Specific expectancies are not always easy to formulate. For example, one may have difficulty generating a specific expectancy in a situation where the desired goal has complex or poorly understood causes. In addition, people often find themselves in situations where there is limited information about the steps necessary to reach the desired goal. In such situations, people may eschew specific expectancies and rely on more generalized expectancies. For example, a college student may struggle to formulate an expectancy for how well he will perform in an organic chemistry class because he has never taken a chemistry class before. Given the lack of specific information, this student may rely on the belief that he is generally a good student to formulate his expectancy for his class performance. That is, he may be optimistic that he will perform well. Even in situations where specific expectancies are formed, generalized expectancies may still exert independent influences on behaviors and psychological well-being (Scheier et al., 1989; Taylor et al., 1992). This generalized expectancy for positive outcomes is the essence of Carver and Scheier's (2002) conceptualization of trait optimism.

Measuring Optimism

Carver and Scheier's (2002) optimism construct has been studied using two versions of a self-report measure. The original measure, called the Life Orientation Test (LOT; Scheier & Carver, 1985), consists of eight items (plus four filler items) to which respondents indicate the extent of their agreement on a 5-point scale (0 = strongly disagree through 4 = strongly agree). Among the scored items, four are positively worded and four are negatively worded.

The LOT was later revised (LOT-R; Scheier, Carver, & Bridges, 1994), resulting in a scale with three positively and three negatively-worded items (plus four filler items). The LOT and the LOT-R are highly correlated (r = 0.95; Scheier et al., 1994), and therefore results using both scales are comparable. The LOT-R has been shown to be internally consistent (alpha = 0.78) and stable over time, with test-retest reliabilities ranging from 0.56 to 0.79 across time spans of 4 months to 28 months (Scheier et al., 1994).

It is worth noting here that some factor analyses of the LOT and the LOT-R have found that the positively- and negatively-worded items load onto two separate factors (e.g., Scheier & Carver, 1985). This has led some researchers to argue that optimism and pessimism are best conceptualized as separate constructs (Chang, D'Zurilla, & Maydeu-Olivares, 1994). In other words, expecting good things is not necessarily the same as not expecting bad things. One could conceivably expect both good and bad things to happen in the future. For the purpose of this chapter, however, we will treat optimism as a unidimensional construct, referring to individuals who score relatively high on the LOT or LOT-R as "optimists" and those who score low as "pessimists." Readers are encouraged to consult a recent study by Segerstrom and colleagues (Segerstrom, Evans, & Eisenlohr-Moul, 2010) for an examination of the dimensionality of optimism as measured by the LOT-R.

It is also worth noting that other measures of optimism are frequently used in research. A popular alternative to the LOT/LOT-R for assessing optimism is the Attributional Style Questionnaire (ASQ; Peterson, Semmel, von Baeyer, Abramson, Metalsky, & Seligman, 1982). Although the construct measured by this scale is frequently called "optimism" in the research literature, it is important to note that the ASQ assesses *explanatory style*, rather than a generalized expectancy. Explanatory style involves how people tend to explain the causes of events in their lives (Peterson & Steen, 2009). Individuals with optimistic explanatory styles make causal attributions that are internal, stable, and global (i.e., general) for positive events and the opposite pattern for negative events. Further discussion of the explanatory style conceptualization of optimism is beyond the scope of this chapter, and interested readers are encouraged to read Peterson and Steen (2009) for more information.

Optimism and Self-Regulation

Defining optimism as a generalized expectancy results in several implications for optimism's role in the self-regulation process, including: (1) psychological responses to adversity, (2) coping behaviors, and (3) goal-directed performance (i.e., success or failure).

Optimism and psychological responses to adversity

Because optimists expect things to turn out well, they should experience a more positively-valenced set of emotions than their pessimistic counterparts, especially when encountering stressors (Carver & Scheier, 2002). Positive emotions are thought to be a result of optimists' appraisals that stressors are challenges that can be successfully overcome. Consequently, they should have more positive and fewer negative emotions during adversity. In contrast, pessimists should experience primarily negative emotions, such as anxiety and despair, in the face of stressors (Carver & Scheier, 1998; Scheier & Carver, 1992).

Research has generally supported the hypothesis that optimists have more positive and less negative emotions. For example, among women diagnosed with breast cancer, greater initial optimism predicted less distress and better quality of life over the subsequent year, even after controlling for disease severity and initial levels of distress (Carver et al., 1994). Similarly, among men undergoing coronary artery bypass surgery, greater initial levels of optimism predicted better mood in the days following surgery and higher quality of life six months later, even when controlling for initial levels of distress and markers of physical health (Scheier et al., 1989). The benefits of optimism on psychological responses have been shown in the context of a variety of other stressors as well, including: the recent birth of a child (Carver & Gaines, 1987), a failed attempt at in vitro fertilization (Litt, Tennen, Affleck, & Klock, 1992), being at risk for AIDS (Taylor et al., 1992), starting college (Brissette, Scheier, & Carver, 2002) or law school (Rand, Martin, & Shea, 2011; Segerstrom, Taylor, Kemeny, & Fahey, 1998), and aging among elderly men (Giltay, Zitman, & Kromhout, 2006).

Optimism and coping

Because optimists appraise problems as being solvable, they should be more likely to utilize coping strategies that acknowledge the reality of the situation and deal directly with the stressors they encounter. In contrast, pessimists should be more likely to deny that the stressor éxists and rely on coping strategies that avoid dealing with the problem, because they are more likely to perceive adverse situations as being unresolvable. Research has generally supported these hypotheses. For example, research among college students has shown that greater optimism predicts greater acceptance of stressors and greater use of active, problem-focused coping efforts to deal with them. In contrast, pessimistic undergraduates are more likely to use denial and attempts to distance oneself from the problem (Aspinwall & Taylor, 1992; Scheier, Weintraub, & Carver, 1986).

When the stressor involves a threat to one's health, optimists are more likely to focus on plans for recovery, information seeking, and reframing the situation in terms of its most positive aspects (Taylor et al., 1992). In contrast, pessimists rely more on avoidance coping, which results in greater distress. For example, among men undergoing coronary artery bypass surgery, optimistic patients were more likely to seek information from their physicians and make plans for recovery and less likely to report feeling helped by efforts at avoiding thinking about their postoperative recovery period (Scheier et al., 1989). Moreover, greater optimism predicted less focus on negative emotions, which in turn predicted better quality of life. Similarly, among couples experiencing failure at in vitro fertilization, greater optimism predicted less reliance on escape as a coping strategy and greater use of benefit finding (Litt et al., 1992).

Optimism's pattern of being positively related to approach coping and negatively related to avoidance coping is consistent across a wide variety of studies. A meta-analysis found optimism to be positively linked with coping efforts aimed at reducing, eliminating, or managing stressors and negative emotions and negatively linked with avoidance strategies (e.g., ignoring, avoiding, or withdrawing; Nes & Segerstrom, 2006). More specifically, Nes and Segerstrom found that greater optimism predicted greater use of problem-focused coping for stressors perceived as controllable and greater use of emotion-focused coping for stressors perceived as uncontrollable. Hence, optimism is associated with a flexible set of coping strategies, depending on the context. This flexibility is important because problem-focused coping may not be adaptive in situations where problems are unresolvable; instead, acceptance of the situation may be adaptive and contribute to greater well-being. In sum, optimists

are more likely to accept a situation and less likely to use denial (Nes & Segerstrom, 2006).

Optimism and goal-directed performance

Because optimists are hypothesized to persist longer in trying to reach goals, optimists should experience greater success at achieving their goals than pessimists. As we noted previously, this is purportedly the result of a self-fulfilling prophecy wherein optimists believe they can succeed, so they expend greater effort trying to accomplish their goal. This greater effort, in turn, increases the chances that the goal will be attained. Although consistent with the overall theory of self-regulation, this particular hypothesis has received mixed support in the empirical literature.

Research has supported the hypothesis that optimists can persist longer at tasks, although optimism's influence may be affected by fatigue and effort (Solberg Nes, Carlson, Crofford, de Leeuw, & Segerstrom, 2011). Among students, there is some evidence that greater optimism predicts better academic success (Rand, 2009). Consistent with the notion that optimism enables individuals to persist at goal-directed activities, greater optimism has been shown to predict undergraduate retention (Nes, Evans, & Segerstrom, 2009). In a study of university freshmen, greater optimism was associated with better faculty ratings of academic performance (Chemers, Hu, & Garcia, 2001). Similarly, a study of military cadets found that greater cadet optimism was associated with greater faculty ratings of leadership potential (Chemers, Watson, & May, 2000). It should be noted, however, that these studies did not rely on grades or other "objective" markers of academic performance. Instead, they relied on more subjective evaluation by faculty.

When grades or other "objective" markers of performance are used, the relationship between trait optimism and success is less clear. For example, one study found that optimistic first-year law students made significantly more money a decade later than their pessimistic peers (Segerstrom, 2007). Alternatively, several studies have failed to find an association between optimism and grades among undergraduates (Aspinwall & Taylor, 1992; Nes et al., 2009) and law students (Rand, Martin, & Shea, 2011; Siddique, LaSalle-Ricci, Glass, Arnkoff, & Díaz, 2006). Similarly, trait optimism among military cadets was not associated with performance on a leadership simulation or other skill-based activities (e.g., marksmanship, land navigation skills; Chemers et al., 2000).

The relationship between optimism and goal-directed performance outside of academics is also inconsistent. For example, higher optimism was related to better athletic performance among skiers (Norlander & Archer, 2002). However, the highest levels of optimism were associated with *poorer* performance among swimmers (Norlander & Archer, 2002). Similarly, greater optimism among entrepreneurs predicted poorer company growth (i.e., revenue and employment) over a two-year period in new business ventures (Hmieleski & Baron, 2009). In contrast, other researchers have found no relationship between employee optimism and job performance (Luthans, Avolio, Avey, & Norman, 2007). One explanation for these inconsistent findings is that optimism may improve performance up to a certain point, but then may impede performance when successful goal attainment becomes too unrealistic (i.e., curvilinear relationship; Hmieleski & Baron, 2009).

Optimism Within the Context of Disability

The influence of optimism within the context of having a disability is a developing area of inquiry, and there is a paucity of research among people with particular types of disabilities (e.g., cognitive, developmental, or emotional/behavioral). The bulk of the evidence regarding the roles of optimism within the context of disability comes from research conducted with people coping with physical impairments that are disabling to varying degrees, including arthritis, Parkinson's disease, hemophilia, and limb amputations. This evidence, as incomplete as it is, still offers insight into the potential influence of optimism in the lives of people with other types of disabilities.

The World Health Organization (2001) has defined disability as a functional mismatch between a person's capabilities and the situation in which they function. Using this definition, the nature of the disability is not as important as the discrepancy created between what the individual is required to do and what s/he can do. This conceptualization meshes well with self-regulation theory in that the impact of a disability is determined by the extent to which it interferes with an individual's ability to pursue meaningful and important life goals. As we articulated previously, optimism may have important implications for people with disabilities in several ways, including psychological responses to adversity, coping, and goal-directed performance.

Optimism and Psychological Responses to Adversity

As we noted previously, optimists generally experience a more positively-valenced set of emotions when encountering stressors. Within the framework of self-regulation theory, a stressor is a perceived interference with a goal pursuit (cf. Lazarus & Folkman, 1984). Optimists are thought to experience more positive emotions in the face of stressors because they are more likely to see the barrier to their goal pursuit as something that can be overcome. Consistent with this hypothesis, research has shown that greater optimism is associated with greater psychological well-being, even during times of stress (Brissette et al., 2002; Rand, Martin, & Shea, 2011). Such research has typically focused on temporary stressors. People with disabilities, however, face a stressor that is chronic and could interfere with multiple goals in several life domains. In this context, optimism may be less beneficial.

The extant research on optimism among individuals with a disability is, however, consistent with the general literature on optimism. Optimistic people with disabilities appear to be more likely to perceive stressors as being manageable. For example, consider people with hemophilia, a hereditary blood clotting disorder that can cause severe joint damage and functional disability. Triemstra and colleagues (1998) found that optimistic people with hemophilia perceived their physical limitations to be less encumbering.

In turn, optimism and the adaptive appraisals it fosters should promote greater psychological well-being among individuals with disabilities. Consistent with this hypothesis, greater optimism among the aforementioned people with hemophilia was associated with a high internal locus of control and less negative affect (Triemstra et al., 1998). A similar association has been found among people with Parkinson's disease, a progressive neurological disorder characterized by movement-related symptoms (e.g., tremors, postural instability). Greater optimism was associated with better perceived quality of life, controlling for the effects of disease-related factors (Gruber-Baldini, Ye, Anderson, & Shulman, 2009). In another cross-sectional study among people who had limb amputations, greater optimism was related to fewer depressive symptoms, greater perceived control, and higher self-esteem (Dunn, 1996).

Optimism is also related to better psychological functioning in the aftermath of a traumatic injury. Quale and Schanke (2010) studied Norwegian inpatients who had recent spinal cord injuries or multiple severe traumas, resulting in functional loss and disability. Patients who were optimistic at admission were less likely to experience symptoms of posttraumatic stress, anxiety, depression, and negative affect at either admission or discharge. In contrast, pessimistic patients were more likely to have psychological reactions characterized by persistent psychological distress at both admission and discharge.

Arthritis is another disease characterized by inflammation, pain, fatigue, and impaired mobility. Despite these characteristics, research has shown that being optimistic predicts better psychological well-being across time. For example, among people with chronic rheumatoid arthritis (mean duration of 12 years), greater optimism at baseline predicted better psychological well-being 16 months later (Brenner, Melamed, & Panush, 1994), even after controlling for the level of disability. Similarly, a study of older adults with osteoarthritis showed that initial optimism predicted less social strain and greater life satisfaction 12 months later (Luger, Cotter, & Sherman, 2009), even after controlling for initial levels of life satisfaction. Finally, in a longitudinal study of people with rheumatoid arthritis, baseline optimism was associated with less depression, less anxiety, and greater life satisfaction a year later, independent of the effects of functional disability and pain (Treharne, Lyons, Booth, & Kitas, 2007).

Thus far, we have reviewed research on optimism in the context of disability resulting from illness or injury. What is the evidence regarding optimism's role in disabilities associated with cognitive functioning? Unfortunately, there is scant research in this area. The sole study we are aware of involved adolescents with cognitive disabilities (i.e., learning disability or intellectual disability). In this study, greater optimism predicted greater life satisfaction, even when accounting for other variables thought to be associated with psychological well-being, such as hope and self-determination (Shogren, Lopez, Wehmeyer, Little, & Pressgrove, 2006).

Optimism and Coping

As is the case with psychological responses to adversity, the relationship between optimism and coping among people with disabilities is not well studied. However, the extant research suggests that optimism is associated with more adaptive coping. Furthermore, these effects have been found in both cross-sectional and longitudinal studies.

For example, optimism has been associated with problem-focused coping in samples of people with multiple chemical sensitivities (MCS). People with MCS suffer a variety of physical symptoms after exposure to low levels of chemicals that are not problematic for most other people. Due to their sensitivities and symptoms, people with MCS often have difficulty maintaining employment and functioning in various environments. Nevertheless, research has suggested that optimism predicts adaptive coping in people with MCS. One study found that optimism was related to less reliance on behavioral disengagement (i.e., avoidance) and more utilization of positive reinterpretation as coping strategies (Davis, Jason, & Banghart, 1998). That is, optimists were less likely to avoid active problem solving and were able to find the benefits to their stressful circumstances. Given the cross-sectional nature of the study, it is unclear whether optimism leads to positive coping behaviors or if positive coping behaviors increase optimism. Nonetheless, other longitudinal studies suggest that optimism is a precursor rather than a consequence of adaptive coping.

A longitudinal association between optimism and beneficial coping practices has been found in people with rheumatoid arthritis. The pain and functional impairment associated with rheumatoid arthritis can have broad effects that lead to work and role disability (Mitchell, Burkhauser, & Pincus, 1988). In the previously discussed study of people with rheumatoid arthritis, initial levels of optimism were positively associated with subsequent problem-focused coping (Brenner et al., 1994). Moreover, this study found evidence consistent with a mediation model wherein optimism led to problem-focused coping, which in turn facilitated better psychological adjustment.

Seeking social support in the midst of dealing with a stressor has been shown to be an effective coping strategy, both in terms of managing psychological distress and for getting assistance in overcoming the obstacles (Cohen & Wills, 1985). Hence, the extent to which optimism facilitates social support can be considered an additional benefit to coping with stressors that should facilitate greater well-being. Indeed, a longitudinal study of people with osteoarthritis found that optimists experienced more social support and less social strain over the course of a year (Luger et al., 2009). Furthermore, this connection between optimism and social support was found to be one of the mechanisms by which optimism influenced life satisfaction.

Optimism and Goal-Directed Performance

Consequent to optimists' positive appraisals and proactive coping styles, they should generate more success in pursuit of their goals. There is an emerging literature examining the relationship between optimism and the ability to work, an important goal for many people with disabilities. Consider people who have cystic fibrosis, a genetic disease characterized by chronic breathing difficulties and frequent chest infections. Because of these symptoms, individuals with cystic fibrosis often have difficulty completing simple, daily tasks, much less maintaining steady employment. In a cross-sectional study of people with cystic fibrosis, half of whom were employed and half of whom were not, greater optimism was associated with a greater number of hours worked (Burker, Sedway, & Carone, 2004).

A large prospective Finnish study suggests that optimism is a protective factor in preventing disability among people with depression (Kronström et al., 2011). In this study, more than 38,000 people without documented disabilities were assessed for optimism. The researchers monitored state records for indication of disability due to depression over a four-year timeframe. Optimistic people were less likely to become disabled due to depression. Moreover, among those who did become disabled as a result of depression, those who were more optimistic were more likely to return to work.

Optimism and Caregivers of People with Disabilities

In addition to being a protective factor for people with disabilities, optimism appears to confer benefits to caregivers of people with disabilities. Identifying and maximizing protective factors for caregivers of people with disabilities is of great importance due to the chronic stress and negative outcomes associated with caregiving. For example, meta-analyses of the physical indicators of well-being in caregivers revealed them to be at greater risk for health problems compared to non-caregivers (Pinquart & Sörensen, 2007; Vitaliano, Zhang, & Scanlan, 2003). Furthermore, caregivers are at greater risk for symptoms of depression and other forms of distress (Pinquart & Sörensen, 2007). Although there is a lack of clear evidence regarding factors that protect caregivers from psychological distress, there are some studies that provide evidence that optimism may be one such protective factor.

Parenting is inherently a stressful endeavor. Parenting a child with a disability presents its own unique set of stressors. Some research has found that parents of children with disabilities are significantly more distressed compared to parents of children without disabilities (e.g., Lach et al., 2009). Not surprisingly, the distress in these parents is related to the severity of the disability in their children (e.g., Grosse, Flores, Ouyang, Robbins, & Tilford, 2009; Plant & Sanders, 2007). Other research has failed to find differences in distress levels among parents with or without children with disabilities (Baker, Blacher, & Olsson, 2005). Parental personality characteristics, such as optimism, may explain why some parents of children with disabilities are more distressed than others. Indeed, initial research has shown that parental optimism may offer protective benefits. For example, children with obstetrical brachial plexus injuries have damage to the nerves that control their arms resulting from difficulties during childbirth. As a result, the child experiences permanent partial or complete paralysis of the arm. McLean and colleagues (2004) conducted a study of mothers of children with obstetrical brachial plexus injuries. In this sample, greater maternal optimism was associated with better maternal psychological adjustment, even when the effects of perceived disability of children were controlled.

In addition to mothers of children with physical disabilities, mothers of children with developmental and intellectual disabilities may also benefit from being optimistic. In a study of parents of preschool children, including children with developmental delays and intellectual disability, optimism was found to be an important influence on maternal well-being and marital adjustment (Baker et al., 2005). Mothers' optimism moderated the relationship between child behavioral problems and their own psychological well-being and between child behavioral problems and marital adjustment. Among optimistic mothers, child behavioral problems did not predict maternal distress or marital maladjustment. In contrast, for pessimistic mothers there was a direct relationship between child behavioral problems on the one hand and maternal distress and marital maladjustment on the other. This relationship may be explained by positive expectancies of mothers, specifically that children's behavior will not exert a negative influence on the future. In addition, this finding may be accounted for by optimistic mothers' use of more problem-focused coping behaviors to maintain well-being and marital satisfaction despite child behavioral problems.

Parental optimism may continue to be an important protective factor even after children with disabilities become adults. For example, among mothers of adult offspring with Down syndrome, schizophrenia, or autism, maternal optimism was associated with better mental and physical health for the mother

(Greenberg, Seltzer, Krauss, Chou, & Hong, 2004). Moreover, maternal optimism was found to mediate the relationship between the quality of the mother-child relationship and maternal psychological well-being (Greenberg et al., 2004). Previous research has shown that the quality of the parent-child relationship reduces caregiver burden and improves caregiver well-being (e.g., Townsend & Franks, 1995). The study by Greenberg and colleagues (2004) demonstrates that the mechanism that creates this relationship is that a high-quality caregiver-child relationship improves caregiver optimism, which in turn leads to greater caregiver well-being.

In addition to providing a better understanding of caregiver well-being, research has uncovered important information about the relationship between caregiver optimism and indicators of well-being among people with disabilities. For example, in caregivers of people with rheumatoid arthritis, research has shown that caregiver pessimism is associated with low self-efficacy in patients (Beckham, Burker, Rice, & Talton, 1995). Furthermore, a higher level of patient-reported physical disability was associated with greater caregiver pessimism. This research was the result of cross-sectional methods, so the directionality of the relationship cannot be assumed. On the one hand, caring for a chronically-ill loved one with greater disability and less perceived self-efficacy may lead to a reduction in dispositional optimism. It is also possible, however, that patient perceptions of self-efficacy and disability are influenced by the caregiver's dispositional optimism via communication of expectancies.

Shedding some light on directionality, researchers have begun to explore the relationship between optimism and indices of well-being in caregivers using longitudinal methods. For example, Lyons and colleagues (2009) conducted a 10-year study examining optimism and role strain in spouses of people with Parkinson's disease. Because of its gradual and progressive nature, people with Parkinson's disease often require little caregiver support in the early stages. As the disease progresses, however, greater assistance is required. In this study, the researchers sampled spouses and people with early-stage Parkinson's disease and followed up with them 10 years later. The study design afforded an opportunity to examine the role of optimism in caregivers before their caregiving demands were high on later indices of well-being. Spouses reporting high levels of optimism at the beginning of the study were less likely to report role strain from worry and increased tension 10 years later. Thus, optimism seemed to provide long-term protection for caregivers with increasing demands.

Future Directions

Although the existing research on optimism among people with disabilities provocatively suggests that optimism may have important influences on psychological well-being, coping behaviors, and goal-related success, there remain several unanswered questions that should guide future research. First, there are relatively few published studies examining optimism within the context of disability, and many of them rely on cross-sectional designs. In order to better understand the causal roles that optimism plays, more longitudinal research is needed among individuals with disability, especially for those whose impairments change significantly over time (e.g., people with Parkinson's disease).

Second, much of the existing research focuses on people with disability due to illness or injury. Because optimism is a cognitive construct, it may function differently in people with disabilities that affect cognition. Hence, more research is needed among individuals with other forms of disability, including developmental, cognitive, and emotional disabilities. Related to this point, future research should pay particular attention to the measurement of optimism. To date, optimism has been assessed via self-report. However, self-reported assessment may not be a valid method of measurement in certain populations. For example, can self-reported optimism be accurately assessed among individuals with cognitive disabilities? There is some preliminary evidence suggesting that it can. For example, Shogren and colleagues (2006) demonstrated that measurement of optimism using the LOT-R among adolescents with and without cognitive disabilities was comparable. However, among the adolescents with cognitive disabilities, the internal consistency of the LOT-R was lower than found among most samples (Cronbach's alpha = 0.56). Hence, more work is needed examining the measurement of optimism as well as its nomological network among populations with cognitive disabilities.

Third, the issue of the dimensionality of optimism deserves more attention. As we mentioned in the section on the measurement of optimism, some scholars have argued that optimism and pessimism might best be conceptualized as separate constructs (Chang et al., 1994). Supporting this view, some research has shown that when assessed separately in people with disability, optimism and pessimism predict different outcomes (Treharne et al., 2007).

Future research may find that one dimension is a more important determinant of well-being than another in certain situations, which would inform efforts at intervention.

Fourth, it is imperative to examine the associations between optimism and important outcomes within the context of other psychological strengths. Positive psychology is a relatively new area of research, and many of the positive psychology constructs have been measured and studied in isolation. To the extent that there is conceptual overlap between optimism and other personality strengths, it will be important to determine the unique roles that optimism plays in well-being, coping, and performance. For example, research has shown that, when assessed concurrently, both optimism and hope (a similar cognitive construct) independently predict life satisfaction (Rand, Martin, & Shea, 2011; Shogren et al., 2006). However, there is also evidence that optimism does not uniquely predict goal-related performance when the influence of other positive psychology constructs is accounted for (Rand, 2009; Rand, Martin, & Shea, 2011).

Fifth, it remains an open question as to whether more optimism is always beneficial. As we noted earlier, there is some evidence that more optimism can actually lead to poorer goal-directed performance (Hmieleski & Baron, 2009; Norlander & Archer, 2002). Given that self-regulation theory posits that greater optimism should improve the likelihood of success, such results are confusing. One resolution that has been suggested is that there may be a curvilinear relationship between optimism and performance (and other important outcomes). That is, more optimism may be beneficial up to a certain point, after which being unrealistically optimistic may become detrimental to one's well-being. For example, research has shown that more optimistic adolescent girls at risk for HIV infection were less likely to seek HIV testing (Goodman, Chesney, & Tipton, 1995). This may be due to an inflated sense of invulnerability to negative outcomes that may go along with the highest levels of optimistic thinking. More research is needed examining the potential negative sequelae to optimism, especially among people with disabilities.

 Finally, can optimism be manipulated? If a certain level of optimism is desirable, can we turn a pessimist into an optimist? Conversely, can extremely negative events turn optimists into pessimists? There is evidence from research with twins that one's optimism is largely inherited at birth (Plomin, Scheier, Bergeman, & Pedersen, 1992). Moreover, early childhood experiences may be important in determining one's outlook on life (Bowlby, 1988; Carver & Scheier, 2002). If optimism is determined largely by genetic and early learning influences, then it is likely that it would be resistant to change in either direction once an individual reaches adulthood. For example, people's subjective well-being, which is strongly associated with optimism, remains stable across time and is not permanently influenced by either positive or negative events (Suh, Diener, & Fujita, 1996). Still, there is reason to believe that people's optimism can be increased. For example, Antoni and colleagues (2001) found that an intervention to help breast cancer patients more effectively manage stress resulted in increases in optimism over the course of 10 weeks. This finding is consistent with the psychotherapy literature that has shown that people's outlooks on life and the world improve following interventions, such as cognitive-behavioral therapy (Cuijpers et al., 2010; Segal, Vincent, & Levitt, 2002). That said, it remains unclear to what extent different interventions permanently alter one's dispositional characteristics, such as trait optimism (Segal, Gemar, & Williams, 1999).

Conclusion

Optimism is a useful construct for understanding individual differences in psychological responses, coping, and goal-directed performance. Subsumed by self-regulation theory, optimistic expectancies help explain why some individuals flourish and others struggle, particularly when facing adversity. Given the stressors associated with disability, optimism is likely an important concept for people with disabilities. However, the extant research on optimism within the context of having a disability is sparse. The emerging literature, however, suggests that optimistic people cope more adaptively, are more likely to achieve important life goals (e.g., being able to work), and enjoy greater well-being. Furthermore, the influences of optimism also extend to caregivers of people with disabilities.

References

Abramson, L. Y., Metalsky, G. I., & Alloy, L. B. (1989). Hopelessness depression: A theory-based subtype of depression. *Psychological Review, 96*(2), 358–372. doi: 10.1037/0033-295x.96.2.358

Abramson, L. Y., Seligman, M. E., & Teasdale, J. D. (1978). Learned helplessness in humans: Critique and reformulation. *Journal of Abnormal Psychology, 87*(1), 49–74. doi: 10.1037/0021-843x.87.1.49

Antoni, M. H., Lehman, J. M., Kilbourn, K. M., Boyers, A. E., Culver, J. L., Alferi, S. M., . . . Carver, C. S. (2001). Cognitive-behavioral stress management intervention decreases the prevalence of depression and enhances benefit finding among women under treatment for early-stage breast cancer. *Health Psychology*, *20*(1), 20–32. doi: 10.1037/0278-6133.20.1.20

Aspinwall, L. G., & Taylor, S. E. (1992). Modeling cognitive adaptation: A longitudinal investigation of the impact of individual differences and coping on college adjustment and performance. *Journal of Personality and Social Psychology*, *63*(6), 989–1003. doi: 10.1037/0022-3514.63.6.989

Atkinson, J. W. (1964). *An introduction to motivation*. Oxford England: Van Nostrand.

Baker, B. L., Blacher, J., & Olsson, M. B. (2005). Preschool children with and without developmental delay: Behaviour problems, parents' optimism and well-being. *Journal of Intellectual Disability Research*, *49*(8), 575–590. doi: 10.1111/j.1365-2788.2005.00691.x

Bargh, J. A., & Chartrand, T. L. (1999). The unbearable automaticity of being. *American Psychologist*, *54*(7), 462–479. doi: 10.1037/0003-066x.54.7.462

Beckham, J. C., Burker, E. J., Rice, J. R., & Talton, S. L. (1995). Patient predictors of caregiver burden, optimism, and pessimism in rheumatoid arthritis. *Behavioral Medicine*, *20*(4), 171–178.

Bowlby, J. (1988). *A secure base: Parent-child attachment and healthy human development*. New York, NY US: Basic Books.

Brenner, G. F., Melamed, B. G., & Panush, R. S. (1994). Optimism and coping as determinants of psychosocial adjustment to rheumatoid arthritis. *Journal of Clinical Psychology in Medical Settings*, *1*(2), 115–134. doi:10.1007/bf01999741

Brissette, I., Scheier, M. F., & Carver, C. S. (2002). The role of optimism in social network development, coping, and psychological adjustment during a life transition. *Journal of Personality and Social Psychology*, *82*(1), 102–111.

Burker, E. J., Sedway, J., & Carone, S. (2004). Psychological and educational factors: Better predictors of work status than FEV1 in adults with cystic fibrosis. *Pediatric Pulmonology*, *38*(5), 413–418. doi: 10.1002/ppul.20090

Carver, C. S., & Gaines, J. G. (1987). Optimism, pessimism, and postpartum depression. *Cognitive Therapy and Research*, *11*(4), 449–462.

Carver, C. S., Pozo-Kaderman, C., Harris, S. D., Noriega, V., Scheier, M. F., Robinson, D. S., Ketcham, A. S., Moffat, F. L., & Clark, K. C. (1994). Optimism versus pessimism predicts the quality of women's adjustment to early stage breast cancer. *Cancer*, *73*(4), 1213–1220.

Carver, C. S., & Scheier, M. F. (1998). *On the self-regulation of behavior*. New York, NY US: Cambridge University Press.

Carver, C. S., & Scheier, M. F. (2002). Optimism. In C. R. Snyder & S. J. Lopez (Eds.), *Handbook of positive psychology*. (pp. 231–243). New York, NY, US: Oxford University Press.

Chang, E. C., D'Zurilla, T. J., & Maydeu-Olivares, A. (1994). Assessing the dimensionality of optimism and pessimism using a multimeasure approach. *Cognitive Therapy and Research*, *18*(2), 143–160. doi: 10.1007/bf02357221

Chemers, M. M., Hu, L.-t., & Garcia, B. F. (2001). Academic self-efficacy and first year college student performance and adjustment. *Journal of Educational Psychology*, *93*(1), 55–64. doi: 10.1037/0022-0663.93.1.55

Chemers, M. M., Watson, C. B., & May, S. T. (2000). Dispositional affect and leadership effectiveness: A comparison of self-esteem, optimism, and efficacy. *Personality and Social Psychology Bulletin*, *26*(3), 267–277. doi: 10.1177/0146167200265001

Cohen, S., & Wills, T. A. (1985). Stress, social support, and the buffering hypothesis. *Psychological Bulletin*, *98*(2), 310–357. doi: 10.1037/0033-2909.98.2.310

Cuijpers, P., van Straten, A., Schuurmans, J., van Oppen, P., Hollon, S. D., & Andersson, G. (2010). Psychotherapy for chronic major depression and dysthymia: A meta-analysis. *Clinical Psychology Review*, *30*(1), 51–62. doi: 10.1016/j.cpr.2009.09.003

Davis, T. H., Jason, L. A., & Banghart, M. A. (1998). The effect of housing on individuals with multiple chemical sensitivities. *The Journal of Primary Prevention*, *19*(1), 31–42. doi: 10.1023/a:1022613324456

Dunn, D. S. (1996). Well-being following amputation: Salutary effects of positive meaning, optimism, and control. *Rehabilitation Psychology*, *41*(4), 285–302. doi: 10.1037/0090-5550.41.4.285

Emmons, R. A. (1992). Abstract versus concrete goals: Personal striving level, physical illness, and psychological well-being. *Journal of Personality and Social Psychology*, *62*(2), 292–300. doi: 10.1037/0022-3514.62.2.292

Feather, N. T. (1982). *Expectations and actions: Expectancy-value models in psychology*. Hillsdale, NJ: Erlbaum.

Giltay, E. J., Zitman, F. G., & Kromhout, D. (2006). Dispositional optimism and the risk of depressive symptoms during 15 years of follow-up: the Zutphen Elderly Study. *Journal of Affective Disorders*, *91*(1), 45–52.

Goodman, E., Chesney, M. A., & Tipton, A. C. (1995). Relationship of optimism, knowledge, attitudes, and beliefs to use of HIV antibody testing by at-risk female adolescents. *Psychosomatic Medicine*, *57*(6), 541–546.

Greenberg, J. S., Seltzer, M. M., Krauss, M. W., Chou, R. J.-A., & Hong, J. (2004). The Effect of Quality of the Relationship Between Mothers and Adult Children With Schizophrenia, Autism, or Down Syndrome on Maternal Well-Being: The Mediating Role of Optimism. *American Journal of Orthopsychiatry*, *74*(1), 14–25. doi: 10.1037/0002-9432.74.1.14

Grosse, S. D., Flores, A. L., Ouyang, L., Robbins, J. M., & Tilford, J. M. (2009). Impact of spina bifida on parental caregivers: Findings from a survey of Arkansas families. *Journal of Child and Family Studies*, *18*(5), 574–581. doi: 10.1007/s10826-009-9260-3

Gruber-Baldini, A. L., Ye, J., Anderson, K. E., & Shulman, L. M. (2009). Effects of optimism/pessimism and locus of control on disability and quality of life in Parkinson's disease. *Parkinsonism & Related Disorders*, *15*(9), 665–669. doi: 10.1016/j.parkreldis.2009.03.005

Hmieleski, K. M., & Baron, R. A. (2009). Entrepreneurs' optimism and new venture performance: A social cognitive perspective. *Academy of Management Journal*, *52*(3), 473–488.

Kronström, K., Karlsson, H., Nabi, H., Oksanen, T., Salo, P., Sjösten, N.,…Vahtera, J. (2011). Optimism and pessimism as predictors of work disability with a diagnosis of depression: A prospective cohort study of onset and recovery. *Journal of Affective Disorders*, *130*(1-2), 294–299. doi: 10.1016/j.jad.2010.10.003

Lach, L. M., Kohen, D. E., Garner, R. E., Brehaut, J. C., Miller, A. R., Klassen, A. F., & Rosenbaum, P. L. (2009). The health and psychosocial functioning of caregivers of children with neurodevelopmental disorders. *Disability and Rehabilitation: An International, Multidisciplinary Journal*, *31*(9), 741–752. doi: 10.1080/08916930802354948

Lazarus, R. S., & Folkman, Susan. (1984). *Stress, appraisal, and coping*. New York: Springer.

Litt, M. D., Tennen, H., Affleck, G., & Klock, S. (1992). Coping and cognitive factors in adaptation to in vitro fertilization failure. *Journal Of Behavioral Medicine*, *15*(2), 171–187.

Luger, T., Cotter, K. A., & Sherman, A. M. (2009). It's all in how you view it: Pessimism, social relations, and life satisfaction in older adults with osteoarthritis. *Aging & Mental Health*, *13*(5), 635–647. doi: 10.1080/13607860802534633

Luthans, F., Avolio, B. J., Avey, J. B., & Norman, S. M. (2007). Positive psychological capital: Measurement and relationship with performance and satisfaction. *Personnel Psychology*, *60*(3), 541–572. doi: 10.1111/j.1744-6570.2007.00083.x

Lyons, K. S., Stewart, B. J., Archbold, P. G., & Carter, J. H. (2009). Optimism, pessimism, mutuality, and gender: Predicting 10-year role strain in Parkinson's disease spouses. *The Gerontologist*, *49*(3), 378–387. doi: 10.1093/geront/gnp046

McLean, L. A., Harvey, D. H. P., Pallant, J. F., Bartlett, J. R., & Mutimer, K. L. A. (2004). Adjustment of Mothers of Children With Obstetrical Brachial Plexus Injuries: Testing a Risk and Resistance Model. *Rehabilitation Psychology*, *49*(3), 233–240. doi: 10.1037/0090-5550.49.3.233

Mitchell, J., Burkhauser, R., & Pincus, T. (1988). The importance of age, education, and combordity in the substantial earnings losses of individuals with symmetric polyarthritis. *Arthritis and Rheumatism*, *31*, 348–357.

Nes, L. S., Evans, D. R., & Segerstrom, S. C. (2009). Optimism and college retention: Mediation by motivation, performance, and adjustment. *Journal of Applied Social Psychology*, *39*(8), 1887–1912. doi: 10.1111/j.1559-1816.2009.00508.x

Nes, L. S., & Segerstrom, S. C. (2006). Dispositional Optimism and Coping: A Meta-Analytic Review. *Personality and Social Psychology Review*, *10*(3), 235–251. doi: 10.1207/s15327957pspr1003_3

Norlander, T., & Archer, T. (2002). Predicting performance in ski and swim championships: Effectiveness of mood, perceived exertion, and dispositional optimism. *Perceptual and Motor Skills*, *94*(1), 153–164. doi: 10.2466/pms.94.1.153-164

Peterson, C., Semmel, A., von Baeyer, C., Abramson, L., Metalsky, G., & Seligman, M. (1982). The Attributional Style Questionnaire. *Cognitive Therapy and Research*, *6*(3), 287–300.

Peterson, C., & Steen, T. A. (2009). Optimistic explanatory style. In S. J. Lopez & C. R. Snyder (Eds.), *Oxford handbook of positive psychology (2nd ed.)*. (pp. 313–321). New York, NY US: Oxford University Press.

Pinquart, M., & Sörensen, S. (2007). Correlates of physical health of informal caregivers: A meta-analysis. *The Journals of Gerontology: Series B: Psychological Sciences and Social Sciences*, *62B*(2), P126–P137.

Plant, K. M., & Sanders, M. R. (2007). Predictors of care-giver stress in families of preschool-aged children with developmental disabilities. *Journal of Intellectual Disability Research*, *51*(2), 109–124. doi: 10.1111/j.1365-2788.2006.00829.x

Plomin, R., Scheier, M. F., Bergeman, C. S., & Pedersen, N. L. (1992). Optimism, pessimism and mental health: A twin/adoption analysis. *Personality and Individual Differences*, *13*(8), 921–930. doi: 10.1016/0191-8869(92)90009-e

Quale, A. J., & Schanke, A. K. (2010). Resilience in the face of coping with a severe physical injury: A study of trajectories of adjustment in a rehabilitation setting. *Rehabilitation Psychology*, *55*(1), 12–22. doi: 10.1037/a0018415

Rand, K. L. (2009). Hope and optimism: Latent structures and influences on grade expectancy and academic performance. *Journal Of Personality*, *77*(1), 231–260. doi: 10.1111/j.1467-6494.2008.00544.x

Rand, K. L., Martin, A. D., & Shea, A. M. (2011). Hope, but not optimism, predicts academic performance of law students beyond previous academic achievement. *Journal of Research in Personality*, *45*(6), 683–686.

Rasmussen, H. N., Wrosch, C., Scheier, M. F., & Carver, C. S. (2006). Self-Regulation Processes and Health: The Importance of Optimism and Goal Adjustment. *Journal Of Personality*, *74*(6), 1721–1747. doi: 10.1111/j.1467-6494.2006.00426.x

Scheier, M. F., & Carver, C. S. (1985). Optimism, coping, and health: assessment and implications of generalized outcome expectancies. *Health Psychology: Official Journal Of The Division Of Health Psychology, American Psychological Association*, *4*(3), 219–247.

Scheier, M. F., & Carver, C. S. (1992). Effects of optimism on psychological and physical well-being: Theoretical overview and empirical update. *Cognitive Therapy and Research*, *16*(2), 201–228. doi: 10.1007/bf01173489

Scheier, M. F., Carver, C. S., & Bridges, M. W. (1994). Distinguishing optimism from neuroticism (and trait anxiety, self-mastery, and self-esteem): A reevaluation of the Life Orientation Test. *Journal of Personality and Social Psychology*, *67*(6), 1063–1078.

Scheier, M. F., Matthews, K. A., Owens, J. F., Magovern, G. J., Sr., Lefebvre, R. C., Abbott, R. A., & Carver, C. S. (1989). Dispositional optimism and recovery from coronary artery bypass surgery: the beneficial effects on physical and psychological well-being. *Journal of Personality and Social Psychology*, *57*(6), 1024–1040.

Scheier, M. F., Weintraub, J. K., & Carver, C. S. (1986). Coping with stress: Divergent strategies of optimists and pessimists. *Journal of Personality and Social Psychology*, *51*(6), 1257–1264. doi: 10.1037/0022-3514.51.6.1257

Segal, Z., Vincent, P., & Levitt, A. (2002). Efficacy of combined, sequential and crossover psychotherapy and pharmacotherapy in improving outcomes in depression. *Journal of Psychiatry & Neuroscience*, *27*(4), 281–290.

Segal, Z. V., Gemar, M., & Williams, S. (1999). Differential cognitive response to a mood challenge following successful cognitive therapy or pharmacotherapy for unipolar depression. *Journal of Abnormal Psychology*, *108*(1), 3–10. doi: 10.1037/0021-843x.108.1.3

Segerstrom, S. C. (2007). Optimism and resources: Effects on each other and on health over 10 years. *Journal of Research in Personality*, *41*(4), 772–786. doi: 10.1016/j.jrp.2006.09.004

Segerstrom, S. C., Evans, D. R., & Eisenlohr-Moul, T. A. (2010). Optimism and pessimism dimensions in the life orientation test-revised: Method and meaning. *Journal of Research in Personality*. *45*(1), 126–129. doi: 10.1016/j.jrp.2010.11.007

Segerstrom, S. C., Taylor, S. E., Kemeny, M. E., & Fahey, J. L. (1998). Optimism is associated with mood, coping, and immune change in response to stress. *Journal of Personality and Social Psychology*, *74*(6), 1646–1655.

Shogren, K. A., Lopez, S. J., Wehmeyer, M. L., Little, T. D., & Pressgrove, C. L. (2006). The role of positive psychology constructs in predicting life satisfaction in adolescents with and without cognitive disabilities: An exploratory study. *The Journal of Positive Psychology*, *1*(1), 37–52. doi: 10.1080/17439760500373174

Siddique, H. I., LaSalle-Ricci, V. H., Glass, C. R., Arnkoff, D. B., & Díaz, R. J. (2006). Worry, Optimism, and Expectations as Predictors of Anxiety and Performance in the First Year of Law School. *Cognitive Therapy and Research, 30*(5), 667–676. doi: 10.1007/s10608-006-9080-3

Solberg Nes, L., Carlson, C. R., Crofford, L. J., de Leeuw, R., & Segerstrom, S. C. (2011). Individual differences and self-regulatory fatigue: Optimism, conscientiousness, and self-consciousness. *Personality and Individual Differences, 50*(4), 475–480. doi: 10.1016/j.paid.2010.11.011

Suh, E., Diener, F., & Fujita, F. (1996). Events and subjective well-being: Only recent events matter. *Journal of Personality and Social Psychology, 70*(5), 1091–1102. doi: 10.1037/0022-3514.70.5.1091

Taylor, S. E., Kemeny, M. E., Aspinwall, L. G., Schneider, S. G., Rodriguez, R., & Herbert, M. (1992). Optimism, coping, psychological distress, and high-risk sexual behavior among men at risk for acquired immunodeficiency syndrome (AIDS). *Journal of Personality and Social Psychology, 63*(3), 460–473. doi: 10.1037/0022-3514.63.3.460

Townsend, A. L., & Franks, M. M. (1995). Binding ties: Closeness and conflict in adult children's caregiving relationships. *Psychology and Aging, 10*(3), 343–351. doi: 10.1037/0882-7974.10.3.343

Treharne, G. J., Lyons, A. C., Booth, D. A., & Kitas, G. D. (2007). Psychological well-being across 1 year with rheumatoid arthritis: Coping resources as buffers of perceived stress. *British Journal of Health Psychology, 12*(3), 323–345. doi: 10.1348/135910706x109288

Triemstra, A. H. M., Van der Ploeg, H. M., Smit, C., Briët, E., Adèr, H. J., & Rosendaal, F. R. (1998). Well-being of haemophilia patients: A model for direct and indirect effects of medical parameters on the physical and psychosocial functioning. *Social Science & Medicine, 47*(5), 581–593. doi: 10.1016/s0277-9536(98)00117-8

Vitaliano, P. P., Zhang, J., & Scanlan, J. M. (2003). Is caregiving hazardous to one's physical health? A meta-analysis. *Psychological Bulletin, 6*, 946–972.

Voltaire. (1759). *Candide, ou L'Optimisme*. Geneva: Cramer.

World Health Organization (2001). *International classification of functioning, disability, and health (ICF)*. Geneva: Author.

6

Social Well-Being and Friendship of People with Intellectual Disability

Joanne Kersh, Laura Corona, *and* Gary Siperstein

Abstract

The chapter demonstrates that a positive psychological perspective on friendships that encompasses universal concepts of belonging, connection, and well-being is important for people with intellectual disability. Evidence suggests that those with intellectual disability, regardless of level of impairment, enjoy close meaningful friendships that fulfill social needs. Much research on the social relationships of people with intellectual disability has focused on social acceptance and positive interactions with typically developing peers; however, new research points to the importance of friendships between people with intellectual disability. The chapter concludes that, for people with intellectual disability, social relationships satisfy an essential human need for belonging and human connection. By focusing on the positive relationships experienced by people with intellectual disability, this chapter adds to a more inclusive positive psychology that embraces and accommodates developmental differences.

Key Words: intellectual disability, friendship, social relationships, adolescents, adults

Social Well-Being and Friendship of People with Intellectual Disability

A significant amount of research and writing has focused on the social inclusion and social acceptance of people with intellectual disability, offering a "macro" perspective of social relationships at the societal level. Although referencing this literature, this chapter adopts a more "micro" perspective, focusing on the relationships of individuals and documenting their unique qualities and benefits. We begin by talking about the concepts of social well-being, belonging, and friendship as they apply broadly to humankind. We then move on to discuss the literature that addresses the social networks and friendships of people with intellectual disability more specifically.

Social Well-Being

The predilection to form social bonds has long been recognized as a defining characteristic of humanity. Perhaps the first recorded acknowledgment of this was made by Aristotle, when he wrote

that "man is by nature a social animal," a sentiment since echoed by numerous philosophers and scholars. Friends are consistently included near the top of people's lists of what is most important in their lives, along with other meaningful relationships, namely those with significant others and family members (Berscheid & Peplau, 1983; Klinger, 1977). As such, friendship and social well-being (i.e., the fulfillment of our universal need to connect with others) are natural constructs to be examined through the lens of positive psychology. Indeed, Martin Seligman, one of the leaders in the field of positive psychology, has recently revised his conceptual model of positive psychology from a focus on happiness to a focus on well-being more broadly, which he has identified as "flourishing" (Seligman, 2011). In this more comprehensive conceptual model, positive relationships are recognized as a critical element—along with positive emotions, engagement, meaning, and achievement—of well-being, without which individuals cannot flourish.

This focus on well-being and the role played by social relationships has increasingly become a prominent concern of those who work with people with intellectual disability. In the decades since policies of deinstitutionalization and mainstreaming brought people with intellectual disability into the public sphere, many policy makers, service providers, and researchers have advocated for social inclusion and integration, based in part on the belief that a network of socially supportive relationships is not only desirable but also a vital necessity (Cummins & Lau, 2003; Forrester-Jones et al., 2006). The emphasis on quality of life (QOL) in the field of intellectual and developmental disabilities research and service provision has also maintained that social relationships are of key importance in the lives of people with disabilities. Among the core domains of QOL (emotional well-being, interpersonal relations, material well-being, personal development, physical well-being, self-determination, social inclusion, and rights), interpersonal relations and social inclusion are the most frequently referenced in the literature (Verdugo, Schalock, Keith, & Stancliffe, 2005). Given the recognized importance of social relationships and belonging in the field of psychology, it is appropriate that social relationships be given a place of prominence in the lives of people with intellectual disability as well.

The Need to Belong

Quality friendships and other positive human connections are undeniable goods in anybody's life. For example, Maslow (1943) described the human need for love and belonging as one of the most basic, secondary only to physical and safety needs. This essentialist view frames an individual's relationships as a basic condition for well-being. There is thus the expectation that, except in the most adverse of conditions, the need to belong will be a driving force in any person's life and, if the basic need for social connectedness is not met, individuals will not be able to achieve a healthy sense of self or attain their full potential. Robust empirical evidence supports the idea that the need for human relationships is universal and innate (see Baumeister & Leary [1995] for a review). Not only do people form social bonds relatively naturally, they tend to resist their dissolution and devote considerable energy and resources to the formation and maintenance of their interpersonal relationships.

Furthermore, there is strong evidence to support an evolutionary basis for the tendency to engage in social relationships. Because early humans were more likely to survive if they existed in groups, "evolution reinforced the preference for strong human bonds by selecting genes that support pleasure in company and produce feelings of unease when involuntarily alone" (Cacioppo & Patrick, 2008). In other words, not only do meaningful relationships and interactions tend to promote positive affective responses, but being deprived of them results in feelings of profound insecurity and painful feelings of loneliness. Significant research has emerged from the field of neuroscience that suggests that the human brain is hardwired to seek out social connections and interactions. For example, neuroimaging has revealed that the brain responds to social pain, such as rejection or loneliness, in much the same way as to physical pain (Cacioppo & Patrick, 2008). Further, the absence of human connection and interaction—in other words, social disconnection or loneliness—has been associated with a range of deleterious neurological outcomes, including the progression of Alzheimer's disease (Wilson et al., 2007). Although there is great variation in the human need for connection (i.e., some are more sensitive to a lack of human contact than others), this need nonetheless appears to be universal.

Indeed, one's social connectedness is closely related to a range of emotional and behavioral outcomes and, in its absence, distinct negative consequences are observed. Generally speaking, people who have close supportive relationships exhibit more positive affective responses such as happiness and contentment (e.g., Diener & Seligman, 2002; Myers, 2000), experience lower levels of stress (Cohen & Wills, 1985), tend to be both mentally and physically healthier (e.g., Cohen, 2004; House, Landis, & Umberson, 1988), and live longer (e.g., Holt-Lunstad, Smith, & Layton, 2010). On the other hand, being rejected or excluded generally leads to distress and a range of powerful negative emotions, such as loneliness, anxiety, and depression (e.g., Weiss, 1973; Cacioppo & Patrick, 2008). Because a sense of belonging is so frequently associated with positive outcomes and its absence with such a wide range of negative outcomes and maladjustment, social connection is recognized not just as something people want, but as a legitimate human need, without which human flourishing cannot be attained (Baumeister & Leary, 1995).

Friendship

A variety of relationship types may fulfill the need to belong in individuals. Certainly, for many people, family members provide a deep sense of connection. For some adults, positive and productive interactions with workmates and colleagues or membership in a meaningful group or club provide opportunities to feel allied with others. For people with disabilities, relationships developed with service professionals and other caregivers are often quite close and assume deep significance (e.g., Campo, Sharpton, Thompson, & Sexton, 1997; Johnson, Douglas, Bigby, & Iacono, 2010). At the most fundamental level, friendships are one of a number of relationships that can satisfy the basic need for human connection and belonging.

Taking a more fine-grained approach, however, there is evidence that the need for belonging and social connection is not singular, but is, in fact, made up of a number of more specific needs, such as the need for affection and love, the need for companionship, the need for intimacy, the need for support, and the need for nurturance (Buhrmester, 1996). Many of these "social needs" appear to carry different significance at varying stages of development. For example, an infant's primary social need is for tender nurturance and security, whereas, during the toddler and preschool years, children develop a need for social input that focuses on play and entertainment. During the early elementary school years, children discover the need for peer acceptance and companionship. Along with the notion that the need to belong is multidimensional and developmental in nature, it has also been suggested that different types of relationships may be particularly effective in meeting specific social needs. Friends appear to be exceptionally well-suited for fulfilling companionship and intimacy needs (Weiss, 1973). In fact, Sullivan (1953) attributed the formation of close friendships ("chumships") in adolescence to the emerging need to form intimate bonds with peers and avoid the debilitating experience of loneliness.

Friendship, widely recognized as an affectionate bond between individuals, appears to be a universal phenomenon, occurring across cultures (Krappmann, 1996) and understood by children as early as toddlerhood (Howes, 1996). Reliance on implicit understanding and imprecise definitions, however, breeds ambiguity and has led to significant challenges in the empirical study of friendship (Bukowski, Newcomb, & Hartup, 1996). Adding greater complexity, there are different degrees or levels of friendship that carry different meanings and significance for the individuals involved. As social scientists, how do we differentiate between a classmate or workmate, an occasional friend, a good friend, and a best friend? How do we operationalize these concepts, and how do we measure the differential impacts of each on individual development and well-being? As Krappman (1996) concluded in his review of cross-cultural perspectives on friendship, friendship is "perhaps the most human of relationships...no relationship is less standardized...no relationship can be realized in richer variation than friendship can be" (p. 37).

For empirical and theoretical purposes, friendship is best understood to be "a close, mutual, and voluntary dyadic relationship" (Rubin, Coplan, Chen, Bowker, & McDonald, 2010, p. 525). Characterized by high levels of reciprocity and perceived equality, friends share a mutual liking of each other and engage in positive interactions in which there exist expectations from both members of the dyad of companionship, security, instrumental help, and emotional support (Bukowski, Motzoi, & Meyer, 2009). This understanding, with its emphasis on reciprocity and choice, distinguishes friendships from other types of close relationships (e.g., with family, coworkers, caregivers), as well as from other peer-group social constructs, such as social acceptance (Asher, Parker, & Walker, 1996; Hughes, Redley, & Ring, 2011; Rubin et al., 2010). Hughes and colleagues (2011) have referred to this as "friendship as commonly understood," reflecting the dominant perspective among social scientists and scholars, and facilitating conclusions and generalizations about the meaning and impact of having friends.

The construct of friendship, however, still leaves considerable latitude for interpretation. For example, the word "friend" is used to describe both the playmates of the preschool years as well as the emotionally close confidantes of adolescence and young adulthood. Hartup and Stevens (1997) designated a useful model for embracing the wide variations that are observed in the expression of friendship across the lifespan, conceptualizing friendship in terms of deep and surface structures. *Deep structure* refers to the social meaning or "essence" of friendship, whereas *surface structure* refers to the regular social interactions that characterize the friendship. Hartup and Stevens identified reciprocity as the deep structure, the essence that is understood as universal and consistent throughout the life course and across contexts and situations. In other words, all friendships are reciprocal, embodied by something shared, at any age and under any circumstances. Surface structure, on the other hand, is manifested in the limitless ways in which friends might interact with each other and is likely to vary with age and situation. The structures are related in that reciprocity, the essence, is expressed through the specific interactions of friendship. Thus, young children experience the reciprocity of friendship by engaging in shared play. The friendships of adolescents and young adults are characterized by the mutual communication of ideas and feelings and the provision of emotional support, as well as by sharing companionable activities (e.g., "hanging out"). Reciprocity in the friendships of adults is often characterized by instrumental support (e.g., helping, doing favors), shared affection, and mutual respect (Hartup & Stevens, 1997; Rawlins, 1992; Shea, Thompson, & Blieszner, 1988). Thus, although friendships are apt to appear very different from each other on the surface, they are universally undergirded by a foundation of mutual attraction and reciprocal benefit. Said another way, all friendships are two-way streets, regardless of how they are paved.

That friendship is both a universal experience but also varied in its form means that the study of friendship is fraught with methodological challenges. For example, friendship is often measured by investigators as a dichotomous variable (friend vs. nonfriend), yet the reality of friendships, as mentioned, generally reflects much more variation. Furthermore, research often depends on self-report, which may result in an overreliance on implicit understandings of friendship. Although self-report data are often appropriate for assessing individual perceptions of friendship quality, they may also sometimes lead to spurious conclusions. For example, almost all children, when asked, will name some peers as "friends," even if they do not actually have friends (Furman, 1996; Parker & Asher, 1993). Although reciprocity is unequivocally acknowledged as a defining characteristic of friendship, investigators may not confirm that a nominated friendship is reciprocated. Yet conclusions in the literature about the salient qualities of friendship, as well as the value of friendship, are generally based on the existence of "good" friendships; that is, friendships that are reciprocated, positive, and close, and that fulfill the requisite social provisions of companionship, intimacy, and support. This can result in an incongruity between the reporting of the existence of friendship on one hand and the anticipated value and benefits of friendship on the other. Because in these pages we are concerned primarily with the value of friendship, we have chosen to focus on research that documents these high-quality, mutual relationships. We refer to these throughout the chapter as "good" or "true" friendships (in contrast to the unreciprocated and unstable relationships that might be considered friendships in name only) because they embody the characteristics inherent in friendships "as commonly understood" (Hughes et al., 2011).

Our goal in the remainder of this chapter is to demonstrate that a positive psychological perspective, one that encompasses universal concepts of belonging, connection, and well-being, is also appropriate and relevant for people with intellectual disability. We suggest that social relationships, including friendships, are similarly important to the flourishing of people with intellectual disability as to anybody else, serving the same broad purpose of supporting social well-being (fulfilling social needs) and contributing to a range of positive outcomes. There is a small but robust body of work that demonstrates that some people with intellectual disability, particularly those with milder impairment, enjoy close meaningful friendships that fulfill the same social needs as they do for their nondisabled peers (e.g., Emerson & Hatton, 2008b). Unfortunately, there is also evidence that people with intellectual disability, in general, are less likely to experience friendships (Emerson & Hatton, 2008a; Solish, Perry, & Minnes, 2010) and more likely to experience social exclusion and isolation than the general population (Bigby, 2008; Cummins & Lau, 2003). There has also been some limited discussion about whether all people with intellectual disability, particularly those with more profound impairments, are capable of engaging in friendship, in the strictest meaning of the word (Hughes et al., 2011). Nonetheless, there is no question that everybody, regardless of functionality, is capable of, worthy of, and ultimately better off for experiencing deep human connections in their lives, and we will explore these ideas in the following pages.

The Social World of People with Intellectual Disability

Although there is a vast literature that addresses the social relationships and friendships of individuals in the general population, perhaps not surprisingly the literature that addresses these constructs in people with intellectual disability is relatively sparse. Small as it may be, however, the literature is varied, exploring topics such as the association between well-being and social relationships for people with intellectual disability (e.g., Lunsky & Benson, 2001; Miller & Chan, 2008), the number and types of relationships included in the social networks of people with intellectual disability (e.g., Barber & Hupp, 1993; Bigby, 1997; Forrester-Jones et al., 2006), and the patterns of social interaction between people with and without intellectual disability (e.g. Siperstein, Leffert, & Wenz-Gross, 1997; Staub, Schwartz, Gallucci, & Peck, 1994). Taken together, this research provides a number of insights into the social worlds of people with intellectual disability.

Social Networks, Social Support, and Well-Being of People with Intellectual Disability

To set the stage, there is support for the notion that relationships play a role in the well-being and QOL of people with intellectual disability. In research with adults with mild intellectual disability, for example, social support has been found to relate to subjective life satisfaction (Miller & Chan, 2008) and QOL (Bramston, Chipuer, & Pretty, 2005; Lunsky & Benson, 2001). A similar association between QOL and social support has been reported for people with profound intellectual disability; for example, in a study that relied on proxy reports made by staff members, QOL was positively related to having a large number of socially supportive staff, family, and friends (Campo et al., 1997). There is also evidence that the absence of social support is related to negative outcomes, most often loneliness, for people with intellectual disability (e.g., Luftig, 1988; McVilly, Stancliffe, Parmenter, & Burton-Smith, 2006a). For example, adults who were identified as the "most lonely" in a study by McVilly and colleagues (2006a) reported dissatisfaction with the size of their social networks and with the frequency with which they saw their friends. Low levels of social support also have been associated with more adjustment problems in children (Wenz-Gross & Siperstein, 1996) and greater depression in adults with mild intellectual disability (Reiss & Benson, 1985). These findings suggest that social connections play a similar role in the lives of people with intellectual disability as they do for people without disabilities.

Beyond demonstrating an association between social support and QOL, researchers have also examined the types of relationships that make up the social networks of people with intellectual disability. In general, there is robust evidence that people with intellectual disability, regardless of their level of impairment, have a range of positive relationships in their lives (e.g., Barber & Hupp, 1993; Bigby, 1997; Forrester-Jones et al., 2006; Johnson et al., 2010). These relationships appear to include a wide variety of people and serve a number of different functions. For instance, Forrester-Jones and colleagues (2006) found that adults with mild to moderate intellectual disability living in a variety of supported living arrangements had an average of 22 social network members providing a range of supports, including spending time together, "looking out for" participants, and helping with domestic tasks. Bigby (1997) reported that older adults living in various forms of supported accommodation generally had relationships with family, caregivers, and other acquaintances, as well as with a "key person" who acted as an advocate and was a consistent, frequent contact in the individual's life.

The Social Networks of People with Profound Intellectual Disability

The results are less clear, however, regarding whether friendships are typically part of the social networks of people with intellectual disability. Before considering the research available on this topic, however, it is prudent to consider the ways in which the severity of an individual's disability may impact a person's capacity for friendships, particularly given the definitions of friendship discussed earlier. Although we maintain that human connection and relationships are universal goods for all people, regardless of disability status, it would be naïve to imply that all people with disabilities are capable of participating in friendships as defined here, characterized by reciprocity, equality, and intimacy (Hughes et al., 2011). Hughes and colleagues (2011) provide a cogent analysis of the ways in which the concept of friendship "as commonly understood" is problematic when applied to people with profound intellectual disability. For adults with significant impairments who may need support in nearly all aspects of day-to-day living and have substantial deficits in their ability to communicate, act intentionally, or even understand the concept of "friend," reciprocity and equity may be unrealistic goals in a relationship.

A case study of a woman with severe intellectual disability and her social network illustrates this well (Johnson et al., 2010). For her part, the young woman engaged in positive interactions with members of her social network, made up of family members, service providers, a former service provider, and peers with intellectual disability, and expressed preferences for some over others. When describing their relationships with the young woman, the members of her social network reported enjoying her company, feeling love toward her, and experiencing personal satisfaction from working with her. It was clear that they generally valued these relationships; nonetheless, their descriptions did not contain the elements of reciprocity, intimacy, or mutual concern and support that are hallmarks of friendship. As Hughes et al. (2011) pointed out, there is little doubt that people with even the most severe disabilities can and do have valuable relationships with strong emotional components, but these relationships may not embody friendship "as commonly understood."

Friendships of People with Intellectual Disability

With the acknowledgment that the severity of an individual's disability may preclude the existence of friendship as defined here, we next consider the research that has addressed the friendships of people with intellectual disability. The following sections discuss a number of investigations that have taken a variety of approaches, including asking people with intellectual disability about their friends, asking proxy respondents about the friendships of people with intellectual disability, and taking an ethnographic approach to document the interactions and experiences that characterize existing friendships. Overall, this work has produced mixed results, with some research demonstrating the existence of friendship and other research suggesting that a lack of friendship is problematic for people with intellectual disability. A related line of research has evaluated the level of social acceptance experienced by people with intellectual disability, as well as the interventions that have been designed to increase this acceptance along with the frequency and quality of social interactions that occur between people with and without disabilities.

Do people with intellectual disability have friends? A small number of studies suggest that friendships are part of the lives of many adolescents and adults with intellectual disability. For example, in a study of adolescents with intellectual disability in special education schools and in self-contained classrooms within mainstream schools, the overwhelming majority of students (about 95%) in both settings reported having friends (Heiman, 2000). Although students in self-contained classrooms reported larger friend networks on average, the vast majority of students in the special education school reported having at least one friend. Similarly, in a sociometric study of friendship patterns among adolescents in a special school for students with intellectual disability, Siperstein & Bak (1989) reported that participants named, on average, four other students as friends. Studies of adults have similarly documented the existence of friendships in the lives of people

with intellectual disability. For example, adults living in both small community homes and a large group facility reported having close meaningful relationships with friends, best friends, and significant others (Barber & Hupp, 1993).

In surveys using proxy respondents, however, researchers have reported somewhat less optimistic findings. In Bigby's (1997) investigation of the social networks of adults with intellectual disability, informants who had a "close, long-term relationship" with the people with intellectual disability provided information about the "supportive ties" in the individuals' lives. On average, the informants listed six members who made up the social network of the individual with intellectual disability, including family, primary caregivers, and church connections. Less than two-thirds (63%) of the informants, however, mentioned a friend as part of the social networks of the people with intellectual disability. Additionally, in a large national survey, *Adults with Learning Difficulties in England 2003/4*, which also utilized proxy respondents, Emerson and colleagues (Emerson, Malam, Davies, & Spencer, 2005) found that 31% of adults with intellectual disability had had no contact with friends in the last year, compared to only 3% of the general population who responded to similar questioning in a separate population-based study (Gordon et al., 2000).

Unfortunately, these studies are difficult to interpret for a variety of reasons. In the studies relying on proxy respondents (Bigby, 1997; Emerson et al., 2005), there was little information about who the proxy respondents were or what their understanding of friendship was (Hughes et al., 2011), making interpretation of results difficult. For example, in the national survey by Emerson and colleagues (2005), because the question asked about contact with friends rather than simply having friends, it is unclear whether those 31% actually had no friends or whether they had friends and never saw them. Regardless, based on the understanding that we have adopted, it is unlikely that someone with whom one has no contact could fulfill the role of friend.

Moreover, in the studies that relied on self-report (Barber & Hupp, 1993; Heiman, 2000), the authors did not report further, potentially important details regarding the friendships, such as who these friends were, the settings in which the friends spent time together, or the frequency with which the individuals were in contact with their friends, thus making it impossible to assess the quality of these "friendships." Additionally, significant variation in personal interpretations of friendship was apparent.

Barber and Hupp (1993) noted that participants in their study sometimes had difficulty deciding how to categorize a particular relationship and that there was great variation in the frequency of interactions with friends and the qualities ascribed to friends. For instance, one of the participants named an individual who had passed away, explaining that the friend "lived in his heart." Furthermore, when asked who their friends were, the answers were sometimes unexpected; a number of the students interviewed by Siperstein and Bak (1989) named one or more adults—including teachers, parents, neighbors, and doctors—as friends. In summary, we note that in these studies the concept of friendship was left open to the interpretation of the (self- and proxy) respondents, without any indication of whether these relationships were actually characterized by reciprocity, equality, and choice, the elements of "true" friendship. Certainly, the nomination of adults (including parents, teachers, and doctors) in the study by Siperstein and Bak (1989) leads us to conclude that the results of these studies may be misleading.

Finally, there is some evidence to suggest that even when people with intellectual disability report having friends, their social needs remain unfulfilled (Heiman, 2000; McVilly et al., 2006a). Among a group of adults with intellectual disability who were classified as the "most lonely" in a study by McVilly and colleagues (2006a), all were able to name someone who they considered a friend, yet this group also reported low levels of regular contact with their "best friend" and expressed dissatisfaction with this infrequency. This again illustrates the wide variations in interpretation of who a friend is, as well as the potential importance of collecting data on the quality of the friendship. Taken collectively, these findings suggest that, similar to the general population of youth who have participated in sociometric studies, adolescents and adults with intellectual disability may also overreport their friendships. Because "having friends" is considered a normative and socially desirable situation, individuals may be motivated to overstate the significance of their existing relationships. For example, there is some evidence that, for people with intellectual disability, proximity may play an inflated role in determining friendship (e.g., Heiman, 2000; Matheson, Olsen, & Weisner, 2007); thus, an acquaintance with whom one has fairly regular contact, but limited interactions, could be interpreted as a friend. It is likely that a variety of factors contribute to the ambiguity in determining the prevalence of friendship relationships in the intellectual disability

community, and, as a result, there is a lack of conclusive empirical evidence to indicate the extent to which people with intellectual disability experience true, meaningful, reciprocate friendships (Hughes et al., 2011).

Do friendships exist between people with and without intellectual disability? A more extensive and robust line of research has investigated the social interactions and relationships between people with and without intellectual disability. In the years since policies of educational inclusion and mainstreaming have become commonplace, there have been high levels of interest in the extent to which people with intellectual disability are integrated into school, work, and community settings. Unfortunately, much of this research has revealed disheartening results, suggesting that many people with intellectual disability experience low levels of social acceptance and friendship when compared to nondisabled peers (Cummins & Lau, 2003; Fishbein, 2002).

A considerable amount of this research has been conducted within the school context and has indicated that students with intellectual disability are less likely to be socially accepted and more likely to be socially rejected than their nondisabled peers (e.g., Larrivee & Horne, 1991; Luftig, 1988; Nabors, 1997; Sale & Carey, 1995; Taylor, Asher, & Williams, 1987). For example, sociometric data from one study demonstrated that typically developing children generally prefer to study with and socialize with other children without disabilities, rather than with their peers with disabilities (Žic & Igric, 2001). In a study conducted in Italy, although elementary school students expressed a willingness to help their peers with disabilities, they were far less inclined to be friends (Nota, Ferrari, & Soresi, 2005). Given this lack of social acceptance, it is not surprising that in a survey of more than 5,000 middle school students from around the United States, only 10% of the students reported having a friend with intellectual disability (Siperstein, Parker, Bardon, & Widaman, 2007).

Interventions to promote friendships between people with and without intellectual disability. In response, a number of interventions have been developed to increase the frequency and quality of social interactions between students with and without intellectual disability, based on the belief that these interactions will benefit students with disabilities both socially and academically and may eventually even lead to friendships (Carter & Hughes, 2005). Some of these interventions employ direct instruction to teach social and communication skills to students with intellectual disability; for instance, using "communication books" to teach appropriate conversational topics and structures (Hunt, Alwell, & Goetz, 1988; Hunt, Alwell, Goetz, & Sailor, 1990). Other successful interventions have involved teaching self-management strategies (Hughes et al., 2002b) and using peers to teach conversational strategies. Successful interventions have resulted in an increased incidence of students with intellectual disability initiating interactions and taking more turns in conversation, as well as increases in peer response and greater variety in the conversations between students with and without intellectual disability (e.g., Hughes et al., 2000; Hughes et al., 2004).

Similarly, interventions focused on increasing contact between students with and without intellectual disability have been successful in increasing the amount of social interactions students with intellectual disability had with nondisabled peers (e.g., Kennedy, Shukla, & Fryxell, 1997; Hughes, Carter, Hughes, Bradford, & Copeland, 2002a). Peer buddy programs, in which students with intellectual disability are paired with peers without intellectual disability, have been shown to promote positive social interactions between students with intellectual disability and their nondisabled peers (Hughes et al., 2001; Marom, Cohen, & Naon, 2007). For example, in one intervention, students with and without intellectual disability were paired either to engage in free-time activities together (e.g., reading magazines) or so that the student without disabilities could assist the student with intellectual disability with an "instructional activity" (e.g., completing worksheets) (Hughes et al., 2002a). Working together in a noninstructional capacity was associated with more social conversations and higher quality interactions.

There is abundant indication, however, that even when social interactions take place and relationships are formed, they are markedly different from relationships between students without disabilities, and are characterized by less verbal communication, collaborative decision making, and affective exchange than are interactions between children without disabilities (Siperstein et al., 1997). Interactions between children with and without intellectual disability often assume a hierarchical structure that is not typically characteristic of friendships or peer interactions between nondisabled children more broadly; that is, the individual without disabilities generally takes the role of leader or instructor or otherwise provides support in their dyadic interactions (Murray-Seegert,

1989; Siperstein et al., 1997; Staub et al., 1994). Moreover, this type of hierarchical helping relationship may also be reinforced by teacher expectations (Staub et al., 1994). Typically developing students have expressed a range of responses to this type of intervention; for instance, some have expressed a sense of personal satisfaction in helping another person or a feeling of being more prepared to handle disability in their own lives (Murray-Seegert, 1989). However, feelings of friendship are rarely mentioned (Staub et al., 1994).

Compared to the number of interventions that take place in school settings, far fewer have been developed for adults with intellectual disability. The interventions that do exist have generally aimed to foster social integration in the workplace (Chadsey & Beyer, 2001; Storey, 2002). Similar to school-based interventions, they have focused mainly on either teaching social skills and behaviors to people with intellectual disability or partnering employees with and without intellectual disability so that the nondisabled employee can provide support (Chadsey & Beyer, 2001). For instance, interventions that have successfully increased frequency and quality of social interactions have focused on coaching adults with intellectual disability on how to appropriately ask questions (Storey & Garff, 1997; Storey, Lengyel, & Pruszynski, 1997) and how to initiate and participate in conversations (Storey & Provost, 1996), as well as teaching more general strategies for engaging in appropriate social behaviors (Collet-Klingenberg & Chadsey-Rusch, 1991).

Interventions that pair employees with and without disabilities for the purpose of support have also had some success in increasing the social interactions of employees with intellectual disability (Lee, Storey, Anderson, Goetz, & Zivolich 1997; Park et al., 1991). In a study that compared a traditional job coach model with a mentor model, employees with mentors had more reciprocal social interactions with nondisabled employees than did those with job coaches (Lee et al., 1997). However, coworker support interventions have not all been successful (e.g., Gaylord-Ross, Park, Johnston, Lee, & Goetz, 1995), and, even when they are, the interventions focus on workplace social interactions, which are not necessarily likely to become friendships.

Moreover, even when interventions do focus directly on fostering friendships between people with and without intellectual disability, such as in the Best Buddies program, the resulting relationships often consist only of periodic meetings and conversations (Hardman & Clark, 2006). In a national survey of the Best Buddies College Program, only 46% of participants with intellectual disability reported speaking with their buddy at least once a month (Hardman & Clark, 2006), and although the majority of people with intellectual disability reported enjoying the experience of participating in the program, it is clear from the infrequency with which many pairs of buddies interacted, as well as the apparent lack of reciprocity, that true friendships cannot be expected to form as a result.

Social acceptance is not the same as friendship. In general, there is considerable indication that many of these interventions are of high quality and have been successful in their aim of increasing positive social contact between people with and without intellectual disability; however, evidence of friendship formation is lacking. Although these interventions are valuable in their potential to encourage and enhance social interactions, these interactions do not constitute the closeness of friendships, in which positive interactions are supplemented by meaningful shared experiences and mutual self-disclosure and concern (Bukowski et al., 2009; Rubin et al., 2010). In fact, broadly speaking, there is powerful evidence to suggest that even when social intervention programs are successful in improving social acceptance, true friendships rarely result (Asher et al., 1996). Despite the circumscribed success of intervention programs, real social integration has remained elusive, and there remains a very low occurrence of friendship between people with and without disabilities, among both youth and adult populations (Kersh, 2011).

Several scholars have warned against conflating the concepts of social acceptance and friendship (see Asher et al., 1996). Although both address the interactions of people with their peers, they are conceptually quite different. Acceptance is a unilateral construct, addressing the extent to which an individual is liked or accepted by his or her peers, and does not account for the dyadic, reciprocal nature of friendship. Although the two constructs are related, they represent very different dimensions of peer social interactions. In other words, although the likelihood of having friends tends to increase with peer acceptance, it is also true that many children who are not well-liked by their peer group have friends, and, conversely, some children who are generally well-liked do not have close friends (Asher et al., 1996). Further, being well-liked and having friends may serve different social needs. More specifically, although being accepted satisfies the developmental need to identify with one's peers and feel a sense of connection to the larger group, forming a friendship meets the needs for intimacy and close companionship. Not only do these needs have different developmental timetables, but they are also associated with different socioemotional outcomes (Sullivan, 1953).

Overall, the research on the social relationships of people with intellectual disability described so far presents an incomplete and unsatisfying story. To summarize, when researchers have asked people with intellectual disability about their friendships, the concept of "friend" is left ambiguous and issues of reciprocity and equality are largely ignored, making it especially difficult to draw clear conclusions about how the word is both interpreted and used by people with intellectual disability or their proxy respondents (Barber & Hupp, 1993; Hughes et al., 2011). Moreover, when documenting various relationships in the lives of people with intellectual disability, research has generally failed to address the question of quality and largely ignored the meaning and value of these relationships for the individuals. Additionally, much of the work that has addressed the peer relationships of people with intellectual disability has focused specifically on interactions between people with and without intellectual disability, which, even when positive, generally do not approximate friendships (Kersh, 2011).

Qualitative studies of friendships of people with intellectual disability. Although we may be ill-equipped to draw conclusions about the extent to which friendships are part of the lives of youth and adults with intellectual disability based on the extant literature, we are more readily able to offer up a picture of what friendships look like for people with intellectual disability when they do occur. The recognition that friendships, although universally signified, are also personally experienced has led to a relatively small but compelling body of work that has explored the friendship experiences of adolescents and adults with intellectual disability in some depth. This work is largely qualitative, using interviews, focus groups, and ethnographic methods to reveal individuals' lived experiences of friendship. Despite some methodological variation, they were all motivated by the conviction that to understand people's experiences, one must ask the individuals themselves. Each of these studies has shown that people with intellectual disability (and other developmental disabilities) do indeed experience true friendships, that they value these relationships very highly, and that, just as we might suppose, these relationships both resemble and differ from those of their typically developing peers (Day &

Harry, 1999; Knox & Hickson, 2001; Matheson et al., 2007; McVilly, Stancliffe, Parmenter, & Burton-Smith 2006b; Randell & Cumella, 2009).

For example, in one particularly rich account of adolescent friendship, Day and Harry (1999) presented a case study of the close friendship that had developed between two girls with mild intellectual disability, aged 17 and 19, who were students in a self-contained special education classroom within a public high school. Day and Harry adopted a phenomenological approach to gain an "insider perspective" of the girls' friendship, spending time with the girls together and conducting in-depth interviews with them individually. Although the majority of the girls' interactions took place in school and over the phone, the authors also helped to arrange and accompanied the pair on an outing to the mall, allowing them to observe the girls in another setting. Day and Harry were able to amass a wealth of rich data and concluded that these girls had developed a friendship that looked a great deal like the friendships of their typically developing peers. They concluded that disability did not compromise the quality of this friendship in any way (and, in fact, may have actually served to strengthen their bond); however, it did contribute to logistical challenges that kept the girls from "spending the kind of time together that would be normative for most individuals of their age in this society" (Day & Harry, 1999, p. 229).

In another investigation of the friendships of teens, Matheson et al. (2007) conducted ethnographic research with 27 adolescents (aged 16–17) with a range of developmental disabilities and functional levels (Stanford-Binet IQ scores ranged from 48 to 105) who were part of a larger longitudinal investigation of the development of these youth and their families. Investigators spent a minimum of 10 hours with each teen in the study and their families, conducted semi-structured interviews that allowed the teens to talk about their friends, and were able to spend time with actual friendship dyads in 19 out of the 27 cases. They found that most of the teens in the study had friendships, regardless of their functioning level. Although they concluded that the friendships they documented tended to be less complex and intense than those of typically developing youth and often needed higher levels of adult facilitation, these friendships were nonetheless deemed to be stable, companionable relationships that were highly satisfying and valued by the teens.

Several studies have focused on the friendships of adults, rather than youth. For example, Knox

and Hickson (2001) interviewed four adults (aged 26–58) with intellectual disability about their friendships. These four lived in varied settings: one lived in a large institutional setting, one had recently moved from an institutional setting to a hostel, and the remaining two lived in apartments—one with two other women and one with his girlfriend. Each of the four described having one or two best friends or "good mates" with whom they felt a particularly close affinity and had maintained relationships over many years. These friendships were deemed to be rich and rewarding, playing a "pervasive and pivotal role" in the lives of the four participants (Knox & Hickson, 2001, p. 287).

McVilly and colleagues (2006b) took another approach to learning about the friendships of adults with intellectual disability, conducting a focus group with 11 members of a self-advocacy association for people with intellectual disability ranging in age from 23 to 50. The focus group was convened to inform another study investigating the loneliness experiences of a separate group of people with intellectual disability, its purpose to give feedback and assist the researchers in interpreting their findings. The group used their own experiences and opinions to evaluate the data presented by the researchers, discussing topics such as the meaning of friendship, the characteristics and importance of best friends, the good and bad aspects of friendships, and the barriers faced in making and keeping friends. Based on the input from this "expert group," the authors concluded that, for many people with intellectual disability, the concept of friendship is meaningful and in fact could be considered "among the most important concerns in their life." Further, they also determined that although the friendships of adults with intellectual disability may require some extra support, they are quite similar to those of adults in the general population.

Finally, another study that put the friendships of adults with intellectual disability in sharp focus was conducted within an "intentional community" in England, in which people with and without intellectual disability live in a communal "village" setting, sharing responsibilities for meeting the needs of the community (Randell & Cumella, 2009). Fifteen adults with intellectual disability took part in in-depth interviews designed to explore their perceptions about their living arrangement and the meaning of their community to them. Although the interviews covered a wide range of topics, including home life, work, recreation, religious beliefs, and views about the intentional community, the results had much to add regarding the role of friendships and social relationships in the lives of people with intellectual disability and were of particular interest because they documented the natural development of these relationships within the context of an egalitarian society. The authors concluded that, given this type of community, which fosters high levels of social interactions among its members, removes logistical barriers such as transportation and safety issues, and discourages the "overt subordination of residents to staff," community members with intellectual disability were easily able to forge and maintain broad social networks, as well as close dyadic friendships, that contributed to a secure and satisfying sense of belonging.

Friendship qualities. Collectively, this work indicates that, in many ways, the friendships of people with intellectual disability resemble the friendships of people in the general population. Certainly, participants were able to name and talk about important friends in their lives, supporting the idea that this type of relationship is salient for people with intellectual disability. On a deeper level, these first-person accounts reveal that when we look closely at the friendships of people with intellectual disability, we generally see the close, positive, reciprocal relationships that typify the idea of friendship "as commonly understood," characterized by the qualities of (a) companionship, (b) intimacy, (c) support, (d) stability, and (e) similarity of characteristics and interests. In the following sections, we describe the findings that support the existence of true friendships for people with intellectual disability, discussing each of these qualities in some detail.

Companionship

One of the most prevalent themes to emerge from the qualitative literature reviewed here is that both youth and adults with intellectual disability value the interactions and activities that they share with their friends. Indeed, for those youth with intellectual disability who took part in these studies, companionship was one of the most noteworthy aspects of their friendships (e.g., Day & Harry, 1999; Heiman, 2000; Matheson et al., 2007). For example, in Day and Harry's (1999) case study of the girls described earlier, although their relationship was largely limited to the school context because of factors relating to both their cultural and disability statuses, the two spent a considerable amount of time together in school and spoke on the phone a few times a week. These friends chatted about boys, clothes, and shopping; they lightheartedly teased each other, joked and laughed together, and described each other and their relationship in affectionate, appreciative terms. The authors concluded that the friendship was characterized by fun, mutual enjoyment, and reciprocal appreciation.

In the ethnographic study of adolescents (Matheson et al., 2007), companionship was the most frequently mentioned theme to emerge from in-depth interviews about friendship. The teens described going to the mall, movies, and football games, as well as eating lunch together. Doing enjoyable, mutually satisfying things together, often in a variety of contexts, was a very important aspect of friendship for these young people, as it is for youth in general. For the youth in this study, companionship and positive interactions were defining features of their friendships, regardless of their functional level, even though the authors deemed other dimensions of these friendships to be less sophisticated and intense than those of their typically developing peers, with less frequency of disclosure, affective support, and conflict management.

Among adults as well, shared experiences and enjoyment of one another's company were salient aspects of friendship. There appears to be a general consensus that it is important for friends to "have fun together" (McVilly et al., 2006b). More specifically, when asked about friendships, adults talked about spending time with friends, enjoying one another's company, and engaging in activities together, such as visiting each other's homes, meeting for a meal or cup of coffee, going to movies, going out to clubs, and meeting regularly to watch a favorite television program (Emerson & McVilly, 2004; Knox & Hickson, 2001; McVilly et al., 2006b; Randell & Cumella, 2009). Thus, among youth and adults alike, sharing mutually enjoyable activities was an important part of friendship, although there seemed to be a greater emphasis on companionship among adolescents. As in the general population, companionship appears to be a more salient aspect of the friendships of youth, whereas adults placed greater emphasis and value on the emotional and instrumental support that their friendships afford. Nonetheless, companionship has been acknowledged as a critical part of any friendship at any life stage. Sharing enjoyable experiences with another sets the stage for friendship to develop, contributing "to a sense of shared history, joint fate, and a perception of investment in the relationship. Thus, shared experiences are the crucible for friendship formation and probably play a large role in cementing friendships" (Asher et al., 1996, p. 390).

Intimacy

Beyond simply spending time together, both adolescents and adults with intellectual disability appear to value the closeness of the relationships they have with their friends. For people with intellectual disability, as for others, there is an intimacy to their relationships with their good friends that involves reciprocal self-disclosure, the exchange of ideas and opinions, and a profound sense of confidence and trust. Although when asked about the meaning of friendship, people with intellectual disability often speak first of companionship, of having someone to share activities and interests, the significance that they place on having a close and trusted confidante cannot be overlooked. For example, Matheson and colleagues (2007) noted that the teens in their study cited intimacy as a reason for their friendship less than might be expected in a sample of typically developing youth, given its emphasis in the literature. However, given the functioning levels of the participants in their study, reflecting a range of cognitive and adaptive skills and developmental trajectories, it is still noteworthy that 30% spontaneously spoke about matters of intimacy and disclosure.

Many of the youth in the studies discussed here recognized and valued the emotional closeness that their friendships afforded. These adolescents with intellectual disability, like their typically developing peers, recognized that their friends are the people with whom they can safely share their private thoughts and secrets (Day & Harry, 1999; Heiman, 2000; Matheson et al., 2007). There was also some recognition that this sharing of experiences and mutual self-disclosure helped to strengthen their relationships. As one adolescent said when talking about his best friend, "I call him my brother because we've been through so much stuff together" (Matheson et al., 2007, p. 325). Day and Harry (1999) also observed a sense of easy intimacy between the adolescent girls in their case study. As one of the girls said, "She knows about me—what I like, what color I like, what kind of subject I like, she knows everything" (p. 224).

Adults with intellectual disability also acknowledged the importance of the closeness in their friendships, stressing the role of communication and trust among friends. Relationships with friends were recognized as closer than with other people in their lives (Knox & Hickson, 2001). As one individual said, "I can tell a lot of things to my friends that I wouldn't tell other people that I know" (Randell & Cumella, 2009, p. 722). In fact, for the adults who took part in the focus group on friendship, this was the most important aspect of their friendships

(McVilly et al., 2006b). They spoke at length about the importance of sharing and trust and agreed that having someone to talk to who accepted them and understood them was what they valued most about their friendships. As one of the participants said, "I just feel better after telling them [about my problems], even when they don't say nothing" (McVilly et al., 2006b, p. 700).

Emotional intimacy is consistently recognized as one of the defining characteristics of friendship in adolescence and adulthood, and the research on the friendships of youth and adults with intellectual disability reveals a comparable emphasis. Although companionship was often mentioned first when people with intellectual disability were asked about their friends, the importance they placed on having a close and trusted confidante was also readily apparent. Even typically developing youth may more readily talk about companionship and shared activities when asked to talk open-endedly about their friendships. It appears that, regardless of individual, developmental, and gender differences, the opportunity to be open and honest with a peer who is also willing to share openly and honestly is universally valued (Asher et al., 1996). Thus, for youth with intellectual disability, just as for their typically developing peers, a relationship characterized by closeness, that provides an atmosphere of comfort and trust, is likely appreciated, even if not explicitly acknowledged.

Support

Pervasive in this qualitative work were the many instances in which participants talked about the roles their friends played in providing help and support in their lives. Heiman (2000) interviewed adolescents with and without intellectual disability and noted that many in both groups defined a "good friend" as a person who helps and/or a person who provides emotional support. Similarly, a number of adolescents interviewed by Matheson and colleagues (2007) mentioned help, support, or acceptance when talking about friendship, citing not only instrumental support, such as assisting the participants in overcoming physical limitations, but also emotional and moral support, including support in social contexts, such as defending participants in the face of teasing or bullying.

The dimension of support emerged as very important in Day and Harry's (1999) case study. The girls revealed that the mutual support in their relationship came, in part, from an understanding of the experiences one another faced. For instance, the girls both came from families who had recently immigrated to the United States and whose cultural identities, although different from one another, were highly significant in their day-to-day lives. This shared "outsider" status and a respect for one another's cultural difference set the stage for a relationship that was characterized by mutual support within a setting of classmates who were not always able or disposed to understand the girls' backgrounds. The shared experience of being students with disabilities in the special education system led to additional instances of understanding and support, which included supporting one another when other students teased them. They would tell each other to "just ignore it" and remind each other that the students who made fun of them were "crazy" or "stupid." In an environment that could otherwise be isolating and lonely, the friendship fostered between these two girls sustained them and provided a great deal of comfort.

The themes of support and mutual concern were also prominent in the studies of friendships of adults with intellectual disability. The members of the focus group (McVilly et al., 2006b) described a friend as a person who can be counted on, as well as a person who is caring and understanding. When asked specifically to describe a best friend, members of the group volunteered that a best friend was someone who was "there when you need them most" and one whom "you can ask them for help and they will always help." Among the four adults interviewed by Knox and Hickson (2001), the topic of mutual concern came up often as participants talked about the types of social support their friendships provided. Various participants brought up ideas of being able to rely on their friends and trusting that their friends would stand up for them and help them in situations of conflict with others. Participants also talked about the instrumental types of help provided by a friend, with tasks such as cooking, budgeting money, and organizing. One man spoke about supporting his friend in his effort to lose weight and helping him stay on his diet. Thus, there was also acknowledgment of the reciprocal nature of the support; just as participants were able to list ways in which their friends helped them, so, too, were they able to name instances in which they helped their friends. This mutual concern for and reliance on one another appeared to be an important source of need fulfillment for these individuals.

The provision of both instrumental and emotional support was a key defining characteristic of friendships for both adolescents and adults. As in any friendship, there exists an expectation that one can turn to one's friends for help when needed and that, in return, an individual is ready and willing to reciprocate that help and support. For people with intellectual disability, their friends offered a valued and important source of support in facing the functional and attitudinal barriers that regularly confront people with intellectual disability. For example, friends provided a safe harbor from peer rejection and from the negative treatment of classmates. Research indicates that, for children who are generally not well-liked by their peers, having a good friend can be a powerful buffer against adjustment problems (Laursen, Bukowski, Aunola, & Nurmi, 2007; Waldrip, Malcolm, & Jensen-Campbell, 2008). Although the studies we reviewed generally did not measure psychosocial outcomes, such as depression, loneliness, and behavior problems, both adolescents and adults did talk about the comfort and reassurance that they were afforded through their friendships.

Stability

Individuals also often talked about their friendships as lasting and consistent parts of their lives. For adults especially, good friendships were often characterized by longevity. For instance, stability and longevity were consistent ideas in the interviews conducted by Knox and Hickson (2001), with participants noting specifically that their friendships had been maintained over a long period of time. Two of the participants (all of whom were over the age of 25) had met in school, whereas another said that he had known his friend "for years." The authors suggested that this longevity could play a role in creating a comfortable and predictable relationship that individuals expect to last, which is a hallmark of friendships and other meaningful relationships. The importance of lasting relationships was also discussed by the focus group participants (McVilly et al., 2006b); although some group members said that "sometimes you know you are best friends straight away" (p. 699), others argued that it was very important for two people to know each other for a long time to consider one another best friends, and many named people they had known since school as their best friends. Similarly, the adults in the intentional community talked about long-term friendships that had developed through years of regularly working and living alongside one another (Randell & Cumella, 2009).

Even among younger people with intellectual disability, stability appeared to be a prominent characteristic of friendship. The friendships of the adolescents interviewed and observed by Day and Harry (1999) had developed naturally due to their daily proximity within their classroom, and one of the girls pointed out that her friend was the only classmate she had known "for a long time." The ongoing and consistent nature of the relationship seemed to provide a space where comfort and intimacy could develop between the girls. Matheson and colleagues (2007) also found that stability was a common theme, endorsed by nearly half of the adolescents in their study of friendship. Friends were described, in part, as individuals whom the adolescents had known for an extended period of time.

For some young people, proximity was the most salient issue in defining friendship; for example, when asked why they nominated a particular peer as a friend, they would respond, "I know him from the park," or "he's been in my class since kindergarten." Matheson and colleagues (2007) noted that more than one-third of the teens in their study mentioned proximity as a reason for choosing their friends. The authors broached the concern that proximity and duration of acquaintance may be a substitute for true interactions in some cases. When individuals talk about their friends in terms of proximity and longevity of acquaintance only—that is, in the absence of other critical dimensions of friendship— it begs the question of whether these relationships can be understood as true friendships. The authors concluded that, although the friendship models of many of the teens in their study conveyed a less complex notion of friendship than would be found among their typically developing peers, nonetheless, these relationships appeared to provide satisfaction and comfort and were often observed to possess elements of reciprocity and endure over time.

Similarity

As alluded to earlier, the mutual concern experienced among friends was often fostered by an understanding born of similarities. To the extent that friends shared experiences in schools and living arrangements, they were able to support one another through challenges that they understood and had overcome themselves. Indeed, echoing a common theme in the broader friendship literature (e.g., Bukowski et al., 2009; Fehr, 2008; Rubin et al., 2010), similarity consistently played a prominent role in these studies of friendships of people with disabilities. Among the adolescents interviewed by Matheson et al. (2007), similarity was mentioned by nearly half of the participants in the course of their discussions of friendship. Among other things, adolescents mentioned that their friends had interests, preferences, and ideas that were similar to their own. These similar interests were borne out in the friends' topics of conversations; one boy stated that he and his best friend enjoyed

talking about the same things—namely, "girls, Britney Spears, NSYNC, and Power Rangers." As has often been noted, when choosing friends, it is not actually opposites that attract but rather similarities. Individuals who can easily identify common ground are more likely to be friends than those who cannot.

The theme of similarity was illuminated effectively in Day and Harry's (1999) case study. As mentioned, one aspect of the girls' friendship was an understanding of each other's circumstances and perspectives, which was in part due to their similarities. Much like the youth in the study by Matheson and colleagues (2007), they found common ground in typical adolescent interests, such as shopping, talking about movies, and gossiping about boys. Moreover, the similarities that resulted from their mutual status as immigrants led to a recognition of their shared values (i.e., the importance of family, respect, and tradition), as well as to a bond that came from the shared experience of being "outsiders" having to negotiate between their native cultural beliefs and traditions and those of the dominant culture. Finally, these girls also found common ground in their disability status, which was related to common experiences of being excluded from school in their countries of origin, encountering difficulties in the process of being placed in the special education system, and coping with peer social rejection. Given these shared experiences, the girls were able to offer support to each other.

Shared disability status as a key factor in determining friendship emerged as a highly visible theme throughout the literature. Both adolescents and adults with intellectual disability (and other developmental disabilities), when asked about their friends, consistently identify others with similar disabilities (Day & Harry, 1999; Emerson & McVilly, 2004; Knox & Hickson, 2001; Matheson et al., 2007; McVilly et al., 2006a; 2006b; Randell & Cumella, 2009). In focus group discussions (McVilly et al., 2006b), when asked about making friends with people who were similar or different, the group collectively agreed that "you can't be friends if they ain't got a disability, sometimes," citing differences, stigma, and teasing as reasons for the difficulty. One participant said "it's because you need to be equal...you need to have an equal say in what you are going to do." The authors suggested that there was a sense of comfort in these "equal" relationships and that they were more likely to last than relationships between an individual with intellectual disability and an individual without disabilities.

Knox and Hickson (2001) noted that their participants did discuss friendships with people without disabilities, but that these friendships seemed to be more superficial and less stable over time. Similarly, because the ethnographic study by Matheson and colleagues (2007) was embedded within a larger longitudinal study, these investigators were able to comment on the subsequent development of the friendships of the teens in their study. They noted that the friendships that existed between teens with developmental disabilities appeared to be more companionable and enduring. They noted, again, the significance of proximity as a defining characteristic of these friendships, observing that the most stable friendships seemed to exist between teens who were less socially proficient, but who were consistently in the same special education classes together.

The account of the friendships that developed in the intentional community (Randell & Cumella, 2009) provided a particularly telling perspective on this point. The authors noted that the friendships about which individuals spoke were largely friendships with other adults with intellectual disability. Relationships with the residents of the village who did not have disabilities (called coworkers) were also considered to be close, important relationships, but the authors observed that these relationships more closely resembled relationships that one has with parents and family members rather than with friends. Thus, even in a setting that emphasized equality and meaningful participation of people with intellectual disability alongside people without disabilities, the friendships that were organically formed and maintained were between people with intellectual disability.

Challenges and barriers to friendship. In addition, another common theme emerged from this collection of studies indicating how the friendships of people with intellectual disability may be unlike those of their nondisabled peers. Specifically, these studies underscored that although true friendships do develop between people with intellectual disability, they are subject to significantly more practical and logistical challenges than are the friendships of people in the general population and thus require more support to sustain them (Knox & Hickson, 2001; Matheson et al., 2007; McVilly et al., 2006a, 2006b; Randell & Cumella, 2009). It was clear that although friendships were highly valued by individuals, there were also challenges to overcome in their formation and maintenance. This was illustrated poignantly by Day and Harry (1999). As mentioned previously, the friendship interactions between the two girls took place primarily in school and over the phone, due to a number of concerns. For instance,

transportation was a difficult challenge to overcome; neither of the girls used public transportation and one needed a wheelchair, so they had to rely on family members to drive them places, which was not always possible. Moreover, the researchers observed that parental permission was also problematic; due to both their disability status and cultural differences, the two girls had little agency to make their own decisions. As a result, they were seldom able to engage in activities outside of school that they might otherwise have chosen to do, such as going to the mall and going to see movies.

The discussion of barriers to friendship was more developed and concrete among adults with intellectual disability. On a broad level, people with intellectual disability recognize many barriers to social interactions and involvement in the community, including deficits in cognitive and adaptive skills and abilities, as well as logistical obstacles. Abbott and McConkey (2006) conducted focus groups with a number of adults with intellectual disability in Ireland who lived in various supported living arrangements. When participants were asked about activities they engaged in or wanted to engage in within the community, the individuals talked about obstacles in the areas of personal abilities and skills, the logistics of their living arrangements, and the community itself. For instance, participants expressed concerns about both a lack of confidence and a lack of certain skills, such as literacy, numeracy, and travel skills, regarding venturing into the community. Additionally, individuals reported having limited access to and information about recreational activities in the community.

Such concerns about opportunities to participate in the community were reiterated in the focus group discussions of self-advocates (McVilly et al., 2006b). As one participant put it, "The older you get the harder it is to make new friends. If you don't have them from school then it's really hard." As mentioned previously, longevity was considered an important characteristic of friendship by people with intellectual disability; most close friendships had lasted for years, and many had begun during their time in school settings. Although this reflects a positive aspect of existing friendships, it also implies a challenge to the formation of new friendships because adults with intellectual disability may have few opportunities after leaving school to meet new people and forge new relationships. Indeed, the participants agreed that the most important places to meet friends were at work, at school, or in continuing education classes (McVilly et al., 2006b). It is easy to imagine that for people with intellectual disability who neither work nor attend school, a lack of opportunity to participate in community activities would limit the potential to make friends.

Logistical difficulties to interacting with friends were also a continuing theme among different groups of people with intellectual disability. Participants suggested that making time and arrangements to spend time with friend was challenging, but recognized that that time was important for maintaining friendships. Nonetheless, travel was consistently problematic, with one participant stating "It's hard when you got too far to travel…mum has to drive and she's got lots of shopping to do and then I can't see my friends" (McVilly et al., 2006b). Other individuals stated the importance of balancing relationships and making time to spend with various friends (Knox & Hickson, 2001). Further, there is evidence that for individuals who live in facilities, having to share accommodations can limit privacy and make it difficult to spend time alone with friends (Abbott & McConkey, 2006).

Taken together, the demonstrated value of friendships along with the numerous challenges in forming and maintaining them suggest a need for support and assistance in these areas. To summarize, people with intellectual disability have reported challenges to making and maintaining friendships related to logistics (transportation, privacy, time), opportunities (few opportunities, lack of awareness of opportunities, restrictions of opportunities by caregivers or staff), and interpersonal difficulties (conflict with friends, self-confidence in meeting new people). In each of these areas, there are possibilities for improvement. In fact, the individuals who spoke about the barriers they faced in their friendships were able to generate a number of possible solutions, for example, practical assistance and training (McVilly et al., 2006b). In terms of practical assistance, transportation was an important need; public transportation was not always a possibility, yet the individuals still desired transport to friends' homes, public places such as movie theaters and shopping centers, and activities sponsored by agencies that catered to people with intellectual disability. Examples of desired training support included advice on how to resolve conflicts, as well as life skills training around travel and literacy (Abbott & McConkey, 2006; McVilly et al., 2006b). Additional means of support mentioned included access to information regarding social activities and events and more freedom to make plans (Abbott & McConkey, 2006).

The Social Well-Being of People with Intellectual Disability: Summary and Synthesis

Some years ago, at a meeting of the Down Syndrome Congress, one of the authors met a new mother of an infant with Down syndrome. Noticing her obvious discomfort, Dr. Siperstein approached her and asked if she was all right. After a few moments, it became clear that she was still trying to come to terms with the news that her child had a disability. He asked if he could answer any questions for her. She looked down at her child, and softly asked, "When my daughter grows up, will she have friends?" Of all the questions she could have asked, of all the concerns she could have voiced, this young mother recognized the absolute necessity of belonging, of feeling connected, of having people with whom one can share one's life, and she feared that her daughter, because of her disability, might suffer social isolation and loneliness. In many ways, we see this chapter as a response to this young mother.

Our best insights into understanding the friendships of people with intellectual disability have come from what people with intellectual disability themselves have told us about their relationships. Although a substantial amount of the work on "friendships" of people with intellectual disability has focused on the promotion of social acceptance and positive interactions with typically developing peers, the literature that has captured the voices of people with disabilities indicates that it might be equally or even more important to ask what can be done to help encourage, support, and sustain friendships among people with intellectual disability. It is also critical to recognize a range of possible relationships and their significance, as it is likely that not all people with intellectual disability, specifically those with more profound impairments, are capable of forging and maintaining true friendships. The literature explored in the preceding pages provides considerable insight into both the friendships that do exist, as well as the circumstances in which they may not.

True Friendships Occur Between People with Intellectual Disability

There is considerable evidence to indicate that when people with intellectual disability do develop friendships, those friendships are likely to be with others with intellectual disability. It has been documented previously that the social networks of people with intellectual disability tend to consist of family members, service providers, and other people with intellectual disability (Romer & Heller, 1983).

Moreover, despite the volume of research that has focused on promoting social interactions and inclusion between people with and without intellectual disability, relationships with people without disabilities are rarely mentioned when people with intellectual disability talk about their friends. On the contrary, the friendships recounted by people with intellectual disability in each of the qualitative studies just discussed are, almost without exception, relationships with other people with intellectual disability. Not only does it seem that friendships between people with intellectual disability are more likely to occur than friendships across disability status, but there is evidence to suggest that they may also be of higher quality (e.g., Emerson & Hatton, 2008a) and more strongly associated with subjective well-being (Emerson & Hatton, 2008b). The authors of several of the studies cited in these pages noted that the friendships shared by people with intellectual disability were more stable and less superficial than were cross-status relationships (e.g., Matheson et al., 2007; McVilly et al., 2006b). It is also apparent that these friendships exert a powerful positive impact on the lives of people with intellectual disability, fulfilling the same essential social needs—namely, companionship, intimacy, and support—as they do for the general population. In general, we know that the fulfillment of these more specific social needs indicates a healthy sense of belonging, which is related to a variety of positive outcomes that signify general well-being and human flourishing (Baumeister & Leary, 1995).

Indeed, it appears that issues of similarity are central to the friendships of people with intellectual disability, just as they are important to those of the general population. In fact, Asher and colleagues (1996) asserted that a general climate of reciprocity and equality between partners signified the "heart of friendship." Clearly, "sharing the socio-cultural identity of being a person with an intellectual disability" (McVilly et al., 2006b, p. 703) is of critical consequence. Yet, a widespread and seemingly exclusive emphasis on social integration and inclusion among the research, education, and service provision communities may send a message of disregard and devaluation concerning the important roles that people with disabilities can play in each other's lives. In fact, Chappell (1994) cautioned two decades ago that to ignore the friendships that develop between people with intellectual disability was potentially damaging to the well-being of these people, both individually and collectively. Recognizing this, Cummins and Lau

(2003) suggested that social connectedness within the community of people with intellectual disability should be acknowledged as an important and desirable objective.

We do not suggest that it is impossible for friendships to develop between people with and without disabilities. Nor do we suggest that efforts and interventions aimed at promoting social acceptance of people with intellectual disability and positive social interactions between people with and without intellectual disability are not valuable. To the extent that social inclusion provides an opportunity for people with intellectual disability to form relationships and develop a sense of belonging within the broader community, the emphasis on integration is not misplaced because pleasant sociable interactions with a variety of people are certainly positive experiences. In light of the evidence here, however, we do suggest that there is generally a low likelihood of "true" friendship developing between people with and without intellectual disability. Although the prevailing emphasis on inclusion and social acceptance is well-intended and has value in its own right, we caution against conflating these efforts with the promotion of friendships for youth and adults with intellectual disability. If we, as (largely nondisabled) researchers and practitioners, truly want to promote human flourishing and well-being for people with intellectual disability, then perhaps we need to reevaluate our assumptions and motivations and refocus our efforts to better understand and endorse the spontaneous, organic relationships that develop between people with intellectual disability when the opportunity is there.

Clearly, the formation and maintenance of these friendships are challenged by a number of unique barriers. People with intellectual disability report logistical difficulties related to transportation, time, and accessibility; limited access to social and recreational opportunities that allow for the chance to meet new people and engage in companionable activities with existing friends; and interpersonal difficulties that arise from both individual social skills deficits and restricted experiences. Taken together, the ubiquity of these challenges on the one hand, coupled with the demonstrated value and benefits of friendship on the other, suggests a pressing need for support and assistance in these areas. To address these challenges, it is essential that the family members, caregivers, and service professionals who are instrumental in the lives of people with intellectual disability recognize the value of meaningful friendships in their lives. Some individuals have suggested that their families and support staff do not recognize the importance of their friendship connections and seem to 'place little priority on helping to facilitate and maintain these relationships (McVilly et al., 2006b). This lack of recognition suggests that friendships shared by people with intellectual disability continue to be devalued in spite of the critical role they appear to play in fostering well-being and QOL. Acknowledging the broad benefits associated with these relationships is the first step to assuring that people with intellectual disability have the tools and support needed to maintain their relationships.

Friendships May Not Occur for Everyone

On the one hand, given that not everybody experiences friendships, it is essential to acknowledge that intellectual disability presents as a spectrum of functional competence and adaptive needs that may have significance for understanding social well-being and the role of relationships in the lives of the individual. There has been some limited discussion about whether all people are capable of achieving friendship. For example, Hughes and colleagues (2011) have argued that the concept of friendship is probably not relevant for people with the most profound disabilities who do not have the capacity for intentional behavior and communication. It is critical to recognize that friendship, as understood in these pages, is, by definition, a reciprocal relationship, the formation and maintenance of which is predicated on a number of specific interpersonal skills and capabilities, including the capacity to be responsive to others' needs for companionship, intimacy, and support (Asher et al., 1996). Thus, we would agree that people with the most significant impairments do not have the functional skills necessary to engage in this type of relationship. However, that does not preclude their need and ability to engage in other types of close relationships and form meaningful bonds. Although all individuals have a basic human need to connect with others, the fulfillment of this need may not always be manifested in friendship. There is evidence to indicate that even people with profound impairments enjoy a range of satisfying, close relationships, for example with family members, trusted service providers, and with "family friends" (e.g., Johnson et al., 2010). These relationships satisfy the needs for love and affection, as well as care and support, and appear to provide people with a general sense of belonging and connection.

Less apparent is whether friendship is a reasonable expectation for people with more moderate intellectual impairment. The literature suggests that people with more moderate intellectual disability are less likely to engage in friendships (e.g., Bigby, 2008; Emerson & McVilly, 2004), but it is not clear whether this is due to limited opportunities or skill deficits. It is likely a combination of the two. There is no doubt that people with intellectual disability, broadly speaking, are challenged by limited opportunities for social engagement. However, if we accept that people with profound impairments do not have the requisite functional skills to engage in true friendship, must we also contemplate the specific social, communication, and adaptive skills that are essential for supporting friendship formation and maintenance?

On the other hand, when it comes to social relationships and friendships, perhaps our thinking needs to be more flexible. We began this chapter with a discussion of how to accommodate broad interpretations and diverse manifestations of friendship under a unifying umbrella. Although we have demonstrated that, in many cases, the friendships shared by people with intellectual disability look very similar to those shared by their nondisabled peers, there is also some suggestion that some individuals, particularly those with moderate impairments, hold a more simplistic intrinsic understanding of friendship. For example, a number of teens in the ethnographic work by Matheson and colleagues (2007) expressed a friendship schema based on long-term proximity (e.g., being in the same class since kindergarten) rather than on the more typical adolescent friendship experiences of companionship, intimacy, and support. Although their "friendships" might not resemble the good friendships described in most of this chapter, nonetheless, they often contained elements of reciprocity and stability and appeared to provide satisfaction and comfort. Thus, lower and more moderate functioning individuals may enjoy relationships with their peers that approximate friendship, even if they don't meet all criteria for friendship "as commonly understood." It is likely that a shared past along with the expectation of regular ongoing encounters can play an important role in nurturing feelings of stability and comfort within the relationship, even if it does not fulfill all the needs of true friendship.

Moreover, if there is both a general need to belong that might be broadly satisfied by any of a number of relationships, as well as more specific social needs that carry developmental significance and are most effectively met by particular members of the social network, then we might assume that these specific needs are not equally salient to all individuals. If these needs are, at least in part, a function of development, then it is plausible to assume that they might also be related to functional level in people with intellectual and developmental disabilities. In that case, it is likely that at diminished levels of functioning, the needs for companionship and intimacy may not be realized, or at least not fully developed. This suggests that for those individuals for whom true friendship may not be possible, it may not be essential either. Instead, at different functional levels, the needs for love and care and affection, for nurturance and support might be considerably more critical, and these needs can be appropriately and satisfyingly met by other social network members.

Conclusion

We conclude that, for people with intellectual disability, as for the broader population, social relationships satisfy an essential human need for belonging and human connection. Although true reciprocal friendships may not be an attainable goal for all, there is no question that everybody is able to engage in other meaningful relationships with family and caregivers that provide love, affection, and a powerful sense of belonging. Regardless of functional capacity, everybody's life is ultimately improved by their connection with others. The exclusion of atypical populations (specifically, people with disabilities) from the mainstream positive psychology literature echoes an inherent bias in much of mainstream psychology (Dykens, 2006) and risks furthering "a skewed and incomplete science" (Hauser-Cram, Warfield, Shonkoff, & Krauss, 2001, p. 4). By focusing on the positive relationships experienced by people with intellectual disability, this chapter contributes to a more accurate and complete understanding of human flourishing, thus reinforcing the model's application to broad populations and contributing to a more inclusive positive psychology that is able to embrace and accommodate developmental differences.

References

Abbott, S., & McConkey, R. (2006). The barriers to social inclusion as perceived by people with intellectual disabilities. *Journal of Intellectual Disabilities, 10,* 275–287.

Asher, S. R., Parker, J. G., & Walker, D. L. (1996). Distinguishing friendship from acceptance: Implications for intervention and assessment. In W. M. Bukowski, A. F., Newcomb, & W. W. Hartup (Eds.), *The company they keep: Friendship in childhood and adolescence* (pp. 366–405). Cambridge, UK: Cambridge University Press.

Barber, D. & Hupp, S. C. (1993). A comparison of friendship patterns of individuals with developmental disabilities. *Education and Training in Mental Retardation, 28,* 13–22.

Baumeister, R. F., & Leary, M. R. (1995). The need to belong: Desire for interpersonal attachments as a fundamental human motivation. *Psychological Bulletin, 117*(3), 497–529.

Berscheid, E., & Peplau, L. A. (1983). The emerging science of relationships. In H. H. Kelley, E. Berscheid, A. Christensen, J. H. Harvey, T. L. Huston, G. Levinger, E. McClintock, Peplau, L. A., & D. R. Peterson (Eds.), *Close Relationships* (pp. 1–19). New York: W. H. Freeman.

Bigby, C. (1997). When parents relinquish care: Informal support networks of older people with intellectual disability. *Journal of Applied Research in Intellectual Disabilities, 10,* 333–344.

Bigby, C. (2008). Known well by no-one: Trends in the informal social networks of middle-aged and older people with intellectual disability five years after moving to the community. *Journal of Intellectual and Developmental Disability, 33*(2), 148–157.

Bramston, P., Chipuer, H., & Pretty, G. (2005). Conceptual principles of quality of life: An empirical exploration. *Journal of Intellectual Disability Research, 49,* 728–733.

Buhrmester, D. (1996). Need fulfillment, interpersonal competence, and the developmental contexts of early adolescent friendship. In W. M. Bukowski, A. F., Newcomb, & W. W. Hartup (Eds.), *The company they keep: Friendship in childhood and adolescence* (pp. 158–185). Cambridge, UK: Cambridge University Press.

Bukowski, W. M., Motzoi, C., & Meyer, F. (2009). Friendship as process, function, and outcome. In K. H. Rubin, W. M. Bukowski, & B. Laursen (Eds.), *Handbook of peer interactions, relationships, and groups* (pp. 217–231). New York: Guilford.

Bukowski, W. M., Newcomb, A. F., & Hartup, W. W. (1996). Friendship and its significance in childhood and adolescence: Introduction and comment. In W. M. Bukowski, A. F., Newcomb, & W. W. Hartup (Eds.), *The company they keep: Friendship in childhood and adolescence* (pp. 1–15). Cambridge, UK: Cambridge University Press.

Cacioppo, J. T., & Patrick, W. (2008). *Loneliness: Human nature and the need for social connection.* New York: W. W. Norton.

Campo, S. F., Sharpton, W. R., Thompson, B., & Sexton, D. (1997). Correlates of quality of life of adults with severe or profound mental retardation. *Mental Retardation, 35,* 329–337.

Carter, E. W., & Hughes, C. (2005). Increasing social interaction among adolescents with intellectual disabilities and their general education peers: Effective interventions. *Research and Practice for Persons with Severe Disabilities, 30,* 179–193.

Chadsey, J., & Beyer, S. (2001). Social relationships in the workplace. *Mental Retardation and Developmental Disabilities Research Reviews, 7,* 128–133.

Chappell, A. L. (1994). A question of friendship: Community care and the relationships of people with and without learning disabilities. *Disability & Society, 9,* 419–424.

Cohen, S. (2004). Social relationships and health. *American Psychologist, 59*(8), 676–684.

Cohen, S., & Wills, T. A. (1985). Stress, social support, and the buffering hypothesis. *Psychological Bulletin, 98*(2), 310–357.

Collet-Klingenberg, L., & Chadsey-Rusch, J. (1991). Using a cognitive-process approach to teach social skills. *Education and Training in Mental Retardation, 26,* 258–270.

Cummins, R. A., & Lau, A. L. D. (2003). Community integration or community exposure? A review and discussion in relation to people with an intellectual disability. *Journal of Applied Research in Intellectual Disabilities, 16,* 145–157.

Day, M., & Harry, B. (1999). "Best Friends": The construction of a teenage friendship. *Mental Retardation, 37,* 221–231.

Diener, E., & Seligman, M. E. P. (2002). Very happy people. *Psychological Science, 13*(1), 81–84.

Dykens, E. M. (2006). Toward a positive psychology of mental retardation. *American Journal of Orthopsychiatry, 76,* 185–193.

Emerson, E., & Hatton, C. (2008a). People with learning disabilities in England (CeDR Research Report 2008:1). Retrieved from ww.lancs.ac.uk/cedr/publications/CeDR 2008-1 People with Learning Disabilities in England.pdf

Emerson, E., & Hatton, C. (2008b). Self-reported well-being of women and men with intellectual disabilities in England. *American Journal on Mental Retardation, 113,* 143–155.

Emerson, E., Malam, S., Davies, I., & Spencer, K. (2005). Adults with learning difficulties in England 2003/4. Retrieved from http://webarchive.nationalarchives.gov.uk/20130107105354/http://www.dh.gov.uk/en/Publicationsandstatistics/Publications/PublicationsStatistics/DH_4120033

Emerson, E., & McVilly, K. (2004). Friendship activities of adults with intellectual disabilities in supported accommodation in Northern England. *Journal of Applied Research in Intellectual Disabilities, 17,* 191–197.

Fehr, B. (2008). Friendship formation. In S. Sprecher, A. Wenzel, & J. Harvey (Eds.), *Handbook of relationship initiation* (pp. 29–54). New York: Psychology Press.

Fishbein, H. D. (2002). *Peer prejudice and discrimination: The origins of prejudice.* Mahwah, NJ: Erlbaum.

Forrester-Jones, R., Carpenter, J., Coolen-Schrijner, P., Cambridge, P., Tate, A., Beecham, J., et al. (2006). The social networks of people with intellectual disability living in the community 12 years after resettlement from long-stay hospitals. *Journal of Applied Research in Intellectual Disabilities, 19,* 285–295.

Furman, W. (1996). The measurement of friendship perceptions: Conceptual and methodological issues. In W. M. Bukowski, A. F., Newcomb, & W. W. Hartup (Eds.), *The company they keep: Friendship in childhood and adolescence* (pp. 41–65). Cambridge, UK: Cambridge University Press.

Gaylord-Ross, R., Park, H. S., Johnston, S., Lee, M., & Goetz, L. (1995). Individual social skills training and coworker training for supported employers with dual sensory impairment: Two case examples. *Behavior Modification, 19,* 78–94.

Gordon, D., Levitas, R., Pantazis, C., Patsios, D., Payne, S., Townsend, P., et al. (2000), *Poverty and social exclusion in Britain.* Retrieved from http://www.jrf.org.uk/sites/files/jrf/185935128x.pdf

Hardman, M. L., & Clark, C. (2006). Promoting friendship through Best Buddies: A national survey of college program participants. *Mental Retardation, 44,* 56–63.

Hartup, W. W., & Stevens, N. (1997). Friendships and adaptation in the life course. *Psychological Bulletin, 121*(3), 355–370.

Hauser-Cram, P., Warfield, M. E., Shonkoff, J. P., & Krauss, M. W. (2001). Children with disabilities: A longitudinal study of child development and parent well-being. *Monographs for the Society for Research in Child Development, 66*(3, Serial No. 266).

Heiman, T. (2000). Friendship quality among children in three educational settings. *Journal of Intellectual and Developmental Disability, 25,* 1–12.

Holt-Lunstad, J., Smith, T. B., & Layton, J. B. (2010). Social relationships and mortality risk: A meta-analytic review. *PLoS Medicine, 7*(7), 1–20. doi:10.1371/jouernal.pmed.1000316

House, J. S., Landis, K. R., & Umberson, D. (1988). Social relationships and health. *Science, 241*(4865), 540–545.

Howes, C. (1996). The earliest friendships. In W. M. Bukowski, A. F., Newcomb, & W. W. Hartup (Eds.), *The company they keep: Friendship in childhood and adolescence* (pp. 66–86). Cambridge, UK: Cambridge University Press.

Hughes, C., Carter, E. W., Hughes, T., Bradford, E., & Copeland, R. S. (2002a). Effects of instructional versus non-instructional roles on the social interactions of high school students. *Education and Training in Mental Retardation and Developmental Disabilities, 37,* 262–272.

Hughes, C., Copeland, S. R., Agran, M., Wehmeyer, M. L., Rodi, M. S., & Presley, J. A. (2002b). Using self-monitoring to improve performance in general education high school classes. *Education and Training in Mental Retardation and Developmental Disabilities, 37,* 262–272.

Hughes, C., Copeland, S. R., Guth, C., Rung, L. L., Hwang, B., Kleeb, G., & Strong, M. (2001). General education students' perspectives on their involvement in a high school peer buddy program. *Education and Training in Mental Retardation and Developmental Disabilities, 36,* 343–356.

Hughes, C., Fowler, S. E., Copeland, S. R., Agran, M., Wehmeyer, M. L., & Church-Pupke, P. P. (2004). Supporting high school students to engage in recreational activities with peers. *Behavior Modification, 28,* 3–27.

Hughes, R. P., Redley, M., & Ring, H. (2011). Friendship and adults with profound intellectual and multiple disabilities and English disability policy. *Journal of Policy and Practice in Intellectual Disabilities, 8*(3), 197–206.

Hughes, C., Rung, L. L., Wehmeyer, M., Agran, M., Copeland, S. R., & Hwang, B. (2000). Self-prompted communication book use to increase social interaction among high school students. *Journal of the Association for Persons with Severe Handicaps, 25,* 153–166.

Hunt, P., Alwell, M., & Goetz, L. (1988). Acquisition of conversation skills and the reduction of inappropriate social interaction behaviors. *Journal of the Association for Persons with Severe Handicaps, 13,* 20–27.

Hunt, P., Alwell, M., Goetz, L., & Sailor, W. (1990). Generalized effects of conversation skill training. *Journal of the Association for Persons with Severe Handicaps, 15,* 250–260.

Johnson, H., Douglas, J., Bigby, C., & Iacono, T. (2010). The pearl in the middle: A case study of social interactions in an individual with a severe intellectual disability. *Journal of Intellectual and Developmental Disability, 35*(3), 175–186.

Kennedy, C. H., Shukla, S., & Fryxell, D. (1997). Comparing the effects of educational placement on the social relationships of intermediate school students with severe disabilities. *Exceptional Children, 64,* 31–47.

Kersh, J. (2011). Attitudes about people with intellectual disabilities: Current status and new directions. In R. M. Hodapp (Ed.), *International Review of Research in Developmental Disabilities, vol. 41* (pp. 199–231). Oxford, UK: Academic Press.

Klinger, E. (1977). *Meaning & void: Inner experience and the incentives in people's lives.* Minneapolis: University of Minnesota Press.

Knox, M., & Hickson, F. (2001). The meanings of close friendship: The views of four people with intellectual disabilities. *Journal of Applied Research in Intellectual Disabilities, 14,* 276–291.

Krappmann, L. (1996). Amicitia, drujba, shin-yu, philia, Freundschaft, friendship: On the cultural diversity of a human relationship. In W. M. Bukowski, A. F., Newcomb, & W. W. Hartup (Eds.), *The company they keep: Friendship in childhood and adolescence* (pp. 19–40). Cambridge, UK: Cambridge University Press.

Larrivee, B., & Horne, M. (1991).Social status: A comparison of mainstreamed students with peers of different ability levels. *Journal of Special Education, 25*, 90–101.

Laursen, B., Bukowski, W. M., Aunola, K., & Nurmi, J. -E. (2007). Friendship moderates prospective associations between social isolation and adjustment problems in young children. *Child Development, 78*(4), 1395–1404.

Lee, M., Storey, K., Anderson, J. L., Goetz, L., & Zivolich, S. (1997). The effect of mentoring versus job coach instruction on integration in supported employment settings. *Journal of the Association for Persons with Severe Handicaps, 22*, 151–158.

Luftig, R. L. (1988). Assessment of the perceived school loneliness and isolation of mentally retarded and nonretarded students. *American Journal on Mental Retardation, 92*, 472–475.

Lunsky, Y., & Benson, B. A. (2001). Association between perceived social support and strain, and positive and negative outcomes for adults with mild intellectual disability. *Journal of Intellectual Disability Research, 45*, 106–114.

Marom, M., Cohen, D., & Naon, D. (2007). Changing disability-related attitudes and self-efficacy of Israeli children via Partners to Inclusion Programme. *International Journal of Disability, Development and Education, 54*, 113–127.

Maslow, A. H. (1943). A theory of human motivation. *Psychological Review, 50*(4), 370–396.

Matheson, C., Olsen, R. J., & Weisner, T. (2007). A good friend is hard to find: Friendship among adolescents with disabilities. *American Journal on Mental Retardation, 112*, 319–329.

McVilly, K. R., Stancliffe, R. J., Parmenter, T. R., & Burton-Smith, R. M. (2006a). "I get by with a little help from my friends": Adults with intellectual disabilities discuss loneliness. *Journal of Applied Research in Intellectual Disabilities, 19*, 191–203.

McVilly, K. R., Stancliffe, R. J., Parmenter, T. R., & Burton-Smith, R. M. (2006b). Self-advocates have the last say on friendship. *Disability & Society, 21*, 693–708.

Miller, S. M., & Chan, F. (2008). Predictors of life satisfaction in individuals with intellectual disabilities. *Journal of Intellectual Disability Research, 52*, 1039–1047.

Murray-Seegert, C. (1989). *Nasty girls, thugs, and humans like us: Social relations between severely disabled and non-disabled students in high school.* Baltimore, MD: Paul H. Brookes.

Myers, D. (2000). The funds, friends, and faith of happy people. *American Psychologist, 55*(1), 56–67.

Nabors, L. (1997). Playmate preferences of children who are typically developing for their classmates with special needs. *Mental Retardation, 35*, 107–113.

Nota, L., Ferrari, L., & Soresi, S. (2005). Elementary school children's willingness to help and be friends with disabled peers. *International Journal on Disability and Human Development, 4*(2), 131–137.

Park, H., Simon, M., Tappe, P., Wozniak, T., Johnson, & Gaylord-Ross. (1991). Effects of coworker advocacy program and social skills training on the social interaction of employees with mild disabilities. *Journal of Vocational Rehabilitation, 1*, 73–90.

Parker, J. G., & Asher, S. R. (1993). Friendship and friendship quality in middle childhood: Links with peer group

acceptance and feelings of loneliness and social dissatisfaction. *Developmental Psychology, 29*, 611–621.

Randell, M., & Cumella, S. (2009). People with an intellectual disability living in an intentional community. *Journal of Intellectual Disability Research, 53*, 716–726.

Rawlins, W. K. (1992). *Friendship matters.* New York: Aldine de Gruyter.

Reiss, S., & Benson, B. A. (1985). Psychosocial correlates of depression in mentally retarded adults: I. Minimal social support and stigmatization. *American Journal of Mental Deficiency, 89*, 331–337.

Romer, D., & Heller, T. (1983). Social adaptation of mentally retarded adults in community settings: A social-ecological approach. *Applied Research in Mental Retardation, 4*, 303–314.

Rubin, K. H., Coplan, R., Chen, X., Bowker, J., & McDonald, K. L. (2010). Peer relationships in childhood. In M. H. Bornstein & M. E. Lamb (Eds.), *Developmental science: An advanced textbook.* (6th ed., pp. 519–570). London: Psychology Press.

Sale, P., & Carey, D. (1995). The sociometric status of students with disabilities in a full-inclusion school. *Exceptional Children, 62*, 6–19.

Seligman, M. E. P. (2011). *Flourish: A visionary new understanding of happiness and well-being.* New York: Free Press.

Shea, L., Thompson, L., & Blieszner, R. (1988). Resources in older adults' old and new friendships. *Journal of Social and Personal Relationships, 5*, 83–96.

Siperstein, G. N., & Bak, J. J. (1989). Social relationships of adolescents with moderate mental retardation. *Mental Retardation, 27*, 5–10.

Siperstein, G. N., Leffert, J. S., & Wenz-Gross, M. (1997). The quality of friendships between children with and without learning problems. *American Journal on Mental Retardation, 102*, 111–125.

Siperstein, G. N., Parker, R. C., Bardon, J. N., & Widaman, K. F. (2007). A national study of youth attitudes toward the inclusion of students with intellectual disabilities. *Exceptional Children, 73*, 435–455.

Solish, A., Perry, A., & Minnes, P. (2010). Participation of children with and without disabilities in social, recreational and leisure activities. *Journal of Applied Research in Intellectual Disabilities, 23*(3), 226–236.

Staub, D., Schwartz, I., Galucci, C., & Peck, C. (1994). Four portraits of friendship at an inclusive school. *Journal of the Association for Persons with Severe Handicaps, 19*, 314–325.

Storey, K. (2002). Strategies for increasing interactions in supported employment settings: An updated review. *Journal of Vocational Rehabilitation, 17*, 231–237.

Storey, K., & Garff, J. T. (1997). The cumulative effect of natural support strategies and social skills instruction on the integration of a worker in supported employment. *Journal of Vocational Rehabilitation, 9*, 143–152.

Storey, K., Lengyel, L., & Pruszynski, B. (1997). Assessing the effectiveness and measuring the complexity of two conversational instructional procedures in supported employment contexts. *Journal of Vocational Rehabilitation, 8*, 21–33.

Storey, K., & Provost, O. (1996). The effect of communication skills instruction on the integration of workers with severe disabilities in supported employment settings, *Education and Training in Mental Retardation and Developmental Disabilities, 31*, 123–141.

Sullivan, H. S. (1953). *The interpersonal theory of psychiatry.* New York: W. W. Norton.

Taylor, A. R., Asher, S. R., & Williams, G. A. (1987). The social adaptation of mainstreamed mildly retarded children. *Child Development*, *58*, 1321–1334.

Verdugo, M. A., Schalock, R. L., Keith, K. D., & Stancliffe, R. J. (2005). Quality of life and its measurement: Important principles and guidelines. *Journal of Intellectual Disability Research*, *49*, 707–717.

Waldrip, A. M., Malcolm, K. T., & Jensen-Campbell, L. A. (2008). With a little help from your friends: The importance of high-quality friendships on early adolescent adjustment. *Social Development*, *17*(4), 832–852.

Weiss, R. S. (1973). *Loneliness: The experience of emotional and social isolation*. Cambridge, MA: The MIT Press.

Wenz-Gross, M., & Siperstein G. N. (1996). The social world of preadolescents with mental retardation: Social support, family environment and adjustment. *Education and Training in Mental Retardation and Developmental Disabilities*, *31* (3), 177–187.

Wilson, R. S., Krueger, S. E., Arnold, J. A., Schneider, J. F., Kelly, L. L., Barnes, Y. T., & Bennet, D. A. (2007). Loneliness and risks of Alzheimer's disease. *Archives of General Psychiatry*, *64*, 234–240.

Žic, A., & Igrić, L. (2001). Self-assessment of relationships with peers in children with intellectual disability. *Journal of Intellectual Disability Research*, *45*, 202–211.

Exercise, Leisure, and Well-Being for People with Disabilities

Jennifer L. Rowland

Abstract

Exercise, leisure, and well-being are terms that are typically applied to general populations, yet people with disabilities have historically faced personal and environmental barriers that have limited their regular exercise participation. Barriers have been within the built and natural environment; economic issues; emotional and psychological problems; equipment inaccessibility; difficulty with the use and interpretation of guidelines, codes, regulations, and laws; and professional knowledge, education, and training issues, among others. This chapter provides information about studies that have focused on ways in which exercise and leisure activities have affected the health status of people with different types of disabilities.

Key Words: exercise, leisure, well-being, quality of life, disability

Exercise, leisure, and well-being are terms that are typically applied to general populations (Caldwell, 2005), yet people with disabilities have historically faced personal and environmental barriers that have limited their regular exercise participation (Rimmer, Rauworth, Wan, Heckerling, & Gerber, 2009). Barriers have been within the built and natural environment; economic issues; emotional and psychological problems; equipment inaccessibility; difficulty with the use and interpretation of guidelines, codes, regulations, and laws; and professional knowledge, education, and training issues, among others (Rimmer, Riley, Wang, Rauworth, & Jurkowski, 2004). This chapter provides information about studies that have focused on ways in which exercise and leisure activities have affected the health status of people with different types of disabilities.

Exercise for People with Disability
Exercise and Spinal Cord Injury

Several studies have focused on spinal cord injury (SCI) and exercise. There appears to be a strong positive effect of exercise for people with SCI

in increasing strength, function, and quality of life (QOL), while also decreasing pain, stress, depression, and anxiety.

A review by Fernhall et al. (2008) found a strong relationship between the number of days a week that a person engages in physical activity and physical work capacity. People with SCI who had higher work capacities were also shown to have improved cholesterol profiles. Wheelchair sports participants had lower levels of reported kidney infections and hospitalizations due to pressure sores compared to their inactive peers. A study in the review also found that an increase in physical work capacity can lead to less physical strain during everyday functional activities. Resistance exercise was found to promote strength, which can improve QOL by aiding in wheelchair propulsion, transfers, and other functional activities that promote independence. Ease of performing daily activities increases in those who have higher levels of physical activity participation.

Martin et al. (2003) studied 34 participants (mean age 38.6 years) who engaged in group exercise twice a week. The exercise sessions included stretching, arm ergometry for aerobic exercise, and resistance training. Outcome measures were determined by a 10-item body satisfaction questionnaire to measure physical self-concept, the Perceived Quality of Life Scale (PQOL). Additional items about satisfaction included time spent out of the house, walking/wheeling activity, amount of sexual activity, and amount of sleep. After the intervention, participants in the exercise group reported less pain and less stress than did those in the control group. There were significant differences between groups in satisfaction with physical function, physical appearance, and depression. Participants in the exercise program reported higher overall QOL compared to those in the control group. There was less reported depression in the exercise group as compared to the control group.

Stevens et al. (2008) also reported a strong positive association between levels of physical activity and ratings of QOL among a sample of 62 participants (aged 18–50) with SCI below the C6 level. When controlling for level of injury, completeness of injury, and time since injury, physical activity was shown to be a predictor of QOL. Outcome measures were the Physical Activity Scale for Individuals with Physical Disabilities (PASIPD) and the Quality of Well-Being Scale.

Hicks et al. (2003) examined physiological measures in addition to quality of life measures among 34 people aged 19–65 years who had been diagnosed with an SCI longer than 1 year. Outcome measures were resting heart rate and blood pressure, arm ergometry heart rate/work ratio, one repetition maximum (1RM) to assess strength (chest press, elbow flexion, shoulder flexion), Perceived Stress Scale (PSS), Centre for Epidemiological Studies Depression Scale (CES-D), pain items from the Short Form-36 Health Survey (SF-36), a 9-item body satisfaction questionnaire to measure physical self-concept, Reported Health Transition subscale from the SF-36, and the PQOL with additional items about satisfaction with time spent out of the house, walking/wheeling activity, amount of sexual activity, and amount of sleep. Twenty-one participants were assigned to the exercise group, and 13 were placed in a wait list group serving as the control group. Those in the exercise group participated 2 days per week in 90- to 120-minute progressive exercise training sessions for 9 months. Participants warmed up with light arm ergometry or laps around an indoor track. Individuals then completed the aerobic training portion, which consisted of arm ergometry for increased periods of time throughout the study.

Resistance training consisted of circuit training with increasing percentages of the 1RM as training progressed. There were no significant differences in resting cardiovascular measures between groups before and after intervention. There was a decrease in heart rate/work ratio during arm ergometry for those in the exercise condition. In the third stage of the arm ergometry protocol, there was an average power output increase of 81.5% in the exercise group. There were significant increases in strength in all muscle groups except for the left anterior deltoid in the exercise group as compared to the control group. There were reported decreases in pain, depression, and stress in the exercise group. Exercisers also reported greater satisfaction with physical appearance, perceived improvements in health, and better overall QOL than the control group.

Muraki et al. (2000) studied 169 men with SCI (mean age 42.7 years) using the Self-rating Depression Scale (SDS), State-Trait Anxiety Inventory (STAI), and Profiles of Mood States (POMS). Participants were assigned to four different groups based on their sports activity level (High Active [more than 3 days a week], Middle Active [1–2 days a week], Low Active [1-3 days a month], No Active [no sports activity]). Depression and anxiety trait scores were the lowest among the participants in the High Active group. When examining depression on the SDS, trait anxiety for STAI, and depression and vigor on the POMS, there were significant differences between groups. There were no significant differences in scores between individuals with paraplegia or tetraplegia. There were no significant differences between people who participated in different modes of sports (wheelchair basketball, wheelchair racing, wheelchair tennis, minor modes).

Exercise and Traumatic Brain Injury

Exercise also appears to have a positive effect on the health status of people with traumatic brain injury (TBI), with evidence pointing to decreased depression, increased reported physical health, and increased exercise self-efficacy.

Gordon et al. (1998) compared 249 people with TBI who were classified as exercisers and nonexercisers to 139 people without disabilities who were classified as exercisers and nonexercisers using Beck Depression Inventory (BDI). Other outcome measures were The Institute for Rehabilitation Research (TIRR) Symptom Checklist domains that included cognitive problems, communication problems, somatic complaints, and behavioral problems the SF-36 Health Survey, Community Integration

Questionnaire (CIQ), and the Craig Handicap Assessment Capacity Technique (CHART). Twenty-three symptoms were reported more frequently in those with a TBI who did not exercise compared to those with a TBI who exercised regularly, and there was a significant difference between groups, with 74% of the symptoms being cognitive. People with TBI who exercised reported less depression than nonexercisers with a TBI based on BDI scores. With the exception of pain, those with a TBI who exercise reported their perceived health status as better. Measures of community participation showed higher levels in the group without disabilities than in those with a TBI. Exercise did not affect the level of community participation in the TBI group, but those who were exercisers did report higher levels of productivity than nonexercisers.

Haworth et al. (2009) examined 44 participants with acquired brain injuries who were assigned to an experimental group (average age 40.9 years) or a standard care group (average age 42.3 years) to assess the effects of an exercise program. Outcome measures were the Exercise Efficacy Scale, Human Activity Profile, SF-36 Health Survey, Hospital Anxiety and Depression Scale, UWIST Mood Adjective Checklist, Motricity Index, Frenchay Arm Test, Rivermead Mobility Index, 10-meter timed walk, and a visual analog scale for perceived benefit. Those in the treatment group participated in an exercise and education group twice a week for 1 month. Exercise included circuit training that targeted strength, cardiovascular health, and mobility. All groups had improvements in all domains of the SF-36, but those in the exercise group experienced more improvement than the control group in the physical and general health domains. These differences were not significant. Although there were no significant differences between groups, there was a moderate reported increase in activity levels in both groups. There was significant improvement in exercise self-efficacy scores. The scores for exercise self-efficacy continued to be higher for the exercise group at a 6-month follow-up. There were no significant improvements in the Motricity Index, Frenchay Arm Test, Rivermead Mobility Index, and 10-meter timed walk test.

EXERCISE AND CHRONIC HEMIPARESIS

Health benefits of exercise for people with neuromuscular disabilities such as chronic hemiparesis appear to be positive. Increased mobility, improved balance, increased ability to perform activities of daily living (ADLs), and decreased depression have all been reported among exercisers.

A study by Macko et al. (2008) involved 22 individuals with chronic hemiparesis over the age of 40 who participated in an adapted physical activity program twice a week for 2 months. Outcome measures were the Berg Balance Scale, 6-minute walk test, Short Physical Performance Battery, Barthel Index, Lawton Scores, Stroke Impact Scale, and Geriatric Depression Scale. The sessions were 60 minutes long and consisted of exercises focused on balance, mobility, and stretching by use of parallel bars and seated exercise. Participants demonstrated improvements in mobility and balance, as evidenced by improvements in performance on the 6-minute walk test and the Berg Balance Scale. Improvement in performance of basic ADLs was also noted after participation in the exercise program. There were also improvements in the Geriatric Depression Scale when the mobility scores increased on the Stroke Impact Scale.

Exercise and Stroke

People with stroke have shown increases in physical functioning, ability to perform ADLs, and increased social participation and functioning as a result of exercise.

Studenski et al. (2005) examined 93 participants who had had a stroke (average age 69.5 years) and were engaged in a 12-week home-based exercise program focusing on strength, balance, and endurance three times a week. Outcome measures were the Barthel Index, Functional Independence Measure, SF-36, Stroke Impact Scale (SIS), and Lawton and Brody Instrumental Activities of Daily Living. Compared to those receiving routine care, participants had significantly higher scores in social functioning on the SF-36 and social participation, upper extremity strength, emotion, and physical functioning on the Stroke Impact Scale. Scores were marginally higher for the exercise group on the Barthel Index, which looks at independence in ADLs. Although many participants experienced benefits directly after the intervention, they were not sustained at the 6-month post-intervention measures.

Exercise and Multiple Sclerosis

People with multiple sclerosis (MS) are among the more frequently studied in regards to health benefits from exercise. The literature supports improvements related to improved QOL; improved mental health; decreased pain, depression, and fatigue; and increased self-efficacy in managing MS as a result of exercise participation.

Rafeeyan et al. (2010) studied participants (mean age 32.6 years) with MS who were engaged in a 1-hour aquatic exercise program 3 days a week for 1 month. Outcome measures were the SF-36 Health Questionnaire and the Quality of Life measure; domains evaluated were spiritual situation, mental health, social function, physical pain, general health, physical efficiency, limitation of the role due to mental health, limitation of the role due to physical problems, and health position. There were improvements in the QOL domains of spiritual situation, mental health, social function, physical pain, general health, physical efficiency, limitation of the role because of mental health, limitation of the role due to physical problems, and health position.

Roehrs and Karst (2004) studied 31 individuals with MS who enrolled in a 12-week 1-hour aquatic exercise program twice a week. Only 15 completed the program due to various reasons, such as exacerbation of symptoms or fear that participation would make it difficult to complete daily tasks. Outcome measures were evaluated using the Expanded Disability Status Scale, the Medical Outcomes Study Short Form 36 (SF-36), and the Multiple Sclerosis Quality of Life Inventory (MSQLI). Domains included fatigue, pain, sexual satisfaction, bladder control, bowel control, visual impairment, perceived cognitive deficits, social support, and mental health. Exercises were determined after a physical therapist evaluated the abilities of the participants. There were significant improvement in the QOL domains of fatigue and social functioning as measured by significant improvements on the Modified Fatigue Impact Scale (MFIS) and Modified Social Support Scale (MSSS) that are parts of the MSQLI. Improvements in mental health functioning were not demonstrated as a result of this exercise program. Some participants were concerned that the program would adversely affect their health, but results showed that there was no negative impact on QOL in terms of physical functioning and general health. Barriers to exercise adherence were transportation problems and availability of a person to assist them during the program.

Motl et al. (2009) studied 292 participants with MS (average age 40.8 years). Participants were given an accelerometer to wear for 7 days, as well as asked to fill out the following questionnaires: Godin Leisure-Time Exercise Questionnaire (GLTEQ), Satisfaction with Life Scale (SWLS), Leeds Multiple Sclerosis Quality of Life Scale (LMSQOL), Patient Determined Disease Steps (PDDS), Fatigue Severity Scale (FSS), Hospital Anxiety and Depression Scale (HADS), Short-form McGill Pain Questionnaire (SF-MPQ), Multiple Sclerosis Self-Efficacy Scale

(MSSE), and Social Provisions Scale. Quality of life was correlated with physical activity. Those with higher levels of activity indicated they had less depression, pain, and fatigue. There were also higher levels of social support and self-efficacy for managing MS in those who reported greater levels of physical activity. The authors state that the relationship between QOL and physical activity is likely indirect. Independent correlates of QOL were pain, fatigue, depression and anxiety, social support, and self-efficacy for managing MS.

Exercise and Children with Disabilities

Children with disabilities are often excluded from mainstream, school-based exercise and after-school sports programs because of inaccessibility (Rowland & Rimmer, 2012). The benefits of exercise participation for children with disabilities can, however, be significant and can include improvements in strength, bone mass, joint structure and function, self-esteem; obesity prevention; and increased ability to perform ADLs.

Oriel et al. (2008) studied 18 children between the ages of 5 and 20 with varied diagnoses of cognitive and/or physical disabilities. Children participated in an 8-week fitness program for 60 minutes once a week. The program consisted of running/walking, stretching, and a physical game or activity. Outcome measures were the Presidential Fitness Test (modified), Energy Expenditure Index (EEI), body mass index (BMI), and Piers-Harris 2 to measure self-concept. Participants tracked the number of positive and negative social interactions encountered during the week. There was a significant increase in the child's ability to perform curl-ups as measured by the Presidential Fitness Test, but there were no other significant improvements in physical fitness measures. Although not statistically significant, fewer children were unable to complete the 1-mile walk/run at post-test compared to pre-test. There were no significant increases in self-concept scores. Parents reported that their children showed increased attention and desire to engage in physical activity, selected healthier food choices, and lost weight.

Murphy and Carbone (2008) reviewed articles related to exercise and children with disabilities and found that improved strength and endurance from physical activity can lead to decreases in injuries and falls, improvement in bone mass, and increased ability to perform daily functional tasks. Exercise can help to improve strength, structure and functioning of joints, and flexibility, and may help to slow overall functional decline. Children with disabilities are more likely to engage in sedentary activity that put them at higher risk for obesity, so participation in sports and physical activity can help to reduce this risk. Participation in sports can help to increase self-esteem, provide opportunities to form social bonds, and improve confidence in performing physical tasks. In children with autism and other developmental disorders, exercise has been shown to decrease fatigue, maladaptive behavior, and stereotypic movements.

Chen and Lin (2011) examined 16 students with visual impairments (aged 15–17) who were engaged in a jump roping exercise protocol 3 times a week for 10 weeks. This consisted of a 10-minute warm-up, eight cycles of 2 minutes of jumping followed by 2 minutes of rest, and a 10-minute cool down (approximately 50 minutes total). Outcome measures were BMI, the PACER test, sit-and-reach, and sit-up. There were no significant changes in BMI or sit-up performance. Participants demonstrated significant improvements in aerobic capacity and sit-and-reach performance.

Long and Rouster-Stevens (2010) reviewed studies focused on exercise and children with juvenile idiopathic arthritis (JIA) and found that children with JIA are more likely to have decreased bone mineral composition as well as muscle atrophy, so engaging in weight-bearing exercises has the potential to help prevent or slow these changes. Those children with higher levels of fitness were better able to perform ADLs.

Although there are mixed results within the literature, different studies have shown improvements in balance, range of motion, strength, health-related quality of life, and decreases in pain because of exercise participation.

Exercise and People with General Physical Disabilities

Potential health benefits of exercise for people with physical disabilities are numerous and are similar to those benefits already identified in other populations: increase strength, flexibility, and QOL, among others.

Eversden et al. (2007) studied 115 participants with rheumatoid arthritis (RA) who either engaged in a hydrotherapy or land-based exercise program 30 minutes per week for 6 weeks. Participants were also issued an optional home exercise program for between sessions. Sessions in both conditions consisted of warming up and stretching, followed by exercises targeting flexibility, joint mobility, and functional activity. The sessions ended with a cool-down, and difficulty of exercises was tailored to each participant's

abilities. Outcome measures were self-reported change in health as measured by an effect of treatment scale (1–7), with 1 = Very much worse, 7 = Very much better; a visual analog scale for pain, a Health Assessment Questionnaire (HAQ), a 10-meter walk speed test, and the Euro-Qol5D (EQ-5D). Scales used within the EQ-5D measure were self-report on health-related quality of life (EQ-VAS) and health status evaluation (EQ-5D utility or index score). Participants in the pool group were more likely to feel "much better" or "very much better" than were those who participated in the land-based program. The self-reported benefits were not reflected in the outcomes of the HAQ, the visual analog scale for pain, the 10-meter walk speed test, or the EQ-5D.

Giacobbi et al. (2008) performed qualitative interviews about the impact of physical activity on health with 26 individuals aged 18–54 with physical disabilities who participated in wheelchair basketball. The semistructured interviews focused on gathering information about the participants' disabilities, occupational or school-related ADLs, perceptions of benefits of physical activity, motivation for maintaining involvement in physical activity, and assessment of their lives. In addition to the interviews, participants were asked to complete the PASIPD. Themes that emerged included physical activity having a positive effect on psychological health, cognitive abilities, emotional health, and self-perception. One participant reported that participating in sports helped her to become more outgoing and social. Another participant commented that she was able to translate the concepts of perseverance and hard work that she used in basketball to other areas of her life. Many participants discussed feeling an increased sense of self-confidence. Participants reported health benefits such as staying in shape, lowering risk of disease, and maintaining a feeling of good health. Eighteen of the 26 participants felt that participation in sports positively influenced physiological domains such as improved sleep, muscle tone development, pain management, and cardiovascular health. Individuals also stated that participating in athletics helped them to promote social opportunities, as well as form connections with people without disabilities by sharing a similar interest.

Wilhite and Shank (2009) also performed qualitative interviews with 12 participants with physical or sensory impairments (aged 29–58) regarding their sports participation. Participants stated that sports helped to increase overall physical functioning and endurance to participate in life activities. Maintaining independence and good health was a motivator within this domain. It was also mentioned that engagement in sports could help increase awareness or manage secondary or psychosocial conditions. Participants discussed the positive impact on self-efficacy, depression, stress, and overall mental well-being. Many participants discussed that sports provided them with chances for socialization. One participant discussed that seeing how independent and capable other athletes were became a personal inspiration. Participants also identified the importance of being able to find support within the community and to identify with other athletes with disabilities.

Rimmer et al. (2009) performed another qualitative analysis of focus groups with 92 women with mobility disabilities. Participants were assigned to one of three groups: (1) an "awareness group," in which they received a brochure on exercise; (2) an individualized exercise program with low levels of support; or (3) an individualized exercise program with high levels of support. Participants in the exercise group with high support had a significant decrease in body weight and BMI, whereas the others did not. This indicates that individuals may need more personal support to help support behavioral change. There were significant increases in physical activity participation reports for both exercise groups. Those in the awareness group experienced an increase in mobility limitations compared to the other groups, but this was not significant.

Exercise and People with Intellectual Disability

Exercise benefits for people with intellectual disability can include increased physical performance, as in the components of balance and strength. Other significant benefits have included weight loss.

Carmeli et al. (2005) studied 22 participants (aged 54–66) with intellectual disability who were engaged in an exercise program 3 days a week for 6 months. Participants were assigned to one of two groups. One group was assigned to a program focusing on strength and balance, and the other received a more general exercise program. The balance intervention was 40–45 minutes and included a warm-up followed by dynamic balance exercises, such as toe-to-heel walking or games with balls and balloons. The 45-minute strength sessions consisted of lower body exercises prescribed according to the American College of Sports Medicine after determining the participants' one-rep maximum. The general exercise program consisted of 45-minute sessions focusing on general gross movements, flexibility, and walking. Outcome measures were the Timed-Up and Go Test (TUGT), Functional Reach Test (FRT), knee flexion and extension strength, a well-being questionnaire, and an adapted questionnaire that looked at the domains of social competence and physical appearance. Both groups experienced significant increases in perceptions of well-being after the exercise intervention. Only the strengthening and balance group experienced increases in physical performance (balance and strength) as compared to those in a generalized exercise program. There were significant increases in the TUGT, FRT, and measures of peak torque.

Wu et al. (2010) studied 146 participants aged 19–67 years with intellectual disability who took part in a physical fitness program consisting of 40 minutes of physical activity 4 days a week. Outcome measures were BMI and physical fitness status (sit-ups, sit-and-reach, shuttle run). There were significant decreases in weight and BMI. Participants also showed improvements in the V-shape sit-and-reach, as well as in the 30- and 60-second sit-up tests but did not demonstrated improvements in the shuttle run.

Carmeli et al. (2009) examined 24 participants (aged 45–55 years) with mild intellectual disability and anxiety who were assigned to either an aerobic exercise group, a leisure activity group, or a control group. Those in the aerobic exercise group participated in three exercise sessions per week over 6 months. Exercises involved the use of an ergometric bicycle or a treadmill. Participants in the leisure group participated in various games and activities over the 6-month period. Outcome measures were domains within the Hamilton Anxiety Scale (HAM-A): anxious mood (worries and anticipates worst), tension (startles, cries easily, restless, and trembling), fears (fear of the dark, fear of strangers, fear of being alone, and fear of animals), depression (decreased interest in activities), somatic complaints of muscles (muscle aches or pains, bruxism), and somatic complaints of sensation (tinnitus, and blurred vision). Significant decreases on the HAM-A scores indicated there were significant decreases in anxiety for participants in both the aerobic and leisure group.

Health Benefits of Leisure Activities for People with Disabilities

As a whole, the literature identifying health benefits of leisure activities for people with disabilities is sparse. The majority of the evidence of health benefits related to leisure activities for populations of people with disabilities is based on qualitative interviews or survey data. The following sections represent a review of the literature relevant to examining the effects of leisure activities on the health of people with disabilities.

Leisure Activities and Spinal Cord Injury

Daniel and Manigandan (2005) examined 25 participants with SCI who were assigned to either a leisure intervention group or a control group. Participants took part in 1-hour leisure group sessions three times per week. These sessions included warming-up with a game, discussion of a previously identified leisure home task, discussion about a topic pertaining to leisure participation, assignment of a homework task, and a relaxing wind-down activity. Outcome measures were the World Health Organization Quality of Life Scale- Brief (WHOQOL-BREF); domains within it included physical health, psychological, social relationships, environment, and the Leisure Satisfaction Scale (LSS). There was a significant increase in all domains of QOL, including the physical health domain within the WHOQOL-BREF. There were no increases in the social relationships measure. There were, however, significant improvements in all areas of the LSS.

Leisure Activities and Cerebral Palsy or Spina Bifida

Specht et al. (2002) performed qualitative interviews with nine participants between the ages of 30 and 50 with cerebral palsy (CP) and spina bifida about how engagement in leisure has affected their overall well-being. A theme emerged that participants felt that engaging in physical activity allowed them to stay active. Others discussed that participation in leisure activities had physical benefits that helped them with completion of other daily activities. Participants reported that engaging in leisure activities had a positive impact on their physical and mental health.

Leisure Activities and Multiple Sclerosis

Khemthong et al. (2008) examined the findings for 60 participants with MS who completed surveys regarding depression, anxiety, stress, fatigue, health, social support, leisure participation, and leisure satisfaction. The specific surveys were the Numeric Rating Scale (NRS), Depression Anxiety Stress Scale (DASS-21), Duke Social Support Index (DSSI), SF-36, Fatigue Impact Scale (FIS), Classification of Leisure Participation (CLP) Scale, and LSS. Results indicated a positive relationship between physical health and physical leisure. A positive association was also found between leisure satisfaction and mental health, and social leisure was a contributing predictor of physical health.

Leisure Activities and Physical Disability

Santiago and Coyle (2004) examined the responses of 170 participants between the ages of 21 and 65 with physical disabilities who completed surveys describing leisure-time physical activity participation, information on secondary conditions, and functional status. Specifically, participants were asked questions about their disability that included secondary conditions, years with disability, health status, functional status, and leisure-time physical activity participation. Seventy-five percent of participants stated that fatigue was a problem for them. Fifty percent or more of participants stated that they experienced joint and muscle pain, depression, access problems, weight problems, sexual dysfunction, mobility problems, physical deconditioning, spasticity, joint and muscle pain, depression, chronic pain, isolation, bowel dysfunction, and bladder dysfunction. Functional status was inversely associated with participation in leisure-time physical activity. There was a significant inverse relationship between participation in leisure-time physical activity and isolation, as well as physical deconditioning after controlling for functional status.

Leisure Activities and Intellectual Disability

Duvdevany and Arar (2004) examined survey responses of 85 adults (aged 18–55 years) with intellectual disabilities. Forty-five of the individuals lived in community residential settings, and 40 lived in foster homes. Outcome measures were a demographic questionnaire, the Quality of Life Questionnaire, the Revised UCLA Loneliness Scale, the Social Relationships List, and a leisure activities list. There were no significant differences in loneliness or number of friends depending on what type of residence the participant lived in. Those who lived in foster homes had significantly higher rates of participation in leisure activities than did those in community residential settings.

Conclusion and Future Directions

Overall, exercise and leisure participation have positive impacts on the health and well-being of people with different types of disabilities. The greatest health benefit of exercise participation for people with disabilities appears to be in improving strength, decreasing depression, and increasing self-reported QOL among samples studied. The impact of specific leisure activities has not been as well studied, however, with most of the findings coming from self-reported survey and qualitative interview data. Information gathered from these reports and interviews indicates that leisure participation can have positive health effects for people with disabilities and therefore should be examined as a possible future direction for health promotion programs among these populations.

The literature that focuses on exercise, leisure, and positive effects for people with disabilities is fairly limited in comparison to that for the general population. However, there are some promising findings that point us in the direction of seeking out accessible exercise options that can potentially improve QOL for people with different types of disabilities. As has been examined in the literature on barriers to exercise, the degree of participation among people with disabilities is affected by a multitude of factors that include a specific individual's personal attributes and their environment.

References

Caldwell, L. L. (2005). Leisure and health: Why is leisure therapeutic? *British Journal of Guidance & Counselling, 33*(1), 7–26.

Carmeli, E., Barak, S., Morad, M., & Kodesh, E. (2009). Physical exercises can reduce anxiety and improve quality of life among adults with intellectual disability. *International SportMed Journal, 10*(2), 77–85.

Carmeli, E., Zinger-Vaknin, T., Morad, M., & Merrick, J. (2005). Can physical training have an effect on well-being in adults with mild intellectual disability? *Mechanisms of Ageing and Development, 126*(2), 299–304.

Chen, C.- C., & Lin, S-Y. (2011). The impact of rope jumping exercise on physical fitness of visually impaired students. *Research in Developmental Disabilities 32*(1), 25–29.

Daniel, A., & Manigandan, C. (2005). Efficacy of leisure intervention groups and their impact on quality of life among people with spinal cord injury. *International Journal of Rehabilitation Research, 28*(1), 43–48.

Duvdevany, I., & Arar, E. (2004). Leisure activities, friendships, and quality of life of persons with intellectual disability: Foster homes vs community residential settings. *International Journal of Rehabilitation Research, 27*(4), 289–296.

Eversden, L., Maggs, F., Nightingale, P., & Jobanputra, P. (2007). A pragmatic randomised control trial of hydrotherapy and land exercises on overall well being and quality of life in rheumatoid arthritis. *BMC Musculoskeletal Disorders, 8*, 23.

Fernhall, B., Heffernan, K., Jae, S. Y., & Hedrick, B. (2008). Health implications of physical activity in individuals with spinal cord injury: A literature review. *Journal of Health and Human Services Administration, 30*(4), 468–502.

Giacobbi Jr., P. R., Stancil, M., Hardin, B., & Bryant, L. (2008). Physical activity and quality of life experienced by highly active individuals with physical disabilities. *Adaptive Physical Activity Quarterly, 25*(3), 189–207.

Gordon, W. A., Sliwinski, M., Echo, J., McLoughlin, M., Sheerer, M. S., & Meili, T. E. (1998). The benefits of exercise in individuals with traumatic brain injury: A retrospective study. *Journal of Head Trauma Rehabilitation, 13*(4), 58–67.

Haworth, J., Young, C. & Thornton, E. (2009). The effects of an 'exercise and education' programme on exercise self-efficacy and levels of independent activity in adults with acquired neurological pathologies: an exploratory, randomized study. *Clinical Rehabilitation, 23*(4), 371–383.

Hicks, A. L., Martin, K. A., Ditor, D. S., Latimer, A. E., Craven, C., Bugaresti, J., & McCartney, N. (2003). Long-term exercise training in persons with spinal cord injury: Effects on strength, arm ergometry performance and psychological well-being. *Spinal Cord, 41*(1), 34–43.

Khemthong, S., Packer, T. L., Passmore, A., & Dhaliwal, S. S. (2008). Does social leisure contribute to physical health in multiple sclerosis related fatigue? *Annual Therapeutic Recreation, 16*, 71–80.

Long, A. R., & Rouster-Stevens, K. A. (2010). The role of exercise therapy in the management of juvenile idiopathic arthritis. *Current Opinion in Rheumatology, 22*(2), 213–217.

Macko, R. F., Benvenuti, F., Stanhope, S., Macellari, V., Taviani, A., Nesi, B., Weinrich, M. & Stuart, M. (2008). Adaptive physical activity improves mobility function and quality of life in chronic hemiparesis. *Journal of Rehabilitation Research & Development, 45*(2), 323–328.

Martin Ginis, K. A., Latimer, A. E., McKechnie, K., Ditor, D. S., McCartney, N., Hicks, A. L., et al. (2003). Using exercise to enhance subjective well-being among people with spinal cord injury: The mediating influences of stress and pain. *Rehabilitation Psychology, 48*(3), 157–164.

Motl, R. W., McAuley, E., Snook, E. M., & Gliottoni, R. C. (2009). Physical activity and quality of life in multiple sclerosis: Intermediary roles of disability, fatigue, mood, pain, self-efficacy and social support. *Psychology, Health, & Medicine, 14*(1), 111–124.

Muraki, S., Tsunawake, N., Hiramatsu, S., & Yamasaki, M. (2000). The effect of frequency and mode of sports activity on the psychological status in tetraplegics and paraplegics. *Spinal Cord, 38*(5), 309–314.

Murphy, N. A., & Carbone, P. S. (2008). Promoting the participation of children with disabilities in sports, recreation, and physical activities. *Pediatrics, 121*(5), 1057–1061.

Oriel, K. N., George, C. L., & Blatt, P. J. (2008). The impact of a community based exercise program in children and adolescents with disabilities: A pilot study. *Fall, 27*(1), 5–20.

Rafeeyan, Z., Azarbarzin, M., Moosa, F. M., & Hasanzadeh, A. (2010). Effect of aquatic exercise on the multiple sclerosis patient's quality of life. *Iran Journal of Nursing & Midwifery Research, 15*(1), 38–42.

Rimmer, J. H., Rauworth, A., Wang, E., Heckerling, & Gerber, B. S. (2009). A randomized control trial to increase physical activity and reduce obesity in a predominantly African American group of women with mobility disabilities and severe obesity. *Preventive Medicine, 48*, 473–479.

Rimmer, J. H., Riley, B., Wang, E., Rauworth, A., & Jurkowski, J. (2004). Physical activity participation among persons with disabilities: Barriers and facilitators. *American Journal of Preventive Medicine, 26*, 419–425.

Rowland, J. L., & Rimmer, J. H. (2012). Feasibility of using active video gaming as a means for increasing energy expenditure in three nonambulatory young adults with disabilities. *Physical Medicine & Rehabilitation, 4*(8), 569–573.

Roehrs, T. G., & Karst, G. M. (2004). Effects of an aquatics exercise program on quality of life measures for individuals with progressive multiple sclerosis. *Journal of Neurologic Physical Therapy, 28*(2), 63–71.

Santiago, M. C., & Coyle, C. P. (2004). Leisure-time physical activity and secondary conditions in women with physical disabilities. *Disability & Rehabilitation, 26*(8), 485–494.

Specht, J., King, G., Brown, E., & Foris, C. (2002). The importance of leisure in the lives of persons with congenital physical disabilities. *American Journal of Occupational Therapy*, *56*(4), 436–445.

Stevens, S. L., Caputo, J. L., Fuller, D. K., & Morgan, D. W. (2008). Physical activity and quality of life in adults with spinal cord injury. *Journal of Spinal Cord Medicine*, *31*(4), 373–378.

Studenski, S., Duncan, P. W., Perera, S., Reker, D., Lai, S. M., & Richards, L. (2005). Daily functioning and quality of life in a randomized controlled trial of therapeutic exercise for sub-acute stroke survivors. *Stroke*, *36*(8), 1764–1770.

Wilhite, B., & Shank, J. (2009). In praise of sport: Promoting sport participation as a mechanism of health among persons with a disability. *Disability and Health Journal*, *2*(3), 116–127.

Wu, C-L., Lin, J-D., Hu, J., Yen, C-F., Yen, C-T., Chou, Y-L., & Wu, P-H. (2010). The effectiveness of healthy physical fitness programs on people with intellectual disabilities living in a disability institution: Six-month short-term effect. *Research in Developmental Disabilities 31*(3), 13–17.

Coping and Disability

Lillian R. Reuman, Chelsea Mitamura, *and* Michele M. Tugade

Abstract

Understanding coping—the behavioral and cognitive efforts one uses to manage the demands of stressful situations—in the face of chronic and acute disability, a potentially burdensome and stressful situation, is a nuanced issue. The complimentary emerging field of positive psychology emphasizes positive emotions and traits as they relate to an individual's capacity for resilience and happiness. The aim of this chapter is to examine processes of coping from a positive psychology perspective, with special attention paid to how certain coping styles (e.g., problem- vs. emotion-focused), positive emotion-based coping strategies (e.g., benefit-finding and optimism), and related factors (e.g., self-esteem, individual differences, and social support networks) may facilitate or impair the lives of people living with disabilities (e.g., arthritis, paraplegia). The authors discuss these constructs in the context of empirical evidence and propose directions for future research.

Key Words: positive psychology, disability, coping, self-regulation

Affecting all individuals, stress and coping are ubiquitous in everyday life. The aim of this chapter is to examine processes of coping from a positive psychology perspective, with special attention given to coping with disability. Historically, psychology research has emphasized obtaining a better understanding of dysfunction or deviant pathology, with a focus on treating mental health deficits once they occur. As a result, efforts to understand human nature have centered around traumatic, non-normative events and the resulting required adjustment. A relatively recent approach in the field, however, has shifted attention from an attempt to understand what's "wrong" to how we can foster healthy outcomes and enhance overall wellness among humans, or focus on what's "right" (Seligman & Csikszentmihàlyi, 2000). The goal of this paradigm shift is to understand the processes, strengths, dispositions, and virtues that make one resilient and able to adapt positively to situations ranging from daily hassles to chronic stressors and traumatic events. *Positive psychology* refers to a complementary field of psychology that focuses on positive emotions, positive individual traits, and positive institutions as they relate to an individual's capacity for resilience and happiness.

A positive psychology framework is adopted in this chapter, which is organized into three parts. First, we describe what coping is and identify different theoretical paradigms used to investigate how people cope with chronic and acute stressors. Second, we define individual differences in psychological resilience and review the literature on how trait resilient individuals cope with stress. In the final sections, we focus more specifically on coping with disabilities. We examine how certain coping styles, individual differences, and social support networks may facilitate or impair the lives of those living with disabilities.

Coping

Coping refers to the behavioral and cognitive efforts that one uses to manage the internal and external demands of stressful situations (Lazarus & Folkman, 1984). More specifically, Folkman and Lazarus (1980) defined coping as "the cognitive and behavioral efforts made to master, tolerate, or reduce external and internal demands and conflicts among them." In this way, coping is defined by a sequence of behavioral and cognitive actions or processes, forming a coping episode.

Problem-Focused Versus Emotion-Focused

Coping can be classified as being either problem-focused or emotion-focused in nature. Problem-focused coping involves activities that focus on directly changing elements of the stressful situation. For example, if an individual loses a job, problem-focused coping might include making a plan of action, such as revamping one's resume and applying broadly to different jobs or obtaining additional training. In contrast, emotion-focused coping involves activities that focus more on modifying one's internal reactions or distress resulting from the stressful situation. Examples of emotion-focused coping might include soothing oneself (e.g., relaxation, listening to music), affective expression (e.g., crying), cognitive processes (e.g., rumination), or disengagement (e.g., denial, withdrawal). To assess problem-focused and emotion-focused coping, one of the most widely used instruments is the Ways of Coping Checklist (Folkman & Lazarus, 1980), which asks respondents to indicate the extent to which they use specific coping strategies to manage or tolerate stressful situations.

Engaged Versus Disengaged

Another distinction among coping strategies is made between engaged versus disengaged coping processes (Moos & Schaefer, 1993). Engaged coping involves approaching a stressor head-on. Engaged coping includes strategies such as acceptance, support-seeking, and cognitive reappraisal. In contrast, disengaged coping involves avoiding one's distress. Disengaged strategies include processes such as denial and wishful thinking. Other forms of disengagement include using alcohol or drugs to cope, which, at excessive levels, can be physically and socially harmful.

Compared to engaged processes, disengagement is often considered a maladaptive form of coping. Although distancing oneself from a stressful situation can offer temporary relief to an individual, the threat remains. For example, if one goes to the movies to avoid feeling anxiety about unpaid bills, the threat of a collection agency still exists after one returns from the movie. In fact, with long-term avoidance, there is less time available to manage the problem at hand. In turn, negative feelings can resurface in the form of intrusive thoughts, often producing a paradoxical increase in distress.

Proactive Versus Reactive

The temporal dynamics of coping have also been modeled. Aspinwall and Taylor (1997) differentiate between proactive and reactive coping processes. Much of the literature focuses on reactive coping, which occurs after a stressful episode has unfolded. The aim of reactive coping is to compensate for loss or alleviate harm that has *already occurred*. In contrast, proactive coping strategies are future-oriented and are aimed at extinguishing a threat in *anticipation* of a stressful episode. Examples of proactive coping include making action plans and using positive reappraisal (appraising a situation as a challenge, rather than a threat). Proactive coping involves building personal resources to thwart possible stressors and facilitate personal growth.

In summary, process models of coping demonstrate the trajectory of the stress and coping response. Indeed, because situations can fluctuate constantly over the course of a lifetime, it is important to investigate how people can navigate their changing environmental conditions. The capacity to cope flexibly and successfully with episodes of adversity and stressful circumstances is described as *psychological resilience*.

Psychological Resilience

Psychological resilience has been characterized by (a) the ability to bounce back from negative emotional experiences and by (b) flexible adaptation to the changing demands of stressful experiences (Block & Block, 1980; Block & Kremen, 1996; Lazarus, 1993). More specifically, Block and Block (1980) defined psychological resilience as "resourceful adaptation to changing circumstances and environmental contingencies, analysis of the 'goodness of fit' between situational demands and behavioral possibility, and flexible invocation of the available repertoire of problem-solving strategies (problem-solving being defined to include the social and personal domains as well as the cognitive)." This definition captures a psychological frame of mind that has been shown to be associated with a variety of behavioral and psychological outcomes.

For several years, developmental researchers and theorists had highlighted various protective factors (e.g., social support networks) that promote healthy outcomes among children exposed to large-scale sources of adversity that have sustained influences throughout the lifetime, such as abuse or poverty (e.g., Rutter, 1987). Beyond adverse situations that can continually affect one's daily life, resilience is also manifested in response to isolated traumatic events (Bonanno, 2005). A resilient response to the death of a loved one, for example, is characterized by flexibility: mild, short-lived disruptions, and a relatively stable, healthy trajectory of healthy functioning over time (Bonanno, 2004). As such, resilience may be more common than previously conceptualized (Bonanno, 2004; Masten, 2001). Indeed, Masten argues that resilience is ordinary, rather than extraordinary. In line with this idea, resilience may be something that all individuals have the capacity to achieve.

Individual Differences in Trait Resilience

Trait resilience is described as the general tendency to modify one's responses effectively to changing situational demands and by having the ability to recover effectively from stressful circumstances (Block & Block, 1980). Resilient individuals may expertly use positive emotions in the coping process, "intelligently" drawing on positive emotions in times of stress (Tugade & Fredrickson, 2002, 2004).

Research indicates that individual differences in trait resilience predict the ability to capitalize on positive emotions when coping with negative emotional experiences. For instance, trait resilient people frequently use humor as a coping strategy (e.g., Werner & Smith, 1992; Wolin & Wolin, 1993), which has been shown to help people cope effectively with stressful circumstances (e.g., Martin & Lefcourt, 1983; Nezu, Nezu, & Blissett, 1988). Likewise, trait resilient children under stress score high on humor generation, compared to less resilient children facing equally high levels of stress (Masten, Best, & Garmezy, 1990). Trait resilient individuals also use other coping strategies that elicit positive emotions to regulate negative emotional situations. For instance, during heightened levels of distress, they engage in relaxation (allowing time to interpret and assess problems), exploration (to consider behavioral alternatives), and hopeful, optimistic thinking (having faith to overcome adversity) as means of regulating negative emotional experiences (Werner & Smith, 1992). Together, these findings indicate that trait resilient people are able to marshal

positive emotions to guide their coping behavior, allowing for the reduction of distress and restoration of perspective.

Trait resilient individuals have been shown to be physiologically resilient as well, and positive emotions appear useful in achieving this outcome (Tugade & Fredrickson, 2004). Theoretical descriptions of psychological resilience indicate that resilient individuals are able to "bounce back" from distressing experiences quickly and efficiently (Carver, 1998; Lazarus, 1993). In line with this theoretical definition, Tugade and Fredrickson (2004) found that although both individuals with low and high levels of resilience experienced equal levels of cardiovascular arousal and subjective negative experience in response to a stressor, highly trait resilient individuals exhibited faster cardiovascular recovery from negative emotional arousal. Additionally, "bouncing back" to cardiovascular baseline levels was partially mediated by resilient people's experiences of positive emotion in the midst of distress (Tugade & Fredrickson, 2004). These findings resonate with theoretical conceptions of resilient individuals, which include their abilities to recognize the effects of stressful situations and to experience positive outcomes despite sources of adversity (Masten, 2001). Furthermore, these findings demonstrate that positive emotions contribute to the ability for resilient individuals to physiologically recover from negative emotional arousal, which can have important health implications. Although it is important to allow negative emotions to unfold so as not to short-circuit the adaptive functions associated with negative emotional experiences, sustained experiences of negative emotional arousal can be associated with long-term cardiovascular illness and disease. In all, these findings linking positive emotions to beneficial coping outcomes indicate that trait resilient people effectively harness positive emotions to their advantage when coping, and they do so with a seeming intuitive sensibility (Tugade & Fredrickson, 2002).

Why are positive emotions important to resilience? According to the broaden-and-build theory (Fredrickson, 1998, 2001), positive emotions can momentarily broaden a person's scope of thought and allow for flexible attention, which in turn can improve one's well-being. Over time, and with repeated experiences of positive emotions, this broadened mindset might become habitual. By consequence, recurrent experiences of positive emotion can increase one's personal resources, including coping resources. Importantly, the arsenal of personal resources produced by positive emotions can be drawn on in times of need, which may have important value in the coping process (Fredrickson, 2000). Research suggests that the experience of positive emotions, in conjunction with effective coping strategies, may determine individual differences in resilience (Fredrickson, 2001). Given that such individual differences exist, it is necessary that we understand the intersection of resilience, positive emotions, and strategic coping strategies as they apply to a specific population of people with disabilities.

Coping with Disability

For our purposes, a working definition of people with disability includes children and adults who experience chronic illness or live with a physical disability on a daily basis. Chronic illness includes medically diagnosed conditions that affect a person over the lifespan. Physical disability includes any impairment caused by injury, birth defect, or illness (Ontario Human Rights Commissions, 2000, as cited in Dahlbeck & Lightsey, 2008). In many cases, chronic illness may lead to restrictions in performing the tasks of daily living. This is known as *functional disability*, one that produces a state that is not only stressful and burdensome, but also is associated with subjective well-being (Robb, Small, & Haley, 2008). These disabilities may include conditions such as cerebral palsy, deafness, amputation, cognitive impairments, autism, and mobility impairments.

Coping Styles

Individuals cope with the aforementioned chronic conditions using a variety of methods. Coping can occur as not only a response (reactive) but also as a proactive (anticipatory) approach to foreseen challenges (Schwarzer & Knoll, 2003). In this vein, the timing and certainty of the event may impact the strategies employed, given that coping is a dynamic process that requires constant reappraisal for the duration of the stressful encounter. Depending on personal preferences, heuristics, and the nature of the stressful situation at hand, individuals adopt various coping strategies. It is important that individuals utilize appropriate coping strategies so as to minimize detrimental consequences and avoid ineffective methods of stress relief, such as substance abuse and social isolation. As physical and mental demands of the disability may fluctuate over the course of the lifetime, adopted coping strategies may shift to better facilitate adjustment (Hudek- Knežević, Kudum, & Maglica, 2005).

Folkman and Lazarus (1980) noted that coping efforts serve two main functions: management of the person-environment relationship and regulation of associated stressful emotions. These functions provide the basis for problem-focused and emotion-focused coping, respectively. As discussed earlier, problem-focused strategies are aimed at solving the problem or reducing the source of the stress, whereas emotion-focused strategies are designed to manage the emotional distress accompanying the given problem. Each category includes both productive and counterproductive coping methods. For example, substance abuse and planning are both problem-focused strategies; however, the latter implies fewer long-term health concerns. Both denial and seeking instrumental social support are emotion-focused methods; however, the former may require considerable effort and debilitate psychological resources over time (Suls & Fletcher, 1985).

Acceptance coping, which involves active cognitive and behavioral efforts to understand a given situation and resolve a stressor by seeking guidance, has been linked to beneficial long-term adaptation to anxiety and improved physical symptoms in ill patients with diseases such as AIDS, diabetes, and heart failure (Dahlbeck & Lightsey, 2008). Conversely, avoidance coping and emotion-oriented coping have been linked to diminished well-being. Avoidance coping involves escape behaviors to avoid thinking about a stressor or its consequences (Ebata & Moos, 1991). Examples of avoidance coping include denial and wishful thinking. However, in select cases, research has shown that emotion-focused coping, which targets the emotional states accompanying a stressor rather than the stressor itself, has been found to lower pain tolerance among children and correlate with poorer adjustment (Piira, Taplin, Goodenough, & von Baeyer (2002).

Expanding on the two main functions of coping posed by Lazarus and Folkman (1984), Livneh, Antonak, and Gerhardt (2000) identified a three-dimensional structure of coping as it relates to adults with disability-related stress. The dimensions assess the degree to which individuals harbor active versus passive, optimistic versus pessimistic, and external- versus internal-oriented coping along a continuum. The first dimension is designed to assess whether the individual is willing to accept the situation or resorts to disengagement. The second dimension aims to illuminate feelings of hope or shades of fatalism. The third dimension encompasses the degree to which individuals seek or accept social support when coping. Conclusions drawn from this study suggest that coping may be hierarchical in nature. Furthermore, findings from the research suggest that coping efforts among people with disabilities may not differ significantly from coping efforts adopted by people without disabilities. Therefore, further research to identify adaptive coping strategies will be beneficial and universally applicable.

Despite the relative utility of widely accepted coping strategies, factors such as personality traits, comorbid medical conditions, temporal differences, and cognitive appraisal may impact adjustment and moderate the individual's ability to cope and thrive with his or her disability (Oaksford, Frude, & Cuddihy, 2005). The following section details these compelling intersections, as well as the environments and support services that appear to facilitate positive adaptation (Tedeschi & Kilmer, 2005).

Positive Emotion-Based Coping Strategies

Research has shown that using positive emotions to cope is an effective way to alleviate negative consequences from adverse emotional events (Tugade & Fredrickson, 2007). In the next section, we discuss different strategies that infuse positive emotional experiences to facilitate coping.

Benefit-Finding and Meaning-Making

One important coping strategy that has been found to be effective at facilitating resilience is the capacity to find positive meaning in negative circumstances (Folkman & Moskowitz, 2000). It has been proposed that finding positive meaning in negative circumstances can cultivate positive emotions and, in turn, prevent and treat problems related to anxiety and depression (Fredrickson, 2001). In the case of disability, a significant facet of successful coping involves finding the positive aspects of a situation and seeing the greater purpose or "meaning" behind it. Janoff-Bulman and Frantz (1997), for instance, suggest that successful adjustment in the face of adversity requires an individual to make sense of the traumatic event and subsequently find some benefit in the experience.

Important processes are associated with positive meaning-making and benefit-finding, which can be especially useful for individuals coping with disabling experiences. Davis and Morgan (2008) propose that finding meaning and/or "growing" from an injury or disability typically requires an individual to follow a specific path to understanding. First, the individual perceives the experience of trauma or

hardship as negatively affecting his or her life goals, identity, and/or worldview. Second, these negative feelings prompt a search for meaning, which includes an effort to understand the trauma and why it has happened to him or her. Third, the practice of making sense of one's predicament leads directly or indirectly to the perception that one has grown (Davis & Morgan, 2008). In this way, an individual may cognitively minimize or mitigate the negative implications of the experience and positively reframe possible consequences to the self, others, and, in a broader context, the world (deRoon-Cassini, de St. Aubin, Valvano, Hastings, & Horn, 2009). Making meaning, thus, may also help the individual determine which resources may be necessary for coping (Schwarzer & Knoll, 2003).

Positive meaning-making and benefit-finding have been shown to be effective strategies for coping with limb loss and amputation. The experience of limb amputation is often characterized by physical, emotional, and social challenges. These personal threats can take a profound toll on individuals and can be associated with lower levels of self-esteem or increases in depressive symptoms. Given the strain often associated with amputation, it is important to examine ways to achieve healthy adjustment to such challenges.

In a study of men who had undergone amputation, three different coping styles were examined: finding positive meaning, dispositional optimism, and perceived control over one's disability. Participants were surveyed about their experience post-amputation, and asked, "Has anything positive or good happened to you as a result of your amputation (yes or no)?" If respondents answered affirmatively, they were asked to elaborate on their response. Results demonstrated that 77% of the 138 participants reported finding positive meaning in their amputation. Examining their open-ended descriptions revealed that 60% reported *finding side benefits* ("I changed to a different occupation"); 35% reported *redefining the event/ reappraising life* ("I think I've become a much better person"); 3% made social comparisons ("I have one leg. What about a person who has no legs?"); 2% forgot negative aspects of the event ("I found that I can still do about everything I did before, only it takes longer to do it"), and less than 1% imagined a worse situation ("I survived; I have a second chance at life"). Findings revealed that finding positive meaning, dispositional optimism, and personal control were each independently associated with lower levels of depressive symptomatology (but not with levels of self-esteem) (Dunn, 1996). Together, these findings indicate that having a favorable outlook can have salutary effects for individuals who have had amputation experiences.

Gallagher and MacLachlan (2000) also reported that, post-amputation, 48% of individuals found positive meaning in their experience and thought something positive had happened as a result of the procedure. In particular, they reported independence gained with an artificial limb, viewing the experience as character building, changing one's attitude toward life, improved coping abilities, financial benefits, elimination of pain, and using it as an opportunity to meet people. Having coped with a major challenge, individuals may commonly report an increased sense of survival and ability to prevail (Tedeschi & Kilmer, 2005).

One explanation for the importance of positive meaning-making and benefit-finding in coping may be that it allows one to reestablish a sense of cognitive coherence about the world. The *just world theory* refers to the human need to believe that everything happens for a reason or that people usually get what they deserve (McParland & Knussen, 2010). Research indicates that individuals who more strongly endorse the just world theory are less susceptible to the negative consequences of disability and more prone to a range of positive outcomes, such as improved mood and increased recovery rate from illness (McParland & Knussen, 2010). In a study of a chronic pain support group, McParland and Knussen (2010) found that stronger just world belief decreased the ability of pain intensity and disability to predict psychological distress.

In this way, it is possible that the more strongly one believes that the world is just, the more one will endeavor to make sense of a negative happening, such as a disability. This motivated cognitive processing, aimed at reducing inconsistency, undoubtedly facilitates the coping process by encouraging engagement in coping strategies. Furthermore, with a stronger just world belief, it is possible that benefit-finding and meaning-making may have a stronger impact on restoring an individual's feelings of perceived control (the belief that one can influence potentially positive or negative outcomes) (Dunn, 1996).

Other researchers have taken an alternative perspective, stating that benefit-finding is an *indicator* of growth and change following a stressful circumstance, rather than being a coping strategy in and of itself. Oaksford et al. (2005) examined their theoretical model of positive coping by measuring five categories of coping (positive escape/distancing, support seeking, humor, cognitive reappraisal, and practical/action-based coping). Participants with lower limb amputation participated in semi-structured interviews that were conducted over 5 years post-amputation. Supporting the positive coping theoretical model, Oaksford et al. (2005) found that reports of positive psychological change post-amputation reflected, rather than resulted from, growth in the aftermath of the traumatic experience. This perspective echoes the recent perspective suggesting that benefit-finding is an indicator of genuine positive adjustment rather than a coping mechanism to protect threatened beliefs.

In the past, benefit-finding has been conceptualized as both an appraisal and as a coping strategy. Park and Folkman (1997) presented a comprehensive theoretical evaluation of the role of meaning-making in the coping process. Within this framework, they conceptualized benefit-finding as an integral part of the meaning-making process and ultimately as a cognitive reappraisal coping strategy. In this way, in the context of an enduring chronic stressor, finding the positive aspects of one's circumstance may be viewed as both a coping mechanism and a product of positive adjustment (Park & Folkman, 1997).

Beyond positive meaning-making and benefit-finding, researchers have identified other strategies that can contribute to psychological well-being and adjustment. Next, we describe positive coping strategies that facilitate resilience in the midst of negative circumstances, such as disability experiences.

Optimism and Hope

Unsurprisingly, research indicates that individuals with higher dispositional optimism show more successful coping in reaction to health threats and significant life transitions. Optimistic outlooks can help people feel better about themselves and therefore cope better with stress (Dunn, 1996). Chronic optimism, or *dispositional optimism,* as a personality factor may also lead to a more adaptive appraisal process.

What mechanism might explain the relation between optimism and well-being? It is possible that optimism is associated with increased positive illusions, which are associated with enhanced well-being, as well as with positive health results in life-threatening illness. In one study, individuals with AIDS who had a more realistic appraisal of their level of control over their disease had decreased survival time as compared to those with positive illusions (Reed, Kemeny, Taylor, Wang, & Visscher,

1994). In this sense, higher levels of optimism may predict better post-stressor adjustment.

Likewise, *hope* refers to a positive motivational state "based on an interactively derived sense of successful (a) agency (goal-directed energy), and (b) pathways (planning to meet goals)" (Snyder, Irving, & Anderson, 1991, as cited in Smedema, Catalano, & Ebener, 2010). High levels of hope have been linked to lower depression, fewer mental health symptoms, improved well-being, more positive thoughts, and more positive therapeutic outcomes (Smedema et al., 2010).

Humor

Using humor to make something seem funny or amusing in times of stress appears to facilitate coping both directly and indirectly (Smedema et al., 2010). First, humor can be used to magnify and maintain positive emotions, resources vital to successful coping (Dunn & Brody, 2008). Second, literature suggests that humor may be a way of reframing uncontrollable or overwhelming distress into something less threatening and more manageable (Smedema et al., 2010). In this manner, making light of a situation may help an individual restore some feelings of control (Rybarczyk, Nicholas, & Nyenhuis, 1997). In individuals with disabilities, a positive relationship has been found among humor, self-concept, and vitality (Smedema et al., 2010).

Gratitude and Savoring

As with benefit-finding, gratitude and savoring require an individual to acknowledge a positive entity in his or her life and appreciate it. Research suggests that recognizing and focusing on things to be grateful for enhances mood, promotes coping behaviors, and leads to self-reported health benefits (Emmons & McCullough, 2003). Gratitude has further been shown to enhance social connections, extend positive emotions, and slow habituation to good things (Dunn & Brody, 2008).

Savoring, learning to enjoy or even enhance an experience, requires an individual to reflect on the nature of a particular pleasure. Empirical evidence suggests that increasing the incidence and reflection of pleasurable experiences reduces negative emotions (Dunn & Brody, 2008).

Savoring can be considered a cognitive form of coping used to maintain and extend positive emotional experiences (Bryant, 1989). Savoring involves conscious awareness of and deliberate attention to one's pleasant experiences (Bryant, 1989). It is also defined as beneficially interpreting positive events by engaging in social behaviors, such as communicating the event to others or celebrating (termed "capitalizing" by Langston, 1994). A theoretical model of savoring proposes that positive emotions are maintained while savoring because one draws attention to feelings (a) in anticipation of upcoming positive events, (b) when appreciating current pleasant events, and (c) when reminiscing about past positive experiences (Bryant, 2003). Consider, for example, a relaxing summer vacation at the beach. Savoring can prolong the duration of positive emotional experiences when thinking about the impending arrival of the airplane that will take you to your summer destination (anticipation), when sharing pleasurable moments with friends or loved ones during your vacation (current pleasant events), and when relishing the memories after returning home (reminiscence) (Bryant, 1989). *Contentment*, an emotion relevant to savoring (Fredrickson, 1998, 2001), resonates with the reminiscence aspect of the savoring process.

Savoring has important implications for coping and well-being. Having a general tendency to savor experiences (measured via the Savoring Beliefs Inventory; Bryant, 2003) appears to benefit individuals across the lifespan. Correlational studies indicate that the tendency to savor predicts subjective well-being for grade school children, adolescents, college students, and the elderly (Bryant, 1989; Meehan, Durlak, & Bryant, 1993). As well, savoring is positively related to favorable advantages in well-being, including self-reported optimism, internal locus of control, self-control behaviors, life satisfaction, and self-esteem; it is negatively correlated with hopelessness and depression (Bryant, 2003). Although studies that empirically test the causal relations between savoring and positive outcomes are needed, these correlational findings lend support to the idea that maintaining positive emotional experiences can have important outcomes for an individual's well-being.

A number of different interventions promote savoring. For example, relaxation therapies and guided meditation practices require participants to engage in thematic imagery exercises that can induce and extend the duration of pleasant experiences. Sessions might include instructions to bring to mind scenes of nature, childhood triumphs, or recent good experiences (Smith, 1990). These techniques can effectively prolong positive emotional experiences and can benefit physical and psychological health (Chesney et al., 2005). Indeed, meditative practices are associated with enhanced subjective quality of life (Shapiro, Astin, Bishop, & Cordova, 2005; Surawy, Roberts, & Silver, 2005), reductions in stress (Kabat-Zinn et al., 1992; Miller, Fletcher, & Kabat-Zinn, 1995; Shapiro, Schwartz, & Bonner, 1998), prevention of disease (Chesney et al., 2005), and improvements in coping and health for both clinical and nonclinical samples (for reviews see Grossman, Niemann, Schmidt, & Walach, 2004; Kabat-Zinn, 1990; Smith, 1990). Together, these studies suggest that regulatory behaviors that help people sustain and maintain positive emotional experiences can be beneficial to health and well-being.

Other Coping Strategies
Control
Locus of control is the tendency to appraise factors that are responsible for, as well as problematic to, outcomes for an individual. Appraisals can either be internal (due to the self) or external (due to the situation). With an internal locus of control, people believe that they are able to exercise effort to yield a specific outcome. Should the outcome be negative or disappointing, the individual is prepared to take responsibility for the result. In contrast, with an external locus of control, a person attributes outcomes to circumstances outside his or her personal responsibility (e.g., luck, fate, situation, another person) (Rotter, 1966).

Having an internal locus of control has been linked to successful outcomes. Results from a study by Oaksford et al. (2005), for instance, point to an internal locus of control as a contributing factor for effective coping. In their study, participants were interviewed about the coping strategies they adopted after lower limb amputation. More than half of the participants attributed their adjustment following an amputation to their appraisal of the event as controllable. Instead of viewing their disability as a catastrophe, these individuals were able to appraise the situation as controllable. Importantly, locus of control has consistently been shown to be associated with adaptation (Bandura, 1977; Carver & Scheier, 2002; Masten, 1999)

Social Comparisons
Social comparison theory (Festinger, 1954) argues that people make comparisons to similar others as a way of evaluating themselves against their social environments. Two types of social comparison exist. With upward social comparison, people evaluate themselves against similar others who are superior to them on a particular dimension (e.g., comparing oneself to an Olympic athlete).

With downward social comparison, people evaluate themselves against similar others who are inferior to them on a particular dimension (e.g., comparing oneself to those less fortunate). People who are ill or have a chronic illness or disability often gain valuable information by using social comparisons: What is the nature of the illness or disability? How effective are treatments? And, how are others coping with the illness or disease? In this way, downward social comparisons may help to reduce negative emotions, thereby helping individuals gain momentary relief. Upward social comparisons, in contrast, can be most effective in the information-gathering or problem-solving stage of coping.

Research shows that people with chronic illness or disability have a tendency to use downward social comparison (Collins, 1996). Conceptualizing oneself in comparison to someone who is worse off on some relevant dimension, such as a disability, often enhances self-esteem and endorses well-being (Dunn & Brody, 2008). It is possible that viewing how one's circumstance could be worse may lead to seeing the positive aspects of the situation or feeling gratitude for what one has retained. This favorable comparison may not be the most socially constructive coping mechanism, but it nonetheless seems effective in the short-term and may be an unavoidable human inclination (Dunn, 1996; Dunn & Brody, 2008).

Goal Striving
In the face of disability, many activities that were previously available to or easy for an individual may become difficult or impossible. In such cases, maintaining goal striving, either by continuing to pursue an activity or goal or by selecting alternative goals, seems to play a significant role in coping with disability.

Research suggests that greater goal engagement was significantly associated with positive but not negative affect (Mackay, Charles, Kemp, & Heckhausen, 2011). Further research has demonstrated the link between greater goal striving and social integration, more autonomy, and better overall productivity in life (Kemp & Vash, 1971).

The Importance of Social Support
Previous research indicates that social relationships and social environment play significant roles in shaping an individual's coping strategies and ability. Various measures of social support have been connected with positive results (e.g., decreased mortality, depression, anxiety, pain; increased self-care) in

individuals with disabilities and chronic illnesses (Franks, Cronan, & Oliver, 2004). *Social support* broadly refers to the resources available to an individual from other individuals or from social networks (López-Martínez, Esteve-Zarazaga, & Ramírez-Maestre, 2008). For individuals with disabilities, this support may come from family, spouses, teachers, online groups, and various community outreach programs, among other sources.

In studying the effects of social support on coping, researchers distinguish between the functional aspects of support (the type of received support), the structural aspects of support (the quantity of available support), and the adequacy of support (perceived accessibility and satisfaction with support) (Neugebauer & Katz, 2004; Obst & Stafurik, 2010; Penninx, Van Tilburg, Deeg, & Kriegsman, 1997). Functional social support has further been classified into emotional support (e.g., intimacy, encouragement, attachment), tangible support (e.g., financial help, material goods, services), and informational support (e.g., information, advice, feedback) (Cobb, 1976; Dean & Lin, 1977; Norbeck, Lindsey, & Carrieri, 1981; Franks et al., 2004). Structural support measures, on the other hand, usually enumerate social ties, frequency of contact (as well as an individual's level of social integration), and the degree to which an individual is embedded within a social network or perceives a stable placement within a community (Mock, Fraser, Knutson, & Prier, 2010; Neugebauer & Katz, 2004).

Although the positive effects of social support on coping and well-being have been documented extensively, the mechanism of these effects remains unclear. Researchers have suggested two means by which social support may influence the coping process. The *direct-effect hypothesis* proposes that social support has a direct, positive effect on psychological health and well-being (Penninx et al., 1998). In this way, social support may provide regular positive experiences and bolster positive affect by providing a set of stable, socially rewarded roles in society (Cohen & Wills, 1985; Franks et al., 2004). In other words, being social may be a coping mechanism in and of itself. The *buffering hypothesis,* on the other hand, proposes that social support mitigates the negative effects of stress by affecting an individual's coping strategies and facility. As follows, social support may augment an individual's personal coping resources (e.g., feelings of mastery, self-efficacy, self-esteem) that facilitate the necessary strength and confidence to successfully manage stress (Franks et al., 2004; Penninx et al., 1997). Alternatively, social support

may influence an individual's choice of coping strategies between active (e.g., positive reframing) and passive (e.g., self-blame) coping, which may subsequently influence his or her emotional well-being (Kim, Han, Shaw, McTavish, & Gustafson, 2010). Finally, supportive others may alleviate the impact of stress assessment by providing solutions to problems, by reducing the perceived magnitude of stressors, or by facilitating healthful behaviors (Cohen & Wills, 1985).

Quality Versus Quantity

As stated, a distinction lies between the quality of one's social support and the quantity of one's social support. Franks, Cronan, and Oliver (2004) aimed to address whether the number of people in an individual's social network, the satisfaction of perceived social support, or the type of received social support predicted individual well-being in a sample of women suffering from fibromyalgia syndrome (a chronic, painful, arthritis-related condition) (Franks et al., 2004). Results indicated that larger social support networks correlated with greater levels of self-efficacy for symptom management. However, higher perceived *quality* of social support correlated with lower levels of depression, helplessness, and mood disturbance, as well as with higher levels of self-efficacy for symptom management and overall psychological well-being (Franks et al., 2004). Therefore, the study suggests that quality of social support plays a more significant role in coping than does quantity of social support, although both aspects appear to be beneficial. Another study reiterated these findings and found that marital closeness moderated the negative psychological effects of functional disability on depression, anxiety, and self-esteem (Mancini & Bonanno, 2006).

Cohen and Wills (1985) suggest that quantity of support may play a more significant role in coping with ordinary levels of stress than in the face of a substantial stressor. Under ordinary levels of stress, social integration may enhance an individual's perception of available external resources. In this way, the perception of increased resources may alleviate stress by reducing the perceived threat of a potential, challenging situation (Mock et al., 2010). However, in the presence of a more significant stressor, such as a chronic illness or a disability, the functional aspects of an individual's relationships, such as intimacy and encouragement, may play a more pivotal role in coping (Cohen and Wills, 1985). In other words, stress and support may interact to produce their outcome on individual coping.

Another study comparing individuals with severe arthritis and people without arthritis indicated that the presence of a partner and having many close relationships (family and household members) had direct, positive effects on depressive symptoms irrespective of arthritis status. Conversely, having many diffuse relationships (friends, neighbors, and acquaintances) and receiving emotional support interacted with arthritis status. These variables had more significant positive effects on individuals with severe arthritis than on people without the disease (Penninx et al., 1997, 1998). The study reinforces both direct and buffering effects of social support on well-being and suggests that the two mechanisms may work concurrently, depending on the form of support measure and significance of the stressor. Cohen and Wills (1985) suggest that using structural support measures typically reveal direct effects, whereas functional measures typically reveal buffer effects (Penninx et al., 1998).

Additional studies support the utility of spouses as a beneficial caretaker for individuals with disabilities. In both case and healthy populations, social support has been shown to have a direct effect on the relationship between stress and depression (Robb et al., 2008). In an effort to identify enduring vulnerabilities that may put an individual at risk for depression when supporting a spouse with a disability, Robb, Small, and Haley (2008) examined these effects in conjunction with individual differences (i.e., gender and personality traits, including neuroticism and extraversion) among older adult couples. Findings revealed that neuroticism both directly affected and moderated the association of physical disability and subjective well-being, regardless of gender. A similar effect was found concerning extraversion among men but not women. Taken together, the study identified social resources as a potentially critical resource for enhancing well-being among husbands caring for a spouse with a disability.

Instrumental Support

A number of studies indicate that instrumental support, actual hands-on assistance by another person, may have more mixed consequences than other forms of social support (Penninx et al., 1998). In a comparative study on the effects of social support on individuals with an assortment of chronic diseases, Penninx et al. (1998) found that instrumental support was consistently associated with more depressive symptoms than were other forms of social support (Penninx et al., 1998). One potential explanation for this correlation may be that

depressed individuals arouse more sympathy from others and therefore receive more instrumental support. Alternatively, it is feasible that extensive instrumental support may arouse feelings of helplessness or dependency, both of which may prompt depression (Penninx et al., 1998).

Although instrumental support may sometimes lead to feelings detrimental to the coping process, it seems that this may depend on the condition of the individual receiving help. Penninx et al. (1997) found that unfavorable effects of instrumental support were nearly absent in individuals with mild or severe arthritis. In another study on individuals with severe arthritis, individuals consistently reported that sufficient help on daily tasks resulted in *less* disability in valued activities (Neugebauer & Katz, 2004). It is possible that the less physically capable an individual is, the more beneficial instrumental support may be. Perhaps, rather than diminishing feelings of fitness, in cases of severe physical impairment, instrumental support moderates impending lifestyle change.

Factors Contributing to Improved Child Support

Because of their developmental maturity, limited understanding, and capacity for resilience, children with disabilities may face unique challenges when seeking support from family and friends. Research shows that the presence of an influential person who believes in them is one of the key factors for promoting resilience among children suffering from a disability (Alvord & Grados, 2005). In a similar vein, children with at least one warm parent are likely to be more resilient. The expression of positive emotions from the child's mother is also related to a child's adjustment.

Group therapy is also an available resource for children. Cognitive behavioral therapy (CBT) groups have been designed for children with the sole intention of destigmatizing the notion of disability. Given that these groups are founded in positive psychology, children may acquire qualities and positive beliefs that allow them to embrace their disability and adapt to their circumstances with a positive outlook. In an attempt to foster resilience, a program through the Positive Psychology Center at the University of Pennsylvania teaches children to become aware of their thoughts and think positively/rationally about negative events.

Internet-Based Social Support

Given the significance of social support in coping, it is imperative for all individuals to have access to relationships and community. In the case of individuals with low mobility, physical barriers can preclude social networking and interaction, which may result in feelings of loneliness and isolation, as well as a lack of access to support information and services (Matt & Butterfield, 2006). Despite the controversy over the positive and negative effects of Internet use in general, it seems that, in the case of disabilities, the pros outweigh the cons. Research into Internet-based support sites reveals that individuals can develop social support and a sense of connectivity through easily accessible computer-mediated communication channels (Obst & Stafurik, 2010).

One study found that membership in disability-specific websites led individuals to feel a sense of community and belonging that was positively correlated with well-being (Obst & Stafurik, 2010). Although the amount of time spent in disability-specific Internet forums was related to levels of reported online sense of community, the time participants spent online was not associated with their perceived offline social support. In this way, it seems that it was not a lack of offline support that prompted individuals to spend more time online but that this time online was an additional coping resource.

Other research has also demonstrated the beneficial effects of exposure to similar others through Internet use (Guo, Bricout, & Huang, 2005). By establishing a social network online with similar others, it is possible that individuals with disabilities may feel a sense of belonging and connection unobtainable in the tangible world. This network may offer unique moral support and personal advice, as well as promote self-reflection and positive change (Obst & Stafurik, 2010).

Self-Esteem

Diener, Suh, Lucas, and Smith (1999) found that satisfaction with life is of great importance for one's well-being, self-esteem, and establishment of productive coping skills. High self-esteem or avoidance of low self-esteem has been found to positively influence health and well-being. Adolescents who actively use more problem-focused coping and less emotion-focused coping have been shown to demonstrate higher self-esteem, a crucial factor for determining psychological adjustment (Dahlbeck & Lightsey, 2008). Results revealed that higher self-esteem and lower emotional reaction coping directly predicted higher life satisfaction and lower anxiety. Higher self-esteem also predicted more use

of acceptance-oriented coping. Alternatively, lower self-esteem has been linked to increased severity of impairment. Therefore, it is important to remember that building positive self-esteem is a crucial component of managing a disability for both children and adults. Therapy focused on teaching coping skills and reducing self-blame may be beneficial for providing people with disabilities with an outlook for life improvement.

As mentioned earlier, an internal locus of control (along with self-control) may allow individuals to adopt more adaptive coping skills, such as positive reframing in lieu of avoidance and denial-based strategies. Individuals with higher self-esteem were more likely to perceive greater control and report using active coping strategies (Major, Richards, Cooper, Cozzarelli, & Zubek, 1998). This sense of control may also facilitate more accurate cognitive appraisals of the situation; a initial appraisal of the situation as less stressful may also facilitate better adjustment.

Conclusion and Future Directions

This chapter reviewed from a positive psychology perspective studies in the literature on coping with illness and disabilities. Our review demonstrates that coping efforts encompass a wide range of cognitive, emotional, and behavioral strategies directed at both external (i.e., environmental) stressors and internal demands and needs. Although some researchers view coping as a global personality trait or dispositional quality, it is by no means an inflexible psychological construct. In fact, coping efforts and behaviors are very much influenced by one's situational context, including the nature, type, duration, prognosis, perception, and severity of the encountered crisis, trauma, or loss. Taken together, the review of the literature indicates that coping can be considered a dynamic process that involves different factors, including the nature, intensity, and extent of the stimulus itself; individual differences; and external resources, such as one's socioeconomic status or social support levels. Additionally, various coping styles have been identified.

Based on the research findings, a number of conclusions and suggestions for future directions can be offered. One possible area of further research might be on the topic of coping flexibility. Coping strategies may be viewed as mostly flexible, integrated, and environmentally attuned efforts that are concerned with both internal and external demands and available resources. Coping flexibility is conceptualized as a good fit between the characteristics of coping strategies and the nature of stressful events (Aldwin, 1994; Linville & Clark, 1989). For effective coping to take place, coping needs to be fine-tuned to meet the specific demands of different stressful situations. Such fine-tuning requires some cognitive ability (Neufeld, 1999). The transactional theory of coping (Lazarus & Folkman, 1984) proposes that cognitive processes "intervene between the encounter [i.e., the stressful situation] and the reaction [i.e., coping responses]" (Lazarus & Folkman, 1984, pp. 22–23). Interestingly, there are individual differences in the capacity to cope flexibly. The cognitive individual difference variable of discriminative facility (Mischel, 1984; Mischel & Shoda, 1995) may explain the process underlying how individuals deploy situation-appropriate or -inappropriate coping strategies when encountering stressful events. Discriminative facility refers to individuals' active appraisals of situational characteristics and their choice among alternative behaviors in response to changing contingencies (Cheng, Chiu, Hong, & Cheung, 2001; Chiu, Hong, Mischel, & Shoda, 1995; Roussi, Miller, & Shoda, 2000; Shoda, 1996). Given the changing situational demands that often accompany experiences of disability, a greater emphasis on the study of coping flexibility could be especially fruitful.

The study of coping with disabilities points to the need to expand the research on positive emotions and coping. The research reviewed in this chapter demonstrated that positive emotions help to facilitate effective coping and resilience for individuals faced with adversity. However, coping with chronic illness or disabilities poses unique challenges. As such, it is important to investigate the factors that might modify the ability or motivation to recruit positive emotions in times of stress. Indeed, additional questions still remain. For whom are positive coping strategies most beneficial? In what contexts might they facilitate or hinder effective coping outcomes? Future research would benefit from further examination of possible individual differences, cultural norms, or situational constraints that may modify the outcomes of using positive emotions in the coping process.

References

Aldwin, C. M. (1994). *Stress, coping, and development: An integrative perspective*. New York: Guilford Press.

Alvord, M. K., & Grados, J. J. (2005). Enhancing resilience in children: A proactive approach. *Professional Psychology: Research and Practice, 36*(3), 238–245.

Aspinwall, L. G., & Taylor, S. E. (1997). A stitch in time: Self-regulation and proactive coping. *Psychological Bulletin, 121*(3), 417–436.

Bandura, A. (1977). Self-efficacy: Toward a unifying theory of behavioral change. *Psychological Review, 84*, 191–215.

Block, J. H., & Block, J. (1980). The role of ego-control and ego-resiliency in the organization of behavior. In W. A. Collins (Ed.), *Development of cognition, affect, and social relations: The Minnesota Symposia on Child Psychology* (Vol. 13, pp. 39–101). Hillsdale, NJ: Erlbaum.

Block, J., & Kremen, A. M. (1996). IQ and ego-resiliency: Conceptual and empirical connections and separateness. *Journal of Personality and Social Psychology, 70*, 349–361.

Bonanno, G.A. (2004). Loss, trauma, and human resilience: Have we underestimated the human capacity to thrive after extremely aversive events? *American Psychologist, 59*, 20–28.

Bonanno, G.A. (2005). Resilience in the face of potential trauma. *Current Directions in Psychological Science, 14*(3), 135–138.

Bryant, F.B. (1989). A four-factor model of perceived control: Avoiding, coping, obtaining and savouring. *Journal of Personality, 57*, 773–797.

Bryant, F.B. (2003). Savoring Beliefs Inventory (SBI): A scale for measuring beliefs about savoring. *Journal of Mental Health, 12*(2), 175–196.

Carver, C. S. (1998). Resilience and thriving: Issues, models and linkages. *Journal of Social Issues, 54*, 245–266.

Carver, C. S., & Scheier, M. F. (2002). Optimism. In C. R. Snyder & S. J. Lopez (Eds.), *Handbook of positive psychology* (pp. 231–243). Oxford, England: Oxford University Press.

Cheng, C., Chiu, C., Hong, Y., & Cheung, J. S. (2001). Discriminative facility and its role in the perceived quality of interactional experiences. *Journal of Personality, 69*, 765–786.

Chesney, M. A., Darbes, L. A., Hoerster, K., Taylor, J. M., Chambers, J. B., & Anderson, D. E. (2005). Positive emotions: Exploring the other hemisphere in behavioral medicine. *International Journal of Behavioral Medicine, 12*(2), 50–58.

Chiu, C., Hong, Y., Mischel, W., & Shoda, Y. (1995). Discriminative facility in social competence. *Social Cognition, 13*, 49–70.

Cobb, S. (1976). Social support as a moderator of life stress. *Psychosomatic Medicine, 38*(5), 300–314.

Collins, R. L. (1996). For better or worse: The impact of upward social comparison on self-evaluations. *Psychological Bulletin, 119*, 51–69.

Cohen, S., & Wills, T. A. (1985). Stress, social support, and the buffering hypothesis. *Psychological Bulletin, 98*(2), 310–357.

Dahlbeck, D. T., & Lightsey, O. R. (2008). Generalized self-efficacy, coping, and self-esteem as predictors of psychological adjustment among children with disabilities or chronic illnesses. *Children's Health Care, 37*(4), 293–315.

Davis, C. G., & Morgan, M. S. (2008). Finding meaning, perceiving growth, and acceptance of tinnitus. *Rehabilitation Psychology, 53*(2), 128–138.

Dean, A., & Lin, N. (1977). The stress-buffering role of social support. *Journal of Nervous and Mental Disease, 165*(6), 403–417.

deRoon-Cassini, T. A., de St. Aubin, E., Valvano, A., Hastings, J., & Horn, P. (2009). Psychological well-being after spinal cord injury: Perception of loss and meaning making. *Rehabilitation Psychology, 54*(3), 306–314.

Diener, E., Suh, E. M., Lucas, R. E., & Smith, H. L. (1999). Subjective well-being: Three decades of progress. *Psychological Bulletin, 125*(2), 276–302.

Dunn, D. S. (1996). Well-being following amputation: Salutary effects of positive meaning, optimism, and control. *Rehabilitation Psychology, 41*(4), 285–302.

Dunn, D. S., & Brody, C. (2008). Defining the good life following acquired physical disability. *Rehabilitation Psychology*, 53(4), 413–425.

Ebata, A. T., & Moos, R.H. (1991). Coping and adjustment in distressed and healthy adolescents. *Journal of Applied Developmental Psychology*, 12(1), 33–54.

Emmons, R. A., & McCullough, M. E. (2003). Counting blessings versus burdens: An experimental investigation of gratitude and subjective well- being in daily life. *Journal of Personality and Social Psychology*, 84, 377–389.

Festinger, L. (1954). A theory of social comparison processes. *Human Relations*, 7, 117–140.

Folkman, S., & Lazarus, R. S. (1980). An analysis of coping in a middle-aged sample. *Journal of Healthy and Social Behavior*, 21(3), 219–239.

Folkman, S., & Moskowitz, J. T. (2000). Positive affect and the other side of coping. *American Psychologist*, 55, 647–654.

Franks, H. M., Cronan, T. A., & Oliver, K. (2004). Social support in women with fibromyalgia: Is quality more important than quantity? *Journal of Community Psychology*, 32(4), 425–438.

Fredrickson, B. L. (1998). What good are positive emotions? *Review of General Psychology: Special Issue: New Directions in Research on Emotion*, 2, 300–319.

Fredrickson, B. L. (March 7, 2000). Cultivating positive emotions to optimize health and well-being. *Prevention and Treatment*, 3, Article 1. Available at http://journals.apa.org/prevention

Fredrickson, B. L. (2001). The role of positive emotions in positive psychology: The broaden-and-build theory of positive emotions. *American Psychologist*, 56(3), 218–226.

Gallagher, P., & MacLachlan, M. (2000). Development and psychometric evaluation of the Trinity Amputation and Prosthesis Experience Scales (TAPES). *Rehabilitation Psychology*, 45, 130–154.

Guo, B., Bricout, J., & Huang, J. (2005). A common open space or a digital divide? A social model perspective on the online disability community in China. *Disability and Society*, 20, 49–66.

Grossman, P., Niemann, L., Schmidt, S., & Walach, H. (2004). Mindfulness-based stress reduction and health benefits: A meta-analysis. *Journal of Psychosomatic Research*, 57(1), 35–43.

Hudek-Knežević, J., Kardum, I., & Maglica, B. K. (2005). The sources of stress and coping styles as mediators and moderators of the relationship between personality traits and physical symptoms. *Review of Psychology*, 12(2), 91–101.

Janoff-Bulman, R., & Frantz, C. (1997). The impact of trauma on meaning: From meaningless world to meaningful life. In M. J. Power & C. R. Brewin (Eds.), *The transformation of meaning in psychological therapies: Integrating theory and practice* (pp. 91–106). New York: Wiley.

Kemp, B., & Vash, C. (1971). Productivity after injury in a sample of spinal cord injured persons: A pilot study. *Journal of Chronic Disease*, 24, 259–275.

Kabat-Zinn, J. (1990). Full catastrophe living: The program of the Stress Reduction Clinic at the University of Massachusetts Medical Center. New York: Dell.

Kabat-Zinn, J., Massion, M. D., Kristeller, J., Peterson, L. G., Fletcher, K. E., Pbert, L., et al. (1992). Effectiveness of a meditation-based stress reduction program in the treatment of anxiety disorders. *American Journal of Psychiatry*, 149, 936–943.

Kim, J., Han, J. Y., Shaw, B., McTavish, F., & Gustafson, D. (2010). The roles of social support and coping strategies in predicting breast cancer patients' emotional well-being: Testing mediation and moderation models. *Journal of Health Psychology*, 15(4), 543–552.

Langston, C. A. (1994). Capitalizing on and coping with daily-life events: Expressive responses to positive events. *Journal of Personality and Social Psychology*, 67, 1112–1125.

Lazarus, R. S. (1993). From psychological stress to the emotions: A history of changing outlooks. *Annual Review of Psychology*, 44, 1–21.

Lazarus, R. S., & Folkman, S. (1984). Stress, appraisal and coping. New York: Springer.

Linville, P. W., & Clark, L. F. (1989). Production systems and social problem solving: Specificity, flexibility, and expertise. In R. S. Wyer Jr. & T. K. Srull (Eds.), *Advances in social cognition* (Vol. 2, pp. 131–152). Hillsdale, NJ: Erlbaum.

Livneh, H., Antonak, R. F., & Gerhardt, J. (2000). Multidimensional investigation of the structure of coping among people with amputations. *Psychosomatics: Journal of Consultation Liaison Psychiatry*, 41(3), 235–244.

López-Martínez, A. E., Esteve-Zarazaga, R., & Ramírez-Maestre, C. (2008). Perceived social support and coping responses are independent variables explaining pain adjustment among chronic pain patients. *The Journal of Pain*, 9(4), 373–379.

Mackay, J., Charles, S. T., Kemp, B., & Heckhausen, J. (2011). Goal striving and maladaptive coping in adults living with spinal cord injury: Associations with affective well-being. *Journal of Aging and Health*, 23(1), 158–176.

Major, B., Richards, C., Cooper, M. L., Cozzarelli, C., & Zubek, J. (1998). Personal resilience, cognitive appraisals, and coping: An integrative model of adjustment to abortion. *Journal of Personality and Social Psychology*, 74(3), 735–752.

Mancini, A. D., & Bonanno, G. A. (2006). Marital closeness, functional disability, and adjustment in late life. *Psychology and Aging*, 21(3), 600–610.

Martin, R. A., & Lefcourt, H. M. (1983). Sense of humor as a moderator of the relation between stressors and moods. *Journal of Personality and Social Psychology*, 45(6), 1313–1324.

Masten, A. S. (1999). Resilience comes of age: Reflections on the past and outlook for the next generation of research. In M. D. Glantz, J. Johnson, & L. Huffman (Eds.), *Resilience and development: Positive life adaptations* (pp. 282–296). New York: Plenum Press.

Masten, A. S. (2001). Ordinary magic: Resilience processes in development. *American Psychologist*, 56, 227–238

Masten, A. S., Best, K. M., & Garmezy, N. (1990). Resilience and development: Contributions from the study of children who overcome adversity. *Development and Psychopathology*, 2(4), 425–444.

Matt, S. B., & Butterfield, P. (2006). Changing the disability climate: Promoting tolerance in the workplace. *American Association of Occupational Health Nurse Journal*, 54, 129–134.

McParland, J. L., & Knussen, C. (2010). Just world beliefs moderate the relationship of pain intensity and disability with psychological distress in chronic pain support group members. *European Journal of Pain*, 14(1), 71–76.

Meehan, M., Durlak, J., & Bryant, F. B. (1993). The relationship of social support to positive life events and subjective mental health in adolescents. *Journal of Community Psychology*, 21, 49–55.

Miller, S. M., Fletcher, K., & Kabat-Zinn, J. (1995). Three-year follow-up and clinical implications of a mindfulness meditation-based stress reduction intervention in the treatment of anxiety disorders. *General Hospital Psychiatry*, 17, 192–200.

Mischel, W. (1984). Convergences and challenges in the search for consistency. *American Psychologist*, *39*, 351–364.

Mischel, W., & Shoda, Y. (1995) A cognitive-affective system theory of personality: Reconceptualizing situations, dispositions, dynamics, and invariance in personality structure. *Psychological Review*, *102*(2), 246–268

Mock, S. E., Fraser, C., Knutson, S., & Prier, A. (2010). Physical leisure participation and the well-being of adults with rheumatoid arthritis: The role of sense of belonging. *Activities, Adaptation & Aging*, *34*(4), 292–302.

Moos R. H., Schaefer J. A. (1993). Coping resources and processes: Current concepts and measures. In L. Goldberger & S. Breznitz (Eds.), *Handbook of stress: Theoretical and clinical aspects* (2nd ed., pp. 234–57). New York: The Free Press.

Neufeld, R. W. J. (1999). Dynamic differentials of stress and coping. *Psychological Review*, *106*, 385–397.

Neugebauer, A., & Katz, P. P. (2004). Impact of social support on valued activity disability and depressive symptoms in patients with rheumatoid arthritis. *Arthritis & Rheumatism: Arthritis Care & Research*, *51*(4), 586–592.

Nezu, A. M., Nezu, C. M., & Blissett, S. E. (1988). Sense of humor as a moderator of the relation between stressful events and psychological distress: A prospective analysis. *Journal of Personality & Social Psychology*, *54*, 520–525.

Norbeck, J. S., Lindsey, K. M., & Carrieri, V. L. (1981). The development of an instrument to measure social support. *Nursing Research*, *30*(5), 264–269.

Oaksford, K., Frude, N., & Cuddihy, R. (2005). Positive coping and stress-related psychological growth following lower limb amputation. *Rehabilitation Psychology*, *50*(3), 266–277.

Obst, P., & Stafurik, J. (2010). Online we are all able bodied: Online psychological sense of community and social support found through membership of disability-specific websites promotes well-being for people living with a physical disability. *Journal of Community & Applied Social Psychology*, *20*(6), 525–531.

Park, C. L., & Folkman, S. (1997). Meaning in the context of stress and coping. *Review of General Psychology*, *1*, 115–144.

Penninx, B. W. J. H., Van Tilburg, T., Deeg, D. J. H., & Kriegsman, D. M. W. (1997). Direct and buffer effects of social support and personal coping resources in individuals with arthritis. *Social Science & Medicine*, *44*(3), 393.

Penninx, B. W. J. H., van Tilburg, T., Boeke, A. J. P., Deeg, D. J. H., Kriegsman, D. M. W., & van Eijk, J. T. M. (1998). Effects of social support and personal coping resources on depressive symptoms: Different for various chronic diseases? *Health Psychology*, *17*(6), 551–558.

Piira, T., Taplin, J. E., Goodenough, B., & von Baeyer, C. L. (2002). Cognitive-behavioral predictors of children's tolerance of laboratory-induced pain: Implications for clinical assessment and future directions. *Behavioral Research Therapy*, *40*, 571–584.

Reed, G. M., Kemeny, M. E., Taylor, S. E., Wang, H. Y. J., & Visscher, B. R. (1994). "Realistic acceptance" as a predictor of decreased survival time in gay men with AIDS. *Health Psychology*, *13*, 299–307.

Robb, C., Small, B., & Haley, W. E. (2008). Gender differences in coping with functional disability in older married couples: The role of personality and social resources. *Aging & Mental Health*, *12*(4), 423–433.

Rotter, J. B. (1966). Generalized expectancies for internal versus external control of reinforcement. *Psychological Monographs*, *80*, 1–28.

Rutter, M. (1987). Psychosocial resilience and protective mechanisms. *American Journal of Orthopsychiatrics*, *57*, 316–331.

Roussi, P., Miller, S. M., & Shoda, Y. (2000). Discriminative facility in the face of threat: Relationship to psychological distress. *Psychology and Health*, *15*, 21–33.

Rybarczyk, B., Nicholas, J. J., & Nyenhuis, D. L. (1997). Coping with a leg amputation: Integrating research and clinical practice. *Rehabilitation Psychology*, *42*(3), 241–255.

Schwarzer, R., & Knoll, N. (2003). *Positive coping: Mastering demands and searching for meaning*. Washington, DC: American Psychological Association.

Seligman, M. E. P., & Csikszentmihàlyi, M. (2000). Positive psychology: An introduction. *American Psychologist*, *55*(1), 5–14.

Shapiro, S. L., Astin, J. A., Bishop, S. R., & Cordova, M. (2005). Mindfulness-based stress reduction for healthcare professionals: Results from a randomized trial. *International Journal of Stress Management*, *12*, 164–176.

Shapiro, S. L., Schwartz, G. E., & Bonner, G. (1998). Effects of mindfulness-based stress reduction on medial and premedical students. *Journal of Behavioral Medicine*, *21*, 581–599.

Shoda, Y. (1996, June). Discriminative facility as a determinant of coping. Paper presented at the 8th Annual Convention of the American Psychological Society, San Francisco.

Smedema, S. M., Catalano, D., & Ebener, D. J. (2010). The relationship of coping, self-worth, and subjective well-being: A structural equation model. *Rehabilitation Counseling Bulletin*, *53*(3), 131–142.

Smith, J. C. (1990). Cognitive-behavioral relaxation training: A new system of strategies for treatment and assessment. New York: Springer.

Snyder, C. R., Irving, L. M., & Anderson, J. R. (1991). Hope and health. In D. R. Forsyth & C. R. Snyder (Eds.), *Handbook of social and clinical psychology: The health perspective* (pp. 285–305). Elmsford: Pergamon Press.

Suls, J., & Fletcher, B. (1985). The relative efficacy of avoidant and nonavoidant coping strategies: A meta-analysis. *Health Psychology*, *4*(3), 249–288.

Surawy, C., Roberts, J., & Silver, A. (2005). The effect of mindfulness training on mood and measures of fatigue, activity, and quality of life in patients with chronic fatigue syndrome on a hospital waiting list: A series of exploratory studies. *Behavioral and Cognitive Psychotherapy*, *33*, 103–109.

Tedeschi, R. G., & Kilmer, R. P. (2005). Assessing strengths, resilience, and growth to guide clinical interventions. *Professional Psychology: Research and Practice*, *36*(3), 230–237.

Tugade, M. M., & Fredrickson, B. L. (2002). Positive emotions and emotional intelligence. In L. Feldman Barrett & P. Salovey (Eds.), *The wisdom of feelings* (pp. 319–340). New York: Guilford.

Tugade, M. M., & Fredrickson, B. L. (2004). Resilient individuals use positive emotions to bounce back from negative emotional experiences. *Journal of Personality and Social Psychology*, *86*(2), 320–333.

Tugade, M. M., & Fredrickson, B. L. (2007). Regulation of positive emotions: Emotion regulation strategies that promote resilience. *Journal of Happiness Studies*, *8*(3), 311–333.

Werner, E., & Smith, R. S. (1992). *Overcoming the odds: High risk children from birth to adulthood*. Ithaca: Cornell University.

Wolin, S. J., & Wolin, S. (1993). Bound and determined: Growing up resilient in a troubled family. New York: Villard.

Adaptive Behavior

Marc J. Tassé

Abstract

Adaptive behavior consists of those skills learned throughout development and performed in response to the expectations placed on us from our community and society at large. Adaptive skills become increasingly more complex with age. Adaptive behavior is defined as the collection of conceptual, social, and practical skills learned by people to enable them to function in their everyday lives. Adaptive behavior is a required diagnostic criterion of all systems defining intellectual and developmental disabilities. Several standardized adaptive behavior scales described in the chapter can be used to assess a person's adaptive behavior for the purpose of either making a diagnosis and/or identifying the educational or interventional goals for the purpose of teaching the person skills that will contribute to independence and improved quality of life.

Key Words: adaptive behavior, adaptive skills, intellectual disability, developmental disabilities, autism spectrum disorders

The construct of adaptive behavior was primarily developed within the field of intellectual and developmental disabilities and thus has its roots firmly planted in the field of disabilities, specifically, intellectual disability. The use of the construct of adaptive behavior in developmental disabilities is a more recent and mostly American phenomenon. "Developmental Disabilities" is a categorization defined in U.S. federal legislation (e.g., Developmental Disabilities Assistance and Bill of Rights Act or DD Act of 2000) not found in traditional diagnostic systems, such as the International Classification of Diseases (ICD-10, World Health Organization, 1992) or the *Diagnostic and Statistical Manual of Mental Disorders* (DSM-IV-TR) (American Psychiatric Association [APA], 2000). According to the DD Act, individuals meeting the eligibility criteria for developmental disabilities must present a lifelong condition that results in significant deficits in three or more of seven specified adaptive behavior domains. These seven adaptive behavior domains or major life activities are self-care, language, learning, mobility, self-direction, independence living, and economic self-sufficiency.

Adaptive behavior consists of those skills that we learn throughout our development and perform in response to expectations placed on us by our community and society at large. Hence, adaptive skills become increasingly more complex with chronological age. In other words, we expect different skills from a child than we do from an adult. Adaptive behavior is defined as the collection of conceptual, social, and practical skills that have been learned by people to enable them to function in their everyday lives (Schalock et al., 2010). The three adaptive behavior domains are defined as:

Conceptual skills: Defined by communication skills, functional academics, and self-direction

Social skills: Defined by such abilities as interpersonal skills, social responsibility, following rules, and self-esteem. Higher order social skills have also been identified to include such elements as gullibility, naïveté, and avoiding victimization.

Practical skills: Consist of basic personal care skills such as hygiene, domestic skills, and health and safety, as well as work skills

Adaptive behavior is a required diagnostic criterion of all systems defining intellectual disability (see American Psychiatric Association, 2000; Schalock et al., 2010; World Health Organization, 1992).

Adaptive skills are also the core component of the functional definition of "developmental disabilities" (see Public Law 106-402: Developmental Disabilities Assistance and Bill of Rights Act, 2000). Furthermore, adaptive behavior is a part of the core features that determine eligibility for U.S. Social Security benefits under the rubric of "intellectual disability." The U.S. Social Security Administration (SSA) convened in 1999 a panel of experts to review the existing literature and propose recommendations to the SSA on criteria to be used to identify and classify individuals as having mental retardation (Reschly, Myers, & Hartel, 2002). Although not meant as a diagnostic system, the resulting report by Reschly, Myers, and Hartel (2002) proposed that the SSA use the same three prongs found in the American Association on Intellectual and Developmental Disabilities (AAIDD) and DSM systems in determining SSA benefits eligibility under the classification of *intellectual disability*. Although there are some minor differences in the three prongs depending on the system consulted, consensus holds that significant deficits in both intellectual functioning and adaptive behavior must be present and that these significant deficits must have originated during the developmental period, generally prior to the age of 18 years.

The AAIDD is generally considered the leading professional authority in defining intellectual disability. First established in 1876, the AAIDD is the oldest interdisciplinary professional association in the field of intellectual and developmental disabilities (Tassé & Grover, 2013), and it has led the field in establishing the definition and diagnostic criteria for intellectual disability for over a century. Since its first definition of intellectual disability in 1905, the AAIDD has revised its definition ten times to reflect ongoing findings of research and improved understanding of this condition. The AAIDD definition of intellectual disability has historically been adopted by all federal and state governments, as well as by the American Psychiatric Association (APA). It was not until the fifth edition of its own diagnostic

manual(Heber, 1959) that the AAIDD required the assessment of adaptive behavior as a criterion for defining intellectual disability.

The APA uses the AAIDD definition and diagnostic criteria of mental retardation in its DSM publications. The DSM first included adaptive behavior in its diagnostic criteria of intellectual disability in its second edition (APA, 1968). In fact, in the DSM-2, the reader is referred to the AAIDD 1961 definition of intellectual disability (Heber, 1961) for a fuller explanation: "Mental retardation refers to subnormal general intellectual functioning which originates during the developmental period and is associated with impairment in either learning and social adjustment or maturation, or both" (DSM-2, p. 14). This reads very similarly to Heber's (1959) definition of adaptive behavior, which he described as maturation, learning, and social adjustment. This alignment persists and is again clearly illustrated in the current edition of the DSM (the DSM-IV-TR). With respect to the adaptive behavior prong, the DSM-IV-TR (APA, 2000) continued its alignment with the AAIDD manual and changed its conceptualization of adaptive behavior to reflect Luckasson and colleagues' (1992) definition of adaptive behavior as being a constellation of ten adaptive skills and significant deficits in adaptive behavior as being limitations in two or more of those adaptive skills: (1) communication, (2) self-care, (3) home living, (4) social skills, (5) community use, (6) self-direction, (7) health and safety, (8) functional academics, (9) leisure, and (10) work. Tassé (2009) concluded that, probably because of a misplaced comma between "health" and "safety," the DSM-IV-TR actually defined adaptive behavior deficits as limitations in two or more of *eleven* adaptive skill areas (APA, 2000).

For all intents and purposes, until about 2010, DSM-IV-TR diagnostic criteria and AAIDD terminology and classifications (Luckasson et al., 1992) were virtually identical, even though many noted that the ten adaptive skill areas were not actually supported by psychometric research (Heal & Tassé, 1999; Spreat, 1999; Thompson, McGrew, & Bruininks, 1999; Widaman & McGrew, 1996). Since the 2010 edition of its terminology and classification manual, the AAIDD has departed from the ten adaptive skills areas to a more psychometrically supported framework of the three adaptive behavior domains mentioned earlier (conceptual skills, social skills, and practical skills) (Luckasson et al., 2002; Schalock et al., 2010).

History of Adaptive Behavior

Initially termed "social competence" and defined by Doll (1953) as "the functional ability of the human organism for exercising personal independence and social responsibility" (p. 10), adaptive behavior was later introduced into the AAIDD (then American Association on Mental Deficiency) definition of intellectual disability in the late 1950s (Heber, 1959). Adaptive behavior was defined by Heber (1959, 1961) as "the effectiveness with which the individual copes with the natural and social demands of his environment. It has two major facets: (1) the degree to which the individual is able to function and maintain himself independently, and (2) the degree to which he meets satisfactorily the culturally-imposed demands of personal and social responsibility" (Heber, 1959, p. 61). Later, Grossman (1973, 1983) reaffirmed the importance of adaptive behavior in the definition and diagnosis of intellectual disability. Grossman's later (1973, 1983) definition of adaptive behavior was a reformulation of Heber's (1959, 1961): "the effectiveness or degree with which individuals meet the standards of personal independence and social responsibility expected for his age and cultural group" (p. 1). Both Heber and Grossman recognized the multidimensionality of adaptive behavior and specified the need to measure three aspects: maturation, leaning, and social adjustment. Interestingly, now, more than 50 years later, the AAIDD has returned to Heber's (1959) original conceptualization of practical, conceptual, and social skills in defining adaptive behavior (see Schalock et al., 2010).

In adding the criterion of concurrent deficit in adaptive behavior to that of deficit of intellectual functioning, the AAIDD stressed that cognitive limitations needed to be sufficiently severe to impact on the individual's ability to perform adequately to societal demands and expectations. In fact, the initial addition of adaptive behavior as a diagnostic criterion was written such that intellectual impairments "resulted" in deficits in adaptive behavior. Nihira (1999) postulated that adaptive behavior was introduced out of concern for increasing the positive aspects associated with the condition of intellectual disability, which could not be easily captured using only the construct of intellectual functioning. In addition, teachers and clinicians have had greater success in teaching and sustaining the learning of adaptive skills than in improving intellectual functioning as measured by IQ tests. Thus, through systematic intervention and personalized supports focused on adaptive skills, it is possible to successfully and positively impact a person's life functioning.

The concept of adaptive behavior better reflects the social characteristics of intellectual disability, reduces the importance placed solely on IQ scores, and decreases the number of "false-positives" that testing returns (Luckasson et al., 2002). Despite these positive implications, there have been numerous debates over the accuracy of adaptive behavior measures, over whether an adaptive behavior assessment should be required in diagnosing intellectual disability, and over which areas of functioning should be included in the assessment of adaptive behaviors.

Relationship Between Intellectual Functioning and Adaptive Functioning

One of the first developers of intelligence testing used the concept of "adaptation" in his definition of intelligence (Binet & Simon, 1905), and, to this day, the two concepts are still sometimes intertwined. Increasingly, however, the broader definition of intelligence is much more focused on mental capabilities and capacity, whereas adaptive behavior is much more focused on the actual performance of skills when needed and in response to societal demands and expectations. The current definition of intelligence adopted by the AAIDD (Schalock et al., 2010) comes from the existing consensus position of prominent intelligence researchers and is defined as follows:

> Intelligence is a very general mental capability that, among other things, involves the ability to reason, plan, solve problems, think abstractly, comprehend complex ideas, learn quickly and learn from experience. It is not merely book learning, a narrow academic or test-taking smarts. Rather, it reflects a broader and deeper capability for comprehending our surroundings—"catching on," "making sense" of things, or "figuring out" what to do. (Gottfredson, 1997, p. 13).

A number of studies have examined the changes that occur in adaptive functioning among adults with developmental disabilities after deinstitutionalization (Felce, de Kock, Thomas, & Saxby, 1986; Fine, Tangeman, & Woodard, 1990; Silverman, Silver, Sersen, Lubin, & Schwartz, 1986). Consistently, a meaningful positive change in adaptive functioning has been reported after moving individuals from a more institutional living environment to a less restrictive community setting (Lakin, Larson, & Kim, 2011). In their review of the literature that included 23 longitudinal studies between 1977 and 2010, Charlie Lakin and his colleagues reported that all but three studies documented adaptive behavior improvements when individuals moved to less restrictive community-based living arrangements. The increase in adaptive behavior was especially marked in the skill areas of self-care, domestic skills, and social skills.

As constructs, intelligence and adaptive behavior are related but distinct (Keith, Fehrmann, Harrison, & Pottebaum, 1987; McGrew & Bruininks, 1990). Thus, discrepancies in the measurement of intelligence and adaptive behavior are to be expected. Not everyone with significant limitations in intellectual functioning will have commensurately limited adaptive behavior and, conversely, not everyone with significant limitations in adaptive behavior will have comparably significant limitations in intellectual functioning. Because of the wide range of measures used for IQ and adaptive functioning, conducting research on children with developmental disabilities and interpreting the results can be challenging, even though some studies have reported a low to moderate correlation between the measures (Harrison & Oakland, 2003; Sparrow, Ciccheti, & Balla, 2005). A much small number of studies have (Carpentieri & Morgan, 1996) demonstrated a high correlation, whereas others have demonstrated that a large portion of the variance (35%) in adaptive functioning among adults with mental retardation can be explained by environmental variables other than intellectual ability (21%; Hull & Thompson, 1980). As a way to examine the relationship between these two constructs, some studies generated tables of values needed for statistical significance between various IQ and adaptive behavior scores. These studies concluded that a difference of at least 10 or more standard points was needed for a statistical difference between the two measures when a 95% confidence level was adopted. Thus, it is not unreasonable to interpret the IQ–Adaptive score discrepancy as indicative of a real underlying difference between cognitive capacity and day-to-day performance. Research findings have tended to document higher correlation between these two constructs in individuals with more severe to profound deficits in intellectual functioning than in those who present with milder impairments in intellectual functioning (Childs, 1982, Sattler 2002).

Information about changes in IQ and adaptive measures over time and their relationship to each other is useful for diagnosing mental retardation, predicting prognosis, and planning treatments.

Many questions, however, remain unanswered. IQ scores appear to be stable over time, yet this may differ somewhat across IQ levels. Changes in adaptive functioning have not been well studied, especially for children with mental retardation. The general consensus in the field is that the IQ and adaptive behavior constructs are distinct but maintain a modest relationship. Thus, adaptive behavior is a construct that provides valuable information about the person's functioning that is not captured by measures of intellectual functioning.

Relationship Between Problem Behavior and Adaptive Behavior

There may be no clear consensus on the definition of problem behavior (Emerson, 2001) but most people knows what it is when it happens. In many cases, a person's environment or surroundings will define which of his or her behaviors are problematic (Emerson, 2001; Einfeld & Aman, 1995). For example, body rocking may not be problematic during leisure time or when a person is engaged in silent reading, but the same behavior may become problematic when it occurs during a vocational task in which repetitive rocking may be disruptive to the work environment. Lowe and his colleagues (2007) categorized problem behavior into four broad groupings including self-injurious behavior, aggression toward persons, destruction of objects, and disruptive behavior.

There is some confusion in the field of developmental disabilities regarding the relationship between problem behavior and adaptive behavior. This confusion has been stoked by standardized adaptive behavior scales that use the term "maladaptive behavior" to represent the construct of problem behaviors. Many standardized adaptive behavior scales (e.g., the Vineland-II, the Scales of Independent Behavior—Revised [SIB-R], the Adaptive Behavior Scale [ABS]) contain sections devoted to the assessment of problem behaviors. None of these instruments uses any of the information obtained from the "problem behavior" scale to compute the assessed person's level of adaptive behavior. This secondary section is instead interpreted separately and used primarily for planning interventions aimed at reducing problem behaviors. At no time is the presence or severity of problem behavior factored into any form of composite score of adaptive behavior. Problem behavior has never been part of any diagnostic criteria of intellectual or developmental disability.

Adaptive behaviors and problem behaviors are two distinct and unrelated constructs that result in their own factor solution (Thompson et al.,

1999; Schalock et al., 2010). As pointed out by Tassé (2009), problem behaviors may at times have a behavioral function that relates to the person's adaptive behavior deficits (e.g., communication), but such behaviors could just as easily relate to co-occurring toothache, ulcers, migraine, depression, schizophrenia, or environmental factors. Thus, Tassé argued that, in some instances, engaging in problem behavior can be interpreted as a sign of good adaptive behavior. Thus, problem behavior has no relevance in making a diagnosis of intellectual disability and, as such, should not be interpreted as part of a person's adaptive behavior.

Assessing Adaptive Behavior

Although the assessment of intellectual functioning has a much longer history than the measurement of adaptive behavior, standardized tests of adaptive behavior have progressed significantly since the first such scale was published (Vineland Social Maturity Scale, Doll, 1936). The first version of the Vineland instrument consisted of items organized into six broad domains (self-help: general, dressing, and eating; self-direction; communication; socialization; motor; and work). Doll (1953) defined the construct of social competence as "the functional ability of the human organism for exercising personal independence and social responsibility" (p. 10). Doll's vision of assessing social competence (what would later be called adaptive behavior) remains ingrained in today's definition of adaptive behavior and associated standardized measures: "Our task was to measure attainment in social competence considered as habitual performance rather than as latent ability or capacity" (Doll, 1953, p. 5). This interpretation is consistent with the AAIDD's current position that the assessment of adaptive behavior be focused on the individual's typical performance and not on maximal ability (see Schalock et al., 2010, 2012). This is a critical distinction from the assessment of intellectual functioning, where best or maximal performance is assessed.

According to Tassé et al. (2012), the main features in assessing adaptive behavior for the purpose of diagnosing mental retardation include the:

- assessment of the individual's typical behavior (and not maximal performance);
- assessment of the individual's present adaptive behavior;
- assessment of the individual's adaptive behavior in relation to societal expectation for his age group and culture;
- use of a standardized adaptive behavior scale that was normed on the general population;
- use of convergence of information; and
- use of clinical judgment.

The AAIDD has further specified:

For the purpose of making a diagnosis or ruling out ID [intellectual disability], a comprehensive standardized measure of adaptive behavior should be used in making the determination of the individual's current adaptive behavior functioning in relation to the general population. The selected measure should provide robust standard scores across the three domains of adaptive behavior: conceptual, social, and practical adaptive behavior. (Schalock et al., 2010, p. 49)

In some cases, it is possible that the use of a standardized assessment instrument will not be possible because a standardized adaptive behavior scale is generally completed using information from a respondent. Multiple adaptive behavior scales can be completed, but generally only one respondent is used to complete the entire scale, per administration procedures.

In the following section, we review six standardized adaptive behavior scales in wide used today. Some of these instruments have been normed on a representative sample of the general population, whereas others have been intentionally normed on a subpopulation of persons with intellectual and developmental disabilities. The former are generally better instruments to use when the reason for evaluation is to assess the person's adaptive behavior to rule-in or rule-out a diagnosis of intellectual disability. The AAIDD has encouraged clinicians to avoid certain instruments that might be appropriate for intervention planning but may not necessarily be appropriate for diagnostic purposes: "[t]he potential user must employ adaptive behavior assessment instruments that are normed within the community environments on individuals who are of the same age grouping as the individual being evaluated" (Schalock et al., 2010, p. 51). Conversely, measures normed on persons with intellectual disability or related developmental disability are perhaps more helpful in identifying an individual's ability level in relation to a target disability population and may yield helpful programmatic adaptive behavior goals.

Hence, adaptive behavior scales are used predominantly for two purposes: (1) to assess an individual's adaptive behavior for the purposes of establishing planning goals for intervention and habilitation; and (2) to assess an individual's adaptive behavior to determine whether significant deficits are present for the purpose of determining if the person meets criteria for a diagnosis of intellectual or developmental disability. Some instruments have been developed to serve both functions, whereas other instruments focus on only one assessment. We briefly describe each of the most commonly used adaptive behavior instruments here, and, at the end of this section, we describe the development and characteristics of the Diagnostic Adaptive Behavior Scale (DABS), the newest standardized measure of adaptive behavior created exclusively for the purpose of assisting in the diagnosis of intellectual disability.

Adaptive Behavior Scale—School Edition

The Adaptive Behavior Scale—School, 2nd edition (ABS-S:2; Lambert, Nihira, & Leland, 1993) is a revision of the original American Association on Mental Deficiency (now know as the AAIDD) ABS-School Edition (Lambert, 1981). The ABS-S:2 was developed for use with individuals between the ages of 3 and 21 years. It has two sections: (1) adaptive behavior and (2) problem behavior. The adaptive behavior section presents 67 items that assess adaptive skills across nine areas and provides standard scores for these skill areas that have a mean of 10 and a standard deviation of 3. Unfortunately, these nine skill areas are not consistent with the skill areas found in the DSM-IV-TR. In addition to the nine skills areas, the ABS-S:2 also provides scoring according to three adaptive behavior domains: personal self-sufficiency, personal-social responsibility, and community self-sufficiency. The ABS-S:2 was normed on two different populations: 2,074 students with intellectual and developmental disabilities and 1,254 students from a representative sample of the general population. The first normative table derived from students with disabilities may be useful for establishing program planning objectives for students with intellectual disability; the other set of standardization data based on the representative sample of students is more appropriately used when trying to establish adaptive functioning for the purpose of ruling in/out a diagnosis of intellectual disability.

The ABS-S:2 is either completed directly by a qualified examiner who also knows the person assessed or via interview with a respondent. The administration time is estimated at approximately 1–2 hours. The ABS-S:2 is a significant improvement on the previous version of the ABS and has reportedly adequate reliability and validity (Harrison, 1998).

Adaptive Behavior Scale— Residential and Community, 2nd Edition

The Adaptive Behavior Scale—Residential and Community, 2nd Edition (ABS-RC:2; Nihira, Leland, & Lambert, 1993) is a revision of the original American Association on Mental Deficiency (now AAIDD) ABS (Nihira, Foster, Shellhaas, & Leland, 1974, 1969). The ABS-RC:2 was normed exclusively on adults with intellectual and developmental disabilities between the ages of 18 and 79 years. The ABS-RC:2 can be useful in identifying relative strengths and weaknesses in adaptive behavior or in relation to other adults with intellectual disability. It can serve as a useful tool for planning interventions. Although the Examiner's Manual claims it can be used for the purpose of making a diagnosis of intellectual disability, this author strongly discourages its use for that purpose because its norms are based entirely on a population with intellectual disability.

The ABS-RC:2 is divided into two sections: (1) adaptive behavior and (2) problem behavior. The adaptive behavior section is divided into ten domains including independent functioning, physical development, economic activity, language development, numbers and time, domestic activity, prevocational/vocational activity, self-direction, responsibility, and socialization. The problem behavior section consists of eight different types of challenging behavior. The ABS-RC:2 can be either completed directly by a qualified examiner who also knows the person assessed or as an interview between a qualified examiner and a respondent. The administration time is estimated at approximately 30 minutes. Harrison (1998) has criticized the ABS-RC:2 for being too similar to the school edition (ABS-S:2). Its psychometric properties, as reported in the Examiner's Manual (Nihira et al., 1993), are adequate.

Adaptive Behavior Assessment System—2nd Edition

The Adaptive Behavior Assessment System—2nd Edition (ABAS-II; Harrison & Oakland, 2003) is a revision of the ABAS, first published in 2000. The ABAS-II contains the same items and structure as the original ABAS (Harrison & Oakland, 2000), but has a revised scoring system aligned with the then recently published AAIDD terminology and classification manual (Luckasson et al., 2002) that provides standard scores according to the conceptual, social, and practical domains, in addition to ten discrete skill areas (communication skills, functional academics, self-direction, social skills, leisure skills, self-care, home living skills, community use, work, health and safety). It also provides an overall composite score.

The ABAS-II provides an individualized measure of adaptive behavior for individuals from birth to 89 years. There are a total of five ABAS-II forms, including parent/caregiver forms for children aged 0–5 years and 5–21 years; teacher forms for children aged 2–5 years and 5–21 years; and an adult form for persons 16–89 years old. The adult form can be completed directly by a respondent (such as a parent) or can be completed as a self-report form by the individual him- or herself. Although the User's Manual (Harrison & Oakland, 2003) estimates the administration time to be approximately 15–20 minutes, it more realistically requires closer to 30–40 minutes to complete the adult form. The ABAS-II is currently the only standardized adaptive behavior scale that provides norms for an adult self-report of adaptive behavior.

Each of the ABAS-II scales provides standard scores (mean = 100; standard deviation = 15) for a full-scale score (General Adaptive Composite) and three domains (Conceptual, Social, and Practical), as well as for nine or ten (if employment skills are scored) skill areas. The ABAS-II has reportedly good psychometric properties (Burns, 2005), with the advantage of providing a scoring scheme that includes both the 10 adaptive skill areas from the DSM-IV-TR (APA, 2000) and the 3 adaptive behavior domains of the AAIDD system (Schalock et al., 2010).

Scales of Independent Behavior—Revised

The Scale of Independent Behavior—Revised (SIB-R; Bruininks, Woodcock, Weatherman, & Hill, 1996) is a revision of an earlier version of the SIB (Bruininks, Woodcock, Weatherman, & Hill, 1984). The SIB-R is a comprehensive standardized adaptive behavior scale that was standardized on a representative sample of individuals from the general population. It was developed for use with individuals from 3 months to 80+ years and consists of three separate forms: Early Development (3 months–8 years), Comprehensive Form (3 months–80 years), and Short Form. The Developmental Form and Short Form are a different subset of 40 items drawn from the full SIB-R instrument. The SIB-R may be administered using either the structured interview or a checklist procedure in which the respondent completes the questionnaire directly.

The SIB-R full form contains two sections: adaptive behavior items and problem behavior items. The adaptive behavior section contains a total of 259 items and yields a total standard score, called the Broad Independence score, and four domain scores in motor skills, social interaction and communication skills, personal living skills, and community living skills. The problem behavior section contains eight distinct challenging behaviors rated for their frequency (0–5) and severity (0–4). The SIB-R requires approximately 60 minutes to complete and may be completed either as a rating scale directly by the respondent or via an interview with a respondent.

Although the reliability and validity psychometric data for the comprehensive form are adequate, the psychometric properties of the Short Form and Developmental Form are questionable (Maccow, 2001).

Inventory for Client and Agency Planning

The Inventory for Client and Agency Planning (ICAP; Bruininks, Hill, Weatherman, & Woodcock, 1986) is a condensed version of the original Scales of Independent Behavior (Bruininks et al., 1984). Compared to its parent scale's 226 adaptive behavior items, the ICAP consists of only 77 items across four domains: motor skills, social and communication skills, personal living skills, and community living skills. In addition to these adaptive behavior items, the ICAP assesses eight broad types of problem behavior. The ICAP was specifically designed to be used to provide information about the person's service needs as a measure for behavior change. It was not meant to be used as a diagnostic tool. With respect to its use in terms of diagnosing intellectual disability, the ICAP is a screening tool.

The ICAP is completed as a rating scale given directly to the respondent, who must know the assessed person for at least 3 months. Its administration is approximately 20 minutes. The Examiner's Manual (Bruininks et al., 1986) reports that the ICAP was developed to be used with individuals "from infancy to adulthood (40 years and older)" (p. 5). The advantage of the ICAP is the resulting "service score," which is a weighted score including 70% of the adaptive behavior level of functioning and 30% of the problem behavior severity to yield a level of service score ranging from 1 to 9, where 1 = total personal care and intense supervision needed to 9 = infrequent to no assistance for daily living. The ICAP has probably been more frequently used as an indirect measure of support needs than as a true scale of adaptive behavior. Its usage has been in decline over the past years, and that trend will not likely change unless a refreshed version with updated norms is released.

Vineland Adaptive Behavior Scale— 2nd Edition

The Vineland Adaptive Behavior Scale—2nd Edition (Vineland-II; Sparrow et al.,, 2005) is probably one of the better known comprehensive standardized adaptive behavior scales. It was first published as the Vineland Social Maturity Scale (Doll, 1953), then revised by Sparrow, Cicchetti, and Balla (1984) as the Vineland Adaptive Behavior Scales. The Vineland II was developed to assess adaptive behavior in individuals from 0 through 90 years. There are four evaluation forms in the Vineland-II: Parent/Caregiver Rating Form (0–90 years), Teacher Form (3–18 years), Survey Form (0–90 years), and Expanded Interview Form (0–90 years). The Survey Forms Manual (Sparrow et al., 2005) recommends using the semistructured interview format of administration when the purpose of assessment is for diagnosis or determining eligibility of services.

The Vineland-II has an extensive and representative normative sample. It has strong psychometric properties. The structure of the Vineland II provides standard scores with a mean of 100 and a standard deviation of 15 for each of the four domains: motor skills (<6 years), daily living skills, communication skills, and socialization. Widaman (2010), in his review of the adaptive behavior instrument, cautions that the Vineland II might have some accuracy issues around the cutoff score range; however, despite this comment, Widaman recommended the Vineland-II as an adaptive behavior assessment instrument of choice when making high-stakes decisions.

Diagnostic Adaptive Behavior Scale

The Diagnostic Adaptive Behavior Scale (DABS; Tassé et al., in press) was designed specifically for the purpose of being a standardized assessment instrument to assist with the diagnosis of intellectual disability. The DABS was designed from its earliest conception to assist in the ruling-in or -out of intellectual disability (formerly mental retardation) by providing a comprehensive assessment of an individual's current adaptive behavior; it is designed to be most precise and reliable at a cutoff score equivalent to 2 standard deviations below the population mean. The DABS was developed based on the conceptual framework of the AAIDD's 2002 and 2010 definitions of adaptive behavior (Luckasson et al.,

2002; Schalock et al., 2010) and measures the three domains of conceptual, social, and practical skills.

The DABS was standardized on a large national sample of typically developing children and adults between the ages of 4 and 21 years (inclusively). The DABS was developed across a period of approximately 7 years. Numerous steps are involved in the development of such a scale, and the interested reader is encouraged to consult the DABS Manual (Tassé et al., in press) for a detailed description of its development and standardization. This section summarizes only essential elements of the scale's development.

The DABS was specifically developed to tap the three domains (conceptual, social, and practical skills) of adaptive behavior based on current factor analytic work and to be a relatively shorter and more efficient assessment instrument that focuses solely on the diagnosis of intellectual disability and not on identifying programming/intervention or support needs. The DABS's item pool includes relevant items that relate directly to the concepts of gullibility, vulnerability, and social cognition (that involve social perception, the generation of strategies for resolving social problems, and consequential thinking)—items often lacking from existing measures of adaptive behavior. One major innovation of the DABS is that it was developed from and has its scoring entirely based on Item Response Theory (IRT).

The DABS consists of a total of 75 items (25 items are administered in each of the three domains) and is administered via a face-to-face interview between a professional (i.e., interviewer) and a respondent (e.g., parent, grandparent, caregiver, teacher, etc.). The estimated administration time for the DABS interview varies slightly depending on the interviewer and number of persons being interviewed simultaneously; on average, DABS administration is approximately 30 minutes. DABS scoring is done using a computerized scoring system that uses IRT algorithms to analyze response patterns and compute a standard score for each of the conceptual, practical, and social skills areas, as well as to generate a composite score. The standard scores have a mean of 100 and standard deviation of 15.

At the time of writing, the DABS was not yet available commercially. It is expected that the AAIDD will make the DABS available in late 2013.

Complements and Alternatives to Standardized Measures

In some instances, the use of a standardized measure of adaptive behavior is either insufficient or impossible. This might occur when there are no or too few respondents available to provide objective information on the assessed person's adaptive behavior, some of the respondents providing the adaptive information can only provide partial information, or the evaluator cannot ensure the proper administration of the instrument per test guidelines. In these instances, alternate sources of adaptive behavior information should be referenced as complementary or alternative sources of a person's adaptive behavior.

The AAIDD Manual (Schalock et al., 2010) and User's Guide (Schalock et al., 2012) recommended using several of the following sources:

- School records
- Medical records
- Previous psychological evaluations
- Driver's and motor vehicle bureau records regarding driving skills
- Employment performance records
- Information from state or federal offices that might hold eligibility information
- Informal interviews with individuals who know the person and have had the opportunity to observe the person in the community

In any event, Schalock and his colleagues (2010) recommend that all evaluations of adaptive behavior follow these guidelines:

- Use multiple types and sources of information to obtain convergence of information regarding the individual's skills and limitations in comparison to same-age peers.
- Always use reasonable caution when weighing qualitative information obtained from respondents—especially in light of conflicting information.
- Always use clinical judgment to guide the evaluation of the reliability of all respondents, as well as possible sources of bias (positive or negative).
- Review and analyze critically all types of information for accuracy and pertinence. One should also ascertain the comparison group when determining ability and limitations. For example, in some special education programs, a 'C' grade denotes something very different in achievement level than a 'C' grade granted in a regular education classroom. (Schalock et al., 2010; p. 48)

Conclusion

Although adaptive behavior is an important construct for the purpose of ruling-in or ruling-out a diagnosis of intellectual disability, it is by far a more important construct because of its value as an outcome measure. Adaptive behavior is what Henry Leland once referred to as the skills that make one "invisible" in society. The more skilled we are in terms of adaptation, the less we stand out. Hence, teaching adaptive skills to persons will equip them to better respond to their community's and society-at-large's expectations of them. These skills are translatable into better coping skills, consumer skills, social interaction, personal healthcare, hygiene, cooking and home-living skills, employment opportunities, and more. When Schalock and his colleagues (2010) assert that, "with appropriate personalized supports over a sustained period, the life functioning of the person with intellectual disability generally will improve" (p. 1), what they are talking about is that person's adaptive behavior. With proper intervention and supports, a person can learn and improve his or her ability to meet society's expectations. This is important because we can teach everyone with intellectual disability—no matter their level of disability—new adaptive skills that will contribute to their improved independence and resulting quality of life.

References

American Psychiatric Association. (1968). *Diagnostic and statistical manual of mental disorders* (2nd ed.). Washington, DC: Author.

American Psychiatric Association. (2000). *Diagnostic and statistical manual of mental disorders* (4th ed., text rev.). Washington, DC: Author.

Arvey, R. D., Bouchard, T. J., Jr., Carroll, J. B., Cattell, R. B., Cohen, D. B., Dawis, R. V., et al. (December 13, 1994). Mainstream science on intelligence. *Wall Street Journal*, p. B1.

Barclay, A. G., Drotar, D. D., Favell, J., Foxx, R. M., Gardner, W. I., Iwata, B. A., et al. (1996). Definition of mental retardation. In J. W. Jacobson & J. A. Mulick (Eds.), *Manual of diagnosis and professional practice in mental retardation* (pp. 13–47). Washington, DC: American Psychological Association.

Binet, A., & Simon, T. (1905). Méthodes nouvelles pour le diagnostic du niveau intellectuel des anormaux. *L'Année Psychologique, 11,* 191–244.

Bruininks, R. H., Hill, B., Weatherman, R., & Woodcock, R. (1986). *Inventory for client and agency planning*. Itasca, IL: The Riverside Publishing Company.

Bruininks, R. H., Woodcock, R., Weatherman, R., & Hill, B. (1996). *Scales of independent behavior—revised*. Chicago, IL: Riverside.

Bruininks, R. H., Woodcock, R. W., Weatherman, R. F., & Hill, B. K. (1984). *Scales of independent behavior: Interviewer's manual*. Allen, TX: DLM Teaching Resources.

Burns, M. K. (2005). Test review of the Adaptive Behavior Assessment System—Second Edition. In R. A. Spies & B. S. Plake (Eds.), *The sixteenth mental measurement yearbook*. Available at the Buros Institute's Test Reviews Online Web site: http://www.unl.edu/buros.

Carpentieri, S., & Morgan, S. B. (1996). Adaptive and intellectual functioning in autistic and nonautistic retarded children. *Journal of Autism and Developmental Disorders, 26,* 611–620.

Childs, R. E. (1982). A study of the adaptive behavior of retarded children and the resultant effects of this use in the diagnosis of mental retardation. *Education and Training of the Mentally Retarded, 17,* 109–113.

Developmental Disabilities Assistance and Bill of Rights Act of 2000 (PL 106-402) http://www.acf.hhs.gov/programs/add/DDACT2.htm

Doll, E.A. (1953). Measurement of social competence: A manual for the *Vineland Social Maturity Scale.* Circle Pines, MN: American Guidance Service, Inc.

Einfeld, S. L., & Aman, M. G. (1995). Issues in the taxonomy of psychopathology in mental retardation. *Journal of Autism and Developmental Disorders, 25,* 143–167.

Emerson, E. (2001). *Challenging behaviour: Analysis and interventions in people with severe intellectual disabilities.* Cambridge, UK : Cambridge University Press.

Felce, D., de Kock., U., Thomas, M., & Saxby, H. (1986). Change in adaptive behavior of severely and profoundly mentally handicapped adults in different residential settings. *British Journal of Psychology, 77,* 489–501.

Fine, M. A., Tangeman, P. J., & Woodard, J. (1990). Changes in adaptive behavior of older adults with mental retardation following deinstitutionalization. *American Journal on Mental Retardation, 94,* 661–668.

Gottfredson, L. (1997). Mainstream science on intelligence: an editorial with 52 signatories, history, and bibliography. *Intelligence, 24,* 13–23.

Grossman, H,. J. (Ed.) (1973). *A manual on terminology and classification in mental retardation* (7th ed.). Washington, DC: American Association on Mental Deficiency.

Grossman, H. J. (Ed.) (1983). *Classification in mental retardation* (8th ed.). Washington, DC: American Association on Mental Deficiency.

Harrison, P. L. (1998). Review of the AAMR Adaptive Behavior Scale-Residential and Community: Second Edition. In J. C. Imparo & B. S. Plake (Eds.), *The thirteenth mental measurement yearbook* (pp. 389–393). Lincoln, NE: Buros Institute of Mental Measurement.

Harrison, P. L., & Oakland, T. (2000). *Adaptive Behavior Assessment System.* San Antonio, TX: Psychological Corp.

Harrison, P. L., & Oakland, T. (2003). *Adaptive behavior assessment system second edition: Manual.* San Antonio, TX: Harcourt Assessment.

Heal, L. W., & Tassé, M. J. (1999). The culturally sensitive individualized assessment of adaptive behavior. In R. L. Schalock (Ed.), *Adaptive behavior and its measurement: Implications for the field of mental retardation* (pp. 185–208). Washington, DC: American Association on Mental Retardation.

Heber, R. (1959). A manual on terminology and classification in mental retardation: A monograph supplement. *American Journal of Mental Deficiency, 64,* 1–111.

Heber, R. (1961). *A manual on terminology and classification in mental retardation* (rev. ed.). Washington, DC: American Association on Mental Deficiency.

Hull, J. T., & Thompson, J. C. (1980). Predicting adaptive functioning of mentally retarded persons in community settings. *American Journal of Mental Deficiency, 85,* 253–261.

Keith, T. Z., Fehrmann, P. G., Harrison, P., & Pottebaum, S. M. (1987). The relationship between adaptive behavior and intelligence: Testing alternative explanations. *Journal of School Psychology, 25,* 31–43.

Lakin, C., Larson, S., & Kim, S. (2011). The effects of community vs. institutional living on the daily living skills of persons with developmental disabilities: Third decennial review of studies, 1977–2010. *Policy Research Brief, 22* (1), Whole issue (available at: http://rtc.umn.edu or http://evidence-basedpolicy.org).

Lambert, N. (1981). *Diagnostic and technical Manual—AAMD adaptive behavior scale—School edition.* Monterey, CA: Publishers Test Service.

Lambert, N., Nihira, K., & Leland, H. (1993). Adaptive Behavior Scale—School, Second Edition. Austin, TX: PRO-ED.

Lowe, K., Allen, D., Jones, E., Brophy, S. Moore, K., & James, W. (2007). Challenging behaviours: Prevalence and topographies. *Journal of Intellectual Disability Research, 51,* 625–636.

Luckasson, R. A., Coulter, D. L., Polloway, E. A., Reiss, S., Schalock, R. L., Snell, M. E., et al. (1992). *Mental retardation: Definition, classification, and systems of supports* (9th ed.). Washington, DC: American Association on Mental Retardation.

Luckasson, R. A., Schalock, R. L., Spitalnik, D. M., Spreat, S., Tassé, M. J., Snell, M. E., et al. (2002). *Mental retardation: Definition, classification, and systems of supports* (10th ed.). Washington, DC: American Association on Mental Retardation.

Maccow, G. (2001). *Test review of the Scales of Independent Behavior—Revised.* In B. S. Plake and J. C. Impara (Eds.), *The fourteenth mental measurements yearbook* [Electronic version]. Available from http://www.unl.edu/buros.

McGrew, K. S., & Bruininks, R. H. (1990). Defining adaptive and maladaptive behavior within a model of personal competence. *School Psychology Review, 19,* 53–73.

Nihira, K. (1999). Adaptive behavior: A historical overview. In R. L. Schalock (Ed.), *Adaptive behavior and its measurement: Implications for the field of mental retardation* (pp. 7–14). Washington, DC: American Association on Mental Retardation.

Nihira, K., Foster, R., Shellhaas, M., & Leland, H. (1969). *AAMD adaptive behavior scale.* Washington, DC: American Association on Mental Deficiency.

Nihira, K., Foster, R., Shellhaas, M., & Leland, H. (1974). *AAMD adaptive behavior scale* (1974 revision). Washington, DC: American Association on Mental Deficiency.

Nihira, K., Leland, H., & Lambert, N. (1993). *AAMR Adaptive Behavior Scales, Residential and Community Edition* (2nd ed.). Austin, TX: Pro-Ed.

Reschly, D. J., Myers, T. G., & Hartel, C. R. (Eds.). (2002). *Mental retardation: Determining eligibility for social security benefits.* Washington, DC: National Academy Press.

Sattler, J. M. (2002). *Assessment of children: Behavioral and clinical applications* (4th ed.). San Diego, CA: Jerome M. Sattler.

Schalock, R. L., Borthwick-Duffy, S. A., Bradley, V. J., Buntinx, W. H. E., Coulter, D. L., Craig, E. M., et al. (2010). *Intellectual disability: Diagnosis, classification, and systems of supports* (11th ed.). Washington, DC: American Association on Intellectual and Developmental Disabilities.

Schalock, R. L., Luckasson, R., Bradley, V., Buntinx, W. H. E., Lachapelle, Y., Shogren, K., et al. (2012). *User's guide to accompany the 11th edition of Intellectual Disability: Definition, Classification, and Systems of Supports.* Washington, DC: American Association on Intellectual and Developmental Disabilities.

Silverman, W. P., Silver, J., Sersen, E. A., Lubin, R. A., & Schwartz, A. A. (1986). Factors related to adaptive behavior changes among profoundly mentally retarded physically disabled persons. *American Journal of Mental Deficiency, 90,* 651–658.

Sparrow, S. S., Cicchetti, D. V., & Balla, D. A. (1984). *Vineland Adaptive Behavior Scales*. Circle Pines, MN: American Guidance Service.

Sparrow, S. S., Cicchetti, D. V., & Balla, D. A. (2005). *Vineland–II: Vineland adaptive behavior scales* (2nd ed.). Minneapolis, MN: Pearson Assessments.

Spreat, S. (1999). Psychometric standards of adaptive behavior assessment. In R. L. Schalock (Ed.), *Adaptive behavior and its measurement: Implications for the field of mental retardation* (pp. 103–118). Washington, DC: American Association on Mental Retardation.

Tassé, M. J. (2009). Adaptive behavior assessment and the diagnosis of mental retardation in capital cases. *Applied Neuropsychology, 16,* 114–123.

Tassé, M. J. & Grover, M. D. (2013). American Association on Intellectual and Developmental Disabilities (pp. 122–125). In F. R. Volkmar (Ed.), *Encyclopedia of autism spectrum disorders.* New York: Springer.

Tassé, M. J., Schalock, R. L., Balboni, G., Bersani, H., Borthwick-Duffy, S. A., Spreat, S., et al. (2012). The construct of adaptive behavior: Its conceptualization, measurement, and use in the field of intellectual disability. *American Journal on Intellectual and Developmental Disabilities, 117,* 291–303.

Tassé, M. J., Schalock, R. L., Balboni, G., Bersani, H., Borthwick-Duffy, S. A., Spreat, S. et al. (in press). *Diagnostic adaptive behavior scale: Manual*. Washington, DC: American Association on Intellectual and Developmental Disabilities.

Thompson, J. R., McGrew, K. S., & Bruininks, R. H. (1999). Adaptive behavior and maladaptive behavior: Functional and structural characteristics. In R. L. Schalock (Ed.), *Adaptive behavior and its measurement: Implications for the field of mental retardation* (pp. 15–42). Washington, DC: American Association on Mental Retardation.

Widaman, K. F. (2010). Review of the Vineland Adaptive Behavior Scales, Second Edition. In R. A. Spies, J. F. Carlson, & K. F. Geisinger (Eds.), *The eighteenth mental measurements yearbook* (pp. 682–684). Lincoln: University of Nebraska Press.

Widaman, K. F., & McGrew, K. S. (1996). The structure of adaptive behavior. In J. W. Jacobson & J. S. Mulick (Eds.), *Manual of diagnosis and professional practice in mental retardation* (pp. 97–110). Washington, DC: American Psychological Association.

World Health Organization (1992). *ICD-10 Classifications of mental and behavioural disorder: Clinical descriptions and diagnostic guidelines*. Geneva: Author.

Self-Determination

Michael L. Wehmeyer *and* Todd D. Little

Abstract

Self-determination is a general psychological construct within the organizing structure of theories of human agency that refers to self- (vs. other-) caused action—to people acting volitionally, based on their own will. Human agency refers to the sense of personal empowerment involving both knowing and having what it takes to achieve goals. Human agentic theories share the meta-theoretical view that organismic aspirations drive human behaviors. An organismic perspective of self-determination that views people as active contributors to, or "authors" of, their behavior, where behavior is self-regulated and goal-directed, provides a compelling foundation for examining and facilitating the degree to which people become self-determined and the impact of that on the pursuit of optimal human functioning and well-being. Further, an organismic approach to self-determination requires an explicit focus on the interface between the self and context. This chapter provides an overview of theoretical frameworks driving efforts to promote self-determination for people with disabilities, examines findings from research pertaining to self-determination and youth and adults with disabilities, and discusses intervention research in the field.

Key Words: self-determination, human agency, causal agency, self-determination theory, volitional action

Positive psychology is the pursuit of understanding optimal human functioning and well-being. Ryan and Deci (2000) asserted that, in this pursuit, researchers must take into account the agentic nature of human action. This chapter overviews self-determination as a general psychological construct within the organizing structure of theories of human agency and examines its application with regard to people with disabilities. Human agency is defined as "the sense of personal empowerment, which involves both knowing and having what it takes to achieve one's goals" (Little, Hawley, Henrich, & Marsland, 2002, p. 390). An agentic person is:

the origin of his or her actions, has high aspirations, perseveres in the face of obstacles, sees more and varied options for action, learns from failures, and

overall, has a greater sense of well being. In contrast, a non-agentic individual can be a pawn to unknown extra-personal influences, has low aspirations, is hindered with problem-solving blinders, often feels helpless and, overall, has a greater sense of ill-being. (Little et al., 2002, p. 390)

Human agentic theories "share the meta-theoretical view that organismic aspirations drive human behaviors" (Little, Snyder, & Wehmeyer, 2006, p. 61). An organismic perspective views people as active contributors to, or "authors" of, their behavior, where behavior is described as self-regulated and goal-directed *action*. Unlike stimulus-response accounts of behavior, actions are defined as purposive and self-initiated activities (Brandtstädter, 1998; Chapman, 1984; Harter, 1999). As outlined by Little, Snyder, and Wehmeyer (2006), human agentic actions are:

a. motivated by biological and psychological needs (Deci & Ryan, 2002; Hawley, 1999; Hawley & Little, 2002; Little et al., 2002).

b. directed toward self-regulated goals that service short- and long-term biological and psychological needs.

c. propelled by understandings of links among agents, means, and ends (Chapman, 1984; Little, 1998; Skinner, 1995, 1996), and guided by general action-control behaviors that entail self-chosen forms and functions (Little, Lopez, & Wanner, 2001; Skinner & Edge, 2002; Vanlede, Little, & Card, 2006).

d. those that precipitate self-determined governance of behavior and development, which can be characterized as hope-related individual differences.

e. triggered, executed, and evaluated in contexts that provide supports and opportunities, as well as hindrances and impediments to goal pursuit.

Further, an organismic approach to self-determination requires an explicit focus on the interface between the self and context (Little et al., 2002). Organisms influence and are influenced by the contexts in which they live and develop. Through this person-context interaction people become agents of their own action.

Self-Determination in Philosophy

The construct's origins lie in philosophy and discourse about the doctrines of *determinism* and *free will*. Determinism is the philosophical doctrine positing that events, such as human behavior, are effects of preceding causes. John Locke (1690) provided a synopsis of the *free will problem*:

> this proposition "men can determine themselves" is drawn in or inferred from this, "that they shall be punished in the other world." For here the mind, seeing the connexion [sic] there is between the idea of men's punishment in the other world and the idea of God punishing; between God punishing and the justice of the punishment; between justice of punishment and guilt; between guilt and a power to do otherwise; between a power to do otherwise and freedom; and between freedom and self-determination, sees the connexion [sic] between men and self-determination. (Locke, 1690)

Locke was a soft determinist; that is, someone who saw both causality and volition or will at work in human behavior. According to Locke, the human mind has the *active* power of beginning or ceasing its own operations as activated by a preference. The exercise of that power is volition or will. Freedom or liberty is "the power to act on our volition, whatever it may be, without any external compulsion or restraint" (Locke, 1690). Human beings act freely insofar as they are capable of translating their mental preferences into actual performance of the action in question (Kemerling, 2000–2001). Freedom is conceptualized as the human capacity to act (or not) as we choose or prefer, without any external compulsion or restraint.

Locke's proposals about the causes of human action as both caused and volitional are important to an organismic theory of self-determination, as is his soft deterministic distinction that it is the *agent* (the person) who is free to act, not the action itself (since it is "caused" by perception or sensation).

Self-Determination in Personality Psychology

In *Foundations for a Science of Personality* (1941), Angyal proposed that an essential feature of a living organism is its autonomy, where autonomous means self-governing or governed from inside. According to Angyal, an organism "lives in a world in which things happen according to laws which are heteronomous (e.g., governed from outside) from the point of view of the organism" (p. 33), and that "organisms are subjected to the laws of the physical world, as is any other object of nature, with the exception that it can oppose self-determination to external determination" (p. 33).

Angyal (1941) suggested that the *science of personality* is the study of two essential determinants to human behavior, autonomous-determinism (self-determination) and heteronomous-determinism (other-determined). Angyal placed primary importance for laying the foundation for a science of personality in the fact that a central process of an organism is the movement toward autonomous determination, noting that "without autonomy, without self-government, the life process could not be understood" (p. 34).

Further, Angyal's (1941) use of the term moved away from the hard determinism that dominated psychology, led by Skinner and operant psychologists, toward a soft determinism that considered the importance of both actor and context. This trend that has continued in efforts to explain human agency, as evidenced by Bandura's (1997) discussion concerning determinism and human agency:

> When viewed from a sociocognitive perspective, there is no incompatibility between freedom and determinism. Freedom is not conceived negatively as exemption from social influences or situational constraints. Rather it is defined positively as the exercise of self-influence to bring about desired results. (p. 7)

Self-determination, as a psychological construct, refers to self- (vs. other-) caused action. It refers to people acting volitionally, based on their own will. Volition is the capability of conscious choice, decision, and *intention* (Gove, 1967). Volitional behavior, then, implies intent. Self-determined behavior is volitional, intentional, and self-caused or self-initiated.

Theories of Self-Determination
Self-Determination Theory

The most visible application of self-determination as a psychological construct has been *Self-Determination Theory* (SDT; Deci & Ryan, 2002), proposed to explain facets of personality and behavioral self-regulation through interactions between innate and environmental determinants within social contexts (Ryan & Deci, 2000). With its basis in various sub-theories (for details see Ryan & Deci, 2002), SDT brings together innate human tendencies, social contexts, and the motivators for human action to illustrate how congruence between one's basic needs and core values spur individual agency that, ultimately, results in overall well-being. SDT proposed three basic psychological needs— competence, autonomy, and relatedness—that are either supported or challenged by social contexts (see Little et al., 2002, for a discussion of how these psychological needs mesh with evolutionary-based biological needs). Much of the research stemming from SDT has focused on ways the social environment creates barriers to the integration of these psychological needs (Ryan & Deci, 2002). The context also contributes to intrinsic and extrinsic motivators that are self-regulated at either conscious or unconscious levels. This perspective views the process of self-regulation as an organizational function that "coordinates" systemic behaviors and serves as a foundation for autonomy and the sense of self (Ryan & Deci, 2004).

Early work on SDT focused on the role of social contexts in supporting or thwarting intrinsic motivation and found that conditions fostering autonomy and competence were positively associated with intrinsic motivation. When extrinsically motivated behaviors were acted on, individuals were more likely to integrate the behavior with core values when the social context supported autonomy, competence, and relatedness (Ryan & Deci, 2000). Recent SDT research has examined the relationship between implicit/explicit motives (conscious or unconscious) and intrinsic/extrinsic motivation (Ryan & Deci, 2004).

As noted, three basic psychological needs (i.e., autonomy, competence, relatedness) are the driving forces in SDT. Satisfying these needs enhance well-being and contribute to the efficacy of other model components (Deci & Ryan, 2000). Within SDT, autonomous actions express integrity and are based on one's core or "higher order values" (Ryan & Deci, 2004). Sometimes outside influences (e.g., social context) force values to conflict, and a choice must be made that reflects the true self. Intrinsic and extrinsic motivation plays a role here, and these motivators are not simply polar opposites (see Walls & Little, 2005). Instead, the rationale and outcome of negotiating and integrating the demands of intrinsic and extrinsic sources of motivation determines the autonomy of an action (Ryan & Deci, 2004). Thus, an autonomous action is one in which the rationale behind an action-response (behavior) to an extrinsic pressure reflects one's core values. Research stemming from SDT has identified conditions that facilitate autonomy and the effect of autonomy on daily functioning and daily life experiences. For example, Sheldon, Ryan, Deci, and Kasser (2004) demonstrated that autonomous motives (e.g., personal identification and enjoyment) and controlled motives (e.g., external rewards and guilt) were associated with higher and lower levels of well-being, respectively.

In SDT, the inherent psychological need for competence refers to the motivation to be effective within environments, which in turn stems from the theory of effectence motivation that describes an innate drive for environmental mastery (Deci & Ryan, 2000; White, 1959). This drive leads to behavioral responses that sustain and augment individual capabilities (Ryan & Deci, 2002). The psychological need for relatedness is the sense of connectedness and belonging with others. This sense is distinct from the status of role identification or group membership, as the focus is on personal perceptions of relatedness instead of goal outcomes (Reis, Sheldon, Gable, Roscoe, & Ryan, 2000). Variously, competence, relatedness, and autonomy needs may compliment each other, or they may conflict (Deci &

Ryan, 2000). More information on SDT research and instruments to assess it can be found at www. std.rochester.edu and www.agencylab.ku.edu.

Functional Model of Self-Determination

Wehmeyer and colleagues (Wehmeyer, 1996a, 2001, 2005) proposed a functional model or theory of self-determination, in which self-determination is conceptualized as a dispositional characteristic based on the *function* a behavior serves for the individual. Self-determined behavior refers to "volitional actions that enable one to act as the primary causal agent in one's life and to maintain or improve one's quality of life" (Wehmeyer, 2005, p. 117). Broadly defined, *causal agency* implies that it is the individual who makes or causes things to happen in his or her life. Causal agency implies more than just causing action, however; it implies that the individual acts with an eye toward *causing* an effect to *accomplish* a *specific end* or to *cause* or *create change*. Bandura (1997) noted that

> In evaluating the role of intentionality in human agency, one must distinguish between the personal production of action for an intended outcome, and the effects that carrying out that course of action produce. Agency refers to acts done intentionally. (p. 3)

All of the theoretical perspectives represented here differentiate between self-determination as self-*caused* action and self-determination as *controlling* one's behavior. As Deci (2004) observed, "the concept of personal control…refers to having control over outcomes" (p. 23). Control is defined as "authority, power, or influence over events, behaviors, situations, or people" (VandenBos, 2007, p. 228). Self-determination is not control over events or outcomes, but the degree to which behavior is volitional and the person is the causal agent.

According to this functional theory, self-determined *actions* are identified by four *essential characteristics*: (1) the person acts *autonomously*, (2) the behavior is *self-regulated*, (3) the person initiates and responds to the event(s) in a *psychologically empowered* manner, and (4) the person acts in a *self-realizing* manner. These essential characteristics refer not to the specific behavior performed, but to the *function* (e.g., purpose) the behavior serves for the individual; that is, whether the action enabled the person to act as a causal agent.

The theory's use of behavioral autonomy draws from two sources: autonomy as synonymous with

individuation and autonomy as roughly synonymous with independence. Developmental psychologists view the process of individuation, or the formation of the person's individual identity (Damon, 1983), as a critical component of social and personality development. Sigafoos, Feinstein, Damond, and Reiss (1988) defined individuation as "a progression from dependence on others for care and guidance to self-care and self-direction" (p. 432), the outcome of which is autonomous functioning or, when describing the actions of individuals achieving this outcome, behavioral autonomy.

Self-regulation is "a complex response system that enables individuals to examine their environments and their repertoires of responses for coping with those environments to make decisions about how to act, to act, to evaluate the desirability of the outcomes of the action, and to revise their plans as necessary" (Whitman, 1990, p. 373). Self-regulated behaviors include the use of self-management strategies (including self-monitoring, self-instruction, self-evaluation and self-reinforcement), goal setting and attainment behaviors, problem-solving and decision-making behaviors, and observational learning strategies.

Psychological empowerment is a construct emanating from the community psychology literature and refers to the multiple dimensions of perceived control (Zimmerman, 1990). Zimmerman and Rappaport (1988) forwarded the construct of psychological empowerment to account for the multidimensional nature of perceived control, which, according to these authors, had been previously treated as if it were a univariate construct (cf. Little, 1998; Skinner, 1995). Thus, according to Zimmerman, through the process of learning and using problem-solving skills and achieving perceived or actual control in one's life (e.g., learned hopefulness), individuals develop a perception of psychological empowerment that enables them to achieve desired outcomes.

Self-realization, a construct proposed by Gestalt psychologists to refer to the intrinsic purpose in a person's life, also has more global meaning related to the "tendency to shape one's life course into a meaningful whole" (Angyal, 1941, p. 355). People who are self-determined are self-realizing in that they use a comprehensive, and reasonably accurate, knowledge of themselves—their strengths and limitations—to act in such a manner as to capitalize on this knowledge. This self-knowledge and self-understanding form through experience with and interpretation of one's environment and are influenced by evaluations of significant others, reinforcement, and attributions of one's own behavior (Little, 1998).

The primary research focus of this functional model has been on people with intellectual disability, although the theory itself is not specific to people with disabilities. Various measures of self-determination from this perspective have been developed for adolescents with disabilities (e.g., Wehmeyer & Kelchner, 1995; Wehmeyer, Kelchner, & Richards, 1996; available at www.beachcenter.org). Moreover, basic tenets of the theory have been validated (e.g., Shogren et al., 2008; Wehmeyer, Kelchner & Richards, 1996; Wehmeyer & Schwartz, 1997, 1998).

Self-Determination as Self-Regulated Problem Solving

In another theoretical model derived from research in education, Mithaug suggested that "self-determination is a form of self-regulation—one that is unusually effective and markedly free of external influence" (Mithaug, Campeau, & Wolman, 1992, p. iii) in which people who are self-determined regulate their choices and actions more successfully than others (Mithaug, 1993; 1996a; 1996b; 1998). Mithaug suggested that individuals are often in flux between existing states and *goal* or desired states. When a discrepancy between what one has and wants occurs, an incentive for self-regulation and action may be operative. With the realization that a discrepancy exists, the individual may set out to achieve the goal or desired state. Because of a previous history of failure, however, individuals may set expectations that are too low or, in some cases, too high.

The ability to set appropriate expectations is based on the individual's success in matching his or her *capacity* with present *opportunity*. Capacity is the individual's assessment of existing resources (e.g., skills, interests, motivation), and opportunity refers to aspects of the situation that allow the individual to achieve the desired gain. Mithaug referred to optimal prospects as *just-right* matches in which individuals are able to correctly match their capacity (i.e., skills, interests) with existing opportunities (e.g., potential jobs). The experience generated during self-regulation, then, becomes a function of the interaction between the person's capacity and opportunity (Mithaug, 1996a). As Mithaug notes, "the more competent we are, the fewer errors we make, and the less time we take, the greater the gain we produce" (p. 156).

Mithaug (1998) also noted that self-determination always occurs in a social context and suggested that the social nature of the concept is worth reviewing because the distinction between self-determination and other-determination is nearly always in play when assessing an individual's prospects for controlling their life in a particular situation. Mithaug and colleagues (Mithaug, Wehmeyer, Agran, Martin, & Palmer, 1998; Wehmeyer, Palmer, Agran, Mithaug, & Martin, 2000) have applied aspects of this theoretical framework to develop an instructional model that enables teachers to increase student self-determination by preparing students to become self-regulated problem solvers. Mithaug and colleagues also have developed a measure of self-determination: the AIR Self-Determination Scale (Wolman, Campeau, Dubois, Mithaug, & Stolarski, 1994), which includes student, teacher, and parent report versions. The scale was normed with 450 students, 80 percent of whom had a disability, most with a cognitive disability. The validated measures yield indicators of opportunity and capacity to self-determine (available at www.ou.edu/zarrow/sdetermination.html).

An Ecological Model of Self-Determination

Abery and colleagues (Abery & Stancliffe, 1996) proposed an ecological model of self-determination that defines the self-determination construct as "a complex process, the ultimate goal of which is to achieve the level of personal control over one's life that an individual desires within those areas the individual perceives as important" (p. 27). The ecological model views self-determination as driven by the intrinsic motivation of all people to be the primary determiner of their thoughts, feelings, and behavior. It may involve, but is not synonymous with, independence and autonomy. Rather, it entails the person determining in what contexts and to what extent each of these behaviors/attitudes will be manifested. Self-determination, accordingly, is the product of both the person and the environment—of the person using the skills, knowledge, and beliefs at his/her disposal to act on the environment with the goal of obtaining valued and desired outcomes. The ecological model was derived from Bronfenbrenner's ecological perspective (1979, 1989), within which people developing and leading their lives is viewed as consisting of four levels: the *microsystem, mesosystem, exosystem,* and *macrosystem* (see Wehmeyer, Abery, Mithaug, & Stancliffe, 2003 for more detail). The ecological model has been empirically evaluated (Abery, McGrew, & Smith, 1995; Stancliffe, Abery, & Smith, 2000).

A Five-Step Model of Self-Determination

Over a three-year research effort, Field and Hoffman (1994) developed a model of self-determination.

That process included: (a) reviewing the literature, (b) conducting interviews, (c) observing students in a variety of school settings, (d) considering internal expertise, and (e) considering external expertise. The model-development process included more than 1,500 student observations and interviews with more than 200 individuals. The model was reviewed by panels of experts (including consumers, parents, educators, and adult service providers) in three states and was revised based on their input. In addition, a national review panel of experts provided input on the model and oversaw the model-development process.

Field and Hoffman (2005) revised the model to clarify and emphasize key elements of self-determination. The revised model highlights the importance of these contributing factors to self-determination:

- understanding of the environment in which one is trying to express self-determination,
- the ability to establish and maintain positive relationships, and
- skill in focusing on goal(s) the individual has set.

As described in this model, self-determination is either promoted or discouraged by factors within the individual's control (e.g., values, knowledge, skills) and variables that are environmental in nature (e.g., opportunities for choice making, attitudes of others). The model addresses both internal, affective factors and skill components that promote self-determination. The model has five major components: *Know Yourself and Your Environment, Value Yourself, Plan, Act, and Experience Outcomes and Learn*. The first two components describe internal processes that provide a foundation for acting in a self-determined manner. The next two components, *Plan* and *Act*, identify skills needed to act on this foundation. One must have internal awareness as well as the strength and ability to act on that internal foundation to be self-determined. To have the foundation of self-awareness and self-esteem but not the skills, or the skills but not the inner knowledge and belief in the self, is insufficient to fully experience self-determination. To be self-determined, one must know and value what one wants and possess the necessary skills to seek what is desired. The final component in the self-determination model is *Experience Outcomes and Learn*. This step includes both celebrating successes and reviewing efforts to become self-determined so that skills and knowledge that contribute to self-determination are enhanced.

Environmental Indicators

As stated above, self-determination is affected by environmental variables as well as by the knowledge, skills, and beliefs expressed by the individual. Field and Hoffman identified nine indicators of environments that support the expression of self-determination (Field & Hoffman, 2001). These quality indicators included:

1. Knowledge, skills, and attitudes for self-determination are addressed in the curriculum, in family support programs, and in staff development.

2. Students, parents, and staff are involved participants in individualized educational decision making and planning.

3. Students, families, faculty, and staff are provided with opportunities for choice.

4. Students, families, faculty, and staff are encouraged to take appropriate risks.

5. Supportive relationships are encouraged.

6. Accommodations and supports for individual needs are provided.

7. Students, families, and staff have the opportunity to express themselves and be understood.

8. Consequences for actions are predictable.

9. Self-determination is modeled throughout the school environment.

Self-Determination as Mastery Motivation and Efficacy Expectations

Powers, Sowers, Turner, Nesbitt, Knowles, and Ellison (1996) conceptualized self-determination as a function of *mastery motivation* (characterized by perceived competence, self-esteem, maintenance of an internal locus of control, and internalization of goals and rewards) and *self-efficacy expectations*. Self-determination is defined as referring to "personal attitudes and abilities that facilitate an individual's identification and pursuit of goals" (p. 292). The promotion of self-determination, within this model, results from experiences and efforts that reduce learned helplessness and promote mastery motivation and self-efficacy expectations. Quite specifically, in this model self-determination is viewed as antithetical to learned helplessness and an *outcome* of promoting mastery motivation and self-efficacy expectations (Powers et al., 1996). Powers and colleagues defined learned helplessness, in accordance with work by Martin Seligman, as an "acquired behavioral disposition characterized by passivity, self-denigration and internalization of devalued social status, perpetuated through permanent, pervasive, internalized negative self-attributions" (pp. 259–260). Learned helplessness is reinforced by "environmental factors that encourage passivity by (1) providing little opportunity for an individual to actively make choices and generate successful responses, (2) communicating expectations of non-involvement or failure, or (3) reinforcing failure or not reinforcing striving" (p. 260). Powers and colleagues identified factors that promote learned helplessness as including overprotection and economic, academic or social deprivation.

Comparatively, self-determination might be construed as an acquired behavioral disposition characterized by self-directed, goal-oriented behavior. This disposition is the outcome of mastery motivation and self-efficacy appraisals and expectations. The former draws from research by Harter (1999) examining how youth acquire a generalized positive disposition toward achievement and striving. Mastery motivation is "characterized by perceived competence, self-esteem, maintenance of an internal locus of control, and internalization of goals and rewards" (Powers et al., 1996, p. 294). Self-efficacy expectations derive from Bandura's (1997) theory of self-efficacy, which, according to these researchers, "provides a detailed framework for understanding specific influences on the development of self-determination" (Powers et al., 1996, p. 294). Briefly, self-efficacy theory postulates two components, outcome expectations (belief about whether a particular behavior will lead to a particular consequence), and personal efficacy expectations (a person's expectations regarding his or her capability to realize a desired behavior within a specific context). Self-efficacy appraisals are impacted by four specific sources: (1) enactive attainment, derived from repeated performance accomplishments; (2) vicarious experiences, observing other's success and effective management of challenges; (3) social persuasion, including encouragement, evaluative feedback, reinforcement, or challenge; and (4) physiological feedback.

Powers and colleagues have developed and field-tested a programmatic effort drawing from the conceptual foundations of mastery motivation and self-efficacy theory, called the TAKE CHARGE model, which is designed to promote adolescent development of self-determination through four primary components: skill facilitation, mentorship, peer support, and parent support. This programmatic effort has been shown to be effective with a wide array of students at risk for learned helplessness, including students with mental retardation (Powers et al., 1996). Sowers and Powers (1995) applied this approach to increase the participation and independence of students with severe disabilities in performing community activities.

Powers, Turner, Matuszewski, Wilson, and Phillips (2001) conducted a controlled field test of the TAKE CHARGE for the Future program with 43 students who had learning, emotional, orthopedic or other health disabilities. Half the students were randomly assigned to the treatment group, while the rest were in a no-treatment group. Powers et al. (2001) used a variety of measures to determine the efficacy of the process, including measures of student involvement in transition planning, student and parent awareness of transition, and family empowerment. Students in the treatment group participated in the TAKE CHARGE for the Future curriculum for 4 months. Upon completion of these instructional activities, students who had received the curriculum showed greater gains in measures of student involvement, parent awareness, and indicators of student empowerment. Powers and colleagues have also used the TAKE CHARGE model to promote the self-determination of young adults with multiple health and other needs.

Causal Agency Theory

Wehmeyer and Mithaug (Wehmeyer, 2004a, Wehmeyer & Mithaug, 2006) proposed *Causal Agency Theory* (CAT) to explain how people become self-determined. CAT attempts to predict how and why people act in such a way as to become *self-* verses *other*-determined. Wehmeyer and Mithaug (2006) refer to the "class of behavioral events" that CAT attempts to explain as *causal events, causal behavior,* or *causal actions.* These function as a means for the person (the causal agent) to achieve valued goals and, ultimately, become more self-determined.

According to CAT, there are a number of "operators" at work that lead to self-determined behavior. These operators involve the capability to perform causal actions or behaviors, subdivided into causal capacity and agentic capacity, and challenges to the organism's self-determination, through causal opportunities or causal threats, which serve as a catalyst to action.

Capability refers to having requisite mental or physical capacity to accomplish a particular task. Two types of capabilities are important to causal agency—*Causal Capability* and *Agentic Capability*. *Causal Capability* refers to the mental or physical capacities that enable a person to cause something to happen. These capacities include *causal capacities*, the knowledge and behavioral skills necessary to express causal capability, and *causal perceptions*, the perceptions and beliefs about oneself and one's environment that are necessary to express causal capability. *Agentic Capability* refers to the mental or physical capacity that enables a person to direct causal action. Agency capability also has two components: *agentic capacity*, the knowledge and skills needed to direct causal action, including self-regulatory and self-management knowledge and the skills that enable persons to address goal states; and *agentic perceptions*, the beliefs about oneself and one's environment that enable one to act.

Wehmeyer and Mithaug (2006) proposed that people are "caused" to implement causal and agentic capabilities in response to challenges that serve as catalysts for causal behavior. A challenge is any circumstance under which one has to engage in the full use of one's abilities or resources to resolve a problem or threat or to achieve a goal or objective. Specifically, causal actions or behaviors are provoked in the organism by two classes of challenges to self-determination: opportunities or threats. *Opportunity* refers to situations or circumstances that provoke the organism to engage in causal action to achieve a planned, desired outcome. Opportunity implies that the situation or circumstance provides a chance for the person to create change or make something happen based upon his or her individual *causal capability*, including both causal capacity and causal perceptions. If a person has the *causal capability* to act on the situation or circumstance, that situation or circumstance can be construed as an opportunity. Opportunities can be "*found*" (unanticipated, happened upon through no effort of one's own) or "*created*" (the person acts to create a favorable circumstance).

The second challenge condition involves situations or circumstances that threaten the organism's self-determination and provoke the organism to exercise causal action to maintain a preferred outcome or to create change that is consistent with one's own values, preferences, or interests, and not the values, preferences, or interests of others. Wehmeyer and Mithaug (2006) also proposed a third operant in CAT: *Causal Affect*. Causal affects are those emotions, feelings, and other affective components that regulate human behavior, including causal behaviors. For example, emotions (a response involving physiological changes as a preparation for action) are often evoked in response to a challenge, be it opportunity (joy, excitement) or threat (anger, anxiety) that serves to heighten or limit the organisms capacity to respond to the challenge.

People who are causal agents respond to challenges (opportunities or threats) to their self-determination by employing causal and agentic capabilities that result in causal action and allow them to direct their behavior to achieve a desired change or maintain a preferred circumstance or situation. Causal capability and agentic capability work together in a complex way to achieve the desired change or maintenance. Briefly, in response to challenges, causal agents use a *goal-generation process* leading to the identification and prioritization of needed actions. The person then frames the most urgent action need in terms of a goal state, and engages in a *goal-discrepancy analysis* to compare current status with goal status. The outcome of this discrepancy analysis is a *goal-discrepancy problem* to be solved. The person next engages in a *capacity-challenge discrepancy analysis* in which capacity to solve the goal discrepancy problem is evaluated. The person maximizes adjustment in capacity (e.g., acquires new or refines existing skills and knowledge) or adjusts the challenge presented to create a "just-right match" between capacity and challenge to optimize the probability of solving the goal discrepancy problem.

Next, the person creates a discrepancy reduction plan by setting causal expectations, making choices and decisions about strategies and methods to reduce the discrepancy between the current status and goal status. When sufficient time has elapsed, the person will engage in a second goal-discrepancy analysis, using information gathered through self-monitoring, to self-evaluate progress toward reduction of the discrepancy between current and goal status. If progress is satisfactory, they will continue implementing the discrepancy reduction plan. If not satisfactory, the person either reconsiders the discrepancy reduction plan and modifies that component or returns to the goal generation process to re-examine the overall goal and its priority and, possibly, cycle through the process with a revised or new goal.

Self-Determination and Disability

Among the first, if not the first, uses of the term self-determination within the disability literature occurred in a chapter by Nirje (1972) in Wolfensberger's (1972) now classic text on the principle of normalization. Nirje (1972) titled his chapter *The Right to Self-Determination* and in the opening paragraph stated:

> One major facet of the normalization principle is to create conditions through which a handicapped person experiences the normal respect to which any human being is entitled. Thus the choices, wishes, desires, and aspirations of a handicapped person have to be taken into consideration as much as possible in actions affecting him. To assert oneself with one's family, friends, neighbors, co-workers, other people, or vis-à-vis an agency is difficult for many persons. It is especially difficult for someone who has a disability or is otherwise perceived as devalued. But in the end, even the impaired person has to manage as a distinct individual, and thus has his identity defined to himself and to others through the circumstances and conditions of his existence. Thus, the road to self-determination is both difficult and all important for a person who is impaired. (p. 177)

Nirje's use of the term suggests, at the least, familiarity with the usage of self-determination as a personality construct. His use of the term, while still pertaining to the *rights* of a particular *group of people* (people with mental retardation), is nonetheless a call for *personal* self-determination or self-governance. His is a call for a wide range of actions that enable people to control their lives and their destinies, including choice over personal activities, control over education, independence, participation in decisions, information upon which to make decisions and solve problems, and so forth. An analysis of Nirje's chapter to determine the types of actions, beliefs, and opportunities that describe self-determination reflects the same breadth and scope seen in the literature today. Nirje (1972) identified making choices, asserting oneself, self-management, self-knowledge, decision making, self-advocacy, self-efficacy, self-regulation, autonomy, and independence (although often not using those terms) as the salient features of personal self-determination.

Nirje's chapter appeared in the same book in which Perske (1972) called for the opportunity for people with mental retardation to experience the "dignity of risk":

> The world in which we live is not always safe, secure and predictable...Every day that we wake up and live in the hours of that day, there is a possibility of being thrown up against a situation where we may have to risk everything, even our lives. This is the way the real world is. We must work to develop every human resource within us in order to prepare for these days. To deny any person their fair share of risk experiences is to further cripple them for healthy living. (p. 199)

These two important calls to action emphasized the *universality* of the desire for control in one's life and one's destiny and over decisions and choices that impact one's life and one's quality of life and illustrate the important link in the use of the term self-determination as it pertains to people with disabilities with *empowerment*.

Self-Determination, Disability, and Empowerment

The focus in disability on self-determination emerged from deeply held convictions pertaining to the rights of people with disabilities to "control" their own lives. Within the context of the disability rights and advocacy movement, the self-determination construct has been imbued with an empowerment and "rights" orientation. Empowerment is, essentially, a process by which people who are marginalized gain power or control. The usage note in the American Heritage Dictionary of the English Language (1994) stated that the mid-17th century use of the term referred to the legal right to invest with authority or to authorize, but that its modern use has shifted to reflect the civil rights agenda in which marginalized people have greater control of their lives and destinies. Both meanings introduce the difficulty in social or educational services efforts "to empower" marginalized people; when understood to mean "to invest with power," such efforts put the loci for that power outside the individual. In the end when one has the power to invest someone else with authority, one also has the power, presumably, to withhold granting that authority. Power and control remain, fundamentally, with the granter. Defining (and describing) "empowerment" is complicated, in large measure because of the lack of consensus as to what terms like "power" and "control" mean.

Despite the ambiguities of defining and acting upon an empowerment framework, empowerment, as a construct, is clearly connected to social and civil rights movements and refers to actions that "enhance the possibilities for people to control their lives" (Rappaport, 1981, p. 15). Cattaneo and Chapman (2010) suggested that one can classify most understandings of empowerment in the literature as reflecting: (1) mastery (e.g., Rappaport, 1987); (2) participation (e.g., Cornell University Empowerment Group, 1989), or (3) as forwarding a meaning pertaining to social good. McWhirter

(1991) defined empowerment consistent with the latter, as "the process by which people, organizations, or groups who are powerless (a) become aware of the power dynamics at work in their life context, (b) develop the skills and capacity for gaining some reasonable control over their lives, (c) exercise this control without infringing up on the rights of others, and (d) support the empowerment of others in their community" (p. 224). Zimmerman (1990) proposed psychological empowerment as referring to multiple dimensions of perceived control, including its cognitive (personal efficacy), personality (locus of control), and motivational dimensions, and linked psychological empowerment to learned hopefulness.

Cattaneo and Chapman (2010) proposed an empowerment process model that defines empowerment as goal achievement, with the construct referring to "an iterative process in which a person who lacks power sets a personally meaningful goal oriented toward increasing power, takes action toward that goal, and observes and reflects on the impact of this action, drawing on his or her evolving self-efficacy, knowledge, and competence related to the goal" (p. 647). The latter, as well as Zimmerman's framing of psychological empowerment, is consistent with current movements emphasizing the promotion of self-determination to enable people who are marginalized to become causal agents in their lives, through mechanisms such as goal setting, the expression of preferences, self-direction of futures planning, involvement in decision making and problem solving activities (Wehmeyer, 2004b).

Self-Determination, Settings, and Environments

It is clear that the environments in which people with disabilities live, learn, work, and play impact self-determination. Three studies (Duvdevany et al., 2002; Wehmeyer, & Bolding, 1999, 2001) compared levels of self-determination among adults with intellectual or developmental disabilities living or working in community-based settings or more restrictive, non-community based settings. Findings showed that participants who lived and worked in community based settings were more self-determined, had greater autonomy, had more choice opportunities, and were more satisfied than participants in congregate, non-community based settings. Similarly, Wehmeyer, Kelchner, and Richards (1995) found that more restrictive living settings were indicators of significantly lower self-determination levels, even when controlling for level of disability. Confirming that there was a causal relationship between environment and self-determination, Wehmeyer and Bolding (2001) found that moving from a more restrictive work or living settings to less restrictive settings resulted in increased self-determination for people with intellectual disabilities (Wehmeyer, & Bolding, 2001).

Intra-Individual Factors and Self-Determination

Findings with regard to the contribution of intra-individual factors—including age, type of disability, gender, and IQ—to self-determination for people with disabilities has linked choice opportunities, self-determination competencies (e.g., choice-making skill, problem-solving skill, etc.), type and size of living residence, positive adaptive behavior, and higher IQ scores to the positive expression of self-determined behavior (Perry & Felce, 2005; Stancliffe, Abery, & Smith, 2000; Wehmeyer & Garner, 2003; Wehmeyer, Kelchner, & Richards, 1995). Pierson, Carter, Lane, & Glaeser (2008) found that the social skills of students with learning disabilities or emotional disturbance contributed significantly to enhanced self-determination. These researchers also found that level and intensity of problem behaviors were not associated with diminished self-determination when social skills and disability label were taken into account. The suggestion from this finding is that problem behavior may be a means to express one's self-determination (e.g., expressing preferences) for students who have no other means to do so. This hypothesis is supported by Shogren, Faggella-Luby, Bae, & Wehmeyer (2004), who reviewed research pertaining to incorporating choice-making as a component of interventions to decrease problem behavior and found that the addition of a choice-making element into an intervention had positive effects on reducing problem behavior.

As to the impact of age on self-determination, Wehmeyer & Garner (2003) found that age did not predict the membership of adults with intellectual and developmental disabilities in a high or low self-determination group, though age did predict membership in a high or low autonomy group, with older people more likely to be in the high autonomy group. In a sample of students ages 15 to 18, Wehmeyer (1996b) found a consistent trend for higher self-determination scores as a function of increased age.

Data pertaining to differences in self-determination by gender are limited, and findings are mixed. Soresi, Nota, and Ferrari (2004) found, in an Italian sample, that men tended to show a higher degree of self-determination than did women. In a second study with a larger Italian sample, Nota, Soresi, Ferrari, and Wehmeyer (2011), researchers also found that males scored higher on multiple domains of a measure of self-determination. With a sample of adolescents in the United States, however, Wehmeyer (1996b) found no significant differences between males and females on overall self-determination scores, although females scored slightly higher than did their male counterparts. Similarly, Wehmeyer & Garner (2003) found no differences on self-determination scores by gender for 300 people with intellectual and developmental disabilities. Shogren and colleagues (2007) also found no gender differences on several measures of self-determination for adolescents with disabilities in the U.S. Nota and colleagues (2011) suggested that gender, as a factor predicting self-determination, is a proxy for cultural and societal issues that vary both among and within countries, and may have limited utility as a predictor outside of the context in which it is examined.

Carter, Lane, Pierson, and Glaeser (2006) studied the self-determination of adolescents with emotional disturbance and learning disabilities from the perspectives of special educators, parents, and students and found lower ratings of self-determination for adolescents with emotional disturbance. Shogren and colleagues (2007) also determined that self-determination status varied as a function of type or level of disability. Generally, students with intellectual disability differed from students with learning disabilities or other health impairments on several, though not all, indicators of self-determination. That, alone, suggests that cognitive ability is a significant predictor of self-determination. This seems, however, to be only partially correct. Students with more severe cognitive disabilities in the Shogren (2007) study also differed from other students on their inclusion in typical classroom settings, and were disproportionately likely to be educated in segregated settings.

These findings speak to the fact that the relationship between self-determination and intelligence is complex. Wehmeyer & Garner (2003) conducted a discriminant function analysis of predictors for self-determination scores for individuals with intellectual disability and found that only choice opportunity (from among four variables, including IQ scores) predicted membership in a high self-determination group, but that IQ predicted the type and size of living or work environments for this population. That is, people with lower IQs were more likely to live or work in larger,

congregate settings, which research has linked to lower self-determination. It appears that IQ was determinant of the types of environments in which people lived or work, which in turn dictated, to a large degree, features such as choice opportunity that, in turn, hinder self-determination.

Nota, Ferrari, Soresi and Wehmeyer (2007) found statistically significant correlations among IQ scores, self-determination, social abilities, and quality of life for individuals with intellectual disability among an Italian sample. IQ scores significantly correlated with self-determination in daily activities, commitments, and decisions, and with social abilities. The correlations between IQ and self-determination, ranging from 0.16 to 0.20) were consistent with correlations between self-determination and IQ scores in other studies, including Wehmeyer & Garner (2003); that is, statistically significant and positive, but not that meaningful in practice. Nota and colleagues also conducted discriminant function analyses examining contributors to self-determination and quality of life scores, including self-determination, and found that of only adaptive behavior and IQ predicted membership in the high quality of life group. This differed from findings from Wehmeyer & Garner (2003), but the latter study explicitly controlled for type of environment (e.g., in congregate settings only), which the Nota study did not.

The Nota and colleagues (2007) discriminant function analysis examining the contribution of IQ score, age, and adaptive behavior scores to self-determination found that only the IQ score predicted membership, with higher IQ scores predicting membership in the high self-determination group. These findings also differed from those described by Wehmeyer & Garner (2003), though they may not represent diametrically opposed findings. In the Wehmeyer & Garner analysis, only choice opportunity (from among four variables, including IQ score) predicted membership in a high self-determination group. Similarly, a discriminant function analysis of autonomous functioning scores conducted by Wehmeyer & Garner found everything but IQ scores as significant predictors, with higher perceptions of choice opportunity being the most powerful predictor. Choice opportunity was not, however, evaluated in the Nota et al. study.

Self-Determination and Adult Outcomes

Findings from several studies have examined the impact of self-determined behavior on adult outcomes for individuals with disabilities. Wehmeyer, Kelchner, and Richards (1996) found significant differences between individuals who were self-determined and those who were not across multiple behavioral indicators of autonomy and perceptions of control. Two studies examining post-school outcomes for students with disabilities (Wehmeyer & Palmer, 2003; Wehmeyer & Schwartz, 1997) showed that students with higher self-determination scores had more positive post-school outcomes (e.g., financial independence and employment) both one and three years post-graduation.

Wehmeyer and Schwartz (1998) found that self-determination contributed to a more positive quality of life for people with intellectual disabilities, with self-determination scores predicting membership in a high quality of life group. This finding was replicated by Lachapelle and colleagues (2005) with 182 adults with mild intellectual disabilities living in community settings in four countries (Canada, United States, Belgium, France). This study found that essential characteristics of self-determination predicted membership in the high quality of life group and that overall self-determination and quality of life were significantly correlated as were subscale scores.

Martorell, Gutierrez-Recacha, Perda, and Ayuso-Mateos (2008) found that, from multiple predictors of positive employment outcomes for people with intellectual disability, self-determination was among the strongest (and, consistent with the previous discussion pertaining to IQ, that IQ scores were not significant contributors to positive employment outcomes).

Self-Determined Career Development Model

Employment has been the focus of several interventions to promote self-determination. For example, Wehmeyer, Lattimore, Jorgensen, Palmer, Thompson, and Schumaker (2003) developed a model to support self-regulated problem solving and goal setting and attainment leading to employment, titled the *Self-Determined Career Development Model* (SDCDM, derived from the Self-Determined Learning Model of Instruction, described subsequently). Multiple studies (Benitez, Lattimore, & Wehmeyer, 2005; Wehmeyer, et al., 2003) have provided evidence that adults with disabilities implementing the SDCDM could set employment-related goals, design an action plan to achieve those goals, and self-regulate goal progress leading to a positive employment outcome. Devlin (2011) implemented the SDCDM with four adults

with intellectual disability, who were able to set and achieve career-related goals in competitive work settings. Wehmeyer, Parent, Lattimore, Obremski, Poston, and Rousso (2009) implemented the SDCDM as a part of a larger employment planning process designed to enable young women with developmental disabilities to set and attain employment goals related to employment in typical work settings.

Self-Determination and School Outcomes

Promoting the self-determination of students with disabilities has become a best practice in special education (Wehmeyer, Abery, et al., 2003; Wehmeyer, Agran, Hughes, Martin, Mithaug, & Palmer, 2007) for several reasons. As described in detail subsequently, self-determination status has been linked to the attainment of more positive academic goals (Konrad, Fowler, Walker, Test, & Wood, 2007; Fowler, Konrad, Walker, Test, & Wood, 2007; Lee, Wehmeyer, Soukup, & Palmer, 2010). As discussed previously, self-determination has been linked to more positive transition outcomes, including more positive employment and independent living outcomes (Martorell et al., 2008; Wehmeyer & Palmer, 2003; Wehmeyer & Schwartz, 1997) and more positive quality of life and life satisfaction (Lachapelle et al., 2005; Nota et al., 2007; Shogren, Lopez, Wehmeyer, Little, & Pressgrove, 2006; Wehmeyer & Schwartz, 1998).

Research across special education disability categories has established the need for intervention to promote self-determination, documenting that students with intellectual disability (Wehmeyer, Agran, et al., 2007), learning disabilities (Field, Sarver, & Shaw, 2003; Pierson et al., 2008), emotional and behavioral disorders (Carter et al., 2006; Pierson et al., 2008), and autism (Wehmeyer & Shogren, 2008) are less self-determined than their non-disabled peers. This research indicates that teachers believe that teaching students to become more self-determined is important (Carter, Lane, Pierson, & Stang, 2008; Thoma, Pannozzo, Fritton, & Bartholomew, 2008; Wehmeyer, Agran, & Hughes, 2000), and there are numerous curricular and instructional models identified to enable them to provide this instructional focus (Test, Karvonen, Wood, Browder, & Algozzine, 2000; Wehmeyer & Field, 2007).

Self-Determination and Academic Performance

School reform efforts associated with No Child Left Behind and associated federal legislation have emphasized the importance, for all students with disabilities, of having access to a challenging academic curriculum. Among several means to achieve such access, Spooner, Dymond, Smith, and Kennedy (2006) stressed the importance of promoting self-determination. Wehmeyer, Field, Doren, Jones, and Mason (2004) noted that efforts to promote self-determination may be beneficial to gaining access to the general education for two reasons. First, most district standards, particularly student achievement standards, include component elements of instruction to promote self-determination, such as goal setting, problem solving, or decision making, as elements of the standard. As such, promoting self-determination, which involves instruction in areas such as these, provides an entry point for gaining access to the general education curriculum for students with severe disabilities and provides a focal point for classroom-wide instruction. Second, it is hypothesized that students who are more self-determined will, in fact, perform more effectively in the general education curriculum. There is a clear evidence base that teaching students to self-regulate learning or teaching students self-directed learning strategies such as self-monitoring or self-instruction has beneficial outcomes for students with severe disabilities in student goal attainment, problem solving, and student engagement (Agran, Blanchard, Hughes, & Wehmeyer, 2002; Agran, Sinclair, Alper, Cavin, Wehmeyer, & Hughes, 2005; Hughes, Copeland, Agran, Wehmeyer, Rodi, & Presley, 2002). Further, the application of instruction to teach and implement these strategies has been validated as effective in promoting standards-based learning for students with severe disabilities (Wehmeyer, Hughes, Agran, Garner, & Yeager, 2003).

Konrad et al. (2007) conducted a review and synthesis of studies that examined the effects of self-determination interventions on academic skills for students with learning disabilities or attention deficit disorders. They found that interventions incorporating efforts to promote self-management, goal setting, and self-advocacy skills were effective in improving academic skills and outcomes.

Wehmeyer and colleagues have provided evidence that teaching students to self-regulate learning using the Self-Determined Learning Model of Instruction (discussed in greater detail subsequently) (SDLMI; Wehmeyer et al., 2000) results in the attainment of goals linked to the general education curriculum (Agran, Wehmeyer, Cavin, & Palmer, 2010; Lee et al., 2010; Palmer, Wehmeyer, Gipson, & Agran,

2004). Lee, Wehmeyer, Palmer, Soukup and Little (2008) used a pre-post test randomized trial control group design to explore the relationship between the SDLMI and access to the general education curriculum. They randomly assigned 42 students with learning disabilities, ADHD, or emotional and behavioral disorders to a SDLMI treatment group or a control (no intervention) group. They found that students in the treatment group who received instruction using the SDLMI were more likely to achieve goals linked to the general education curriculum. More recently, Shogren, Palmer, Wehmeyer, Williams-Diehm, and Little (2012) conducted cluster or group-randomized trial control group study examining the impact of intervention using the SDLMI on student academic and transition goal attainment and on access to the general education curriculum for 312 students with intellectual disability and learning disabilities. Findings support the efficacy of the model for both goal attainment and access to the general education curriculum, though students varied in the patterns of goal attainment as a function of type of disability.

Intervention to Promote Self-Determination

Several studies have established the efficacy of interventions to promote self-determination. In a meta-analysis of single subject and group subject design studies, Algozzine, Browder, Karvonen, Test, and Wood (2001) found evidence for the efficacy of instruction to promote component elements of self-determined behavior, including self-advocacy, goal setting and attainment, self-awareness, problem-solving skills, and decision-making skills. Cobb, Lehmann, Newman-Gonchar, and Alwell (2009) conducted a narrative meta-synthesis—a narrative synthesis of multiple meta-analytic studies—covering seven existing meta-analyses examining self-determination and concluded that there is sufficient evidence to support the promotion of self-determination as effective.

Wehmeyer, Palmer, Shogren, Williams-Diehm, and Soukup (2010) conducted a randomized trial control group study of the effect of interventions to promote self-determination on the self-determination of high school students receiving special education services under the categorical areas of intellectual disability and learning disabilities. Students in the treatment group ($n = 235$) received instruction using a variety of instructional methods to promote self-determination and student involvement in educational planning meetings over three years, while students in the control group ($n = 132$) received no such intervention. The self-determination of each student was measured using two instruments, The Arc's Self-Determination Scale (Wehmeyer & Kelchner, 1995) and the AIR Self-Determination Scale (Wolman et al., 1994) across three measurement intervals. Using latent growth curve models to examine differences in self-determination across control and treatment groups, Wehmeyer and colleagues (2013) found that students with cognitive disabilities who participated in intervention to promote self-determination over a three-year period showed significantly more positive patterns of growth in their self-determination scores than did students not exposed to interventions to promote self-determination during the same time period.

Self-Determined Learning Model of Instruction

The SDLMI (Mithaug et al., 1998; Wehmeyer, Palmer et al., 2000) was developed to enable teachers to teach students to self-regulate learning and is based on the component elements of self-determination, the process of self-regulated problem solving, and research on student-directed learning. This intervention has been implemented to promote greater access to the general education curriculum for students with disabilities, as well as to promote goal setting and attainment skills and enhance self-determination. The SDLMI is appropriate for use with students with and without disabilities across a wide range of content areas and enables teachers to engage students in the totality of their educational program by increasing opportunities to self-direct learning and, in the process, to enhance student self-determination.

Implementation of the model consists of a three-phase instructional process. Each instructional phase presents a problem to be solved by the student. The student solves each problem by posing and answering a series of four *Student Questions* per phase that students learn, modify to make their own, and apply to reach self-selected goals. Each question is linked to a set of *Teacher Objectives*. Each instructional phase includes a list of *Educational Supports* that teachers can use to enable students to self-direct learning. In each instructional phase, the student is the primary agent for choices, decisions, and actions, even when eventual actions are teacher-directed.

The *Student Questions* are constructed to direct the student through a problem-solving sequence in each instructional phase. The solutions to the

problems in each phase lead to the problem-solving sequence in the next phase. Teachers implementing the model teach students to solve a sequence of problems to construct a means-ends chain—a causal sequence—that moves them from where they are (an actual state of not having their needs and interests satisfied) to where they want to be (a goal state of having those needs and interests satisfied). To answer the questions in this sequence, students must regulate their own problem solving by setting goals to meet needs, constructing plans to meet goals, and adjusting actions to complete plans. Thus, each instructional phase poses a problem the student must solve (*What is my goal? What is my plan? What have I learned?*) by, in turn, solving a series of problems posed by the questions in each phase. The four questions differ from phase to phase but represent identical steps in the problem-solving sequence. That is, students answering the questions must: (1) identify the problem, (2) identify potential solutions to the problem, (3) identify barriers to solving the problem, and (4) identify consequences of each solution. These steps are the fundamental steps in any problem-solving process, and they form the means-end problem-solving sequence represented by the *Student Questions* in each phase and enable the student to solve the problem posed in each instructional phase.

Wehmeyer, Palmer, et al. (2000) conducted a field test of the SDLMI with 21 teachers responsible for the instruction of adolescents receiving special education services in two states, who identified a total of 40 students with mental retardation, learning disabilities, or emotional or behavioral disorders. The field test indicated that the model was effective in enabling students to attain educationally valued goals. In addition, there were significant differences in pre- and postintervention scores on self-determination, with postintervention scores more positive than preintervention scores.

Agran, Blanchard, and Wehmeyer (2000) conducted a study using a single subject design to examine the efficacy of the SDLMI for adolescents with severe disabilities. Students collaborated with their teachers to implement the first phase of the model and, as a result, identified one goal as a target behavior. Prior to implementing the second phase of the model, teachers and researchers collected baseline data on student performance of these goals. At staggered intervals subsequent to baseline data collection, teachers implemented the model with students, and data collection continued through the end of instructional activities and into a maintenance phase. As before, the model enabled teachers to teach students educationally valued goals. In total, 17 of the participants achieved their personal goals at or above the teacher-rated expected outcome levels. Only two students were rated as indicating no progress on the goal.

Two recent studies have established causal evidence for the efficacy of the SDLMI to promote self-determination, access to the general education curriculum, and transition-related goals. Wehmeyer, Shogren, Palmer, Williams-Diehm, Boulton, & Little (2012) conducted a randomized trial control group study of the efficacy of the SDLMI to promote self-determination. Data on self-determination using multiple measures was collected with 312 high school students with cognitive disabilities, half in a control and the other half in a treatment group, and determined that students in the treatment group had significantly higher levels of self-determination as a function of receiving instruction with the model. As discussed previously, Shogren and colleagues (2013) similarly document the efficacy of the SDLMI on student academic and transition goal attainment and access to the general education curriculum.

Interventions to Promote Student Involvement and Self-Determination

Research documents the positive impact of efforts to promote student involvement in educational and transition planning (Martin, Van Dycke, Christensen, Greene, Gardner, & Lovett, 2006; Mason, Field, & Sawilowsky, 2004; Test, Mason, Hughes, Konrad, Neale, & Wood, 2004) on more positive transition and self-determination related outcomes.

Test and colleagues (2004) conducted an extensive review of the literature pertaining to student involvement and determined that students across disability categories can be successfully involved in transition planning, and a number of programs, including those mentioned subsequently, are effective in increasing student involvement. Martin, Marshall, and Sale (2004) conducted a three-year study of middle, junior, and senior high school Individualized Education Program (IEP) meetings and found that the presence of students at IEP meetings had considerable benefits, including increasing parental involvement and improving the probability that a student's strengths, needs, and interests would be discussed. Research (Mason et al., 2004; Wehmeyer, Agran, & Hughes, 2000) has found that

teachers value student involvement, though they fall short of actually implementing practices to promote this outcome.

ChoiceMaker Self-Determination Transition Curriculum and Program

The *ChoiceMaker Self-Determination Transition Curriculum* (Martin & Marshall, 1995) consists of three sections: (1) Choosing Goals, (2) Expressing Goals, and (3) Taking Action. Each section contains two to four teaching goals and numerous teaching objectives addressing six transition areas. Included are: (1) an assessment tool, (2) Choosing Goals lessons, (3) the Self-Directed IEP, and (4) Taking Action lessons. The program includes a criterion-referenced self-determination transition assessment tool that matches the curricular sections. The Choosing Goals lessons enable students to learn the necessary skills and personal information needed to articulate their interests, skills, limits, and goals across one or more self-selected transition areas. The Self-Directed IEP lessons enable students to learn the leadership skills necessary to manage their IEP meetings and publicly disclose their interests, skills, limits, and goals identified through the Choosing Goals lessons. Rather than be passive participants at their IEP meetings, students learn to lead their meetings to the greatest extent of their ability. These lessons teach students 11 steps for leading their own staffing.

The Taking Action materials enable students to learn how to break their long-range goals into specific goals that can be accomplished in a week. Students learn how they will attain their goals by deciding: (1) a standard for goal performance, (2) a means to get performance feedback, (3) what motivates them to do it, (4) the strategies they will use, (5) needed supports, and (6) schedules. There have been several studies examining the efficacy of the *ChoiceMaker* materials (Allen, Smith, Test, Flowers, & Wood, 2001; Cross, Cooke, Wood, & Test, 1999; Snyder, 2002; Snyder & Shapiro, 1997) documenting positive effects on student self-determination, skills in goal setting and leadership, and student involvement in educational planning.

Whose Future Is It Anyway? A Student-Directed Transition Planning Program

Whose Future is it Anyway? (WFA, Wehmeyer, Lawrence, Kelchner, Palmer, Garner, & Soukup, 2004) consists of 36 sessions introducing students to the concept of transition and transition planning and enabling students to self-direct instruction related to (1) self- and disability-awareness; (2) making decisions about transition-related outcomes; (3) identifying and securing community resources to support transition services; (4) writing and evaluating transition goals and objectives; (5) communicating effectively in small groups; and (6) developing skills to become an effective team member, leader, or self-advocate.

The materials are student-directed in that they are written for students as end users. The level of support needed by students to complete activities varies a great deal. Some students with difficulty reading or writing need one-on-one support to progress through the materials; others can complete the process independently. The materials make every effort to ensure that students retain this control while at the same time receiving the support they need to succeed.

Students are encouraged to work on one session per week during the weeks between their previous transition planning meeting and the next scheduled meeting. The final two sessions review the previous sessions and provide a refresher for students as they head into their planning meeting. Wehmeyer & Lawrence (1995) conducted a field test of the process, providing evidence of the impact of the process on student self-determination, self-efficacy for educational planning, and student involvement. More recently, Wehmeyer, Palmer, Lee, Williams-Diehm, & Shogren (2011) conducted a randomized-trial, placebo control group designed to study the impact of intervention with the WFA process on self-determination and transition knowledge and skills, finding that instruction using the WFA process resulted in significant, positive differences in self-determination when compared with a placebo-control group, and that students who received instruction gained transition knowledge and skills. Similarly, Lee, Wehmeyer, Palmer, Williams-Diehm, Davies, & Stock (2011) conducted a randomized-trial study of the impact of the WFA process both with and without the use of technology, and determined significant gains in self-determination and transition knowledge and skills as a function of instruction with WFA.

Conclusions

The application of the self-determination construct to people with disabilities is one area within positive psychology that has received considerable attention. The research provides evidence that people with disabilities are less self-determined than their non-disabled peers, but that if provided with opportunities to learn the skills enabling them to become more self-determined and provided supports that emphasize self-determination, youth and adults with disabilities can become more self-determined. It is important to reemphasize that the fact that people with disabilities are less self-determined than their non-disabled peers is not a statement about the capacity of people with disabilities to become more self-determined, but instead an indictment of the lack of opportunities to learn and practice skills leading to greater self-determination. Enhanced self-determination status has been linked to more positive adult and school-related outcomes, including more positive employment and independent living outcomes and more positive educational goal attainment. Promoting self-determination has become best practice in special education, and there is sufficient evidence that adolescents with disabilities can learn skills such as goal setting, problem solving, and decision making that enable them to become more self-determined young people.

Future Directions

Despite the progress of the past several decades, there are still areas of need with regard to future research and practice. Measurement of self-determination is an area of need for future research and development. There are two widely used norm-referenced assessments of self-determination—*The Arc's Self-Determination Scale* (SDS, Wehmeyer & Kelchner, 1995) and the *AIR Self-Determination Scale* (AIR, Wolman et al., 1994)—that have been normed with students with disabilities, as well as one measure that includes both criterion- and norm-referenced components—the Self-Determination Assessment Battery (Field, Hoffman, and Sawilowsky, 2004). These measures have provided impetus to the field, but are limited in their scope (e.g., not normed for use with or appropriate for students without disabilities) and utility. There is a significant need for new norm-referenced measures of self-determination that can be used with students with and without disabilities and, eventually, with adults with and without disabilities.

A few interventions, such as the SDLMI, have been evaluated using research designs that allow for causal attribution, but there remains a need for both the development of interventions to promote global self-determination and the evaluation of these and other interventions using robust research designs that can both determine the efficacy of the intervention and identify and isolate mediating and moderating variables that impact such interventions.

Third, although considerable progress has been made with regard to efforts to promote the self-determination of youth with disabilities, similar such efforts focused on adults with disabilities are limited. There is a need to develop and evaluate interventions that enable adults with disabilities to become more self-determined that adhere to principles of adult learning. Walker and colleagues (2011) and Wehmeyer and colleagues (2011) have argued that such efforts must be conducted in a social-ecological framework, recognizing that many such efforts will focus on the environments, contexts, and settings in which people with disabilities live, learn, work and play and taking into account the importance of the social context for adult-based interventions.

Fourth, there is a need for more research on component elements of self-determined behavior, such as goal setting, problem solving, and decision making for adolescents and adults with disabilities. There are far too few interventions, assessments, and supports focused at this level of practice. Relatedly, research with particular disability populations is needed to identify what components are most important for that group.

Finally, there is a need for more research with related positive psychological constructs with people with disabilites. There are logical theoretical links between such important positive psychological constructs as hope, optimism, happiness, life satisfaction and well being, and so forth that need to be examined in the context of self-determinaion and people with disabilities.

References

Abery, B., McGrew, K., & Smith, J. (1995). *Validation of an ecological model of self-determination for children with disabilities. Technical Report #2*. Minneapolis, MN University of Minnesota, Institute on Community Integration.

Abery, B. H. & Stancliffe, R. J. (1996). The ecology of self-determination. In D. J. Sands & M. L. Wehmeyer (Eds.), *Self-determination across the life span: Independence and choice for people with disabilities* (pp. 111–145). Baltimore: Paul H. Brookes.

Agran, M., Blanchard, C., & Wehmeyer, M. L. (2000). Promoting transition goals and self-determination through student self-directed learning: The Self-Determined Learning Model of Instruction. *Education and Training in Mental Retardation and Developmental Disabilities, 35*(4), 351–364.

Agran, M., Blanchard, C. Hughes, C., & Wehmeyer, M. L. (2002). Increasing the problem-solving skills of students with severe disabilities participating in general education. *Remedial and Special Education, 23*, 279–288.

Agran, M., Sinclair, T., Alper, S., Cavin, M., Wehmeyer, M., & Hughes, C. (2005). Using self-monitoring to increase following-direction skills of students with moderate to severe disabilities in general education. *Education and Training in Developmental Disabilities, 40*, 3–13.

Agran, M., Wehmeyer, M., Cavin, M., & Palmer, S. (2010). Promoting active engagement in the general education classroom and access to the general education curriculum for students with cognitive disabilities. *Education and Training in Autism and Developmental Disabilities, 45*(2), 163–174.

Algozzine, B., Browder, D., Karvonen, M., Test, D.W., & Wood, W.M. (2001). Effects of intervention to promote self-determination for individuals with disabilities. *Review of Educational Research, 71*, 219–277.

Allen, S.K., Smith, A.C., Test, D.W., Flowers, C., & Wood, W.M. (2001). The effects of "Self-Directed IEP" on student participation in IEP meetings. *Career Development for Exceptional Individuals, 4*, 107–120.

American Heritage Dictionary of the English Language, The (1992). New York: Houghton Mifflin Company.

Angyal, A. (1941). *Foundations for a science of personality*. Cambridge, MA: Harvard University Press.

Bandura, A. B. (1997). *Self-efficacy: The exercise of control*. New York: W.H. Freeman and Co.

Benitez, D., Lattimore, J., & Wehmeyer, M.L. (2005). Promoting the involvement of students with emotional and behavioral disorders in career and vocational planning and decision-making: The Self-Determined Career Development Model. *Behavioral Disorders, 30*, 431–447.

Brandtstädter, J. (1998). Action perspectives on human development. In R. M. Lerner (Ed.), *Theoretical models of human development. Volume 1 of the Handbook of child psychology* (5th ed., pp. 807–863), Editor-in-chief: W. Damon. New York: Wiley.

Bronfenbrenner, U. (1979). *The ecology of human development: experiments by nature and design*. Cambridge MA: Harvard University Press.

Bronfenbrenner, U. (1989). Ecological systems theory. *Annals of Child Development, 6*, 187–249.

Carter, E.W., Lane, K.L., Pierson, M.R., & Glaeser, B. (2006). Self-determination skills and opportunities of transition-age youth with emotional disturbance and learning disabilities. *Exceptional Children, 72*(3), 333–346.

Carter, E.W., Lane, K.L., Pierson, M.R., & Stang, K.K. (2008). Promoting self-determination for transition-age youth: Views of high school general and special educators. *Exceptional Children, 75*(1), 55–70.

Cattaneo, L.B., & Chapman, A.R. (2010). The process of empowerment: A model for use in research and practice. *American Psychologist, 65*(7), 646–659.

Chapman, M. (1984). Intentional action as a paradigm for developmental psychology: A symposium. *Human Development, 27*(3-4), 113–144.

Cobb, B., Lehmann, J., Newman-Gonchar, R., & Allwell, M. (2009). Self-determination for students with disabilities: A narrative metasynthesis. *Career Development for Exceptional Individuals, 32* (2), 108–114.

Cornell University Empowerment Group (1989). Empowerment and family support. *Networking Bulletin, 1*(2), 1–23.

Cross, T., Cooke, N.L., Wood, W.M., & Test, D.W. (1999). Comparison of the effects of MAPS and ChoiceMaker on students' self-determination skills. *Education and Training in Mental Retardation and Developmental Disabilities, 34*,499–510.

Damon, W. (1983). *Social and personality development*. New York: W.W. Norton and Co.

Deci, E. L. (2004). Promoting intrinsic motivation and self-determination in people with mental retardation. In H. Switzky, L. Hickson, R. Schalock, & M.L. Wehmeyer, (Eds.) *Personality and motivational systems in mental retardation: Vol. 28, International Review of Research in Mental Retardation* (pp. 1–31). San Diego, CA: Academic Press.

Deci, E. L. & Ryan, R. M. (2000). The "what" and "why" of goal pursuits: Human needs and the determination of behavior. *Psychological Inquiry, 11*, 227–268.

Deci, E.L., & Ryan, R. M. (2002). *Handbook of self-determination research.* Rochester, NY: University of Rochester Press.

Devlin, P. (2011). Enhancing job performance. *Intellectual and Developmental Disabilities, 49*(4), 221–232.

Duvdevany, I., Ben-Zur, H. and Ambar, A. (2002) Self-determination and mental retardation: is there an association with living arrangement and lifestyle satisfaction? *Mental Retardation, 40*, 379–89.

Field, S., & Hoffman, A. (1994). Development of a model for self-determination. *Career Development for Exceptional Individuals, 17*, 159–169.

Field, S., & Hoffman, A. (2001). *Teaching with integrity, reflection, and self-determination.* Working Paper. Detroit: Wayne State University.

Field, S., & Hoffman, A. (2005). *Steps to Self-Determination,* 2nd edition Austin, TX: ProEd.

Field, S., Sarver, M.D., & Shaw, S.F. (2003). Self-determination: A key to success in postsecondary education for students with learning disabilities. *Remedial and Special Education, 24*(6), 339–349.

Fowler, C.H., Konrad, M., Walker, A.R., Test, D.W., & Wood, W.M. (2007). Self-determination interventions' effects on the academic performance of students with developmental disabilities. *Education and Training in Developmental Disabilities, 42*(3), 270–285.

Gove, P.B. (1967). *Webster's Third New International Dictionary of the English Language Unabridged.* Springfield, MA: Merriam-Webster.

Harter, S. (1999). *The construction of the self: A developmental perspective.* New York, NY: Guilford press.

Hawley, P. H. (1999). The ontogenesis of social dominance: A strategy-based evolutionary perspective. *Developmental Review, 19*, 91–132.

Hawley, P. H., & Little, T. D. (2002). Evolutionary and developmental perspectives on the agentic self. In D. Cervone & W. Mischel (Eds.), *Advances in personality science.* New York, NY: Guilford press.

Hughes, C., Copeland, S. R., Agran, M., Wehmeyer, M. L., Rodi, M. S., & Presley, J. A. (2002). Using self-monitoring to improve performance in general education high school classes. *Education and Training in Mental Retardation and Developmental Disabilities, 37*, 262–271.

Kemerling, G. (2000–2001). John Locke. Philosophy Pages http://www.philosophypages.com/locke/g0.htm. Accessed October 17, 2006.

Konrad, M., Fowler, C.H., Walker, A.R., Test, D.W., & Wood, W.M. (2007). Effects of self-determination interventions on the academic skills of students with learning disabilities. *Learning Disabilities Quarterly, 30*(2), 89–113.

Lachapelle, Y., Wehmeyer, M. L., Haelewyck, M. C., Courbois, Y., Keith, K. D., Schalock, R., Verdugo, M. A. & Walsh, P. N. (2005). The relationship between quality of life and self-determination: an international study. *Journal of Intellectual Disability Research, 49*, 740–744.

Lee, S.H., Wehmeyer, M.L., Palmer, S.B., Soukup, J.H., & Little, T. D. (2008). Self-determination and access to the general education curriculum. *The Journal of Special Education, 42*, 91–107.

Lee, S.H., Wehmeyer, M.L., Soukup, J.H., & Palmer, S.B. (2010). Impact of curriculum modifications on access to the general education curriculum for students with disabilities. *Exceptional Children, 76*(2), 213–233.

Lee, Y., Wehmeyer, M., Palmer, S., Williams-Diehm, K., Davies, D., & Stock, S. (2011). The effect of student-directed transition planning using a computer-based reading support program on the self-determination of students with disabilities. *Journal of Special Education, 45*, 104–117.

Little, T. D. (1998). Sociocultural influences on the development of children's action-control beliefs. In J. Heckhausen & C. S. Dweck (Eds.), *Motivation and self-regulation across the life span* (pp. 281–315). New York: Cambridge University Press.

Little, T. D., Hawley, P. H., Henrich, C. C., & Marsland, K. (2002). Three views of the agentic self: A developmental synthesis. In E. L. Deci and R. M. Ryan (Eds.), *Handbook of self-determination research* (pp. 389–404). Rochester, NY: University of Rochester press.

Little, T. D., Lopez, D. F., & Wanner, B. (2001). Children's action-control behaviors (Coping): A longitudinal validation of the behavioral inventory of strategic control. *Anxiety, Stress, and Coping, 14*, 315–336.

Little, T. D., Snyder, C. R., & Wehmeyer, M. (2006). The agentic self: On the nature and origins of personal agency across the lifespan. In D. K. Mroczek & T. D. Little (Eds.). *Handbook of personality development* (pp. 61–80). Mahwah, NJ: LEA.

Locke, J. (1690). *An essay on human understanding.* (http://www.ilt.columbia.edu/projects/digitexts/locke/understanding/title.html Accessed on December 29, 2011).

Martin, J.E., & Marshall, L.H. (1995). ChoiceMaker: A comprehensive self-determination transition program. *Intervention in School and Clinic, 30*,147–156.

Martin, J.E., Marshall, L.H., & Sale, P. (2004). A 3-year study of middle, junior high, and high school IEP meetings. *Exceptional Children, 70*, 285–297.

Martin, J.E., Van Dycke, J.L., Christensen, W.R., Greene, B.A., Gardner, J.E., & Lovett, D.L. (2006). Increasing student participation in IEP meetings: Establishing the Self-Directed IEP as an evidenced-based practice. *Exceptional Children, 72*(3), 299–316.

Martorell, A., Gutierrez-Recacha, P., Perda, A., & Ayuso-Mateos, J.L. (2008). Identification of personal factors that determine work outcome for adults with intellectual disability. *Journal of Intellectual Disability Research, 52*(12), 1091–1101.

Mason, C., Field, S., & Sawilowsky, S. (2004). Implementation of self-determination activities and student participation in IEPs. *Exceptional Children, 70*, 441–451.

McWhirter, E. H. (1991). Empowerment in counseling. *Journal of Counseling & Development, 69*, 222–227.

Mithaug, D. E. (1993). *Self-regulation theory: How optimal adjustment maximizes gain.* Westport, CT: Praeger.

Mithaug, D. (1996a). *Equal opportunity theory.* Thousand Oaks, CA: Sage Publications.

Mithaug, D. (1996b). The optimal prospects principle: A theoretical basis for rethinking instructional practices for self-determination. In D. J. Sands & M. L. Wehmeyer (Eds.), *Self-determination across the life span: Independence and choice for people with disabilities* (pp. 147–165). Baltimore: Paul H. Brookes.

Mithaug, D. (1998). Your right, my obligation? *Journal of the Association for Persons with Severe Disabilities*, 23, 41–43.

Mithaug, D., Campeau, P., & Wolman, J. (1992). *Self-determination assessment project*. Unpublished grant proposal.

Mithaug, D., Wehmeyer, M. L., Agran, M., Martin, J., & Palmer, S., (1998). The self-determined learning model of instruction: Engaging students to solve their learning problems. In M. L. Wehmeyer & D. J. Sands (Eds.), *Making it Happen: Student Involvement in Educational Planning, Decision-Making and Instruction* (pp. 299–328). Baltimore: Brookes Publishers.

Nirje, B. (1972). The right to self-determination. In W. Wolfensberger, (Ed.), *Normalization: The principle of normalization* (pp. 176–200). Toronto: National Institute on Mental Retardation.

Nota, L., Ferrrari, L., Soresi, S., & Wehmeyer, M.I. (2007). Self-determination, social abilities, and the quality of life of people with intellectual disabilities. *Journal of Intellectual Disability Research*, 51, 850–865.

Nota, L., Soresi, S., Ferrari, L., & Wehmeyer, M.I. (2011). A multivariate analysis of the self-determination of adolescents. *Journal of Happiness Studies*, 12(2), 245–266.

Palmer, S.B., Wehmeyer, M.L., Gipson, K., & Agran, M. (2004). Promoting access to the general curriculum by teaching self-determination skills. *Exceptional Children*, 70, 427–439.

Perry, J. & Felce, D. (2005) Correlation between subjective and objective measures of outcome in staffed community housing. *Journal of Intellectual Disability Research*, 49, 278–287.

Perske, R. (1972). The dignity of risk. In W. Wolfensberger (Ed.), *Normalization: The principle of normalization in human services* (pp. 194–200). Toronto, Ontario, Canada: National institute on Mental Retardation.

Pierson, M.R., Carter, E.W., Lane, K.L., & Glaeser, B.C. (2008). Factors influencing the self-determination of transition-age youth with high-incidence disabilities. *Career Development for Exceptional Individuals*, 31(2), 115–125.

Powers, L.E., Sowers, J., Turner, A., Nesbitt, M., Knowles, E., & Ellison, R. (1996). TAKE CHARGE! A model for promoting self-determination among adolescents with challenges. In L.E. Powers, G.H.S. Singer, & J. Sowers (Eds.), *On the road to autonomy: Promoting self-competence in children and youth with disabilities* (pp. 291–332). Baltimore: Paul H. Brookes Publishing Co.

Powers, L.E., Turner, A., Matuszewski, J., Wilson, R., & Phillips, A. (2001). TAKE CHARGE for the future: A controlled field-test of a model to promote student involvement in transition planning. *Career Development for Exceptional Individuals*, 24, 89–103.

Rappaport, J. (1981). In praise of a paradox: A social policy of empowerment over prevention. *American Journal of Community Psychology*, 9, 1–25.

Rappaport, J. (1987). Terms of empowerment/exemplars of prevention: Toward a theory for community psychology. *American Journal of Community Psychology*, 15, 121–148.

Reis, H. T., Sheldon, K. M., Gable, S. L., Roscoe, J., & Ryan, R. M. (2000). Daily well-being: the role of autonomy, competence, and relatedness. *Personality and Social Psychology Bulletin*, 26, 419–435.

Ryan, R. M., & Deci, E. L. (2000-). Self-determination theory and the facilitation of intrinsic motivation, social development, and well-being. *American Psychologist*, 55, 68–78.

Ryan, R. M., & Deci, E. L. (2002). An overview of self-determination theory: An organismic-dialectical perspective. In E. L. Deci & R. M. Ryan (Eds.), *Handbook of self-determination research* (pp. 3–36). Rochester, NY: University of Rochester press.

Ryan, R. M., & Deci, E. L. (2004). Autonomy is no illusion: Self-determination theory and the empirical study of authenticity, awareness, and will. In J. Greenberg, S. L. Koole & T. Pyszczynski (Eds.), *Handbook of experimental existential psychology* (pp. 449–479). New York: The Guilford Press.

Sigafoos, A. D., Feinstein, C. B., Damond, M., & Reiss, D. (1988). The measurement of behavioral autonomy in adolescence: The Autonomous Functioning Checklist. In C. B. Feinstein, A. Esman, J. Looney, G. Orvin, J. Schimel, A. Schwartzberg, A. Sorsky & M. Sugar (Eds.), *Adolescent Psychiatry, Volume 15* (pp. 432–462). Chicago: University of Chicago Press.

Sheldon, K. M., Ryan, R. M., Deci, E. L., & Kasser, T. (2004). The independent effects of goal contents and motives on well-being: It's both what you pursue and why you pursue it. *Personality and Social Psychology Bulletin*, 30, 475–486.

Shogren, K., Faggella-Luby, M., Bae, S.J., & Wehmeyer, M.I. (2004). The effect of choice-making as an intervention for problem behavior: A meta-analysis. *Journal of Positive Behavior Interventions*, 6, 228–237.

Shogren, K. A., Lopez, S. J., Wehmeyer, M. L., Little, T. D., & Pressgrove, C. L. (2006). The role of positive psychology constructs in predicting life satisfaction in adolescents with and without cognitive disabilities: An exploratory study. *Journal of Positive Psychology*, 1, 37–52.

Shogren, K., Palmer, S., Wehmeyer, M.I., Williams-Diehm, K., & Little, T. (2012). Effect of intervention with the *Self-Determined Learning Model of Instruction* on access and goal attainment. *Remedial and Special Education*, 33(5), 320–330.

Shogren, K. A., Wehmeyer, M. L., Palmer, S. B., Soukup, J. H., Little, T. D., Garner, N. & Lawrence, M. (2007). Examining individual and ecological predictors of the self-determination of students with disabilities. *Exceptional Children*, 73, 488–509.

Shogren, K.A., Wehmeyer, M.L., Palmer, S.B., Soukup, J.H., Little, T., Garner, N., & Lawrence, M. (2008). Understanding the construct of self-determination: Examining the relationship between The Arc's Self-Determination Scale and the American Institute for Research Self-Determination Scale. *Assessment for Effective Instruction*, 33, 94–107.

Skinner, E. A. (1995). *Perceived control, motivation, and coping*. Beverly Hills, CA: Sage.

Skinner, E. A. (1996). A guide to constructs of control. *Journal of Personality and Social Psychology*, 71(3), 549–570.

Skinner, E. A., & Edge, K. (2002). Self-determination, coping, and development. In E. L. Deci and R. M. Ryan (Eds.), *Handbook of Self-Determination Research* (pp. 297–338). Rochester, NY: University of Rochester press.

Snyder, E.P. (2002). Teaching students with combined behavioral disorders and mental retardation to lead their own IEP meetings. *Behavioral Disorders*, 27, 340–357.

Snyder, E.P., & Shapiro, E.S. (1997). Teaching students with emotional/behavioral disorders the skills to participate in the development of their own IEPs. *Behavioral Disorders*, 22, 246–259.

Soresi, S., Nota, L., & Ferrari, L. (2004). Autodeterminazione e scelte scolastico-professionali: uno strumento per l'assessment [Self-determination and school-career choices: an instrument for the assessment]. *Giornale Italiano di Psicologia dell'Orientamento*, 5, 26–42.

Sowers, J., & Powers, L. (1995). Enhancing the participation and independence of students with severe physical and multiple disabilities in performing community activities. *Mental Retardation*, *33*, 209–220.

Spooner, F., Dymond, S.K., Smith, A., & Kennedy, C.H. (2006). What we know and need to know about accessing the general curriculum for students with significant cognitive disabilities. *Research and Practice for Persons with Severe Disabilities*, *31*(4), 277–283.

Stancliffe, R. J., Abery B. H., & Smith, J. (2000). Personal control and the ecology of community living settings: Beyond living-unit size and type. *American Journal on Mental Retardation*, *105*, 431–454.

Test, D. W., Karvonen, M., Wood, W. M., Browder, D., & Algozzine, B. (2000). Choosing a self-determination curriculum: Plan for the future. *Teaching Exceptional Children*, *33*, 48–54.

Test, D.W., Mason, C., Hughes, C., Konrad, M., Neale, M., & Wood, W. (2004). Student involvement in individualized education program meetings. *Exceptional Children*, *70*, 391–412.

Thoma, C.A., Pannozzo, G.M., Fritton, S.C., Bartholomew, C.C. (2008). A qualitative study of preservice teachers" understanding of self-determination for students with significant disabilities. *Career Development for Exceptional Individuals*, *31*(2), 94–105.

VandenBos, G. R. (2007). *APA Dictionary of Psychology*. Washington, DC: APA.

Vanlede, M., Little, T. D., & Card, N. A. (2006). Action-control beliefs and behaviors as predictors of change in adjustment across the transition to middle school. *Anxiety, Stress, and Coping*, *19*, 111–127.

Walker, H.M., Calkins, C., Wehmeyer, M., Walker, L., Bacon, A., Palmer, S. …Johnson, D. (2011). A social-ecological approach to promote self-determination. *Exceptionality*, *19*, 6–18.

Walls, T. A. & Little, T. D. (2005). Relations among personal agency, motivation, and school adjustment in early adolescence. *Journal of Educational Psychology*, *97*, 23–31.

Wehmeyer, M. L. (1996a). Self-determination as an educational outcome: Why is it important to children, youth and adults with disabilities? In D.J. Sands & M.L. Wehmeyer (Eds.), *Self-determination across the life span: Independence and choice for people with disabilities* (pp. 15–34). Baltimore, MD: Paul H. Brookes.

Wehmeyer, M. L. (1996b). A self-report measure of self-determination for adolescents with cognitive disabilities. *Education and Training in Mental Retardation and Developmental Disabilities*, *31*, 282–293.

Wehmeyer, M. L. (2001). Self-determination and mental retardation. In L. M. Glidden (Ed.), *International review of research in mental retardation* (Vol 24, pp. 1–48). San Diego, CA: Academic Press.

Wehmeyer, M.L. (2004a). Beyond self-determination: Causal Agency Theory. *Journal of Developmental and Physical Disabilities*, *16*, 337–359.

Wehmeyer, M.L. (2004b). Self-determination and the empowerment of people with disabilities. *American Rehabilitation*, *28*, 22–29.

Wehmeyer, M. L. (2005). Self-determination and individuals with severe disabilities: Reexamining meanings and misinterpretations. *Research and Practice in Severe Disabilities*, *30*, 113–120.

Wehmeyer, M.L., Avery, B., Matthau, D.E., & Stancliffe, R.J. (2003). *Theory in self-determination: Foundations for educational practice*. Springfield, IL: Charles C Thomas Publisher, LTD.

Wehmeyer, M.L., Abery, B., Zhang, D., Ward, K., Willis, D., Amin, W.H. … Walker, H. (2011). Personal self-determination and moderating variables that impact efforts to promote self-determination. *Exceptionality*, *19*, 19–30.

Wehmeyer, M. L., Agran, M., & Hughes, C. (2000). A national survey of teachers' promotion of self-determination and student-directed learning. *Journal of Special Education*, *34*, 58–68.

Wehmeyer, M.L., Agran, M., Hughes, C., Martin, J., Mithaug, D.E., & Palmer, S. (2007). *Promoting self-determination in students with intellectual and developmental disabilities*. New York: Guilford Press.

Wehmeyer, M. L., & Bolding, N. (1999). Self-determination across living and working environments: A matched-samples study of adults with mental retardation. *Mental Retardation*, *37*, 353–363.

Wehmeyer, M. L., & Bolding, N. (2001). Enhanced self-determination of adults with mental retardation as an outcome of moving to community-based work or living environments. *Journal of Intellectual Disability Research*, *45*, 1–13.

Wehmeyer, M.L., & Field, S. (2007). *Self-determination: I nstructional and Assessment Strategies*. Thousand Oaks, CA: Corwin Press.

Wehmeyer, M.L., Field, S., Doren, B., Jones, B., & Mason, C. (2004). Self-determination and student involvement in standards-based reform. *Exceptional Children*, *70*, 413–425.

Wehmeyer, M.L., & Garner, N. W. (2003). The impact of personal characteristics of people with intellectual and developmental disability on self-determination and autonomous functioning. *Journal of Applied Research in Intellectual Disabilities*, *16*, 255–265.

Wehmeyer, M.L., Hughes, C., Agran, M., Garner. N., & Yeager, D. (2003). Student-directed learning strategies to promote the progress of students with intellectual disability in inclusive classrooms. *International Journal of Inclusive Education*, *7*, 415–428.

Wehmeyer, M. L., & Kelchner, K. (1995). *The Arc's Self-Determination Scale*. Arlington, TX: The Arc National Headquarters.

Wehmeyer, M. L., Kelchner, K., & Richards. S. (1996). Essential characteristics of self-determined behaviors of adults with mental retardation and developmental disabilities. *American Journal on Mental Retardation*, *100*, 632–642.

Wehmeyer, M., Lattimore, J., Jorgensen, J., Palmer, S., Thompson, E., & Schumaker, K.M. (2003). The Self-Determined Career Development Model: A pilot study. *Journal of Vocational Rehabilitation*, *19*, 79–87.

Wehmeyer, M.L., & Lawrence, M. (1995). Whose future is it anyway? Promoting student involvement in transition planning. *Career Development for Exceptional Individuals*, *18*, 69–83.

Wehmeyer, M., Lawrence, M., Kelchner, K., Palmer, S., Garner, N., & Soukup, J. (2004). *Whose future is it anyway? A student-directed transition planning process* (2nd ed.). Lawrence, KS: Beach Center on Disability.

Wehmeyer, M. L., Lopez, S., & Shogren, K. (2005). *The Adolescent Self-Determination Scale*. Lawrence, KS: Author.

Wehmeyer, M. L., & Mithaug, D. (2006). Self-determination, causal agency, and mental retardation. In L. M. Glidden (Series Ed.) & H. Swtizky (Vol. Ed), *International Review of*

Research in Mental Retardation: Vol. 31 Current Perspectives on Individual Differences in Personality and Motivation in Persons with Mental Retardation and Other Developmental Disabilities (pp. 31–71). San Diego, CA: Academic Press.

Wehmeyer, M. L., & Palmer, S. (2003). Adult outcomes for students with cognitive disabilities three-years after high school: The impact of self-determination. *Education and Training in Developmental Disabilities, 38*(2), 131–144.

Wehmeyer, M. L., Palmer, S. B., Agran, M., Mithaug, D. E., & Martin, J. (2000). Teaching students to become causal agents in their lives: The self-determining learning model of instruction. *Exceptional Children, 66*, 439–453.

Wehmeyer, M.L., Palmer, S.B., Lee, Y., Williams-Diehm, K., & Shogren, K.A. (2011). A randomized-trial evaluation of the effect of Whose Future is it Anyway? on self-determination. *Career Development for Exceptional Individuals, 34*(1), 45–56.

Wehmeyer, M.L., Palmer, S., Shogren, K., Williams-Diehm, K., & Soukup, J. (2013). Establishing a causal relationship between interventions to promote self-determination and enhanced student self-determination. *Journal of Special Education, 46*, 195–210. doi:10.1177/0022466910392377

Wehmeyer, M.L., Parent, W., Lattimore, J., Obremski, S., Poston, D., & Rousso, H. (2009). Promoting self-determination and self-directed employment planning for young women with disabilities. *Journal of Social Work in Disability and Rehabilitation, 8*(3-4), 117–131.

Wehmeyer, M. L., & Schwartz, M. (1997). Self-determination and positive adult outcomes: A follow-up study of youth with mental retardation or learning disabilities. *Exceptional Children, 63*, 245–255.

Wehmeyer, M. L. & Schwartz, M. (1998). The relationship between self-determination, quality of life, and life satisfaction for adults with mental retardation. *Education and Training in Mental Retardation and Developmental Disabilities, 33*, 3–12.

Wehmeyer, M.L., & Shogren, K. (2008). Self-determination and learners with autism spectrum disorders. In R. Simpson & B. Myles (Eds.), *Educating Children and Youth with Autism: Strategies for Effective Practice* (2nd Ed.)(pp. 433–476). Austin, TX: ProEd Publishers, Inc.

Wehmeyer, M.L., Shogren, K., Palmer, S., Williams-Diehm, K., Little, T., & Boulton, A. (2012). The impact of the Self-Determined Learning Model of Instruction on student self-determination. *Exceptional Children, 78*(2), 135–153.

White, R. W. (1959). Motivation reconsidered: The concept of competence. *Psychological Review, 66*, 297–333.

Whitman, T. L. (1990). Self-regulation and mental retardation. *American Journal on Mental Retardation, 94*, 347–362.

Wolfensberger, W. (1972). *Normalization: The principle of normalization*. Toronto: National Institute on Mental Retardation.

Wolman, J., Campeau, P., Dubois, P., Mithaug, D., & Stolarski, V. (1994). *AIR Self-Determination Scale and user guide*. Palo Alto, CA: American Institute for Research.

Zimmerman, M. A. (1990). Toward a theory of learned hopefulness: A structural model analysis of participation and empowerment. *Journal of Research in Personality, 24*, 71–86.

Zimmerman, M.A. & Rappaport, J. (1988). Citizen participation, perceived control, and psychological empowerment. *American Journal of Community Psychology, 16*, 725–750.

Self-Determined Learning

Dennis E. Mithaug

Abstract

Self-determined learning is a function of three interacting factors: self-interest that, which motivates thinking and responding; self-regulation that, which controls and coordinates that thinking and responding; and persistence of repeated adjustment to results that maximizes learning. This chapter presents evidence that when these patterns are present early in childhood, prospects for later success are greatly improved. However, this rarely occurs for children youth with disabilities, as results from national longitudinal studies of special education outcomes indicate. Instead, in special education classrooms, students are more likely to follow directions to learn than to self-regulate to learn. The recommended solution is based on self-determined learning theory that explains how self-interest, self-regulation, and persistent adjustment maximize learning and self-instruction pedagogy that teaches these behaviors. The chapter concludes that study skills classes available in schools nationwide provide key opportunities for special education teachers to help students with disabilities become self-determined learners.

Key Words: self-determined learning, self-interest, self-regulation, persistent adjustment, special education achievement outcomes, self-determined learning theory, maximizing learning, self-instruction pedagogy, self-regulation cards, study skills classes

Most of what we learn in life is self- not teacher-determined; it is learning that serves our interests, whatever they may be, and it is controlled by us as we adjust to new circumstances and make the unpredictable predictable and the undesirable desirable. The learning determined by teachers is usually in classrooms and short lived, confined to the hours we spend receiving advice, directions, and feedback. It is learning from structured opportunities, often limited in relevance and application to changing circumstances in daily life. Even so, this mode of learning dominates instructional practice by focusing on what teachers can do to improve their instruction so that they understand what learners should do and when they've done it correctly. This chapter focuses on the learning that occurs when teachers are not present for direct instruction.

The first part describes self-determined learning. The second describes what occurs when it is absent or occurs too infrequently to make a difference in adjustment to challenge. The third shows how self-determined learning theory, its self-instruction principles, and learning to learn strategies help children and youth with disabilities learn how to learn. The last part identifies a nationwide educational opportunity for teachers to deliver this type of instruction to the students who need it the most.

What Is Self-Determined Learning?

The three factors that define self-determined learning are *self-interest, self-regulation*, and *persistent adjustment*. When learners exhibit them together, they are engaged in self-determined learning. When any of the three are absent, children are less engaged in self-determined learning, but are more likely engaged in a version of other-directed learning, with another person determining the interests to be served, the behaviors to be emitted, or the adjustments to be made. Self-determined learning occurs when an individual's interests drive the regulation of thoughts and actions required to produce desired outcomes. By contrast, other-determined learning is direction-delivered instruction about the thoughts and actions required for a learner to learn. The difference is the agent in control. In teacher-determined learning, teachers are the controllers; in self-determined learning, students are.

The Interest Factor

Learner interest in the behaviors and outcomes of what is to be learned is necessary for learning to occur. Indeed, there are shades and degrees of self-interest present in all such pursuits. Figures 11.1 through 11.5 represent some variations. Figure 11.1 illustrates the least motivating situation, with the learner being required to emit uninteresting behaviors to produce outcomes that are also of marginal interest. Little learning is likely in these situations. Figure 11.2 is slightly more appealing, with the learner required to emit behaviors to produce required outcomes that ultimately lead to an intrinsically valuable outcome. An example of this is when we take uninteresting courses in order to graduate and get a degree. We learn what we must but little else. Figure 11.3 represents a substantially more interesting situation, with intrinsically valuable outcomes resulting from behaviors that are not particularly interesting. The work-then-play contingency in

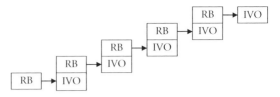

Figure 11.3 Suboptimal self-determined learning: Required Behaviors (RB), Intrinsically Valuable Outcomes (IVO).

effect at home, school, and work is a good example. Required behaviors provide access to intrinsically valuable outcomes. Motivation to learn depends on the consequences of acting in a prescribed way.

Figure 11.4 is closer to optimal, with intrinsically motivating behaviors producing immediate outcomes that are marginally valuable to the learner. People who enjoy interacting with others may be intrinsically motivated to sell insurance, used cars, or men's shoes because those jobs require social interactions that are enjoyable, although the required result, making a sale, is not. The pay check at the end of the month is also motivating. Even so, there is enough that is intrinsically valuable to motivate learning. Figure 11.5 represents the most powerful of these contingencies. Here, the behaviors are intrinsically motivating and the outcomes are intrinsically valuable. People pursuing their talents in jobs they love are usually self-determined learners. The behaviors required to produce learning are intrinsically rewarding, as are the results of those behaviors. Musicians enjoy practicing to perfect their skills as much as they enjoy displaying their talents at concerts. Baseball players enjoy hitting, throwing, and

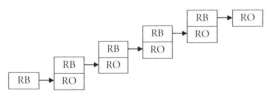

Figure 11.1 Other-determined learning: Required Behaviors (RB) and Required Outcomes (RO).

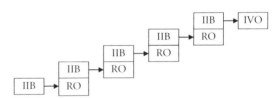

Figure 11.4 Optimal self-determined learning: Intrinsically Interesting Behaviors (IIB) Required Behaviors (RB), Intrinsically Valuable Outcome (IVO).

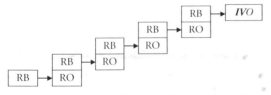

Figure 11.2 Suboptimal self-determined learning: Required Behaviors (RB), Required Outcomes (RO), Intrinsically Valuable Outcome (IVO).

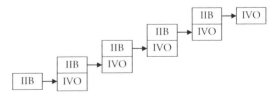

Figure 11.5 Optimal self-determined learning: Intrinsically Interesting Behaviors (IIB) and Intrinsically Valuable Outcomes (IVO).

catching baseballs as well as using those skills to win baseball games and earn money.

This is how intrinsic interests define what is self-determined learning and what isn't. Learners become self-determined to the extent that they make connections between a learning requirement and their interests, a condition teachers often strive to establish when they assign work that is consistent with student interests. Some go a step further by allowing students to choose topics that reflect their interests, with the purpose of provoking as much intrinsic motivation as possible for the learning ahead.

The Self-Regulation Factor

But interests alone do not produce learning. The right behaviors must occur in the right way. This is likely when teachers give good directions and guidance, or when learners have good self-regulation skills. Either way, the behaviors required for learning occur purposefully and correctly rather than impulsively, erratically, randomly, and inaccurately, as is often the case among young children who lack sufficient control to learn on their own. According to several studies, children who fail to develop necessary self-control levels end up as adults unable to learn sufficiently to get what they need or want later in life. This was the finding of the now classic study by Mischel, Shoda, and Rodriguez (1989), who conducted the Marshmallow Test to assess the self-control of 4-year-olds. They found that some children were able to resist the impulse to grab marshmallows when they were available and other children were not. The first group became known as *waiters* and the second as *grabbers*. In a follow-up of these children more than a decade later, Mischel and his colleagues found that grabbers were poor self-regulators and were seen by others as being stubborn, overactive, envious, jealous, easily upset, and troubled with low self-esteem. In contrast, the waiters, who were good self-regulators early on, were later seen as competent, self-assertive, socially adjusted, adaptable in difficult situations, dependable, and academically successful.

In a related longitudinal follow-up study, Duckworth and Seligman (2006) reported on the self-regulation behaviors of 140 eighth-grade students and a replication study involving 186 eighth graders. They wanted to determine whether IQ scores and levels of self-discipline correlated with academic achievement. Using several measures, including self-reports, parent reports, teacher reports, and questionnaires about final grades, school attendance, achievement-test scores, and others, they found that self-discipline measured in the fall accounted for more than twice as much variance as IQ for final grades, high school selection, school attendance, hours spent doing homework, hours spent watching television (inversely), and time of day students began their homework. This relationship also held when there were controls for grades, test scores, and measured IQ. Indeed, self-discipline was twice as robust as IQ in predicting achievement, with a 0.67 correlation between self-discipline and grade point average (GPA) compared to a 0.32 correlation between IQ and GPA. A regression analyses also indicated that self-discipline accounted for twice as much variance in GPA as did IQ. The researchers concluded that students were more likely to fall short of reaching their full intellectual potential because of failures in self-discipline than because of limitations in intellectual capacity.

In another longitudinally study, Moffitt (2011) evaluated the self-control of 1,037 children born in 1972 and 1973 in Dunedin, New Zealand. They collected data on levels of attention, persistence, and impulsiveness in a variety of settings. Then they conducted a follow-up of the children when they reached 32 years of age and found that, after controlling for factors such as intelligence and socioeconomic status, those with lower self-control levels as children were more likely as adults to have poor health, be single parents, depend on drugs or alcohol, have difficulties with money, and possess a criminal record. In another study evaluating the self-control characteristics of 509 pairs of British twins born in 1994 and 1995, theses researchers found that the twin with less self-control at age 5 was more likely to be smoking, behaving badly, and struggling in school at age 12. Moffitt concluded that the more self-control a child exhibited, the better adjusted that child was as an adult.

The Persistence Factor

This third characteristic of self-determined learning is sometimes equated with "determination," in the sense being steadfast, unswerving, and perhaps even stubborn in the face of hardship or difficulty. This is not the meaning intended here. During self-determined learning, persistence refers to the *continuous regulation of thoughts and actions* to produce a desired outcome. Learners with this capability persist in the regulation of their thoughts and actions until they find a pattern that produces the outcome they seek. Self-interest is their motivation, self-regulation is their problem solving, and persistent adjustment is their means of discovering what works and what doesn't. This is what they learn. These patterns of behavior were not evident among children who failed the Marshmallow Test. They failed to regulate their behaviors persistently to reach the more distant goals set by the waiters. They acted immediately to get what they wanted. The waiters, by contrast, engaged in various patterns of persistent adjustment of wait responding to reach more ambitious goals.

In nearly every school, there are a few such students who spend a significant amount of time practicing a talent, sport, or subject area of interest. These learners are self-determined in that they persistently adjust their thoughts and actions to get to some distant end point. Although they are a minority in most schools, they are well represented among those who achieve and succeed throughout life. They are also well represented in historical accounts of the rich and famous, as Napoleon Hill (1960) first described them more than half century ago:

> What mystical power gives to men of persistence the capacity to master difficulties? Does the quality of persistence set up in one's mind some form of spiritual, mental, or chemical activity which gives one access to supernatural forces? Does Infinite Intelligence throw itself on the side of the person who still fights on, after the battle has been lost, with the whole world on the opposing side?
>
> These and many other similar questions have arisen in my mind as I have observed men like Henry Ford, who started at scratch, and built an industrial empire of huge proportions, and little else in the way of a beginning but persistence. Or, Thomas A. Edison, who, with less than three months of schooling, became the world's leading inventor and converted persistence into the talking machine, the moving picture machine, and the incandescent light, to say nothing of half a hundred other useful inventions.
>
> I had the happy privilege of analyzing both Mr. Edison and Mr. Ford, year by year, over a long period of years, and therefore, the opportunity to study them at close range, so I speak from actual knowledge when I say *that I found no quality save persistence, in either of them, that even remotely suggested the major source of their stupendous achievement.* (p. 49; emphasis added)

The Learning to Learn Problem

Given this understanding of self-determined learning, we might expect an absence of the capacity to self-direct and persist to relate to underachievement among students with and without disabilities. This appears to be the case as well. Zimmerman and Martinez-Pons (1986), for example, studied this relationship between self-regulation and achievement in secondary general education students and found that students with high levels of self-regulation were 93% more likely to be in a high achievement groups than were students lacking those capabilities. Whitman (1990) similarly observed that students with disabilities lacked the "complex response system that enables individuals to examine their environments and their repertories of responses for coping with those environments, to make plans (decisions) about how to act, to evaluate the desirability of the outcomes of their actions, and to revise their plans as necessary" (p. 373). Eisenberger, Conti-D'Antonio, and Bertrando (2000) made similar observations of students with learning disabilities:

> Students with learning disabilities may not approach tasks with a plan of action nor be able to estimate accurately how much time a task will require. Some of these students may exhibit disorganized thinking and have problems in planning, organizing, and controlling their lives in academic and social settings. Their school performance, when compared with their ability, may be poor. This issue may be evidenced on report cards that are rife with Ds and Fs. The work that they do may be incomplete or of poor quality. They may attribute their lack of work to personal feelings, require adult intervention and "help" before making an attempt, or avoid tasks completely by treating teachers and other adults as enemies to fight. They often have no strategies for comprehending, retrieving, or using information. They may have a tendency to complete only work that is effortless and openly complain if work requires effort. They behave as though they have no influence over how they live their lives. These are students who have not developed self-efficacy, they don't believe that they have the abilities needed to produce quality work through sustained effort. Because these students approach difficult tasks without self-efficacy, they make very poor use of their capabilities. (pp. 33–34)

Studies of the relationship between disability and self-regulation support these assertions. In one comparison, students from general and special education classes played a computer game that provided repeated opportunities to plan, act, monitor, evaluate, and adjust to meet self-set goals. The results indicated that students from general education classes were significantly more effective self-regulators than were students from special education classes (Mithaug

& Mithaug, 2003). In another study that surveyed these behaviors in 450 students with and without disabilities across several states, Mithaug, Campeau, and Wolman (2003) reported that teacher ratings of self-regulation behaviors (self-planning, self-monitoring, self-evaluating, and self-adjusting) were significantly higher for students without disabilities than for students with disabilities. Silfen (2009) also found that the self-regulation behaviors of 151 fourth-grade students from ethnically diverse neighborhoods in a New York City elementary school explained more than 70% of the variance in class placements. Students receiving lower self-regulation scores were more likely to be enrolled in special education classes. In fact, self-regulation and self-determination indicators were better predictors of class placement than were background characteristics such as age, learning disability, underachievement, and school adjustment. Students scoring lower on self-determination indicators were also more likely to be placed in special education classes. Caraher (2010) reported related findings in a study of general and special education teachers who assessed their students' levels of engagement, self-regulation, and achievement. He found that teacher reports of student levels of self-regulation were the most robust predictors of achievement. And although student engagement was not a significant predictor of achievement, it predicted more that 34% of the variance in self-regulation, which was a significant predictor. Student-directedness and use of unmodified curricula were also significant predictors of self-regulation.

Studies such these clarify the importance of findings from the national longitudinal follow-up studies of special education progress, which include the 1991 National Longitudinal Transition Study (NLTS), the 2000 Special Education Elementary Longitudinal Study (SEELS, 2007), and the 2001 National Longitudinal Transition Study (NLTS2). Figures 11.6 through 11.9 were constructed from online data tables available from the NLTS2 study to profile the self-regulation behaviors of students with disabilities nationally. Figure 11.6 presents percentages of students with disabilities by grade level who frequently engage in five self-regulation behaviors: how often these students complete homework on time, perform up to their ability, persist on a task, seek help to improve, and work independently. As indicated in the chart, only about 30% frequently exhibit these behaviors, with those levels decreasing somewhat from first to twelfth grades. The data in Figure 11.7 comparing these behaviors for students with disabilities in special and general education classes indicate that students are more likely to exhibit self-regulation behaviors in general than in special education classes. Figure 11.8 indicates that students with disabilities are more likely to follow directions than do things on their own even when difficult, a pattern that is constant across grade levels. Indeed, these students are twice as likely to follow directions (teacher-directed behaviors) than do things on own even when difficult (self-regulated behaviors). Overall, about a fourth of students with disabilities exhibit self-regulated

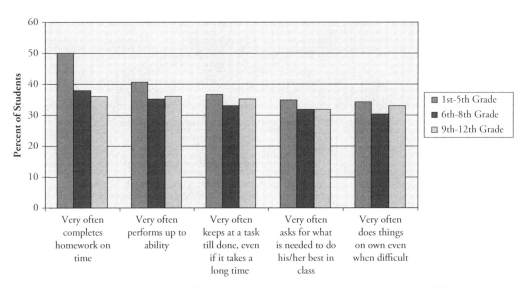

Figure 11.6 Self-regulated learning capabilities of students with disabilities by grade level constructed from NLTS2 data tables.

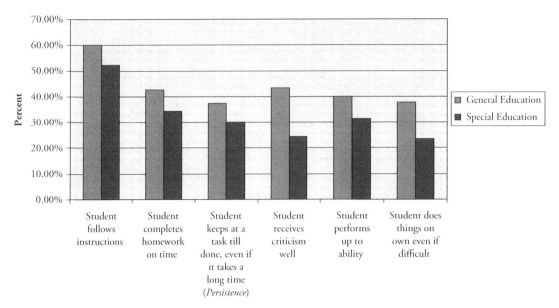

Figure 11.7 Percent of students with disabilities in general and special education classes exhibiting different types of self-regulated engagement during instruction.

behaviors frequently. Finally, Figure 11.9 comparing self-regulated behaviors of students with disabilities in special and general education classes indicates that (a) students with disabilities are more likely to exhibit self-directed behavior in general education classes than in special education classes across all grade levels, and (b) these patterns persist as students advance in grade. In other words, the tendency to follow directions rather than engage in

self-determined behavior persists across grade levels for students with disabilities.

Another analysis of factors affecting the learning and achievements of children and youth with disabilities is available in a summary of findings reported by Blackorby, Knokey, Wagner, Levine, Scheiller, and Sumi (2007) entitled "What makes a difference?" Based on these results, I constructed the schematic in Figure 11.10 to illustrate significant

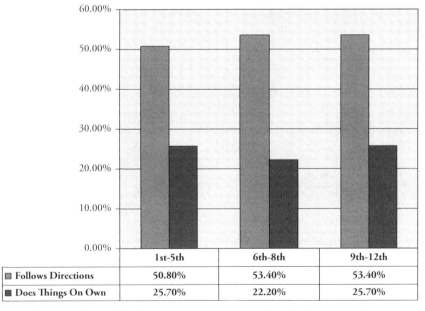

	1st-5th	6th-8th	9th-12th
Follows Directions	50.80%	53.40%	53.40%
Does Things On Own	25.70%	22.20%	25.70%

Figure 11.8 Percent of students with disabilities by grade level who very often follow directions and do things on own even when difficult (from NLTS2 data tables).

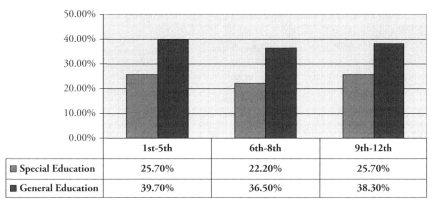

	1st-5th	6th-8th	9th-12th
■ Special Education	25.70%	22.20%	25.70%
■ General Education	39.70%	36.50%	38.30%

Figure 11.9 Percent of students with disabilities by grade level in special and general education classes who very often do things on own even when difficult (from NLTS2 data tables).

correlations between instructional practices and achievements of students with disabilities nationally. The upper row represents general education practices and the lower row represents special education practices. The middle row represents academic achievements, and the two indicators on the right represent employment and high school graduation outcomes. The solid arrows connecting practices and outcomes represent significant correlations, broken arrows indicate indirect associations, and X-ed arrows indicate a lack of association. As these data illustrate, the main achievement correlates are with general

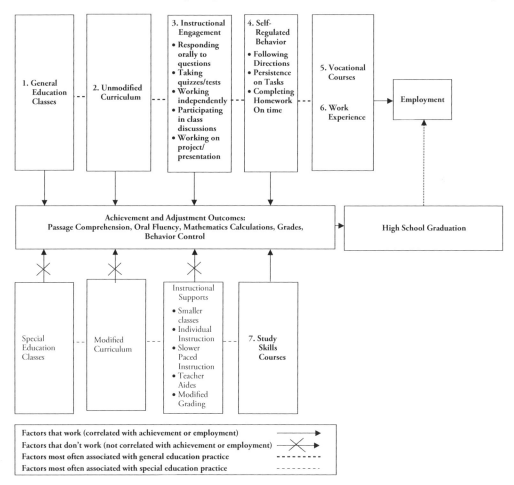

Figure 11.10 Schematic for school factors that work and don't work in terms of associations with the achievement, adjustment, and employment experience by children and youth with disabilities.

education: taking general education classes, learning from an unmodified curricula, being engaged during instruction, and exhibiting self-regulated behavior. These experiences correlated with one or more of the achievement indicator in the center box. Vocational courses and work experience correlated with employment outcomes, as indicated at the right in the figure. The most important finding, which I will return to later, is that the study skills courses usually taught by special education teachers correlated with one of the achievement indicators in the center box. However, none of the other special education practices were achievement correlates.

Solving the Learning to Learn Problem

Although these findings are sobering, they are not surprising given that significant achievement requires a level of persistent, sustained engagement that many students, especially those in special education, do not often exhibit. As noted in the previous section, these students are more likely to follow instructions than engage in self-regulated adjustments and to exhibit this preference for instruction-following in special than in general education classes. This is a problem my colleagues and I have studied for more than two decades; our findings have resulted in the development of approaches that help parents encourage self-determined learning in children and youth with and without disabilities at home (Mithaug, 1991, Palmer & Wehmeyer, 2002), promote self-determination across the lifespan for children and youth with disabilities (Sands & Wehmeyer, 1996), encourage student-directed learning through instruction of self-determination skills (Agran, 1997; Agran, Blanchard, & Wehmeyer, 2000), encourage teachers to establish self-determined learning opportunities in classrooms (Wehmeyer, Palmer, Agran, Mithaug, & Martin, 2000), promote self-determined learning in secondary youth with disabilities (Wehmeyer, Agran, Palmer, Martin, & Mithaug, 2003), infuse self-determined learning during Individual Education Plan (IEP) development and school-to-work transitions (Martin & Marshall, 1996; Wehmeyer et al., 2004), and assist adults with severe disabilities learn to direct their learning and adjustments to community jobs (Mithaug, Martin, Husch, Agran, & Rusch,1988; Martin, Mithaug, Oliphint, Husch, & Frazier, 2002).

We have also developed a rationale in theory and practice to explain self-determined learning (Mithaug, Mithaug, Agran, Martin, & Wehmeyer, 2003; see also Chapter 11, as well as a pedagogy of self-instruction

Table 11.1 Self-Determined Learning Theory

1. The closer to optimal the opportunities for experiencing gain, the more likely the regulation of expectations, choice, and actions to produce gain.

2. The more often the regulation of expectations, choices, and actions to produce gain, the more likely it is that adjustments optimize as expectations, choices, actions, and results become adaptive, rational, efficient, and successful.

3. The closer to optimal the adjustments to an opportunity, the more persistent is the engagement to produce gain, the greater is the feeling of control over gain production, and the closer to maximum is the learning from that adaptation.

4. Therefore, the closer to optimal the opportunities for experiencing gain, the more persistent is the engagement, the greater is the sense of control, and the closer to maximum is the learning (Mithaug, Mithaug, Agran, Martin, & Wehmeyer, 2003).

that guides its practice (Mithaug, Mithaug, Agran, Martin, & Wehmeyer, 2007). Our work is based on a vast body of research published from 1967 to the present and summarized in Mithaug, Mithaug, Agran, Martin, and Wehmeyer (2007), which shows self-management and self-regulation research to be substantially greater in depth and scope than comparable research on direct instruction, which tends to dominate special education instruction.

The *self-determined learning theory* presented in Table 11.1 describes this basis. The sequence of events leading to learning maximization is described in four propositions. According to the first, a self-determined learning cycle is provoked by the optimality of an opportunity to gain something from self-engagement. When that opportunity is optimal (when it matches the learner's interests and capabilities), the learner regulates expectations, choices, and actions to produce a desired outcome. The second proposition describes the effects of repeated episodes of this setting of expectations, making choices, and taking action to produce results: the more frequently they occur, the more experienced the learner becomes, and the greater are the improvements in those expectations, choices, and responses. The third proposition describes how this persistent (repeated) engagement leads to optimal adjustments that maximize learning. When learners persist in their adjustments to results, they gain increased control of their learning and, over time, they maximize their learning from the pursuit, as indicated in the last proposition of the theory.

Of course, this only occurs when learners are fully in control of their expectations, choices, actions, and results When another person controls those events, the learning is not self-determined. It is other-determined. The problem is that when teachers control learning over long periods of time, students are at risk of never learning to learn on their own. Increasingly, they become dependent on teacher directions to learn. In our view, this is what happens to students in special education classes in which teacher-directed instruction dominates. Students learn to follow directions rather than to learn how to learn.

The Self-Instruction Principles

Choice Principle: The more valuable and doable a learning opportunity, the more likely the learner will engage the opportunity to produce an expected result. Self-instruction pedagogy solves this problem by translating the four propositions of self-determined learning theory into practices teachers can use to help students become self-determined learners (Mithaug et al., 2007). The four principles of the pedagogy identify key components of that instruction. The first, on choice opportunities, reminds teachers that learners are most likely to self-engage when they perceive their learning challenges to be both valuable and doable. Practically speaking, this means giving students choices on what they will learn by encouraging them to pick from a menu of options the one that *best matches their interests and capabilities.* This procedure has two purposes. First, it provokes self-engagement because choice opportunities allow student to match what is available with what they like and can do. Second, it provokes a process of discovering for themselves what they like and what they can do on their own.

Self-Regulation Principle: The more often learners use strategies to set expectations, make choices, and respond to opportunities, the more likely they will produce results that match their expectations. The next step is to provide supports learners can use as they act on their choices to regulate their expectations, choices, and actions. These supports include (a) a list of goal options to choose from to produce results they expect, (b) a choice of what they will do to meet those expectations, and (c) a self-monitoring and self-evaluation routine that allows them to record what they do and evaluate what they accomplish.

Matching Principle: The more often learners compare their results with their expectations after responding to a learning opportunity, the more often they adjust their expectations, choices, and actions in subsequent attempts to learn from the opportunity. The third principle explains what happens when students compare the results of their behavior with their expectations for that outcome. These comparisons provoke adjustments in subsequent expectations, choices, and behaviors. For example, when they get matches between their expectations and results, they are provoked into setting higher expectations and making more ambitious plans. On the other hand, when they fail to produce a match, they are provoked into lowering expectations, improving responses, or both and then repeating the process until they find a combination that produces a match. Either way, engagement in learning becomes a cycle that occurs again and again until matches occur. Of course, when they fail to make comparisons to learn what matches and what doesn't, they exhibit the opposite pattern: disengagement and learning avoidance. This is why *making a comparison between expectations and a result is necessary*. It perpetuates cycles of choosing-regulating-adjusting that lead to the maximization of engagement and learning.

Persistence Principle: The more often learners adjust their expectations, choices, and actions to produce results they seek from that opportunity, the closer to maximum is their learning from that opportunity. The fourth principle describes the net effect of cyclical patterns of choosing, responding, evaluating, and adjusting, which is the maximization of learning. When students adjust to results repeatedly, they move successively closer to their goals (expectations), with each adjustment becoming a stepping stone to the next in a process that gradually transforms a once challenging opportunity to an increasingly manageable one. Over time, these repeated adjustments inch closer to the desired end until the once unknown becomes a known quantity, a familiar situation, an actual experience. This is learning maximization. It is a direct function of the learners' *persistent adjusting* of expectations, choices, and actions as described in the following sections.

Learning to Learn Strategies

Self-instruction pedagogy translates these principles into practice through student use of printed words and pictures on self-regulation cards they carry with them as reminders of what to do to produce results that match their expectations. This section of the chapter provides examples of these approaches, which were inspired by two classic self-determined learning studies by Stevenson and Fantuzzo (1984, 1986) that demonstrated remarkable effects for young school-aged children who generalized their learning across all possible situation and time gradients. In these studies, a "self-determined and self-administered" strategy was printed on cards students carried with them to regulate their behavior as they learned on their own. The cards reminded them to (a) set goals for the number of problems they expected to complete accurately, (b) count and record the number of problems they actually completed, (c) compare the number they completed with their goal, and (d) reward themselves when they met their goal. After they mastered use of the cards during training, they used them for several weeks and, in the process, generalized their self-determined learning across all 16 possible generalization gradients.

In a related study, Mithaug and Mithaug (2003) investigated whether the directedness of instruction on use of these self-regulation cards affected the learner's use of the strategy. The study compared teacher-directedness with student-directedness during strategy instruction sessions for young children with severe disabilities. During teacher-directed instruction, the teacher used a self-regulation card to instruct students to set of goals, assign work to be completed, and then record and evaluate results. During student-directed instruction, the teacher prompted students to use the card by emitting self-regulation behaviors to set goals, decide what work to assign themselves, and then respond and evaluate results. In both conditions, students selected items from a prize box for correct "yes" responses circled on cards, indicating matches between what they said they would do on the cards and what they did. The results indicated that students emitted more frequent self-determined behaviors during free time that followed student-directed instruction than during free time that followed teacher-directed instruction. The findings were consistent with the proposition that too much teacher-directed instruction depresses and discourages self-determined learning.

The following examples illustrate several self-instruction approaches used to teach self-determined learning to students and adults with disabilities. The sample cards in these demonstrations consist of single sheets of paper learners use to identify their interests, set goals, make plans, monitor work, evaluate results, and adjust behaviors for next-time learning episodes. One of these includes an employment contract adults with severe disabilities used in a supported employment project. The last two are for use by teachers and parents to help children at home and school engage in self-determined learning.

SELF-DETERMINED LEARNING CARDS

Self-determined learning is provoked when learners use reminder cards that have pictorial and/or written indicators of the self-regulation sequence to follow to complete learning tasks. The cards indicate what to do and when. They are comparable to the daily shopping and to-do lists we use to get tasks completed in a timely manner. In this application, they remind learners of the self-regulation steps to follow as they repeat the learning cycles needed for learning and mastery. They provide cues for setting goals for subjects to engage, specifying the plan to accomplish each goal, recording what is accomplished, evaluating results, and setting new goals based on those evaluations. One section of the card provides cues for setting goals, another for making plans to reach goals, a third for monitoring the completion of plans, a fourth for evaluating results, and a fifth section provides cues for delivering rewards when completed work matches the work planned. The last section provides cues for adjusting goals for the next cycle, which requires a new card. Each cycle requires a card (cue sheet).

The design of the cards varies according to student needs and capabilities. The one illustrated in Figure 11.11 has all of the components and is easy to follow. Four of the self-regulation strategies are represented in the left to right columns, and the topics to be learned are represented in rows by subject matter. Students set goals in the first column, make plans in the second, monitor actions taken on plans in the third column, and evaluate results in the fourth. The two bottom row cells are for self-rewards to be delivered when goals are met and for setting new goals based on results.

Figure 11.11 illustrates this format. Students begin by setting their goal for subjects to work in the first column. Then they indicate what they will accomplish in second column. In the third column, they indicate the work they accomplished, and, in the fourth, they indicate whether they met their goal for each subject. In the seventh row of the last two columns, they evaluate their accomplishments by indicating the number of matches between what they planned and what they accomplished. In the last row of columns three and four, they indicate the number of goals they plan to meet next time. In this example, the student met four goals and plans to meet five goals next time. This step connects the current self-determined learning card with the next card to be completed the following day.

When students complete successive learning cycles using a new card each time, they give themselves repeated opportunities to adjust their goals, plans, and responses as they learn what they are capable of accomplishing in the time allotted. At the same time, they learn to regulate their work more accurately by making the adjustments needed to do exactly what they

	Sample Self-Determined Learning Card		
Is My Goal Reading?	**What Will I Do in Reading?**	**What Did I Do In Reading?**	**Did I Match (Meet) My Goal?**
Yes	Read 1 chapter in book	Chapter 1 in book	**YES** No
Is My Goal Math?	**What Will I Do in Math?**	**What Did I Do In Math?**	**Did I Match (Meet) My Goal?**
Yes	Complete a math worksheet	Nothing	Yes **NO**
Is My Goal Science?	**What Will I Do in Science?**	**What Did I Do In Science?**	**Did I Match (Meet) My Goal?**
No	Nothing	Science Worksheets	Yes **NO**
Is My Goal Social Studies?	**What Will I Do in Social Studies?**	**What Did I Do In Social Studies?**	**Did I Match (Meet) My Goal?**
No	Nothing	Nothing	**YES** No
Is My Goal Writing?	**What Will I Do in Writing?**	**What Did I Do in Writing?**	**Did I Match (Meet) My Goal?**
Yes	Write a Journal entry	Journal entry	**YES** No
Is My Goal Other Activity?	**What Will I Do in Other Activity?**	**What Did I Do In Other Activities?**	**Did I Match (Meet) My Goal?**
No	Nothing	Nothing	**YES** No
		Number of Goals Met (Matches)?	4
		Number of Met Goals (Matches) Next Time?	5

Figure 11.11 Sample of self-determined learning card.

say they will do. The main instructional goal here is *accurate self-regulation*. Its achievement is motivated by the learner's desire to accumulate "yes's", which teachers reward as well. In other words, external reinforcement is contingent on accurate self-regulation and not on the number of assignments completed or the number of assignments completed correctly. The goal is for students to regulate their behaviors so accurately and consistently that they are able to learn what they say they will learn. Finally, there is no need for additional reinforcement because with this type of learning the match contingency is sufficient. Accomplishing what you say you will accomplish is one of the most powerful of reinforcers. It is intrinsically motivating. It is also liberating in that students no longer depend on teachers for praise. In time, the match contingency becomes the central motivational force for learning, which is evident when learners are provoked to adjust again and again—to persist in their adjustments—until the outcomes they produce match the outcomes they expect. This is the seed of self-determined learning.

SELF-DETERMINED EMPLOYMENT CARDS

This version of the self-determined learning card was developed in a supported employment program that served more than 750 adults with severe disabilities from 1988 and 1999, including 234 persons with development disabilities, 113 adults with severe learning disabilities, 145 persons with chronic mental illness, 61 persons with traumatic brain injury, 102 with physical disabilities, and 96 with other disabilities (Mithaug, Martin, Husch, Agran, & Rusch, 1988; Martin & Mithaug, 1990). The approach was also used in school-to-work transition programs serving school-aged youth with disabilities (Martin, Oliphint & Weisenstein,1994; Martin et al., 2002). The central feature of these programs was the consumer-directed practices developed for job searches, employment preparation, on the job training, and work performance. All participants in the employment program prepared themselves using self-determined learning cards, similar to those described earlier. The self-instructions on the cards reminded them what to

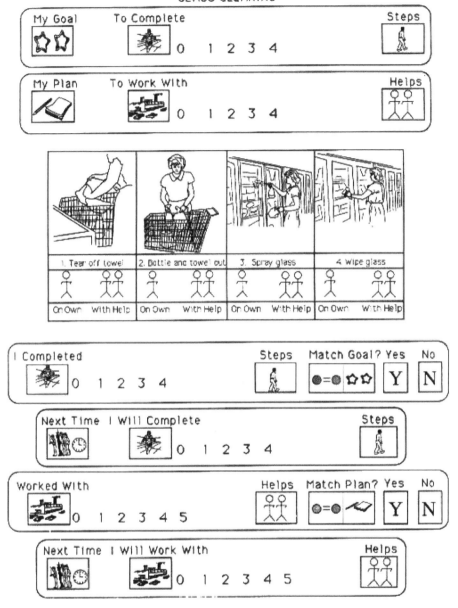

Figure 11.12 Using self-regulation cards to learn self-regulated adjustments. Reprinted with permission from Mithaug, Martin, Agran, & Rusch, 1988.

do to be successful at work. The cards were sheets of paper attached to clip boards they carried when on the job. The sheets displayed pictures, drawings, and brief phrases for setting goals, making plans, following key steps to complete tasks, and self-evaluating and self-adjusting after completing each card.

Figure 11.12 illustrates one of the cards used to help consumers with severe disabilities learn to complete a four-step glass cleaning task at a discount store. They completed "My Goal" by circling the number of steps they planned to take to complete the task. They

did the same for "My Plan," indicating the number of helps they expected from the supervisor to complete the task. The pair of stick figures signified two people together: one receiving and the other giving help. Next, they commenced work by referring to the drawings and corresponding phrases for each step. After completing a step, they recorded the completion by circling whether they finished the task "On Own" (one stick figure) or "With Help" (two stick figures). Next they indicated the number of steps they completed in "I completed…Steps." Marked

"Yes or "No" if they "Matched their "Plan?", and then "Next Time I will Complete.... Steps." They repeated similar evaluation and adjustment statements for helps received. During instruction, the trainer substituted instructional cues with the following reminder questions:

Before consumers begin work, the trainer asked:

"What is your goal?"
"How many steps will you complete?"
"What is your plan?"
"How many helps will you need?"

While the worker worked, the trainer provided cues and consequences as needed for the worker to complete the task correctly. After the worker completed the task, the trainer asked:

"How many steps did you complete?"
"Did you meet your goal?"
"How many steps will you complete next time?"
"Did you complete your plan?"
"How many helps will you need next time?"

Self-Determined Learning Model of Instruction

The instructional model for self-determined learning helps teachers and parents promote this type of learning at school and at home (Mithaug,

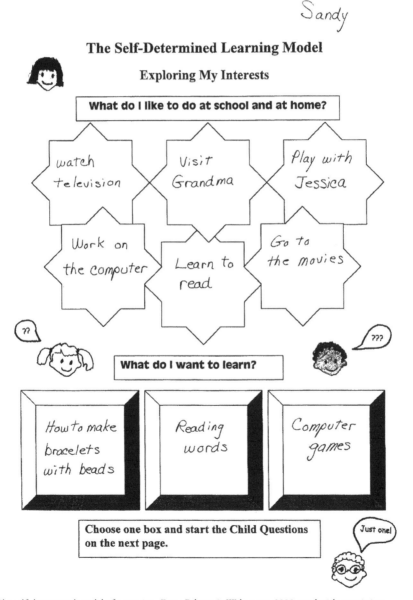

Figure 11.13 The self-determined model of parenting. From Palmer & Wehmeyer, 2002, used with permission.

Wehmeyer, Agran, Martin, & Palmer, 1998; Wehmeyer, 2007; Wehmeyer et al., 2000, 2003). Described in detail in Wehmeyer and Little's "Self-Determination (Chapter 24)," the *self-directed learning model of instruction* (SDLMI) illustrates instructional phases that lead to self-determined learning. The model has three parts, each posing a different set of problems for students to solve and a series of questions to provoke engagement and answers. The questions are consistent with self-regulation problem solving.

The self-determined learning model for parents of children with disabilities was constructed by Palmer and Wehmeyer (2002). It has similar steps, with an introductory component requiring learners to explore their interests as they make connections between what they like and what they want to learn. The second component helps children set goals based on interests, the third provokes action to meet that goal,

and the fourth prompts adjustments to results. The self-interest component motivates children to choose what they want to learn. This exploration phase encourages children to answer questions about what they like to do at school and home and what they want to learn. Based on these expressions of interests, they set goals to advance an interest in what they want to learn, what they know about the topic now, what must change to learn what they don't know, and what they will do to produce that outcome. In the Take Action phase, they specify what they can do to learn what they don't know, what could prevent them from taking that action, what they can do to remove those obstacles, and when they will take that action. In the last phase, they adjust their goal by responding to questions about what actions they took, what obstacles they removed, what changed about what they don't know, and whether they learned what they wanted to know. Figures 11.13 through 11.16 illustrate

Figure 11.14 The self-determined model of parenting phase 1: Set a goal. From Palmer & Wehmeyer, 2002, used with permission.

Figure 11.15 The self-determined model of parenting phase 2: Take action. From Palmer & Wehmeyer, 2002, used with permission.

each phase, showing how the questions and sample answers lead to self-determined learning.

A Singular Opportunity

This chapter described self-determined learning in terms of three factors that interact to produce learning: self-interest that motivates thinking and responding, self-regulation that controls and coordinates thinking and responding, and persistent adjustment to results that indicates learning. Next, the chapter presented evidence that when this pattern is present early in childhood, prospects for success later in life are greatly improved. The problem then posed was that this type of learning rarely occurs among children and youth with disabilities, as research and data from national longitudinal studies show. According to the national findings, students with disabilities are more likely to follow directions than to self-regulate. Moreover, analyses of factors associated with their achievement levels nationwide indicate that special education instruction fails to correlate with those outcomes, with the one exception being *study skills courses* (see Figure 11.10), which correlate significantly with an achievement outcome. This finding is important for two reasons. One is that nearly all elementary and secondary schools nationwide offer these courses, which are usually taught by special education teachers. The other is that these courses are strategically situated to develop the self-determined learning capabilities all students need to regulate their use of content-specific strategies that increase learning

Sandy

Phase 3, Adjust Goal

Name _Sandy_   Date _November 2_

Problem to Solve: **What have I learned?**

9. **What actions have I taken?**

I wrote my words 10 times each day. I said them a lot.

10. **What barriers have been removed?**

I remember to study every night before I watch Television.

11. **What has changed about what I don't know?**

What's new?

I know more words now. Instead of 5, I know more words on our word List.

12. **Do I know what I want to know?**

Yes? No?

Yes!

Here's how I feel about what I did!

I like to learn things. It was fun!

Figure 11.16 The self-determined model of parenting phase 3: Adjust goal. From Palmer & Wehmeyer, 2002, used with permission.

in general education courses. In the passage below, Levine and Wagner's (2003) description of study skill classes illustrates the basis of this singular opportunity for students to learn how to learn so they can control, direct, and determine their own achievements at school. The caveat, of course, is what is missing from this description of study skills classes: a singular focus on self-determined learning.

> Special education classes that focus on study skills have a different mix of students than academic-subject classes and a different purpose; hence, classroom practices also are significantly different in many respects.... Students with disabilities in study skills classes have teachers who use individualized instruction more than whole-group or small-group instruction. Most

of these classes are taught without a specific curriculum so that classroom activities can be adapted to individual students' needs. Yet half of the students in these classes have teachers who use textbooks, worksheets, and workbooks often, and about one third are frequently taught by using other print materials. Reflecting the individualized emphasis, *the majority of students work independently more than they are involved in any other classroom activity. More students in study skills classes than in other types of classes use computers for word processing or creating spreadsheets as part of their independent work.* Although one of five students in study skills classes experience school-based instruction outside of their classrooms, they rarely experience community-based activities or field trips (pp. 8–17; emphasis added)

References

Agran, M. (1997). *Student-directed learning: Teaching self-determination skills.* Pacific Grove, CA: Brookes-Cole.

Agran, M., Blanchard, C., & Wehmeyer, M. (2000). Promoting transition goals and self-determination through student self-directed learning. The self-determined learning model of instruction. *Education and Training in Mental retardation and Developmental Disabilities, 35,* 351–364.

Blackorby, J., Knokey, A. -M., Wagner, M., Levine, P., Schiller, E., & Sumi, C. (2007). *What makes a difference: Influences on outcomes for students with disabilities.* Menlo Park, CA: SRI International. Available at http://policyweb.sri.com/cehs/publications/seels-w1w3overview.pdf

Caraher, P. J. (2010). *Teacher survey of the relationship between student self-regulation and achievement among students with and without disabilities in an urban setting.* Unpublished doctoral dissertation, Teachers College Columbia University, New York.

Duckworth, A. L., & Seligman, M. E. P. (2006). Self-discipline outdoes IQ in predicting academic performance of adolescents. *Psychological Science, 16*(12), 939–944.

Eisenberger, J., Conti-D'Antonio, M., Bertrando, R. (2000). *Self-efficacy: Raising the bar for all students.* Larchmont, NY: Eye on Education.

Hill, N. H. (1960). *Think and grow rich.* New York: Ballantine Books.

Levine, P., & Wagner, M. (2003). *Secondary school students' experiences in special education classrooms.* Menlo Park, CA. SRI International. Available at http://www.nlts2.org/reports/2003_12/nlts2_report_2003_12_ch8.pdf

Martin, J. E., & Marshall, L. (1996). ChoiceMaker: Infusing self-determination instruction into the IEP and transition process. In D. J. Sands, & M. L. Wehmeyer (Eds.), *Self-determination across the life span* (pp. 215–236). Baltimore: Paul H. Brookes

Martin, J. E., & Mithaug, D. E. (1990). *Consumer-directed placement.* In F. R. Frusch (Ed.), *Supported employment: Models, methods, and issues* (pp. 87–110). De Kalb, IL: Sycamore.

Martin, J. E., Mithaug, D. E., Oliphint, J. H., Husch, J. V., & Frazier, E. S. (2002). *Self-directed employment: A handbook for transition teachers and employment specialists.* Baltimore: Paul H. Brookes.

Martin, J. E., Oliphint, J. H., & Weisenstein, G. R. (1994). ChoiceMaker: Transitioning self-determined youth. *Rural Special Education Quarterly, 13,* 16–23.

Mischel, W., Shoda, Y., Rodriguez, M. L. (1989). Delay of gratification in children. *Science, 244,* 4907; Research Library pp. 933–938.

Mithaug, D. E. (1991). *Self-determined kids: Raising satisfied and successful children.* Lexington, MA: Lexington Books.

Mithaug, D. E., Campeau, P. L. & Wolman, J. M. (2003). *Assessing self-determination prospects among students with and without disabilities.* Mahwah, N.J.: Lawrence Erlbaum

Mithaug, D. E., Martin, J. E., Husch, J. V., Agran, M., & Rusch, F. R. (1988). *When will persons in supported employment need less support?* Colorado Springs, CO: Ascent Publications.

Mithaug, D. E., Mithaug, D. K., Agran, M., Martin, J. E., & Wehmeyer, J. L. (2003). *Self-determined learning theory: Construction, verification, and evaluation.* Mahwah, NJ: Lawrence Erlbaum.

Mithaug, D. E., Mithaug, D. K., Agran, M., Martin, J. E., & Wehmeyer, J. L. (2007). *Self-instruction pedagogy: How to teach self-determined learning.* Springfield, Ill: Charles C. Thomas.

Mithaug, D. E., Wehmeyer, M. L., Agran, J., Martin, J., & Palmer, S. (1998). The self-determined learning model of instruction: Engaging students to solve their learning problems. In M. Wehmeyer & D. J. Sands (Eds.), *Making it happen: Student involvement in educational planning, decision-making, and instruction* (pp. 299–328). Baltimore: Paul Brooks Publishing Co.

Mithaug, D. K., & Mithaug. D. E. (2003). Effects of teacher-directed versus student-directed instruction on self-management of young children with disabilities. *Journal of Applied Behavior Analysis, 36*(1), 133–136.

Moffitt, T. E., Arseneault, L., Belsky, D., Dickson, N., Hancox, R. J., Harrington, H.,…Caspi, A. (2011). A gradient of childhood self-control predicts health, wealth, and public safety. *Proceedings of the National Academy of Sciences, 108*(7), 2693–2698.

National Longitudinal Transition Study-2 (NLTS2). (2007). Menlo Park, CA. SRI International. Available at http://www.nlts2.org/index.html

Palmer, S. B., & Wehmeyer, M. L. (2002). *A parent's guide to the self-determined learning model of instruction for early elementary students.* Lawrence, KS: The Beach Center on Disability.

Sands, D. J., & Wehmeyer, M. L. (1996). *Self-determination across the life span: Independence and choice for people with disabilities.* Baltimore: Paul H. Brookes.

Special Education Elementary Longitudinal Study (SEELS). (2007). Menlo Park, CA. SRI International. Available at http://www.seels.net/grindex.html

SEELS Data Tables. (2007). Menlo Park, CA. SRI International. Available at http://www.seels.net/search/datatableOverview.htm

Silfen, M. (2009). *The relationship between underachievement and learning disabilities in special education.* Unpublished doctoral dissertation, Teachers College Columbia University, New York.

Stevenson, H. C., & Fantuzzo, J. W. (1984). Application of the "generalization map" to a self-control intervention with school-aged children. *Journal of Applied Behavior Analysis, 17,* 203–212.

Stevenson, H. C., & Fantuzzo, J. W. (1986). The generality of social validity of a competency-based self-control intervention for underachieving students. *Journal of Applied Behavior Analysis, 19,* 269–276.

Wehmeyer, M. L. (2007). How students direct their learning. In D. E. Mithaug, D. K. Mithaug, M. Agran, J. E. Martin, & J. L. Wehmeyer (Eds.), *Self-determined learning theory: Construction, verification, and evaluation* (pp. 88–105). Springfield, IL: Charles C. Thomas.

Wehmeyer, M. L., Agran, M., Palmer, S. B., Martin, J. E., & Mithaug, D. E. (2003). The effects of problem-solving instruction on the self-determined learning of secondary students with disabilities. In D. E. Mithaug, D. K. Mithaug, M. Agran, J. E. Martin, & J. L. Wehmeyer (Eds.), *Self-determined learning theory: Construction, verification, and evaluation* (pp. 158–171). Mahwah, NJ: Lawrence Erlbaum Associates.

Wehmeyer, J., Lawrence, J., Kelchner, K., Palmer, S., Garner, N., & Soukup, J. (2004). *Whose future is it anyway? A student-directed transition planning program.* Lawrence, KS: Beach Central on Disability.

Wehmeyer, M. L., Palmer, S., Agran, J., Mithaug, D. E., & Martin, J. (2000). Promoting causal agency: The self-determined learning model of instruction. *Exceptional Children, 66,* 439–453.

Whitman, T. L. (1990). Development of self-regulation in persons with mental retardation. *American Journal on Mental Retardation, 94*(4), 373–376.

Zimmerman, B. J., & Martinez-Pons, M. (1986). Development of a structured interview for assessing student use of self-regulation learning strategies. *American Educational Research Journal, 23,* 614–628.

Understanding Hope in Individuals with Disabilities

Cindy L. Buchanan *and* Shane J. Lopez

Abstract

Hope is a positive psychology construct that provides an excellent platform to study and enhance the lives of people with disabilities. This chapter will describe hope, specifically focusing on Snyder's take on the hope construct. The benefits of high levels of hope will be examined as will the influence of high levels of hope on an individual's ability to cope with daily challenges and stressors. Psychometrically sound measurement tools for assessing hope in individuals' lives will be described. Finally, the chapter will discuss novel interventions to increase hope in individuals, highlighting interventions that have implications for use with individuals with disabilities.

Key Words: hope theory, Hope Scale, agency, pathway, Snyder

The psychological buoyancy required to overcome obstacles and navigate barriers is necessary to live well with a disability. Accordingly, setting goals and effectively working toward them is an essential element of everyday life and long-term thinking for individuals with disabilities. Despite the need to understand how people with disabilities cope with daily challenges and pursue wellbeing, research regarding people with disabilities has primarily focused on deficits and the multitude of problems that arise because of these deficits (Shogren, Wehmeyer, Pressgrove, & Lopez, 2006). Little attention has been paid to coping, positive traits or characteristics, and wellbeing. Though the field of psychology has grown and diversified dramatically over the years by balancing psychology's view of humankind and promoting optimal human functioning along the way, little emphasis within positive psychology has focused on individuals with disabilities until now.

Psychological practice has done a better job of focusing on what is right with people with disabilities, but there is more work to do. Schools, hospitals, workplaces, and mental health clinics have all incorporated interventions into their respective institutions so as to enhance positive constructs and individual lives (Snyder & Lopez, 2002). It is important to applaud these developments, as each and every intervention adds yet another layer of data to a growing body of information and literature upon which the field at large can build. But few of these interventions have been conducted with individuals with cognitive or physical disabilities (Clark, Olympia, Jensen, Heathfield, & Jensen, 2004; Grant, Ramcharan, & Goward, 2003; McCullough & Huebner, 2003; Wehmeyer, 2004). Because positive psychology itself does indeed accentuate the positive aspects of humankind (e.g., hope) while it also acknowledges the struggles of all individuals, such interventions are especially ideal for individuals with disabilities.

One stream of positive psychology research in particular—the hope theory—provides an excellent platform to study and enhance individual lives among people with disabilities. This chapter examines the past and future of hope-related interventions for this specific population. This chapter will examine definitions that were the precursors of

Snyder's hope theory and describe the underpinnings of hope theory. Considered by many to be the most comprehensive, Snyder's take on the hope construct—its history and development—will be outlined in detail. Additionally, childhood antecedents of hope will be explained, as will the primary scales for measuring hope. An examination of what hope predicts and how high levels of hope benefit will help locate the theory in its contemporary application among all populations. Finally, the recent shift in the field of measuring hope will be explained along with descriptions of novel interventions for increasing hope. Finally, this chapter will make suggestions for infusing hope theory into practice and research.

Precursors to the Hope Theory

A short review of the previous theories of hope is crucial to help illustrate the significant focus on this construct. While G. R. "Rick" Snyder is widely considered the father of the hope theory, other theorists prior to Snyder focused on the concept of hope as well. They theorized that hope was primarily centered on a person's positive expectancies for attaining goals and viewed hope as, chiefly, the perception that goals were attainable (Snyder et al., 1997).

One of the earliest scholarly definitions of hope is credited to Mowrer (1960). He described hope as an emotion that occurred in rats when they encountered a stimulus that was linked with something pleasurable. Mowrer's animal research also highlighted an aspect of fear (the antithesis of hope) by which animals experience a type of dread that decreases their activity level and causes them to stop moving toward their goal pursuits. Erikson (1964) continued the work but took a slightly different approach. Whereas Mowrer's research showed us the debilitating effects of fear upon goal attainment, Erikson developed a definition of hope that went the other direction, describing hope as "the enduring belief in the attainability of fervent wishes" (Erikson, 1964, p. 118). Breznitz (1986), the next major researcher to tackle the question of hope, focused his work on the powers that hope can exhibit over hurdles in one's life. He examined the relationship between hope and life stressors, warning that hope could actually enable people to overlook unpleasant facts surrounding their stress. A contemporary of Breznitz, Marcel (1978) further defined hope based on the coping skills and techniques of war prisoners; he concluded that hope gives people the power to cope with helpless circumstances (Godfrey, 1987). Shortly thereafter, Averill, Caitlin, and Chon (1990) proposed that

hope is necessary when goals are perceived as reasonably achievable, controllable, important, and acceptable at social and moral levels.

Just as the fundamental definition of hope itself has morphed and changed over the last 50 years, so too have the ways we seek to measure that hope in individuals. One of the first scales developed to measure hope was derived from Stotland's (1969) model of hope. In this pioneering project, Stotland (1969) investigated the role of expectancies and cognitive schemas, proposing that hope is present when one's perception of goal attainment is high. Based on this definition, the Hope Scale (Erickson, Post, & Page, 1975), a questionnaire that included 20 questions about general and common goals, was created. While this measurement tool was an important development in the history of hope research, it is rarely used today to examine levels of hope in individuals due to the small amount of supporting research. Stotland's work demonstrated that hope was an objective, measurable aspect of human life.

Soon, more scales were designed to measure hope. In 1979, Gottschalk focused his Hope Scale on an examination of 5-minute segments of spoken words. Through content analysis, he dissected individual speech and isolated individual statements around hope. The scale fit well with his conceptualization that people with hope have positive expectancies about outcomes and that this hope causes people to move through psychological problems in a more seamless manner. The measure was found to have positive correlations with achievement and human relations.

To examine the basic tenets of hope, Miller and Powers (1988) created another measurement. They proposed that hope is multifaceted and composed of multiple components: satisfaction with self, satisfaction with others, and satisfaction with life in addition to the avoidance of hope threats and the anticipation of a future. The Miller Hope Scale (Miller & Powers, 1988) sought to assess these three factors and took the form of a self-reported measure on a five-point Likert continuum. This work examined multiple components of hope; however, the findings suggested a lack of scale reliability and validity.

Staats (1989) theorized that hope involves the interaction between expectations and wishes. To test this theory, several measurement tools were created to measure both the cognitive and affective aspects of Staats' definition of hope, one of which is the Expected Balance Scale (Statts, 1989). This scale includes 18 items with responses given to a 5-point Likert scale. In addition, Staats and Stassen developed another measurement tool, the Hope Index (Staats & Stassen, as cited in Staats, 1989), which measures the cognitive aspects of hope and targets particular events and the outcome of those events. The Hope Index includes 16 items that ask individuals to rate the degree of "wish this to occur" and "expect this to occur" on a 6-point Likert scale (0 = Not at all to 5 = Very much). The Hope Index is broken down into four subscales: Hope-Self, Hope-Other, Wish, and Expect.

Taken as a whole, the measurement of hope has advanced significantly over the last few decades, from Stotland to Staats. One may observe that all of them are based on the common assumption that hope, as a positive construct, serves human functioning in a meaningful way. Moreover, the various scales used to measure levels of hope seek to harness the most crucial information about hope in an attempt to—simply—devise the best intervention for each individual. Although all the various definitions of hope vary from each other slightly, they all contribute in some form to the core components of the current hope theory.

Hope Theory

Understandably, as the field of positive psychology has grown and research has deepened our understanding of hope, a complete conceptualization of hope was not fully established until Snyder's hope theory. Given the variety of definitions of hope and scales that measure it throughout the past six decades, a brief history of Snyder's hope theory will illustrate a similar evolution, illustrate the importance of this model, and provide additional details relevant to the theoretical model of hope.

The most generally accepted definition of hope within the field of positive psychology is as follows: "a cognitive set involving the belief in one's capabilities to produce workable routes to goals (the pathway component), as well as the self-related beliefs about initiating and sustaining movement toward those goals (the agency component)" (Snyder, 1994, p. 401). In this definition and through subsequent research, Snyder and his colleagues (2000) asserted that purposive human actions are goal-directed, and they extended the conception of hope itself to include both pathway and agency components of thinking. Additionally, Snyder (1995) emphasized that these components of thinking not only exist, but that human beings perform extensive cognitive analyses of both pathway and agency components as they move toward goals.

What exactly do we mean by "agency" and "pathway"? Pathway thinking, also known as waypower,

is one's perceived capacity to produce many routes to desired goals (Snyder, 1994). Pathway thinking, therefore, is the ability to devise strategies to get to one's desired goals. To attain imagined goals, people must be able to perceive that they can produce effective routes to their goals. This requires that various possible routes are imaginable, by an individual, in order for that person to attain a goal. In addition, pathway thinking includes a personal appraisal of one's capability to conceive multiple and effective routes to a desired goal.

The second component of hope is referred to as agency thinking, the cognitive energy or willpower that allows an individual to move toward a goal (Snyder, 1995). Agency, or willpower thinking, is the perceived capability to sustain energy as you move in the direction of desired goals (Snyder, 1994). It also includes the ability to maintain that energy until that goal is reached (Snyder, 2000). Agency thinking, therefore, also can be viewed as the process of thoughts or perceptions that help one begin and continue to move along a chosen pathway. Frequently associated with agency thinking are self-affirming statements or thoughts such as "I know I can do this." For hope to exist both components are necessary—neither pathway nor agency is sufficient alone for the existence of hope (Michael, 2000).

Clearly, goals are central to hope theory. Indeed, goals themselves present the end product of the aforementioned pathway and agency components of thinking. One could even say that goals serve as motivators for action and catalysts for success. But all goals are not created equal. For people to continue movement along their selected pathways, sufficient value must be attached to a goal for the pursuit to be meaningful. In Snyder's hope theory (2000), a goal can be anything that an individual desires to experience, generate, obtain, accomplish, or become, but goals may be either significant, lifelong pursuits or they may be small everyday stirrings. Plus, the perceived likelihood of goal attainment falls on a similar spectrum, varying from very low to very high. As defined previously, pathway and agency thinking are therefore crucial to how we think about both hope and goals; they are the components of hope, and they are the ways by which individuals reach these goals. Summarily, hope needs both waypower and willpower; it requires both the goal-directed energy (agency) toward a goal and the perceived capacity to envision workable routes toward that goal (pathway).

Not all goal pursuits are simple. In fact, a person may encounter an obstacle or stressor that could potentially block his or her actual goal pursuit. Snyder's hope theory proposes that obstacles or stressors are evaluated based on one's overall level of hope and past experiences with navigating difficult obstacles. Individuals with high hope should be able to explore a variety of possible pathways to their goals and then continue to use their agency thinking to stay motivated toward their goal despite encountering obstacles. People with low hope might not be able to develop those alternative pathways to their goals, and they would then also lack agency thinking to stay motivated toward their goals. That lack, in turn, impedes their goal pursuits.

Other positive psychology constructs, such as optimism (Scheier & Carver, 1985), self-efficacy (Bandura, 1982), and problem-solving (Heppner & Peterson, 1982), give differently-weighted emphases to goals or to future-oriented agency-related or pathway-related processes. Snyder's hope theory equally emphasizes all of these goal-pursuit components in a parsimonious, cohesive, and unique manner (Snyder, 1994). Although related to constructs such as optimism, self-efficacy, and problem solving (due to their collective focus on motivation and expectancies), hope measures something quite different and has theoretical distinctions from its other positive counterparts (Snyder, 2000).

An examination of the childhood antecedents of hope will help to differentiate between these theories. Additionally, a more detailed understanding of the development of hope can help to illustrate the impacts of childhood disability on hope development.

Development of Hope in Childhood

Snyder's (1994) theory of hope posits that it is a learned cognitive set about goal thinking instead of a hereditary trait passed down from one's parents. Individuals build pathways and agency goal-directed thinking from the time of birth (Snyder, Cheavens, & Sympson, 1997). It is proposed that hopeful thoughts (pathway and agency thoughts) are established by the age of two or three. Pathways and agency thinking is taught by parents and learned from ongoing life experiences in early childhood. Pathway thinking is related to children learning about external stimuli, cause-and-effect linkages between events, and focusing on specific goals that will satisfy their needs and desires. Agency thoughts develop a bit later than pathway thoughts because they require additional insights into the self as the originator of actions (Snyder, Cheavens, & Sympson, 1997). They require a child to have a self-recognition of the self as a part of the process that initiates action toward goals.

A child's experiences during his or her early years sets the stage for future hopeful thinking. During preschool, childhood, and adolescence, children must learn to navigate obstacles that are placed in the way of their goal pursuits. Often the ability to navigate obstacles is learned from parents and other significant adults in a child's environment. These adults model hopeful thinking, provide feedback on overcoming obstacles to goals, and reinforce working toward goals (Kliewer & Lewis, 1995; Snyder et al., 1997). Snyder and his colleagues (1997) posited that a child's level of hope should be stable across childhood developmental periods.

Measuring Snyder's Hope

In adults, the construct of hope is measured using the Hope Scale (Snyder et al., 1991), the State Hope Scale (Snyder et al., 1996) and the Revised Snyder Hope Scale (Shorey et al., 2009). In children, the construct of hope is measured using the Children's Hope Scale (Snyder et al., 1997). All of these hope scales are used to determine agency thinking and pathways thinking (Lopez et al., 2000). While there is not a specific Hope Scale designed for children or adults with disabilities, all four existing measurement tools have potential positive application across all populations and the children's version of the measure has been specifically validated for use with people with disabilities.

Hope Scale

The first self-report measure was created by Snyder and colleagues (Snyder et al., 1991) to measure the trait of hope in people 16 or older. They developed a 12-item measure, which included four items related to agency thinking, four items related to pathway thinking, and four distracter items. The measure asked individuals to answer each item on an 8-point Likert continuum (1 = Definitely false to 8 = Definitely true). The resulting scores on the Hope Scale were treated as continuous variable with higher total scores indicating a greater amount of hope. An example pathways item is "I can think of many ways to get out of a jam," and an example agency item is "I energetically pursue my goals."

The internal consistency of the Hope Scale is generally in the 0.80 range and test-retest reliabilities of 0.80 or above at time periods of 8 to 10 weeks (Snyder et al., 1991). Concurrent validity of the Hope Scale has been found with correlations to similar positive constructs such as optimism, self-esteem, and expected control. Negative correlations have been found between hopelessness and depression. Additionally, factor analysis has supported the two-factor structure of the Hope Scale (Babyak, Snyder, & Yoshinobu, 1993).

State Hope Scale (SHS)

The State Hope Scale (SHS; Snyder et al., 1996) was developed to assess here-and-now goal-directed thinking in people 16 and older. It is comprised of six items, which include three items related to agency thinking and three items related to pathways thinking. Each of the items is answered on an 8-point Likert continuum (1 = Definitely false to 8 = Definitely true). A total score, an agency score, and a pathways score can be derived from the scale. An example pathways thinking item is, "There are lots of ways around any problem that I am facing now," and an example agency item is, "At the present time, I am energetically pursuing my goals." The internal consistency of the SHS is quite high with alphas in the 0.90 range. Concurrent validity of the SHS has been found with correlations to state indices of negative affect. Additionally, factor analysis has supported the two-factor structure of SHS (Snyder et al., 1996).

Revised Snyder Hope Scale (RHS)

The Revised Snyder Hope Scale (Shorey et al., 2009) was developed to measure the three facets of hope in adults. It is comprised of 18 items, which include six agency thinking-related items, six pathways thinking-related items, and six goal-related items. A total scores and subscale scores for agency, pathways, and goals are derived from the measure. The internal consistency of the RHS range are 0.91, 0.82, 0.79, and 0.80 for the total score, agency, pathways, and goals subscales, respectively (Gallagher & Lopez, 2009).

Children's Hope Scale (CHS)

This scale measures levels of hope as reflected by agency and pathway thinking (Snyder et al., 1997). The CHS is comprised of three pathway and three agency items. Scores can be calculated for each of the pathway and agency subscales and for the total hope score. The total hope score ranges from six to 36, with higher scores indicating higher levels of hope. The scale has demonstrated satisfactory psychometric properties. The internal consistency of the scale has been measured using Cronbach alphas for the total score ranging from 0.72 to 0.86 with the median alpha of 0.77 (Snyder et al., 1997). The test-retest reliabilities have assessed the temporal stability of the scale, and reasonable results have been found at 1-week, 1-month, and 3-month intervals (Snyder et al., 1997; Valle, Huebner, & Suldo, 2006). Validity has been assessed in a multitude of ways: convergent validation studies, predictive and incremental validation studies, and discriminate validation studies (Edwards, Ong, & Lopez, 2007; Edwards, Rand, Lopez, & Snyder, 2007; Snyder et al., 1997). This scale has been used with a variety of populations (e.g., physically and psychologically healthy children from public schools, boys diagnosed with attention-deficit/hyperactivity disorder, children with various medical problems, children under treatment for cancer or asthma, child burn victims, adolescents with sickle-cell disease, and early adolescents exposed to violence) aside from healthy children populations (Berg, Rapoff, Snyder, & Belmont, 2007; Snyder et al., 1997).

Initial factor analysis from 75 middle school-aged students with mild cognitive disabilities indicate that the CHS yielded one factor with an eigenvalue greater than 1.0, accounting from 57% of the variance (Shogren, Lopez, et al., 2006). The scale again demonstrated satisfactory psychometric properties. Research has shown that the CHS has adequate reliability and validity for use with individuals with intellectual disabilities; the Cronbach alpha value for this scale was 0.89 for a sample of 75 students with cognitive disabilities (Shogren, Lopez, et al., 2006). The CHS demonstrated satisfactory psychometric properties in the study of 20 middle school students with disabilities (Buchanan, 2008). The internal consistency of the scale was measured using Cronbach alphas for the total score. The alphas ranged from 0.80 to 0.90, which make these scores for children with disabilities similar to the past reliability findings presented above (Valle, Huebner, & Saldo, 2006).

Another crucial aspect of hope theory is not only that the various hope scales measure if hope merely exists before and after an intervention, but hope theory also emphasizes the importance of addressing varying levels of hope in individual lives. Multiple studies have done exactly that; they have found significant differences in outcomes of and characteristics between low- and high-hope individuals (Gilman, Dooley, & Florell, 2006; Snyder, Cheavens, & Michael, 2005). An examination of the benefits of high levels of hope and, conversely, the drawbacks of low levels of hope will be examined.

Hope and Its Benefits

The characteristics associated with people with high levels of hope are ultimately positive in scope and beneficial in life. High hope has been associated with greater well-being, coping, and the regulation of emotional distress (Irving et al., 2004). Hope is also associated with perceived competence and self-esteem and negatively associated with depression (Snyder et al., 1997). High-hope individuals are more optimistic about the future and have a greater perceived purpose in life (Feldman & Snyder, 2000). In the area of athletic performance, those who have higher levels of hope are more successful even when controlling for physical ability (Curry, Snyder, Cook, Ruby, & Rehm, 1997).

As mentioned in the discussion of how we define hope itself, high-hope individuals are also more likely to develop alternative pathways to important goals when obstacles occur. These goals are known as "stretch goals" in that they are slightly more difficult than previously attained goals (Snyder et al., 2003). People with high hope (especially high agency subscale scores) are also more likely to attain their goals (Feldman, Rand, & Kahle-Wrobleski, 2009). People with high hope are also more likely to select more difficult goals and be able to clearly conceptualize their goals (Snyder et al., 1997).

Students with high hope scores tend to have greater reported scholastic and social competences; these findings hold true even when controlling for intellectual ability and self-esteem (Onwuegbuzie, 1999; Onwuegbuzie & Snyder, 2000). In addition, students with high hope are more likely to effectively use feedback to improve their performance (Onwuegbuzie & Snyder, 2000). In college-aged students, high Hope Scale scores taken at the start of college predict better cumulative grade point averages and college retention (Snyder et al., 2002). Students with low hope experience high levels of anxiety in test taking situations (Onwuegbuzie, 1999). They are also prone to self-doubt, a clear interference with studying and test taking (Michael, 2000). Consequently, students with low hope have a more difficult time in school.

In addition to academic success, there are health benefits associated with high levels of hope. Those with higher levels of hope are more likely to utilize self-management strategies and health-promoting behaviors (Chi, 2007; Hollis, Massey, & Jevne; 2007; Maikranz, Steele, Dreyer, Stratman, & Bovaird, 2007). Higher hope is even related to lower distress in children with sickle cell disease (Kliewer & Lewis, 1995) and burns (Barnum et al., 1998). Barnum et al. (1998), in their study of 29 adolescent burn survivors, found that higher hope predicted lower externalizing behaviors and higher

global self-worth. The findings from this study suggest that high-hope adolescents are able to adapt their goals and behaviors even in significantly challenging times. In dealing with stressful situations where higher levels of coping are needed, individuals with higher hope seem to have superior outcomes in comparison to their lower-hope counterparts (Barnum et al., 1998). Hope even helps us when we get bad news. Individuals who report higher levels of hope after a diagnosis of cancer also report fewer physical symptoms, less pain, and a higher quality of life (Tsui-Hsia, Meei-Shiow, & Tsung-Shan, 2003; Vellone, Rega, Galletti, & Cohen, 2006). Along those same lines, hope can contribute to a greater sense of control over a disease and result in better coping outcomes related to medical illnesses (Back, Arnold, & Quill, 2003; Clark, 2002; Duggleby et al., 2007; Taylor & Brown, 1994; Taylor, Kemeny, Bower, Gruenewald, & Reed, 2000). High hope also may be beneficial to caregivers. In a study by Venters-Horton and Wallander (2001), high-hope mothers were found to be considerably more capable of maintaining their emotional balance in times of high stress related to their child's condition.

Relating to psychological health, people with higher hope scores tend to report fewer psychological problems and, generally speaking, have a more encouraging outlook concerning their lives (Carifo & Rhodes, 2002). Hope has been related to positive mood and as one of the most important determinants of recovery from mental health problems (Deegan, 1988; Farran, Herth, & Popivich, 1995; Kwon, 2002). Hope also has been proposed as one of the common factors related to change in psychological treatment (Snyder et al., 2000).

Elliott and Kurylo (2000), in their case study of a female with a newly acquired spinal cord injury, discussed the notion that the agency component had palliative effects soon after the disability onset. Additionally, they found that pathways thinking seemed to enable the patient to find meaning and resume social roles in life. Similar in topic but differing in scope and methodology, Dorsett (2010) examined the adjustment to spinal cord injuries in 46 adults from a qualitative perspective. Semistructured interviews were conducted at discharge from the hospital; at 6, 12, 24, and 36 months post-discharge; and again at 10 years post-discharge. Although not measured using the standardized hope measures, the results supported the conclusion that 73% of participants acknowledged hope as a primary factor that helped them cope after their injury. Specifically, hope emerged as the most significant theme as the individuals coped with and adjusted to their spinal cord injuries.

Hope also was examined in another sample of individuals with spinal cord injuries in a 2010 study. This time 87 participants took part in a study designed to examine hopefulness and life satisfaction (Kortte, Gilbert, Gorman, & Wegener, 2010). The findings indicated that individuals with spinal cord injuries who self-reported higher levels of hope tended to have greater life satisfaction at the time of their admission to the acute, inpatient rehabilitation service. Additionally, the individuals with higher levels of hope tended to have greater life satisfaction at the 3-month follow-up from discharge from the rehabilitation service. Clearly, these findings suggest that hope plays a role in post-rehabilitation subjective well-being for individuals with spinal cord injuries.

Shogren, Lopez, and colleagues (2006) examined the relationship between hope, optimism, self-determination, locus of control, and life satisfaction in adolescents with and without cognitive disabilities. Participants included 285 students without cognitive disabilities and 75 students with cognitive disabilities in grades seven to 12. Results were similar for both groups of youth with hope, optimism, locus of control, and self-determination being strongly correlated. Additionally, hope and optimism predicted life satisfaction in both the adolescents with and without cognitive disabilities. Thus, hope is a significant predictor of life satisfaction in youths with and without cognitive disabilities (Shogren, Lopez, et al., 2006). It is fair to say that in general, people with or without disabilities with higher hope reported greater levels of life satisfaction.

Lackaye and Margalit (2006) explored the relationship between hope, loneliness, mood, and academic self-efficacy in students with learning disabilities (LD). Four comparison groups of students without LD (high average, high achievers, low average, low achievers) were utilized to examine these constructs in children at different achievement levels. The participants were a mix of 571 seventh-grade students (292 boys and 279 girls). These students included 124 children with LD (75 boys and 49 girls) who attended general education classes and 447 students without LD (217 boys and 230 girls) who attended the same classes. The findings indicated that students with LD had lower levels of hope than the high-average and high achievement groups of their fellow students, but there was no difference between students with LD in the levels of hope from the low-average or low achievers. In this study, students with LD showed lower levels

of achievement, academic self-efficacy, and positive mood. Specifically, the hope comparison revealed that students with LD differ from the two high-achievement subgroups but not from the low-average or low-achievement subgroup on levels of hope.

Lackaye, Margalit, Ziv, and Ziman (2006) continued to explore the experiences of students with LD. To further understand how children with LD experience hope, the researchers investigated 123 students with LD and 123 non-LD students matched by school grades, grade level, and gender. They found again that students with LD reported lower levels of hope than their peers. The researchers proposed that students with LD have decreased beliefs in their competence and a decreased ability to change frustrating realities that they encounter on a daily basis.

Studies examined the role of hope in the lives of people with disabilities. For example, Elliott and his colleagues (1991) considered levels of hope in 57 people who had traumatically-acquired severe physical disabilities and found that people with higher levels of hope experienced lower levels of depressive symptoms. Elliott and colleagues found that both the agency and pathway components of hope theory were associated with less depressive behavior and psychosocial adjustment among persons with acquired spinal cord injuries (Elliott, Witty, Herrick, & Hoffman, 1991). Another study of adults, Jackson and colleagues (1998), looked at levels of hope in 63 American military veterans who were blinded during service. This study found that higher levels of hope were associated with fewer depressive symptoms and higher levels of self-reported ability. The final conclusion was that higher levels of hope are positively associated with more functional abilities among individuals with visual impairments entering a rehabilitation program (Jackson et al., 1998).

A qualitative study of the experience of college students with disabilities was conducted (Buchanan, unpublished manuscript) to understand how they overcome the many obstacles they must face in order to be successful in college. The participants were six college freshman who were enrolled in a freshman orientation course, which was designed specifically for students with disabilities. Of the six students, three were women and three were men with an age range of 18–22. The students in this study represented a range of disabilities: attention-deficit hyperactivity disorder (1), learning disabilities (2), physical disability (1), pervasive developmental disorder (1), and chronic health disorder (1). Using a brief, semi-structured interview protocol, the interview included questions specific to goal setting and college experiences. Those with high hope were able to develop goals relating to academic and social factors of their college success. All participants had goals related to succeeding in college. They dealt with these obstacles by developing alternative pathways and tried a variety of strategies to facilitate their success, including visiting with their professors, joining study groups, finding tutors, and studying in environments conducive to learning (such as the library). Hope seems to play an important role in the college experience of college students with disabilities.

Hope Interventions

After recognizing the multitude of benefits that increased levels of hope have for individuals, researchers began to develop specific interventions to increase these levels in their mental health clients, hospital patients, and students. One of the first interventions aimed at increasing hope in children was developed by McDermott and colleagues (1997). This program consisted of eight weekly sessions with first- through sixth-grade students at a culturally diverse elementary school. Students were presented with information about hope and goal-setting each week for 30 minutes. These elementary students had the chance to learn how to apply hope concepts into their own lives. Appraisal of the program was conducted through comparing pre-test and post-test hope scores for the intervention group to a control group of students, and results demonstrated that there were modest gains. In addition, teacher ratings of students' levels of hope were significantly higher at post-test, suggesting that they perceived increases in their students' levels of hopeful thinking.

After the first intervention showed benefits, researchers decided to create a systematic manualized curriculum to instill hope in children. The first of these was created by Pedrotti, Lopez, and Krieshok (2000); their intervention was developed for seventh graders and was designed to enhance hope through five weekly, 45-minute sessions. Groups consisting of eight to twelve students were formed, and two graduate students facilitated each. With a control group was established for comparison, the program was designed to enhance hope in these youths by teaching them about the hope model.

Before the first session, all participants were administered the CHS (Snyder et al., 1997). In order to control for initial variance in hope across the control and experimental groups, initial levels of hope were analyzed (Pedrotti, Lopez, & Krieshok, 2000). At the conclusion of the program, the CHS was again administered to the junior high students. After comparison to the control group's scores on the same CHS, the participants in the program were found to have significantly higher levels of hope. The findings indicated that the program enhanced the hope in these children; moreover, results of a six-month follow-up study indicated that the participants in the experimental group maintained the gains of higher levels of hope. These findings point to the strength of the curriculum as a long-term, beneficial intervention for instilling hope in junior high students.

Following the study with the junior high students, a similar program was created to enhance hope for elementary school students (Edwards & Lopez, 2000). Over two years, the five-session program was implemented with two different fourth-grade cohorts. Each year, the sessions were preceded and followed by the administration of the CHS (Snyder et al., 1997). While the evaluation via the CHS of this five-session program did not include a control group, a comparison of means at pre-test and post-test demonstrated significant gains in hope scores for the fourth-grade students.

Group therapy focused on goal setting and increasing the production of pathways and agency has provided benefits to depressed older adults and to college-aged distressed adults by reducing depressive and anxious symptoms while also increasing levels of hope (Cheavens et al., 2001; Cheavens et al., 2006; Klausner et al., 1998). Formal and informal hope strategies have been created to develop relationship skills and improve client and therapist interactions in therapy (Lopez et al., 2004; Worthington et al., 1997). Another application of the hope theory was implemented with outpatients at a community mental health center (Irving et al., 2004). These outpatients were given a pretreatment therapy preparation intervention based on the hope theory in addition to the typical treatment of their particular community mental health center. Afterwards, the outpatients who received the pretreatment hope intervention were compared with individuals who did not receive the intervention. It was found that the outpatient clients who were given the hope theory intervention improved significantly (as compared to the control group). These types of therapies, therapies based on hope, have been evaluated in individual settings (Lopez et al., 2000; Lopez et al., 2004), with couples (Worthington et al., 1997), and in groups (Klausner et al., 1998).

Hope interventions are beneficial for students in general education. Conceivably, students with disabilities could benefit from similar programs that help to instill hope in their lives as well. Initial findings from the hope scale validation studies suggest that hope can be measured effectively in diverse groups of youths; the findings also show that students with disabilities have marginally lower levels of agency as compared to students without disabilities (Snyder et al., 1997; Shogren, Lopez, et al., 2006). Considering the fact that students with disabilities have never been the target population for these interventions and that those with low levels of hope benefited the most from such interventions, hope enhancement strategies may be appropriate for students with special needs. Some pilot work has been done in this area. Based on the interventions in schools to increase hope developed by Pedrotti, Lopez, and Krieshok (2000), an intervention was conducted in a middle school specifically focused on improving the lives of students with disabilities (Buchanan, 2008). While students who receive special education services may have been a part of previous studies, demographic data on disability status was never collected. This was the first time that the middle-school-based hope intervention was specifically targeted to students receiving special education services. The first study of this intervention with students receiving special education suggested that the program could be successfully modified, but it did not enhance hope on the first attempt.

Another novel intervention for instilling hope in children with LD was conducted in middle schools in Israel (Kotzer & Margalit, 2007). The researchers wished to identify predictors of success among adolescents with LD who participated in a self-advocacy program. The program, "The Road to Myself," was developed as a virtually-supported intervention geared at training self-advocacy skills among students with LD over the course of an entire academic year. The program consisted of both classroom activities and virtual-based discussions to develop students' self-awareness and insight into their abilities, competences, and difficulties while also improving their ability to advocate for their own personal needs. Using the Internet extensively for distance education, the four main topics for the intervention and for the classroom activities were promoting self-awareness, exploring the personal meaning of LD, identifying coping strategies, and experimenting with self-advocacy at school—all key tenets of the hope theory.

The participants in the study included 374 adolescents with and without LD, students of seventh to ninth grade, at 15 schools across Israel. The adolescents were divided into three groups matched by age and gender with 111 of the adolescents with

LD participating in the 5-month virtual-supported intervention. The other adolescents were placed in the two comparison groups: 115 adolescents with LD who did not participate in the program and 148 adolescents without LD who did not participate in the program. A Hebrew adaptation (Lackaye & Margalit, 2006) of the Children's Hope Scale was given to the all of the adolescents, and after the intervention, higher hope scores were found for the students who participated in the program (as compared to their scores on the hope scale prior to the intervention). In addition, there was significant improvement on hope scores when compared with the two comparison groups. These results suggest that the intervention contributed to changes in the levels of hope of children while also supporting that hope plays a significant role in the functioning of children with LD.

Conclusion

The construct of hope has enjoyed a long history of development and refinement. Definitions have morphed into the comprehensive and detailed one that Snyder developed and continues to evolve as many more researchers investigate the construct. For now, hope can be measured accurately in children with disabilities using the CHS. The scale has been shown to have adequate reliability and validity when utilized with samples of children with disabilities. In adults, hope can be measured with three scales (the Hope Scale, the SHS, RHS), which have potential for clinical applications with adults with disabilities. Interventions created to increase levels of hope work across a wide variety of populations including individuals with disabilities. Existing hope interventions can be modified for use with individuals with disabilities. Likewise, novel interventions to increase levels of hope have been created for individuals with disabilities and have shown initial levels of success. There is room for tailored interventions for tailored groups using the basic tenets of the hope theory. Ultimately, continued focus on individuals with disabilities needs to be a central next step within the hope theory.

References

Averill, J. R., Catlin, G., & Chon, K. K. (1990). *Rules of hope.* New York: Springer-Verlag.

Babyak, M., Snyder. C. R., & Yoshinobu, L. (1993). Psychometric properties of the Hope Scale: A confirmatory factor analysis. *Journal of Research in Personality, 27,* 154–169.

Back, A. L., Arnold, R. M., & Quill, T. E. (2003). Hope for the best, and prepare for the worst. *Annals of Internal Medicine, 138,* 439–442.

Bandura, A. (1982). Self-efficacy mechanism in human agency. *American Psychologist*, *37*, 122–147.

Barnum, D. D., Snyder, C. R., Rapoff, M. A., Mani, M. M, & Thompson, R. (1998). Hope in social support in the psychological adjustment of pediatric burn survivors and matched controls. *Children's Health Care*, *27*, 15–30.

Berg, C. J., Rapoff, M. A., Snyder, C. R., & Belmont, J. M. (2007). The relationship of children's hope to pediatric asthma treatment adherence. *The Journal of Positive Psychology*, *2*, 176–184.

Breznitz, S. (1986). The effect of hope on coping with stress. In M. H. Appley & P. Trumball (Eds.), *Dynamics of stress: Physiological, psychological, and social perspectives* (pp. 295–307). New York: Plenum.

Buchanan, C. L. (2008). Making hope happen for students receiving special education services. Dissertation Abstracts International: Section B: The Sciences and Engineering.

Buchanan, C. L. (unpublished manuscript). Hope and independence: A qualitative study of college freshmen with disabilities.

Carifo, J., & Rhodes, L. (2002). Construct validities and empirical relationships between optimism, hope, self-efficacy, and locus of control. *Work*, *19*, 12–136.

Cheavens, J., Gum, A., Feldman, D. B., Michael, S. T., & Snyder, C. R. (2001, August). *A group intervention to increase hope in a community sample.* Poster presented to the American Psychological Association, San Francisco.

Cheavens, J., Feldman, D. B., Gum, A., Michael, S. T., & Snyder, C. R. (2006). Hope therapy in a community sample: A pilot investigation. *Social Indicators Research. Special Issue: Subjective Well-Being in Mental Health and Human Development Research Worldwide*, *77*, 61–78.

Chi, G. C. (2007). The role of hope in patients with cancer. *Oncology Nursing Forum*, *34*(2), 415–424.

Clark, D. (2002). Between hope and acceptance: The medicalisation of dying. *British Medical Journal*, *324*, 905–907.

Clark, E., Olympia, D. E., Jensen, J., Heathfield, L. T., & Jensen, W. R. (2004). Striving for autonomy in a contingency-governed world: Another challenge for individuals with developmental disabilities. *Psychology in the Schools*, *41*, 143–153.

Curry, L. A., Snyder, C. R., Cook, D. L., Ruby, B. C., & Rehm, M. (1997). The role of hope in student-athlete performance and sport achievement. *Journal of Personality and Social Psychology*, *73*, 257–267.

Deegan, P. (1988). Recovery: The lived experience of rehabilitation. *Psychosocial Rehabilitation Journal*, *11*(4), 11–19.

Dorsett, P. (2010). The importance of hope in coping with severe acquired disability. *Australian Social Work*, *63*(1), 83–102.

Duggleby, W. D., Degner, L., Williams, A., Wright, K., Cooper, D., Popkin, D., et al. (2007). Living with hope: Initial evaluation of psychosocial hope intervention in older palliative home care patients. *Journal of Pain and Symptom Management*, *33*(3), 247–257.

Edwards, L. M., & Lopez, S. J. (2000). Making Hope Happen for Kids. Unpublished protocol.

Edwards, L. M., Ong, A. D., & Lopez, S. J. (2007). Hope measurement in Mexican American youth. *Hispanic Journal of Behavioral Sciences*, *29*, 225–241.

Edwards, L. M., Rand, K. L., Lopez, S. J., & Snyder, C. R. (2007). Understanding hope: A review of measurement and construct validity research. In A. Ong and M. van Pulmen (Eds.), *Oxford handbook of methods in positive psychology: Series in positive psychology* (pp.83–95). New York: Oxford University Press.

Elliott, T. R., & Kurylo, M. (2000). Hope over acquired disability: Lessons from a young woman's triumph. In C. R. Snyder (Ed.), *Handbook of hope: Theory, measures, and applications* (373–386). San Diego, CA: Academic Press.

Elliott, T. R., Witty, T. E., & Herrick, S. (1991). Negotiating reality after physical loss: Hope, depression, and disability. *Journal of Personality and Social Psychology*, *61*(4), 608–613.

Erickson, R. C., Post, R. D., & Paige, A. B. (1975). Hope as a psychiatric variable. *Journal of Clinical Psychology*, *31*, 324–330.

Erikson, E. H. (1964). *Insight and responsibility.* New York: Norton.

Farran, C. J., Herth, K. A., & Popivich, J. M. (1995). *Hope and hopelessness: Critical clinical constructs.* Thousand Oaks, CA: Sage.

Feldman, D. B., Rand, K. L., & Kahle-Wrobleski, K. (2009). Hope and goal attachment: Testing a basic prediction of hope theory. *Journal of Social and Clinical Psychology*, *28*, 479–497.

Feldman, D. B., & Snyder, C. R. (2000). The State Hope Scale. In J. Malby, C. A. Lewis, and A. Hill (Eds.), *A handbook of psychological tests* (pp. 240–245). Lampeter, Wales, UK; Edwin Mellen Press.

Gallagher, M. W., & Lopez, S. J. (2009). Positive expectancies and mental health: Identifying the unique contributions of hope and optimism. *The Journal of Positive Psychology*, *4*(6), 548–556.

Gilman, R., Dooley, J., & Florell, D. (2006). The first study of the Multidimensional Students' Life Satisfaction Scale. *Social Indicators Research*, *52*, 135–160.

Godfrey, J. J. (1987). *A philosophy of human hope.* Dordrecht, Germany: Martinus Nijhoff.

Grant, G., Ramcharan, P., & Goward, P. (2003). Resilience, family care, and people with intellectual disabilities. In L. M. Glidden (Ed.), *International review of research in mental retardation* (Vol. 26, pp. 135–173). San Diego, CA: Academic Press.

Heppner, P. P. & Petersen, C. H. (1982). The development and implications of a personal problem-solving inventory. *Journal of Counseling Psychology*, *29*, 66–75.

Hollis, V., Massey, K., & Jevne, R. (2007). An intentional use of hope. *Journal of Allied Health*, *36*, 52–56.

Irving, L. M., Cheavens, J., Snyder, C. R., Gravel, L., Hanke, J., Hilberg, P., & Nelson, N. (2004). The relationship between hope and outcomes at pre-treatment, beginning, and later phases of psychotherapy. *Journal of Psychotherapy Integration*, *14*, 419–443.

Jackson, W. T., Taylor, R., Palmatier, A., Elliott, T., & Elliott, J. L. (1998). Negotiating the reality of visual impairment: Hope, coping, and functional ability. *Journal of Clinical Psychology in Medical Settings*, *5*, 173–185.

Klausner, E. J., Clarkin, J. F., Spielman, L., Pupo, C., Abrams, R., & Alexopoulos, G. S. (1998). Late-life depression and functional disability: The role of goal-focused group psychotherapy. *International Journal of Geriatric Psychiatry*, *13*, 707–716.

Kliewer, W. & Lewis, H. (1995). Family influences on coping processes in children and adolescents with sickle cell disease. *Journal of Pediatric Psychology*, *20*, 511–525.

Kortte, K. B., Gilbert, M., Gorman, P., & Wegener, S. T. (2010). Positive psychological variables in the prediction of life satisfaction after spinal cord injury. *Rehabilitation Psychology*, *55*(1), 40–47.

Kotzer, E., & Margalit, M. (2007). Perception of competence: Risk and protective predictors following an e-self-advocacy intervention for adolescents with learning disabilities. *European Journal of Special Needs Education, 22*(4), 443–457.

Kwon, P. (2002). Hope, defense mechanisms, and adjustment: Implications for false hope and defensive hopelessness. *Journal of Personality, 70,* 207–231.

Lackaye, T. D., & Margalit, M. (2006). Comparisons of achievement, effort, and self-perceptions among students with learning disabilities and their peers from different achievement groups. *Journal of Learning Disabilities, 39*(5), 432–446.

Lackaye, T. D., Margalit, M., Ziv, O., & Ziman, T. (2006). Comparison of self-efficacy, mood, effort, and hope between students with learning disabilities and their non-LD-matched peers. *Learning Disabilities Research & Practice, 21*(2), 111–121.

Lopez, S. J., Floyd, R. K., Ulven, J. C., & Snyder, C. R. (2000). Hope therapy: Helping clients build a house of hope. In C. R. Snyder (Ed.), *Handbook of hope: Theory, measures, and applications* (pp. 123–150). San Diego: CA: Academic Press.

Lopez, S. J., Snyder, C. R., Magyar-Moe, J. L., Edwards, L. M., Pedrotti, J. T., Janowski, K., Turner, J. L., & Pressgrove, C. (2004). Strategies for accentuating hope. In P. A. Linley & S. Joseph (Eds.), *Positive Psychology in Practice* (pp. 388–404). New York, NY: John Wiley & Sons.

Maikranz, J. M., Steele, R. G., Dryer, M. L., Stratman, A. C., & Bovaird, J. A. (2007). The relationship of hope and illness-related uncertainty to emotional adjustment and adherence among renal and liver transplant recipients. *Journal of Pediatric Psychology, 32,* 571–581.

Marcel, G. (1978). *Homo Viator: Introduction to a metaphysic of hope* (E. Craufurd, Trans.). Gloucester, Mass.; Peter Smith. (Original work published 1944).

McCullough, G. C., & Huebner, E. S. (2003). Life satisfaction reports of adolescents with learning disabilities and normally achieving adolescents. *Journal of Psychoeducational Assessment, 21,* 311–324.

McDermott, D., Hastings, S. L., Gariglietti, K. P., Gingerich, K., Callahan, B., & Diamond, K. (1997). A cross-cultural investigation of hope in children and adolescents. *Resources in Education,* CG028078.

Michael, S. T. (2000). Hope conquers fear: Overcoming anxiety and panic attacks: In C. R. Snyder (Ed.), *Handbook of hope: Theory, measures, and applications* (pp. 355–378). San Diego, CA: Academic Press.

Miller, J. F. & Powers, M. J. (1988). Development of an instrument to measure hope. *Nursing Research, 37*(1), 6–10.

Mowrer, O. H. (1960). *Learning theory and behavior.* New York: Wiley.

Onwuegbuzie, A. J. (1999). Statistics anxiety among African American graduate students: An affective filter? *Journal of Black Psychology, 25,* 189–209.

Onwuegbuzie, A. J., & Snyder, C. R. (2000). Relationship between hope and graduate students' studying and test-taking strategies. *Psychosocial Reports, 86,* 803–806.

Pedrotti, J., Lopez, S. J., & Krieshok, T. K. (2000). Making hope happen: A program for fostering strengths in adolescents. Unpublished protocol.

Scheier, M. F., & Carver. C. S. (1985). Optimism, coping, and health: Assessment and implications of generalized outcome expectancies. *Health Psychology, 4,* 219–247.

Shogren, K. A., Lopez, S. J., Wehmeyer, M. L., Little, T. D., & Pressgrove, C. L. (2006). The role of positive psychology constructs in predicting life satisfaction in adolescents with and without cognitive disabilities: An exploratory study. *The Journal of Positive Psychology, 1*(1), 37–52.

Shogren, K. A., Wehmeyer, M. L., Pressgrove, C. L., & Lopez, S. J. (2006). The application of positive psychology and self-determination to research in intellectual disability: A content analysis of 30 years of literature. *Research and Practice for Persons with Severe Disabilities, 31*(4), 338–345.

Shorey, H. S., Little, T., Rand, K., Snyder, C. R., Monsson, Y., & Gallagher, M. W. (2009). *Validation of the Revised Snyder Hope Scale (HS-R2): The will, the ways, and now the goals for positive future outcomes.* Unpublished manuscript, University of Kansas, Lawrence.

Snyder, C. R. (1994). *The psychology of hope: You can get there from here.* New York: Free Press.

Snyder, C. R. (1995). Conceptualizing, measuring, and nurturing hope. *Journal of Counseling and Development, `73,* 355–360.

Snyder, C. R. (2000). *Handbook of hope: Theory, measures, and applications.* San Diego, CA: Academic Press.

Snyder, C. R., Cheavens, J. S., & Michael, S. T. (2005). Hope theory: History and elaborated model. In J. A. Eliott (Ed.), *Interdisciplinary perspectives on hope* (pp. 101–118). Hauppauge, NY: Nova Science Publishers.

Snyder, C. R., Cheavens, J., & Sympson. S. C. (1997). Hope: An individual motive for social commerce. *Group Dynamics, Theory, Research, and Practice, 2,* 107–118.

Snyder, C. R., Harris, C., Anderson, J. R., Holleran, S. A., Irving, L. M., Sigman, S. T., Yoshinobu, L., Gibb, J., Langelle, C., & Harney, P. (1991). The will and the ways: Development and validation of an individual-differences measure of hope. *Journal of Personality and Social Psychology, 60,* 570–585.

Snyder, C. R., Hoza, B., Pelham, W. E., Rapoff, M., Ware, L., Danovsky, M., Highberger, L., Rubinstein, H., & Stahl, K. (1997). The development and validation of the Children's Hope Scale. *Journal of Pediatric Psychology, 22,* 399–421.

Snyder, C. R., Ilardi, S., Michael, S. T., & Cheavens, J. (2000). Hope theory: Updating a common process for psychological change. In C. R. Snyder & R. E. Ingram (Eds.), *Handbook of psychological change: Psychotherapy, processes, and practices for the 21st century* (pp. 128–153). New York: John Wiley & Sons.

Snyder, C. R. & Lopez, S. J. (2002). *Handbook of positive psychology.* New York: Oxford University Press.

Snyder, C. R., Lopez, S. J., Shorey, H. S., Rand, K. L., & Feldman, D. B. (2003). Hope theory, measurements, and applications to school psychology. *School Psychology Quarterly, 18*(2), 122–139.

Snyder, C. R., Shorey, H., Cheavens, J., Pulvers, K. M., Adams III, V. H., & Wiklund, C. (2002). Hope and academic success in college. *Journal of Educational Psychology, 94,* 820–826.

Snyder, C. R., Sympson, S. C., Ybasco, F. C., Borders, T. F., Babyak, M. A., & Higgins, R. L. (1996). Development and validation of the state hope scale. *Journal of Personality and Social Psychology, 70,* 321–335.

Staats, S. R. (1989). Hope: A comparison of two self-report measures for adults. *Journal of Personality Assessment, 53,* 366–375.

Stotland, E. (1969). *The psychology of hope.* San Francisco: Jossey-Bass.

Taylor, S. E., & Brown, J. D. (1994). Positive illusions and well-being revisited: Separating fact from fiction. *Psychological Bulletin, 116*(1), 21–27.

Taylor, S. E., Kemeny, M. E., Bower, J. E., Gruenewald, T. L., & Reed, G. M. (2000). Psychological resources, positive illusions, and health. *American Psychologist, 55*(1), 99–109.

Tsui-Hsia, H., Tsung-Shan, L., & Tsung-Shan, T. (2003). The relationship between pain, uncertainty, and hope in Taiwanese lung cancer patients. *Journal of Paint Management, 26,* 835–842.

Valle, M. F., Huebner, E. S., & Suldo, S. M. (2006). An analysis of hope as a psychological strength. *Journal of School Psychology, 44,* 393–406.

Vellone, E., Rega, M. L., Galletti, C., & Cohen, M. Z. (2006). Hope and related variables in Italian cancer patients. *Cancer Nursing, 29,* 356–366.

Venters-Horton, T., & Wallander, J. L. (2001). Hope and social support as resilience factors against psychological distress of mothers who care for children with chronic physical conditions. *Rehabilitation Psychology, 46*(4), 382–399.

Wehmeyer, M. L. (2004). Self-determination and the empowerment of people with disabilities. *American Rehabilitation, 28,* 22–29.

Worthington, E. L., Hight, T. L., Ripley, J. S., Perrone, K. M., Kurusu, T. A., & Jones, D. R. (1997). Strategic hope-focused relationship enrichment counseling with individuals. *Journal of Counseling Psychology, 44,* 381–389.

Family Perspectives on Child Intellectual Disability: Views from the Sunny Side of the Street

Jan Blacher, Bruce L. Baker, *and* Lauren D. Berkovits

Abstract

Research published over the past two decades has underscored the power of positivity, whether in the form of positive perceptions, optimism, positive coping, or even positive illusions. Such positive perspectives have been shown to be powerful influences on child rearing. This chapter focuses on family perspectives of disability, with an emphasis on the positive impact of raising such a child. The chapter presents the conceptual underpinning for studying positive impact, including related constructs such as optimism, as well as methodological considerations for understanding its interpretation, including three views of positive impact: (1) the low negative view, (2) the common benefits view, and (3) the special benefits view. In addition, findings are presented from a longitudinal study of parents of children with and without intellectual disability that support a theory of positivity as a key underpinning of resilience. The chapter also considers the application of this conceptualization of positive impact across cultures and disability types.

Key Words: parenting, positive impact, positive emotions, optimism, positivity

Historical Context

The study of families and disability, particularly of intellectual disability (ID), has a fairly recent history. Of particular note is the shift in family research from a focus almost exclusively on negative outcomes to a consideration of positive ones. This focus was catalyzed by Ann Turnbull and colleagues in 1993, with their book that addressed cognitive coping and disability (Turnbull, Patterson, Behr, Murphy, Marquis, & Blue-Banning, 1993). In 2002, Blacher and Baker mined the publication archives of the American Association on Mental Retardation (now the American Association of Intellectual and Developmental Disabilities) from its founding in 1876 and drew together a representative volume of family research that can potentially drive current efforts:

As we move into the 21st century, we hope that these now historical papers on family adjustment and coping continue to inspire studies that replicate,

elaborate, and update the work of the past. The impact of the child with retardation on the family must change as the political climate in the United States changes, as the service delivery system expands or contracts according to the winds of the economy, as genetics research leads to amelioration or even elimination of some disorders, and as definitions of retardation evolve. Families are now not only visible but key players. (Blacher & Baker, 2002, p. 39)

With the emergence of a focus on the family raising a child with ID came the realization that this involved both positive and negative dimensions. This was probably first articulated by Crnic, Friedrich, and Greenberg (1983), who proposed a model for the study of families that presented a more positive view of family outcome to balance more negative perspectives so predominant in the literature. In this chapter, we first examine the historical context from which a positive perspective on coping and adjustment has emerged, and then present some empirical and conceptual approaches to the study of positive family perceptions and disability. We then illustrate these themes with findings from the Collaborative Family Study (CFS) that began in 1999 (Crnic, Baker, Blacher, & Edelbrock, original PIs), wherein we have, to date, followed children with or without ID and their families from child age 3 through 13 years. Although the stressors these families have faced are very real, this street also has its sunny side, and that is where our story will focus.

Conceptual Underpinnings of "Positive Impact"

Considerations of the positive impact of raising a child with a disability are grounded in the broader theories of positive psychology. It is useful to review these perspectives as they have informed both the design and interpretation of much of the work related to disability. There are parallels to be drawn, for example, between caregivers (mothers) of children with ID and daily care needs or behavioral challenges faced by individuals who care for family members with chronic or severe illness. In both cases, caregivers likely experience heightened levels of daily stress. Although prolonged stress results in known physiological detriments to bodily systems, such as the cardiovascular and hormonal systems, possibly leading to clinical levels of depression, positive emotions have been found to buffer against these negative effects (Folkman, 2008; Folkman & Moskowitz, 2000; Tugade, Fredrickson, & Barrett, 2004). Thus, there has been a push in the last several decades to attend as well to positive affect and the beneficial outcomes that can buffer stressful experiences.

Coexisting Positive and Negative Emotions

There are many reports of people experiencing positive emotions alongside strong negative emotions in the midst of stressful events such as serious illness or chronic conditions (Aspinwall & MacNamara, 2005; Folkman, 1997; Folkman & Moskowitz, 2000, 2004). These positive states can occur in those individuals suffering from a malady or condition, or in those who care for them, and they provide appropriate parallels to research with parents raising children with disabilities. For example, studies in the 1990s that focused on caregivers of men with advanced stages of AIDS found that these caregivers experienced high levels of positive affect despite concurrently high levels of negative states and depressive symptomatology. Scores rarely dropped more than a third of a standard deviation below community norms of positive states even during more stressful periods of the illness course (Folkman, 1997). Folkman and Moskowitz's (2000) review presents many other studies that also find high levels of positive emotion in individuals who themselves experienced chronic illness, pain, and stress. Although this might be unexpected, positive emotions can coexist with negative states during times of distress and thus provide protective functions. For instance, a certain degree of negative emotion may actually help a caregiver focus on the stressor in hopes of figuring out a solution or finding relief. Meanwhile, positive emotions can provide a break from the distress caused by the illness and help to replenish personal and interpersonal resources needed for continued tolerance of the situation.

Positive Coping

Several coping methods have been proposed to describe how these beneficial positive emotions arise during intense stress. As coping efforts are likely to be utilized during times of increased negative affect, positive emotions as both a form and outcome of coping can help to explain the co-occurrence of negative and positive emotional states during these stressful life experiences. *Positive reappraisal* is a coping strategy in which an individual cognitively reframes the situation in order to maintain an optimistic point of view despite a largely negative event. For example, although taking care of a seriously ill loved one causes stress, sadness, and exhaustion, it can also be viewed as a way to show one's care and love for the other.

Meaning-focused coping is another coping style wherein persons draw on their internal beliefs and values in order to cope with the stress at hand. They find positive meaning or enjoyment from events that are typically viewed as ordinary occasions (e.g., time with friends or receiving a compliment) (Folkman, 2008; Folkman & Moskowitz, 2000, 2004). Careproviders and even those with the illness might be more likely to seek out or remember these islets of happiness when trying to cope with large amounts of stress.

Several other types of coping have also been described as leading to positive affect and greater sense of well-being. In a large meta-analytic review, *benefit-finding* coping, defined as the identification of positive changes as a result of a stressful event, was found to predict lower levels of depression and greater rates of positive well-being (Helgeson, Reynolds, & Tomich, 2006). *Problem-focused* coping, giving rise to feelings of success and self-efficacy as smaller daily tasks are completed, can counteract the more overarching hopelessness or helplessness caregivers feel in response to an inability to improve their ill partners' long-term outcomes (Folkman & Moskowitz, 2000). Folkman (1997) also found that at each of four time points in the months surrounding their HIV-positive partners' death (two before and two after the death), caregivers' levels of positive reappraisal and problem-focused coping were positively correlated with positive affect, above and beyond the previous month's positive affect and the other types of coping. These studies involving individuals with HIV and their loved ones provide a methodologically sophisticated context for evaluating the importance of positivity.

Self-regulation of one's goals can also be conceptualized in the context of coping, including disengagement from goals that are no longer attainable and reengagement with new, more adaptive goals (Wrosch, Scheier, Miller, Schulz, & Carver, 2003). Wrosch and colleagues (Wrosch et al., 2003) reported that among typical undergraduate students, both goal disengagement and goal reengagement were related to greater sense of well-being, measured as lower levels of perceived stress, lower levels of intrusive thoughts, and higher levels of self-mastery. Replicated among parents of children undergoing cancer treatment, lower levels of depressive symptomatology were found among those parents who were able to disengage from previous goals and reengage in new goals as required by their children's illness.

Health Benefits of Positivity

In addition to benefits to caregivers, meaning-focused coping results in better illness trajectories among patients themselves (Taylor, Kemeny, Reed, Bower, & Gruenewald, 2000). These benefits have been shown to include maintenance of T-cell levels among HIV-positive men mourning a friend or partner and longer survival after having a heart attack or being diagnosed with AIDS (Peterson, 2000). Beyond these coping strategies, positive illusions about the progress or outcome of their illnesses offered additional benefits to the health of patients (Folkman, 2010; Taylor et al., 2000). Overly positive views of the self, exaggerated sense of control over life events, and unrealistic optimism make up the cognitive basis for positive illusions (Taylor & Brown, 1988). These illusions might include beliefs of being able to control one's illness or beliefs that the illness has been cured, despite medical evidence to the contrary. There are several processes through which these positive illusions might improve one's

health. For example, positive illusions might help to improve the physiology related to the illness, promote better health habits, and increase medical care utilization (Taylor, 2010; Taylor et al., 2000). In one study described by Taylor and colleagues, men who were less optimistic about their HIV progression, but who were not yet experiencing any HIV-related symptoms, had an earlier onset of symptoms as compared to men who had positive expectations about their prognosis (Taylor et al., 2000). This difference existed even though the more negative expectations were more realistic of the patients' prognoses, suggesting that some deviation from reality in the face of negative circumstances can be protective. Additionally, positivity could result in more social support for patients, with positive emotional states aiding in forming better social relationships, and greater self-efficacy helping patients to recruit social support from others. This greater support, in turn, leads to improvements in the patients' overall health and well-being (e.g., Seeman, 1996; Taylor, 2010).

The extensive, early work on coping with aspects of HIV as cursorily reviewed here provided direction for conceptualizing and understanding parental coping with children with ID. However, in contrast to a medical diagnosis, a child's developmental delay (DD) does not have as clear an objective negative outcome; parents' strong positive beliefs regarding parenting a child with delays may be realistic rather than illusory (Paczkowski & Baker, 2008). In trying to understand the positive impact of child disability on parents (mainly mothers), we must also consider inherent personality traits that can affect the lens through which parents view the caregiving experience. The literature on "optimism" is a good place to start.

Optimism and Its Relationship to Positive Impact

Optimism can be defined as a relatively stable individual difference variable that reflects generalized positive expectancies about the future (Scheier & Carver, 1985). In other words, optimists have a favorable outlook on life and are disposed to believe that good things will happen. To maintain such positive beliefs, optimists rely on a sense of positive evaluation of the social context and its ability to provide necessary support. As a result, optimistic people are more likely to display continued effort in the face of adversity and stress (Karademas, 2006; Olason & Roger, 2001; Scheier & Carver, 1985).

Parents themselves tend to recognize the value of maintaining a positive orientation. Findings from general research on optimism suggest ways that having an optimistic outlook may be linked to parenting children with developmental disabilities. First, optimists may have an advantage in dealing with threatening events from their preference for more adaptive coping strategies. Optimists are more likely to engage in problem solving and seeking social support (Dougall, Hyman, Hayward, McFeeley, & Baum, 2001). In addition, they effectively modulate their anger and patience, as well as manage their children more appropriately (Koenig, Barry, & Kochanska, 2010). Despite the extraordinary challenges faced by families of children with developmental disabilities, many parents maintain high dispositional optimism and develop effective coping strategies (Bayat, 2007; Meirsschaut et al., 2010). In fact, Judge (1998) reported that although parents of children with disabilities used a variety of coping strategies, their problem-focused coping that emphasized efforts to seek social support, actively solve the problem, and maintain a positive outlook on life was the most adaptive.

To the extent that dispositional optimism leads parents to emphasize their children's positive behavior, there may be generalized benefits to family relationships. There is evidence that optimistic parents have an attentional bias for their child's positive behaviors (Segerstrom, 2001), redefining difficult behaviors in more positive terms (e.g., high energy) (Koenig et al., 2010). For some parents of children with developmental disabilities, acknowledgment of children's positive behaviors has resulted in more positive affect in the parent–child relationship (Coplan et al., 2002). Ekas, Lickenbrock, and Whitman (2010) studied a sample of 119 mothers of children with autism spectrum disorders (ASD). They found that higher levels of optimism were associated with increased positive outcomes (increased positive affect, life satisfaction, and psychological well-being) and decreased negative outcomes (decreased depression, parenting stress, and negative affect).

Overall, research on optimism has shown that maternal optimism can influence parenting of children with and without developmental disabilities. With typically developing children, maternal optimism is associated with positive affect, sensitivity, and a lack of detachment. With children with developmental disabilities, maternal optimism is related to increased positive affect and decreased negative affect. Optimism may be related to parenting behaviors through adaptive coping strategies, as well as through an attentional bias for children's positive behaviors.

Raising a Child with Intellectual Disability: No Denying Stress

Although we are focusing in this chapter on the positive aspects of raising a child with ID, there is no denying that there are many challenges along the way. Although these are numerous and, to some extent, depend on the nature of the disability and of family circumstances, some negative experiences may be omnipresent. We will briefly review parenting stress, given the extensive study of this domain, the pervasiveness and chronicity of stress, and the promise of positive perspectives to reduce stress levels.

Stress is the product of many interrelated challenges. These begin, of course, with parenting challenges from the child's cognitive limitations, social skill deficits, and behavior problems. These families experience excessive caretaking demands, financial burden, and restrictions on leisure activities and social lives, as well as disruptions of family plans (Gunn & Berry, 1987; Rodrigue, Morgan, & Geffken, 1992). In addition, there are the restraints imposed on the parents' and siblings' time availability and social lives. Financial burdens often have emanative effects on the family; for example, when one parent must spend more time at home and the other needs to spend more time at work (Brandon, 2007). A much less explored but ultimately major source of stress for many families is the seemingly endless burden of securing appropriate services and the frustrations engendered by the service system itself.

Parenting Stress

Not surprisingly, parents of children with an ID experience increased stress, especially in domains related to child rearing (Baker, Blacher, Kopp, & Kraemer, 1997; Blacher & Baker, 2002; Crnic, Friedrich, & Greenberg, 1983; Fidler, Hodapp, & Dykens, 2000; Orr, Cameron, Dobson, & Day, 1993, Minnes, 1988). There is also evidence for increased maternal depression (Olsson & Hwang, 2001).

In our CFS (Collaborative Family Study), we have examined, longitudinally, the relationship between family factors and the onset, exacerbation, and amelioration of behavior problems and mental disorders, as well as the development of social competence in children with or without ID. The study initially recruited 225 families of 3-year-old children with DDs ($n = 92$) or typical cognitive development ($n = 133$). Families were then assessed annually at child ages 3 through 9 years, and again at ages 13 and (ongoing) 15 years. (Note: In early childhood, we use the term *developmental delay*; subsequently, we classify children using both IQ and adaptive behavior and use the term *intellectual disability*). Measurement has involved in-home observation of naturalistic family interactions; center-based observations of mother–child interactions in problems solving, clean up, and free-play situations; assessments of child intelligence, adaptive behavior, and social skills; interviews with mothers and youths; and batteries of parent, teacher, and, more recently, youth self-report measures. From these, we have brought into focus a picture of the variety of family experiences and child outcomes in families raising a child with or without ID.

Again, there is no denying stress. We have found parenting stress levels as early as child age 3 years to be significantly higher when a child has a DD in contrast to families raising children with typical cognitive development (Baker, Blacher, Crnic, & Edelbrock, 2002). Moreover, we have found that the parent stress levels and the difference between the two groups of families were highly stable over the subsequent year, to child age 4 (Baker et al., 2003). This is consistent with many other reports (e.g., Baker et al., 1997; Crnic et al., 1983; Fidler et al., 2000). For example, Hauser-Cram and colleagues (2001) followed children with delays from infancy through 10 years of age, finding increasing parental stress such that, by age 10, four times as many parents were reporting stress in the clinical range as parents in the nondisabled comparison sample.

Stress and Physical Health

Although there has been considerable study of the mental health of parents (primarily mothers) raising a child with DDs, much less is known about the impact on mothers' physical health. Research on chronic stress suggests that, over time, the stressors these mothers face may negatively affect their physical well-being (Taylor, Repetti, & Seeman, 1997). To date, there has been little study of perceived physical health in mothers of children raising children with or without delayed development. In one study, we examined mothers' self-perceived physical health at child ages 3, 4, and 5 years, in a sample of 218 families raising a child with or without DDs. We found that mothers of children with delayed development at age 3 reported poorer concurrent and subsequent physical health than did demographically similar mothers of children with typical development (TD) (Eisenhower, Baker, & Blacher, 2009).

In subsequent analyses, we examined mothers' health at annual assessments from child age 3 through 9 years (Eisenhower, Blacher, & Baker,

2013). The self-perceived physical health of mothers raising children with DD across early and middle childhood was consistently poorer than that of mothers raising children with TD. Latent growth curve (LGC) analysis indicated that both groups showed similar, linear health trajectories over time. This pattern suggests that the poorer well-being facing mothers of children with DD, most often observed in measures of psychological well-being, extends to these mothers' physical health as well.

If poorer physical health is evident in the early years of raising a child with disabilities, what might the effects of chronic stress across a lifetime be? Although this has not been studied extensively, one provocative line of research from Blackburn, Epel, and colleagues has focused on mechanisms of how stress, especially chronic stress, gets "under the skin" and impacts health and aging at the cellular level. In short, telomeres are the protective caps on the ends of chromosomes that are a measure of cell age and thus health. Telomere length can serve as a biomarker of a cell's biological (vs. chronological) "age." The researchers found that perceived stress and chronicity of stress were significantly associated with higher oxidative stress, lower telomerase activity, and shorter telomere length in immune system cells, which are known determinants of cell senescence and longevity (Epel, Blackburn, Lin, Dhabhar, Adler, et al., 2004). They examined biomarkers of cellular aging that are strong predictors of longevity among mothers, aged 20–50 years, raising children with various physical or developmental disabilities (e.g., autism, cerebral palsy, chronic illnesses) compared to mothers of children with TD. Although there was no overall difference between mothers of children with and without disabilities, mothers reporting chronic perceived parenting stress had aged 9–17 years more than those who perceived low parenting stress, according to the biomarkers of cellular aging. Mothers' self-reported perceptions of stress were the strongest predictor of cellular aging. As the authors pointed out, longitudinal studies in which telomere length is assayed repeatedly are needed to directly test whether the rate of telomere shortening in persons with higher levels of reported stress is actually faster than in those with low stress. Ultimately, studies of whether interventions to reduce stress can slow the process of telomere shortening would be pivotal.

A Key Source of Parent Stress

It is no surprise that parents raising a child with an ID experience heightened and chronic stress. The early psychodynamic perspectives on families spoke of "chronic sorrow" (Olshansky, 1962) and similar psychological effects from the very fact of the child's disability, and, for years, variations of this view were the predominant perspectives on the family (Blacher & Baker, 2002). Over time, scholars in this field broadened their perspective to incorporate the multitude of sources of potential stress. Moreover, although there has been little study of this, it would seem that the sources of stress change—or at least are weighted differently—developmentally. Wikler's (1986) classic cross-sectional study of parent stress supported her view that stress levels rise and fall according to the developmental stages and demands that parents face, with the highest stress at the outset of adolescence and transition to young adulthood.

In subsequent studies primarily of children, an interesting and consistent finding has been that the parents' heightened stress is strongly related to the extent of the child's behavior problems (Hodapp et al., 1998; Stores et al., 1998). Floyd and Phillippe (1993) reported that parents of school-aged children with delayed development spent more time issuing commands and working to gain compliance, and they experienced more behavior management struggles and coercive parent–child interactions than other parents. Moreover, it appears that the heightened parenting stress is more attributable to these child behavioral challenges than to the presence of cognitive delays per se.

In studies from our CFS, we examined this question of parent-reported stress and child behavior problems in 225 families of 3-year-old children with or without DDs. Even at this young age, children with DDs were three times as likely to have clinical levels of behavior problems as children with typical cognitive development (Baker, et al., 2002). Child behavior problems were highly related to parents' stress levels, not only in the families of children with DDs but also in the families of children with TD. Indeed, in the families of children with DD, when behavior problems were accounted for statistically, the extent of cognitive delay no longer accounted significantly for variance in stress (Baker et al., 2002).

Two subsequent CFS studies examined related questions: First, what is the continuity of the "behavior problems/parenting stress" relationship across childhood? Second, what is the evidence for a causal relationship between behavior problems and stress? It is logical that child behavior problems are contributing to parenting stress, but it is also possible that highly stressed parents may engage in parenting behaviors that are less growth-promoting, that

may be relevant to the emergence, or exacerbation, of behavior problems (Crnic & Greenberg, 1987)?

In the first study, we followed 205 of the families in the Baker et al. 2002 study (described earlier) from child age 3 to 4 (Baker et al., 2003). Mother and father reports of child behavior problems and of parenting stress were highly stable across time, and both were consistently higher in parents of children with DD. Despite the high stability of behavior problems and parent stress over time, we conducted hierarchical regression analyses to see how each variable assessed earlier predicted changes in the other by age 4. Child behavior problems at age 3 and changes in behavior problems over the 1-year period contributed significantly to changes in parenting stress. Looking at the opposite direction of effect in separate regressions, parenting stress at 36 months and changes in parenting stress over the 1-year period were associated with increases in child behavior problems. In these analyses, child DD did not explain significant variance in parenting stress. These findings were consistent with the notion that maladaptive child behavior and parenting stress have a mutually escalating effect on each other, following the often proposed, but less studied, transactional models (Greenbaum & Auerbach, 1998; Sameroff & Chandler, 1975; Sameroff & Mackenzie, 2003).

In the second study, drawing on annual assessments at child ages 3 through 9 years, we conducted cross-lagged panel analyses to investigate the bidirectional effects of child behavior problems and parenting stress across these seven time points (Neece, Green, & Baker, 2012). These analyses included families who had complete data for at least two time points. There were six sets of cross-lagged effects tested in these models (e.g., behavior problems at age 3 predicting stress at age 4 and stress at age 3 predicting behavior problems at age 4, and so on). Most paths from one year to the next—for behavior problems to stress and for stress to behavior problems—were significant for mothers and fathers. These findings supported the bidirectional hypothesis. They were particularly interesting, given the high stability of both child behavior problems and parenting stress over time, which affords little change to predict. Moreover, these transactional effects did not differ by the presence or absence of child disability.

This heightened stress concomitant with child behavior challenges has also been found in families raising children with autism, although the body of research on this topic is far more limited. Children with ASD are generally described as having a strong negative impact on the overall well-being of their families. In fact, many studies find that children with ASD have a greater negative impact on their families than other children with developmental disabilities (Eisenhower, Baker, & Blacher, 2005). Research studies exploring the negative impact of having a child with ASD focus on domains such as parenting stress, marital strain, and poor parental mental health, which are generally found to relate to the daily stressors surrounding raising a child with ASD (Rodrigue, Morgan, & Geffken, 1990; Sanders & Morgan, 1997). However, the positive impact these children may have on their families has been largely ignored, relegated only to the occasional study that finds families able to cope or develop positive relationships "in spite of autism." When the family experiences are studied more completely, it is clear that family members perceive a mix of negative and positive effects of having a child with ASD and that these positive experiences are an important factor in considering the family experiences, adaptations, and interventions surrounding ASD.

Studies exploring these factors often use qualitative interviews to understand the full family experience of ASD. One such study found that parents of children with ASD view a range of benefits associated with raising their children, including becoming more aware about people with disabilities, learning tolerance and compassion, and learning to slow their lives down and appreciate smaller things (Myers, Mackintosh, & Goin-Kochel, 2009). Parents also discussed appreciating their children's uniqueness, feeling blessed by their children, and feeling as if their spiritual life, marriage, and family have been enriched and strengthened by the experience of raising their children (Myers et al., 2009). Parents expressed these positive views in addition to the hardships and stressors that come along with raising their children. Siblings also hold this dialectical view of their brothers and sisters with ASD, describing their siblings' negative impact on the family (e.g., disruption to daily routines, aggression), as well as positive outcomes of living with their sibling (e.g., fun times spent together, pride over their accomplishments, teaching them to care about others) (Petalas, Hastings, Nash, Dowey, & Reilly, 2009).

In sum, there is no denying that raising a child with cognitive or developmental disabilities is stressful for parents. However, there is evidence that, at least for preschool and early school-aged children, the cognitive disability is less of an influence than the behavior problems that are more prevalent in children with DDs. Thus, one way to ease parenting stress would be to employ a dual focus in early intervention program on ways to reduce both parenting stress and child behavior problems. It is possible, also, that the positive domains we will now consider in greater detail provide some balance to the heightened parenting stress or even serve as a buffer to it. A parent with a more positive perspective of the child in the family, with higher optimism, and/or with more positive parenting behavior may experience lower stress in response to the same level of child-rearing challenges.

The Other Perspective: Positive Impact

Despite the growing body of knowledge, the disability field lacks theoretical models that fully address positivity, and, in fact, there is a lack of conceptual clarity as to what is meant by *positive impact* or related terms (Blacher & Baker, 2007). Fortunately, there is an emerging literature on positive impact, with some research on families and disability taking a "more positive and less negative" approach, to paraphrase Helff and Glidden (1998). In this section, we propose three levels at which one could view and assess the positive impact of a child on his or her family.

The first is a view that positive impacts can be implied by the absence of negative ones. In this "low negative" view, positive impacts would be inferred if the parent reported low scores on measures of adverse well-being, such as stress or depression (Taunt & Hastings, 2002). However, even though measures of adverse well-being are likely to be negatively correlated with more direct measures of positive impact, parents may simultaneously report both negative and positive perceptions. A two-factor model of caregiving appraisal proposed in the gerontology field (Lawton, Moss, Kleban, Glicksman, & Rovine, 1991) and further developed with aging parents of adult children with ID (Pruchno, Patrick, & Burant, 1996) views positive and negative emotional states not as polar opposites but, rather, as partially independent and as having different antecedents.

The second view of positive impact is that, despite their child's disability, parents experience many of the same joys of child rearing that are experienced by families of children without a disability. In this "common benefits" view, positivity would be demonstrated by evidence that parents report the same types and extent of positive experiences related to child rearing that are reported by parents of children without disabilities. The third, a "special benefits" view, holds that, because of the disability, the family experiences unique benefits not necessarily experienced by parents of children without disabilities. The common benefits view has received relatively little attention, whereas a number of studies have purported to address the special benefits view (Hastings & Taunt, 2002; Sandler & Mistretta, 1998; Stainton & Besser, 1998). However, study methods have often confused the two views. Typical of these, Stainton and Besser (1998) asked families only the question: "What are the positive impacts you feel your son or daughter with an intellectual disability has had on your family?"

The domains of impact that come out of such studies are, however, important to note. For example, Hastings and Taunt (2002) found parent responses included having increased sensitivity and tolerance, a changed perspective on life, improved family dynamics, and opportunities to learn new information. Identifying such themes is helpful, especially in conceptualizing additional controlled studies. However, conclusions must be tempered not only because of the positive bias in the way questions were asked, but also because, without adequate control groups, we cannot know whether these are, indeed, special benefits or experiences also shared by families raising children with typical cognitive development (e.g., common benefits).

A central problem in advancing our research in this area is that there are few standardized measures of positive impacts. Measures of stress—or negative impact—abound, and from the "low negative" view considered earlier, one might consider low scores to be positive. However, in addition to the conceptual limitations (as it is certainly possible to hold both positive and negative perceptions simultaneously), there is a drawback to many of the measures themselves. The scales primarily used by family disability researchers, such as the widely used Questionnaire on Resources and Stress (QRS; Holroyd, 1985), the QRS-short form (Friedrich, Greenberg, & Crnic, 1983), or the Kansas Inventory of Parental Perceptions (Behr, Murphy, & Summers, 1992) have a strong disability focus and are not appropriate for use with families who have typically developing children, thus precluding comparisons. Moreover widely used measures that are not disability specific (e.g. Parenting Stress Index; Abidin, 1990), include ratings of many negative child characteristics and then infer from those that parents are stressed (as opposed to more directly assessing the domain of interest: stress).

Evidence from the Collaborative Family Study

We turn to some views from the sunny side of the street in our research program, briefly mentioned earlier. In this section, we will draw from a variety of measures to speak to the positive domains of parenting that we are considering in this chapter: positive parenting, dispositional optimism, and positive perceptions of the child's impact on the family.

Positive Parenting

Resilience is functioning that is much better than expected in the face of challenges. Stories of individuals who have made notable achievements in spite of early disadvantage are inspirational (Taylor, 2010). The two requisite conditions that must be present for resilience are (1) a significant threat or difficult circumstance and (2) positive adaptation (Luthar, Cicchetti, & Becker, 2000). Although most resilience research has focused on children who grow up to do far better than their origins would predict, our particular interest here is in resilient parenting—mothers and fathers who show positive parenting in the face of child ID and other risk factors. Positive parenting has been found to be a strong protective factor for children's outcomes under normal circumstances (Vanderbilt-Adriance & Shaw, 2008; Burchinal, Roberts, Zeisel, Hennon, & Hooper, 2006) with even greater benefits in the face of child risk (Greenberg & Crnic, 1988).

In a recent study, Blacher, Baker, and Kaladjian (in press) reported that parents of children with Down syndrome demonstrated higher levels of positive parenting behavior than did parents of children with autism, cerebral palsy, or undifferentiated DD at ages 3, 4, and 5 years. Positive parenting was scored from videotaped mother–child interactions during free play, problem-solving tasks, and clean-up at our child age 3- and 5-year center visits. Coders used the Parent-Child Interaction Rating Scale (PCIRS; Belsky, Crnic, & Woodworth, 1995) that yields negative and positive parenting composites established through factor analyses. The positive parenting score is the sum of four dimension scores: positive affect (verbal and behavioral expression of positive regard or affect, warmth, and affection); sensitivity (maternal behavior is child-centered and developmentally appropriate); stimulation of cognition (attempts to foster the child's cognitive growth at a developmentally appropriate level), and detachment (reverse coded—marked nonresponsiveness and a lack of awareness of the child's needs). Thus, although we could successfully code positive and negative parenting, it was important to understand why some parents manage to be effective in their parenting

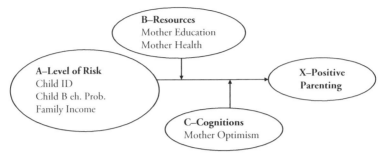

Adaptation of ABCX model (Hill, 1949; 1958)

B–Resources
Mother Education
Mother Health

A–Level of Risk
Child ID
Child B eh. Prob.
Family Income

X–Positive Parenting

C–Cognitions
Mother Optimism

Figure 13.1 Risk and protective factors for resilient parenting. Reprinted with permission from Ellingsen & Baker, 2012.

interactions with the child despite facing formidable challenges.

Another CFS study examined more closely some factors that moderated the relationship of risk factors and positive parenting (Blacher, Baker, & Ellingsen, 2012; Ellingsen & Baker, 2012), using an adaptation of Hill's (1958) ABCX model of stress. The relationship between level of child risk and positive parenting was examined in 232 families. Using regression analyses, we indicated the relationship of child risk to positive parenting and the possible moderation of this relationship by parent resources and cognitions. As shown in Figure 13.1, the risk index was comprised of (1) child ID; (2) child clinical level behavior problems; and (3) family low income (below 2 times poverty level). We found that each of these risk indicators had a significant negative relationship to positive parenting and that, taken together, positive parenting decreased as the risk score increased from 0 (no risk) to 3 (all three risks).

As possible moderators of the child risk–positive parenting relationship, we examined parent resources (mother's education, mother's health) and cognitions (dispositional optimism). At child age 3, the relationship between level of risk and positive parenting, although still significant, was reduced when the moderators were accounted for; education and optimism each accounted for significant variance. At child age 5, all three moderators accounted for significant variance, so much so that the risk score no longer related significantly to positive parenting (Ellingsen & Baker, 2012). Thus, in these analyses, the mothers who "beat the odds" and had positive parenting despite child and family risk factors were those with some combination of higher education, better health, and greater dispositional optimism. There are, of course, many other factors that might promote positive parenting in the face of risk, and hopefully researchers will explore these possible protective factors.

Dispositional Optimism

As reviewed previously, dispositional optimism is a personality characteristic that individuals bring with them to the parenting experience. This propensity to see events in a positive or pessimistic way is likely to affect, and perhaps be affected by, the parenting experience. We have explored both of these questions: To what extent, if any, is dispositional optimism affected by the experience of raising a child with ID? Does high optimism or, conversely, pessimism, relate to how well parents cope with the stresses of parenting?

We have measured dispositional optimism using a simple and widely used self-report measure, the Life Orientation Test—Revised (LOT-R; Scheier, Carver, & Bridges, 1994). This is a 6-item scale (with four additional filler items). Sample items are "In uncertain times, I usually expect the best," and, "If something can go wrong for me, it will" (reverse coded). Respondents indicate the extent of agreement on a 5-point Likert scale from 0 (Definitely disagree) to 4 (Definitely agree). The LOT-R has high internal reliability.

In one set of analyses, we examined parents' dispositional optimism across early and middle childhood, using scores at child ages 3, 6, and 9 years (Blacher et al., 2012). Parent optimism scores were quite stable across these assessments in early and middle childhood, and the group mean scores for parents of children with ID versus TD were also highly stable, supporting the view of optimism as a trait variable. In reference to our first question, of whether raising a child with ID can affect dispositional optimism, the answer appears to be: not much. Although the means for mothers and fathers of children with ID were slightly lower, the differences were not statistically significant.

We have examined the possible protective role of optimism at child ages 3 and 4 years, considering

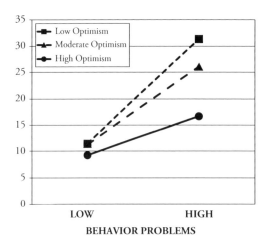

Figure 13.2 Child behavior problems and parenting stress: Optimism as a moderator. Reprinted with permission from Baker, Blacher, & Olsson, 2005.

whether it moderated the strong relationships between child behavior problems and parenting stress (Baker, Blacher, & Olsson, 2005). Figure 13.2, from that article, shows evidence of moderation: When child behavior problems were low, mothers' stress was low regardless of optimism. When child behavior problems were high, however, mothers with high optimism reported only a modestly higher level of stress, whereas pessimistic mothers (low optimism) reported a much higher level of stress.

Dispositional optimism, then, appears to be a protective factor in child-rearing situations that are likely to increase parenting stress. We have argued that early intervention programs could concentrate not only on enhancing parents' teaching skills and behavior problem management, but also on parents' belief systems toward increasing dispositional optimism. Although optimism is a trait, it certainly can be changed (Seligman, 2002). For example, the most successful psychological treatment for depression is cognitive behavior therapy, a major component of which is helping people to identify negative thought patterns and to develop more optimistic cognitive styles (Abramson et al., 2000; Shatté et al., 2000). We have noted that there may be promise in adding a similar component to early intervention programs, especially those enrolling mothers of young children with very challenging behaviors (Baker et al., 2005).

Positive Perceptions

A third domain of "positivity" is the most direct: Asking parents about the positive impacts they perceive their child to have on the family.

Following from the three perspectives on positive impact that we have presented earlier (low negative, common benefits, and special benefits), our studies that follow have focused on the common benefits view, using a measure of positive impact that is applicable to the parents of any child and then examining whether parents of children with ID and TD differ in their perceptions.

We have used the "positive impact" subscale of the Family Impact Questionnaire (FIQ; Donenberg & Baker, 1993). This seven-item scale is introduced by: "We would like to know what impact your child has had on your family compared to the impact other children his/her age have on their families." Sample items are: "I enjoy the time I spend with my child more," and, "My child makes me feel more energetic." Parents respond to six items on a 4-point scale: not at all, somewhat, much, or very much. The seventh item states, "Compared with other children my child's age, the impact of my child on our family is," with a 7-point scale (much less positive, less positive, slightly less positive, about the same, slightly more positive, more positive, and much more positive).

We studied perceived positive impact in families of 92 children with DD and 122 children with typical cognitive development who had complete data at ages 3, 4, and 5 years (Blacher & Baker, 2007). Interestingly, neither mothers nor fathers of children with DD differed in expressed positive impact from parents of children with TD. Positive impact, however, was a significant moderator of the strong relationship between child behavior problems and parenting stress. We conducted three regression analyses, for mothers at child age 3, 4, and 5, to examine the contribution of positive impact to parent stress. The dependent variable was the negative impact score on the FIQ. Child behavior problems and positive impact accounted for significant variance in each analysis, as did the interaction term (behavior problems × positive impact). Figure 13.3 shows a representative picture of this interaction, in this case at child age 3. When behavior problems were low, stress (negative impact) was low and the level of positive impact did not matter. However, with high behavior problems, we see the same finding as with dispositional optimism: mothers reporting greater positive impact of the child on the family reported lower negative impact (stress) than did mothers who perceived less positive impact. Contrary to expectations, dispositional optimism and perceived positive impact of the child are not significantly correlated; they appear to be relatively separate types of positive

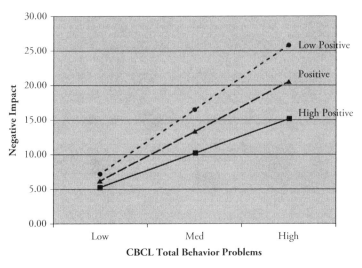

Figure 13.3 Child behavior problems and parenting stress: Positive impact as a moderator. Reprinted with permission from Blacher & Baker, 2007.

perceptions. We repeated these analyses for fathers with much the same findings.

We should note, however, that there seems to be a positive bias in our measure of positive impact. As in Garrison Keeler's fictional town Lake Woebegone, where "all the children are above average," mothers of children with TD or ID mostly reported that they viewed their child's impact on the family as more positive compared to children in other families.

Culture and Positive Impact

In our explorations of positive impact and optimism, the emphasis was on comparisons of children with ID versus typical cognitive development, to determine whether having a child with ID put families at risk of lower positivity or a less optimistic outlook. Generally speaking, it did not. However, it is important to consider families in context and to broaden the lens to include "culture," a domain that can be easily overlooked. Here, we use the term "culture," even though it is synonymous with ethnicity in our analyses that have examined positivity in Anglo and Latino families. This is in part because the growing literature on Latino families suggests some uniformity in beliefs, values, and practices. We present here three examples in which parent perceptions of positive impact of their child with ID differed quite dramatically by culture.

First, Blacher and McIntyre (2006) examined well-being in 282 parents of young adults with ID; 132 of those were Latina mothers and 150 were Anglo mothers. Although the Latina mothers had significantly lower education and income, and were

significantly more likely to be single parents and to score higher in depressive symptomatology, their perceptions of negative impact of the young adult did not differ from those of the more advantaged Anglo mothers. What was most striking, though, is that their perceptions of positive impact on the FIQ (Donenberg & Baker, 1993) were significantly higher than those of the Anglo mothers.

Building on this finding, Blacher and Baker (2007) examined positive impact in a sample of mothers and fathers from the CFS. As noted, using the whole sample of 214 families who had complete data, parents of children with delays reported almost the same positive impact as did parents of children with TD. However, this masked important differences between the Anglo and Latino groups. When the sample was divided by culture as well as by child delay status, the findings were quite surprising. With typically developing children, Anglo and Latino mothers and fathers reported about the same extent of positive impact. However, when their children had DDs, the Anglo parents reported lower positive impact whereas the Latina parents reported higher positive impact. This interaction between cultural group and delay status was significant for mothers and marginally significant for fathers. Figure 13.4 shows this effect for mothers. This interaction mirrored the large and significant cultural difference reported in Blacher and McIntyre's (2006) parents of young adults.

Subsequently, we sought to determine whether culture as a moderator of the child status-positive impact relationship was long-lasting or merely reflective of dynamics during early childhood (Blacher, Begum, Marcoulides, & Baker, in press). We developed

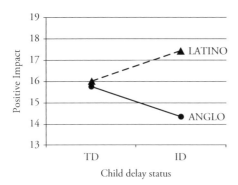

Figure 13.4 Child delay status and mothers' positive impact: Culture as a moderator. From Blacher & Baker, 2007.

trajectories of positive impact from 219 mothers over seven annual CFS time points (child ages 3–9 years). We used latent growth modeling and two predictors: culture (Anglo, Latino) and child disability status (ID, TD). Consistent with the earlier reported findings that were not analyzed using time-sensitive models (Blacher & Baker, 2007), we anticipated finding initial differences by ethnic or cultural group. However, we advanced no hypothesis about trajectory from early through middle childhood. On average, at age 3, Anglo mothers reported significantly lower initial positive impact values than did Latino mothers when their children had ID. Too, growth trajectories reflected a general decline in positive impact for Anglo mothers, but not for Latino mothers. Across all time points, Latino mothers had higher scores on positive impact, regardless of whether they had a child with ID or a typically developing child.

How do parents of children with intellectual delays emerge on the sunny side of the street? We will consider three probable reasons why Latina mothers may report more positive impact, and possibly more optimism, about raising a child with a disability. First, it is likely that their attributions focus on an external locus of control (Blacher & McIntyre, 2006). Chavira, Lopez, Blacher, and Shapiro (2000) interviewed 129 Latina mothers of children with DDs regarding incidents in which their child exhibited a behavior problem. They reported that mothers' attributions of control or responsibility were related to their responses. In particular, mothers who attributed high responsibility to the child were significantly more likely to report negative emotions (anger and frustrations) and harsh/aggressive behavioral reactions than mothers who attributed low responsibility. However, most Latina mothers viewed their child as not being responsible for his or her behavior problems. From an educational perspective, this

belief that the child's behavior challenges were not endemic paves the way for more effective intervention. If behavior problems were attributed to internal or child-driven causes, then parents might have little hope of being able to intervene effectively (Coplan et al., 2002; Mills & Rubin, 1992).

A second dynamic underlying the greater positive impact endorsed by Latina mothers pertains to religion. It is true that religion and spirituality provide a way to make sense of having a child with a disability, even in non-Latino families (Lee, 2009; Poston & Turnbull, 2004) and in families who have children with autism without ID (Ekas, Whitman, & Shivers, 2009). In a study by Skinner, Correa, Skinner, and Bailey (2001), 68% of Latinos reported that they believed their child was a blessing sent from God as a sign of their worthiness as parents.

Along with attribution and religion, there are some cultural beliefs that influence the positive perceptions of some Latina mothers raising children with ID. For example, Blacher and McIntyre (2006) attributed their paradoxical finding that Latina mothers reported more depressive symptoms but also more positive impact to *marianismo*. Although certainly not endorsed by all, or even most, Latina mothers, *marianismo* reflects the self-sacrifices that some women feel they must make for their children, to give much more than they receive (Altarriba & Santiago-Rivera, 1994; Gill & Vazquez, 1996). This belief may also underscore the reason why Latina mothers reported contradictory feelings of grief and joy in child rearing, hopes and fears for the child's future (Larson, 1998), and possibility also account for their high level of acceptance of their child with ID. Positive perceptions and acceptance can protect them from some of the negative aspects of disability or of their life circumstances (Taylor, 1983; Zuniga, 2004). Thus, the overwhelming historical emphasis in the families and disability literature on stress and adjustment difficulties on the part of mothers in adapting to their children with ID (Blacher & Baker, 2002) may have less relevance to contemporary Latino families.

In the United States, Latino families are the largest and fastest growing cultural group. That Latino mothers have different values about child rearing and different attitudes toward disability, despite their more widespread economic hardship, suggests a special kind of resilience. We note the overall level of optimism found among the parents of the CFS, and especially the lessons we can learn from Latina mothers. Clearly, these parents are resilient—they are themselves at-risk but have beaten the odds and will likely raise their children with ID with good, or better than expected, outcomes. In preparing this chapter, we were reminded of Ann Masten's (2001) description of the ordinariness of resilience. Even though she studied children rather than parents and parenting, she purported that resilience derived from ordinary functions of the human adaptation systems, which are inherently quite protective. "Threats" to these adaptive systems are those that compromise these protective systems. For too long, our field has viewed the mere presence of an ID as a "threat."

Conclusion

From these varying views of the family experience we can see that child rearing is at once filled with hurdles to be overcome and highlights to be savored. Some families may find themselves more resilient than others, where resilience may depend not only on the extent of risk but also on the resources available to the family. It is reflected not only in parental behaviors (e.g., positive parenting) but in personality traits (e.g., dispositional optimism) that prepare parents to face challenges and in positive perceptions of the child's role in the family. Finally, resilience is not independent of cultural values and practices. In the case of our Latina mothers, perhaps resilience and adaptability toward their child with ID is simply ordinary rather than extraordinary. We need to develop models to understand further the positive, adaptive systems of these mothers and to provide the scaffolding for all families to foster protective factors within their social context.

Acknowledgments

This paper was based on the activities of the Collaborative Family Study, supported by the Eunice Kennedy Shriver National Institute of Child Health and Human Development, Grant number: 34879-1459 (Drs. B. L. Baker, J. Blacher, & Keith Crnic PIs). We also acknowledge the Institute for Education Sciences, Grant number R324A110086, J. Blacher, PI, and the SEARCH Family Autism Resource Center at UC Riverside. As in all of our work, we are grateful to the many children and families for their participation, and to the dedication and expertise of the students, staff, and colleagues involved.

References

Abidin, R. R. (1990). *Parenting Stress Index manual* (3rd ed.). Charlottesville, VA: Pediatric Psychology Press.

Abramson, L. Y., Alloy, L. B., Hankin, B. L., Clements, C. M., Zhu, L., Hogan, M. E., & Whitehouse, W. G. (2000). Optimistic cognitive styles and invulnerability to depression. In J. E. Gillham (Ed.), *The science of optimism and hope: Research essays in honor of Martin E. P. Seligman* (pp. 75–98). Philadelphia, PA: Templeton Foundation Press.

Altarriba, J., & Santiago-Rivera, A. L. (1994). Current perspectives on using linguistic and cultural factors in counseling the Hispanic client. *Professional Psychology: Research and Practice*, 25(4), 388–397. doi:10.1037/0735-7028.25.4.388

Aspinwall, L. G., & MacNamara, A. (2005). Taking positive changes seriously. *Cancer*, 104(S11), 2549–2556. doi:10.1002/cncr.21244

Baker, B. L., Blacher, J., Crnic, K., & Edelbrock, C. (2002). Behavior problems and parenting stress in families of three-year-old children with and without developmental delays. *American Journal on Mental Retardation*. 107(6), 433–444. doi:10.1352/0895-8017(2002)107<0433:BPAPSI>2.0.CO;2

Baker, B.L., Blacher, J, Kopp, C.B., & Kraemer, B. (1997). Parenting children with mental retardation. *International Review of Research in Mental Retardation*, 20, 1–45. doi:10.1016/S0074-7750(08)60174-3

Baker, B.L., Blacher, J., & Olsson, M.B. (2005). Preschool children with and without developmental delay: Behaviour problems, parents' optimism and well-being. *Journal of Intellectual Disability Research*, 49(8), 575–590. doi:10.1111/j.1365-2788.2005.00691.x

Baker, B. L., McIntyre, L. L., Blacher, J., Crnic, K., Edelbrock, C., & Low, C. (2003). Pre-school children with and without developmental delay: Behaviour problems and parenting stress over time. *Journal of Intellectual Disability Research*, 47(4-5), 217–230. doi:10.1046/j.1365-2788.2003.00484.x

Bayat, M. (2007). Evidence of resilience in families of children with autism. *Journal of Intellectual Disability Research*, 51(9), 702–714. doi:10.1111/j.1365-2788.2007.00960.x

Behr, S. K., Murphy, D. L., & Summers, J. A. (1992). *User's manual: Kansas Inventory of Parental Perceptions (KIPP)*. Lawrence, KS: Beach Center on Families and Disability.

Belsky, J., Crnic, K., & Woodworth, S. (1995). Personality and parenting: Exploring the mediating role of transient mood and daily hassles. *Journal of Personality*, 63(4), 905–929. doi:10.1111/j.1467-6494.1995.tb00320.x

Blacher, J., & Baker, B. L. (2002). *Families and mental retardation: A collection of notable AAMR journal articles across the 20th century*. Washington, DC: American Association on Mental Retardation.

Blacher, J., & Baker, B. L. (2007). Positive impact of intellectual disability on families. *American Journal of Mental Retardation*, 112(5), 330–348. doi:10.1352/0895-8017(2007)112[0330:PIOIDO]2.0.CO;2

Blacher, J., Baker, B. L., & Kaladjian, A. (2012). Syndrome specificity and mother-child interactions: Examining positive and negative parenting across contexts and time. *Journal of Autism and Developmental Disorders*. Advance online publication. doi:10.1007/s10803-012-1605-x

Blacher, J., Begum, G., Marcoulides, G., & Baker, B. L. (in press). Longitudinal perspectives of child impact on families: Relationship to culture and disability status. *American Journal on Intellectual and Developmental Disabilities*.

Blacher, J., Baker, B. L., & Ellingsen, E. (2012, July). *Still resilient after all these years: Parents raising children with intellectual disability*. Paper presented at the International Association for the Scientific Study of Intellectual Disabilities Word Congress, Halifax, Nova Scotia.

Blacher, J., & McIntyre, L. L. (2006). Syndrome specificity and behavioural disorders in young adults with intellectual disability: Cultural differences in family impact. *Journal of Intellectual Disability Research*, *50*(3), 184–198. doi:10.1111/j.1365-2788.2005.00768.x

Brandon, P. (2007). Time away from "smelling the roses": Where do mothers of children with disabilities find time to work? *Social Science and Medicine*, *65*(4), 667–679. doi:10.1016/j.socscimed.2007.04.007

Burchinal, M., Roberts, J. E., Zeisel, S. A., Hennon, E. A., & Hooper, S. (2006). Social risk and protective child, parenting, and child care factors in early elementary school years. *Parenting: Science and Practice*, *6*(1), 79–113. doi:10.1207/s15327922par0601_4

Chavira, V., López, S. R., Blacher, J., & Shapiro, J., (2000). Latina mothers' attributions, emotions, and reactions to the problem behaviors of their children with developmental disabilities. *Journal of Child Psychology and Psychiatry*, *41*(2), 245–252. doi:10.1017/S0021963099005144

Coplan, R. J., Hastings, P. D., Lagacé-Séguin, D. G., & Moulton, C. E. (2002). Authoritative and authoritarian mothers' parenting goals, attributions, and emotions across different childrearing contexts. *Parenting: Science and Practice*, *2*(1), 1–26. doi:10.1207/S15327922PAR0201_1

Crnic, K. A., Friedrich, W. N., & Greenberg, M. T. (1983). Adaptation of families with mentally retarded children: A model of stress, coping, and family ecology. *American Journal of Mental Deficiency*, *88*(2), 125–138.

Crnic, K. A., & Greenberg, M. T. (1987). Transactional relationships between perceived family style, risk status, and mother-child interactions in two-year-olds. *Journal of Pediatric Psychology*, *12*(3), 343–362. doi:10.1093/jpepsy/12.3.343

Donenberg, G., & Baker, B. L. (1993). The impact of children with externalizing behavior on their families. *Journal of Abnormal Child Psychology*, *21*(2), 179–198. doi:10.1007/BF00911315

Dougall, A. L., Hyman, K. B., Hayward, M. C., McFeeley, S., & Baum, A. (2001). Optimism and traumatic stress: The importance of social support and coping. *Journal of Applied Social Psychology* *31*(2), 223–245. doi:10.1111/j.1559-1816.2001.tb00195.x

Eisenhower, A. S., Baker, B. L., & Blacher, J. (2005). Preschool children with intellectual disability: Syndrome specificity, behaviour problems, and maternal well-being. *Journal of Intellectual Disability Research*, *49*, 657–671. doi:10.1111/j.1365-2788.2005.00699.x

Eisenhower, A. S., Baker, B. L., & Blacher, J. (2009). Children's delayed development and behavior problems: Impact on mothers' perceived physical health across early childhood. *Social Science and Medicine*, *68*(1), 89–99. doi:10.1016/j.socscimed.2008.09.033

Eisenhower, A., Blacher, B., & Baker, B. L. (2013). Mothers' perceived physical health during early and middle childhood: Relations with child developmental delay and behavior problems. *Research in Developmental Disabilities*, *34*(3), 1059–1068. doi: 10.1016/j.ridd.2012.12.002

Ekas, N. V., Whitman, T. L., & Shivers, C. (2009). Religiosity, spirituality, and socioemotional functioning in mothers of children with autism spectrum disorder. *Journal of Autism and Developmental Disorders*, *39*(5), 706–719. doi:10.1007/s10803-008-0673-4

Ekas, N. V., Lickenbrock, D. M., & Whitman, T. L. (2010). Optimism, social support, and well-being in mothers of children with autism spectrum disorder. *Journal of Autism and Developmental Disorders*, *40*(10), 1274–1284. doi:10.1007/s10803-010-0986-y

Ellingsen, R., & Baker, B. L. (2012). *Resilient parenting of preschool children at developmental risk*. Unpublished manuscript, Department of Psychology, UCLA, Los Angeles, CA.

Epel, E. S., Blackburn, E. H., Lin, J., Dhabhar, F. S., Adler, N. E., Morrow, J. D., & Cawthon, R. M. (2004). Accelerated telomere shortening in response to life stress. *Proceedings of the National Academy of Sciences*, *101*(49), 17312–17315. doi:10.1073/pnas.0407162101

Fidler, D. J., Hodapp, R. M., & Dykens, E. M. (2000). Stress in families of young children with Down syndrome, Williams syndrome, and Smith-Magenis syndrome. *Early Education and Development*, *11*(4), 395–406. doi:10.1207/s15566935eed1104_2

Floyd, F. J., & Phillippe, K. A. (1993). Parental interactions with children with and without mental retardation: Behavior management, coerciveness, and positive exchange. *American Journal on Mental Retardation*, *97*(6), 673–684.

Folkman, S. (1997). Positive psychological states and coping with severe stress. *Social Science & Medicine*, *45*(8), 1207–1221. doi:10.1016/S0277-9536(97)00040-3

Folkman, S. (2008). The case for positive emotions in the stress process. *Anxiety, Stress & Coping*, *21*(1), 3–14. doi:10.1080/10615800701740457

Folkman, S. (2010). Stress, coping, and hope. *Psychooncology*, *19*(9), 901–908. doi:10.1002/pon.1836

Folkman, S., & Moskowitz, J. T. (2000). Positive affect and the other side of coping. *American Psychologist*, *55*(6), 647–654. doi:10.1037/0003-066X.55.6.647

Folkman, S., & Moskowitz, J. T. (2004). Coping: pitfalls and promise. *Annual Review of Psychology*, *55*, 745–774. doi:10.1146/annurev.psych.55.090902.141456Z

Friedrich, W. N., Greenberg, M. T., & Crnic, K. (1983). A short-form of the Questionnaire on Resources and Stress. *American Journal of Mental Deficiency*, *88*(1), 41–48.

Gill, R. M., & Vazquez, C. I. (1996). *The Maria paradox: How Latinas can merge old world tradition with new world self-esteem*. New York: G. P. Putnam's Sons.

Greenbaum, C. W., & Auerbach, J. G. (1998). The environment of the child with mental retardation: Risk, vulnerability, and resilience. In J. A. Burach, R. M. Hodapp & E. Zigler (Eds.), *Handbook of Mental Retardation and Development* (pp. 583–605). Cambridge: Cambridge University Press.

Greenberg, M. T., & Crnic, K. A. (1988). Longitudinal predictors of developmental status and social interaction in premature and full-term infants at age two. *Child Development*, *59*(3), 554–570. doi:10.2307/1130557

Gunn, P., & Berry, P. (1987). Some financial costs of caring for children with Down Syndrome at home. *Journal of Intellectual and Developmental Disability*, *13*(4), 187–194. doi:10.3109/13668258709049921

Hastings, R. P., & Taunt, H. M. (2002). Positive perceptions in families of children with developmental disabilities. *American Journal on Mental Retardation*, *107*(2), 116–127. doi:10.1352/0895-8017(2002)107<0116:PPIFOC>2.0.CO;2

Hauser-Cram, P., Warfield, M. E., Shonkoff, J. P., & Krauss, M. W. (2001). Children with disabilities: A longitudinal study of child development and parent well-being. *Monographs of the Society for Research in Child Development*, *66*(3), 1–114. doi:10.1111/1540-5834.00151

Helff, C. M., & Glidden, L. M. (1998). More positive or less negative? Trends in research on adjustment of families rearing children with developmental disabilities. *Mental Retardation*, *36*(6), 457–464. doi:10.1352/0047-6765(1998)036<0457:MPOLNT>2.0.CO;2

Helgeson, V. S., Reynolds, K. A., & Tomich, P. L. (2006). A meta-analytic review of benefit finding and growth. *Journal of Consulting and Clinical Psychology*, *74*(5), 797–816. doi:10.1037/0022-006X.74.5.797

Hill, R. (1958). Generic features of families under stress. *Social Casework*, *49*, 139–150.

Hodapp, R. M., Fidler, D. J., & Smith, A. C. M. (1998). Stress and coping in families of children with Smith-Magenis syndrome. *Journal of Intellectual Disability Research*, *42*(5), 331–340. doi:10.1046/j.1365-2788.1998.00148.x

Holroyd, J., (1985). *Questionnaire on Resources and Stress Manual*. Unpublished manuscript, University of California, Los Angeles, Neuropsychiatric Institute, Los Angeles, CA.

Judge, S. L. (1998). Parental coping strategies and strengths in families of young children with disabilities. *Family Relations*, *47*(3), 263–268. doi:10.2307/584976

Karademas, E. C. (2006). Self-efficacy, social support and well-being: The mediating role of optimism. *Personality and Individual Differences*, *40*(6), 1281–1290. doi:10.1016/j.paid.2005.10.019

Koenig, J. L., Barry, R. A., & Kochanska, G. (2010). Rearing difficult children: Parents' personality and children's proneness to anger as predictors of future parenting. *Parenting: Science and Practice*, *10*(4), 258–273. doi:10.1080/15295192.2010.492038

Larson, E. (1998). Reframing the meaning of disability to families: The embrace of paradox. *Social Science and Medicine*, *47*(7), 865–875. doi:10.1016/S0277-9536(98)00113-0

Lawton, M. P., Moss, M., Kleban, M.H, Glicksman, A., & Rovine, M. (1991). A two-factor model of caregiving appraisal and psychological well-being. *Journal of Gerontology: Psychological Sciences*, *46*(4), 181–189. doi:10.1093/geronj/46.4.P181

Lee, G. K. (2009). Parents of children with high functioning autism: How well do they cope and adjust? *Journal of Developmental and Physical Disabilities*, *21*(2), 93–114. doi:10.1007/s10882-008-9128-2

Luthar, S. S., Cicchetti, D., & Becker, B. (2000). The construct of resilience: A critical evaluation and guidelines for future work. *Child Development*, *71*(3), 543–562. doi:10.1111/1467-8624.00164

Masten, A. S. (2001). Ordinary magic: Resilience processes in development. *American Psychologist*, *56*(3), 227–238. doi:10.1037/0003-066X.56.3.227

Meirsschaut, M., Roeyers, H., & Warreyn, P. (2010). Parenting in families with a child with autism spectrum disorder and a typically developing child: Mothers' experiences and cognitions. *Research in Autism Spectrum Disorders*, *4*(4), 661–669. doi:10.1016/j.rasd.2010.01.00289

Mills, R. S. L., & Rubin K. H. (1992). A longitudinal study of normative maternal cognitions and beliefs about social behaviors. *Merrill-Palmer Quarterly*, *38*, 494–512.

Minnes, P. M. (1988). Family resources and stress associated with having a mentally retarded child. *American Journal on Mental Retardation*, *93*(2), 184–192.

Myers, B. J., Mackintosh, V. H., & Goin-Kochel, R. P. (2009). "My greatest joy and my greatest heart ache:" Parents' own words on how having a child in the autism spectrum has affected their lives and their families' lives. *Research in Autism Spectrum Disorders*, *3*(3), 670–684. doi:10.1016/j.rasd.2009.01.004

Neece, C. L., Green, S. A., & Baker, B. L. (2012). Parenting stress and child behavior problems: A transactional relationship across time. *American Journal on Intellectual and Developmental Disabilities*, *117*(1), 48–66. doi:10.1352/1944-7558-117.1.48

Olason, D. T., & Roger, D. (2001). Optimism, pessimism and "fighting spirit": A new approach to assessing expectancy and adaptation. *Personality and Individual Differences*, *31*(5), 755–768. doi:10.1016/S0191-8869(00)00176-8

Olshansky, S. (1962). Chronic sorrow: A response to having a mentally defective child. *Social Casework*, *43*(4), 190–193.

Olsson, M. B., & Hwang, C. P. (2001). Depression in mothers and fathers of children with intellectual disability. *Journal of Intellectual Disability Research*, *45*(6), 535–543. doi:10.1046/j.1365-2788.2001.00372.x

Orr, R. R., Cameron, S. J., Dobson, L. A., & Day, D. M. (1993). Age-related changes in stress experienced by families with a child who has developmental delays. *Mental Retardation*, *31*(3), 171–176.

Paczkowski, E., & Baker, B. L. (2008). Parenting children with developmental delays: The role of positive beliefs. *Journal of Mental Health Research in Intellectual Disabilities*, *1*(3), 156–175. doi:10.1080/19315860801988392

Petalas, M. A., Hastings, R. P., Nash, S., Dowey, A., & Reilly, D. (2009). "I like that he always shows who he is": The perceptions and experiences of siblings with a brother with autism spectrum disorder. *International Journal of Disability, Development and Education*, *56*(4), 381–399. doi:10.1080/10349120903306715

Peterson, C. (2000). The future of optimism. *American Psychologist*, *55*(1), 44–55. doi:10.1037/0003-066X.55.1.44

Poston, D. J., & Turnbull, A. P. (2004). The role of spirituality and religion in family quality of life. *Education and Training in Mental Retardation and Developmental Disabilities*, *39*(2), 95–108.

Pruchno, R. A., Patrick, J. H., & Burant, C. J. (1996). Mental health of aging women with children who are chronically disabled: Examination of a two-factor model. *Journal of Gerontology: Social Sciences*, *51B*(6), S284–S296. doi:10.1093/geronb/51B.6.S284

Rodrigue, J. R., Morgan, S. B., & Geffken, G. R. (1992). Psychosocial adaptation of fathers of children with autism, Down syndrome, and normal development. *Journal of Autism and Developmental Disorders*, *22*(2), 249–263. doi:10.1007/BF01058154

Rodrigue, J. R., Morgan, S. B., & Geffken, G. (1990). Families of autistic children: Psychological functioning of mothers. *Journal of Clinical Child Psychology*, *19*(4), 371–379. doi:10.1207/s15374424jccp1904_9

Sameroff, A. J., & Chandler, M. J. (1975). Reproductive risk and the continuum of caretaking casualty. In F. D. Horowitz, M. Hetherington, S. Scarr-Salapatek, & G. Siegel (Eds.), *Review of child development research* (vol. 4, pp. 187–244). Chicago: University of Chicago Press, 1975.

Sameroff, A. J., & Mackenzie, M. J. (2003). Research strategies for capturing transactional models of development: The limits of the possible. *Development and Psychopathology*, *15*(3), 613–640. doi:10.1017/S0954579403000312

Sanders, J. L., & Morgan, S. B. (1997). Family stress and adjustment as perceived by parents of children with autism or Down syndrome: Implications for intervention. *Child & Family Behavior Therapy*, *19*(4), 15–32. doi:10.1300/J019v19n04_02

Sandler, A. G., & Mistretta, L. A. (1998). Positive adaptation in parents of adults with disabilities. *Education and Training in Mental Retardation and Developmental Disabilities*, *33*(2), 123–130.

Scheier, M. F., & Carver, C. S. (1985). Optimism, coping, and health: Assessment and implications of generalized outcome expectancies. *Health Psychology*, *4*(3), 219–247. doi:10.1037/0278-6133.4.3.219

Scheier, M. F., Carver, C. S., & Bridges, M. W. (1994). Distinguishing optimism from neuroticism (and trait anxiety, self mastery, and self-esteem): A reevaluation of the Life Orientation Test. *Journal of Personality and Social Psychology*, *67*(6), 1063–1078. doi:10.1037/0022-3514.67.6.1063

Seeman, T. E. (1996). Social ties and health: The benefits of social integration. *Annals of Epidemiology*, *6*(5), 442–451. doi:10.1016/S1047-2797(96)00095-6

Segerstrom, S. C. (2001). Optimism and attentional bias for negative and positive stimuli. *Personality and Social Psychology Bulletin*, *27*(10), 1334–1343. doi:10.1177/01461672012710009

Seligman, M. E. P. (2002). *Authentic happiness: Using the new positive psychology to realize your potential for lasting fulfillment.* New York: Simon and Schuster.

Shatté, A. J., Gillham, J. E., & Reivich, K. J. (2000). Promoting hope in children and adolescents. In J. E. Gillham (Ed.), *The science of optimism and hope: Research essays in honor of Martin E. P. Seligman* (pp. 215–234). Philadelphia: Templeton Foundation Press.

Skinner, D. G., Correa, V., Skinner, M., & Bailey, D. B. (2001). Role of religion in the lives of Latino families of young children with developmental delays. *American Journal on Mental Retardation*, *106*(4), 297–313. doi:10.1352/0895-8017(2001)106<0297:RORITL>2.0.CO;2

Stainton, T., & Besser, H. (1998). The positive impact of children with an intellectual disability on the family. *Journal of Intellectual and Developmental Disability*, *23*(1), 57–70. doi:10.1080/13668259800033581

Stores, R., Stores, G., Fellows, B., & Buckley, S. (1998). Daytime behaviour problems and maternal stress in children with Down's syndrome, their siblings, and non-intellectually disabled and other intellectually disabled peers. *Journal of Intellectual Disability Research*, *42*(3), 228–237. doi:10.1046/j.1365-2788.1998.00123.x

Taunt, H. M., & Hastings, R. P. (2002). Positive impact of children with developmental disabilities in their families: A preliminary study. *Education and Training in Mental Retardation and Developmental Disabilities*, *37*(4), 410–420.

Taylor, S. E. (1983). Adjustment to threatening events: A theory of cognitive adaptation. *American Psychologist*, *38*(11), 1161–1173. doi:10.1037/0003-066X.38.11.1161

Taylor, S. E. (2010). Mechanisms linking early life stress to adult health outcomes. *Proceedings of the National Academy of Sciences*, *107*(19), 8507–8512. doi:10.1073/pnas.1003890107

Taylor, S. E., & Brown, J. D. (1988). Illusion and well-being: A social psychological perspective on mental health. *Psychological Bulletin*, *103*(2), 193–210. doi:10.1037/0033-2909.103.2.193

Taylor, S. E., Kemeny, M. E., Reed, G. M., Bower, J. E., & Gruenewald, T. L. (2000). Psychological resources, positive illusions, and health. *American Psychologist*, *55*(1), 99–109. doi:10.1037/0003-066X.55.1.99

Taylor, S. E., Repetti, R. L., & Seeman, T. (1997). Health psychology: What is an unhealthy environment and how does it get under the skin? *Annual Review of Psychology*, *48*, 411–447. doi:10.1146/annurev.psych.48.1.411

Tugade, M. M., Fredrickson, B. L., & Barrett, L. F. (2004). Psychological resilience and positive emotional granularity: Examining the benefits of positive emotions on coping and health. *Journal of Personality*, *72*(6), 1161–1190. doi:10.1111/j.1467-6494.2004.00294.x

Turnbull, A. P., Patterson J. M, Behr, S., Murphy, D., Marquis, J., & Blue-Banning, M. (1993). *Cognitive coping, families, & disability.* Baltimore, MD: Paul H. Brookes.

Vanderbilt-Adriance, E., & Shaw, D. S. (2008). Protective factors and the development of resilience in the context of neighborhood disadvantage. *Journal of Abnormal Child Psychology*, *36*(6), 887–901. doi:10.1007/s10802-008-9220-1

Wikler, L. M. (1986). Periodic stresses of families of older mentally retarded children: An exploratory study. *American Journal of Mental Deficiency*, *90*(6), 703–706.

Wrosch, C., Scheier, M. F., Miller, G. E., Schulz, R., & Carver, C. S. (2003). Adaptive self-regulation of unattainable goals: Goal disengagement, goal reengagement, and subjective well-being. *Personality and Social Psychology Bulletin*, *29*(12), 1494–1508. doi:10.1177/0146167203256921

Zuniga, M. (2004). Latino children and families. In R. Fong (Ed.), *Culturally competent practice with immigrant and refugee children and families* (pp. 183–201). New York: Guilford Press.

Resilience and Disability: Concepts, Examples, Cautions, and Prospects

Christopher Murray *and* Bonnie Doren

Abstract

Although the concept of resilience is related to positive psychology in the sense that both focus on the promotion of competence, resilience refers to the process of adapting to or overcoming risk, whereas positive psychology is concerned mainly with competence enhancement among all individuals. This chapter provides an overview of the concepts of risk, promotive, and protective factors and reviews research documenting risk and protection among children and youth with disabilities. It then examines the applicability of these concepts to a prevention and intervention agenda within the field of disability generally and within special education specifically. Recommendations include documentation of ecological risk factors that are predictive of negative developmental outcomes, documentation of both promotive and protective factors that serve to enhance competence and buffer the negative effects of risk, and implementation and evaluation of risk reduction and protection enhancement prevention and intervention efforts for children, youth, and adults with disabilities.

Key Words: resilience, students with disabilities, coping, prevention

At the biological level 100,000 genes are required to transform an egg cell into an adult human body, each gene expressing itself in precise degrees at precise times in precise locations. It may take far more than 100,000 events to produce the complex psychological functioning of the adult human, integrating a wide variety of environmental experiences with a wide variety of developing capacities.

—*Sameroff, 2000, p. 309*

The concept of "resilience" has captivated the attention and imagination of human beings for many years. It almost seems central to human nature to be attracted to stories of strength in the face of adversity. Until relatively recently, such accounts were relegated primarily to individual stories of courage, strength of spirit, and seemingly miraculous recovery from or resistance to illness. However, beginning in the 1960s, a small number of social

scientists, influenced heavily by the field of epidemiology, began to systematically document evidence of "resilience" through retrospective and prospective longitudinal studies of "high risk" children, youth, and adults (Elder, 1974; Farrington, 2003; Garmezy, 1987, 1991; Moskovitz, 1983; Werner & Smith, 1989). These works proved so illuminating that they spawned the field of developmental psychopathology—a field dedicated not only to understanding pathology but also to understanding competence, adaptation to adverse conditions, etiology, and normative functioning (Achenbach, 1974; Garmezy, Masten, & Tellegen, 1984; Sameroff, 2000). Developmental psychopathology, in turn, contributed heavily to the now burgeoning fields of prevention science (Lerner, 2001), positive youth development (Damon, 2004), and positive psychology (Seligman & Csikszentmihályi, 2000).

Not surprisingly, early evidence of resilience within the social sciences was greeted with enthusiasm, and book titles such as *Vulnerable but Invincible*, and *The Invulnerable Child* juxtaposed views of pathology on the one hand, with apparent super human capacities on the other. Although certainly captivating, this early exuberance for the *extra*ordinary was problematic because it implied that only those with exceptional abilities could withstand insult. Rather, as noted by Masten (2001):

> Resilience does not come from rare and special qualities, but from the everyday magic of ordinary, normative human resources in the minds, brains, and bodies of children, in their families and relationships, and in their communities. (p. 238)

Thus, the processes that promote resilience are in and around all of us, and the potential to draw on these resources in times of stress is not reserved for (or bestowed upon) the few, but is instead available to all. Moreover, resilience is a process, and individuals who demonstrate adaptive outcomes in the face of stress at one point in time may, at other times, experience maladaptive outcomes (Zimmerman & Arunkumar, 1994). Therefore, terms and concepts such as "invincible" are at the same time both overly restrictive and overly optimistic.

The purpose of this chapter is to provide a brief overview of risk and resilience and to explore evidence of the effectiveness of recent interventions designed to promote "resilience" among children and youth. Although the examples we draw on often include populations without disabilities, our primary aim is to draw attention to the potential application of these concepts to the field of disability generally and to special education specifically. Resilience has not been studied widely within special education to date, perhaps because this field has historically required an implicit and explicit adoption of organismic views of development. However, evidence of resilient children, youth, and adults with disabilities certainly exists; strategies for understanding and promoting resilience among high-stress populations is currently emerging in the areas of reading and behavior, and developing further understanding about the application of a resilience framework has important implications for those interested in promoting competence among all vulnerable children and youth, including those with disabilities.

Ecological Models and Developmental Systems Theory

Resilience is not a fixed attribute but instead represents processes that reside in individuals and their environments. Therefore, understanding resilience requires one to consider integrative theoretical models of human development including ecological models (Bronfenbrenner & Morris, 2006) and systems theories (Ford & Lerner, 1992). Although an in-depth exploration of these theories is beyond the scope of this chapter, both highlight the importance of developmental contextualism by specifying the important role exchanges among biological, maturational, and ecological contexts play in shaping the developmental trajectories of children and youth. In addition to providing the forum for development generally, these same systems provide opportunities for protection during times of stress. Resilience describes the effective functioning of basic adaptive systems (e.g., positive attachments) under adverse conditions. All systems have the capacity to develop, or draw on, this adaptive functioning through a compilation of resources at the individual (e.g., biological) and ecological (e.g., families, peers, schools, and communities) levels. Under conditions of adversity, these adaptive systems can serve to restore competence in development (Sameroff, 2000; Sroufe, 2009; Yates & Masten, 2004).

Ecological and developmental systems theories also highlight the interactive nature of the individual and the multiple contexts he or she encounters. Developmental experiences represent more than direct inputs and instead represent transactions between individual and contextual systems, as well as interactions between contextual systems themselves (Lynch & Cicchetti, 1998). Thus, not only are individuals shaped by these contexts—they also shape them. Bronfenbrenner and Morris (2006) observed that "behavioral dispositions can set proximal processes in motion and sustain their operation" (p. 810) when describing the role individuals play in promoting, or inhibiting, opportunities for positive or negative developmental experiences within the microsystem. Evidence of such transactions has now been demonstrated by researchers studying parent–child interactions (Bugental & Shennum, 1984; Patterson, Forgatch, Yoerger, & Stoolmiller, 1998), teachers–student interactions (Berry, 2012; Nelson & Roberts, 2000), and in the dynamics of peer relationships (Poulin, Dishion, & Burraston, 2001). In addition to transactions between the developing individual and contexts, contexts themselves can interact. For example, Whipple, Evans, Barry, and Maxwell (2010) found that the detrimental effects of school-level risk factors on student performance were higher in neighborhoods defined as moderately risky than in neighborhoods with either high or low levels of risk, suggesting a

※ Ecological model of risk
↳ Framework for the chapter

unique interactive relationship between schools and neighborhoods. Lenzi et al. (2012) found that social support from peers partially mediated the effects of neighborhood cohesion on prosocial behavior among adolescents. That is, although supportive neighborhood contexts were an important predictor of prosocial behavior, some of these effects operated through the increased availability of supportive peers within such contexts (Lenzi et al., 2012). From an ecological-systems perspective, such complexities are the norm, not the exception. As observed by Cicchetti and Toth (1997):

> [r]eductionistic efforts to delimit unitary, main effects causes of maladaption or psychopathology are inadequate. Such linear models of causality deny the complexity of development and the mutually influencing nature of constitutional, biological, psychological, environmental, and sociological influences over time. (p. 319)

Although ecological systems models have been widely adopted in other fields, they are less widespread among educators generally and among special educators specifically. However, most special educators recognize that developmental trajectories and outcomes can be influenced by students' experiences within classrooms, homes, peer groups, and communities, and they also recognize that the specific individual characteristics, dispositions, and histories that students bring to these contexts can affect opportunities, supports, and outcomes within them.

Risk

Resilience is not possible without risk. Although we recognize that the field of positive psychology is concerned primarily with the promotion of competence among all children, youth, and adults, along with the premise that deficit models have been the dominant zeitgeist in psychology for far too long (Seligman & Csikszentmihályi, 2000), currently, in all societies, children and youth are exposed to varying levels of risk, and some of these risks are predictive of maladaptive outcomes. Risks take many forms and include (but are not limited to) genes transmitted to individuals prior to birth; prenatal environmental insults; perinatal complications; exposure to toxins during critical developmental periods throughout the lifespan; experiences within the contexts of families, such as physical or sexual abuse; experiences within peer relationships, such as bullying and deviancy training; disorganized and dangerous schools; exposure to violence, drugs, and alcohol within communities; and broader societal risks, including exposure to poverty and lack of adequate health care. Exposure to these and many other risk factors are reliably, and inversely, related to healthy development.

In general, to qualify as a risk factor, the individual characteristic or experience must temporally precede a specific negative outcome of interest and must also be a potent (i.e., clinically or policy significant) predictor of that outcome (Kraemer et al., 1997). Kramer et al. (1997) proposed different classes of risk factors, including *malleable* or variable risk factors (e.g., parent management practices), as well as less flexible or *fixed* markers (e.g., genes, race). Moreover, according to Kramer et al. (1997) variable risk factors that have been shown to alter the likelihood of experiencing a specific outcome following experimental manipulation are causal risk factors. An understanding of risk is essential because the concept of resilience is inextricably tied to risk by virtue of the fact that resilience describes the process of adapting to, coping with, disrupting, or overcoming risk (Masten, 2001).

The Complexities of Risk

A general observation within the field of developmental psychology has been that it is more difficult to attain positive outcomes as the number of risks experienced accumulates (Gutman, Sameroff, & Eccles, 2002; Stouthamer-Loeber, Loeber, Wei, Farrington, & Wikstrom, 2002). The concept of cumulative or additive risk refers to the phenomenon of being exposed to multiple risk factors. In their now classic study of families in Philadelphia, Sameroff, Bartko, Baldwin, Baldwin, and Seifer (1998) provide a clear illustration of cumulative risk and downward trending adjustment by charting exposure to an increasing number of risk factors related to parent characteristics, family process variables, peers, and communities on one axis, and adjustment on five developmental outcomes (i.e., psychological adjustment, academic performance, self-competence, problem behavior, activity involvement) on the other. Their findings were striking. Trends on all of the adjustment indicators studied (i.e., psychological adjustment, academic performance, etc.) showed virtually identical patterns of decline as the number of risk factors experienced accumulated, and there was an approximately 1.5–2 standard deviation difference between youth exposed to one risk factor and those exposed to nine risk factors. The findings from this study illustrate how exposure to increasing amounts of stress—in this case within families, peers, and communities— can lead to rather dramatic declines in adjustment across multiple domains of functioning.

Although it makes sense that there should be a linear relationship between exposure to an accumulating number of risks and poor adjustment, it has also proved difficult to reliably predict various cognitive, behavioral, and social outcomes based solely on an understanding of risk. This challenge may be due in part to findings suggesting that there can be nonlinear, multiplicative, and threshold relationships between risk and adjustment (Durlak, 1998; Greenberg, Speltz, DeKlyen, & Jones, 2001). For example, Rutter (1979) examined the cumulative effects of risk associated with childhood psychiatric disorder and found that having any one of six risk factors did not increase the likelihood of disorder beyond having no risk. However, having any two risk factors increased the chances of a psychiatric disorder fourfold and having any four risk factors increased the chances of psychiatric disorder tenfold.

An additional challenge to understanding risk is related to the finding that risk factors often cluster together (Jessor, 1993) and, over time, can interact with or augment one another in unexpected ways. For example, children who live in poverty are more likely to be exposed to a greater number of risks related to variety of negative outcomes than are children from middle or upper income backgrounds (Stouthamer-Loeber et al., 2002). Moreover, early exposure to poverty can have a compounding negative effect on other risks, such that difficulties "cascade" and spill over to create new risk experiences (Egeland, Carlson, & Sroufe, 1993) or have negative effects at critical developmental time points and lead to compounding detrimental effects at later points in time (Appleyard, Egeland, van Dulmen, & Sroufe, 2005).

Yet another challenge to understanding the relationships between risk exposure and outcomes is related to the principles of equifinality and multifinality (Cicchetti & Rogosch, 1996). *Equifinality* refers to phenomena of different developmental experiences (including risks) leading to similar outcomes (Ford & Learner, 1992). Thus, a specific risk factor or factors may reliably predict a consequent disorder for one individual, but an entirely different set of risk factors may predict the *same* disorder for a different individual. The principle of *multifinality* refers to the fact that the same risk factor (e.g., abuse) or set of risk factors (e.g., low IQ, abuse, and peer deviancy training) can lead to different disorders or outcomes.

Because of these challenges in understanding risk, few maladaptive outcomes are completely understood or are fully explained by any single or set of risk factors regardless of how comprehensive the list. Instead, risk factors increase the *likelihood* of experiencing a disorder or maladaptive outcome, but rarely fully explain them.

Disability and Risk

Students with disabilities are more likely to experience exposure to a variety of risk factors including poor cognitive and academic performance (Lackaye & Margalit, 2006; Reid, Gonzalez, Nordness, Trout, & Epstein, 2004; Wagner, Newman, & Cameto, 2004), high rates of externalizing behavior problem (Douma, Dekker, Ruiter, Tick, & Koot, 2007; Haager & Vaughn, 1995; Werner, 1993), low self-esteem and poor self-images (Maag & Reid, 2006; Manikam, Matson, Coe, & Hillman, 1995; Raviv & Stone, 1991; Whitaker & Read, 2006), poor social skills (Haager & Vaughn, 1995; Most & Greenbank, 2000; Swanson & Malone, 1992; Vaughn, Zaragoza, Hogan, & Walker, 1993), poor peer relationships (Guevremont & Dumas, 1994), and poor relationships with adults (Murray & Greenberg, 2001; Nelson & Roberts, 2000). Moreover, students with disabilities are more likely than their peers to live in high-poverty environments (Aud, KewalRamani, & Frohlich, 2011; Sherman, 1994), and such environments include a greater number of risks (Egeland et al., 1993). Students with disabilities who live in poverty are particularly susceptible to experiencing a range of poor outcomes (Blackorby & Wagner, 1996; Wagner et al., 2005).

Although there is some variability in the levels of risk experienced by students with disabilities depending on specific disability classification (Caffrey & Fuchs, 2007; Lane, Carter, Pierson, & Glaeser, 2006), children and youth with disabilities in all categories are faced with myriad challenges and risks that portend later difficulties adjusting to schools, communities, and society (Barclay & Doll, 2001; Benz, Yovanoff, & Doren, 1997; French & Conrad, 2001; Halpern, Yovanoff, Doren, & Benz, 1995). In one of the only long-term, lifespan investigations of the associations among disability, risk, and outcomes in students with disabilities, Werner and Smith (1992) found that children with learning disabilities (LD) had a higher prevalence of risks at birth (e.g., low birthweight, lack of parental support and warmth) that were associated with additional challenges in early adolescence and young adulthood (e.g., poor academic achievement, higher discipline

Ecological systems/levels can play a role

referrals, lower involvement in school, poor social and family life) compared to a matched control group without disabilities (Werner & Smith, 1992). Hartzell and Compton (1984) conducted a 10-year follow-up of students with LD to examine risk factors associated with poor academic and social success during late adolescence and adulthood (age range in sample was 15–27 years old at follow-up). This study focused primarily on individual-level risks, and findings indicated that severity of disability, having a disability in mathematics, hyperactivity, and being placed into a special education setting were all risks associated with poorer academic and social adjustment over time.

Using data from the National Longitudinal Study of Adolescent Health, Svetaz, Ireland, and Blum (2000) investigated risk factors associated with emotional well-being among adolescents with and without LDs. Findings from this analysis indicated that adolescents with LD were twice as likely as youth without disabilities to experience emotional distress (24% vs. 12%) and suicide attempts (4% vs. 2%), and were slightly more likely to report involvement in violent behaviors (31% vs. 25%). Risk factors that contributed to these elevated rates of emotional and behavioral difficulties among youth with LD included factors at the individual (i.e., early sexual intercourse, carrying a weapon, and substance use), family (suicide attempt by family member), and school (i.e., trouble in school, failing a grade) levels. Using the same data set, Blum, Kelly, and Ireland (2001) found that youth with LDs, emotional disabilities, and those with mobility impairments were more likely to engage in health-compromising behaviors including suicide attempts, regular tobacco use, alcohol use, and early sexual intercourse (before the age of 12) than were a national comparison group of youth without disabilities. Moreover, risk factors at the individual (e.g., appears old for age, belief in an early death, somatic complaints), family (e.g., gun available in the home), and school (i.e., repeated a grade) levels were associated with these health-compromising outcomes.

Although this research makes an important contribution to the relationships among disability, risk, and adjustment, limited research exists that examines the mechanisms by which these risks exert their influence on each other and on the likelihood of future difficulties among students with disabilities. An important goal of future research in the field of special education is to continue to identify risk factors but to also examine transactional risk *processes* that are predictive of outcomes among this population. Such research should extend beyond students' individual characteristics and the characteristics of schools (i.e., teachers and classrooms) because meaningful risk experiences are likely to be found across a range of ecological contexts and in interactions within and between these contexts (Bronfenbrenner & Morris, 2006; Whipple et al., 2010). Moreover, there is also a need for carefully planned *prospective* studies among students with disabilities. One of the limitations of the research just reviewed is that the questions asked regarding students with disabilities were often asked after data had already been gathered and therefore these data were not originally planned to evaluate the potentially unique developmental experiences of students with disabilities.

Promotive and Protective Factors and Processes

Whereas risk factors are reliable predictors of negative developmental outcomes, promotive and protective factors are individual skills or contextual experiences that reliably predict positive developmental outcomes. Sameroff et al. (1998) defined promotive factors as skills and processes that are the polar opposite of risk factors. Thus, if low self-esteem is a risk factor, high self-esteem could be viewed as a promotive factor. Other researchers classify promotive factors or "assets" as skills and experiences that are predictive of positive adjustment for *all* individuals, regardless of risk exposure (Keating, Dowdy, Morgan, & Noam, 2011; Leffert et al., 1998; Yates & Matsen, 2004). For example, supportive and caring parent–child relationships, prosocial experiences with peers, and high-quality educational experiences are beneficial for all children and youth, regardless of their particular risk experiences or vulnerabilities.

Whereas promotive factors and assets have broad benefits, *protective* factors are reliable predictors of positive adjustment in the presence of known risk factors (Garmezy et al., 1984). Thus, another reason why it is difficult to fully understand or predict a particular outcome based solely on an understanding of risk is that other *positive* individual traits and/or social and contextual experiences are often also present in the lives of children, and these protective factors and processes may serve to (a) decrease dysfunction directly, (b) interact with the risk factor to buffer the negative effects of risk exposure, or (c) serve to disrupt the chain of events between risk factor(s) and negative outcomes (Coie et al., 1993). In all cases, by definition, protective factors reduce the likelihood that risk exposure will result in a consequent disorder or negative outcome. When these conditions are present, "[r]esilience describes patterns of positive adaptation that reflect the normative operation of fundamental developmental processes under non-normative conditions" (Yates & Matsen, 2004 p. 536).

The most common strategy for distinguishing between promotive factors/assets and protective factors is to compare main effects to interactions (moderation). If a particular predictor variable (supportive parent–child relationship) has a main effect on a particular outcome (prosocial behavior) (a) regardless of underlying risk exposure *and* (b) in the presence of an interaction term between risk and the protective factor of interest, then that variable would provide evidence that the predictor was a promotive factor or asset. Alternatively, if the beneficial effects of parent–child relationships on prosocial behavior were moderated by risk status (i.e., interaction) such that they were more beneficial for children identified as high-risk (on a predefined risk factor for negative behavior) than for children defined as low-risk (on the same predefined risk factor), then that would provide evidence that the variable was a protective factor. That is, the protective effects of supportive parent–child relationships were evident for some (high-risk) but not all (low-risk) children.

As with risk factors, and consistent with a systems perspective, protective factors may reside in the individual (e.g., IQ, self-regulation, positive temperament), in the family (supportive parent–child relationships, authoritative parenting style, effective parent management practices), in schools (high-quality classroom/school experiences, supportive teacher–student relationships), or communities (participation in extracurricular activities, mentoring programs) (Durlak, 1998; Elder, 1974; Garmezy, 1991; Hardaway, McLoyd, & Wood, 2012; Hawkins, Catalano, & Miller, 1992; Jessor, 1993; Rutter, Maughan, Mortimore, & Ouston, 1979; Werner & Smith, 1989). Moreover, protective factors and processes can and do accumulate (cumulative), they can interact with one another, and they can also represent transactional relationships in the sense that they may shape and be shaped by interactions with one another (DiRago & Vaillant, 2007). Additionally, over time, protective factors may augment one another in unexpected ways (e.g., the Matthew effect).

Disability and Resilience

A growing number of researchers in the field of special education have begun to examine the applicability of a resilience framework to explain variations in outcomes experienced by individuals with disabilities (Raskind, Goldberg, Higgins, & Herman, 1999; Werner & Smith, 1992). This work has resulted in the identification of a set of potential protective factors that are similar to those identified in other fields, along with recommendations for further research to identify additional protective factors among children, youth, and adults with disabilities (Keogh & Weisner, 1993; Margalit, 2003; Morrison & Codsen, 1997; Wong, 2003). Understanding the factors that protect against the negative effects of risk among children and youth with disabilities is important because it contributes to a comprehensive understanding of adjustment within this population and can provide an empirical starting point for interventions.

In addition to gathering data on risk factors, these studies also examined protective factors among youth with disabilities. For example, Werner and Smith (1992) explored developmental factors and processes that were associated with successful outcomes for a high-poverty sample of individuals with LDs in adulthood (e.g., employed, life satisfaction). This life-course investigation revealed a progression of factors that began with positive infant temperament along with parent educational status, leading to positive and supportive interactions between the child and his or her parents, peers, and teachers in early childhood. These positive social interactions, in turn, were associated with individual skills such as greater autonomy, problem-solving ability, self-efficacy, and self-esteem in early and late adolescence. Moreover, these protective factors and processes experienced during childhood and adolescence were associated with lower emotional distress, a greater number of emotionally supportive relationships, and positive work, school, and community adjustment outcomes during adulthood.

Hartzell and Compton (1984) followed students with LD for approximately 10 years after initial diagnosis and identified protective factors associated with academic and social success among adolescents and adults with LD. These factors included IQ, psychosocial functioning (social relationships), family functioning, positive family support, private tutoring, and other interests including sports (Hartzell & Compton, 1984). Blum et al. (2001) examined protective factors associated with *reductions* in health-compromising behaviors (i.e., suicide attempts; use of alcohol, tobacco, and drugs; early intercourse) among adolescents with LD, emotional disabilities, and mobility impairments and found that protective factors that reduced the likelihood of involvement in these behaviors included (a) individual student characteristics (i.e., religiosity, appears young for age, high self-esteem), (b) experiences within families (i.e., family connectedness, parental presence, parental expectations, activities with parents, and lives with both parents), and (c) experiences within schools (i.e., school connectedness, higher grade point averages). Svetaz et al. (2000), reported a similar set of individual, family, and school-related protective factors that reduced the likelihood of experiencing emotional distress and problem behaviors among adolescents with LD.

Finally, in one of the few investigations to evaluate the cumulative effects of multiple protective factors on outcomes, Alriksson-Schmidt et al. (2007) investigated the relationships among life stress, protective processes, and quality of life among youth with physical disabilities. These researchers found that having just one of any three protective factors (i.e., social competence, high family functioning, or good peer relationships) did not moderate the effects of stress on adjustment. However, the presence of all three protective factors significantly reduced the negative effects of stress on quality of life (Alriksson-Schmidt et al., 2007).

In addition to the findings just described, evidence from several additional prospective and retrospective studies highlights a set of protective factors that appear to be particularly salient for individuals with disabilities who, as adults, experience positive employment, postsecondary education, and community adjustment. These factors include (a) awareness and acceptance of one's disability, (b) identifying and implementing strategies to work around limitations/challenges related to disability, (c) a focus on strengths, (c) purposefully choosing environments and using social resources that optimize performance, (d) supportive relationships with mentors, (e) participation and successful completion of core high school English and math courses, and (f) a mastery versus performance goal orientations (Goldberg, Higgins, Raskind, & Herman, 2003; Hall, Spruill, & Webster, 2002; Miller, 2002; Rogers, Muir, & Evenson, 2003; Spekman et al., 1992). Taken together, these initial correlational findings on protective factors and processes provide a rich starting point for causal research designed to test the efficacy of these protective processes in prevention and intervention trials.

Application

In this section, we provide an overview of several prevention and intervention efforts designed to build resilience. These examples are drawn from a diverse research base across various developmental periods including childhood, adolescence, and adulthood. Our goal in this section is not to provide a comprehensive review of all interventions that have implications for resilience, but is instead to identify several examples to illustrate how various researchers have attempted to promote resilience through models that are predicated on a clear understanding of risk and protective factors. In doing so, we were also cognizant of the importance of identifying efforts that have targeted individual, family, school, and community levels to highlight applications of a prevention and intervention framework based on ecological systems theories.

Individual Level (War)

Children, youth, and adults exposed to war and other forms of disaster have certainly experienced extreme conditions, and studying resilience within such contexts provides an opportunity to develop insights regarding the effectiveness of efforts to build the capacity for positive adaptation under extremely adverse conditions (Brick, Goodman, Tol, & Eggerman, 2011; Miller, Grabelsky, & Wagner, 2010). In an effort to counter the trauma of exposure to violence within the context of war, Wolmer and colleagues (Wolmer, Hamiel, & Laor, 2011; Wolmer, Hamiel, Barchas, Slone, & Laor, 2011) developed and implemented a school-based resilience training program for children in Israel. This intervention can be delivered by teachers and consists of 14 manualized activities designed to teach cognitive control and cognitive restructuring pertaining to the regulation of negative thoughts and emotions, relaxation techniques, and mental imagery.

Wolmer, Hamiel, Barchas et al. (2011) implemented this curriculum in a study of approximately 2,500 students in grades 3–5 in northern Israel following the 2006 Lebanon war. All students had been exposed to rocket attacks (approximately 4,000 rockets were launched); approximately half ($n = 983$) were provided with the 14-week resilience training while the others ($n = 1,152$) served as a wait list control. Data gathered directly following the intervention (9 months after attacks) and again 3 months later (12 months after attack) revealed that the intervention group showed fewer symptoms of post-traumatic stress disorder (PTSD) and fewer disordered moods than did students in the control group at both time points. Moreover, approximately half as many students in the experimental group met the criteria for PTSD (5% vs. 10%) suggesting the practical significance of this effort.

In an extension of this model to a primary prevention effort, Wolmer, Hamiel, and Laor (2011) evaluated the preventive effects of the same curriculum with approximately 1,500 fourth- and fifth-grade students from 55 classrooms in southern Israel. Classrooms and schools were selected because of their proximity to the Gaza Strip; approximately half of the classrooms received the full intervention whereas the others served as a control group. Approximately 3 months after the intervention, students in both groups were exposed to a 3-week conflict (Operation Cast Lead) that included sustained rocket and mortar attacks. Following this conflict, students in both conditions completed measures of post-traumatic stress reaction and a stress/mood scale. Findings indicated that students in the intervention condition experienced fewer negative stress/mood difficulties, significantly lower scores on the PTSD reaction scale (on all four factors on the measure), and fewer intervention students met the diagnostic criteria for PTSD (7% vs. 11%).

Findings from this program of research indicate that it is possible to promote adjustment and reduce maladaptive outcomes through efforts focused on promoting *individual* coping skills within the context of a school-based, teacher-led curriculum. Additionally, the approach taken by Wolmer, Hamiel, and Laor (2011) and Wolmer, Hamiel, Barchas et al. (2011) to promote individual protective skills was shown to be effective as both a primary prevention effort (Wolmer, Hamiel, & Laor, 2011) and secondary intervention effort (Wolmer, Hamiel, Barchas et al., 2011).

Family Level (Divorce)

In an effort to promote resilience to mental health problems among children from divorced families, Wolchik et al. (2000) developed and evaluated a family-focused intervention designed to promote children's positive adaptation following divorce. These researchers first demonstrated that divorce was predictive of a host of negative long-term outcomes including clinical levels of mental health problems, teen pregnancy, and school dropout (Wolchik et al., 1992; Wolchik, Mackinnon, & Sandler, 2009). They then developed an intervention that targeted mothers and addressed known family correlates (risk and protective factors) of both negative and adaptive outcomes following divorce. These processes included interactions between parents and children, such as mother–child relationship (i.e.,

family fun time, one-on-one time, catch 'em being good), effective discipline (i.e., clear and consistent expectations, parental monitoring), and father–child contact (i.e., removal of visitation obstacles), as well as individual skills to reduce interparental conflict (i.e., anger management).

In two separate randomized control trials (Wolchik et al., 2009), the positive effects of this training on the hypothesized mechanisms of the intervention (i.e., mother–child relationships, effective discipline, and father–child conflict), as well as on the beneficial effects on children's internalizing and externalizing symptomatology, were demonstrated. These effects were moderated by child and family initial levels of functioning such that the intervention was most beneficial for children and families who had the poorest functioning (greatest need) at baseline. Moreover, a 3-month, 6-month, and 6-year follow-up of the initial intervention revealed that although the magnitude of the effects observed at post-test and at the first follow-up (3 month) were relatively modest, effect sizes 6 years after initial implementation were considerably larger, thus suggesting that positive initial effects at one developmental time point provided access to additional environmental resources, thereby amplifying positive effects over time (Wolchik et al., 2009).

The findings from this work on families is important because it demonstrates how intervention efforts can be conceptualized and delivered to target family processes. Similar strategies to affect change in family processes have recently been implemented in schools, and the early results of these efforts are promising (Stormshak et al., 2011). Moreover, one of the unique features of the Wolchik et al. (2007) research is that they followed intervention participants for an extended period following initial intervention. Results at these follow-up time points indicated that initial modest effects were often amplified over time, thus lending support to a "cascading pathways model" whereby initial access to protective resources at a critical developmental stage, or following a critical event, contributed to new opportunities to access resources, and, over time, these opportunities had additive beneficial effects for participants.

School Level (Delinquency Prevention)

The social development model (SDM, Hawkins & Catalano, 1992) is a school-based risk reduction and protection enhancement delinquency prevention program based on known risk and protective factors related to delinquency. The SDM blends social control theory (Hirschi, 1969) and social learning theories (Bandura, 1977) and theorizes that providing students with opportunities to develop supportive attachments to prosocial adults and conventional institutions (e.g., schools) prevents later deviant behavior. In SDM, these bonds are developed by providing students with (a) skills for developing supportive attachments/bonds, (b) opportunities to use those skills to develop supportive attachments/bonds, and (c) recognition for prosocial behavior. Access to these processes provides students with opportunities to learn and internalize prosocial norms and behaviors, thus reducing delinquent behavior (Catalano et al., 2004).

A number of investigators have utilized the SDM to prevent and reduce rates of delinquency among both low- and high-risk youth (Catalano et al., 2004; Eggert, Thompson, Herting, Nichols, 1994; O'Donnell, Hawkins, Catalano, Abbot, & Day, 1995). O'Donnell et al. (1995) investigated the effects of an SDM intervention that included cognitive problem-solving skills training, parent training, and teacher training among fifth and sixth graders from low-income backgrounds. Students in the intervention group received training in communication skills, emotional understanding, and problem solving. Parents received training that included positive behavior management techniques, communication strategies, and strategies for positively supporting students' academic work in school. Teachers received training in communication strategies, classroom management techniques, and cooperative learning. Thus, although the model is school-based, intervention targets include individual students, their parents, and teachers. Results from the O'Donnell et al. (1995) intervention indicated that the program enhanced protective factors among participants, as evidenced by stronger attachments to teachers and schools among students in the intervention condition. These heightened attachments were accompanied by improvements in social competence and academic grades. In a 5-year follow-up study, Catalano et al. (2004) reported that eleventh and twelfth graders who had participated in the intervention during middle school maintained stronger attachments to teachers, greater academic achievement, and had lower rates of school dropout than did youth in the control condition during middle school. Furthermore, an increase in teacher attachments between grades 7 and 12 were positively associated with higher grade point averages and negatively associated with grade repetition, school misbehavior, school dropout, and suspensions/expulsions. Following these same youth into adulthood, Hawkins, Kosterman, Catalano, Hill, and Abbott (2008) reported that as adults (27 years old), youth who had participated in the SDM intervention condition had fewer mental health problems and higher socioeconomic status than did adults who were in the control condition during middle school.

Taken together, results from this line of inquiry on the SDM provide an excellent example of how protective factors at multiple levels of a student's microsystem can be targeted in a school-based prevention model. By concurrently targeting students' individual skills, opportunities with parents, and interactions with teachers, this model promotes synergistic effects across multiple contexts.

Community Level (Drug and Alcohol Prevention)

Communities that Care (CTC, Hawkins & Catalano, 1992) is a community-based prevention model designed to prevent drug and alcohol use by concurrently targeting reductions of known risk factors related to substance use and promoting access to known protective factors (Arthur, Briney, Hawkins, Abbott, Weiss, & Catalano, 2007). The model utilizes a community mobilization framework and an iterative process that includes (a) involvement of key community leaders; (b) the formation of a community board; (c) assessment of community risk, protection, and relevant outcomes related to substance abuse; (d) prioritization of factors to be targeted; and (e) the selection and implementation of empirically based interventions to reduce risk and provide protection within targeted communities (Hawkins & Catalano, 1992).

An important question to ask with the CTC model is whether these steps, particularly the selection and implementation of empirically based interventions, would be adopted by communities in community mobilization efforts? Fagan, Arthur, Hanson, Briney, and Hawkins (2011) addressed this question through an evaluation of implementation fidelity in 24 communities in seven states. Interviews and surveys of community leaders and program implementers indicated that CTC communities were more likely than control communities to adopt evidence-based prevention and intervention strategies and that these programs reached a greater number of community participants in the prevention versus the control condition.

With regard to effects on developmental outcomes, two large-scale investigations have evaluated the effects of CTC on the reduction of risk factors and substance use. Feinberg, Greenberg, Osgood, Sartorius, and Bontempo (2007) evaluated the effects of the model on risk reduction and substance use outcomes in a large quasi-experimental investigation in Pennsylvania. These researchers studied these effects in more than 225 school districts in communities where the CTC model was being implemented (135 intervention) and in communities where the model was not implemented (90 control). Because data were gathered from students, effects were evaluated by grade level and included students in sixth, eighth, tenth, and twelfth grades. Overall, significant and beneficial effects were found on approximately 12% of the risk and outcome variables studied, with the strongest effects observed for students in early adolescence.

In a second evaluation, Oesterle, Hawins, Fagan, Abbott, and Catalano (2010) examined the effects of CTC on substance use in communities that had been implementing the model for approximately 3 years (N = 12) and in communities (N = 12) not implementing the model but who were matched with intervention communities on several key variables including size of the community, state, race and ethnicity, socioeconomic status, and crime rates. Overall, communities using the CTC model showed positive effects for reductions in substance use (main effect) and reductions in alcohol and tobacco use among youth who were at higher risk at baseline due to prior alcohol and tobacco use.

Cautions and Future Directions

The models described here provide a glimpse into the potential application of a resilience framework to practice. However, several cautions are also in order, as highlighted in a recent issue of the *American Psychologist* (vol. 66, January 2011). This special issue was dedicated to a resilience training program for the U.S. military called Comprehensive Soldier Fitness (CSF), developed by Martin Seligman, one of the founders of positive psychology (Seligman & Csikszentmihályi, 2000; Seligman & Pawelski, 2003). The CSF program is designed to reduce the negative psychological effects of the experiences of war among U.S. combat soldiers through resiliency training. The training focuses on building resilience through strengthening social-emotional skills (e.g., self-awareness, self-regulation, optimism, etc.), mental toughness (e.g., identifying thoughts and triggering events, energy management, minimizing catastrophic thinking, fighting counterproductive thoughts, etc.), identifying character strengths (identifying strengths in self and others), and

strengthening relationships (constructive responding, praise, and communication styles) (Reivich, Seligman, & McBride, 2011). Although limited data exist to support the effectiveness of the program, it has already been widely adopted (Cornum, Matthews, & Seligman, 2011).

In a later issue of the same journal (vol. 66, October, 2011), comments on the special issue on CSF were published (Dyckman, 2011; Eidelson, Pilisuk, & Soldz, 2011; Krueger, 2011; Phipps, 2011). Commenters raised important questions and concerns about the concept of resilience training in the military, including basic questions about the morality of training soldiers to be "psychologically resilient." As one commenter noted

> Can we use resilience training and other forms of stress inoculation to immunize our soldiers against the stresses of war? Should we? War is horrific and exposes its participants to the most gruesome of terrors. A response of distress and repugnance would seem to be the most natural and even adaptive reaction. If we can train our soldiers to experience more death, destruction, and depredation with less distress, is that a positive outcome? (Phipps, 2011, p. 641)

Almost three decades ago, Garmezy (1987) raised similar questions about studying resilient children and youth from high-poverty backgrounds. His comments, however, extended beyond implications for individuals and also included the potential social and political implications of such an agenda.

> The concept of protective factors is potentially a political weapon. Resilient children and the countless numbers of successful adults who demonstrate their escape from poverty and disadvantage, can be used by political advocates of an ideological viewpoint that holds the resiliency of some to be proof of its possession by all: that anyone can emulate such achievements if they only try harder. (Garmezy, 1987, p. 171)

These examples are important because they illuminate some of the challenges inherent in studying resilient children, youth, and adults. Should wartime soldiers and impoverished children be taught to be psychologically resilient, and should such resilience be celebrated? Or, should greater resources and effort be devoted to preventing the need for resilience by eliminating soldiers' exposure to war and children's exposure to poverty? Should policymakers, generals, soldiers, and the public be exposed to preventive interventions that teach conflict resolution, problem solving, and processes that promote peace so that soldiers are spared the detrimental psychological consequences of war? Should all members of our society be taught principles of social justice, sustainability, and the equitable distribution of resources to eliminate children's exposure to poverty? Such questions lead naturally to implications for a research agenda, one that focuses on primary prevention rather than rehabilitation.

Primary Prevention and Competence Enhancement: Positive Psychology

In our view, and we expect in the view of most readers of this chapter, primary prevention efforts should always be at the forefront of efforts to promote healthy development among all members of a society, including those with disabilities. Such efforts begin with the documentation of the associations between exposure to risk/stress (casual risk factors) and consequent negative outcomes (e.g., exposure to war and mental health problems, exposure to poverty and consequent rates of school dropout, exposure to childhood maltreatment and depression) and then proceed to reduce or prevent exposure to those causal risk factors that appear most likely to produce unfavorable outcomes. Such efforts also recognize the important role *promotive* factors and assets play in contributing to positive health and well-being among all individuals and seek to increase access to such factors and processes.

Not only does primary prevention offer the best approach from a public health perspective, but, according to Cicchetti and Toth (2007), such efforts can also provide opportunities for scientific understanding of the underlying mechanisms associated with positive development:

[I]f the developmental course is altered as a result of the implementation of preventive interventions and the risk for negative outcomes is reduced, then prevention research helps to specify processes that are involved in the emergence of psychopathology or other negative developmental outcomes. As such, prevention research can be conceptualized as true experiments in altering the course of development, thereby providing insight into the etiology and pathogenesis of disordered outcomes. (p. 499)

From this perspective, one can imagine a research agenda within the discipline of disability that focuses broadly on prevention and health promotion and includes areas such as academic skills, social relationships, emotional and behavioral adjustment, physical health, school completion, and post-school adult outcomes. Although such efforts are beginning to emerge in multitiered frameworks within the field of special education, these models are in their infancy and should be extended beyond reading and behavior.

Challenges (or opportunities) for such an agenda include the operationalization of socially relevant and clinically significant outcomes, the identification of potent (and malleable) causal risk factors that are clearly linked with the outcome(s) of interest, the identification of promotive factors that enhance opportunities for competence, and the consequent development, implementation, and evaluation of preventive and competence-enhancement efforts that concurrently focus on risk reduction and health promotion. Although such an agenda seems daunting, similar proposals were made almost two decades ago by Hill Walker and colleagues (Walker et al., 1996) in relation to school-wide models of positive behavior supports. In recent years, the field of special education has begun to adopt this perspective as it has slowly moved from a focus on remediation to one of prevention and empowerment. Examples of this paradigm shift are particularly evident in early childhood special education (Shonkoff & Phillips, 2000; Woolfson, 1999) and in multitiered prevention models in elementary schools (e.g., Response to Intervention [RTI] and school-wide positive behavior support [SWPBS]).

Because risks reside in individuals, in their environments, and in the transactions and processes that occur among these systems, preventive efforts that target risk, promotive, and protective factors at *multiple levels* are more likely to produce desirable outcomes than are efforts that focus on only one level (individual) or one context (schools) (Taylor, Eddy, & Biglan, 1999). Evidence for this claim has now been demonstrated by researchers studying multicomponent efforts to prevent conduct problems and delinquency (Catalano et al., 2004; Conduct Problems Prevention Research Group, 2011), efforts that have compared the strength of interventions that focus solely on the individual with those that include both an individual and family component (Lochman & Wells, 2004), and efforts to intervene in the microsocial interactions (transactions) between children and adults (Dishion, Nelson, & Kavanaugh, 2003).

Secondary and Tertiary Intervention: Promoting Resilience

Although our view is that primary prevention should be the goal of all policymakers, social scientists, educators, and families, we are also not so naive to think that the needs of all individuals can or will be met through primary prevention efforts. Nor are we optimistic that sufficient resources can or will be devoted to preventing exposure to all social ills, we are not ignorant of the fact that herculean efforts have already been made to prevent exposure to wide-scale societal stressors such as poverty, and we also recognize that such efforts are, in some cases, only marginally successful (National Center for Children in Poverty, 2009). Therefore, for the foreseeable future, there will continue to be a need for secondary and tertiary interventions. Efforts at these levels target children and youth who are already exposed to risk and/or are displaying symptoms of disorder. Like primary prevention efforts, interventions at these levels should seek to reduce exposure to known risks but should also target the enhancement of protective factors that have been shown to interact with risk in ways that promote positive adaptation.

The field of special education has a long history of serving children and youth at these levels, and the concept of special education itself could easily be classified as a secondary or tertiary intervention. Within emerging multitiered school-wide efforts, secondary and tertiary interventions are designed for groups or individuals who are not responsive to universal prevention efforts at tier I (Institute of Educational Sciences [IES], 2009). However, interventions recommended and delivered at these levels are rarely based on protective factors and processes gleaned from carefully conceived *prospective* longitudinal studies of risk and protective processes among students with disabilities but instead are more likely to emerge from correlational data (in the best-case scenario) or researchers' "best guesses" about how to produce change in nonresponsive students. Such strategies include small-group instruction, increased time receiving instruction, implementation of increasingly individualized instruction, functional behavioral plans, or an expansion of services and supports. Although these efforts have been shown to be effective for some students (IES, 2009), labeling research in this area as "evidence-based" is, to a high degree, dependent on one's definition of evidence. Moreover, with a few exceptions (cf. Conduct Problems Prevention Research Group, 2011; NICHD, 2004; Stormshak et al., 2011; Walker et al., 1996), such efforts are generally confined to the context of schools and do not seriously consider strategies to affect other sources of support within and beyond students' microsystem.

As illustrated in the quote at the beginning of this chapter (Sameroff, 2000), human development is undeniably complex, and efforts to produce desired developmental outcomes, particularly among the most vulnerable children and youth, are likely to be equally complex. Therefore, just as further research is needed in the field of special education to develop a deeper understanding of the developmental pathways that influence the progression and course of risks and promotive factors to frame a primary prevention/ competence-enhancement agenda for people with disabilities (Margalit, 2003; Morrison & Cosden, 1997; Young, Green, & Rogers, 2008), additional research is also needed to understand protective processes and the mechanisms that buffer individuals with disabilities from experiencing their currently elevated levels of negative developmental outcomes (Walker et al., 1996). Such research will provide greater opportunities to develop interventions for already affected children and youth, interventions that are based not only on hypotheses about what might work, but also on an understanding of the individual and ecological processes that differentiate high-risk successful and unsuccessful children and youth. The implementation and evaluation of interventions based on this understanding, in turn, will cycle back to further inform consequent secondary and tertiary intervention efforts (Cicchetti & Toth, 2007).

One of the great strengths of the field of special education is the applied nature of our work. Equally impressive is our ability to aggressively act on problems with practical solutions. Some might argue that devoting more attention to understanding risk, promotive, and protective processes will detract from a focus on action—on helping those in need, and quickly. We would counter that developing insights about the interactive nature of developmental experiences and processes among children and youth with disabilities, the adaptive functioning of individuals with disabilities in the face of adversity, and the consequent application of this knowledge to prevention and intervention trials offers the only reasonable foundation for developing a comprehensive, scientifically sound, research and practice agenda devoted to promoting healthy adjustment and outcomes among children, youth, and adults with disabilities.

References

Achenbach, T. (1974). *Developmental psychopathology.* New York: Wiley.

Alriksson-Schmidt, A. I., Wallander, J., & Biasini, F. (2007). Quality of life and resilience in adolescents with a mobility disability. *Journal of Pediatric Psychology, 32,* 370–379.

Appleyard, K., Egeland, B., van Dulman, M. H., & Sroufe, L. A. (2005). When more is not better: The role of cumulative risk in child behavior problems. *Journal of Child Psychology & Psychiatry*, *46*, 235–245.

Arthur, M. W., Briney, J. S., Hawkins, D. J., Abbott, R. D., Weiss, B. I., & Catalano, R. F. (2007). Measuring risk and protection in communities using the Communities that Care youth survey. *Evaluation and Program Planning*, *30*, 197–211.

Aud, S., KewalRamani, A., & Frohlich, L. (2011). *America's youth: Transitions to adulthood* (NCES 2012-026). U.S. Department of Education, National Center for Education Statistics. Washington, DC: U.S. Government Printing Office.

Bandura, A. (1977). *Social learning theory.* London: Prentice Hall.

Barclay, J. R., & Doll, B. (2001). Early prospective studies of the high school dropout. *School Psychology Quarterly*, *16*, 357–369.

Benz, M. R., Yovanoff, P., & Doren, B. (1997). School-to-work components that predict postschool success for students with and without disabilities. *Exceptional Children*, *63*, 151–165.

Berry, D. (2012). Inhibitory control and teacher-child conflict: Reciprocal associations across the elementary-school years. *Journal of Applied Developmental Psychology*, *33*, 66–76.

Blackorby, J., & Wagner, M. (1996). Longitudinal postschool outcomes of youth with disabilities: Findings from the national longitudinal transition study. *Exceptional Children*, *62*, 399–413.

Blum, R. W., Kelly, A., & Ireland, M. (2001). Health-risk behaviors and protective factor among adolescents with mobility impairments and learning and emotional disabilities. *Journal of Adolescent Health*, *28*, 481–490.

Brick, C., Goodman, A., Tol, W., & Eggerman, M. (2011). Mental health and childhood adversities: A longitudinal study in Kabul, Afghanistan. *Journal of the American Academy of Child & Adolescent Psychiatry*, *50*, 349–363.

Bronfenbrenner, U., & Morris, P. A. (2006). The bioecological model of human development. In R. M. Lerner & W. Damon (Eds.), *Handbook of child psychology: Vol. 1. Theoretical models of human development* (pp. 793–828). Hoboken, NJ: John Wiley & Sons.

Bugental, D. B., & Shennum, W. A. (1984). Difficult children as elicitors and targets of adult communication patterns: An attributional-behavioral transactional analysis. *Monographs of the Society for Research in Child Development*, *49*(1), serial no. 205.

Caffrey, E. & Fuchs, D. (2007). Differences in performance between students with learning disabilities and mild mental retardation: Implications for categorical instruction. *Learning Disabilities Research & Practice*, *22*, 119–128.

Catalano, R. F., Haggerty, K. P., Oesterle, S., Fleming, C. B., & Hawkins, J. D. (2004). The importance of bonding to school for healthy development: Findings from the social development research group. *Journal of School Health*, *74*, 252–261.

Cicchetti, D., & Rogosch, F. A. (1996). Equifinality and multifinality in developmental psychopathology. *Development and Psychopathology*, *8*, 597–600.

Cicchetti, D., & Toth, S. L. (1997). Transactional ecological systems in developmental psychopathology. In S. Luthar, J. Burack, D. Cicchetti, & J. Weisz (Eds.), *Developmental psychopathology: Perspectives on adjustment, risk, and disorder* (pp. 317–349). Cambridge, UK: Cambridge University Press.

Cicchetti, D., & Toth, S. L. (2007). Developmental psychopathology and preventive intervention. In W. Damon & R. M. Lerner (Eds.), *Handbook of child psychology v. 4 child*

psychology in practice (pp. 497–547). Hoboken, NJ: John Wiley & Sons.

Coie, J. D., Watt, N. F., West, S. G., Hawkins, J. D., Asarnow, J. R., Markman, H. J., et al. (1993). The science of prevention: A conceptual framework and some directions for a national research program. *American Psychologist*, *48*, 1013–1022.

Conduct Problems Prevention Research Group. (2011). The effects of the Fast Track preventive intervention on the development of conduct disorder across childhood. *Child Development*, *82*, 331–345.

Cornum, R., Matthews, M. D., & Seligman, M. E. (2011). Comprehensive soldier fitness: Building resilience in a challenging institutional context. *American Psychologist*, *66*, 4–9.

Damon, W. (2004). What is positive youth development? *Annals of the American Academy of Political and Social Science*, *591*, 13–24.

DiRago, A. C., & Vaillant, G. E. (2007). Resilience in inner city youth: Childhood predictors of occupational status across the lifespan. *Journal of Youth and Adolescence*, *36*, 61–70.

Dishion, T. J., Nelson, S. E., & Kavanaugh, K. (2003). The family check-up with high risk young adolescents: Preventing early onset substance use by parent monitoring. *Behavior Therapy*, *34*, 553–571.

Douma, J. C. H., Dekker, M. C., Ruiter, K. P. D., Tick, N. T. & Koot, H. M. (2007). Antisocial and delinquent behaviors in youths with mild or borderline disabilities. *American Journal on Mental Retardation*, *112*, 207–220.

Durlak, J. A. (1998). Common risk and protective factors in successful prevention programs. *American Journal of Orthopsychiatry*, *68*, 512–520.

Dyckman, J. (2011). Exposing the glosses in Seligman and Fowler's [2011] straw-man arguments. *American Psychologist*, 644–645.

Egeland, B., Carlson, E., & Sroufe, L. A. (1993). Resilience as a process. *Development and Psychopathology*, *5*, 517–528.

Eggert, L. L., Thompson, E. A., Herting, J. R., & Nichols, L. J. (1994). Preventing adolescent drug abuse and high school dropout through an intensive school based social network development program. *American Journal of Health Promotion*, *8*, 202–215.

Eidelson, R., Pilisuk, M., & Soldz, S. (2011). The dark side of comprehensive soldier fitness. *American Psychologist*, *66*, 643–644.

Elder, G. H. (1974). *Children of the great depression: Social change in life experiences.* Chicago: University of Chicago Press.

Fagan, A. A., Arthur, M. W., Hanson, K., Briney, J. S., & Hawkins, J. D. (2011). Effects of Communities that Care on the adoption and implementation fidelity of evidence-based prevention programs in communities: Results from a randomized control trial. *Prevention Science*, *12*, 223–229.

Farrington, D. P. (2003). Key results from the first forty years of the Cambridge Study in delinquent development. In T. Thornberry & M. Krohn (Eds.), *Taking stock of delinquency: An overview of findings from contemporary longitudinal studies* (pp. 137–183). New York: Kluwer Academic/Plenum Publishers.

Feinberg, M. E., Greenberg, M. T., Osgood, D. W., Sartorius, J., & Bontempo, D. (2007). Effects of the communities that care model in Pennsylvania on youth risk and problem behaviors. *Prevention Science*, *8*, 261–270.

Ford, D. H., & Learner, R. M. (1992). *Developmental systems theory: An integrative approach.* Newbury Park: Sage.

French, D. C., & Conrad, J. (2001). School dropout as predicted by peer rejection and antisocial behavior. *Journal of Research on Adolescence, 11*, 225–244.

Garmezy, N. (1987). Stress, competence, and development: Continuities in the study of schizophrenic adults, children vulnerable to psychopathology, and the search for stress-resistant children. *American Journal of Orthopsychiatry, 57*, 159–174.

Garmezy, N. (1991). Resiliency and vulnerability to adverse developmental outcomes associated with poverty. *American Behavioral Scientist, 34*, 416–430.

Garmezy, N., Masten, A., & Tellegen, A. (1984). The study of stress and competence in children: A building block for developmental psychopathology. *Child Development, 55*, 97–111.

Goldberg, R. J., Higgins, E. L., Raskind, M. H., & Herman, K. L. (2003). Predictors of success in individuals with learning disabilities: A qualitative analysis of a 20-year longitudinal study. *Learning Disabilities Research and Practice, 18*, 222–236.

Greenberg, M. T., Speltz, M. L., DeKlyen, M., & Jones, K. (2001). Correlates of clinic referral for early conduct problems: Variable- and person-oriented approaches. *Development and Psychopathology, 13*, 255–276.

Gutman, L. M., Sameroff, A. J., & Eccles, J. S. (2002). The academic achievement of African American students during early adolescence: An examination of multiple risk, promotive, and protective factors. *American Journal of Community Psychology, 30*, 367–399.

Guevremont, D. C., & Dumas, M. C. (1994). Peer relationship problems and disruptive behavior disorders. *Journal of Emotional and Behavioral Disorders, 2*, 164–172.

Haager, D., & Vaughn, S. (1995). Parent, teacher, peer, and self-reports of the social competence of students with learning disabilities. *Journal of Learning Disabilities, 28*, 206–215.

Hall, C. W., Spruill, K. L., & Webster, R. E. (2002). Motivational and attitudinal factors in college students with and without learning disabilities. *Learning Disability Quarterly, 25*, 79–86.

Halpern, A. S., Yovanoff, P., Doren, B., & Benz, M. R. (1995). Predicting participation in postsecondary education for school leavers with disabilities. *Exceptional Children, 62*, 151–164.

Hardaway, C. R., McLoyd, V. C., & Wood, D. (2012). Exposure to violence and socioemotional adjustment in low-income youth: An examination of protective factors. *American Journal of Community Psychology, 49*, 112–126.

Hartzell, H. E., & Compton, C. (1984). Learning disability: 10-year follow-up. *Pediatrics, 74*, 1058–1064.

Hawkins, J. D., & Catalano, R. F. (1992). *Communities that care: Action for drug prevention.* San Francisco: Jossey Bass.

Hawkins, J. D., Catalano, R. F., & Miller, J. Y. (1992). Risk and protective factors for alcohol and other drug problems in adolescence and early adulthood: Implications for substance abuse and prevention. *Psychological Bulletin, 112*, 64–105.

Hawkins, J. D., Kosterman, R., Catalano, R. F., Hill, K. G., & Abbott, R. D. (2008). Effects of social development intervention in childhood 15 years later. *Archives of Pediatric and Adolescent Medicine, 162*, 1133–1141.

Hirschi, T. (1969). *Causes of delinquency.* Berkeley, CA: University of California Press.

Institute of Educational Sciences. (2009). *Assisting students struggling with reading: Response to Intervention and multi-tier intervention for reading in the primary grades. A practice guide.* (NCEE 2009-4045). Washington, DC: U.S. Department of Education. Retrieved from http://ies.ed.gov/ncee/wwc/publications/practiceguides/

Jessor, R. (1993). Successful adolescent development among youth in high-risk settings. *American Psychologist, 48*, 117–126.

Keating, M., Dowdy, E., Morgan, M. L., & Noam, G. G. (2011). Protecting and promoting: An integrative conceptual model for healthy development of adolescents. *Journal of Adolescent Health, 48*, 220–228.

Keogh, B. K., & Weisner, T. (1993). An ecocultural perspective on risk and protective factors in children's development: Implications for learning disabilities. *Learning Disabilities Research and Practice, 8*, 3–10.

Kraemer, H. C., Kazdin, A. E., Offord, D. R., Kessler, R. C., Jensen, P. S., & Kupfer, D. J. (1997). Coming to terms with the terms of risk. *Archives of General Psychiatry, 54*, 337–343.

Krueger, J. J. (2011). Shock without awe. *American Psychologist, 66*, 642–643.

Lackaye, T. D., & Margalit, M. (2006). Comparisons of achievement, effort, and self-perceptions among students with learning disabilities and their peers from different achievement groups. *Journal of Learning Disabilities, 39*, 432–446.

Lane, K. L., Carter, E., Pierson, M. R., & Glaeser, B. C. (2006). Academic, social, and behavioral characteristics of high school students with emotional disturbances or learning disabilities. *Journal of Emotional and Behavioral Disorders, 14*, 108–117.

Leffert, N., Benson, P. L., Scales, P. C., Sharma, A. R., Drake, D. R., & Blyth, D. A. (1998). Developmental assets: Measurement and prediction of risk behaviors among adolescents. *Applied Developmental Science, 2*, 209–230.

Lenzi, M., Vieno, A., Perkins, D. D., Pastore, M., Santinello, M., & Mazzardis, S. (2012). Perceived neighborhood social resources as determinants of prosocial behavior in early adolescence. *American Journal of Community Psychology, 50*, 37–49.

Lerner, R. M. (2001). Promoting promotion in the development of prevention science. *Applied Developmental Science, 5*, 254–257.

Lochman, J. E., & Wells, K. C. (2004). The Coping Power Program for preadolescent boys and their parents: Outcome effects at the 1-year follow-up. *Journal of Consulting and Clinical Psychology, 72*, 571–578.

Lynch, M., & Cicchetti, D. (1998). An ecological-transactional analysis of children and contexts: The longitudinal interplay among child maltreatment, community violence, and children's symptomology. *Development and Psychopathology, 10*, 235–257.

Maag, J. W., & Reid, R. (2006). Depression among students with learning disabilities: Assessing the risk. *Journal of Learning Disabilities, 9*, 3–10.

Manikam, R., Matson, J. L., Coe, D. A., & Hillman, N. (1995). Adolescent depression: Self-reports to intellectual and adaptive functioning. *Research in Developmental Disabilities, 16*, 349–364.

Margalit, M. (2003). Resilience model among individuals with learning disabilities: Proximal and distal influences. *Learning Disabilities Research and Practice, 18*, 82–86.

Masten, A. (2001). Ordinary magic: Resilience processes in development. *American Psychologist, 56*, 227–238.

Miller, M. (2002). Resilience elements in students with learning disabilities. *Journal of Clinical Psychology, 58*, 291–298.

Miller, J., Grabelsky, J., & Wagner, K. C. (2010). Psychosocial capacity building in New York: Building resiliency with construction workers assigned to ground zero after 9/11. *Social Work with Groups, 33,* 23–40.

Morrison, G. M., & Cosden, M. A. (1997). Risk, resilience, and adjustment of individuals with learning disabilities. *Learning Disability Quarterly, 20,* 43–60.

Moskovitz, S. (1983). *Love despite hate: Child survivors of the holocaust and their adult lives.* New York: Schocken Books.

Most, T., & Greenbank, A. (2000). Auditory, visual, and auditory-visual perceptions of emotions by adolescents with and without learning disabilities and their relationship to social skills. *Learning Disabilities Research and Practice, 15,* 171–178.

Murray, C., & Greenberg, M. T. (2001). Relationships with teachers and bonds with school: Social-emotional adjustment correlates for children with and without disabilities. *Psychology in the Schools, 38,* 25–41.

National Center for Children in Poverty. (2009). *Low-income children in the United States: National and state trend data, 1998-2008.* New York: Mailman School of Public Health, Columbia University.

Nelson, R. J., & Roberts, M. L. (2000). Ongoing reciprocal teacher-student interactions involving disruptive behaviors in general education classrooms. *Journal of Emotional and Behavioral Disorders, 8,* 27–37.

NICHD Early Child Care Research Network. (2004). Multiple pathways to early academic achievement. *Harvard Educational Review, 74,* 1–29.

O'Donnell, J., Hawkins, J. D., Catalano, R. F., Abbot, R. D., & Day, L. E. (1995). Preventing school failure, drug use, and delinquency among low-income children. *American Journal of Orthopsychiatry, 65,* 87–100.

Oesterle, S., Hawkins, J. D., Fagan, A. A., Abbott, R. D., & Catalano, R. F. (2010). Testing the universality of the effects of the Communities that Care prevention system for preventing adolescent drug use and delinquency. *Prevention Science, 11,* 411–423.

Patterson, G. R., Forgatch, M. S., Yoerger, K. L., & Stoolmiller, M. (1998). Variables that initiate and maintain an early-onset trajectory for juvenile offending. *Development and Psychopathology, 10,* 531–547.

Phipps, S. (2011). Positive psychology and war: An oxymoron. *American Psychologist, 66,* 641–642.

Poulin, F., Dishion, T. J., & Burraston, B. (2001). 3-Year iatrogenic effects associated with aggregating high-risk adolescents in cognitive-behavioral preventive interventions. *Applied Developmental Science, 5,* 214–224.

Raskind, M. H., Goldberg, R. J., Higgins, E. L., & Herman, K. L. (1999). Patterns of change and predictors of success in individuals with learning disabilities: Results from a twenty-year longitudinal study. *Learning Disabilities Research and Practice, 14,* 35–49.

Raviv, D., & Stone, A. (1991). Individual differences in the self-image of adolescents with learning disabilities: The roles of severity, time of diagnosis, and parental perceptions. *The Journal of Learning Disabilities, 24,* 602–611.

Reid, R., Gonzalez, J. E., Nordness, P. D., Trout, A., & Epstein, M. H. (2004). A meta- analysis of the academic status of students with emotional/behavioral disturbance. *Journal of Special Education, 38,* 130–143.

Reivich, K. J., Seligman, M. E., & McBride, S. (2011). Master resilience training in the U.S. Army. *American Psychologist, 66,* 25–34.

Rogers, S., Muir, K., & Evenson, C. R. (2003). Signs of resilience: Assets that support deaf adults' success in bridging the deaf and hearing worlds. *American Annals of the Deaf, 148,* 222–232.

Rutter, M. (1979). Protective factors in children's responses to stress and disadvantage. In M. W. Kent & J. E. Rolf (Eds.), *Primary prevention of psychopathology: Vol. 3. Social competence in children.* (pp. 49–74). Hanover, NH: University Press of New England.

Rutter, M., Maughan, B., Mortimore, P., & Ouston, J. (1979). *Fifteen thousand hours: Secondary schools and their effects on children.* Cambridge, MA: Harvard University Press.

Sameroff, A. J. (2000). Developmental systems and psychopathology. *Development and Psychopathology, 12,* 297–312.

Sameroff, A. J., Bartko, W. T., Baldwin, A., Baldwin, C., & Seifer, R. (1998). Family and social influences on the development of child competence. In M. Lewis & C. Feiring (Eds.), *Families, risk, and competence* (pp. 161–205). Mahwah, NJ: Lawrence Erlbaum Associates.

Seligman, M. E., & Csikszentmihályi, M. (2000). Positive psychology: An introduction. *American Psychologist, 55,* 5–14.

Seligman, M. E., & Pawelski, J. O. (2003). Positive psychology: FAQs. *Psychological Inquiry, 14,* 159–163.

Sherman, A. (1994). *Wasting America's future: The children's defense fund report on the costs of child poverty.* Boston: Beacon Press.

Shonkoff, J. P., & Phillips, D. A. (2000). *From neurons to neighborhoods: The science of early childhood development.* Washington, DC: National Academy Press.

Spekman, N. J., Goldberg, R. J., & Herman, K. L. (1992). Learning disabled children grow up: A search for factors related to success in the young adult years. *Learning Disabilities Research and Practice, 7,* 161–170.

Sroufe, L. A. (2009). The concept of development in developmental psychopathology. *Child Development Perspectives, 3,* 178–183.

Stormshak, E. A., Connell, A. M., Veronneau, M., Myers, M., Dishion, T. J., Kavanaugh, KI., et al. (2011). An ecological approach to promoting early adolescent mental health and social adaptation: Family-centered intervention in public middle schools. *Child Development, 82,* 209–225.

Stouthamer-Loeber, M., Loeber, R., Wei, E., Farrington, D. P., & Wikstrom, P. H. (2002). Risk and promotive effects in the explanation of persistent serious delinquency in boys. *Journal of Consulting and Clinical Psychology, 70,* 111–123.

Svetaz, M. V., Ireland, M., & Blum, R. (2000). Adolescents with learning disabilities: Risk and protective factors associated with emotional well-being: Findings from the National Longitudinal Study of Adolescent Health. *Journal of Adolescent Health, 27,* 340–348.

Swanson, L. H., & Malone, S. (1992). Social skills and learning disabilities: A meta- analysis of the literature. *School Psychology Review, 21,* 427–433.

Taylor, T. K., Eddy, J. M., & Biglan, A. (1999). Interpersonal skills training to reduce aggression and delinquency: Limited evidence and the need for an evidence-based system of care. *Journal of Clinical Child and Family Psychology Review, 2,* 169–182.

Vaughn, S., Zaragoza, N., Hogan, A., & Walker, J. (1993). A four-year longitudinal investigation of the social skills and behavior problems of students with learning disabilities. *Journal of Learning Disabilities, 26,* 404–412.

Wagner, M., Newman, L., & Cameto, R. (2004). *Changes over time in the secondary school experiences of students with disabilities.* A report from the National Longitudinal Transition Study-2 (NLTS2). Menlo Park, CA: SRI International.

Wagner, M., Newman, L., Cameto, R., Garza, N., & Levine, P. (2005). *After high school: A first look at the postschool experiences of youth with disabilities.* A report from the National Longitudinal Transition study-2 (NLTS2). Menlo Park, CA: SRI International.

Walker, H. M., Horner, R. H., Sugai, G., Bullis, M., Sprague, J. R., Bricker, D., et al. (1996). Integrated approaches to preventing antisocial behavior patterns among school-age children and youth. *Journal of Emotional and Behavioral Disorders, 4,* 194–209.

Werner, E. E. (1993). Risk and resilience in individuals with learning disabilities: Lessons learned from the Kauai Longitudinal Study. *Learning Disabilities Research and Practice, 8,* 28–34.

Werner, E. E., & Smith, R. S. (1989). *Vulnerable but invincible: A longitudinal study of resilient children and youth.* New York: Adams, Bannister & Cox.

Werner, E. E., & Smith, R. S. (1992). *Overcoming the odds: High risk children from birth to adulthood.* Ithaca, NY: Cornell University Press.

Whipple, S. S., Evans, G. W., Barry, R. L., & Maxwell, L. E. (2010). An ecological perspective on cumulative school and neighborhood risk factors related to achievement. *Journal of Applied Developmental Psychology, 31,* 422–427.

Whitaker, S., & Read, S. (2006). The prevalence of psychiatric disorders among people with intellectual disabilities: An analysis of the literature. *Journal of Applied Research in Intellectual Disabilities, 19,* 330–345.

Wolchik, S. A., Ramirez, R., Sandler, I. N., Fisher, J. L., Balls, P., & Brown, C. (1992). Inner city, poor children of divorce: Negative divorce-related events, problematic beliefs and adjustment problems. *Journal of Divorce and Remarriage, 19,* 1–20.

Wolchik, S. A., Schenck, C. E., & Sandler, I. N. (2009). Promoting resilience in youth from divorced families: Lessons learned from experimental trials of the New Beginnings Program. *Journal of Personality, 77,* 1833–1868.

Wolchik, S. A., West, S. G., Sandler, I. N., Tein, J., Coatsworth, D., & Lengua, L. (2000). An experimental evaluation of theory-based mother and mother-child programs for children of divorce. *Journal of Consulting and Clinical Psychology, 68,* 843–856.

Wolmer, L., Hamiel, D., Barchas, J. D., Slone, M., & Laor, N. (2011). Teacher-delivered resilience-focused interventions in schools with traumatized children following the second Lebanon War. *Journal of Traumatic Stress, 24,* 309–316.

Wolmer, L., Hamiel, D., & Laor, N. (2011). Preventing children's posttraumatic stress after disaster with teacher-based intervention: A controlled study. *Journal of the American Academy of Child & Adolescent Psychiatry, 50,* 340–348.

Woolfson, L. H. (1999). Using a model of transactional developmental regulation to evaluate the effectiveness of an early intervention programme for pre-school children with motor impairments. *Child: Care, Health and Development, 25,* 55–79.

Wong, B. Y. (2003). General and specific issues for researchers' consideration in applying the risk and resilience framework to the social domain of learning disabilities. *Learning Disabilities Research and Practice, 18,* 68–76.

Yates, T. M., & Masten, A. S. (2004). Fostering the future Resilience theory and the practice of positive psychology. In P. Alex & J. Stephan (Eds.), *Positive psychology in practice* (pp. 521–539). Hoboken, NJ: Wiley.

Young, A., Green, L., & Rogers, K. (2008). Resilience and deaf children: A literature review. *Deafness and Education International, 10,* 40–55.

Zimmerman, M. A., & Arunkumar, R. (1994). Resiliency research: Implications for schools and policy. *Society for Research in Child Development: Social Policy Report, 8,* 1–19.

Problem Solving and Decision Making

Linda Hickson *and* Ishita Khemka

Abstract

This chapter explores the implications of problem-solving and decision-making theory and research for a positive psychology of disability, focusing on the social/interpersonal aspects of these domains as they pertain to people with intellectual disabilities (ID) and autism spectrum disorders (ASD). Intervention approaches shown to improve the decision-making performance of adults (i.e., ESCAPE-DD) and adolescents (i.e., PEER-DM) are described. Building on past theory and research, the chapter introduces a new theoretical model that highlights alternative pathways of decision processing. The model represents a major shift in prevailing views of decision making that provides a supportive structure for building a repertoire of effective decision-making skills. The chapter concludes that progress in research and theory on problem solving and decision making can contribute to a positive psychology of disability that promises to improve the quality of interpersonal experiences and social relationships of people with ID or ASD.

Key Words: abuse, autism spectrum disorder, decision making, intellectual disability, peer pressure, problem solving

The purpose of this chapter is to explore the implications of problem-solving and decision-making theory and research for a positive psychology of disability. Although the broad domains of problem solving and decision making encompass myriad activities ranging from handling the problems of everyday living to solving complex mathematical problems to making high-stakes economic decisions, this chapter focuses on the social/interpersonal aspects of these domains as they pertain to people with intellectual disability (ID) or autism spectrum disorders (ASD). In an effort to gain an integrated understanding of how people with these diagnostic labels handle challenging social situations, we will consider a broad range of theory and research including emerging work on the neurobiological bases of these processes. Because people with ID or ASD are highly vulnerable to abuse and victimization (see Hickson, Khemka, Golden, & Chatzistyli,

2008; Fisher, Moskowitz, & Hodapp, 2012) and because the effective handling of problem-solving and decision-making situations that involve risks or threats to safety or well-being can be pivotal in reducing this vulnerability, many of the research applications used by ourselves and others have focused on self-protection. However, our overall purpose in this work is to identify new ways to understand, support, and enhance positive and proactive problem solving and decision making in people with ID or ASD in the interest of enabling their increased engagement in positive and satisfying interpersonal relationships and improved quality of life.

Underpinnings of Social Problem Solving and Decision Making in People with Disabilities

This section provides a snapshot of some of the social limitations attributed to people with ID or

ASD. Current understandings of the nature of the social limitations are considered from the perspective of their implications for problem solving and decision making in social/interpersonal situations, including situations involving risk taking, peer pressure, and victimization. This discussion is followed by a consideration of issues regarding the definition of problem solving and decision making.

Social Limitations Associated with Intellectual Disability and Autism Spectrum Disorders

A variety of social limitations have been attributed to people with ID or ASD, some of which may contribute to their vulnerability in situations requiring problem solving and decision making. Social limitations are central to the definitions of both ID and ASD. The American Association on Intellectual and Developmental Disabilities (AAIDD, 2010) defined ID as "characterized by significant limitations both in intellectual functioning and in adaptive behavior as expressed in conceptual, *social*, and practical adaptive skills." The *Diagnostic and Statistical Manual of Mental Disorders* (DSM-IV-TR; American Psychiatric Association, 2000) defined autistic disorder as involving qualitative impairments in *social interaction*, communication, and restrictive, repetitive patterns of behavior. A social limitation is necessary for a diagnosis of ASD, but not for a diagnosis of ID, which requires limitations in only one of the three areas of adaptive behavior.

Nevertheless, Leffert, Siperstein, and Widaman (2010) have pointed out that social limitations have always held a prominent place in the definition of ID, perhaps because "the social skills domain is highly saturated with cognition" (p. 169). In fact, Greenspan and his colleagues (Greenspan, Switzky, & Granfield, 1996) have advocated redefining ID as a disorder of everyday intelligence, which is comprised of social and practical intelligence. Accordingly, Greenspan and Love (1997) asserted that social intelligence is the cognitive underpinning of social competence, which consists of "one's ability to understand interpersonal situations and transactions and to use that understanding to assist one in achieving desired interpersonal outcomes" (p. 311). The three domains of social intelligence in Greenspan's 1979 model are social sensitivity, social insight, and social communication.

Greenspan, Loughlin, and Black (2001) highlighted the importance of credulity and gullibility in the social vulnerability of people with ID. They argued that a tendency toward credulity and gullibility is a central feature of the ID prototype and the basis of their need for protection. Credulity involves believing something despite scanty evidence, and gullibility is vulnerability to being tricked or manipulated. A key aspect of making sense of social situations is the accurate interpretation of another's intentions. However, there is evidence that people with ID are less accurate at this than are people without ID (e.g., Leffert, Siperstein, & Millikan, 2000).

More recently, Greenspan, Switzky, and Woods (2011) have focused on a "common sense deficit," involving a failure to appreciate the existence and seriousness of risk, as the core feature of ID. Accordingly, they emphasized the diagnostic importance of information about the quality of an individual's decisions and his or her vulnerabilities in social situations.

Van Nieuwenhuijzen, Orobio de Castro, Wijnroks, and Vermeer (2009) reported that children with mild ID or "borderline intelligence" showed "poorer social skills, fewer social peer interactions, less acceptance by peers, and more rejections by peers." Although Kasari and Bauminger (1998) reported similar social difficulties in children with ID, they cautioned that social abilities are likely to differ with etiology. Well-known examples are the tendency for people with fragile-X syndrome to exhibit shyness and avoidance of eye contact, in contrast to the tendency for people with Williams syndrome to show high levels of friendliness toward strangers (Dykens, 2001; Semel & Rosner, 2003).

A variety of social limitations have also been reported to characterize individuals on the autism spectrum. In one study, Channon, Charman, Heap, Crawford, and Rios (2001) compared adolescents and young adults with Asperger syndrome with typically developing adolescents and young adults on their responses to a series of questions on an everyday problem-solving task (e.g., how to deal with a neighbor with noisy dogs). The performance of the Asperger syndrome group was significantly below that of the typically developing group on the quality of their solutions, problem appreciation, and the social appropriateness of their solutions.

Based on clinical observations of impaired decision making and goal-directed behavior in ASD, South, Dana, White, and Crowley (2011) underscored the importance of studying decision making and risk taking in ASD. They compared children and adolescents with ASD with typically developing children and adolescents on a task in which subjects were told that the computer would blow up a virtual balloon according to how many pumps they gave it. If they gave it too many pumps, it would explode and they would lose all of their points for that round. Although they found no overall group differences on this risk-taking task, they did find differences in the relationship between risk taking and anxiety, which was associated with increased risk taking in the ASD group but not in the typically developing group. It was suggested that, "rather than causing functioning to shut down, high anxiety in the ASD group leads to increased motivation due to a fear of failure." The typically developing group appeared to be more concerned with reward.

After reviewing the available literature on social skills of people with Asperger syndrome and high-functioning autism (IQ in the average range), Rao, Beidel, and Murray (2008) reported that their social skills limitations included difficulties interpreting social cues, inappropriate emotional response, and difficulty understanding the perspectives of others. They pointed out, however, that one limitation of the entire body of research is that there is no common definition of social skills, which, depending on the definition, may or may not include social problem solving.

Only a few studies have directly explored possible qualitative differences in the social limitations associated with ID and ASD. In an effort to identify the diagnostic criteria that were most likely to distinguish between children diagnosed with both ASD and ID and children diagnosed with ID only, Hartley and Sikora (2010) compared the two groups on a battery of instruments that spanned the diagnostic criteria for ASD. They found that the diagnostic criteria most likely to distinguish between the two groups were in the social relatedness domain, indicating that children who met criteria for ASD were more likely than children who met criteria for ID only to exhibit failure to develop peer relationships, lack of seeking to share, and lack of social/emotional reciprocity.

Embregts and van Nieuwenhuijzen (2009) compared boys with ASD and mild to borderline ID and boys with mild to borderline ID without ASD to a group of typically developing boys. They found that both the ASD group and the typically developing group generated more assertive responses and fewer submissive responses than the ID group, suggesting that the boys with ASD were more socially competent in some ways than the boys with only ID.

In a meta-analysis review of studies comparing people with ID and people with ASD on theory of mind (ToM) tasks, Yirmiya, Erel, Shaked, and Solomonica-Levi (1998) found that both people with ID and people with ASD performed more poorly than typically developing individuals on ToM mind tasks. However, people with ASD performed significantly less well than people with ID, suggesting that it is "the severity of the impairment in theory of mind abilities rather than the impairment itself [that] is unique to autism" (p. 291). Although there is ample evidence of social limitations of people with ID and people with ASD that may contribute to their difficulties with social problem solving and interpersonal decision making, the extent to which these limitations differ qualitatively has not been fully explored.

Definitions of Problem Solving and Decision Making

To date, the literature does not reveal clear distinctions between the definitions of social problem solving and interpersonal decision making, nor does it reflect consensus on the definition of either construct. In fact, most discussions of social problem solving and interpersonal decision making indicate considerable overlap between these two task domains. For example, in identifying both problem-solving and decision-making skills as key components of self-determination, Wehmeyer and Shogren (2008) viewed decision-making skills as embedded in the problem-solving process. Wehmeyer, Shogren, Zager, Smith, and Simpson (2010) defined problem solving broadly as a "task for which a solution is not known or readily apparent" (p. 478) and went on to state that "decision making, like problem solving, is a systematic process that involves coming to a judgment about which solution is best at a given time" (p. 479).

Writing in the context of the national effort to improve "functional health literacy," Frauenknecht and Black (2010) expressed concern about inconsistency and confusion in the definition of problem solving and decision making. They attempted to resolve the confusion by defining social problem solving as "a multidimensional, cognitive-affective-behavioral process that enables an individual to generate and select systematically from potential alternatives for a problem encountered in daily living." In accord with Wehmeyer and Shogren (2008), they asserted that decision making is subsumed within the problem-solving process, but it does not constitute the entirety of the problem-solving process. Frauenknecht and Black underscored the importance of problem solving by suggesting that it is the sine qua non of behavior change programs for youth.

Izzo, Pritz, and Ott (1990) also emphasized the central importance of problem solving and decision making, pointing out that employers need workers who have mastered these skills. They went on to advocate for explicit instruction in problem solving and decision making as part of the curriculum to prepare students for the workplace, especially in classrooms including special needs learners. Their definition of problem solving included the following components (1) state the problem, (2) list the choices that are available, (3) identify the consequences of each choice, and (4) select the choice that best meets immediate as well as long-term needs (p. 25). However, Izzo et al.'s definition of problem solving is quite similar to Wilson and Kirby's (1984) definition of decision making. According to them, the decision-making process entails the following skills: defining the decision to be made, educating oneself (gathering facts and generating alternatives), considering options, identifying a choice, designing a plan to carry out the decision, and evaluating the decision.

D'Zurilla, Maydeu-Olivares, and Gallardo-Pujol (2011) defined problem solving more broadly as the "general coping strategy by which a person attempts to develop effective coping responses for specific problematic situations in everyday living" (p. 142). According to their model, which also has relevance to interpersonal decision making, social problem-solving outcomes are largely determined by two processes: (1) problem orientation (cognitive-emotional process that serves a motivational function) and (2) problem-solving style (cognitive and behavioral activities by which a person tries to understand problems and find effective solutions). Their model specifies two problem orientations: (1) positive, which involves appraising problems as a challenge, believing that problems are solvable, and believing in one's own ability to solve problems successfully; and (2) negative, which involves viewing problems as a threat to well-being, doubting one's own ability to solve problems successfully, and easily becoming frustrated and upset. The D'Zurilla et al. model also specified three problem-solving styles: (1) rational (the rational, deliberate, and systematic application of problem-solving skills), (2) impulsive/careless (attempts to apply problem-solving strategies that are narrow, impulsive, careless, hurried, and incomplete), and (3) avoidant (involving procrastination, passivity, inaction, and dependency).

Some researchers have drawn a distinction between problem solving as a well-defined problem and decision making as an ill-defined problem (Short & Evans, 1990; Simon, 1974). As we noted in (Hickson & Khemka, 1999), well-defined problems typically include clear specifications of initial states, goal states, and/or rules to minimize the distance between the two states. Ill-defined problems lack one or more of these components. Typically, problem-solving tasks include a specification of at least the initial state and the goal state, with or without rules on the generation of possible alternatives, but decision-making tasks typically lack a clearly defined goal state and rules on how to proceed.

Further examination of the literature suggests other possible distinctions between problem solving and decision making, often in terms of the types of situations targeted and the types of questions asked about the situation. Social problem-solving situations often involve interpersonal dilemmas ranging from benign to hostile, with a stated goal, and a request for alternative means to attain that goal. Interpersonal decision-making situations more typically involve an open-ended situation, often one involving risk or danger, and a request for one best way to handle the situation.

Although it is important to be aware of these definitional issues, in light of the inconsistencies and overlap between the constructs of problem solving and decision making, we will not attempt to draw a sharp distinction between these two task domains in this chapter. Instead, we will consider relevant research pertaining to both constructs while maintaining a theoretical focus on decision making in order to provide continuity with our previous work. In our previous models of decision making (see Hickson & Khemka, 1999,; 2001; Khemka & Hickson, 2006), as well as in our new model proposed later in this chapter, we have interpreted decision making somewhat broadly as being a goal-driven process, drawing on elements from previous research and theory on problem solving and decision making. We have assumed that at the start of the decision-making process, identifying and defining the problem (and hence recognizing that a decision has to be made) are essential components that must occur before solution strategies can be engaged. Since our decision-making research has been primarily in the context of hypothetical interpersonal and social situations, often involving uncertainty and urgency, the frequently included end steps of implementing the decision and evaluating its success are not formally expressed in our models but are implied for decisions that are recursive or long term. In the present survey of research studies involving adults and adolescents, we draw on both the problem-solving and decision-making literatures as needed in order to advance understanding of the role of problem solving and decision making in the social difficulties faced by people with ID or ASD as a basis for designing effective interventions.

Theoretical Perspectives on Decision Making

The study of human decision making has been evolving with contributions from a number of disciplines over many years. These contributions have ranged from providing mathematical and econometric models of decision-making processes to the study of bounded rationality and descriptive reasoning, along with stage-based and intuitive models of decision making. In particular, the past few decades have seen widespread applications of these theories in economics, operations research, and medicine, and, through these disciplines, to the social sciences. As a result, the study of collective and individual decision making in social/interpersonal situations has embodied several prevalent concepts and models with additional components that exert significant influence on interactive or relation-based types of decision making (Doyle & Thomason, 1999). Additionally, the newer emerging fields of cybernetics and neuroscience have also shed light on the biological and cognitive nature of decision makers' processes, thereby providing a deeper look at the neural underpinnings, or the "hardwiring," of an individual's decision-making systems.

In this section, we provide an overview of the main theories that have guided much of decision-making research, leading into some of the newer paradigms of thinking and ideas of a multifaceted approach to decision making, especially in the context of real-life decision tasks and unpredictable decision situations.

Rational Choice Theory

Rational choice theory, also known as *choice theory* or *rational action theory*, is a dominant paradigm in microeconomic models for understanding and modeling economic and social behavior. It is also widely represented in modern political science, sociology, and philosophy. Referred to as *normative models of decision making* (e.g., expected utility theory), these theories provide prescriptive functions or decision rules that serve as the norm or rational standards on which individuals (and societies) base their decisions. The primary rule or assumption underlying decision making is that individuals operatively seek rationality in their preferences, expressed in their exhaustively seeking the most cost-effective means to achieve a specific goal by comparing the costs and benefits of different courses of action.

Since people want to get the most useful products at the lowest price, they will judge the benefits of a certain object (e.g., how useful it is or how attractive it is) compared to similar objects. Then they will compare prices (or costs). In general, people will choose the object that provides the greatest reward at the lowest cost. According to rational choice theory, decision makers remain stable and consistent in their motivations to maximize expected utility or payoffs of outcomes. Although the models used in rational choice theory are diverse, all assume (with some minor differences) that individuals choose the best action according to unchanging and stable preference functions (i.e., if decision makers prefer or rank one alternative above another, then they would tend to prefer or rank them identically on all other occasions in which these possible alternatives are available) (Fischhoff, 1982).

The idea of rational choice, in which people maximize utility by comparing the costs and benefits of certain actions, is easy to see in economic theory. However, observations of decision making within the field of behavioral economics present enough evidence to suggest that actual human behavior often deviates from or goes against such an axiomatic notion of "pure economic rationality" and that more realistic theories of human action are needed to fully explain decisions, even in the context of economic tasks (Galotti, 2002).

Standard prescriptive decision-making models based on probabilities of outcomes and payoffs are limited in explaining decision making in real-life situations. Pragmatic decision constraints, such as resource limitations or presence of multiple goals, may result in the need for various kinds of planning, as opposed to a strictly prescribed rule. To make rational calculations or predictions, it is implicitly assumed that decision makers have somewhat idealized cognitive abilities, including foresight. However in reality, most individuals do not resemble such an ideal in their everyday decision making and may be limited in their ability or have incomplete knowledge to adequately handle all the processing demands needed to adhere to a normative choice. Because rational choice theory does not account for individual motivation, its usefulness for understanding interpersonal interactions, in which goals are not as clear as they may be in business behaviors, is fairly limited.

Descriptive Theories

Descriptive decision making theories (e.g., Tversky and Kahneman's [1979] prospect theory) addressed many of the limitations tied to the unrealistic and intractable assumptions of rational choice theories and promulgated a more plausible concept of bounded versus absolute rationality. Tversky and Kahneman (1974) were among the first to challenge the central notion of rational choice theory of complete logical thinking across decisions and presented empirical data to show that individuals are highly susceptible to the effects of "framing" (i.e., the manner or context in which options are presented, resulting in a decision bias).

In contrast to rational choice theory, descriptive theories use cognition to delineate how people reach decisions in the face of certain and uncertain events. They suggest that individuals make decisions by evaluating the utility of alternative courses of action relative to a reference point (typically, outcomes below the reference point are viewed as losses and not desirable; outcomes above the reference point are perceived as gains and hence desirable). Decision makers may also attach extra value to items that they already own compared to similar items owned by others. The weights or values ascribed to the different attributes of a problem depend on the framing of the decision problem (as either gains or losses) and affect the way the decision is approached. Descriptive decision theories support the view that decision makers will selectively reduce the processing demands of a decision to manageable levels by adjusting for a satisfactory rather than an optimal choice (as prescribed in rational choice theory) and thereby "satisficing" in accord with reasonable constraints on one's capacity for decision making and level of aspiration (Selten, 2001; Simon, 1957; Simon et al., 1986).

Stage-Based Theories

A large number of decision-making theories follow a stage-based or process view of decision making and define the steps or stages through which a decision maker may proceed to arrive at a decision outcome in a specific situation. The focus is not on prediction of outcomes or maximizing the decision output but on understanding how individuals engage in a decision-making process. In delineating the process, the theories (e.g., Byrnes, 1998; Gumpel, 1994; Janis & Mann, 1977) outline a fairly well-sequenced progression of steps, with minor variations, to illustrate how a decision maker deliberatively proceeds from the stages of identifying a problem to making a reasoned choice through careful consideration and evaluation of alternatives. Although the stepwise models advocate

for the deliberation of all of the components in the specified order, research findings suggest that decision makers broadly operate within the parameters of the frameworks defined by these theories, but may not always follow, or be efficient in completing, all of the components in the process, especially in the recommended order (see Byrnes, Miller, & Reynolds, 1999). Therefore, Galotti (2002) argued for a "phase-based" approach as an alternative to a stepwise approach, to allow for variation in the order as long as the key phases were attended to.

Role of Motivational and Goal-Related Processes

Decision makers do not hold stable motivational states in interpersonal contexts (as predicted in normative theories) and are likely to have varied personal and/or social goals motivating their decision engagement and outcomes. In an interpersonal context, decisions may be influenced by differing motivations depending on the relationship of the decision maker with the other(s) and the nature of the ensuing interaction(s). In relationship studies (e.g., Lewicki & Litterer, 1985; Walster, Walster, & Bershcheid, 1978), individuals have been found to value different goals for themselves (e.g., equity vs. inequality) in response to positive versus negative relationships and the nature of the dispute context (personal vs. business). It is necessary to address the role of an individual's sense of morals or ethics in decision making and to investigate the nature or validity of decision motivations (why we want what we want) so that decision makers are not restricted to given and inexplicable wants or goals (as in strict rational choice theories) but can benefit from changing motivations to adaptively adjust their preferences and choices and maximize their best interest in specific social or interpersonal environments. Many researchers (e.g., Argyle, 1991; Byrnes, 1998; Fiske, 1992; Kruglanski, 1989, Kuhl, 1986) have highlighted that motivation and goal-related processes in decision making are important not only because these elements make decision behavior more purposeful and personally desirable but because they also interact with the cognitive reasoning or the information processing parts of decision making to ensure that the search process and the final decision outcomes are effective and reflective of desired goals.

Role of Emotional and Intuitive Processes

Most decision-making theories do not specify the role of individual and situational influences on decision making, such as beliefs, emotions, or culture. This limits their applicability to the decision-making processes in real-life and interactive social interpersonal situations. The importance of incorporating emotional processes within models of decision making is well established (see De Martino, Kumaron, Seymour, & Dolan, 2006). Evidence from the field of neuroscience linking decision making to an amygdala-based emotional system is also growing (e.g., De Martino et al., 2006; Kahneman & Frederick, 2007). Similarly, neuropsychologists have studied the impact of limitations in emotional control and reasoning capacities of people on their ability to successfully resolve everyday problems (e.g., Rath, Simon, Langenbahn, Sherr, & Diller, 2003). It is assumed that during problem solving or decision making, the initial process of problem orientation is largely attitudinal or affective in nature.

The importance and influence of beliefs, values, and stereotypic behavior in the decision-making process has been widely discussed in the literature (Camic, 1992; Etzioni, 1988; Hastie & Dawes, 2000; Higgins & Bargh, 1987; Hogarth, 1994; Meneghetti & Seel, 2001; Stein, & Welch, 1997). Research on decision heuristics provides explanations for how individuals use "mental shortcuts" or "biases" based on their beliefs, values, or habits to circumvent the use of detailed decision rules and to simplify the decision process to a limited set of viewpoints or expectations. Decisions are also based on individual evaluations of past and possible future events and the psychological consequences to the decision maker of those events. Personal beliefs integrate with people's personal histories and their subjective reactions to decision making experiences to influence decision outcomes. Researchers have drawn on attribution theories (e.g., Fiske, 1986; Schank & Abelson, 1977) and locus of control mechanisms to explain how people process information and interpret situations differentially during decision making based on their individual beliefs and values. The mediating beliefs relate to preexisting schemas of self and other individuals (Fiske and Taylor 1991) and influence decision engagement and style. Fishbein and Ajzen's (1975) theory of reasoned action and Bandura's (1977, 1997) self-efficacy theory illustrate how cognitions related to decision making are influenced by individual perceptions of control and feelings of self-efficacy. Therefore, the concept of "self" as a decision maker is central to psychological understandings of decision-making phenomena.

Concurrently, the literature also supports the premise that decision-making processes possess a strong cultural component that might influence the decision style, perceptions, and attitudes of decision makers (Adler, 1991; Brake, Walker, & Walker, 1995). Culture dictates preferences (ethics and values) in life and influences how individuals and groups think, behave, and communicate and thus solve their problems (Hofstede, 2001; Schein, 1992). Meneghetti and Seel (2001) have proposed a four-step decision process that helps to deal with cultural and ethical dilemmas in the business environment. Culture-based decision-making studies are still relatively sparse, although the cultural components of decision-making behavior are well recognized.

In situations of decision making under uncertainty, as is often the case in social situations when the information available to the decision maker may be ambiguous, incomplete, or uncertain, the ability to integrate emotional contextual information into the decision process serves as a useful heuristic. In situations of high emotional intensity or time pressure, individuals have been known to completely bypass the decision-making process, failing to obtain or evaluate even the most basic information necessary to make any informed choices (Janis & Mann, 1977). Hoch, Kunreuther, and Gunther (2001) maintained that in uncertain and unexpected situations decision makers will often disregard logical models of choice and that their variations in decision behavior may not find any theoretical basis in normative thinking (models). The uncertainty of outcomes can influence decision makers to disregard any formal processes of thinking (or estimating probabilities) in unusual ways.

The primacy of intuitive reasoning (in contrast to formal, planful thinking) during decision making is also well documented. "Intuitions" or "instinctual judgments" serve as a "satisficing" tool to quickly narrow the decision process to a few accessible solutions rather than launching a thorough investigation of all applicable alternatives in search of an optimal solution (Kay, 2002). Remarks by decision makers such as "acted on one's guts" or "followed my heart" exemplify the intuitive approach commonly reported.

Dual-Process Theory

Kahneman (2003, 2011) has explored the differential roles played by intuition-based and reasoning-based modes of decision making. Although these two modes have often been referred to as system 1 (intuition-based) and system 2 (reasoning-based) (e.g., Kahneman, 2003, 2011;

Stanovich, 1999), we are persuaded by Stanovich's (2011) rationale for his recent shift to type 1/type 2 terminology to avoid the implication that the two systems map directly onto two specific brain systems. For the sake of consistency, we have chosen to use the terms type 1 and type 2 to refer to these dual processes throughout this chapter, regardless of the terminology used in the work being cited. According to these dual process theories, the type 1 intuition-based heuristic processes are fast, autonomous, and effortless whereas the reasoning-based, analytic type 2 processes are slower, effortful, and deliberately controlled (e.g., Kahneman, 2011; Stanovich, 2011). According to Kahneman (2003, 2011), because intuition-based thoughts are highly accessible and come to mind quickly, they tend to control judgments and preferences unless they are corrected or overridden by type 2 processes. Most decisions are based on intuitive impressions and therefore readily available. People can make quick decisions based on their intuitive thoughts unless they are deliberately controlled or overridden by slower, effortful, inputs from the reasoning-based system (Kahneman, 2003, 2011; Stanovich, 2010, 2011).

Recently, Stanovich (2010, 2011) has elaborated on the dual process model, expanding it into a tripartite model consisting of autonomous type 1 processing and two levels of analytic type 2 processing, the *algorithmic* level and the *reflective* level. Processing at the algorithmic level is characterized by the stepwise processes involved in carrying out mental tasks. Its key function is to sustain the processing of the "decoupled secondary" representations involved in the hypothetical thinking required for generating and evaluating possible alternative courses of action. Processing at the reflective level involves goal processes and thinking dispositions or cognitive style. The key function of reflective processing is to interrupt autonomous processing and put out the call for the hypothetical reasoning activities needed to come up with a better solution or course of action. Interestingly, algorithmic processes are correlated with intelligence, but reflective processes are not. Accordingly, Stanovich (2011) suggested that the continuous process disruptions associated with ID would be most apparent in the domain of algorithmic processing. He went on to speculate that the more discontinuous process disruptions associated with ASD might be manifested in type 1 processing.

Taking into account the unique perspectives and scope of the decision-making theories just reviewed,

it is apparent that these theories are limited in their overall explanatory or descriptive understanding of social and interpersonal decision making, especially with respect to people with ID or ASD. For a fuller explanation, a broader, more nuanced approach that takes into consideration the interaction of individual psychological, social, and situational elements may impart additional value. In a later section, we discuss the interdependency of the basic processes of cognition, emotion, and motivation in decision making and their interaction with situational and contextual factors. We present our new decision-making model as it has evolved in response to new and emerging paradigms that demand a multidisciplinary approach to the study of decision making and the findings of our decision-making studies with people with ID or ASD over the past 15 years. However, first we present an overview of relevant research on the decision-making performance of people with disabilities and consider the implications of certain developmental processes.

Decision Making in People with Disabilities

Insights about the biological or psychological bases of problem-solving and decision-making behaviors of people with disabilities, as informed by a growing body of neuroscience research, are reflected on in this section in an effort to gain a fuller perspective on the possible sources of problem-solving and decision-making difficulties experienced by people with ID or ASD. First, however, a brief examination of aspects of decision making in people with ADHD is included as a glance into the complex role of emotion and inhibitory factors in everyday decision making that may pose similar challenges for people with ID or ASD.

Decision Making in Individuals with Attention Deficit Hyperactivity Disorder

Examination of the decision-making difficulties observed of people with attention deficit hyperactivity disorder (ADHD) provides useful insights into the processes involved in everyday decision-making tasks. People with ADHD have been noted to have difficulties in decision making because of their impairments in planning, attention, and response inhibition, which are characteristic of their neuropsychological condition. Ernst et. al (2003) noted that people with ADHD tend to respond differently to rewards and punishment (favoring short-term gain in spite of long-term consequences) and that such differences in the regulation of their motivation may alter their approach to decision-making tasks in everyday life, in comparison to people without ADHD. Various studies have highlighted regions in the brain that function differently in people with ADHD, especially during decision-making tasks (see Doya, 2008). In a study examining adults with ADHD during a decision-making task involving a choice between high- or low-risk gambles, differences were observed in regions of the brain that are involved in "complex cognitive-emotional processes" (Ernst et al., 2003, p. 1066). The differences observed in people with ADHD were also related to their difficulties in using prior experience to make rational decisions; they tended to use their most recent decision-making experiences (the availability heuristic) instead of doing a more accurate search for evidence that would help achieve their goal (Baron, 2008). Evans (2003, 2008) has utilized Stanovich's 1999 dual-process theory, highlighting how the cognitive functions of the brain work at either an autonomous, intuitive level (type 1 processing) or at a more deliberative, analytical level (type 2 processing) to explain difficulties in decision making for people with ADHD. For rational decision making, type 2 processes must be able to override type 1 processes when it is optimal to the individual. However, for people with ADHD, it appears that during decision-making tasks the type 2 processes may be too weak to override the strength of the type 1 signals, resulting in more impulsive and less rational decision making. Examination of the possible links between neuropsychological impairments and difficulties with the type 2 processes involved in rational decision making in people with ADHD helps illuminate possible patterns of limitations of people with ID or low-functioning ASD, for whom overlapping difficulties in areas such as attention, impulse control, working memory, or inability to generalize learning from past experiences may play a role in decision making.

Decision Making of People with Intellectual Disability and Autism Spectrum Disorders

People with ID typically exhibit serious limitations in important decision-making skills, often jeopardizing their health and safety in situations that pose a risk of harm (Hickson & Khemka, 1999, 2001; Jenkinson, 1999; Jenkinson & Nelms, 1994; Khemka & Hickson, 2006; Tymchuk, Yokota, & Rahbar, 1990; Wong, Clare, Holland, Watson, & Gunn, 2000). Past research on social problem solving and decision making has indicated that people with ID typically fail to apply a systematic (type 2) process, tending to rely on solutions from their past experience that may or may not result in effective action in new situations. Furthermore, when these individuals do attempt to apply a multistep process, they often encounter a range of difficulties, including limited risk awareness and comprehension of potentially threatening situations, a failure to generate alternative courses of action, a failure to consider the possible consequences of each alternative, and selection of minimally effective or ineffective courses of action (e.g., Castles & Glass, 1986; Healey & Masterpasqua, 1992; Hickson & Khemka, 1999; Jenkinson & Nelms, 1994; Khemka & Hickson, 2006; Smith, 1986; Tymchuk, Yokota, & Rahbar, 1990; Wehmeyer & Kelchner, 1994).

Research on social problem solving and decision making in people with ASD is quite limited. Most of these studies have restricted their attention to participants whose IQs fall in the average or above average range, focusing on participants with Asperger syndrome (AS) or high-functioning autism (HFA) (e.g., Bernard-Opitz, Srira, & Nakhoda-Sapuan, 2001; Hillier, Fish, Cloppert, & Beversdorf, 2007). Although these studies have addressed a broad range of social skills that sometimes have included aspects of problem solving or decision making, they have often used the terms *social skills* and *social problem solving* interchangeably, making it difficult to draw clear conclusions from this body of work (e.g., Boujarwah, Hong, Arriaga, Abowd, & Isbell, 2010). One study that did include students with ASD representing a wider range of cognitive functioning (verbal IQ 57–101) suggested that the generation of alternatives may be an area of particular difficulty for people with ASD because of their well-documented issues with flexibility. The authors of this study, Ruble, Willis, and Crabtree (2008), reported that more than half of their participants improved in their ability to generate multiple solutions to problems after participating in a cognitive-behavioral social skills group.

In an often-cited study by DeMartino, Harrison, Knafo, Bird, and Dolan (2008), young adults with ASD showed significantly less sensitivity to a contextual framing effect (financial tasks presented in either a gain or a loss frame) in a decision task and revealed a more logical pattern of choice making, akin to rational norm-based thinking, in comparison to young adults with typical development. Although the pattern of choice for the people with ASD demonstrated logical consistency, it implied reduced behavioral flexibility and a difficulty with incorporating emotional cues into the decision process. Psychophysiological evidence collected in this study (skin conductance response measuring emotional sensitivity) corroborated evidence from previous studies by DeMartino et. al. (2006) and Kahneman and Frederick (2007) that pointed toward a potential core neurobiological impairment in ASD that interfered with the ability to integrate emotional context easily into the decision-making process. This impairment is noted to assume considerable importance during social interactions in situations of uncertainty, when information about others is often ambiguous and the need to absorb emotional contextual information into the decision process outweighs the need for standard inferential reasoning processes. For optimal decision making in uncertain social environments, the ability to incorporate a broad range of contextual cues into the decision process is interpreted to operate as an "affect heuristic" that allows the decision maker to evaluate multiple sources of critical and subtle information and to make rapid responses without having to necessarily engage in a demanding or enhanced analytic process (Stanovich and West, 2002). On this basis, a failure by people with ASD to deploy an affect heuristic in complex and uncertain social contexts might limit their intuitive reasoning mechanisms and thereby their social competence.

In our own work with people with ID, we have attempted to look at the entirety of the decision-making process in an effort to better understand key points in the process that may pose barriers to effective real-life decision making and as a basis for designing pivotal interventions. In our initial study in this area, we asked adults with and without ID what the protagonist should do in a series of vignette situations in which the protagonist was faced with a decision involving the possibility of interpersonal conflict, physical harm, or sexual assault. We found that the adults with mild and moderate ID recommended effective decisions that appeared to be in the best interest of the protagonist only 50% of the time, compared with adults without ID who recommended effective decisions 91% of the time (Hickson, Golden, Khemka, Urv, & Yamusah, 1998). In a subsequent study, adults with mild and moderate ID provided direct, prevention-focused decision responses to video-simulated abuse situations only 45% of the time (Khemka & Hickson, 2000). Hickson, et al. (2008) reported, in a related study, that women with ID and a history of abuse were more likely than women with ID but

without a history of abuse to employ passive/avoidant decision-making strategies that tend to be less effective than more active strategies for dealing with the immediate situation and preventing repetition of the abuse.

Developmental Perspectives on Decision Making and Risk Taking

Our recent decision-making studies with people with ID or ASD during the adolescent period (see Khemka & Hickson, 2006; Khemka, Hickson, Casella, Acceturi, & Rooney, 2009) underscore the need to look at the developmental and maturational aspects of decision making in association with underlying biological and/or neurological structures that inform decision-making patterns and functioning during critical periods of development. In light of the growing body of neuroscience research and knowledge about brain development, understanding of adolescent behavior has taken on new significance, especially in reflecting on why adolescence may be a critical and sensitive period characterized by heightened vulnerability to risk taking and peer victimization. Next, we examine a few findings from the developmental literature that bring to light certain distinctive features of adolescent functioning and that have contributed to our own increased understanding of the factors involved in decision making and risky behavior during this period.

Even though the connections between maturational brain processes and adolescents' behavioral and emotional development are still putative and not fully known, there is considerable evidence to suggest that the changes, beginning early and continuing into the late adolescent years, occur noticeably in functions relating to emotion regulation, response inhibition, and calibration of risk-reward. Also pertinent to our overall understanding of risky behavior during this period are the widespread observations that adolescents' experience of arousal, motivation, and emotion (an impact of puberty-related maturation) develops before their ability to regulate these feelings. This disjunction between adolescents' growing affective experiences and lags in regulatory competence is a contributing factor to their risky or impulsive behaviors—where the affect urges them to go forward in embracing newer, perhaps sensational opportunities when they may not be fully equipped to handle the new opportunities without risking harm. Martin, Kelly, Rayens, Brogli, Brenzel, Smith, and Omar (2002) found a significant correlation between puberty maturation and sensation seeking and risk taking in a large group of young adolescents (aged 11–14 years). There was no significant correlation between chronological age and sensation-seeking and risk-taking behaviors.

In a dual-systems model of adolescent risk taking, Steinberg (2010) has identified two distinct systems that interact during adolescence: a cognitive control system and a socioemotional system. The cognitive control system influences long-term planning and the ability to inhibit impulsive behavior and develops gradually over a longer period of time; however, the socioemotional system, responsible for reward seeking and sensation seeking, asserts itself and peaks abruptly during adolescence. The differing time tables of these changes make adolescence, especially mid-adolescence, a time of heightened vulnerability to risky and reckless behavior. Paralleling Kahneman's (2011) proposition of dual types of thinking (automatic and intuitive type 1 processing or deliberative and effortful type 2 processing), it appears that type 2 thinking, akin to the cognitive control system functions, may develop later in adolescence and that type 1 thinking, analogous to the socioemotional system functions that generate more impulsive and "acting-without-thinking" behavior, may dominate decision-making behavior during early adolescence. In our own research with adolescents with ID (e.g., Khemka & Hickson, 2006; Khemka, et al., 2009), we have found indications of decision making reflecting hypervigilant and less planful thinking, with a predominant type 1 thinking pattern and with little evidence of type 2 thinking in the form of deliberative decision making.

Many advances in developmental neuroscience (see Casey, Giedd, & Thomas, 2000; Keating, 2004; Spear, 2000) have pointed to sizeable changes in both the structure and functional aspects of brain development throughout the course of adolescence, specifically in multiple regions of the prefrontal cortex, with rapidly expanding linkages to the whole brain leading to enhanced connectivity and communication among different brain regions. These changes support improvements in various aspects of executive functioning, including metacognition, long-term planning, self-regulation, and the coordination of affect and cognition, thus resulting in increases in adolescents' efficiency of information processing and reasoning. Martin et al. (2002) and Spear (2000) have also highlighted that there is improved connectivity between regions of the prefrontal cortex and several areas of the limbic system during adolescence, a restructuring that further shapes the ways in which individuals evaluate and respond to risk and reward. Whatever the

underlying processes, during early adolescence, there is broad consensus that adolescents show perceptible improvements in deductive reasoning and enhanced efficiency and capacity for information processing (Wigfield, Byrnes, & Eccles, 2006). As a result of these gains, the core of the change between late childhood and middle adolescence is expressed in adolescents becoming more planful and abstract thinkers, more self-regulated, and more self-directed.

The need for increased individual regulation of affect and behavior in accordance with long-term goals and consequences carries important implications for those adolescents for whom such regulatory demands may already be an inherent challenge. For instance, adolescents with ID or ASD may be slow in their maturation, may lack the cognitive capacity or be limited in their emotional awareness, and may need extra regulatory structure and added supports (and for much longer into their lifespan) than their counterparts without disabilities, for whom regulatory supports may become less necessary with increasing age.

Interplay of Cognition, Emotion and Motivation in the Risky Decision Making of Adolescents

For a long time, the plausible explanation for the impulsive or risky decision-making behaviors of adolescents was thought to be cognitive in nature, in that adolescents lacked adequate cognitive skills relevant to decision making or had difficulty fully knowing or estimating the consequences of risky behavior (Tobler, 1986). Furby and Beyth-Marom (1992) theorized that adolescents' predisposition to risk taking was largely tied to their deficient cognitive skills that would be needed to make good decisions. This speculation has since been widely debated and now there is considerable evidence (Benthin, Slovic, Moran, Severson, Mertz, & Gerrard, 1995; Fischhoff, Parker, Downs, Palmgren, Dawes, & Manski, 2000; Martin et al., 2002; Steinberg, 2007) to confirm that, in real-life situations, adolescents engage in risk-taking decisions despite understanding very well the consequences of their actions and the risks involved. Research shows that young people are actually well aware of their vulnerability and can estimate some of their risks quite reasonably (Fischhoff et. al, 2000; Reyna & Adam, 2003; Reyna & Farley, 2006). Sometimes, adolescents are known to display an optimistic bias in thinking that they are at less risk than their peers, but adults are inclined to the same bias, rendering this bias unable to explain why adolescents take risks that adults avoid (Reyna & Farley, 2006). Keating (2004) reports that studies of people's responses to hypothetical dilemmas involving the perception and appraisal of risk show few reliable age differences in their risk perception abilities after middle adolescence, but that studies of actual risk taking indicate that adolescents are significantly more likely to engage in risky decision making than are adults (Arnett, 1992). This suggests that adolescents make decisions not simply by rationally calculating relative risks and consequences of their behaviors, but heavily weight their choices on their individual subjective experiences, such as feelings and social influences. Developmentally, it is hypothesized that adolescents (16 and older) may share the same logical competencies as adults, but their varying psychosocial capacities (e.g., impulse control or sensation seeking) and social-emotional experiences (e.g., peer influence) may lead to decision-making differences between adults and adolescents in real-life (Steinberg & Cauffman, 1996).

Further, individuals' social perspective taking (i.e., the ability to look at things from another person's perspective) is also shown to increase in adolescence (Wainryb, Shaw, Laupa, & Smith, 2001). The extent to which adolescents exercise more advanced social perspective taking with time depends on their intellectual ability for social reasoning (cognitive functioning), but also on their desires, motives, and interests (social and emotional reactivity) in response to particular social situations. Knowledge of intentionality of behavior is an equally important social processing skill that increases developmentally and can influence the framing of a decision-making situation.

Role of Affective Factors in Risky Decision Making

As described by Bechara, Demasio, Demasio, and Lee (1999), many day-to-day decisions regarding what to do in response to a particular situation are made at the level of "gut-feeling" rather than through a deliberative process of evaluating risks or prospects of outcomes. These gut feelings or intuitions seem to be products of the affective systems in the brain that operate at levels largely outside the individual's conscious or controlled awareness. Loewenstein and Lerner (2002) have provided an interesting framework to visualize the impact of intense emotions on risky decision making. They described cognitive processes that individuals engage in when making a decision with potential long-term risky consequences (e.g., smoking, alcohol abuse, unprotected

sex, participation in dangerous activities, serious offending) as being either "cold" or "hot." Cold cognitive processes are thinking processes under conditions of low emotion and/or arousal, whereas hot cognition refers to thinking under conditions of strong feelings or high arousal. In real-life situations, the hot cognitions perhaps play an important role in risky choices as adolescents confront major unpredictable and emotionally laden dilemmas in their social interactions.

The role of emotions, both positive (Fredrickson, 1998; Isen, 2000) and negative, in decision making and risk taking has been well established. The study of emotions is more pressing during adolescence as, developmentally, this is a time when the experience of extreme moods and emotions is more likely to occur, in contrast to childhood and adulthood (Arnett, 1992; Buchanan, Eccles, & Becker, 1992).

Emerging findings (see Martin et al., 2002) within the field of affective neuroscience denote that affective influences on behavior are impacted by puberty and maturation during adolescence and that these feelings are further formed in relation to the new social experiences that adolescents developmentally engage in as they begin to become more independent and experience new drives, motivations, and strong emotions (Richards, Crowe, Larson, & Swarr, 1998). As the social arena of adolescents broadens, peer relationships become increasingly important, dyadic close friendships develop, cliques or group memberships are formed, and romantic interests gain attention (see Lashbrook, 2000).

Role of Social Contextual Factors in Risky Decision Making

New advances in adolescent development research have focused on cognitive development as it plays out socially and, in particular, as it influences decision-making ability and risk taking. One of the most important and influential influences on risky behaviors, and one that has been widely studied during adolescence, is the influence of peers, peer pressure, or peer group effects (see Chassin, Hussong, & Beltran, 2009; Clark & Loheac, 2007; Monahan, Steinberg, & Cauffman, 2009; O'Brien, Albert, Chein, & Steinberg, in press). Much-cited studies on adolescents' risk-taking behavior (e.g., Moffitt, 1993) suggest that adolescents' decisions are directly influenced by the presence of peers. Risk taking in adolescence under peer influence appears to reflect efforts to redress adolescents' inflated emotional feelings of sensitivity to social status and a desire to impress peers (Moffitt, 1993).

Neuroimaging studies validate that when adolescents make decisions under the influence of peers, there is heightened activity in those areas of the brain that are associated with valuation of rewards (Chein, Albert, O'Brien, Uckert, & Steinberg, 2010). Given that adolescents hold elevated reward value for peer interactions, the presence of peers heightens their sensitivity to the potential reward value of risky behaviors (as opposed to potential harm), which in turn influences subsequent decisions about risk. This reward-sensitive motivational state may bias the adolescents' decisions toward greater risks since adolescents' cognitive control brain functions are not yet fully developed to regulate heightened reward-sensitivity and promote more deliberative decision making. The peer effects are so robust that adolescents will often override their rational thinking and undertake risky behaviors in the presence of peers, but may be more risk averse and make deliberate choices (less impulsive) in the same situations when peers are absent.

The presence of peers increases risk taking among adolescents but not adults. Interestingly, in a study by Gardner and Steinberg (2005), the mere presence of peers was found to double the amount of risk taking in which adolescents engaged; however, for adult counterparts, no such impact was noticed in the presence of peers. Findings of several studies (Andrade & Walker, 1996; Steinberg and Monahan, 2007; Sumter, Bokhurst, Steinberg, & Westenberg, 2009) substantiate that the ability to resist peer influence increases developmentally during the course of adolescence, especially between ages 14 and 18 (Steinberg & Monahan, 2007). This ability to resist peer influence coincides with adolescents' increasing psychosocial maturity, which results in more impulse control, responsibility, and self-awareness. This allows older adolescents to become more discerning and have a lower tendency to follow others without thinking and therefore to become less susceptible to peer influence in general.

Further, the strength of the peer group influence may be moderated by the sex of the adolescent and the group composition of her or his peer group. For instance, Clark and Loheac (2007) found strong peer group effects for alcohol use, particularly with respect to the male peer group. Similarly, Sumter et. al. (2009) noticed that general resistance to peer influence peaked at mid-adolescence and that girls, relative to boys, were more resistant to peer influence. Studies by Case and Katz (1991), Clark and Loheac (2007), Gaviria and Raphael (2001), and Norton, Costanza, and Bishop (1998) have presented evidence to suggest that social interactions and participation in risky behaviors are likely to be confounded by contextual effects, such as peer group variables relating to specific school or neighborhood characteristics.

An empirically validated theory of risk taking in adolescence, called the *fuzzy-trace theory*, elucidates how people's emotions (intuitions or biases) shape the way they represent, retrieve, and process information when making decisions (Reyna, Lloyd, & Brainerd, 2003). The theory posits that mature decision makers rely on simplified, gist mental representations of information and choices (qualitative, intuitive processing) as opposed to a more detailed or deliberate weighting of choices through risk evaluation (analytical processing). *Gist* refers to the meaning an individual derives from information based on her or his knowledge, understanding, culture, and developmental level (e.g., Reyna, 1996, 2004; Reyna & Farley, 2006). The reliance on intuitive, gist-based processing increases with development (e.g., Brainerd & Reyna, 2007) and as individuals acquire greater expertise in a domain (e.g., Reyna & Lloyd, 2006). In the context of risk-taking, the theory suggests that going with the bottom-line, "core gist" of a decision (representing risk as categorically present or absent) generally leads to less risk taking than does adopting a more deliberative process of evaluating choices (high or low risk analysis). Here, the reliance on intuitive thinking validates Kahneman's (2011) suggestion that, with adequate practice and skill development, the type 1 intuitive rapid processing of thoughts can be trained for correctness and as the "skill eventually develops, the intuitive judgments and choices that quickly come to mind will mostly be accurate" (p. 416).

Role of Neurological Factors in Risky Decision Making

Decision making requires extended neural networks comprised of different brain functions for different aspects of decision making. There is evident interaction among the numerous brain areas during different processes relating to evaluation of stimuli or anticipation of rewards during a decision making task. Gleichgerrcht, Ibáñez, Roca, Torralva, and Manes (2010) have suggested three main systems as being involved in decision making: a "stimulus encoding system," an "action selection system," and an "expected reward system." The initial stimulus encoding system is important during the framing stages of decision making; the action selection system is involved in learning and subjective value encoding, including exploring actions and voluntary choices; and the expected reward system is involved in reward learning and prediction of errors. The different activities of these systems activate strong associations at dominant neural points across a coordinated network, along with modulating other related responses such as emotional learning (in the amygdala), learning the subjective value of objects (dependent on the midbrain dopamine level), and reinforcement-guided decision making (linked with the prefrontal cortex). For a more detailed summary of activities and corresponding critical brain areas, see Gleichgerrcht et al. (2010).

As a result of emerging neuroscience research, specific underlying neural bases critical to social decision making are becoming clear. For instance, as explicated by Gleichgerrcht et al. (2010), decision-making tasks involving consideration of the preferences or choices of others seem to require functioning of brain areas that are associated with ToM, such as the paracingulate cortex, striatum insula cortex, and orbitofrontal cortex. According to these researchers, moral decision making seems to be associated with activity in different parts of the brain (mainly orbitofrontal and dorsolateral prefrontal cortex, cingulated cortex, precuneus, and temporoparietal junction). When complex decisions are being made, greater activity in the insula and posterior cingulated cortex occurs to modulate the activity of the prefrontal cortex. Conversely, simpler choices engage the parietal areas during decision making. The complexity of the neural involvement is such that any impaired brain functioning, due to neurological damage or disease, will naturally impact healthy (effective) decision-making performance. These advances carry implications for the study of cognitive-related processes and impairments from a neurological, brain-related perspective when examining decision-making performance in people with ID or ASD.

With a growing body of scientific data establishing that the risk-taking nature of adolescence is a developmentally normative phase in the lifespan, efforts to intervene and train are common. Given that many adolescents have the capacity to control their risk taking, efforts need to be under taken to foster their ability to channel sensation-seeking drives toward safer activities. The distinction between types of thinking, ranging from automatic to a slower, analytic processing, with each serving different functions, is pertinent to individual differences among decision makers. Taken as a whole,

the research findings in this area suggest that different types of interventions will be needed and that a one-size-fits-all approach to reducing risky behaviors and vulnerability to negative peer influences is likely to be unsuccessful.

Next, we propose a comprehensive decision-making research model and discuss methodological issues in the study of decision making. This new model builds and elaborates on previous versions of our decision-making research model and draws on research with people with ID or ASD, as well as on the recent cognitive psychology and neuroscience research and theory reviewed in previous sections. Compared with previous versions, our new model reflects a more nuanced understanding of biological and developmental influences on decision-making performance and its development.

A Decision-Making Model for Research and Training

Given the complexity of human decision making, especially in social situations of uncertainty, ambiguity, or time pressure, it is hard to propose a single convergent model that can predict the decision-making process in its entirety or fully account for the final decision outcome. We propose an updated working model of decision making that can be used at an explanatory level to address the decision-making behavior of individuals across a wide variety of social decision-making situations, ranging from everyday friendship preferences to more complex interpersonal relationships that may involve abuse, negative peer pressure, or bullying. In the model, we illustrate different pathways that individuals may follow in their decision making and highlight the various factors that impinge on these pathways and the ultimate decision output. The model includes a decision-making strategy that provides an overall schema of how one might engage in a decision-making process in a planful, reasoned way by using a sequenced, step-by-step approach.

Building on earlier versions of our decision-making model (see Hickson & Khemka, 1999, 2001; Khemka & Hickson, 2006), it is argued that decision making is a complex mental function influenced by the multiple interactive processes of cognition, motivation, and emotion. These processes each operate separately to provide unique inputs in the decision-making process, but, at various stages, they interact with each other to determine the final decision output. Because an individual's decision in relation to a particular situation or problem is determined by a range of cognitive, motivational, and

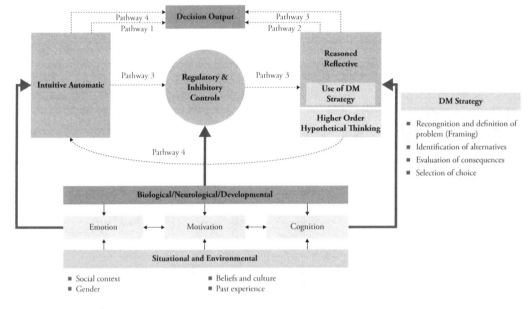

Figure 15.1 Pathways of decision processing.

emotional processes, we posit that, depending on the nature of the decision and the characteristics of the decision maker, different decisions reflect different levels of engagement of these basic processes. Various external stimuli also impinge on the decision-making process, resulting in different patterns of behavior organization within the model. Some of the salient influences pertain to situational and environmental factors that define the decision-making context, as well as the properties of the decision to be made.

Next, we present the model (see Figure 15.1) and describe the constituent elements that inform the decision-making process and the resulting pathways of decision processing.

Pathways of Decision Processing

A decision maker can follow several different pathways when processing a decision problem and generating a decision output (the final decision outcome). In the model, we illustrate the different pathways that can be generated during decision making. *Pathway 1*: The first, most automatic decision processing pathway can be pursued with little or no effort and is based on an intuitive or gist-based recognition of one's feelings, leading to a fast but emotionally laden decision response. *Pathway 2*: For

certain decisions, the processing is centered almost entirely on a calculated, reasoned/reflective pathway of thinking (such as in mathematical problems), and there is no margin for intuitive gut responding. A central feature of this pathway is the higher order hypothetical thinking necessary for speculation and the generation and evaluation of alternatives during decision making. *Pathway 3*: A third pathway also leads to a reasoned/reflective type of processing, but as a result of mediating regulatory mechanisms inhibiting initial intuitive responding and allowing for an eventual effortful and purposeful monitoring of thoughts and actions. *Pathway 4*: Finally, there are individual decisional feedback loops that develop over time as consequential evidence from repeated decision-making experiences accumulates. The feedback and experience from reasoned/reflective decision processing provides a more lucid and informed understanding of the automatic nature of responding such that, over time, a new pathway of decision processing evolves to create a strengthened and adaptive type of intuitive decision processing in the form of a learned heuristic or a mental short-cut. Klein's (1998) description of emergency workers, who function as expert decision makers on a regular basis as part of their jobs, suggests that they rely heavily on this fourth pathway to build up a repertoire of effective decision actions that they can draw on and implement rapidly under the extreme time pressure and high-stakes conditions of emergency situations.

The pathways of decision processing are shaped by basic psychological processes, executive control mechanisms, and other external factors, as discussed later. The basic processes of cognition, emotion, and motivation have a strong primary or direct influence (shown in bold arrows in Figure 15.1) on the pathways of decision processing or interact with each other to exert indirect or secondary influence on decision making (shown in simple, gray arrows in Figure 15.1). We conjecture that emotional factors play a dominant role in triggering an intuitive, automatic type of decision processing, whereas cognitive systems are foremost in reasoned/reflective decision thinking. The regulatory or executive control system that modulates the experience of emotional arousal and leads to impulse control and response inhibition in favor of more reasoned/reflective processing is largely dependent on an individual's biological or neurological make up, as well as on developmental factors such as age, maturity, and disability. The biological, neurological, and developmental markers carry an overriding, robust influence on the regulatory capacity of the decision maker and control the flow of decision processing from intuitive to reasoned thinking. In addition to the dominant effects of the underlying processes on the pathways, there are recognizable indirect effects of the relatedness among the processes on the direction and strength of the decision-processing pathways. For instance, appraisal of a decision-making situation requires cognitive processing but is also guided by the amount of emotional intensity (hot or cold cognitions) triggered by the particular stimulus situation, indicating an overlap between the emotional-cognitive systems to create a secondary impact on decision processing. Similarly, developmental factors could have a bearing on the quality of cognitive processing. Value attached to the desirability or likelihood of a particular option may vary among decision makers, influencing how decision processing is approached and the final decision outcome is assessed.

Basic Processes of Cognition, Motivation, and Emotion

COGNITION

The cognitive aspects of decision making broadly include stimulus encoding, generation and evaluation of alternatives, and action selection. Stimulus encoding involves knowledge and awareness of decision-making situations and comprehension of the decision problem, including estimation of risk. Cognitive inputs are needed to recognize signs of abuse or positive versus negative peer pressure or to identify associated feelings that may trigger a specific understanding of the situation or problem at hand. The generation and evaluation of alternative courses of action requires consequential thinking, and action selection entails consideration of goal preferences (motivational inputs) to make a final decision. Depending on the complexity of the decision task, hypothesizing and comprehending alternative courses of action and their potential consequences necessitates higher order cognition, coordinated in an analytical space that may involve demands for sustained attention and working memory. Rational cognitive participation during decision processing is exemplified in the use of a sequenced strategy for decision making and its effective application and generalization to novel decision-making situations. A four-step decision-making strategy that is applicable in a wide range of situations is described in a later section.

MOTIVATION

Motivational inputs that contribute to the processing of information are derived from individual perceptions of control and feelings of self-efficacy or self-empowerment and individual goal priorities. Establishing goal priorities requires identifying and ranking preferences, sometimes including the balancing of competing goals. Goal priorities and self-empowerment interact with each other to produce different types, or degrees, of motivational input that affect the extent and direction of information processing during decision making. Decision making is essentially a goal-driven process. For instance, when evaluating the desirability of the possible consequences of alternatives, one's goals set the standards on which to base decisions. Using goals as the rules on how to proceed, decision makers seek the most optimal course of action to meet the desired goals. Motivational engagement and decisional style or commitment varies with an individual's own perceptions of his or her self-efficacy or empowerment.

EMOTION

Emotional processes are described as certain psychological states that play a role in the coordination of cognition, internal physiology (intensity of feelings, experience of arousal) and external behavior (reactionary impulses). Levels of emotional intensity of thoughts provoked by a decision-making situation bias behavior and hence decision processing across a range of decision styles (e.g., avoidant, hypervigilant, impulsive, vigilant).

The emotional experience of a decision maker is calibrated by many intervening factors, including cognitive and situational ones. For example, the emotional responses elicited by the way options are framed often results in a lack of logical consistency in human decision making. Viewing a decision problem and its prospects as either loss or gain (a cognitive interpretation) may lead to varying emotional responses to the decision situation and, in turn, to selection of a specific pathway for decision processing. The ability to meaningfully integrate emotional contextual information into the decision process functions as a powerful heuristic in decision making, especially in situations of uncertainty or ambiguity. This ability becomes particularly crucial when making decisions in social environments, in which multiple subtle contextual cues carry critical information. We believe that competence in dealing with social uncertainty involves deployment of affect heuristics and trade-offs with more analytic and effortful reasoning. To that extent, the model supports training on the use of multiple pathways of decision processing, including emotional intuitive processing, with continuous feedback and learning from actual decision-making experiences.

Biological, Neurological, and Developmental Factors

The individual characteristics and personality of the decision maker play an important part in shaping her or his interaction with the decision-making situation and the ensuing level of involvement and engagement with the decision-making process. Each decision maker is characterized by particular biological and neurological characteristics, which define the extent and type of regulatory competence the individual can exercise when confronted with a decision-making situation. The level of inhibitory control applied by the decision maker at the initial stages dictates the pathway of decision-making processing ultimately selected by the individual.

Decision making requires extended neural networks, comprised of different brain functions for different aspects of decision making. There is evident interaction among the numerous brain areas during different processes relating to evaluation of stimuli or anticipation of rewards during a decision-making task. The neural bases underlying social decision

making are tapped differentially depending on the type of decision-making task. For example, when complex decisions are being made, greater activity in the insula and posterior cingulated cortex occurs to modulate the activity of the prefrontal cortex (Gleichgerrcht et. al, 2010). Conversely, simpler choices engage the parietal areas during decision making. The complexity of the neural involvement is such that any impairment or differences in brain functioning, due to neurological damage or impairment, will naturally compromise the efficiency of neurological inputs available for successful inhibitory control and the selection of optimal pathways of decision processing toward thoughtful and effortful reasoning. For example, psychological impairments associated with ADHD impede the planning, inhibition, and executive control mechanisms, making people with ADHD more likely to adopt hypervigilant and rushed pathways of decision processing. Among people with ID, the selection of planful, reasoned/reflective decision pathways may be difficult to follow or complete efficiently because they may have attention or comprehension difficulties. Also, analytic decision processing may require the use of working memory and higher cognitive processing linked with hypothetical reasoning and judgment, making it challenging for people with gaps in understanding, including difficulty assimilating feedback from past choices (and mistakes) for future processing of decisions.

Biological or genetic dispositions are manifested in individual personality or cognitive styles that can then play influential roles in decision processing—ranging from being impulsive or avoidant, to displaying a more analytic, rational, and planful style of responding.

Developmental characteristics linked with age and puberty fundamentally impact the level of inhibition control exercised during decision processing. In particular, adolescent development is tied to elevated sensation seeking and discrepant calibration of reward–risk, making youth more likely to follow the pathways of intuitive, emotional responding. Corresponding to cognitive control system functions, analytic decision behaviors appear to develop later in adolescence, whereas corresponding to socioemotional system functions, impulsive and acting-without-thinking behaviors tend to dominate early adolescence.

The model recognizes that biological changes and resulting socioemotional maturity variations during the adolescent developmental period may lead to differently maturing regulatory systems (emotional, cognitive, and behavioral) and therefore a range in decision processing, risk taking, and social vulnerability.

Regulatory/Executive Control

Given that decision making is a complex mental process that requires the coordination of several simultaneous processes, executive functions are important in the selection and processing of decision pathways. Executive functions such as forward planning, anticipation, judgment, reasoning, long-term memory, and working memory are critical to the initial processing of decision information and setting up the decision problem for solution. Specifically, they help establish the level of impulse control and emotional regulation needed for effective decision making.

Situational and Environmental Factors

The inherent belief system, values, and cultural preferences of the decision maker individualize the nature of participation in the decision-making process, both in terms of dictating level of decisional engagement and in establishing goal preferences. Environmental features can be enabling (and hence motivating) in certain decisions or may pose obstacles in others. For instance, in situations involving peers, the presence of peers may bias adolescents toward making risky choices by increasing the salience of the potential immediate reward of a risky decision. The presence of peers may function to subvert an initiated reasoned process of decision making or completely undermine the inhibitory control process, resulting in the decision maker yielding to a risky, emotional decision-processing pathway.

The feedback from any decision alters the experience and expectation of the decision maker at two separate levels. At one level, there are external consequences of a decision (depending on how the external environment is changed), and, at another, there are internal consequences of a decision (how the decision maker feels or adapts to the decision). The psychological consequences of an event to a decision maker have an important impact over time because the feedback is internalized by the decision maker and used in future processing of decisions. This feedback loop is underscored in the model as a mechanism for informing and strengthening the pathways of intuitive decision processing as a result of experiential learning from activity in alternative, nonintuitive pathways. The model, in this important regard, interprets decision making as a "dynamic"

process, with inherent changes occurring over time either due to the previous actions of the decision maker or due to events that are outside of the control of the decision maker (and hence a consequence of the decision feedback). Decision preferences change to the extent that people are able to use their experiences to undertake more adaptive pathways of decision processing and make better decisions over time.

Depending on certain stimulus properties of the decision-making situation, there may be a low or high level of emotional processing. The interaction of situational influences with emotional processes to impact decision making is evident in social interpersonal situations involving peer victimization, bullying, or abuse, in which automatic reactions and emotional intensity may be activated.

The model also suggests that situational and environmental factors could impact motivational aspects of decision making. The presence or absence of factors in the environment (such as opportunities for self-empowerment or encounters with coercive tactics) may foster an independent or an avoidant decision making style, respectively.

A Decision-Making Strategy

Our model includes a four-step decision-making strategy for reasoned/reflective decision processing that we have employed with success in our intervention studies (to be described in the next section). The components of the strategy entail (1) defining the problem and recognizing the need to make a decision, (2) identifying alternative choice options, (3) identifying and evaluating possible consequences of each alternative using a goal-driven decision rule, and (4) selecting the best alternative to make a decision. Implementing a plan to execute a decision and evaluating the effectiveness of the decision are not emphasized as separate steps in the sequenced strategy but are implicit in real-life decision making. In reality, individuals may not completely follow the step-by-step strategy to reach an ideal process in everyday decision making. However, repeated practice with the decision-making sequence provides rehearsal with decision appraisal, the process of generating and evaluating alternative choice options and thereby achieving much greater awareness of the choice–consequence links and potentially leading to a more informed and reflective approach to the decision-making process for decisions in real life. The decision-making strategy helps individuals to examine decision situations with new tools and be more aware of utilizing their intuitive or analytical thinking to choose a course of action. Also, as shown in the next section, instruction in when and how to apply the decision-making strategy can promote self-empowerment and self-protection, as well as positive attitudes and positive psychologies for safe and satisfying interpersonal relationships.

To summarize, our model represents a major shift in prevailing views of decision processing and training for adults and adolescents with ID or ASD, going beyond the advocacy of any one specific process to a broader framework that focuses on the integrated advancement of multiple components or skills for effective decision making, rather than through the rote training of any one isolated skill domain. Our model, by delineating the multilayered processes underlying decision-making performance, provides a supportive structure for building a repertoire of skills for effective decision-making

Interventions to Improve Decision Making

A key question that arises with regard to developmental and individual differences in decision making is when, and even whether, to provide interventions aimed at improving decision-making effectiveness. Traditionally, interventions have typically consisted of cognitive training to teach a stepwise process based on sequential, stage-based models of decision making. New theoretical challenges to existing models, however, have raised the question of if and when effective decision making requires the employment of a rational, deliberative process. As some have suggested (Kahneman, 2003; Klaczynski, 2001), many successful decisions rely on intuitive type 1 processes. In those instances, conscious, rational type 2 processes are used only to monitor and support decisions that have been arrived at by rapid, preconscious processes. Klaczynski, Byrnes, and Jacobs (2001) have questioned whether interventions should teach people to always use rational, deliberative approaches. Instead, they underscored the need to determine the conditions under which conscious, analytic decision-making approaches are likely to lead to more effective decisions than unconscious or "heuristic" approaches.

Most past efforts to improve the effectiveness of decision making and social problem solving of people with disabilities have been limited in scope, focusing on only certain components of the process. Although some studies monitored the number of steps completed, most focused on a single component of the process (e.g., Vaughn, Ridley, & Cox, 1983). Many past studies focused on the generation of possible solutions

to problem-solving situations in which a goal was pre-specified (e.g., Browning & Nave, 1993; Castles & Glass, 1986; Martella, Marchand-Martella, & Agran, 1993; Park & Gaylord-Ross, 1989). However, two recent studies reported promising improvements in overall problem solving for participants with ID after participation in broad-based training programs. Using a single-subject research design with three participants, Anderson and Kazantzis (2008) reported improved problem-solving effectiveness for two participants and improved social acceptability of problem solutions for one participant after training that included sessions on decision-making effectiveness, decision-making social acceptability, and decision-making consequences. No clear distinction was made between problem solving and decision making in this study. In another recent study that used a group experimental design with youth with borderline intelligence (some with IQs below 70), Nestler and Goldbeck (2011) reported that participants who received a 3-month social competence intervention showed significantly greater improvement than did students in a control group on a problem-solving measure of cognitive competence that involved responding to hypothetical situations but not on a role-play measure of problem-solving competence or on a self-report measure of social interactions with peers. This study highlights the difficulty, almost universally reflected in this body of research, in documenting generalization to real-life situations.

Interventions to Improve Decision Making of Adults with Intellectual Disability and Autism Spectrum Disorders

Initiating consideration of the role of motivational factors in decision-making training, Khemka (2000) assessed the relative effectiveness of two approaches for teaching women with mild and moderate ID to apply a decision-making strategy in handling abuse situations. The 36 women were randomly assigned to one of three conditions: (1) a traditional cognitive strategy approach, (2) an integrated cognitive strategy and motivational approach, and (3) a no-intervention control condition. Although both intervention approaches were effective relative to the control condition, the approach that addressed both the cognitive and motivational aspects of decision making was superior to the approach that addressed only the cognitive aspects of decision making on measures of self-decision making and locus of control.

Building on Khemka's (2000) intervention, we developed and evaluated the Effective Strategy-Based Curriculum for Abuse Prevention and Empowerment (ESCAPE), which was designed to empower women with ID to become effective decision makers equipped with the tools to protect themselves against abuse. The ESCAPE curriculum was designed, in accord with earlier versions of our decision-making model (Hickson & Khemka, 1999; Hickson & Khemka, 2001), to emphasize the interplay of the cognitive, motivational, and emotional components of decision making. The ESCAPE curriculum consists of 12 instructional lessons (units 1 and 2) and six support group sessions (unit 3) designed for small-group instruction with an instructor/facilitator. Unit 1 is designed to teach key concepts of abuse as a basis for identifying situations that might require careful, deliberative decision making. The focus of unit 2 is to apply priority goals (i.e., safety and independent action) and to teach and provide guided practice in applying a four-step decision-making strategy to hypothetical situations involving abuse. Unit 3 consists of support group sessions in which participants have opportunities to apply the decision-making strategy to situations in their own lives. In accord with dual-process theory, participants are encouraged to apply spontaneous, intuitive (type 1) approaches in situations that do not involve abuse (e.g., "Mike and Elise have been coworkers for many years. One day, Mike asks Elise for a date. What should Elise do?"). However, in problem situations that do involve abuse (e.g., "Trisha's uncle often visits her family. Whenever, he comes to family parties, Trisha's uncle forces Trisha into a bedroom and touches her private parts. What should Trisha do?"), participants are taught to systematically apply a four-step decision-making strategy by answering the following questions: (1) Is there a problem (involving abuse)? (2) What are my choices (alternative ways to handle the problem)? (3) What could happen if…. (for each alternative)? And, (4) What is the best thing for _____ to do in this situation? As can be seen, this approach addresses when and how to apply a systematic type 2 reasoned/reflective approach involving hypothetical, algorithmic processing to consider possible alternatives and their potential consequences, and which, according to Stanovich (2011), is the ability most likely to be impaired in people with ID. Instructional approaches employed to facilitate decision-making strategy acquisition and generalization include modeling, prompting, fading of prompts, visuals (including activity sheets and a decision-making flow chart), and a variety of interactive activities.

In a study to evaluate the effectiveness of the ESCAPE curriculum, 36 women with mild and moderate ID were randomly assigned to either an intervention group or a wait-list control group. Results revealed that the women who received the ESCAPE curriculum performed significantly better than the women in the control group on measures of empowerment, knowledge of abuse, and decision making in hypothetical situations of abuse (Khemka, Hickson, and Reynolds, 2005). Exit interviews conducted with the women in the intervention group provided anecdotal reports of a real-life impact for some of the women, who made comments such as, "It helped me a lot to help myself" or "It helped me with decisions when I have a bad relationship" or "We can stand up for ourself" (Hickson, Khemka, Will, & Golden, 2002).

The original ESCAPE curriculum was subsequently modified and expanded so that it would be applicable to men as well as women with developmental disabilities. The efficacy of this revised, ESCAPE-DD version of the curriculum was evaluated in a recent study involving 58 adults with mild and moderate ID, some of whom had secondary diagnoses of ASD (Hickson, Khemka, Golden, & Chatzistyli, 2012). Participants were randomly assigned to either an intervention group, which received the 12 instructional lessons (units 1 and 2) of ESCAPE-DD or to a wait-list control group that was given delayed access to the curriculum on completion of post-testing. The intervention group did not differ from the control group in either age or IQ at the outset of the study. Subjects completed individual pre- and post-tests consisting of six vignettes depicting situations involving sexual, physical, and verbal abuse. After each vignette was read to them, subjects were asked to respond to one comprehension question ("What is happening in this story?") and one decision-making question ("What should _____ do?").

Results indicated that, on the post-test, subjects in the intervention group produced significantly more comprehension responses that accurately identified situations as involving abuse or violation than did subjects in the control group. Subjects in the intervention group also produced significantly more decision-making responses reflecting attempts to avoid or escape from the abuse than did subjects in the control group. Overall, approximately 84% of the intervention group's post-test responses constituted reasonable attempts to avoid or escape from the abuse situation, whereas only 63% of the control group's post-test responses represented such attempts. When responses to the decision-making questions were categorized further to look at responses that indicated an effort to be *safe now* by verbally resisting, physically fleeing, or calling for *immediate* help to avoid or escape from the threatened or ongoing abuse, a significant difference favoring the intervention group was found. This finding suggested that adults who participated in the intervention were producing more responses with the potential to actually stop the abuse from happening than were the adults in the control group.

Interventions to Improve Decision Making of Adolescents with Intellectual Disability and Autism Spectrum Disorders

Given the importance of peer group influences on adolescent social interactions and hence their interpersonal decision-making skills (e.g., Gardner & Steinberg, 2005), our recent work with adolescents has emphasized the study of decision making in the context of peer pressure. Most studies in the developmental literature have focused on the negative effects of peer influence during adolescence in terms of risky behaviors or peer victimization. Only a few researchers have acknowledged the impact of neutral or positive peer pressure (Barry & Wentzel, 2006; Ellis & Zarbatany, 2007; Steinberg & Silverberg, 1986). In our research, we have chosen to take a broad view of peer influence that includes both positive and negative peer pressure, with the goal of not only preventing risky decision making, but also of fostering age-appropriate pro-social interactions and positive personal relationships. As Mounts and Steinberg (1995) have pointed out, norms and values may vary across adolescent peer groups, and sometimes the influence of peers can be adaptive, encouraging socially desirable behavior (e.g., positive peer pressure to do well in school, avoid drugs, not rush into sexual relationships). Accordingly, in the decision-making scenarios used in our adolescent studies (e.g., Khemka, Hickson, Zealand, & Mallory, 2011), we have attributed motives to peers that manifest in a positive or pro-social manner (e.g., encouraging peer to finish homework before going out), as well as motives that are clearly negative (e.g., pressuring peer to use drugs).

Our research studies involving adolescents have aimed to expand current understandings of the mechanisms through which adolescents with ID or ASD approach interpersonal decision-making situations involving potentially risky choices and peer pressure (e.g., Khemka & Hickson, 2006; Khemka et al., 2009). In our most recent initiative (Khemka, et al., 2011), we have designed and implemented a six-session intervention, Peers Engaged

in Effective Relationships: A Decision-Making Approach (PEER-DM), to provide adolescents with a decision-making strategy for handling situations involving peer pressure. The first four lessons of PEER-DM are designed to teach the concepts of positive peer pressure (e.g., "Pam's friend Susan is respectful of Pam's need to finish her important homework and encourages Pam to finish it before they meet at the park") and negative peer pressure (e.g., "Janet's classmate, Chris, says 'Hey, no one is in this auditorium! Let's smoke in here'") to establish goal priorities and to increase feelings of self-empowerment as a basis for recognizing situations of negative peer pressure in which systematic type 2 reasoned/reflective processing may be needed to handle the situation effectively. Lessons 5 and 6 are focused on teaching and providing guided practice with a four-step decision-making strategy that provides a schema for handling problem situations involving negative peer pressure, including bullying. According to this four-step decision-making strategy, once the problem has been identified as one involving negative peer pressure and the core gist of the problem has been represented (step 1), the decision maker is instructed to proceed in a deliberate way to generate possible options for how to handle the situation (step 2). Possible consequences of each hypothetical choice option are then considered and weighed against previously established goals (e.g., safety and not getting into trouble) (step 3). The evaluation of hypothetical alternatives and their possible consequences leads to the selection of the final decision outcome (step 4). A visual decision-making chart with stick-on choice options is provided to scaffold the hypothetical processing required in the generation and evaluation of possible alternatives, processes likely to pose difficulties for people with ID or ASD.

Emotion and motivation interact with cognition at every stage of the decision-making strategy, from encoding/representing the problem, to generating possible choice options, to retrieving and applying goals to evaluate alternative choice options, to then arriving at a decision. The encoding stage integrates emotion into the decision process by distinctly increasing the salience of emotion cues ("Is there positive/negative peer pressure? Is this a situation to approach/avoid? Should we give it a thumbs up or thumbs down?") and identifying the discrete feeling state likely to be experienced by a person in the situation (e.g., unhappy, angry, sad). The evaluation of choice options brings motivational input into the decision process by establishing important goals that serve as a basis against which hypothetical consequences of alternative choice options are assessed. Additionally, the decision maker is prompted to select an independent and empowered choice option for the final decision ("Is the decision maker acting on his/her own?"). The cognitive elements are embedded throughout and probed in terms of comprehending and framing the problem, estimating the links between possible choice options and consequences, and evaluating the final decision. In this way, the interactions among cognitive, emotional, and motivational factors in a specific situational context (e.g., negative peer pressure) are interwoven in the design of the training strategy.

Preliminary data from a randomized experimental study with 28 adolescents with ID, ASD, and other developmental disabilities (e.g., multiple disabilities, other health impaired) support the effectiveness of the PEER-DM intervention (Khemka et al., 2011). The group that received instruction ($n = 13$) in the use of a decision-making strategy was more likely than a wait-list control group ($n = 15$) to produce effective decision-making responses involving active attempts to resist negative pressure, either by negotiation, direct refusal, or reporting.

To take a preliminary look at the performance of adolescents with ASD relative to that of adolescents with intellectual and developmental disabilities on measures relevant to decision making, we split the sample of 28 students into two groups according to whether students had received a diagnosis of ASD and compared their performance. Ten adolescents (nine male/one female) with diagnoses of ASD and 18 adolescents (twelve male/six female) with other intellectual and developmental disabilities diagnoses made up the groups. Although the subjects with ASD did not differ significantly from those with intellectual and developmental disabilities at the time of pre-test in age or CREVT-2 Receptive Vocabulary age-equivalent scores, the subjects with ASD had significantly higher IQs and CREVT-2 Expressive Vocabulary age-equivalent scores than the subjects with intellectual and developmental disabilities.

In spite of their higher IQs and expressive vocabulary scores, the subjects with ASD did not differ significantly from subjects with intellectual and developmental disabilities on any of our pre-test decision-making measures, which included a self-report measure of decision-making style, as well as measures of effective decision making and accurate anticipation of possible consequences in response to a series of vignette situations involving peer pressure. On a pre-test measure of goal

priorities, however, subjects with ASD rated *having many friends* as being less important than did subjects with intellectual and developmental disabilities, and subjects with ASD rated *having a boyfriend/girlfriend* as less important than did subjects with intellectual and developmental disabilities. In spite of their cognitive strength in general intelligence and expressive vocabulary, the ASD group performed similarly to the intellectual and developmental disabilities group on the decision-making measures, suggesting that their decision-making performance was depressed relative to their general ability and that the social vulnerability of the ASD group may be heightened by motivational and affective factors at play in decision making, perhaps reflected in the reduced importance they placed on goals involving friendships and relationships. More research is clearly needed to gain a fuller understanding of decision making in people with ASD. The recognition that underlying biological mechanisms can mediate decision-making behaviors in social situations suggests that advances in research are needed so that we can have a better understanding of the nature of decision making in people with ASD so that we can improve the specificity of targeted interventions.

Conclusion

Research on problem solving and decision making has much to contribute to a positive psychology of disability. Although the emphasis in some of our studies has been on effective decision making for the purpose of avoiding abuse or peer victimization, decision making plays a pivotal role in sustaining the positive, healthy relationships that are associated with well-being. Kahneman (2011) has pointed out the need to distinguish between *happiness* experienced on a day-to-day basis and *life satisfaction* that is associated with the achievement of long-term goals. In the disability field, it is the line of research exploring quality of life that has most directly addressed issues pertaining to well-being. Among the key dimensions of quality of life identified by an international panel of experts are several that directly pertain to social/interpersonal problem solving and decision making, including interpersonal relationships, emotional well-being, social inclusion, and rights (Schalock et al., 2002). Although, to date, the guiding principles for providing services and supports to people with disabilities have focused on the individual (e.g., self-determination, independence, person-centered planning), there have been recent admonitions to address the frequent isolation of people with intellectual and developmental disabilities and to consider their need for belonging and improved social relationships (Clegg & Lansdall-Welfare, 2009). It is our vision that interventions, designed in accord with our most recent model (described in this chapter) and aimed at increasing decision making-effectiveness, can provide people with flexible repertoires of decision-making approaches to help them to gain access to a better quality of life and, ultimately, to happiness and long-term life satisfaction.

Overall, research by ourselves and others provides strong support for the notion that the best way to prevent abuse and victimization is to foster and support the kinds of positive, healthy friendships and intimate relationships that contribute to day-to-day happiness and long-term life satisfaction. Both ESCAPE-DD and PEER-DM were designed to define and foster positive relationships as the desirable goal state. In PEER-DM, the emphasis on positive peer pressure reflects an effort to capitalize on the elevated reward value of peer interactions during adolescence (see Chein et al., 2010). In ESCAPE-DD, healthy relationships are featured as the alternative to the loneliness and isolation that is believed to exacerbate vulnerability to abuse. In a recent study (Hickson, Khemka, Golden, & Chatzistyli, in press), we found that experienced support professionals working in both the developmental disabilities field and the domestic violence/sexual assault field agreed that the need to be liked or wanted and a desire for friends or intimate relationships are key factors that contribute to vulnerability to abuse in adults with developmental disabilities.

We do, however, acknowledge the need for caution in promoting relationship behaviors that are usually considered positive. As noted by McNulty and Fincham (2012), sometimes behaviors that are generally viewed as positive and beneficial in relationships (e.g., forgiveness) can contribute to increased vulnerability in abusive relationships. Furthermore, although people in long-term, committed relationships tend to be happier, fear of aloneness may sometimes result in people staying in abusive relationships (Myers, 2000).

Since our studies have been done in the context of hypothetical or simulated (via video) situations, we can only speculate that our measures are indicative of developing competence and the ability to apply acquired decision-making skills in real-life situations. Although our measures provide a reasonable assessment of how well an individual may be prepared to handle a decision-making task, they are only modest indicators of how decisions in real-world situations will be made. Actual decision-making performance may be affected additionally by emotional, psychosocial, or contextual factors (e.g., friend vs. stranger or presence of a peer vs. an authority figure) (Steinberg, 2004). In a hypothetical decision-making task, individuals may not fully experience the same emotional arousal/intensity or social impact as might unfold in a real-life situation (e.g., risky situation in presence of peers). To get a more accurate measure of decision-making functioning in real-life, everyday settings, more research using in vivo or authentic measures and observations is clearly needed.

Future Directions

As we move forward with research and theory on social problem solving and decision making, we recommend increased attention to several factors that may exert a powerful influence on problem-solving and decision-making performance.

Future studies should consider the possibility that culture and ethnicity may influence various aspects of problem-solving and decision-making performance in predictable and unpredictable ways. An example is provided by the findings of a study by Padilla-Walker and Bean (2009) that compared youth from various ethnic backgrounds on their responsiveness to peer influence. It was found that youth with non-European ethnic backgrounds (e.g., Asian and Hispanic) were less responsive to peer influence than were youth who came from European ethnic backgrounds.

Another important factor to consider is etiology. In particular, Dykens (2006) has noted that strengths associated with certain genetic syndromes may contribute to happiness and well-being. These include the positive personalities of many people with Down syndrome and the visual-spatial strengths of people with Prader-Willi syndrome. In a recent study, Jawaid, Riby, Owens, White, Tarar, and Schulz (2012) contrasted the social cognition profiles of people with Williams syndrome, characterized by "hyperfriendliness," and people with ASD, characterized by "social withdrawal." The authors went on to discuss how both of these profiles were associated with different patterns of social vulnerability and impaired decision making. In an effort to address the vulnerability of women with Williams syndrome, we conducted an exploratory project aimed at adapting our ESCAPE curriculum to address the specific learning characteristics of women with Williams syndrome (Hickson, Khemka, Collado, Spillane, & Wang, 2004). We observed that, although the visual-spatial and attention difficulties associated with Williams syndrome posed challenges to the women's ability to benefit from the original version of the ESCAPE curriculum, we were able to tailor a version of the curriculum, ESCAPE-WS, that addressed these issues and resulted in improved decision-making performance.

Finally, future studies on problem solving and decision making should explore the contributions of decision making style to type 2 thinking. According to Stanovich (2011), hypothetical, algorithmic thinking is correlated with IQ, but thinking dispositions and style are not. It will be important to gain a fuller understanding of how style influences problem solving and decision making for people with different etiologies. For instance, it has been suggested (see Bernard-Opitz et al., 2001) that the type 1 thinking of people with ASD may be restricted by a lack of flexibility associated with that disorder. It has also been noted that the lack of an affect heuristic in people with ASD contributes to an inability to use emotional context to facilitate decision making. Most importantly, because style is not correlated with cognitive ability, it may offer a fruitful focus area for future intervention research on problem solving and decision making in people with ID or ASD.

Although there is growing evidence of the influence of emotion on the decision making of individuals without disabilities, more applied research is required to see if emotion operates similarly in people with ID—and especially in people with ASD, with their typically high levels of anxiety—and how the effects vary developmentally across different age groups (children, adolescents, and adults). Additionally, it is important to examine how personal feelings, moods, and psychological factors interact with decision-making performance for those people with specific ID syndromes or ASD profiles who may have a biological predisposition toward greater mood swings, depression, impulsivity, or aggressive tendencies.

As we look to the future of research on social problem solving and decision making in people with ID or ASD, a major challenge lies in the need to integrate research from biological and neuroscience perspectives with findings emerging from cognitive and behavioral studies during the very normative, but precarious, stage of adolescent development and throughout the lifespan. Clearly, much work remains to be done to apply this burgeoning body of research and theory in ways that can improve the quality of the interpersonal experiences and social relationships of people with ID or ASD.

References

AAIDD Ad Hoc Committee on Terminology and Classification. (2010). *Intellectual disability: Definition, classification, and systems of supports* (11th ed.). Washington, DC: Author.

Adler, N. J. (1991). *International dimensions of organization behavior* (2nd ed.). Boston: PWS-Kent Publishing Company.

American Psychiatric Association. (2000). *Diagnostic and statistical manual of mental disorders* (4th ed., text rev.). Washington, DC: Author.

Anderson, G., & Kazantzis, N. (2008). Case studies and shorter communications. *Behaviour Change, 25*, 97–108.

Andrade, M. G., & Walker, M. B. (1996). Conformity in the Asch task as a function of age. *Journal of Social Psychology, 136*(3), 367–372.

Argyle, M. (1991). A critique of cognitive approaches to social judgment and social behavior. In J. P. Forgas (Ed.), *Emotion and social judgments* (pp. 161–181). Oxford, England: Pergamon Press.

Arnett, J. (1992). Reckless behavior in adolescence: A developmental perspective. *Developmental Review, 12*, 339–373.

Bandura, A. (1977). *Social learning theory*. Englewood Cliffs, NJ: Prentice-Hall.

Bandura, A. (1997). *Self-efficacy: The exercise of control*. New York: W. H. Freeman and Company.

Baron, J. (2008). *Thinking and deciding* (4th ed.). New York: Cambridge University Press.

Barry, C. M., & Wentzel, K. R. (2006). Friend influence on prosocial behavior: The role of motivational factors and friendship characteristics. *Developmental Psychology, 42*, 153–163.

Bechara, A., Damasio, H., Damasio, A., & Lee, G. P. (1999). Different contributions of the human amygdala and ventromedial prefrontal cortex to decision-making. *Journal of Neuroscience, 19*(13), 5473–5481.

Benthin, A., Slovic, P., Moran, P., Severson, H., Mertz, C. K., & Gerrard, M. (1995). Adolescent health-threatening and health-enhancing behaviors: A study of word association and imagery. *Journal of Adolescent Health, 17*, 143–152.

Bernard-Opitz, V., Srira, N., & Nakhoda-Sapuan, S. (2001). Enhancing social problem solving in children with autism and normal children through computer-assisted instruction. *Journal of Autism and Developmental Disorders, 31*, 377–398.

Boujarwah, F. A., Hong, H., Arriaga, R. I., Abowd, G. D., & Isbell, J. (2010). Training social problem solving skills in adolescents with high-functioning autism. *Pervasive Health*, 1–9.

Brake, T., Walker, D. M., & Walker, T. (1995). *Doing business internationally: The guide to cross-cultural success*. New York: Irwin.

Brainard, C. J., & Reyna, V. F. (2007). Explaining developmental reversals in false memory. *Psychological Science, 18*, 442–448.

Browning, P. L., & Nave, G. (1993). Teaching social problem solving to learners with mild disabilities. *Education and Training in Mental Retardation, 28*, 309–317.

Buchanan, C. M., Eccles, J. S., & Becker, J. B. (1992). Are adolescents the victims of raging hormones: Evidence for activational effects of hormones on moods and behavior at adolescence. *Psychological Bulletin, 111*, 62–107.

Byrnes, J. P. (1998). *The nature and development of decision-making: A self-regulation model*. Mahwah, NJ: Erlbaum.

Byrnes, J. P., Miller, D. C., & Reynolds, M. (1999). Learning to make good decisions: A self-regulation perspective. *Child Development, 70*(5), 1121–1140.

Camic, C. (1992). The matter of habit. In M. Zey (Ed.), *Decision making: Alternatives to rational choice theory* (pp. 185–232). Newbury Park, CA: Sage Publications.

Case, A. C., & Katz, L. F. (1991). The company you keep: The effects of family and neighborhood on disadvantaged youths. *NBER Working Papers 3705, National Bureau of Economic Research, Inc.*

Casey, B. J., Giedd, J., & Thomas, K. (2000). Structural and functional brain development and its relation to cognitive development. *Biological Psychology, 54,* 241–257.

Castles, E. E., & Glass, C. R. (1986). Training in social and interpersonal problem solving skills for mildly and moderately mentally retarded adults. *American Journal of Mental Deficiency, 91,* 35–42.

Channon, S., Charman, T., Heap, J., Crawford, S., & Rios, P. (2001). Real-life-type problem-solving in Asperger's syndrome. *Journal of Autism and Developmental Disorders, 31,* 461–469.

Chassin, L., Hussong, A., & Beltran, I. (2009). Adolescent substance use. In R. M. Lerner & L. Steinberg (Eds.), *Handbook of adolescent psychology* (3rd ed., pp. 723–763), Hoboken, NJ: Wiley.

Chein, J., Albert, D., O'Brien, L., Uckert, K. & Steinberg, L. (2010). Peers increase adolescent risk taking by enhancing activity in the brain's reward circuitry. *Developmental Science, 14,* 1–10.

Clark, A. E., & Loheac, Y. (2007). It wasn't me, it was them! Social influences in risky behavior by adolescents. *Journal of Health Economics, 26,* 763–784.

Clegg, J., & Landsall-Welfare, R. (2009). From autonomy to relationships: Productive engagement with uncertainty. *Journal of Intellectual Disability Research, 54,* 66–72.

De Martino, B., Harrison, A. N., Knafo, S., Bird, G., & Dolan, R. J. (2008). Explaining enhanced logical consistency during decision making in autism. *The Journal of Neuroscience, 28,* 10746–10750.

De Martino, B., Kumaran, D., Seymour, B., & Dolan, R. J. (2006). Frames, biases, and rational decision-making in the human brain. *Science, 313,* 684–687.

Doya, K. (2008). Modulators of decision making. *Nature Neuroscience, 11,* 410–416.

Doyle, J., & Thomason, R. (1999). Background to qualitative decision theory. *AI Magazine, 20*(2), 55–68.

Dykens, E. M. (2001). Personality and psychopathology: New insights from genetic syndromes. In H. N. Switzky (Ed.), *Personality and motivational differences in persons with mental retardation* (pp. 283–317). Mahwah, NJ: Erlbaum.

Dykens, E. M. (2006). Toward a positive psychology of mental retardation. *American Journal of Orthopsychiatry, 76*(2), 185–193.

D'Zurilla, T. J., Maydeu-Olivares, A., & Gallardo-Pujol, D. (2011). Predicting social problem solving using personality traits. *Personality and Individual Differences, 50,* 142–147.

Ellis, W. E., & Zarbatany, L. (2007). Peer group status as a moderator of group influence on children's deviant, aggressive, and prosocial behavior. *Child Development, 78,* 1240–1254.

Embregts, P., & van Nieuwenhuijzen, M. (2009). Social information processing in boys with autistic spectrum disorder and mild to borderline to intellectual disabilities. *Journal of Intellectual Disability Research, 53,* 922–931.

Ernst, M., Kimes, A. S., London, E. D., Matochik, J. A., Eldreth, D., Tata, S., et al. (2003). Neural substrates of decision making in adults with attention deficit hyperactivity disorder. *American Journal of Psychiatry, 160,* 1061–1070.

Etzioni, A. (1988). *The moral dimension: Towards a new economics.* New York: The Free Press.

Evans, J., St. B. T. (2003). In two minds: Dual-process accounts of reasoning. *Trends Cognitive Science, 7,* 454–459.

Evans, J. St. B. T. (2008). Dual-processing accounts of reasoning, judgment and social cognition. *Annual Review of Psychology, 59,* 255–278.

Fischhoff, B. (1982). Debiasing. In D. Kahneman, P. Slovic, & A. Tversky (Eds.), *Judgement under uncertainty: Heuristics and biases* (pp. 422–444). New York: Cambridge University Press.

Fischhoff, B., Parker, A. M., Downs, J., Palmgren, C., Dawes, R., & Manski, C. F. (2000). Teen expectations for significant life events. *Public Opinion Quarterly, 64*(2), 189–205.

Fishbein, M., & Ajzen, I. (1975). *Belief, attitude, intention and behavior: An introduction to theory and research.* Reading, MA: Addison-Wesley.

Fisher, M. H., Moskowitz, A. L., & Hodapp, R. M. (2012). Vulnerability and experiences related to social victimization among individuals with intellectual and developmental disabilities. *Journal of Mental Health Research in Intellectual Disabilities, 5,* 32–48.

Fiske, A. P. (1992). The four elementary forms of sociality: Framework for a unified theory of social relations. *Psychological Review, 99,* 689–723.

Fiske, S. T. (1986). Schema-based versus piecemeal politics: A patchwork quilt, but not a blanket, of evidence. In R. R. Lau & D. O. Sears (Eds.), *Political cognition* (pp.127–158). Hillsdale, NJ: Lawrence Erlbaum Associates, Inc.

Fiske, S. T., & Taylor, S. E. (1991). *Social cognition* (2nd ed.). New York: McGraw Hill.

Frauenknecht, M., & Black, D. R. (2010). Is it social problem solving or decision-making? Implications for health education. *American Journal of Health Education, 41,* 112–123.

Fredrickson, B. L. (1998). What good are positive emotions? *Review of General Psychology, 2,* 300–319.

Furby, L., & Beyth-Marom, R. (1992). Risk taking in adolescence: A decision-making perspective. *Developmental Review, 12,* 1–44.

Galotti, K. M. (2002). *Making decisions that matter: How people face important life choices.* Mahwah, NJ: Erlbaum.

Gardner, M., & Steinberg, L. (2005). Peer influence on risk taking, risk preference, and risky decision making in adolescence and adulthood: An experimental study. *Developmental Psychology, 41,* 625–635.

Gaviria, A., & Raphael, S. (2001). School-based peer effects and juvenile behavior. *Review of Economics and Statistics, 83*(2), 257–268.

Gleichgerrcht, E., Ibanez, A., Roca, M., Torralva, T., & Manes, F. (2010). Decision-making cognition in neurodegenerative diseases. *Nature Reviews Neurology, 6,* 611–623.

Greenspan, S. (1979). Social intelligence in the retarded. In N. R. Ellis (Ed.), *Handbook of mental deficiency: Psychological theory and research* (2nd ed., pp. 483–531). Hillsdale, NJ: Erlbaum.

Greenspan, S., Loughlin, G., & Black, R. S. (2001). Credulity and gullibility in people with developmental disorders: A framework for future research. *International Review of Research in Mental Retardation, Vol. 24,* 101–135.

Greenspan, S., & Love, P. F. (1997). Social intelligence and developmental disorder: Mental retardation, learning disabilities, and autism. In W. E. MacLean, Jr. (Ed.), *Ellis handbook of mental deficiency, psychological theory and research* (pp. 311–342). Mahwah, NJ: Lawrence Erlbaum Associates.

Greenspan, S., Switzky, H., & Granfield, J. (1996). Adaptive behavior, everyday intelligence and the constitutive definition of mental retardation. In A. F. Rotatori, J. O. Schwenn, & S. Burkhardt (Eds.), *Advances in special education* (vol. 10, pp. 1–24). Greenwich, CT: JAI Press.

Greenspan, S., Switzky, H. N., & Woods, G. W. (2011). Intelligence involves risk-awareness and intellectual disability involves risk-unawareness: Implications of a theory of common sense. *Journal of Intellectual and Developmental Disability, 36*, 246–257.

Gumpel, T. (1994). Social competence and social skills training for persons with mental retardation: An expansion of a behavioral paradigm. *Education and Training in Mental Retardation and Developmental Disabilities, 29*, 194–201.

Hartley, S. L., & Sikora, D. M. (2010). Detecting autism spectrum disorder in children with intellectual disability: Which DSM-IV-TR criteria are most useful? *Focus on Autism and Other Developmental Disabilities, 25*, 85–97.

Hastie, R., & Dawes, R. M. (2000). *Rational choice in an uncertain world: The psychology of judgment and decision making.* Thousand Oaks, CA: Sage Publications.

Healey, K. N., & Masterpasqua, F. (1992). Interpersonal cognitive problem solving among children with mild mental retardation. *American Journal on Mental Retardation, 96*, 367–372.

Hickson, L., Golden, H., Khemka, I., Urv, T., & Yamusah, S. (1998). A closer look at interpersonal decision making in adults with and without mental retardation. *American Journal on Mental Retardation, 103*, 209–224.

Hickson, L., & Khemka, I. (1999). Decision making and mental retardation. In L. M. Glidden (Ed.), *International review of research in mental retardation, Vol. 22* (pp. 227–265). San Diego: Academic Press.

Hickson, L., & Khemka, I. (2001). The role of motivation in the interpersonal decision making of people with mental retardation. In H. N. Switzky (Ed.), *Personality and motivational differences in persons with mental retardation* (pp. 199–255). Mahwah, NJ: Erlbaum.

Hickson, L., Khemka, I., Collado, J., Spillane, A., & Wang, P. (2004). *Adapting ESCAPE for women with Williams syndrome.* Paper presented at the 10th International Professional Conference on Williams Syndrome, Grand Rapids, MI.

Hickson, L., Khemka I., Golden, H., & Chatzistyli, A. (2008). Profiles of women with mental retardation with and without a documented history of abuse. *American Journal on Mental Retardation, 113*, 133–142.

Hickson, L., Khemka I., Golden, H., & Chatzistyli, A. (in press). Views and values of developmental disabilities and domestic violence/sexual assault support professionals regarding the prevention and handling of situations of abuse. *Journal of Policy and Practice in Intellectual Disabilities.*

Hickson, L., Khemka, I., Golden, H., & Chatzistyli, A. (March, 2012). *Impact of ESCAPE-DD on the comprehension and self-protective decision-making of adults with intellectual disabilities.* Poster presented at the Gatlinburg Conference on Research and Theory in Intellectual and Developmental Disabilities, Annapolis, MD.

Hickson, L., Khemka, I., Will, G., & Golden, H. (2002). *Evaluation of a decision-making curriculum designed to empower women with mental retardation to resist physical, sexual, and verbal abuse.* Annual Convention of the American Association on Intellectual and Developmental Disabilities, Chicago, IL.

Higgins, E. T., & Bargh, J. A. (1987). Social cognition and social perception. In M. R. Rosenzweig & L.W. Porter (Eds.), *Annual review of psychology* (pp.369–425). Palo Alto, CA: Annual Reviews.

Hillier, A., Fish, T., Cloppert, P., & Beversdorf, D. Q. (2007). Outcomes of a social and vocational skills support group for adolescents and young adults on the autism spectrum. *Focus on Autism and Other Developmental Disabilities, 22*, 107–115.

Hoch, S. J., Kunreuther, H. C., & Gunther, R. E. (2001). *Wharton on making decisions.* New York: John Wiley & Sons, Inc.

Hofstede, G. (2001). *Culture's consequences: Comparing values, behaviors, institutions, and organizations across nations* (2nd ed.). Thousand Oaks, California: Sage Publications, Inc.

Hogarth, R. M. (1994). *Judgment choice: The psychology of decision.* Chichester, England: John Wiley & Sons, Ltd.

Isen, A. (2000). Positive affect and decision making. In M. Lewis & J. M. Haviland-Jones (Eds.), *Handbook of emotions* (pp. 417–435). New York: Guilford Press.

Izzo, M. V., Pritz, S. G., & Ott, P. (1990). Teaching problem-solving skills: A ticket to a brighter future. *Journal for Vocational Special Needs Education, 13*, 23–26.

Janis, I., & Mann, L. (1977). *Decision making: A psychological analysis of conflict, choice, and commitment.* New York: The Free Press.

Jawaid, A., Riby, D. M., Owens, J., White, S. W., Tarar, T., & Schulz, P. E. (2012). 'Too withdrawn' or "too friendly": Considering social vulnerability in two neuro-developmental disorders. *Journal of Intellectual Disability Research, 56*, 335–350.

Jenkinson, J. C. (1999). Factors affecting decision-making by young adults with intellectual disabilities. *American Journal on Mental Retardation, 104*, 320–329.

Jenkinson, J. C., & Nelms, R. (1994). Patterns of decision-making behaviour by people with intellectual disability: An exploratory study. *Australia and New Zealand Journal of Developmental Disabilities, 19*, 99–109.

Kahneman, D. (2003). A perspective on judgment and choice: Mapping bounded rationality. *American Psychologist, 58*, 697–720.

Kahneman, D. (2011). *Thinking, fast and slow.* New York: Farrar, Straus, and Giroux.

Kahneman D., & Frederick S. (2007). Frames and brains: Elicitation and control of response tendencies. *Trends in Cognitive Sciences, 11*, 45–46.

Kasari, C., & Bauminger, N. (1998). Social and emotional development in children with mental retardation. In J. Burack., R. M. Hodapp, & E. Zigler (Eds.), *Handbook of mental retardation and development* (pp. 411–433). New York: Cambridge University Press.

Kay, J. (August 20, 2002). Beware the pitfalls of over-reliance on rationality: Attempting to shoehorn complex decisions into the framework of classical theory can be a mistake. *The Financial Times*, p.9.

Keating, D. P. (2004). Cognitive and brain development. In R. J. Lerner & L. D. Steinberg (Eds.), *Handbook of adolescent psychology* (pp. 45–84). New York: Wiley.

Khemka, I. (2000). Increasing independent decision-making skills of women with mental retardation in simulated interpersonal situations of abuse. *American Journal on Mental Retardation, 105*, 387–401.

Khemka, I., & Hickson, L. (2000). Decision making by adults with mental retardation in simulated situations of abuse. *Mental Retardation, 38*, 15–26.

Khemka, I., & Hickson, L. (2006). The role of motivation in the decision making of adolescents with mental retardation. In L. M. Glidden & H. N. Switzky (Eds.), *International review of research in mental retardation* (vol. 31, pp. 73–115). Amsterdam: Elsevier.

Khemka, I., Hickson, L., Casella, M., Accetturi, N., & Rooney, M. E. (2009). Impact of coercive tactics on the decision making of adolescents with intellectual disabilities. *Journal of Intellectual Disability Research, 53*(4), 353–362.

Khemka, I., Hickson, L., & Reynolds, G. (2005). Evaluation of a decision-making curriculum designed to empower women with mental retardation to resist abuse. *American Journal on Mental Retardation, 110,* 193–204.

Khemka, I., Hickson, L., Zealand, R., & Mallory, S. (March, 2011). *Impact of an intervention to increase effective decision making by adolescents with intellectual and developmental disabilities in situations involving peer pressure.* Poster presented at the Gatlinburg Conference on Research and Theory in Intellectual and Developmental Disabilities, San Antonio, TX.

Klaczynski, P. A. (2001). Analytic and heuristic processing influences on adolescent reasoning and decision making. *Child Development, 72,* 844–861.

Klaczynski, P. A., Byrnes, J. P., & Jacobs, J. E. (2001). Introduction to the special issue: The development of decision-making. *Applied Developmental Psychology, 22,* 225–236.

Klein, G. (1998). *Sources of power: How people make decisions.* Cambridge, MA: MIT Press.

Kruglanski, A. W. (1989). *Lay epistemics and human knowledge: Cognitive and motivational bases.* New York: Plenum.

Kuhl, J. (1986). Motivation and information processing. In M. Sorrentino & E. T. Higgins (Eds.), *Handbook of motivation and cognition* (pp. 404–434). New York: The Guilford Press.

Lashbrook, J. T. (2000). Fitting in: Exploring the emotional dimension of adolescent peer pressure. *Adolescence, 35*(140), 747–757.

Leffert, J., Siperstein, G., & Millikan, E. (2000). Understanding social adaptation in children with mental retardation: A social-cognitive perspective. *Exceptional Children, 66,* 530–545.

Leffert, J. S., Siperstein, G. N., & Widaman, K. F. (2010). Social perception in children with intellectual disabilities: The interpretation of benign and hostile intentions. *Journal of Intellectual Disability Research, 54,* 168–180.

Lewicki, R. J., & Litterer, J. A. (1985). *Negotiation in business.* Homewood, IL: R.D. Irwin.

Loewenstein, G., & Lerner, J. S. (2002). The role of affect in decision making. In R. Davidson, K. Scherer, & H. Goldsmith (Eds.), *Handbook of affective science* (pp. 619–642). New York: Oxford University Press.

Martella, R. C., Marchand-Martella, N. E., & Agran, M. (1993). Using a problem-solving strategy to teach adaptability skills to individuals with mental retardation. *Journal of Rehabilitation, 34,* 58–68.

Martin, C. A., Kelly, T. H., Rayens, M. K., Brogli, B. R., Brenzel, A., Smith, W. J, et al. (2002). Sensation seeking, puberty, and nicotine, alcohol and marijuana use in adolescence. *American Academy of Child and Adolescent Psychiatry, 41* (12), 1495–1502.

McNulty, J. K., & Finchman, F. D. (2012). Beyond positive psychology: Toward a contextual view of psychological processes and well-being. *American Psychologist, 67*(2), 101–110.

Meneghetti, M. M., & Seel, K. (2001). Ethics and values in the nonprofit organization. In T. D. Connors (Ed.), *The nonprofit handbook: Management* (579–609). New York: John Wiley& Sons, Inc.

Moffitt, T. E. (1993). Adolescence-limited and life-course-persistent anti peer pressure social behavior: A developmental taxonomy. *Psychological Review, 100,* 674–701.

Monahan, K., Steinberg, L., & Cauffman, E. (2009). Affiliation with antisocial peers, susceptibility to peer influence, and desistance from antisocial behavior during the transition to adulthood. *Developmental Psychology, 45,* 1520–1530.

Mounts, N. S., & Steinberg, L. (1995). An ecological analysis of peer influence on adolescent grade-point-average and drug use. *Developmental Psychology, 31,* 915–922.

Myers, D. G. (2000). The funds, friends, and faith of happy people. *American Psychologist, 55*(1), 56–67.

Nestler, J., & Goldbeck, L. (2011). A pilot study of social competence group training for adolescents with borderline intellectual functioning and emotional and behavioural problems. *Journal of Intellectual Disability Research, 55,* 231–241.

Norton, B., Costanza, R., & Bishop, R. C. (1998). The evolution of preferences: Why "sovereign" preferences may not lead to sustainable policies and what to do about it. *Ecological Economics, 24,* 193–211.

O'Brien, L., Albert, D., Chein, J., & Steinberg, L. (in press). Adolescents prefer more immediate rewards when in the presence of their peers. *Journal of Research in Adolescence.*

Padilla-Walker, L. M., & Bean, R. A. (2009). Negative and positive peer influence: Relations to positive and negative behaviors for African American, European American, and Hispanic adolescents. *Journal of Adolescence, 32*(2), 323–337.

Park, H. S., & Gaylord-Ross, R. (1989). A problem-solving approach to social skills training in employment settings with mentally retarded youth. *Journal of Applied Behavior Analysis, 22,* 373–380.

Rao, P. A., Beidel, D. C., & Murray, M. J. (2008). Social skills interventions for children with Asperger's syndrome or high-functioning autism: A review and recommendations. *Journal of Autism and Developmental Disorder, 38,* 353–361.

Rath, J., Simon, D., Langenbahn, D., Sherr, R. L., & Diller, L. (2003). Group treatment of problem-solving deficits in outpatients with traumatic brain injury: A randomized outcome study. *Neuropsychological Rehabilitation, 13,* 461–488.

Reyna, V. F. (1996). Conceptions of memory development, with implications for reasoning and decision making. *Annals of Child Development, 12,* 87–118.

Reyna, V. F. (2004). How people make decisions that involve risk. A dual-processes approach. *Current Directions in Psychological Science, 13,* 60–66.

Reyna, V. F., & Adam, M. B. (2003). Fuzzy-trace theory, risk communication, and product labeling in sexually transmitted diseases. *Risk Analysis, 23,* 325–342.

Reyna, V. F., & Farley, F. (2006). Risk and rationality in adolescent decision making: Implications for theory, practice, and public policy. *Psychological Science in the Public Interest, 7,* 1–44.

Reyna, V. F., & Lloyd, F. (2006). Physician decision making and cardiac risk: Effects of knowledge, risk perception, risk tolerance, and fuzzy processing. *Journal of Experimental Psychology: Applied, 12,* 179–195.

Reyna, V. F., Lloyd, F. J., & Brainerd, C. J. (2003). Memory, development, and rationality: An integrative theory of judgment and decision-making. In S. Schneider & J. Shanteau (Eds.), *Emerging perspectives on judgment and decision research* (pp. 201–245). New York: Cambridge University Press.

Richards, M. H., Crowe, P. A., Larson, R., & Swarr, A. (1998). Developmental patterns and gender differences in the experience of peer companionship during adolescence. *Child Development, 69,* 154–163.

Ruble, L. A., Willis, H., & Crabtree, V. (2008). Social skills group therapy for autism spectrum disorders. *Journal of Clinical Case Studies, 7,* 287–300.

Schalock, R. L., Brown, I., Brown, R., Cummins, R. A., Felce, D., Matikka, L., et al. (2002). Conceptualization, measurement, and application of quality of life for persons with intellectual disabilities: Report of an international panel of experts. *Mental Retardation, 40*(6), 457–470.

Schank, R. C., & Abelson, R. P. (1977). *Scripts, plans, goals, and understanding: An inquiry into human knowledge structures.* Hillsdale, NJ: Lawrence Erlbaum Associates.

Schein, E. (1992). *Organizational culture and leadership.* San Francisco: Jossey-Bass.

Selten, R. (2001). What is bounded rationality? In G. Gigerenzer & R. Selten (Eds.), *Bounded rationality: The adaptive toolbox* (pp. 13–36). Cambridge, MA: The MIT Press.

Semel, E., & Rosner, S. R. (2003). *Understanding Williams syndrome: Behavioral patterns and interventions.* Mahwah, NJ: Erlbaum.

Short, E. J., & Evans, S. W. (1990). Individual differences in cognitive and social problem-solving as a function of intelligence. In N. W. Bray (Ed.), *International review of research in mental retardation*, Vol. 16 (pp. 89–123). San Diego: Academic Press.

Simon, H. A. (1957). *Administrative behavior* (2nd ed.). New York: Macmillan.

Simon, H. A. (1974). How big is a chunk? *Science, 183,* 482–488.

Simon, H. A., Dantzig, G. B., Hogarth, B., Plott, C. R., Raiffa, H., Schelling, T. C., et al. (1986). *Decision making and problem solving: Report of the research briefing panel on decision making and problem solving by the National Academy of Sciences.* Washington, DC: National Academy Press.

Smith, D. C. (1986). Interpersonal problem-solving skills of retarded and non-retarded children. *Applied Research in Mental Retardation, 7,* 431–442.

South, M., Dana, J., White, S. E., & Crowley, M. (2011). Failure is not an option: Risk taking is moderated by anxiety and also by cognitive ability in children and adolescents diagnosed with an Autism spectrum disorder. *Journal of Autism and Developmental Disorders, 41,* 55–65.

Spear, P. (2000). The adolescent brain and age-related behavioral manifestations. *Neuroscience and Biobehavioral Reviews, 24,* 417–463.

Stanovich, K. E. (1999). *Who is rational? Studies of individual differences in reasoning.* Mahwah, NJ: Erlbaum.

Stanovich, K. E. (2010). *Decision making and rationality in the modern world.* New York: Oxford University Press.

Stanovich, K. E. (2011). *Rationality & the reflective mind.* New York: Oxford University Press.

Stanovich, K. E., & West, R. F. (2002). Individual differences in reasoning: Implications for the rationality debate? (pp. 421–440). In T. Gilovich, D. W. Griffin, D., & D. Kahneman (Eds.), *Heuristics and biases: The psychology of intuitive judgment.* New York: Cambridge University Press.

Stein, J. G., & Welch, D. A. (1997). Rational and psychological approaches to the study of international conflict: Comparative strengths and weaknesses. In N. Geva & A. Mintz (Eds.), *Decision making on war and peace: The cognitive-rational development* (pp. 51–80). Boulder, CO: Lynne Rienner Publishers, Inc.

Steinberg, L. (2004). Risk-taking in adolescence: What changes and why? *Annals, New York Academy of Sciences, 1021,* 51–58.

Steinberg, L. (2007). Risk taking in adolescence: New perspectives from brain and behavioral science. *Current Directions in Psychological Science, 16*(2), 55–59.

Steinberg, L. (2010). A dual systems model of adolescent risk-taking. *Developmental Psychobiology, 52,* 216–224.

Steinberg, L., & Cauffman, E. (1996). Maturity of judgment in adolescence: Psychosocial factors in adolescent decision making. *Law and Human Behavior, 20,* 249–272.

Steinberg, L., & Monahan, K. C. (2007). Age differences in resistance to peer influence. *Developmental Psychology, 43*(6), 1531–1543.

Steinberg, L., & Silverberg, S. B. (1986). The vicissitudes of autonomy in early adolescence. *Child Development, 57,* 841–851.

Sumter, S. R., Bokhorst, C. L., Steinberg, L., & Westenberg, P. M. (2009). The developmental pattern of resistance to peer influence in adolescence: Will the teenager ever be able to resist? *Journal of Adolescence, 32,* 1009–1021.

Tobler, N. (1986). Meta-analysis of 143 adolescent prevention programs: Quantitative outcome results of program participants compared to a control or comparison group. *Journal of Drug Issues, 16,* 537–567.

Tversky, A., & Kahneman, D. (1974). Judgment under uncertainty: Heuristics and biases. *Science, 185*(4157), 1124–1131.

Tversky, A., & Kahneman, D. (1979). Prospect theory: an analysis of decision under risk. *Econometrica, 47,* 263–292.

Tymchuk, A., Yokota, A, & Rahbar, B. (1990). Decision making abilities of mothers with mental retardation. *Research in Developmental Disabilities, 11,* 97–109.

Van Nieuwenhuijzen, M., Orobio de Castro, B., Wijnroks, L., Vermeer, A., & Matthys, W. (2009). Social problem-solving and mild intellectual disabilities: Relations with externalizing behavior and therapeutic context. *American Journal on Intellectual and Developmental Disabilities, 114,* 42–51.

Vaughn, S. R., Ridley, C. A., & Cox, J. (1983). Evaluating the efficacy of an interpersonal skills training programs with children who are mentally retarded. *Education and Training of the Mentally Retarded, 18,* 191–196.

Wainryb, C., Shaw, L. A., Laupa, M., & Smith, K. (2001). Children's, adolescents', and young adults' thinking about different types of disagreements. *Developmental Psychology, 37,* 373–386.

Walster, E., Walster, G. W., & Bershcheid, E. (1978). *Equity: Theory and research.* Boston: Allyn and Bacon, Inc.

Wehmeyer, M. L., & Kelchner, K. (1994). Interpersonal cognitive problem-solving skills of individuals with mental retardation. *Education and Training in Mental Retardation and Developmental Disabilities, 29,* 265–278.

Wehmeyer, M. L., & Shogren, K. (2008). Self-determination and learners with autism spectrum disorders. In R. Simpson & B. Myles (Eds.), *Educating children and youth with autism: Strategies for effective practice* (2nd ed., pp. 433–476). Austin, TX: Pro-Ed Publishers, Inc.

Wehmeyer, M. L., Shogren, K. A., Zager, D., Smith, T.E. C., & Simpson, R. (2010). Research-based principles and practices for educating students with autism: Self-determination and social interactions. *Education and Training in Autism and Developmental Disabilities, 45*(4), 475–486.

Wigfield, A., Byrnes, J. P., & Eccles, J. (2006). Development during early and middle adolescence. In P. A. Alexander & P. H. Winne (Eds.), *Handbook of educational psychology, 2nd ed.* (pp. 87–114). Mahwah, NJ: Lawrence Erlbaum Associates.

Wilson, P., & Kirby, D. (1984). *Sexuality education: A curriculum for adolescents.* Santa Cruz, CA: Network Publications.

Wong, J. G., Clare, I. C. H., Holland, A. J., Watson, P. C., & Gunn, M. (2000). The capacity of people with a "mental disability" to make a health care decision. *Psychological Medicine, 30,* 295–306.

Yirmiya, N., Erel, N., Shaked, M., & Solomonica-Levi, D. (1998). Meta-analyses comparing theory of mind abilities of individuals with autism, individuals with mental retardation, and normally developing individuals. *Psychological Bulletin, 124,* 283–307.

Forgiveness, Gratitude, and Spirituality

William Gaventa

Abstract

Forgiveness, gratitude, and spirituality are separate yet intertwined. Forgiveness has long been seen as a spiritual, if not religious process. Forgiveness and gratitude play fundamental roles in changing the perception, approach, and responses to disability by the individuals themselves, their families, professionals, caregivers, friends, and communities. Spirituality and/or religious beliefs and practice can initiate both forgiveness and gratitude but also can be harmful and isolating. All three are focus areas for an increasing amount of scientific research, particularly on the impact of forgiveness and spirituality on health and well-being. People with intellectual and developmental disabilities can also be agents of forgiveness and gratitude, as well as demonstrate a capacity for other dimensions of spirituality. The power of all three encourages using the potential of spirituality as a source of support and inclusion, particularly when it comes to overcoming barriers of participation and attitude.

Key Words: forgiveness, gratitude, spirituality, intellectual and developmental disability, health, attitude, religion, participation, professional role

The Challenge and Relationship

Exploring the dimensions of forgiveness, gratitude, and spirituality as themes in positive psychology and their relationship to, or manifestation in, the arena of disability could easily be done in depth in separate discussions; each of these dimensions of human life are both broad in scope and deep in history and literatures of their own. But these three dimensions also have a long history of dynamic relationship with one another through the rich diversity of ways in which spirituality and religious traditions deal with both forgiveness and gratitude as fundamental components of human life and the lives of faith for individuals, communities, and cultures.

The challenge, then, is putting these dimensions, or positive psychological constructs, in the kind of rational order that psychological research and writing, based in the broader arena of scientific inquiry and research, would prefer and prescribe. Beliefs, attitudes, and actions shape both forgiveness and

gratitude. Some would say they are ways of being involving profound mystery; for others, they symbolize deep faith and spirituality; for still others, they are concepts that are profoundly irrational: "How can one forgive in this or that circumstance, given what has happened to them or been done to them? I could not do that." "They don't have anything in terms of wealth, material goods, or typical human ability or capacity, but they seem to be so incredibly grateful for what they have and joyful in their approach to life. I could not do that." "I would never choose to be in that position, or more specifically, be a parent of a child with a disability or be disabled myself."

When one mixes spirituality and religion with scientific perspectives, one is then considering relationships that have never been marked by easy collaboration and partnership. In fact, that intersection has often been fraught with great mistrust and conflict, both founded and unfounded, as both camps attempt, in similar and dissimilar ways, to explore the human condition, understand the human story, and come to terms with the nature of life itself. Both stances involve intellect, belief, reason, passion, feeling, and attitude. Enter disability—and the ways in which both scientific and religious perspectives have both helped and harmed human understandings of disability—and one is soon in a maze where the way through often seems impossible and with little promise of reward (no matter the amount of cheese) on the other end.

A discussion of this mix of the spiritual and the scientific is precisely what this chapter is going to attempt because one cannot reasonably or honestly ignore the ways that forgiveness, gratitude, and spirituality manifest themselves in the lives of people with disabilities and their families. None of the three necessarily comes first, because one's spirituality or religious faith does not always lead to forgiveness and/or gratitude, even though those two qualities are central tenets of most religious traditions in belief, ritual, symbol, actions, and songs. Nor does gratitude necessarily lead to forgiveness and spirituality, or forgiveness to gratitude, or forgiveness and gratitude to spirituality. These certainly can be possible paths, as exemplified by the work of pioneer forgiveness scholar and researcher Robert Enright (Rocca, 2011). In psychological terms, one might say they are all interrelated, intertwined, dynamic processes, just as a Christian theologian might try to explain his or her experience of different dimensions of the divine and holy and their relationship using the construct of the Trinity. But, certainly, these processes have all been connected to core human understandings and experiences of compassion—more matters of the heart than the head—and are clearly components of human life and spirit experienced by people with disabilities, their families, and those who care for, work with, and support them as both friends and professionals.

I will come at this from my own background as a clergyman, one whose life has been graced by finding my own call and vocation in the arena of disability. I and others have tried both to find and utilize language that enables communication, understanding, and collaboration between "secular" human services and "faith-based" ministries and supports. Sometimes that feels like cross-cultural interpretation, with the same inherent frustrations but also with the same excitement about making new connections. In doing so, finding areas of intersection has meant trying to find points of unity in the diversity of ways that varied human sciences and human faith traditions see and address matters of the spirit

and tap its potential for the kinds of support that can lead to the flourishing of individuals, families, service systems, and communities.

Foundational Understandings: What Do We Mean by Forgiveness, Gratitude, and Spirituality?
Forgiveness

First, forgiveness is commonly understood as giving up, laying aside, or letting go of feelings of anger, resentment, guilt, or a claim to requital or revenge, or—what seems rational and common sense to many—responding to others in equal measure to what was done to you. That, however, is tremendously problematic. Stated clearly in Mahatma Gandhi's famous quote (with words that just happen to be famous constructs and metaphors of disability), "If we practice an eye for an eye, and a tooth for a tooth, soon the whole world will be blind and toothless."[1] Stated anew by poet Robert Frost (1949) in his poem, *Star-splitter*:

> If one by one we counted people out
> For the least sin, it wouldn't take us long
> To get so we had no one left to live with
> For to be social is to be forgiving

Its communal power is at the heart of nonviolence as a political process and in reconciliation processes, such as those found in the South African Truth and Reconciliation Tribunals. It can mean forgetting and reconnection, or it can mean forgiving a person or people but not the act. According to Bishop Desmond Tutu (1999):

> In forgiving, people are not being asked to forget. On the contrary, it is important to remember, so that we should not let atrocities happen again. Forgiveness does not mean condoning what has been done. It means taking what has happened seriously…drawing out the sting in the memory that threatens our entire existence.

One can forgive others or oneself. Forgiveness can also be an act in community, or between parts of a community or between nations. It has been understood as duty, virtue, joyful response, and/or as gift, but not usually as a rule because one cannot make someone forgive. It can be freely given or given in response to a confession, a request, plea, or process. As John Dryden said: "Reason to rule, mercy to forgive. The first is law, the last prerogative." (Dryden, http://forgivenessweb.com.)

In most religious traditions, forgiveness flows from the deity or an understanding of what is at the heart of the universe. Because we have been forgiven by God, deity, or the grace at the heart of life itself, our call is to pass that on to others (Briggs, 2008). It can thus be a response of gratitude for the grace, wonder, and mystery at the heart of life, leading to humility from being forgiven, and then forgiving one's own mistakes and others. "The secret of forgiving everything is to understand nothing" (Shaw, http://forgivenessweb.com.).

Forgiveness is also an exploding area of scientific inquiry, pioneered by developmental psychologist Dr. Robert Enright at the University of Wisconsin, assisted by funding from the Templeton Foundation, and now a field unto itself, with input from others like Dr. Frederic Luskin at Stanford. The field has developed institutes, conferences, and publications related to arenas of therapy, health, human services, politics, and religion. In the secular arenas of science, forgiveness is usually seen as choice process and is focused on the ends rather than the means (Briggs, 2008). Enright notes: "Now forgiveness is well established as a scientific, foundational area of moral development. Most people who take at least a peek under the tent of forgiveness will realize that the scientific studies show meaningful results with emotionally healthy people, once they forgive" (Enright, 2008). Luskin's empirical research has led to findings on its power and health benefits (Luskin, 2002). Succinctly summarizing the research, Ken Briggs writes that "[h]olding onto gripes and accusations can make you sick" (Briggs, 2008, p. 34).

Gratitude

Interestingly for me, in some of the research and reading done for this chapter, I saw very little reference to scientific inquiry into what it means "to be forgiven," to be recipient rather than agent and chooser, which we will explore later as a key dimension in the experience of disability.

For most of us, gratitude is the immediate response to forgiveness, perhaps after being stunned and amazed. We all know something about the power of being forgiven and, conversely, the sometimes demonic power of guilt that eats from within or comes in the form of anger and resentment or fear of punishment from others. In those religious traditions in which forgiveness flows from God, gratitude for that gift is what calls one to forgive another as part of a renewed commitment to righteousness. That call is both invitation and imperative, as, for example, in Jesus' answer to Peter about how many times we should forgive—"seventy times seven"— and in the parable in which he tells the story of the

master servant who begs for forgiveness and a grace period from his master because of his debts, yet turns around and demands, in the harshest terms, immediate payment from servants beneath him who owe him money. When the other servants complain to the master, he throws the master servant into jail (Matthew 18:21–35). The master servant is far too like what happens in hierarchical human organizations when a person gets called on the carpet for his or her "debts." Alternatively, in the most famous of Christian prayers, the call to "forgive us our trespasses (debts) as we forgive those who trespass against us" follow a lines of gratitude: "Give us this day our daily bread." (http://www.lords-prayer-words.com/lord_traditional_king_james.html)

Gratitude is profoundly connected to the concept of *gift*, not to something one has earned, worked for, or deserved. In fact, gratitude is often a feeling of thanks in oneself for gifts and graces received when you feel you deserved something much worse or nothing at all, and a giving of thanks to others and to God for that gift. "Grace is getting something you don't deserve, and mercy is not getting something that you do deserve" (Arnott, http://forgivenessweb.com.).

Like forgiveness, gratitude is belief, attitude, and action. Both can be learned and practiced. Both can be explored as processes but neither is an entitlement, product, or definitive outcome. Gratitude is a response and a choice. Gratitude is most certainly connected to positive feelings and experiences. It can also be or become a perspective, a construct, through which one views the world, allowing one to see the very gift and wonder of life itself, as well as its pain and suffering. Buddhism teaches that it comes from our own enlightenment, recognizing the attitudes that cause our very experience of pain and suffering. Gratitude is fundamental to individual optimism and to interpersonal relationships. Being taken for granted, or, more significantly for the area of disability, being seen (or seeing oneself) as someone who primarily elicits sorrow, regret, avoidance, or dismissal in others, is far too common. Gratitude thus might been seen as the opposite to a construct that only sees deficit. Gratitude can envision and celebrate strengths, capacities, or gifts whereas an opposite construct might only see deficit, disease, and curse as core components of what it means to experience disability. Those attitudes become stereotypes, embedded in traditions and cultures. They become concrete and thus form a fundamental part of the World Health Organization's definition and construct of disability discussed in Chapter 2 of this book.

Spirituality

A precise definition for spirituality is even harder to come by than one for forgiveness or gratitude. As noted, forgiveness and gratitude are so often connected with spiritual and religious processes and responses. Too often, all three are seen simply as matters of the heart and belief more than of reason, yet the premise of this chapter and much of the research on forgiveness is that it also involves intellectual/psychological constructs that can come from a multitude of sources. Speaking out of the vast and varied dimensions of spirituality, one might look at this volume's exploration of positive psychology and disability and claim that most of the psychological constructs included are also matters of the spirit or spirituality (e.g., hope, courage, resilience, optimism happiness, friendship, and coping skills). Spiritual traditions have been sources of empowerment, lifestyle satisfaction, purpose, adaptive behavior, self-concept, and, certainly, social capital and social inclusion.

In the past 20 years, there has also been growing interest in research on spirituality and its relationship to psychological, physical, and social well-being. Spirituality has been differentiated from religion as being a part of all of human nature and cultures, with religions being varied constructs and traditions in which spirituality has been expressed, understood, and nurtured. It may be universal in scope, but spirituality is lived out in particular ways. Social work, psychiatry, psychology, nursing, and medicine are but a few of the human service disciplines and sciences that have been part of that exploration, not just in terms of its relationship to outcomes for patients but also to the ways that spirituality simply is part, whether approved or not, of the integration of professional and human. Two examples are the work centered at the Duke University Center for Theology and Health and the George Washington University Institute for Spirituality and Health.[2]

The exploration of spirituality as a construct for positive psychology and its proven or potential relationship to health and well-being cannot, however, overlook the ways that constructions of spirituality within religious traditions have been a source of both psychological and physical harm, especially in the arena of disability. In the growth of psychiatry and psychology after Freud and others, spirituality and religion were too often seen as a symptom rather than a resource. A pastoral acquaintance of mine, recovering from and coping with a life-long psychiatric disorder, noted once that "in the world of mental health, my interest in faith makes me a patient, and in my religious community, my mental illness makes me a stranger."

Additionally, individuals, parents, and professionals who live and work with disability have far too frequently experienced attitudes and practices that are insensitive, theologically questionable, and at times simply spiritual abusive. Ask a group of individuals with disabilities and/or their families to tell you their "faith stories." Many will talk about the importance and power of their faith and faith communities. Others will tell stories of attitudes and actions that wounded them deeply, especially because they happened in a community or relationship in which they expected far different responses from the "people of God." Some religious answers to the question of "Why did this happen?" such as "the sins of the parents" have too often heightened blame, guilt, and/or social isolation, at its worst leading to exclusion, scapegoating, and outright murder. In the same vein, in response to disability, when lack of healing or cure is blamed on someone's lack of faith, spirituality again becomes a tool of wounding rather than of support, balm, or healing.[3]

Those experiences can obviously lead to anger, resentment, guilt, and despair, as well as to rejection of the values or beliefs that someone thought were held in common with the sources of that wounding. There are all kinds of ways to respond to those experiences, such as demonstrating completely different interpretations of scriptures, traditions, or theological practices. One of my favorites is a story of a man with a disability who was simply fed up with strangers and acquaintances saying to him, "My brother, if your faith was strong enough, you could be healed." One day his response became, "My brother, if your faith was strong enough, you could cure me."

One might note, to be fair, that scientific explanations or treatments in the past century, if not before, have also occasionally led to the same results. Eugenics led to extermination. Initial causes of autism, such as "refrigerator mothers," led to increased blame or guilt. Failure to improve or grow has more than once been laid at the feet of the lack of parental initiative or not following the "right" plan or therapy. Prognosis has led to withdrawal of treatments because of assumptions (beliefs) about quality of life.

Paradoxically, the more we learn about disability, the more we also know that some forms of intellectual and developmental disabilities are caused by human "sins," either individually (e.g., fetal alcohol syndrome) or collectively (environmental factors that impact pregnancy and birth). I will never forget an experience I had as a young chaplain of a residential facility in upstate New York, hearing a family direct intense anger at a wonderfully competent and compassionate young pediatric neurologist after the avoidable death of their 26-year-old daughter. I could not understand, partly because they were a family that rarely visited. But at one point in the tirade, I realized the anger was directed at "you, doctor, who caused the disability by misuse of forceps at her birth." Her death peeled away the cover over the resentment and anger that had been neither forgiven nor forgotten.

Spirituality is then a part of both religion and science, each with its own beliefs and faith in constructs of what is real and true. Both spiritual and scientific traditions have done things that have meant, or should have meant, asking for forgiveness. Both have been profound sources of gratitude for help, healing, and recovery. Part of the issue is that there are different understandings of "truth." Parker Palmer (1986) noted that in the arena of science, a truth can be proven false and replaced by another truth. In human relationship and spirituality, a truth may be met by a different truth, and both be true to certain individuals, cultures, or spiritual traditions. In conversations with John Swinton, a pastoral theologian in Scotland who has worked on theological understandings of learning disabilities, mental illness, autism, and Alzheimer disease, he noted that, in the realm of science, good equates to observable, truth to measurable, and beauty to replicable.

Both arenas struggle with questions of cause, control, responsibility, and power, with their underlying themes of reason, freedom, and choice, all of which relate to forgiveness and gratitude. Ethicist and theologian Hans Reinders (2000) asks whether (a) a society that is founded on the valued constructs of reason, freedom, and choice can ever actually see people with intellectual and developmental disabilities as human beings with full dignity and full rights, given the underlying assumptions about their capacity for reason and choice; and (b) whether those constructs can fully explain the motivations, most often spiritual, that lead people into and sustain their care for people that others (e.g., Peter Singer) may think are of no utilitarian use?

For the purposes of this chapter, I define or use constructs of spirituality in ways I have written about in other places (Gaventa, 2005, 2006). Spirituality can been seen as a twofold construct, the meanings and sources of which enable one to cope with the struggles of life, and, also as what is seen or experienced as most true (then sacred or holy) in individual and communal lives. Spirituality

can also be defined as connection, a connection with self, with others, with community, with time (past and present), with place (holy sites), and with the Divine. The focus on connection, of course, immediately demonstrates the core role of forgiveness. Spiritual questions are at the heart of the core values in intellectual and developmental disability, values such as:

- *Independence*, the usual Western answer to what it means to be a person and individual, a value not held as highly in other cultures.
- *Productivity*, our answer to "Why am I?", the answer to which is the purpose of one's life, what I am to do, or who I am to be in order to be in my life's journey.
- *Inclusion*, the subversive question in opposition to the first: "Whose am I?" To whom, not necessarily "where," do I belong?
- *Self-determination*, "What choice, power, and control do I have in my life?"

The answers to these questions lie at the heart of our individual spirituality, our collective spiritual traditions, and/or our collective cultural and social values.

With those foundations laid, then, let's turn to the ways that the dynamic, living constructs of forgiveness, gratitude, and spirituality can be manifest and addressed within the experience and construct of disability.

Forgiveness and Disability

The experience of disability can be rife with anger, guilt, resentment, shame, blame, and scapegoating projections. Those are often basic human responses to the question of "Why?" Why this accident? Why this disaster? Why this cancer? In disability: Why me? Why my child? Whose fault was it? Why has this happened and my expectations about life been overturned? There are core assumptions being made that someone or something was responsible and/or that they (or I) could have controlled life so that "it" would not have happened. A common assumption is that bad things happen because of bad people. If one asks, "What was the title of Rabbi Harold Kushner's (1981) famous book, prompted by his son's unusual disability?" they usually answer *Why Bad Things Happen to Good People*," when, if fact, the title is *When Bad Things Happen to Good People*. Bad things are going to happen to everyone, sometimes made better or worse by our underlying expectations and interpretations.

The "Why?" question, though, is not just at onset or diagnosis. Why are people avoiding me? Why did they do that? Why am I, my child, my friends, or my family excluded? Why can't they see beyond my diagnosis? Why do I have no job or friends? Why can't the school, government, church, or other social institution do more? Why are professionals sometimes so wrong or so distant? Why can't I find a doctor who will see my child or family member? Why does he or she have to get sick or die? The list goes on. All of the resulting feelings of anger, blame, guilt, and resentment then lead to how one should or could respond. Anger channeled in the right directions is, as we all know, a creative and powerful force that can lead to change. But forgiveness is also a possible and important step: forgiveness of self, forgiveness of others, and/or forgiveness of organizations and whole communities.

In religious and theological perspectives, it may also involve forgiving God. When the Divine gets thrown into the mix with all of the why questions, one is faced with ancient and current struggles with the theistic question: "Why did God do this?" For punishment? A test? A blessing? To help me learn what is most important? Is suffering redemptive? Is disability a spiritual gift (Brock, 2011)? Was it God's will? Or did God have anything to do with it? If not, whose fault was it? Who can fix it?

There are various typologies for dealing with the question of the Divine's role in suffering, and rich explorations of that question make up in the histories of all major faith traditions. Clergyman and chaplain David Patterson (1970), who worked with people with cerebral palsy and their families, posits a framework with two axes crossing at the origin of the suffering. On axis has "God as the author" on one end and "God as not the author" on another, or, in other words, "Is God the source, and to what extent is God responsible for it?" The other has "beneficial to the sufferer" on one end and "harmful to the sufferer on the other"; that is, what is the perceived value of this experience to the person or persons involved? These frame four broad theological perspectives and spiritual attitudes on suffering:

1. If God is the author, and it is harmful, then suffering is retribution, punishment to me for something.

2. If God is the author, but it is experienced as beneficial or helpful, in either the short or long run, then suffering is experienced as redemptive, or done for me.

3. If God is not the source, but it is still perceived as beneficial, then suffering can be providential (i.e., God did not cause it, but my

faith has deepened and there have been untold gifts coming from this experience).

4. If God is not the source, and it is harmful, then suffering is absurd. And I then need to seek to eliminate it.

Like any typology, Patterson's point is not to say these are the only potential answers, but he goes on to explore how each of them are found in the Judeo-Christian tradition and Biblical story, thus serving as a real caution against thinking that there is any one answer or meaning to be found in suffering for people of faith in those traditions.

In psychological and spiritual traditions, those feelings and questions are also recognized as part of any grieving or coping process. The wider and deeper question is how one moves beyond those feelings to forgiveness and then, possibly, to gratitude. I am making several core assumptions:

1. That the process, like grief and mourning, is not completely rational, nor can it be ordered, planned, and/or controlled in a series of defined steps. A true "scientific" answer does not necessarily mean the other feelings or questions are answered. There are theories and understandings about a variety of processes or steps, including the different versions of the steps of grief and mourning. Robert Enright (2001) has developed a 20-step process for people choosing to work toward forgiveness. Judaism has a long and deep history of thinking about forgiveness and an annual 10-day ritual for repentance (seeking forgiveness) every year in the period between Rosh Hashanah and Yom Kippur known as *Aseret Y'mai Teshuva*: Ken Briggs outlines it as:

• Step 1. Regret: Realize the extent of the damage and feel sincere regret.
• Step 2. Cessation: Immediately stop the harmful action.
• Step 3. Confession: Articulate the mistake and ask for forgiveness.
• Step 4. Resolution: Make a firm commitment not to repeat it in the future.

Briggs (2008) notes further that, in Judaism, "the only one who can start the forgiveness process is the offender, and only the offended one can let go of the wrong, but if a plea is made three times, and the offended does not forgive, then it is their fault" (p. 19).

Again, it is important to remember that those processes serve primarily as guides that have come from long experience and can be immensely helpful to those involved, but they are not cause and effect; the outcome is not a given.

2. Particular answers cannot be prescribed, only found and claimed, and sometimes they never happen. Early in my career, a mother of a child with a disability told me she had used the book *J. B.*, a modern poetic rendering of the story of Job, with whom many have identified over centuries. "Like Job," she said, "I asked question after question, refusing to believe that it was my fault. It was not till I got the point where I realized Job never really got an answer to question that I, like Job, was able to move on."

3. A specific answer can be harmful or helpful, depending on the person and context. Think, for example, of the two poems that have floated around parent networks for decades, the author-unknown *Heaven's Very Special Child* and Emily Kingsbury's *Trip to Holland*. As a clergyman, I have often had to refrain from wincing both verbally and physically when I have heard people tell me how much they appreciated the former. The poem essentially says that one can come to believe that disability may be God's will for that person and for me as a parent. That can mean "This is the only sense of purpose I can understand and that helps me to get over the anger and align myself with God's role and/or purpose in my life." Conversely, the very same answer can mean repressed anger and deep, deep resentment toward God or others who have told them that. "It's God's will and I cannot say otherwise or be angry. I just have to accept it." Those who profess to help others with those questions and feelings need to be very careful that they do not take away an answer that may be helpful to another just because that is not what the helper can believe. Conversely, as noted in Patterson's typology, the helper can perhaps enable others to see different interpretations and meanings of the same answer within their own religious, spiritual, or philosophical traditions, or, in this case, offer *A Trip to Holland* as an alternative appreciated by many other parents as capturing their experience.

4. The most important thing is that those feelings have ways to be expressed, heard, and/or acted out, which varies greatly by cultural, religious, and scientific practices. Ritual, symbol, story, sacred scripture, beliefs, traditions, habits, and customs all can be avenues of expression. Friends, professionals, colleagues, other parents of children with disabilities, other people with disabilities, support groups and advocacy groups, communities, literature, song, and often unexpected sources may be sources of relief, revelation, comfort, and closure or provide the capacity to move on.

In my own Judeo-Christian tradition, for example, people are often surprised to discover that the Bible is full of stories expressing anger, blame, resentment, and questions, sometimes directed at others, often directed at God, in people and passages often seen as the very pillars of faith. Ken Briggs (2008) starts his book with the comment that the Bible begins with a grudge, God's anger at Adam and Eve, both for their action and for their blaming others for that action. Forgiveness and gratitude frame the Biblical story. In addition to Job, there's a whole book named for the universal practice of lamenting a loss, and multitudes of Psalms poetically spew despair, anger, resentment, blame, and questions before arriving at a resolution, often a form of gratitude not for a particular answer, but for the experience of being heard, of remembering past and present blessings, and for the promise of God's presence on the journey.

Who will hear my feelings and questions? Who will repent and ask for forgiveness for actions that may have hurt me? Those are not just issues at birth, diagnosis, or onset, but throughout one's life with disability, just as they are typical and normal for others struggling with other factors impacting their health, safety, and well-being. As noted, anger is not simply a negative emotion, but often a very appropriate response to the actions of others, a response that has fueled advocacy and social change. But, as many well know, unacknowledged guilt, unheard anger, uncollaborated answers, mistakes or actions unacknowledged in honest and remorseful ways, and simply limited human skills and systems can all lead to blame and anger that takes the forms of extreme conflict, lawsuits, blame of particular people and practices (e.g., vaccinations), and more.

The 10-day *teshuva* (meaning "return") process could, one might imagine, serve as description of what human service professionals in the arena of disability services and other organizations might call "continuous quality improvement." Far too often, however, those processes and procedures do not end in a sense of freedom, reconciliation, relief, or joy, perhaps because they do not include or allow asking for forgiveness but rather become the means by which someone takes the blame or new procedures (or rules) are established that sometime heighten anxiety and fear. One might wonder about the impact of bringing more of the spirit of repentance and/or forgiveness back into the process.

Forgiveness, along with resolution and/or reconciliation, can also come from both expected and unexpected sources, moments of choice and moments of complete serendipity, unanticipated support and compassion, and unexpected revelations or reframing of the very questions that led to the anger or guilt in the first place. Parents and/or people with disabilities reverse the "Why?" question, asking "Why not me?" and then go on to explore their journey in fellowship with so many others who have faced or are facing similar situations in their own lives.

Forgiveness and Gratitude

The act of forgiveness of self, others, a divinity, or the universe is one that can flow from gratitude as well as from repentance, especially in spiritual traditions. The gratitude is for being forgiven for our faults, sins, or mistakes, over and over again, and for the recognition that no one is perfect. The central prayer in Christianity asks "Forgive us our debts (sins) as we forgive our debtors (those who sin against us)." The power of the experience of being forgiven, by God or others, is experienced as gift, with all of its possible layers of joy, relief, liberation, and/or blessing.

As noted earlier, the more recent research on the power of forgiveness usually focuses on the impact on the forgiver, on the ways that forgiveness can free one from repressed anger, tension, and stress, thus relieving one of those internal burdens and then helping the forgiver to reconnect with others who may have been the source or target of that anger, blame, or resentment. In other words, it explores the choice and agency of the forgiver, such as a parent or a person with a disability, for forgiving one's self, others, or God.

That points to an obvious gap in this exploration that needs attention and naming: the agency and power of people with disabilities as forgivers, and the experience of being forgiven by them. The glaring omission in some of the writing and thinking about forgiveness within the construct of disability is the often amazing capacity of people with intellectual and developmental disabilities, in particular, but others as well, to be forgivers in ways that one might say approach the powers attributed to a deity, forgiving so-called typical people over and over again. This occurrence can be attributed to all kinds of sources, such as the lack of perception of the ways in which they have been mistreated; the hunger for relationship, acceptance, and connection

with others; the relationship of intellect with the memory and time; or, as Jean Vanier might say, the deep simplicity of their own spirituality and life in the world of relationships, the present, and joys of day-to-day living.

This acknowledgment is not a denial of the power of being wounded, or of the anger and resentment that are turned inward into depression, nor of those expectations and practices that too often stifle the opportunities and capacities for people with intellectual and developmental disabilities to express anger or be empowered by it. But we who live, befriend, work with, and care for many with intellectual and developmental disabilities have our own stories of being deeply moved by someone's ability to forgive, to not hold grudges, to maintain a sense of joy and gratitude we cannot imagine ourselves doing in the face of the struggles and barriers they face day to day and throughout their lives. I return to this topic in the final section because it relates especially to what I see as a need for professionals who work in the arena of disability to be more honest about their own gratitude for the gifts they have been given, including forgiveness, from the very people they serve and support. That capacity for forgiveness too often ends up falling under the construct of the "specialness" of people with intellectual and developmental disabilities, so all of us who seek to move beyond that description to a self- and public image of being "just like everyone else" need to find other ways that describe and acknowledge that characteristic, gift, and power.

Let me give an example that relates to anger and forgiveness. In the fall of 2010, Hans Reinders and I were at a conference sponsored by Peaceful Living, a Mennonite-based service provider in eastern Pennsylvania. The first day was an exploration of the power of friendship and spirituality. One direct support staff professional told the story of a person she supports who had been known for his outbursts (i.e., behavioral expressions) of anger at any number of things that happened that were not to his liking, one of them being rain. One of his unique laments and expressions was "Off with God's head!" Although something of an initial shock to this staffer, whose religious faith was very important to her, she also realized that he had very little connection with family or others outside of the agency. She invited him to attend her church, and they began to go regularly. He developed some friendships, enjoyed the services, and, gradually, as more attention was paid to the spirituality of his life, his outbursts and behavior problems diminished. (This is an anecdotal observation that I have heard repeatedly and one that begs for some valid research.) One rainy day she was struck by the fact he was not going into a fit of anger. She asked him what he thought was happening, and his new explanation was that "God just forgot to turn off the faucet."

The willingness of parents, family members, friends, and even people with other forms of disability to talk or write about their own sense of gratitude is not so hidden. Over time, it has come in so many forms. People talk and write about their own movement from anger and resentment over what life has dealt them to acceptance, forgiveness, and, indeed, gratitude. As noted, gratitude can come from anger and resentment being heard, a resolution or reframing of one's core questions, and revelations coming from unexpected places. Reframing personal experience, attitudes, and direction has been a core gift of parent support networks and advocacy groups.

When people talk about the "blessings" of their child with a disability in the lives of their families, friends, and communities, they are talking about lessons of gratitude. When others say, "I wish the disability had never happened, but I cannot imagine my life without my child, my friend, or even my disability because of what I have learned and received from them," they are talking about gratitude. The shift is sometimes a result of sources of unanticipated support or radical acceptance. It may be a discovery or revelation of a sense of purpose. It can come from an attitudinal shift, a realization that others have worse problems than they do—variations of the same sentiment so famously expressed by Leo Tolstoy that "I complained because I had no shoes until I met a man who had no feet."

There are any number of ways of exploring this journey both within and outside of the realm of disability. Sociologist and ethicist Arthur Frank (1995) explores what he calls the three narratives of illness in our society. The first is that of cure and recovery, the one lauded in the press and sought by all kinds of healing sciences, alternative medicines, and indeed spiritual practices. The second is what happens when healing does not happen as planned or hoped for, producing the narrative of chaos, when personal values and beliefs are upended or deemed worthless and life is then not worth living. This experience and these attitudes can lead to judgments about the absence of quality of life for people with any form of disability, but particularly for people with multiple intellectual, developmental, or acquired disabilities (e.g., "I would not want to live in that condition"). But there is a third alternative

narrative, one Frank describes in a word this chapter has already used, that of *journey*, an unexpected and new path in one's life that can bring both hardships and the discovery of new meaning, gifts, and purpose. It is "a road I did not choose, but now, on it, I am making all kinds of important discoveries." In the spiritual traditions, of course, the image of a journey and discovery in the face of suffering is the core of many faith traditions, from the young Buddha's Enlightenment to the 23rd Psalm. Arthur Frank's next book is closely related to gratitude, *The Renewal of Generosity: Illness, Medicine, and How to Live* (Frank, 2004).

Parker Palmer is another author and teacher who has explored spirituality in a number of its manifestations in understanding community, education, and vocation. At a 1986 conference on inclusion in Rochester, New York, his keynote speech explored understandings of community and hospitality and how, in the major spiritual traditions, "hospitality to the stranger" was a call and obligation, not simply because a host might sometime be a stranger him- or herself, but because of the gifts that might come to the host through the stranger. He then went on to talk about the ways that people with intellectual and developmental disabilities, as strangers to many in our society, "puncture our illusions" about the very fabric of life. That may feel less like a gift than a "disillusioning experience," but he goes on to note that it is indeed a favor because it brings us closer to the nature of truth. The four illusions he explores are that we cannot ever fully understand another person, that we cannot ever fully understand ourselves, that love can be earned by effort and works, and, finally, that we can escape vulnerability, limitation, and death.

For many people with disabilities and their families, their spiritual or faith tradition has been the context and source of their gratitude, embracing profound moments of personal transformation. Two of the most succinct expressions of that gratitude have come to me through young adults with autism.

First, Cal Montgomery (1999), a woman I met online after an introduction by a colleague: We started a discussion about spirituality and faith and then, one day, she asked if she could send me a prayer she had written. "Sure," I said, with no inkling of what was to come. The piece, which became an article entitled *Thanksgiving/Easter 1998,* was a reflection on her life, a journey that had included institutionalization, but it was written as a prayer because of the power of being accepted by a congregation in ways that transformed her usual expectations of social exclusion. As she notes in a number of places, she had always heard and experienced that the "Kingdom of God was open to all…except me." This time, there was no "except."

Then, most recently, a blog entry by Jacob Artson a young man with autism: In it, he talks about the profound spark that came from a doctor who looked at him with a smile rather than a frown, leading to his beginning to believe in himself. Another source he cites was his family's unwavering belief that he was a child of God and then his own experience of God and the Torah. Then he says:

> Finally, Judaism has taught me the importance of gratitude. For much of my life, my existence was controlled by autism. Autism was at the root of every experience I had or didn't have. I lived with constant anger at my disability and fear that it would isolate me forever. Then one day several years ago, my wonderful physician and mentor, Dr. Ricki Robinson, asked me what is the opposite of anger. I realized that it is not the absence of anger, but rather acceptance, laughter, and joy. I also realized that fear and anger just produces more fear and anger, while acceptance brings connection to God and humanity. For many years I have been praying for God to cure my autism and wondering why God didn't answer my prayer. I realized at that point that I had been praying for the wrong reason. I started to pray for strength to accept autism and live with joy, laughter, and connection. My prayers were answered more richly that I ever imagined! Sometimes I still hate autism, but now I love life more than I hate autism. (Artson, 2011)

A personal premise in this exploration of gratitude and disability is that receiving the gifts of people with intellectual and developmental disabilities, such as their expressions of gratitude and our own gratitude for them, is one of the major sources propelling the evolution of the definition of disability away from a complete focus on deficit and deficiency as residing within the individual. As with the whole field of positive psychology, *disability* is recognition of strengths and capacities as well as deficits. That recognition is fueled by personal experiences of gratitude for being gifted by the lives of individuals with disabilities, as well as by a variety of theoretical constructs. For many of us, the compelling nature of those gifts has given us a vocation and purpose.

Gratitude has taken other forms in the evolution of scientific and research perspectives. Ann Turnbull and colleagues at the Beach Center (Summers, Behr, & Turnbull, 1988) coined the phrase and started research on the "positive contributions of people with intellectual and developmental disabilities." Gifts and strengths led to new forms of planning for services and supports, all under the umbrella of "person-centered planning," that recognized and built from gifts and strengths both within the individual and his or her circles of supports, as well as tapping most of the constructs of positive psychology explored in this book. The PATH Process (Planning Alternative Tomorrows with Hope) (Forest, O'Brien, & Pearpoint, 1998) is one that also captures the image of the journey. Linked with an about-face in approaches to urban planning, community development, and community building, the concept is now known under the rubric of "asset-based community development" (McKnight & Kretzmann, 1993), which works from "capacity visions" that built community from assets and strengths rather than simply trying to erase problems and deficits by pouring in other assets and resources from the outside.

Spirituality: Beginning, Process, Renewal

The spirit and experience of forgiveness and gratitude, including attitude, response, and chosen action, can lead people of all kinds (individuals with disabilities, families, friends, caregivers, professionals, scientists, and theologians) to reexamine core constructs in both psychology and theology. Positive psychology, among other movements already mentioned, is one such response. So is the increasing amount of work being done in religious and spiritual traditions to rediscover and describe the ways that disability has been treated in those traditions and/or helped to shape understanding about them. Constructs being examined include:

• What does it means to be human, with all of its vulnerabilities in addition to its strengths and powers?
• What really are healing, cure, and/or health?
• How can one really talk about community unless everyone is included?
• What defines our understandings of truth, power, choice, reason, and control?

We could cite others. One of them must be the construct of what it means to be professional and how professionals can recognize, deal with, and utilize matters of the heart and spirit, as well as theories from the intellect and lessons from the head. The honest recognition and expression of the power of forgiveness coming toward us and the gifts of gratitude we have experienced, seen, and felt, is one step toward that reframing.

A second construct relates to exploring the spiritual journey undergone by many when it comes to encountering or acquiring disability. Coming to advocacy, commitment, and community is not just a process of understanding the dimensions of disability and learning how best to respond, treat, serve, or support others. It is, as Arthur Frank might say, a spiritual journey. Long ago, as a young chaplain in a residential facility seeking to build connections and relationships with and for people with intellectual and developmental disabilities, I had a conference conversation with Fr. John Aurelio, a fellow chaplain in upstate New York. He told me that, in his own ministry, in those areas, he thought people moved from fear to pity to anger to love. That process and construct described much of my journey, and it has resonated with many others.

The idea of a journey also frames the evolution of social attitudes and services, both public services and congregational ministries. The movement is from fear that led to avoidance and exclusion, to pity (special services for special people) to anger (by people with disabilities and their families leading to advocacy, but also in others as "we" get to know "them" and hear their stories of injustice and unnecessary struggle), and finally to love, a mutuality that occurs when one recognizes that one may be helping a person or family with a disability, but that they are also giving back gifts that one now, in turn, wants others in the community to see and experience, as well as a gift for one's own personal growth. Can professionals learn new and appropriate ways to thank the people they support for the gifts they have received through them? People with disabilities, like all of us, need to know that their lives have made a difference, in positive ways, to others and the community/world in which they live. Their lives are mostly ones of seeking services and being recipients, rather than being invited, asked, or challenged to use their gifts in service to others or, as people of faith, to the Divine.

At a June 2011 discussion about spiritual supports sponsored by the Virginia Partnership with People with Disabilities, the state's University Center of Excellence in Developmental Disabilities, Nicole Cossu, a young woman with cerebral palsy heard me talk about that progression and said, "That's my journey as well." I asked her to write it in an e-mail so I would not forget her words: "Fear: of not being accepted as a person. Pity: feeling sorry for myself. Anger: Angry at God and asking myself "Why me?" and finally my favorite, Love. Loving yourself as a person, a special creation of God, in my

case, a princess. I hope this helps." I, the consultant and "expert," received a gift once again.

Third, this journey needs to include ways that professionals and others can explore spirituality with the people they serve and support. Service systems need to follow-up by enabling supports in that dimension of life as part of responding to people's choices, hopes, and dreams. There have been several barriers to doing so, including:

- misunderstandings of "church/state" restrictions related to public funding,
- confusion because of the huge number of spiritual traditions and expressions,
- legitimate and valued professional practice to keep others from being hurt by unhelpful constructs and actions (e.g., proselytizing),
- a subsequent awareness—and fear—of the power of faith and religion in cultures and communities, and, finally,
- a lack of skills in how to collaborate effectively with spiritual leaders and communities to utilize that power and potential for the good.

Countering those barriers in many areas of human service and health care, there is growing research on the role of spirituality and development of processes for "spiritual assessments" to be included with interdisciplinary approaches and supports. One of them is George Fitchett's (1993) 7 × 7 model of spiritual assessment, one within a seven-fold range of holistic dimensions for assessments and support that draws in other constructs in positive psychology (Table 16.1).

Table 16.1 George Fitchett's (1993) 7 × 7 model of spiritual assessment (adapted from source).

Holistic Assessment	Spiritual Assessment
Biological (Medical) Dimension	Belief and Meaning
Psychological Dimension	Vocation and Obligations
Family Systems Dimension	Experience and Emotion
Psycho-Social Dimension	Courage and Growth
Ethnic/Racial/Cultural Dimension	Ritual and Practice
Social Issues Dimension	Community
Spiritual Dimension	Authority and Guidance

Another simpler and easy to remember spiritual assessment comes from Dr. Christina Puchalski (www.gwish.org) at the George Washington Institute on Spirituality and Health. The FICA process has four areas of questions that can be explored both quickly and/or in depth:

• *Faith*: Preference, choice, tradition, identity. Do you consider yourself a person of faith, or are you religious?

• *Influence and Importance*: How important is it to you? How does it influence your daily life?

• *Communal expression*: What form does it take, if any? Would you like it to?

• *Assistance*: How can I/we assist you to address this part of your identity as part of your treatment or supports?

Person-centered planning processes, including all of a person's areas of interest, hopes, and supports, also become a natural and obvious way of addressing needs and interests related to spirituality, which may or may not have anything to do with involvement in faith communities. This can mean letting a person invite people from one's faith community or others to whom one turns for guidance and authority into those planning processes. The impact of having a number of people in one's life, from family and friends to social networks to professionals, is a tremendous asset to individuals with disabilities and their families.

Assessing or engaging spiritual supports is a life-long process. Reaching out for spiritual support (or spiritual supports reaching toward a parent or person) may occur at the physical, psychological, and spiritual crisis of diagnosis and onset. It can also occur in periods of transition, as a counterbalance to times of isolation into segregated services to enhance community inclusion, as a resource for building networks as a young adult seeks employment, or simply as one community place where gifts can be shared and contributions recognized through volunteer and leadership roles. Rituals of transition and community belonging, such as First Communion, confirmation, and Bar or Bat Mitzvahs (see, for example, the documentary *Praying with Lior*; Trachtman, 1998) can be amazing and wonderful community ceremonies that contribute to psychological and spiritual well-being, personal identity, and social connections. Spirituality can be a component in building culturally sensitive supports and an area of supports that contribute, in many ways, to someone's right to choice and self-determination, as well as to their quality of life. Finally, spiritual supports can be a crucial resource at multiple points of loss and grief.

Addressing spiritual supports effectively also means recognizing that faith communities are developing a huge variety of resources and strategies for including people with disabilities and their families. All of those communities, of course, have regular forms of individual and communal acts of forgiveness and gratitude. Theologians and others are building a growing body of literature coming out of the intersection of spirituality, theology, and disability. Writers and researchers in both spiritual supports and other human service disciplines are beginning to explore the role of spirituality and spiritual supports in the lives of people with intellectual disabilities and their families. As hinted in this chapter, intriguing areas include exploring the impact of spiritual supports on "challenging behaviors" and quality of life. Parents and professionals in other disciplines are developing resources to guide agencies, families, and faith communities in the development of spiritual supports through partnership and collaboration (Carter, 2007).

Fourth, I would offer the psychological construct or human dimension of spirituality as one that professionals in many of the human sciences and services can utilize to reframe their own understanding of what it means to be "professional." "Professional" should mean understanding and skills, but it does not mean having all the answers, never being wrong, or holding most of the power and control. It is, as most know, an identity that includes intellect, theory, and heart, such as compassion and empathy, but it can also mean acknowledging the ways that our own spirituality is integrated and infused in our professional roles. What motivates and sustains us? Does assessment and professionalism always imply objectivity and distance, rather than, as the Latin root to assessment means, "sitting next to," an affirmation of the gift and need for trusted, vulnerable, intimate, and long-term presence (Hilsman, 1997)?

One of the greatest and most powerful strengths and gifts a professional can give others is his or her belief and faith in the capacity of the person they are supporting and serving, a gift that can precede as well as come from professional and personal gratitude for the gifts received from those who professionals support and serve. Pastoral theologian Henri Nouwen (1983), who spent the last ten years of his life living at Daybreak, the L'Arche communities in Toronto, says it profoundly in his book entitled *Gracias*:

> The great paradox of ministry, therefore, is that we
> minister above all with our weakness, a weakness
> that invites us to receive from those to whom we go.
> The more in touch we are with our need for healing

and salvation, the more open we are to receive in gratitude what others have to offer us. The true skill of ministry is to help fearful and often oppressed men and women become aware of their own gifts, by receiving them in gratitude. In a sense, ministry becomes the skill of active dependency: willing to be dependent on what others have to give but often do not realize they have.

Coming from a completely different discipline, participatory research and practices in international community and economic development, Robert Chambers (1999) asserted that the hardest task for any program seeking to facilitate self-determination and empowerment of those in need is not that of "putting the last first" but, as his title asks, *Whose Reality Counts? Putting the First Last*. In other words, it is learning how to relinquish power and control and get out of the way.

Gratitude for gifts received is one character trait and skill that the relatively new construct of positive psychology brings to professional identity and supports. The core construct, or one might say "belief," of positive psychology is that social and scientific constructs too often limit and disable others rather than allying with their capacities to survive, grow, and flourish. Positive psychology, old and new traditions of religious faith, and ancient and modern practices and expressions of spirituality all have the potential to collaborate in ways that (a) can help us forgive others and ourselves; (b) help us repent, in the Talmudic *teshuva* meaning of that term, of theories, practices, and policies that have been far too misguided at times; and (c) help all of us, including people with intellectual and developmental disabilities, their families, and friends, be grateful for the gifts that everyone brings to relationships of care, support, and love.

Notes

1 Forgiveness quotes are from http://forgivenessweb.com..
2 http://www.spiritualityandhealth.duke.edu/ and http://www.gwish.org.
3 I am intentionally using the word "healing" again, because explorations of spirituality and healing, even psychological healing, note the distinction between healing and cure.

References

Artson, J. (2011). You have probably never met anyone like me. Available at http://mentschen.org/2011/03/22/you-have-probably-never-met-anyone-like-me.

Briggs, K. (2008). *The power of forgiveness* (p. 10). Based on the documentary, *The power of forgiveness*, by Martin Doblemeir. Minneapolis: Fortress Press.

Brock. B. (2011). Is disability a spiritual gift? Unpublished paper distributed at the Third Conference of the European Society for the Study of Theology and Disability. University of Aberdeen, Scotland.

Carter, E. (2007). *Including people with disabilities in faith communities: A guide for service providers, families, and congregations*. Baltimore: Brookes Publishing.

Chambers, R. (1999). *Whose reality counts? Putting the first last*. London: Intermediate Training Technology Publications.

Dryden, J. Quotation from The Forgiveness Web. http://www.forgivenessweb.com/RdgRm/Quotationpage.html Accessed 01/29/2013

Enright, R. (2001). *Forgiveness is a choice*. Washington DC: American Psychological Association.

Enright, R. (2008). Forgiveness as a field of inquiry. In Briggs, K. (Ed.), *The power of forgiveness* (pp. 52–53). Minneapolis: Fortress Press.

Fitchett, G. (1993). *Assessing spiritual needs: A guide for caregivers*. Minneapolis: Augsburg/Fortress Press.

Forest, M., O'Brien, J., & Pearpoint, J. (1998). *PATH: Planning positive possible futures*. Toronto: Inclusion Press.

Frank, A. (1995). *The wounded storyteller: Body, illness, and ethics*. Chicago: University of Chicago Press.

Frank, A. (2004). *The renewal of generosity: Illness, medicine, and how to live*. Chicago: University of Chicago Press.

Frost, R. (1949). *Complete Poems of Robert Frost*. New York: Holt, Rinehart and Winston.

Gaventa, W. (2005). A place for all of me and all of us: Rekindling the spirit in services and supports. *Mental Retardation, 43*(1), 48–54.

Gaventa, W. (2006). Defining and assessing spirituality and spiritual supports: Moving from benediction to invocation. In H. Switzky & S. Greenspan (Eds.), *What is mental retardation: Ideas for an evolving disability in the 21st century* (pp. 151–166). Washington, DC: American Association on Intellectual and Developmental Disabilities.

Hilsman, G. (1997). Spiritual pathways: One response to the current standards challenge. *Vision. Newsletter of the National Association of Catholic Chaplains*. June, pp. 8–9.

Kushner, H. (1981). *When bad things happen to good people*. New York: Random House.

Luskin, F. (2002). *Forgive for good. A proven prescription for health and happiness*. San Francisco: Harper Press.

Mcknight, J., & Kretzman, J. (1993). *Building communities from the inside out: A path toward finding and mobilizing a community's assets*. Evanston, IL: Northwestern University.

Montgomery, C. (1999). Thanksgiving/Easter 1998. *Journal of Religion, Disability, and Health, 3*(2), 5–14.

Nouwen, H. (1983). *Gracias: A Latin America journal*. New York: Harper and Row.

Palmer, P. (1986). Keynote address, Merging Two Worlds Conference. Rochester, New York. CD available from Bill Gaventa, bill.gaventa@umdnj.edu.

Patterson, D. (1970). *Helping your handicapped child*. Minneapolis: Augsburg Press.

Reinders, H. (2000). *The future of the disabled in liberal society*. South Bend, IL: University of Notre Dame Press.

Rocca, F. Forgiveness expert explores religious dimension. *Christian Century*, March 22, 2011.

Summers, J. A., Behr, S. K., & Turnbull, A. P. (1988). Positive adaptation and coping skills of families who have children with disabilities. In G. H. S. Singer & L. K. Irvin (Eds.), *Support for caregiving families: Enabling positive adaptation to disability* (pp. 27–40). Baltimore, MD: Brookes Publishing.

Trachtman, I. (2008). *Praying with Lior*. Ruby Pictures.

Tutu, D. (1999). *No future without forgiveness*. New York: Doubleday.

Career Development and Career Thoughts

Salvatore Soresi, Laura Nota, Lea Ferrari, *and* Teresa Maria Sgaramella

Abstract

Positive psychology, counseling psychology, and psychology of integration can form the basis for a new way of thinking about the development of and professional planning for individuals with disabilities. An examination of important journals on career counseling, rehabilitation, and positive psychology showed that few research studies are actually interested in career counseling and that little consideration has been given by vocational guidance practitioners to the problems perceived by individuals with disabilities. Referring to the sociocognitive model, learning theory, and the more recent life design approach, this chapter focuses on the way people represent work and their own future and on how vocational guidance and disability experts could collaborate with these individuals to plan an adequate and satisfactory professional future for themselves.

Key Words: positive psychology, career counseling, vocational guidance, inclusion, disability, satisfaction, career development, sociocognitive, learning theory, life design

The new century is characterized by factors of globalization, internationalization, and rapid technological progress. These phenomena will inevitably and significantly influence the ways in which people perform and experience their jobs. In fact, jobs are now less well-defined and predictable, and work transitions occur more frequently and present more difficult challenges (Savickas et al., 2009) than ever before. In the richest countries, and especially in Western countries, over the past decade only 40% of workers have been regularly employed, with the remaining 60% being employed at contract work, especially short-term or subcontract jobs or through outsourcing (Savickas, 2008). Against this background, the idea of a linear professional career, with initial training, a brief period devoted to work inclusion, and the subsequent attainment of a stable position with an open-ended contract, becomes, if not unrealistic, at least very difficult to realize (Kuijpers, Schyns, & Scheerens, 2006).

This working reality seems to be characterized especially by the following factors:

1. *Internet-based technology.* The Internet has drastically changed people's way of communicating, buying, and working. In recent years, the labor market has massively resorted to Internet management—and will increasingly do so in the future—organized around networks and using less rigid hierarchies built on partnership and aliases.

2. *Multiethnicity.* Our societies are becoming increasingly more multiethnic, and people's cultural references will become increasingly heterogeneous, even in those countries that traditionally have not been affected by immigration and multiculturalism. Those who wish to actively and productively participate in these contexts must learn to be inclusive and respect diversity in the workplace.

3. *Global competition.* Global competition is particularly noticeable in production and

trading. That said, not only do manufacturing processes tend to migrate toward the East, but also those business activities that do not require face-to-face interactions with clients or that involve considerable spreading and processing of information (Cascio, 2010). This not only has reduced job vacancies, but has also significantly changed the types of jobs available. Job seekers need to have high skill levels and specific knowledge and competencies that only years of training can guarantee. People from disadvantaged sociocultural backgrounds and those who, for a number of reasons, have few abilities at their disposal will find it increasingly difficult to access the world of work in the future.

This new scenario demands that young people be more proactive when planning their futures, constructing their professional lives, and acquiring "occupational adaptability"—that is, the ability to deal adaptively with changes using versatility, flexibility, time perspective, and optimism (Savickas, 2005; Savickas et al., 2009).

In today's economic climate, we see evidence of the "butterfly effect"; that is, a butterfly fluttering its wings in one part of the world could, through cause and effect, produce a hurricane in another. In the realm of career development, these butterfly effects are more likely to be environmental and financial crises. But, as volatile as the present global economic and structural system is, it also can afford us the opportunity to think about career development from a more optimistic and positive perspective when planning and constructing a quality future for people with disabilities; like the butterfly effect, the smallest and earliest interventions and changes could trigger positive, potentially important developments over time.

Being able to think in terms of the butterfly effect within the domains of education and rehabilitation is appropriate because it can enhance the positivity, confidence, and hope of people who are engaged in increasing the levels of autonomy, self-determination, and participation for people with disabilities. Without underestimating the effects of an individual's past experiences and contexts (family, school, work, social) and the presence of disability, and also taking into account the limits of our rehabilitation abilities, the butterfly effect can keep us from falling into the trap of negativity and increase the sense of possibility and hope (Bussolari & Goodell, 2009; Soresi & Nota, 2010).

All this is important because people with disabilities must be encouraged to think more about the future, rather than concentrate on the past or on the barriers and obstacles they encounter every day because of impairments. Paying too much attention to obstacles is not very helpful when the main focus should be on vocational guidance and professional planning, which need the mobilization of resources, opportunities, and possibilities that have to be sought and created when they are not readily available.

With reference to vocational guidance and work inclusion, this means that a considerable change of course is necessary, given the limited interest to date in working opportunities for people with disabilities. In many places, people with disabilities are still considered unable to look after themselves, unable to be productive, and even less able to make autonomous choices or pursue professional projects that can be satisfactory from a personal and social point of view.

Having a disability has often resulted in less than advantageous options from career counseling and guidance, options typified by special settings, "segregated" learning experiences, and the bureaucracy of educational, social, and healthcare service systems. These interactions and limited opportunities often serve to reduce the development of social, problem-solving, and decisional competencies (Luzzo, Hitchings, Retish, & Shoemaker, 1999) and to entail less exposure to different work role models and fewer opportunities to undertake efficacious exploration activities (Szymanski, 1999).

Positive psychology, counseling psychology, and a psychology of integration and inclusion can form the basis for a new way of thinking about career development and professional planning for people with disabilities.

As evidenced by this text, positive psychology is fostering change in the focus of research with regard to people with cognitive, sensory, and motor disabilities. If, traditionally, research on people with disabilities has been primarily focused on functional deficits and on the negative outcomes that ensue from these deficits (e.g., learned helplessness, negative perceptions of control, and academic failure), positive psychology, as a component of the "emerging disability paradigm" (Schalock, 2004, p. 204), stimulates a new conception of personal well-being in these people. There is a growing body of research on promoting strengths in adolescents with disabilities (Clark, Olympia, Jensen, Heathfield, & Jenson, 2004; Grant, Ramcharan, & Goward, 2003; McCullough & Huebner, 2003) that suggests that positive psychology is undergirding an emphasis on the importance of building on positive characteristics as a means to promote more positive outcomes for adolescents, both with and without disabilities.

Within a psychology of vocational guidance, Savickas (2003) has already noted that what positive psychology pays attention to in fact characterizes the core of the developing professional identity and that many pioneering works have already highlighted that educational and career success leads to better quality of life. Eggerth (2008) underlined the fact that attention devoted to job satisfaction, to goal directedness and goal attainment, to work—which affects so many life areas—and to the fact that these aspects are all related to general well-being, should allow vocational psychology to be viewed as central to positive psychology. Results from a meta-analysis have showed a significant correlation (0.44) between job and life satisfaction (Tait, Padgett, & Baldwin, 1989). Although that correlation is not causation, when we reflect on the several life areas influenced by work, it would seem that job satisfaction plays a significant role in non–work-related life satisfaction.

Wolf-Branigin, Schuyler, and White (2007) emphasize that developing a positive attitude toward employment provides a vital link to work readiness and that an essential component of developing a positive career attitude in adolescents with disabilities is to put these youths on an age-appropriate trajectory similar to that of their peers without disabilities. The intervention components are aimed at building resilience in the adolescents involved, and the authors addressed resilience using a strength-based perspective to prepare adolescents who may have to face serious difficulties as adults with the necessary ability to recover from and cope with stress.

In describing career counseling approaches for young adults with disabilities, Dunn and Brody (2008) suggested that it is important to assess not only student limitations but also individual strengths and the environment in which a young person lives and functions. A psychology of inclusion argues for the unquestioned superiority of inclusive environments over those modalities that envisage "separate" or "special" ways of dealing with the career issues of individuals with disabilities and in providing vocational guidance and professional training (Nota, Soresi, Ferrari, & Wehmeyer, 2007; Soresi, 2007a; Soresi, Nota, & Wehmeyer, 2011). Promoting inclusion requires access to and the possibility of being part of the community where one lives; at the same time, inclusion must pay attention to the way of life and needs of all of the community's members (Bunning & Horton, 2007).

Furthermore, promoting the inclusion of people with disabilities requires considering the type and level of participation needed in relation to the person's life phase: school inclusion is obviously related to child development and adolescence, and work inclusion to adult life.

In the next sections, we first examine to what extent research in rehabilitation is actually interested in career counseling and how much consideration vocational guidance practitioners give to the problems perceived by people with disabilities. Then we focus on the way people represent work and their own future and on how vocational guidance and disability experts could collaborate to help people with disabilities plan an adequate and satisfactory professional future for themselves.

Choice and Thoughts about the Future of People with Disabilities

To enable people with disabilities to make choices about and realize their professional and work lives, vocational guidance must be able to personalize its interventions so that they are congruent with the characteristics and needs of those who receive them. In line with this conviction, the International Conference of the International Association for Educational and Vocational Guidance (IAEVG) held in Padua, Italy in 2007 made "diversity" its core issue. In delivering the greetings of the Italian Society for Vocational Guidance (SIO) and of the University of Padua, Salvatore Soresi (Soresi, 2007b) noted that *diversity* can refer to very obvious differences, like gender differences or those due to disability or learning difficulties, but can also refer to differences due to socioeconomic, ethnic, cultural, religious, and linguistic reasons. Some of these conditions describe people who have been traditionally labeled as "special types," placed at the extremes of the Gaussian curve and mostly excluded from the standardization samples of our assessment instruments and professional planning. In addition, the idea of diversity must encompass both differences so conspicuous that one would be particularly shortsighted not to see them, as well as others more subtle, which need decidedly remarkable sensitivity and observational acuity to be recognized. Those who express a professional interest in knowing and helping people must be sensitive to even the smallest and best disguised differences and must use approaches, assessment procedures, and interventions capable of responding to them in a personalized way. This must be considered the *normality of vocational guidance* (Soresi & Nota, 2010).

At the International Conference a few years ago, the debate among scholars was lively and productive. But how much of this debate can be seen in the scientific literature? To find out, we looked at three different types of scientific journals:

1. Those especially devoted to vocational guidance and professional development

2. Those addressing issues associated with disability and rehabilitation, given that inclusion and job placement are the most operationally tangible indicators of successful rehabilitative and inclusionary programs (Cappa et al., 2003; Cicerone, 2005)

3. Those that bring together the scientific contributions inspired by positive psychology, which, by emphasizing people's potentials, strengths, optimism, aspirations, interests, and hopes, should pay attention also to those individuals who have limitations and difficulties

When available, the impact factor, a quantitative index used to compare journals and reflecting the average number of times articles from a journal have been cited normally in the past 3 years, is reported. The following journals were examined:

1. With regard to vocational guidance and professional development:

• *The Journal of Vocational Behavior* (*JVB*), which, since 1971, has published empirical, methodological, and theoretical articles that expand knowledge about vocational choice and vocational adjustment across the lifespan. Topics covered are general categories of career choice, implementation, and vocational adjustment and adaptation (impact factor: 2.604).

• *The Career Development Quarterly* (*CDQ*), which is the official journal of the National Career Development Association (NCDA). Topics covered are career counseling, individual and organizational career development, work and leisure, career education, career coaching, and career management (impact factor: 1.345).

• *Journal of Career Assessment* (*JCA*), which, since 1993, has published articles focusing on the processes and techniques by which counselors gain understanding of the individual faced with making informed career decisions. Topics covered are the various techniques, tests, inventories, rating scales, interview schedules, surveys, and direct observational methods used in scientifically based practice to provide an

improved understanding of career decision making (impact factor: 1.639).

• *Journal of Career Development* (*JCD*), which, since 1972, has published articles focusing on career development theory, research, and practice. Topics covered are career education, adult career development, career development of special needs populations, career development and the family, and career and leisure (impact factor: 1.050).

Two other journals were included because they represented the European point of view: the *British Journal of Guidance and Counselling* (*BJGC*) and the *International Journal for Educational and Vocational Guidance* (*IJEVG*):

• Since 1973, the *BJGC* has published articles focusing on theory and practice of guidance and counseling, the provision of guidance and counseling services training, and professional issues (impact factor: 0.403).

• The *IJEVG* promotes the importance of educational and vocational guidance throughout the international community. Since 2001, it has published articles focusing on work and leisure, career development, career counseling and guidance, and career education.

With regard to the issues associated with disability, we examined the following four journals:

• *Journal of Intellectual Disability Research* (*JIDR*), published in association with the International Association for the Scientific Study of Intellectual and Developmental Disabilities (IASSIDD). Issues range from clinical case reports to experimental studies on cognitive and functional profiles, to theoretical analyses, experimental studies, pathological reports, and biochemical investigations (impact factor: 1.596).

• *American Journal on Intellectual and Developmental Disabilities* (*AJIDD*; formerly the *American Journal on Mental Retardation*). The *AJIDD* publishes critical research in biological, behavioral, and educational sciences (impact factor: 2.507).

• *Intellectual and Developmental Disability* (*IDD*), published by the American Association on Intellectual and Developmental Disabilities (AAIDD). Issues dealt with range from life science biology and neuroscience to behavioral and health sciences as they relate to intellectual and related disabilities (impact factor: 1.13).

• *Brain Injury*, which began publication in January 1997. The journal focuses on neuropsychological rehabilitation and, more generally, on rehabilitation therapy. It involves all aspects of acquired brain injury, from basic scientific research and assessment methods to rehabilitation and outcome (impact factor: 1.750).

We also examined four representative journals of rehabilitation:

• *Rehabilitation Counseling Bulletin* (*RCB*), a journal devoted to rehabilitation therapy, which started in January 1990. It publishes articles, commentary, essays, reviews, and research articles addressing and examining all aspects of rehabilitation counseling, the presentation of innovative techniques or applications, debates on controversies challenging the profession, and essays on important ethical dilemmas when counseling clients, as well as articles on clinical problem solving in case micromanagement (impact factor: 0.74).

• *Rehabilitation Psychology*, which debuted in 1954, is the official journal of Division 22 (Rehabilitation Psychology) of the American Psychological Association. Its objective is to develop the science and practice of rehabilitation psychology by addressing the biological, psychological, social, environmental, and political factors that affect the functioning of persons with disabilities or chronic illness (impact factor: 1.676).

• *Journal of Vocational Rehabilitation* (*JVR*), which, since 1994, has covered major areas of vocational rehabilitation. Its emphasis is on articles that have immediate application for rehabilitation professionals providing direct services to people with disabilities. The *JVR* is associated with the Association for Persons in Supported Employment (APSE).

• *Disability and Rehabilitation*, established in 1978, is an international journal that works to encourage a better understanding of disability and of rehabilitation science, as regards the practice and policy aspects of the rehabilitation process (impact factor: 1.395).

With regard to journals that focus on positive psychology themes, we selected the three guild journals included in PsycINFO:

• *The Journal of Positive Psychology* (*JPP*) is an interdisciplinary journal started in 2006;

it focuses on the science and application of positive psychology. Topics covered are human strengths and virtues, personal and social well-being, and the application of positive psychology to psychotherapy and counseling, teaching, and coaching.

• *The Journal of Happiness Studies* is an interdisciplinary journal that, since 2000, has published articles on the scientific understanding of subjective well-being. Topics covered are cognitive evaluations of life, such as life satisfaction; affective enjoyment of life, such as mood level; appraisal of life-as-a-whole, such as job-satisfaction; and the perceived meaning of life (impact factor: 2.104).

• *The International Journal of Qualitative Studies on Health and Well-Being* (*QHW*) is an interdisciplinary journal that, since 2006, has published articles using rigorous qualitative methodology that are of significance for issues related to human health and well-being.

Using PsycINFO, we examined all articles published by each journal from 2000 to 2010. To identify contributions on disability, we used the following three keywords: *disabilities* (including reading disabilities, learning disabilities, sensory disabilities, disabilities, disability, multiple disabilities, developmental and acquired disabilities, physical and cognitive disabilities), *mental retardation*, and *handicap*. To identify the contributions focused on career counseling and professional development, we used the following four keywords: *vocational* (included vocational education, vocational counselors, vocational rehabilitation, vocational maturity), *career* (or occupations), *job* (or occupation), and *interests* (included occupational interests). We combined our keywords (e.g., *career counseling* AND *career development in individuals with disabilities*) to begin our search.

After identifying articles that addressed the interaction among vocational guidance, career counseling, and disability, we read the abstracts to see which contributions explicitly referred to the constructs of interest for positive psychology. In so doing, we followed the work of Hart and Sasso (2011) and Lopez et al. (2006), who deem the following constructs as particularly representative of this perspective: (1) resilience; (2) happiness; (3) life satisfaction; (4) character, strengths, and virtues; (5) meaning and purpose in life; (6) flourishing/thriving; (7) good life; and (8) life worth living. Although the results of our research are not comprehensive of all the literature, we believe that they are representative of a large body of research on positive psychology that taps both career counseling and the fields of professional development, disability, and rehabilitation.

The data collected confirm that the major journals on positive psychology pay little attention to disability issues. Indeed, only four such articles appeared among the 582 published in the period we examined (0.7%; see Table 17.1). More attention seems to have been paid to professional development in general (31 articles [5.3%]). However, none of these articles addressed the issue of career counseling and professional development for people with disabilities.

With regard to vocational guidance journals, over the 10-year period considered, we found only 11 articles (0.5%) that focused simultaneously on issues of vocational guidance and issues of disability among the total 2,225 published (see Table 17.1).

After reading the abstracts, we agreed that only 5 of the 11 articles actually focused on positive psychological themes and that only 3 of the 8 categories identified were used. One article in the *JVB* focused on employee satisfaction and was included in the Life Satisfaction category. One article in the *JCA* that focused on dysfunctional career thoughts and adjustment and an article in the *BJGC* on job-seeking self-efficacy were included in the Resilience category. One article in the *JCD* and one in the *CDQ* that focused on meaning of work were included in the Meaning and Purpose in Life category. The same criterion was then used in the second part of the search for works in the literature.

The scant amount of contributions found in the literature we had selected, published in different journals and in different years, prevent us from considering incremental trends over the past few years in studies seeking to address the vocational

guidance issues of individuals with disabilities. We could, however, address this by resorting to the positive psychology constructs represented. Pursuing this line of inquiry, a similar picture emerged from the analysis of the published articles in the journals we had selected as regards disability and rehabilitation issues.

The total number of papers focused on positive psychology, career/vocational guidance, and disability was 17 out of 7,088 (0.24 %), excluding those papers that dealt with the analysis of supported employment.

As can be seen in Table 17.2, more articles were found in the rehabilitation journals. Most of these either described the profiles of youths and adults with disabilities rather than positive psychology dimensions, or they analyzed some variables affecting the development of the dimension considered. Only 3 out of 13 articles focused on training programs. In two cases, positive psychology dimensions were used as outcome measures and, in one case, as the content of the training activities.

Although it seems apparent that interest has been low in the issues we are dealing with, it may be a good omen for the future that most of the relative contributions (13 out of 17) were published in the past 4 years (Table 17.3).

Three main themes were found. According to the classification system of Hart and Sasso (2011) and Lopez et al. (2006), the most frequent themes drawn from positive psychology were *character, strengths, and virtues* (seven papers), mostly in the rehabilitation journals; *meaning and purpose in life* (six papers), across all journals; and *resilience* (four papers) in the rehabilitation journals. The main themes from career guidance were *career exploration, thoughts, success,* and *decision*. Positive psychology

Table 17.1 **Number of articles published in the decade 2000–2010 on vocational guidance and career counseling and on professional development with persons with disabilities**

	JVB	CDQ	JCA	JCD	BJGC	IJEVG	JPP	The Journal of Happiness Studies	QHW	Total
Articles published in the decade 2000–2010	739	317	318	223	477	151	179	308	95	2,807
Articles interested in vocational guidance and disability	1	4	2	3	1	0	0	0	0	11

JVB, The Journal of Vocational Behavior; CDQ, Career Development Quarterly; JCA, Journal of Career Assessment; JCD, Journal of Career Development; BJGC, British Journal of Guidance and Counselling; IJEVC, International Journal for Educational and Vocational Guidance; QHW, International Journal of Qualitative Studies on Health and Well-Being.

Table 17.2 Number of articles focusing on positive psychology and career counseling in the rehabilitation and in the disability journals analyzed

	RCB	JVR	Rehab. Psych.	Disability and Rehab.	JIDR	AJIDD*	IDD**	Brain Injury	Total
Total number of articles published in the journal	382	490	600	2,276	839	512	562	1,427	7,088
Articles focused on career counseling, positive psychology, and disability	3	6	2	2	1	1	0	2	17

* Previously *American Journal of Mental Retardation*; ** previously *Mental Retardation*.
RCB, Rehabilitation Counseling Bulletin; JVR, Journal of Vocational Rehabilitation; JIDR, Journal of Intellectual Disability Research; AJIDD, American Journal on Intellectual and Developmental Disabilities; IDD, Intellectual and Developmental Disability.

dimensions were involved as predictors of successful vocational development after acquired disabilities in five studies and mainly occurred in journals focused on research in disability.

The overall picture is rather discouraging: those authors publishing in the most highly credited international journals do not seem very interested in positive psychology as it relates to the future of individuals with disabilities nor to their vocational development and professional planning. The reasons for this may vary, such as dealing with and facilitating the work inclusion of these individuals without thinking it necessary to resort first to vocational guidance actions, assuming that vocational guidance deals only with people who have many options from which to choose, and further assuming that this is not the case for people with disabilities.

As far as we are concerned, the field should not forget—both at the research and support planning levels—that the issues of work inclusion and vocational guidance have at least one common area of interest that includes (a) analyzing the individual's wishes, strengths, and occupational expectations; and (b) verifying the characteristics and possibilities of the labor market in a given territory. Both dimensions have to be carefully considered. In addition,

Table 17.3 Number of articles focusing on positive psychology and career counseling per year and themes in the rehabilitation and disability journals analyzed

	JIDR	AJIDD*	IDD**	Brain Injury	RBC	JVR	Rehab. Psych.	Disability and Rehab.
2000								
2001								
2002						1		
2003		1		1	1			
2004								
2005								
2006								
2007							1	
2008					2	3		
2009	1					1	1	
2010				1		1	1	1

*Previously *American Journal of Mental Retardation*; **previously *Mental Retardation*.
JIDR, Journal of Intellectual Disability Research; AJIDD, American Journal on Intellectual and Developmental Disabilities; IDD, Intellectual and Developmental Disability ; RBC, Rehabilitation Counseling Bulletin; JVR, Journal of Vocational Rehabilitation.

if these individuals have the right to prepare themselves to make choices and start professional lives (as regards training, vocational guidance, and occupations), then joint and early action should be taken that actively includes their participation, that of their families, and of the rehabilitation and educational professionals involved. If this is accomplished, career counseling becomes more than simply reciting a person's limited competencies, and the focus instead shifts to more than just job placement (Fabian & Leisener, 2005).

In light of what is highlighted by positive psychology, by research on inclusion, and by recent models that analyze issues of vocational guidance, such as those proposed in social cognitive theory (Lent, 2005; Lent, Brown, Nota, & Soresi, 2003), by the Life Design Group (Savickas et al., 2009), and by other scholars (e.g., Blustein [2006] and Gysbers, Heppner, & Johnston [2009]), it is crucial to identify factors that can affect the professional development of individuals with disabilities and the conditions that must be created to favor their full participation in social and working life. An increasing number of research studies and the revision of existing theoretical models to include those situations experienced by individuals with disabilities or impairments would not only make our reflection on vocational guidance less limited but would also enhance the scientific validity and social relevance of this discipline.

Choice and Thoughts about People with Disabilities: Research Constructs and Data

We believe that vocational guidance that takes into account the supports and accommodations needed for success by people with disabilities should become the norm and, in turn, should benefit from research in vocational psychology (Soresi, Nota, Ferrari, & Solberg, 2008). Currently, however, not many theoretic models within vocational psychology have undergone empirical validation in persons with disabilities (Shahnasarian, 2001).

This is not particularly surprising considering that, as already discussed, not much research deals with the issues addressed here. We were, however, able to find some studies that suggested examining vocational guidance and career counseling for people with disabilities. These studies take inspiration mainly from three important approaches: social cognitive theory (Lent, Brown, & Hackett, 1994), learning theory of career choice and counseling (Mitchell & Krumboltz, 1996), and the life design model.

The Social Cognitive Model

The social cognitive model pivots around the self-efficacy construct, which is assumed to play a crucial role with regard to choice making. People tend to develop interests, including professional ones, in activities they believe they are good at (self-efficacy) and that will allow them to achieve positive results (outcome expectations). On the other hand, people tend to avoid or dislike activities at which they feel incompetent and in which they think they will achieve negative results. Together with self-efficacy and outcome expectations, interests contribute to the choice of activities to carry out (e.g., university majors or professional courses), which, in turn, can support a person in achieving his or her goals. Goals and actions can be affected by contextual influences that may either facilitate or hinder the achievement of one's own goals (Lent, 2007).

Moreover, self-efficacy beliefs play a mediating role in other important components of decision making and academic and professional achievement (Lent et al., 2003; Lent, Brown, Tracey, Soresi, & Nota, 2006).

Data support the influence of self-efficacy on interests and real integration into the world of work in students with learning difficulties, problem behaviors, and psychiatric disorders (Regenold, Sherman, & Fenzel, 1999; Willis, 2002). People with disabilities also seem sensitive to interventions aimed at increasing their efficacy beliefs (Conyers & Szymanski, 1998).

Ochs and Roessler (2004) used the Career Decision Self-Efficacy Scale-Short Form (CDSES-SF; Betz & Taylor, 2001) and the Career Decision-Making Outcome Expectations (CDMOE; Betz & Voyten, 1997) to explore dynamics central to the intention to engage in career exploratory behavior in youths with learning disabilities. The significant, moderate correlational relationships found between and among the constructs of the social cognitive career theory (i.e., career decision self-efficacy and academic and career outcome expectations) confirmed the pattern of relationships found among general and special education high school students (Ochs & Roessler, 2001), undergraduate students (Betz & Voyten, 1997), and middle school students (Fouad & Spreda, 1996), thus suggesting that the constructs are relevant to understanding and facilitating the career development process, independent of disability status. More specifically, the authors found that career decision self-efficacy and career outcome expectations contributed significantly to exploratory intentions in both the special and general education sample.

Lower levels of self-efficacy beliefs are found also among persons with learning difficulties (Soresi & Nota, 2011), and they are the best predictors of their professional interests (Panagos & DuBois, 1999). In this regard, it must be recalled that, within social cognitive theory, interests are seen in light of Holland's (1997) proposed classification, the RIASEC model. The types of interests considered are:

- *Realistic* preferences for activities involving the use of objects, tools, and machinery
- *Investigative* preferences for reality observation and use of scientific procedures of analysis and verification
- *Artistic* preferences for creative abilities that can be verbal, musical, expressive, and the like
- *Social* preferences for activities occurring in contact with others to help, educate, inform, or care for them
- *Enterprising* preferences for activities that influence others in order to gain personal advantages
- *Conventional* preferences for systematic activities and/or data elaboration and storing

Based on the RIASEC model, Nota, Ginevra, and Carrieri (2010) have examined, among other things, the assumptions of social cognitive theory that self-efficacy beliefs could actually predict interests, including the interests of people with disabilities. These researchers involved 129 young adults with intellectual disability. They administered the My Future Preferences structured interview (Soresi & Nota, 2007a), consisting of four parts, with a total of 42 items scored on a 3-point Likert Scale, to investigate career interests and career self-efficacy beliefs. The authors found that, regardless of gender and level of intellectual disability, participants tended to show greater preference and self-efficacy beliefs for occupations in the conventional, realistic, social, and artistic areas, thus showing a less restricted range of interests and self-efficacy beliefs than expected. At the same time, they observed that self-efficacy beliefs were predictive of interests and concluded that, among people with disabilities, there was a relationship among developing self-efficacy beliefs in the ability to do certain activities, being actually able to master these activities, and feeling an interest in such activities (Lent, 2005; Lent et al, 1994; Nota & Soresi, 2000).

In a recent study, Carrieri and Sgaramella (2011) analyzed variables affecting self-efficacy and interests for occupations, trying to parcel out the relationship between these constructs and knowledge about jobs.

Thirty-five adults (22 men and 13 women) with a diagnosis of mild or moderate intellectual disability took part in this study. Knowledge about 12 different occupations, grouped according to Holland's coding scheme, was examined along several dimensions: knowledge perception, familiarity with occupation, training time, earnings, and skills required using the Job Knowledge Interview (JKI; Nota & Soresi, 2009a). A correlational analysis showed that interests and self-efficacy beliefs positively correlated with level of knowledge about occupations. This pattern seems particularly high for well-known jobs; that is, for occupations for which respondents are able to provide more information. The relationship observed among knowledge, interests, and self-efficacy beliefs underlines the importance of an accurate job analysis activity during the vocational assessment process and the relevance of increasing knowledge about occupations in order to enhance self-efficacy.

Learning Theory

Learning theory is another approach that can be used to probe the issues of choice and professional planning. As espoused by Krumboltz and colleagues (Krumboltz, 2009; Mitchell & Krumboltz, 1996), learning theory attributes great importance to so-called dysfunctional thoughts. In this approach, the limitations experienced by people with disabilities can also affect the development of irrational ideas about the self and external reality, which can, in turn, negatively influence the effectiveness of their career choice processes. Doubts about themselves and perceived social expectations can produce a dissonance that increases indecision and prolongs decision times.

The Career Thoughts Inventory (CTI; Sampson, Peterson, Lenz, Reardon, & Saunders, 1996) has been used in most research to examine the impact of "dysfunctional" ideas on the career choice of people with disabilities. This is a 48-item questionnaire that assesses a general index of dysfunctional thinking that can inhibit decision making and career problem solving. It also assesses a series of factors, such as inability to initiate and continue the career decision-making process (Decision Making Confusion Scale); the anxiety that can ensue from perceived difficulty in engaging in specific career choice (Commitment Anxiety Scale); and the inability to balance the input from significant others with one's own preferences, which is expressed through *deresponsibilization* with decision making (External Conflict Scale). The research studies in this area do not yield entirely compatible results.

Strauser, Lustig, Keim, Ketz, and Malesky (2002), for instance, found that students with and without disabilities involved in job placement activities did not show different levels of dysfunctional thinking. Conversely, Dipeolu, Reardon, Sampson, and Buckhead (2002) studied college students with and without learning disabilities and found that those students with disabilities produced fewer dysfunctional career thoughts, had less commitment anxiety, and experienced less confusion about vocational decisions than did their peers without disabilities.

In a nonexperimental descriptive study, Lustig and Strauser (2003) investigated the career thoughts of 132 people with disabilities, classified in three groups: those with dysfunctional thoughts, external conflict, or productive thoughts. Participants characterized by productive thoughts about career showed less decision-making confusion, less commitment anxiety, and less external conflict. The authors emphasized that individuals with similar scores exhibited generally productive approaches to making career decisions, understood how to make a career decision, and typically found the process of making a career decision manageable, independent of disability status. More recently, Yanchak, Lease, and Strauser (2005) compared dysfunctional career thoughts and perceptions of vocational identity in individuals with different types of disabilities and examined whether the relation of career thoughts with vocational identity was moderated by the type of disability. They found that people with physical disabilities showed fewer dysfunctional thoughts than those with cognitive disability, especially with regard to decision-making confusion and external conflict. At the same time, however, they also found that these two groups did not present any differences in perceived vocational identity as measured on the instrument My Vocational Identity (Holland, Daiger, & Power, 1980) and that having a physical or intellectual disability did not affect the way in which dysfunctional thoughts were associated with vocational identity. This led the authors to suggest that individuals may change with regard to their level of dysfunctional thoughts based on their disability, but the way in which the thoughts are associated with vocational identity is similar and is not influenced by the disability itself.

In this vein, researchers at the University of Padua have examined the role played by irrational ideas in the professional outcome of people with and without disabilities. The project involved 54 adults with intellectual disabilities, 25 men and 29 women (mean age = 35.54, standard deviation [SD] = 8.56), and 49 adults without disabilities, 22 men and 27 women (mean age = 32.45, SD = 6.48). They answered the questionnaire Thinking about the Future (Soresi & Nota, 2007b), which measures irrational ideas about the self and the future, and the Job Satisfaction Survey (Spector, 1985, 1997), which measures job satisfaction. Regression analyses showed that job satisfaction was predicted in both groups by propensity to improve oneself and strengthen one's competencies, with 10.3% of variance explained for persons with disabilities and 13.3% for persons without disabilities. Job satisfaction was also predicted by perception of uncertainty and insecurity, with 21.5% of variance explained. These results suggested that thinking it is important to constantly strengthen one's abilities over time and trying to improve by facing problem situations is related to greater perceptions of satisfaction about the environment and work relationships and the financial rewards one does or does not receive. We think these data are interesting not only because they encourage us to resort to more functional ideas of the self and how to represent the future, but also because they are equally shared by people with and without disabilities.

The Life Design Approach

The third model, the life design approach, emphasizes the role of adaptability and time perspective, as well as people's concept of work. This approach (Savickas et al., 2009) maintains that analyzing only attitudes and interests to predict success in a given occupation can be misleading. In fact, the notion that such features can remain stable seems to be no longer generally agreed on because of the swift and massive changes that have taken place in the world of work and education over the past decades. The life design approach emphasizes the strategies necessary for professional planning, problem-solving abilities, the ability to manage socially and financially complex situations, and the skills needed to deal with multiple, changeable, and complex decisional chains that are further complicated by interdependent and nonlinear causalities. Special attention is paid to career adaptability, which is defined as the propensity to suitably deal with developmental tasks to get ready to and participate in a working role, as well as to adapt to unexpected requests ensuing from changes in the world of work and in working conditions (Savickas, 2005). It involves dealing with the professional tasks and role transitions that people have to face and, as a result, the coping strategies needed to deal with these changes. In other words, it focuses on the process through which people actively build their professional lives while they simultaneously face changes and take into consideration the social context in which they live (Karaevli & Hall, 2006; Savickas, 2005).

Savickas (2005, 2010) maintained that career adaptability develops along the following dimensions: (a) concern about the future (by being positively future oriented and feeling concerned about it; being inclined to plan for the future by putting together past, present, and future); (b) career control, by thinking that the future can be controllable to some extent and that it is important to be persistent; (c) career curiosity (i.e., the propensity to explore the environment to acquire information on the self and on the outer world); (d) confidence in one's own abilities, by handling the challenges and overcoming the obstacles and barriers people encounter in pursuing their goals; and (e) cooperation (the ability to cooperate with others in an ever-changing world, sharing and acting for one's own good and that of others to increase the chances of improving the context one lives in) (Nota, Ginevra, & Soresi, 2012; Savickas et al., 2009).

To study this dimension in depth, the Career Adaptability International Collaborative Group was founded in Berlin in 2008 and has investigated the process of making career transitions. It is a large research group that has expanded knowledge on the construct of adaptability and professional transition processes. Its members come from 17 countries and are currently engaged in cross-cultural discussions on instruments that can be used for assessment. Scientists at the University of Padua laboratory have investigated the relationship between adaptability and quality of life in people with and without disabilities in the wake of results obtained by Hirschi (2009), who had emphasized the association between former and current levels of satisfaction experienced by adolescents. We involved 43 participants with intellectual disability (mean age = 34.42; SD = 8.39; 20 women and 23 men) and as many participants without disabilities (mean age = 33.09; SD = 8.92) matched for age, gender, and activities carried out. We asked them to fill out the Satisfaction with Life Scale (SWLS, Pavot & Diener, 1993) and the Career Adapt-Abilities Inventory in its Italian version (Soresi, Nota, & Ferrari, 2012). In both groups, the higher the level of adaptability, the higher the level of satisfaction about quality of life experienced. Further, adaptability has been found to be a significant predictor of quality of life and explained 14% of variance in the group with disabilities and 24% in the group without disabilities.

Among the variables that favor adequate professional planning and that are considered important in the life design approach (Savickas et al., 2009) is the issue of time perspective, which was defined by Savickas (1991) as a mental picture of past, present, and future and as a personal experience of time. This construct is characterized by connection between past, present, and future and also by optimism and hope about the possibility of achieving goals; it denotes the sense of connectedness among events across time. Wolf and Savickas (1985) found that youths who show high levels of time perspective usually attribute their success to their own efforts and abilities and their failures to low levels of commitment. The authors observed that "a more integrated time perspective relates to a facilitative attributional pattern" that "facilitates achievement motivation (i.e., task initiation and persistence) and performance" (p. 477). Ferrari, Nota, and Soresi (2010) found that individuals with greater continuity, who consider the future in a nonfragmented way and project themselves positively into it, see their future as more attainable and are more likely to set career goals, plan, feel in charge of their future, and create conditions for their success by applying themselves in school. Time perspective, therefore, can be considered a prerequisite for making an advantageous choice from the very beginning.

In this connection, Nota, Ferrari, Ginevra, and Soresi (2012) asked 100 adults (mean age = 32.38; SD = 6.36, 54 men and 46 women), 50 with disabilities and 50 without disabilities, matched for age, gender, and activities carried out, to answer the My Present and My Future interview (Soresi & Nota, 2007a). The following sentences were asked: "In five years' time, I would like very much to be and be able to do…" and "In ten years' time, I would like very much to be and be able to do…." In classifying the answers, the main categories emerging in the two groups related to work, private life, and quality of life. A very interesting finding was that about half of the people involved attributed to work an important role in quality of life, and this was so for persons with (42%) and without (52%) disabilities, even if the former group seemed to aim at jobs requiring less training (22% vs. 10%), such as school caretaker, carpenter, waiter/waitress. The participants also said that they would like to have stable relationships (persons with disabilities 8% vs. persons without 14%; i.e., "being a mother and look after my children," "having a wife") and to have hobbies for their leisure time (6% for both persons with and without disabilities). People with disabilities thought it was particularly important to pursue higher levels of autonomy and independence (20% for persons with disabilities vs. 2% for persons without). Such a pattern of results is confirmed also after examining the answers given to the question concerning the more distant future ("In ten years' time I would like very much to be and be able to do…").

Attention to the prospect of having a satisfactory personal and professional life also emerged when studying 35 university students with sensory (20 students) or motor (15) disabilities who participated in a vocational guidance activity organized by the LaRIOS Laboratory (Sgaramella, 2011). In this research, the answers given to questions drawn from the My Present and My Future interview (Soresi & Nota, 2007a) were analyzed. Work was the primary goal for 45% of students with disabilities and for 75.6% for students without disabilities. Additionally, 35% of students with disabilities referenced generic well-being goals and only 17.5% were characterized by absence of plans about career development. A more detailed analysis was carried out on variables that might interfere with the realization of future career plans. Students in both groups reported that lack of motivation, limited interests, or wrong choices may interfere with realization of future plans (32.4% for students with disabilities and 24.2% for students without disabilities). Outer conditions, such as health problems and social attitudes, were perceived as the most frequent external barriers. Students with disabilities ascribed a similar relevance to both personal abilities (20%) and external supports (19%), whereas nearly half of the students without disabilities mentioned personal abilities as facilitating conditions for realizing their career plans (54.05%). The results highlight similarities and differences in career time perspective for students with sensory/motor disabilities and underline the relevance for both groups of career guidance programs aimed at emphasizing and increasing abilities, facilitating realization of preferred activities, and providing means for achieving one's potential. A high proportion of students with disabilities were future oriented (i.e., referred to specific career plans); for instance "I know it will be difficult but I hope I'll find a job in line with my study course," and "in ten years I think I'll have a permanent job and a family."

In general, these results seem to indicate that youths, whether with or without disabilities, share the same wishes and hopes about their future and give importance to essential aspects of their life,

such as having a satisfactory job and experiencing positive family relationships.

The life design perspective emphasizes the active role people play in building their lives and in giving meaning to their choices. Therefore, to answer the question "How may individuals best design their own lives in the human society in which they live?" (Savickas et al., 2009, p. 241), we have to examine more deeply individuals' ideas about work, study, and leisure time and the meaning they attribute to life in terms of these complex aspects. With regard to a definition of work, in his psychology-of-working framework, Blustein (2006) has underlined that work is a social and cultural multidimensional construct that holds a central role in people's lives. It is a means to achieve survival and power, establish social connections, and enhance self-determination (Blustein, 2008; Cohutinho, Dam, & Blustein, 2008). It also has a crucial impact on psychological health and well-being (Blustein, 2008). Middle class and better educated people in modern Western societies see work not only as a means to produce financial advantages, but also as a way to personal realization, to fulfill interests and values, and to use their abilities (Helms & Cook, 1999; Riverin-Simard, 1991; Wilson, 1996). Poorer people, working class people, and people with less education do not often see work as an intrinsically interesting activity and think they have little opportunity for vocational choice (Chaves et al., 2004). Ferrari et al. (2009) underlined that adolescents consider work as associated with economic and psychological advantages and with satisfaction of social values. In addition, work is defined in terms of positive (pleasant, enjoyable, interesting) and negative (tiring, requires sacrifices, etc.) characteristics. Individuals with a more articulate concept of work show better school achievement, tend to use self-regulation strategies, and can gather information when facing a choice. This outcome seems to suggest an association with greater adaptability and the development of a flexible and sophisticated sense of work (Chaves et al., 2004).

It is not clear that youths with disabilities hold similar perceptions of the multifaceted role of work. One study investigating the work concepts of people with intellectual disability was conducted by Cinamon and Gifsh (2004), who interviewed a group of young people with mild intellectual disability (IQ 60–70) attending special high schools. The authors examined the participants' notions of work ("What is your definition of work?" and "Why do people work?"), their knowledge about the reality of work ("What kind of jobs do you know about?" "How should a working person behave?"), and their interests ("Is there any particular job you would like to do?" "Why would you like this job?"). Results revealed that the participants mostly considered work as a source of income or as a way to avoid staying at home with nothing to do and feeling lonely. Moreover, participants had knowledge of only a limited number of occupations, although they were aware of the role that their interests and abilities could play in their school career choices. Most individuals stated that it was important to get to work on time and to be well-groomed and cordial. None considered work as an opportunity for self-realization, as a means to favor social affiliation, or as a way to improve their own knowledge and skills. Neumayer and Bleasdale (1996) examined a group of 30 adults with intellectual disability and obtained highly similar results. Specifically, the questions "What does work mean to you?" and "Is working important to you? Reasons?" elicited answers referring to the fact that working served to make money or gave a person something to do. Most of the participants who were working reported that they would like to change jobs by expressing their personal interests and requesting to be considered for a future job interview. The authors investigated the participants' ideas concerning leisure as a characterizing quality of life factor ("What do you like doing in your free time?"). Participants listed various activities, such as "helping other people," "listening to music," "watching television," "knitting," "getting together with people," "dancing," "working on the computer," "bowling," "going to the cinema," "exercising," and "taking an afternoon nap."

In the wake of these findings, Ferrari, Nota, and Soresi (2008) conducted a study involving 144 participants: 48 participants with intellectual disability, 48 adults without disabilities of the same chronological age as the disabled participants, and 48 adolescents without disabilities of the same mental age as the disabled participants. The authors observed that people with disabilities showed a poorer concept of work, partly distorted by excessive attention to its positive aspects and by scant attention to aspects related to commitment and sense of responsibility. On the other hand, they also mentioned some aspects more often mentioned by participants without disabilities, such as that work allows one to earn money, can enhance a sense of personal satisfaction, and helps avoid boring and unpleasant situations. As for other at-risk categories, in this group it is vital to pay attention to the individual's notion of work

and to encourage a deeper knowledge of working life. It is therefore crucial to promote the capacity to distinguish among the various advantages that work can offer, the commitment work requires, and the different responsibilities that different types of jobs entail. These abilities can be developed by stimulating an analysis of various jobs and by facilitating decisional processes as well.

In analyzing these theoretical models and research conducted on persons with and without disabilities, some basic relationships have been found to be valid for all people. Even though further research and confirmations are needed, preliminary results seem to suggest that the following hold true for people with and without disabilities:

• Thinking themselves able to do some tasks (self-efficacy beliefs) affects the preferences people have about some professional activities (interests), and such perceptions are related to the experiences they make and the knowledge that is stimulated.

• Irrational or dysfunctional thoughts, like thinking one is not a motivated person or able to learn, or that others can make better decisions than oneself, are associated with higher levels of indecision, decisional difficulties, and lower levels of satisfaction.

• The propensity to think "actively" about the future, perceive some sort of responsibility in making it happen, and have confidence in one's own planning ability (adaptability) seems to be related to a better quality of life.

To sum up, even people who were once considered unable to choose and pursue advantageous goals do represent the future for themselves, formulate hypotheses, and have hopes, and, in all that, they also show a certain amount of realism.

Vocational Guidance Actions for People with Disabilities

In our work in career counseling and vocational guidance, we have often emphasized the need to implement rigorously planned interventions that are also legitimized from a scientific and theoretical perspective (Soresi, 2000; Soresi & Nota, 2010). Obviously, this also applies when the career counselor is dealing with persons with disabilities. The literature for professional development emphasizes that personalization is important for every individual. In vocational guidance, as in other psycho-pedagogical areas, diversity—and thus the need to adapt actions to the characteristics of those individuals who are the targets of our professional attention—is the norm. A good indicator of a career practitioners' professionalism is certainly his or her ability to respond to unique personal needs, expectations, and aspirations. Based on this fact, and after proposing a definition of vocational guidance, we will consider some vocational guidance programs that could be successfully implemented, especially in inclusive settings, with persons with disabilities.

What Is Vocational Guidance?

Vocational guidance cannot be seen as a simple operation of diagnosis and classification, nor of superficial and often delayed prognoses. Vocational guidance should promote individuals' actions capable of producing changes in their vocational lives. It can no longer confine itself to intervening at transition times or to making predictions or suggestions on the basis of present appraisal. From the perspective of life design counseling, vocational guidance must be interested in people's future far in advance of when they have to handle the difficulties of transitions, so that their range of opportunities can be increased and special attention can be paid to at-risk situations (Savickas et al., 2009; Soresi & Nota, 2010).

Vocational guidance and career counseling should act in such a way that, during the process, possibilities are enhanced to access the education, information, and conditions that increase vocational development. In doing so, it might be important to aim at the construction of relationships that can originate positive processes that trigger optimism, create a propensity to action, enhance the handling of difficult situations, and promote a sense of efficacy and the ability to analyze reality from diverse viewpoints without being trapped by stereotyped views.

Moreover, vocational guidance should be acknowledged for its preventive role, involving not only professional career counselors, but other people who also play critical roles in child development. The efficacy of vocational guidance could be measured by considering its ability to produce significant changes in the life story conclusions of many individuals— particularly those who seem already predestined to an easily predicted or anticipated outcome (Soresi et al., 2008)—by fostering adaptability, activity, and intentionality.

Efforts in that direction must be intensified so that vocational guidance can acquire scientific and ethical depth, legitimization, social relevance, and preventive value. For this it must (a) be started very early in life, using gradual but continuous programs; (b) be adequately planned so as to be congruent with the different worldviews or contextual environments

of targeted individuals and respectful of the characteristics of the participants; (c) be able to lessen the inhibiting power of obstacles, to remove both personal and social barriers and difficulties; (d) be respectful of individual and cultural differences and adjust to them without hegemonic pretense, with the paramount objective of promoting empowerment, self-determination, and quality of life; and (e) anticipate and stimulate the involvement and participation of those who, because of their own authentic interest (primarily parents and teachers) or because of their own or institutional goals (social and work agencies), could contribute to the spreading of a preventive view of vocational guidance.

Features of Vocational Guidance Interventions

Based on the model to which career counselors anchor their interventions, on the type of client, and on the career problem he or she presents, diverse vocational guidance activities can be implemented. No matter what activity is actually carried out, it must be clear that the idea of action and personalization is implicit in vocational guidance and that success will be more likely with the active involvement of the person for whom the plans are made and inclusive actions are planned.

Vocational guidance that aims at improving the abilities needed for choice and professional realization needs to enable people with disabilities, as early as possible, to:

• Perform self-evaluations and early explorations of the worlds of training and of work
• Know and discuss the "laws" that regulate the so-called professional development and the educational and training environments
• Increase problem-solving abilities in order to facilitate adequate information processing operations and the activation of executive control processes on the actions the person must carry out (gathering information on the self, on the training and labor sectors; processing, storing, and memorizing the most important information; making use of the information gathered in the different steps of career decision making; planning and implementing the choices made).

To realize personalized career guidance intervention, it is paramount that instruments used to implement specific assessment activities on key dimensions in choice and professional planning projects have been validated with persons with disabilities. Some of these instruments have been put together in portfolios, such as Optimist (Soresi & Nota, 2001a), Clipper (Soresi & Nota, 2003), Astrid (Soresi & Nota, 2007a), and Astrid-OR (Soresi & Nota, 2007b), which are all accompanied by manuals for their use. In particular, Astrid contains self- and other-evaluation instruments to be used with individuals with intellectual disability and allows both normative comparisons and criterion assessments. The dimensions considered (both for self- and other-evaluation) concern self-determination, concept of work, interests and professional self-efficacy, perception of barriers and supports, decision and self-confidence, decisional ability, and professional expectations. Along with the description of the variables being investigated, these portfolios include indications for their application and scoring, examples of reports that can be drafted, and indications for the interventions that could and should be realized.

Finally, these interventions have particular importance if they are implemented (as happens with students without disabilities) in typical and integrated school settings. Integrating and involving students without disabilities in such training, planning small-group educational activities, and using teaching techniques that emphasize active participation and strong realism cannot but give a sense of normality to what is proposed and increase the feeling of involvement and motivation in adolescents with disabilities (Nota & Soresi, 2004a,b; Soresi & Nota, 2001b).

Within this perspective, in addition to vocational guidance activities aimed at increasing vocational development, what is often needed most to increase participation is the involvement of significant others who share the same life environments, such as parents, teachers, schoolmates, and service providers. It is important to encourage these stakeholders to support the participation of people with disabilities over time, emphasizing personalization and the abilities needed to overcome biases and stereotypes (Soresi, 2007b).

Such reflections are in line with what Dunn and Dougherty (2005) and Lopez and Edwards (2008) maintained about the rehabilitative actions to be carried out from the perspective of positive psychology. These authors believe it is necessary to engage people in career counseling and vocational guidance through interventions that can enhance human strengths and character and that also emphasize virtues like wisdom, courage, tenacity, perseverance, forgiveness, creativity, and the ability to love. It is necessary to encourage people to engage in responsible behavior toward others by being civil, altruistic, caring, and tolerant, especially toward individuals who face greater difficulties. A positive psychology of rehabilitation should not simply focus on treatment issues or adaptation to disability; it should make the most of people's psychological and social strengths to maintain or boost psychological and physical well-being and to prevent pathology.

Considering some of the variables we have discussed to this point, such as efficacy beliefs and human agency, some programs covered in the literature have been implemented, albeit to a limited extent, with people with disabilities.

Recently, Gorzkowski, Kelly, Klaas, and Vogel (2010) conducted a study in which positive psychology dimensions were used to identify factors that enhance resilience and to compile suggestions for vocational rehabilitation programs. The study was conducted on 97 girls (aged 7–17 years) with an acquired disability (spinal cord injury [SCI]) who had been injured at least 1 year prior to the study. Because of employment barriers, girls with SCI, similar to other women with disabilities, have limited opportunities to experience the self-esteem benefits that come with economic independence (Nosek, Howland, Rintala, Young, & Chanpong, 2001). The authors showed that participating in positive job-related activities—defined as routine tasks that help build job skills—increased quality of life and well-being. Exposure to chores, household responsibilities, volunteer work, and part-time jobs provided these youths with experiences and skills that can be applied to future careers. The authors hypothesized that higher scores on social and job-related participation predicted lower depression and higher quality of life. Overall, it was found that a broader context of social participation and an increased frequency of job-related participation were related to lower levels of depression and to increased quality of life. They suggested that participation in social and job-related activities is relevant to building resilience against future obstacles and to preparing girls for a smooth transition to adulthood.

Breeding (2008) conducted a well-designed proactive intervention study on 20 youths and adults with a variety of disabilities. All participants were given pre- and post-test measures on the Career Decision Self-Efficacy Scale (CDMSE; Betz & Taylor, 2001), which provides information related to gathering occupational information, goal selection, making plans for the future, and problem solving, and on the Work Locus of Control Scale (WLCS; Spector 1988), a measure of control beliefs in work settings. The control group received traditional vocational assessment activities (initial interview, standard functioning and interest assessment), whereas the treatment group received the Work-Interest Profile for Rehabilitation Counseling (WIPRC, Power, 2000; see also Aiken, 2003) intervention. The WIPRC helps clients solve ambivalence by providing a structured method to gain contextual self-understanding related to work interests through direct counselor intervention. In that study, for instance, using questions and directed descriptions, clients were helped to focus and increase their knowledge on a detailed definition of the individual work personality codes; on current legislative opportunities for participation, informed choice, and self-determination; on the exploration of occupations across all functional capacity levels, with the identification of occupations of highest interest; and on identification of a personal profile according to Holland's personality codes (Realistic, Investigative, Artistic, Social, Enterprising, and Conventional), rank ordering the top 10 occupations of interest. Post-test measures showed no significant gain in the empowerment-related variables under investigation (i.e., career decision self-efficacy, work-related locus of control) for those receiving traditional vocational assessment activities, whereas significant gains were found in the group for which proactive assessment was used on overall career decision self-efficacy measures, as well as on specific measurement subscales (i.e., occupational information and problem solving ability). The author concluded that career decision self-efficacy may be enhanced in the assessment setting through proactive interventions designed to increase related contextual self-understanding and career development activities (e.g., finding interesting occupations, accurately assessing personal abilities, selecting a training or career goal). As the author suggests, empowerment-focused rehabilitation counseling should involve deliberate action to foster meaningful participation, informed decision making, and self-determination.

There are, as well, some programs that have not been tested with persons with disabilities, but which involve specific adaptations and personalization and could therefore be used in inclusive settings and involve both adolescents with and without disabilities.

Kush and Cochran (1993), for example, devised a program aimed at helping people think of themselves as the actors of their own actions, experience internal locus of control, choose short- and long-term goals, plan their actions, and monitor their progress. The program is divided into three steps: the first aims at helping participants learn their own interests, strengths (abilities and aptitudes), and values. This is made easier by use of an accompanying booklet, which parents can consult together with their children. The second aim is devoted to the various phases of decision making, and the third examines and suggests the operations that must be activated to plan the actions necessary to carry out the decision. The program was tested with high school adolescents and recorded improved responsibility in youths approaching the issue of choice.

Drawing on Bandura (1995, 1997) we devised an intervention, *First commandment: I believe in myself... also because it is in my interest* (Nota & Soresi, 2000), which fosters adolescents' self-reflection and ability to analyze behaviors and experienced situations. It also encourages them to recognize the cognitive processes that are implied in controlling negative thoughts and in decision making, to manage some negative emotional states, to plan and set goals, and to select more adaptive ways to analyze and manage difficult situations and choices. The instrument envisages a number of meetings for personalized supervision with each adolescent involved in the intervention in order to verify and support the efforts made to strengthen self-efficacy beliefs in a specific area. It is composed of 14 didactic units:

1. Introduction to the course and presentations
2. Self-efficacy beliefs
3. How to evaluate one's self-efficacy beliefs
4. We are all different... also as regards self-efficacy
5. How to develop self-efficacy beliefs
6. Self-efficacy, objectives, and aspirations
7. Self-efficacy and professional interests
8. Learning and human behavior
9. Choice and analysis of one's objectives
10. Pursuing one's objectives
11. Choice of models
12. Social persuasion and self-efficacy
13. How to get reinforcements and gratifications
14. How to plan to increase one's self-efficacy beliefs

To verify the efficacy of the intervention, the questionnaire "How Much Confidence Do I Have in Myself?" (Soresi & Nota, 2003), which investigates middle school students' self-efficacy beliefs, was used both at pre- and post-test with experimental and control groups. Results indicated that youths receiving the curriculum reported higher levels of self-efficacy about their choice abilities; their abilities to manage difficult situations; to complete difficult, demanding tasks; and to be successful (Nota, Soresi, & Ferrari, 2008).

Addressing dysfunctional thoughts, Yanchak et al. (2005) maintained that it is important to work with students with learning difficulties to develop abilities to search for occupational information (e.g., job descriptions) and to categorize the information according to work preferences (e.g., outdoor work vs. indoor work). This type of exercise allows students to make career decisions based on concrete occupational information. Decisional abilities should be stimulated by starting with simple career decisions (e.g., designating work preferences) that can increase individuals' confidence in their ability to make more complex career decisions. Counselors should also plan some activities to encourage self-awareness and knowledge of assets, limitations, and preferences, especially functional limitations related to disability type. These should be realized by emphasizing personalization, because a person's vocational identity can be influenced by many factors. For example, a person with mobility impairment may be afraid to establish specific career goals because he or she is worried about transportation or accommodation issues. In addition, because professional identity is closely related to ego identity (Raskin, 1994), confusion about roles may seriously affect career decision making. People who have recently acquired physical disabilities often find it extremely difficult to integrate their disability into their self-identity (Cook, 1998).

Nota and Soresi (1999) devised the program Choice for the Future: No Problem! This intervention aims at increasing school-career decision levels. In devising it, they took inspiration from the research studies on career problem solving carried out by Peterson, Sampson, Reardon, and Lenz (1996) and on career decision making by Gati (1986, 1998). These studies emphasized that, to make conscious and adequate school-career decisions, it is necessary to have, on the one hand, sufficient knowledge about one's own personal characteristics and training and working realities and, on the other, the ability to classify such knowledge, as well as to possess adequate and efficacious decisional processes. In the specific case studied, the intervention was intended to increase students' knowledge of themselves and their professional interests, professional self-efficacy beliefs, academic abilities, professional values, and professional reality. The objective was also to increase knowledge on a range of at least 200 occupations and on the characteristics of the professional approach routes to these occupations. Participants

were taught to set themselves a professional goal while considering the knowledge acquired and to identify several options (professional activities) that would allow them to pursue their objectives, while taking into consideration the information acquired and their specific explorations. Last, they were taught to choose, through the use of compensatory decisional strategies, the most advantageous of the options they had already identified. The intervention consists of 15 didactic units:

1. Presentation of the program
2. Professional interests
3. Efficacy beliefs and professional interests
4. Own school abilities
5. Professional values
6. Own professional characteristics
7. Thoughts about the future
8. Professions and areas of professional interest
9. High schools and areas of professional interest
10. Decision and indecision when facing a school-career choice
11. Professional goals
12. Comparison of options and professional choice
13. Realization of decisions
14. Information sources and possible problems
15. Summing up and conclusion

To verify the efficacy of the intervention with middle school students, the instrument Ideas and Attitude on School-Career Future (Soresi & Nota, 2001a) was used both at pre- and post-test with both experimental and control groups. Results indicated that youths receiving the Choice for the Future: No Problem! program reported higher levels of assurance associated with self-knowledge and academic/vocational reality, higher levels of commitment to and involvement in choice, and better confidence in their own decisional abilities (Nota & Soresi, 1999). In this case, too, by taking into account Yanchak et al.'s (2005) suggestions, specific adjustments and personalization can be devised to implement this intervention with adolescents with disabilities.

A program we are especially proud of is "Plans, Itineraries and Possible Steps... for Your Vocational Projects" (Soresi et al., 2009). It has been tried out with adolescents without disabilities and is presently being tested in inclusive contexts with students with and without disabilities.

The idea underlying this project is that career counselors should select a series of "steps" to be implemented following the list shown in Table 17.4;

Table 17.4 Working session of the "Plans, Itineraries, and Possible steps…for your vocational projects"

- **An important premise:** learn to make choices and plan your future

- **Knowing and rearranging your ideas on the world of work**
  - *The concepts of work, study, and free time*
  - *The analysis of work*
  - *Vocational stereotypes and commonplaces*

- **Knowing yourself to like yourself**
  - *Self-efficacy beliefs*
  - *Vocational interests*
  - *Vocational values*

- **Extending your possibilities**
  - *Open-mindedness, chance, and planning*
  - *Curiosity and exploration*
  - *Creativity*

- **Setting off on the right foot and with grit**
  - *Optimism*
  - *Irrational ideas and "thoughts against" (positive thinking)*
  - *Self-determination*

- **Coping with barriers, difficulties, and problems**
  - *Adolescents' concerns and problems*
  - *From problems to goals*
  - *Decisional strategies*

- **Projecting into the future**
  - *Time perspective and the book of your life*
  - *Vocational goals*
  - *Transition times*

- **Self-regulation: An extra instrument for building your future**
  - *Self-regulation*
  - *Managing your time*
  - *Efficacious studying*

- **Staying with others in a positive and productive way**
  - *Assertiveness at school, at work, and in free time*
  - *How to defend yourself from others*
  - *How to look for help, alliances, and collaborations*

- **Presenting and proposing yourself adequately and efficaciously**
  - *There's only one of me!*
  - *How to prepare for a job interview*
  - *How to write your curriculum vitae.*

this list is based on the characteristics of the people involved, on one's own specific competencies, and on what is considered important by counselors and participants. Such an intervention should be articulated over a number of meetings (we try to have at least 10) and be aimed at strengthening the knowledge and abilities identified as important both by counselors and the clients/users. The training materials used in all the sessions have been compiled into a book, which is available to counselors and clients (Soresi et al., 2009).

For each session, the materials are presented in a series of "packages" called *didactic units*. Each unit includes (a) a brief presentation that describes the aim and contents of the didactic unit, so that participants can decide if that unit is of interest or use to them); (b) a theoretical introduction (under the heading "*a few theoretical nuggets*"), which enlightens participants on what today's international research suggests about the different issues that each didactic unit will cover; (c) some examples and applications (under the heading "*from theory to practice*"), which help the client to make actual use of the theoretical nuggets presented earlier; and (d) drills and suggestions that intend to consolidate and increase client's abilities. It is important to reiterate that people can learn to make choices and decisions and can develop and improve their abilities to formulate plans and realize projects. These skills are analyzed in the program by using the "*Important things I could do…and the sooner I do them…the better!*" section. Each didactic unit ends with a questionnaire ("*I test myself on…*") that summarizes the main issues dealt with in that unit. The aim of the questionnaire is to stimulate verification and consolidation of learning and to allow the client to monitor the route he or she is taking.

Moreover, to encourage further reflection on the activities carried out in each didactic unit, adolescents are given a list of thoughts, proverbs, and sayings to choose from that best describe and represent what they have learned in each meeting. Table 17.5 shows examples of thoughts, proverbs, and sayings, and Figure 17.1 illustrates the materials we developed to promote reflection.

Using these materials, several programs were devised, one of which aimed at strengthening the self-determination and professional planning abilities of a group of 13 adolescents. Qualitative and quantitative analyses were carried out to test the efficacy of the training program. Normative data analysis has underlined that, by the end of training, participants showed higher levels of self-determination to

Table 17.5 Examples of thoughts, proverbs, or sayings

A Thought a Day Keeps Pessimism Away

Every morning when you get up take this page and read a thought.

"Then close your eyes, take a deep breath, and let yourself be inspired by what you have read. Let yourself be run over, engulfed by that thought, and by everything that comes out of it and by what it implies. Let your day be influenced by the sentence you have read, let the hours go by under the banner of that thought. You will find that little by little its effects will soon be felt" (Ballerini, 2009, p. 7).

1. No other day will be like today. (Soho Takuan)

2. Every joy is destined to the happy heart: The sky is full of shadows for those who always wear a hat. (Chinese proverb)

3. There is no road to happiness, happiness is the road. (Buddha)

4. Every difficulty has an opportunity. (Demosthenes)

5. You cannot stop the birds of anxiety and worry from flying over your head, but you can stop them from building their nest there. (Chinese proverb)

6. If you change your attitude toward things, you will change things. (Emil Cioran)

7. Finding important things in life does not mean that you must give up all the others. (Paulo Coelho *Brida*)

8. It is better to believe yourself an acrobat than a dwarf.

9. If at first you don't succeed, you must try and try again.

10. It's all water under the bridge.

11. . . . .

12. . . . .

make decisions without external influences both as concerned school-career choices and leisure. They also showed higher levels of career adaptability and satisfaction. The qualitative analysis of their hopes for the future revealed that the adolescent participants' career goals had become clearer and more articulated, they had outlined the steps needed to achieve their goals, and they attributed more importance to school-career choices and the possibility of self-determination. Overall, compared to preintervention, participants showed an attitude of hope

and confidence in the future and said that they were more inclined to invest in training.

One general characteristic of our program is its use of small-group sessions. Working with groups of participants allows the intervention to be carried out on a larger number of individuals, which makes it less expensive. Moreover, because students can see that others are experiencing the same difficulties as themselves, it helps them consider their situation in a less negative way. Last, techniques that encourage more active participation (e.g., role-play, homework) and that consider real-life difficult situations open the possibility for adolescents to consider many examples of the efficacious management of interpersonal situations that are useful to decision making (Brown & Ryan Krane, 2000; Whiston, 2002).

Involvement of Significant Others: Parents and Teachers

In this context, as well as in other counseling and educational contexts, success is much more likely if support is provided by parents, who, when properly involved, can further promote the professional identity development of their child with disability (Dawn, 2011; Mpofu & Wilson, 2004; Wolf-Branigin et al., 2007, Yanchak et al., 2005) and guarantee greater generalization of the abilities learned during vocational guidance activities. The idea of devising parent-focused training comes from the realization that some parents may find it difficult to accept that their children are becoming adults and that they have the potential to be employed. Others may tend to think that work is only "a way to keep their children busy"; these parents have little confidence in the decisional and productive abilities of their child and may even hinder the search for a job for fear of losing rights and/or Social Security benefits (Coakley, Holmbeck, Friedman, Greenley, & Thill, 2002; Soresi, Nota, & Ferrari, 2007). Counselors should take into account that these parents' wishes can sometimes conflict with the goals of intervention, and they should develop for parents specific informational and educational activities centered on revisiting the idea of work for persons with disabilities and the actions that these parents can take to promote in their child an enhanced sense of self-determination as they approach adulthood, one that favors and supports efficacious work inclusion. Parents should be shown, for example, the crucial issues that are examined with an undecided or insecure individual during career counseling and what they could do to support their children in similar situations.

Envelope for vocational guidance materials

Ticket N. 1

(hand to the "driver", to the "tour operator")

Name and Surname of the "traveler into the future" ____________
Date of filling out ____________
Place of the Course ____________

Fill out

1. **I think the most important thing I learned today is** ....
2. **The most important thing I still would like to learn about how to continue my journey toward the future is** ....
3. **What I liked best today is** ....
4. **During today's meeting I happened to think of** ....
5. **What I will remember best about today is** ....

... a thought a day keeps pessimism away!

Among the vocational guidance materials inside the envelope you have certainly not missed the long list of proverbs, sayings and positive thoughts.

1. Examine them and write down below those that you would associate to the issue of interests. Pick as many as you like, but in any case at least than three:
....

Figure 17.1 Materials used to favor reflections (developed by the authors)

As an example, at the LaRIOS laboratory, Department of Developmental and Socialization Psychology, University of Padua, a group of parents have proposed a program composed of the following didactic units:

1. Overview of the course
2. Career choice and vocational development
3. Self-efficacy beliefs and interests
4. How to make decisions
5. How and when to speak of vocational guidance in the family
6. How to help one's child focus on his or her career goals
7. Irrational ideas
8. How to help one's child get information on vocational options
9. How to help one's child choose among options
10. How to support one's child's self-determination

Teachers

In addition to parents, teachers also play an important role in the life of individuals with disabilities. Alston, Bell, and Hampton (2002) have emphasized that, typically, neither parents nor teachers of individuals with learning disabilities adequately encourage

2. Reflecting on the proverbs, sayings and thoughts that you have just written down, which would you choose as the 'leader' or 'standard-bearer'?
....
Why did you choose that? ....

3. In addition to recalling the issue of interests, the proverbs, sayings and thoughts you have just written down maybe go well together also for other reasons. In your opinion, which could they be?
....
....
....
....

4. If you have filled out the questionnaire "I test myself on vocational interests", write in the boxes corresponding to the questions the number you have given as an answer.

I test myself on vocational interests

1	2	3	4	5	6	7	8
☐	☐	☐	☐	☐	☐	☐	☐

5. If you have followed the suggestions you have been given in these days, you should have chosen some proverbs, sayings or thoughts to use often. Did you do that?
If you did, write them down on this form together with the effects you think they have had on you.

Chosen thought: ....
Effects it has caused ....
....
....
Chosen thought: ....
Effects it has caused ....
....
....
Chosen thought: ....
Effects it has caused ....
....
....
Chosen thought: ....
Effects it has caused ....
....
....
Chosen thought: ....
Effects it has caused ....
....
....

Figure 17.1 (Continued)

these youths to continue with studies that emphasize science or engineering courses because they anticipate difficulties for the student. The idea that the world of work reserves little space for individuals with disabilities, and the propensity to see disability as "something a person has" (as if it was a disease), as a permanent "negative trait," or as a sort of inadequacy that makes people unable to look after themselves and make vocational choices, can diminish efforts to facilitate professional development in students with disabilities and can lower expectations for these students. To discourage such tendencies, teachers should be given specific in-service training that enhances their ability

to see the potential of individuals with disabilities and to support their actions and their efforts.

To examine how teachers represent the future of students with intellectual disabilities, Nota and Soresi (2009b) asked 72 inclusive public school teachers to describe in writing their perception of the future for a hypothetical student with Down syndrome. The authors found that only a minority predicted that such a student would be working in a competitive inclusive setting and that he or she would be self-determining as regards to his or her future. These teachers paid greater attention to the restrictions that disability can imply, and the results reveal a certain tendency to refer to a more traditional way of perceiving disability, one more greatly focused on limitations and deficits (Fabian & Liesener, 2005).

Bearing in mind the research results coming from the vocational guidance field, it seems clear that working toward the professional development of persons with disabilities—in addition to being essential to the overall development of the individual—requires the realization of several conditions, among which are early intervention, personalized services, and concerted action that includes schools, communities, significant others, parents, and teachers. We believe that these conditions are the most important challenges that vocational guidance must face if its role is not to be confined to simply giving support to individuals but promote a supportive and inclusive context (Soresi & Nota, 2010).

Conclusion

Thus far, we have considered the need to offer people with disabilities opportunities to reflect on their professional future by devising the necessary supports to help them realize their aspirations. Here, we underline the importance of quality training in vocational guidance that should be provided for those scholars and practitioners who focus on rehabilitation and social and work inclusion. We believe that the developers of training courses for vocational guidance and rehabilitation practitioners should draw on the assumptions put forward in positive psychology and the vocational sciences to devise materials and curricula that teach counselors how to provide quality services and interventions for this population.

When vocational guidance scholars deal with the career choices of people with disabilities, especially when working in collaboration with services and practitioners that facilitate the development of personal and social autonomy, they should not limit their work to exclusively describe the characteristics, potentials, and preferences of these individuals or the expectations that the different contexts (i.e., parents, teachers) could have. Rather, as Savickas (2007) maintains, they should address ways to help these persons construct their own professional future by teaching them what is necessary to successfully surmount obstacles and barriers.

To respond to these needs, and in consideration of recent recommendations for vocational guidance coming from the European Commission and the Organization for Economic Cooperation and Development, the University Network for Innovation in Guidance (Erasmus Academic Network—NICE), which includes 44 European universities, has been established. The network has been charged with setting up conclusive guidelines on university training in vocational guidance, which European countries will be required to follow. The project envisages the training of vocational guidance practitioners who can help individuals facing issues such as the risk of exclusion from the world of work because of social or cultural disadvantages; going through significant transitions in difficult conditions; having poor personal and occupational planning abilities; having poor propensity to training and in-service training; having low self-efficacy beliefs; facing stereotypes and prejudice; and overcoming social, cultural, and financial barriers. In line with these guidelines, the Italian Network–University Training in Vocational Guidance has been created. Its aim is to make a significant contribution to the development of career guidance in harmony with the European priorities of lifelong learning and lifelong career guidance, in order to train career counselors to work with both individuals and groups, addressing different contexts and the individuals that characterize them socially, economically, and politically. Thus, career counselors will be able to carry out preventive interventions and reduce contextual factors that characterize various barriers (Nota & Ferrari, 2011). This university-based vocational guidance training project includes some specific modules on vocational guidance for individuals with disabilities (at least 40 hours of training) that will address the following: (a) new criteria of analysis on the life conditions of individuals with disabilities (medical as well as ecological-behavioral, sociological, and neuropsychological model; definitions and international classification of disabilities—World Health Organization [WHO] documents, International Classification of Functioning [ICF]; inclusion, integration, and social participation processes); (b) vocational guidance models tested for individuals with disabilities and assessment procedures and instruments to analyze the determinants of career choice (procedures and instruments to assess interests, self-efficacy beliefs, career values, decisional strategies, indecision, adaptability, time perspective, concept of work, study and leisure, self-determination, skills, career barriers and career supports, qualitative procedures); and (c) vocational guidance interventions (procedures of personalized counseling for individuals with disabilities; interventions to strengthen self-determination and decisional abilities of individuals with disabilities; vocational guidance interventions in inclusive school settings; interventions that involve significant others—parents, teachers, social-health service providers—to facilitate professional development). The final part is devoted to inclusion actions within educational and professional contexts.

This type of training should guarantee that career counselors, in addition to possessing the competences necessary to supply guidance and supports to the single individual, should also be able to (a) generate a new culture of career guidance and career development in significant settings (schools, communities, work contexts, health and social services) and as regards important figures (teachers, parents, employers, colleagues, health and social service providers, etc.); (b) analyze the training, work, and community settings frequented by individuals at risk (drop-out youths, immigrants, persons with disabilities, etc.); (c) develop and maintain multiple forms of communication and collaboration with users, professionals, and diverse services; (d) select and analyze risk factors; (e) plan, implement, and realize screening activities aiming at the early detection of risk situations; and (f) plan, implement, and realize early interventions with the selected individuals at risk. To reduce the obstacles and barriers that some people perceive in planning their own future, primary (searching for and eradicate causes), secondary (early diagnosis of at-risk situations), and tertiary (timely intervention on the diagnosed situations) prevention interventions are necessary.

Last, we would like to point out that those who train rehabilitation and vocational guidance and career counseling practitioners should, we believe, envisage specific modules aiming at training in the field. Such modules should favor the analysis of the new definitions of disability and of those theories and approaches that have the strongest empirical relevance, as well as describe the actions that should be implemented. This type of training would help practitioners to work toward guaranteeing users/clients adequate professional development and also help them to collaborate with career counselors to create projects on lifelong career learning for individuals with disabilities.

Sharing the goals and aims of vocational guidance from an inclusive perspective and paying attention to the strengths and possibilities of individuals with disabilities could favor greater cooperation and connection between practitioners and the services.

By working as a team, all professionals, no matter their specialty, will then focus their actions on helping individuals with disabilities achieve a good future quality of life by involving them in choosing habilitation and rehabilitation objectives and also by supporting them in keeping their expectations high as regards their social and professional goals.

References

Aiken, L. R. (2003). *Psychological testing and assessment* (11th ed.). Boston: Person Educational.

Alston, R. J., Bell, T. J., & Hampton, J. L. (2002). Learning disability and career entry into the sciences: A critical analysis of attitudinal factors. *Journal of Career Development, 28*, 263–275.

Bandura, A. (1995). *Self-efficacy in changing societies.* New York: Cambridge University Press.

Bandura, A. (1997). *Self-efficacy: The exercise of control.* New York: W. H. Freeman.

Betz, N. E., & Taylor, K. M. (2001). *Manual for the Career Decision Self-Efficacy Scale and CDMSE-Short Form.* Unpublished manuscript, Ohio State University, Columbus, OH.

Betz, N. E., & Voyten, K. K. (1997). Efficacy and outcome expectations influence career exploration and decidedness. *Career Development Quarterly, 46*, 179–189.

Blustein, D. L. (2006). *The psychology of working: A new perspective for career development, counseling and public policy.* London: Lawrence Erlbaum Associates.

Blustein, D. L. (2008). The role of work in psychological health and well-being: A conceptual, historical, and public policy perspective. *American Psychologist, 63*, 228–240.

Breeding, R. R. (2008). Empowerment as a function of contextual self-understanding. The effect of Work Interest Profiling on Career Decision Self-Efficacy and Work Locus of Control *Rehabilitation Counseling Bulletin, 51*, 96–106.

Brown, S. D., & Ryan Krane, N. E. (2000). Four (or five) sessions and a cloud of dust: Old assumptions and new observations about career counseling. In S. D. Brown & R. W. Lent (Eds.), *Handbook of counseling psychology* (3rd ed., pp. 740–766). New York: Wiley.

Bunning, K., & Horton, S. (2007). "Border crossing" as a route to inclusion: A shared cause with people with a learning disability? *Aphasiology, 21*, 9–22.

Bussolari, C. J., & Goodell, J. A. (2009). Chaos theory as a model for life transitions counseling: Nonlinear dynamics and life's changes. *Journal of Counseling & Development, 87*, 98–107.

Cappa, S. F., Benke, T., Clarke, S., Rossi, B., Stemmer, B., & van Heugten C. M. (2003). EFNS guidelines on cognitive rehabilitation: report of an EFNS Task Force. *European Journal of Neurology, 10*, 11–23.

Carrieri, L., & Sgaramella, T. M. (2011, September). Knowledge about jobs, interests and self-efficacy beliefs in young adults with intellectual disability. Paper session presented at the International Conference on Vocational Designing and Career Counseling. Challenges and New Horizons, Padova, Italy.

Cascio, W. F. (2010). The changing world of work. In P. A. Linley, S. Harrington & N. Garcea (Eds.). *Oxford handbook of positive psychology and work* (pp. 13–23). New York: Oxford University Press.

Chaves, A. P., Diemer, M. A., Blustein, D. L., Gallagher, L. A., DeVoy, J. E., Casares, M. T., & Perry, J. C. (2004). Conceptions of work: The view from urban youth. *Journal of Counseling Psychology, 51*, 275–286.

Cicerone K. (2005). Evidence-based practice and the limits of rational rehabilitation. *Archives of Physical Medicine and Rehabilitation, 86*, 1073–1074.

Cinamon, R. G., & Gifsh, L. (2004). Conceptions of work among adolescents and young adults with mental retardation. *Career Development Quarterly, 52*, 212–224.

Clark, E., Olympia, D. E., Jensen, J., Heathfield, L. T., & Jenson, W. R. (2004). Striving for autonomy in a contingency-governed world: Another challenge for individuals with developmental disabilities. *Psychology in the Schools*, *41*, 143–153.

Coakley, R. M., Holmbeck, G. N., Friedman, D., Greenley, R. N., & Thill, A. W. (2002). A longitudinal study of pubertal timing, parent-child conflict, and cohesion in families of young children with spina bifida. *Journal of Pediatric Psychology*, *27*, 461–473.

Cohutinho, M. T., Dam, U. C., & Blustein, D. L. (2008). The psychology of working and globalization: A new perspective for a new era. *International Journal for Educational and Vocational Guidance*, *8*, 5–18.

Conyers, L., & Szymanski, E. M. (1998). The effectiveness of an integrated career intervention on college students with and without disabilities. *Journal of Postsecondary Education and Disability*, *13*, 23–34.

Cook, D. (1998). Psychosocial impact of disability. In R. L. Parker & E. M. Szymanski (Eds.), *Rehabilitation counselling: Basic and beyond* (pp. 303–326). Austin, TX: PRO-ED.

Dawn C. L. (2011). A proposed integrative model for enhanced career development for young adults with disabilities. *Adultspan Journal*, *10*, 24–34.

Dipeolu, A., Reardon, R., Sampson, J., & Burkhead, J. (2002). The relationship between dysfunctional career thoughts and adjustment to disability in college students with learning disabilities. *Journal of Career Assessment*, *10*, 413–427.

Dunn, D. S., & Dougherty, S. B. (2005). Prospects for a positive psychology of rehabilitation. *Rehabilitation Psychology*, *50*, 305–311.

Dunn, D. S., & Brody, C. (2008). Defining the good life following acquired physical disability. *Rehabilitation Psychology*, *53*, 413–425.

Eggerth, D. E. (2008). From theory of work adjustment to person-environment correspondence counseling: Vocational psychology as positive psychology. *Journal of Career Assessment*, *16*, 60–74.

Fabian, E. S., & Liesener, J. J. (2005). Promoting the career potential of Youth with disabilities. In S. D. Brown & R. W. Lent (Eds.), *Career development and counseling: Putting theory and research to work* (pp. 551–572). Hoboken, NJ: John Wiley & Sons.

Ferrari, L., Nota, L., & Soresi, S. (2008). Conceptions of work in Italian adults with intellectual disability. *Journal of Career Development*, *34*, 438–464.

Ferrari, L., Nota, L., & Soresi, S. (2010). Time perspective and indecision in young and older adolescents. *British Journal of Guidance & Counselling*, *38*, 61–82.

Ferrari, L., Nota, L., Soresi, S., Blustein, D., Murphy, K. A., & Kenna A. C. (2009). The idea of working in adolescents about to make a school-career choice. *Journal of Career Assessment*, *17*, 99–115.

Fouad, N. A., & Spreda, S. L. (1996). Translation and use of a career decision making self efficacy instrument for middle school students. *Journal of Vocational Education Research*, *21*, 67–86.

Gati, I. (1986). Making career decisions: A sequential elimination approach. *Journal of Counseling Psychology*, *33*, 408–417.

Gati, I. (1998). Using career-related aspects to elicit preferences and characterize occupations for a better person-environment fit. *Journal of Vocational Behavior*, *52*, 343–356.

Gorzkowski, J. A., Kelly, E. H., Klaas, S. J., & Vogel, L. C. (2010). Girls with spinal cord injury: Social and job-related participation and psychosocial outcomes. *Rehabilitation Psychology*, *55*, 58–67.

Grant, G., Ramcharan, P., & Goward, P. (2003). Resilience, family care, and people with intellectual disabilities. In Glidden, L. M. (Ed.), *International review of research in mental retardation*, vol. 26. (pp. 135–173). San Diego, CA: Academic Press.

Gysbers, N. C., Heppner, M. J., & Johnston, J. A. (2009). *Career counseling: Contexts, process and techniques.* Alexandria, VA: American Counseling Association.

Hart, K., & Sasso, T. (2011). Mapping and teaching positive psychology: Canadian and American perspectives. *Canadian Psychology*, *52*, 82–92.

Helms, J., & Cook, D. A. (1999). *Using race and culture in counseling and psychotherapy: Theory and process.* Needham Heights, MA: Allyn & Bacon.

Hirschi, A. (2009). Career adaptability development in adolescence: Multiple predictors and effect on sense of power and life satisfaction. *Journal of Vocational Behavior*, *74*, 145–155.

Holland, J. L. (1997). *Making vocational choices: A theory of vocational personalities and work environments.* (3rd ed.). Odessa, FL: Psychological Assessment Resources.

Holland, J. L., Daiger, D. C., & Power, P. G. (1980). *My Vocational Situation* Palo Alto, CA: Consulting Psychologists Press.

Karaevli, A., & Hall, D. T. (2006). How career variety promotes the adaptability of managers: A theoretical model. *Journal of Vocational Behavior*, *69*, 359–373.

Krumboltz, J. D. (2009). The happenstance learning theory. *Journal of Career Assessment*, *17*, 135–154.

Kuijpers, M. A. C. T., Schyns, B., & Scheerens, J. (2006). Career competencies for career success. *Career Development Quarterly*, *55*, 168–178.

Kush, K., & Cochran, L. (1993). Enhancing a sense of agency through career planning. *Journal of Counseling Psychology*, *40*, 434–439.

Lent, R. W. (2005). Social cognitive view of career development and counseling. In S. D. Brown & R. W. Lent (Eds.), *Career development and counseling: Putting theory and research to work* (pp. 101–127). New York: John Wiley and Sons.

Lent, R. W. (2007). Restoring emotional well-being: A theoretical model. In M. Feuerstein (Ed.), *Handbook of cancer survivorship* (pp. 231–247). New York: Springer.

Lent, R. W., Brown, S. D., & Hackett, G. (1994). Toward a unifying social cognitive theory of career and academic interest, choice, and performance. *Journal of Vocational Behavior*, *45*, 79–122.

Lent, R. W., Brown, S. D., Nota, L., & Soresi, S. (2003). Testing social cognitive interest and choice hypotheses across Holland types in Italian high school students. *Journal of Vocational Behavior*, *62*, 101–118.

Lent, R. W., Brown, S. D., Tracey, T. J. G., Soresi, S. & Nota, L. (2006). Development of interests and competency beliefs in Italian adolescents: An exploration of circular structure and bidirectional relationships. *Journal of Counseling Psychology*, *53*, 181–191.

Lopez, S. J., & Edwards, L. M. (2008). The interface of counseling psychology and positive psychology: Assessing and promoting strengths. In S. D. Brown & R. W. Lent (Eds.), *Handbook of counseling psychology* (4th ed., pp. 86–99). Hoboken, NJ: John Wiley & Sons.

Lopez, S. J., Magyar-Moe, J. L., Peterson, S. E., Ryder, J. A., Krieshok, T. S., O'Byrne, K. K., & Fry, N. A. (2006).

Counseling psychology's focus on positive aspects of human functioning. *Counseling Psychologist, 34*, 205–227.

Lustig, D. C., & Strauser, D. R. (2003). An empirical typology of career thoughts of individuals with a disability. *Rehabilitation Counseling Bulletin, 46*, 98–107.

Luzzo, D. A., Hitchings, W. E., Retish, P., & Shoemaker, A. (1999). Evaluating differences in college students' career decision making on the basis of disability status. *Career Development Quarterly, 48*, 142–156.

McCullough, G., & Huebner, E. S. (2003). Life satisfaction reports of adolescents with learning disabilities and normally achieving adolescents. *Journal of Psychoeducational Assessment, 21*, 311–324.

Mitchell, L. K., & Krumboltz, J. D. (1996). Krumboltz's learning theory of career choice and counselling. In D. Brown, L. Brooks, et al. (Eds.), *Career choice and development* (3rd ed., pp. 223–280). San Francisco, CA: Jossey Bass.

Mpofu, E., & Wilson, K. B. (2004). opportunity structure and transition practices with students with disabilities: The role of family, culture, and community. *Journal of Applied Rehabilitation Counseling, 35*, 9–16.

Neumayer, R., & Bleasdale, M. (1996). Personal lifestyle preferences of people with an intellectual disability. *Journal of Intellectual & Developmental Disability, 21*, 91–114.

Nosek, M. A., Howland, C., Rintala, D. H., Young, M. E., & Chanpong, G. F. (2001). National study of women with physical disabilities: Final report. *Sexuality and Disability, 19*, 5–40.

Nota, L., & Ferrari, L. (2011, May). Italian network university training in vocational guidance. Paper session presented at the NICE Conference, Heidelberg.

Nota, L., Ferrari, L., Ginevra, M.C., & Soresi, S. (2012, September). La prospettiva temporale in un gruppo di persone con disabilità intellettiva [Time perspective in a group of individuals with intellectual disability]. Paper session presented at the National Conference of the Italian Association of Psychology, Chieti, Italy.

Nota, L., Ginevra, M. C., & Carrieri, L. (2010). Interests and self-efficacy beliefs among young adults with intellectual disability. *Journal of Policy and Practice in Intellectual Disabilities, 7*, 250–260.

Nota, L., Ginevra, M. C., & Soresi, S. (2012). The Career and Work Adaptability Questionnaire (CWAQ): A first contribution to its validation. *Journal of Adolescence, 35*, 1557–1569.

Nota, L., & Soresi, S. (1999). L'indecisione scolastico-professionale nella scuola media [School/career indecision in junior school]. *Supplement to Psicologia e Scuola, 95*, 191–200.

Nota, L., & Soresi, S. (2000). *Autoefficacia nelle scelte* [Self-efficacy and school-career choice]. Firenze: Giunti-Organizzazioni Speciali.

Nota, L., & Soresi, S. (2004a). Vocational guidance for persons with intellectual disability. In J. A. Rondal, A. Rasore Quartino, & S. Soresi (Eds.), *The adult with Down Syndrome. A new challenge for society* (pp. 265–276). London: Whurr.

Nota, L., & Soresi, S. (2004b). Improving the problem-solving and decision-making skills of a high indecision group of young adolescents: A test of the "Difficult: No Problem!" training. *International Journal for Educational and Vocational Guidance, 4*, 3–21

Nota, L., & Soresi, S. (2009a, June). *Valutare le conoscenze professionali: lo strumento "Quanto conosci le professioni?"* [Evaluating career knowledge: The instrument "How much do you know jobs?"]. Paper session presented at the XI Congresso Nazionale Orientamento alla Scelta: Ricerche, Formazioni, Applicazioni, Padova, Italy.

Nota, L., & Soresi, S. (2009b). Ideas and thoughts of Italian teachers on the professional future of persons with disability. *Journal of Intellectual Disability Research, 53*, 65–77.

Nota L., Soresi, S., & Ferrari, L. (2008). "Premier principe: je crois en moi…parce que c'est aussi dans mon intérêt": une formation pour renforcer les sentiments d'efficacité. *L'Orientation Scolaire et Professionnelle, 37,* 113–134.

Nota, L., Soresi, S., Ferrari, L., & Wehmeyer, M. L. (2007). Self-determination, social abilities, and the quality of life of people with intellectual disabilities. *Journal of Intellectual Disability Research, 51*, 850–865

Ochs, L. A., & Roessler, R. T. (2001). Students with disabilities: How ready are they for the 21st century? *Rehabilitation Counseling Bulletin, 44*, 170–176.

Ochs, L. A., & Roessler, R. T. (2004). Predictors of career exploration intentions: A social cognitive career theory perspective. *Rehabilitation Counseling Bulletin, 47*, 224–233.

Panagos, R., & DuBois, D. L. (1999). Career self-efficacy development and students with learning disabilities. *Learning Disabilities Research & Practice, 14*, 25–34.

Pavot, W., & Diener, E. (1993). Review of the Satisfaction with Life Scale. *Psychological Assessment, 5*, 164–172.

Peterson, G. W., Sampson, J. P., Jr., Reardon, R. C., & Lenz, J. G. (1996). Becoming career problem solvers and decision makers: A cognitive information processing approach. In D. Brown & L. Brooks (Eds.), *Career choice and development* (3rd ed.) (pp. 423–475). San Francisco, CA: Jossey-Bass.

Power, P. W. (2000). *A guide to vocational assessment* (3rd ed.). Austin, TX: PRO-ED.

Raskin, P. M. (1994). Identity and the career counseling of adolescents: The development of vocational identity. In S. L. Archer (Ed.), *Interventions for adolescent identity development* (pp. 155–173). Thousand Oaks, CA: Sage Publications.

Regenold, M., Sherman, M. F., & Fenzel, M. (1999). Getting back to work: Self-efficacy as a predictor of employment outcome. *Psychiatric Rehabilitation Journal, 22*, 361–367.

Riverin-Simard, D. (1991). *Career and social classes*. Montreal: Meridian Press.

Sampson, J. P., Peterson, G. W., Lenz, J. G., Reardon, R. C., & Saunders, D. E. (1996). *Career Thoughts Inventory: Professional manual*. Odessa, FL: Psychological Assessment Resources.

Savickas, M. L. (1991). Career time perspective. In D. Brown & L. Brooks, *Career counseling techniques* (pp. 236–249). Boston: Allyn & Bacon.

Savickas, M. L. (2003). Toward a taxonomy of human strengths: Career counseling's contribution to positive psychology. In W. B. Walsh (Ed.), *Counseling psychology and optimal human functioning* (pp. 229–249). Mahwah, NJ: Lawrence Erlbaum Associates Publishers.

Savickas, M. L. (2005). The theory and practice of career construction. In S. D. Brown & R. W. Lent (Eds.), *Career development and counseling: Putting theory and research to work* (pp. 42–70). New York: Wiley.

Savickas, M. L. (2007). Internationalisation of counseling psychology: Constructing cross-national consensus and collaboration. *Applied Psychology: An International Review, 56*, 182–188.

Savickas, M. L. (2008). Helping people choose jobs: A history of the guidance profession. In J. Athanasou & R. Van Esbroeck (Eds.), *International Handbook of Career Guidance* (pp. 97–113). Amsterdam: Kluwer.

Savickas, M. L., Nota, L., Rossier, J., Dauwalder, J. P., Duarte, M. E., Guichard, J., et al. (2009). Life designing: A paradigm for career construction in the 21st century. *Journal of Vocational Behavior, 75,* 239–250.

Savickas, M. L. (2010, July). *Career adaptability: Cross-cultural examination of a model and measure.* Paper session presented at the 27th International Congress of Applied Psychology, Melbourn, Australia.

Schalock, R. L. (2004). The concept of quality of life: What we know and do not know. *Journal of Intellectual Disability Research, 48,* 203–216.

Sgaramella, T. M. (2011, September). *Time perspective, future goals and intervening conditions in university students with sensory or motor disability: patterns and suggestions for career guidance programs.* Paper session presented at the International Conference on Vocational Designing and Career Counseling. Challenges and New Horizons, Padova, Italy.

Shahnasarian, M. (2001). Career rehabilitation: Integration of vocational rehabilitation and career development in the twenty-first century. *Career Development Quarterly, 49,* 275–283.

Soresi, S. (2000). La personalizzazione dell'attività di orientamento [Personalized career guidance]. In S. Soresi (Ed.), *Orientamenti per l'orientamento* [Vocational Guidance and counselors] (pp. 22–28). Firenze, Italy: Giunti-Organizzazioni Speciali.

Soresi, S. (2007a). Quando orientare è difficile? Suggerimenti per la personalizzazione degli interventi di orientamento [When career counseling is difficult? Suggestions for the personalization of vocational guidance interventions]. In S. Soresi (Ed.), *Orientamento alle scelte: Rassegne, ricerche, strumenti ed applicazioni* [Vocational guidance and choice: reviews, researches, instruments and applications] (pp. 331–346). Firenze: Giunti-Organizzazioni Speciali.

Soresi, S. (2007b). *Psicologia delle disabilità* [Psychology of disability]. Bologna: Il Mulino.

Soresi, S., & Nota, L. (2001a). *Portfolio Optimist per l'orientamento dagli 11 ai 14 anni* [Portfolio Optimist for vocational guidance from 11 to 14 years of age]. Firenze: ITER-Organizzazioni Speciali.

Soresi, S., & Nota, L. (2001b). *La facilitazione dell'integrazione scolastica* [Facilitating school inclusion]. Pordenone: Erip Editrice.

Soresi, S., & Nota, L. (2003). *Portfolio Clipper per l'orientamento dagli 15 ai 19 anni* [Portfolio Clipper for vocational guidance from 15 to 19 years of age]. Firenze: ITER-Organizzazioni Speciali.

Soresi, S., & Nota, L. (2007a). *ASTRID Portfolio per l'assessment, il trattamento e l'integrazione delle disabilità— ORIENTAMENTO* [ASTRID Portfolio for the assessment, the treatment and the inclusion of disabilities—vocational guidance]. Firenze: Organizzazioni Speciali.

Soresi, S., & Nota, L. (2007b). *ASTRID-OR: Portfolio per l'assessment, il trattamento e l'integrazione delle disabilità.* [ASTRID-OR: a portfolio for the assessment, the intervention and the inclusion of disabilities]. Firenze: Organizzazioni Speciali.

Soresi, S., & Nota, L. (2010). *Sfide e nuovi orizzonti per l'orientamento. Vol. I* [Challenges and new horizons for vocational guidance. Vol. I]. Firenze, Italy: Giunti OS.

Soresi, S., & Nota, L. (2011). *L'orientamento in persone con difficoltà di apprendimento: Il ruolo di alcuni processi cognitivi* [Career counseling for persons with learning disabilities: the role of some cognitive and non-cognitive processes]. *Giornale Italiano di Psicologia dell'Orientamento* [Italian Journal of Vocational Guidance], *12*(2), 31–44.

Soresi S., Nota, L., & Ferrari L. (2007). Considerations on supports that can increase the quality of life of parents of children with disability. *Journal of Policy & Practice in Intellectual Disabilities, 4,* 248–251.

Soresi, S., Nota, L., & Ferrari, L. (2012). Career Adapt-Abilities Scale-Italian Form: Psychometric properties and relationships to breadth of interests, quality of life, and perceived barriers. *Journal of Vocational Behavior, 80,* 705–711.

Soresi, S., Nota, L., Ferrari, L., & Solberg, S.V. H. (2008). Career guidance for persons with disabilities. In J. Athanasou & R. Van Esbroeck (Eds.), *International handbook of career guidance* (pp. 405–417). Amsterdam: Kluwer.

Soresi, S., Nota, L., Ferrari, L., Sgaramella, M. T., Ginevra, M. C., & Carrieri, L. (2009). *Progettazioni, itinerari e passi possibili di orientamento* [Plans, itineraries and possible steps in career guidance]. Firenze: Giunti O.S.

Soresi, S., Nota, L., & Wehmeyer, M. L. (2011). Community involvement in promoting inclusion, participation, and self-determination. *International Journal of Inclusive Education, 15,* 15–28.

Spector, P. E. (1985). Measurement of human service staff satisfaction: Development of the Job Satisfaction Survey. *American Journal of Community Psychology, 13,* 693–713.

Spector, P. E. (1988). Development of the work locus of control scale. *Journal of Occupational Psychology, 61,* 335–340.

Spector, P. E. (1997). *Job satisfaction: Application, assessment, causes, and consequences.* Thousand Oaks, CA: Sage.

Strauser, D. R., Lustig, D. C., Keim, J., Ketz, K., & Malesky, A. (2002). Analyzing the differences in career thoughts based on disability status. *Journal of Rehabilitation, 68,* 27–32.

Szymanski, E. M. (1999). Disability, job stress, and the changing nature of careers, and the career resilience portfolio. *Rehabilitation Counseling Bulletin, 42,* 279–289.

Tait, M., Padgett, M. Y., & Baldwin, T. T. (1989). Job and life satisfaction: A reevaluation of the strength of the relationship and gender effects as a function of the date of the study. *Journal of Applied Psychology, 74,* 502–507.

Whiston, S. C. (2002). Application of the principles: Career counseling and interventions. *Counseling Psychologist, 30,* 218–237.

Willis, S. (2002). The relationship of social cognitive variables to outcomes among young adults with emotional disturbance. Unpublished doctoral dissertation, University of Maryland, College Park.

Wilson, W. J. (1996). *When work disappears: The world of the new urban poor.* New York: Random House.

Wolf, F. M., & Savickas, M. L. (1985). Time perspective and causal attributions for achievement. *Journal of Educational Psychology, 77,* 471–480.

Wolf-Branigin, M., Schuyler, V., & White, P. (2007). Improving quality of life and career attitudes of youth with disabilities: Experiences from the Adolescent Employment Readiness Center. *Research on Social Work Practice, 17,* 324–333.

Yanchak, K.V., Lease, S. H., & Strauser, D. R. (2005). Relation of disability type and career thoughts to vocational identity. *Rehabilitation Counseling Bulletin, 48,* 130–138.

Self-Regulation and Disability

Dale H. Schunk *and* William D. Bursuck

Abstract

Self-regulation (self-regulated learning) refers to learning that results from students' self-generated thoughts and behaviors that are systematically oriented toward their learning goals. Various theories have been proposed to account for self-regulation including operant and social cognitive theories. Common features of theories include an emphasis on learner activity, the cyclical nature of self-regulation, and motivation to instigate and sustain self-regulation. Much research has explored the development of self-regulatory skills by students with disabilities. Research is summarized that investigated the self-regulatory activities of self-monitoring, self-instruction, goal setting, and self-regulated strategy development. Based on theory and research evidence, implications for educational practice are discussed, and recommendations are made for future research in the areas of curricular integration, cultural differences, and learning with technology.

Key Words: self-regulation, self-efficacy, self-instruction, goal setting, motivation

Self-regulation (or *self-regulated learning*) refers to learning that results from students' self-generated thoughts and behaviors that are systematically oriented toward the attainment of their learning goals (Zimmerman, 2000). Self-regulated learning involves goal-directed activities that students instigate, modify, and sustain, such as attending to instruction, cognitively processing information, rehearsing and relating new learning to prior knowledge, believing that one is capable of learning, and establishing productive social relationships and work environments (Zimmerman & Schunk, 2004). Self-regulated learning fits well with a central feature of cognitive theories of learning that students actively contribute to their learning and exercise control over attainment of their learning goals. Research evidence supports the point that self-regulatory processes influence learners' achievement cognitions, behaviors, and emotions (Schunk & Zimmerman, 2008; Zimmerman & Schunk, 2011).

Self-regulation is a key component of the construct of self-determination (see chapter by Wehmeyer & Little, this volume). However, theories of self-regulated learning do not address the dispositional aspects of self-determination, including the ability to act autonomously in a self-realizing, psychologically-empowered manner (Wehmeyer et al., 2011). Thus, dispositional issues are not addressed in this chapter.

We review relevant theories and research on self-regulation among students with disabilities and provide implications for educational practice and recommendations for future research. While the field of disability studies includes a broad range of disabilities, our discussion focuses on students with high-incidence disabilities (e.g., learning disabilities, emotional and behavior disorders, mild intellectual disabilities) and attention deficit and hyperactivity disorders (ADHD) because most research on self-regulation has addressed these populations of students. Principles of self-regulation, however, also are applicable to students with other disabilities such as students on the autism spectrum or students with moderate-to-severe intellectual disabilities. More research is needed on these students.

Developing self-regulation skills among students with disabilities is an important educational goal. Research shows that students with disabilities and ADHD are likely to experience difficulties with self-regulation (Barkley, 1997; Hallahan & Mercer, 2002), and can be helped to develop self-regulatory capabilities that lead to higher motivation, achievement, and beliefs about their capabilities (Schunk & Zimmerman, 2008). These gains are critical for all students but especially for students with disabilities who, relative to their peers without disabilities, often achieve at lower levels and hold lower perceptions of their capabilities (Licht & Kistner, 1986). The problem is compounded if teachers react to students with disabilities based on their presumed characteristics (e.g., lower ability) rather than on what students actually do (Bryan & Bryan, 1983), which can negatively affect students' motivation if they believe that teachers do not expect much from them. Low self-efficacy can adversely affect student performance on a range of tasks within multiple contexts (Lodewyk & Winne, 2005) and may contribute to significant life-adjustment problems later on (Bear, Kortering, & Braziel, 2006; Gerber, Ginsberg, & Reiff, 1992), including dropping out of school at higher rates (Cameto, Levine, & Wagner, 2004), enrolling in postsecondary education in lower numbers (Newman, Wagner, Cameto, & Knokey, 2009), and having higher rates of unemployment (Newman et al., 2009) and lower rates of living independently (Wagner, Newman, Cameto, Garza, & Levine, 2005).

We initially discuss some assumptions of theories of self-regulation, after which we explain two theories of self-regulation that have been applied to students with disabilities: operant and social cognitive. With this theoretical background in place, we discuss self-regulation research that examined the operation of self-regulatory processes during learning. The chapter concludes with implications of the theory and research for educational practice and suggestions for future research.

Theories of Self-Regulation
Assumptions

Theory and research on academic self-regulation was prompted by investigations into individuals' behavioral self-control in such areas as personal management and task completion (Karoly & Kanfer, 1982). Self-regulation researchers have explored whether the same self-regulatory processes improve academic learning, motivation, and achievement (Zimmerman, 2001).

Regardless of perspective, theories stress common features (Zimmerman, 2001). One is that individuals are self-regulated to the extent that they are behaviorally, cognitively, and motivationally active in their own learning and performance. A second feature is that self-regulation is a cyclical process comprising feedback loops (Lord, Diefendorff, Schmidt, & Hall, 2010). Persons set goals and monitor their progress toward them. They respond to this self-monitoring, as well as to external feedback, in ways to attain their goals, such as by working harder or changing their strategy. A third common feature is an emphasis on why persons choose to self-regulate. Effective self-regulation requires not only knowing what to do and how to do it but also regulating one's motivation and emotional involvement (Pintrich, 2000; Schunk & Zimmerman, 2008).

Operant Theory

The views of operant theorists about self-regulation derive primarily from the theory and research by Skinner (1953). Operant (voluntary) behavior is emitted in the presence of discriminative stimuli, or those to which people may respond. Whether behavior becomes more or less likely to occur in the future depends on its consequences. Behaviors that are reinforced (followed by positive consequences) are more likely to be repeated, whereas those punished (followed by negative consequences) are less apt to occur.

Operant theorists have studied how individuals establish discriminative stimuli and reinforcement contingencies (prescribed consequences for various behaviors; Brigham, 1982). Self-regulated behavior involves choosing among alternative courses of action (Mace, Belfiore, & Shea, 1989), typically by deferring an immediate reinforcer in favor of a different and usually greater future reinforcer. From the perspective of operant theory, one decides which behaviors to regulate, establishes discriminative stimuli for their occurrence, evaluates performance in terms of whether it matches the standard, and administers reinforcement (Mace, Belfiore, & Hutchinson, 2001). The key self-regulation activities are self-monitoring, self-instruction, and self-reinforcement.

Self-monitoring

Self-monitoring refers to deliberate attention to some aspect of one's behavior, and often is accompanied by recording its frequency or intensity (Mace et al., 2001). People cannot regulate their actions if they are not aware of what they do. Behaviors can be assessed on such dimensions as quality, rate, quantity, and originality. While working on a problem set, students may periodically assess their work to determine how quickly they are completing it and whether their answers are correct. One can engage in self-monitoring in such diverse areas as motor skills (e.g., how fast one runs the 100-meter dash), art (e.g., how original one's pen-and-ink drawings are), and social behavior (e.g., how much one interacts at social functions).

Often students must be taught to self-monitor (Belfiore & Hornyak, 1998; Lan, 1998). Methods include narrations, frequency counts, duration measures, time-sampling measures, behavior ratings, and behavioral traces and archival records (Mace et al., 1989). *Narrations* are written accounts of behavior and the context in which it occurs. Narrations can range from detailed to open-ended. *Frequency counts* are used to record instances of specific behaviors during a given period (e.g., number of times a student turns around in his or her seat during a 30-minute seatwork exercise). *Duration measures* record the amount of time a behavior occurs during a given period (e.g., number of minutes a student studies during 30 minutes). *Time-sampling measures* divide a period into shorter intervals and record how often a behavior occurs during each interval. A 30-minute study period might be divided into six 5-minute periods, where for each 5-minute period students record whether they studied the entire time. *Behavior ratings* require estimates of how often a behavior occurs during a given time (e.g., always, sometimes, never). *Behavioral traces* and *archival records* are permanent records that exist independently of other assessments (e.g., number of pages completed or problems solved correctly).

In the absence of self-recording, people's memories of successes and failures become selective, and their beliefs about outcomes may not faithfully reflect actual outcomes. Self-recording often yields surprising results. Students having difficulties studying who keep a written record of their activities may learn they are wasting most of their study time on nonacademic tasks.

Two important self-monitoring criteria are regularity and proximity (Bandura, 1986). *Regularity* means observing behavior continually rather than intermittently, such as by keeping a daily record rather than recording behavior once a week. Nonregular observation requires accurate memory

and often yields misleading results. *Proximity* means observing behavior close in time to its occurrence rather than long afterwards. It is better to write down what we do at the time it occurs rather than waiting until the end of the day to reconstruct events.

In addition to self-monitoring overt behaviors, students also can be taught to self-monitor their attention (Harris, Graham, MacArthur, Reid, & Mason, 2011). For example, students can learn to self-assess and self-record whether they are attending to and working on the task. The self-monitoring of attention has been shown in research to improve students' attention and academic achievement (Harris et al., 2011).

Self-monitoring places responsibility for assessment on the person doing the monitoring (Belfiore & Hornyak, 1998). Self-monitored responses are consequences of behaviors, and like other consequences affect future responding. Self-recordings are immediate responses that serve to bridge the relation between preceding behavior and longer-term consequences (Mace & West, 1986). Students who monitor their completion of assignments provide themselves with immediate reinforcers that link their prior work and distant consequences such as teacher praise and high grades (Harris, Graham, Mason & Friedlander, 2008; Mace et al., 2001). Research also shows that self-monitoring can, by itself, lead to behavioral improvements (Belfiore & Horynak, 1998). Reid, Trout, and Schartz (2005) reviewed the research literature on self-regulation interventions among children with ADHD. Self-monitoring alone and in combination with self-reinforcement often was a component of effective interventions.

Self-instruction

Self-instruction refers to discriminative stimuli that set the occasion for self-regulatory responses leading to reinforcement (Mace et al., 1989). One type of self-instruction involves arranging the environment to produce discriminative stimuli. Students who realize they need to review class notes the next day might write themselves a reminder before going to bed. The written reminder serves as a discriminative stimulus to review, which makes reinforcement (e.g., a good grade on a quiz) more likely.

Another type of self-instruction takes the form of statements that serve as discriminative stimuli to guide behavior. Self-instructional statements have been used to teach a variety of academic, social, and motor skills. Verbalizing statements keeps students focused on a task, which may be especially beneficial for learners with attention deficits. Kosiewicz, Hallahan, Lloyd, and Graves (1982) used the following self-instruction procedure to improve the handwriting of a student with learning disabilities:

- Say aloud the word to be written.
- Say the first syllable.
- Name each of the letters in that syllable three times.
- Repeat each letter as it is written down.
- Repeat steps 2 through 4 for each succeeding syllable.

Other researchers also have found statement verbalization to assist students to learn and apply a strategy to improve their performances. Using the Self-Regulated Strategy Development program (discussed later in this chapter), Reid and Lienemann (2006) had teachers explain and demonstrate use of a writing strategy by verbalizing and applying statements such as "What is my goal?" and "What is my next step?" Schunk and Rice (1987) taught students with reading disabilities a comprehension strategy, and students verbalized the individual steps prior to applying them, such as "Read the questions" and "Read the passage to find out what it is mostly about."

Self-reinforcement

Self-reinforcement is the process whereby people provide themselves with reinforcement contingent on performing a response, and the reinforcement increases the likelihood of future responding (Mace et al., 1989). Although research shows that reinforcement contingencies improve academic performance (Bandura, 1986), it is unclear whether self-reinforcement is more effective than externally administered reinforcement (such as given by a teacher). Studies investigating self-reinforcement often contain problems that make it difficult to discern the isolated effects of this intervention (Brigham, 1982). In academic settings, the reinforcement contingency usually occurs in classrooms that include instruction and rules. Students typically do not work on materials when they choose but rather when told to do so by the teacher. Students may stay on task primarily because of the teacher's classroom control rather than because of reinforcement.

Self-reinforcement is hypothesized to be an effective component of self-regulated behavior (O'Leary & Dubey, 1979), but the reinforcement may be more important than its agent (self or others). Although self-reinforcement may enhance behavioral maintenance

over time, explicitly providing reinforcement may be more important while self-regulation skills are being learned. In the Reid and Lienemann (2006) project, students also verbalized self-reinforcing statements (e.g., "I like that part!").

In summary, the operant theory activities of self-monitoring, self-instruction, and self-reinforcement have been shown to promote students' academic behaviors. At the same time, by focusing only on behavior, operant theory ignores the cognitive and motivational aspects of self-regulation. Operant theory defines motivation in behavioral terms as the increased rate or duration of behavior, but this neglects the important cognitive and affective components of motivation such as beliefs and emotions. Behavioral methods are effective in the short term for increasing on-task behaviors, but self-regulation becomes more important over the longer term such as in finishing school or obtaining a job. Social cognitive theory offers a more elaborate perspective that includes goals and actions that extend beyond the immediate.

Social Cognitive Theory

The principles of social cognitive theory have been applied extensively to self-regulation (Bandura, 1997, 2001; Pintrich, 2004; Pintrich & Zusho, 2002; Zimmerman, 2000; Zimmerman & Schunk, 2004). From a social cognitive perspective, self-regulation involves learner choices as captured in Zimmerman's (1998) conceptual framework comprising six areas that one can self-regulate: motives, methods, time, outcomes, physical environment, and social environment. Self-regulation is possible to the extent that learners have choices in one or more of these areas. When all aspects of a task are predetermined, students may learn, but the source of control is external (i.e., teachers, parents, computers).

Reciprocal interactions

Bandura's (1986) social cognitive theory serves as the conceptual framework for social cognitive perspectives on self-regulation. According to Bandura (1986), human activities involve reciprocal interactions between personal, behavioral, and social/environmental factors (Figure 18.1). This reciprocity is exemplified with an important construct in Bandura's theory: *self-efficacy*, or beliefs about one's capabilities to learn or perform behaviors at designated levels (Bandura, 1997). Research shows that students' self-efficacy beliefs (personal factor) influence such behaviors as choice of tasks, persistence,

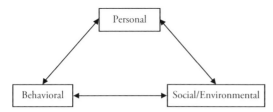

Figure 18.1 Reciprocal interactions in social cognitive theory

effort, and achievement (Schunk & Pajares, 2009). In turn, students' behaviors modify their self-efficacy. For example, as students work on tasks, they note their progress toward their learning goals (e.g., completing sections of a term paper). Progress indicators convey to students that they are capable of performing well, which enhances self-efficacy for continued learning.

The interaction between self-efficacy and social/environmental factors has been demonstrated in research on students with learning disabilities. As noted earlier, many such students hold low self-efficacy for performing well (Licht & Kistner, 1986), and persons in students' social environments may react to them based on attributes typically associated with them rather than based on students' behaviors (Bryan & Bryan, 1983). Teachers may judge such students as less capable than average learners and hold lower academic expectations for them, even in content areas where students with learning disabilities are performing adequately. In turn, teacher feedback can affect self-efficacy. Persuasive statements (e.g., "I know that you can do this") can raise self-efficacy.

Students' behaviors and learning environments influence one another. For example, when teachers present information, they may ask students to direct their attention to a visual. Environmental influence on behavior occurs when students attend to the visual without much conscious deliberation. Students' behaviors often alter the instructional environment. If teachers ask questions and students give incorrect answers, the teachers may reteach some points rather than continue the lesson.

A key assumption of social cognitive theory is that people desire to develop a sense of *agency,* or the belief that they can exert a large degree of control over important events in their lives (Bandura, 1997). This sense of agency (and related concepts such as empowerment, self-determination, and mastery; Cattaneo & Chapman, 2010) manifests itself in intentional acts, cognitive processes, and self-regulation. Self-efficacy is a central process affecting

one's sense of agency. Other key processes discussed in this chapter are goals, assessments of goal progress, modeling, and self-instruction.

Processes of self-regulated learning

The classical social cognitive view of self-regulation conceptualized it as involving self-observation, self-judgment, self-reaction (Bandura, 1986; Kanfer & Gaelick, 1986). These processes are not mutually exclusive but rather interact. While observing aspects of one's behavior, one may judge them against standards and react positively or negatively. One's evaluations and reactions set the stage for additional observations of the same behavioral aspects or others. These processes also do not operate independently of the learning environment; environmental factors can assist the development of self-regulation.

Self-observation is substantially similar to self-monitoring described earlier (Harris et al., 2011; Zimmerman, 2011). Self-observation is important because students need to know what they actually do.

Self-judgment refers to comparing present performance with one's goal. The belief that one is making goal progress enhances self-efficacy and sustains motivation. Students who find a task to be easy may think that they set their goal too low and may set it higher the next time. Further, knowing that similar others performed a task can promote self-efficacy and motivation since students may believe that if others can succeed they can as well (Schunk & Pajares, 2009). Students who perceive they have not made acceptable progress should not become discouraged if they feel efficacious about succeeding and believe that a different strategy will produce better results.

Self-reactions to goal progress can affect motivation (Bandura, 1986). Students who judge goal progress as acceptable and anticipate satisfaction from goal attainment should feel efficacious about continuing to improve and motivated to complete the task. Negative evaluations will not necessarily decrease self-efficacy and motivation if students believe they are capable of improving, such as by working harder. Evaluations are not intimately tied to level of performance. Some students are content with a B in a course, whereas others want only an A. Assuming that people believe they are capable of improving, higher goals lead to greater effort and persistence than do lower goals (Locke & Latham, 2002).

Cyclical nature of self-regulation

The interaction of personal, behavioral, and social/environmental factors during self-regulation is a cyclical process because these factors typically change during learning and must be monitored (Bandura, 1986; 1997; Zimmerman, 2000, 2011). Such monitoring leads to changes in an individual's strategies, cognitions, affects, and behaviors.

This cyclical nature is captured in Zimmerman's (2000) three-phase self-regulation model. The *fore-thought* phase precedes actual performance and refers to processes that set the stage for action. The *performance (volitional) control* phase involves processes that occur during learning and affect attention and action. During the *self-reflection* phase—which occurs after performance and during pauses—people respond evaluatively to their efforts.

Various self-regulatory processes come into play during the different phases (Table 18.1; Zimmerman, 2011). In the forethought phase, learners set goals, engage in strategic planning, and develop a sense of self-efficacy for learning and attaining their goals. Performance control involves implementing learning strategies that affect motivation and learning, as well as self-monitoring and self-recording one's performances. During periods of self-reflection, learners evaluate their goal progress, make attributions for their outcomes, decide whether to continue or alter their strategies, and set new goals as needed. Self-efficacy is enhanced as learners note their goal progress.

Research supports the validity of these three phases and substantiates the hypothesized processes that occur during them. DiBenedetto and Zimmerman (2010) studied the self-regulation processes of high school students who were high, average, or low achievers in science. Compared with students who were average- or low-achieving, high achievers employed more self-regulatory processes during each of the three phases, spent more time studying science, and displayed higher achievement. Teaching students to engage in self-regulation in all three phases has desirable

Table 18.1 Key Processes in Self-Regulation Phases

Phase	Key Processes
Forethought	Goal setting, strategy planning, development of self-efficacy for learning
Performance control	Strategy application, self-monitoring, self-recording
Self-reflection	Progress evaluation, attributions, continue or change strategy, goal setting, enhancement of self-efficacy for continued learning

effects on motivation and performance (Cleary, Zimmerman, & Keating, 2006).

Social to self progression

Schunk and Zimmerman (1997) postulated that self-regulation develops initially from social sources and shifts to self sources in a series of levels. At the outset, novice learners acquire learning strategies most rapidly from teaching, modeling, coaching, task structuring, and encouragement (Zimmerman, 2000). At this *observation* level, learners can induce the major features of learning strategies from observing models; however, most of them also need practice to fully incorporate the skill into their behavioral repertoires. Accuracy can be improved if models provide guidance, feedback, and social reinforcement during practice. During participant (mastery) modeling (Bandura, 1986), models repeat aspects of the strategy and guide enactment based on learners' imitative accuracy.

Learners attain an *emulation* level of skill when their performances approximate the general form of the model's. Observers are not copying the model but rather are imitating general patterns or styles. For example, they may imitate the type of question that the model asks but not mimic the model's words.

The source of learning skills is primarily social (external) for the first two levels but shifts to self (internal) influences at more advanced levels as learners internalize skills and self-regulatory processes. The third, *self-control* level, is characterized by learners' ability to use strategies independently while performing transfer tasks. Students' use of strategies becomes internalized but is affected by representational standards of modeled performances (e.g., covert images and verbal meanings) and self-reinforcement processes (Bandura, 1986).

When students reach a *self-regulation* level of academic skill, they can adapt strategies to changes in personal and situational conditions (Bandura, 1986). Learners can initiate use of strategies, incorporate adjustments based on features of situations, and are motivated to achieve by goals and self-efficacy. Learners choose when to use particular strategies and adapt them to changing conditions with little or no guidance from models.

Reciprocal interactions are evident throughout the phases. In the early stages of learning, for example, teachers who observe problems in learners' performances offer correction, learners who do not fully comprehend how to perform a skill or strategy at the emulation level may ask teachers for assistance, and learners' performances affect their self-efficacy. More advanced learners mentally and overtly practice skills and seek out teachers, coaches, and tutors to help refine their skills.

Social influences do not disappear with advancing skill acquisition. Although learners at the self-control and self-regulation phases use social sources less frequently, they nonetheless continue to rely on them (Zimmerman, 2000). Self-regulation does not mean social independence but rather increasing internalization and self-direction of one's learning. Although it is possible to learn on one's own, self-teaching does not fully capitalize on the benefits of the social environment on learning.

Self-Regulation Research

This section reviews some key areas of academic self-regulation research on students with disabilities. A comprehensive review is beyond the scope of this chapter; readers are advised to consult other sources (Bandura, 1986, 1997; Boekaerts, Pintrich, & Zeidner, 2000; Schunk & Zimmerman, 2008; Zimmerman & Schunk, 2011). We review research in the following areas relevant to the development of academic self-regulation skills by students with disabilities: self-monitoring, self-instruction, goals, and self-regulated strategy development.

Self-Monitoring

The effects of self-monitoring have been studied extensively among students with disabilities (Mace et al., 1989; Reid, 1996). Although studies differ in the type of self-monitoring implemented (e.g., self-monitoring of attention or performance), the research generally supports its use for helping students maintain task engagement and improve their academic performances (Reid, 1996).

Reid and Harris (1993) taught children with learning disabilities a strategy for studying spelling, and provided instruction on procedures for self-monitoring spelling performance and for self-monitoring their attention to the spelling tasks. Instruction of self-monitoring performance improved spelling achievement; both self-monitoring procedures improved on-task behaviors (e.g., pronouncing and checking words in the spelling list; focusing eyes on the spelling work).

Belfiore and Hornyak (1998) implemented a self-monitoring program for homework completion among students with disabilities enrolled in an after-school program. Students were taught to monitor steps involved in homework and its overall accuracy. Results showed that the self-monitoring improved frequency of homework turned in on time and its overall accuracy relative to the teacher monitoring that previously had been in effect.

Schunk (1983) found benefits of monitoring with children during mathematics learning. Although these children were not identified as having learning disabilities, they were evaluated by their teachers as having extreme difficulties learning mathematical skills. Self-monitoring students recorded their progress at the end of each session; external monitoring students had their progress recorded by an adult; no-monitoring students were not monitored and did not self-monitor. Self- and external monitoring enhanced self-efficacy and achievement equally well and better than did no monitoring. Effects of monitoring did not depend on session performance because the three conditions did not differ in work completed during self-directed practice. The key was monitoring of progress rather than who performed it.

Self-Instruction

Researchers have examined how self-instructional statements affect achievement outcomes of students with disabilities. These self-instructions often have been verbalized by learners as they perform the appropriate behaviors during academic learning. To become part of students' self-regulatory repertoires, the self-instructions must be internalized, often through overt-to-covert fading. Research supports the effectiveness of self-instructions in promoting students learning, motivation, and self-regulation.

For example, Schunk and Cox (1986) investigated how self-instruction influenced the self-efficacy and learning of subtraction skills of students with disabilities. Middle school students received instruction and practice opportunities over several sessions. During the problem solving, the continuous verbalization group verbalized aloud subtraction solution steps and their application to problems; a second (discontinued verbalization) group verbalized aloud only during the first half of the instructional program; and a third group did not verbalize. Continuous verbalization led to higher self-efficacy and skill than the other two conditions, which did not differ. It is possible that when instructed to no longer verbalize aloud, discontinued verbalization students had difficulty internalizing the instructions and did not utilize covert instructions to self-regulate their performances. For self-instructions to become internalized, students may need to be taught to fade overt verbalizations to a covert level.

In a series of studies, Schunk and Rice (1984, 1985, 1987, 1992, 1993) investigated how self-instructions of listening and reading comprehension strategies affected children's self-regulation, motivation, and achievement. The participants in these studies were students with language disabilities. For example, Schunk and Rice (1984) gave children in grades 2–4 instruction and practice in listening comprehension. An adult model verbalized and applied a listening comprehension strategy that included specific steps (e.g., "What is it I have to do?" "I must find the correct picture."). Half of the children in each grade verbalized the steps prior to applying them to questions; the other half received instruction but did not verbalize the steps. Self-verbalization led to higher self-efficacy across grades and promoted performance among third- and fourth-grade students. Perhaps the demands of verbalization, along with those of the comprehension task, were too complex for the second graders. They may have focused primarily on the comprehension task, which could have interfered with applying the steps.

In a follow-up study (Schunk & Rice, 1985), children in grades 4–5 received instruction and practice in reading comprehension. Within each grade, half of the students verbalized strategic steps prior to applying them to passages (e.g., "Read the questions." "Look for key words."). Verbalization led to higher reading comprehension and self-efficacy. Children also judged the importance of causal attributions (i.e., perceived causes) for their performances. Children who had verbalized the steps placed more importance on ability as a cause of their successes than did students who had not verbalized. This finding suggests that verbalization may enhance self-efficacy through its effects on ability attributions.

Other studies showed that children's self-regulation during comprehension learning was improved by having them fade verbalizations from an overt to a covert level (Schunk & Rice, 1993) and by verbally stressing to children the importance of using the strategy to improve their learning (Schunk & Rice, 1987, 1992). Taken together, the research by Schunk and Rice on children with language disabilities provides strong support for the point that self-instruction can help students self-regulate their academic performances and enhance their motivation and learning.

Goals

Goals are an integral part of self-regulation, and goal setting is a key component of the forethought phase in Zimmerman's (2000) model. Researchers have investigated how the properties of goals affect learning, motivation, and self-regulation (Locke & Latham, 2002). For goals to foster self-regulation, learners must believe they are making progress on their goals. Perceptions of progress may be facilitated by providing learners with explicit feedback (Schunk & Pajares, 2009).

Tollefson, Tracy, Johnsen, Farmer, and Buenning (1984) implemented a program to teach junior high students with disabilities to set realistic achievement goals. The content area for each student was either mathematics or spelling depending on the student's area of greater academic difficulty. Each week for four weeks students selected 10 words or problems from a list of 20 that teachers judged to be moderately difficult. Students set a goal of a number to get correct on a test given the following week and were given a study plan to accomplish the goal. Following each test, they recorded their scores, evaluated them against their goals, and changed study plans if desired. Results showed that the goal-setting treatment significantly increased students' accuracy of goal setting and their attributions for their successes and difficulties to effort. They also were less likely to attribute their outcomes to factors beyond their control (e.g., luck, task difficulty).

The participants in a study by Schunk (1985) were sixth-grade students classified as having learning disabilities in mathematics. Over several sessions, children received subtraction instruction that included practice opportunities. Some children set short-term (proximal) performance goals each session, others had comparable goals assigned to them by the teachers, and children in a third condition neither set nor received goals. Compared with no goals, proximal goals led to higher student motivation during the sessions. Children who set their own goals demonstrated the highest self-efficacy and subtraction achievement. Participation in goal setting can raise learner commitment, which can produce an initial sense of self-efficacy for learning and enhance motivation and learning.

Schunk and Rice (1989, 1991) compared the effects of learning process goals with those of product goals among children with reading disabilities. Students participated in a comprehension strategy instruction program comprising modeled instruction, guided practice, and independent practice. For each session, some students received a product goal of answering comprehension questions, whereas others were given a process goal of learning to use the strategy. In the Schunk and Rice (1989) study, students in a third condition received no goal but were advised to work productively; in the Schunk and Rice (1991) study, children in a third condition received the process goal and periodic feedback on their goal progress.

Schunk and Rice (1989) found that compared with the no-goal group, students in the goal conditions demonstrated higher self-efficacy, and that process-goal students displayed higher achievement. The results of the Schunk and Rice (1991) study showed that children who received process goals and feedback demonstrated higher self-efficacy and achievement compared with students in the other two conditions. Collectively, these results attest to the importance of process goals for promoting achievement outcomes. By highlighting their progress in learning, the feedback also helped to substantiate children's self-efficacy for performing well.

Self-Regulated Strategy Development

Self-Regulated Strategy Development (SRSD) is an intervention program designed to teach students strategies for completing academic tasks (Harris, Graham, & Mason, 2006). It includes many of the components discussed in this chapter, such as instruction and practice on self-regulation strategies (e.g., goal setting, self-monitoring, effort expenditure) designed to improve academic performance and motivation. SRSD utilizes teacher modeling of strategies, collaborative peer group practice, and independent practice, where assistance (*scaffolding*) is gradually faded out. SRSD includes general and specific strategies, as well as motivational components (e.g., self-reinforcement).

SRSD has been applied to different academic content including writing (Harris et al., 2006), reading (Mason, 2004), and mathematics (Fuchs et al., 2003). Research has shown that SRSD has a positive effect on students' learning, motivation, and self-regulated strategy use (Harris et al., 2006). Here we describe its application to writing; some adaptations of the procedure typically are necessary depending on the type of students, content area, and specific skills addressed.

Reid and Lienemann (2006) applied SRSD to elementary children identified as having ADHD. The specific academic task addressed was story writing. Students were taught to set goals, monitor their performances, instruct themselves and manage their effort expenditure, use the strategy, and other behaviors. Performance improvements were made explicit with self-monitoring and graphing. After students were taught the strategies, instruction gradually shifted responsibility for their use to the students. Feedback and instructional support were individualized; students moved through the instruction and practice at their own pace.

Participants received 30-minute instructional sessions until they could achieve the criterion of independently writing a story with seven parts. These essential parts were identified with the mnemonic WWW, What = 2, How = 2: *Who* are the main characters? *Where* does the story take place? *When* does the story take place? *What* do the main characters want to do? *What* happens next? *How* does the story end? *How* do the main characters feel? In addition to this writing mnemonic, SRSD also used a planning mnemonic to help students plan narrative stories: POW—"*Pick* my ideas," "*Organize* my notes," and, "*Write* and say more."

In the first part of the intervention—Develop Background Knowledge—students were introduced to the planning and story writing mnemonics as the teacher explained them and then had students explain them and their importance. The teacher then modeled by reading stories aloud and having students pick out the seven parts.

In the second stage of instruction—Discuss It—students continued to pick out story parts from stories the teacher read to them. Students then followed the same procedure in analyzing stories they had written to determine whether they had included all seven parts. They completed charts graphing the number of parts and number of words their stories included.

During the third stage, Model It, the teacher explained and demonstrated the use of the POW and the WWW, What = 2, How = 2 strategies by generating a story with student input that included all elements. As ideas were generated, the teacher wrote them on a planning sheet that included prompts for the seven parts of a good story. The teacher verbalized statements to help generate ideas; for example, problem definition (e.g., "What is my goal?"), planning (e.g., "What is my next step?"), self-evaluation (e.g., "Does that make sense?"), self-reinforcement (e.g., "I like that part!"), and coping (e.g., "I'm almost done!"). The teacher discussed with students the importance of verbalizing these statements, after which students created self-statements to use while writing.

The Support It stage was collaborative as teacher and students jointly wrote a story using the mnemonics and graphic organizers. Students wrote the story and then verified that all seven elements were included. To develop their beliefs about the importance of strategy use, the teacher asked students how the strategies helped them write better stories.

During the final Independent Performance stage, students wrote stories independently after receiving a story prompt. When they finished, they graphed the number of story parts and number of words in the story.

Results of the intervention showed that students gained significantly in number of story parts addressed and number of words in stories. Maintenance tests given 3 and 6 weeks after the Independent Performance stage showed that gains were maintained.

This application of SRSD and others have shown that it not only benefits learners' knowledge and use of strategies for performance and motivation but also facilitates maintenance and generalization of self-regulated strategy use beyond the original learning setting (Harris et al., 2011). Although SRSD studies have not evaluated students' self-regulation development according to the levels of development postulated by Zimmerman (2000), the project descriptions show that the observation, emulation, and self-control levels are addressed, and the results suggest that students often may attain the self-regulation level.

Implications for Practice

The theory and research on academic self-regulation discussed in this chapter have implications for educational practice (Table 18.2). It seems clear that students with disabilities should be taught methods for self-regulating their cognitions, motivation, and behaviors, and be given opportunities to practice these skills by embedding them within actual academic tasks.

Zimmerman's (2000) model offers guidance on how to proceed with instruction, and the SRSD program illustrates an application. Teachers initially explain and demonstrate self-regulatory processes such as setting goals, deciding which strategy to use, and monitoring performance outcomes (observation). Students then practice with guidance, coaching, and feedback from the teacher (emulation), after which they practice independently inside and

Table 18.2 Implications for Practice of Self-Regulation Theory and Research

Teach self-regulation and provide opportunities for learners to practice

Assist students as they learn to adapt self-regulation skills

Have students set goals and monitor progress

Foster desirable attributions by students

Incorporate forethought, performance control, and self-reflection into instruction

outside of class (self-control). This latter practice allows students to internalize processes so they can employ them on their own.

To fully attain self-regulation, however, students must be able to adapt self-regulation methods to changing environmental and task conditions. Goal setting, for example, is useful on all types of academic tasks, but the type of goal and its difficulty will vary for each student depending on the content area. Thus, students should be encouraged to practice their self-regulation skills in different content areas and shown through teacher modeling, guidance, and feedback, how to make needed adaptations.

The roles of goal setting and self-monitoring of progress are especially important for motivation and achievement. As students monitor their progress toward their goals and perceive that they are making progress, this perception helps to strengthen their self-efficacy and motivation for continued learning. Progress can be monitored mentally or students can keep records, such as with lists where they check off tasks as they complete them. Such progress self-evaluations are beneficial for all learners and especially for students with disabilities, many of whom have encountered academic difficulties and who may doubt their capabilities to succeed. Although students benefit from teacher scaffolding that helps them succeed, independent practice is needed to develop self-efficacy and self-regulation.

Another suggestion is to ensure that students make desirable attributions for their academic outcomes. Students who have experienced learning difficulties may believe that they lack the ability to perform well, which can negatively affect motivation (Licht, Kistner, Ozkaragoz, Shapiro, & Clausen, 1985). Teachers can assist by showing students how their work has improved as a result of their effort and use of self-regulatory skills—factors they can control. Providing attributional feedback to students for their successes and difficulties that highlights these controllable factors can help to sustain motivation and their self-efficacy for learning.

Finally, we recommend that attention be given during instruction to the three phases of self-regulation (Zimmerman, 2000): forethought, performance control, and self-reflection. Students with disabilities may be inclined to move quickly to the performance phase without giving adequate forethought to processes such as setting goals and deciding which strategy to use. They also may not be inclined to pause during performance and engage in self-reflection, such as assessing their task progress, deciding whether to continue their approach or change, and judging their self-efficacy for learning. These phases can be built into instructional sequences as teachers can have students engage in forethought planning before they begin and then having them periodically stop to self-reflect.

Future Research Directions

Research on academic self-regulation with students with disabilities has advanced tremendously in the past few years, and we expect this trend to continue. In this section we suggest some profitable areas for future research, which will contribute to our understanding of the operation of self-regulation processes among students with disabilities and have implications for educational practice.

Self-Regulation and Curricular Integration

Research is needed on self-regulation in curriculum areas. When self-regulatory processes are linked with academic content, students learn how to apply them in learning contexts. It is worthwhile to teach students to set goals, organize their schedules, rehearse information to be remembered, and the like, but such instruction may not transfer beyond the context in which it is provided.

In the past few years, researchers increasingly have investigated the effects on learning and motivation of incorporating self-regulation instruction into academic curricula (Schunk & Zimmerman, 2008; Zimmerman & Schunk, 2011). For example, research has shown that students' motivation, learning, self-regulation, and achievement can be improved in such diverse content areas as reading, writing, science, and mathematics, and that students can be taught to adapt self-regulatory processes for use on academic content outside of the instructional context (Zimmerman & Schunk, 2011).

We recommend that this research direction be expanded. Additional studies are needed to determine how the teaching of self-regulatory skills can be modified to fit different situations. For example, many schools are employing a *Response to Intervention* (RTI) framework that calls for the systematic use of increasingly intensive, evidence-based interventions, or instructional tiers, as a means for deciding whether a learning disability exists (Fuchs & Deshler, 2007). RTI also involves prevention, as the provision of high-quality, evidence-based instruction in the less-intensive tiers may prevent more serious academic difficulties from occurring (Bursuck & Damer, 2011). The teaching of self-regulated learning should have a place within all RTI tiers, but it remains for researchers to determine just how instruction in self-regulated learning can be effectively integrated into RTI models. For example, instruction in self-regulation is usually delivered in small groups or one to one while the least intensive tier, tier 1—the tier most important for preventing future learning difficulties—is usually delivered within larger instructional groups. Research is needed on how self-regulation can be effectively taught within larger instructional groupings. The potential impact of training in self-regulation on rates of students identified as learning disabled is another research question of interest.

In general, studies that show how self-regulated learning can be used in different situations have the added benefit of showing students the value of self-regulation for their learning, motivation, and academic performance. Students who learn strategies but feel they are not especially useful are not likely to use them. From a motivational perspective, students who believe they can effectively use strategies to learn and perform better are apt to hold high self-efficacy for learning, which strengthens their motivation for continued learning (Schunk & Pajares, 2009).

Self-Regulation Across Cultures

Most investigations of self-regulation among students with disabilities have been conducted in Western cultures. As interest in self-regulation has grown, researchers have explored the operation of self-regulatory processes in non-Western cultures. This trend is promising, and we recommend more international self-regulation research.

It is risky to assume that self-regulatory processes operate much the same way in students regardless of culture. Cultures reflect the values, traditions, and beliefs that affect the behaviors of social groups and their ways of perceiving their social environments (McInerney, 2011). It is erroneous to believe that individuals in different cultures hold the same meanings for the elements of self-regulated learning. For example, Chinese and Japanese cultures emphasize education, effort, and high achievement standards, and children in these cultures are expected to fulfill their parents' ambitions for them (McInerney, 2008). These students perform well in the type of structured situations common in their cultures, but may not display high levels of self-regulated behavior in less-structured situations. The types of self-regulated strategies discussed in this chapter (e.g., goal setting, self-monitoring, self-instruction) may not be strategies that Chinese and Japanese students are skilled in employing.

This is not to suggest that students in non-Western cultures do not display self-regulation. Effort expenditure, for example, is valued in Chinese and Japanese cultures (McInerney, 2008). Self-regulation covers not only cognitive strategies but emotional and motivational ones as well, of which the self-regulation of effort and persistence is critical. An expanded level of international research will identify the prevalent self-regulation strategies in different cultures and ways that students with disabilities employ them productively to promote their learning and achievement.

Self-Regulation During Learning with Technology

The last several years have witnessed a rapid explosion of technology in instruction with students with disabilities. Technology has the potential to facilitate learning in ways that formerly were unknown. Compared with only a few years ago, today's students can experience simulations of events and environments, receive instruction from and communicate with others at long distances, and interact with large knowledge bases and expert tutoring systems.

Challenges for researchers are to determine which self-regulation strategies are helpful for learning from technology and how to teach students these strategies and raise their motivation for using them. Computer-based learning environments have many advantages over traditional instruction, but they typically lack the external controls found in traditional settings (e.g., teachers keeping students on task). It seems that many self-regulation strategies would be critical for learning in the absence of external regulation.

Research also is needed on how technology may help to improve students' self-regulated learning. Azevedo and colleagues have shown how hypermedia learning environments can be structured to foster learners' self-regulated learning in such key areas as planning, knowledge activation, metacognitive monitoring, and self-reflection (Azevedo, 2005; Azevedo & Cromley, 2004; Azevedo, Johnson, Chauncey, & Graesser, 2011). This type of research is needed on students with disabilities.

Conclusion

Self-regulation has become an integral topic in the study of human learning. Developing self-regulation skills among students with disabilities can improve their learning, motivation, and achievement. More research and intervention studies will show how to best improve their self-regulatory skills and will contribute to our understanding of the role of self-regulation in their educational success.

References

Azevedo, R. (2005). Using hypermedia as a metacognitive tool for enhancing student learning? The role of self-regulated learning. *Educational Psychologist, 40*, 199–209.

Azevedo, R., & Cromley, J. G. (2004). Does training on self-regulated learning facilitate students' learning with hypermedia? *Journal of Educational Psychology, 96*, 523–535.

Azevedo, R., Johnson, A., Chauncey, A., & Graesser, A. (2011). Use of hypermedia to assess and convey self-regulated learning. In B. J. Zimmerman & D. H. Schunk (Eds.), *Handbook of self-regulation of learning and performance* (pp. 102–121). New York: Routledge.

Bandura, A. (1986). *Social foundations of thought and action: A social cognitive theory.* Englewood Cliffs, NJ: Prentice Hall.

Bandura, A. (1997). *Self-efficacy: The exercise of control.* New York: Freeman.

Bandura, A. (2001). Social cognitive theory: An agentic perspective. *Annual Review of Psychology, 52*, 1–26.

Barkley, R.A. (1997). Behavioral inhibition, sustained attention, and executive functions: Constructing a unifying theory of ADHD. *Psychological Bulletin, 121*, 65–94.

Bear, G.G., Kortering, L.J., & Braziel, P. (2006). School completers and non-completers with learning disabilities: Similarities in academic achievement and perceptions of self and teacher. *Remedial and Special Education, 27*, 293–300.

Belfiore, P. J., & Hornyak, R. S. (1998). Operant theory and application to self- monitoring in adolescents. In D. H. Schunk & B. J. Zimmerman (Eds.), *Self- regulated learning: From teaching to self-reflective practice* (pp. 184–202). New York: Guilford Press.

Boekaerts, M., Pintrich, P. R., & Zeidner, M. (Eds.) (2000). *Handbook of self-regulation.* San Diego: Academic Press.

Brigham, T. A. (1982). Self-management: A radical behavioral perspective. In P. Karoly & F. H. Kanfer (Eds.), *Self-management and behavior change: From theory to practice* (pp. 32–59). New York: Pergamon.

Bryan, J. H., & Bryan, T. H. (1983). The social life of the learning disabled youngster. In J. D. McKinney & L. Feagans (Eds.), *Current topics in learning disabilities* (Vol. 1, pp. 57–85). Norwood, NJ: Ablex.

Bursuck, W.D., & Damer, M. (2011). *Teaching reading to students who are at risk or who have disabilities* (2nd ed.). Boston, MA: Pearson.

Cameto, R., Levine, P., & Wagner, M. (2004). *Transition planning for students with disabilities: A special topic report of findings from the National Longitudinal Study-2 (NLTS2).* Menlo Park, CA: SRI International. Available at http://www.nlts2.org/reports/2004_11/nlts2_report_2004_11_complete.pdf

Cattaneo, L. B., & Chapman, A. R. (2010). The process of empowerment: A model for use in research and practice. *American Psychologist, 65*, 646–659.

Cleary, T. J., Zimmerman, B. J., & Keating, T. (2006). Training physical education students to self-regulate during basketball free throw practice. *Research Quarterly for Exercise and Sport, 77*, 251–262.

DiBenedetto, M. K., & Zimmerman, B. J. (2010). Differences in self-regulatory processes among students studying science: A microanalytic investigation. *International Journal of Educational and Psychological Assessment, 5*(1), 2–24.

Fuchs, D., & Deshler, D. D. (2007). What we need to know about responsiveness to intervention (and shouldn't be afraid to ask). *Learning Disabilities Research and Practice, 22*, 129–136.

Fuchs, L. S., Fuchs, D., Prentice, K., Burch, M., Hamlett, C. L., Owen, R., Hosp, M., & Jancek, D. (2003). Explicitly teaching for transfer: Effects on third-grade students' mathematical problem solving. *Journal of Educational Psychology, 95*, 293–305.

Gerber, P. J., Ginsberg, R., & Reiff, H. B. (1992). Identifying alterable patterns in employment success for highly successful adults with learning disabilities. *Journal of Learning Disabilities, 25*, 475–487.

Hallahan, D. P., & Mercer, C. D. (2002). Learning disabilities: Historical perspectives. In R. Bradley, L. Danielson, & D. P. Hallahan (Eds.), *Identification of learning disabilities: Research to practice* (pp.1–67). Mahwah, NJ: Erlbaum.

Harris, K. R., Graham, S., MacArthur, C. A., Reid, R., & Mason, L. H. (2011). Self- regulated learning processes and children's writing. In B. J. Zimmerman & D. H. Schunk (Eds.), *Handbook of self-regulation of learning and performance* (pp. 187–202). New York: Routledge.

Harris, K. R., Graham, S., & Mason, L. H. (2006). Improving the writing, knowledge, and motivation of struggling young writers: Effects of Self-Regulated Strategy Development with and without peer support. *American Educational Research Journal, 43*, 295–340.

Harris, K. R., Graham, S., Mason, L. H., & Friedlander, B. (2008). *Powerful writing strategies for all students.* Baltimore: Brookes.

Kanfer, F. H., & Gaelick, K. (1986). Self-management methods. In F. H. Kanfer & A. P. Goldstein (Eds.), *Helping people change: A textbook of methods* (3rd ed., pp. 283–345). New York: Pergamon.

Karoly, P., & Kanfer, F. H. (Eds.) (1982). *Self-management and behavior change: From theory to practice.* New York: Pergamon.

Kosiewicz, M. M., Hallahan, D. P., Lloyd, J., & Graves, A. W. (1982). Effects of self- instruction and self-correction procedures on handwriting performance. *Learning Disability Quarterly, 5*, 71–78.

Lan, W. Y. (1998). Teaching self-monitoring skills in statistics. In D. H. Schunk & B. J. Zimmerman (Eds.), *Self-regulated learning: From teaching to self-reflective practice* (pp. 86–105). New York: Guilford Press.

Licht, B. G., & Kistner, J. A. (1986). Motivational problems of learning-disabled children: Individual differences and their implications for treatment. In J. K. Torgesen & B. W. L. Wong (Eds.), *Psychological and educational perspectives on learning disabilities* (pp. 225–255). Orlando: Academic Press.

Licht, B. G., Kistner, J. A., Ozkaragoz, T., Shapiro, S., & Clausen, L. (1985). Causal attributions of learning disabled children: Individual differences and their implications for persistence. *Journal of Educational Psychology, 77*, 208–216.

Locke, E. A., & Latham, G. P. (2002). Building a practically useful theory of goal setting and task motivation: A 35-year odyssey. *American Psychologist, 57*, 705–717.

Lodewyk, K. R. & Winne, P. H. (2005). Relations among the structure of learning tasks, achievement, and changes in self-efficacy in secondary students. *Journal of Educational Psychology, 97*, 3–12.

Lord, R. G., Diefendorff, J. M., Schmidt, A. M., & Hall, R. J. (2010). Self-regulation at work. *Annual Review of Psychology, 61*, 543–568.

Mace, F. C., Belfiore, P. J., & Hutchinson, J. M. (2001). Operant theory and research on self-regulation. In B. J. Zimmerman & D. H. Schunk (Eds.), *Self-regulated learning and academic achievement: Theoretical perspectives* (2nd ed., pp. 39–65). Mahwah, NJ: Erlbaum.

Mace, F. C., Belfiore, P. J., & Shea, M. C. (1989). Operant theory and research on self- regulation. In B. J. Zimmerman & D. H. Schunk (Eds.), *Self-regulated learning and academic achievement: Theory, research, and practice* (pp. 27–50). New York: Springer-Verlag.

Mace, F. C., & West, B. J. (1986). Unresolved theoretical issues in self-management: Implications for research and practice. *Professional School Psychology, 1*, 149–163.

Mason, L. H. (2004). Explicit self-regulated strategy development versus reciprocal questioning: Effects on expository reading comprehension among struggling readers. *Journal of Educational Psychology, 96*, 283–296.

McInerney, D. M. (2008). The motivational roles of cultural differences and cultural identity in self-regulated learning. In D. H. Schunk & B. J. Zimmerman (Eds.), *Motivation and self-regulated learning: Theory, research, and applications* (pp. 369–400). New York: Taylor & Francis.

McInerney, D. (2011). Culture and self-regulation in educational contexts: Assessing the relationship of cultural group to self-regulation. In B. J. Zimmerman & D. H. Schunk (Eds.), *Handbook of self-regulation of learning and performance* (pp. 442–464). New York: Routledge.

Newman, L., Wagner, M., Cameto, R., & Knokey, A.M. (2009). *The post-high school outcomes of youths with disabilities up to 4 years after high school. A report from the National Longitudinal Transition Study-2 (NLTS2) (NCSER 2009-3017).* Menlo Park, CA: SRI international. Available at: http://www.nlts2.org/reports/2009_04/nlts2_report_2009_04_complete.pdf

O'Leary, S. G., & Dubey, D. R. (1979). Applications of self-control procedures by children: A review. *Journal of Applied Behavior Analysis, 12*, 449–466.

Pintrich, P. R. (2000). The role of goal orientation in self-regulated learning. In M. Boekaerts, P. R. Pintrich, & M. Zeidner (Eds.), *Handbook of self-regulation* (pp. 451–502). San Diego: Academic Press.

Pintrich, P. R. (2004). A conceptual framework for assessing motivation and self- regulated learning in college students. *Educational Psychology Review, 16*, 385–407.

Pintrich, P. R., & Zusho, A. (2002). The development of academic self-regulation: The role of cognitive and motivational factors. In A. Wigfield & J. S. Eccles (Eds.), *Development of achievement motivation* (pp. 249–284). San Diego: Academic Press.

Reid, R. (1996). Research in self-monitoring with students with learning disabilities: The present, the prospects, the pitfalls. *Journal of Learning Disabilities, 29*, 317–331.

Reid, R., & Harris, K. R. (1993). Self-monitoring of attention versus self-monitoring of performance: Effects on attention and academic performance. *Exceptional Children, 60*, 29–40.

Reid, R., & Lienemann, T. O. (2006). Self-Regulated Strategy Development for written expression with students with attention deficit/hyperactivity disorder. *Exceptional Children, 73*, 53–68.

Reid, R., Trout, A. L., & Schartz, M. (2005). Self-regulation interventions for children with attention deficit/hyperactivity disorder. *Exceptional Children, 71*, 361–377.

Schunk, D. H. (1983). Progress self-monitoring: Effects on children's self-efficacy and achievement. *Journal of Experimental Education, 51*, 89–93.

Schunk, D. H. (1985). Participation in goal setting: Effects on self-efficacy and skills of learning-disabled children. *Journal of Special Education, 19*, 307–317.

Schunk, D. H., & Cox, P. D. (1986). Strategy training and attributional feedback with learning disabled students. *Journal of Educational Psychology, 78,* 201–209.

Schunk, D. H., & Pajares, F. (2009). Self-efficacy theory. In K. R. Wentzel & A. Wigfield (Eds.), *Handbook of motivation at school* (pp. 35–53). New York: Routledge.

Schunk, D. H., & Rice, J. M. (1984). Strategy self-verbalization during remedial listening comprehension instruction. *Journal of Experimental Education, 53,* 49–54.

Schunk, D. H., & Rice, J. M. (1985). Verbalization of comprehension strategies: Effects on children's achievement outcomes. *Human Learning, 4,* 1–10.

Schunk, D. H., & Rice, J. M. (1987). Enhancing comprehension skill and self-efficacy with strategy value information. *Journal of Reading Behavior, 19,* 285–302.

Schunk, D. H., & Rice, J. M. (1989). Learning goals and children's reading comprehension. *Journal of Reading Behavior, 21,* 279–293.

Schunk, D. H., & Rice, J. M. (1991). Learning goals and progress feedback during reading comprehension instruction. *Journal of Reading Behavior, 23,* 351–364.

Schunk, D. H., & Rice, J. M. (1992). Influence of reading-comprehension strategy information on children's achievement outcomes. *Learning Disability Quarterly, 15,* 51–64.

Schunk, D. H., & Rice, J. M. (1993). Strategy fading and progress feedback: Effects on self-efficacy and comprehension among students receiving remedial reading services. *Journal of Special Education, 27,* 257–276.

Schunk, D. H., & Zimmerman, B. J. (1997). Social origins of self-regulatory competence. *Educational Psychologist, 32,* 195–208.

Schunk, D. H., & Zimmerman, B. J. (Eds.) (2008). *Motivation and self-regulated learning: Theory, research, and applications.* New York: Taylor & Francis.

Skinner, B. F. (1953). *Science and human behavior.* New York: Macmillan.

Tollefson, N., Tracy, D. B., Johnsen, E. P., Farmer, A. W., & Buenning, M. (1984). Goal setting and personal responsibility training for LD adolescents. *Psychology in the Schools, 21,* 224–233.

Wagner, M., Newman, L., Cameto, R., Garza, N., & Levine, P. (2005). *After high school: A first look at the postschool experiences of youth with disabilities. A report from the National Longitudinal Transition Study-2 (NLTS2).* Menlo Park, CA: SRI International.

Wehmeyer, M. L., Abery, B. H., Zhang, D., Ward, K., Willis, D., Hossain, W.A., Balcazar, F., Ball, A., Bacon, A., Calkins, C., Heller, T., Goode, T., Dias, R., Jesien, G. S., McVeigh, T., Nygren, M. A., Palmer, S. B., & Walker, H. M. (2011). Personal self-determination and moderating variables that impact efforts to promote self-determination. *Exceptionality, 19:* 19–30.

Zimmerman, B. J. (1998). Developing self-fulfilling cycles of academic regulation: An analysis of exemplary instructional models. In D. H. Schunk & B. J. Zimmerman (Eds.), *Self-regulated learning: From teaching to self-reflective practice* (pp. 1–19). New York: Guilford Press.

Zimmerman, B. J. (2000). Attaining self-regulation: A social cognitive perspective. In M. Boekaerts, P. R. Pintrich, & M. Zeidner (Eds.), *Handbook of self-regulation* (pp. 13–39). San Diego, CA: Academic Press.

Zimmerman, B. J. (2001). Theories of self-regulated learning and academic achievement: An overview and analysis. In B. J. Zimmerman & D. H. Schunk (Eds.), *Self- regulated learning and academic achievement: Theoretical perspectives* (pp. 1–38). Mahwah, NJ: Erlbaum.

Zimmerman, B. J. (2011). Motivational sources and outcomes of self-regulated learning and performance. In B. J. Zimmerman & D. H. Schunk (Eds.), *Handbook of self- regulation of learning and performance* (pp. 49–64). New York: Routledge.

Zimmerman, B. J., & Schunk, D. H. (2004). Self-regulating intellectual processes and outcomes: A social cognitive perspective. In D. Y. Dai & R. J. Sternberg (Eds.), *Motivation, emotion, and cognition: Integrative perspectives on intellectual functioning and development* (pp. 323–350). Mahwah, NJ: Erlbaum.

Zimmerman, B. J., & Schunk, D. H. (Eds.) (2011). *Handbook of self-regulation of learning and performance.* New York: Routledge.

Disability Studies/Disability Culture

Brenda Jo Brueggemann

Abstract

This chapter addresses three primary questions: *What is disability culture? What is disability studies? How do these two interact?* Disability culture is explored as a movement "from the inside out," one focused on issues of choice, power, language, and identity/community. Disability studies is articulated as a political and interdisciplinary field, and four key areas of scholarly and activist focus (and the connection between them) that take place within the field are examined: questioning previous and developing models of disability (social, medical, identity); refiguring representation; restructuring worldview concepts such as normal, different, deviant; and understanding disability as positioned within diversity and identity. The productive and creative potential, and the limiting and denigrating reality, of categorizing disability/disabilities is considered. Finally, future directions and key questions for both disability studies and disability culture are outlined.

Key Words: disability studies, disability culture, identity, representation, normal, diversity, aesthetics

The Chicken or the Egg?

Disability studies and disability culture are two pieces of a circle that tie back into themselves, where one's tail becomes the other's head and vice versa. Like the "chicken or the egg" paradox (which came first?), it is hard to set one in front of the other or to determine, for example, if disability studies has grown up and out from disability culture or if disability culture has arisen from (or at least alongside) disability studies. Instead, it becomes perhaps more important to acknowledge that they exist in a closely coupled, twin-like relationship and that they are both very much part of a "positive psychology" and nonpathological approach to disability and to the lives of disabled people.

In a groundbreaking 1996 book for both disability studies and disability culture, *The Rejected Body: Feminist Philosophical Reflections on Disability*, author Susan Wendell promised that "if disabled

people were truly heard [without sentimentalizing], an explosion of knowledge of the human body and psyche would take place" (p. 274). From many perspectives, as outlined in this chapter, it looks as if this explosion is now under way and, in its positive, constructive aftermath, we are also witnessing the establishment and growth of two twinned—shared but separate—elements: disability culture and disability studies. For the purposes of organizational clarity, this chapter first outlines disability culture and then maps, at more length, the terrain of disability studies. Its conclusion rewraps those two strands into one ball of colorful twine using the categorization of disability (collective identity, community) into disabili*ties* (individualized, multiple) as a merging model. The chapter concludes by delineating future directions that present some of the problems that remain, issues to be addressed, and terrains to be traveled in the promising, and positive, intersections between disability studies and disability culture.

Disability Culture: From the Inside Out

Although there are many markers that show people with disabilities in the United States joining in community (and, thus, potential culture) throughout the 1960s and 1970s, and although the American Deaf community lays claims to "Deaf Culture" from the early to mid-1800s (Krentz, 2000; Van Cleve, 2007; Van Cleve & Crouch; 1989), one of the earliest explicit references to a thing called "disability culture" is from historian and activist Steven Brown (n.d.). In a 7-minute video from the "It's Our Story" Project—part 9 of 12—Brown narrates his own memories and sense of the development of the idea (and term) "Disability Culture." In his mini oral history, Brown chronicles the role of *The Disability Rag* newspaper/magazine and its editor, Mary Johnson; psychologist and scholar, Carol Gill; and Judy Heumann, disability activist and former assistant secretary of the U.S. Department of Education. He also mentions how, in those early days of the late 1980s and early 1990s, every time he dared to ask people to talk about the idea of *disability culture* he received passionate responses, both celebrating and rejecting the idea (from people with disabilities themselves).

One of the earliest explicit published references to *disability culture* is from poet and performer Cheryl Marie Wade. She writes in a 1994 piece, "Disability Culture Rap," published in *The Ragged Edge*: "So what's this disability culture stuff all about? It's simple/ it's just 'This is disability. From the inside out'" (p. 17). (Later, a performance piece created from, stylized on, and expanded from this original printed text. It is, as of this writing, available on YouTube in two parts that total roughly 22 minutes [Wade, 2010].)

Wade's poetic "inside out" reference is largely based on the idea of claiming (one's own identity) rather than naming or being named (having one's condition named by others, particularly medical, rehabilitative, employment, or educational others). From "inside out" is about valuing the disability experience from inside the person who lives it and tells, it rather than valuing "case studies" of that person delivered by people outside the experience. As such, "inside out" is typically a nonpathological, positive approach to the condition (impairment) and experience (disability) one lives in through different contexts and situations. In a similar "from the inside out" move, one of the first major anthologies of writing by people with disabilities was edited by Kenny Fries in 1997 and took, as its title, the same view: *Staring Back: The Disability Experience from the Inside Out*. Some of the pulses of Wade's 1992 rap/

poetry/performance piece might serve well as categories to further explicate a thing called "Disability Culture": choice, power, language, and identity.

Choice

The questions of *choice* in disability culture are many. The twinned movements of disability rights and disability culture have often centered on the power, autonomy, and agency that comes with choosing: Where will we live? How will we live? Who will live with us? Who will "take care" of us? How will we be treated, seen, known?

These questions of choice arise in importance largely because so many disabled people have lived institutional/ized lives, in which choice was minimal at best and completely denied or violently overtaken at worst. Key movements in disability culture and activism have operated around such choices: ADAPT, Not Dead Yet (2012), the Independent Living Movement, and perhaps even the Autistic Students Advocacy Network (ASAN).

ADAPT, as just one example, originally began in Denver, Colorado, in 1983, and was, in its initial skin, a grassroots organization that took action to get wheelchair accessible lifts on Denver city buses; the acronym stood, at that time, for Americans Disabled for Accessible Public Transit. In its current iteration, ADAPT now articulates itself as "a national grass-roots community that organizes disability rights activists to engage in nonviolent direct action, including civil disobedience, to assure the civil and human rights of people with disabilities to live in freedom" (ADAPT, 2012; http://www.adapt.org/) This morphing of the organization—in key words (that still manage to match the ADAPT-able acronym) and in goals—reflects the shifting terrain of disability rights and disability culture from the 1980s through the 1990s and into the first decades of the 2000s.

Power

Much like the central concern with issues of choice, the access to, engagement with, and even taking of power much occupies disability culture and disability rights movements and activism from at least the 1980s forward. Regaining power (and autonomy, as well as choice)—a central tenet of the Independent Living Movement—has been a pulse for both the development of disability culture and disability studies. Power to rebalance, revert, and reconfigure the oppression of those with disabilities, as well as the narrative, linguistic, political, and historical power to tell, find, and make your own history and heroes, your own policies, your own story—all of these potential powers sit at the foundation of the current, building work of both disability studies and disability culture.

Language

The importance of the repeated phrase, "pass the word," in Cheryl Marie Wade's "Disability Culture Rap" is that the phrase signifies, in a kind of chorused repetition, the power of language itself—in telling the story and keeping the story going. This storytelling and sharing builds a foundation for disability culture. Likewise, the ability to make one's own terms (names) and to claim and define those terms is an essential feature of language used with power. In contemporary disability culture, the power to name and claim often takes the form of "talking back" as disabled individuals take up their own words and ideas to define themselves.

The disability rights movement (DRM) increased and encouraged the affirmation and celebration of disability identity. It emphasized the importance of disabled people and their allies "talking back" to their oppressors, insisting on their basic civil rights, and demanding access to full participation in society. A significant part of the DRM and the development of a discernible disability culture has been the strategic and proud adoption of formerly negative and exclusionary rhetoric and imagery—terms such as "crip(ple)" and "gimp"—as a form of powerful celebration and affirmation. As Mitchell and Snyder put it, "As opposed to substituting more palatable terms, the ironic embrace of derogatory terminology has provided the leverage that belongs to openly transgressive displays" (Mitchell & Snyder, 2000, p. 35). Being a cultural outsider actually lends a significant amount of power to the outsider, who is then in a position to critique the inner core of the social order that has excluded her.

One simple but important gesture has been the adoption of the term "crip" as a way to denote membership in a disability culture that embraces its outsider status and celebrates the uniqueness, joys, and challenges of being a disabled person. Thus, Robert McRuer's important volume on disability studies in the humanities is titled *Crip Theory* and makes connections to the similar transgressive logic of the gay rights movement's adoption of "queer" as a positive term of value.

Identity

Disability identity—individual or collective— is often forged through multiple melding streams: through art (practices and products), through representing one's own models and heroes or heroines, through telling one's own history, through foregrounding one's own preferred cultural representations, and through individuals collecting themselves into community.

DOCUMENTARY FILMS BY DISABILITY ADVOCATES

One good example of disability culture being both created and illustrated is through documentary films made by (or with) disability advocates in the late 20th and early 21st centuries. These films effectively celebrate models and heroes/heroines, tell history "from the inside out," and are also often artistically interesting. These documentaries explore individuals' or particular groups' experiences, disability rights issues, community formation, and specific topics that are important to disability experience and identity, such as sexuality, family, and assistive technology. As disabled people have organized into a political group to pass laws such as the Americans with Disabilities Act (in 1990; amended in 2008), a disability community and culture have formed that are both reflected in and fostered by documentaries by disabled people.

For example, Billy Golfus's documentary *When Billy Broke His Head...And Other Tales of Wonder* devotes attention to Billy's quest to find individuals who are part of the disability community (Golfus, 1994). Another documentary that is itself a critical look at disability rights, representations of disability, and being both female and disabled is *Leibe Perla*. This film chronicles the friendship between Perla Ovitz and Hannelore Witkofski, two women of short stature. Perla is a Nazi concentration camp survivor, and Hannelore is a German academic anthropologist who is helping Perla find in the archives a degrading video that Dr. Josef Mengele made of Perla's family during the war (Rozen & Kowarsky, 1999). One strength of films made by disabled people about disability is that their perspectives become widely available to viewing audiences, and, in this way, disability culture is better shared, understood, and valued.

At the same time that some disability documentaries have influenced culture within communities of disabled people, some recent films also explicitly seek to communicate disability experiences to nondisabled viewers. There is no clear line between films that are intended for disabled people and those that are not, but some documentaries have caught the attention of nondisabled viewers on a large scale. Two examples are *Murderball* and *Through*

Deaf Eyes. Because both films were produced by well-known networks (*Murderball* by MTV Films and *Through Deaf Eyes* by PBS), large numbers of viewers who might not otherwise seek out documentaries on disability have encountered them. The films include information on quadriplegia (in *Murderball*; Shapiro, Mandel, & Rubin, 2005) and on the history of deafness and Deaf culture in America (in *Through Deaf Eyes*; Garey & Hott, 2007) that members outside of the quadriplegic and the Deaf communities would probably not already know. These films use documentary as a medium to educate and inform nondisabled audiences about specific experiences with disability with which those audiences would otherwise be unfamiliar.

ONLINE COMMUNITY, PERSONAL NARRATIVES, AND "SPEAKING BACK"

Another example of a community and of a growing cultural practice that forges and advances disability identity is the use of online communities and personal narratives. Disabled individuals increasingly use online spaces to speak back to an able-bodied, one-size-fits-all world. As autobiography scholar G. Thomas Couser (2009) has commented, the affordances that digital media lend to those with disabilities are not widely available within the strictures of the publishing industry. Book presses, especially popular presses, often publish "typical," formulaic narratives—such as the triumph narrative, or the sentimental/pity-me narrative, or the gift-from-God narrative—when the topic involves disability. Accounts that disembark from these formulas are not as marketable. As a result, many disabled people who advocate a social approach to disability, rather than a medical approach, find themselves relegated to the blogosphere.

The affordances of blogging and other online, community-based spaces for people with disabilities are innumerable. The Internet has the potential to bridge physical distance. For many disabled individuals, online spaces might be the first—and only—spaces in which they can communicate with those who have similar disabilities. Additionally, digital technologies often represent assistive technologies for disabled users. Some individuals, for example, might find social networking technology a more "natural" communication space than face-to-face or phone encounters, for any variety of reasons: computer interfaces might present less sensory overload; it might be easier to interpret another person's emotions via instant messenger and emoticons; the individual might primarily communicate through text or use video conferencing technology and sign language; and a certain anonymity is afforded to online spaces, making Internet communities a potentially safer space for disclosing one's disability.

In addition to recognizing the affordances of online technologies to disabled users, digital humanists have recently focused their research on blogging communities and their contributions to disability studies and activism. Blogger *cripchick* focuses on disability rights and its relationship to other rights movements, including queer activism and social justice. The late Laura Hershey frequently blogged on issues relating to healthcare reform, accessibility within vocational and educational contexts, and media representations of disability. Of note was Hershey's use of online spaces to encourage offline, face-to-face protests against Jerry Lewis and the annual MDA Telethon.

Blogging has played a vital role in the formation of the *neurodiversity movement*, a term that, although originally used to refer to Autistic culture (and that was coined variously by Jim Sinclair and Judy Singer in the 1990s), has evolved to include all manners and expressions of neurological diversity (e.g., dyslexia, Tourette syndrome, depression, Down syndrome, etc.). In late 2007, the New York University (NYU) Child Study Center released its infamous "Ransom Notes" ad campaign, a series of fictional notes written from kidnappers claiming to have ADHD, Asperger's syndrome, and autism, among other mental disabilities. The blatant statement that neurological disabilities imprison and hold hostage these children sparked outcry from a number of neurodiversity bloggers, including autistic adults and parents of autistic children. Disability groups including ASAN, ADAPT, TASH, and Autism Network International collaborated in the development of an online petition and e-mail campaign that eventually resulted in NYU rescinding the ads and offering a public apology.

But blog hubs and other online disability communities have not been limited to activism or collective protest. Quite arguably, online spaces have contributed to the proliferation of broader disability culture, playing host to many highly regarded, disability-oriented scholarly and literary journals. *Disability Studies Quarterly*, the first journal in the field of disability studies, was made open-access and free to the online public in 2006. Other notable online disability journals, with literary and artistic forms as their focus, include *Wordgathering*, *Breath & Shadow*, and *Hyperlexia*. These journals have published works by Jim Ferris, Laura Hershey, Laurie Lambeth, and Petra Kuppers, among others.

The shared practices and narratives being produced widely by people with disabilities—whether online, in journals, in academic or trade presses, or in film and video—often feature content focusing on oppression, power, language, and choice.

Disability Studies: A Political and Interdisciplinary Field

Disability studies is, in and of itself, just one of those shared practices that arises from or is allied with disability culture. The field's oldest journal is *Disability Studies Quarterly (DSQ)*, founded in 1985; as a key academic marker of a field under development, *DSQ* appeared roughly a decade after three powerful and connected events: the signing of the 1973 Rehabilitation Act (which included the important but unsigned "Section 504"); the passage of Public Law 94-142, the Education for All Handicapped Law of 1975; and the famous "504 Sit-in" that began on April 5, 1977. Many of these pivotal (U.S.) disability rights protests are outlined in Sharon Barnartt and Richard Scotch's 2001 book, *Disability Protests: Contentious Politics, 1970–1999*. Ten years later, in 2011, PBS helped produce *Lives Worth Living*, a documentary film by Eric Neudel, that uses an "oral history" format as it "traces the development of consciousness of these [disability rights] pioneers who realized that in order to change the world they needed to work together. Through demonstrations and inside legislative battles, the disability rights community secured equal civil rights for all people with disabilities" (http://www.pbs.org/independentlens/lives-worth-living/film.html).

Fifteen to twenty years ago, it would have been impossible to talk or write about the field of disability studies as anything but an emerging field. As Pamela Cushing and Tyler Smith point out in a longitudinal study of the field published in *DSQ* in 2009:

> In the last two decades the field of Disability Studies (DS) has made an impressive ascent into a position of academic recognition.... We discovered a proliferation of degrees and courses as well as new DS research centers, speakers' series, journals and special issues that speak to the vital pockets of interest in the field.

Here, I briefly outline the ascent, recognition, and proliferation that the Cushing and Smith survey refers to by centering on four principal poles of study or critical approaches. The foundational premise for disability studies, circulated widely in the past 10–15 years, is that disability is not a state of bodily impairment, inadequacy, failing, misfortune, or excess—that it is not about marking the things gone "wrong" with the body. Rather, disability, as it is conceived in disability studies, is a culturally composed (and shared) narrative of the body, a narrative that is similar to the ways we have come to understand the identities (and fictions) of race and gender. In this view, disability is more about ideology than it is about biology. Yet, too, it is still, importantly and unfortunately, a study of the unequal distribution of power, material and economic resources, and status (class, etc.) within both social and architectural environments.

The work that disability studies has done in the past 10–20 years primarily has been to:

- Question current and dominant/longstanding models of disability
- Study carefully how the representation of disability works (both self- and other-generated representations)
- Interrogate the language and concepts we have "typically" used to understand our bodies and minds ("healthy" ones as well as "troubled," "disabled," "deviant," "abnormal," "average," "normal," and "aberrant" bodies and minds)
- Consider disability as a component of diversity and identity studies (along with fields such as women's and gender studies, queer studies, Latino/a studies, Native American studies, and African-American studies) while also working to circumvent the "pop-bead" additive (and + and + and) structure of such studies

Disability Studies Questions Models of Disability

For much of the history of studying the physical or mental conditions of disability, models that characterize disability as an *abnormal* condition have been used. For example, the medical field (including psychology) has historically and largely approached disability and illness as something to be removed from an individual in order to restore or rehabilitate that person back to health. Likewise, in our education system and philosophy, we have in the past excluded people with disabilities from "regular" classrooms or from most kinds of public education, whereas separate institutions for educating these (aberrant) students were (and probably still are) very popular. "Special education" classes for students who fall outside the range of "normal" were in abundance following passage of the important Public Law 94-142 "Education of All Handicapped

Law" in 1975. Many people with disabilities have now internalized these "deficit" and "included but still separate" models as the only way to understand and respond to their disability. And although many good things have come from these medical, rehabilitation, and educational approaches to disability, disability studies has pointed out ways in which these models could be revised and rethought in a more positive, valuing, experience-validating way.

One of the major contributions that disability studies has made is to put forth the idea that disability is, both simply and profoundly, part of what it means to be human. Rather than an abnormal condition, disability is a part of life. If we think of our bodies and minds as functioning differently throughout our lives (since the abilities of bodies and minds certainly do shift as we age), disability becomes an issue, an identity, and a condition that affects almost every person and almost every aspect of life. Current disability studies scholars have suggested new models for understanding disability.

For example, the social model of disability views disability as a consequence of *barriers*, both physical and cultural, in environment and context. This social model offers the idea that the environment and our attitudes toward disability should be changed (rather than necessarily fixing the individual with a disability) so that all disabled people can participate more fully in society. Another example of the social model at work is the rights-based model of disability, which understands disabled people as a group deserving human and civil rights. From within the social model, disability rights activists have gathered to counter ableism in the same way that racism and sexism have been addressed and analyzed; as such, an identity-based model for disability has been developed through disability studies.

This new(er) model—based on identity and power (or claiming), rather than on being labeled, named, or oppressed—is not, however, without critique. As many scholars have begun to critically suggest: yes, disability is/can be socially constructed, but the material consequences of impairment and its suffering and degradation are quite prevalent and must continue to be acknowledged, studied, interrogated, and alleviated.

SOCIAL AND MEDICAL MODELS

Without some important events (protests, activist moments) of the 1960s, it might not be possible to explain the idea of models of disability. Both the civil rights movement and second-wave feminism set a precedent for disabled people to demand equal

rights in the face of widespread prejudice. Advocates of racial and ethnic minorities and of women had developed a substantial critique of prejudice based on constructs stating that members of these marginalized groups are not marginalized because of anything inherent to members of the groups, but rather because of misguided beliefs about these individuals and groups. Those attitudes and assumptions, and the actions they motivate, are the product of historical trends, social conventions, and sometimes false ideas about minority groups and their members.

In 1966, sociologists James L. Berger and Thomas Luckmann published *The Social Construction of Reality*, which argues that *all* social patterns are based on concepts that people develop over a long history of group interactions and the roles that members of a society imagine for themselves and for others. Berger and Luckmann's explanation of the relative nature of both knowledge and social conventions provided a firm foundation for contemporary civil rights advocates. Although ideas about the social construction of reality and knowledge have been around for millennia, beginning in the 1960s, many minority groups embraced what has come to be called *social constructionism*. Social constructionism is an important backdrop for thinking about models of disability. If knowledge about society and its members is flexible, then we can emphasize different parts of the disability experience in ways that lead to very different conclusions about what disability means and how we ought to interact with disability—as both condition and experience/identity—in our world.

For example, if we think of disability as a mostly a medical "condition gone wrong" state of the body or mind, we are seeing it through the lens of a medical model of disability. Under this medical model paradigm, disability is mostly a *condition* of human bodies, and it typically marks a *deficit or lack* in the human body that belongs to *the individual* whose body it is. The medical model imagines disability as a departure from the normative functioning of healthy human bodies. Further, in this model, medical professionals are primarily (if not solely) best equipped to address disability, and they do so as they would other illnesses and diseases. In the event that the medical professional cannot provide a cure, the disability is considered "chronic" or, in instances where an individual was born with his or her disability, "congenital."

The medical model is perhaps the dominant paradigm for thinking about disability today, both in the United States and around the globe. Its most substantial counterpart is the social model.

Under the social model, disability is—both simply and profoundly—socially constructed. Inaccessible buildings, inflexible educational systems aimed at students who learn only in certain system-dominated ways, prejudicial attitudes held by society at large, and sometimes certain policies or laws actually *disable* people with certain types of bodies. And then, too, if disability is a social product, people's bodies are not *inherently* defective or ill. Rather, bodies do not have attached qualitative values, but only the potential to participate or not participate in the life of a society, depending on how that society is arranged.

Artists who think according to the social model might produce works that thematize or directly represent problems of access and prejudice—and these productions often contribute significantly to the shaping and size of the thing called "disability culture." Many contemporary autobiographies and memoirs written by disabled people provide good examples of social model approaches, such as Stephen Kuusisto's *Planet of the Blind*, in which he describes the liberating experience of training with a guide dog in order to enable confident movement on busy city streets not designed with blind people in mind. Working with a dog in harness, he says, "For the first time I feel the sunken lanes under my feet. The street is more my own. I belong here. . . . The harness is a transmitter, the dog is confident. . . . I am choosing to be blind in a forceful way" (Kuusisto, 1998, p. 171). In Kuusisto's case, adapting his environment by traveling with a service animal empowers him to navigate the world confidently, although still quite differently than do sighted people.

Similarly, Georgina Kleege opens her 1999 collection of essays, *Sight Unseen*, with the eye-catching claim, "Writing this book made me blind" (p. 1). She goes on to explain that she did not, in effect, lose her sight in the process of writing this book, but rather that, in the essays that follow, her exploration of the historical, cultural, linguistic, and media representations of blindness brought her to proudly claim for herself the identity of "blind." John Hockenberry also explores the socially constructed nature of his own disability in "Fear of Bees," a frequently reprinted essay from his 1995 book *Moving Violations*. In answer to a question frequently put to him—"people want to know what I want to be called"—Hockenberry opens this essay with a nearly three-page rant about the "names" for his life and "condition" that are often complex and contradictory. He writes, for example, "I am a former food stamp recipient. I am in the 35% tax bracket. I am part of the disability rights movement. I am a sell-out wannabe TV star media scumbag who has turned his broken back on other crips" (p. 88).

Legal scholars and historians working with the social model might survey legislation directed at people with disabilities and discover the ways that political systems have disabled people at different points in history. For instance, in his *Why I Burned My Book and Other Essays on Disability* (2003), Paul K. Longmore analyzes the progression of disability rights activism through the lens of the social model: "The movement of disabled Americans has entered its second phase. The first phase has been a quest for civil rights, for equal access and equal opportunity. . . . The second phase is a quest for collective identity" (p. 221). Here Longmore's argument is that disability rights activists, starting with New York City's League of the Physically Handicapped in the 1930s, use the social model to argue for accommodations and access to employment opportunities and public places.

BUILDING A NEW IDENTITY-BASED MODEL

In the field of disability studies, the medical and social models are probably best known and most discussed—and often pitted in tension with each other. This pitting of the two models against each other also produces, at times, a false and unproductive binary since, as many in disability studies are now suggesting, the placement of "medical" versus "social" can bracket off the real pain and material reality of "impairment" from the lived experience of "disability" as it is socially constructed. Setting the two models at odds with each other also falsely suggests that there is nothing social (or socially constructed) about a medical model itself or, too, that medicine and medical ways of thinking are somehow outside our everyday social spheres.

Disability studies has offered other important and useful ways of thinking about disability, particularly in the form of an identity model. Within an identity model, having a disability is a marker of membership in a minority identity, much like gender or race. Yet, in order to think through an identity model, we must have an operative definition of what constitutes disability (or doesn't), no matter how complex or conflicted that definition might be, and this definition must allow for both individual and collective/community experience.

In an identity model, disability is primarily defined by a certain type of experience in the world—a social and political experience that is shaped by the effects of a social system not designed with disabled people typically in mind. Although this (disability) experience is honored as "individual," it more often than not has some resonance with others who may be or become part of one's identity group. Because a disability identity model depends on the way that the social system is organized as the producer of that (individual) experience, it largely depends on the social model. The difference between the social model and the identity model is that the latter claims disability as a positive identity, a way to identify oneself and to be part of a community, in a way that the former, by definition, does not. Once someone has claimed disability as a positive identity marker, it becomes more feasible and desirable to produce art (and thus, to create further "disability culture") that celebrates human variation than it would be under either a medical or a social model.

For example, Simi Linton's *Claiming Disability* (1998) explains and celebrates disability identity as "the social and political circumstances that have forged [disabled] people as a group" (p. 4), and her memoir *My Body Politic* (2007) is an ebullient celebration of disability identity. Again, although the identity model owes much to the social model, it is less interested in the ways that environments, policies, and institutions disable people and more interested in forging a positive definition of disability identity based on experiences and circumstances that have created a recognizable minority group called "people with disabilities" or, variously, "disabled people."

It is not suggested here that these three models (medical, social, identity) are exclusive of one another, or even that these are the only models of disability, or that one is clearly preferable to the others for disability studies. Additional models that have circulated historically and that are extant today bear significant impact on the ways we have thought about and reacted to/interacted with "disability" (e.g., a moral model, a charity model, and an economic model). On a theoretical or instructional level, it might be possible to separate these models, as has been done here—and it is exactly this kind of theoretical work that disability studies often takes up. But when these models actually engage with "disability culture," we find that such cultural and artistic productions almost always draw on multiple models of disability, whether unconsciously or by design.

Refiguring Representation

There are at least three primary ways that the general construct of representation has been "opened up" through exploration from disability theorists, activists, and artists. The first way that disability studies has expanded conversations about representation is in its study of literature and art. In the late 1990s and early 2000s, as disability studies was really gaining ground as a field, scholars such as G. Thomas Couser, Rosemarie Garland-Thomson, David Mitchell, and Sharon Snyder pointed to the ways in which disabled characters in literature are often used to represent negative ideas, such as evil, guilt, or tragedy. And, regardless of what they are specifically meant to represent, disabled characters often function only as literary devices, rather than providing realistic portrayals of people living with disability. Consider, for example, how Captain Hook's disability (in *Peter Pan*) serves as a signal that he is a villain and should be feared, or how Tiresias' blindness (in *The Odyssey*) is often explained by literary scholars as a marker of his insight and wisdom and also repurposed frequently in Western literature (by Dante, Lord Tennyson, T. S. Eliot, and Gustave Flaubert, for example). In all of these cases, disability itself is not represented but is used to deliver some other message. Disability studies scholars have pointed out how disability is often used in literature and art to complicate and challenge these (very limited) representations.

These complications and challenges bring us to the second way that disability studies has influenced our understanding of representation, which is through disabled individuals speaking for themselves about their experiences (rather than being spoken about by caregivers or medical professionals). Disability activists have often used the phrase "Nothing about us without us," (see Charlton, 2000), thus capturing the idea that disabled people should be active participants in creating the literature, art, laws, policies, and history about disability. This simple idea—that disabled people are the authority on their own experiences—has marked effects on the way disability is represented.

Finally, the third way that disability studies has expanded our understanding of representation is through the creation of works of art as cultural artifacts. Such works of art help create a shared disability experience because people are able to identify with artwork and memoirs. We could look to the contemporary poems of Jim Ferris or the "Circle Stories" paintings (and others) by Riva Lehrer as examples. We could also turn to the 2010 special issue of *DSQ* that is focused on disability poetry, or the VSA (Very Special Arts) national Disability Film Festival, or even the October 2012 Turner

Broadcasting Systems (TBS) focus on disability films in film history. But we could also easily look only to comments left by Amazon.com reviewers in response to memoirs about disability. Memoirs about living with disability are artifacts that define a community of people, and they are signs of a shared disability identity.

Restructuring Worldviews

Language infuses the experience, identity, and understanding of disability. Likewise, and in a parallel crossing, disability concepts infuse our language. Students in disability studies often marvel, for example, over the sheer number and weight of disability-laden phrases and metaphors in our language (*blind justice, fall on deaf ears, lame idea, crippling traffic, disabled vehicle, blind-sided, sweetly mute,* etc.), as well as on the equally weighty nomenclature of the endless acronyms that circulate in "disability world" (ADA, IEP, TAB, IDD, DD, PDD, ADAPT, DALY, UNCRPD, LD, PWD, etc.). Language shapes worldviews, and vice versa. And the disability experience richly illustrates the nexus of language and worldviews; this is perhaps nowhere more evident than in our contemporary culture's constructions of the terms *normal, difference,* and *deviance*.

NORMAL

We might often assume that we have an idea of what it means to be "normal." We might expect, for example, a normal college student to be between the ages of 18 and 22; we may believe that we can recognize whether a person falls into the range of normal height and weight; and we think we have an understanding of what type of food is normally served at breakfast and not at dinner. We also generally accept that being normal has positive value, and, as a result, it can be difficult to step back from our assumptions and think critically about what our culture values as normal and why.

However, in recent years, disability studies scholars have begun doing just that: they are following gender and race studies scholars who have turned their attention to whiteness and heterosexual relationships as allegedly unmarked identities. In the same way, disability studies scholars are interested in normalcy as an unmarked, previously unquestioned category.

Disability studies scholars have become interested in the concept of *normal* as something that is difficult to pin down. Not only does it change over time and across cultures (just think of the style of jeans considered "normal" 50 years ago

as opposed to now!), but it is incredibly difficult to actually be a "normal" person in every sense of the word. Rosemarie Garland-Thomson (1996) coined the term "normate" to describe what is understood as the definitive, generalizable human being—that which is thought to be normal. The power of Garland-Thomson's term is that only a small minority of real people could be considered normates, because almost all people deviate in some way from whatever their culture deems normal (p. 8). In Robert McRuer's (2008) book, *Crip Theory,* he lists traits that make up the normate in American culture, including proper dimensions of height and weight, freedom from chronic illness, Euro-American standards of beauty, and heterosexuality, among other things (p. 245). Lennard Davis's (2002) historical perspective (which follows on his 1995 book, *Enforcing Normalcy*) considers what it means to be normal, and it adds another dimension to Garland-Thomson's and McRuer's works by showing that what defines the normate is different in every culture: "the idea of a norm is less a condition of human nature than it is a feature of a certain kind of society" (p. 3). According to Davis, we learn what is normal in our own culture through many positive representations of normal characters and negative representations of abnormal characters in books, movies, TV shows, and other cultural objects. Davis calls this process of equating normal with positive traits "enforcing normalcy" (p. 12), and that concept was, in fact, the title of his first disability studies book, published in 1995.

Although it can be useful to question what is normal, it is not always practical to question the reasons why one thing is understood as normal and another is not. For standardized tests, medical diagnoses, and school applications to be useful, an agreed upon normal range of performance is necessary. On the other hand, disability studies provides a different perspective on how such standardized tests, for example, define their range of normal scores. Disability studies asks questions such as: Who decides what counts as normal and what does not? What are some of the consequences of being labeled abnormal? In a given scenario, what does normal look like? How does normal/abnormal circulate historically and socially in art, literature, and media? Who benefits from thinking in terms of normal and abnormal?

As this last question suggests, disability studies scholars are interested in where the boundary between normal and abnormal is drawn, and, furthermore, how firm that boundary is. In the same way that the boundary between a novel and a novella is not always clear, a neat circle cannot be drawn to include everything that counts as normal and exclude everything abnormal. In the same way that Joseph Conrad's *Heart of Darkness* is not clearly a novel or a novella, certain bodily behaviors and traits inevitably straddle the boundary line between normal and abnormal. The boundary between normal and abnormal is not fixed, but one that can be blurred or redrawn. Furthermore, creating a category of "normal" means that everything outside of the category's boundaries is "abnormal"; if we only focus on what lies inside the circumscribed boundary lines of the "normal" circle, we ignore whatever lies without.

The stakes involved in ignoring novels and focusing on novellas (or vice versa) are relatively low. However, if we substitute novellas with "normal people" and novels with "abnormal people," the results could be more damaging. For example, if our government and social programs focused only on normal individuals and excluded any individuals deemed abnormal, the stakes would obviously be much higher. In Nazi Germany, those deemed abnormal were not quietly excluded but forcibly sterilized, experimented on, and killed—a testament to the power that cultural understandings of normalcy can have (Davis, 2002, p. 10).

For most of art's history, a tension between normality and abnormality within an individual has created an aesthetic. Consider the beautiful, limbless Venus de Milo or the haunting, ambiguously gendered Mona Lisa. The history of art's reliance on both normality and abnormality to create beauty highlights the central place that abnormality plays in the very fabric of what it means to be human. Some scholars and activists in disability studies have adopted the acronym TAB (temporarily able-bodied) as a reminder that we will all become disabled if we live long enough. Disability studies, as a reaction against a history of excluding "abnormal" people from society, shifts the focus to those excluded from normalcy—those who lie outside the circle's boundary. It becomes possible, then, using a disability studies framework, to understand disability as a human condition and as something more normal and inevitable than being able-bodied.

DIFFERENCE AND DEVIANCE

The question raised by the use of the TAB acronym—"Are we all disabled?"—is particularly interesting for disability studies because it asks us to ponder where the boundary lies between being disabled and able-bodied. An alternative to separating the world and human traits into normal and abnormal is to conceptualize all human variation as lying on a continuum of difference. This alternative viewpoint can remove the stigma and negative value judgments that are so often associated with "abnormal" bodies and minds, and instead views difference as simply part of being human.

These viewpoints have been very useful to scholars in disability studies who research the cultural value placed on disability. By viewing all human characteristics on a continuum of difference, we can then conceptually separate *deviance,* which accepts a firm boundary between normal and abnormal and assigns a negative value to abnormality and disability, from *difference,* which is a neutral view of variation as a key component of humanity. One way to distinguish between these views regarding abnormality and disability is to consider that the *difference* model has a neutral value, whereas the *deviance* model has a negative value. Think, for instance, of the difference between saying, "That man has one leg," and saying, "Unfortunately, that poor man only has one leg." The first statement is underwritten by a difference model, and the second by a deviance model. Disability studies scholar and creative writer Kenny Fries has linked the difference model to Darwin's theory of natural selection. In *The History of My Shoes and Darwin's Theory of Evolution* (2007), Fries creatively and convincingly weaves his own (disability) experience with the development of Darwin's theory of evolution to illustrate how Darwin's ideas yield insights into how disability fits into (and is natural in) culture.

Viewing disability as difference allows for positive, or at least neutral, attitudes toward disability to be adopted. Since, in our culture, disability is largely understood as deviance from the norm, it can be difficult for disabled people to advocate for their experiences as different but not necessarily negative. The Deaf community is an apt example of this: many Deaf people do not consider themselves disabled, but rather argue that they are distinguished not primarily by an inability to hear, but by their use of a separate language (American Sign Language) that allows them to communicate without needing to hear. This attitude toward Deafness as difference can be seen, for example, in parts of the PBS documentary *Through Deaf Eyes*. Interviewee Summer Crider claims, at one point in this film, "I don't view myself as having a disability.... I function like any other hearing person can. My deafness does not deprive me of anything. I can do anything

I want. Except maybe sing." Perhaps, as I suggest in "The Tango: What Deaf Studies and Disability Studies Do," the Deaf community's eagerness to separate itself from the disabled community indicates that disability still has deviant status and is still viewed as negative by the Deaf community (Brueggemann, 2010).

In an attempt to counter the deviance viewpoint of disability, scholars in disability studies have begun focusing on and placing positive value on the experiences of disabled people. Simi Linton (1998), in her foundational book *Claiming Disability*, places value on the disability experience by "centering" it; she writes about disability as the norm and indicates that able-bodied people are abnormal by referring to them as the "nondisabled" (p. 13). Likewise, James Charlton's 1999 book *Nothing About Us Without Us: Disability Oppression and Empowerment* serves up in its title, borrowed originally from Central European foreign relations, a phrase that has become central to the disability right movement.

Some examples of deliberately centering disability can be found in Riva Lehrer's (2004) paintings, titled *Circle Stories*. Each painting in this collection features a disabled activist, scholar, or artist whose identity—including his or her disability—is the focal point. Authors such as Nancy Mairs, Raymond Luczak, and Kenny Fries also make disability a focal point in their writing, as have postmodern critical theorists such as Fredric Jameson, Gilles Deleuze, and Felix Guattari, whose theories rely on schizophrenia as a model for understanding humanity. Although Jameson, Deleuze, and Guattari are not centering disability for the reasons that Linton and other disability activists are (to make attitudes toward disability more positive), they are similarly redefining a disabled, schizophrenic mind as the norm, rather than as deviant or abnormal. Finally, as another major cultural artifact that recently centered—quite provocatively—around disability, London's Trafalgar Square was recently home to Marc Quinn's statue of Alison Lapper, which publicly displayed a disabled (and pregnant) body as its focal point. What all of these examples show is that centering disability changes its value—and this centering and value-changing is part and parcel of both disability studies and disability culture.

Positioning and/in Diversity and Identity

This key contribution of disability studies is also an example of how nonmedical models can lead to new understandings of disability. When the rights-based model is used to approach ideas about disability or people with disabilities, then having a disability becomes a community-making identifier for a group of activists working to redress ableism. Because the disability rights movement in America has followed a similar trajectory to the civil rights movement and the feminist movement, disability is now often grouped with other university studies of identity groups. For example, at the Ohio State University, disability studies is an active part of the Diversity and Identity Studies Collective at Ohio State (DISCO), and the ADA Coordinator's Office is housed now in the Office of Diversity and Inclusion, reporting to the Provost's Office. Increasingly, disability is being understood as part of who one is, not as simply a condition one has. In large part because of disabled people writing and speaking about their own experiences (which creates disability culture), disability is being thought of as part of one's identity, rather than as a biological fact—similar to how we understand what it means to be a woman or an African American.

Indeed, an entirely new discipline has been formed under the name "disability studies" to study disability from the perspective of disabled people and in ways outside of the view of the medical field. This new discipline has moved the creation of knowledge about disability outside of the social and medical sciences and has brought attention to the need for interdisciplinary studies of disability issues.

There are twin components to disability and (or as) identity: first, in identity politics and second, in identity studies. Within the frame of identity politics, disability as a political reality and experience wraps itself heavily and historically in educational practices, policy development, and now, too, in legal mandates. Or, as performance artist Cheryl Marie Wade quips near the opening of the Mitchell and Snyder film, *Vital Signs: Crip Culture Talks Back*, "There's a politics to your disability whether you realize it or not" (Mitchell & Snyder, 1995). The very problem of *identifying* disability based on the Americans with Disabilities Act (ADA)—for policy development or legal enforcement—is the center of a collection of pieces edited by Ruth O'Brien, *Voices from the Edge: Narratives about the Americans with Disabilities Act* (2004). Disability is also a big political and economic business these days, figuring significantly in global development efforts. One only has to look at the broad and deep array of information and initiatives the World Bank now devotes to disability on its website. As global development and attention to identifying disability politically and economically continues to take place, we will surely see more literary, artistic, and historical evidence of disability—both as it is uncovered historically and as it is advanced for the present and future—within cultural fabrics around the globe.

And, in this uncovering and advancement, the component of disability as identity and in identity studies will likely also grow. The ways disability serves, and looks like, other areas of "identity studies" (women's studies, ethnic studies, queer studies, etc.) will continue to be explored. Already, Robert McRuer's book *Crip Theory: Cultural Signs of Queerness and Disability* and Michael Davidson's article "Phantom Limbs: Film Noir and the Disabled Body" (2010) analyze similarities in representations of disability and queerness. Jonathan Metzl's *The Protest Psychosis: How Schizophrenia Became a Black Disease* (2010) examines relationships between race and diagnoses of mental disorders, and Rosemarie Garland-Thomson's book (and much of her work at large), *Extraordinary Bodies: Figuring Physical Disability in American Culture and Literature*, brings feminist theory, among other things, into conversation with disability studies.

This relationship of disability to identity is one of prepositions: identifying *for*, identifying *as*, identifying *about*, identifying *with* and *against*. In identifying *for*, we must consider the purposes, stances, and arguments made for identifying disability in relation to one's audiences and contexts. The many discussions of "passing" now taken up in disability studies—concerning the negotiation of outing, hiding, managing, revealing, or cloaking of one's disability in any given situation or with any given audience or relationship—are examples of identifying *for*. Right alongside stories and strategies for "passing" are trenchant considerations of "faking" disability, malingering, posing. These, too, are moments of identifying *for* certain personal and social purposes. Classic pieces in disability literature that illuminate the passing/faking dynamics can be found in Irving Kenneth Zola's *Missing Pieces* (2003); Brueggemann's "On (Almost) Passing" (2007); Kleege's entire essay collection *Sight Unseen* (the book that begins with the double entendre, "Writing this book made me blind"); and Stephen Kuusisto's alternate moments of comfort and resistance on his *Planet of the Blind*; or even Achim Nowak's toggling essay "Disclosures" (2004; about passing and outing with HIV status) in the O'Brien *Voices from the Edge* collection.

Identifying *as* marks a position of *claiming* disability—of reinscribing the naming, labeling, and categorization often imposed on one's self in a new and now self-conscious, prideful, political, and personal positioning in relationship to a community of (disabled) others. Some disability dance and disability performance art moves in this moment as well: Petra Kuppers's performance and poetic work, Alice Sheppard's dance (along with all of AXIS Dance Company), Jim Ferris's poetry. Simi Linton's memoir *My Body Politic* stands as a manifesto for the identifying *as* position when she revises the popular and often enforced "overcoming" narrative of disability life by writing into one of "coming over"— coming over to claim an identity and membership in a vibrant and satisfying "disability community" and "disability culture."

The tension between identifying *with* and identifying *against* any (also dominant) disability identity position occurs often, for example, in ongoing debates about deafness as (or not as) a disability. The Susan Burch and Alison Kafer collection *Deaf and Disability Studies: Interdisciplinary Perspectives* (2010) substantially explores this particular with/against debate. Similarly, several of John Hockenberry's essays in his collection *Moving Violations* position him as vacillating between the *with* and *against* identification of disability; "Fear of Bees" is perhaps his best-known essay in this vein. Henry Alex Rubin and Dana Adam Shapiro's popular 2005 documentary *Murderball*, about Mark Zupan and the U.S. Paralympic Quad Rugby team, exhibits yet another oscillating personal and political identification with and against disability: the men on the rugby team are comfortable with their physically disabled bodies, but they are equally adamant that they must be distinguished from people who compete in the Special Olympics.

The debates surrounding disability identity provide a means into the debates surrounding disability studies as a field. As Simi Linton (1998) asks—*what is, and what is not, disability studies?*

Categorizing Disability: Enabling Study, Producing Culture

Much like the interweave of multiple models of disability that make up the work and production of both disability studies and disability culture, the categorizing of various kinds of disabilities and physical/mental/sensory experiences has also been a source of (disability) study and a site of (disability) cultural production. One of the primary ways disability has been imagined—and studied—is through its potential and various categorizations. To categorize is to arrange something into further (smaller) classes and subsets, to characterize and describe something by additional labeling and descriptive or sometimes prescriptive detailing. And disability—in experience, imagination, and identification and in social, medical, identity, moral, and economic models—has been historically and extensively labeled, arranged, characterized, and placed in subsets.

The act of categorizing disability has served many purposes in both disability studies and disability culture. First among these purposes is to focus the study and understanding of the larger category of disability so that we can grasp at least some smaller part of the whole. Placing certain kinds of disabilities (and the people who are labeled with those disabilities) alongside certain genres of art, literature, cultural production, or historical moments helps sharpen the study of that genre, that historical moment, that disability. For example: autobiography by blind people (such as Stephen Kuusisto's *Planet of the Blind* and *Eavesdropping* and Georgina Kleege's *Sight Unseen*), performance art (in sign language) by deaf people, visual art by people with cognitive disabilities (such as Judith Scott's sculptures), fiction or poetry by people presumed to be mentally unstable, narratives by polio and post-polio survivors (like Anne Finger's *Elegy for a Disease* [2006]), photography by developmentally disabled adults, dance performed by people who use wheelchairs, films about Vietnam War veterans (for example, *Born on the Fourth of July* (Stone, 1989) or *Coming Home* [Ashby, 1978]), art workshops for disabled veterans—all of these, and more, are examples of the ways in which categorizations of disability can populate the field of disability studies.

Historically, the study and understanding of disability has also been characterized as a way to manage certain kinds of bodies in institutions of science, medicine, education, and rehabilitation. These institutional classifications—schools and "asylums" for people who are blind, deaf, cognitively disabled, "crippled," "insane," epileptic, and the like—have also, however, brought people together who sometimes develop artistic, cultural, or literary practices or whose shared existence in an institutional place offers a kind of ready-made historical site of study or a place of cultural production. As such, the purpose of categorizing disabled people for institutional management and (re)habilitation can also provide us with a historical tracing of an era, show us a shared social attitude (about that disability), illuminate the practice of public policy about disability,

exemplify medical practices aimed at that kind of disability/difference, and illustrate timely methods of education and rehabilitation. Categorizing, then, not only creates a confined space in which to study a disability or a group of people with a certain disability, but it also opens up our perspectives about policies, practices, and attitudes in a society at large.

The categorization of disability also opens up a space for shared experience and the identification of oneself to one's own self, to others, and among others. This categorizing moment happens when *naming* disability (having been named and categorized, by others, as one with a certain kind of disability and exhibiting certain kinds of traits or life experiences because of that disability) becomes a moment of *claiming* disability (one's own taking of the name). Although so much of disability identification is predicated on oppression and (shared) negative experiences, the categorization and lump-summing of certain kinds of disabilities alongside certain kinds of artistic, literary, or historical practices can and does produce more positively framed art, literature, historical events, and practices. For example, the performative nature of American Sign Language has made deaf performance a recognizable genre and a cultural space in which deafness is central both to form and content and in which disability is often favorably represented.

Primary categorizations of disability that inform both disability studies and disability culture typically occur along the lines related to the physical, cognitive, sensory, mental/psychological, behavioral, intellectual, or developmental, and in relation to disease. Many of these categorizations can, and, of course, do significantly overlap (much like the models of disability). Physical disability—in history, art, and literature, as well as in culture at large—often becomes the category that most people imagine when they think of "disability." The power of the wheelchair symbol is global and pervasive, even though the number of people worldwide who use wheelchairs is not a particularly high percentage of the total population of people with disabilities. Physical disability serves as significant marker and metaphor in our culture, literature, art, and representation, as is articulated in key texts about disability in the humanities: David Mitchell and Sharon Snyder's collection *The Body and Physical Difference: Discourses of Disability* (1995); Rosemarie Garland-Thomson's *Extraordinary Bodies: Figuring Physical Disability in American Culture and Literature*; Carrie Sandahl and Philip Auslander's *Bodies in Commotion: Disability and Performance* (2005); and the literary collection edited by Kenny Fries, *Staring Back: The Disability Experience from the Inside Out* (which, ironically enough, features a blurred image of a person using a wheelchair from a side view—not staring back but being gazed on by the audience of the text).

In particular, popular personal narratives or memoirs around disability also center on physical difference: Nancy Mairs's classic *Waist High in the World: A Life among the Nondisabled* (1996) and John Hockenberry's *Moving Violations: War Zones, Wheelchairs, and Declarations of Independence* are two notable examples. The domination of physical disability as marker and primary metaphor also appears, for example, in (deaf) writer/performer Terry Galloway's well-known piece "The Performance of Drowning" (which appears in her memoir, *Mean Little Deaf Queer* [2009]) when she "fakes" a limp across the "crippled kids camp" stage to win her swimming award. By doing this, Galloway identified herself as having a "valid" disability that others would recognize and on which they would confer sympathy.

Similarly, performance artist Robert DeFelice tells us in the *Vital Signs: Crip Culture Talks Back* documentary video that he's never really understood what the wheelchair symbol was about and confesses that he felt "confused" as a kid when he was asked to wear a t-shirt with a wheelchair symbol to "show his pride." Finally, physical disability also dominates heavily in contemporary representations of and attention to prosthetic devices—as in the considerable media attention to double amputee/fashion model/Paralympic record holder/speaker Aimee Mullins's relationship with her prosthetic legs, especially as the subject of several remarkable TED talks (Mullins, 2009a,b), or the James Gandolfini documentary film *Alive Day Memories: Home from Iraq*.

Cognitive disability—sometimes categorized as intellectual or developmental disability—also occupies considerable space in our literary and historical/cultural imagination. The heavy disability weight of cognitive disability (and the Eugenics-era generated category of "feeblemindedness"), often anchored in and associated with the eugenics movement, is well-documented in James Trent's important study *Inventing the Feeble Mind: A History of Mental Retardation in the United States* (1995), or in more recent work such as Allison Carey's *On the Margins of Citizenship: Intellectual Disability and Civil Rights in Twentieth-Century America* (2009) or Susan Burch and Hannah Joyner's *Unspeakable: The Junius Wilson Story* (2007). Popular film portrays cognitive disability as well in major films such as *Forrest Gump*

(Zemeckis, 1994), *Radio,* or *Simon Birch*, or in successful made-for-TV movies like *Riding the Bus with My Sister* (based on Rachel Simon's memoir by the same name). Many of the literary, artistic, historical, and cultural documents around "developmental disability" often raise, with a particular pointedness, the parent question—namely, what is the role of parents of children (and adults) with cognitive, intellectual, or developmental disabilities in the representations of those people (and their disabilities) in the literary, artistic, historical record? And, perhaps because the further categorization of "verbal/nonverbal" also occurs within this domain, the preponderance of texts by parents of children with Down syndrome or children labeled on the autism spectrum beg this question often.

Sensory disability, as it is categorized, studied, and represented in disability studies and disability culture, works most often under the powerful gaze, for better or worse, turned on Helen Keller, who was deaf-blind. Keller is huge in our cultural mind's eye view of sensory disability: from her own multiple autobiographical texts (*The Story of My Life* [2003], *The World I Live In* [2003], *Midstream* [1969], *My Later Life*) to multiple film and documentary representations of her work (*The Miracle Worker* play and film; see Penn, 1962) to multiple biographies (perhaps too numerous to list or example) to collections and scholarly monographs around her life and interests (see especially those by Kim Nielsen in the last decade) or even to the collection of (largely dark parody) Helen Keller jokes. (See also Kleege, 2006; Nielson, 2004, 2005, 2209, 2012).

Blind musicians also carry a considerable tune in this categorization. Just a sampling includes Jose Feliciano, Ray Charles, Ronnie Milsap, the Blind Boys of Alabama, Stevie Wonder, Andrea Bocelli, and a number of early blues musicians who carried "blind" as part of their performance name: Blind Blake, Blind Lemon Jefferson, Blind Boy Fuller, Blind Willie Johnson, Blind Willie McTell, and more. From at least Tiresias, the blind prophet of Greek mythology, forward, blindness can be cited often metaphorically or in character within literature; José Saramago's novel *Blindness* (1997; also made into a 2008 film) and the famous H. G. Wells story "In the Country of the Blind" (2004) are two significant examples. Blindness in film also finds categorical figuration in such classic films as *A Patch of Blue* (Green, 1965) and *Magnificent Obsession* (Sirk, 1954) or *Scent of a Woman* (for which Al Pacino won an Academy Award as Best Actor in 1992 [Brest, 1992]).

Deafness, another major sensory disability, appears less often in the arts and humanities. In fact, Helen Keller's own deafness more often than not takes a sensory backseat to her blindness. Carson McCullers's deaf protagonist in *The Heart Is a Lonely Hunter* (2000) remains a classic example of deaf characterization in fiction, whereas recent fictional accounts of major deaf characters by Melanie Rae Thon (*Sweet Hearts*; 2000), T. C. Boyle (*Talk Talk* [2006]), David Lodge's autobiographical fiction, *Deaf Sentence* [2009], or even Brian Selznick's graphic young adult novel, *Wonderstruck* (2011; with double deaf characters and a visual-print twinned narrative), for example, also extend the categorical possibilities. Yet films in which deaf characters appear—more often than not in a plot that pits them against music in some way—are also a part of our cultural imagination (and categorization) of sensory disability: *Children of a Lesser God* (Raines, 1986; for which Marlee Matlin, deaf actress, won an Oscar in 1986); *Jenseits der Stille* (Beyond Silence [Link, 1996]), winner of the Oscar for Best Foreign Film in 1996; *Mr. Holland's Opus* (Herek, 1995); and others. The recent rise of "Deaf cinema"—film made by deaf people and often (although not always) featuring deaf experiences or themes—is also apparent through several national and international Deaf film festivals. Deaf autobiographies—along with all autobiographies by people of any categorical disability—seem to be notably on the rise in the last decade or so: Gallaudet University Press currently features 28 titles in their "autobiography" category.

Mental and/or psychological disability (the loose popular cultural category of "madness") can further be categorized as mental disorder, mental disability, psychiatric disorder, mood disorder, and mental illness. Charlotte Perkins Gilman's classic short story "The Yellow Wallpaper" (1997) is perhaps a foundational literary text here. Edgar Allan Poe's "Tell-Tale Heart" (1843) also represents the category, as do more recent works such as Ken Kesey's *One Flew Over the Cuckoo's Nest* (in both novel and film adaptation), Susanna Kaysen's *Girl, Interrupted* (again in both text [1994] and film), Sylvia Nasar's biography of Nobel Prize-winning mathematician John Nash, *A Beautiful Mind* (1998; also in film), and Kay Redfield Jamison's important psychologist-as-bipolar memoir, *An Unquiet Mind* (1996). Artists who have been placed (in current times) or retro-diagnosed in this category are abundant: Sylvia Plath, Vincent Van Gogh, and Antonin Artaud, to name a few. In fact, with only a little excavation, it would be fairly easy to uncover this category almost everywhere in our cultural, literary, and artistic history.

Less apparent but still perhaps pervasive is the categorical representation of disability in relation to "disease" or "illness." Sociologist Erving Goffman's classic treatises on *Stigma: Notes on the Management of Spoiled Identity* (1963) and *Asylums: Essays on the Social Situation of Mental Patients and Other Inmates* (1961) illustrate the ways in which "disability" is interwoven into the fabric of our cultural management of our own (and other's) illness, disease, and difference. Several of cultural critic Susan Sontag's works—as she herself encountered cancer—also now point to the complex fabric between disability and illness/disease. Sociologist Arthur Frank's exploration of the "recovery" from cancer in *The Wounded Storyteller* (1997) often adapts well to disability studies in the humanities scholarship, and key or perhaps canonical memoirs about cancer are also often read in disability studies classes. Chief among these cancer narratives are Audre Lorde's *The Cancer Journals* (1980) and the more recent graphic novel by Harvey Pekar and Joyce Brabner, *Our Cancer Year* (1994).

Future Directions, Key Questions

The largest problems in disability studies are definitional and, as it were, also then territorial as well as rhetorical (caught up in motivation and intent). Although scholars in disability studies might often agree about the field's premises and its openly political goals, they often disagree about other issues, including what the field's most pressing questions are, how those questions should be framed, and who is best suited to answer them. This is to say nothing of actually *answering* those questions.

Selected here are some of the most pressing issues and controversies in the field, especially as reflected in major journals like *DSQ* and the *Journal of Literary and Cultural Disability Studies* (JLCDS), as well as on the well-trafficked Disability Studies in the Humanities (DS-HUM) listserv.

Nothing About Us Without Us?

The expression *nothing about us without us* is pervasive in the political DRM. It is also prevalent, although less so, in disability studies in the academy. In essence, the phrase means that no action should be taken or utterance made regarding disability without the consent, authorization, or origination (i.e., originating with) of disabled people concerned with the action or utterance in question. In both political and academic contexts, the principle of *nothing about us without us* is important first as a corrective to a long history of disabled people being spoken about in public discourse by educators, doctors, legislators, and family members, but rarely being authorized to speak for themselves, except in private settings and to highly limited audiences. *Nothing about us without us* is also important because it ensures that political and intellectual work on disability bears in mind the perspectives and interests of the real people to whom disability is always related. In other words, the phrase—and the idea behind it—makes clear that disability is not a concept that can be abstracted from people, but a *way* of being a person.

The issue of disabled people's perspectives remaining front and center in the field is an important one for all work in disability studies, however, as a principle, *nothing about us without us* raises difficult questions about who works in the field and on what basis those people derive their right to do that work, as well as their authority in doing it.

For example, can one only work in disability studies and engage disability issues if one is disabled oneself? Or, are there ways of representing a disability perspective without actually being disabled? To say that one can only really "do" disability studies or present a disability perspective if one is disabled is almost certainly a misstep. The first reason is that demanding that someone be disabled to "do" disability studies immediately raises the difficult question of what "counts" as disability and how disabled is "disabled enough" to qualify someone. If a non-disabled historian breaks his leg and use crutches for a month before surgery that requires him to use a wheelchair for three months, can he only then work in the field of disability history? If so, can he work in the field permanently or only while he is experiencing disability? Moreover, can he only write about the history of mobility impairment and people affected by it, or can he also write about the history of blindness?

Another reason that requiring disability (or impairment) for work in the field is probably undesirable is that it creates barriers that undercut the cooperative origins of the field and the political movement of which it is a part. Much of what made the DRM successful was the willingness of its pioneers to draw support from any possible source, especially cross-disability alliances and coalitions of other minority groups. Moreover, just because someone is disabled does not mean that person can speak to the perspective of people with disabilities at large. Disability identities are myriad and diverse,

and although there is some common political experience among disabled people, even that experience depends on what particular disability identity one has. In the same way that it would not make sense to say that only people of Japanese descent can do work in Japanese history, it does not seem that being disabled is a useful criterion for working in disability studies.

Finally, requiring disability status sends the field straight back to the medical model, in which a certain "diagnosis" certifies our rights to be, perform, have authority or agency (or therein, too, denies those rights). A better interpretation of *nothing about us without us* might be to say that having a disabled "us" present in any work "about" disability means that anyone desiring to produce work embraced by disability studies should be educated about disability perspectives and perhaps employ a critical disability studies framework. This would mean that anyone, regardless of the status of her or his body, could create art scholarship that represented disabled bodies or discussed disability issues. However, claiming the title "disability studies" would obligate that person to consider her or his subject from the perspective of disability rights.

As disability studies continues to develop its critical, cultural, and artistic scope and scene, artists and scholars will need to make sure they especially promote the work of disabled colleagues, as well as educate colleagues and students about the field's activist aims. This approach will go some way toward ensuring that disabled people's interests are not overlooked in the interest of artistic or academic achievement or self-promotion—in short, that nothing will happen in the field without disabled people's consent, authorization, or origination.

Complex Representations

At the heart of the DRM and central then to disability studies and disability culture as well, as indicated even by the resonant phrase *nothing about us without us*, are issues of representation (as discussed earlier). Numerous disability communities have embraced the *nothing about us without us* message of self-determination, inclusion, representation, and equality. Whether during the course of protests, in op-ed articles and personal blogs, or in everyday life (at work, school, or in local communities), disability advocates, authors, and artists are more often than not, at root, concerned with representation.

In the field of disability studies, representation is a multifaceted concept. In the context of civil and social rights, we might consider representation as a matter of *speaking*, in the broadest sense of the word. Disability studies scholars routinely ask: *How* is disability being represented? *Who* is doing the representing? And *for what purpose* is representation taking place? These core representational questions are not to be taken lightly. In our particular, 21st-century moment, we can barely go a day without encountering *something* that invokes—and represents—disability in some way. Whether on our Facebook walls, the evening news, or the latest episode of *Glee*, representations of disability abound. Along with these representations come the attitudes, values, and experiences of those who are doing the representing. As we attempt to analyze the proliferation (and sheer magnitude) of these representations, disability studies asks us to consider (and reconsider) the following questions:

- *For* whom are we speaking?
- *About* whom are we speaking?
- *With* whom are we speaking?
- Are *we* speaking?

Disability/Aesthetics

The basic question of disability aesthetics, one that is posed in both disability studies and disability culture, is: What is the relationship between disability and the concept of beauty? Disability aesthetics is especially alive to the question of who determines the definition of beauty and the beauty of particular objects. For scholars in disability studies, even seemingly benign value judgments like those about beauty are politically charged. Especially since so many art objects represent human bodies, the determination of artistic beauty is often closely related to the determination of acceptable bodies. Consequently, definitions of beauty are often (some would go so far as to say always and inevitably) political. Bodies are so much a part of aesthetics that Tobin Siebers, in his book *Disability Aesthetics* (2010), modifies 18th-century German philosopher Alexander Baumgarten's definition of aesthetics to offer as his definition of the field, "the [study of] the way some bodies feel in the presence of other bodies" (p. 1). Disability aesthetics explores the effects that disabled bodies have on both disabled and nondisabled bodies.

Architecture, for example, makes the relationship between body and beauty clear. The history of architecture is largely an inaccessible history, because many buildings prominently feature stairs, narrow doorways and hallways, heavy doors, and other features that make them difficult or impossible to navigate for wheelchair users or other people with physical disabilities. However, more than just being designed in ways that prohibit disabled people's access, buildings with such features are thought of as beautiful. Calls for retrofitting buildings for accessibility and for constructing new buildings according to principles of accessibility sometimes elicit objections that accessible features decrease the buildings' beauty. Such objections rely on objective definitions of beauty, insisting that, somehow, stairs are more beautiful than sloped entryways, narrow doors more beautiful than wide ones, and so on.

Disability aesthetics would enter this conversation with two observations: first, that the association of beauty and inaccessibility is conventional rather than inherent to inaccessible features; and second, that the association actually constitutes oppression of disabled people and perpetuates prejudices against them. If, for whatever reason, buildings had always been constructed with ramps, no-step entries, wide doorways, and doors with low handles, we might actually find ourselves objecting to the kinds of inaccessible features that characterize most of the buildings we encounter today. A simple thought experiment like this demonstrates that there is no necessary connection between beauty and inaccessibility. It also demonstrates that there *is* a necessary connection between oppression and the argument that inaccessible buildings are more beautiful than accessible ones: people whose bodies require accessible design are implicated in the lesser aesthetic value of accessibly designed buildings. Therefore, people whose bodies require accessible design are inherently less beautiful than people whose bodies do not require accessible design.

Scholars interested in disability aesthetics argue persuasively that, far from being the opposite of beauty, disability is an important part of how we understand beauty, especially in the contemporary period. Siebers points out that the *Venus de Milo*'s disabled body is one of the world's treasured artworks, whereas Nazi propaganda art depictions of idealized, "perfect" bodies only enter discussions of art as an example of the tacky or tasteless. In contemporary art, Siebers asks, "To what concept, other than the idea of disability, might be referred modern art's love affair with misshapen and twisted bodies, stunning variety of human forms, intense representation of traumatic injury and psychological alienation, and unyielding preoccupation with wounds and tormented flesh?" (Siebers, 2010, p. 4). Depictions of disabled bodies feature prominently in film, literature, and visual art, and disability is increasingly represented as a form of beauty, the distinction of disabled bodies drawing attention to the remarkable diversity of human beings even as we share universal experiences of love and longing, suffering and success.

In sum, the existence of disability insistently raises questions about the relationship between bodies and beauty. Disability aesthetics asserts that any definition of beauty is necessarily political, since it must say something about what kinds or proportions of bodies are beautiful. Consequently, disability aesthetics is an important addition to any consideration of beauty in art and design, urging us to remember that our bodies and backgrounds condition our assumptions about beauty and to make explicit those implicit influences on our understanding of aesthetics.

Placing Disability Studies Within the Academy

As a developing academic field, disability studies can be difficult to locate. We might find ourselves asking what department teaches disability studies. Or we might wonder if a person can get a degree in disability studies. Depending on where you go to ask these questions, the answers differ. This situation arises because many different disciplines deal with particular issues related to disability, and because disability studies departments are just beginning to be developed. Because the study of disability intersects with so many academic disciplines and historical and contemporary topics, the study of disability is happening in a range of different departments on college campuses.

When we begin thinking about *where* disability studies is located, one recurring and crucial question comes up: "Who can study disability?" This question is important because it can be answered in different ways. For example, in the arts and humanities, unlike in the medical field, the answer has been that disabled people are the experts on their own experiences.

This dual location for disability studies (both within and outside the university) is a fundamental issue when we think about locations for disability studies because the goals of activism and of academic studies are sometimes at odds with one another. And when we think of disability studies being both within and outside the university, the question of who can or should study disability becomes especially tricky. Does a person have to be disabled to study disability? If not, does he or she need to have a personal connection to disability? Given that earning a degree gives a person certain prestige that is not accorded

to disability activists—who are often disabled—is it right for able-bodied people to study disability? Furthermore, given that few people with disabilities are employed in higher education, can disability studies in the university responsibly hire able-bodied people? These questions start to outline the inherent issues with disability studies being located both within and outside the university and with questions of who can study disability in the university.

Another effect of disability studies expanding within other departments is its interdisciplinary nature, and a remaining question for the field is how best to continue to support and nourish that interdisciplinarity. Although interdisciplinarity positively affects the research done in disability studies in many ways, the knowledge base in the field becomes extremely vast and potentially difficult for individual scholars to stay informed about. Evidence of the interdisciplinarity of disability studies can be seen in the field's primary journal, *DSQ*; the publication currently has four accepted citation formats and two editors, each from different disciplines. Being an interdisciplinary study can also pose problems for the field's growth, given the current structure of most universities. For example, it can be difficult to secure funding or financial support for disability studies because it is dispersed across many departments. It may also be difficult to hire faculty who have interdisciplinary training.

Disability and/as Identity Studies

Disability constitutes, calls forth, and even claims an identity. And, too, disability studies is part of—yet also different from—identity studies in the academy. How disability (and disability studies) is—or isn't—an identity (or part of identity studies) stakes out one of the most significant issues for disability studies today. Disability is an experience in which individuals are connected to others—and to themselves—by some identification (or not) over their disability. Thus, disability identification comes from a consideration of how one's disability is understood, expressed, and shared both as an impairment and as a social construction. That is, we know "disability"—our own, others', our family members'—through the way it is multiply identified *to* us, *for* us, and *by* us. This multifaceted identification occurs as a (medical) impairment and also as a social (and familial, political, historical, geographical, experiential) element.

As discussed earlier, much of the scholarship on disability studies has sprouted from an idea of and affiliation with disability as a construct of identity (and identity studies)—as an act and art of identifying. One would only need to look at the introductions to many of the key texts published on disability studies in the past 15 years to put a finger on this identity pulse. In narrative and linguistic sum and short, disability and/as an identity issue is also closely aligned to disability and/as representation (see the earlier discussion on representation).

Disability studies is also like other areas of identity studies in that it concerns itself heavily with the key question: *why identify?* And, from this central question, the experiential, political, economic, individual, and community reasons for disability identification (or, too, for hiding/passing at one's identification) form a considerable core of the field's "study." Much of the critical work within disability studies that focuses on the act, affordances, risks, and processes of "passing" (as disabled or as "normal") is also largely answering the question, *why identify?* and *how (do we? should we?) identify?*

And, too, for all the affinities drawn here between disability and/as identity, there are also meaningful ways in which disability is not as, like, or part of identity or identity studies; questions about the affordances and drawbacks of disability and/as identity will continue to occupy disability studies.

Multiple Critical Frames

As an interdisciplinary field, disability studies does not have a central critical-theoretical or disciplinary frame. Disability studies complements (teaches to, learns from) already existing work in gender, sexuality, race, and class studies. As can be seen from a search of disability studies-focused scholarship in the arts and humanities over the past decade, it intersects well with and can even enhance the study of genre (literary and artistic forms), and it can align with, illuminate, or complicate various other critical theories often employed in the arts and humanities: feminist theory, queer theory, Marxism, literary criticism, historicism, and social constructionism, to name but a few. It spans literary periods and languages. It engages in what Sharon Snyder (2002) has called "infinities of form" in *Disability Studies: Enabling the Humanities* (p. 173).

Disability studies employs many other critical apparatuses to make its meanings. *Disability Studies Quarterly*, the oldest journal in the field and arguably the journal of record for the field, publishes articles from a significant number of fields and not only permits, but even encourages (cross) disciplinary citation formats as an illustration of the field's critical/framework diversity; authors submitting

manuscripts to *DSQ* can follow the style of any one of a number of accepted academic, disciplinary organizations, so long as they employ one style consistently: American Psychological Association (APA) style, Modern Language Association (MLA) style, the *Chicago Manual of Style,* or the like.

The overall field of disability studies breaks itself into (at least) six further critical domains, with active scholarship represented in each area: (1) representations of disability (in literature, art, popular media, film, etc.); (2) educational perspectives and studies of disability; (3) sociological and psychological perspectives (which offer some of the earliest theoretical work on disability); (4) a historical approach to studying disability; (5) political representations and policy development/studies; and (6) rehabilitation/medical/clinical perspectives. The intersections and conflicts between these six critical domains will continue to invigorate—and perplex—disability studies scholarship for years to come.

New and different models for disability studies—and thinking about disability in America and around the globe—are being considered. Considering disability as both a national and a global civil and human rights issue, for example, has been advanced by both the World Health Organization and the World Bank in the past decade, and the United Nations Convention on the Rights of People with Disabilities (UNCRPD) is circulating around the globe and seeing compelling numbers of parties-states ratifying it, whereas new scholarship resulting from that global circulation reaches the submission desk of *DSQ* almost daily now. Likewise, scholarship that arises from disability studies in the arts and humanities has employed disability as a powerful tool, frame, or insight to (re)think such concepts as aesthetic "value" (Siebers, 2010) or "normalcy" and "normate" (Davis, 2006; Garland-Thomson, 1996) or "betweenity" as identity (Brueggemann, 2009) or "body politic" (Linton) or "identity politics" (McRuer, 2006; Davis, 2002) or "accessibility" (Price, 2009) or, in corpus, "embodiment" (Hall, 2002; Imrie, 1998; Kuppers, 2003). Disability, in sum, enables insights, and this illumination is, in effect, the impact of its work in disability studies and disability culture.

References

ADAPT. (2012). http://www.adapt.org/. Accessed November 14, 2012.

Ashby, H. (Director). (1978). *Coming home* [Motion picture]. United States: Jerome Hellman Productions.

Barnartt, S. N., & Scotch, R. K. (2001). *Disability protests: Contentious politics, 1970–1999*. Washington, DC: Galludaet University Press.

Berger, P. L., & Luckmann, T. (1966). *The social construction of reality*. New York: Doubleday.

Boyle, T. C. (2006). *Talk talk*. New York: Penguin.

Brest, M. (Director) (1992). *Scent of a woman* [Motion picture]. United States: City Light Films.

Brown, S. (n. d.). "It's our story: Part 9 of 12: The origins of disability culture." http://www.youtube.com/watch?v=H0myf8gp1lM. Accessed November 14, 2012.

Brueggemann, B. J. (2007, October). On (almost) passing. *College English*, 59(6), 647–660.

Brueggemann, B. J. (2009). *Deaf subjects: Between identities and places*. New York: New York University Press.

Brueggemann, B. J. (2010). The tango: Or, what Deaf studies and disability studies do-do. In S. Burch & A. Kafer (Eds.) *Deaf and disability studies: Interdisciplinary perspectives* (pp. 245–265). Washington, DC: Gallaudet University Press.

Burch, S., & Joyner, H. (2007). *Unspeakable: The story of Junius Wilson*. Chapel Hill: The University of North Carolina Press.

Burch, S., & Kafer, A. (Eds.). (2010). *Deaf and disability studies: Interdisciplinary perspectives*. Washington, DC: Gallaudet University Press.

Carey, A. (2009). *On the margins of citizenship: Intellectual disability and civil rights in twentieth-century America*. Philadelphia, PA: Temple University Press.

Charlton, J. (2000). *Nothing about us without us: Disability oppression and empowerment*. Berkeley: University of California Press.

Couser, G. T. (2009). *Signifying bodies: Disability in contemporary life writing*. Ann Arbor: University of Michigan Press.

Cushing, P., & Smith, T (2009). A multinational review of English-language disability studies degrees ad courses. *Disability Studies Quarterly*, 29(3). Retrieved from http://dsq-sds.org/article/view/940/1121.

Davidson, M. (2010). Phantom limbs: Film noir and the disabled body. In S. Chivers & N. Markotic (Eds.), *The problem body: Projecting disability on film* (pp. 43–66). Columbus: Ohio State University Press.

Davis, L. J. (1995). *Enforcing normalcy: Disability, deafness, and the body*. New York: Verso.

Davis, L. J. (2002). *Bending over backwards: Disability, dismodernnism, and other difficulty positions*. New York: New York University Press.

The disability rights and independent living movement. (2010). Berkeley, CA: The Regents of the University of California. http://bancroft.berkeley.edu/collections/drilm/. Accessed November 14, 2012.

Finger, A. (2006). *Elegy for a disease: A personal and cultural history of polio*. New York: St. Martin's.

Frank, A. (1997). *The wounded storyteller*. Chicago, IL: University of Chicago Press.

Fries, K. (Ed.). (1997). *Staring back: The disability experience from the inside out*. New York: Plume.

Fries, K. (2007). *The history of my shoes and Darwin's theory of evolution*. New York: Carroll & Graf.

Garland-Thomson, R. (1996). *Extraordinary bodies*. New York: Columbia University Press.

Gilman, C. P. (1997). *The yellow wallpaper and other stories* (first published in 1892). Mineola, NY: Dover.

Green, G. (Director) (1965). *A patch of blue* [Motion picture]. United States: Filmways Pictures.

Goffman, E. (1961). *Asylums: Essays on the social situation of mental patients and other inmates*. New York: Doubleday.

Goffman, E. (1963). *Stigma: Notes on the management of spoiled identity*. New York: Simon and Schuster.

Golfus, B. (1994). *When Billy broke his head…and other tales of wonder*. Boston, MA: Fanlight Productions.

Herek, S. (Director). (1995). *Mr. Holland's opus* [Motion picture]. United States: Hollywood Pictures.

Galloway, T. (2009). *Mean little deaf queer*. Boston, MA: Beacon Press.

Gandolfini, J. (Director). (2007). *Alive day memories: Home from Iraq* [Motion picture]. New York: Attaboy Films/HBO Documentary Films.

Garey, D., & Hott, L. (2007). *Through deaf eyes*. Washington DC: WETA & PBS Productions.

Hall, K. Q. (Ed.) (2002). Special issue on Feminist Disability Studies, *NWSA Journal*, 14(3), vii–xiii.

Hockenberry, J. (1995). *Moving violations: War zones, wheelchairs, and declarations of independence*. New York: Hyperion.

Imrie, R. (1998). Oppression, disability, and access in the built environment. In T. Shakespeare (Ed.), *The disability reader: Social science perspectives* (pp. 129–146). London: Cassell.

Jamison, K. R. (1996). *An unquiet mind: A memoir of moods and madness*. New York: Random House.

Kayston, S. (1994). *Girl, interrupted*. New York: Vintage.

Keller, H. (1969). *Midstream: My later life*. New York: Greenwood.

Keller, H. (2003). *The story of my life*. New York: Norton.

Keller, H. (2003). *The world I live in*. (R. Shattuck, Ed.). New York: New York Review of Books.

Kleege, G. (1999). *Sight unseen*. New Have, CT: Yale University Press.

Kleege, G. (2006). *Blind rage: Letters to Helen Keller*. Washington DC: Gallaudet University Press.

Krentz, C. (Ed.). (2000). *A mighty change: An anthology of deaf American writing, 1816–1864*. Washington, DC: Gallaudet University Press.

Kuusisto, S. (1998). *Planet of the blind*. New York: Delta.

Kuppers, P. (2003). *Disability and contemporary performance: Bodies on edge*. New York: Routledge.

Lehrer, R. (2004). *Circle stories*. Chicago, IL: Chicago Cultural Center

Link, C. (Director). (1996). *Jenseits der Stille (Beyond Silence)* [Motion picture]. Germany: Arte.

Linton, S. (1998). *Claiming disability: Knowledge and identity*. New York: New York University Press.

Linton, S. (2007). *My body politic*. Ann Arbor: University of Michigan Press.

Lodge, D. (2009). *Deaf sentence*. New York: Penguin.

Longmore, P. K. (2003). *Why I burned my book and other essays on disability*. Philadelphia, PA: Temple University Press.

Lorde, A. (1980). *The cancer journals*. San Francisco, CA: Aunt Lute Books.

Mairs, N. (1996). *Waist-high in the world: A life among the nondisabled*. Boston, MA: Beacon Press.

McCullers, C. (2000). *The heart is a lonely hunter* (first published 1940). New York: First Mariner Books.

McRuer, R. (2006). *Crip theory: Cultural signs of queerness and disability*. New York: New York University Press.

Metzl, J. (2010). *The protest psychosis: How schizophrenia became a black disease*. Boston, MA: Beacon Press.

Mitchell, D., & Snyder, S. (Directors). (1995). *Vital signs: Crip culture talks back*. Fanlight Productions.

Mitchell, D., & Snyder, S. *The body and physical difference: Discourses of disability*. Ann Arbor: University of Michigan Press.

Mitchell, D., & Snyder, S. (2000). *Narrative prosthesis: Disability and the dependencies of discourse*. Ann Arbor: University of Michigan Press.

Mullins, A. (2009a). It's not fair having 12 pairs of legs. TED Talk. http://www.ted.com/talks/aimee_mullins_prosthetic_aesthetics.html. Accessed November 14, 2012.

Mullins, A. (2009b). The opportunity of adversity. TED Talk. http://www.ted.com/talks/aimee_mullins_the_opportunity_of_adversity.html. Accessed November 14, 2012.

Nasar, S. (1998). *A beautiful mind*. New York: Touchstone.

Neudel, E. (Director). (2011). *Lives worth living* [Motion picture]. Natick, MA: Storyline Motion Pictures.

Nielson, K. E. (2004). *The radical lives of Helen Keller*. New York: New York University Press.

Nielson, K. E. (Ed.). (2005). *Helen Keller: Selected writings*. New York: New York University Press.

Nielson, K. E. (2009). *Beyond the miracle worker: The remarkable life of Anne Sullivan Macy and her extraordinary friendship with Helen Keller*. Boston, MA: Beacon Press.

Nielson, K. E. (2012). *A disability history of the United States*. Boston, MA: Beacon Press.

Not dead yet: The resistance. (2012). http://www.notdeadyet.org/. Accessed November 14, 2012.

Nowak, A. (2004). Disclosures. In R. O'Brien (Ed.), *Voices from the edge: Narratives about the Americans with Disabilities Act* (pp. 55–69). Oxford, UK: Oxford University Press.

O'Brien, R. (Ed.) (2004). *Voices from the edge: Narratives about the Americans with Disabilities Act*. Oxford, UK: Oxford University Press.

Pekar, H., & Brabner, J. (1994). *Our cancer year*. New York: Four Walls Eight Windows.

Penn, A. (Director). (1962). *The miracle worker* [Motion picture]. United States: Playfilm Productions.

Poe, E. A. (1843). *The tell-tale heart*. Retrieved from http://xroads/virginia.edu-hyper/poe/telltale.html (original work published 1843). Accessed November 14, 2012.

Price, M. (2009). Access imagined: The construction of disability in conference policy documents. *Disability Studies Quarterly* 29(1). Retrieved from http://www.dsa-sds.org/article/view/174/174. Accessed November 14, 2012.

Raines, H. (Director). (1986). *Children of a lesser god* [Motion picture]. United States: Paramount Pictures.

Rozen, S., & Kowarsky, E. (1999). *Liebe Perla*. England: Eden Productions.

Sandahl, C., & Auslandar, P. (Eds.). (2005). *Bodies in commotion: Disability and performance*. Ann Arbor: University of Michigan Press.

Saramago, J. (1997). *Blindness*. (J. Sager, Trans.). Orlando, FL: Harcourt.

Selznick, B. (2011). *Wonderstruck: A novel in words and pictures*. New York: Scholastic.

Siebers, T. (2010). *Disability aesthetics*. Ann Arbor: University of Michigan Press.

Sirk, D. (Director). (1954). *Magnificent obsession* [Motion picture]. United States: Universal.

Shapiro, D., Mandel, J., & Rubin, H.-A. (2005). *Murderball* [Motion picture]. New York: Lions Gate Home Entertainment.

Snyder, S., Brueggemann, B.J., & Garland-Thomson, R. (2002). *Disability studies: Enabling the humanities*. New York: Modern Language Association Press.

Stone, O. (Director). (1989). *Born on the fourth of July* [Motion picture]. United States: Ixtlan.

Thon, M. R. (2000). *Sweet hearts*. New York: Simon & Schuster.

Trent, J. W. (1995). *Inventing the feeble mind: A history of mental retardation in the United States*. Berkeley: University of California Press.

Van Cleve, J. V. (Ed.). (2007). *The deaf history reader*. Washington, DC: Gallaudet University Press.

Van Cleve, J. V., & Crouch, B. (1989). *A place of their own: Creating the deaf community in America*. Washington DC: Gallaudet University Press.

Wade, C. M. (1994). "Disability culture rap." In B. Shaw (Ed.), *The ragged edge: The disability experience from the pages of the first fifteen years of The Disability Rag* (pp. 15–18). Louisville, KY: Advocado Press.

Wade, C. M. (2010). "Disability culture rap, parts 1 & 2." http://www.youtube.com/watch?v=j75aRfLsH2Y and http://www.youtube.com/watch?v=WTO2vn0dkaU. Accessed November 14, 2012.

Wells, H. G. (2004). *The country of the blind, and other stories* (original work published 1911). Retrieved from http://www.gutenberg.org/ebooks/11870.

Wendell, S. (1996). *The rejected body: Feminist philosophical reflections on disability*. New York: Routledge.

Zemeckis, R. (Director). (1994). *Forrest Gump* [Motion picture]. United States: Paramount Pictures.

Zola, I. K. (2003). *Missing pieces: A chronicle of living with a disability*. Philadelphia, PA: Temple University Press.

PART 3

Systems that Support Positive Psychology and Disability

Positive Behavior Support: Foundations, Systems, and Quality of Life

Glen Dunlap, Donald Kincaid, *and* Donald Jackson

Abstract

Positive behavior support (PBS) is an approach for helping people overcome behavioral challenges by developing a functional understanding of environmental influences and using that understanding to establish and implement interventions designed to build interpersonal competencies, reduce problem behaviors, and improve a person's quality of life. This chapter describes the foundations of PBS, discusses the relationship of PBS to applied behavior analysis and positive psychology, and provides examples of PBS at the level of the individual, the family, and in school-wide applications.

Key Words: positive behavior support, quality of life, positive psychology, problem behavior

Positive behavior support (PBS) is a term that has come to be used widely to refer to systematic, data-based applications of multicomponent procedures designed to encourage adaptive, pro-social behaviors and reduce problem behaviors. Derived from and still closely aligned with applied behavior analysis (ABA) (Dunlap, 2006), PBS emerged in the late 1980s as an approach characterized by an emphasis on instructional procedures, an avoidance of interventions that involved pain or stigmatization, and an insistence that all interventions be based on an understanding of a person's life circumstances, preferences, and goals (Horner et al., 1990). As PBS developed, its definition was elaborated and various authors began to articulate a growing number of essential, descriptive elements (Bambara & Kern, 2005; Janney & Snell, 2000). In 2002, Carr and his colleagues delineated nine features that defined PBS (Carr et al., 2002). The authors acknowledged that none of the features is unique to PBS and that many practitioners affiliated with other approaches may well subscribe to these guidelines, but that, in

aggregate, the features serve to distinguish PBS. These features are:

1. *Comprehensive lifestyle change and improved quality of life* (QOL) as the ultimate and obligatory goals of intervention;

2. A recognition that interventions and supports must be seen and implemented from a longitudinal, *lifespan perspective*;

3. A focus on *ecological validity*, meaning that strategies of intervention and support must be relevant to, and effective in, real-life settings and situations;

4. An insistence that *principal stakeholders* (such as parents, teachers, friends, employers, siblings) *function as collaborators and partners* in the development and implementation of PBS;

5. An emphasis on the *social validity* of procedures and outcomes;

6. An understanding that effective, longitudinal support requires *systems change and multicomponent interventions*;

7. A comprehensive *emphasis on prevention* and an acknowledgment that functional (proactive) intervention occurs when problem behaviors are not present;

8. An appreciation and utilization of knowledge derived from *various types of methodological practices*, and, correspondingly;

9. A pragmatic appreciation for the contributions of *multiple theoretical perspectives*.

The influences that combined to create PBS are many. They include the social and civil rights movements of deinstitutionalization and inclusion (Bambara, 2005), the conceptual and methodological framework and procedural foundations of ABA (Cooper, Heron, & Heward, 1987), and pivotal research contributions in the areas of functional equivalence, functional analysis, instructional design, and the influence of contextual variables. The scientists responsible for these key empirical findings typically used single-subject experimental designs (Gast, 2010; Kennedy, 2004) to analyze and examine the effectiveness of environmental factors in producing socially significant behavior change. Increasingly, however, PBS researchers are using the full range of research methods to explore influences, develop useful assessments and interventions, and evaluate the efficacy and replicability of specific and broad-based behavior support strategies.

The purpose of this chapter is to elucidate some of the foundations of PBS and to emphasize the contextual circumstances in which PBS arose, developed, and is defined. Context is vital to PBS because the viability of the approach has always been dependent on its efficacy in the full range of environments and circumstances in which people live, learn, work, play, and interact with one another. Major themes in PBS highlighted in this chapter include its focus on the individual, its appreciation of the individual's life within the context of systems (e.g., families, schools), and the need to undertake behavior support with a broad perspective on an individual's QOL.

The first section provides a discussion of the historical, conceptual, and procedural foundations of PBS. Following the consideration of foundations are separate reflections on the relationship between PBS and ABA and positive psychology. The section that follows describes some applications of PBS in the contexts of individual behavior analysis, family systems, and schools. The chapter concludes with some summary observations related to PBS, context, and the overall enterprise of supports for improved human functioning.

Foundations of Positive Behavior Support
Historical and Conceptual Foundations

Prior to the 1980s, the practice of behavior management (or behavior modification) was based heavily on contingency management strategies whereby the prescription for behavior problems would entail: (a) positive reinforcement for behaviors different from and often incompatible with the problem behavior, and (b) extinction or punishment for the problem behavior. This approach worked well to reduce the problem behaviors of many individuals, but it was often inadequate for the chronic problem behaviors of people with significant and complex challenges, including many people with severe intellectual disability. In such cases where common contingency management practices were insufficient, the tendency was often to increase the intensity or potency of the consequences. Instead of praise or tokens, the positive reinforcers would be elevated to candy or other distinctively preferred items, and they would be delivered on a dense schedule. Similarly, the consequences for problem behaviors escalated from planned ignoring or mild timeouts to more intensive and often painful punishers, such as hand slaps, noxious smells, water sprays, and, for the most severe behaviors, contingent electric shock. In the 1970s and early 1980s, it had become commonplace for treatment programs for people with severe disabilities and problem behaviors to include contingencies for the delivery of aversive consequences (Guess, Helmstetter, Turnbull, & Knowlton, 1987).

This tendency to use aversive consequences and to rely extensively on contingency management began to change in the early 1980s. This change was due initially to the complaints of disability rights advocates who argued that the use of aversive techniques was incompatible with the growing movements of inclusion and deinstitutionalization. Simply stated, procedures that involved extensive physical contact and/or the infliction of pain would not be accepted in typical community settings such as restaurants, stores, parks, or inclusive schools. On a more basic level, advocates also asserted that aversive procedures were inconsistent with implicit standards of decency regarding human interactions (see Singer, Gert, & Koegel, 1999). In short, by the mid-1980s, a chorus of concern had galvanized against the use of aversive consequences for controlling the problem behaviors of individuals with disabilities. A major social and civil rights movement had formed to stop aversive interventions and to find new, effective strategies for addressing the challenge of problem behaviors. By 1987, the federal government had directed resources to the quest for "nonaversive" options of behavior management (Risley, 1999).

Although advocacy movements provided the necessary impetus, PBS could not have emerged without a solid conceptual and methodological foundation. That foundation was provided primarily by the practical discipline of ABA (Baer, Wolf, & Risley, 1968) and the psychology of instrumental (operant) learning (Skinner, 1953). Of essential importance were the basic principles of learning (e.g., reinforcement, stimulus control), the four-term contingency model (Dunlap, Harrower, & Fox, 2005), the research methods of quasi-experimental and experimental time series designs (Bailey & Burch, 2002; Kennedy, 2004), and the pragmatic focus that characterized ABA (Dunlap, 2006). These features combined to produce a considerable body of empirical findings pertaining to the analysis and manipulation of environmental variables and the employment of those variables to yield improvements in the efficacy of behavioral interventions.

By the early 1980s, important developments in applied behavior analytic research had established the groundwork that enabled an evolution of behavior support technology (Dunlap, Carr, Horner, Zarcone, & Schwartz, 2008). One development came from studies illustrating the functional properties of problem behaviors, showing that problem behaviors could be interpreted often as a means of communication. That is, in most cases, problem behaviors could be seen as "functionally equivalent" to adaptive methods of expression and were maintained by the same contingencies of reinforcement (Carr, 1977). Thus, if the purpose (function) of the problem behavior was understood, and if a functionally equivalent alternative behavior could be taught and maintained, then the problem behaviors could be replaced by more desirable alternatives and aversive consequences would be unnecessary. These studies led to practical technologies of functional analysis and functional assessment (Iwata, Dorsey, Slifer, Bauman, & Richman, 1994; O'Neill et al., 1997) and highly effective educational strategies for developing appropriate, communicative alternatives to problem behaviors (Carr et al., 1994; Durand, 1990; Evans & Meyer, 1985). The conceptual and practical implications of this line of research provided a critical foundation for PBS and were key factors in pushing behavior management beyond the confines of contingency management.

Simultaneously, a complementary line of applied research was demonstrating how substantially the environmental context influenced occurrences of problem behavior. Numerous observations showed how individuals' problem behaviors occurred in the presence of some stimuli and not in the presence of other stimuli (Haring & Kennedy, 1990). The same studies illustrated how omitting or ameliorating pertinent events in the environment could prevent problem behaviors and increase desirable behaviors (Dunlap & Kern, 1996; Luiselli, 2006). This research delivered another foundational element and critical principle to PBS—that the design of the environment is an essential variable in understanding and resolving problem behaviors.

Procedural Foundations

From its origins in ABA and advocacy, the procedures of PBS developed substantially over the past 20 years. As mentioned, strategies derived from the practical science of ABA and the conceptual framework of learning (operant) theory provided the starting point. In addition, however, a set of procedural elements were embraced that served to establish the contextual circumstances for producing outcomes that were most valued by consumers. Some of these procedural elements are viewed as foundational to the PBS approach (Carr et al., 2002), including: (a) a collaboration with principal stakeholders, (b) a commitment to ecological and social validity that places a high priority on contextual fit (Albin, Lucyshyn, Horner, & Flannery, 1996), (c) an acknowledgment that effectiveness often requires interventions that are comprehensive rather than delimited, and (d) accountability based on evaluations of the lifestyle and QOL outcomes for participating individuals. These foundations of PBS may be considered procedural in that they shape how PBS is applied in practice.

Although authors from many disciplines have alluded to a need for collaboration with key stakeholders, PBS has specifically developed its training and direct support approaches to strengthen and promote involvement in the PBS process by families, teachers, friends, community members, and, importantly, the person receiving PBS (Dunlap et al., 2000; Fox, Vaughn, Dunlap, & Bucy, 1997). Positive behavior support is an approach based on collaborative "partnerships," which is in clear contrast to the more traditional "expert" or "professionally driven" consultation model (Carr, 1997). Providing choices and respecting decisions of team members are essential to implementation of effective behavioral supports.

This commitment to contextual fit is evident in the emphasis on providing PBS approaches that are ecologically and socially valid. *Ecological validity* refers to the need for interventions to be relevant to and effective in real-life settings and situations (Dunlap, 2006). *Social validity* refers to whether the people implementing or observing the implementation of the procedures believe that they are appropriate for the circumstances (e.g., location, the severity of the behavior problem, and the severity of intervention approach) (Schwartz & Baer, 1991; Wolf, 1978). Thus, contextual fit refers to whether the identified interventions fit into the routines, resources, structures, and values of the intervention agents and whether they are considered appropriate and effective by those agents (Albin et al., 1996)

This contextual fit issue is reflected in the PBS commitment to both macro- and micro-analysis of contextual issues. The development of a wide range of effective functional assessment tools and strategies (Scott et al., 2004; Sugai et al., 2000; Umbreit, Ferro, Liaupsin, & Lane, 2007) has been instrumental in providing the PBS practitioner with critical information about the antecedents, setting events, behaviors, and consequences and the relationships between each. This collection of data specific to the identified student or individual's behavior is critical for determining the central question of "Why is this behavior occurring?"

In addition to this micro-level functional assessment of how behavior is impacted by antecedents, setting events, and consequences, PBS emphasizes a broadened scope of functional assessment to include the impact of lifestyle issues and social contexts on problem behavior (Dunlap & Kincaid, 2001; Fox et al., 1997). Strategies such as person-centered planning have assisted practitioners and teams in understanding the impact of issues such as relationships, productivity, inclusion, self-advocacy, self-determination, choice-making, and social and cultural norms on the QOL of individuals who also have problem behaviors (Kincaid & Fox, 2002). Conducting a functional assessment to understand why an individual's problem behavior is occurring is an integral part of the PBS process. No less important is understanding how such problem behavior actually "makes sense," given the context of the person's life. Such a comprehensive understanding of the person, his life and his behavior, can be essential to motivating and supporting typical intervention agents such as parents and teachers.

The comprehensive understanding of the interaction of the person's past and current environment with his or her problem behavior necessarily leads to the understanding that a successful support system for the focus person will likely require comprehensive supports that include antecedent or environmental arrangements, changes in teaching approaches, and modifications in the type and delivery of consequences. Occasionally, a comprehensive functional assessment will identify a simple problem that may be solved immediately with an environmental or lifestyle adaptation. However, in the majority of cases, a complex and challenging array of life circumstances, which may have existed for many years, will be found to be maintaining an equally complex and challenging array of problem behaviors. Within a PBS framework, such situations are not solved by finding a more powerful aversive consequence to suppress the problem behavior but by providing the support to implement multicomponent interventions that alleviate the lifestyle and environmental stressors promoting problem behavior (Carr et al., 1999; Lucyshyn, Albin, & Nixon, 1997).

Since multicomponent interventions are intended to impact an array of problem behaviors and life circumstances, the evaluation of the success of PBS approaches must also address a wide array of outcomes for the individual (Kincaid, Knoster, Harrower, Shannon, & Bustamante, 2002; Knoster & Kincaid, 2005). It will always be important to show that the multicomponent interventions actually decrease some dimension of problem behavior, such as its frequency, duration, or intensity. However, it will seldom be sufficient to show that, as a result of this array of interventions, only the frequency of problem behaviors has decreased. Within a PBS paradigm, it would also be important to measure whether any alternative, positive behaviors also increased in frequency, duration, or intensity. It may also be necessary to measure whether the person achieved important QOL goals. For instance, does the person have more friends or a better job after intervention? Is the person living a more inclusive and self-determined life than prior to the PBS process? Although it is difficult to measure QOL outcomes with precision (Kincaid et al., 2002), attempts have been made to evaluate the extent to which comprehensive, multicomponent PBS interventions can produce these vital effects. Later in this chapter, we describe a multiyear investigation of PBS in which multiple outcomes were examined, including QOL (Dunlap, Carr, Horner, et al., 2010). First, however, it is useful to conclude our description of PBS' foundations by commenting on some relationships between PBS and two important perspectives on interventions for problem behaviors. We consider ABA because it is a well-established discipline that was the major foundation from which PBS arose, and we consider positive psychology because it emerged more recently as an important and influential orientation that has important areas of congruence with PBS.

Positive Behavior Support and Applied Behavior Analysis

As we have acknowledged, PBS was derived directly from ABA and continues to share many of its conceptual and methodological underpinnings. Indeed, some authors have offered thoughtful arguments stipulating that PBS should not be viewed as a distinct discipline because it is essentially a manifestation or extension of ABA (Carr & Sidener, 2002, Wacker & Berg, 2002). There is merit in this position because many PBS procedures, including the essential strategies of functional assessment and intervention, are indisputably taken from the principles, technology, and field research traditions of ABA. At the level of direct implementation, a great deal of PBS *is* ABA, and it is acknowledged that the practices of many behavior analysts are fully consistent with PBS.

Still, other authors assert that it is important to view PBS as a unique approach, largely because it is the only identified approach explicitly distinguished as being based on and defined by characteristics that are not routinely absorbed in other disciplines, such as ABA (Carr et al., 2002). Some of these characteristics have compelled the development and/or adoption of core strategies that are central to PBS that may be unprecedented in other behavioral traditions. For instance, the commitment to ecological validity, collaboration, and lifestyle outcomes has occasioned the incorporation of person-centered planning and systems analysis in the routine armamentarium of PBS (Kincaid & Fox, 2002). Similarly, from both a conceptual and methodological perspective, the PBS pledge to lifestyle and lifespan outcomes requires consideration of new frameworks and expanded techniques of analysis than have been common heretofore in the literature of behavioral interventions (e.g., Risley, 1996). From this realization comes the PBS regard for multiple methodological and theoretical contributions, as well as the opinion that the further development of PBS may well constitute an evolution into a new applied science (Carr et al., 2002).

In the past decade, there has been a good deal of discussion about the position of PBS with respect to ABA, and some of this discussion has been contentious (e.g., Johnston, Foxx, Jacobson, Green, &

Mulick, 2006). However, the dominant perspective regarding the relationship is that (a) the procedural and conceptual foundations of PBS are largely, although not entirely, those of ABA (Dunlap, 2006); (b) many specific intervention strategies are common to PBS and ABA; but (c) there are enough important distinctions that separate labels and terminology are warranted (Dunlap et al., 2008). For the most part, when addressing particular strategies or techniques of intervention, the approaches are common to PBS and ABA. In the discussion to follow, a number of general strategies and specific procedures are reviewed under the auspices of PBS. It is clear, however, that most of these strategies and procedures are also clearly (and appropriately) associated with ABA, and there is no intent to imply any kind of special proprietorship.

Positive Behavior Support and Positive Psychology

Given the fact that both approaches have the word "positive" in their titles, perhaps it is not surprising that PBS and positive psychology have much in common. Nevertheless, the differences in origins and focus populations make the similarities in their characteristics somewhat striking. Carr (2007), in his presidential address for the Association for Positive Behavior Support, first highlighted this alignment, arguing that positive psychology is a field with particular importance and relevance to the work of PBS. He pointed out the similarities of key defining features and argued that positive psychology could be a significant resource for ideas about both assessment and intervention strategies for PBS.

Positive psychology has been defined as "an umbrella term for the study of positive emotions, positive character traits, and enabling institutions" (Seligman, Steen, Park, & Peterson, 2005; p. 410). Carr (2007) connected these core elements of positive psychology to critical features of PBS: positive emotions relates directly to the PBS concept of QOL; positive character traits involves building personal competence and skills in the PBS world; and enabling institutions is reflected in PBS by the strong emphasis on environmental redesign. Like PBS, positive psychology shifts the focus from deficits and pathology to strengths, abilities, and virtues (Seligman & Csikszentmihályi, 2000; Shogren, Wehmeyer, Buchanan, & Lopez, 2006).

Several key characteristics of PBS are also prominent in positive psychology. For example, the PBS emphasis on comprehensive lifestyle change and improved QOL has a conspicuous parallel in positive psychology's focus on the personal traits of subjective well-being, optimism, happiness, and self-determination (Seligman & Csikszentmihályi, 2000). A significant area of research in both disciplines is the relationship of social connections to personal competence, happiness, and life satisfaction. Another commonality involves the PBS emphasis on the longitudinal perspective as a guiding principle of intervention. Positive psychology also argues that a full appreciation for positive psychological processes, particularly long-lasting well-being and QOL, requires this longitudinal orientation (Seligman & Csikszentmihályi, 2000; Vaillant, 2000).

Another central characteristic of PBS is ecological validity, or the need to ensure that strategies of intervention and support are relevant and effective in real-life settings (Carr et al., 2002). Similarly, positive psychology considers it essential to address the social context in which people and experiences are embedded and to study the influence of positive communities and positive institutions. To fully understand how "individual strengths unfold over an entire life span," positive psychology argues for the need to look "at behavior in its ecologically valid social setting" (Seligman & Csikszentmihályi, 2000, p. 8).

The conception of the role of the individual is important in positive psychology. Individuals play a central role as decision makers, expressing choices and preferences, taking initiative, self-organizing, and being self-directed (Seligman & Csikszentmihályi, 2000; Shogren et al., 2006). In PBS, the role of the individual is embedded within the concept of social validity (Wolf, 1978), in which the individual and related stakeholders (parents, educators, etc.) are participants and decision-makers with respect to the goals of interventions (whether goals are aligned with personal priorities and preferences), the processes of intervention (their practicality, desirability, goodness of fit), and the outcomes of the intervention (its perceived effectiveness in terms of problem behaviors and impact on QOL) (Carr et al., 2002). And, analogously, PBS focuses on an educative orientation to intervention. Rather than emphasizing the reduction of problem behaviors, the stress is placed on building skills that make problem behavior irrelevant. Positive psychology stresses that interventions with families and community institutions need to "develop climates that foster...strengths" (Seligman & Csikszentmihályi, 2000, p. 8) and emphasizes strategies for "systematically building competency, not on correcting weakness" (Seligman & Csikszentmihályi, 2000).

Applications of Positive Behavior Support

In the relatively brief time of its existence, PBS has been applied at different levels of analysis. In the following section, examples from three levels are discussed: the level of the individual, the level of the family system, and the level of whole schools.

Individual level

The initial and still-prevalent focus of PBS has been on assessment and intervention for problem behavior (and, more broadly, problems of behavioral adaptation) exhibited by individuals, especially people with disabilities (Dunlap, Horner, Sailor, & Sugai, 2009). The model of PBS for people with severe and chronic problem behaviors generally consists of five steps: (a) the establishment of a team of support providers; (b) agreement on short-term and long-term goals pertaining to building competencies, enhancing QOL, and reducing problem behaviors; (c) conducting relevant assessments, including a comprehensive functional assessment of problem behaviors; (d) development and implementation of a multicomponent behavior support plan; and (e) evaluation of the effects of the intervention, with modifications of the plan as indicated by the progress monitoring and fidelity data.

Many studies have been published demonstrating positive effects of PBS implementation, the majority of which have used single-subject experimental designs to document causal relations between implementation of PBS interventions and improvements in an individual's behavior; however, the literature also includes a number of randomized group designs (e.g., Iovannone et al., 2009). Syntheses of the literature on PBS have demonstrated a number of replicated findings relevant to PBS with individuals (Carr, Horner et al., 1999; Dunlap & Carr, 2007). First, functional assessment is useful for identifying controlling variables, and interventions based on such assessments can be effective in reducing problem behaviors. Second, the teaching of alternative skills and the manipulation of identified antecedent influences can produce rapid behavior change without resorting to punishing or invasive procedures. Third, multicomponent and assessment-based interventions can lead to substantial and durable lifestyle improvements.

Although the beneficial effects of PBS have been documented extensively, the majority of studies have examined behavior change in relatively circumscribed and short-term contexts. However, the goal of PBS is to help produce lifestyle, QOL changes that would represent long-term and broad-based benefits. For such changes to occur, the behavior support plan would need to be implemented by typical agents (teachers, parents, etc.) in the full range of a person's regular environments (schools, work, home). An example of such a large-scale, longitudinal investigation was described recently by Dunlap, Carr, Horner, Koegel, Sailor, Clarke, and colleagues (2010). This descriptive study is summarized in the following paragraphs.

The Dunlap, Carr et al. (2010) study was conducted at five sites in diverse geographical locations around the United States. Thirty participants were enrolled in the study, although complete datasets covering baseline and 2 years of intervention were available for 21. By design, the participants were diverse in age (3–39 years), diagnosis (e.g., autism, mild to profound intellectual disability, at-risk for emotional disabilities), ethnicity, and residential status (home, publicly funded residence). However, all participants displayed severe problem behavior and were identified as requiring intensive and extensive supports.

All participants were provided with comprehensive PBS services that followed the standard model for individualized, multicomponent, assessment-based interventions. The participants' team members (e.g., teachers, parents, residential support staff) implemented the interventions, with members of the research team facilitating the process. In all cases, baseline measures were followed by person-centered planning, comprehensive functional assessments, and team-driven development of behavior support plans designed for implementation in all settings in which problem behavior occurred. Team meetings were scheduled periodically to review data and make adjustments to the support plans as needed.

A large amount and variety of data were obtained for each participant on an individualized basis. Data elements included standardized tests, direct observations, structured interviews, detailed journal entries, and functional assessments. Comprehensive data were obtained at baseline and periodically thereafter, with some measures being collected annually, semi-annually, or on an as-needed basis. Ultimately, data were assembled in portfolios to capture the participant's status during 2–3 months of baseline and then for Year 1 and Year 2 of intervention. Data elements for each of the three periods were identified as relating to levels of problem behavior, levels of PBS implementation, and six dimensions of QOL. Independent raters were then appointed to review the extensive portfolios and assign a rating for each time period. Integrity of PBS implementation was

rated for each year on a 5-point scale ranging from full and systematic implementation in all relevant settings with a high level of fidelity (score of 5) to very little implementation in relevant settings with no evidence of fidelity (score of 1). Problem behavior and the six dimensions of QOL were scored on a 9-point scale for each year, with the scale indicating the degree of improvement over the year of intervention relative to baseline. Therefore, the task of the raters was to obtain a thorough description of the participants' status during the baseline period and then use the 9-point scale to rate the degree of improvement or deterioration. A score of 5 indicated no change relative to baseline; scores above 5 indicated that, overall, the participant's status was improved, and scores below 5 indicated that the status had worsened. More than 90% of the scores were generated by two independent raters, and interrater agreement for all variables was 89% or higher.

The results of this descriptive study must be characterized as "modest" but encouraging. First, across the 21 participants, the extent of PBS implementation yielded average ratings of 3.40 for Year 1 and 3.57 for Year 2. A score of 3 was defined as PBS being implemented "in more than one environment with some effort to be consistent but without indications of integrity over extended periods of implementation (moderate fidelity)." This was unsurprising as it is not realistic to expect full implementation in all settings for 24 hours per day for every day of the year. But it is encouraging that natural intervention agents were able to sustain efforts of behavior support and that there was a slight increase in fidelity in the second year of implementation.

Ratings for problem behavior on a 9-point scale averaged 6.5 in Year 1 and 6.9 for Year 2. Because a score of 5 indicates no change relative to baseline, these scores are indicative of some improvement, with Year 2 again showing gains beyond those seen in Year 1.

Ratings for QOL were scored on six distinct domains. The domains were material well-being, health and safety, social well-being and interpersonal competence, emotional and affective well-being, leisure/recreation, and personal well-being. These domains were derived from the literature and carefully defined so as to be mutually exclusive. Logically, it would seem likely that some of the domains would covary with levels of problem behavior. For example, the definition of "personal well-being" included indicators of independence, self-determination, and choice, all of which are common objectives of PBS. However, other domains, such as "material well being," might not be expected to be affected by PBS implementation. The results were somewhat surprising. On average, all of the six domains showed improvement relative to baseline in Year 1, and they showed even greater improvement over the course of Year 2. These data are depicted in Figure 20.1.

It should be acknowledged that these gains in the domains of QOL are relatively modest. Most of the scores were between 6 and 7 on a 9-point scale and, of course, there was considerable variability. It is also important to emphasize that these data are not experimental, so it is risky to assign any causal interpretation. Indeed, the explanation for a link between PBS implementation and changes in QOL would be difficult to elucidate. However, the findings from the study are of interest because they are some of the only data that reflect attempts to measure QOL in the context of longitudinal implementation of PBS.

Family Systems

A significant area of concern for behavioral practitioners is the occurrence of problem behaviors displayed by children (Dunlap et al., 2006), especially in home and family contexts. Numerous authors have described the importance of addressing such problem behaviors by considering their occurrence in light of the overall functioning of family systems (Turnbull & Turnbull, 2000, 2001). Such family-centered assessment and behavior support has been a conspicuous theme of PBS research and practice (Lucyshyn, Dunlap, & Albin, 2002). In particular, support pertaining to children's problem behaviors at the family level has emphasized the

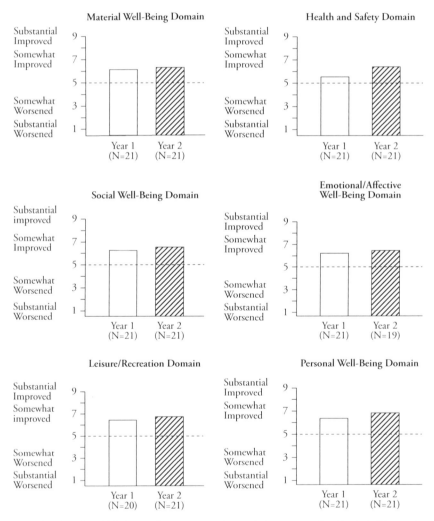

Figure 20.1 Means of each quality of life domain for participants (N = 21) for Years 1 and 2. The dashed lines indicate the level at which no change from baseline was evident. Descriptions of the study and definitions of the quality of life domains are in Dunlap et al., 2010. Figure is reprinted with permission of the Council for Children with Behavioral Disorders.

need to (a) include family members as key participants in the process of assessment and intervention planning and (b) help resolve problem behaviors by helping families function more effectively. Although these considerations have been noted in work prior to PBS, they have been manifested prominently in recent PBS research and practice (Lucyshyn et al., 2002). These two manifestations of family context are evident in the following two illustrations.

The first example is from a case study reported by Vaughn and her colleagues (1997) concerning a boy with serious problem behaviors in home and community settings. Jeffrey was 9-years-old and was diagnosed with multiple and severe disabilities, including Cornelia de Lange syndrome, accompanied by extreme problem behaviors such as head banging, aggression, and screaming. Jeffrey's mother and principal caregiver, Millie, participated as a full member of the PBS team charged with conducting functional assessments and designing a support plan. Assessment data were gathered from reports by all family members and from direct observations of Jeffrey in common, problematic community routines (fast-food restaurant, bank, grocery store). Millie provided the key voice in identifying the contextual circumstances associated with Jeffrey's most severe problem behaviors, and she was instrumental in selecting intervention components (Vaughn et al., 1997). The team depended on Millie to identify the components that would not only be consistent with the assessment data, but would also be feasible in the everyday circumstances of the family's routines. The data showed that Jeffrey's problem behaviors in the three community contexts were resolved to the point that Millie and her family could engage in the routines without difficulty. As a co-investigator on this family-centered PBS support project, Millie also provided qualitative data that offered insights into the various stresses and challenges experienced by the family prior to and during the entire process of PBS (Fox et al., 1997). Such data may help future program developers and applied researchers develop family-centered interventions that are more sensitive to families' concerns, the vicissitudes of the behavior support process, and the potential of parent–professional partnerships (Fox, Vaughn, Wyatte, & Dunlap, 2002). The case study of Jeffrey and Millie served as an illustration of these contextual aspects of family-centered work in PBS.

The second illustration highlights the value of working directly with family systems to establish a durable context for resolving young children's problem behaviors. This approach seeks to support families by building on family strengths, adding competencies to parents' repertoires, and ameliorating family problems through a myriad of individualized support options (Dunlap & Fox, 1999b). By strengthening family systems and family functioning, it is anticipated that children who are part of the family systems will be less vulnerable to those environmental challenges that can provoke problem behaviors. Furthermore, families with improved functioning are expected to be better able to implement behavior support programs with consistency and focus. These assumptions were manifested in the Individualized Support Project (ISP) (Dunlap & Fox, 1999a), in which families with young children with severe problem behaviors were provided assistance, training, and support with an emphasis on the development and implementation of family-centered PBS. The results of the program included significant reductions in the children's problem behaviors, as well as long-lasting lifestyle gains for the children and their families (Dunlap & Fox, 1999a; Fox, Benito, & Dunlap, 2002; Scandariato, 2002). The ISP program is one of many family-centered PBS efforts that address problem behaviors by enhancing the family context in which children live, develop, and learn to behave.

School-wide and Program-wide Applications

Although much of the research that formed the empirical support for PBS was developed through discovery and application of basic principles of behavior as applied to individuals with problem behaviors, there has always been an awareness that each child and adult functions in very complex community environments. These complex environments provide the context in which PBS interventions flourish or fail. Thus, the success of PBS approaches for a child or adult may depend more on the impeding or promoting contextual variables in critical social systems than on the precision of an individual behavior support plan (Hieneman & Dunlap, 2000).

Nowhere is the importance of social context variables more evident than in schools. Positive behavior support can be applied at multiple levels in schools to effectively support all students, including those with serious problem behaviors (George, Harrower, & Knoster, 2003; Lewis & Sugai, 1999; Weigle, 1997). This commitment to a multitiered system of student support has resulted in (at a minimum) a three-tiered model of support that emphasizes, first, developing a core or primary curriculum for addressing the needs of all students to gain social competencies (tier 1 or universal supports). The second tier of support is provided to students who are not responding adequately to the primary interventions (tier 2, targeted or supplemental supports). These students may exhibit repeated minor or major behavior problems that require targeted support. Finally, there may be between 1% and 5% of students in a school who, even with effective tier 1 and 2 supports, require more intensive and individualized PBS approaches (tier 3 or individualized and intensive supports). A useful graphic describing this multitiered system of student support for academics and behavior within a problem-solving framework is illustrated in Figure 20.2.

At tier 1 (universal), the presence of effective classroom and school-wide supports creates a necessary context for all students to achieve behavioral success. School-wide or universal PBS is the application of evidence-based strategies and systems to assist schools to increase academic performance, increase safety, decrease problem behavior, and establish positive school cultures (Office of Special Education Programs Center on Positive Behavior Support, 2004; Sugai et al., 2000). At the level of the entire school, school-wide PBS (SWPBS) advocates for a

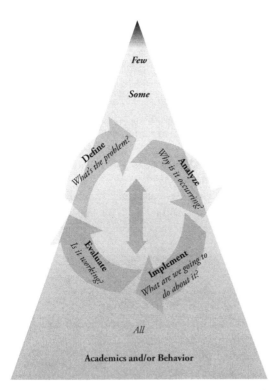

Figure 20.2 The three-tiered model of academic and behavioral supports is depicted, along with the problem-solving steps to address the needs of students at universal (tier 1), supplemental (tier 2), and intensive (tier 3) levels.

preventative, teaching, and reinforcement approach for addressing behavior problems. For instance, teaching and reinforcing appropriate expectations and rules for all students can have a significant impact on students with even the most severe problem behavior. The implementation of effective school-wide behavior support practices can create a more positive school climate and culture and provide school personnel with additional tools and skills to teach and recognize appropriate behavior from all students, including students with very difficult behavior. Implementation of an effective school-wide system can also reduce the resources (time, funds, personnel, etc.) that had been applied ineffectively to the entire student population. As a result, there may be fewer students who require more intensive behavior supports and more adequate resources at the school level to address the curricular, instructional, and behavioral needs of those students who still require targeted/supplemental or individual adaptations.

Extension of this SWPBS system can further enhance the functioning of classrooms by increasing academic engagement and minimizing disruptive behavior (Hieneman, Dunlap, & Kincaid, 2005). Although limited research is available on classroom PBS systems, such systems should extend the strategies of universal PBS into the classroom, support delivery of supplemental interventions for groups of students, and accommodate individual intervention for students requiring greater support. Classroom-based PBS can draw from some well-articulated classroom intervention strategies (Colvin & Lazar, 1997; Darch & Kameenui, 2004; Jackson & Panyan, 2002; Sprick, Garison, & Howard, 1998; Westling & Fox, 2004) that may address contextual variables in the classroom to promote students' academic and behavioral success. In addition, extension of strategies from the school-wide system (clearly articulated rules, established routines, effective teaching of expected behavior, effective rewards for positive behavior, and consistent responses to inappropriate behavior) will establish a context in which positive peer behavior and appropriate social relationships is the expected norm and not the exception.

Tier 2 or targeted and supplemental supports are intended for those 15–30% of students who are not responsive to a tier 1 system of support. Many evidence-based practices have been employed to support students at tier 2, including self-management, social skills instruction, peer support, and token economies. Although many of these practices may be evident in a plethora of social skills training programs that target this population, many of these programs have not been subjected to rigorous scientific validation. Some of the more common approaches that are represented in peer-reviewed journals include Check In/Check Out (Fairbanks, Sugai, Guardino, & Lathrop, 2007; McIntosh, Campbell, Carter, & Dickey, 2009; Simonson, Myers, & Briere, 2011), the Behavior Education Program (Crone, Horner, & Hawken, 2004; Hawken, MacLeod, & Rawlings, 2007), Check and Connect (Anderson, Christenson, Sinclair, & Lehr, 2004; Lehr, Sinclair, & Christenson, 2004; Sinclair, Christenson, & Thurlow, 2005), and Check, Connect and Expect (Cheney et al., 2009). These programs, as well as other effective tier 2 interventions, share some basic features that make them effective and appropriate tier 2 supports. These intervention components include (a) being continuously available for student enrollment; (b) being quickly and easily accessible; (c) requiring minimal time commitment from classroom teachers; (d) requiring skill sets needed by classroom teachers that can be easily learned; (e) aligning with school-wide expectations; (f) supporting all staff/faculty to be aware of the intervention(s) and their roles in the process; (g) implementing consistently with most students, but with some flexibility; and (h) selecting interventions matched to the function of the student's behavior.

If effective universal and supplemental PBS systems are implemented with fidelity, fewer students may need a more intensive problem-solving approach that would be characterized as a tier 3 (individualized) PBS system. However, there will always be a few students in a school who will need individual support ranging from a brief teacher consultation to a traditional functional assessment and behavior intervention planning process. The success of any of these individual support approaches is likely based on several contextual variables such as (a) the collaborative relationship between consultants and teachers or teams, (b) the ability to adapt the PBS plan to the classroom to meet the needs of the individual student, and (c) the skill level and willingness of the teacher who will be the primary intervention agent.

One standardized model of school-based intervention that addresses each of the above contextual variables is Prevent-Teach-Reinforce (PTR) (Dunlap, Iovannone, Wilson et al., 2010; Dunlap, Iovannone, Kincaid et al, 2010). Prevent-Teach-Reinforce is a manualized approach for individualizing the process of assessment and intervention for specific students who display serious patterns of problem behavior. The initial PTR research with 245 students in grades K–8 found that students who received the PTR intervention had significantly higher social skills and academic engaged time and significantly lower problem behavior when compared with students who received services as usual. In addition, teachers gave high social validity ratings to the intervention, indicating that they approved of the process and would likely utilize the strategies in the future (Iovannone et al., 2009). Prevent-Teach-Reinforce has also been found to be effective with students with autism in general education settings (Strain, Wilson, & Dunlap, 2011) and is currently being studied with young children in preschool settings.

An extension of the SWPBS approach into the early childhood educational settings has been termed Program-Wide Positive Behavior Support (PWPBS; Hemmeter, Fox, Jack & Broyles, 2007) and is built on the Teaching Pyramid Model, which is similar to the SWPBS three-tiered model of support. The Teaching Pyramid (Dunlap & Fox, 2009; Fox, Dunlap, Hemmeter, Joseph, & Strain, 2003) is designed to build social competence and prevent problem behaviors in young children. The Teaching Pyramid is four-level support system of which the first two levels correspond to universal practices that impact all children. These practices include the development of responsive and positive relationships with children and all support providers and the provision of high-quality environments (Fox & Hemmeter, 2009). The secondary tier in the Teaching Pyramid is the explicit instruction in teaching social emotional skills. The final tier of the teaching pyramid model involves the implementation of intensive, individualized interventions. Although the tiers of support in the program-wide model correspond closely to those in the school-wide model, the successful application of these supports at an early childhood level requires much greater attention to issues around family involvement, establishing all three tiers of support initially in the environment, and developing an effective system for data collection that addresses both implementation fidelity and child outcomes. Such a program-wide system can produce meaningful outcomes for children (i.e., reducing referrals for problem behavior, increasing prosocial behaviors, improved transitioning, increased participation), as well as for staff (i.e., improved satisfaction, reduced turnover, increased confidence in supporting all students).

Although SWPBS and PWPBS approaches are being implemented in more schools and programs, their further expansion within all schools is impacted by state and district policies that provide barriers or opportunities for successful implementation of PBS strategies with students in general education settings.

For instance, the extension of "zero tolerance" philosophies to a wide range of problem behaviors establishes a district context for removal of students with severe problem behaviors. Such policies tend to decrease the commitment of schools and personnel to adapt classrooms and develop effective individual interventions since the perception exists that "we can send this student somewhere else." Similarly, a lack of commitment to the concept and implementation of an inclusive model of education for students with disabilities and problem behaviors is likely to result in students who require classroom or individual adaptations being removed from general education settings and placed in self-contained or alternative center schools. Such policies and practices restrict the capacity of districts to develop the full range of PBS supports in general education settings because the removal of students from those settings is an immediate convenience but ineffective in promoting the academic and behavioral success of students with problem behavior.

Conclusion

Positive behavior support is an approach that is rapidly growing in its range of applications and in its empirical, research-based support. Positive behavior support emerged from ABA in the mid 1980s and, since then, has established substantial constituencies in the realms of disabilities, early intervention, schools, and many other arenas concerned with helping people acquire more adaptive and more fulfilling behavior.

In this chapter, we have examined the conceptual and procedural foundations of PBS, and we have described examples and applications of PBS with respect to individualized support, families, and schools. Although a great deal of research remains to be conducted, it is clear that PBS has become an established approach for developing, designing, and implementing interventions that can be effective while maintaining sensitivity and respect for individuals' autonomy and self-determination.

References

Albin, R. W., Lucyshyn, J. M., Horner, R. H., & Flannery, K. B. (1996). Contextual fit for behavior support plans. In L. K. Koegel, R. L. Koegel, & G. Dunlap (Eds.), *Positive behavioral support* (pp. 81–98). Baltimore: Brookes.

Anderson, A. R., Christenson, S. L., Sinclair, M. F., & Lehr, C. A. (2004). Check and Connect: The importance of relationships for promoting engagement with school. *Journal of School Psychology, 32*, 95–113.

Baer, D. M., Wolf, M. M., & Risley, T. R. (1968). Some current dimensions of applied behavior analysis. *Journal of Applied Behavior Analysis, 1*, 91–97.

Bailey, J. S., & Burch, M. R. (2002). *Research methods in applied behavior analysis.* Thousand Oaks, CA: Sage Publications.

Bambara, L. (2005). Evolution of positive behavior support. In L. Bambara & L. Kern (Eds.), *Individualized supports for students with problem behaviors: Designing positive behavior plans* (pp. 1–24). New York: Guilford Press.

Bambara, L., & Kern, L. (Eds.) (2005). *Individualized supports for students with problem behaviors: Designing positive behavior plans.* New York: Guilford Press.

Carr, E. G. (1997). The evolution of applied behavior analysis into positive behavior support. *Journal of the Association for Persons with Severe Handicaps, 4*, 208–209.

Carr, E. G. (2007). The expanding vision of positive behavior support: Research perspectives on happiness, helpfulness, hopefulness. *Journal of Positive Behavior Interventions, 9*, 3–14.

Carr, E. G. (1977). The motivation of self-injurious behavior: A review of some hypotheses. *Psychological Bulletin, 84*, 800–816.

Carr, E. G., Dunlap, G., Horner, R. H., Koegel, R. L., Turnbull, A. P., Sailor, W. et al. (2002). Positive behavior support: Evolution of an applied science. *Journal of Positive Behavior Interventions, 4*, 4–16.

Carr, E. G., Horner, R. H., Turnbull, A., Marquis, J., Magito-McLaughlin, D., McAtee, M. et al. (1999). *Positive behavior support as an approach for dealing with problem behavior in people with developmental disabilities: A research synthesis.* AAMR Monograph.

Carr, E. G., Levin, L., McConnachie, G., Carlson, J. I., Kemp, D. C., & Smith, C. E. (1994). *Communication-based interventions for problem behavior: A user's guide for producing behavior change.* Baltimore, MD: Brookes.

Carr, J. E., & Sidener, T. M. (2002). On the relation between applied behavior analysis and positive behavioral support. *The Behavior Analyst, 25*, 245–253.

Cheney, D., Stage, S., Hawken, L., Lynass, L., Mielenz, C., & Waugh, M. (2009). A 2-year outcomes study of the Check, Connect, and Expect intervention for students at risk for severe behavior problems. *Journal of Emotional and Behavioral Disorders, 17*, 226–243

Colvin, G., & Lazar, M. (1997). *The effective elementary classroom: Managing for success.* Longmont, CO: Sopris West.

Cooper, J. O., Heron, T. E., & Heward, W. L. (1987). *Applied behavior analysis.* Upper Saddle River, NJ: Merrill.

Crone, D., Horner, R., & Hawken, L. (2004). *Responding to problem behavior in schools: The behavior education program.* New York, Guilford.

Darch, C., & Kameenui, E. (2004). *Instructional classroom management: A proactive approach to behavior management* (2nd ed.). Upper Saddle River, NJ: Pearson-Merrill Prentice Hall.

Dunlap, G. (2006). The applied behavior analytic heritage of PBS: A dynamic model of action-oriented research. *Journal of Positive Behavior Interventions, 8*, 58–60.

Dunlap, G., & Carr, E. G. (2007). Positive behavior support and developmental disabilities: A summary and analysis of research. In S. L. Odom, R. H. Horner, M. Snell, & J. Blacher (Eds.), *Handbook of developmental disabilities* (pp. 469–482). New York: Guilford Publications.

Dunlap, G., Carr, E. G., Horner, R. H., Koegel, R. L., Sailor, W., Clarke, S. et al. (2010). A descriptive, multi-year examination of positive behavior support. *Behavioral Disorders, 35*, 259–293.

Dunlap, G., Carr, E. G., Horner, R. H., Zarcone, J., & Schwartz, I. (2008). Positive behavior support and applied behavior analysis: A familial alliance. *Behavior Modification, 32*, 682–698.

Dunlap, G., & Fox, L. (1999a). A demonstration of behavioral support for young children with autism. *Journal of Positive Behavior Interventions, 1*, 77–87.

Dunlap, G., & Fox, L. (1999b). Supporting families of young children with autism. *Infants and Young Children, 12*, 48–54.

Dunlap, G., & Fox, L. (2009). Positive behavior support and early intervention. In Sailor, W., Dunlap, G., Sugai, G., and Horner, R. (Eds.), *Handbook of positive behavior support* (pp. 49–72). New York: Springer.

Dunlap, G., Harrower, J., & Fox, L. (2005). Understanding the environmental determinants of problem behaviors. In L. Bambara & L. Kern (Eds.), *Individualized supports for students with problem behaviors: Designing positive behavior plans* (pp. 25–46). New York: Guilford Press.

Dunlap, G., Hieneman, M., Knoster, T., Fox, L., Anderson, J., & Albin, R. W. (2000). Essential elements of inservice training in positive behavior support. *Journal of Positive Behavior Interventions, 2*, 22–32.

Dunlap, G., Horner, R. H., Sailor W., & Sugai, G. (2009). Origins and history of positive behavior support. In W. Sailor, G. Dunlap, G. Sugai, & R. H. Horner (Eds.), *Handbook of positive behavior support* (pp. 3–16). New York: Springer.

Dunlap, G., Iovannone, R., Kincaid, D., Wilson, K., Christiansen, K., Strain, P., & English, C. (2010). *Prevent-Teach-Reinforce: A school-based model of individualized positive behavior support.* Baltimore, MD: Paul H. Brookes.

Dunlap, G., Iovannone, R., Wilson, K., Kincaid, D., & Strain, P. (2010). Prevent-Teach-Reinforce: A standardized model of school-based behavioral intervention. *Journal of Positive Behavior Interventions, 12*, 9–22.

Dunlap, G., & Kern, L. (1996). Modifying instructional activities to promote desirable behavior: A conceptual and practical framework. *School Psychology Quarterly, 11*, 297–312.

Dunlap, G., & Kincaid, D. (2001). The widening world of functional assessment: Comments on four manuals and beyond. *Journal of Applied Behavior Analysis, 34*, 365–377.

Dunlap, G., Strain, P. S., Fox, L., Carta, J. J., Conroy, M., Smith, B., et al. (2006). Prevention and intervention with young children's challenging behavior: A summary and perspective regarding current knowledge. *Behavioral Disorders, 32*, 29–45.

Durand, V. M. (1990). *Severe behavior problems: A functional communication training approach.* New York, Guilford Press.

Evans, I. M., & Meyer, L. H. (1985). *An educative approach to behavior problems: A practical decision model for interventions for severely handicapped learners.* Baltimore, MD: Paul H. Brookes Publishing Co.

Fairbanks, S., Sugai. G., Guardino, D., & Lathrop, M. (2007). Response to intervention: Examining classroom behavior support in second grade. *Exceptional Children, 73*, 288–310.

Fox, L., Benito, N., & Dunlap, G. (2002). Early intervention with families of young children with autism and problem behaviors. In J. Lucyshyn, G. Dunlap, & Albin, R. W. (Eds.), *Families and positive behavior support: Addressing problem behaviors in family contexts* (pp. 251–269). Baltimore, MD: Paul H. Brookes.

Fox, L., Dunlap, G., Hemmeter, M. L., Joseph, G. E., & Strain, P. S. (2003). The teaching pyramid: A model for supporting social competence and preventing challenging behavior in young children. *Young Children, 58*, 48–52.

Fox, L., & Hemmeter, M. L. (2009). A programwide model for supporting socialemotional development and addressing challenging behavior in early childhood settings. In Sailor, W., Dunlap, G., Sugai, G., & Horner, R. (Eds.), *Handbook of positive behavior support* (pp. 177–202). New York: Springer.

Fox, L., Vaughn B. J., Dunlap, G., & Bucy, M. (1997). Parent-professional partnership in behavioral support: A

quantitative analysis of one family's experience. *Journal of the Association for Persons with Severe Handicaps, 22*, 198–207.

Fox, L., Vaughn, B., Wyatte, M. L., & Dunlap, G. (2002). "We can't expect other people to understand": The perspectives of families whose children have problem behavior. *Exceptional Children, 68*, 437–450.

Gast, D. L. (2010). *Single subject research methodology in behavioral sciences.* New York: Routledge.

George, H., Harrower, J., & Knoster, T. (2003). School-wide prevention and early intervention: A process for establishing a system of school-wide behavior support. *Preventing School Failure, 47*(4), 170–176.

Guess, D., Helmstetter, E., Turnbull, H. R., & Knowlton, S. (1987). *Use of aversive procedures with persons who are disabled: An historical review and critical analysis.* Seattle, WA: The Association for Persons with Severe Handicaps.

Haring, T. G., & Kennedy, C. H. (1990). Contextual control of problem behavior in students with severe disabilities. *Journal of Applied Behavior Analysis, 23*, 235–243.

Hawken, L., MacLeod, S., & Rawlings, L. (2007). Effects of the Behavior Education Program (BEP) on office discipline referrals of elementary school students. *Journal of Positive Behavior Interventions, 9*, 94–101.

Hemmeter, M., Fox, L., Jack, S., & Broyles, L. (2007). A program-wide model of positive behavior support in early childhood settings. *Journal of Early Intervention, 29*, 337–355.

Hieneman, M., & Dunlap, G. (2000). Factors affecting the outcomes of community-based behavioral support: I. Identification and description of factor categories. *Journal of Positive Behavior Interventions, 2*, 161–169.

Hieneman, M., Dunlap, G., & Kincaid, D. (2005). Positive support strategies for students with behavioral disorders in general education settings. *Psychology in the Schools, 42*, 779–794.

Horner, R. H., Dunlap, G., Koegel, R. L., Carr, E. G., Sailor, W., Anderson, J., Albin, R. W., & O'Neill, R. E. (1990). Toward a technology of "non-aversive" behavioral support. *Journal of the Association for Persons with Severe Handicaps, 15*, 125–132.

Iovannone, R., Greenbaum, P., Wei, W., Kincaid, D., Dunlap, G., & Strain, P. (2009). Randomized control trial of a tertiary behavior intervention for students with problem behaviors: Preliminary outcomes. *Journal of Emotional and Behavioral Disorders, 17*, 213–225.

Iwata, B., Dorsey, M., Slifer, K., Bauman, K., & Richman, G. (1994). Toward a functional analysis of self-injury. *Journal of Applied Behavior Analysis, 27*, 197–209. (Reprinted from *Analysis and Intervention in Developmental Disabilities, 2*, 3–20, 1982).

Jackson, L., & Panyan, M. V. (2002). *Positive behavioral support in the classroom: Principles and Practices.* Baltimore, MD: Paul H. Brookes Publishing Co.

Janney, R., & Snell, M. E. (2000). *Behavioral support.* Baltimore, MD: Paul H. Brookes Publishing Co.

Johnston, J. M., Foxx, R. M., Jacobson, J. W., Green, G., & Mulick, J. A. (2006). Positive behavior support and applied behavior analysis. *Behavior Analyst, 29*, 51–74.

Kennedy, C. H. (2004). *Single-case designs for educational research.* New York: Allyn & Bacon.

Kincaid, D., & Fox, L. (2002). Person–centered planning and positive behavior support. In S. Holburn & P. M. Vietze (Eds.), *Person–centered planning. Research, practice, and future directions* (pp. 29–50). Baltimore, MD: Paul H. Brookes.

Kincaid, D., Knoster, T., Harrower, J. Shannon, P., & Bustamante, S. (2002). Measuring the impact of positive behavior support. *Journal of Positive Behavior Interventions*, *4*, 2, 109–117.

Knoster, T., & Kincaid, D. (2005). Long-term supports and ongoing evaluation. In L. Bambara and L. Kern (Eds.), *Individualized supports for students with problem behaviors: Designing positive behavior plans*. New York: Guilford, 303–333.

Lehr, C. A., Sinclair, M. F., & Christenson, S. L. (2004). Addressing student engagement and truancy prevention during the elementary years: A replication study of the Check & Connect model. *Journal of Education for Students Placed At Risk*, *9*(3), 279–301.

Lewis, T. J., & Sugai, G. (1999). Effective behavior support: A systems approach to pro-active school-wide management. *Focus on Exceptional Children*, *31*, 1–24.

Lucyshyn, J. M., Albin, R. W., & Nixon, C. D. (1997). Embedding comprehensive behavioral support in family ecology: An experimental, single-case analysis. *Journal of Consulting and Clinical Psychology*, *65*, 241–251.

Lucyshyn, J. M., Dunlap, G., & Albin, R. W. (Eds.). (2002). *Families & positive behavior support: Addressing problem behavior in family contexts*. Baltimore, MD: Paul H. Brookes.

Luiselli, J. K. (Ed.). (2006). *Antecedent intervention: Recent developments in community focused behavior support*. Baltimore, MD: Paul H. Brookes.

McIntosh, K., Campbell, A. L., Carter, D. R., & Dickey, C. R. (2009). Differential effects of a tier two behavioral intervention based on function of problem behavior. *Journal of Positive Behavior Interventions*, *11*, 68–81.

Office of Special Education Programs Center on Positive Behavior Support. (2004). *School-wide positive behavior support: Implementers' blueprint and self-assessment*. Eugene, OR: Technical Assistance Center on Positive Behavioral Interventions and Supports.

O'Neill, R. E., Horner, R. H., Albin, R. W., Storey, K., Sprague, J. R., & Newton, J. S. (1997). *Functional assessment of problem behavior: A practical assessment guide*. Pacific Grove, CA: Brooks/Cole.

Risley, T. R. (1996). Get a life! In L. K. Koegel, R. L. Koegel, & G. Dunlap (Eds.), *Positive behavioral support* (pp. 425–437). Baltimore, MD: Paul H. Brookes.

Risley, T. R. (1999). Foreword: Positive behavioral support and applied behavior analysis. In E. G. Carr et al., *Positive behavior support for people with developmental disabilities: A research synthesis* (pp. xi–xiii). Washington, DC: American Association on Mental Retardation.

Scandariato, K. (2002). They're playing our song: Our family's involvement in the Individualized Support Project. In J. Lucyshyn, G. Dunlap, & Albin, R. W. (Eds.), *Families and positive behavior support: Addressing problem behaviors in family contexts* (pp. 243–249). Baltimore, MD: Paul H. Brookes.

Schwartz, I. S., & Baer, D. M. (1991). Social validity assessments: Is current practice state of the art? *Journal of Applied Behavior Analysis*, *24*, 189–204.

Scott, T. M., Bucalos, A., Liaupsin, C., Nelson, C. M., Jolivette, K., & DeShea, L. (2004). Using functional behavior assessment in general education settings: Making a case for effectiveness and efficiency. *Behavioral Disorders*, *29*, 189–201.

Seligman, M. E., & Csikszentmihályi, M. (2000). Positive psychology: An introduction. *American Psychologist*, *55*, 5–14.

Seligman, M. E., Steen, T. A., Park, N., & Peterson, C. (2005). Positive psychology progress: Empirical validation of interventions. *American Psychologist*, *60*, 410–421.

Shogren, K. A., Wehmeyer, M. L., Buchanan, C. L., & Lopez, S. J. (2006). The application of positive psychology and self-determination to research in intellectual disability: A content analysis of 30 years of literature. *Research & Practice for Persons with Severe Disabilities*, *31*, 338–345.

Simonson, B., Myers, D., & Briere, D. (2011). Comparing a behavioral check-in/check-out (CICO) intervention to standard practice in an urban middle school setting using an experimental design. *Journal of Positive Behavior Interventions*, *13*, 31–48.

Sinclair, M. F., Christenson, S. L., & Thurlow, M. L. (2005). Promoting school completion of urban secondary youth with emotional or behavioral disabilities. *Exceptional Children*, *71*(4), 465–482.

Singer, G. H. S., Gert, B., & Koegel, R. L. (1999). A moral framework for analyzing the controversy over aversive behavioral interventions for people with severe mental retardation. *Journal of Positive Behavior Interventions*, *1*, 88–100.

Skinner, B. F. (1953). *Science and human behavior*. New York: Macmillan.

Smull, M., & Burke Harrison, S. (1992). *Supporting people with severe reputations in the community*. Alexandria, VA: National Association of State Mental Retardation Program Directors.

Sprick, R. S., Garrison, M., & Howard, L. (1998). *CHAMPS: A proactive and positive approach to classroom management*. Longmont, CO: Sopris West.

Strain, P., Wilson, K., & Dunlap, G. (2011). Prevent-Teach-Reinforce: Addressing problem behaviors of students with autism in general education classrooms. *Behavioral Disorders*, *36*, 160–171.

Sugai, G., Horner, R. H., Dunlap, G., Hieneman, M., Lewis, T. J., Nelson, C. M., et al. (2000). Applying positive behavior support and functional behavioral assessment in schools, *Journal of Positive Behavior Interventions*, *2*, 131–143.

Turnbull, A. P., & Turnbull, H. R. (2000). Achieving "rich" lifestyles. *Journal of Positive Behavior Interventions*, *2*, 190–192.

Turnbull, A. P., & Turnbull, H. R. (2001). *Families, professionals, and exceptionality: Collaborating for empowerment*. Upper Saddle River, NJ: Prentice Hall.

Umbreit, J., Ferro, J., Liaupsin, C., & Lane, K. L. (2007). *Functional behavioral assessment and function-based intervention: An effective, practical approach*. Upper Saddle River, NJ: Prentice-Hall.

Vaillant, G. E. (2000). Adaptive mental mechanisms: Their role in a positive psychology. *American Psychologist*, *55*, 89–98.

Vaughn B. J., Dunlap, G., Fox, L., Clarke, S., & Bucy, M. (1997). Parent-professional partnership in behavioral support: A case study of community-based intervention. *Journal of the Association for Persons with Severe Handicaps*, *22*, 185–197.

Wacker, D. P., & Berg, W. K. (2002). PBS as a service delivery system. *Journal of Positive Behavior Interventions*, *4*, 25–28.

Weigle, K. L. (1997). Positive behavior support as a model for promoting educational inclusion. *Journal of the Association for Persons with Severe Handicaps*, *22*, 36–48.

Westling, D. L., & Fox, L. (2004). *Teaching persons with severe disabilities* (3rd. ed.). Columbus, OH: Prentice Hall/Merrill Publishing.

Wolf, M. M. (1978). Social validity: The case for subjective measurement, or how behavior analysis is finding its heart. *Journal of Applied Behavior Analysis*, *11*, 203–214.

21

Supports and Support Needs

James R. Thompson *and* Yuwadee Viriyangkura

Abstract

A supports paradigm provides a basis for uniting the efforts of researchers, policymakers, and practitioners whose work is focused on services to children and adults with disabilities. The premise of this paradigm is that the most salient difference between people with and without disabilities is their needs for different types and intensities of support in order to fully participate in and contribute to society. Historical foundations and current trends in disability services are reviewed in relation to a supports paradigm. Research findings and critical issues associated with measuring support needs are summarized. Finally, ways that information on supports and support needs can be used to guide planning and decision making at individual and systems levels are presented.

Key Words: supports, support needs assessment, person-centered planning, intellectual disability, resource allocation

What supports do people need to have their basic needs met? What supports are needed to provide people with opportunities for meaningful experiences on a regular basis? What supports can help people establish positive relationships with others? Does everyone need and use the same types of supports? Do people differ in regard to the intensity of support they need?

Because concepts associated with supports and support needs resist simple definitions and descriptions, answers to these questions are not as straightforward as they might first appear. For instance, determining what constitutes supports must be clear. Are supports any type of assistance from any external source, whether it is help from other people, help from animals, or help from machines? Do supports include internal processes such as mnemonics that one might use to remember critical information? Furthermore, what is meant by "support needs?" Are support needs limited to assistance that is needed to assure that Maslow's (1943) lowest-level human needs (e.g., safety, shelter, daily

nourishment) are satisfied, or is the concept of support needs relevant to higher-order needs, including the need for self-actualization? If so, what is meant by "meaningful experiences" and "positive relationships?" Certainly, what might be meaningful and positive to one individual may not be particularly fulfilling to another.

Despite the complexity inherent in understanding people's needs for support, the premise that having extraordinary support needs is the most salient characteristic of people with disabilities is gaining acceptance. The International Classification of Functioning, Disability, and Health (ICF) model of disability put forth by the World Health Organization (WHO, 2001) maintains that human functioning is influenced by two factors: health factors (broadly defined) that are internal to an individual and environmental/contextual factors that are external to a person. When factors internal to a person (e.g., medical conditions, problem behaviors, skill deficits, functional limitations) are not well aligned with factors external to a person (i.e., the demands of the environment), ineffectual human functioning results and corresponding needs for support are evident. The availability of supports that are tailored to a person's unique support needs will significantly influence the extent to which a person participates in and contributes to society.

Conceptual Foundations
Supports Paradigm

Several socio-ecological models of disability have been proposed where disability is conceptualized as a misalignment between a person and his or her environmental context (e.g., see Pledger, 2003; Switzky & Greenspan, 2006). Although discussing distinctions between different socio-ecological models is beyond the scope this chapter, due to the emphasis placed on the relational nature of the person and the environment, the major implication of these models is the need to arrange personalized systems of supports that improve human functioning and quality of life.

For the purposes of this chapter, "supports paradigm" will be used as an umbrella term for conceptualizations of disability that underscore the importance of understanding people by their support needs instead of their deficits, and for organizing human service systems so that time and energy are directed toward identifying people's support needs and then matching them with supports that effectively address those needs. According to Schalock (2011a), a supports paradigm "focuses on the provision of a person-centered system of supports that enhances human functioning" (p. 234). Butterworth (2002) noted "the New Supports Paradigm suggests that individuals should first, without restriction, define the lifestyles they prefer and the environments they want to access. Their goals and priorities then become the basis for intensity and types of support they need to succeed in those environments" (p. 85).

In his classic book, *The Structure of Scientific Revolutions*, Kuhn (1962) indicated that paradigms are conceptual frameworks for understanding critical concepts in a scientific field. Collective research findings in a scientific field provide the foundation for current paradigms. When new research findings emerge that reveal that an existing paradigm provides inadequate explanations for observed phenomena, then a scientific revolution or paradigmatic shift occurs. A new paradigm is developed that provides more satisfactory explanations (i.e., one that has less anomalous research findings).

Kuhn (1962) focused on scientific progress in the natural sciences, and a case can be made that

social sciences fields do not have unifying paradigms based on how Kuhn used the term. However, a broader definition of paradigm is a shared worldview that underlies theories, drives research, and is applicable to professional practices, public policies, and service delivery. And it is this broader type of paradigm that is relevant to applied, interdisciplinary, and multidimensional fields such as disability related human service fields.

The purpose of this chapter is to convey how a supports paradigm provides a basis for uniting the efforts of researchers, policymakers, and practitioners whose work is focused on services to children and adults with disabilities. Extraordinary supports that are used by people with disabilities are distinguished from the types of supports that are used by the general population. Historical foundations and current trends in disability services are reviewed in relation to a supports paradigm. Research findings and critical issues on measuring support needs are summarized. Finally, ways that information on supports and support needs can be used to guide decision making at the individual and systems levels are presented.

Contrasting Conceptualizations of Disability

Pledger (2003) suggested that there were two basic disability paradigms: an old paradigm referred to as the medical model where disability is understood in terms of functional loss and impairment (Rothman, 2010), and the new paradigm based on a socio-ecological understanding of disability with which a supports paradigm is clearly associated (Butterworth, 2002). How might understanding people with disabilities through a traditional, deficit-based medical paradigm be different than understanding people through a supports paradigm? Consider the case of a person who uses a wheelchair for mobility.

A medical model, deficit-based understanding of a wheelchair user would focus on what limbs are affected, the etiology of the condition (e.g., cerebral palsy, spinal cord injury), and what the person cannot do effectively or efficiently. In its purest form, a medical model of disability directs time and energy toward finding a cure. In the absence of a cure, services are directed toward teaching skills that result in an individual becoming more capable.

In the context of a medical model of disability, personal independence is equated with being less reliant on others for assistance. If a person can walk several kilometers without assistance, then that person is considered to be more independent than a person who could walk only 10 meters without assistance, but this person would be more independent than someone who could not walk at all without assistance. The rejection of the medical model by people active in the disability rights movement is apparent in Shapiro's (1993) account of the life of disability activist Ed Roberts. According to Shapiro: "Roberts redefined independence as the control a disabled person had over his life. Independence was measured not by the tasks one could perform without assistance, but by the quality of one's life with help" (p. 51).

Considering the same person who uses a wheelchair for mobility through the lens of a supports paradigm would result in a much different understanding of the person. Like the medical model, there would be consideration of what the person cannot do efficiently and effectively, but attention would also be paid to what the person can do. That is, a supports paradigm is strength-based because it calls for as much consideration of a person's relative strengths in relationship to the demands of the environment as it does for consideration of a person's functional limitations. Searching for a cure is not a logical implication of a supports paradigm, because supports are not intended to fix the individual. Rather, what needs fixing is the misalignment between the person and the environment, and supports are intended to bridge the gap between "what is and what can be" (Schalock et al., 2010, p. 111). Supports do not fix the person; rather, supports empower a person to fully participate in the same settings and activities that the general population accesses and values. Like the medical model, a supports paradigm calls for teaching and learning new skills, as long as the skills are useful in settings and activities in which the individual desires to participate.

A critical distinction between a supports paradigm and the traditional medical model of disability is the emphasis placed on environmental modification and/or adaptation. For example, a universally designed, barrier-free/accessible setting is a type of support that enables people who use wheelchairs to fully access physical environments. If a setting is not accessible, then another type of support could be used in the form of personal assistants who are able to physically maneuver a wheelchair user around inaccessible settings. A supports paradigm calls for problem solving until a solution to a support need is identified.

However, the quality of the two support options outlined in this scenario is not comparable from a wheelchair user's perspective. Support from personal assistants would be far more intrusive, and therefore far less desirable, than supports embedded in an accessible environment. According to a supports paradigm, the perspectives of support users are paramount in assessing the quality and appropriateness of support options.

Although understanding people through a supports paradigm has many advantages over the medical model of disability, in the applied, interdisciplinary, and multidimensional field of disability services it is clear neither conceptual approach provides definitive guidance for all activities. Historically, even people and systems firmly entrenched in medical conceptualizations of disability have recognized the need to arrange environmental accommodations and adaptations. Likewise, although a supports paradigm is not focused on curing people with disabilities, the staunchest proponents for supports-based thinking welcome efforts to find cures and treatments for specific conditions (e.g., the effects of phenylketonuria [PKU] can be mitigated through diet) as well as efforts to prevent disabilities from occurring (e.g., public education about the dangers of alcohol use during pregnancy). Therefore, practices associated with the medical model are not always wrong, and practices associated with a supports paradigm are not always right. Rather, there is a time and place to apply practices associated with both conceptual models. Although new, more sophisticated models of disability may provide a framework that reconciles the tension between socio-ecological and medical models (e.g., see Rothman, 2010), it will always be vital to remain aware of implications for practice based on conceptual principles in order to thoughtfully discern when certain practices are appropriate and when they are misguided.

The Support Needs of People With and Without Disabilities
Extraordinary Support Needs

If adopting a supports paradigm is essential to understanding people with disabilities, then the most important distinction between people with and without disabilities is the extraordinary supports that people with disabilities need that the general population does not need (Thompson et al., 2009). It is critical to clarify how extraordinary supports differ, in terms of type and intensity, from the everyday (i.e., non-extraordinary) supports that are used by others in society in their homes, schools, work places, and public areas such as stores and parks. However, any attempt to establish a precise boundary where the "extent of extraordinary support" begins that separates people with disabilities from those without disabilities will be fraught with difficulty. But this is true whenever a psychological construct is used as a basis for determining disability.

Like other psychological constructs, the level of a person's support needs (just as the level of a person's motivation or shyness) must be inferred because it is not directly observable. Using anything other than a biological marker (e.g., karyotype test to diagnose trisomy 21) for disability determination introduces a degree of uncertainty into the diagnostic process. Whether a standard deviation score on an IQ test is utilized to diagnose intellectual disability (ID), a visual acuity score based on a Snellen chart is used to distinguish "normal vision" from low vision (and low vision from blindness), or a mental status examination is applied to diagnose depression, there are going to be borderline cases and any cut-off point that is chosen will not be entirely satisfactory.

The development of reliable and valid measures of people's support needs (see Hennike, 2002; Hennike, Myers, Realon, & Thompson, 2006; Riches, Parmenter, Llewellyn, Hindmarsh, & Chan, 2009a; 2009b; Thompson et al., 2004a; Thompson et al., 2012) is in its infancy, and it is not yet sufficiently advanced for the purposes of disability diagnosis. However, thoughtful consideration of the nature of supports and people's support needs can shed light on how valid distinctions may be made between people with and without extraordinary support needs. Three important considerations are the nature of supports needed to participate in an interdependent society, how long extraordinary supports are needed, and the age of an individual.

Extraordinary Supports in an Interdependent Society

Interdependence has always defined the human condition. People are emotionally and economically dependent on one another, and everyone needs and uses an array of supports. Not only do people depend on one another for support, people use a wide range of tools for support every day, ranging from simple tools such as a shovel to till soil to complex machines such as an automobile for transportation.

Although using multiple supports is universal in an interdependent society, some people use supports that are either quite different than others or they use supports in a different way than others. For example, millions of people use a tablet computer on a daily basis for organization, entertainment, and communication purposes. However, very few have augmentative communication software loaded on their tablet computer and use their tablet computer as their primary mode for face-to-face communication. There are many people who own dogs, and in many cases their dogs are an important source of emotional support. But, relatively few people have guide dogs that they need for mobility around their communities. Extraordinary support needs are evident when someone uses supports to participate in an interdependent society that are qualitatively and/or quantitatively different than the supports used by the vast majority of others in society.

Chronicity of Support Needs

Whether or not supports are needed on a relatively short- or long-term basis is essential to determining if support needs should be considered to be extraordinary. People experiencing an acute illness may need intense supports for a short period of time that others in society do not need. However, disabilities should not be equated with temporary health conditions. For example, a woman who is placed on bed rest due to complications during her pregnancy may need intensive supports. However, because her pregnancy is a transitional condition, her extraordinary support needs are temporary.

Chronicity of extraordinary support needs a key indicator of disability in a supports paradigm. People with disabilities' need for extraordinary supports is an enduring feature of their daily lives, and it is neither an episodic event nor a temporary state. Therefore, evidence of extraordinary support needs requires documentation that a person has experienced a long-term state of interacting with their environment that has been characterized by needing supports that are different from what most others in society require.

Age Considerations
SUPPORT NEEDS AND THE ELDERLY

The fact that most people experience some loss of physical and/or mental function in their later years of life provides the logic underlying the adage that most people are only "temporarily able-bodied." It is important, however, to understand that coping with advancing age is not the same as experiencing a lifelong disability. If an 80-year-old person needs extraordinary support because he or she uses a wheelchair, then extraordinary support is needed for purposes of mobility, not because of advancing age, per se. A different 80-year-old person may not have any extraordinary support needs in terms of mobility.

A positive correlation between the presence of disability and age does not mean that the supports needed by people with disabilities are the same as those needed by older people. The continued presence of healthy, relatively young people with disabilities residing in facilities intended for elderly people with nursing care needs (Stancliffe et al., 2011) provides a reminder of the types of undesirable outcomes that result when there is a failure to distinguish the needs of people with disabilities from the elderly.

Although the support needs of people with disabilities and the elderly are different, the trend of providing older adults with technologies and other supports that enable them to stay in their own homes is a prime example of how a supports paradigm is applicable to eldercare services. Providing supports that enable elderly people to function in their homes has been justified partially on the premise that that human dignity is associated with taking reasonable risks (Teel, 2011). It is interesting that the same "dignity of risk" argument has been a tenant of the deinstitutionalization movement for people with ID for many years (Perske, 1972).

SUPPORT NEEDS AND CHILDREN

On the other end of the age spectrum are infants. Infants cannot survive without total support from others, but this does not mean that all infants have disabilities based on a supports paradigm. Evidence of extraordinary support needs must be considered in the context of same-aged peers, and chronicity of support needs must be factored in once again. For typically developing infants, the need for intensive support will gradually dissipate as they reach developmental milestones and acquire skills in walking, talking, eating, and so forth. However, until adulthood is reached, children will continue to need additional supports that typically functioning adults do not need due to limited life experiences as well as legal restrictions. For example, 3-year-old children need to be monitored on a regular basis for safety reasons, and although 15-year-olds do not need constant monitoring, they still require supports that adults do not need because they are more vulnerable to exploitation. Because support needs are confounded with age, determining whether children have extraordinary support needs requires that their support needs be compared to support needed by typically developing peers of the same age.

Intellectual Disability and Support Needs
AAIDD's Definition of Intellectual Disability

Although a supports paradigm is applicable to all disability populations, it has been embraced fully

by many researchers and practitioners in the field of ID. The American Association on Intellectual and Developmental Disabilities (AAIDD) has stimulated research and practice related to support needs assessment and planning through the terminology, definition, and classification manuals they published over the past 20 years (see Luckasson et al., 1992; Luckasson et al., 2002; Schalock et al., 2010). Evidence of a supports paradigm can be seen in the most recent manual's five assumptions that "clarify the context from which the definition arises and indicate how the definition must be applied" (Schalock et al., 2010, p. 6). The five assumptions are: (1) limitations in present functioning must be considered within the context of community environments typical of the individual's age peers and culture; (2) valid assessment considers cultural and linguistic diversity as well as differences in communication, sensory, motor, and behavioral factors; (3) within an individual, limitations often coexist with strengths; (4) an important purpose of describing limitations is to develop a profile of needed supports; and (5) with appropriate personalized supports over a sustained period, the life functioning of the person with ID generally will improve." (pp. 11–12).

The AAIDD has provided leadership in much of the conceptual work relevant to a supports paradigm, including providing definitions of supports and support needs. According to the AAIDD, *supports* are "resources and strategies that aim to promote the development, education, interests, and personal well-being of a person and that enhance individual functioning" (Schalock et al., 2010, p. 110), and *support needs* refer to "a psychological construct referring to the pattern and intensity of supports necessary for a person to participate in activities linked with normative human functioning" (Schalock et al., 2010, p. 110).

Historical Trends in Intellectual Disability

A supports paradigm is best considered to be a "bottom up" conceptual model, because it emerged from theoretical perspectives, policy initiatives, and research findings that have been prominent over the past five decades. A supports paradigm did not prompt the emergence of the normalization principle, deinstitutionalization policies, access to education policies, individual budgets, supported employment, supported living, or inclusive education, but rather it is a logical outgrowth of these historical and contemporary trends.

NORMALIZATION

The principle of normalization was introduced in the 1960s and has been arguably the most important theoretical perspective in the field of ID. Normalization called for patterns and conditions of everyday life for people with ID that are as close as possible to those valued by the general population. The key implication of normalization was that people with disabilities should be living, working, and recreating in the same environments that the general population used and valued. Additionally, people with ID should be provided with chronologically age appropriate opportunities, because the life experiences, attitudes, and behaviors of adults are quite different from those of children. Interacting with people with ID who are permitted to assume valued social roles in society and in a manner that is consistent with their chronological ages reduces stigmatization and affords people greater personal dignity and respect (Nirje, 1969; Wolfensberger, 1972). A key implication of the normalization principle was the importance of focusing efforts on how to support people with ID in age appropriate, socially valued, community settings and activities.

DEINSTITUTIONALIZATION AND ACCESS TO EDUCATION POLICIES

Public policies encouraging deinstitutionalization (Braddock, Hemp, & Rizzolo, 2008; Chowdhury & Benson, 2011) and access to public education (Ferguson, 2008; U.S. Department of Education, 2011) have been major priorities throughout the world. In accordance with a supports paradigm, these policies have directed public funding and professional practice toward arranging supports for people living in the community and learning in local schools. Research findings showing better outcomes for people living in the community compared to large congregate settings (e.g., see Hamelin, Frijters, Griffiths, Condillac, & Owen, 2011) and the development of innovative materials and strategies that educators can use to support children with disabilities in general education classrooms (e.g., Jorgensen, McSheehan, & Sonnenmeier, 2010; Mastropieri & Scruggs, 2010) have confirmed the wisdom of these two key policy initiatives.

INDIVIDUAL BUDGETS

The movement toward providing public funding directly to people with disabilities and their families as opposed to funding programs that are administered by service provider organizations gives people opportunities to "shop" for services that meet their needs (Stancliffe & Lakin, 2005). Braddock et al. (2008) reported that 24 U.S. states had programs where cash payments or vouchers are provided directly to families to purchase supports for a member with a disability. Funding people instead of programs by creating individualized budgets based on a person's support needs is not only aligned with the supports paradigm, but it also has the potential to create a more responsive and efficient human service system.

FROM PROGRAMS TO SUPPORTS

Over the past 50 years there has been a tremendous expansion in not-for-profit, community-based organizations whose mission is to provide services to persons with disabilities. Initially, these organizations were charged with creating programs for groups of people (Kiernan, Gilmore, & Butterworth, 1997). Because provider organizations were charged with serving groups and were not organized to meet the support needs of individuals, people with disabilities had no choice other than to accept whatever opportunities a group program offered. Unfortunately, these options almost always segregated people with ID from others in their community. For instance, if a person needed a job and a local vocational services program offered the opportunity to complete subcontracted piecework such as packaging parts for a small engine, then the person either packaged parts or did not work. If a person needed housing and the community residential service provider offered housing in group homes with 15 residents, then the only option for a person was to live in a large group home. If a recreation program offered a group bowling outing on Saturday mornings, then bowling was the only game in town for Saturday morning; it did not matter if a person preferred to participate in a different sport.

Traditionally, educational programs for children with disabilities were also organized in a manner that limited choices and resulted in segregation from other children. Special classrooms were established based on disability categorical label. For example, if a child was diagnosed with blindness, then he or she attended a special class or special school for children who are blind or visually impaired. Children diagnosed with mild ID attended a different class than children with moderate or severe ID, and they certainly attended a different class than students without disabilities. Multi-categorical classrooms eventually became more common and included students with different disability diagnoses. However, students in these classrooms remained separated from typically developing peers (Mastropieri & Scruggs, 2010; Giangreco, 2011; Winzer, 1993).

Program-based adult services targeted to groups are still prevalent (Braddock et al., 2008; Martinez-Leal et al., 2011), and special classrooms that only include students with disabilities (Ferguson, 2008; U.S. Department of Education, 2011) are common. However, since the late 1970s there have been steady calls for approaches that are more consistent with a supports paradigm. Supports-based approaches focus on tailoring supports to the needs and preferences of people with disabilities and their families. Individuals with disabilities determine the types of settings and activities in which they want to participate, and the onus is on a service provider organization or school system to work with people with disabilities and their families in identifying and arranging needed supports. Although a supports paradigm is applicable to all areas of life, the growth of supported employment, supported living, and inclusive education makes these domains of life particularly well suited to illustrate the evolution from providing from program-based services for groups to arranging personalized systems of supports for individuals.

SUPPORTED EMPLOYMENT

Traditionally there were two options for people with disabilities in terms of employment—competitive employment or sheltered employment. Competitive employment was the option for people who could work on a job without any extraordinary, long-term supports. Vocational rehabilitation (VR) systems provided "time limited" assistance to people with disabilities who needed short-term assistance in order to become competitively employed (Clark & Kolstoe, 1995). An example of a "time limited" service was "on the job training," where an employer would not be required to pay the worker a full wage during a training period and the employee would receive some additional assistance in order to learn a job. Another common "time limited" VR service was job placement assistance, where people with disabilities received assistance during a job search (Noble & Conley, 1989).

Sheltered employment was reserved for people who could not find or maintain employment in a competitive job for whatever reason (e.g., they could not work fast enough to meet the production standards of employers). The purpose of sheltered employment was to provide an accommodating work setting where people without competitive employment skills could function successfully.

Another purpose was to prepare people for competitive employment by teaching them proper work habits and skills. For years sheltered workshops were considered to be the ultimate back-up plan for anyone who could not maintain employment in a competitive job (Clark & Kolstoe, 1995).

Sharp criticism of the sheltered employment model began in the early 1980s and has continued to the present day. Critics pointed out that most sheltered workshops do not have enough subcontract work to keep people occupied for a full work day, and when paid work is not available then workers must complete simulated work (e.g., assembling and disassembling flashlights) or have "down time" where they are engaged in other activities (e.g., watch a movie). Regardless of whether work is paid or simulated, critics charged that work assignments in sheltered workshops are qualitatively different than work assignments in jobs in the community. Therefore, sheltered employees are not provided with experiences that are likely to prepare them for competitive employment. Data have consistently verified that the vast majority of sheltered employees earn very low wages and very rarely move into competitive jobs (Bellamy, Rhodes, & Albin, 1986; National Disability Rights Network, 2011; Rogan & Rinne, 2011).

Today, few people would claim that sheltered employment is a desirable vocational outcome, and many question whether sheltered employment programs should even be considered as viable employment alternative at all. The U.S. Department of Labor (2012) recently reported the term "Work Center" is preferred over "Sheltered Workshops." "Work centers no longer refer to themselves as 'sheltered workshops' nor do they perceive themselves as offering 'sheltered' employment" (Sheltered Workshop or Work Center, para 1). This change in language reflects the reality that many community-based vocational service organizations are trying to convert from providing sheltered employment to providing integrated employment services. According to Rogan and Rinne (2011), "most rehabilitation services organizations have added integrated employment to their array of services while maintaining sheltered day services" (p. 250).

Supported employment is an alternative to sheltered and competitive employment. It is different than sheltered employment because supported employees work on paid jobs in community work settings alongside the general population. It differs from competitive employment and traditional VR services because it is assumed that supported employees need ongoing supports that other employees do not need in order to maintain employment. A critical assumption of the supported work approach is that all individuals, regardless of the nature or extent of their disabilities, can work in jobs in the community if provided with adequate support (Wehman, Inge, Revell, & Brooke, 2007). An organization providing integrated employment services must locate and/or modify meaningful jobs in the community and provide supports at a job site (Mank, 1997). The supported employment approach is consistent with a supports paradigm because it focuses on extraordinary supports (i.e., ongoing supports) to bridge the gap between the person (i.e., supported employee) and the demands of the environment (i.e., community job setting and competitive job tasks).

SUPPORTED LIVING

Deinstitutionalization policies moved tens of thousands of people with ID and related developmental disabilities out of large institutions and prevented the admission of many more. In the U.S., the total number of residents in state-operated institutions dropped from 194,650 in 1967 to 36,650 in 2007, although progress was not uniform across the 50 states. Nine states had reduced their institutional populations to zero, but 13 states continued to have more than 1,000 institutional residents (Scott, Lakin, & Larson, 2008).

Martinez-Leal et al. (2011) reported similar findings in Europe. Sweden and Norway completely closed residential institutions for people with ID and related developmental disabilities, and the U.K. has made considerable progress. Although other countries have made more modest progress, the overall number of people in large residential institutions in Europe has been steadily decreasing. According to Young, Sigafoos, Suttie, Ashman, and Grevell (1998), Australia's progress has lagged behind the U.S. and the U.K. Nevertheless, deinstitutionalization has been a global phenomenon.

Deinstitutionalization also spurred the development of community residential services. Unfortunately, eliminating institutions is not the same as creating opportunities for supported living in communities. Taylor (2001) pointed out that community-based residential programs were arranged along a continuum "where the most restrictive placements were also the most segregated and offered the most intensive services; the least restrictive placements were the most integrated and independent and offered the least intensive services" (p. 17). When people have no choice in terms of the type of house in which they live, how their home is decorated and

what things are in it, with whom they live, or what to do when they are at home, then simply residing in community residence may have no advantages over residing an institution. Lakin, Hayden, and Abery (1994) voiced concerns about the disparate quality of community residential alternatives by observing that "elements of institutional living are still all too evident" (p. 15). It does not matter where people are geographically residing if they have little control over their housing options and lifestyle choices.

Antithetical to the "institution in the community" is the concept of supported living. Key features of supported living include choice and self-determination in type of housing, housemates, and support providers, as well as home-ownership (Breihan, 2007; Feinstein, Levine, Lemanowicz, Sedlak, Klein et al., 2006; Lakin et al., 1994). Supported living arrangements are consistent with a supports paradigm because they focus on providing personalized supports that enable people to live in their own homes as members of their communities. In a study of supported living in the U.S., Braddock et al. (2008) defined supported living as "housing in which individuals choose where and with whom they live, in which ownership is by someone other than the support provider (such as the individual, family, landlord, or housing cooperative), and in which the individual has a personalized support plan that changes as his or her needs or abilities change" (p. 36). They reported that public spending on supported living grew steadily in the U.S. since the early 1990s but has continued to lag behind spending for institutions as well as for traditional, community-based residential services.

INCLUSIVE EDUCATION

Today's inclusive education movement has its roots in the mainstreaming movement of the 1960s and 1970s. At that time mainstreaming referred to moving students from their home classrooms, which were self-contained classrooms, to general education settings for portions of the day. Sometimes that meant simply being alongside other children in common areas of the school such as the playground and cafeteria; other times it meant participating in non-academic subjects such as music, art, and physical education; and still other times it meant coming into the general education classroom for instruction in core academic areas such as reading, math, and science (Giangreco & Putman, 1991; MacMillan, 1977). Dailey (1974) confirmed that mainstreaming meant different things to different people when he conducted telephone interviews with more than 80 prominent special educators in the early 1970s and discovered that mainstreaming was defined and described in wide variety of ways.

During the 1980s and 1990s, there were two significant movements in the U.S. promoting the inclusion of students with disabilities in general education classrooms. The Regular Education Initiative (REI; Reynolds, Wang, & Walberg, 1987) was concerned primarily with children from high-incidence or "mild" disability populations and placed emphasis on modifying academic instruction and curricula to meet student needs. The "full inclusion" movement was focused mostly on students with severe disabilities. Proponents of full inclusion voiced a civil rights argument, that it was discriminatory to exclude children from general education classroom because of disability characteristics, when advocating for their position (Stainback & Stainback, 1984).

Although these brief descriptions do not do justice to the progress made in developing instructional strategies and classroom accommodations through the REI and full inclusion movements, perhaps the most important shift from the mainstreaming movement of the earlier decades was that students with disabilities were no longer regarded as visitors to general education classrooms. Rather, it was assumed that students with disabilities belonged in general education schools and classrooms in the first place, and it was the responsibility of educators to expand the capacity of general education classrooms to educate diverse learners in meaningful ways. In this shift of thinking, the supports paradigm had been embraced because the focus was no longer on preparing students to participate in the mainstream. Rather, the student-environment misalignment was what needed to be addressed. General education settings needed to be changed by inserting special education supports into them. These included individual student accommodations; adaptations of classroom lessons, materials, and routines; opportunities for classroom teachers to collaborate with teachers with expertise in special education; and the movement of specific supports (e.g., modified equipment, teacher aides) from special classrooms into general education classrooms (e.g., see Janney & Snell, 2011; Mastropieri & Scruggs, 2010).

The inclusive education movement transformed special education services from a place where children with disabilities went in order to get the help they needed to learn to an array of supports that were embedded in classrooms attended by all children. The focus was on changing the general education environment to one where all students had meaningful opportunities to learn. By the mid-1990s, Snell and Drake (1994) concluded that "disability labels may still be necessary for eligibility, but a profile of each student's needed supports is essential" (p. 406). Although most educators acknowledged that they did not know how to meaningfully include every child in every general education classroom during every minute of every school day, there was consensus that no child should be pulled out of the general education without a strong educational justification (Brown et al., 1991; Fuchs & Fuchs, 1994).

The United Nation's 2008 Convention on the Rights of Persons with Disabilities declaration calling for all nations to assure an inclusive education system at all levels for all students (UNESCO, 2009) is evidence of today's consensus regarding the desirability of access to general education schools and classrooms for children with disabilities. Consistent with the supports paradigm, educators have moved away from asking "Should we include children with disabilities in general education classrooms?" to asking "How do we expand the capacity of general education classrooms to meaningfully educate a diverse student population, including students who learn at different speeds and in different ways?"

A better term for inclusive education may be supported education, because the essential feature of inclusive education is providing students with the supports they need to be successful. However, the term inclusive education has become so established in educators' minds that changing the name would undoubtedly cause more confusion than increase clarity. Today, the development of methods and strategies associated with inclusive education have progressed to the point that it is not enough to physically include students in classrooms simply for "exposure to the general education curriculum" or for "socialization." Students with disabilities must participate in learning activities with peers in general education classrooms and acquire meaningful skills. Additionally, students with disabilities must be actively engaged in the life of their school community by participating in daily or periodic events (school assemblies, holiday gatherings, dances, etc.), non-academic subjects (art, music, physical education, etc.), and co-curricular activities (clubs, school plays, etc.; Carter, Hughes, Guth, & Copeland, 2005; Janney & Snell, 2011).

Measuring Support Needs
Measurement to Knowledge

Progress in any field is often contingent on the capacity to measure key constructs of interest. The

Dutch physicists Heike Onnes had the words "Door meten tot weten" ("Through measurement to knowledge") placed over each of his laboratory doors as a reminder that a key to understanding something is to be able to measure it (Laesecke, 2002). The modern world could not function without reliable and valid ways to measure natural phenomena. For example, if there were no way to reliably and validly measure temperature, it would be necessary to rely on people's impressions of concepts such as hot, cold, and lukewarm. Precise measures of temperature have enabled advances in fields as diverse as transportation, health care, and cooking. According to the developer of the Kelvin Scale, William Thomson, "when you can measure what you are speaking about, and express it in numbers, you know something about it; when you cannot measure it, when you cannot express it in numbers, your knowledge is of a meager and unsatisfactory kind" (Sydenham, 2003).

The social sciences differ in important ways from the natural sciences, and there will never be as precise as a measure for support needs as there are for concepts such as mass, electrical current, speed, etc. However, the capacity to accurately measure critical concepts in the field of human services for people with disabilities has the potential to greatly enhance understanding of the nature of people's interactions with their environment, their needs for support, and their quality of life.

Descriptions of three scales that purport to measure support needs have been published in the professional literature: the *North Carolina Support Needs Assessment Profile* (*NC-SNAP*), the *Instrument for Classification and Assessment of Support Needs* (*I-CAN*), and the *Supports Intensity Scale* (*SIS*). Each scale's features and psychometric qualities are briefly reviewed. Guscia, Harries, Kirby, Nettelbeck, and Taplin (2005; 2006) and Guscia, Harries, Kirby, and Nettelback (2006) reported psychometric findings regarding a fourth scale, the *Service Need Assessment Profile*. However, very little additional information could be found regarding this scale, and it does not appear that it is widely used.

Scales that Measure Support Needs

NC-SNAP

The *NC-SNAP* was developed under the auspices of the Murdoch Center Foundation with guidance from the North Carolina Developmental Disability Policy Advisory Work Group. Initial descriptions of the *NC-SNAP* (Hennike, 2002) and *SIS* (Thompson et al., 2002) were reported in the professional literature at about the same time. It appears that the *NC-SNAP* was not developed as a tool to assist in developing personalized support plans with people with disabilities, but rather was created to inform resource allocation at the systems level as an alternative to an adaptive behavior scale, the *Inventory for Client and Agency Planning (ICAP*; Bruininks, Hill, Weatherman, & Woodcock, 1986). The *NC-SNAP* includes 11 items in three domains: Daily Living, Health Care, and Behavioral. Each item is rated on a Likert-type scale, ranging from 1 (essentially independent) to 5 (receives 24-hour per day continuous, intensive, and specialized assistance). A score is "obtained for each domain by selecting the highest score marked for that domain. The overall score is equivalent to the highest domain score" (Hennike et al., 2006, p. 204).

Hennike et al. (2006) reported reliability data from a study using two researchers and 80 people with disabilities. The coefficients for test-retest reliability and interrater reliability were 0.92 and 0.86 respectively. They assessed concurrent validity by comparing *NC-SNAP* scores to a "supports intensity level" score that was generated from information regarding the supports people currently received, and they reported a coefficient of 0.72.

I-CAN

Researchers at the University of Sydney's Centre for Developmental Disability Studies developed the *I-CAN* to provide "an innovative, rigorous and robust system of identifying and classifying support needs of people with disabilities, based on the conceptual framework promulgated by the World Health Organization through the ICF" (Riches et al., 2009a, p. 328). The *I-CAN* is administered through a semi-structured process that involves collecting qualitative and quantitative data. Information gathered from an *I-CAN* assessment can be used at the individual and systems planning levels. The *I-CAN* consists of ten domain scales, four of which are included under a "Health and Well Being" section and the other six included in an "Activities and Participation" section. Items are rated on two 6-point Likert-type scales according to frequency and level of support needs.

Riches et al. (2009a; 2009b) collected data on 1,012 persons, most of whom were people with ID or multiple disabilities. Data were collected on the first three versions of the *I-CAN* (there is now a new version), and the authors concluded that their instrument "demonstrated acceptable reliability and validity" (Riches et al., 2009b, p. 349). Specifically, data were reported in regard to interrater reliability (coefficients ranged from 0.96 to 1.00), test-retest reliability (coefficients ranged from 0.05 to 0.93 at 1 year and 0.01 to 0.94 at 2 years), concurrent validity with the *ICAP* (coefficients ranged from −0.39 to −0.62), and predictive validity (prediction of daytime support was $R^2 = 0.40$ and 24-hour support was $R^2 = 0.27$).

SIS

The *SIS* was developed by a committee appointed by the Board of Directors of AAIDD and was published in 2004. As alluded to earlier, starting with its 9th-edition definition and classification manual published in 1992 (Luckasson et al., 1992), the AAIDD had embraced a supports paradigm and sought to develop tools and materials that would advance the paradigm in professional practice. The standardized portion of the instrument is made up of 49 items related to life activities in six subscales. There are also eight items included in a supplemental scale focused on self-advocacy and self-determination. Finally, 29 items are related to support needed to either maintain or improve medical conditions, or prevent negative or damaging consequences from challenging behaviors (Thompson et al., 2004a). The scale is administered through a semi-structured interview with at least two respondents who are very familiar with the person being assessed (Thompson et al., 2004b).

Scores from the standardized section of the *SIS* generate two indices of support needs. The *SIS Support Needs Index* is a composite score that reflects a person's overall intensity of support needs relative to adults with ID and related developmental disabilities. The *SIS Support Needs Profile* provides a graphic display of a person's relative support needs across six support domains: Home Living, Community Living, Lifelong Learning, Employment, Health and Safety, and Social Activities (Thompson et al., 2004b). The *SIS* is the only support needs assessment scale that provides norm-referenced scores that allow comparison of a person's intensity of support needs relative to a standardization sample of adults with ID and related developmental disabilities.

Psychometric data were reported in the *SIS Users Manual* on a sample of 1,306 people. Findings showed strong internal reliability/consistency (coefficients ranged from 0.86 to 0.99), fair interrater reliability (coefficients ranged from 0.35 to 0.79), strong test-retest reliability (coefficients ranged from 0.52 to 0.82), and strong concurrent validity with the *ICAP* (coefficients ranged from −0.23 to −0.68; Thompson et al., 2004b).

The *SIS* has been the focus of a considerable amount of additional psychometric investigation since its publication. Thompson, Tassé, and McLaughlin (2008) investigated interrater reliability under the condition that interviewers had to have completed at least a half-day training session on how to administer and score the *SIS*, and investigated how having different interviewers and different respondents affected interrater reliability. Data from the trained interviewers produced interrater reliability coefficients that were considerably higher than those reported in the *SIS Users Manual* (Thompson et al., 2004b) under three conditions: *inter-interviewer* reliability (pairs of *SIS* scores generated from different interviewers who interviewed the same respondents), *inter-respondent* reliability (pairs of *SIS* scores generated from the same interviewer who interviewed different respondents on two different occasions), and *mixed interrater reliability* (pairs of *SIS* scores generated from the different interviewers who interviewed different respondents). The pattern of reliability coefficients were virtually identical for all three conditions, with subscale coefficients ranging from 0.51 to 0.90, and composite score coefficients ranging from 0.85 to 0.90. The researchers suggested that, because assessing support needs requires an interviewer to engage in probing and clarifying with respondents, the *SIS* and other support needs assessment scales may require training above that required by assessment measures that have been traditionally completed by practitioners (e.g., adaptive behavior scales).

The *SIS* has been translated into 13 languages (personal communication, A. L. McElhinney, December 31, 2011), and psychometric data have been published on seven of the translated versions. Buntinx (2011) compared psychometric findings from the Dutch (Buntinx, Van Unen, Speth, & Groot, 2006), Italian (Cottini, Fedeli, Leoni, & Croce, 2008), Spanish (Verdugo, Arias, Ibanez, & Schalock, 2010), and French (Lamoureux-Hebert & Morin, 2008) translations and concluded: (a) the *SIS* maintained very high internal consistency throughout all translations; (b) according to criteria proposed by Cicchetti and Sparrow (1981) for adaptive behavior scales, the interrater reliability is in the "good" range or better (i.e., coefficients 0.65 or higher) in all translated versions; (c) concurrent and construct validity was strong, with all translated versions showing negative correlations with adaptive behavior scores ranging from −0.59 to −0.73, and high subscale inter-correlations ranging from 0.51 to 0.91; and (d) there were only small differences in means and standard deviations of *SIS* raw scores, and these differences were likely related to sample characteristics.

Additional investigations have examined the construct the *SIS* is measuring. Wehmeyer, Chapman, Little, Thompson, Schalock et al. (2009) collected data on 274 subjects and reported that *SIS* scores contributed significantly to a model predicting levels of support needs. They concluded that the *SIS* measured a different construct than what was measured by assessments of personal competence. Weiss, Lunsky, Tassé, and Durbin (2009) investigated the predictive capacity of the *SIS* and found that *SIS* scores predicted clinician rankings of support need.

The factor structure of the *SIS* has also been of interest to researchers. In separate factor analytic studies, Kuppens, Bossaert, Buntinx, Molleman, Van den Abbeele et al. (2010) and Verdugo, Arias, Ibanez, and Gomez (2006) confirmed a six-factor structure based on the six subscales of the *SIS*. However, Bossaert, Kuppens, Buntinx, Molleman, Van den Abeele et al. (2009) completed a confirmatory factor analysis using *SIS* scores from a population with diverse disability characteristics, and found that the six-factor *SIS* subscale structure was not supported. Their data supported a multidimensional, four-factor model with the following four dimensions: Personal and Social, Community Living, Daily Living, and Work. In exploratory factor analysis studies where *SIS* scores and adaptive behavior scores were included in the same data set, Harries, Guscia, Kirby, Nettelbeck, and Taplin (2005) and Brown, Ouellette-Kuntz, Bielska, and Elliott (2009) reported that their data supported a single-factor structure.

Critical Issues in Support Needs Measurement

As the supports paradigm becomes more fully embraced and the importance of aligning activities associated with assessment, planning, implementation, and outcome evaluation becomes more prominent, it is likely that additional support needs measurement scales will emerge. The introduction of new and different ways to measure support needs will likely lead to advances in understanding the nature of people's support needs. Although IQ tests have a checkered history to say the least (e.g., see Gould, 1981), there is little doubt that much of the progress in understanding human intelligence would not have been possible without measures of intelligence. Contemporary models of intelligence (e.g., Cattell and Horn's Fluid and Crystallized Abilities; hierarchical factorial models proposed by Vernon, Guilford, and Gustafsson, Carroll's Three-Stratum

Model) are based on data from IQ tests (Wasserman & Tulsky, 2005). Likewise, progress in understanding adaptive behavior coincided with the introduction of increasing numbers of adaptive behavior scales (Thompson, McGrew, & Bruininks, 1999; Widaman & McGrew, 1996). New support needs assessment scales will undoubtedly make new contributions or in some manner represent an improvement over scales that came before.

ESTIMATING SUPPORT NEEDS

Whether a support needs assessment should be limited to only those activities in which a person currently participates has become a matter of debate. Arnold, Riches, and Stancliffe (2011) recently argued, "the measurement of support needs must be based on an assessment of the *individual* in the context of their *specific* environment, not support needed for some standardized set of activities" (p. 260). They charged, "it is problematic that supports needs assessments such as the Support (*sic*) Intensity Scale (*SIS*; Thompson et al., 2004[a]) ask how much support is needed for an activity, even when the person does not normally complete this activity in their environment" (p. 260).

However, Arnold et al. (2011) do not suggest how a norm-referenced support needs score could be generated without a standard set of items/ activities. Regardless of the construct on which a measurement tool is focused, it would seem to be impossible to meaningfully compare people's scores without the assurance that their scores were based on the same item set. For instance, if one person's height is measured using meters that are 80 centimeters long, and another person's height is measured using meters that are 120 centimeters long, then the two people's heights cannot be compared based on "meters," since in this case a meter does not contain a standard set of items.

Although a norm-referenced support needs score may be of little use when developing support plans for individuals, the availability of norm-referenced scores are essential if equity is a concern when deciding on how to distribute finite public funds to provide supports for people with disabilities. If it is true that people have different intensities of support needs, and if it is true that these differences should be considered when allocating public funds, then reliable and valid norm-referenced support needs scores are needed.

Moreover, asking respondents to envision people with disabilities engaging in activities with supports in which they are not currently involved has the potential to promote creative thinking and problem solving. Case workers in Alberta, Canada have started including a list of activities from the *SIS* that are "most important to the individual" in their assessment reports to remind planning teams to consider specific activities when developing annual support plans, and the activities may or may not be ones in which the person is currently engaged (Schalock, 2011b). In an article about how a team of nurses from Ireland were using the *SIS*, the nurses reported, "As each item is scored to reflect what supports would be necessary if the person was to be successful in a given area it prompts the individual to consider other goals that had not previously been identified" (Swanton, Walsh, O'Murchu, & O'Flynn, 2010, p. 8).

Riches et al. (2009a) also criticized the *SIS* because the scale requires respondents to estimate support needs for activities that a person has not yet had an opportunity to do. Citing a finding from Guscia et al. (2005), they claimed that "initial attempts to administer the scale in Australia have proven difficult, as raters have encountered problems making ratings" (p. 328) based on educated guesses. However, upon reviewing the article (i.e., Guscia et al., 2005) that Riches et al. cited, no reference to administering the *SIS* was found. In fact, there was no mention of the *SIS* at all in the article. However, in a different article published in 2006 where Guscia was the lead author (i.e., Guscia, Harries, Kirby, Nettelbeck et al.) that was not included in Riches et al.'s (2009a) reference list, there was a paragraph in the discussion section referring to the ease of administration of the *SIS* and two other assessment scales. Here, Guscia, Harries, Kirby, Nettelbeck et al. noted that the *SIS* was different from the two other assessment scales used in their study because the *SIS* required respondents to estimate the relative intensity of support required by an individual when there had not been an opportunity to directly observe him or her in an activity. They reported that "this approach tended to cause confusion for informants" (p. 154) who were 19 care workers from Australian institutions.

Although Guscia, Harries, Kirby, Nettelbeck et al. (2006) did not expand on why their respondents were confused, it is not surprising that institutional employees might be puzzled when asked to estimate people's support needs for the community activities that are included on the *SIS*. It is likely that many of them had not had opportunities to observe the people they were rating outside of an institutional setting. Assuming Riches et al. (2009a)

were actually referring to Guscia, Harries, Kirby, Nettelbeck et al.'s (2006) study (and not the article they cited), their conclusion that the *SIS* was difficult to administer appears tenuous. Guscia and colleagues only provided an anecdotal report from a small sample of institutional employees. Moreover, reports from respondents that items requiring estimation were confusing is not quite the same as asserting the scale was difficult to administer.

On the other hand, it could be argued that moving respondents out of their comfort zone might be a useful byproduct of the *SIS* assessment process. The *SIS* was not developed for the convenience and comfort of assessors, and if administering the *SIS* forced staff members to envision people engaged in a variety of life activities that they had not had prior opportunities to experience, then that that could be considered a good reason to administer the scale. If the confusion that the respondents reported stemmed from cognitive dissonance due to contrasting visions of people living lives in the community with supports instead of lives inside an institution, then participating in the SIS interview may have served a useful purpose. The status quo does not change unless people begin to envision something different than the current state of affairs.

Finally, it is important to remember that although Guscia, Harries, Kirby, Nettelbeck et al.'s (2006) respondents reported that estimating people's support needs was confusing, this does not mean that the items were unreliable or invalid. As the studies cited earlier show, the psychometric properties of the *SIS* have been robust across countries and cultures. In summary, although good people can have different views regarding the desirability of including items on support needs assessment scales that require respondents to estimate a person's support needs, at this time there is no empirical basis to reject scales with these types of items.

POPULATIONS OTHER THAN ADULTS WITH ID

Current support needs scales were developed for and field tested on adult populations of persons with intellectual and related developmental disabilities. However, Guscia, Harries, Kirby, Nettelbeck et al. (2006) investigated the construct and criterion validity of the *SIS* for a group of 31 persons with a primary disability of physical disability, neurological disability, or acquired brain injury, and their findings provided preliminary support for using the *SIS* with these populations. Bossaert et al. (2009) examined the psychometric properties of the *SIS* with a large sample of people with primary disabilities that included physical disabilities, sensory disabilities, autism, psychiatric disorders, and acquired brain injury. They concluded that a subset of *SIS* items had strong reliability and construct validity.

A children's version of the *SIS* has been developed, and data are currently being collected on children with ID between the ages of 5 and 15. It has two sections, the *Support Needs Scale* and *Exceptional Medical and Behavioral Needs*. The section from which norm-referenced indices will be generated, the *Support Needs Scale*, includes 61 life activities grouped into seven subscales: (1) Home Life Activities, (2) Community and Neighborhood Activities, (3) School Participation Activities, (4) School Learning Activities, (5) Health and Safety Activities, (6) Social Activities, and (7) Advocacy Activities. Each of the 61 items is rated across two support dimensions: Type (the nature of supports) and Time (how much total daily time is needed to provide supports) (Thompson et al., 2012). Because age is a confounding factor when assessing the support needs with children, separate norms are being developed for children of different ages.

Planning Supports for People with Disabilities

Advances in developing tools for support needs assessment have been encouraging during the ten years since Hennike (2002) and Thompson et al. (2002) first reported on their scales. Equally encouraging have been advances in person-centered planning (PCP) processes, where people's strengths and needs are explored within the context of their future hopes and dreams.

Person-Centered Planning Processes

Person-centered planning (PCP) processes are being used throughout the world (Claes, Van Hove, Vandevelde, van Loon, & Schalock, 2010; Robertson et al., 2007). These team-planning processes focus on identifying people's preferences, strengths, support needs, and goals in order to establish a collective vision of a desirable future life for a person. "Goals" in PCP processes are not achievement-oriented goals based on behavioral objectives, but instead refer to desired life experiences and conditions. Certainly, learning new skills can be included in a collective vision for the future, but increasing personal competence is not the focus per se.

With PCP processes, implementation plans are intended to lead to personal outcomes that are aligned with the collective vision. Time and energy are invested in arranging whatever supports are needed to achieve these outcomes. PCP is never initiated without involving the person who is the focus of planning efforts, and his or her family. In many instances, people with disabilities lead the process (Butterworth, Steere, & Whitney-Thomas, 1997; Nicoll & Flood, 2005; O'Brien & O'Brien, 2002).

Some of the better known PCP processes include *MAPS, ELP, PATH*, and the *PICTURE Method. MAPS* was developed at McGill University in Montreal, and it was originally an acronym for the "McGill Action Planning Strategy" before become known as "Making Action Plans." The process requires a facilitator, who is charged with leading a planning group through a series of eight questions, and a recorder responsible for documenting responses on a flip chart using both pictures and text. *MAPS* concludes by specifying action items, including what needs to be done, when it needs to be done, and who is responsible for following through (Vandercook, York, & Forest, 1989; Wells & Sheehey, 2012). In comparison to other PCP processes, Wells and Sheehey (2012) and Westling and Fox (2009) reported that *MAPS* is especially useful when planning with children.

Michael Smull (2000) and his colleagues developed the *Essential Lifestyle Planning* or *ELP* approach. An important assumption of *ELP* is that planning for a person is an ongoing activity, not an episodic event. Therefore, it is assumed plans are always going to need to be refined based on implementation issues and both planned and unplanned outcomes. Also, planning is a continuous process because people and circumstances are constantly changing. *ELPs* are developed through an iterative process of listening, learning, and acting.

PATH (Pearpoint, O'Brien, & Forest, 1998) begins with visioning activities where desired dreams and outcomes are identified. It is based on the premise that a person must know where he or she is going before making a plan on how to get there. Therefore, the *PATH* approach requires a team to work backwards from the desired end point (known as the "North Star"). The planning process moves from the North Star all the way back to the current day, and steps are identified that can be acted on right away.

Holburn, Gordon, and Vietze's (2007) *PICTURE Method* emphasizes differences between the person's life now and the person's desired life in the future, and the discrepancy between "now" and "the future" becomes the focus for planning. Compared to other PCP approaches, the *PICTURE Method* places more emphasis on involving paid service providers and using tools such as structured observations and questionnaires.

Evaluating PCP Processes

Until recently there were few attempts to systematically investigate the outcomes of PCP processes. Among the many challenges that interested researchers had to navigate were the absence of a universal definition of a PCP process, the diversity of processes used by practitioners, and difficulties in assuring that processes were implemented with fidelity (Claes et al., 2010; Robertson et al., 2007). Osborne (2005) went so far as to charge that PCP processes could not be scientifically evaluated because they were characterized by fuzzy goals and fuzzy outcomes.

However, research findings supporting the efficacy of PCP processes have started to emerge in peer-reviewed journals. Claes et al. (2010) completed a comprehensive review of professional literature and located 15 studies reporting empirical findings on the effectiveness of PCP processes. Although cautioning that the body of evidence for PCP is weak in regard to criteria for evidence-based research, they concluded that PCP has a positive, but moderate, effect on personal outcomes.

Perhaps the most comprehensive study to date was reported by Holburn, Jacobson, Schwartz, Flory, and Vietz (2004). These researchers conducted a longitudinal follow-up study that investigated the life experiences and conditions of 20 person-centered planning participants with ID and problem behavior who had moved out of a large institution. The outcomes of these individuals were superior when compared with those of a matched contrast group who received traditional planning services. Moreover, there was evidence that PCP processes enhanced team roles, commitment to a shared vision, and promoted both identification of and solutions to barriers to community living.

Proponents of PCP processes have warned that it can be difficult to immediately address all of the goals and dreams that are identified. Because PCP processes encourage participants to think positively about the person and his or her prospects, and many even have specific ground rules of not constraining discussion during a planning meeting by introducing perceived barriers such as lack of funding (Butterworth et al., 1997), some goals may need to be tempered when it comes time to develop specific action plans. Holburn and Cea (2007) cautioned against "excessive positivism" where goals are so lofty that incremental steps never get made and meaningful change in a person's life doesn't result.

Individualized Support Plans

The goal of person-centered planning is for planning teams to arrive at a unified vision of a person's life going forward. The support needs assessment scales discussed earlier are intended to assess a person's need for extraordinary supports. Thompson et al. (2009) suggested that planning teams make use of both types of information for the purpose of designing and implementing an "optimistic and realistic plan of action" (p. 141). Thompson et al.'s planning model rests on the premise that an intermediate, action-based plan is needed as a balance between long-term goals and specific activities that are going to be initiated right away. Although there is nothing sacrosanct about a 12-month timeframe, assessing what was and was not accomplished during the past year, and identifying what needs to be accomplished in the coming year, appears to be a sensible timeframe to assure that planning teams are provided a reasonable opportunity to get their work off the ground without allowing plans that are unsuccessful to linger. Additionally, annual planning has been a traditional requirement for many disability related human service organizations.

An annual planning process adopted from Thompson et al. (2009) is shown in Figure 21.1 and includes assessment, planning, implementation, monitoring, and evaluation components. The first component requires implementing a PCP process so that personal preferences are identified and a long-term vision of desired life experiences is developed that drives all planning efforts. The second component requires assessment of support needs, which can be completed by using a support needs assessment scale such as the *SIS* or *I-CAN*. The first two components do not need to be completed each year. However, every year planning teams should review information from the most recent PCP process and the most recent support needs assessment and determine whether the information reflects a person's current goals and circumstances. If there has been a significant change in a person's life since the last PCP process or supports needs assessment was completed, then it would be important to initiate Components #1 and/or #2. However, in most cases, Components #1 and #2 are activities that need to be completed only once every 3 to 5 years.

Information from the first two components is used to guide the development of Component #3, an unambiguous, annual plan that specifies the settings and activities in which a person will be engaged during a typical week, and the types and intensity of support that will be provided (and by whom).

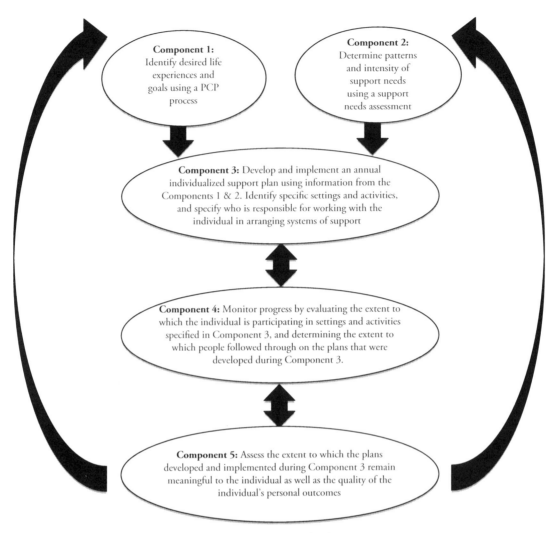

Figure 21.1 Five-Component Assessment, Planning, Implementation, and Evaluation Process

Adapted with permission from: Thompson, J. R., Bradley, V., Buntinx, W. H. E., Schalock, R. L., Shogran, K. A., Snell, M. E., Wehmeyer, M. L., et al. (2009). Conceptualizing supports and the support needs of people with intellectual disability. *Intellectual and Developmental Disabilities, 47*, 135–146.

The fourth component, monitoring, requires planning teams to schedule periodic follow-up meetings (e.g., monthly, quarterly) to review the correspondence between what the annual plan called for and what has actually come to pass. The key question to ask is a simple one: Did people follow through on what they agreed to do? Based on the congruence between what was planned and what actually happened, the planning team may decide to go back to Component #3 and develop a more workable annual plan.

The final component, evaluation, addresses the extent to which a person's desired life experiences (i.e., outcomes) have actually come to pass as the result of the planning team's efforts, as well as his or her quality of life. Personal preferences and priorities can change over time, and completing the evaluation component will assure that annual plans remain relevant to a person's needs. Component #5 may trigger a return to Component #1 (PCP process) and/or Component #2 (support needs assessment).

A case study of a provider organization in the Netherlands that uses information from a PCP process, support needs assessment, and personal outcome evaluation as a basis for an ongoing assessment, planning, implementation, and evaluation process was provided by van Loon, Claes, Vandevelde, Van Hove, and Schalock (2010). This case study reinforced Smull's (2000) assertion that planning is indeed an ongoing process, and both creativity and perseverance are needed in order to develop responsive annual plans that result in meaningful life experiences and outcomes. However, perhaps the most important lesson illustrated from this case study is that a service provider organization can adopt a systematic process that integrates assessment, planning, implementation, and evaluation activities. A systematic process can serve to facilitate change in an organization's culture from one that provides program-based services to one that arranges personalized systems of supports for individuals.

Aggregated Support Needs Assessment Data

Support needs assessment information is not only of value when planning with individuals, but aggregated results are useful when planning and making decisions at the systems level. Although there are undoubtedly multiple applications of aggregated support needs assessment data for disability service organizations, government agencies, and policymakers, the following four ways to analyze and use group data have been proposed: Descriptive analysis, Covariate analysis, Funding analysis, and Resource allocation (Fortune & Bershadsky, 2011; Fortune, LeVelle, Meche, Severance, Smith et al., 2008; Thompson et al., 2004b).

Descriptive analysis

Descriptive analysis refers to using descriptive statistics (e.g., frequency distributions, measures of central tendency such as mean and mode scores, variability indicators such range scores and standard deviations) to concisely summarize the support needs characteristics of a specific group or population. A descriptive analysis of support needs assessment data can reveal distributions of populations by support needs level, needs in specific domains of support, and exceptional medical and behavioral support needs. Daily time commitments for providing different types of supports can be determined, and areas to target for consumer education and professional development can be informed (Thompson et al., 2004b).

Covariate analysis

Covariate analysis allows for interpreting outcome data in the context of population differences in regard to support needs (Thompson et al., 2004b). For example, if a government agency wanted to provide incentives to work centers based on their progress in converting employees from sheltered employment to supported employment jobs, aggregated support needs assessment data could be used to investigate the relationship between outcome differences and population differences in regard

to support needs among various work centers. For instance, if one organization had placed 75% of its clients into supported employment jobs and another organization had placed 60%, a covariate analysis of support needs assessment information and employment outcomes would reveal if these two organizations served people with similar intensities of support needs. Such information would be critical to the government agency providing incentives, because the agency would want to know if the organization with more supported employees was providing human services to a population with less intense support needs. Without this information, the incentive program may not serve to encourage supported employment, but may unintentionally serve to encourage work centers to target only people with relatively less intense support needs for supported employment jobs.

Funding analyses

As mentioned earlier, the traditional "government to service provider" model of funding has been questioned by many who advocate for individual budgets, where funds go directly to the person with disability and his or her family. Regardless of how the money flows, there is a need for public funds to be distributed equitably so that each person is treated fairly. If it is true that people with disabilities are a heterogeneous population, and that some people have more complex support needs than others, then it is reasonable to conclude that it may require more funding to meet the needs of people with relatively more intense support needs than people with relatively less intense support needs. Equity and fairness should not be confused with everyone getting the same amount of funds. Additional values driving funding systems include individualization (funds should be tailored to a person's unique needs), flexibility (funds should be adaptable to a person's changing circumstances), empowerment (funds should provide people with options), cost-effectiveness (funds should be spent in a manner that provides the most benefit possible, in ways that are the most responsive to people needs), and transparency (the method for determining how funds are distributed is evident to all) (Fortune et al., 2008; Stancliffe & Lakin, 2005).

Although a thorough discussion of the complexities of funding decisions is beyond the scope of this chapter, aggregated data from support needs assessment scales can be used to compare measures of intensity of support needs with funding amounts that people receive (Thompson et al., 2004b; Fortune

& Bershadsky, 2011; Fortune et al., 2008). The purpose of this analysis would be to identify people who may be relatively "underfunded" or "overfunded." Of course, in most jurisdictions it would be argued that very few, if any, people are overfunded in the sense of receiving excess financial resources to meet their needs. However, the purpose of a funding analysis is to promote a more equitable system, and this may entail assuring that everyone gets an equally inadequate amount of funds in order to prevent people getting a grossly inadequate amount.

Resource allocation

Using support needs assessment data in developing resource allocation algorithms has been of special interest to governmental agencies that make funding decisions. Fifteen U.S. states, two Canadian provinces, and one European country have either incorporated *SIS* scores into a funding formula or are in the process of developing such an algorithm. So far, experiences with funding algorithms that include the *SIS* make it clear that *SIS* scores can be useful in creating a more equitable means for distributing public funds. Moreover, with proper monitoring of assessors, the *SIS* is not a scale that is easily manipulated (Fortune & Bershadsky, 2011; Fortune et al., 2008).

However, no support needs assessment score should be the only determinant of funding levels. When the *SIS* was first published, its authors cautioned against any attempt to use *SIS* in a regression-line manner to establish funding amounts, where increasingly higher *SIS* scores would automatically translate to progressively higher amounts of funding. "One needs to appreciate the complexity of cause-effect relationships among support needs, funding levels, and outcomes. In this regard, *SIS* data will provide only one 'piece of the puzzle'" (Thompson et al., 2004b, p. 89). This guideline would apply to all other support needs assessment scales as well, because support needs are only one of many factors that contribute to cost variations (Fortune & Bershadsky, 2011; Fortune et al., 2008).

Conclusion

According to a supports paradigm, disability is not an invariant trait within a person, but rather is a state of functioning that creates needs for different types and intensities of supports than those that are needed by people from the general population. Over the past five decades, considerable progress has been made in understanding people by their support needs. There are many cases where personalized systems of supports have empowered people to live dignified and purposeful lives as citizens who fully participate in and contribute to their communities.

However, the evolution from a program-based human service system to an individualized supports-based system is far from finished. Well-established approaches to providing individualized supports, such as supported employment, supported living, and inclusive education, continue to be less common than traditional group services such as sheltered employment, congregate living in large group homes, and schooling in special education classrooms (Braddock et al., 2008; Ferguson, 2008; Martinez-Leal et al., 2011; U.S. Department of Education, 2011). Although new approaches and materials applicable to understanding people by their support needs have been developed, including support needs assessment scales and PCP processes, additional research evidence is needed to determine the extent of benefits that can be derived from using these new tools and processes. A supports paradigm may be transforming human services to people with disabilities, but more work is needed before it can be claimed that that service system has been transformed.

References

Arnold, S. R. C., Riches, V. C., & Stancliffe, R. J. (2011). Intelligence is as intelligence does: Can additional support needs replace disability? *Journal of Intellectual & Developmental Disability*, 36, 254–258. doi:10.3109/13668 250.2011.617732

Bellamy, G. T., Rhodes, L. E., & Albin, J. M. (1986). Supported employment. In W. Kiernan & J. Stark (Eds.), *Pathways to employment for adults with developmental disability* (pp. 129–138). Baltimore, MD: Paul H. Brookes.

Bossaert, G., Kuppens, S., Buntinx, W., Molleman, C., Van den Abeele, A., & Maes, B. (2009). Usefulness of the Supports Intensity Scale (SIS) for persons with other than intellectual disabilities. *Research in Developmental Disabilities*, 30, 1306–1316.

Braddock, D., Hemp, R., & Rizzolo, M. K. (2008). *State of the state in developmental disabilities (7th ed.)*. Washington, DC: American Association on Intellectual and Developmental Disability.

Breihan, A. W. (2007). Who chooses service providers? The spread of consumer choice, 1992-2004. *Intellectual and Developmental Disabilities*, 45, 365–372.

Brown, H. K., Ouellette-Kuntz, H., Bielska, I., & Elliott, D. (2009). Choosing a measure of support need: Implications for research and policy. *Journal of Intellectual Disability Research*, 53, 949–954. doi:10.1111/j.1365-2788.2009.01216

Brown, L., Schwarz, P., Udvari-Solner, A., Kampschroer, E., Johnson, F., Jorgensen, J., & Gruenewald, L. (1991). How much time should students with severe intellectual disabilities spend in regular classrooms and elsewhere? *JASH*, 16, 39–47.

Bruininks, R. H., Hill, B. K., Weatherman, R. F., & Woodcock, R. W. (1986). *Inventory for Client and Agency Planning*. Itasca, IL: Riverside.

Buntinx, W. (2011). *Supports Intensity Scale psychometric properties: Similarities and differences between original U.S. versions and Dutch, Italian, French, and Spanish translations.* Lecture presented on June 9, 2011 at the SIS Post-conference Workshop at the 35th Annual Meeting of the American Association on Intellectual and Developmental Disabilities, St. Paul, MN.

Buntinx, W., Van Unen, F., Speth, W., & Groot, W. (2006). The Supports Intensity Scale in the Netherlands: Psychometric properties and applications in practice. *Journal of Applied Research in Intellectual Disabilities, 19*, 246.

Butterworth, J. (2002). Programs to supports. In R. L. Schalock, P. C. Baker, & M. D. Croser (Eds.), *Embarking on a new century: Mental retardation at the end of the 20th century* (pp. 83–100). Washington, DC: American Association on Mental Retardation.

Butterworth, J., Steere, D. E., & Whitney-Thomas, J. (1997). Using person-centered planning to address personal quality of life. In R. L. Schalock (Ed.), *Quality of Life (vol. 2)* (pp. 5–24). Washington, DC: American Association on Mental Retardation.

Carter, E. W., Hughes, C., Guth, C., & Copeland, S. R. (2005). Factors influencing social interaction among high school students with intellectual disabilities and their general education peers. *American Journal on Mental Retardation, 110,* 366–377.

Chowdhury, M., & Benson, B. A. (2011). Deinstitutionalization and quality of life of individuals with intellectual disability: A review of the international literature. *Journal of Policy and Practice in Intellectual Disabilities, 8,* 256–265.

Cicchetti, D. V., & Sparrow, S. S. (1981). Developing criteria for establishing interrater reliability of specific items: Applications to assessment of adaptive behavior. *American Journal of Mental Deficiency, 86,* 127–137.

Claes, C., Van Hove, G., Vandevelde, S., van Loon, J., & Schalock, R. L. (2010). Person-centered planning: Analysis of research and effectiveness. *Intellectual and Developmental Disabilities, 48,* 432–453.

Clark, G. M., & Kolstoe, O. P. (1995). *Career development and transition education for adolescents with disabilities (2nd ed.).* Needham Heights, MA: Allyn & Bacon.

Cottini, L., Fedeli, D., Leoni, M., & Croce, L. (2008). La Supports Intensity Scale nel panorama riabilitativo italiano: Standardizzazione italiana e procedure psicometriche. *AJMR Italian Edition, 6,* 21–38.

Dailey, R. F. (1974). Dimensions and issues in '74: Tapping into the special education grapevine. *Exceptional Children, 40,* 503–507.

Feinstein, C. S., Levine, R. M., Lemanowicz, J. A., Sedlak, W. C., Klein, J., & Hagner, D. (2006). Home ownership initiatives and outcomes for people with disabilities. *Journal of the Community Development Society, 37,* 1–7.

Ferguson, D. L. (2008). International trends in inclusive education: The continuing challenge to teach each one and everyone. *European Journal of Special Needs Education, 23,* 109–120. doi:10.1080/08856250801946236

Fortune, J., & Bershadsky, J. (2011). *Issues to consider when implementing resource allocation using SIS.* Lecture presented on June 9, 2011 at the SIS Post-conference Workshop at the 35th Annual Meeting of the American Association on Intellectual and Developmental Disabilities, St. Paul, MN.

Fortune, J., LeVelle, J., Meche, S., Severance, D., Smith, G., & Stern, J. et al. (2008). SIS resource allocation: Four papers on issues and approaches. *AAIDD SIS White Paper Series* (R. L. Schalock, J. R. Thompson, & M. J. Tassé, Eds.).

Washington, DC: American Association on Intellectual and Developmental Disabilities.

Fuchs, D., & Fuchs, L. S. (1994). Inclusive schools movement and the radicalization of special education reform. *Exceptional Children, 60,* 294–309.

Giangreco, M. F. (2011). Educating students with severe disabilities: Foundational concepts and practices. In M. E. Snell & F. Brown (Eds.), *Instruction of students with severe disabilities* (7th ed., pp. 1–30). Upper Saddle River, NJ: Pearson Education/Prentice-Hall.

Giangreco, M. F., & Putnam, J. W. (1991). Supporting the education of students with severe disabilities in regular education environments. In L. H. Meyer, C. A. Peck, & L. Brown (Eds.), *Critical issues in the lives of people with severe disabilities* (pp. 245–270). Baltimore, MD: Paul H. Brookes.

Gould, S. J. (1981). *The Mismeasure of Man.* New York, NY: Norton.

Guscia, R., Harries, J., Kirby, N., & Nettelbeck, T. (2006). Rater bias and the measurement of support needs. *Journal of Intellectual & Developmental Disability, 31,* 156–160. doi:10.1080/13668250600876459

Guscia, R., Harries, J., Kirby, N., Nettelbeck, T., & Taplin, J. (2006). Construct and criterion validities of the Service Need Assessment Profile (SNAP): A measure of support for people with disabilities. *Journal of Intellectual & Developmental Disability, 31,* 148–155. doi:10.1080/13668250600876459

Guscia, R., Harries, J., Kirby, N., Nettelbeck, T., & Taplin, J. (2005). Reliability of the Service Need Assessment Profile (SNAP): A measure of support for people with disabilities. *Journal of Intellectual & Developmental Disability, 30,* 24–30. doi:10.1080/13668250500033144

Hamelin, J. P., Frijters, J., Griffiths, D., Condillac, R., & Owen, F. (2011). Meta-analysis of deinstitutionalization adaptive behavior outcomes: Research and clinical implications. *Journal of Intellectual & Developmental Disability, 36,* 61–72. doi:10.3109/13668250.2010.544034

Harries, J., Guscia, R., Kirby, N., Nettelbeck, T., & Taplin, J. (2005). Support needs and adaptive behaviors. *American Journal on Mental Retardation, 110*(5), 393–404.

Hennike, J. M. (2002). DD-SNAP. *Exceptional Parent, 32,* 56–57.

Hennike, J. M., Myers, A. M., Realon, R. E., & Thompson, T. J. (2006). Development and validation of a needs-assessment instrument for persons with developmental disabilities. *Journal of Developmental and Physical Disabilities, 18,* 201–217.

Holburn, S., & Cea, C. D. (2007). Excessive positivism in person-centered planning. *Research & Practice for Persons with Severe Disabilities, 32,* 167–172.

Holburn, S., Gordon, A., & Vietze, P. M. (2007). *Person-centered planning made easy: The PICTURE method.* Baltimore, MD: Paul H. Brookes.

Holburn, S., Jacobson, J. W., Schwartz, A. A., Flory, M. J., & Vietz, P. M. (2004). The Willowbrook futures project: A longitudinal analysis of person-centered planning. *American Journal on Mental Retardation, 109,* 63–76.

Janney, R. E., & Snell, M. E. (2011). Designing and implementing instruction for inclusive classes. In M. E. Snell & F. Brown (Eds.), *Instruction of students with severe disabilities* (7th ed., 224–256). Upper Saddle River, NJ: Merrill/Prentice-Hall.

Jorgensen, C. M., McSheehan, M., & Sonnenmeier, R. M. (2010). *The beyond access model: Promoting membership, participation, and learning for students with disabilities in the general education classroom.* Baltimore, MD: Paul H. Brookes.

Kiernan, W. E., Gilmore, D. S., & Butterworth, J. (1997). Integrated employment: Evolution of national practices. In W. E. Kiernan & R. L. Schalock (Eds.), *Integrated employment: Current status and future directions* (pp. 17–29). Washington, DC: American Association on Mental Retardation.

Kuhn, T. S. (1962). *The structure of scientific revolutions.* Chicago, IL: University of Chicago.

Kuppens, S., Bossaert, G., Buntinx, W., Molleman, C., Van den Abbeele, A., & Maes, B. (2010). Factorial validity of the Supports Intensity Scale (SIS). *American Journal on Intellectual and Developmental Disabilities, 115,* 327–339.

Laesecke, A. (2002). Through measurement to knowledge: The inaugural lecture of Heike Kamerlingh Onne (1882). *Journal of Research of the National Institute of Standards and Technology, 107,* 261–277.

Lakin, K. C., Hayden, M. F., & Abery, B. H. (1994). An overview of the community living concept. In M. F. Hayden & B. H. Abery (Eds.), *Challenges for a service system in transition: Ensuring quality community experiences for persons with developmental disabilities* (pp. 3–22). Baltimore, MD: Paul H. Brookes.

Lamoureux-Hebert, M., & Morin, D. (2008). *French translation of the Supports Intensity Scale.* Washington, DC: American Association on Intellectual and Developmental Disabilities.

Luckasson, R., Borthwick-Duffy, S., Buntinx, W. H. E., Coulter, D. L., Craig, E. M., Reeve, A., . . . Tassé, M. J. (2002). *Mental retardation: Definition, classification, and systems of supports (10th ed.).* Washington, DC: American Association on Mental Retardation.

Luckasson, R., Coulter, D. L., Polloway, E. A., Reese, S., Schalock, R. L., Snell, M. E., . . . Stark, J. A. (1992). *Mental retardation: Definition, classification, and systems of supports (9th ed.).* Washington, DC: American Association on Mental Retardation.

MacMillan, D. L. (1977). *Mental retardation in school and society.* Boston, MA: Little, Brown and Company.

Mank, D. (1997). Systems change strategies for integrated employment: A blueprint for the future. In W. Kiernan & Schalock (Eds.), *Integrated employment: Current status and future directions* (pp. 107–120). Washington, DC: American Association on Mental Retardation.

Martinez-Leal, R., Salvador-Carulla, L., Linehan, C., Walsh, P., Weber, G., Van Hove, G. . . . Kerr, M. (2011). The impact of living arrangements and deinstitutionalization in the health status of persons with intellectual disability in Europe. *Journal of Intellectual Disability Research, 55,* 858–872. doi: 10.1111/j.1365-2788.2011.01439.x

Maslow, A. H. (1943). A theory of human motivation. *Psychological Review, 50,* 370–396.

Mastropieri, M. A., & Scruggs, T. E. (2010). *The inclusive classroom: Strategies for effective differentiated instruction (4th ed.).* Upper Saddle River, NJ: Pearson Merrill/Prentice Hall.

National Disability Rights Network, (2011). *Segregated & exploited: The failure of the disability service system to provide quality work.* Washington, DC: National Disability Rights Network.

Nicoll, T., & Flood, K. (2005). Self advocates leading person centred planning. *Learning Disability Practice, 8*(1), 14–17.

Nirje, B. (1969). The normalization principle and its human management implications. In R. Kugel & W. Wolfensberger (Eds.), *Changing patterns in residential services for the mentally retarded* (pp. 179–195). Washington, DC: President's Committee on Mental Retardation.

Noble, J. H., & Conley, R. W. (1989). The new supported employment program: Prospects and potential problems. In W. E. Kiernan & R. L. Schalock (Eds.), *Economics,* *industry, and disability: A look ahead* (pp. 207–222). Baltimore, MD: Paul H. Brookes.

O'Brien, C. L., & O'Brien, J. (2002). The origins of person-centered planning: A community of practice perspective. In S. Holburn & P. M. Vietze (Eds.), *Person-centered planning: Research, practice, and future directions* (pp. 3–28). Baltimore, MD: Paul H. Brookes.

Osborne, J. G. (2005). Person-centered planning: A faux fixe in the service of humanism? In J. W. Jacobson, R. M. Foxx, & J. A. Mulick (Eds.), *Controversial therapies for developmental disabilities: Fad, fashion, and science in professional practice* (pp. 313–329). Mahwah, NJ: Lawrence Erlbaum Associates.

Pearpoint, J., O'Brien, J., & Forest, M. (1998). *PATH: Planning alternative tomorrows with hope.* Ontario, Canada: Inclusion.

Perske, R. (1972). The dignity of risk and the mentally retarded. *Mental Retardation, 10,* 24–27.

Pledger, C. (2003). Discourse on disability and rehabilitation issues: Opportunities for psychology. *American Psychologist, 58,* 279–284. doi:10.1037/0003-066X.58.4.279

Reynolds, M. C., Wang, M. C., & Walberg, H. J. (1987). The necessary restructuring of special and regular education. *Exceptional Children, 53,* 391–398.

Riches, V. C., Parmenter, T. R., Llewellyn, G., Hindmarsh, G., & Chan, J. (2009a). I-CAN: A new instrument to classify support needs for people with disability: Part I. *Journal of Applied Research in Intellectual Disabilities, 22,* 326–339. doi:10.1111/j.1468-3148.2008.00466.x

Riches, V. C., Parmenter, T. R., Llewellyn, G., Hindmarsh, G., & Chan, J. (2009b). The reliability, validity and practical utility of measuring supports using the I-CAN instrument: Part II. *Journal of Applied Research in Intellectual Disabilities, 22,* 340–353. doi:10.1111/j.1468-3148.2008.00467.x

Robertson, J., Emerson, E., Hatton, C., Elliott, J., McIntosh, B., Swift, P., . . . Joyce, T. (2007). Person-centred planning: Factors associated with successful outcomes for people with intellectual disabilities. *Journal of Intellectual Disability Research, 51,* 232–243. doi:10.1111/j.1365-2788.2006.00864.x

Rogan, P., & Rinne, S. (2011). National call for organizational change from sheltered to integrated employment. *Intellectual and Developmental Disabilities, 49,* 248–260. doi: 10.1352/1934-9556-49.4.248

Rothman, J. C. (2010). The challenge of disability and access: Reconceptualizing the role of the medical model. *Journal of Social Work in Disability & Rehabilitation, 9,* 194–222. doi:10.1080/1536710X.2010.493488

Schalock, R. L. (2011a). The evolving understanding of the construct of intellectual disability. *Journal of Intellectual & Developmental Disability, 36,* 227–237.

Schalock, R. L. (2011b). *The SIS as an international tool: Learning from one another.* Lecture presented on June 9, 2011 at the SIS Post-conference Workshop at the 35th Annual Meeting of the American Association on Intellectual and Developmental Disabilities, St. Paul, MN.

Schalock, R. L., Borthwick-Duffy, S., Bradley, V. J., Buntinx, W. H. E., Coulter, D. L., Craig, E. M., . . . Yeager, M. H. (2010). *Intellectual disability: Definition, classification, and systems of supports (11th ed.).* Washington, DC: American Association on Intellectual and Developmental Disabilities.

Scott, N., Lakin, K. C., & Larson, S. A. (2008). The 40th anniversary of deinstitutionalization in the United States: Decreasing state institutional populations, 1967-2007. *Intellectual and Developmental Disabilities, 46,* 402–405. doi:10.1352/2008.46:402-405

Shapiro, J. P. (1993). *No pity: People with disabilities forging a new civil rights movement*. NY: Times Books.

Smull, M. W. (2000). *Listen, learn, act*. Annapolis, MD: Support Development Associates.

Snell, M. E., & Drake, G. P. (1994). Replacing cascades with supported education. *Journal of Special Education, 27*, 393–409.

Stainback, W., & Stainback, S. (1984). A rationale for the merger of special and regular education. *Exceptional Children, 51*, 102–111.

Stancliffe, R. J., & Lakin, K. C. (2005). *Cost and outcomes of community services for people with intellectual disabilities*. Baltimore, MD: Paul H. Brookes.

Stancliffe, R. J., Lakin, K. C., Larson, S., Engler, J., Taub, S., & Fortune, J. (2011). Choice of living arrangements. *Journal of Intellectual Disability Research, 55*, 746–762. doi:10.1111/j.1365-2788.2010.01336.x

Switzky, H. N., & Greenspan, S. (2006). Summary and conclusions: Can so many diverse ideas be integrated? Multiparadigmatic models of understanding mental retardation in the 21st century. In H. N. Switzky & Steve Greenspan (Eds.), *What is Mental Retardation?* (pp. 341–358). Washington, DC: American Association on Mental Retardation.

Swanton, S., Walsh, S., O'Murchu, R., & O'Flynn, P. (2010). A tool to determine support needs for community life. *Learning Disability Practice, 13*(8), 24–26.

Sydenham, P. (2003). Relationship between measurement, knowledge and advancement. *Measurement, 34*, 3–16.

Taylor, S. J. (2001). The continuum and current controversies in the USA. *Journal of Intellectual & Developmental Disability, 26*, 15–33. doi:10.1080/13668250020032741.

Teel, A. S. (2011). *Alone and invisible no more*. White River Junction, VT: Chelsea Green.

Thompson, J. R., Bradley, V. J., Buntinx, W. H. E., Schalock, R. L., Shogren, K. A., Snell, M. E., & Wehmeyer, M. L. (2009). Conceptualizing supports and the support needs of people with intellectual disability. *Intellectual and Developmental Disabilities, 47*, 135–146.

Thompson, J. R., Bryant, B., Campbell, E. M., Craig, E. M., Hughes, C., Rotholz, D. A.,…Wehmeyer, M. (2004a). *Supports Intensity Scale (SIS)*. Washington, DC: American Association on Mental Retardation.

Thompson, J. R., Bryant, B., Campbell, E. M., Craig, E. M., Hughes, C., Rotholz, D. A.,…Wehmeyer, M. (2004b). *The Supports Intensity Scale (SIS): Users manual*. Washington, DC: American Association on Mental Retardation.

Thompson, J. R., Hughes, C., Schalock, R. L., Silverman, W., Tassé, M. J., Bryant, B.,…Campbell, E. M. (2002). Integrating supports in assessment and planning. *Mental Retardation, 40*, 390–405.

Thompson, J. R., McGrew, K. S., & Bruininks, R. H. (1999). Adaptive and maladaptive behavior: Functional and structural characteristics. In R. L. Schalock (Ed.), *Adaptive behavior and its measurement: Implications for the field of mental retardation* (pp. 15–42). Washington, DC: American Association on Mental Retardation.

Thompson, J. R., Tassé, M. J., & McLaughlin, C. A. (2008). Interrater reliability of the Supports Intensity Scale (SIS). *American Journal on Mental Retardation, 113*, 231–237.

Thompson, J. R., Wehmeyer, M. L., Hughes, C., Copeland, S. R., Little, T. D., Obremski, S.,…Tassé, M. J. (2012). *Supports Intensity Scale for Children Field Test Version 2.0*. Unpublished assessment instrument.

UNESCO. (2009). Inclusive education: The way of the future. Geneva: United Nations Educational, Scientific and Cultural Organization (UNESCO). Retrieved from http://www.ibe.unesco.org/en/ice/48th-ice-2008/final-report.html

U.S. Department of Education. (2011). *30th Annual report to Congress on the implementation of the Individuals with Disabilities Education Act, 2008*. VA: U.S. Department of Education.

U.S. Department of Labor. (2012). Wage and hour division (WHD). Retrieved from http://www.dol.gov/whd/FOH/ch64/64k00.htm

van Loon, J., Claes, C., Vandevelde, S., Van Hove, G., & Schalock, R. (2010). Assessing individual support needs to enhance personal outcomes. *Exceptionality, 18*, 193–202. doi:10.1080/09362835.2010.513924

Vandercook, T., York, J., & Forest, M. (1989). The McGill Action Planning System (MAPS): A strategy for building the vision. *Journal of the Association for Persons with Severe Handicaps, 14*, 205–215.

Verdugo, M., Arias, B., Ibanez, A., & Gomez, S. (2006). Validation of the Spanish version of the Supports Intensity Scale. *Journal of Applied Research in Intellectual Disabilities, 2006, 19*, 274.

Verdugo, M., Arias, B., Ibanez, A., & Schalock, R. L. (2010). Adaptation and psychometric properties of the Spanish version of the Supports Intensity Scale (SIS). *American Association on Intellectual and Developmental Disabilities, 115*, 496–503. doi:10.135/1944-7558-115.6.496

Wasserman, J. D., & Tulsky, D. S. (2005). A history of intelligence assessment. In D. P. Flanagan & P. L. Harrison (Eds.), *Contemporary intellectual assessment: Theories, tests, and issues (2nd ed.)* (pp. 3–22). New York, NY: Guilford.

Wehman, P., Inge, K. J., Revell, W. G., & Brooke, V. A. (2007). *Real Work for Real Pay: Inclusive Employment for People with Disabilities*. Baltimore: Brookes Publishing Co.

Wehmeyer, M., Chapman, T. E., Little, T. D., Thompson, J. R., Schalock, R., & Tassé, M. J. (2009). Efficacy of the Supports Intensity Scale (SIS) to predict extraordinary support needs. *American Journal on Intellectual and Developmental Disabilities, 114*, 3–14.

Weiss, J. A., Lunsky, Y., Tassé, M. J., & Durbin, J. (2009). Support for the construct validity of the Supports Intensity Scale based on clinician rankings of need. *Research in Developmental Disabilities, 30*, 933–941. doi:10.1016/j.ridd.2009.01.007

Wells, J. C., & Sheehey, P. H. (2012). Person-centered planning: Strategies to encourage participation and facilitate communication. *Teaching Exceptional Children, 44*(3), 32–39.

Westling, D. L., & Fox, L. (2009). *Teaching students with severe disabilities (4th ed.)*. Upper Saddle River, NJ: Pearson Education/Prentice-Hall.

Widaman, K. F., & McGrew, K. S. (1996). The structure of adaptive behavior. In J. W. Jacobson & J. A. Mulick (Eds.), *Manual of diagnosis and professional practice in mental retardation* (pp. 97–110). Washington, DC: American Psychological Association.

Winzer, M. A. (1993). *The history of special education: From isolation to integration*. Washington, DC: Gallaudet University Press.

Wolfensberger, W. (1972). *Normalization: The principle of normalization in human services*. Toronto, Canada: National Institute on Mental Retardation.

World Health Organization (WHO). (2001). *International classification of functioning, disability, and health*. Geneva, Switzerland: Author.

Young, L., Sigafoos, J., Suttie, J., Ashman, A., & Grevell, P. (1998). Deinstitutionalisation of persons with intellectual disabilities: A review of Australian studies. *Journal of Intellectual & Developmental Disability, 23*, 155–170.

Supported Employment

Paul Wehman, Vicki Brooke, Stephanie Lau, *and* Pamela Targett

Abstract

As large institutions began to downsize and individuals with severe disabilities moved back to their communities, the need arose for improved disability service programs for these citizens. The result was an increase in sheltered workshops and day-activity programs that offered consistency, security, and safety, much like the institutional settings these individuals had recently left. At the same time, a new philosophical approach known as *normalization* emerged. This was followed by an increase in residential and community-based employment services and government-funded small demonstration projects to test *supported employment* (SE) as a means to assist disabled individuals gain and maintain real jobs. The 1986 Rehabilitation Act Amendments provided funding for SE services through the National Vocational Rehabilitation system. This chapter briefly reviews the history of SE and offers guidance on targeted populations. A review of the philosophy and values associated with best practices follows, and the chapter concludes by describing model implementation.

Key Words: employment, disability, supported employment, vocational rehabilitation

This chapter offers an overview of the supported employment (SE) model for people with severe disabilities. It begins with a discussion of the concept and history of SE. This is followed by an examination of the values and best practices associated with this approach. In later sections, the reader is led through the various components involved in services delivery: assessment, job development, on-the-job site training, and long-term follow-along or retention services. The chapter concludes with some ideas on future directions for research.

Concept and History of Supported Employment

Supported employment can be traced back to the 1970s, when many communities across the United States were actively discussing how to create and deliver community-based services for people with disabilities. During this period, many large residential institutions around the country were downsizing, and, as a result, people with more severe disabilities were returning to their local communities. As this was occurring, public leaders struggled to ramp up a host of new services to meet the needs of people leaving these institutions. Many communities were unprepared and struggled with establishing community supports for people with disabilities. In communities where existing disability service programs had openings, people with severe disabilities gained access to such programs as day support services, including sheltered workshops, adult activity centers, and day treatment programs designed to serve people with intellectual or psychiatric disabilities. Many of these programs mirrored the same philosophy as institutions: programs were designed based on consistency, security, and safety. These programs provided very limited opportunities for people with severe disabilities to obtain meaningful, community-based employment.

A Philosophical Shift

Hand-in-hand with the deinstitutionalization process was a new philosophical approach to the delivery of human services for people with disabilities known as *normalization*. Wolfensberger's (1977) refined definition of normalization focused on enabling people with disabilities to lead lives that are valued by other members of the community. During the late 1970s and the 1980s, normalization quickly became accepted as the guiding philosophy for the majority of human service programs and services in the United States, and it can be directly linked to the significant increase in the number of community programs serving people with disabilities, including residential services and community-based employment programs. In the 1990s, a focus on individual empowerment began to be viewed as the driving force behind the development, implementation, and evaluation of human services. This was a natural evolution that ultimately occurred because of the immense importance and positive effect that normalization had on people and programs.

Legislative Changes

In 1975, with the passage of the Education for All Handicapped Children Act, known as P.L. 94-142, organizations began to review their services and structure. The Act mandated, for the first time, that the U.S. public school system provide a free, appropriate education for all children, irrespective of the nature or severity of a child's disability. The disability movement took on a civil rights agenda, and there was discussion and congressional concern regarding the exclusion of millions of children with disabilities from public education and inappropriate educational programs for more children with disabilities who had gained access to the public schools (U.S. Commission on Civil Rights, 1983). The Act made reference to transition services and the importance that students with disabilities leaving the public education system have available to them an adult services program that emphasized employment, as well as a host of other support activities. This emphasis on transition services focused national attention on what young people finishing school needed as they moved into the community as young adults. There was a clear and important emphasis placed on obtaining real jobs in the community.

There was also the sense that people with disabilities could do more and could work in the community but that a service technology or system to support this advancement did not exist. The next reform came in the late 1970s and early 1980s,

when small employment demonstration projects, located in isolated areas across the country, tested the concept of *supported employment*. In 1984, the Developmental Disabilities Act (P.L. 98-527) made the first actual reference to SE. As a direct result of this legislation, SE became part of formal rehabilitation terminology, although the Act did not allocate funds to provide services in the community. Although this was a positive acknowledgment of the employability of people with disabilities, resources were not given to states and/or communities to create SE service programs.

The Rehabilitation Act Amendments of 1986 (P.L. 99-506) was the first legislation in which SE was referenced that also provided funding for the service. The national Vocational Rehabilitation (VR) system is funded through the Rehabilitation Act, and these 1986 amendments established a formula grant that made SE services funding available to every state in the country. Consequently, employment support agencies began searching for information on how to set up an SE program that was consistent with the definition of such a service that originated in these 1986 amendments. In 1998, the Reauthorization of the Rehabilitation Act retained the core definition of SE that appeared in the original 1986 Amendments. Today, efforts continue to target specific areas of the legislation that need further federal language clarification. Who is appropriate for SE services? Who are persons with the most significant disabilities? Who is SE intended to service? How are services delivered? What is social integration, and how is it measured? Does competitive work involve payment of minimum wage or above? What is the nature of ongoing supports?

Target population The federal legislation is clear: SE is for people with significant disabilities who are in need of ongoing supports and who have no work history or an interrupted and/or intermittent employment record. Although SE has been in place for at least 20 years, people and organizations still struggle to determine who this program is intended to serve. The legislation gives guidance on how to select a target audience for SE.

Confusion has arisen over the term *significant disability* because different programs and services define these terms in various ways. For example, could someone have a master's degree and still have a significant psychiatric disability? The answer is yes, and much of this confusion has been mitigated in the last few years through adult service organizations (such as developmental disability and VR agencies) accepting proof of disability from prior special education services or from the Social Security Administration's disability determination process. Still, issues persist when discussing a person's intermittent work history, in which, for example, a person works for 3–4 months, is not successful, drops out of the employment market, and then comes back several months later. For some people, this repeated pattern of failed employment is key to their intermittent work history. People with this pattern are eligible to receive SE services because they need support in selecting an appropriate job with the right combination of workplace supports.

Integrated work settings. From the beginning, SE was intended to occur in typical, competitive employment work settings. At times, there has been an interest in blurring these lines and attempting to redefine what is meant by a competitive employment work setting. For example, a prominent sheltered workshop provider decided to move its hospital kit assembly task out of the workshop and back into the company contracting with the workshop for this service. The company has a total of 58 employees, which includes 14 people from the workshop. These 14 people have a work area in the back of the warehouse, isolated from other employees in terms of physical proximity, break schedule, and room assignment. This is, obviously, not an example of a typical, competitive work setting. The intent of the legislation was for SE to mirror a typical work setting, including opportunities to interact with people other than paid service providers and maintaining a ratio of people with disabilities to nondisabled coworkers that reflects national population proportions.

Determining what constitutes an integrated work setting can be difficult when an SE program secures employment for multiple people at a single site, as seen in the previous example. When SE organizations negotiate with an employer during the hiring process and end up redesigning a position that, in fact, isolates the new employee with a disability from his or her coworkers (e.g., by taking work breaks at a different time from everyone else or receiving a paycheck from an organization other than the business), then the employment support program has provided a disservice to this employee because it impedes integration. The legislative intent was for SE services to occur in business settings where people with disabilities are working and interacting with coworkers who are not associated with an SE program.

Competitive employment. Similar to ambiguities in defining an integrated work setting are some issues related to what is meant by *competitive employment*. The definition of what constitutes competitive employment has changed over time. In the initial legislation, the 1986 Rehabilitation Act Amendments, competitive employment was defined as a job that involved 20 hours or more of work. The reference to a specific number of hours of work for SE was dropped when the regulations were amended in the early 1990s. It was hoped that by dropping the hours-worked regulation, it would increase the number of people with the most significant disabilities entering SE. In fact, in far too many organizations across the country, people with disabilities are underemployed because it is easier to obtain a 5-hour a week job versus a 30- or 40-hour a week position. When the hour regulations were dropped, the clear intent was that a plan would be put into place for each person, gradually increasing total hours worked; in most cases, this did not occur. Currently, competitive work is seen as being full- or part-time employment that is consistent with the work goals of the person and for which wages paid are commensurate with coworkers earning at or above minimum wage.

Ongoing support services. The final component of the SE definition is the provision of long-term supports. As stated previously, the notion of long-term supports is a component of the SE definition that makes this service unique among a variety of different service models. It involves a commitment to the employee throughout her job tenure. Over time, once the employee has become stabilized in his or her job, the employment specialist (ES) would continue to provide, at a minimum, twice monthly contacts. The number and focus of these contacts are individually tailored to the needs of the employee. The services can occur at or away from the job site, and exactly how services are delivered are directed by the employee. Many people with psychiatric disabilities and/or traumatic brain injuries, who have mastered their job duties but seem to struggle with employer or coworker relationships, for example, have requested that support services be provided away from the job site to reduce the stigma of having an ES. Ultimately, the employee should drive this process, with the ES respecting his or her concerns and wishes. Regardless of where long-term supports are delivered, they are presented to the employee and employer in a two-step sequential process: time-limited and extended services, both of which are addressed in the VR legislation. The time-limited phase is generally a 60-day assessment of the employee's job stability and satisfaction. Once this initial hurdle is cleared, there is a general ongoing assessment of the initial employment situation with a primary focus of assisting the person to maintain or advance his or her career, which may or may not occur in the business setting.

It is important to note that the core definition of SE has not changed since its inception. Legislation has attempted to refine the language more clearly to improve SE outcomes and to improve the impact of SE in the lives of people with disabilities. Consistent with national trends, SE stays focused on a very personal and supports-driven approach to employment services, with the individual directing his or her own career path.

A final piece of federal legislation that provided for the advancement of community-based services and, specifically, SE is the Medicaid Home and Community-Based Services (HCBS) waiver program established by Congress in 1981 (P.L.97-35). The HCBS legislation, better known simply as the Medicaid Waiver program, identifies SE as an appropriate means for assisting a person's eligibility for Medicaid Waivers services. For several years, individual states struggled with their unique definitions of Waiver services and funding formulas for how state Wavier funds could be expended to support people with significant disabilities. Today, in many state across the country, Waiver dollars have far surpassed the traditional VR program in providing funding for competitive employment services for people with significant disabilities. This funding stream provides community rehabilitation programs with another source to support the employment of people with disabilities.

Ultimately, SE services vary from state to state and from community to community. This is due in part to the voices of people with disabilities, individual organizational executives, program mangers, ESs, and community leaders who attempt to match the expectations contained in legislation with specific target populations in need of employment supports. It is important to recognize this variability of SE among communities and even within a community from situation to situation. Despite these individual differences, it is important to return to the legislation and focus on the population for whom SE is intended to serve.

Core Values of Supported Employment

Supported employment emphasizes the benefits derived by people with significant disabilities from having opportunities for real, integrated work as a primary option. All parties involved benefit from competitive employment. Such employment provides the person with a disability with a real job,

benefits, and the dignity that arises from gainful employment. The employer gets a good employee and receives specialized support for employee job acquisition and retention. The family is able to see their newly employed family member in a fully competent role in the workplace. Finally, taxpayers spend less money than they would to support the individual in a long-term segregated day program. Several difficulties, however, remain: why do the vast majority of people with intellectual, physical, psychiatric, and sensory disabilities remain in segregated day treatment programs? What values are service providers and advocates following? And what are the indicators that best reflect quality employment outcomes?

The answers to these questions lie partially in the inability of advocates and people with disabilities to adequately marshal their collective efforts to increase work opportunities. Adult service systems using segregated services remain deeply entrenched, as they have for decades. Changing this way of providing services is extremely difficult, particularly in times of reduced funding resulting from a recessionary economy. Hence, there is an overwhelming need to market the positive attributes of SE intended to serve people with significant disabilities. Table 22.1 provides a brief description of nine values that have guided SE efforts since the early 1980s.

These values reflect the themes discussed at the beginning of this chapter that have been increasingly reflected in rehabilitation legislation: presumption of employment, person-centered control, commensurate wages, adequate supports, interdependence, and connecting within the community. These the underlying values should be reflected in a quality employment program for people with significant disabilities. It is only by having a clear vision and an articulated set of core values that individual organizational members are able to consistently make decisions and conduct business in a manner that, over time, stays true to the mission of the organization.

Almost three decades ago, initial published reports began to appear on SE as a means to assist people with significant disabilities become competitively employed. During these past 30 years, we have learned a great deal about what works in SE. Many challenging implementation issues and persistent philosophical differences among practitioners persist, and these serve to create major barriers to the original intent and full implementation of SE. Still, there are clear indicators marking the progress achieved in developing the supports used by many people with significant disabilities to live

Table 22.1 Supported Employment Values

Values	Values Clarification
A firm conviction that:	
Presumption of Employment	Everyone, regardless of the level or the type of disability, has the capability and right to a job.
Competitive Employment	Employment must occur within the local labor market in regular community businesses.
Self Determination and Control	People with disabilities must choose and regulate their own employment supports and services, which will ultimately lead to career satisfaction.
Commensurate Wages & Benefits	People with disabilities should earn wages and benefits equal to those of coworkers performing the same or similar jobs.
Focus on Capacity & Capabilities	People with disabilities should be viewed in terms of their abilities, strengths, and interests rather than their disabilities.
Importance of Relationships	Community relationships both at and away from work lead to mutual respect and acceptance.
Power of Supports	People with disabilities need to determine their personal goals and receive assistance in assembling the supports necessary to achieve their ambitions.
Systems Change	Traditional systems must be changed to support self-determination, which is vital to the integrity of supported employment.
Importance of Community	People need to be connected to the formal and informal networks of a community for acceptance, growth, and development.

and work more fully integrated within their home communities. The positive news is that deinstitutionalization has resulted in a significant decrease in people living in large, state-run congregate settings. Further, large, sheltered workshops have opted to either downsize or close, with selective reallocation of funds targeted from segregated programs to integrated services. Most important, people with disabilities have established themselves as a significant voice via the statutes and advocacy movement in influencing the policies and services that affect their lives.

Another step forward occurred at the turn of the 21st century, when evidence-based research in SE for persons with psychiatric disabilities established a set of practices whereby the individual seeking employment is guided through the career process by an ES and other members of the mental health treatment team. Key among these evidence-based practices was the long-held SE cornerstone belief in a rapid job search. In fact, competitive employment discussions across all disabilities that are focused on needed supports or how to assist people to become self-determined or self-directed have become commonplace. The use of SE, supported education,

and supported living, when intertwined with the philosophical depth of self-determination, effectively marries supports as a programmatic strategy with self-determination as a philosophical foundation that reaches out to all people with significant disabilities.

The use of trained ESs, informed coworkers, mentors, and technology specialists, together with civil rights legislation such as the Americans with Disabilities Act (ADA), have greatly enhanced the employment possibilities for people with significant disabilities. The number of people participating in SE in the United States has dramatically increased. Historically, the vast majority of these people were once confined to adult activity centers, day treatment programs, sheltered workshops, nursing homes, or institutions. A strict continuum-of-care model was in effect that required people to (often very slowly, if at all) move through each stage before being permitted to advance to the next less restrictive level of care. Competitive employment became an unlikely future goal as long as they participated in segregated center-based activities. Fostered by the ADA, the growth of competitive employment outcomes over the past couple of decades through the use of SE has been an important milestone in the movement toward full community integration of people with a disability, both at work and elsewhere in their lives. The ADA was the reason the Supreme Court upheld the Olmstead case (*Olmstead v. L. C.*, 1999; Legal Information Institute, 2002), a major community integration landmark decision.

Federal funding of employment service is critically important to increasing opportunities for achieving competitive employment outcomes by people with significant disability. A significant change occurred in 2001, when the Rehabilitation Services Administration (RSA) of the U.S. Department of Education amended the regulations governing the publicly funded state VR program to redefine the term *employment outcome* to mean *an individual with a disability working in an integrated setting*. For decades, under the VR program, *extended employment* (sometimes referred to as *nonintegrated* or *sheltered employment*) was an approved potential employment outcome for people with disabilities who received VR services. Because extended or sheltered employment utilizes nonintegrated work settings, the redefining of an employment outcome for a VR participant to mean "work in an integrated setting" removes extended or sheltered employment as an approved potential employment outcome for VR service recipients. As noted, another major source of funding for SE is through the Medicaid Waiver program, managed by individual state mental developmental disabilities agencies. Increasingly, states are gaining a strong understanding of how to use their state-based Waiver program to fund competitive employment for people with significant disabilities. In some states, Waiver programs are the major funder of SE services.

Yet, despite these historic changes and the availability of federal and state funds, are people with significant disabilities readily accessing competitive employment? When we examine the current status of day services, treatment, and employment, we must ask, is competitive employment readily available to people with significant disabilities? All too often, the clear answer is no. National reports dramatically demonstrate that, for far too many people with significant disabilities, the dominant work experience continues to be in nonintegrated settings.

So, what has the field learned over the past 30 years about what is needed for people with significant disabilities to live with independence? The demystification of disability is the most significant contribution generated through the evolution of SE and other programs that define themselves in a context of supports. Too often and with too many

people in our society, perceptions related to disability are immediately linked to descriptors such as "handicapped," "dependent," and "less qualified." The power of SE is in its focus on the abilities of people with disabilities to be valued and productive in a competitive employment situation, consistent with the positive psychology focus emphasized throughout this text. Supported employment reduces the impact of disability, even if only during the workday.

For example, consider Roseanne, a woman with a significant physical and intellectual disability. Roseanne has very limited speech and requires some personal assistance services throughout the day. When Roseanne works at a department store placing security scanners on the compact discs in the electronics department, she earns $8.20 an hour, receives health benefits, and participates in the profit sharing plan. With supports at work, Roseanne reduces or neutralizes the effects of her disability label. She is, in fact, a valued employee, and her disability is a nonissue during the workday. In the eyes of her coworkers and manager, Rosanne works her shift, performs her job duties, receives above-average evaluations, and generally is not seen as having a disability because her coworkers and employers depend on her to complete her work assignments. Unfortunately, once Rosanne's work shift ends, she is dependent on and at the mercy of the local transit systems that serves people with physical disabilities. Once she wheels out of the department store, she must again "put on her label" and be dependent. The more the concepts of supports can permeate not only the human service system, but also communities and society as a whole, the more people with disabilities like Rosanne will become infused into the mainstream of community life.

Customized Employment: An Evolutionary Development

As an outgrowth of SE, the U.S. Department of Labor, Office of Disability and Employment Policy (ODEP) introduced *customized employment* (CE) in 2002 using the following definition:

> Customized employment is a means for individualizing the employment relationship between employees and employers in ways that meet the needs of both. It is based on an individualized determination of the strengths, needs, and interests of the person with a disability, and is also designed to meet the specific needs of the employer. It may include employment developed through job carving, self-employment or entrepreneurial initiatives, or

other job development or restructuring strategies that result in job responsibilities being customized and individually negotiated to fit the needs of individuals with a disability. Customized employment assumes the provision of reasonable accommodations and supports necessary for the individual to perform the functions of a job that is individually negotiated and developed. (Federal Register, June 26, 2002, vol. 67. no. 123 pp 43154 -43149)

Like SE, customized employment is based on an individualized determination of the strengths, needs, and interests of the person with a disability, while also meeting the stated needs of the employer. Customized employment attempts to engage the business community, one employer at a time, through informational interviewing and negotiation, ensuring that the needs of both the employer and the job seeker are met through an employment agreement. This approach calls for a departure from the traditional labor market–driven approach to employment and seeks a more personal and customized match to employment.

Earlier adopters of the CE approach have identified some of the defining features of this employment approach. Table 22.2 highlights each strategy, along with a corresponding description. As Table 22.2 shows, one of the real cornerstones of CE is the *discovery process* strategy (Callahan & Condon, 2007). During discovery, the community rehabilitation service provider attempts to get a clear idea of the person seeking employment through interviews, observations, paid work experience, and meetings with family and friends. Over a period of weeks, the *ideal conditions for employment* emerge for the job seeker, and this newly developed vocational profile then guides the entire employment process. Another key strategy in CE is the *informational interviewing process*. Guided by the vocational profile, the community rehabilitation service provider makes a list of possible places of employment where other community members with similar interests and talents work. Then, the service provider contacts appropriate community businesses to explore and tour business sites. Over time, the employer begins to serve as a "career counselor," assisting with information without promise or obligation of employment.

Self-Employment

Self-employment, as defined by customized employment practices, supports people with significant disabilities to start their own businesses. For many, this may seem like uncharted territory, and,

Table 22.2 Features of a Customized Employment Approach

Feature	Description of Feature
Discovery Process	Starting with the individual as the source of information for exploring potential employment options Targeting individualized job goals to negotiate based on the needs, strengths, and interests of the job seeker
Informational Interviewing	Identifying specific job duties or employer expectations that are negotiated with employers
Job Negotiation	Meeting the unique needs of the job seeker and the discrete, emerging needs of the employer Starting with the individual as the source of information for exploring potential employment options
Employment Support	Offering representation, as needed, for job seekers to assist in negotiating with employers
Integration	Occurring in integrated, noncongregate environments in the community or in a business alongside people who do not have disabilities
Self Employment	Creating employment through self-employment and business ownership
Funding and Support	Facilitating and coordinating individual supports and funding options to meet individual employment situations, such as one stop/career centers, vocational rehabilitation (VR), Medicaid, community rehabilitation programs (CRPs), public schools, Social Security (SSA), families, and other community partners (Griffin & Hammis, 2005; Callahan, 2004; Condon & Brown, 2005)

Adapted with permission from Griffin & Hammis, 2005; Callahan, 2004; Condon & Brown, 2005.

until recently, self-employment was viewed as an employment goal only for those people with disabilities who had a business background and/or were thought capable of designing and implementing a business plan. For many people, particularly people with cognitive disabilities, self-employment was not viewed as an attainable goal, usually because of the perception that anyone owning a business must be able to run the company independently. Most business owners without disabilities, however, are "interdependent" on others to assist them in day-to-day operations. For instance, an accountant is hired to maintain the company books or a sales staff is used to market and distribute products. Business owners with disabilities can hire staff to assist with business operations just like any other business owner, as well as obtain other supports necessary for them to be gainfully self-employed. What is vitally important is to identify each individual's strengths and talents, as well as support needs, while assembling a team to facilitate self-employment. Self-employment is all about customized supports. The basics are a business plan, a solid marketing plan, management skills, and capital. Where the entrepreneur can lead the way and where support is needed will vary among persons and situations. Some individuals may need more assistance with start-up activities; others may need support with operations; still others may need ongoing assistance using a variety of workplace supports (Inge, 2007).

Resource Ownership

Resource ownership is another form of CE and involves identifying a resource that a person with a disability can offer to a company. The person purchases and, subsequently, owns the equipment or property and is paid wages by the business that has hired him or her. If the individual moves to another position, the resource still belongs to him or her. Resource ownership can empower a person with a disability and provide an advantage when he or she is negotiating a customized position with an employer. Ultimately, resource ownership might lead to self-employment and an individual eventually owning his or her business (Inge, 2007).

Providing Quality Employment Services

Prior to the turn of the 21st century, the field was occupied with conducting research demonstration projects highlighting the employability of people with significant disabilities. Today, few people would argue that, with the right supports, people

with significant disabilities can and are achieving real competitive employment all across the country. What, then, is standing in the way of success? Are we destined to repeat the mistakes of early implementation efforts of SE with new customized employment efforts? We have already seen that with poor implementation, people with disabilities end up securing employment in stereotypical food-service or janitorial jobs in SE and in vending machine stocking and greeting cards businesses in customized employment. As a field dedicated to improving the employment outcomes of people with disabilities, it is important to determine what type of organization best delivers high-quality employment services. What do these organizations look like? How are services delivered? How are individual workplace support needs best assessed and delivered?

Key to success in providing quality employment services to people with significant disabilities is ensuring that the job seeker is at the center of the process. Decisions from selecting the community rehabilitation service provider and job coach to identifying the type and level of workplace supports must be made by the individual seeking employment support. The following section provides a brief description of core indicators of a high-quality employment support program for people with significant disabilities. These core indicators take into consideration the regulatory meaning of SE and customized employment while providing guidance on how to implement them at the community application level. Table 22.3 contains 10 quality indicators that can serve as effective measures for high-quality community rehabilitation programs.

The 10 indicators presented in Table 22.3 address quality standards for employment programs from a variety of critical perspectives. The first perspective is the point of view of those people with disability who turn to an SE program for support in securing and retaining a job. Do people served by the SE program consistently achieve truly meaningful job outcomes? Who selects these jobs, and do these employment opportunities reflect informed customer choice and control? The indicators must also reflect the employer perspective. Are employers satisfied with the work produced by individuals in SE and the quality of the ongoing support services received from the SE program? The indicators also must be responsive to those agencies funding the SE program. Does the provider have a well-coordinated job retention support system in place, and does the program's management information system accurately track and monitor employment outcomes?

Table 22.3 Quality Indicators for Supported Employment Programs

Quality Indicator	Example Functional Measures for Indicator
Meaningful Competitive Employment in Integrated Work Settings	Employee with a disability is hired, supervised, and paid directly by business where job setting is located; receives wages/benefits commensurate with nondisabled coworkers.
Informed Choice, Control, and Satisfaction	Employee selects own service provider and job coach; selects job and work conditions; is satisfied with job and supports.
Level and Nature of Supports	Program is skilled in identifying workplace support options and developing workplace support options.
Employment of People with Truly Significant Disabilities	Program is serving individuals whose intermittent competitive work history, disability profile, functional capabilities, and other barriers to employment are truly reflective of people who need ongoing workplace supports to retain employment.
Amount of Hours Worked Weekly	Program is achieving employment outcomes at 30 or more hours per week consistently. Individuals receiving support are satisfied with their hours of competitive employment.
Number of Persons from Program Working Regularly	Program currently has a majority of its participants working in competitive employment. Individuals receiving support are satisfied with their program of services.
Well-Coordinated Job Retention System	Program maintains regular contact with its employed customers to monitor job stability and can respond effectively to both planned and unplanned job retention support needs. Program re-places individuals who do not retain employment.
Employment Outcome Monitoring and Tracking System	Program maintains an information system that provides information readily to its customers on employment status, longevity, wages, benefits, hours of employment, and jobs.
Maximizing Integration and Community Participation	Employees with a disability work in jobs where the work environment facilitates physical and social interaction with coworkers. Employees are satisfied with the quality of their work and community integration.
Employer Satisfaction	Program is viewed as an employment service agency rather than a human service provider. Employers are seen as a customer of the service, and the program designs policies and procedures that are responsive to the business community

Finally, the combined set of indicators must serve as a means for self-assessment by the SE program itself to help identify areas of strength that can be used in marketing and areas that need priority attention for improvement.

The 10 quality indicators are derived from the core values of SE and from documented best practices critical to ongoing job success. In measuring the quality of an SE outcome, it is critically important that observable, functional measures be defined. For example, the first indicator, *meaningful competitive employment in integrated work settings*, reflects the core value that SE places on competitive work.

Functionally, the true quality of a competitive employment job opportunity is reflected in the wages and benefits paid to the person with a disability and how he or she is hired, supervised, and paid in relation to the business in which the job is located. The second quality indicator, *informed choice, control, and satisfaction*, is derived from the core value of self-determination and control by the person with a disability. Functionally, control is measured by the relationship and degree of satisfaction of the individual in SE with his or her service provider, job coach, support services, and employment setting. In the discussion that follows, each of the 10 indicators recommended in Table 22.3 is described in terms of its importance as a quality measure for an SE program. The research documenting the best practice content of a number of the indicators is referenced. Probe questions that functionally define the key features of each indicator are also provided.

Meaningful Competitive Employment in Integrated Work Settings

A person in SE works in a competitive job in an integrated work setting. What, in fact, characterizes the true quality of competitive work in an integrated setting? The preamble to the 1997 Vocational Rehabilitation regulatory announcement frames paid employment in integrated settings in the context of the *parity principle* by asking the question "Is the experience of the person with a disability at parity with the experiences of the nondisabled coworker?" (Federal Register, February 11, 1997). The importance of this parity principle is supported by the research of David Mank and his associates on the positive relations of typical employment features and coworker involvement with higher wage and integration outcomes for individuals in SE (Mank, Cioffi, & Yovanoff, 1997, 1999, 2000). Consideration of the parity of experiences between the worker with a disability and the nondisabled coworker leads directly to the following questions as functional indicators of the quality of the paid employment outcome:

- How is the person with a disability hired? Is he or she hired by the business where the work is being performed, or is he or she an employee of an employment services organization?
- How is the person with a disability supervised? Is he or she supervised by an employee of the business where the work is being performed or by an employee of an employment service organization?
- Is the person with a disability paid wages *and* benefits comparable to those of coworkers who are not disabled?
- Does the employee with a disability have the same career advancement opportunities within the worksite as coworkers who are not disabled? Does he or she have equal access to resources at the workplace, such as Employee Assistance Programs?
- Is there full social access to coworkers who are not disabled, and is there an absence of a congregation of persons with disabilities within the work site?

The goal of SE was never to simply find jobs for people with significant disabilities. Rather, the focus of quality SE dictates that services result in meaningful employment outcomes for customers.

A meaningful employment outcome is a job with career possibilities. A worker at a job site who is actually the employee of an outside service provider has limited career opportunities. Most people are not interested in dead-end positions. As with other members of the labor force, people with disabilities are interested in jobs in which they can build their resumes and/or employment positions and potentially grow with a company. Meaningful employment outcomes for individuals in SE are jobs that have full parity with other jobs within the workplace in terms of how people are hired, supervised, and compensated; the opportunities they have to interact with coworkers; and the access they have to job advancement and career opportunities.

Informed Choice and Control

The opportunity to make choices concerning employment, living arrangements, and recreation has been limited or nonexistent for many people with disabilities (Gilson, 1998). It has become increasingly evident that the powerlessness and lack of direction frequently felt by people with disabilities are related to attitudes and practices of service providers, caregivers, funding agencies, and society in general, rather than because of any true limitations resulting from an individual's disability (Brooke, Wehman, Inge, & Parent, 1995; Browder, Wood, Test, Karvonen, & Algozzine, 2001; Wehman, 1981). High-quality SE programs avoid this trap by empowering their customers to make choices and take control of their career paths. A critical factor in assessing the overall quality of an SE program is analyzing the data to determine if the service's customers have choice over the process and are truly in control of their rehabilitation outcomes. Organizations that support choice and control shape their service delivery practices by the wants and needs of their customers. Key features or quality indicators of an SE program would assess informed choice and control by reviewing the following questions to determine the level of involvement by customers:

- Who selected the service provider?
- Who selected the job coach?
- Who accepted the job?
- Does the customer like the job?
- Is the customer satisfied with the service?
- Is the customer able and willing to retain the job?

Customers of SE must be in a position to not only choose their service provider and employment support personnel, but also to have some measure of control over the services they seek. Supported employment customers must be free to participate in SE services by choosing a service provider and ES, by accepting or declining a specific job, or by electing to resign or continue employment with a particular company without fear of reprisal. Informed choice and control must be a key feature of any employment support service assisting people with significant disabilities in their search for employment. Customer choice is a core principle of the Workforce Investment Act (WIA) of 1998 (Public Law 105-202) that established one-stop career centers. Customer choice is also a core principle of the Social Security Administration's Ticket to Work established by the Ticket to Work and Work Incentives Improvement Act of 1999 (TWWIIA; Public Law 106-170).

Level and Nature of Supports

Supported employment is perhaps best characterized as employment with ongoing supports. Key to the career success of people with significant disabilities is the unique arrangements of the necessary supports that will assist each customer of SE in obtaining and maintaining competitive employment (Brooke, Inge, Armstrong, & Wehman, 1997). Detailed job analysis, identification and use of community and workplace supports, systematic instruction, compensatory strategies, orientation training, and workplace accommodations have always been the cornerstones of a well-developed plan of support (Inge, 1997; Parent, Wehman, & Bricout, 2001). The term *natural supports* was first noted in federal policy in the 1992 Rehabilitation Act Amendments (P.L.102-569) that included "natural supports" as a possible source of ongoing (Sec. 7.33.C. vii) and extended services (Sec. 635, 6.C. vii). Yet quality SE service providers must move beyond the language provided in federal policy and attempt to provide the exact type and intensity of support necessary across all aspects of their services. For example, an ES should not provide any more or less support than actually necessary to assist the SE customer in obtaining, learning about, or maintaining employment. Supported employment providers, in consultation with their customers, should always approach a task through the least intrusive approach and only move to a more intrusive level of support if it is the desire of the customer and is needed to achieve the desired outcome. As discussed in, the SE customer must be in control of selecting his or her own supports. The following quality indicators can be used to assess a program's ability to provide the appropriate level and nature of support to achieve the desired employment outcome:

• Do customers assist in selecting the support option?

• Does the program advocate moving from a least intrusive level of support to a more intrusive support option based on customer need?

• Does the program have staff skilled at identifying possible workplace support options?

• Are program staff members skilled at matching support options to the learning style of their customers?

• Does the program have staff skilled at interviewing employers and coworkers to gauge their interest and willingness to provide supports?

• Are staff members sufficiently skilled to predict which support option will result in the greatest level of independence for the customer?

• Does program staff begin thinking about fading supports from the first day employment?

Identifying, selecting, and facilitating supports that promote independence and employment stability is a complex task with multiple factors that must be considered. Working with the SE customer, the ES must be skilled at analyzing data results, along with supervisor and coworkers comments, to determine the exact nature and level of intensity of support that will best match the employment situation. When this process is done correctly, SE customers are assured a high-quality SE service.

Employment of People with Truly Significant Disabilities

The 1986 Amendments to the Rehabilitation Act of 1973 included Title VI-C, which designated SE as a program. However, it was not until the 1992 Reauthorization of the Rehabilitation Act (P.L. 102-569) that the regulations made major changes to the eligibility provisions and included language that clearly stated that the programs were designed for people with the *most* significant disabilities. Supported employment was never intended to serve the typical VR customer. Rather, this service option was created for those people who experience truly significant disabilities and who traditionally were not able to obtain competitive employment through VR services. P.L. 102-569 further describes customers of SE as those individuals who have obtained intermittent employment but have not been successful in maintaining competitive employment and who need long-term support to achieve competitive employment.

Supported employment service providers need to work with potential customers and rehabilitation counselors to ensure that the organization is marketing their service to the appropriate audience (Green & Brooke, 2001). Employment service organizations can analyze this quality indicator by determining who is accessing their services and by reviewing the following questions:

- What are the customers' primary and secondary disabilities?
- What are the customers' functional capabilities?
- What are the customers' prior work or service histories?
- What other characteristics have presented a barrier to employment for the customers?
- How do SE customers compare with those individuals accessing other rehabilitation services?

These indicators should provide a clear and concise picture of the customers who are being served through SE services. The service provider needs to match these results to the federal regulations to determine if they are truly serving people with the most significant disabilities, the group for whom SE services are intended.

Amount of Hours Worked Weekly

The number of hours worked weekly is a critical quality indicator for an SE program, for a number of reasons. First, on an individual customer basis, hours of weekly employment establish the base for a number of meaningful employment outcomes. Lower hour, part-time jobs are usually characterized by lower pay and limited benefits. In comparison, employment of 30 or more hours per week brings better access to higher wages and potential benefits, such as health coverage, vacation and sick leave, and insurance coverage. Higher hours of weekly employment also improve access to work-related training provided through the employer and to social interaction with coworkers. From a program perspective, supporting a high percentage of customers in lower hour jobs creates a variety of possible strains on the program. What are the programs funded responsibilities for helping its customers fill nonwork hours? Many funding agencies require a certain level of program involvement per week; lower hours of employment can create situations in which programs turn to more center-based, segregated services to fill hours. This practice perpetuates center-based services, ties down staff who could be shifted to supporting customers in the community,

and creates confusion among program participants and their families as customers move back and forth between community-integrated work and set-apart, center-based services.

On a customer-to-customer basis, hours worked per week should reflect the preferences and choices of each individual. An individual might choose to work under 30 hours a week because of concerns over maintaining Social Security Disability Benefits, because of work preferences, and/or because of work tolerances reflecting the residual effects of the disability and the supports needed for that person to work. For example, an individual who needs personal assistance services at work might have limited hours of this service available and will therefore work a more limited number of hours. Overall, however, the hours of weekly employment consistently achieved by participants are a valid indicator of the quality of an SE program. Programs can analyze this quality indicator by using data on hours of weekly employment to answer the following questions:

- What is the average hours of weekly competitive employment for program participants?
- What percent of program participants work in competitive employment over 30 hours per week or under 20 hours per week?
- For those participants working competitively under 30 hours per week, how many hours of alternative programming are provided weekly?
- What is the satisfaction level of participants with their hours of weekly competitive employment?

Supported employment programs that have a high percentage of customers working consistently under 30 hours a week (or working sporadic hours from week to week, back and forth above and below 30 hours) are not achieving quality employment outcomes. State funding agencies, such as VR and mental retardation/developmental disabilities (MR/DD) offices, can reward the achievement of employment outcomes of 30 hours or more per week with funding incentives. Vocational rehabilitation counselors should strongly push for employment outcomes of over 30 hours a week and should provide the funding support needed to achieve such outcomes.

Number of People from the Program Working Regularly

Earlier in this chapter, reference was made to the approximate 3:1 ratio of noncompetitive to competitive work outcomes for people served by

MR/DD agencies nationally (Braddock, Hemp, Parish, & Rizzolo, 2002). A high number of people with significant disabilities have very limited access to competitive employment. The negative impact of nonemployment on the lives of people with disabilities is substantial. Participation in noncompetitive work programs by people with a disability severely limits earnings. It restricts personal choices, both in terms of available resources and opportunities. It creates unnecessary dependency and perpetuates the myths and stereotypes related to disability and nonproductivity. Maintaining noncompetitive programs locks down resources within more segregated settings, resources that are needed to provide community-integrated workplace supports.

Identifying the number of people from a program working regularly should not be limited to just those people who are in the SE program. Many SE programs are a component offering of larger agencies who provide multiple services, sometimes including noncompetitive employment services (Wehman, Revell, & Kregel, 1998). The true measure of the quality of SE outcomes achieved by a program is reflected in the percent of people in its overall enrollment who are working regularly in competitive employment. In an enrollment of 100 people, if 75 are involved in noncompetitive activities and 25 are working regularly in competitive employment, this program is stuck at the national 3:1 ratio and fails this quality indicator. However, if this same program establishes a clearly stated conversion goal and begins making steady progress toward having a majority of its participants working in competitive employment, then it is making clearly observable progress. Programs can analyze the quality of their efforts to support their customers in working regularly in competitive employment by using data to answer the following questions:

• What is the average number of program enrollees presently working in competitive employment?
• What percent of program enrollees work regularly in competitive employment?
• For each of the last 3 years, what percent of program enrollees worked regularly in competitive employment?
• What is the satisfaction level of participants with their program of services?

A number of factors influence the services offered by programs that provide SE services. The continuation of noncompetitive employment services can reflect federal-, state-, and community-level funding policies and precedents; pressure from families of people with disabilities to maintain these services; pressure from the boards and administrators to maintain traditional missions and services; and/or lack of confidence by program staff in their ability to support competitive employment outcomes for people with significant disabilities. However, quality SE programs have demonstrated that each of these prohibitive factors can be overcome. The number of people working regularly in competitive employment is truly a critical quality indicator for an SE program.

Well-Coordinated Job Retention System

The provision of ongoing supports as long as needed after employment is the core characteristic of SE that differentiates it from other employment models. There is strong evidence that the maintenance of ongoing supports after employment is a characteristic of successful SE programs that generate better employment outcomes (Bond et al., 2001). Well-coordinated job retention systems provide ongoing individualized supports that assist the employee with a disability in areas such as structuring needed workplace accommodations, monitoring and assessing job stability, adjusting supports to address changing needs both at and away from the job site, and providing other supports that enhance job retention (Ridgway & Rap, 1998). Well-coordinated job retention systems provide replacement assistance in situations of job loss or job enhancement.

Supported employment providers face a substantial challenge in operating a well-coordinated job retention system that extends into the extended services phase of SE services after the time-limited funding from VR ends. Although very few studies have focused on extended services, there is evidence that many SE providers have very limited access to funding for extended services. Extended services funding provided to agencies frequently does not cover the cost of providing these services, and monthly follow-along services are often funded from other program revenues (West, Johnson, Cone, Hernandez, & Revell, 1998). This limited commitment of funding agencies to extended services continues despite the findings from a recent study citing clear evidence that maintaining employment supports well into the job tenure and beyond the limited period of VR funding is often critical to addressing work-related problems. This same study noted the increases in the contact time that occur in extended services during the 3- to 6-month tenure in employment to address non–work-related problems and career advancement interests (West, Wehman, & Revell, 2002). Although funding for job retention services continues to be a problem for SE agencies, it is clear that the most successful SE programs are those that can operate a well-coordinated job retention service.

Programs can analyze the quality of their job retention efforts for customers working in competitive employment by answering the following questions:

• What percent of individuals placed into employment retain their jobs for less than 90 days; for 90–180 days; for more than 180 days?

• What is the replacement rate for those individuals who do not retain employment, and what is the average timespan between job loss and replacement?

• For those individuals placed into employment who do not retain their jobs, what are the specific reasons for separation from employment?

• Does the program maintain a job retention contact schedule with its employed customers that involves regular contact to monitor job stability?

• Is there clearly identifiable extended services funding in place with the program that supports both planned and unplanned responses to retention issues?

Employment Outcome Monitoring and Tracking System

Traditionally, SE programs have developed standards, objectives, and processes in an effort to build and promote quality SE services. Program managers and staff design standards and indicators to assist in gauging the success of their program services. The typical areas assessed include philosophy, mission, administration, fiscal management, image, community resources, personnel, job or career development, job training and support, long-term supports, and employee relations.

With many programs, the primary reason for organizational assessment is to meet an agency's need for SE provider certification. This certification is required to become a local vendor for SE and to qualify for state or local funding. However, most SE organizations recognize the need for assessing quality and are committed to providing excellent services. Yet many SE personnel report that collecting and analyzing data on quality indicators are unrealistic expectations. For this reason, some programs have stopped assessing and collecting the data

necessary for an accurate assessment of the overall quality of their service organization.

Collecting and analyzing data on SE service outcomes does not have to be difficult or time consuming. Without accurate and consistent data, it is impossible to accurately assess the quality of an SE program, particularly in the core quality indicators of serving persons with significant disabilities, achieving meaningful employment outcomes, customer choice and employer satisfaction, and job retention. Programs can analyze the quality of their employment outcome monitoring and tracking system through answering these questions:

• Does the program maintain a longitudinal, data-based information system that contains accurate and up-to-date information for program participants on employment status and longevity, wages, benefits, hours of weekly employment, and types of jobs?

• Is information on employment outcomes for participants reported in a format that makes it readily accessible for review by current and prospective program participants, funding agency representatives, potential employers, and other community partners (i.e., one-stop centers, benefit planners, independent living centers)?

• Does the program regularly track and report on the satisfaction of participants with the services they receive and the employment outcomes they achieve?

Maximizing Integration and Community Participation

Integration and community participation are important outcome measures of quality services. The idea that people with significant disabilities can and should work in regular business environments and participate fully in the life of their communities is the guiding philosophy behind SE. Work is a highly valued activity in American culture, and it offers wage earners numerous benefits. Having a job and paying taxes can enhance an individual's status in the community and offer the employee an opportunity to interact with coworkers and develop a host of relationships at work and in the community.

Multiple factors can be examined when determining if an employee is integrated in the workplace and participating in the community. Analyzing a business site to determine if the company offers an opportunity for integration is important, as is the need to repeat the analysis periodically as the customer becomes more familiar to his or her coworkers. In addition, the employee's work area, work hours, and satisfaction level play an important role in assessing a customer's integration and community participation. A negative answer to any of the following questions could be an indicator that intervention is necessary to improve the overall quality of the employment situation and, consequently, the services of the SE program:

- Does the company offer opportunities for physical and social integration, such as common break areas and company social functions?
- Does the employee's work area facilitate physical and social interactions through close proximity of coworkers, shared responsibilities, unrestricted communication, and the like?
- To what extent is the customer integrated? Does he or she work and socialize with others or in isolation?
- In what activities does the customer engage in the community, such as going out with friends, participating in clubs and groups, and the like?
- Is the customer satisfied with the job and the level of community integration?

Employer Satisfaction

Supported employment service providers must not view themselves as human service providers, but rather as employment service agencies that provide valued and needed services to employers. The language must be business to business; the message must be clear: "Our company will fill your personnel needs!" This approach to business presents the service, as well as the person with a significant disability, in a competent and respectful manner. In addition, it focuses the organization's resources on the business community and is designed to satisfy employment needs (Green & Brooke, 2001).

Job placement personnel with rehabilitation programs are still fairly hidden from the business community. Businesses looking to recruit and hire people with disabilities often can't seem to find rehabilitation programs in their community, nor do they know how to recruit people with disabilities who want to work (Peck & Kirkbride, 2001). It is fair to say that most rehabilitation professionals assisting people with disabilities in obtaining employment do not see themselves as customer representatives with direct responsibility for building ongoing relationships with the business community. Yet the task of customer relationship building should be the primary responsibility for all rehabilitation personnel. Programs can measure the quality of their service

to employers by reviewing the following quality indicators:

- Does the SE program develop business profiles, complete with business culture notations and language specific to the identified business?
- Does the SE program provide staff development education that trains rehabilitation personnel to use business-friendly language?
- Has the SE program established a sense of urgency that is responsive to the business community?
- Does the SE program do community outreach and provide training on disability awareness?
- Does the SE program serve as liaison between the business community and people with disabilities?
- Does the SE program involve the business community in the development of the organization's policy?

These indicators ensure that the community rehabilitation program is developing strong strategies for developing productive business relationships. As well, these are the key areas that businesses consider as roadblocks to productive relationships with rehabilitation programs (Egan, 2001).

Critical Importance of Supported Employment Quality Indicators

The development and evolution of SE over the past 20 years has witnessed a move from an embryonic level of episodic, university-based interventions to increasing numbers of community rehabilitation programs focusing on using workplace and related supports to help people with significant disabilities achieve competitive employment outcomes. In recent years, further expansion has occurred into other countries, which are implementing SE as a means of improving career opportunities and competitive employment for persons with significant challenges.

As positive and exciting as these developments are, as occurs with most innovative programs, there can be and usually is a gradual deterioration of the standards of quality under which the innovation was originally designed. In the case of SE, the speed with which new programs have been implemented (Wehman et al., 1998) has led to increasing levels of unevenness in program quality. Furthermore, and perhaps more disturbing, many community programs are simply adding on to their segregated services a small SE segment that does not have significant impact on many consumers. The use of the quality indicators described in this chapter will increase awareness of what an appropriate framework of excellence should be. These indicators provide benchmarks from which programs, consumers, families, and funding agencies can determine the validity of given employment programs.

It is not unreasonable to have standards of accountability that can answer the question "Is the program doing what it purports to do?" The 10 quality indicators are easily operationalized behaviorally so that those stakeholders who are interested in affirming the validity of a given SE program will have tools to use in assessing the program. Yet the question remains: How do values become translated into real operational quality indicators for programs to guide themselves? What are the benchmarks by which program staff, consumers, and advocates can discern the value of one program over another? These questions take on special merit when one considers, for example, the emergence of the TWWIIA, a program intended to financially empower individuals who receive Social Security Disability Benefits to utilize funding from the Social Security Administration to select their own employment program and pay for needed services and supports. What core indicators of quality competitive employment services can be used by a person with a disability holding a Ticket to Work, a funding agency seeking to positive employment outcomes for the dollars spent on services, or an employment service agency seeking to measure its effectiveness and improve its services? The 10 quality indicators described in this chapter can be utilized in assessing the quality of an SE program.

Research

For many years, people with severe disabilities were served within a continuum model of VR that included day centers, sheltered workshops, and transitional work programs. The premise behind this approach was to teach people with disabilities the skills needed to become "ready to work." However, movement out of these segregated settings into employment in the community rarely took place. Eventually, the system came under criticism and SE developed as a response. Over the years, the SE approach developed from small group models (i.e., enclaves and mobile work crews) to today's individualized approach. Through the years, an SE approach has been used to assist people with severe disabilities gain and maintain "real work for real pay" (Wehman & Kregel, 1985; Wehman, 2013). Although initially conceived as an employment support service for people with intellectual disability, SE

has also been instrumental in assisting people with mental illness (Bond, 2004; Bond et al., 2001b), traumatic brain injury (Wehman, Targett, West, & Kregel, 2005), autism (Howlin, Alcock, & Burkin 2005; Wehman, Smith, & Schall 2009), cerebral palsy, physical disabilities (Inge, 2001), and other disabilities (Wehman, 2013). Today, we know that, with the right type, level, and intensity of support, many people with intellectual disability can and are becoming competitively employed in their communities (Wehman, 2013). What follows is a literature review highlighting some of the ways that individualized SE is used across major disability categories.

Cognitive and Developmental Disabilities

Supported employment was originally conceived as a service for people with severe intellectual and developmental disabilities. There was a boom period in the 1980s and 1990s when SE flourished. At this time, extensive research emerged to prove the efficacy of the individual approach to serving these individuals. Some of the highlights from this literature follow.

Many benefits are gained by people with developmental disabilities working in integrated employment settings. These include higher wages, greater independence and economic self-sufficiency, greater integration with people without developmental disabilities in the workplace and the community, and more opportunities for choice and self-determination, as well as expanded career options and increased job satisfaction (Wehman, 2013).

Wehmeyer (1994) reported that people in SE felt a greater sense of control over their lives than did those within a sheltered setting or unemployed. He also found that reported levels of sense of control and quality of life were significantly lower among people within a sheltered setting than among those in integrated employment.

Griffin, Rosenberg, & Cheyney (1996) noted that individuals (*n* = 200) involved in SE reported higher self-esteem and higher job satisfaction than did individuals in a sheltered employment setting. Gliner and Sample (1996) found that people within a sheltered employment group scored significantly lower on measures of quality of life, environment control, and community integration.

In 1999, Cimera reviewed 21 costs studies and found that, at the individual level, the cost–benefit ratio was almost always positive, regardless of level of disability. Later, Cimera (2007a & 2007b) investigated the cumulative costs for supported versus sheltered employment for people with intellectual disability. Again, SE was shown to be more cost effective. In a newly released study, Cimera (2010) took a comprehensive look at 231,204 supported employees funded by VR throughout the entire United States from 2002 to 2007. One remarkable finding extrapolates to more than $1.5 billion dollars in cost benefits from SE if applied to the total number of the U.S. population with disabilities served in segregated day placements. However, the author notes that SE services must ensure that individuals served are earning decent wages to support themselves.

Since its inception, SE has assisted people with significant intellectual and cognitive disabilities to achieve positive employment outcomes (Wehman et al., 2007; Wehman, 2013). However, challenges persist. For instance, the percentage of individuals in integrated employment supported by state developmental disability agencies declined between 2001 and 2008 (Rusch & Braddock, 2004; Winsor & Butterworth, 2008).

Physical Disability

There is some research related to SE for people with more severe physical disabilities. When serving people with physical disability on the job site, interventions typically focus less on training on specific job tasks and more on adaptations of the work environment, job duties, and support for the employee, and on establishing relationships with the supervisor and coworkers (Inge, 2001). The use of adaptations and support strategies in an SE approach have been well described (Sowers & Powers, 1991; Wood, 1988; Inge & Targett, 2006). Sharpton and West (1991) summarized the approach for ES to use when offering on-the-job support to people with severe physical disabilities: "If a work skill or task can be taught, teach it, if it can't be taught adapt it; if it can't be taught or adapted, support it" (p. 16). Some examples of workplace support strategies that may prove useful are offered in Table 22.4.

Table 22.4 Work Supports for People with Physical Disability

Redesign sequence of task to eliminate problematic steps by determining alternate means to task completion.

Rearrange workspace to maximize access to work materials or change worker position to make work easier to do.

Fabricate or purchase assistive devices or equipment to alleviate problems associated with work-related difficulties (i.e., movement, work speed etc.).

Sensory Disability

There is limited SE research for this category. The concerns of the Deaf-Blind community were perhaps first expressed in the text *Supporting Young Adults Who Are Deaf-Blind in Their Communities* (Everson, Burwell, & Killam, 1995). There, the authors reported that the data on SE programs nationally indicate that people who are deaf-blind and have other multiple impairments are not gaining access to services in proportion to their numbers. Their exclusion appears to be caused by programmatic and personnel barriers in SE.

Emotional or Behavioral Disability

Over the years, SE has been used to assist people with severe mental illness, which should help inform service delivery for young people with emotional and/or behavioral difficulties (EBD). From the research, a number of principles consistently related to better employment outcomes were identified (Becker, Swanson, Bond, & Merrens, 2008; Bond, Becker, Drake, & Vogler, 1997; Bond, Becker et al., 2001; Salyers, Becker, Drake, Torrey, & Wyzik, 2004). Later, this led to the development of evidence-based SE that mirrors the earlier Individual Placement and Support model (Becker et al., 2008, Bond, McHugo, Becker, Rapp, & Whitley, 2008). The seven principles that emerged as indicators of successful programs are noted in Table 22.5.

Autism

Some examples of an SE approach have been described for people with autism spectrum disorders (ASD) in the literature (e.g., Hillier et al., 2007a; Howlin et al., 2005; Nesbitt, 2000, Wehman, Datlow-Smith, & Schall, 2009; Lawer, Brusilovsky, Salzer, & Mandell, 2009; Schaller & Yang, 2005). Additionally, case studies conducted with adults with ASD provide tremendous insight regarding vocational needs (Wehman et al., 2009; Hurlbutt & Chalmers, 2002; Hurlbutt & Chalmers, 2004, Müller et al., 2003).

From this and other research, best practices in supporting people with ASD have emerged. These include (1) assistance with job placement (Schaller & Yang, 2005) and consideration of match (Howlin et al., 2005; Müller et al., 2003); (2) supportive supervisors and coworkers (Bolman, 2008; Hagner & Cooney, 2005; Hillier et al., 2007a; Howlin et al., 2005; Nesbitt, 2000; Müller et al., 2003); (3) providing on-the-job supports (Hillier et al., 2007; Lawer et al., 2009; Smith, Hagner, & Cooney, 2005); (4) making workplace modifications

Table 22.5 Quality Indicators Associated with Best Practices in Supported Employment Specifically for People with Mental Illness

All clients are encouraged to consider employment and are offered supported employment, but the client ultimately determines if and when to participate. Eligibility is not based on factors (i.e., readiness, abstinence, etc.) that have excluded people from employment services.
Supported employment is integrated with mental health treatment. The team usually includes the psychiatrist, caseworker, employment specialist, and other people who relate to the person.
Supported employment is regular employment—real work for real pay. Employment specialists assist people with obtaining competitive employment.
Emphasis is on a rapid job search. Lengthy prevocational assessment, evaluation, training, practice, and preparation do not take place. Together, the employment specialist and the job seeker develop an employment plan that is consistent with his or her work goals, and the plan is revised over time if needed.
Job search efforts are geared to locate or create work that matches the jobseeker's preferences, strengths, experiences, and unique challenges. Job finding, disclosure of mental illness, and job supports follow clients' preferences and choices.
Follow-along supports are ongoing (Bond and Kukla, 2008). The types and amounts of support vary and must be individualized to the unique situation on hand (Bond, Becker, & Drake et al., 2001).
Benefits counseling is used to educate individuals on the effect of earnings on benefits (Bond, 2004).

(Fast, 2004; Hagner & Cooney, 2005; Müller et al., 2003; Nuehring & Sitlington, 2003); (5) enhancing predictability at work (Foley & Staples, 2003; Hagner & Cooney, 2005; Hume & Odom 2007; McClannahan, MacDuff, & Krantz 2002); and (6) providing ongoing long-term support (Hillier et al., 2007a; Howlin et al., 2005; Müller et al., 2003). Notably, these are all essential ingredients in an individualized approach to SE.

Implementation of Supported Employment

Up to this point, the history of supported employment, core values, quality indicators and research has been reviewed. The remainder of the chapter provides an takes a brief look at the components associated with implementing the indivualized approach to supported employment: assessment, job development, job site training and support and job retention.

Job Seeker Assessment and Profile

A critical first step in SE is the development of a job seeker employment profile. Information for the profile is compiled through a variety of interviews, observations, and information-gathering activities, with the aim of capturing a comprehensive representation of the individual, including his or her interests, skills, and desires. This process is not meant to screen people out of services but rather to find out as much as possible about the individual seeking employment. The job seeker profile helps to establish a foundation that will guide job development, job site training, long-term supports, and the career advancement activities that follow. When the job seeker profile directs job development, the goal will not only be employment, but employment that offers the job characteristics and opportunities that best match the person's preferences and lifestyle. A strong job match along multiple factors will likely increase job satisfaction, job retention, and job advancement (Wehman, Inge, Revell, & Brooke, 2007).

Commonly, individuals referred to SE have previously been evaluated for service eligibility by the state VR office. Although informative, a job seeker profile cannot be built on these evaluations and test results alone. The purpose, procedures, instruments, and context of previous evaluations must be considered when using results to form part of the profile. Each employment environment is uniquely different. The closed testing environment, in which many of these evaluations take place, may not reflect the actual needs of a particular job. In contrast, a functional description of a job seeker's abilities and support needs allows an ES to identify and create supports specific to the job. An example functional description would be "can read digital clock, low perception of passage of time, requires prompts to transition to new tasks, and can follow one-step directions with a verbal or picture cue."

Two methods of functional assessment include situational and community assessments. Both assessments require the individual to participate in nonmanufactured environments or tasks. By using real activities and locations, it is possible for the individual to express preferences, skills, and abilities that otherwise would not be possible in a controlled testing environment.

A situational assessment provides a job seeker with the opportunity to perform work tasks in real work environments in the community (Inge, 2007; Wehman, Revell, & Brooke, 2003). Generally, the situational assessment is conducted for a 4-hour period in two or three different types of jobs in the community that are representative of the local labor market. However, the guideline for the length of the assessment depends on the job seeker's desired work-day; if an individual wishes to work full time, then the situational assessment should reflect a full day of work. The businesses chosen as situational assessments site should be dictated by the interests of the job seeker. This includes field of interest, as well as job tasks and job environment. It is also possible that an individual may voice a preference (e.g., working with pets), but retract that preference once exposed to the actual job and tasks. Situational assessments are especially important when working with individuals who have no career preference. These assessments allow the individual to "try out" a variety of job task. The knowledge that they are not obliged to continue with any of the assessments and will have the assistance of an ES, if necessary, may empower some job seekers to step outside of their comfort zone and attempt previously daunting tasks. This is especially important for job seekers who have low self-esteem due to past employment experience.

Whereas situational assessments are structured work assessments, community assessments provide the opportunity to observe the job seeker in his or her preferred environment, whether work related or not (Brooke et al., 1997). Community assessments provide the opportunity for the ES to identify personality traits and preferences that will aid in securing a strong job match. Questions to consider include: how does the job seeker conduct him- or herself in a crowd or react to environmental stimuli such as background noise or climate fluctuations? Is the job seeker gregarious or introspective? Would the job seeker thrive in a people-oriented position, or would such interactions be distracting? These assessments offer the opportunity for ESs to identify similar factors in each environment enjoyed by the individual. Employment opportunities with similar environmental factors will likely encourage higher job satisfaction and retention.

Opportunities to observe an individual are not limited to the strict confines of the situational or community assessment. For example, conversing during travel time or while waiting for transportation often offers a multitude of opportunities to learn about an individual's preferences. Often, the job seeker profile continues to develop through such casual interactions during both the situational assessment phase and the job development phase.

Job satisfaction is often dictated by more than simply pay, and assessments allow an individual to identify and communicate his or her preferred work environment and job tasks. It is also important to understand that an assessment cannot be considered a failure. If a job seeker is not able to complete the tasks assigned to him or her in a situational assessment, it can still be considered a learning experience for both the ES and the job seeker. This is also true of a community assessment. If a location is chosen based on assumed preferences and proves to not be a stimulating environment, it provides more information for the ES when identifying businesses for job development.

Job Development

Career planning via assessment activities provides information that steers job development. After the job seeker with disability has had the opportunity to express his or her job expectations, preferences, and abilities, and the ES has seen first-hand the job seeker's strengths, abilities, and potential support needs (via various assessment activities), job development can begin in earnest.

Job development involves engaging in various activities to help the job seeker gain employment. This requires making the right connection between the job seeker and an employer. Some job-seeking activities may also offer the opportunity for career exploration; new insights about abilities, aspirations, and other factors may be added to the individual's personal vocational goal to further develop the customer profile. In many ways, job development is the natural extension of career planning. Although there is no one best way to develop a job, two recommended strategies and techniques will be highlighted in this section. Some principles to guide these practices are offered in Table 22.6.

Benefits to Business

To develop a job, the ES must not only understand the preferences, abilities, and support needs of the job

Table 22.6 Principles to Guide Job Development

The vast majority of jobs are not advertised, so tap into the hidden job market.

Personal networks and professional contacts should be tapped to develop employer contacts.

The amount of time spent in job development impacts how quickly a person locates a work opportunity.

Finding ways to make ongoing business connections and establishing partnerships with business can enhance effectiveness.

Job development requires understanding an employer's needs. Job development is based on an exchange of knowledge. The employer learns about the job seeker, and the job seeker and employment specialist learn about the workplace. This information can lead to compromise (developing a job).

Job development takes place one person at a time.

The process of breaking jobs down into their key components and reassigning those pieces in more efficient ways and other techniques to negotiate work must be understood.

When negotiating a job description, social inclusion is an important factor to consider.

seeker but must also understand what the individual has to offer to the business. Without this knowledge, the ES will not be able to talk intelligently to employers or exude the confidence needed to move toward the primary goal—a job offer. Therefore, before going out and meeting with businesses, ESs should understand how their services benefit businesses.

Luecking, Fabian, and Tilson (2004) reminded ESs to think of employers as customers and to give them choices. They recommended preparing a menu of options for employers to consider. For instance, one could offer a bigger labor pool to help reduce employment cost or perhaps educational materials or training on disability awareness topics. Even when an employer does not have an immediate work opportunity, ESs have the chance to set the stage for a long-term partnership if they can offer something the business values, such as options to reduce recruitment and staffing costs, create new work structures designed to enhance workplace productivity, enhance a diverse workforce, offer new employee training assistance, and offer education and resources on disability- and employment-related topics. Employment specialists should spend some time thinking about their program's features and what they have to offer prior to

meeting with businesses. Considering the answers to the following questions will help the ES prepare:

- Why should a business want to work with the provider?
- Why should the business employ the job seeker?
- What services does the ES offer?
- How will the business, the community, and society benefit?
- What concerns will the business have, and how will these be addressed?
- What will be used to help convey the message to employers (i.e., brochures, video, job seeker portfolio, tax incentive information, etc.)?

Although the primary goal of job development is to assist the job seeker with gaining work, an opportunity may not be immediately available. In such instances, ESs should consider other things employers have to offer. For example, perhaps they can serve on an advisory committee, provide expertise and insight about their industry, give feedback or advice on marketing materials and ways to approach employers, or allow job seekers to tour the business site. If a position is not readily available, but the employer appears interested in SE, consider developing a situational assessment site at the business location.

Employment specialists should keep in mind that not receiving an immediate work opportunity still leaves the door open for building relationships. If an organization is not interested or is unwilling to hire at the time, then ESs should at least leave the employer with a positive first impression in case they want to reach out to them later. Time may be needed to build rapport and gain the trust necessary to form a working relationship that eventually leads to employment opportunities.

Generating Leads

There are a number of ways to generate leads for employer contacts. Common methods are looking in the Yellow Pages, reading the business section of the newspaper, and driving around to see what businesses exist in an area. When an identified business is contacted using this method, the ES makes a *cold call*. In other words, the ES has had no prior contact with anyone in the targeted business. In job development, as much as possible, the ES should try to avoid making cold calls. One way to achieve this is through networking. The ES can make casual connections, formal connections, business connections, and referred connections when networking.

Networking taps into the hidden job market. To network successfully, ES should broaden his or her business connections. This will also help the ES become known in the business community. The following are examples of a few approaches:

1. Consider joining an organization whose membership is mainly employers (e.g., the Chamber of Commerce).

2. Draw on the job seekers' network. The ES can ask the job seeker and his or her family who they know. While inquiring, the ES should also inquire about places the person and family frequent, such as stores, restaurants, churches, and other places where the job seeker is a customer or member. When contacting people within the job seeker's network, the ES can create new contacts and extend the job seeker's original network. If the job seeker lacks a social network, consider ways to develop one (i.e., take a class, attend a cultural event like a play or lecture, participate in a hobby club, attend church socials, volunteer, go to sports events, etc.).

3. Consider tapping the service organization's network. Who does the organization purchase services or supplies from? What about other employees: where do they shop, or where do their family members work? Who can coworkers connect the ES with?

4. Make regular presentations on an ongoing basis. The presentation should be of interest and value to the audience and not necessarily about the role of ESs unless this is of particular interest to the group.

5. Get media attention. For example, offer to be interviewed on the radio or in local newspapers or other publications. When trying to find ways to broaden business connections, the ES should use any approach that will put him or her closer to employers.

Job Creation

Many people who access SE will not be able to qualify for existing jobs. This may be due to an inability to perform certain functions of the job or for other reasons. In addition, existing jobs may be advertised to the public, which means that the job seeker would be competing with everyone else who is looking for work. To help circumvent such issues, ES focus on tapping into the hidden job market and creating jobs.

Tapping into the hidden job market means contacting employers to learn about their business needs rather than contacting a business because it is known to be hiring (via advertisements or human resource listings). There are many advantages to this approach, including the fact that it opens up the entire business world as a possible contact.

There are a number of ways to go about creating a job. One possible way to do so is described here. The first step is for the ES to ensure that he or she fully understands the job seeker's abilities, needs, and desires. This critical step guides the process. In addition, the ES should develop a brief statement that introduces the job seeker to potential employers. The introduction should include information about the job seeker's positive personality traits, potential work skills, and comments on any life or work experiences. The ES should also be able to describe in simple terms what supports the job seeker might need. As needed this verbal introduction can be accompanied by a fuctional resume or other documents (ie. letters of references from work experiences, pictures of person working in work experience etc . . .) to share with employers.

Next, the ES should brainstorm ideas on businesses to contact, including those with which he or she already has a relationship. Then, contacts are made to arrange an appointment for an informational interview. During this interview, the ES should ask questions to learn more about the business, in the hopes of finding ways to bring value to the business through hiring the job seeker. Questions like how is business going and how do you do what you do should get initial talks with an employer started. As the conversation progresses the ES must be prepared to ask additional follow up questions.. Asking releveant and intelligent questions helps establish the ES credibility. If an employer feels the ES is genuinely interested in his needs and concerns, it may inspire enough confidence to move forward with talks about a specific job seeker or an ongoing relationship with the service provider. It is important to keep in mind that informational interviews provide the opportunity for employers and the ES to build a relationship without the expectation of an imminent job offer, although this technique does often results in an offer of employment (Griffin, Hammis, & Geary, 2007).

During the interview, if all goes well, the ES can ask for a chance to learn even more about a job by interviewing department heads and/or shadowing workers. A tour is another way to get information about a company. Observations and questions about the business may encourage conversations about the possibilities of creating a job. For example, a new job could support a recently created department, a position may be created to reduce the load on employees who are overworked and receiving overtime, or a position could evolve from combining the marginal duties of professional staff to form an entry-level job, thus freeing up existing staff up to attend to their areas of expertise. Sometimes, an opportunity to spend additional time learning about the business may immediately follow the initial appointment; usually, this will take place at a future meeting. The goal of the informational interview is to learn more business operations, various occupations within an organization, and to negotiate a job for the job seeker. When this happens, a job is created.

During this process, the ES needs some systematic way to gather information. A workplace and job analysis can be used for this purpose. To complete an analysis, the ES learns about the specific job tasks or functions for various positions to determine, for example, the general flow or routine and the goal or outcome of the work being performed. Then, for each job duty identified, investigations on how it is currently being accomplished are conducted. For example, what procedures are followed, and what materials and/or types of equipment are used? Work pace and standards of production should also be considered in addition to the types of interactions required with coworkers. For example, is task completion dependent on others? Do coworkers seem friendly and helpful to one another? A very important but often overlooked aspect of this analysis is observing the informal social interactions and relationships at work. What is the management style? What shared social customs, norms, and expectations exist among the workers that define the workplace culture? Is it positive?

Even if an ES has experience and knowledge of various types of occupations, an analysis is still recommended because workplaces and how jobs are performed vary from one business to the next: the only way to learn about the workplace is to spend some time there talking to workers and making observations. This will provide the information necessary to speak to the employer about the possibility of creating a job.

If the ES is able to come up with some ideas for a job, and the employer is amenable to take the matter under consideration, then the job seeker is contacted to discuss the position and find out about his or her interest in pursuing it. To begin, an informal comparison between the job seeker's previously expressed preferences and personal strengths in relation to the proposed job can take place. This comparison will also shed light on workplace supports that the person may require should he or she be hired. If the job seeker is interested, a proposal for hire is presented to the employer. If the job seeker is not interested, the ES should investigate why. Is it a fear of going to work, transportation concerns, or a dislike of certain job duties? This information

should be added to the job seeker's profile and noted when developing jobs in the future.

Job Site Training and Support

A unique design of SE is the use of job site training rather than extensive pre-employment assessment, training, and counseling. The rapid job search and on-site training approach are critical components of successfully implemented SE (Bond et al., 2001). The shortcoming of traditional pre-employment training is that it does not consider potential natural supports and natural cues in the work environment. The process by which an individual is trained to complete a specific task may not be the most appropriate in a given environment, and unlearning those skills may prove difficult. In contrast, an ES creates an instructional program based on the work environment, job tasks, job seeker's support needs, employer's support needs, and the demands of the workplace in order to select the least intrusive method for providing supports (Wehman, 2001). The least intrusive method will refrain from segregating the job seeker and encourage interaction between the job seeker and other staff or customers.

Observation of the work environment and first-hand knowledge of the job tasks allows an ES to create a work-specific job duty analysis. Based on the job duty analysis, an ES can create a task analysis and sequence that specifies the components of each job duty. A task analysis and sequence allows an ES to identify how the tasks should be organized or modified to ensure success. The task analysis should be composed of observable behaviors and can also be used as a means of identifying when the job seeker masters various skills (Inge, Wehman, Revell, & Brooke, 2007). Developing a job and task analysis of each skill serves as the foundation for job site training. Once established, the ES can use the task analysis to determine which skills the individual has mastered and which will require further instruction. Additionally, the job analysis affords the ES the opportunity to analyze the worksite and identify the natural cues and supports that are available to the job seeker.

The use of natural or existing supports and cues in the work environment can determine the job seeker's success. Examples of natural supports include a coworker who acts as a mentor, a supervisor who monitors work performance, and employee training opportunities (Inge, 2007). These resources may not already exist, or the job seeker may not know how to access them; it is often the role of the ES to facilitate these supports and help develop relationships between the jobseeker and his or her coworkers. Employment specialists should be cautious to avoid creating an unnecessary dependence on any coworker. The goal is for the job seeker to integrate as independently as possible, and the use of natural cues can offer the job seeker a higher level of independence in the workplace.

A *natural cue* represents some feature of the work environment, job tasks, or activities that signals an employee what to do next (Inge, 2007). Natural cues are sensory cues that often exist in the work environment and are not added by the ES. Examples include telephone rings, doorbells, and placement of work materials (e.g., mail in an "in" box, dirty dishes on an unoccupied table). An ES should ensure that the job seeker knows how to correctly respond to these natural cues and should provide instruction if necessary. If a cue needs to be highlighted or added to the environment, approval must be granted by the supervisor. This ensures that the supervisor and coworkers are aware of the cue and its purpose. It is also possible that other coworkers will find the added cue useful and adopt its usage as well. Integration and social interaction in the workplace is a factor in job satisfaction, and the use of natural supports and cues means that an individual interacts with his or her coworkers and their work environment. If these natural supports and cues are not tapped, the job seeker may feel isolated and detached.

An individual may require more intensive instruction to complete tasks independently. Adding compensatory strategies to a job site training can enhance a job seeker's ability to learn and perform independently (Inge, 2007). The exact design of the compensatory strategy will be specific to the job seeker and the work environment. As with cues in the workplace, all strategies should be approved and discussed with supervisors and relevant staff. For example, if the job seeker cannot remember the sequence of his or her tasks, the ES might decide to introduce a written list, a video or voice recording, a picture process list, an assignment board, or a flowchart. But the job seeker may not be able to read written steps, and the supervisor may be opposed to the use of visual/audio devices for safety reasons. In this scenario, a posted picture list or flowchart would be least intrusive. This strategy adds the additional step of referencing the chart between tasks, but it also promotes independence and reduces reliance on the ES or coworkers for prompts.

Once job duties are determined, task analysis designed, and natural supports, cues, and compensatory strategies identified, the ES should design a systematic instructional program and *fading plan* with input from the job seeker, supervisor, and coworkers.

The components of an instructional program include (1) training objective, (2) data collection guidelines, (3) prompting procedures, (4) reinforcement procedures, and (5) compensatory strategies (Brooke et al., 1997). The training objectives are those identified in the job duty and task analysis. These objectives should be observable and include the criteria used to evaluate performance. For example, an objective may be for the employee to independently identify the correct sheet for a hotel bed using a color-coded system. Data collection should be systematic and include information on prompts used and job performance. Data collection helps an ES identify if a specific training strategy is working, and it will continue through initial job site training into the long-term supports phase. Prompting procedures should always begin with the least intrusive prompt, such as indirect verbal instruction. The most appropriate prompt may vary for each employee. Collecting data on prompt procedures will assist an ES in identifying if the training strategy is successful. Ideally, an individual should progress from more intrusive prompts to the least intrusive prompt to correct response without any prompts. The inability of a job seeker to move through that continuum may mean that a change in training strategy or a compensatory strategy is required. It is important to understand that task analysis, natural supports, cues, and strategies are not fixed in stone. All are liable to change, depending on the employee and employer needs.

Motivation is unique to each worker. What is reinforcing to one person is not necessarily reinforcing to another. During job site training the best reinforcers are those that naturally occur in the workplace like pay, coworker and supervisor praise. However, sometimes this will not be enough and the ES will need to identify artificial reinforcers to help the new hire learn the job or improve work performance. The ES can learn about reinforcers by talking to the new hire and those who know him best. The important point to remember about adding reinforcement on the job is to build a structure to reduce the need for the reinforcement before the ES fades away from the job site.

Compensatory strategies also should be in place as soon as possible to allow for training consistency. It is important to note that strategies should be systematic and data driven. If the training objectives are not being met by the job seeker, the ES should be flexible about adopting new strategies and adjusting the instructional plan as needed.

Sometimes, in spite of efforts to change the instructional program, modify the workplace, or add assistive technology devices and services, the customer still has difficulty performing a job duty (Inge, 2007). In these instances, the ES may need to negotiate a change in job duties; the ES should be prepared to explain how a change in job duties is beneficial to the employer, as well as to the job seeker. Any changes in responsibilities that require new learning will necessitate the implementation of a new instructional program.

Once the job seeker has learned to perform the necessary skills independently, the ES must ensure that performance to company standards continues under naturally occurring supervision and reinforcement (Inge, 2007). Fading from the workplace will mostly occur naturally as the job seeker masters skills and if the ES has incorporated the supervisor and coworkers into the instructional program design from the first day of employment. Fading as quickly as possible, but systematically, is important to avoid either job seeker or employer reliance on the ES, and the fading plan should be a component of the instructional program design. Once the ES begins to fade from the workplace, it is important to communicate the fading process to both the job seeker and employer and to make it clear that the ES will return to the job site if needed. Similar to the instructional program, the fading program should also be flexible and adjusted to meet the needs of the employer and job seeker. Typically, the ES will fade first during a particular time of day or during tasks when the job seeker demonstrates mastery. Should job performance drop, the ES should adjust fading to compensate for lost productivity and identify additional needed cues or instructional strategies. If all parties are involved in designing the fading program, it is more likely that both the job seeker and employer will take ownership of job-related duties and supervision.

Job site training involves the direct instruction of job duties and related nonvocational skills. The ES's role here is to facilitate the job seeker's successful work performance; be available to support the job seeker, supervisor, and coworkers; and fade systematically from the workplace as quickly as possible. Once the job seeker is capable of independently completing his or her job duties under naturally occurring supervision, the ES moves into the *follow-along phase*, during which the goal is job retention or advancement.

Job Retention

Another unique tenet of SE is the maintenance of consistent service and support over the course of an individual's employment tenure (Revell & Inge,

2007). The continuation of services is vital for job retention and career advancement; the nature and amount of support will vary from person to person and business to business. Factors that influence both the level and type of supports that are ultimately used are related to employment satisfaction, expanding job duties, and career development in a variety of corporate cultures.

Generally, supports fall into one of two categories: employment-specific supports and individual or community supports (Brooke et al., 1997). Employment supports are those supports and/or services that are directly related to the employee's job. These supports may include job task training, service coordination, orientation and mobility, employer and/or coworker support, and job accommodation (including assistive technology). Individual and community supports are supports that are arranged and delivered away from the workplace. They include areas that, if left unresolved, directly or indirectly impact employment stability. Supports in this category include housing and/or personal living situation, leisure, financial support, transportation, and relationships.

When the ES fades from the workplace, it signals that the job seeker has mastered those specific job tasks in that specific work environment; however, the workplace is a dynamic environment, and the needs of the employer and employee are subject to change. Should job tasks change, or if there is a change in management or staff, the ES will need to return to the work environment to support the employee in learning the new job task and/or developing new relationships. In circumstances where management changes, new management supports and relationships may need to be developed. Employment specialists can assist with these transition periods by supporting the employee's disclosing to new management and by reviewing and establishing new supports in the workplace.

To maintain service consistency, it is imperative to maintain regular contact with the both the supported employee and the employer. Establishing a plan for regular communication will allow the ES and the customer to be proactive in their approach to new situations and events. Quality service dictates that the ES works closely with the employer and supported employee to plan for predictable or upcoming changes in the work environment (Brooke et al., 1997). The ES must also monitor the satisfaction level of both the employer and the supported employee. If either party is dissatisfied with work production or job duties, it is likely that problems on the worksite will develop and the quality of the relationship among all parties will degrade.

For most people, a natural consequence of employment is a desire for expanded job responsibilities and a possible change in career goals. Becoming a valued employee is an important goal for supported employees, and expanding their job responsibilities is an excellent way to accomplish this goal. Employment specialists can initiate discussion with the employer or supported employee to identify areas for future development. It is important to remember that the decision to expand job duties is based on the employee's desire and ability to increase his or her work scope and on the company's need or interest to increase work performance. When job expansion occurs, it may require the ES to return to the job site for a period of time. Although natural supports and cues may already be in use, new job responsibilities may require the addition of new supports and cues.

A natural inclination is to assume that long-term supports regarding job retention are limited to the workplace, employer satisfaction, and employee job satisfaction. However, changes to the supported employee's personal situation can also affect job retention. The ES should discuss these factors with the supported employee on a regular basis and be prepared to supply long-term supports there, too, if needed. For example, an employee may need new transportation options should he or she move and no longer have access to previous transportation methods.

Even the most effective job site training cannot guarantee job retention when personal or employment factors change. Long-term supports increase job retention by maintaining communication with the employer and employee that continually assesses work quality and satisfaction. When possible, the ES should be proactive and, as with job site training, be prepared to implement the least intrusive systematic instructional program necessary.

Conclusion

This chapter provided an overview of how an SE approach can be used to assist people with severe disabilities in gaining and maintaining work in their communities. When the values of SE are embraced and best practices are followed by competent ES staff individuals with the most significant support needs will go to work in their communities in real jobs for real pay.

References

Americans with Disabilities Act (ADA) of 1990. PL 101-336, 42 U.S.C. §§ 12101 et seq.

Becker, D., Swanson, S., Bond, G., & Merrens, M. (2008). Evidenced-Based Supported Employment Fidelity Review Scale and Manual. Concord, NH: Dartmouth College, Dartmouth Psychiatric Research Center.

Bolman, W. M. (2008). Brief report: 25-year follow-up of a high-functioning autistic child. Journal of Autism and Developmental Disorders, 38, 181–183.

Bond, G. R. (2004). Supported employment: Evidence for an evidence-based practice. Psychiatric Rehabilitation Journal, 27, 345–359.

Bond, G. R., & Kukla, M. (2008). Service intensity and job tenure in supported employment. In P. Wehman, J. Kregel, & V. Brooke (Eds.), Research in review (pp. 145–155). Richmond, VA: Virginia Commonwealth University.

Bond, G. B., Becker, D. R., Drake, R. E., Rapp, C. A., Meisler, N., Lehman, A. F., Bell, M. D., & Blyler, C. R. (2001). Implementing supported employment as an evidenced-based practice. Psychiatric Services, 52(3), 313–322.

Bond, G. R., Becker, D. R., Drake, R. E., & Vogler, K. M. (1997). A fidelity scale for the Individual Placement and Support model of supported employment. Rehabilitation Counseling Bulletin, 40(4), 265–284.

Bond, G., McHugo, G., Becker, D, Rapp, C. & Whitley, R. (2008). Fidelity of supported employment: Lessons learned from the National Evidence-Based Practice project. Psychiatric Rehabilitation Journal, 31(4), 300–305.

Braddock, D., Hemp, R., Parish, S., & Rizzolo, M. (2002). The state of the states in developmental disabilities: 2002 study summary. Boulder: University of Colorado, Coleman Institute for Cognitive Disabilities and Department of Psychiatry.

Brooke, V., Inge, K. J., Armstrong, A., & Wehman, P. (1997). Supported employment handbook: A customer-driven approach for persons with significant disabilities. Richmond: Virginia Commonwealth University Rehabilitation Research and Training Center on Workplace Supports and Job Retention.

Brooke, V., Wehman, P., Inge, K., & Parent, W. (December, 1995). Toward a customer-driven approach of supported employment. Education and Training in Mental Retardation and Developmental Disabilities, 24, 308–320.

Browder, D., Wood, W., Test, D., Karvonen, M., & Algozzine, B. (2001). Reviewing resources on self-determination: A map for teachers. Remedial and Special Education, 22(4) 233–244.

Callahan, M. (2004). Fact sheet on customized employment. Retrieved from www.t-tap.org.

Callahan, M., & Condon, E. (2007). Discovery: The foundation of job development. In C. Griffin, D. Hammis, & T. Geary (Eds.), The job developer's handbook: Practical tactics for customized employment (pp. 23–33). Baltimore: Paul H. Brookes Publishing Co.

Condon, E., & Brown, K. (2005). It takes a village (or at least several partners) to transition a student from school to work. Missoula, MT: Rural Institute/University of Montana.

Cimera, R. E. (2007a). The cumulative cost-effectiveness of supported and sheltered employees with mental retardation. Research and Practice for Persons with Severe Disabilities, 32(4), 247–252.

Cimera, R. E. (2007b). The cost of supported employment in Wisconsin (FY 2002—FY 2005). Journal of Vocational Rehabilitation, 26(2), 97–104.

Cimera, R. (2010). Supported employment's cost-efficiency to taxpayers: 2002 to 2007, Research and Practice for Persons with Severe Disabilities, 34(2), 13–20.

Cimera, R. E., & Rusch, F. R. (1999). The cost-efficiency of supported employment programs: A review of the literature. *International Review of Research in Mental Retardation, 22,* 175–225.

Developmental Disabilities Act (1984). PL 98-527.

Education for All Handicapped Children Act (1975). PL 94-142, 20 U.S.C. § § 1400 *et seq.*

Egan, K. (2001). Staffing companies opening new doors to people with disabilities. *Journal of Vocational Rehabilitation, 16,* 93–96.

Everson, J. M., Burwell, J., & Killam, S. G. (1995). Working and contributing to one's community: Strategies for including young adults who are deaf-blind. In J. M. Everson (Ed.), *Supporting young adults who are deaf-blind in their communities. A transition planning guide for service providers, families and friends* (pp. 131–158). Baltimore: Paul H. Brookes Publishing Co.

Fast, Y. (2004). *Employment for individuals with Asperger syndrome or nonverbal learning disability: Stories and strategies.* London and Philadelphia: Jessica Kingsley.

Federal Register, (June 26, 2002). 67(123), 43154-43149. 34 CFR 361.

Federal Register (February 11, 1997). 62(28), 6311. 34 CFR 361.

Foley, B. E., & Staples, A. H. (2003). Developing augmentative and alternative communication (AAC) and literacy interventions in a supported employment setting. *Topics in Language Disorders, 23*(4), 325–343.

Gilson, S. F. (1998). Choice and self-advocacy: A consumer's perspective. In P. Wehman & J. Kregel (Eds.), *More than a job: Securing satisfying careers for people with disabilities* (pp. 3-23). Baltimore, MD: Paul H. Brookes.

Gliner, J. A., & Sample, P. (1996). A multimethod approach to evaluate transition into community life. *Evaluation and Program Planning, 19,* 225–233.

Green, H., & Brooke, V. (2001). Greater success through new partnerships: The business connection. In. Wehman, P. (Ed.), *Supported employment in business: Expanding the capacity of workers with disabilities* (pp. 23-34). St. Augustine, FL Training Resource Network.

Griffin, C. C., & Hammis, D. (2005). *The contradictions of leadership: Making customized employment work.* Fact Sheet retrieved from www.t-tap.org

Griffin, C., Hammis, D., & Geary, T. (2007). *The job developer's handbook: Practical tactics for customized employment.* Baltimore, MD: Paul H. Brookes.

Griffin, D. K., Rosenberg, H., & Cheyney, W. A. (1996). Comparison of self-esteem and job satisfaction of adults with mild mental retardation in sheltered workshops and supported employment. *Education and Training in Mental Retardation and Developmental Disabilities, 31*(2), 142–150.

Hagner, D., & Cooney, B. F. (2005). "I do that for everybody": Supervising employees with autism. *Focus on Autism and Other Developmental Disabilities, 20*(2), 91–97.

Hillier, A., Campbell, H., Mastriana, K., Izzo, M., Kool-Tucker, A., Cherry, L., et al. (2007a). Two-year evaluation of a vocational support program for adults on the autism spectrum. *Career Development for Exceptional Individuals, 30*(1), 35–47.

Hillier, A., Fish, T., Cloppert, P., & Beversdorf, D. Q. (2007b). Outcomes of a social and vocational skills support group for adolescents and young adults on the autism spectrum. *Focus on Autism and Other Developmental Disabilities, 22*(2), 107–115.

Howlin, P., Alcock, J., & Burkin, C. (2005). An 8 year follow-up of a specialist supported employment service for high-ability adults with autism or Asperger syndrome. *Autism: The International Journal of Research & Practice, 9*(5), 533–549.

Hume, K., & Odom, S. (2007). Effects of an individual work system on the independent functioning of students with autism. *Journal of Autism and Developmental Disorders, 37,* 1166–1180.

Hurlbutt, K., & Chalmers, L. (2002). Adults with autism speak out: Perceptions of their life experiences. *Focus on Autism and Other Developmental Disabilities, 17*(2), 103–111.

Hurlbutt, K., & Chalmers, L. (2004). Employment and adults with Asperger Syndrome. *Focus on Autism and Other Developmental Disabilities, 19*(4), 215–222.

Inge, K. (1997). Job site training. In V. Brooke, K. Inge, A. Armstrong, & P. Wehman (Eds.), *Supported employment handbook: A customer-driven approach for persons with significant disabilities.* Richmond: Virginia Commonwealth University, Rehabilitation Research and Training Center on Workplace Supports.

Inge, K. (2001). Supported employment for individuals with physical disabilities. In P. Wehman (Ed.), *Supported employment in business: Expanding the capacity of workers with disabilities.* St. Augustine, Florida: Training Resource Network, Inc.

Inge, K. J. (2007). Demystifying customized employment for individuals with significant disabilities. *Journal of Vocational Rehabilitation, 26*(1), 63–66.

Inge, K., & Targett, P. (2006). Assistive technology and job accommodation. In P. Wehman, K. Inge, G. Revell, and V. Brooke (Eds.), *Real work for real pay: Inclusive employment for people with disabilities.* Baltimore: Paul H. Brookes Publishing Co.

Inge, K. J., Wehman, P., Revell, W. G., & Brooke, V. (2007) Supported employment and workplace supports. In P. Wehman, K. Inge, W. G. Revell, & V. Brooke (Eds.), *Real work for real pay* (pp. 139–162). Baltimore, MD: Paul H. Brookes.

Lawer, L., Brusilovskiy, E., Salzer, M. S., & Mandell, D. S. (2009). Use of vocational rehabilitative services among adults with autism. *Journal of Autism and Developmental Disorders, 39,* 487–494.

Legal Information Institute. (2002). *Olmstead v. L. C.* (98–536). Available at http://supct.law.cornell.edu/supct/html/98-536.ZS.html

Luecking, R. G., Fabian, E. S., & Tilson, G. P. (2004). *Working relationships: Creating career opportunities for job seekers with disabilities through employer partnerships.* Baltimore: Paul H. Brookes Publishing Co., Inc.

Mank, D., Cioffi, A., & Yovanoff, P. (1997). An analysis of the typicalness of supported employment jobs, natural supports, and wage and integration outcomes. *Mental Retardation, 35*(3), 185–197.

Mank, D., Cioffi, A., & Yovanoff, P. (1999). Impact of co-worker involvement with supported employees on wage and integration outcomes. *Mental Retardation, 37*(5), 383–394.

Mank, D., Cioffi, A., & Yovanoff, P. (2000). Direct support in supported employment and its relation to job typicalness, coworker involvement, and employment outcomes. *Mental Retardation, 38*(6), 506–516.

McClannahan, L. E., MacDuff, G. S., & Krantz, P. J. (2002). Behavior analysis and intervention for adults with autism. *Behavior Modification, 26*(1), 9–26.

Müller, E., Schuler, A., Burton, B. A., & Yates, G. B. (2003). Meeting the vocational support needs of individuals with

Asperger Syndrome and other autism spectrum disabilities. *Journal of Vocational Rehabilitation, 18*(3), 163–185.

Nesbitt S. (2000). Why and why not? Factors influencing employment for individuals with Asperger syndrome. *Autism, 4*(4), 357–369

Nuehring, M. L., & Sitlington, P. L. (2003). Transition as a vehicle: Moving from high school to an adult vocational service provider. *Journal of Disability Policy Studies, 14*(1), 23–35.

Olmstead v. L. C. (1999).119 Supreme Court 2176.

Parent, W., Wehman, P., & Bricout, J. (2001). Supported employment and natural supports. In. Wehman, P. (Ed.), *Supported employment in business: Expanding the capacity of workers with disabilities* (pp. 93-112). St. Augustine, FL Training Resource Network.

Peck, B., & Kirkbride, L. T. (2001). Why businesses don't employ people with disabilities. *Journal of Vocational Rehabilitation, 16,* 71–75.

Public Law 105-202. (1998). Workforce Investment Act of 1998, 105th Congress, Washington, DC.

Rehabilitation Act Amendments. (1986). PL 99-506, 29 U.S.C. §§ 701 et seq.

Rehabilitation Services Administration. (2001). *Rehabilitation cases in selected work status at closure.* Unpublished report. Washington, DC: Author.

Revell, W. G., & Inge, K. J. (2007). Customized employment: Funding consumer-directed employment outcomes. *Journal of Vocational Rehabilitation, 26*(2), 123–127.

Ridgway, P., & Rap, C. (1998). *The active ingredients in achieving competitive employment for people with psychiatric disabilities: A research synthesis.* Lawrence: University of Kansas, School of Welfare.

Rusch F. R., & Braddock D. (2004). Adult day programs versus supported employment (1988–2002): Spending and service practices of mental retardation and developmental disabilities state agencies. *Research and Practice for Persons with Severe Disabilities, 29*(4), 237–242.

Salyers, M., Becker, D. R., Drake, R. E., Torrey, W. C., & Wyzik, P. (2004). A ten-year follow-up of supported employment. *Psychiatric Services,* 55, 302–308.

Schaller, J., & Yang, N. K. (2005). Competitive employment for people with autism: Correlates of successful closure in competitive and supported employment. *Rehabilitation Counseling Bulletin, 49*(1), 4–16.

Sharpton, W. R., & West, M. (1991). Severe and profound mental retardation. In P. McLaughlin & P. Wehman (Eds.), *Handbook of developmental disabilities: A guide to best practices* (pp. 16–29). Austin, TX: PRO-ED.

Sowers, J., & Powers, L. (1991). *Vocational preparation and employment of students with physical and multiple disabilities.* Baltimore: Paul H. Brookes Publishing Co.

Ticket to Work and Work Incentive Improvement Act (TWWIIA). (1999). PL 106-170, 42 U. S. C. §§ 1305, et seq.

U.S. Commission on Civil Rights. (1983). *Accommodating the spectrum of individuals with disabilities.* Washington, DC: Author.

Wehman, P. (1981). *Competitive employment: New horizons for severely disabled individuals.* Baltimore, MD: Paul H. Brookes.

Wehman, P. (2013). *Life beyond the classroom* (5th ed.). Baltimore, MD: Paul H. Brookes.

Wehman, P., Inge, K. J., Revell, W. G., & Brooke, V. A. (2007). *Real work for real pay: Inclusive employment for people with disabilities.* Baltimore, MD: Paul H. Brookes Publishing Co.

Wehman, P., & Kregel, J. (1985). A supported work approach to competitive employment for individuals with moderate and severe handicaps. *The Journal of the Association for Persons with Severe Handicaps, 10,* 3–11.

Wehman, P., Revell, W. G., & Brooke, V. (2003). Competitive employment: Has it become the "first choice" yet? *Journal of Disability Policy Studies, 14*(3), 163–173.

Wehman, P., Revell, G., & Kregel, J. (1998). Supported employment: A decade of rapid growth and impact. *American Rehabilitation, 24*(1), 31–43.

Wehman, P., Smith, M., & Schall, C. (2009). *Transition from school to adulthood for youth and young adults with autism: Growing up in the real world.* Baltimore: Paul Brookes Publishing Co.

Wehman, P., Targett, P., West, M., & Kregel, J. (2005). Productive work and employment for persons with traumatic brain injury: What have we learned after 20 years? *Journal of Head Trauma Rehabilitation, 20,* 115–127.

Wehmeyer, M. L. (1994). Employment status and perceptions of control of adults with cognitive and developmental disabilities. *Research in Developmental Disabilities, 15*(2), 119–131.

West, M., Johnson, A., Cone, A., Hernandez, A., & Revell, G. (1998). Extended employment support: Analysis of implementation and funding issues. *Education and Training in Mental Retardation and Developmental Disabilities, 33,* 357–366.

West, M., Wehman, P., & Revell, G. (2002). Extended services in supported employment: What are providers doing? Are customers satisfied? In D. Dean, P. Wehman, & J. Kregel (Eds.), *Achievements and challenges in employment services for people with significant disabilities: A longitudinal impact of workplace supports.* Richmond: Virginia Commonwealth University, Rehabilitation Research and Training Center on Workplace Supports.

Winsor, J., & Butterworth, J. (2008). Participation in integrated employment and community-based non work services for individuals supported by state disability agencies. *Intellectual and Developmental Disabilities, 46*(2), 166–168.

Wolfensberger, W. (1977). The normalization principle, and some major implications to architectural-environmental design. In M. J. Bednar (Ed.), *Barrier-free environments* (pp. 135–169). Stroudsburg, PA: Dowden, Hutchinson & Ross.

Wood, W. (1988). Supported employment for persons with physical and disabilities. In P. Wehman & M.S. Moon. *Vocational rehabilitation and supported employment* (pp. 341–363). Baltimore, MD: Paul H. Brookes.

Family Quality of Life

Caya Chiu, Kathleen Kyzar, Nina Zuna, Ann Turnbull, Jean Ann Summers, *and* Vivi Aya Gomez

Abstract

Family quality of life (FQOL) shares a mutual goal with positive psychology in its emphasis on strengths and the enhancement of well-being. This chapter reviews trends in family research related to family quality of life in the disability field and draws parallels with the positive psychology field in terms of a gradual evolution from a negative to a positive orientation. This evolutionary progress is highlighted in terms of reviewing current research (published after 2000) within a FQOL theoretical framework, with a focus on systemic factors, family-unit factors, individual-level factors, family and individual support, and outcomes. Recommendations are provided for future research that will contribute to enhancing FQOL in families who have children with disabilities.

Key Words: family quality of life, family, systemic factors, family-unit factors, individual-member factors, support factors, supports

The purposes of this chapter are to (a) highlight general research trends from family literature on families who have children with disabilities in light of key tenets in the positive psychology field, (b) review and situate selected research within a family quality of life (FQOL) theoretical framework, and (c) provide suggestions for future research to increase the likelihood that such research will be a catalyst for enhancing FQOL.

Trends in Family Research Related to Family Quality of Life

The definition of FQOL as an outcome is as follows: "Family quality of life is a dynamic sense of well-being of the family, collectively and subjectively defined and informed by its members, in which individual and family-level needs interact" (Zuna, Summers, Turnbull, Hu, & Xu, 2010, p. 262). The concept of FQOL for families who have a child with a disability is well rooted in the precepts of positive psychology. Two lines of inquiry that have emerged over the past two decades undergird interest in and

conceptualization of FQOL. The first is an increasing recognition of the capacity for positive adaptation and strengths of families who have children with disabilities. The second is the shift in understanding disability within the context of the person's environment, his or her support needs, and available resources as opposed to describing the characteristics or needs of a person or a family as inherent deficits residing *within* the person or family. We will briefly summarize these two lines of inquiry to set the stage for a more in-depth exploration of the components of the FQOL theory.

Past research examining the impact of disability on families was based on assumptions of negativity, with studies examining stress and depression, divorce, and maladjustment (Bowlby, 1960; Solnit & Stark, 1961; Wolfensberger, 1967). In the decades that followed, researchers began to highlight the positive outcomes experienced by families in having a child with a disability (Summers, Behr, & Turnbull, 1988; A. P. Turnbull, Turbiville, & Turnbull, 2000). Findings that are more recent have prompted researchers to reexamine their assumptions of disability negatively impacting families. For example, researchers conducting studies of siblings have found less conflict, greater warmth, and in general a more positive attitude of typically developing siblings toward their brothers or sisters with a disability (Fisman et al., 1996; Kaminsky & Dewey, 2001; Stoneman, 2005). Similarly, the results from a meta-analysis on impact of disability on marital well-being revealed that the relationship between the birth of a child with a disability and the assumption of inevitable marital strain was not warranted, as the child's disability had only a small effect ($d = 0.21$) on rates of marital strain (Risdal & Singer, 2004). Research that focuses solely on negativity may have implications for family outcomes, too. Some researchers have argued that a focus on negative assumptions and stereotypes may lead to a failure to recognize strengths and to customize services that are appropriate for families, especially those from diverse backgrounds (Harry, Klingner, & Hart, 2005).

Within the same time frame, a specialized field of psychology (i.e., positive psychology) was emerging in which researchers began to focus on positive development, strengths, coping strategies, and health as a basis for building both research and therapeutic approaches (Seligman & Csikszentmihályi, 2000). Within the field of disability, a similar positive emphasis occurred. For example, Antonovsky (1987) coined the term "salutogenesis" to describe the process of focusing on factors contributing to health rather than disease. Studies within the family literature also highlight the shift toward a positive framework to examine disability. For example, Summers and colleagues (1988) reviewed family narratives and empirical studies addressing the positive adaptation and coping strengths of families. Based on their review, they recommended cognitive adaptation theory (Taylor, 1983) as a conceptual framework for a positive orientation to family research. Cognitive adaptation theory hypothesizes that three dimensions of cognitive adaptation mediate adjustment to challenging events: attributing a cause for the event, establishing a sense of mastery or control over the event and over one's life more broadly, and enhancing one's self-esteem. Moreover, A. P. Turnbull and colleagues (1993) edited a book examining cognitive coping theory and research in family studies and the disability field as a way to enhance family strengths and adaptation. Chapters in that book reported on the development of a psychometrically sound measure addressing the three components of cognitive adaptation theory (Behr & Murphy, 1993) and on a family research agenda focusing on the application of cognitive adaptation

theory. Similarly, Scorgie and Sobsey (2000) identified "transformations" or life-changing experiences of parents of children with disabilities. They defined both *personal transformation* and *relational transformation*. Personal transformation often meant that the family members gained new roles—in the family, community, and in their careers—that led to newly acquired traits, such as an ability to speak out and advocate for the child with a disability, or new convictions and faith. Relational transformation for the families referred to changes in the ways parents and family members of children with disabilities related to other people. Parents in the study reported stronger marriages, healthy family outcomes, and acquisition of new friendship networks with other families who had children with disabilities.

Unfortunately, these inquiries into potential positive impacts represent a very small minority of the overall body of literature on families and disability. Helff and Glidden (1998) recommended a positive approach in studying families of children with disabilities. In their analysis of more than 60 research articles in disability research, they concluded that although there has been a shift toward less negativity, there has not been a move toward greater positivity. Almost a decade later, A. P. Turnbull, Summers, Lee, and Kyzar (2007a) found the same lack of inquiry into positive outcomes for families of children with disabilities in their literature review of family outcomes. Their review specifically examined outcomes of family well-being, family functioning, family adaptation, and FQOL. These authors identified only 28 articles that focused on a positive (or at least neutral) family outcome over the decade from 1997 to 2007. The lack of research on potential positive outcomes may be due to a lack of measurement tools available to probe for such outcomes (A. P. Turnbull et al., 2007a). As a result, family and disability researchers have focused on exploring the conceptualization and measurement of more value-neutral outcomes (in lieu of "stress" or "depression") as contrasted to conducting research using positive-oriented outcomes.

The movement toward a focus on the positive, strengths-based potential of family research occurred in parallel to the second emerging trend relevant to positive psychology: the conceptualization and definition of disability as an environmentally relevant construct rather than as an inherent characteristic residing within an individual. This ecological view regards disability as a product of the interaction of the person and the environment, and thus highlights the need for defining disability in terms of the intensities of support required for the individual to experience a meaningful life (Luckasson et al., 1992, 2002; Schalock et al., 2010). This perspective has led to an ecological basis for reconstructing the definition and classification of intellectual disability (Luckasson et al., 1992) and the development of a measurement tool called the Supports Intensity Scale. This tool identifies the level of supports needed for individuals with disabilities to function in their environments (Thompson et al., 2009) and to the development of outcome measures to examine the impact of those supports expressed as individual quality of life (Schalock, 2004; Schalock & Verdugo, 2002). Thus, family and disability researchers who were seeking a more positive orientation to exploring family outcomes adapted the concept of *individual* quality of life to the consideration of *family* quality of life (FQOL).

In the early 2000s, family disability researchers began to focus their attention on the development of FQOL measures. This work originally began with the conceptualization of FQOL via qualitative research (Aznar & Castañón, 2005; Poston et al., 2003). Later, these research teams utilized findings from their qualitative investigations to develop and test FQOL measures (Hoffman, Marquis, Poston, Summers, & Turnbull, 2006; Issacs et al., 2007); we describe these measures later in the chapter.

Having developed measurement tools, the next step in the evolution of the concept of FQOL was the development of a theory explaining variations in FQOL. Consistent with the ecological orientation of quality of life studies in general, an effective theory requires a framework for exploring and explaining the impacts of the various external environmental factors that could influence FQOL as an outcome. Zuna and colleagues (2010) proposed an initial theory of FQOL intended to explain why and how FQOL varies among families of children with disabilities. The FQOL theory (Zuna et al., 2010) identifies a series of concepts, constructs, and variables and proposes a set of propositions that provide simplistic examples of the theory process. It identifies systemic factors including societal values, policies, systems, and programs. The model also includes variables such as demographics (e.g., age, income, and ethnicity) and the internal characteristics of the family (e.g., family cohesion and adaptability) and of individuals (e.g., health, behavior). But its primary purpose is to describe how these constructs and variables might interact with each other to predict FQOL. In this way, the FQOL theory is reflective of the focus on the view of disability as residing primarily within the environment and therefore is an appropriate model to use for the purposes of this chapter.

Figure 23.1 is an overview of FQOL theory from Zuna et al. (2010) and forms the organizational

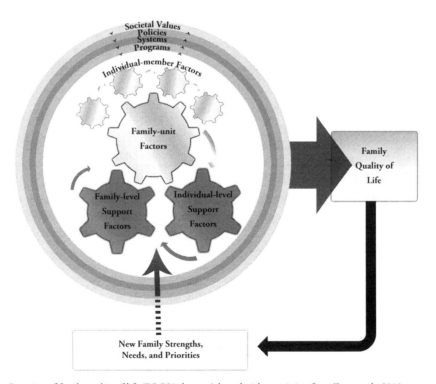

Figure 23.1   Overview of family quality of life (FQOL) theory. Adapted with permission from Zuna et al., 2010.

framework for the remainder of the chapter. Specifically, the theoretical framework posits that

> [Systemic factors] directly impact individual and family-level supports, services, and practices. Individual-member concepts (i.e., demographics, characteristics, and beliefs) and family-unit concepts (i.e., dynamics and characteristics) are direct predictors of FQOL and also interact with individual and family-level supports, services, and practices to predict FQOL. Singly or combined, the model predictors result in a FQOL outcome that produces new family strengths, needs, and priorities which re-enter the model as new input resulting in a continuous feedback loop throughout the life cycle. (Zuna et al., 2010, p. 269)

As explained previously, our intention in this chapter is to review and highlight research aligned with this FQOL theory. As such, the remaining sections of this chapter include (a) a description of the search procedures and criteria for article inclusion; (b) a discussion of the outer circles, or systemic factors influencing FQOL; (c) a description of FQOL outcomes, individual and family-unit factors, and program variables that influence FQOL; and (d) recommendations for how FQOL theory can be used to generate a research agenda that is aligned with the precepts of positive psychology.

Review of Research within Family Quality of Life Theory
Research Review Procedures

We conducted a keyword search in two major databases (i.e., PsycInfo, PubMed) and one search engine (Google Scholar). We used the following inclusion criteria for selecting articles: (a) the terms "family quality of life" or "quality of life" were in the abstract or title, (b) the sample included family members of individuals with disabilities from birth to 21 years, and (c) the article was published after 2000 in a peer-reviewed journal or a book chapter and was written in English.

Systemic Factors

Systemic factors within the FQOL theory include societal values, policies, systems, and programs and represent the macro-environment within which people with disabilities and families live their lives. Recognition of the powerful impact of systemic factors is essential in transforming an understanding of disability from a deficits model residing within a person to a supports model operating within one's environment. Table 23.1 identifies six key literature

sources related to systemic factors and highlights key points related to each. These literature sources comprise articles and chapters that are policy analyses, literature reviews, and/or conceptual reviews, and they have as a common theme the analysis of systemic factors within a FQOL conceptualization. A note of explanation is in order here in terms of literature sources related to systemic factors. Only one of the six literature sources cited met the inclusion criteria stated earlier. We expanded our search criteria to include articles in which "family quality of life" or "quality of life" was in the article but not in the title or abstract.

Societal Values

Regarding societal values, H. R. Turnbull and Stowe (2001) have elucidated three constitutional principles they suggest should drive policies, systems, and programs:

- *Life.* The value placed on human existence in terms of the sanctity or inherent worth of an individual's life and a family's life
- *Liberty.* The value that everyone in society is entitled to specific freedom (e.g., freedom of speech, freedom from unreasonable search and seizure, and freedom to generally pursue life without undo interference from others)
- *Equality.* The value that each individual has the same access, opportunities, and benefits as other citizens, without regard to traits such as disability.

In addition to constitutional principles, H. R. Turnbull and Stowe (2001) also identified three ethical principles that are representative of societal values. These ethical principles include

- *Family as foundation.* The value that families are the core unit of society and are the first, most enduring, and most important entity to which children relate
- *Dignity.* The value of treating others with respect and esteem, even in situations in which there are significant clashes in values and actions
- *Community.* The value of citizens having the right to be part of a greater social whole, with recognition of being a full citizen of society at all levels

Policies

Within the disability field, there is consensus at the policy level on 18 key core concepts of disability policy as an important framework to evaluate

Table 23.1 Systemic factors literature highlights

Author/Year/Type of Article	Key Points
A. P. Turnbull, Brown, & Turnbull, 2004 *Conceptual analysis*	• Sociopolitical trends impacting families include changing demographics reflecting greater diversity, deflated national economy, and devolution of government rights from federal to state-local levels. • Sociopolitical trends within the disability field include stronger emphasis on outcomes, a new paradigm of disability focusing on its social construction, and the consolidation of federal legislation codifying rights for individuals with disabilities and their families. • Family quality of life (FQOL) is consistent with the new paradigm of disability. • A new paradigm analytical framework for enhancing FQOL holds that enhanced FQOL results when core concepts of disability policy shape policy; policy, in turn, shapes services at the federal, state, and local levels (education, human and social services, and healthcare); services are delivered through family–professional partnerships; and the result is enhanced FQOL. • To improve FQOL, there is a need for programmatic research including policy analysis, explanatory research, and program evaluation.
H. R. Turnbull, Beegle, & Stowe, 2001 *Policy analysis*	• The authors extensively reviewed federal statutes and judicial case law, as well as conducted interviews and focus groups with individuals having policy-related expertise (policymakers, administrators, professionals, and families) in order to identify and confirm the core concepts of disability policy. The 18 core concepts include antidiscrimination, individualized and appropriate services, classification, capacity-based services, empowerment/participatory decision-making, service coordination and collaboration, protection from harm, liberty, autonomy, privacy and confidentiality, integration, productivity and contribution, family integrity and unity, family centeredness, cultural responsiveness, accountability, professional and system capacity-building, and prevention and amelioration.
H. R. Turnbull & Stowe, 2001 *Policy analysis*	• The authors identify nine principles to organize the 18 core concepts identified in the previous entry. They organized these nine principles into three larger categories—constitutional, ethical, and administrative. • The three constitutional principles include life, liberty, and equality. • The three ethical principles include dignity, family as foundation, and community. • The administrative principles include capacity, individualization, and accountability.
Turnbull et al., 2004 *Conceptual analysis; literature review*	• This chapter was part of the proceedings of the 2003 national conference entitled "Keeping the Promises: National Goals, State of Knowledge, and Research Agenda for Persons with Intellectual and Developmental Disabilities." It was co-authored by members of the Family Task Group of that national conference. • An overarching policy goal related to family support is as follows: To support the caregiving efforts and enhance the quality of life of all families so that families will remain the core unit of American society. • The overarching policy goal has five associated goals related to family–professional partnerships, community participation, access to services and supports, sufficiency of public and private funding, and access to state-of-art knowledge. • The authors highlight key research aligned with the overarching and associated goals, along with recommendations for future research and knowledge translation to accomplish goals.

(Continued)

Table 23.1 Systemic factors literature highlights (continued)

Author/Year/Type of Article	Key Points
A. P. Turnbull et al., 2007b *Conceptual analysis; literature review*	• Empirically, the authors document a current gap in policy and practice related to family support at the early childhood level through the presentation of data on the decline in the number of families receiving family services, the attainment of family outcomes, and the perceptions of families regarding service adequacy. Data revealed a downward trend in the percentage of families receiving family support and the fact that families reported more satisfaction with child-related supports/services rather than family-related supports and services. • Conceptually, the authors reviewed three sets of recommendations from national organizations and consortia—Early Childhood Outcomes Center, Division of Early Childhood, and National Goals Conference. All three organizations/consortia identified family outcomes, but none was specific about the types of services and supports that should be available to meet the outcomes. • An analysis of four federal statutes revealed a primary focus on individuals with disabilities rather than families as the beneficiary focus, lack of clear requirements for family support, and no accountability provisions for family outcomes.
Wang & Brown, 2009 *Conceptual analysis; literature review*	• The National Goals Conference policy goal of supporting the caregiving effort of families served as the policy basis for the authors describing the work of two international research teams in terms of their conceptualization, measurement, and application of FQOL. • One team, headquartered at the Beach Center on Disability at the University of Kansas, developed the Beach Center Family Quality of Life Scale (included in Table 23.8). • The second team, based in Canada with international colleagues, developed the Family Quality of Life Survey (described in Table 23.8). • Both teams shared the vision of using the quality of life tools as the basis for a family needs assessment in order to identify the specific nature of family support that would be most advantageous in enhancing families' quality of life.

policies, programs, and outcomes (H.R. Turnbull, Beegle, & Stowe, 2001). Although space prevents the inclusion of a definition of all 18 core concepts, definitions for five of the core concepts are included in Table 23.2. Although there is consensus on the identification of these core concepts, this consensus has not led to the enactment of federal policies that adequately advance FQOL outcomes. A. P. Turnbull and colleagues (2007c) reviewed four federal statutes that authorize services to children and youth with disabilities—the Individuals with Disabilities Education Act (IDEA), the Developmental Disabilities Assistance and Bill of Rights Act, the Children's Mental Health Act, and the Maternal and Title V of the Social Security Act –Maternal and Child Health Services Block Grant. Their analysis revealed that these policies primarily focus on outcomes for children and involve families as a means to the achieving child outcomes. Part B of the IDEA is the only individually enforceable piece of legislation with respect to family support. The authors conclude that "with respect to family supports and services,

policy is more aspirational than individually enforceable" (A. P. Turnbull et al., 2007b, p. 201). Policies primarily focus on the expectation that families and professionals should work together in partnership in the delivery of services (the "how" of service delivery) but do not focus on the specific family support that should be programmatically delivered (the "what" of service delivery).

In 2003, more than 200 national experts in the field of developmental disabilities convened to establish national goals for individuals with disabilities and their families; they also proposed a research agenda aligned with those goals (Lakin & Turnbull, 2005). This conference was sponsored by 10 federal agencies and numerous private professional and advocacy organizations, as well as by several universities. Of the 12 Task Groups, one focused specifically on family support. The Family Support Task Group recommended an overarching goal and five associated goals to reflect what U.S. "policy promises" should be to families who have members with disabilities. Table 23.3 highlights these six goals. The overarching policy goal

Table 23.2 Definitions of five of 18 disability core concepts

Core Concept	Definition
Autonomy	Statutes, generally known as "civil rights acts," make it illegal to discriminate against a person with a disability solely by reason of the person's disability. A person with a disability or the person's family has a right to consent, refuse to consent, withdraw consent, or otherwise control or have choice over what happens to him or her. Sometimes the concept of autonomy is expressed as "independence," "self-determination," or "full participation."
Empowerment/participatory decision making	These are the means by which a person or family or a duly appointed surrogate secures what he or she wants from a service provider system; the means is through participation with the system in consenting (see "autonomy") or otherwise participating in the decision-making processes by which the services that will be received are planned, developed, implemented, and evaluated.
Individualized and appropriate services/capacity-based services	These services are specially tailored to meet the needs and preferences of individuals with disabilities and their families. The evaluation of the unique strengths and needs of a person with a disability or the person's family is the basis for capacity-based services. It includes a person- or family-directed evaluation of their resources, priorities, and concerns and their identification of the services necessary to enhance their various capacities. The term reflects the "strengths" perspective and rejects the "pathology" perspective.
Family integrity and unity	Policy presumes in favor of preserving and strengthening the family as the core unit of society. That policy is reflected in services that maintain the family intact, assure responses to all family members, and respond to the family based on its cultural, ethnic, linguistic, or other socioeconomic traits and choices. Related are the concepts of family centeredness and cultural responsiveness.
Service coordination and collaboration	Activities assist individuals with disabilities or their families to access and then to benefit from services from more than one provider system (interagency) or within a single provider system (intra-agency).

Table 23.3 Overarching goal and five associated goals to "Leave No Family Behind" model

- *Overarching goal*: To support the caregiving efforts and enhance the quality of life of all families so that families will remain the core unit of American society.

- *Goal A*: To ensure family–professional partnerships in research, policy making, and the planning and delivery of supports and services so that families will control their own destinies with due regard to the autonomy of adult family members with disabilities to control their own lives.

- *Goal B*: To ensure that families fully participate in communities of their choice through comprehensive, inclusive, neighborhood-based, and culturally responsive supports and services.

- *Goal C*: To ensure that services and supports for all families are available, accessible, appropriate, affordable, and accountable.

- *Goal D:* To ensure that sufficient public and private funding will be available to implement these goals and that all families will participate in directing the use of public funds authorized and appropriated for their benefits.

- *Goal E*: To ensure that families and professionals have full access to state-of-the-art knowledge and best practices and that they will collaborate in using knowledge and practices.

focuses squarely on enhancing FQOL. The five associated goals are all means to the end of families receiving the support required to achieve a positive FQOL outcome. The authors used this policy framework to review more than 30 research studies that align with designated goals and to make recommendations for a policy-relevant future research agenda (Lakin & Turnbull, 2005). This research review pointed out the gap between policy goals and the general body of family research, which tended to focus on inherent limitations of individuals with disabilities as contrasted to research that would move policy ahead with an ecological interpretation of disability.

Systems

A. P. Turnbull, Brown, and Turnbull (2004) proposed an analytical framework strongly aligned to the FQOL systemic factors. Figure 23.2 depicts their analytical framework. The theory of change derived from this analytical framework related to the impact of systemic factors on FQOL outcomes as follows:

• Core concepts of disability policy and overarching generic principles should shape policy (statutes, regulations, and court cases) at federal, state, and local levels and across the three strands of education, social services, and healthcare.

• Policy shapes service delivery structures and processes at the federal, state, and local governmental level and across the three strands of education, human and social services, and healthcare.

• Enhanced FQOL results when policies and services are infused with the core concepts and principles, provide for horizontal implementation (service coordination), and are delivered through partnerships.

• Family quality of life domains or indicators should influence and be integral to core concepts and principles, so that, in turn, the core concepts' and generic principles' impact on policies and services will advance FQOL.

• Accordingly, there should be an unbroken loop in the relationship among core concepts and generic principles, policies, services, and FQOL outcomes. (A. P. Turnbull et al., 2004, p. 68)

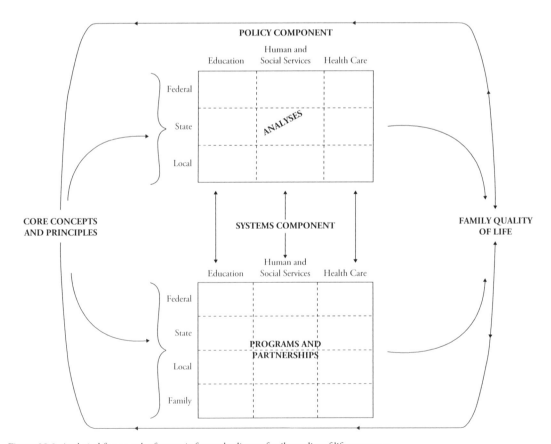

Figure 23.2 Analytical framework of systemic factors leading to family quality of life outcomes.

Programs

Wang and Brown (2009) made recommendations for an FQOL emphasis in the service system of social work and in the programs embedded in that system (this is the one article in this section that met the original search criteria of having "family quality of life" in the title). Their recommendations for the field of social work included using FQOL tools to assess families' overall satisfaction with their family lives, identifying strengths and needs in family domains, recognizing that some families report satisfaction when they still need support, considering both current and future family needs, focusing on the family unit and not solely on a single member, recognizing that there can sometimes be an uneven pattern of satisfaction across FQOL domains, and partnering with families in service delivery and accountability.

SUMMARY

In summary, although research has begun to address the systemic factors of societal values, policy, systems, and programs, significant progress is needed in shaping societal values related to the constitutional principles of life, liberty, and equality, as well as to the ethical principles of families as foundation, dignity, and community. Further, substantial policy, system, and program enhancements are needed to increase the likelihood that the analytical framework represented in Figure 23.1 leads to positive FQOL outcomes.

Family-Unit Factors

Family-unit factors, depicted in Figure 23.2, are descriptions of the family unit or interactions within the family unit as experienced by the members who identify themselves as a family, regardless of their biological or marital relationships. The connection of the family-unit cog to all other cogs also illustrates how family-unit factors (i.e., family characteristics and family dynamics) interact with other variables in the model. Table 23.4 highlights methodology and relevant findings of four key literature sources related to family-unit factors. No studies on family dynamics were found using our search criteria.

Family characteristics embody how the family can be collectively described as a whole. Some examples of family characteristics are family income, size of family, family geographic location, religious preference, and family structure. Among these characteristics, researchers have investigated family income and its impact on FQOL and found a positive correlation. Park, Turnbull, and Turnbull (2002) reviewed

the existing literature on poverty prior to 2000 and found it has a negative impact on health (e.g., medical, dental, and psychological conditions), productivity (e.g., how well the families could participate in desirable daily activities), emotional well-being, family interaction, and physical environment (e.g., housing condition and neighborhood).

This line of research was followed by Wang, Mannan, Poston, Turnbull, and Summers (2004a). In their study, families receiving early childhood services responded to a FQOL survey and demographic survey. Family income was found to be a significantly positive predictor of only mothers' FQOL; that is, mothers in families with higher family income have higher FQOL satisfaction ratings. Family quality of life was also found to correlate highly with the fathers' satisfaction with services, despite not being significant in the path analysis. However, the interaction between family income and severity of disability was not found to be a strong predictor of FQOL for either mothers or fathers. The inconsistency of findings from this study with past literature may be explained by the small and homogeneous sample (e.g., residents from one state in the United States).

Similarly, Hu, Wang, and Fei (2011b) found that families in China with higher family income reported higher FQOL. These authors also found significance related to the relationship of housing conditions and FQOL. Larger living spaces were found to be associated with higher FQOL (as compared to smaller spaces, such as a crowded apartment).

In addition to family income, researchers have also examined spirituality and religion in families of children with disabilities and found families highly valued these activities. Poston and Turnbull (2004) recruited individuals with disabilities, their parents, or siblings from both urban and rural settings to participate in either a focus group or interview. Qualitative responses from this diverse group indicate that families considered spiritual beliefs (i.e., having faith, using prayer, and attributing meaning to disability) important to their emotional well-being and overall FQOL. Families also emphasized that when the religious community accepted their child with disabilities, it positively impacted their participation in religious communities.

Family dynamics can be defined as aspects of interactions and ongoing relationships among two or more family members. For families of individuals with disabilities, family cohesion, communication, or adaptability can also impact family quality of life. We found no studies examining the influence of family dynamics on FQOL outcomes based on the

Table 23.4 Family-unit factors literature highlights

Author (s) /Year/ Type of Article	Relevant Variable within FQOL Theory	Methodology	Relevant Findings
Park, Turnbull, & Turnbull, 2002 *Literature review*	Family characteristics (family income)	• *Publication selection criteria:* Not reported	• Challenge for families of children with disabilities in poverty to achieve high FQOL: • Health: Undernutrition during pregnancy, malnutrition, limited healthcare access. • Productivity: Families in poverty have limited resources to support children's learning and recreational activities. • Physical environment: Poor housing conditions and crowded homes in a undesirable neighborhood environment, with issues such as crime and violence • Emotional well-being: Encompasses positive thinking, stress level, and happiness in family quality of life (FQOL). Families in poverty report more stress and lower self-esteem. Having a child with disabilities adds more stress to their life. • Family interaction: Negative parent–child interaction (less sensitivity and satisfaction in parenting) and sibling interactions (caregiving burden) between typically developing sibling and the sibling with disabilities
Wang et al., 2004b *Quantitative study*	Family characteristics (family income)	• *Measure:* Beach Center FQOL Scale • *Sampling procedures:* Convenience • *Participants:* 130 fathers & 234 mothers of families in early childhood programs	• Statistically, family income is a predictor of FQOL only for mothers. • The interaction effect between family income and severity of disability is not significant. • Mothers with higher income and a child with less severe disability are more likely to report higher FQOL. • Fathers' FQOL scores are not significantly different based on family income.
Poston & Turnbull, 2004 *Qualitative study*	Family characteristics (religious preference)	• *Data source:* Interviews and focus groups • *Sampling procedures:* Convenience • *Participants:* 187 parents and siblings of individuals with a disability; 8 individuals with intellectual and developmental disabilities, families of children without disabilities, service providers and administrators	• Families perceive spirituality well-being and participation in religious communities impact FQOL. The spiritual beliefs, activities, and social supports enable family members to overcome their challenges. • Having spiritual beliefs helps parents to have faith, to use prayer, and to attribute meaning to disability. • The extent to which the religious communities accept the child with disability can impact FQOL, in which families feel supported spiritually and emotionally.
Hu et al., 2011b *Quantitative study*	Family characteristics (family income)	• *Measure:* Translated Beach Center FQOL Scale • *Sampling procedures:* Stratified • *Participants:* 442 families (mostly parents, some grandparents [$n = 15$] and others [$n = 4$]) of individuals with intellectual disabilities across lifespan	• Family income and housing condition are significant predictors FQOL outcomes.

search criteria for this chapter. Nevertheless, research has documented that family dynamics impact family outcomes measured by constructs similar to FQOL (e.g., family well-being, family resilience) (Bayat, 2007; Conger & Conger, 2002). Given the placement of family dynamics in the FQOL theory that we highlight in this chapter (Zuna et al., 2010), future research should test the relationship of family dynamics in relationship to the FQOL construct.

As introduced earlier, Table 23.4 includes a summary of the research literature examining the relationship between family-unit factors and FQOL. Poston and Turnbull (2004) examined the variables that families valued as a positive attribute (e.g., spiritual well-being) or perceived as important to them. The remaining three studies utilized independent variables that researchers targeted for inclusion in the study and that described families (e.g., family income) regardless of families' perceived importance of these variables as positively impacting their FQOL. With the exception of the one literature review (Park et al., 2002), parents were the majority of participants in the three research studies. Of the three studies, two employed the Beach Center FQOL Scale to quantitatively measure FQOL (Hu et al., 2011b; Wang et al., 2004a), and one utilized qualitative measurements (Poston & Turnbull, 2004).

SUMMARY

In summary, family-unit factors (i.e., family characteristics, family dynamics) can impact the members' perceptions toward their FQOL. Family income is the major family characteristic that has been researched to date. Additional family characteristics (e.g., family geographic location, family structure) are important to consider, as is an emphasis on family dynamics (e.g., communication, adaptability), which has not received attention in the FQOL literature. Family-unit factors exhibit bidirectional interaction with the individual-member factors.

Individual-Member Factors

Individual-member factors are illustrated as several smaller cogs above the family-unit cog in Figure 23.1. Each member within the family unit has his or her own demographics, characteristics, and beliefs. Table 23.5 highlights key aspects of six publications related to individual-member factors.

Demographics, such as age, gender, education levels, ethnicity, geographic location, and employment status are basic traits of a family member. Research has revealed a differential relationship

between type of disability and FQOL. For example, R. I. Brown, MacAdam-Crisp, Wang, and Iarocci (2006) compared Canadian families of children with no disabilities (control group), children with autism, and children with Down syndrome. Findings from this study revealed that the control group had significantly higher FQOL scores than either of the two disability groups. Further, the Down syndrome group had higher scores than the autism group. More recently, Jackson, Wegner, and Turnbull (2010) conducted a study that includes families of children with hearing impairment. Families perceived deafness as having greater impact on the emotional well-being domain, followed by parenting, family interaction, health, and finally financial well-being.

Residential arrangement for individuals with a disability is another example of a demographic variable (i.e., where one lives). One research group found that FQOL tends to increase after the out-of-home placement of an adolescent or adult family member with an intellectual disability (Werner, Edwards, & Baum, 2009). Werner and colleagues (2009) interviewed parents and siblings before and after the families arranged for the individuals with disabilities to live in full-time residences. In general, family emotion, experience, and relationships become more positive after the change. Families felt relieved and less exhausted or stressed after the out-of-home placement. Sibling relationships (between siblings with and without disabilities) improved as the member with disability moved out of home. Families' lives also became less restricted as members felt freer to pursue personal goals. However, family members reported guilt and worry about the individuals with disabilities.

As compared to demographics, characteristics are more complex traits within a person, such as severity of disability, behavior of the individual with a disability, parental depression, or sibling health conditions. In one study, fathers and mothers of children with less severe disabilities reported higher FQOL (Wang et al., 2004b). A recent study found that families of individuals with disabilities and behavioral problems negatively affected families' FQOL (R. I. Brown, Gelder, Primrose, & Jokinen, 2011). Researchers interviewed parents of children with diagnoses of both intellectual disability and behavioral challenges in either an individual interview or focus group. Parent participants expressed concerns about behavior problems such as sleep problems, recognition of danger, escaping behaviors, aggression toward self and others, tantrums, and lack of

Table 23.5 Individual-member factor literature highlights

Author (s) /Year/ Type of Article	Relevant Variable within FQOL theory	Methodology	Relevant Findings
R. I. Brown et al., 2006 *Mixed method study*	Individual demographics (type of disability)	• *Measure and data source:* FQOL Survey 2000 and interviews • *Sampling procedures:* Convenience • *Participants:* 69 families with a child with developmental disabilities (i.e., Down syndrome and autism) in Canada. 18 families of children with no disability.	• Satisfaction scores were much greater in the families where no child has a disability, yet the trends across domains are similar. • Families raised concerns over a lack of sufficient support from disability-related services, especially with obtaining respite and gaining opportunities for career development and education among the primary caregivers
Jackson, Wegner, & Turnbull, 2010 *Quantitative study*	Individual demographics (type of disability)	• *Measure:* Beach Center FQOL Scale 2003 • *Sampling procedures:* Convenience • *Participants:* Family members of 207 children (aged 0–6) with hearing impairment	• Families of children with hearing impairment reported being generally satisfied with all areas of family life. • Instead, families noted lower satisfaction in the areas of emotional well-being, time demands, financial well-being, and support for the child who is deaf. Specific items with lower observed satisfaction included having time to pursue individual interests, having support to relieve stress, getting support from local agencies, having support for the child to be included in the community, and having a way to take care of expenses.
Werner, Edwards, & Baum, 2009 *Qualitative study*	Individual characteristics (residential arrangement)	• *Data source:* Semistructured interviews • *Sampling procedures:* Convenience • *Participants:* 16 family members (parents and siblings) of 17 individuals (aged 13–55) with intellectual disabilities	• After placement, most families reported positive emotional changes (from exhaustion to happiness/hopefulness), better family relationship, and enhanced FQOL. • More families expressed worries such as concern over the health and safety of the family member with intellectual disability after placement than before placement, even when the family member had been placed many years ago.
Wang et al., 2004b *Quantitative study*	Individual characteristics (severity of disability)	• *Measure:* Beach Center FQOL Scale • *Sampling procedures:* Convenience • *Participants:* 1,372 participants (individuals with mild, moderate, severe, and profound intellectual disabilities and mental illness across lifespan and their caregivers, including staff and family)	• Severity of disability is a strong predictor of FQOL for both fathers and mothers of individuals with disabilities. • There is no statistically significant interaction between severity of disability and family income for the impact on FQOL.

Study	Variables	Methodology	Key findings
R. I. Brown et al., 2011 *Qualitative study*	Individual characteristics (behavioral problems)	• *Data source:* Semistructured individual interviews and focus groups • *Sampling procedures:* Convenience • *Participants:* 23 parents of children (6–19 years) with multiple diagnoses in out-of-home placement	• Parents and siblings indicate positive changes for the whole family after the out-of-home placement. • The child with a disability and challenging behaviors requires much greater support from services and community if they are to survive and enjoy a good quality of life.
Walton-Moss, Gerson, & Rose, 2005 *Qualitative study*	Individual characteristics (Severity of disability) Individual beliefs (Perspective toward disability)	• *Data source:* Interview • *Sampling procedures:* Convenience • *Participants:* 17 families of an individual with mental illness (i.e., schizophrenia, bipolar disorder, or major depression) • *Data analysis:* Descriptive and qualitative analyses	• Based on their responses, families were categorized into three groups "doing-well," "stable," "hanging on." • "Hanging on" families of individuals with more severe disabilities encountered more behavioral issues and unexpected events that disrupt their daily life. • "Stable" families tend have better coping strategies to minimize impact of the disability. In general, they reported satisfaction of family life. • "Doing well" families reported the least restriction and were the most optimistic among the three groups.

coping strategies. They described those behaviors as having negative impacts on family life (e.g., limited family outings, negative impact on siblings/marital relationship and emotional well-being, property destruction at home).

Finally, beliefs are attributions of meaning, expectations, or understanding of a phenomenon. One example of a belief is how one understands the family member's disability in terms of how it will impact family dynamics. Thus, families' perceptions of disability also influence FQOL outcomes. Walton-Moss, Gerson, and Rose (2005) categorized families of an individual with mental illness into three groups and found family members who reported "doing-well" tended to accept mental illness as part their family life and be more optimistic about the future.

Of the six studies presented in this section, only two (Jackson et al., 2010; Walton-Moss et al., 2005) provided families with the opportunity to reflect on positive and challenging aspects of the impact of disability on their family. Four studies (R. I. Brown et al., 2006; R. I. Brown et al., 2011; Wang et al., 2004b; Werner et al. 2009) utilized variables that described the individual with a disability (e.g., type of disability, severity of disability, child behavior, geographic location of person). In contrast, the Werner et al. study did not take into account the residential preferences of the person with a disability but rather focused on the perspectives of family members about the residential placement of the family member with a disability. This raises an important issue. From whose frame of reference should disability be interpreted? More research is necessary to examine how interests align and compete between and among family members, with an emphasis placed on how to balance the needs of all members.

SUMMARY

In summary, recent research shows that a specific family member's disability type/living location (demographic), disability severity/problem behaviors (characteristics), and how family members view disability (beliefs) can interact with family-unit factors and impact FQOL. Research has largely focused in this area, given the history of approaching disability as deficits within the individual. Two of the most frequently researched individual-member factors are type of disability and presence of behavior problems. We did not locate any research that focused on positive characteristics or empowering beliefs of individuals in terms of their connection to FQOL outcomes.

Family-Level and Individual-Level Support Factors

As discussed earlier in this chapter, FQOL is grounded in the assumption that disability is a natural part of the human experience by situating disability within a holistic and positive perspective of family functioning and well-being. Similarly, the support paradigm is in the process of gradually shifting the field from a focus on a *deficits* model residing within a person or family to a supports model assessing and providing *supports* within the person's or family's environment (Luckasson et al., 1992; Schalock et al., 2010; Thompson et al., 2009). Within-the-person variables cannot be changed easily by the service system or other agents included in a family's support network; on the contrary, *support* can be influenced by leveraging funding and implementing programs on behalf of families. Thus, a critical question is: What individual and family support is significantly related to FQOL? In this section, we discuss (a) the nature of support and (b) key points from conceptual papers and research studies highlighting the relationship of support to FQOL.

Nature of Supports

The concept of support has no consistent definition within the disability field. As we indicated at the beginning of the chapter, the term "supports" is defined as "resources and strategies that aim to promote the development, education, interests, and personal well-being of a person and that enhance individual functioning" (Schalock et al., 2010, p. 109). The focus here is clearly on the individual with a disability and does not mention the family. Alternatively, another concept is family support, defined most recently as follows:

> Family Support is defined as a set of strategies directed to the family unit but that ultimately benefit the individual with ID/DD [intellectual disability/developmental disability]. Family Support strategies are intended to assist family members, who have a key role in the provision of support and guidance to their family member with ID/DD. These strategies are designed, implemented and funded in a flexible manner that addresses the emotional, physical, and material well-being of the entire family. (National Agenda on Family Support Summit, 2011)

This definition focuses largely on the support to family members who, in turn, provide assistance to the individual with a disability. A coherent conceptualization across the levels of individual and family support is paramount.

Kyzar, Turnbull, Summers, and Aya (2012) reviewed two decades of family research (1990–2010) documenting the relationship of family support to family outcomes for families of children with moderate to severe disabilities. Findings showed that instruments used to measure family support focused on the support source (e.g., friends, neighbors, professionals) and the type of support. Kyzar and colleagues utilized support typologies put forth by the National Agenda on Family Support (2011) and McWilliam and Scott (2001) as the framework for analyzing support typologies assessed in the research literature. Findings showed that emotional, physical, material/instrumental, and informational typologies were assessed across the studies. Table 23.6 lists definitions emerging from the analysis for each support type.

Some authors discuss *support* as "informal" resources (i.e., assistance from friends or other unpaid sources) (Correa, Bonilla, & Reyes-MacPherson, 2011; Zuna et al., 2010) and *services* as "formal" resources. For the purposes of this chapter, we conceptualize formal *and* informal resources not as "services and supports" but rather as only support. Our reason for not including the term "services" is that families and individuals with disabilities receive support (i.e., emotional, physical, material/instrumental, informational) from a variety of sources, which may include professional services but also include support received from friends, extended and immediate family members, and others. Therefore, the distinction between services and supports (formal or informal) is blurred; services are a *source* of support but the construct is *support*. In the following section, we review articles that met our inclusion criteria for this review. In this review, we refer to "services and supports" only in cases where the authors made this distinction to retain integrity in report of the findings.

FAMILY AND INDIVIDUAL SUPPORTS TO FAMILY QUALITY OF LIFE

Table 23.7 includes a summary of the papers focusing on family and individual support factors. We report the type of articles (quantitative, conceptual, or literature review), variables relevant to FQOL theory (both individual- and family-level support, family support, and individual support), and support typologies examined (emotional, physical, material/instrumental, or informational). A total of 11 articles met the review criteria. Two main themes emerged from the articles: conceptual papers promoting FQOL as an outcome of support or research studies examining the relationship of support to FQOL. Six papers were research studies. Five papers examined both individual and family support; an additional four articles focused on family support only; two studies examined individual support only. The papers addressed informational, material/instrumental, and emotional support. We found no articles examining the impact of physical support on FQOL. Three papers used the general term "services" to refer to support, and one study used the term "service providers." Due to the small number of research articles that resulted from our literature searches relating to this component of the theory (i.e., six) and the high overlap in papers examining the relationship of both family and individual support to FQOL (i.e., five), we report family and individual support factors in the same section of this chapter. (Alternatively, according to the FQOL theory, family support factors and individual support factors are represented in two separate cogs.) Because of space limitations on the table, we did not include findings of the articles; therefore, the remainder of this section includes a report of key findings.

Table 23.6 Definitions for support types

Type of Support	Definition
Emotional support	Assistance related to improving psychosocial functioning in terms of reducing stress and improving a positive orientation of feelings
Physical support	Assistance related to improving physical health (e.g., health checks, nutrition) or daily living skills of the family member with a disability (e.g., helping child with toileting, eating, moving around his environment)
Material/ instrumental support	Assistance related to improving access to adequate financial resources and the completion of necessary tasks (e.g., transportation to doctor's appointments, child care enabling the parents to work, assistance with housework so the family can spend time together)
Informational support	Assistance related to improving knowledge from verbal or written materials presented either online, through print, or on video that leads to improved decision making

Table 23.7 Family and individual support factors literature highlights

Author (s) /Year/ Type of Article	Relevant Variable within family quality of life (FQOL) theory	Methodology	Support Typology
Papers Promoting FQOL as an Outcome of Supports			
Dunst & Bruder, 2002 *Quantitative study*	Individual and family supports	• *Research Design:* Survey research • *Measure:* Questionnaire • *Participants:* 879 early-intervention program practitioners and parents of children with disabilities	Service coordination, early intervention, and natural environments
Kober & Eggleton, 2009 *Conceptual paper*	Individual supports	n/a	Outcomes achieved by service providers
Summers et al., 2005 *Conceptual paper*	Individual and family supports	n/a	Services
H. R. Turnbull et al., 2003 *Conceptual paper*	Individual and family supports	n/a	Individualized Family Service Plans and Individualized Education Plans
Research Examining the Relationship of Support to FQOL			
Feldman & Werner, 2002 *Quantitative study/ experimental*	Family supports	• *Measure:* Family Quality of Life Questionnaire • *Research design:* Experimental; random assignment to treatment and control group • *Participants:* 34 mothers, one father, and one grandmother	Informational (i.e., parent training), Material/Instrumental (e.g., behavioral treatment plans)
Schippers & van Boheemen, 2009 *Qualitative study*	Individual supports	• *Data source:* Case study • *Sampling procedures:* Convenience • *Participants:* Nine young adults (18–23 years) with intellectual disabilities	Material/Instrumental, informational
Summers et al., 2007 *Quantitative study*	Individual and family supports	• *Measure:* Beach Center FQOL Scale • *Sampling procedures:* Convenience • *Participants:* 180 families (176 mothers) of children (aged 0–5) receive early childhood services in a Midwestern State	Perceptions of early childhood services

Study	Support type	Details	Support categories
Soresi et al., 2007 *Quantitative study/ experimental*	Family support (parent training)	• *Measure:* Questionnaire, My Life as a Parent • *Research design:* Experimental; random assignment to treatment and control group • *Participants:* 32 parents of children with a disability (16 mothers and 16 fathers)	Emotional, material/instrumental, informational
Abedi & Vostanis, 2010 *Quantitative study/ experimental*	Family support (quality of life therapy)	• *Measure:* Quality of Life Inventory • *Research design:* Experimental; random assignment to treatment and control group • *Participants:* 49 mothers of children with obsessive-compulsive disorder	Emotional, material/instrumental, informational
Friend et al., 2009 *Literature review*	Family support	• *Publication selection criteria:* Included intervention studies in the field of early intervention (birth to 3 services) or early childhood focusing on families of children with disabilities or families of children who were at-risk for disability published between 1995 and 2005. Search terms included variations of family outcomes or parent training terms (see article for a full list of key terms) and names of leading researchers • *Study sample size:* 26	Emotional, material/instrumental, informational
Saito & Turnbull, 2007 *Literature review*	Individual support	• *Publication selection criteria:* Included quantitative or qualitative studies, published between 1985 and 2005, study focus was on families' perspectives about AAC practices, sample mostly included AAC users (children) who were younger than 21 years. Search terms included variations of "augmentative and alternative communication," "assistive technology," and "parent/family." • *Study sample size:* 13	Material/instrumental

Of the papers promoting FQOL as an outcome of supports, Dunst and Bruder (2002) was the only research report; in this study, families and service providers rated FQOL as an important outcome for service coordination, receiving services in natural environments, and early intervention services. The remaining papers (Kober & Eggleton, 2009; Summers et al., 2005; H. R. Turnbull, Turnbull, Wehmeyer, & Park, 2003) were conceptual in nature. These papers cited the need to hold systems and programs (systemic factors) responsible not only to the child, but also to the family. On the whole, authors argued that FQOL is favorable to other family outcomes as a measure of assessing the benefits of support to families because it is multidimensional; this is appropriate for the context of disability, which affects multiple aspects of family life, and provides for a positive frame for understanding disability within the context of family life.

We report the findings of the research examining the relationship of support to FQOL according to research design: three papers were experimental in nature, with random assignment to treatment and control groups; one utilized qualitative methods; one reported descriptive data; and two were literature reviews. The three experimental studies showed positive effects of support on FQOL. The support provided included parent training focused on behavioral interventions (Feldman & Werner, 2002), parent training focused on increasing coping and problem solving strategies (Soresi, Nota, & Ferrari, 2007), and a quality of life therapy promoting family strengths (Abedi & Vostanis, 2010). Feldman and Werner (2002) reported that the treatment group demonstrated significantly less "family life disruptions" than did the control group (p. 81). Soresi, Nota, and Ferrari (2007) found that those parents who participated in the intervention reported improved "knowledge, use of appropriate educational principles, increased levels of well-being, and ultimately satisfaction" (p. 250). Finally, the quality of life therapy implemented by Abedi and Vostanis (2010) resulted in significantly increased quality of life scores as compared to the control group. The study utilizing qualitative methods (Schippers & van Boheemen, 2009) was a case study exploring the effects of community participation and partnerships on FQOL. The researchers utilized a paid "intermediary," or a professional who provided "personal support consistent with family needs" (p. 21) as the agent promoting community participation and partnerships. The main findings of this study were that an intermediary was crucial in both individual and family quality of life, particularly in achieving community and social inclusion. The purpose of the one descriptive study included in the review (Summers et al., 2007) was to examine the relationship of families' perceptions of the adequacy of early childhood services to FQOL. Additionally, these authors explored family–professional partnerships as a mediator of the relationship between service adequacy and FQOL. In this study, families' perceptions of services were significantly related to FQOL, and partnerships partially mediated the effects of service adequacy on FQOL. Finally, two papers reported literature reviews related to the association of family support to FQOL. Saito and Turnbull (2007) reviewed research examining families' perceptions of augmentative and alternative communication (AAC) use for their child. Findings indicated that "AAC practices encompass multiple FQOL domains including family interaction, parenting, physical/material well-being, disability-related services, and emotional well-being" (p. 62). Friend, Summers, and Turnbull (2009) reviewed intervention literature in early childhood research to determine trends in family support and the associated FQOL domains. Articles included in their review evaluated parent training programs, general family-centered practice models offering comprehensive systems of supports, peer support, two-generation programs (i.e., programs focused on both the child with a disability and the family), and respite care.

SUMMARY

The papers included in this review varied in terms of their focus; however, they could be characterized as either promoting FQOL as an outcome of support or researching the relationship of support to FQOL. The fact that we found only six studies reporting FQOL in original research points to the need for more research, as the impact of support on FQOL is a major consideration in improving outcomes for families, as depicted in the FQOL theory. Clearly, more research is needed.

Family Quality of Life Outcome

We turn now to a discussion of FQOL as an outcome, as shown in Figure 23.1. The majority of empirical studies published in the past 10 years centered on conceptualization, development, and validation of FQOL outcome measures. These measures result in a de facto definition of FQOL as consisting of families' perception about aspects or domains of FQOL, such as physical and material well-being, family interaction and relationships, emotional well-being, parenting, influence of values, community interaction, and leisure and recreation. Although leaders in the individual and FQOL fields have recommended that quality of life measures be used to evaluate program practices and supports (Kober & Eggleton, 2009; Verdugo & Schalock, 2009), the use of these measures has primarily been restricted to research studies rather than to program accountability.

MEASURES

Hu, Summers, and Turnbull (2011a) analyzed quantitative instruments published in peer-reviewed journal during 1980–2009 that contains keywords of *family quality of life*, *quality of family life*, *family satisfaction and disab** and *family well-being and disab** via 25 databases; they found five disability-related instruments developed to measure family outcomes. Among the five instruments, we highlight two measures used for measuring FQOL outcomes in eight of the 12 quantitative/mixed method studies included in their review. The first instrument, the Family Quality of Life Survey-2006 (hereafter referred to as the FQOL Survey) (I. Brown et al., 2006) has both quantitative and qualitative components. Since initiation of the International Family Quality of Life Project in 1997, the FQOL Survey has been translated into 16 languages and used in 20 countries. Second, the Beach Center Family Quality of Life Scale (hereafter referred to as the Beach Center FQOL Scale) (Hoffman et al., 2006) is a quantitative scale that includes a factor structure of five domains. It has been used in diverse geographical areas of the United States and three other countries (Balcells-Balcells, Giné, Guàrdia-Olmos, & Summers, 2011; Bekir, 2011; Hu et al., 2011b). Although the two surveys differ in length, completion time, and design, both tools have the ultimate purpose of improving FQOL and have been used primarily with families whose members have developmental disabilities. We identified similarities in development process of the two instruments as follow:

- *Items and domains generation.* The instruments were grounded in quality of life literature and discussions with stakeholders (i.e., families, service organizations, and researchers) from diverse cultural backgrounds. After the research teams developed and organized items based on the discussion, stakeholders participating in Participatory Action Research committees, focus groups, and/or individual interviews reviewed and provided feedback for the initial version (Issacs et al., 2007; Poston et al., 2003).

- *Instrument revision.* Researchers collected quantitative and qualitative data through field tests to evaluate psychometrics and to revise instruments. Results from the pilot study of FQOL Survey during 2000–2004 in Australia, Canada, Israel, South Korea, and Taiwan were used to revise the survey (I. Brown et al., 2006). The Beach Center FQOL Scale was field tested in multiple states in the United States (Hoffman et al., 2006; Park et al., 2003).

- *Use in diverse cultures.* Researchers used translation/back-translation methods to ensure the accuracy of the translated instrument. Verdugo, Cordoba, and Gomez (2005) interviewed respondents to test the content validity and structure. Results from confirmatory factor analysis conducted by researchers in Spain, China, and Nigeria indicated the translated instruments can be used in various countries with high validity (Balcells-Balcells et al., 2011; Hu et al., 2011b; Isaacs et al., 2011).

We summarize the description and scale structure of the two measures in Table 23.8 (Issacs et al., 2011; Mannan, Summers, Turnbull, & Poston, 2006; Rillotta, Kirby, & Shearer, 2010; Zuna, Selig, Summers, & Turnbull, 2009).

THEMES OF OUTCOME DATA

Table 23.9 highlights six recent publications that examine FQOL outcomes; the countries represented across these six studies include the United States, Canada, Australia, South Korea, Taiwan, Spain, Slovenia, China, and Belgium. In this section, we provide a brief description of the key study characteristics and provide an overview of the themes extracted from our review.

Participants in these studies were mostly parents, predominantly mothers; this continues to be a concern in family study research because the perspectives of all family members are not obtained. However, Wang et al. (2006) found that no differences existed in FQOL ratings across mothers and fathers. Less is known about differences in FQOL ratings among other family members (e.g., siblings, grandparents). The children included in these six studies had various disabilities (e.g., intellectual disabilities, autism, and Down syndrome).

Findings from the selected studies revealed themes on four topics: culture, material well-being, emotional well-being, and family-centered support. With respect to culture, a need exists to examine further the impact of culture on the relationship

Table 23.8 Information of Family Quality of Life (FQOL) Survey-2006 and Beach Center FQOL Scale

Instrument	Description	Scale Structure
FQOL Survey-2006 (I. Brown et al., 2006) Available at: http://www.surreyplace.on.ca/Education-and-Research/research-and-evaluation/Pages/International-Family-Quality-of-LifeProject.aspx	*Purpose:* • To measure FQOL of families with one or more members with ID/DD • To understand the needs and state of FQOL *Length:* • 39 pages *Time for completion (self-administration):* • 45 min *Reliability:* • Standardized item scores Cronbach's α = 0.53 to 0.85 (three countries) • Nine domains Cronbach's α = 0.75 *Validity:* • Nigeria (4 factors): χ^2 (27) = 69.34, p <.001, CFI = 0.85, RMSEA = 0.11 • Three-country (Australia, Canada, and the U.S.): χ^2 (27) = 55.328, p <.001, CFI = 0.93, RMSEA = 0.06	*Sections (3):* • Demographics information • Nine areas of family life in six dimensions, • Overall impressions of family quality of life. *Domains (9):* • Health, Finances, Family Relationships, Support from Other People, Support from Disability-Related Services, Influence of Values, Careers and Planning for Careers, Leisure and Recreation, and Community Interaction *Dimensions (6):* • Importance (1= hardly important at all, 3 = somewhat important, and 5 = very important) • Opportunity, Initiative, and Attainment (1 = hardly any, 3 = some, and 5 = great many) • Stability (1 = greatly decline, 3= stay about the same, and 5 = greatly improve) • Satisfaction (1 = very dissatisfied, 3= neither satisfied nor dissatisfied, and 5 = very satisfied) *FQOL items (54):* • Example: All things considered, how satisfied are you with the practical and emotional support your family gets from other people, excluding service providers? (1 = very dissatisfied, 3 = neither satisfied nor dissatisfied, and 5 = very satisfied) *Response format:*
Beach Center FQOL Scale Hoffman et al., 2006 Available at: http://beachcenter.org/resource_library/beach_resource_detail_page.aspx?Type=Tool&intResourceID=2391	*Purpose:* • To measure family perceptions of satisfaction on different domains of FQOL • To evaluate family services *Length:* • 2 pages *Time for completion (self-administration):* • 20 minutes *Reliability:* • Cronbach's α = 0.88. • Test-retest reliability: All correlations were significant at 0.01. • Correlations between time points: 0.60 to 0.77 *Validity:* • Item-level overall FQOL importance: χ^2 (270) = 617.28, p <.001, CFI = 0.87, RMSEA = 0.07 • The convergent validity: The Family APGAR and Family Interaction domain, r (87) = 0.68, p <.001 • The Family Resource Scale and Physical/Material Well-Being domain, r = 0.60, p <.001, n = 60	*Section (1):FQOL* *Domains (5):* • Family Interaction, Parenting, Emotion Well-being, Physical/Material Well-Being, Disability-Related Services *Dimension(1):* • Satisfaction (1 = very dissatisfied, 3= neither satisfied nor dissatisfied, and 5 = very satisfied) • Importance is a dimension of the older version and no longer one of the dimensions on the current scale. Nevertheless, some researchers continue to use this dimension. *FQOL items (25):* • Example: Family members help the children learn to be independent. (1 = very dissatisfied, 3 = neither satisfied nor dissatisfied, and 5 = very satisfied)

between systemic factors (i.e., societal values, policies, programs, systems) and FQOL outcomes. Impact of the systemic factors on different FQOL satisfaction scores at the family level across countries also remains unclear. Although a causal relationship cannot be assumed, the difference in FQOL scores across countries suggests the importance of examining how disability is perceived across countries and the impact this may have on the development of disability policies, systems, and programs to provide support to individuals and families. Only one study (R. I. Brown, Hong, Shearer, Wang, & Wang, 2010) proposed that lower FQOL scores (i.e., South Korea and Taiwan) may be associated with society's view of disability and, in turn, may be related to lack of appropriate services. Families in Slovenia also reported relatively low satisfaction when compared generally to the FQOL scores reported in the international studies described previously. Families in Belgium reported medium to high satisfaction (R. I. Brown et al., 2010; Schmidt & Kober, 2010; Steel, Poppe, Vandevelde, Van Hove, & Claes, 2011). One of the researchers speculated that the lower FQOL findings in some countries may be due to a more negative view toward disability in those cultures and therefore may result in fewer types and sources of support for families of children with disabilities (R. I. Brown et al., 2010).

The second theme focuses on material well-being. In general, families considered material well-being (e.g., transportation, financial sufficiency) as the most important FQOL domain (R. I. Brown et al., 2010; Hu et al., 2011b; Schmidt & Kober, 2010; Summers et al., 2007). Nevertheless, family reports of satisfaction levels of material well-being have been inconsistent across studies. Families of younger children in one study reported the highest satisfaction with this domain (Summers et al., 2007). Nevertheless, when families of older individuals with disabilities are included in another study, the results showed less satisfaction with financial (material) well-being (R. I. Brown et al., 2010).

The third theme addresses emotional well-being. Researchers using the Beach FQOL Scale found that families have consistently been least satisfied with their emotional well-being (Hoffman et al. 2006; Summers et al., 2007; Wang et al., 2004b, 2006; Zuna et al., 2009). The summary of the six highlighted studies (Table 23.9) illustrates that emotional well-being or the desire for emotional support continues to be a high need expressed by families. R. I. Brown and associates (2010) found

that families with low internal/external FQOL needed additional emotional support. Steel and colleagues (2011) found that the domain "support from others" had the lowest attainment and lowest satisfaction. Although families reported receiving as much instrumental as emotional support, they tended to consider support from informal sources as a favor and refrained from asking for help (Steel et al., 2011, p. 9). The authors speculated that families may feel guilty or feel that requesting emotional support is an imposition. Finally, Schmidt and Kober (2010) reported that families declared a need for a variety of sources of support, of which emotional support was highly important. The inability to draw definitive conclusions about these findings related to emotional support illustrates the point we made in the previous section regarding support: clarifying the distinction between what is an outcome and what is a predictor of that outcome will enable research to identify which products and sources of support may product optimal outcomes with respect to emotional well-being.

The fourth and final theme in our research review addressed family-centered support, which is a method of service delivery that recognizes families as unique entities and emphasizes family–professional partnership (Law et al., 2005). In this research, families expressed the need for family-centered support, which is strongly associated with FQOL outcomes (Giné, Gràcia, Vilaseca, & Balcells, 2010; Schmidt & Kober, 2010; Summers et al., 2007). Although relatively fewer Australian, Canadian, Taiwan, and Korean families reported being satisfied or very satisfied with support from the disability-related services, Belgian families expressed high satisfaction on support from the services in contrast to low satisfaction on supports from friends and community (R. I. Brown et al., 2010; Steel et al. 2011).

Conclusion

As depicted in Figure 23.1, FQOL outcomes are constantly influenced by and interact with systemic (e.g., culture), family-unit, individual-member, family support, and individual support factors. Researchers in various countries have developed, validated, and used measures to study FQOL outcomes in the domains of physical and material well-being, family interaction and relationships, emotional well-being, parenting, influence of values, community interaction, and leisure and recreation. Among all domains, material and emotional well-being are the most studied.

Table 23.9 International family quality of life (FQOL) outcome literature highlights

Author (s) /Year/ Type of Article	Nation(s)	Methodology	Findings
Summers et al., 2007 *Quantitative study*	U.S.	• *Measure*: Beach Center FQOL Scale • *Sampling procedures*: convenience • *Participants*: 180 families (176 mothers) of children (aged 0–5) receive early childhood services in a Midwestern state	• Families considered emotional well-being the least important and with the lowest satisfaction. • Families considered physical/material well-being the most important and with the highest satisfaction. • Service adequacy, mediated by family–professional partnership, was a significant predictor of FQOL.
R. I. Brown et al., 2010 *Quantitative study*	Australia, Canada, South Korea, and Taiwan	• *Measure*: Satisfaction dimension of the FQOL survey 2006 • *Sampling procedures*: Convenience • *Participants*: • Australia: 55 families of people with intellectual disabilities (ID) including some with Down syndrome (DS) and a few with autism • Canada: 51 families of children with disabilities (DS, $n = 33$; autism, $n = 18$; and contrast ($n = 18$) • South Korea: 81 families of children with DS and autism • Taiwan: 83 families of children with autism	• Australia: Internal FQOL domains (e.g., family relation) have higher FQOL score as compared to external FQOL domains (e.g., financial well-being). Younger parents report higher satisfaction as compared to older (55+) parents. • Canada: Findings are consistent with the Australian study. Families reporting low internal/external FQOL need additional emotional support and/or direct personal support. In terms of type of disability, DS group has higher score than autism group. The contrast (with no disability) group reported relatively high score. • Taiwan/South Korea: Participants reported relatively low FQOL as compared to Australian and Canadian data. Only one domain (family relations) is considered satisfied by most Korean respondents. The lowest three domains for both countries are disability-related services, support from other people, and spiritual/cultural beliefs. • The authors concluded that the lower FQOL scores may be associated with society's view toward disability, and consequently, the lack of appropriate social services as well as financial problems. But it could also be because the Taiwanese sample consisted of parents of a child with autism.
Gine et al., 2010 *Qualitative study*	Spain	• *Data source*: Focus group • *Sampling procedures*: Purposive • *Participants*: 5 mothers of people with ID and 2 fathers of people with ID (age of people with ID ranges from 16 to 42)	• Variables impacting FQOL: • Age of people with ID, behavior problems, and services in place • Residential area (urban vs. rural) • Parents' knowledge of services • Family interaction (needing place and time to meet and share needs/supports

Study	Country	Methods	Findings
Schmidt & Kober, 2010 *Mixed method study*	Slovenia	• *Measure and data source:* Translated and adapted of FQOL Survey 2006 (six domains selected out of the nine domains) and interview • *Sampling procedures:* Convenience • *Participants:* 20 families of children (7–14 years) from northeastern Slovenia (10 with children with intellectual disabilities and developmental issues and 10 with children with ID and behavior issues) • *Data analysis:* Descriptive; *t* test; qualitative analysis was not mentioned	• Slovene families have lower FQOL compared to international averages. • Families of children with ID with developmental issues reported higher FQOL score as compared to families of children with ID with behavioral issues. • Financial well-being is significantly correlated to FQOL. • Slovene families need services (i.e., trained and committed professionals, better educational system), emotional supports, instrumental supports, and consider needs of the family unit important.
Hu et al., 2011b *Quantitative study*	China	• *Measure:* Translated Beach Center FQOL Scale • *Sampling procedures:* Stratified • *Participants:* 442 families (mostly parents, some grandparents [*n* =15] and some others [*n* = 4]) of people (age 0–18+) with ID	• Families of various housing conditions (i.e., crowded, small, medium, and large living space) have different FQOL. • Families with different major transportation means (i.e., walking, biking) have different FQOL. • Family income and severity of disability are significant predictors of FQOL.
Steel et al., 2011 *Mixed method study*	Belgium	• *Measure:* Translated FQOL Survey-2006 • *Sampling procedures:* Purposive • *Participants:* 25 parents (24 mothers, a father) of individuals (aged 3–28) with disabilities (ID- [*n* = 9], ID+ASD- [*n* = 8], ASD- [*n* = 1], DS- [*n* = 9])	• Belgian families reported medium to high FQOL, but there is considerable variation in individual scores. • Health, family relationships, and support from the services are the domains with highest attainment and satisfaction. In contrast, support from others is the domain with lowest attainment and satisfaction score, whereas leisure and community interaction have low attainment scores. • Service: The majority of parents expect current services to stay the same (77.3 %). Nevertheless, families still reported unmet need of services (40%) because available services (mostly child-centered) do not equate to attainable, accessible, and affordable services. • Support: Families received equal emotional and instrumental support from relatives and sometimes experienced difficulties in communicating with relatives. They reported receiving more emotional support from friends and neighbors than professionals did. Families consider supports from families and friends a favor and refrain from asking help.

Table 23.10 Future research topics consistent with family quality of life (FQOL) theory

Terminology	Definition and Examples	Potential Research Topics
Systemic factors		
Societal Values	Constitutional and ethical principles that drive policies, systems, and programs	• How do the societal values in different countries influence the strengths of families?
Policies	Laws influenced by core concepts that shapes service delivery	• How do policies in different countries compare and contrast in terms of the provision of the four types of family support?
Systems	A collection of interrelated networks organized to meet the various needs of society	• What professional development would be most effective in preparing service providers to identify and build on family strengths?
Programs	Formally and informally organized entities provide services and supports to an identified population	
Family-unit factors		
Family characteristics	Traits or descriptors of the family as a whole (e.g., family income, size of family, family geographic location, religious preference, or family form)	• Which family-unit variables are strong predictors of positive FQOL? • Are there interaction effects of family-unit variables in predicting positive FQOL?
Family dynamics	Aspects of interactions and ongoing relationships among two or more family members (e.g., family cohesion, communication, or adaptability)	• What types of family support are most effective in addressing family-unit variables in order to achieve positive FQOL outcomes?
Individual-member factors		
Demographics	Basic traits (e.g., age, type of disability, gender, education levels, ethnicity, employment status)	• Which individual-member variables are strong predictors of positive FQOL? • Are there interaction effects of family-unit and individual-member variables in predicting FQOL that have implications for the provision of family support?
Characteristics	Multidimensional traits (e.g., behavior of the individual with a disability, parents' depression, sibling health condition)	• What are the strengths of individuals with disabilities that are most predictive of positive FQOL outcomes?
Beliefs	Attributions of meaning, expectations, or understanding of a phenomenon (e.g., understanding the family member's disability)	
Support factors		
Family-unit level support	Educational, social, behavioral, and health-related activities expected to improve family outcomes (e.g., support from extended families)	• What types and sources of family support are most effective in improving FQOL? • How do the effects of types of support vary among families of children with different degrees of severity of disability and across lifespan stages?
Individual-level support	Educational, social, behavioral, and health-related activities expected to improve individual outcomes (e.g., being matched with a mentor-parent, parent training)	• What are the relationships of different sources of support (e.g., friends, extended or nucleus family members, professionals) to specific domains of FQOL (e.g., parenting, emotional well-being, physical well-being)?

Directions for Future Research

An analysis of research aligned with the FQOL theory documents that researchers have developed psychometrically sound measures of FQOL as an outcome and have begun to investigate relationships between different variables and FQOL for families with individuals with disabilities, primarily with intellectual disabilities. Given the recent emergence of FQOL as a research topic and the extensive effort required to develop sound measures, the current research literature is lacking in studies that examine FQOL as an outcome of providing support to individuals with disabilities, as well as to the family unit. Rather than a focus on the impacts of the provision of support, most current studies are descriptive in that they investigate the relationship between individual and family factors and FQOL outcomes.

We recommend two major foci for future research related to FQOL that align with the field of positive psychology. The first is to focus on the strengths of families who have children with disabilities as contrasted to focusing only on their needs and challenges. Interestingly, U.S. legislation passed in the early 1980s required that family resources, priorities, and concerns be identified and specified on individualized family support plans for infants and toddlers with disabilities. The concept of family resources, which has been interpreted to mean family strengths, has never been actualized within the disabilities field. Currently, no measures of family strengths have been developed and validated with families who have children with disabilities. Future research analyzing family strengths and the relationship of family strengths to FQOL outcomes is an important future direction.

A second important research direction is focusing on providing family support as a means to improve FQOL. Family support strategies intend to assist family members who have key roles in the provision of support and guidance to their family member with intellectual or developmental disabilities. These strategies are designed, implemented, and funded in a flexible manner that addresses the emotional, physical, and material well-being of the entire family. (Table 23.6 includes definitions of different types of support to families who have children with severe disabilities.)

Table 23.10 identifies possible research topics tied to these two themes, according to the factors and *especially the interaction of factors* within the FQOL theory. Consistent with the framework of this chapter, we believe that the FQOL theoretical framework can be helpful in generating future research, organizing the new knowledge gained from research, and moving forward the provision of support to families.

In summary, we see major consistencies between the precepts of positive psychology and the precepts within the FQOL research area. The shared focus on strengths and the enhancement of well-being are mutual goals around which the potential exists for research in FQOL to benefit tremendously from the advancements made within the positive psychology field.

References

Abedi, M. R., & Vostanis, P. (2010). Evaluation of quality of life therapy for parents of children with obsessive-compulsive disorders in Iran. *European Children and Adolescent Psychiatry, 19*, 605–613.

Antonovsky, A. (1987). *Unravelling the mystery of health: How people manage stress and stay well.* San Francisco: Jossey-Bass.

Aznar, A. S., & Castañón, D. G. (2005). Quality of life from the point of view of Latin American families: A participative research study. *Journal of Intellectual Disability Research, 49*, 784–788. doi: 10.1111/j.1365-2788.2005.00752.x

Balcells-Balcells, A., Giné, C., Guàrdia-Olmos, J., & Summers, J. A. (2011). Family quality of life: Adaptation to Spanish population of several family support questionnaires. *Journal of Intellectual Disability Research,* doi: 10.1111/j.1365-2788.2010.01350.x

Bayat, M. (2007). Evidence of resilience in families of children with autism. *Journal of Intellectual Disability Research, 51*, 702–714.

Behr, S. K., & Murphy, D. L. (1993). Research progress and promise: The role of perceptions in cognitive adaptation to disability. In A. P. Turnbull, J. A. Patterson, S. K., Behr, D. L. Murphy, J. G. Marquis, & M. J. Blue-Banning (Eds.), *Cognitive coping, families, and disability* (pp. 151–163). Baltimore: Brookes.

Bekir, F. M. (2011). *The examination of the family quality of life perceptions of mothers who have children with disabilities* (Unpublished doctoral dissertation). Anadolu University The Graduate School Educational Sciences, Turkey.

Bowlby, J. (1960). Grief and mourning in infancy and early childhood. *Psychoanalytic Study of the Child, 15*, 1–9.

Brown, I., Brown, R., Baum, N. T., Isaacs, B. J., Myerscough, T., & Neikrug, S. (2006). *Family quality of life survey: Main caregivers of people with intellectual or developmental disabilities.* Toronto: Surrey Place Centre.

Brown, R. I., Gelder, S., Primrose, A., & Jokinen, N. S. (2011). Family life and the impact of previous and present residential and day care support for children with major cognitive and behavioral challenges: A dilemma for services and policy. *Journal of Intellectual Disability Research, 55*, 904–917.

Brown, R. I., Hong, K., Shearer, J., Wang, M., & Wang, S. (2010). Family quality of life in several countries: Results and discussion of satisfaction in families where there is a child with a disability. In R. Kober (Ed.), *Enhancing the quality of life of people with intellectual disability. From theory to practice* (pp. 255–264). Dordrecht: Springer.

Brown, R. I., MacAdam-Crisp, J., Wang, M., & Iarocci, G. (2006). Family quality of life when there is a child with a developmental disability. *Journal of Policy and Practice in Intellectual Disabilities, 3*(4), 238–245.

Conger, R. D., & Conger, K. J. (2002). Resilience in Midwestern families: Selected findings from the first decade of a prospective, longitudinal study. *Journal of Marriage and Family, 64,* 361–373.

Correa, V. I., Bonilla, Z. E., & Reyes-MacPherson, M. E. (2011). Support networks of single Puerto Rican mothers of children with disabilities. *Journal of Child Family Studies, 20,* 66–77, doi: 10.1007/s10826-010-9378-3

Dunst, C. J., & Bruder, M. B. (2002). Valued outcomes of service coordination, early intervention, and natural environments. *Exceptional Children, 68,* 361–375.

Feldman, M. A., & Werner. S. (2002). Collateral effects of behavioral parent training on families of children with developmental disabilities and behavior disorders. *Behavior Interventions, 17,* 75–83.

Fisman, S., Wolf, L., Ellison, D. Gillis, B., Freeman, T., & Szatmari, P. (1996). Risk and protective factors affecting adjustment of siblings of children with chronic disabilities. *Journal of American Academy of Child & Adolescent Psychiatry, 35* (11), 1532–1541.

Friend, A., Summers, J. A., & Turnbull, A. P. (2009). Impacts of family support in early childhood intervention research. *Education and Training in Developmental Disabilities. 44*(4), 433–470.

Giné, C., Gràcia, M., Vilaseca, R., & Balcells, A. (2010). Quality of life of the families of people with intellectual disability in Spain. In R. Kober (Ed.), *Enhancing the quality of life of people with intellectual disability. From theory to practice* (pp. 349–361). Dordrecht: Springer.

Harry, B., Klingner, J. K., & Hart, J. (2005). African American families under fire: Ethnographic views of family strengths. *Remedial and Special Education, 26*(2), 101–112.

Helff, C. M., & Glidden, L. M. (1998). More positive or less negative? Trends in research on adjustment of families rearing children with developmental disabilities. *Mental Retardation, 36,* 457–464.

Hoffman, L., Marquis, J., Poston, D., Summers, J. A., & Turnbull, A. (2006). Assessing family outcomes: Psychometric evaluation of the Beach Center Family Quality of Life Scale. *Journal of Marriage and Family, 68,* 1069–1083.

Hu, X., Summers, J., & Turnbull, A. (2011a). The quantitative measurement of family quality of life: A review of available instruments. *Journal of Intellectual Disability Research,* doi: 1 0.1111/j.1365-2788.2011.01463.x

Hu, X., Wang, M., & Fei, X. (2011b). Family quality of life of Chinese families of children with intellectual disabilities. *Journal of Intellectual Disability Research,* doi: 10.1111/j.1 365-2788.2011.01391.x

Isaacs, B., Wang, M., Samuel, P., Ajuwon, P., Baum, N., Edwards, M., & Rillotta, F. (2011). Testing the factor structure of the Family Quality of Life Survey—2006. *Journal of Intellectual Disability Research,* doi: 10.1111/j.1365-2788.2 011.01392.x

Issacs, B., J., Brown, I., Baum, N., Myerscough, T., Neikrug, S., Roth, D.,…Wang, M. (2007). The international family quality of life project: Goals and description of a survey tool. *Journal of Policy and Practice in Intellectual Disabilities, 4,* 177–185.

Jackson, C. W., Wegner, J. R., & Turnbull, A. P. (2010). Family quality of life following early identification of deafness. *Language, Speech, & Hearing Services in Schools, 41,* 194–205.

Kaminsky, L., & Dewey, D. (2001). Siblings relationships of children with autism. *Journal of Autism and Developmental Disorders, 31*(4), 399–410.

Kober, R. &, Eggleton, I. (2009). Using quality of life to evaluate outcomes and measure effectiveness. *Journal of Policy and Practice in Intellectual Disability, 6*(1), 40–51.

Kyzar, K. B., Turnbull, A. P., & Summers, J. A. (2012). The relationship of family support to family outcomes: A synthesis of key findings from research on severe disability. *Research & Practice for Persons with Severe Disabilities, 37*(1), 31–44.

Law, M., Teplicky, R., King, S., King, G., Kertoy, M., Moning, T., et al. (2005). *Family-centered service: Moving ideas into practice. Child: Care, Health and Development, 31*(6), 633–642.

Lakin, K. C., & Turnbull, A. P. (Eds.). (2005). *National goals and research for persons with intellectual and developmental disabilities.* Washington, DC: American Association on Mental Retardation.

Luckasson, R., Borthwick-Duffy, S., Buntinx, W. H. E., Coulter, D. L., Craig, E. M., Reeve, A.,…Tassé, M. J. (2002). *Mental retardation: Definition, classification, and systems of supports* (10th ed.). Washington, DC: American Association on Mental Retardation.

Luckasson, R., Coulter, D. L., Polloway, E. A., Reese, S., Schalock, R. L., Snell, M. E., et al. (1992). *Mental retardation: Definition, classification, and systems of supports* (9th ed.). Washington, DC: American Association on Mental Retardation.

Mannan, H., Summers, J. A., Turnbull, A., & Poston, D. (2006). A review of outcome measures in early childhood programs. *Journal of Policy and Practice in Intellectual Disabilities, 3,* 219–228.

McWilliam, R. A., & Scott, S. (2001). A support approach to early intervention: A three-part framework. *Infants and Young Children, 13*(4), 55–66.

National Agenda on Family Support Summit (2011, March). Retrieved from www.famliysupportagenda.com

Park, J., Hoffman, L., Marquis, J., Turnbull, A., Poston, D., Mannan, H.,…Nelson, L. (2003). Toward assessing family outcomes of service delivery: Validation of a family quality of life survey. *Journal of Intellectual Disability Research, 47,* 367–384.

Park, J., Turnbull, A. P., & Turnbull, H. R. (2002). Impacts of poverty on quality of life in families of children with disabilities. *Exceptional Children, 68,* 151–170.

Poston, D., Turnbull, A., Park, J., Mannan, H., Marquis, J., & Wang, M. (2003). Family quality of life: A qualitative inquiry. *Mental Retardation, 41,* 313–328.

Poston, D. J., & Turnbull, A. P. (2004). Role of spirituality and religion in family quality of life for families of children with disabilities. *Education and Training in Developmental Disabilities, 39,* 95–108.

Rillotta, F., Kirby, N., & Shearer, J. (2010). A comparison of two family quality of life measures: An Australian study. In R. Kober (Ed.), *Enhancing the quality of life of people with intellectual disability. From theory to practice* (pp. 305–348). Dordrecht: Springer.

Risdal, D., & Singer, G. H. (2004). Marital adjustment in parents of children with disabilities. *Research and Practice for Persons with Severe Disabilities, 29*(2), 95–103.

Saito, Y., & Turnbull, A. (2007). Augmentative and alternative communication practice in the pursuit of family quality of life: A review of the literature. *Research & Practice for Persons with Severe Disabilities, 32*, 50–65.

Schalock, R. L. (2004). The concept of quality of life: What we know and do not know. *Journal of Intellectual Disability Research, 48*, 203–216.

Schalock, R. L., Borthwick-Duffy, S. A., Bradley, V. J., Buntinx, W. H., Coulter, D. L., Craig, E. M.,.... Yeager, M. H. (2010). *Intellectual disability: Definition, classification and systems of supports* (11th ed.). Washington DC: American Association on Intellectual and Developmental Disabilities.

Schalock, R. L., & Verdugo, M. A. (2002). *Handbook on quality of life for human service practitioners.* Washington, DC: American Association on Mental Retardation.

Schippers, A., & Boheemen, M. (2009). Family quality of life empowered by family-oriented support. *Journal of Policy and Practice in Intellectual Disabilities. 6*, 19–24.

Schmidt, M., & Kober, R. (2010). Quality of life of families with children with intellectual disabilities in Slovenia. In R. Kober (Ed.), *Enhancing the quality of life of people with intellectual disability. From theory to practice* (pp. 363–376). Dordrecht: Springer.

Scorgie, K., & Sobsey, D. (2000). Transformational outcomes associated with parenting children with disabilities. *Mental Retardation, 38*(3*)*, 195–206.

Seligman, M., & Csikszentmihályi, M. (2000). Positive psychology: An introduction. *American Psychologist, 55*, 5–14.

Solnit, A. J., & Stark, M. H. (1961). Mourning and the birth of a defective child. *Psychoanalytic Study of the Child, 16*, 523–537.

Soresi, S., Nota, L., & Ferrari, L. (2007). Considerations on supports that can increase the quality of life of parents of children with disabilities. *Journal of Policy and Practice in Intellectual Disabilities, 4*, 248–251.

Steel, R., Poppe, L., Vandevelde, S., Van Hove, G., & Claes, C. (2011). Family quality of life in 25 Belgian families: Quantitative and qualitative exploration of social and professional support domains. *Journal of Intellectual Disability Research,* doi: 10.1111/j.1365-2788.2011.01433.x

Stoneman, Z. (2005). Siblings of children with disabilities: Research themes. *Mental Retardation, 43*(5), 339–350.

Summers, J. A., Behr, S. K., & Turnbull, A. P. (1988). Positive adaptation and coping strengths of families who have children with disabilities. In G. H. S. Singer & L. K. Irvin (Eds.), *Support for caregiving families: Enabling positive adaptation to disability* (pp. 27–40). Baltimore, MD: Brookes.

Summers, J. A., Marquis, J., Mannan, J., Turnbull, A., Fleming, K., Poston, D.,.... Kupzyk, K. (2007). Relationship of perceived adequacy of services, family-professional partnerships, and family quality of life in early childhood of life in early childhood service programmes. *International Journal of Disability, Development, and Education, 54*, 319–338.

Summers, J. A., Poston, D. J., Turnbull, A. Marquis, J., Hoffman, L. Mannan, J., & Wang, M. (2005). Conceptualizing and measuring family quality of life. *Journal of Intellectual Disability Research, 49*, 777–783.

Taylor, S. E. (1983). Adjustment to threatening life events: A theory of cognitive adaptation. *American Psychologist, 38*, 1161–1173.

Thompson, J. R., Bradley, V. J., Buntinx, W. H., Schalock, R. L., Shogren, K. A., Snell, M. E., & Yeager, M. H. (2009). Conceptualizing supports and the support needs of people with intellectual disability. *Intellectual and Developmental Disabilities, 47*(2), 135–146, doi: 10.1352/1934-9556-47.2.135

Turnbull, A. P., Brown, I., & Turnbull, H. R. (2004). *Families and people with mental retardation and quality of life: International perspectives.* Washington, DC: American Association on Mental Retardation.

Turnbull, A. P., Patterson, J. M., Behr, S. K., Murphy, D. L., Marquis, J. G., & Blue-Banning, M. J. (Eds.). (1993). *Cognitive coping, families, and disability: Participatory research in action.* Baltimore, MD: Paul H. Brookes.

Turnbull, A. P., Summers, J. A., Lee, S., & Kyzar, K. (2007a). Conceptualization and measurement of family outcomes associated with families of individuals with intellectual disabilities. *Mental Retardation and Developmental Disabilities, 13*, 346–356.

Turnbull, A. P., Summers, J. A., Turnbull, R., Brotherson, M. J., Winton, P., Roberts, R., & Snyder, P. (2007b). Family supports and services in early intervention: A bold vision. *Journal of Early Intervention, 29*(3), 187–206.

Turnbull, A. P., Turbiville, V., & Turnbull, H. R. (2000). Evolution of family-professional partnership models: Collective empowerment as the model for the early 21st century. In S. J. Meisels & J. P. Shonkoff (Eds.), *Handbook of early intervention* (pp. 630–650). New York: Cambridge University Press.

Turnbull, H. R., Beegle, G., & Stowe, M. S. (2001). The core concepts of disability policy affecting families who have children with disabilities. *Journal of Disability Policy Studies, 12*(3), 133–143.

Turnbull, H. R., & Stowe, M. J. (2001). A taxonomy for organizing the core concepts according to their underlying principles. *Journal of Disability Policy Studies, 12*(3), 177–197.

Turnbull, H. R., Turnbull, A., Wehmeyer, M L., & Park, J. (2003). A quality of life framework for special education outcomes. *Remedial and Special Education, 24*, 67–74.

Verdugo, M. A., Cordoba, L., & Gomez, J. (2005). Spanish adaptation and validation of the family quality of life survey. *Journal of Intellectual Disability Research, 49*, 794–798.

Verdugo, M. A., & Schalock, R. L. (2009). Quality of life: From concept to future applications in the field of intellectual disabilities. *Journal of Policy and Practice in Intellectual Disabilities, 6*, 62–64.

Walton-Moss, B., Gerson, L. & Rose, L. (2005). Effects of mental illness on family quality of life. *Issues in Mental Health Nursing, 26*, 627–624.

Wang, M., & Brown, R. (2009). Family quality of life: A framework for policy and social service provisions to support families of children with disabilities. *Journal of Family Social Work, 12*, 144–167.

Wang, M., Mannan, H., Poston, D., Turnbull, A., & Summers, J. A. (2004a). Parents' perceptions of advocacy activities and their impact on family quality of life. *Research & Practice for Persons with Severe Disabilities, 29*, 144–155.

Wang, M., Summers, J. A., Little, T., Turnbull, A., Poston, D., & Mannan, H. (2006). Perspectives of fathers and mothers of children in early intervention programmes in assessing family quality of life. *Journal of Intellectual Disability Research, 50*, 977–988.

Wang, M., Turnbull, A., Summers, J. A., Little, T., Poston, D. J., Mannan, H., & Turnbull, R. (2004b). Severity of disability and income as predictors of parents' satisfaction with their family quality of life during early childhood years. *Research & Practice for Persons with Severe Disabilities, 29*, 82–94.

Werner, S., Edwards, M., & Baum, N. T. (2009). Family quality of life before and after out-of-home placement of a family member with an intellectual disability. *Journal of Policy and Practice in Intellectual Disabilities, 6,* 32–39.

Wolfensberger, W. (1967). Counseling the parents of the retarded. In A. A. Baumeister (Ed.), *Mental retardation: Appraisal, education, and rehabilitation* (pp. 329–400). Chicago: Aldine.

Zuna, N. I., Selig, J. P., Summers, J. A., & Turnbull, A. P. (2009). Confirmatory factor analysis of a family quality of life scale for families of kindergarten children without disabilities. *Journal of Early Intervention, 31,* 111–125.

Zuna, N., Summers J. A., Turnbull A. P., Hu, X., & Xu S. (2010). Theorizing about family quality of life. In R. Kober (Ed.), *Enhancing the quality of life of people with intellectual disability. From theory to practice* (pp. 241–278). Dordrecht: Springer.

Education

Sharon L. Field

Abstract

Over the past 25 years, a growing emphasis has been placed on wellness, prevention, and strengths-based research and practice in both special education and psychology. Within special education, this positive focus has been organized around the concepts of normalization, inclusion, quality of life, and self-determination. The dominant organizing concepts in positive psychology have focused on happiness, subjective well-being, categorization and optimization of character strengths, and self-determination theory. This emerging positive orientation is in sharp contrast to the traditional disease- or deficit-based models prevalent in both fields. This chapter provides specific examples of how research in positive psychology and wellness-based special education practice has impacted educational services for students with disabilities in the areas of assessment, educational planning, behavioral management and support, and curriculum. Information exchange and collaboration between researchers focused on positive practice in both fields is recommended.

Key Words: positive psychology, special education, self-determination, prevention, wellness, youth development

The purpose of special education is to provide instruction to meet the needs of students with disabilities. By definition, *dis*ability is focused on a negative trait; that is, something inherent to the individual that denotes a lack of ability or a deficit. Students qualify for special education services based on their disability category, and such services have been organized around the remediation of student deficits. This negative orientation has been called into question. Educators and policy makers are increasingly debating the degree to which students with disabilities need distinctive, specialized instruction targeted to address their specific identified deficit areas or if they should be educated in typical education settings, where they interact with students with diverse abilities and instructional decisions are made primarily on the basis of their abilities and strengths.

As these questions are debated within the field of special education, there has been a movement within the field of psychology to incorporate the strengths-based, wellness orientation of positive psychology. This movement toward a more positive approach in psychology is in reaction to traditional thought within the field, which has typically had a negative focus that emphasized disease and deficit.

The conversations and controversies regarding deficit versus positive orientation have been similar within the two fields and seem to have run on a parallel path. There has been some intersection as findings from positive psychology have informed and contributed to the steadily progressing focus within the field of special education on strengths, wellness, and inclusion for students with disabilities.

Emerging Positive Focus in the Fields of Special Education and Psychology

Because they have typically been defined by their deficits, individuals with disabilities have frequently faced the negative, fearful perceptions of others. As a result, people with disabilities were often isolated from more typical and positive aspects of society. Relegated to living within institutions, their living conditions were typically horrific and there was little that could be considered positive about the experience. With the deinstitutionalization and normalization movement that began in the 1960s and '70s, a step toward the possibility of a more positive quality of life for persons with disabilities was initiated. A key issue throughout the special education literature since deinstitutionalization has been discussion of the degree to which students with disabilities should be served in same or separate settings as students without disabilities. Although many issues cut across this key topic, the most fundamental of these issues is whether one is working from a medical, deficit-based model or a more ecological, strengths-based approach. Historically, the medical model, in which individuals' disabilities are diagnosed, defined, and treated, has been dominant.

The key concepts of normalization set forth by Nirje (1969) contributed to the deinstitutionalization movement and had an enormous impact on special education services. Nirje's normalization principle emphasized the importance of "making available to [persons with mental retardation] the patterns and conditions of everyday life which are as close as possible to the norms and patterns of mainstream society" (Nirje, 1976, p. 363). Inherent in this principle is a focus on a person's strengths, rather than on their weaknesses or limitations. As the normalization principle infused itself throughout special education practice, ecological, as opposed to medical, frameworks were increasingly used to structure educational and support services for students with disabilities. Ecological frameworks define disability as a function of the relationship between the characteristics of individuals and the demands and supports of the environment in which they are interacting. Within an ecological framework, attributes of the individual can be viewed with more neutrality because the degree to which characteristics are seen as positive or negative are a function of the environment within which the individual is interacting and not simply internal to the individual. From an ecological perspective, individual strengths and weaknesses are therefore seen as more transient and malleable. The deinstitutionalization and normalization movements provided a foundation for a more positive approach to disability and allowed a focus on strengths and wellness, rather than shining a light solely on limitations.

As the normalization and deinstitutionalization movements were occurring, interest in and advocacy for the quality of life experienced by people with disabilities became an important concept. A focus on providing educational services for students with disabilities that promote quality of life, rather than just remediating deficits, emerged. The quality-of-life concept is another example of the movement toward well-being that is consistent with the aims of positive psychology. Schalock (1996; Chapter 4 this volume) described eight core principles that contribute to quality of life, and he posited that quality of life will be enhanced when basic needs are met according to these principles. These core elements include emotional well-being, interpersonal relations, material well-being, personal development, physical well-being, self-determination, social inclusion, and rights.

The Self-Determination Initiative

The most direct intersection between special education and positive psychology can be seen within the self-determination movement in special education and the study of Self-Determination Theory (Ryan & Deci, 2000; see also Chapter 10, this volume) in positive psychology. A focus on self-determination in special education was initiated in the late 1980s as part of the normalization movement. People with disabilities, parents, advocates, and educators began to question the lack of opportunity that persons with disabilities often had to make determinations about their futures. According to Ward (1992): "Self-determination, which includes self-actualization, assertiveness, creativity, pride, and self-advocacy, must be part of the career development process that begins in early childhood and continues throughout adult life" (p. 389).

A self-determination focus is particularly evident in the movement within special education concerned with improving the transition from school to adulthood. Typical traits of adulthood include increased self-reliance and greater control over one's destiny. The emphasis on improving self-determination, which included the development of curricular and instructional strategies, emerged as students with disabilities, their families, educators, and service providers explored how to best help students make successful transitions to adult roles.

The concept of self-determination as applied to special education was set in motion during the early 1990s as part of a federal initiative from the U.S. Department of Education (Ward & Kohler, 1996). Federal funding was provided to researchers and practitioners across the country to examine how the concept of self-determination could be applied within educational programming for students with disabilities, with the hope of creating more successful outcomes in their transitions from school to work and community life.

The initiative came about partially in response to reviews of follow-up data on graduates of special education programs, which revealed that these graduates were experiencing high rates of unemployment, low incomes, little access to postsecondary education, and low levels of community participation after they left the P–12 setting. The follow-up studies, which were conducted with the first cohorts of students who had the benefit of special education services throughout their P–12 experience, were disappointing to many students, parents, professionals, and other advocates who had hoped that access to free and appropriate public education would have much more positive effects on attainment of positive adult outcomes (Field, Martin, Miller, Ward, & Wehmeyer, 1998). Another factor that fueled the development of self-determination as an organizing concept for special education programming was advocacy by those concerned with the civil rights of persons with disabilities (Ward, 1996). The phrase "nothing about me without me" was frequently used by adults with disabilities to convey the importance of promoting self-determination throughout all services for persons with disabilities, as a fundamental right and an expression of respect for the dignity and worth of persons with disabilities.

Several models of self-determination were developed with funding from the federal initiative. The work of researchers in the field of positive psychology, most notably Edward Deci and Richard Ryan, was influential in the development of these models. Self-Determination Theory (SDT) as developed by Deci and Ryan (described in detail in Chapter 10) is a theory of motivation and personality development. It is concerned with how individuals' natural or intrinsic tendencies to behave in effective and healthy ways can best be supported. The primary purpose of the development of self-determination models within special education was to drive instructional interventions, rather than to describe psychological processes as Deci and Ryan sought to do. Therefore the self-determination models and materials developed within special education tended to focus more on identifying those behaviors associated with self-determination that can be taught or encouraged, rather than on analyzing motivation and other basic psychological constructs.

The models of self-determination developed under the federal initiatives both reflected and contributed to a philosophical shift within the field of special education to a focus on increased involvement, respect, and dignity for the individuals with disabilities served by special education, goals that are highly consistent with positive psychology. The models also provided a foundation for the development of multiple assessment, instructional, and planning strategies that are now used with students. Those models are described in detail in Chapter 10, but because one model has directed much of our own work in this area, it will be described here.

A Five-Step Model of Self-Determination

According to Field and Hoffman (1994), self-determination is either promoted or discouraged by factors within the individual's control (e.g., values, knowledge, skills) and variables that are environmental in nature (e.g., opportunities for choice making, attitudes of others). This model (Field and Hoffman, 1994; Hoffman & Field, 2005) is depicted in Figure 24.1.

The model has five major components: Know Yourself and Your Environment, Value Yourself, Plan, Act, and Experience Outcomes and Learn. The first two components describe internal processes that provide a foundation for acting in a self-determined manner. The next two components, Plan and Act, identify skills needed to act on this foundation. According to this model, to be self-determined, one must have internal awareness, as well as the strength and ability to act on that internal foundation. To have the foundation of self-awareness and self-regard but not the skills, or the skills but not the inner knowledge and belief in the self, is insufficient to fully experience self-determination. To be self-determined, one must know and value what one wants and possess the necessary skills to seek what is desired. The final component in the Field and Hoffman self-determination model is Experience Outcomes and Learn. This step includes both celebrating successes and reviewing efforts to become self-determined so that skills and knowledge that contribute to self-determination are enhanced.

As stated earlier, self-determination is affected by environmental variables as well as by the knowledge, skills, and beliefs expressed by the individual. Field and Hoffman identified nine indicators of environments that support the expression of

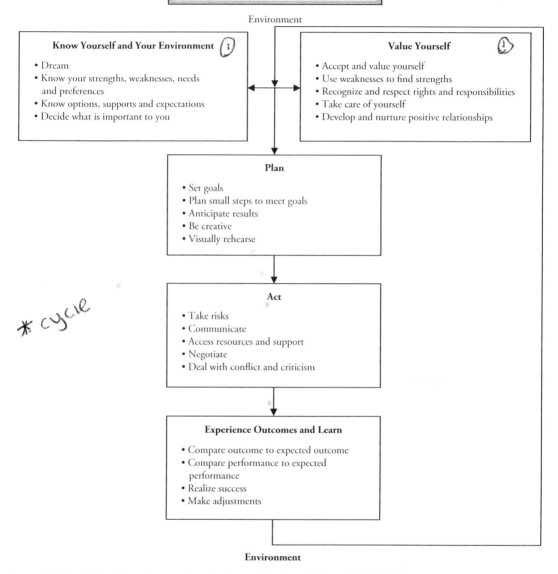

Environment

Know Yourself and Your Environment (i)

- Dream
- Know your strengths, weaknesses, needs and preferences
- Know options, supports and expectations
- Decide what is important to you

Value Yourself (!)

- Accept and value yourself
- Use weaknesses to find strengths
- Recognize and respect rights and responsibilities
- Take care of yourself
- Develop and nurture positive relationships

Plan

- Set goals
- Plan small steps to meet goals
- Anticipate results
- Be creative
- Visually rehearse

* cycle

Act

- Take risks
- Communicate
- Access resources and support
- Negotiate
- Deal with conflict and criticism

Experience Outcomes and Learn

- Compare outcome to expected outcome
- Compare performance to expected performance
- Realize success
- Make adjustments

Environment

Figure 24.1 Model of self-determination. Adapted with permission from Hoffman & Field (1994).

self-determination (Field & Hoffman, 2002). These quality indicators include:

1. Knowledge, skills, and attitudes for self-determination are addressed in the curriculum, in family support programs, and in staff development.

2. Students, parents, and staff are involved participants in individualized educational decision making and planning.

3. Students, families, faculty, and staff are provided with opportunities for choice.

4. Students, families, faculty, and staff are encouraged to take appropriate risks.

5. Supportive relationships are encouraged.

6. Accommodations and supports for individual needs are provided.

7. Students, families, and staff have the opportunity to express themselves and be understood.

8. Consequences for actions are predictable.

9. Self-determination is modeled throughout the school environment.

Emerging Trends

As a result of research and advocacy, self-determination is now widely accepted as a recommended practice in special education programming (e.g., Kohler & Field, 2003). Researchers have asserted that self-determination should not be viewed as a separate component, course, or activity within special education. Instead, they have suggested that self-determination has the greatest potential to have positive effects for students when it is seen as a central organizing concept throughout all aspects of educational programming and services for students with disabilities.

Self-determination is one of several major areas within the practice of special education where it is evident that an orientation toward positive psychology theory and practice has had an impact. Normalization, inclusion, quality of life, and strengths-based approaches are also representative of an increased orientation toward more positive practices in education for students with disabilities. Examples of specific ways in which these positive practices have had an impact on practice in special education are discussed in upcoming sections. These areas of practice include assessment, educational planning, behavioral management and support, and curriculum.

Assessment

The way in which assessment of students with disabilities' knowledge and skills is conducted in school settings has changed significantly in a manner that is consistent with key tenets of positive psychology. Over the past two decades, assessment practices have moved toward placing an emphasis on students' strengths rather than identifying deficits. Furthermore, educators have increasingly considered the impact of the environment and instructional strategies on students' performance in addition to assessing students' abilities. This broader focus in assessment acknowledges that students may exhibit varied levels of strength and ability in different contexts and that it may be best to alter instruction or the environment to capitalize on students' strengths rather than simply trying to remediate perceived "deficits" that reside in students. Finally, there has been a marked movement toward involving students in an integral manner in the educational planning process. Increased involvement in the educational planning process demonstrates a shift in the way that students with disabilities are viewed in the educational system; they are increasingly being perceived as strong and important individuals whose voices are central to the planning process. This is in sharp contrast to earlier years in the field of special education, when students with disabilities were viewed as dependent, having little to no ability to contribute to educational planning discussions and the assessment data used in those discussions.

Assessment Requirements

The Individuals with Disabilities Education Improvement Act (IDEIA) requires that appropriate, measurable postsecondary goals be included in the Individualized Education Plan (IEP) for students who are 16 years of age, or younger if appropriate. The goals are to be "based on the individual child's *needs*, taking into account the child's *strengths, preferences and interests*" (34 CFR 300.43 (a)] [20 U.S.C. 1401(34). This requirement affirms the importance of positive, strengths-based assessment within the transition process in education for students with disabilities. It is a proactive approach that requires schools to take action to help students identify and express their needs, strengths, preferences, and interests. Involving students in the assessment of their strengths provides the foundation for developing effective instructional programs.

Students as Team Members in the Assessment Process

By actively involving students in assessment, valuable information can be gathered, student and family ownership of assessment results is increased, and support for student self-determination is demonstrated. In addition, because positive attributes (e.g., understanding of one's strengths and weaknesses, belief in oneself, ability to make choices and decisions based on self-awareness) are important life skills that students need to be successful throughout their lives, educators are increasingly choosing to include these skills in assessment so that appropriate instructional programs, supports, and accommodations can be provided.

Students can help formulate questions to be answered through assessment, and they should have input into the assessment design. Student and family involvement at the beginning of the assessment process helps increase the commitment of these key participants. It also helps ensure that key factors from the perspective of students and parents are taken into account.

If students' input about their educational goals is to be accurate and meaningful, they need substantial preparation prior to their IEP meetings. This preparation should include participation in data collection prior to the meeting. Simply asking students while they are at the meeting what they would like to do after high school is not sufficient. They may lack the experience necessary to make an informed choice, and, furthermore, they may not have enough time or presence when they are in a meeting with several adults to provide a thoughtful response. Therefore, they need to participate in a variety of assessment practices prior to participating in IEP meetings.

Assessment Strategies

There are several ways that specific assessment strategies are being used in special education settings. These strategies, provided below, have a grounding in positive psychology, and are being used in a manner that promotes student involvement. They focus on students' strengths and take into consideration the context in which the student is performing, as well as the knowledge and skills demonstrated by the individual.

ANALYSIS OF BACKGROUND INFORMATION

Educators have long relied on review of student records to gather important assessment information about students. Increasingly, there has been a focus on reviewing students' files with an eye toward positive attributes. For example, Field and Hoffman (2007) suggested that educators should peruse the file for

- information about the student's needs, strengths, preferences, and interests (e.g., interest inventory results, accommodations needed, observed strengths);
- documentation of the student's prior involvement in educational and transition planning (e.g., IEP meetings attended; whether the student was involved in setting goals); and
- data about student characteristics related to self-determination, such as self-awareness, confidence, planning and decision-making skills, risk taking, communication, and evaluative skills (e.g., teacher or parent observations, self-determination assessment results).

INTERVIEWS

Interviews with students, family members, and other pertinent individuals are often used to gather information about a student's strengths, as well as about his or her preferences, interests, goals, and past experiences. One of the advantages of interviews is that they provide a way to more clearly determine students' perceptions. In addition, when interviewers find a student's response confusing, they are able to ask additional questions that lead

to an approach that creates a broader understanding and is less likely to lead to a deficit approach.

In their discussion of interviewing techniques, Sitlington and Clark (2007) recommended the use of person-centered planning strategies in transition assessment. Person-centered planning relies heavily on interviewing students and then having students interview people who are close to them to gather information that is useful for the planning process. The person-centered planning process helps strengthen the student voice in educational planning, and it provides an opportunity for students to expand and practice acting on their strengths. Person-centered planning places the student at the center of the process and builds a support network of individuals around the student. Clearly delineated procedures for conducting person-centered planning build on a student's strengths, support student self-determination, and create an ongoing circle of support for the student to assist him or her in achieving stated goals. Feedback from those who have used person-centered planning procedures indicates that such planning meetings often take more time than typical meetings, but the time is perceived as well spent.

CURRICULUM-BASED ASSESSMENT

Curriculum-based assessment techniques have gained popularity in recent years. In curriculum-based assessment, data are collected on student performance that is directly connected to curriculum content. Several of the self-determination instructional packages (e.g., Hoffman & Field, 2005; Martin & Marshall, 1995) include assessment instruments that measure specific skills taught within the respective curricula.

Portfolio assessment is one type of curriculum-based assessment that is particularly aligned with key tenets in positive psychology. The portfolio approach allows students to take control of the assessment process and to design a plan by which they can collect meaningful data on their progress toward achieving their goals and on their self-determination skill development. Portfolio assessment offers a method to design assessment so that the student is clearly at the center of the process. Portfolios can be used to help track student progress toward self-selected goals or the growth of specific strengths. Portfolio assessment has worked well in conjunction with instructional programs in which students set and work toward goals as part of their participation in the curriculum. More information on procedures for designing and implementing portfolio assessment can be found in Sitlington and Clark (2006).

* an accumulation of a variety of work

PERFORMANCE SAMPLES

Performance samples provide an opportunity for students to perform specific tasks (typically a sample of representative tasks) while being systematically observed. Performance samples can be commercially or locally developed. When using performance samples, it is important for students to be included in the assessment process design and to understand why they are participating in the selected activities. Performance samples can be used to gather information on students' needs, strengths, interests, and preferences by carefully observing for these variables while students are completing tasks and by interviewing students about their reactions to the work samples. Work samples can also be constructed to replicate specific skills associated with key signature strengths. When using work samples, one should remember that students may not demonstrate skills in the same ways in natural environments as they do in the replicated setting. It is also critical to obtain information from students regarding their perceptions of the tasks presented to them. When used in conjunction with other assessment data, performance samples can provide valuable information about students' strengths, challenges, and interests.

BEHAVIORAL OBSERVATION TECHNIQUES

Behavioral observation is an authentic assessment strategy. Observations provide an opportunity to assess applied skills in natural environments. However, they can also be affected by the perceptions and biases of the observer. Using a systematic approach for observing student behavior (e.g., narrative recording, time sampling, rating scales) can help minimize the effect of observer bias. A key ingredient in using behavioral observation techniques successfully is a clear definition of the behaviors to be observed. Using a strengths-based approach, it is also highly important that students be active participants in helping to identify the behavior(s) selected for observation and in developing the observation plan.

SITUATIONAL ASSESSMENT

Situational assessment can help students find an appropriate fit between their strengths and needs and potential future settings. Exploring a variety of optional post-school environments and helping students reflect on their reactions to these environments is essential if students are to provide informed input for their educational plans about their needs, strengths, interests, and preferences. For example, if a student is asked what kind of a job she would like after graduation, and the only job she has ever been exposed to is in the school cafeteria, it is quite likely that she will say she wants to work in food service, whether or not that is what she prefers. If students are exposed to a wide variety of post-school options but aren't supported to reflect on their experiences, they also may have difficulty making informed decisions about their goals.

Standardized Instruments

Several standardized instruments are available to assess knowledge and skills related to positive youth development. The primary use of these instruments is to ascertain the degree to which students possess the knowledge, skills, and beliefs that support their self-determination and other character strengths. These instruments can be used to compare student performance over time and to evaluate the effectiveness of instructional programs. A sampling of instruments follows.

THE ARC'S SELF-DETERMINATION SCALE

The Arc's Self-Determination Scale (Wehmeyer & Kelchner, 1995) is a student self-report measure designed for use by adolescents with disabilities, particularly students with mild cognitive and learning disabilities. The 72-item scale measures overall self-determination and the domain areas of autonomy, self-regulation, psychological empowerment, and self-realization. The primary purpose of the instrument is to help students with disabilities assess their strengths and limitations related to self-determination and to provide a tool for students and teachers to use together to determine goals and instructional programming for self-determination.

One suggested use of the Arc's Self-Determination Scale is to stimulate discussion about the student's reactions to the items. Another use of the scale is to score it and compare students' total, domain, and subdomain scores with the scale norms. This analysis can be used to compare students' individual strengths and weaknesses across the self-determination domain areas measured by the instrument. The Arc's Self-Determination Scale and information about how to obtain the procedural guidelines, which describe administration and scoring procedures, can be found online at the University of Kansas Beach Center on Disability website at http://www.beachcenter.org.

CHOICEMAKER SELF-DETERMINATION ASSESSMENT

ChoiceMaker (Martin & Marshall, 1995) is a curriculum-based assessment and planning tool intended for use with middle to high school students with emotional or behavioral disabilities and mild or moderate learning problems. It measures student skills and opportunities presented to students to use those skills in three areas: choosing goals, expressing goals, and taking action. The assessment has three parts. The first part is a rating scale of (a) student skills related to self-determination and (b) opportunities at school to perform each of the self-determination-related skills. Student skills and opportunities are rated on a scale of 0–4. The second part is an assessment profile. The student skills and school opportunities ratings are recorded on a form on which similarities and differences in scores can be easily seen. The third part of the assessment offers potential objectives and goals that can be used for specific areas identified through assessment.

SELF-DETERMINATION ASSESSMENT BATTERY, SECOND EDITION

The Self-Determination Assessment Battery (Hoffman, Field, & Sawilowsky, 2004) consists of five instruments that can be used alone or in combination. The Self-Determination Assessment Battery measures cognitive, affective, and behavioral factors related to self-determination from the perspectives of the student, parent, and teacher. Instruments are the Self-Determination Knowledge Scale (an objective test of knowledge related to self-determination concepts), the Self-Determination Student Scale (a self-report instrument that measures affective and cognitive aspects of self-determination), the Self-Determination Observation Checklist (a behavioral checklist for use by classroom teachers), and the Teacher and Parent Perception Scales, on which teachers or parents rate their student or son or daughter on a 5-point Likert-type scale on a variety of behaviors, abilities, and skills associated with self-determination. (note: The Teacher Perception Scale is also known as the Counselor/Educator Perception Scale as it can be completed by any professional, such as counselors, psychologists, who interact with the student.)

Just as students are being rated from three different perspectives (i.e., the student, teacher, and parent), they are also being assessed in three different areas: cognition/knowledge, behavior, and affect. Examining the differences in these three aspects of self-determination may help determine appropriate interventions. Data from the instruments can be used to stimulate discussion in educational planning meetings. They also can provide information that helps to identify appropriate educational interventions. The Self-Determination Student Scale, Counselor/Educator Perception Scale

and Parent Perception Scale are available as web-based assessments from www.ealyeducation.com. The Self-Determination Knowledge Scale is published as part of the *Steps to Self-Determination* curriculum published by ProEd (www.proedinc.com). The Self-Determination Observation Checklist and further information about development of the Self-Determination Assessment Battery can be found at http://www.coe.wayne.edu/selfdetermination or by contacting sdtalk@wayne.edu.

AIR SELF-DETERMINATION SCALE

The AIR Self-Determination Scale (Wolman, Campeau, Dubois, Mithaug, & Stolarski, 1994) is based on theoretical work by Mithaug and colleagues (see Wehmeyer, Abery, Mithaug, & Stancliffe, 2003). The AIR Self-Determination Scale measures individual capacity for and opportunity to practice self-determination through educator, student, and parent forms of the scale. The results from each of these three perspectives can be used to develop a profile of a student's level of self-determination and to identify (a) areas of strength and areas needing improvement, (b) educational goals and objectives, and (c) strategies to increase student capacity and students' opportunities to become self-determined. More information about the AIR Self-Determination Scale can be found at the University of Oklahoma Zarrow Center for Learning website at http://www.ou.edu/zarrow/sdetermination.html.

VALUES IN ACTION (VIA) YOUTH INVENTORY FOR YOUTH

The VIA Youth Inventory (Park & Peterson, 2006) is a self-report survey that measures 24 strengths of character. It includes four subscales: temperance strengths (e.g., prudence, self-regulation), intellectual strengths (e.g., love of learning, curiosity), theological strengths (e.g., hope, religiousness, love), and other-directed (interpersonal) strengths (e.g., kindness, modesty). It was designed to be used with youth between the ages of 11 and 17. The VIA Youth Inventory is comprised of 198 questions and takes about 40–50 minutes to complete. Park and Peterson (2006) suggested that the VIA Youth Inventory can help students identify their "signature strengths" relative to their other strengths and that helping youth identify and capitalize on their strengths can help them achieve a psychologically more fulfilling life.

Response to Intervention

To help students maximize their performance, the Response to Intervention (RTI) framework is a model that combines assessment and intervention to better understand what supports or hinders student performance. It is widely used as a multilevel prevention system. RTI focuses on identifying learning and/or behavioral problems at an early stage so that the likelihood of special education placement, which requires a student to have a defined disability, can be lessened. This focus on prevention within RTI, as well as its ecological orientation, makes it consistent with positive psychology theory and practice.

Screening, progress monitoring, data-based decision making, and use of multiple levels of prevention are core elements of RTI. Screening with the use of brief assessments is implemented on a school-wide basis to identify students who are at risk of poor learning outcomes. The progress of students who have been so identified through screening is then monitored to estimate rates of improvement, whether or not they are making adequate progress, and to compare the efficacy of different forms of instruction for individual students. A key tenet of RTI is the use of data-based decision making at all levels of prevention.

RTI uses three levels of prevention. The primary level is intended to be used with all students. At this level, evidence-based, differentiated instruction is provided, and screening tools are used to identify those students who may be at risk for poor learning outcomes. The purpose of the secondary prevention level of RTI, which is also conducted within the general education classroom, is to assess the reaction of students who have been identified through screening as being at risk for poor learning outcomes to targeted, supplemental, small-group instruction. Assessment at this level is diagnostic so that the types of instruction and strategies that are most successful for individual students can be identified. At the tertiary prevention level, students who have not responded well to instructional interventions provided at either the primary or secondary level are provided with intensive, supplemental, small-group or individual instruction within a general education setting. Again, diagnostic tools are used to assess students' reactions to different interventions.

Although RTI is used to identify learning problems, it is still consistent with positive psychology practice because it has a primary focus on preventing further learning problems. Also, it is used to assess how different instructional and environmental modifications can be made to help students maximize their strengths. It doesn't focus on remediating deficits in students. For more information on RTI, see www.rti4success.org.

Educational Planning

The IDEIA sets forth the expectation that students will be centrally involved in the transition planning process. The act requires that local education agencies invite students with disabilities to attend their IEP meeting if transition services are considered at that meeting.

This requirement to have students involved in their educational planning promotes respect for the strengths and contributions that students with disabilities can bring to planning meetings. This strengths-based focus makes it consistent with the discipline of positive psychology.

To meet the legislative and perceived best-practice requirement to have students integrally involved in their educational planning process, several schools have begun to implement specific instruction to prepare students for active participation in and leadership of their educational planning process.

Many instructional programs are available to help prepare students for participation in the IEP process. Examples of skills addressed in these programs include helping students anticipate what to expect at meetings, identifying goals they would like to achieve, and developing assertive communication skills. Examples of two of these curricula are provided below.

The ChoiceMaker Self-Directed IEP curriculum (Martin, Marshall, Maxson, & Jerman, 1993) is targeted toward helping students acquire knowledge and skills that will give them a stronger voice in the IEP planning process. The Self-Directed IEP includes lesson plans and videos aimed at (a) helping students become comfortable and familiar with the IEP process, (b) assisting students to make decisions about input they would like to provide to the process, and (c) developing skills that allow students to chair and participate in educational planning meetings.

The curriculum delineates those skills and in-school opportunities for students that contribute to increased self-determination in the three phases of the IEP process: choosing goals, expressing goals, and taking action. Specific teaching goals and objectives are described for each of these three major aspects of the IEP. For example, the first teaching goal under "Choosing Goals" is "student understanding." This goal is operationalized via three teaching objectives: "Indicate goal-setting purpose and component," "Identify student rights," and "Identify goal-setting roles and timelines." The curriculum includes 10 teaching goals and 62 teaching objectives. The lessons are intended to be infused into existing coursework.

The Self-Advocacy Strategy for Education and Transition Planning (Van Reusen, Bos, Schumaker, & Deshler, 2002) was designed specifically to promote increased student involvement in the educational and transition planning process. The Self-Advocacy Strategy was designed to be taught to small groups of students over a 1- to 2-week period for approximately 45 minutes per day. Students are taught to use the following five-step strategy in the IEP conference:

1. "I" = Inventory your strengths, weaknesses you need to improve, goals and interests, and choices for learning
2. "P"= Provide your inventory information
3. "L" = Listen and respond
4. "A" = Ask questions
5. "N" = Name your goals

The five steps form the acronym IPLAN, which becomes a mnemonic tool for students.

Table 24.1 provides information about several programs available to help students with disabilities proactively develop communication and leadership skills for educational planning meetings.

Instructional Strategies

The strategies used to help students acquire knowledge and skills can emanate from a remedial, deficit orientation or from a wellness and strengths-based philosophy. Several types of instructional strategies used in special education services are consistent with the wellness, strengths-based focus of positive psychology. These strategies are further described here.

Behavioral Management and Support

Applied behavioral analysis (ABA) has long been used as a key tool by special educators to modify and shape student behaviors. Although there are varied opinions as to whether the use of ABA is consistent

Table 24.1 Student involvement programs

Program	Evaluated with	Authors	Publisher
Self-Directed IEP	Students with emotional and behavioral disorders, intellectual disability	Martin, Marshall, Maxson, & Jerman (1993)	Sopris West http://www.sopriswest.com
Next S.T.E.P.	Students with learning disabilities	Halpern, Herr, Wolf, Lawson, Doren, & Johnson (2000)	PRO-ED, Inc. http://www.proedinc.com
Whose Future Is It Anyway?	Students with intellectual disability, learning disabilities, other health impairments	Wehmeyer, Lawrence, Kelchner, Palmer, Garner, & Soukup (2004)	Beach Center on Disability http://www.beachcenter.org
Whose Future Is It?	Students with intellectual disability, learning disabilities, other health impairments	Wehmeyer & Palmer (2012)	Modified software version of Whose Future Is It Anyway? Attainment Company http://www.attainment-company.com
The Self-Advocacy Strategy	Students with learning disabilities	Van Reusen, A. K., Bos, C. S., Schumaker, J. B., & Deshler, D. D. (2002).	Edge Enterprises, P. O. Box 1304, Lawrence, KS 66044
TAKE CHARGE for the Future	Students with learning disabilities, other health impairments, emotional and behavioral disorders	Powers, L.E., Ellison, R., Matuszewski, J., & Turner, A. (2004)	Portland State University, Regional Research Institute http://www.rri.pdx.edu/index.php
A Student's Guide to the IEP	No formal evaluation, designed for students across disability categories	McGahee-Kovac (2002)	National Information Center for Children and Youth with Disabilities http://www.nichcy.org

with principles of positive psychology, work in this area has clearly laid a foundation for subsequent interventions, such as positive behavioral supports that are rooted in principles related to positive psychology. Applied behavioral analysis has been defined as "systemic application of behavioral principles (e.g., antecedent, behavior, consequence) to change student learning and behavior to a meaningful degree" (Kavale & Forness, 2000). Because ABA has been shown to have strong effect sizes in meta-analytic research, it is considered an evidence-based practice (Burns & Ysseldyke, 2009). In a study on the use of evidence-based practices, Burns and Ysseldyke (2009) found that approximately 70% of their survey respondents, which included a national random sample of special education teachers and school psychologists, reported that they used ABA with their students at least weekly.

According to Baer, Wolf, and Risley (1968), ABA is *applied* (i.e., addresses problems that improve people's lives), *behavioral* (i.e., observable, clearly delineated, measurable events), *analytical* (i.e., demonstrates cause and effect relationships between behavior and environment), *technological* (i.e., can be reproduced by others), *systematic* (i.e., incorporates basic behavioral principles such as reinforcement and stimulus control), *effective* (focuses on magnitude and social importance of change), and has *generality* (e.g., creates change that is sustained across people, time, and settings).

Some within the field of positive psychology have expressed concern about the use of strategies based on behavioral principles because of the negative effects that such interventions may have on intrinsic motivation. Deci (2004) cited several studies that found that events experienced by individuals as controlling (i.e., they felt pressure to perform in specific ways) decreased intrinsic motivation. They also found that events that were perceived as autonomy supportive (i.e., provided encouragement for self-initiation and choice) maintained or enhanced intrinsic motivation. Deci further specified that tangible rewards, threats of punishment, evaluations, deadlines, imposed goals, and good player awards all tended to be experienced by individuals as controlling and to therefore undermine intrinsic motivation. Deci elaborated on this issue by explaining that the manner in which performance-contingent consequences were administered also made a difference in how controlling or autonomy-supportive these methods were perceived to be.

Deci (2004) provided substantial evidence to support that intrinsic motivation leads to higher quality learning, which magnifies concerns about the use of ABA within a positive psychological framework. For example, Deci, Schwartz, Sheinman, and Ryan (1981) found that students in more autonomy-supportive classrooms demonstrated greater curiosity, more independent mastery attempts, and higher self-esteem than did students in more controlling classrooms.

Positive behavior support (PBS) is a form of behavioral intervention rooted in the ABA techniques that emerged in special education in the mid-1980s. The field of PBS has grown significantly since that time, in both research and practice. Positive behavior support emerged partially because of concerns about overuse of aversive procedures and ABA's focus on consequent-based interventions (DelPizzo-Cheng, LaRue, Sloman, & Weiss, 2010). Although both PBS and ABA have a foundation in behavioral science, PBS incorporates a specific emphasis on quality of life, normalization, and consumer choice. These are all concepts that are consistent with and reflective of the emerging trends in special education and positive psychology on dignity, respect, and wellness.

The PBS approach has been widely adopted in special education services. It offers a three-tiered approach that includes prevention of problem behavior through environmental modifications, specialized instruction at a group level for students identified as at risk, and assessment and treatment of problem behavior on an individual basis. According to DelPizzo et al. (2010), PBS is rooted in ABA, the normalization/inclusion movement, and person-centered values. Positive behavior support represents a movement in behavioral strategies toward a focus that is more consistent with positive psychology. However, it is still centered on identifying problem behaviors or deficits. In addition, it utilizes behavioral principles that, as described earlier, can undermine intrinsic motivation, a key concept in positive psychology.

Given the need to help students develop behavior that will be viewed as acceptable in a variety of environments, it may not always be possible to implement instruction to promote positive behavior in a manner that is completely autonomy supportive and will support intrinsic motivation, as suggested by Deci (2004). When it is necessary to use strategies that may be perceived as controlling (i.e., those done to reach a specific outcome), such as teacher approval or another type of reward, it is important to help students work toward increased autonomy by supporting the processes of internalization and integration. According to Deci (2004), internalization involves students taking ownership of regulatory processes so the behavior no longer requires an external contingency. Integration is a process through which internalized values and regulatory processes become part of one's sense of self. Deci states that internalization and integration take place within the experience of relatedness, competence, and autonomy. According to Deci (2004), the integrative process may be more or less effective as a function of the degree to which people experience relatedness, competence, and autonomy while performing the behavior. If more integration occurs, the behavior will be considered more self-determined; if less integration occurs, the behavior will be perceived as being more other-controlled.

Wehmeyer and Field (2007) discussed several key concepts related to effective implementation of behavioral strategies so they are as consistent as possible with supporting the development and expression of a positive, wellness orientation in students. They suggested that teachers engage in partnership with students to identify target behaviors that students want to work toward. They also recommended that positive reinforcement should be used to encourage positive behaviors rather than using punishment to extinguish negative behaviors. In addition, they stated that reinforcement techniques should encourage appropriate student experimentation and risk-taking, suggesting that it is important to reinforce successive approximations of desired behaviors, based on the starting level for each student.

Modeling and Mentoring

Research has demonstrated that modeling is a powerful instructional strategy (Bandura, 1986). Modeling can be used as a direct instructional strategy (e.g., using role models to demonstrate a specific positive attribute) or an indirect strategy (e.g., encouraging students to learn vicariously by observing teachers and other adults in the school who consistently model positive behaviors). Several special and general education programs have established mentorship programs to support student learning by observing and interacting with adult role models. These programs help students gain knowledge and skill in a manner that is both autonomy-focused and relationship supportive.

Cooperative Learning

Cooperative learning is an instructional strategy that is both relationship-focused and autonomy-supportive and is therefore consistent with tenets of positive psychology. Cooperative learning increases the availability of peer role modeling experiences and helps students learn collaboration skills. The effectiveness of cooperative learning has been well established in the literature (Johnson, Johnson, & Holubec, 2008).

Coaching

Coaching emerged in the 1990s as a model to help individuals in corporate settings achieve their goals. Many teachers in K–12 schools have demonstrated interest in coaching models and have begun to implement similar practices. Often, the services provided by teachers in classrooms are not coaching, as it is specifically designated within the major coaching models. Rather, teachers are increasingly using coaching-inspired strategies to provide support to students in a manner that is individualized, competence-building, autonomy-supportive, and relationship-focused.

Many definitions of coaching have been provided in the literature. Here is one definition that incorporates many commonly accepted features of coaching:

> In a co-active coaching relationship the agenda comes from the client, not the coach.... The relationship is entirely focused on getting the results clients want. They set the agenda. The coach's job is to make sure the agenda doesn't get lost.... This is different from consulting, for example, where the consultant brings specialized expertise and very often sets the agenda for the relationships. Co-active coaching is not about the coach's content, or the coach's expertise, or giving solutions (Whitworth, Kimsey-House, & Sandahl, 1998, pp. 4–5)

According to Byron and Parker (2002), several beliefs are evident throughout the array of coaching definitions and frameworks. These include (a) using questioning as a primary communication tool, (b) working from a belief base that clients or students usually possess the capacity to develop their own solutions, (c) explicitly deciding on communication and logistical components of the coaching relationship that are mutually agreed on by the coach and the client, and (d) emphasizing the importance of breaking goals into small steps and working to achieve those goals one step at a time. The concept of coaching is highly consistent with positive psychology and deserves careful consideration and further research to determine its value as a positive strategy to help students with and without disabilities achieve positive outcomes.

Student-Directed Learning Strategies

Student-directed learning is used to teach students how to change and regulate their behavior (Agran, King-Sears, Wehmeyer, & Copeland, 2003). The major emphasis in student-directed learning is on the student. Student-directed learning is often used as an umbrella term to include self-regulation, self-management, and self-control strategies (Wehmeyer & Field, 2007). Student-directed learning is rooted in the principles of ABA. However, in student-directed learning, students use behavioral principles to solve problems and make changes as *they* choose to do so. Strategies used within student-directed learning are antecedent cue regulation, self-monitoring, self-instruction, self-evaluation, and self-reinforcement. Self-directed learning helps students take more responsibility for their learning process. Meichenbaum and Biemiller (1998) stated

> In contrast to the less self-directed students, the highly self-directed students can accomplish academic tasks more successfully, and can explain their performance to others. They assume a higher level of responsibility for task accomplishment and achieve a higher level of mastery. (p. 57)

The Self-Determined Learning Model of Instruction was developed by Wehmeyer, Palmer, Agran, Mithaug, and Martin (2000) as an instructional tool to enable students to become causal agents in their lives. It is based on component elements of self-determination, self-regulated problem solving, and research on student-directed learning. Student questions used in the model are designed to guide students through a problem-solving sequence that leads to the next phase. The Self-Determined Learning Model is based on theory in the problem-solving and self-regulation research literature that suggests that there is a means-end problem-solving sequence that needs to be followed in order for any person's actions to satisfy his or her needs and interests. The strategies within this model are autonomy supportive and therefore should lead to greater intrinsic motivation. For more information on the Self-Determined Learning Model of Instruction, see Wehmeyer et al. (2000).

Curriculum

Government mandated testing of students has had an enormous effect in recent years on the curriculum offered in public schools for students with and without disabilities. The movement to conduct standards-based testing and to use the results of those tests to make major decisions about the effectiveness and trajectory of schools and, in some cases, the graduation or other high-stakes outcomes of students, has been highly controversial. As a focus on preparing students to perform well on tests has come to the forefront, many parents, educators, and researchers have raised questions about the effects that this emphasis on externally imposed standards has on students, families, and teachers.

Damon (2008) provided a vivid description of the effects that the current mandated testing focus is having on students and schools:

> The standardized tests that schools in the United States use today have little to do with advancing standards of excellence in learning, understanding, or gaining useful knowledge. Instead, the tests that we rely on to determine whether a student is learning (and whether a school is doing its job well) are used to provide evidence for those who wish to evaluate the student or the school system. The tests are intended to have "high stakes" for student and schools. As such, the tests draw attention away from other educational priorities, in particular the core missions of encouraging the acquisition of active knowledge and a lifelong love of learning. Often squeezed entirely out of the school day are questions of meaning and purpose that should underlie every academic exercise. In place of these broader goals, the main objective of the classroom becomes imparting a rapid familiarity with facts, names, places, and formulas that students have little interest or skill in applying to problems beyond the classroom. (p. 111)

Damon's concerns were echoed by psychologist Madeleine Levine as she elaborated on how prevalent is the pressure to conform to externalized standards in schools. Levine (2006) stated that

> What looks like a healthy assimilation into the family and community—getting high grades, conforming to parents' and community standards, and being receptive to the interests and activities valued by others—can be deceptive. Kids can present as models of competence and still lack a fundamental sense of who they are. Psychologists call this the "false self," and it is highly correlated with a number of emotional problems, most notably depression. (p. 11)

As is apparent from these quotes, many aspects of the mandated testing movement appear to be inconsistent with a positive psychology orientation. The testing movement is often focused on identifying deficits (e.g., schools or students who do *not* meet externally identified standards). In addition, standardized testing places pressure on students and teachers to conform to externally imposed standards, which is the antithesis of self-determination. Finally, and perhaps most disturbingly, some see it as contributing to an increase in mental health deficits, such as depression and apathy, in students.

Using Deci and Ryan's Self-Determination Theory, which identifies competence, autonomy, and relatedness as basic psychological needs that must be met in order to achieve higher degrees of wellness, it is clear that the mandated testing movement seeks to satisfy only one of these needs: competence. However, as educators struggle to meet the demands of mandated testing, they often find that this quest to promote test-taking competence in students is often pursued at the expense of autonomy and relatedness. Alternatively, there are also examples of schools that offer students choice, autonomy, and community but fail to place an emphasis on the acquisition of specific knowledge and skills. Many educators who are committed to the use of positive psychology in schools are grappling with the question of how to promote the satisfaction of all three of these needs (i.e., competence, autonomy, relatedness) for students through a school's curriculum offerings rather than addressing one of these needs at the expense of others.

Curriculum Approaches Consistent with Positive Psychology

Several curriculum approaches used in special education services are consistent with the tenets of positive psychology, and they are described here.

INDIVIDUALIZED, RELEVANT CURRICULUM

Clark, Field, Patton, Brolin, and Sitlington (1994) claimed that curriculum must be tailored to meet the needs and goals of individual students. The concept of individualization has been particularly relevant in the area of life skills instruction. Students with disabilities often have a need to develop practical life skills (e.g., transportation skills, leisure awareness, vocational skills) while they are still in school or they will not be adequately prepared for their next environment. This can, at times, result in conflict for schools that organize their curriculum solely around academic competencies addressed in government-mandated testing programs. The student-centered perspective on

curriculum advocated by Clark et al. is clearly conducive to a positive psychology orientation when it is built on students' strengths and when students have the opportunity to be involved in determining their instructional needs. Clark et al. (1994) stated

> Given our current knowledge of existing programs and the need for addressing adult outcomes, it is difficult to imagine that academic content programming would be provided as the only option for many students. Three guiding principles for considering the curriculum needs of any student with a disability before limiting a student's options in any instructional delivery system are suggested: Utilize the notion of "subsequent environment as attitude" (Polloway, Patton, Smith, & Rodrique, 1991); Consider for each individual the notion that time for learning is short and that school time cannot afford to be wasted or taken lightly; re-evaluate what we are doing with students on a regular basis.

QUESTIONING AND CONVERSATION

Damon (2008) asserted that adults in schools need to share with students stories of their own search for purpose. Furthermore, Damon claims that adults need to ask students to explore the "why" and "for what purpose" about all that they do. He stated that every part of the curriculum should be taught with "why?" squarely in the foreground. He also emphasized the importance of community involvement for youth to help students learn that they can make a difference.

SPECIFIC POSITIVE STRENGTHS-BASED CURRICULA

Several curricula are aimed at helping students believe that they can make a difference. For example, Steps to Self-Determination (Hoffman & Field, 2005) is a curriculum based on the Field and Hoffman (1994, 2005) model of self-determination described earlier in this chapter. The curriculum is experientially based, allowing students to establish and work toward goals as they acquire the knowledge and skills delineated in the model. Students develop a belief that they can make a difference by actually defining and *achieving* goals that are important to them. The curriculum was designed to be used in integrated environments (i.e., including students with and without disabilities). It can be infused into existing coursework or taught as a separate class or extracurricular activity. With flexible scheduling, it can be infused into standards-based coursework. Teachers participate in the curriculum with students so that they can act as role models and create a collaborative classroom climate. Parents or other significant persons in students' lives also participate in the curriculum to support students' efforts.

There are many more curricula aimed at helping students with disabilities develop knowledge and skills related to self-determination. The majority of these curricula have been designed so that they can be infused into academic content. Additional information about these curricula are available at the University of North Carolina-Charlotte website for the Self-Determination Synthesis project at http://www.uncc.edu/sdsp.

In addition to the self-determination curricula developed through special education initiatives, several additional curricula rooted in positive psychology are available to special educators. One example is the Penn Resiliency Program (PRP), developed by Martin Seligman. The major goal of the PRP is to increase students' ability to handle day-to-day problems that are common during adolescence. The PRP promotes optimism by teaching students to think more realistically and flexibly about problems they encounter; PRP also teaches assertiveness, creative brainstorming, decision making, relaxation, and several other coping skills. (For more information on the PRP, see www. authentichappiness.com.)

Conclusion

An increased focus over the past 25 years on wellness, prevention, and strengths-based research and practice are evident in both special education and psychology. Within special education, this emerging positive orientation has been organized around the concepts of normalization, inclusion, quality of life, and self-determination. The dominant organizing concepts in psychology have focused on happiness, subjective well-being, categorization and optimization of character strengths, and self-determination theory. Research in these fields has often run on parallel tracks. At times, there has been an intersection between the two fields, with research in positive psychology benefitting the field of special education and vice-versa.

The movement toward positive practice is now well-ingrained in both fields. Increased dialogue in psychology and special education could promote an increased rate of progress in both fields. For example, Deci (2004) suggested that special education self-determination interventions and evaluations would benefit from use of a process model (such as the Self-Determination Theory) to add greater specificity to the research process. In addition, the rate of progress in positive psychology could be increased by incorporating findings from the special education literature on positive psychology-related concepts and interventions. Although a major shift has occurred within psychology and special education to incorporate wellness and prevention-based practices, this shift is still in its infancy, and deficit or disease models are still pronounced in both fields. Increased collaboration by researchers interested in positive practice could help to accelerate the development of positive practices in both fields.

References

Agran, M., King-Sears, M, Wehmeyer, M. L., & Copeland, S. R. (2003). *Teachers' Guides to Inclusive Practices: Student-Directed Learning Strategies*. Baltimore: Paul H. Brookes.

Baer, D., Wolf, M., & Risley, R. (1968). Some current dimensions of applied behavior analysis. *Journal of Applied Behavior Analysis, 1*, 91–97.

Bandura, A. (1986). *Social foundations of thought and action: A social cognitive theory*. Englewood Cliffs, NJ.

Burns, M. K., & Ysseldyke, J. E. (2009). Reported prevalence of evidence-based instructional practices in special education. *The Journal of Special Education, 43*(1), 3–11.

Byron, J., & Parker, D. R. (2002). College students with ADHD: New challenges and directions. In L. C. Brinckerhoff, J. M. McGuire, & S. F. Shaw, S. F. (Eds.), *Postsecondary education and transition for students with learning disabilities* (pp. 335–367). Austin, TX: PRO-ED.

Clark, G. M., Field, S., Patton, J. R., Brolin, D. E., & Sitlington, P. L. (1994). Life skills instruction: A necessary component for all students with disabilities. *Career Development for Exceptional Individuals, 17*(2), 125–133.

Damon, W. (2008). *The path to purpose: Helping our children find their calling in life*. New York: Free Press.

Deci, E. L. (2004). Promoting intrinsic motivation and self-determination in people with mental retardation. In H. N. Switzky (Ed.), *Personality and motivational systems in mental retardation, vol. 28* (pp. 1–29). San Diego: Elsevier Academic Press.

Deci, L., Schwartz, A. J., Sheinman, L., & Ryan, R. M. (1981). An instrument to assess adults' orientations toward control versus autonomy with children: Reflections on intrinsic motivation and perceived competence. *Journal of Educational Psychology, 73*, 642–650.

DelPizzo-Cheng, E., LaRue, R. H., Sloman, K., & Weiss, M. J. (2010). ABA and PBS: the dangers in creating artificial dichotomies in behavioural intervention. *Behavior Analyst Today, 10*, 428.

Field, S. & Hoffman, A. (1994). Development of a model for self-determination. *Career Development for Exceptional Individuals, 17*(2), 159–169.

Field, S., & Hoffman, A. (2002). Preparing youth to exercise self-determination: quality indicators of school environments that promote the acquisition of knowledge, skills and beliefs related to self-determination. *Journal of Disability Policy Studies, 13*, 113–118.

Field, S., & Hoffman, A. (2007). Self-determination in secondary transition assessment. *Assessment for Effective Intervention, 32*(3), 181–190.

Field, S, Martin, J., Miller, R., Ward, M., & Wehmeyer, M. (1998). *A practical guide to teaching self-determination.* Reston, VA: Council for Exceptional Children.

Halpern, A.S., Herr, C.M., Doren, B., & Wolf, N.K. (2000). *NEXT S.T.E.P.: Student Transition and Educational Planning Second Edition.* Austin, TX: ProEd.

Hoffman, A., & Field, S. (2005). *Steps to self-determination,* 2nd ed. Austin, TX: ProEd.

Hoffman, A., Field, S. & Sawilowsky, S. (2004). *Self-determination assessment battery,* 2nd ed. Detroit, MI: Center for Self-Determination and Transition, College of Education, Wayne State University.

Johnson, D., Johnson, R., & Holubec, E. (2008). *Cooperation in the classroom.* Edina, MN: Interaction Book Company.

Kavale, K. A., & Forness, S. R. (2000). Policy decision in special education: The role of meta-analysis. In R. Gersten, E. P. Schiller, & S. Vaughn (Eds.), *Contemporary special education research: Synthesis of the knowledge base on crucial instructional issues* (pp. 281–326). Mahway, NJ: Lawrence Erlbaum.

Kohler, P., & Field, S. (2003).Transition focused education: Foundation for the future. *Journal of Special Education,37*(3), 174–183.

Levine, M. (2006). *The price of privilege.* New York: Harper Collins.

Martin, J. E., & Marshall, L. H. (1995). *ChoiceMaker Self-Determination Instructional package.* Longmont, CO: Sopris West.

Martin, J. E., Marshall, L. H., Maxson, L., & Jerman, P. (1993). *ChoiceMaker: The self-directed IEP.* Longmont, CO: Sopris West.

McGahee-Kovac, M. (2002). *A student's guide to the IEP.* Washington, DC: National Information Center for Children and Youth with Disabilities.

Meichenbaum, D., & Biemiller, A. (1998). *Nurturing independent learners: Helping students take charge of their learning.* Cambridge, MA: Brookline Books.

Nirje, B. (1969). The normalization principle and its human management implications. In R. Kugel & W. Wolfensberger (Eds.), *Changing patterns in residential services for the mentally retarded* (pp. 181–195). Washington, DC: President's Committee on Mental Retardation.

Nirje, B. (1976). The normalization principle and its human management implications. In M. Rosen, D. R. Clark, & M. S. Kivitz (Eds.), *The history of mental retardation: Collected papers* (vol. 2, pp. 363–376). Baltimore, MD: University Park Press.

Park, N., & Peterson, C. (2006). Moral competence and character strengths among adolescents: The development and validation of the Values in Action Inventory of Strengths for Youth. *Journal of Adolescence 29*(6), 891–909.

Powers, L.E., Ellison, R., Matuszewski, J., & Turner, A. (2004). *TAKE CHARGE for the future.* Portland, OR: Portland State University Regional Resource Center.

Ryan, R. M., & Deci, E. L. (2000). Self-determination theory and the facilitation of intrinsic motivation, social development, and well-being. *American Psychologist, 55*(1), 68–78.

Schalock, R. L. (1996). Reconsidering the conceptualization and measurement of quality of life. In R. Schalock (Ed.), *Quality of life: Conceptualization and measurement* (vol. I; pp. 123–139). Washington, DC: American Association on Mental Retardation.

Sitlington, P. L., & Clark, G. M. (2006). *Transition education and services for students with disabilities,* 4th ed. New York: Pearson Education.

Sitlington, P. L., & Clark, G. M. (2007). The transition assessment process and IDEIA 2004. *Assessment for Effective Intervention, 32*(3), 133–142.

Van Reusen, A. K., Bos, C. S., Schumaker, J. B., & Deshler, D. D. (2002). *The self-advocacy strategy for enhancing student motivation and self-determination.* Lawrence, KS: Edge Enterprises.

Ward, M. J. (1992). Introduction to secondary special education and transition issues. In F. R. Rusch, L. DeStefano, J. Chase-Rusch, L. A. Phelps, & E. Szymanski (Eds.), *Transition from school to adult life: Models, linkages and policy* (pp. 387–389). Sycamore, IL.: Sycamore.

Ward, M., & Kohler, P. (1996) Teaching self-determination: Content and process. In L. E. Powers, G. H. S. Singer, & J. Sowers (Eds.), *On the road to autonomy* (pp. 275–290). Baltimore: Paul H. Brookes.

Wehmeyer, M. L., & Palmer, S. (2012). *Whose future is it?* Verona, WI: Attainment Company.

Wehmeyer, M. L., Abery, B., Mithaug, D. E., & Stancliffe, R. J. (2003). *Theory in self-determination: Foundations for educational practice.* Springfield, IL: Charles C Thomas Publisher.

Wehmeyer, M. L., & Field S. L. (2007). *Self-determination and instructional and assessment strategies.* Thousand Oaks, CA: Corwin Press.

Wehmeyer, M. L., & Kelchner, K. (1995). *The Arc's Self-Determination Scale.* Arlington, TX: The Arc National Headquarters.

Wehmeyer, M., Lawrence, M., Kelchner, K., Palmer, S., Garner, N., & Soukup, J. (2004). *Whose future is it anyway? A student-directed transition planning process* (2nd ed.). Lawrence, KS: Beach Center on Disability.

Wehmeyer, M. L., Palmer, S. B., Agran, M., Mithaug, D. E., & Martin, J. E. (2000). Promoting causal agency: The Self-Determined Learning Model of instruction. *Exceptional Children, 66*(4), 439–453.

Whitworth, L., Kimsey-House, H., & Sandahl, P. (1998). *Co-active coaching: New skills for coaching people toward success in work and life.* Palo Alto, CA: Davies-Black Publishing.

Wolman, J. M., Campeau, P. L., DuBois, P. A., Mithaug, D. E., & Stolarski, V.S. (1994). *AIR Self-Determination Scale and user guide.* Stanford, CA: American Institute on Research.

Aging with Disability

Tamar Heller *and* Lieke van Heumen

Abstract

This chapter provides a life course framework and describes a model of aging well with a disability that takes into account the supports and the social-environmental context of the lives of people with disabilities. It then examines the demographic context of aging into and with a disability. Next, the chapter focuses on several key aspects in the context of positive psychology: disability identity, self-determination, and social connectedness. It concludes with challenges to studying positive psychology among adults aging with disability.

Key Words: aging, disabilities, positive psychology

Research on aging adults with disabilities often focuses on age-related losses in functioning and on ways to prevent decline. A focus on positive psychology provides a different perspective and framework. This perspective focuses on determinants of positive emotions and strength and on ways of increasing meaningfulness in life as one ages. In examining positive psychological processes in aging among persons with disabilities, one must take a life course approach because new experiences cumulatively build on earlier life experiences.

This chapter provides a life course framework and describes a model of aging well with a disability that takes into account the supports and the social-environmental context of the lives of people with disabilities. Next, it examines the demographic context of aging into and with a disability. Then, the chapter focuses on several key aspects in the context of positive psychology: disability identity, self-determination, and social connectedness. It concludes with challenges to studying positive psychology among adults aging with disability.

Providing a Life Course Framework
Contemporary Conceptualization and Life Course Approach to Aging

Aging is a complex and dynamic process that can only be understood by considering it from multiple perspectives that take into account different developmental forces. Physiological changes are often overemphasized in explanations of aging even though their effects are intertwined with psychological and sociocultural forces. Psychological or behavioral forces include all internal perceptual, cognitive, emotional, and personality factors that affect development. Sociocultural forces include interpersonal, societal, cultural, and ethnic factors. It is important to note that chronological age is not a meaningful indicator of aging. Aging is affected by experiences that occur with the passage of time, not by time itself. In other words, aging is the result of time- or age-dependent processes, not of age itself (Cavanaugh, 1999; Dannefer & Settersten Jr., 2010).

An adequate understanding of aging and what it means for an individual to grow old requires knowledge of the lifelong context in which different developmental forces occur (Cavanaugh, 1999; Elder Jr., Kirkpatrick Johnson, & Crosnoe, 2004). The life course perspective has therefore emerged as a key arena of scholarship for understanding aging (Dannefer, 2011; Elder Jr. et al., 2004). This perspective explicitly acknowledges that aging is a lifelong process that occurs from birth through death. Individuals construct their own life course through the choices and actions they take within the opportunities and constraints of history and social circumstances (Elder Jr. et al., 2004). Circumstances, events, and behavior earlier in life (and prenatally) influence human development at older ages. Importantly, the life course of individuals is shaped by cohort-historical factors (Elder Jr. et al., 2004; Marshall, 1996; Passuth & Bengtson, 1988). These are events or circumstances that most people in a specific culture experience at the same point in time and that can endow a generation with an unique identity (Cavanaugh, 1999). Developmental antecedents and the consequences of life transitions, events, and behavioral patterns can vary according to their timing in a person's life (Cavanaugh, 1999; Elder Jr. et al., 2004). Birth cohorts can age in different ways if they have different experiences at different times in their lives and follow different pathways as a consequence (Elder, 2001). Individuals born during the 1920s in Europe, for example, and who actively experienced World War II likely had very different memories than their brothers and sisters who were too young to be exposed to the harsh circumstances of the war. Additionally, the war might have impacted these individuals' education and the start of their working and family life. Hence, when compared to younger cohorts, this older generation was influenced differently by these historic circumstances throughout their lives.

Furthermore, human lives and experiences cannot be adequately represented when removed from relationships with significant others because lives are lived interdependently, within a network of shared relationships. Often, individuals are affected by larger social changes through the impact such changes have on their interpersonal contexts within more micro-level settings (Elder Jr. et al., 2004). During the Iowa farm crisis in the 1980s for example, economic hardship affected child development in negative ways largely because it increased the depressive feelings of parents (Conger & Elder Jr., 1994).

Universal changes occur for all people as they age, but the rates and nature of change are different based on tremendous variability in individual circumstances, opportunities, and experiences across

the lifespan (Heller & Marks, 2006; Kelley-Moore, 2010; Mosqueda, 2004). As a consequence, cohorts of people become more heterogeneous as they age (Dannefer, 1987). This heterogeneity is reflected in the intersection of aging and disability.

Contemporary conceptualization and life course approach to disability. Disability is a complex process, one that is multidimensional, dynamic, biopsychosocial, and interactive in nature. It is not a dichotomous phenomenon of presence or absence or a static condition, although it is often characterized as such (Ferrucci, Koh, Bandinelli, & Guralnik, 2007; Kelley-Moore, 2010; Zola, 1993). Historically, people with disabilities have been isolated from general society, which has restricted their opportunities to participate on an equal basis with others. Barriers and disabling factors include environments, attitudes, institutions, discourses, policies, and practices. A key in the struggle against the historical oppression and exclusion of people with disabilities is the challenge of overmedicalizing accounts of disability. The global politics of disability rights has launched social explanations of disability in which disability is operationalized as the relationship between people with impairment and a disabling society (Shakespeare, 2006).

Even though the number of people aging with lifelong disability is increasing, little research has addressed aging with a lifelong disability from a life course perspective (Jeppsson Grassman, Holme, Taghizadeh Larsson, & Whitaker, 2012; Kelley-Moore, 2010; Parker Harris, Heller, & Schindler, 2012; Priestley, 2003; Yorkston, McMullan, Molton, & Jensen, 2010). Most of the research and scholarship on disability has been grounded in age-related approaches. Disability among younger persons, mid-life adults, and older adults is frequently considered independently, with little cross-fertilization of ideas or acknowledgment of life course processes (Kelley-Moore, 2010).

A life course approach that addresses disability issues across generations and through various life stage transitions is useful to inform and further our understanding of disability (Irwin, 2001; Parker Harris et al., 2012). Disability can be experienced differently at different stages of life (Parker Harris et al., 2012), and there are significant differences in the life experiences of different age cohorts of persons with disabilities. Children with disabilities born in 2013 have significantly more opportunities in life than they would have had in the past. A life course approach to disability highlights how disabling societies and practices affect the circumstances, experiences, and opportunities of people with disabilities of different generations in different ways throughout the life course (Goodley, Armstrong, Sutherland, & Laurie, 2003; Parker Harris et al., 2012; Priestley, 2003).

A life course approach is of particular importance in creating insight into the experiences of persons aging with a lifelong disability. The inequalities that many persons with disabilities experience have the tendency to become more pronounced during the process of aging (Phillipson & Baars, 2007), accumulating to a more severe disadvantage that poses risks to health, wealth, and well-being and further differentiating the experiences of cohorts over time (Alkema & Alley, 2006; Biggs & Daatland, 2004). In many ways, the experiences of older adults with disabilities are likely to be very different from their nondisabled peers because they experienced segregation, discrimination, and oppression for decades.

It is important to note that the social constructions of age and the life course intersect with the experience of disability. The social meanings of age structure the life course through age expectations, (in)formal sanctions, and social timetables (Elder Jr. et al., 2004). There exists an emphasis on the importance of early- and mid-life roles in determining achievement and value in society; thus, becoming disabled early in life can affect some of these roles, such as that of being a spouse, parent, or employee (Zink, 1992). The inability to achieve normatively expected roles such as these can greatly influence perceptions of social worth and identity (Kelley-Moore, 2010; Zink, 1992). Unwittingly, families can also be a significant agent in generating stereotypes about persons with disabilities by informally discouraging particular life choices such as marriage, parenthood, independent living arrangements, or educational opportunities (Johnson, Traustadottir, Harrison, Hillier, & Sigurjonsdottir, 2001). Given the numerous factors that contribute to understanding disability within a life course approach (Parker Harris et al., 2012), we cannot make generalized statements about the "disabled life course" or "disability experience" (Priestley, 2001).

Unraveling the Discourse on Disability and Aging

Traditionally, the aging literature has been dominated by an emphasis on aging as a period of decline and loss in function (Achenbaum, 2005; Minkler, 1990). Hence, the discourse about aging and disability is dominated by the perspective that functional decline is a normative part of the human aging process leading inevitably and irreversibly to

disability. However, disablement is not an inevitable consequence of growing old, and chronological age does not represent a set of homogenous risks of disablement (Kelley-Moore, 2010).

The field of aging has spent years trying to disabuse others of the idea that age equals loss and disability (Ansello, 1988; Riley & Bond, 1983). Normal aging has been described as encompassing those age-related changes that are expected and inevitable and in understanding that changes that cause disease or inability to function are not part of aging (Mosqueda, 2004). However, the attempts to differentiate between normal aging and disease processes or disabilities also have an important downside. Attempts to stress "healthy" and "successful" aging have sometimes had the effect of reinforcing negative attitudes and prejudice toward those older adults who are in fact disabled, and this negative perception is often shared by older people themselves (J. Kennedy & Minkler, 1998, 1999; Minkler, 1990; Minkler & Fadem, 2002).

Aging well with a disability. For persons who are aging *with* disability rather than aging *into* disability, the common conceptualization of "successful aging" as aging without a disability is exclusionary. Conversely, the *supports-outcomes model of aging well* is a model that provides a vehicle for understanding aging with a disability from a life course perspective (Heller, 2004). This model combines discourse on disability with gerontological theory and describes that positive outcomes of aging for this population are related to independence, quality of life, physical and emotional well-being, and community inclusion. It stipulates that these outcomes depend on capabilities; physical and emotional health; physical functioning; environment, including home, work, and other community surroundings; and the amount and kind of support that persons receive. Overall functioning results from the interaction of people's capabilities, their environments, and the type and extent of individualized support provided to them. The model emphasizes that aging well evolves from exercising self-determination to create a successful and productive life.

Desirable environments are seen to possess three main characteristics: opportunities for fulfilling people's needs; possibilities for fostering physical, social, material, and cognitive well-being; and prospects for realizing a sense of stability, predictability, and control. The physical, social, and attitudinal environments within the home, community, and society therefore play a large role in aging well. Supports may come from a variety of sources including people, technology, and services. Supportive resources are grouped around seven key areas: companionship from family and friends, financial planning, employee assistance, emotional and behavioral support, in-home living assistance, community access and use, and health promotion and care. These supports fluctuate throughout the lifespan. Effective supports employ consumer-directed, person-centered models (Heller, 2004).

As they age, people with disabilities experience unique physical and psychosocial changes, as well as changes in their social and physical environments. A central feature of aging well has been described as adaptations to these changes that reflect individual choices and goals (Bigby, 2004). It is therefore important to consider those aspects of self-determination that provide support and opportunities for people with disabilities as they age (Heller, 2004). The supports-outcomes model of aging well indicates important factors to consider in exploring aging in this population. It also provides insight into the unique challenges that older persons with disabilities face with regards to aging well on their own terms in comparison to other older adults.

Demographic Context of Aging

There has been an increase in overall life expectancy at birth worldwide due to improved health and social care (Alley & Crimmins, 2010; Kelley-Moore, 2010; Kemp & Mosqueda, 2004; Kinsella, 2000; Sheets, 2011; Victor, 2010). In the United States, life expectancy increased from 47 years in 1900 to about 78 years in 2009 (Administration on Aging, 2009). During the past half century, the world's population aged significantly (Kemp & Mosqueda, 2004; Kinsella, 2000; Sheets, 2011) in both absolute and relative terms (Victor, 2010). The longevity of the population has led to an increase in the number of older persons. Not only is the population becoming increasingly older, the cohort of older people worldwide is larger than ever before in history. In the past century, while the total American population tripled (including those over 65 years of age), the population of older adults increased elevenfold (U.S. Bureau of the Census, 1996). This combination of larger, older cohorts and of smaller, younger cohorts due to decreased fertility that has resulted in the overall population aging (Alley & Crimmins, 2010; Victor, 2010).

In addition to the growth in both absolute and relative terms of the world's older population, the older population itself is aging (Victor, 2010). According to Harper (2006), that part of the population aged 80 years and over is the fastest growing segment of the world's population. This is caused by the reduction in late-age mortality rates and by the increased absolute size of this birth cohort in the post-World War I "baby boom." The "baby booms" or "birth bulges" following the ending of both World Wars can be explained by increased survival rates relative to previous generations (Victor, 2010).

Population aging is a feature of both developed and less developed nations, even though demographic aging was initially closely linked to the Western industrial world. Overall, the developed world demonstrates the highest relative percentage of its population in the older age groups. However, in absolute terms, the majority of older people live in developing nations (Victor, 2010). It is estimated that by 2050, there will be 2 billion people aged 60 years and over, and 75% will live in the countries of the developing world (Harper, 2006).

The intersection of aging and disability. Trends in disability have best been mapped and analyzed for older age groups (Institute of Medicine (IOM), 2007a). The prevalence of disability among people over age 65 rapidly increased during the 20th century in industrialized nations. People aging with a disability form a growing proportion of the population (Sheets, 2005). In the United States, in 2000, 42% of the population 65 years of age and older reported some type of long-lasting condition or a disability (U.S. Bureau of the Census, 2004). A prominent conceptualization of aging and disability has made a distinction between people with early-onset disabilities, who are said to "age with disability," and people with mid- or late-life onsets, who are said to experience "disability with aging" (Putnam, 2007; Verbrugge & Yang, 2002) or to "age into disability."

Drawing this distinction is helpful in organizing knowledge or in thinking through issues that affect people with lifelong disabilities; however, this should not become an end in itself (Bigby, 2004). Disability and aging are dynamic processes that interact in complex ways across the entire lifespan (Verbrugge & Yang, 2002; Yorkston et al., 2010), and various different pathways lead to the intersection of aging and disability.

The group of persons with disabilities over age 65 includes a growing number of people with congenital or early-onset impairments who are living into later years (Ansello & Janicki, 2000; Heller & Marks, 2006; Kelley-Moore, 2010; Kemp & Mosqueda, 2004; Priestley, 2003) and a growing number of people living longer who acquire impairments in their later years (Lightfoot, 2007; Priestley, 2003). This last group includes people who experience an acute health event such as stroke, spinal cord injury, or a hip fracture later in life and those who experience a decline in functioning resulting from the cumulative effects of multiple health conditions associated with aging (Kelley-Moore, 2010; Yorkston et al., 2010). Persons with early-onset disabilities will also often acquire additional impairments in old age (Priestley, 2003). The fact that impairments can be temporary or permanent, stable or cyclical, and vary in severity and prognosis further complicates the conceptualization of aging and disability.

Psychosocial differences may spring from the differing age of onset of a disability, which affects the way in which the individual interacts with the larger social environment, including family, work, and the health care system (Institute of Medicine (IOM), 2007b; Jeppsson Grassman et al., 2012; Kelley-Moore, 2010; Verbrugge & Yang, 2002; Yorkston et al., 2010). Individual differences work in combination to create distinct pathways of physical and psychological health (Yorkston et al., 2010). With the infusion of the population of people aging with a lifelong disability, the types of disability-related conditions and impairments among the older population overall will broaden. This means that the experiences of disability that people bring with them into old age will create a more heterogeneous older population (Putnam, 2007).

The aging and disability experiences interact, influence, and shape each other not only through physiological changes, but through social experiences as well (Kelley-Moore, 2010). The social constructions of disability and age influence practices, policies, and research, and, hence, individual lives. Both old age and disability can be viewed as organic and naturalized characteristics of individuals (Achenbaum, 2005; Baars, Dannefer, Phillipson, & Walker, 2006; Chappell, Goodley, & Lawthom, 2001; Dannefer, 2011; Goodley & Rapley, 2001, 2002), but this approach limits the application of supports (Kane & Kane, 2005; Sheets, 2005) and environmental adaptations to improving quality of life. Also, because both old age and disability are devalued social conditions to be avoided, postponed, or denied, there are common sources of prejudice and discrimination against older adults and people with disabilities (Alkema & Alley, 2006; Sheets, 2005). People with disabilities and older people are often considered dependent and incompetent and are systematically denied the right to participate in making decisions about how they will live their lives (Stone, 2002); thus those who both older

and disabled may have a doubly diminished social status (Bigby, 2004; Breitenbach, 2001). Examples of issues important to both groups of older adults, with and without disabilities, are the availability of affordable residential options, long-term support needs, family caregiver support, accessible transportation, access to health care, economic stability and security, and consumer-direction in services and support. Despite these similarities, much of the research, policy, practice, and advocacy efforts between the aging and disability fields are distinct (Lightfoot, 2007; Sheets, 2005).

Prevalence and incidence of disease and disability among the older population. There is a persistent view that the aging of the population will inevitably lead to an enormous increase in the number of older persons with disabilities who will drain resources by requiring substantial care (Kelley-Moore, 2010). Dementia, for example, is often described as a demographic and economic nightmare (Basting, 2003). In this view, population aging is confused with individual disablement processes and concludes that it is the aging process itself that leads inevitably to disability. There is no debate that certain aspects of physiological aging increase the risk of disablement at older ages. Yet these processes are too frequently treated as the only explanatory factor for disability in older age. Since changes in the human genome that may affect aging and/or disability are very slow to occur and operate only through natural selection, these do not explain the relatively rapid changes in the age distribution of disability that has occurred over the past century. Little attention has been given to the social environment in which disability develops and to the influence of social structural factors (Kelley-Moore, 2010; Verbrugge & Jette, 1994).

Prevalence rates of disability across age groups only provide a static picture and can lead to erroneous causal explanations linking aging to disability processes. The spike of disability at the oldest ages occurs because the risk of mortality is high, and many older adults are experiencing terminal declines in function. It should be called into question whether end-of-life processes are truly the same as disablement, even when functional impairments are equivalent (Diehr & Patrick, 2003; Kelley-Moore, 2010).

Trends of higher prevalence of disability among the older population and trends showing persons with disabilities living longer are occurring at the same time that disability incidence has been reported to be declining in the general population of persons over age 65 (Crimmins, 2004; Putnam, 2007). The higher prevalence of disability in the older population refers to the increase in the total number of persons with disability in this segment of the population. In contrast, the lower incidence of disability among older persons refers to a decrease in the number of new occurrences of disability among the older population. Today, persons over age 65 have a lower risk of developing a new disability or of experiencing a loss in functioning than in the past. One explanation is that having a disease has become less disabling; improved treatments and diagnosis in older adults have certainly led to an increased life expectancy for those with a disease (Crimmins, 2004; Kelley-Moore, 2010), as well as to a delay in the progression of disease to disability (Crimmins, 2004). Despite this estimated lower incidence of disability among the older population, the prevalence of diseases among older persons did increase in recent years because these older adults have survived a number of diseases that once would have been fatal, and they have lived long enough to acquire additional conditions (Kelley-Moore, 2010). This decrease in incidence does not counter the effect of increased survival (Crimmins, 2004).

Period and cohort factors can help explain trends and differences in disease and disability among various age groups of older adults. Recent older cohorts had healthier younger lives than did previous cohorts (Crimmins, 2004). For example, people born before the decline in deaths from infectious diseases took place are exposed to the late-life consequences of a lifetime burden of infectious conditions (Alley & Crimmins, 2010). Additionally, a number of improvements in health, such as a reduction in risk from smoking and a lowering of cholesterol, have only been noted since the 1980s and 1990s. For some indicators, trends have differed by age within the older population, with more improvement for younger cohorts (Crimmins, 2004).

Aging of persons with disabilities. The medical and social factors leading to the increase in longevity of the overall population have also significantly increased the lifespan of people with disabilities. In general, until approximately the 1970s, persons with disabilities faced lower life expectancies than their nondisabled peers (Kemp & Mosqueda, 2004; Sheets, 2011). In 1945, an able-bodied person could expect to live about 55 years; in contrast, a person who sustained a spinal cord injury had a life expectancy of just 2 years following the injury, and a person with Down syndrome could expect to only live into the early teenage years (Carmeli, Merrick, Kessel, Masharawi, & Carmeli, 2003; Kemp & Mosqueda, 2004). Fortunately, these disparities

have been reduced (Kemp & Mosqueda, 2004). People with spinal cord injury are now expected to live approximately 85% of a normal lifespan, which equals a life expectancy of 68 years (Kemp, 2005; Kemp & Mosqueda, 2004). The most significant increase in life expectancy is reported for individuals with Down syndrome (Haveman et al., 2009), who now regularly live to be 56 years old, on average (Carmeli et al., 2003). Although life expectancy for persons with intellectual disabilities has significantly increased over the past few decades, it has remained lower than the estimated life expectancy for the general population (Haveman et al., 2009). Persons with moderate or severe intellectual disabilities live into their late 60s and late 50s, respectively. In comparison, the life expectancy of adults with mild intellectual disabilities equals 74 years and is rapidly approaching near parity with the general population (Bittles et al., 2002; Haveman et al., 2009).

For the first time in history, large numbers of persons with disabilities are living into older adulthood (Mosqueda, 2004). Aging with a lifelong disability is therefore a relatively new trend. This phenomenon is particularly striking in countries like Germany and Austria. In October 1939, Hitler authorized a euthanasia program targeted at people with disabilities (Emerson, 2005). Tragically, only a few individuals with disabilities survived this systematic killing during the Nazi regime, and persons from birth cohorts before 1945 are almost nonexistent today in the disability statistics of those countries subjected to Nazi rule (Haveman & Stöppler, 2004). Although statistics on the population of middle-aged and older adults who are aging with disability are limited, it is estimated that 12 million individuals in the United States currently comprise this population, and this number is believed to be growing (Kemp & Mosqueda, 2004; Torres-Gil & Putnam, 2004). Because people with early-onset disability who recently aged into older adulthood constitute the first generation of this group, limited knowledge is available about how this group ages (Kemp & Mosqueda, 2004).

Of the different groups of people aging with a disability, people with intellectual disabilities make up the largest and best-studied group (Bigby, 2004; Janicki & Ansello, 2000). They also form one of the most vulnerable groups of older people aging with disability (Bigby, 2000). The absolute numbers of older people with intellectual disabilities are small, and they constitute a small proportion of the general older population. Thus, there exists a danger that their specific needs are neglected amid demands of larger groups (Bigby, 2004).

Health and functioning of aging adults with disabilities. Health and functioning are important factors in aging well. People who are aging with disabilities often experience a multitude of age-related functional, medical, and psychological problems that tend to occur earlier than in people without disabilities (Heller & Marks, 2006; Kemp & Mosqueda, 2004). Persons with intellectual disabilities, for example, have on average twice as many health problems than the general public (van Schrojenstein Lantman de-Valk & Noonan-Walsh, 2008). Because this is the first time in history that large numbers of people with disabilities are living into middle age and beyond, it is unknown what to expect and what to accept. There is a tendency to accept changes in health and function as inevitable outcomes of aging or the primary disability, but some changes that are common are not inevitable (Heller & Marks, 2006; Mosqueda, 2004). It is important to improve the current situation, in which several accessibility barriers exist that prevent people with disabilities from receiving appropriate health care, including health care provider's lack of knowledge (Ansello & Janicki, 2000; van Schrojenstein Lantman-de Valk, 2009), a complex bureaucracy, and physical and societal attitudinal barriers (Heller & Marks, 2006; Lightfoot, 2007). There is a need for more evidence-based practice standards in the area of health care for older people with disabilities, as well as more well-trained medical professionals who specialize in providing health care services to this population (Lightfoot, 2007).

The Experiences of Old Age and Disability and Disability Identity

People who age with disabilities and those who acquire disabilities at older ages generally perceive themselves and are perceived by others as being very different from one another (Breitenbach, 2001) despite some common challenges and similar needs on a functional level. Older people with impairments are less likely than younger people to be considered "disabled" since aging processes are commonly associated with the onset of impairment and hence impairment is seen as "normal" (Kelley-Moore, Schumacher, Kahana, & Kahana, 2006; Priestley, 2003). This fuels lowered expectations for independence and self-directed care (Kelley-Moore, 2010). Even older adults themselves frequently accept these diminished social expectations and "normative" deteriorations in health (Priestley, 2003).

Furthermore, it has been suggested that persons who experience impairments later in life are less likely to develop a "disability-rooted" identity. Those who have already experienced many life domains, such as education and employment, as able-bodied persons may be less likely to orient their sense of self around the ability (or inability) to fulfill these social roles, thus reducing the perception of themselves as having a disability (Breitenbach, 2001; Kelley-Moore, 2010; Kelley-Moore et al., 2006; Priestley, 2003; Zink, 1992). Indeed, a study by Verbrugge and Yang (2002) using data collected from the 1994–1995 National Health Interview Survey Disability Supplement, the first large-scale probability survey of disability among U.S. community-dwelling persons of all ages, found that individuals with child-onset disabilities have a much stronger disability identity than do individuals with adult-onset disabilities. An insider's perspective of the experience of persons aging with a long-term disability is very limited (Zarb, 1993a, 1993b; Zarb & Oliver, 1993). A series of empirical studies done by Zarb and Oliver (1993) on aging with a physical disability in the United Kingdom is an exception to this void. These authors examined the personal experiences of aging people who acquired their impairment in childhood or early adulthood, and they placed an emphasis on the importance of subjective experience and meaning in furthering an understanding of aging with a disability. They describe how the biographies of people who are both aging and disabled incorporate both an "aging" and a "disability" career. Prior experience of disability is an important factor in shaping people's perceptions of aging, whereas their experience of aging also influences changing perceptions of disability. The authors found that many older people with disabilities feel that their needs, and even their existence, have been overlooked (Zarb, 1993a, 1993b; Zarb & Oliver, 1993).

A unique study of the experiences of people aging with physical disability by Yorkston et al. (2010) found that the process of aging with disability was characterized by multiple pathways. These older adults with spinal cord injury, post-polio syndrome, or multiple sclerosis indicated that some pathways, including positive psychosocial adjustment and medical advancements, were favorable, whereas other pathways, including physical decline, were not. The study found the co-existence of a high quality of life in the presence of physical decline, a finding consistent with gerontological literature indicating that some elements of the aging experience, such as declining physical function, may have a progressive course with age whereas others, such psychological well-being and general quality of life, may not. It also confirms what is called the "disability paradox" (Albrecht & Devlieger, 1999), the discrepancy between changes in physical functioning and quality of life over time. Participants in the study indicated that they were uncertain about whether they would have the resources to cope with future change, but they did describe themselves as having a number of positive attributes, such as being "resilient." They wished to maintain control over decisions in their lives with the support of those in their social network and the health care community.

A participatory study by Brown and Gill (2009) on the experiences and perspectives of aging women with intellectual and developmental disabilities found that they held mostly negative views associated with getting older. Most of the women emphasized physical perceptions of aging and interpreted getting ill and dying as part of the aging process. Aging was associated with disability, the lack or loss of functional abilities, and debilitation. They also expressed being confronted with the loss of loved ones, such as parents, friends, or siblings. On probing, some of the women identified more positive aspects of aging, such as "getting discounts" and the idea that older people "deserve more respect." Brown and Gill also found that the words and attitudes of family members and peers significantly shaped how the women came to understand both aging and disability experiences (Brown & Gill, 2009).

It has also been suggested that, for persons with intellectual disabilities, chronological age might not have the same meaning and relevance as for other older adults. These persons experience problems with the concept of time marked by a strong present orientation and difficulties with dates and numbers (Booth & Booth, 1996) related to the severity of their impairment (Sharpe, Murry, McKenzie, Quigley, & Patrick, 2001). Milestones such as reaching 50, 60, or 70 are probably meaningless for persons who are able to count only to twenty (Haveman et al., 2009). Functional aging is much more important for persons with intellectual disabilities. If adults with intellectual disabilities at advanced chronological age begin to notice difficulty with walking, seeing, hearing, eating, and talking, they may start to feel old (Haveman, 2004; Haveman et al., 2009). Urlings et al. (1993) documented in a qualitative study of older people with intellectual disabilities that only for individuals over 70 is aging is a major topic of interest. They were able to relate the decline of self-help skills and the anxiety of becoming physically ill and bedridden to

the perceived concept of aging. Growing old and dying were major issues for these older adults.

Dementia. Dementia is one of the most common impairments in older people and is commonly understood as a terrifying illness. It is almost entirely seen as a loss by persons affected by it (Beard, Knauss, & Moyer, 2009). The thought of being insane, deranged, and lost forever in confusion is terrifying to many people (Kitwood, 1997). Additionally, many people dread becoming a burden to others (Basting, 2003, 2009). This reflexive fear is a problem because it worsens the experience of dementia. The source of this fear is that people with dementia are thought to lose their individuality and "selfhood" (Basting, 2003, 2009).

Assumptions that persons with dementia cannot lead meaningful lives or enjoy a high quality of life are pervasive and powerful. Those who have dementia are often subjected to ageism in its most extreme form, being categorized as incompetent, ugly, and burdensome (Kitwood, 1997). To shed light on the question of whether living with dementia involves the suffering that is feared, it is important to listen to the voices of people who live with it. Knowledge of the experiences of persons with dementia is also important for creating effective and respectful supports. A literature review by de Boer et al. (2007) on studies including the perspective of persons with dementia gives no solid support to the pervasive assumption that dementia is primarily and necessarily a state of dreadful suffering. The experiences of persons with dementia yield a more subtle picture. Although the impact of dementia and the experiences of loss resulting in multiple negative emotions such as fear, insecurity, confusion, or disbelief cannot be denied, it has been found that people do not undergo dementia as "passive sufferers," but use coping strategies to deal with its challenges. Dementia is often a process with an insidious onset and gradual progression, allowing the person to adapt and adjust to his or her changing situation. As a result, the actual experiences of the disease can deviate, in a positive manner, from anticipatory beliefs. People with dementia have expressed that being able to take part in activities, along with friendships and feelings of belonging or attachment, are important aspects of their quality of life. Despite the impact of the disease, most people diagnosed with dementia try to continue to live in the best possible way (de Boer, Dröes, Jonker, Eefsting, & Hertogh, 2010; de Boer et al., 2007).

Life histories of older adults with disabilities. The subjective well-being of older adults is not only determined by what they experience today, but also by what happened to them in the past and their retrospective view on those life events (Westerhof, Dittman-Kohli, & Thissen, 2001). *Life review* has been described as a means to age successfully (Butler, 1963), and retrieving memories is an important activity in the last stages of life (Erikson, 1997). Talking about their lives is a way for older people to make peace with themselves and their accomplishments. Talking about their lives can also provide insight into how they have become the person they are today (van den Brandt-van Heek, 2011). In addition, older adults have wisdom to share with younger generations through telling their stories, and, as people grow older, the issue of generativity may increasingly move to the front and center of the life story (McAdams, 2001).

Life story research is important because it puts a human face on aging and growing old and produces emancipatory and empowering knowledge, hence fighting stereotypes and prejudice against older persons (Bornat, 2002; Estes, Biggs, & Phillipson, 2003; Jamieson, 2002; Minkler, 1998). The individual experiences of older persons with disabilities throughout their lives may throw light on forgotten or hidden aspects of past experience, bringing to the foreground lives that have been marginalized, disregarded, and downgraded (Bornat, 2002). Gray (1997), for example, assisted Herbert (Bertie) Lawford in telling his story of life in Church Hill House Hospital in England. Bertie was admitted to Church Hill House in August 1934, when he was 9. He was told he was going for a day at the seaside. He lived there for the next 60 years. His memories include hard physical work on the farm or scrubbing and polishing the wards and of the "boys," who were grown men by then, always having to walk two by two whenever out of the institution's grounds, a practice that persisted until the 1960s (Emerson, 2005).

One rare example of the life history approach used with people with disabilities is a study by Caldwell (2010), in which he interviewed thirteen leaders in the self-advocacy movement for individuals with developmental disabilities regarding factors that contributed to their leadership development. Through their stories, he was able to capture the central stories of their lives, including the formation of their identities, leadership development, and beliefs. In addition, the study pointed to the critical role that involvement in the self-advocacy movement played in the lives of these self-advocates. The community and connection with peers allowed for personal and collective resistance to oppression and the formation of a positive disability identity (Caldwell, 2010). Furthermore, these seasoned leaders had a strong desire to pass on their history and the lessons they had learned to younger self-advocates.

The problem is that the collective voices of older people with disabilities, their views on aging, how they would like to be supported to lead a better quality of life, and what they regard as successful aging are rarely included in the body of research in the field. This silence makes it difficult to counter negative assumptions and means that the views of others tend to dominate the agenda of successful aging and the nature of support to achieve it (Bigby, 2004).

Social connectedness among aging adults with disabilities. Social relationships and social support are important elements in how people define their life quality and happiness (Barrera, 2000; Bigby, 2004; C. H. Kennedy, 2004). Research has demonstrated that satisfaction of the fundamental human need to develop close, long-lasting, and supportive relationships (Baumeister & Leary, 1995) is associated with positive physical and psychological health outcomes. The reverse is true when persons experience social isolation and a lack of social support (Antonucci, Akiyama, & Sherman, 2007; Baumeister & Leary, 1995; Berkman, Ertel, & Glymour, 2011; Broese van Groenou & van Tilburg, 2007; Cohen & Syme, 1985; Due, Holstein, Lund, Modvig, & Avlund, 1999; Hogan, Linden, & Najarian, 2002; Knipscheer & Antonucci, 1990; Stevens, Martina, & Westerhof, 2006; Wills & Shinar, 2000). Social well-being is of particular importance for older adults because they rate social relationships among the most important determinants of aging well (Cavanaugh, 1999). Social relations have been increasingly recognized as a critical element in the well-being of older people (Antonucci et al., 2007) and a lifetime of social inclusion, of engagement with one's community, as central to promoting healthy aging (Janicki & Breitenbach, 2000). The social networks of older people are shaped by the lives they have lived (Knipscheer & Antonucci, 1990). People enter old age with a personal network that reflects earlier circumstances and transitions affecting their opportunities and individual needs and choices to maintain and develop supportive relationships (Antonucci & Knipscheer, 1990; Broese van Groenou & van Tilburg, 2007).

People with disabilities face a different social reality than do persons without disabilities (Hopps, Pepin, Arseneau, Frechette, & Begin, 2001). The prevailing social and cultural attitudes and physical barriers constitute important obstacles to the social integration of people with disabilities and the development of relationships across the life course (Hopps et al., 2001; McConkey, 2005; Pabst, 2006). Relationships exist in social geographies and the spaces people use and occupy. Issues such as housing, finances, transport, mobility, and the experience of public and segregated spaces all play a key role in understanding the context of social relations for persons with disabilities (Power, 2010; Walsh & LeRoy, 2004). Persons with intellectual disabilities, for example, face a mix of patronization, fear, an unwillingness to understand "nonstandard" forms of communication, and a strong sense of "difference" in public life (Hall & Kearns, 2001). Others have low expectations of persons with intellectual disabilities and devalue the importance of their relationships (Bigby, 2002, 2003). Many people with intellectual disabilities still live secluded lives (Power, 2010), and their interaction with the community is often regulated and controlled by professionals (Parker Harris et al., 2012). The social relations at work in the sheltered workshop or the group home are not those that promote autonomy and self-esteem (Power, 2010). Many persons with intellectual disabilities are in a "double-bind" of marginalization, experiencing exclusion from and abjection and discrimination within the very social spaces that are the key markers of social inclusion policy (Hall, 2005).

One of the issues facing people aging with disabilities is that their need for assistance with daily activities may increase as they get older (McNoll, 2004). Families play a pivotal role in meeting the increased needs for care by persons with disabilities as they age (Heller & Caldwell, 2006; Kemp & Mosqueda, 2004; Mosqueda, 2004). With longer life expectancy, parents have a longer period of responsibility and are more likely to face dealing with their own aging in addition to the aging of their adult children (Heller, 1999; Heller & Caldwell, 2006; Heller, Caldwell, & Factor, 2007; Heller & Marks, 2006). It is now also more common for adults with disabilities to provide support to their aging family members (Heller et al., 2007), and there is a greater likelihood of the person with a disability outliving his or her parents (Heller & Caldwell, 2006; Heller et al., 2007) and needing new residential options. Adults with disabilities who live in out-of-home residences are likely to need supports to "age in place" (Heller, 2004).

Self-determination. Older adults with disabilities typically have had few opportunities to exercise self-determination in their lives (Heller, Sterns, Sutton, & Factor, 1996), and they experience substantial discrimination on the basis of age (Bigby, 2004; Walker & Walker, 1998). Self-determination has been recognized as an important element of aging well (Heller, 2004; Heller et al., 2010). Older adults with disabilities have the same rights to personal growth as do others, and they are entitled to expression through self-advocacy of what they will do with their own lives (Ansello & Janicki, 2000). However, the population of older adults with disabilities faces some unique challenges and disabling barriers in exercising choice and control over their own lives, and their voices and experiences are underrepresented (Priestley, 2003).

Those older adults who acquire disability as they age—and therefore do not evolve with disability as a presence in their younger life—are at risk of not being appropriately accommodated in the way that people with preexisting disabilities might be because of their political activism and identification with the disability cause (Sheets, 2005). Nevertheless, there are systematically low expectations for all older people with disabilities (Harris, 2010; Hogg, Moss, & Cooke, 1988; Kelley-Moore, 2010; Walker & Walker, 1998) regardless of whether the impairment was acquired early or late in life. Such views become self-fulfilling prophecies (Bigby, 2004), in particular in older adults with intellectual disabilities who often have little understanding and skills to express their desires.

Research has demonstrated the efficacy of assertiveness training and decision-making training in developing these individuals' choice-making skills (Heller et al., 1996). There is increasing evidence that older people with intellectual disabilities become more independent, learn new skills, acquire new interests, and want to lead active lives (Bigby, 2004; Buys et al., 2008; Edgerton, 1994; Krauss & Seltzer, 1994). Indeed, for people regarded as "slow learners," longer lives can mean greater opportunities for personal growth, constructive training, and life experience and more time to achieve self-determination (Bigby, 2000; Breitenbach, 2001; Heller & Caldwell, 2006; Kelley-Moore, 2010). Also, education and training of staff, as well as systemic changes, are important strategies for increasing self-determination and choice for individuals and for combating ageism (Bigby, 2004). Social policies of deinstitutionalization and support in the community potentially increase the opportunities and scope for self-determination and decision making (Wong, Clare, Gunn, & Holland, 1999).

Aging people with lifelong disabilities move beyond traditional skills development or job programs (Bigby, 1997), and retirement from these work experiences becomes a more common expectation (Ansello & Janicki, 2000). Similar to many older adults in the general population, many older adults with disabilities prefer to continue working as long as possible and desire obtaining better-paying jobs in the community (Heller, 1999). A major ongoing concern is that, despite aspirations for continuing inclusion, older people with disabilities experience few opportunities to participate in meaningful day and leisure activities of their choice (Bigby, 2005).

Quality of life can be increased by learning what older people seek and facilitating opportunities for them to meet their needs and aspirations (Schroots & Birren, 2001) and by questioning taken-for-granted practices (Hamilton, 2009). Individualized person-centered (future) planning of supports has therefore been recognized as of central importance because it can give individuals with intellectual disabilities a voice and provide them with knowledge and opportunities to make choices as they age (Heller & Caldwell, 2006). The rationale for person-centered planning is even stronger for older adults because people become more heterogeneous as they age, and hence one-size-fits-all policies and practices simply fail (Ansello & Janicki, 2000). Individualized supports potentially provide powerful mechanisms to counter negative stereotypes and to ensure that older people with intellectual disabilities are being recognized as persons of worth (Bigby, 2004).

Conclusion

In future research, an increased emphasis on life course perspectives is important. Many persons with disabilities experienced an accumulation of restricted opportunities and major inequalities throughout their life course that affects their aging process in ways different from their nondisabled peers. It is important to realize that the experiences and needs of future generations might be different because they will have lived their lives in different circumstances with likely more opportunities.

Most of the research to date on aging and disability focuses on cross-sectional data and does not take into account the impact of early experiences or the cumulative and dynamic nature of aging. Furthermore, this research rarely examines the lived experiences of people with disabilities and those aspects of their lives that bring meaningfulness, happiness, and joy. Life history research could address this dynamic aspect. Another is the use of longitudinal data that includes interviews with

and observations of people with disabilities in their social and physical environments. Knowledge of the patterns of aging with disability in the context of one's changing environment is critical for providing the medical, rehabilitative, and psychosocial supports needed for aging well.

Future Directions

Positive psychology within a life course and disability studies framework offers a promising line of research. This type of research can answer questions regarding the lifelong influences that result in aging well for people with disabilities. The largely neglected outcomes that need to be studied include meaning in one's life and feelings of positive identity, happiness, self-esteem, and empowerment. Few studies have examined the dynamic impact of social-environmental factors on these outcomes for people with disabilities throughout their lives.

There are many challenges to this type of research. One is measuring these outcomes, particularly among people with limited cognitive abilities. Second, longitudinal data are difficult to collect over a period of many years. Third, few evidence-based interventions to increase positive well-being have been tested that can be disseminated widely to change practice and policies. Hence, many opportunities exist to forge new research territory to explore the pathways to aging well among individuals with disabilities.

Acknowledgments

This document was produced under grant number H133B080009 awarded by the U.S. Department of Education's National Institute on Disability and Rehabilitation Research to the Rehabilitation Research and Training Center on Aging with Developmental Disabilities-Lifespan Health and Function at the University of Illinois at Chicago. The contents of this article do not necessarily represent the policy of the U.S. Department of Education and should not be assumed as being endorsed by the U.S. federal government.

References

Achenbaum, W. A. (2005). Ageing and changing: International historical perspectives on ageing. In M. L. Johnson, V. L. Bengtson, P. G. Coleman, & T. B. L. Kirkwood (Eds.), *The Cambridge handbook of age and ageing* (pp. 21–29). Cambridge, UK: Cambridge University Press.

Administration on Aging. (2009). A Profile of Older Americans: 2009. Retrieved November 13, 2011, from http://www.aoa. gov/AoARoot/Aging_Statistics/Profile/index.aspx

Albrecht, G. L., & Devlieger, P. J. (1999). The disability paradox: high quality of life against all odds. *Social Science & Medicine, 48,* 977–988.

Alkema, G. E., & Alley, D. E. (2006). Gerontology's future: An integrative model for disciplinary advancement. *Gerontologist, 46,* 574–582.

Alley, D., & Crimmins, E. (2010). Epidemiology of aging. In D. Dannefer & C. Phillipson (Eds.), *The SAGE handbook of social gerontology* (pp. 75–95). London: Sage.

Ansello, E. F. (1988). The intersecting of aging and disabilities. *Educational Gerontology, 14*(5), 351–365.

Ansello, E. F., & Janicki, M. P. (2000). The aging of nations: Impact on the Community, the family and the individual. In M. P. Janicki & E. F. Ansello (Eds.), *Community supports for aging adults with lifelong disabilities* (pp. 3–18). Baltimore, MD: Paul H. Brookes.

Antonucci, T. C., Akiyama, H., & Sherman, A. M. (2007). Social networks, support, and integration. In J. E. Birren (Ed.), *Encyclopedia of gerontology, 2nd edition* (pp. 531–541). Oxford: Academic Press.

Antonucci, T. C., & Knipscheer, C. P. M. (1990). Social network research: Review and perspectives. In C. P. M. Knipscheer & T. C. Antonucci (Eds.), *Social network research: Substantive issues and methodological issues* (pp.161–173). Amsterdam/Lisse: Swets & Zeitlinger, B.V.

Baars, J., Dannefer, D., Phillipson, C., & Walker, A. (2006). Introduction: Critical perspectives in social gerontology. In J. Baars, D. Dannefer, C. Phillipson, & A. Walker (Eds.), *Aging, globalization and inequality. The new critical gerontology* (pp. 1–14). Amityville, NY: Baywood.

Barrera, M. J. (2000). Social support research in community psychology. In J. Rappaport & E. Seidman (Eds.), *Handbook of community psychology* (pp. 215–245). New York: Kluwer Academic/Plenum.

Basting, A. D. (2003). Looking back from loss: Views of the self in Alzheimer's disease. *Journal of Aging Studies, 17,* 87–99.

Basting, A. D. (2009). *Forget memory: Creating better lives for people with dementia.* Baltimore, MD: Johns Hopkins University Press.

Baumeister, R. F., & Leary, M. R. (1995). The need to belong: Desire for interpersonal attachments as a fundamental human motivation. *Psychological Bulletin, 117*(3), 497–529.

Beard, R. L., Knauss, J., & Moyer, D. (2009). Managing disability and enjoying life: How we reframe dementia through personal narratives. *Journal of Aging Studies, 23,* 227–235.

Berkman, L. F., Ertel, K. A., & Glymour, M. M. (2011). Aging and social intervention: Life course perspectives. In R. H. Binstock & L. K. George (Eds.), *Handbook of aging and the social sciences* (pp. 337–351). San Diego: Academic Press.

Bigby, C. (1997). When parents relinquish care: Informal support networks of older people with intellectual disability. *Journal of Applied Research in Intellectual Disabilities, 10*(4), 333–344.

Bigby, C. (2000). *Moving on without parents.* Baltimore, MD: Paul H. Brookes.

Bigby, C. (2002). Social roles and informal support networks in mid life and beyond. In P. Noonan Walsh. & T. Heller (Eds.), *Health of women with intellectual disabilities.* Oxford: Blackwell.

Bigby, C. (2003). The evolving informal support networks of older adults with learning disability. In M. Nolan (Ed.), *Partnerships in family care* (pp. 167–182). Berkshire: McGraw-Hill Education.

Bigby, C. (2004). *Ageing with a lifelong disability: A guide to practice, program and policy issues for human services professionals.* Philadelphia, PA: Jessica Kingsley.

Bigby, C. (2005). Growing old. Adapting to change and realizing a sense of belonging, continuity and purpose. In G. Grant, P. Goward, M. Richardson, & P. Ramcharan (Eds.), *Learning disability. A life cycle approach to valuing people* (pp. 663–684). Maidenhead: New York: Open University Press.

Biggs, S., & Daatland, S. (2004). Ageing and diversity: a critical introduction. In S. Biggs & S. Daatland (Eds.), *Ageing and diversity: Multiple pathways and cultural migrations* (pp. 1–12). Bristol: Policy Press.

Bittles, A. H., Petterson, B. A., Sullivan, S. G., Hussain, R., Glasson, E. J., & Montgomery, P. D. (2002). The influence of intellectual disability on life expectancy. *Journals of Gerontology Series A: Biological Sciences and Medical Sciences, 57*(7), M470–M472.

Booth, T., & Booth, W. (1996). Sounds of silence: Narrative research with inarticulate subjects. *Disability & Society, 11*(1), 55–69.

Bornat, J. (2002). Doing life history research. In A. Jamieson & C. Victor (Eds.), *Researching ageing and later life: the practice of social gerontology.* Buckingham: Open University Press.

Breitenbach, N. (2001). Ageing with intellectual disabilities: discovering disability with old age: same or different? In M. Priestley (Ed.), *Disability and the life course: Global perspectives.* Cambridge: University Press.

Broese van Groenou, M., & van Tilburg, T. (2007). Network analysis. In J. E. Birren (Ed.), *Encyclopedia of gerontology.* Amsterdam: Academic Press.

Brown, A. A., & Gill, C. (2009). New voices in women's health: Perceptions of women with intellectual and developmental disabilities. *Intellectual and developmental disabilities, 47*(5), 337–347.

Butler, R. N. (1963). The life review: An interpretation of reminiscence in the aged. *Psychiatry, 26*(65–76).

Buys, L., Boulton-Lewis, G. M., Tedman-Jones, J. S., Edwards, H. E., Knox, M. F., & Bigby, C. (2008). Issues of active ageing: Perceptions of older people with lifelong intellectual disability. *Australasian Journal on Ageing, 27*(2), 67–71.

Caldwell, J. (2010). Leadership development of individuals with developmental disabilities in the self-advocacy movement. *Journal of Intellectual and Developmental Disabilities, 54,* 1004–1014.

Carmeli, E., Merrick, J., Kessel, S., Masharawi, Y., & Carmeli, V. (2003). Elderly persons with intellectual disability: a study of clinical characteristics, functional status, and sensory capacity. *Scientific World Journal, 3,* 298–307.

Cavanaugh, J. C. (1999). Theories of aging in the biological, behavioural and social sciences. In J. C. Cavanaugh & S. K. Whitbourne (Eds.), *Gerontology: An interdisciplinary perspective* (pp. 46–357). Oxford: Oxford University Press.

Chappell, A. L., Goodley, D., & Lawthom, R. (2001). Making connections: The relevance of the social model of disability for people with learning difficulties. *British Journal of Learning Disabilities, 29*(2), 45–50.

Cohen, S., & Syme, S. L. (1985). Issues in the study and application of social support. In S. Cohen & S. L. Syme (Eds.), *Social support and health* (pp. 3–22). New York: Academic Press.

Conger, R. D., & Elder Jr., G. H. (1994). *Families in troubled times: Adapting to change in rural America.* Hawthorne, NY: Aldine de Gruyter.

Crimmins, E. M. (2004). Trends in the health of the elderly. *Annual Review of Public Health, 25*(79–98).

Dannefer, D. (1987). Aging as intracohort differentiation: accentuation, the Matthew effect and the life course. *Sociological Forum, 2*, 211–236.

Dannefer, D. (2011). Age, the life course, and the sociological imagination: Prospects for theory. In R. H. Binstock & L. K. George (Eds.), *Handbook of aging and the social sciences* (pp. 3–16). San Diego: Academic Press.

Dannefer, D., & Settersten Jr., R. A. (2010). The study of the life course: Implications for social gerontology. In D. Dannefer & C. Phillipson (Eds.), *The SAGE handbook of social gerontology* (pp. 3–19). London: Sage.

de Boer, M. E., Dröes, R. M., Jonker, C., Eefsting, J. A., & Hertogh, C. M. (2010). The lived-experiences of early-stage dementia and the feared suffering: An explorative survey. *Tijdschrift voor Gerontologie en Geriatrie, 41*(5), 194–203.

de Boer, M. E., Hertogh, C. M. P. M., Droes, R., Riphagen, I. I., Jonker, C., & Eefsting, J. A. (2007). Suffering from dementia—the patient's perspective: A review of the literature. *International Psychogeriatrics, 19*(6), 1021–1039.

Diehr, P., & Patrick, D. L. (2003). Trajectories of health for older adults over time: Accounting fully for death. *Annals of Internal Medicine, 139*, 416–420.

Due, P., Holstein, B., Lund, R., Modvig, J., & Avlund, K. (1999). Social relations: Network, support and relational strain. *Social Science and Medicine, 48*, 661–673.

Edgerton, R. B. (1994). Quality of life issues: Some people know how to be old. In M. M. Seltzer, M. W. Krauss, & M. P. Janicki (Eds.), *Life course perspectives on adulthood and old age* (pp. 53–66). Washington DC: AAMR.

Elder, G. H. (2001). Lifecourse. In G. L. Maddox (Ed.), *The encyclopedia of aging* (pp. 593–596). New York: Springer.

Elder Jr., G. H., Kirkpatrick Johnson, M., & Crosnoe, R. (2004). The emergence and development of life course theory. In J. T. Mortimer & M. J. Shanahan (Eds.), *Handbook of the life course* (pp. 3–22). New York: Springer.

Emerson, E. (2005). Models of service delivery. In G. Grant, P. Goward, M. Richardson, & P. Ramcharan (Eds.), *Learning disability: A life cycle approach to valueing people* (pp. 108–127). New York: Open University Press.

Erikson, E. (1997). *The life cycle completed*. New York: W. W. Norton.

Estes, C. L., Biggs, S., & Phillipson, C. (2003). Conclusion: Future tasks for a critical gerontology. In C. L. Estes, S. Biggs & C. Phillipson (Eds.), *Social theory, social policy and ageing* (pp. 145–153). Berkshire: Open University Press.

Ferrucci, L., Koh, C., Bandinelli, S., & Guralnik, J. M. (2007). Disability, functional status and activities of daily living. In J. E. Birren (Ed.), *The encyclopedia of gerontology, 2nd edition* (pp. 427–436). Oxford: Academic Press.

Goodley, D., Armstrong, D., Sutherland, K., & Laurie, L. (2003). Self-advocacy, "learning difficulties," and the social model of disability. *Mental Retardation, 41*(3), 149–160.

Goodley, D., & Rapley, M. (2001). 'How do you understand 'learning difficulties'? Towards a social theory of impairment. *Mental Retardation, 39*, 229–232.

Goodley, D., & Rapley, M. (2002). Changing the subject: Postmodernity and people with learning difficulties. In M. Corker & T. Shakespeare (Eds.), *Disability/postmodernity: Embodying disability theory* (pp. 127–139). London: Continuum.

Gray, G. (1997). *A long day at the seaside*. Windsor: Reedprint.

Hall, E. (2005). The entangled geographies of social exclusion/inclusion for people with learning disabilities. *Health and Place, 11*(1), 107–115.

Hall, E., & Kearns, R. (2001). Making space for the "intellectual" in geographies of disability. *Health and Place, 7*(3), 237–246.

Hamilton, C. (2009). "A Story to Tell": Learning from the life-stories of older people with intellectual disabilities in Ireland. *British Journal of Learning Disabilities, 37*(4), 316–322.

Harper, S. (2006). *Ageing societies*. London: Hodder Arnold.

Harris, J. C. (2010). Developmental perspective on the emergence of moral personhood. In Feder Kittay E. & L. Carlson (Eds.), *Cognitive disability and its challenge to moral philosophy* (pp. 55–74). West Sussex: John Wiley & Sons Ltd.

Haveman, M. (2004). Disease epidemiology and aging people with intellectual disabilities. *Journal of Policy and Practice in Intellectual Disabilities, 1*(1), 16–23.

Haveman, M., Heller, T., Lee, L. A., Maaskant, M. A., Shooshtari, S., & Strydom, A. (2009). *Report on the state of science on health risks and ageing in people with intellectual disabilities*: IASSID Special Interest Research Group on Ageing and Intellectual Disabilities/Faculty Rehabilitation Sciences, University of Dortmund.

Haveman, M., & Stöppler, R. (2004). *Altern mit geistiger Behinderung*: Kohlhammer Verlag.

Heller, T. (1999). Emerging models. In S. S. Herr & G. Weber (Eds.), *Aging, rights and quality of life. Prospects for older people with developmental disabilities* (pp. 149–166). Baltimore: Paul H. Brookes.

Heller, T. (2004). Aging with developmental disabilities: Emerging models for promoting health, independence, and quality of life. In B. J. Kemp & L. Mosqueda (Eds.), *Aging with a disability: What a clinician needs to know* (pp. 213–233). Baltimore, MD: Johns Hopkins University Press.

Heller, T., & Caldwell, J. (2006). Supporting aging caregivers and adults with developmental disabilities in future planning. *Mental Retardation, 44*(3), 189–202.

Heller, T., Caldwell, J., & Factor, A. (2007). Aging family caregivers: Policies and practices. *Mental Retardation and Developmental Disabilities Research Reviews, 13* (2), 136–142.

Heller, T., & Marks, B. (2006). *Aging in encyclopedia of disability* (vol. 1). Thousand Oaks, CA: Sage.

Heller, T., Schindler, A., Palmer, S., Wehmeyer, M., Parent, W., Jenson, R., et al. (2010). Self-Determination across the life span: Issues and Gaps. *Exceptionality, 19*(1), 31–45.

Heller, T., Sterns, H., Sutton, E., & Factor, A. R. (1996). Impact of person-centered later life planning training program for older adults with mental retardation. *Journal of Rehabilitation, 62*, 77–83.

Hogan, B. E., Linden, W., & Najarian, B. (2002). Social support interventions Do they work? *Clinical Psychology Review, 22*, 381–440.

Hogg, J., Moss, S., & Cooke, D. (1988). *Ageing and mental handicap*. Cambridge: Cambridge University Press.

Hopps, S. L., Pepin, M., Arseneau, I., Frechette, M., & Begin, G. (2001). Disability related variables associated with loneliness amongst people with disabilities. *Journal of Rehabilitation*, July/August/September, 42–48.

Institute of Medicine (IOM). (2007a). Disability trends. In M. J. Field & A. M. Jette (Eds.), *The future of disability in America* (pp. 65–97). Washington, DC: National Academies Press.

Institute of Medicine (IOM). (2007b). *The future of disability in America*. Washington, DC: National Academies Press.

Irwin, S. (2001). Repositioning disability and the life course: A social claiming perspective. In M. Priestley (Ed.), *Disability and the life course: Global perspectives* (pp. 15–25). Cambridge: Cambridge University Press.

Jamieson, A. (2002). Theory and practice in social gerontology. In A. Jamieson & C. Victor (Eds.), *Researching ageing and later life. The practice of social gerontology* (pp.7–19). Buckingham/Philadelphia: Open University Press.

Janicki, M. P., & Ansello, E. F. (2000). Supports for community living. Evolution of an aging with lifelong disabilities movement. In M. P. Janicki & E. F. Ansello (Eds.), *Community supports for aging adults with lifelong disabilities* (pp. 529–548). Baltimore, MD: Paul H. Brookes.

Janicki, M. P., & Breitenbach, N. (2000). *Aging and intellectual disabilities—Improving longevity and promoting healthy aging: Summative report*. Geneva: World Health Organization.

Jeppsson Grassman E., Holme, L., Taghizadeh Larsson A., & Whitaker, A. (2012). A long life with a particular signature: Life course and aging for people with disabilities. *Journal of Gerontological Social Work, 55*, 95–111.

Johnson, K., Traustadottir, R., Harrison, L., Hillier, L., & Sigurjonsdottir, H. B. (2001). The possibility of choice: Women with intellectual disabilities talking about having children. In M. Priestley (Ed.), *Disability and the life course: Global perspectives* (pp. 206–218). Cambridge, MA: Cambridge University Press.

Kane, R. L., & Kane, R. A. (2005). Ageism in healthcare and long-term care. *Generations, Fall*, 49–54.

Kelley-Moore, J. A. (2010). Disability and ageing: The social construction of causality. In D. Dannefer & C. Phillipson (Eds.), *The SAGE handbook of social gerontology* (pp. 96–110). London: Sage.

Kelley-Moore, J. A., Schumacher, J. G., Kahana, E., & Kahana, B. (2006). When do older adults become "disabled"? Social and health antecedents of perceived disability in a panel study of the oldest old. *Journal of Health and Social Behavior, 47*, 126–141.

Kemp, B. J. (2005). Aging with disability: What the rehabilitation professional and the consumer need to know. *Physical Medicine and Rehabilitation Clinics of North America, 16*(1), 1–18.

Kemp, B. J., & Mosqueda, L. (2004). Introduction. In B. J. Kemp & L. Mosqueda (Eds.), *Aging with a disability: What the clinician needs to know* (pp. 1–5). Baltimore, MD: Johns Hopkins University Press.

Kennedy, C. H. (2004). Research on social relationships. In E. Emerson, C. Hatton, T. Thompson, & T. R. Parmenter (Eds.), *The international handbook of applied research in intellectual disabilities* (pp. 297–309). Sussex: John Wiley & Sons Ltd.

Kennedy, J., & Minkler, M. (1998). Disability theory and public policy: implications for critical gerontology. *International Journal of Health Services, 28*(4), 757–776.

Kennedy, J., & Minkler, M. (1999). Disability theory and public policy: Implications for critical gerontology. In M. Minkler & C. L. Estes (Eds.), *Critical gerontology. Perspectives from political and moral economy* (pp. 91–108). Amityville, NY: Baywood.

Kinsella, K. (2000). Demographic dimensions of global aging. *Journal of Family Issues, 21*(541), 541–558.

Kitwood, T. (1997). *Dementia reconsidered: The person comes first*. Maidenhead: Open University Press.

Knipscheer, C. P. M., & Antonucci, T. C. (Eds.). (1990). *Social network research: substantive issues and methodological issues*. Amsterdam/Lisse: Swets & Zeitlinger, B.V.

Krauss, M. W., & Seltzer, M. M. (1994). Taking stock: Expected gains from a life-span perspective on mental retardation. In M. M. Seltzer, M. W. Krauss, & M. P. Janicki (Eds.), *Life course perspectives on adulthood and old age* (pp. 213–220). Washington DC: AAMR.

Lightfoot, E. (2007). Disability. In J. A. Blackburn & C. N. Dulmus (Eds.), *Handbook of gerontology: Evidence-based approaches to theory, practice, and policy* (pp. 201–229). Hoboken, NJ: John Wiley & Sons.

Marshall, V. W. (1996). The state of theory in aging and the social sciences. In R. H. Binstock & L. K. George (Eds.), *Handbook of aging and the social sciences* (vol. 4th ed., pp. 12–30). San Diego: Academic Press.

McAdams, D. P. (2001). The psychology of life stories. *Review of General Psychology, 5*(2), 100–122.

McConkey, R. (2005). Promoting friendships and developing social networks. In G. Grant, P. Goward, M. Richardson, & P. Ramcharan (Eds.), *Learning disability. A life cycle approach to valuing people* (pp. 469–490). New York: Open University Press.

McNoll, M. A. (2004). Family and caregiving issues. In B. J. Kemp & L. Mosqueda (Eds.), *Aging with a disability: What the clinician needs to know* (pp. 68–83). Baltimore, MD: Johns Hopkins Press.

Minkler, M. (1990). Aging and disability: Behind and beyond the stereotypes. *Journal of Aging Studies, 4*(3), 245–260.

Minkler, M. (1999). Introduction. In M. Minkler & C. L. Estes (Eds.), *Critical gerontology. Perspectives from political and moral economy* (pp. 1–13). Amityville, NY: Baywood.

Minkler, M., & Fadem, P. (2002). "Successful aging": A disability perspective. *Journal of Disability Policy Studies, 12*(4), 229–235.

Mosqueda, L. (2004). Psychological changes and secondary conditions. In B. J. Kemp & L. Mosqueda (Eds.), *Aging with a disability* (pp. 35–47). Baltimore, MD: Johns Hopkins University Press.

Pabst, M. K. (Ed.). (2006). *Encyclopedia of disability* (Vol. 1). Thousand Oaks, CA: Sage.

Parker Harris, S., Heller, T., & Schindler, A. (2012). Introduction, background and history. In T. Heller & S. P. Harris (Eds.), *Disability through the life course* (pp. 1–38). Thousand Oaks, California: Sage.

Passuth, P. M., & Bengtson, V. L. (1988). Sociological theories of aging: Current perspectives and future directions. In J. E. Birren & V. L. Bengtson (Eds.), *Emergent theories of aging* (pp. 333–355). New York: Springer.

Phillipson, C., & Baars, J. (2007). Social theory and social aging. In J. Bond, S. M. Peace, F. Dittman-Kohli, & G. Westerhof (Eds.), *Ageing in society: European perspectives on gerontology* (pp. 68–84). London: Sage.

Power, A. (2010). The geographies of interdependence in the lives of people with intellectual disabilities. In V. Chouinard, E. Hall & R. Wilton (Eds.), *Towards enabling geographies: 'Disabled' bodies and minds in society and space* (pp. 107–122). Farnham, Surrey: Ashgate.

Priestley, M. (Ed.). (2001). *Disability and the life course: Global perspectives*. Cambridge: Cambridge University Press.

Priestley, M. (2003). *Disability. A life course approach*. Cambridge, UK: Polity Press.

Putnam, M. (Ed.). (2007). *Aging and disability. Crossing network lines*. New York: Springer.

Riley, M. W., & Bond, K. (1983). Beyond ageism: Postponing the onset of disability. In M. W. Riley & B. B. H. K. Bond (Eds.), *Aging in society: Selected reviews of recent research* (pp. 243–252). Hillsdale, NJ: Lawrence Erlbaum Associates.

Schroots, J. J. F., & Birren, J. E. (2001). The study of lives in progress: Approaches to research on life stories. In G. D. Rowles & N. E. Schoenberg (Eds.), *Qualitative gerontology: Perspectives for a new century* (pp. 51–65). New York: Springer.

Shakespeare, T. (2006). The social model of disability. In L. J. Davis (Ed.), *The disability studies reader* (pp. 197–204). New York: Routledge.

Sharpe, K., Murry, G. C., McKenzie, K., Quigley, A., & Patrick, S. (2001). A matter of time. *Learning Disability Practice, 3*(6), 10–13.

Sheets, D. (2005). Aging with disabilities: Ageism and more. *Generations, 29*(3), 37–41.

Sheets, D. (Ed.). (2011). *International encyclopedia of rehabilitation*. Buffalo, NY: Center for International Rehabilitation Research Information and Exchange.

Stevens, N. L., Martina, C. M. S., & Westerhof, G. J. (2006). Meeting the need to belong: Predicting effects of a friendship enrichment program for older women. *Gerontologist, 46*(40), 495–502.

Stone, S. D. (2002). Disability, dependence, and old age: Problematic constructions. *Canadian Journal on Aging, 22*(1), 59–67.

Torres-Gil, F., & Putnam, M. (2004). The politics of aging with a disability: Health care policy and the shaping of a public agenda. In B. J. Kemp & L. Mosqueda (Eds.), *Aging with disability* (pp. 262–279). Baltimore, MD: Johns Hopkins University Press.

U.S. Bureau of the Census. (1996). *65+ in the United States*. Washington D.C.: U.S. Government Printing Office.

U.S. Bureau of the Census. (2004). We the People: Aging in the United States. Retrieved from http://www.census.gov/prod/2004pubs/censr-19.pdf

Urlings, H., Haveman, M., Maaskant, M., Van Schrojenstein Lantman-de Valk, H., Claessens, M., & Kessels, A. (1993). Qualitative research on ageing: How do mentally retarded persons themselves experience the ageing process. In M. Schuurman & D. Flikweert (Eds.), *Research on mental retardation in the Netherlands* (pp. 200–205). Utrecht: BBI/NGBZ.

van den Brandt-van Heek, M. (2011). Asking the right questions: enabling persons with dementia to speak for themselves. In G. Kenyon, E. Bohlmeijer, & W. L. Randall (Eds.), *Storying later life. Issues, investigations and interventions in narrative gerontology* (pp. 338–353). Oxford: Oxford University Press.

van Schrojenstein Lantman-de Valk, H. M. J. (2009). Healthy persons with intellectual disabilities in an inclusive society. *Journal of Policy and Practice in Intellectual Disabilities, 6*(2), 77–80.

van Schrojenstein Lantman de-Valk, H. M. J., & Noonan-Walsh, P. (2008). Managing health problems in people with intellectual disabilities. *British Medical Journal* (337), 1408–1412.

Verbrugge, L. M., & Jette, A. M. (1994). The disablement process. *Social Science and Medicine, 38*, 1–14.

Verbrugge, L. M., & Yang, L. (2002). Aging with disability and disability with aging. *Journal of Disability Policy Studies, 12*(4), 253–267.

Victor, C. (2010). The demography of aging. In D. Dannefer & C. Phillipson (Eds.), *The SAGE handbook of social gerontology* (pp. 61–74). London: Sage.

Walker, A., & Walker, C. (1998). Normalisation and 'normal' ageing: The social construction of dependency among older people with learning difficulties. *Disability & Society, 13*(1), 125–142.

Walsh., P. N., & LeRoy, B. (2004). *Women with disabilities aging well: A global view*. Baltimore: Paul H. Brookes.

Westerhof, G. J., Dittman-Kohli, F., & Thissen, T. (2001). Beyond life satisfaction: Lay conceptions of well-being among middle-aged and elderly adults. *Social Indicators Research, 56*(2), 179–203.

Wills, T. A., & Shinar, O. (2000). Measuring perceived and received social support. In S. Cohen, L. G. Underwood, & B. H. Gottlieb (Eds.), *Social support measurement and intervention: A guide for health and social scientists* (pp. 86–135). New York: Oxford University Press.

Wong, J. G. W. S., Clare, I. C. H., Gunn, M. J., & Holland, A. J. (1999). Capacity to make health care decisions: Its importance in clinical practice. *Psychological Medicine, 29*(2), 437–446.

Yorkston, K. M., McMullan, K. A., Molton, I., & Jensen, M. P. (2010). Pathways of change experience by people aging with disability: A focus group study. *Disability and Rehabilitation, 32*(20), 1697–1704.

Zarb, G. (1993a). The dual experience of ageing with a disability. In J. Swain, V. Finkelstein, S. French, & M. Oliver (Eds.), *Disabling barriers–enabling environments* (pp. 186–195). London: Sage.

Zarb, G. (1993b). 'Forgotten but not gone.' The experience of aging with a disability. In S. Arber & M. Evandrou (Eds.), *Ageing, independence and the life course* (pp. 27–45). London: Jessica Kingsley.

Zarb, G., & Oliver, M. (1993). *Ageing with a disability: What do they expect after all these years?* London: University of Greenwich.

Zink, J. B. (1992). Adjusting to early- and late-onset disability: A personal perspective. In E. F. Ansello & N. N. Eustis (Eds.), *Aging and disabilities: Seeking common ground* (pp. 111–114). Amityville, NY: Baywood.

Zola, I. K. (1993). Disability statistics: What we count and what it tells us. *Journal of Disability Policy Studies, 4*(2), 9–39.

PART 4

Specific Populations
and Positive Psychology

A Positive Psychology of Physical Disability: Principles and Progress

Dana S. Dunn, Gitendra Uswatte, Timothy R. Elliott, Alissa Lastres, *and* Brittany Beard

Abstract

This chapter proposes a rationale for a positive psychology of physical disability, one in which theoretical constructs serve theory development, operationalization, investigation, and theory testing. It then reviews levels of analysis for exploring positive psychology's link to physical disability and discusses select positive precursors, research-based principles, and key themes for building a positive psychology of physical disability. It argues for comprehensive theory and models for conducting rigorous research linking positive psychological constructs to psychosocial and behavioral aspects of physical disability. It then reviews nascent research concerning a neuropsychological basis for resiliency following disabling injury, and closes by identifying future directions for a positive psychology of physical disability.

Key Words: physical disability, positive psychology, rehabilitation psychology, person-environment relation, insider-outsider perspectives, resiliency, constraint-induced movement therapy

Throughout recorded history, and probably before, man has been intrigued by the possibility that the outward characteristics of physique might in some way be a guide to the inner nature of man, his temperament, his character, his personality. It is not difficult to understand how such a deep-seated belief might become established.

—*Wright (1983, p. xviii)*

It appears that rehabilitation psychology and positive psychology share similar underlying philosophies and goals; primarily, they seek to empower individuals to enhance what is good rather than attend to what is adverse in their lives.

—*Chou, Lee, Catalano, Ditchman, & Wilson (2009, p. 208)*

Positive psychology, the science dedicated to understanding and promoting human strengths, seeks to enhance psychological and physical well-being (e.g., Aspinwall & Staudinger, 2003; Keyes & Haidt, 2003; Lopez & Snyder, 2009; Seligman, 2011). This approach is in direct contrast to the heretofore predominant, negatively focused disease model defining the greater discipline of psychology since the late 1940s (e.g., Gillham & Seligman, 1999; Peterson, 2006; Seligman, 2002; Seligman & Csikszentmihályi, 2000). Positive psychology emphasizes maintaining well-being and preventing pathology before it happens, and its theories and practices presume the elements for a good and fulfilling life are either present or obtainable. Consequently, positive psychology holds great promise for understanding people's health and happiness in daily life. But what are this nascent field's implications for coping with particular health challenges, such as physical disability?

Physical disability refers to acute or chronic limitations of bodily function resulting from *impairment* to an organ (e.g., brain injury) or bodily system (e.g., vision). Physical disability can be acquired through accident, trauma, or disease, or it can be a congenital condition. The normative process of aging, too, can be a source of physical disability. As a term, then, "physical disability" entails a broad range of possible challenges involving or resulting from compromises to people's physiques, that is, their physical selves (e.g., Wright, 1983). Hearing loss caused by a brain tumor is an example of physical disability, as is spinal cord injury (and accompanying paralysis) following a motorcycle accident, or the physiological and behavioral consequences of depression following cardiovascular problems, such as heart attack or stroke.

But physical disability is not merely intrapersonal, it is also an interpersonal phenomenon. Physical disability entails interactions between people with disabilities and nondisabled individuals, in which the roles of being perceiver or perceived are routinely exchanged (Dunn, 2010). And, as social psychology amply demonstrates, behavior is often influenced by situational factors—not exclusively other people—present in the environment (e.g., Lewin, 1935; Ross & Nisbett, 1991). Beyond the impairing aspect of physical disability, then, there is also the reality of what are sometimes referred to as *handicapping* conditions or circumstances (Wright, 1983). Existing barriers, whether architectural (e.g., absence of ramps or elevators) or attitudinal (e.g., prejudice, stigma), can "handicap" people with disabilities (e.g., Wang & Dovidio, 2011).

In this chapter, we propose a rationale for a positive psychology of physical disability, one in which theoretical constructs can serve theory development, operationalization, investigation, and theory testing. We begin by reviewing some levels of analysis for examining positive psychology's link to disability. We then discuss select positive precursors, research-based principles from rehabilitation psychology indicating that an emphasis on exploring positive aspects of physical disability is not new. These principles are followed by a consideration of some key themes potentially relevant to building a positive psychology of physical disability. We then turn to the need for comprehensive theories and models for conducting rigorous research linking positive psychology to physical disability, followed by discussion of a research example reviewing a neuropsychological basis for resiliency following disabling injury. The chapter's closing section identifies future directions for psychologists, researchers, and practitioners interested in creating a positive psychology of physical disability.

As we wrote this chapter, we were mindful of the reality that physical disability is becoming an increasing concern for many Americans due to the return of veterans from wars in Iraq and Afghanistan. There is serious discussion, even debate, in the psychological community regarding what sort of therapies to provide to these service men and women (e.g., Caplan, 2011). We believe that a positive psychological approach to ameliorating the negative consequences of acquired physical disability will provide needed help to our fellow citizens, their families, and the institutions and agencies that serve them.

Why a Positive Psychology of Physical Disability?

Why establish a positive psychology of physical disability? We argue that the answer to this question is straightforward: The empirical base of positive psychology provides a complementary framework for rehabilitation psychology and, more specifically, for research dealing with physical disability (e.g., Chou et al., 2009; Seligman, Steen, Park, & Peterson, 2005). Dunn and Dougherty (2005, p. 309), for example, claimed that the prospects for a positive psychology of rehabilitation were "excellent." They did so by linking positive psychology's three levels of analysis (e.g., Gillham & Seligman, 1999; Seligman & Csikszentmihályi, 2000)—subjective experiences, personality traits, and positive public virtues—with research and practice issues germane to disability. These levels of analysis provide different points of entry for researchers interested in examining ways to help people with physical disabilities maintain or identify strengths while also managing weaknesses. We consider each level and representative research topics in brief.

Subjective Experiences

This subjective level of analysis considers people's attitudes or values connected to the past (e.g., satisfaction with life, reported well-being; e.g., Diener, 1984), the present (e.g., positive emotions, such as happiness or flow; Csikszentmihályi, 1990; Tugade & Frederickson, 2004), or the future (e.g., optimism, hope; Scheier & Carver, 1992; Snyder, 1994). Although they can be enduring, subjective accounts are often reactive to life changes or critical incidents, such as the onset, consequences, and adjustment to physical disability. During rehabilitation, for example, a person's subjective appraisals can play a prominent role in recovering strength and function following a physically disabling injury (e.g., Snyder, 1994). Such positive appraisals, in turn, may well provide protection against depression or other forms of negative affect that can disrupt rehabilitative or therapeutic progress (Seligman & Csikszentmihályi, 2000).

Personality Traits

The trait or individual level of analysis represents a stable or ongoing arena in which responses to disability can be explored. Relevant personality traits are often also considered to be strengths or evidence of character and even virtue (e.g., Aspinwall & Staudinger, 2003; Peterson & Seligman, 2004). Sample traits include creativity, perseverance, tenacity, wisdom, love, courage, and forgiveness, among others (see Peterson & Seligman for a comprehensive list). Disability researchers have consistently argued that identifying, enhancing, and encouraging the development of personal strengths can promote mental and physical recovery following disabling events (Wright, 1983; Wright & Fletcher, 1982; Wright & Lopez, 2002). One fruitful approach could be to identify traits that predict favorable adjustment to chronic illness and physical disability.

Positive Public Virtues

How can societal influences be used to promote people's strengths? This level of positive psychological analysis is also referred to as being devoted to positive, often community-based, institutions. Positive psychologists suggest that people should be educated as well as encouraged to promote community values such as altruism, civic-mindedness, and tolerance (Peterson, 2006; Seligman & Csikszentmihályi, 2000). Establishing engaging and healthy places to work is a related concern (e.g., Luthans & Youssef, 2009). Compared to subjective experiences and personality traits, however, to date, less research has been conducted in this arena. Nonetheless, advocacy by or on behalf of people with disabilities, such as the disability rights movement (e.g., Charlton, 1998) and the 1990 Americans with Disabilities Act (ADA), should be considered as part of this level of analysis.

Clearly, positive psychology's basic levels of analysis complement psychological research concerning rehabilitation issues and physical disability. Yet positive perspectives—precursors to present-day positive psychology—have long been an important part of research on physical disability within rehabilitation psychology. We suggest that investigators interested in constructive approaches linking the study of well-being to physical disability should recognize the role of these positive precursors—connected theoretical, empirical, and practice-oriented perspectives—drawn from literature.

Positive Precursors from Rehabilitation Psychology

Rehabilitation psychology studies and applies psychological knowledge toward improving the lives of people with disabilities and chronic health conditions to promote health, socialization, independence, choice, and general well-being. This subfield of the wider discipline has always had a salutary focus. To support this claim, we review four positive precursors: three classic perspectives (persons in situations, insider-outsider perspectives, value-laden beliefs and principles) and one recent formulation (the good life) specifically linked to acquired physical disability.

Persons in Situations

As already noted, whether tangible or intangible, situational factors can create handicapping conditions for people with physical disabilities. At the same time, understanding the power of the situation on behavior (also known as the *person-environment relation*) can be turned to positive advantage to appreciate the actual experience of disability. The profound analysis of the person in the situation was first identified by social psychologist Kurt Lewin (1890–1947).

Relying on ideas drawn from Gestalt psychology (Marrow, 1977), Lewin (1951) argued that social perception relies on holistic rather than elemental processes and that people's inferences about others are subjective, not objective. His analysis proposed that neither the psychological forces typically attributed to nature (e.g., temperament, traits, intelligence) nor nurture (e.g., rules and routines linked to experiences in the social world) can completely account for people's behavior. Instead, Lewin posited that the interaction between these personal and situational factors is the guiding force that shapes the unique behavior of individuals (Nisbett, 1980).

Lewin (1935) created a field theory wherein behavior is said to be a function of both the person and his or her psychological environment, or the so-called *life space*. He represented this relationship using a quasi-mathematical formulation, where $B = f(P, E)$, or behavior is a function of the person and his or her perceived environment. An important feature of this analysis is that the person's own interpretation of the social world (i.e., cognition) and strength to take action (i.e., motivation) serve as influential behavioral determinants (for classic, theoretical discussions linking field theory to the psychological impact of physical disability, see

Barker, Wright, Meyerson, & Gonick [1953] and Dembo, Leviton, & Wright [1956]).

Both rehabilitation psychology and social psychology implicitly share this Lewinian perspective and tradition of the person in the situation (Dunn, 2010; 2011). Where physical disability is concerned, two important qualities regarding a Lewinian analysis emerge. First, casual observers routinely overlook situational influences, assuming instead that a person's perceived qualities, such as a personality trait, a physical disability, or a cognitive impairment, among other possibilities, are the source of his or her behavior. Where social inference is concerned, casual observers downplay environmental forces and instead make attributions that are dispositionally based, a general problem well documented in social psychology (e.g., Gilbert & Malone, 1995; Ross, 1977). By discounting or missing contextual influences, perceivers explain the actions of others by focusing on these often incidental but salient personal factors, leading to potentially erroneous conclusions about people and explanations for their behavior. When encountering persons with disabilities, nondisabled people—including psychologists and medical professionals—need to remind themselves of the interpretive pitfalls posed by the presence of handicapping conditions.

A second influential quality is that a Lewinian analysis will frequently reveal that environmental constraints (e.g., presence of stairs, narrow doors) generate greater behavioral restrictions for people with physical disabilities than do the disabilities themselves (Dembo, 1982). Thus, a positive (re) interpretation is that problems associated with disability are often found in the environment and not the person or his or her impairment per se and that dispositional analyses are often misguided. People with and without disabilities should be prompted to remember that characteristics of the environment are likely to encourage or inhibit behavior much more than any perceived qualities attributed to personality, physical disability, or both.

Insider-Outsider Perspectives

Beyond engaging in dispositional analyses, nondisabled observers frequently assume they have an implicit understanding of life with a physical disability, a psychological interpretation known as the *insider-outsider distinction* (Dembo, 1969; Shontz, 1982; Wright, 1991). In essence, nondisabled observers (so-called *outsiders*) assume that they know what disability must be like—a life-changing, all encompassing preoccupation that

leads people with disabilities (so-called *insiders*) to be forever focused on their own physical, mental, and emotional states. Outsiders believe that insiders live limited existences marked by low quality of life and few pleasures or opportunities, remaining largely focused on those things they cannot accomplish due to their impairments. In reality, for most insiders, disability is simply one aspect of their lives among many and, in all likelihood, not the central one, meaning that the presence of a physical disability need not preclude a meaningful and full life (e.g., Dunn, 1994, 2009, 2010; Dunn, Uswatte, & Elliott, 2009; Smith, Lowenstein, Jankoviz, & Ubel, 2009; Ubel et al., 2001).

What is the source of this negatively biased conclusion? As already acknowledged, a failure to consider the effect of situational factors on behavior is a typical source. Another may be that the divergent perspectives of outsiders and insiders result from the formers' cognitive confusing of the experience of *becoming* disabled (i.e., accidents and trauma are both acute and salient) with already *being* a person with a disability (i.e., living with a chronic, if not necessarily comprehensive, condition; e.g., Kahneman, 1999, 2000; see also, Dunn, 2009, 2010). Wright (1988, 1991) also suggested that a *fundamental negative bias* may be operating, in which people attend more to pessimistic information linked to disability than to any optimistic information, even when the latter is more accurate. Ample research supports this claim, demonstrating that bad news readily trumps the impact of good news in social life (Baumeister, Bratlavsky, Finkenauer, & Vohs, 2001).

Yet, outsiders can be taught to adopt the perspective of insiders for a short time, a shift illustrated in the rehabilitation literature as the "mine/thine problem" (Wright, 1975; see also, Wright & Lopez, 2002). In the context of a sensitizing exercise, nondisabled outsiders are prompted to reflect on their own self-identified disabilities or handicaps, which can be physical, mental, or emotional in nature. These self-reported disabilities are then paired randomly with those shared by other participants; subsequently, each participant is given the opportunity to claim her original disability or the alternate and to then explain the choice. Wright (1983) claimed that various participant samples (e.g., college students, children, parents, hospital staff members, medical and rehabilitation professionals, teachers) consistently yielded the same result: People reclaim their own disability, a pattern that holds true even when the self-reported conditions are limited exclusively to physical disabilities. In Wright's work, the percentages of people who reclaimed their own disability ranged between 62% and 95% across different samples. Recent research replicated and extended these findings, revealing that individuals are likely to reclaim their own disabilities even when given the (imagined) opportunity to exchange them for less severe disabilities (see Dunn, Fisher, & Beard, 2012, 2013).

Wright (1983) argued people retain their own disability for various reasons (e.g., familiarity, coping, self-identity) that highlight the distinct "span of realities" (p. 48) of insiders and outsiders. Thus, with guidance, people can learn that, instead of being labeled a burden, physical disability can be seen as a familiar, comforting, or even beneficial quality to the affected individual. Physical disability, then, can be construed as another (sometimes positive) part of a person's life, one that is rarely so negative that it is wished away. As Wright (1983, p. 159) wrote, "[a] disability can become an inextricable part of one's identity and one's life. To cast it aside can signal too basic a restructuring and relinquishing of aspects and values that are too important."

Value-Laden Beliefs and Principles

The nature of an affected individual's response to living with disability clearly matters. Social responses to physical disability, too, can be positive or negative, and the availability of philosophical and practical guidelines can promote the former approach. Wright (1972) advocated that people with disabilities, psychologists and rehabilitation professionals, students, and other interested parties should familiarize themselves with and enact a set of "value-laden beliefs and principles." The 20 beliefs and principles (a slightly updated version appears in the preface to Wright [1983]) offer a constructive and positive affirmation of the worth and dignity of people with disabilities (see Dunn & Elliott, 2005). Space constraints preclude a point-by-point presentation of the beliefs and principles, but a summary of key themes found therein will illustrate their positive relevance to professional encounters with people with disabilities: (a) no matter how severe their disabilities may be, people deserve to be treated with respect, dignity, and encouragement; (b) social and environmental variables have profound influences on adjustment to disability; (c) every individual has singular, personal qualities and assets that can inform and help rehabilitation therapy; (d) there are benefits associated with enlisting people with disabilities themselves to act as "co-managers" of their treatment; and (e) psychological issues are present throughout rehabilitation experiences.

There is an empowering spirit embedded in the beliefs and principles that implicitly recognizes the psychological import of the person-in-the-situation analysis and insider-outsider perspectives. Similarly, the values and beliefs reduce the tendency to objectify people with disabilities by casting them as partners in the process of navigating their health challenges and helping them to flourish in all areas of their lives. These three positive precursors, then, provide a solid foundation for pursuing a good life with acquired physical disability.

The Good Life Following Acquired Physical Disability

Recently, Dunn and Brody (2008) reviewed empirical and theoretical perspectives regarding attitudes and behaviors that might constitute living a good life following the onset of acquired physical disability. The term "good life" is meant to incorporate a critical evaluation of choices that make life worth living. The term was specifically chosen as a means to portray a broad definition for living with disability. A now considerable literature reveals that, compared to the list of possible candidates, relatively few variables actually predict even moderate levels of happiness, an important aspect of a good life (for one recent and thorough review, see Diener & Biswas-Diener [2008]). For example, higher income and education, youth, and even physical attractiveness have little impact on people's happiness, whereas being married, extraverted, or conscientious act as somewhat stronger predictors.

To encourage researchers interested in exploring the good life following acquired physical disability, Dunn and Brody (2008) focused on three related elements drawn from the literature in positive psychology: positive connections to other people, positive personal qualities, and life regulation qualities (e.g., Compton, 2005; Lopez & Snyder, 2009; Seligman, 2002; Snyder & Lopez, 2002). *Positive connections* can involve establishing and maintaining close relationships with other people, thereby providing opportunities to socialize or offer help (tangible aid, emotional comfort), among other possibilities. Cultivating *positive personal qualities* leads to developing or heightening existing strengths, such as savoring pleasant experiences (Bryant & Veroff, 2007), having a good sense of humor, and expressing genuine gratitude to others (e.g., Emmons & McCullough, 2003). Being generative (i.e., giving back by sharing one's skills with others), performing activities that promote "flow" states (i.e., fully engaging, absorbing experiences; Csikszentmihályi,

1990), and taking time to pursue recreational activities that add balance to daily life represent examples of *life regulation qualities*. Pursuing one or more activity options from the three good life categories of behaviors is not a recipe for well-being per se, but presents a means to develop psychological resources, including positive affect, which can broaden perspectives (e.g., Fredrickson, 1998), enhance cognition and problem solving (e.g., Isen, 2004), provide meaning (e.g., King, Hicks, Krull, & Del Gaiso, 2006), and sharpen coping skills (e.g., Folkman & Moskowitz, 2000). The good life framework is one approach to exploring ways that positive psychology can inform the study and treatment of physical disability.

Some Key Themes for a Positive Psychology of Physical Disability

Links between the study of physical disability issues and positive psychology are apparent. Beyond the positive precursors reviewed in the previous section, what constructs have rehabilitation researchers and positive psychologists developed that potentially can be leveraged for a positive psychology of disability? There are several potential candidates, some classic, others contemporary. These include adjustment issues, exploring assets, positive growth after disability, value changes, and the potential of positive emotions. We briefly introduce each one.

Adjustment, Adaptation, and Coping

Adjustment, *adaption*, and *coping* are common terms used to characterize how individuals deal with the onset and consequences of life with acquired physical disability. When using these terms, researchers need to be careful to avoid referring to persons with disabilities as "victims" of trauma or fate. Failure to do so reinforces widely held beliefs that people with disabilities are miserable, dependent, and incapable of making decisions for themselves, which leads to their objectification (Fine & Asch, 1988; Shontz, 1982). Thus, researchers should not construe well-being linked to adjustment as the absence of physical disability (e.g., Dunn, 2010; Fine & Asch, 1988). Instead, the focus should be on *disability acceptance*, in which the chronic condition becomes accepted as a non-devalued part of the individual's self-concept (e.g., Wright, 1983).

A related constructive approach to examining adjustment issues is found in *reality negotiation*, in which individuals rely on cognitive strategies that promote favorable beliefs about the self in situations that threaten self-esteem and well-being (Elliott, Witty, Herrick, & Hoffman, 1991; Snyder, 1989; Dunn, 1996). Adapting to disabling circumstances becomes a process of coming to terms with actions that can no longer be performed by, for example, making excuses (engaging in protective behaviors) and seeking out situations that foster what can be accomplished or performed (self-enhancing behaviors).

Assets

No physical disability, however severe, can eliminate all of one's assets or the chance to acquire new ones (Dunn & Dougherty, 2005; Wright, 1983). *Assets* are tangible or psychological resources (e.g., intellectual, physical, social, or professional skills; personal strengths or qualities; social support; goals; material goods; sense of humor, tenacity) that aid in the development and maintenance of people's identities (Dunn, 2010; Dunn, Uswatte, & Elliott, 2009). Emphasizing lost assets resulting from disability (i.e., what a person is no longer able to do) can be counterproductive, potentially leading to feelings of hopelessness or inadequacy. Focusing on assets that remain or can be attained during rehabilitation leads to positive emotions that promote positive growth and resiliency (e.g., Keany & Glueckauf, 1993).

Positive Growth Following Disability

People who experience disabling circumstances endure a variety of changes, some of which indicate positive, psychological growth. *Positive growth* can include, but is not limited to, increased personal strength, finding new purpose in life, reinterpreting negative events in a positive manner, and enhanced interpersonal relationships (for a review, see Tedeschi & Calhoun [2004]). Previously, such positive reactions were viewed as inaccurate, likely defensive, portrayals of people's actual experience. These responses are now largely accepted as ordinary, adaptive, and candid psychological expressions (Dunn, Uswatte, & Elliott, 2009). For example, there is compelling evidence that, on occasion, personal suffering can lead to positive self-insight (Davis & Nolen-Hoeksema, 2009; Lechner, Tennen, & Affleck, 2009). Examples of positive growth can include perceptual changes (e.g., increased feelings of self-reliance or self-confidence), relationship changes (e.g., closer connections to family and friends), and life priority changes (e.g., reduced concern with material goods or status concerns).

Positive growth is not the only term in the literature used to describe the positive affect occurring subsequent to unfavorable life experiences. Other terms include *stress-related growth* (Park, Cohen, & Murch, 1996), *benefit-finding* (McMillen & Cook, 2003), *post-traumatic growth* (Tedeschi & Calhoun, 2004; Vash, 1981; Wright, 1983), and *adversarial growth* (Linley & Joseph, 2004, 2005).

Consider an example: Evidence suggests that some cognitive activity directed toward finding benefits or positive meaning in otherwise adverse circumstances can allow people to enhance their level of well-being (e.g., Dunn, Uswatte, & Elliott, 2009). One study found that among a group of men and women who had amputations, the majority found side benefits associated with their physical disability (Dunn, 1996). These "side benefits" represent individuals' abilities to assimilate the disability into their lives advantageously, which may be an indicator of disability acceptance. An important point is that it is not *what* the participants attribute as positive that allows them to reap the benefits; the mere *act* of seeking something positive may promote heightened well-being (see also Taylor [1983]).

Values and Value Change

Do people's values—personal principles deemed to be important to daily life, including guiding worldviews—change in response to disability? Keany and Glueckauf (1993), for example, explored the relationship between value change and feelings of loss following disability. These researchers focused primarily on value changes in relation to the acceptance of disability, arguing that during the initial period following a trauma, affected individuals mourn over values believed to be lost (cf. Wright, 1983). Following this mourning, a positive outcome occurs when people's "scope of values" enlarges; that is, they recognize the worth of other values (i.e., beyond those presumed to be lost). Thus, a person initially concerned by a presumed loss of physical attractiveness due to disability might eventually elect to focus on other values (e.g., family, friends, career, hobbies). One research challenge identified by Keany and Glueckauf (1993), however, is identifying valid measures of value change related to disability acceptance.

Positive Emotions

Emotions are short-lived feelings, usually acute responses to positive or negative events. Emotions tend to be uncontrollable and are routinely accompanied by a variety of physiological changes (e.g.,

increased heart rate). Until relatively recently (Fredrickson, 1998), psychological research emphasized the study of negative emotions, which focus attention to dealing with threats, over positive ones. Positive emotions are pleasant affective reactions to events that promote connections with others, including subjective states such as happiness, joy, gratitude, and contentment. When people experience positive emotions, they feel favorable toward others and very often about what they are thinking about or doing behaviorally. Emotional states are not mutually exclusive, however; people can simultaneously experience positive and negative emotions, even under upsetting circumstances (Folkman & Moskowitz, 2000).

Folkman and Moskowitz (2000) theorize, for example, that positive emotions provide humans with respite from negative emotions, a release that helps to maintain coping efforts by refreshing psychological resources. Fredrickson's (1998) influential broaden-and-build theory, however, states that positive emotions broaden people's awareness outside themselves, which facilitates the building of personal assets, including coping responses. Although these two theories differ slightly, both address the benefits of positive emotions in terms of the psychological assets people may possess. The existing literature relevant to physical disability issues ascribes numerous benefits to positive emotions, including reductions in pain, improved immune functioning, reduced inflammatory responses to stress, and effective emotion regulation (Ehde, 2010). Studies also suggest that positive emotions predict posttraumatic growth and resiliency, although the intensity of the positive emotions appears to be less beneficial than the amount of time spent experiencing the positive affect (Ehde, 2010; Lyubomirsky et. al., 2005).

The Need for Theory and Models for a Positive Psychology of Physical Disability

Unlike the rich theoretical perspectives that guide much of the contemporary research in positive psychology, the bulk of the empirical study of persons with disabilities concerns issues of interest to health service providers, health delivery systems, and vested policymakers (including consumers of these services). This research, particularly the work conducted by funded collaborative projects housed in medical schools, has "produced reams of means and standard deviations divorced from any theoretical context" (Elliott & Frank, 2000, p. 649). The clinical rehabilitation literature informs us that depressive symptoms may be related to the use of indwelling catheters and increased antidepressant use, and higher levels of subjective well-being are associated with younger age, less pain, good health, mobility, and lower depression scores.

Unfortunately, these clinical findings do not give us any information about behavioral or social mechanisms that may account for these relationships in a fashion that could provide testable and potentially refutable predictions about future behavior under general or specific conditions or how to make logical choices about intervention strategies. Psychological theories are necessary to understand the ways in which people with disabilities experience optimal adjustment (Dunn & Elliott, 2008).

Clinical rehabilitation research relies on interdisciplinary collaborations that place a high premium on practical services and products. Esoteric, jargonized academic theories that are difficult to communicate to colleagues from other disciplines are often viewed suspiciously as impractical or professionally self-serving (Elliott & Rath, 2012). Market pressure and expectations for accountability (and reimbursement) have compelled health care services (including rehabilitation) to reach consensus in the definitions and measurement of important outcomes. Interestingly, this results in a greater appreciation of consumer-driven outcome measures to benefit patients, clinicians, researchers, service delivery systems, and policymakers. This movement has resulted in the emerging Patient Report Outcomes Measurement Information System (PROMIS; http://www.nihpromis.org/default.aspx), funded by the National Institutes of Health, in which the feasibility and applicability of measures across a variety of chronic health conditions are rated. Measures of "Illness Impact Positive" in the PROMIS will include indicators of positive growth, benefit finding, and meaning in response to the condition.

The recognized value for consumer-oriented outcome measures for health services is theoretically intriguing, as it acknowledges the importance of subjective reports of adjustment (although it does not necessarily convey respect for the mechanisms that influence self-reported adjustment). In addition, this movement is congruent with the influential *International Classification of Functioning, Disability and Health* (ICF) developed by the World Health Organization (WHO, 2011). Reminiscent of a Lewinian field-theory perspective, the ICF advocates a greater appreciation of the environmental context in which disability occurs, and it prescribes assessment of the degree to which an individual engages in desired activities and participates in normative social and personal roles (and of the environmental barriers to and facilitators of activity and participation; Lollar, 2008).

Although the ICF is not a psychological theory—indeed, it is described as a "workable compromise between medical and social models" of disability (World Health Organization, 2011; p. 5)—psychologists can easily operationalize "activities" and "participation" into constructs vital to positive psychology theories. For example, in one critical review of happiness research, Lyubomirsky et al. (2005) argue that *intentional activities*—ones that are behavioral, volitional, and cognitive—account for a greater degree of variance in happiness and well-being (as much as 40%) than do circumstantial factors (e.g., marriage). Consistent with this position, longitudinal research has found that persons who have greater functional impairments following traumatic brain injury—implying these persons would be associated with decreased ability to engage to participate in desired activities—experienced greater declines in life satisfaction over the first 5 years of disability than did those who had fewer functional impairments (Resch et al., 2009). Moreover, marital status did not affect these trajectories, but higher family satisfaction had a positive effect on life satisfaction among those with more functional ability (Johnson et al., 2010). The behavioral and social mechanisms that promote activity and participation (or restrict them; see Mausbach et al., 2011) and their subsequent role in positive adjustment are ripe for theory-driven investigation.

In the next section, we illustrate how a strong theory can be used to guide a research program that culminates in an intervention to promote skill acquisition that enhances participation in desired activities (and, in the process, reduce functional limitations) and facilitate subjective well-being among individuals who have incurred a disability.

A Neurophysiological Basis for Resiliency Following Disabling Injury

For many, psychological adaptation to a disabling condition is marked by resiliency. Unless magic is truly at work, the remarkable capacity to make large shifts in patterns of thought and behavior has to have a physiological basis in the central nervous system (CNS). One CNS process that has been shown to underlie how organisms alter their behavior in response to changes in their abilities or environment is *neuroplasticity*, which is defined here as changes in the organization of activity or structure of the adult CNS that involve multiple neurons.

For most of the 20th century, the dominant view was that the organization of activity and structure of the human CNS was largely fixed after the closing of critical windows for developmental changes in childhood (Kaas, 1995, p. 735). Over the past three decades, this view has been replaced by one that depicts the adult CNS as an organ capable of substantial change (e.g., see reviews by Buonomano & Merzenich, 1998; Uswatte & Taub, 2010; Uswatte, Taub, Mark, Perkins, & Gauthier, 2010).

Accumulating evidence indicates that brain regions can expand when there is an increase in use of the functions they represent. Neurogenesis seems to be experience-dependent, as enriched environments and exercise increase its likelihood (Gould, 2007; van Praag, Kempermann, & Gage, 2000). An increase in cortical representation areas has been observed in the auditory cortex of blind persons and is thought to be due to increased reliance on audition for information about their environment (Elbert et al., 2002). Blind persons receive the same amount of auditory stimulation as those who are sighted. Therefore, cortical reorganization is not merely a passive response to increases in sensory stimulation, but rather it depends on the behavioral relevance of input into the nervous system and the attention devoted to it. This property would appear to permit the brain to adapt itself to the functional demands placed on an individual. This type of CNS change has been termed "input-increase" or "use-dependent" neuroplasticity.

Principles for Harnessing Neuroplasticity for Making Therapeutic Changes: Constraint-Induced Therapy as a Model

Few rehabilitation treatments for chronic CNS disease have actually been shown in a controlled manner to benefit real-world behaviors. The approach with the most evidence of efficacy is *constraint-induced movement* therapy (CI therapy) for rehabilitating use of the more-impaired arm in stroke survivors (Ottawa Panel et al., 2006). The treatment, which is provided over 10 to 15 consecutive weekdays, involves (a) intensive task practice with the more-impaired arm, (b) restraint of the less-impaired arm for 90% of waking hours, and (c) a "transfer package" of behavioral techniques to induce and reinforce adherence to the prescription to increase use of the more-impaired arm in the home environment (Taub et al., 1993, 2006). In

two separate single-site controlled trials, CI therapy, compared to two types of placebo interventions, produced prolonged improvement in use of the more-impaired arm in daily life in older adults more than 1 year after stroke (Taub et al., 1993, 2006). In addition, CI therapy has been shown to be superior to customary care in a large, blinded, randomized, multisite clinical trial of CI therapy for mild to moderate weakness of the more-impaired arm in individuals 3–9 months after stroke (Wolf et al., 2006). Participants in the CI therapy group ($n = 106$) showed significantly larger gains in real-world use of the more-impaired arm up to 1 year after treatment than did participants who were permitted access to any care available on a clinical basis ($n = 116$). CI therapy group participants also showed significant improvements in quality of life up to 2 years after treatment.

Several aspects of the clinical gains following CI therapy deserve attention from students of resiliency. First, the gains in real-world use of the more-impaired arm are very large. For example, effect sizes range from 1.6 to 2 for everyday use of the more-impaired arm produced by CI therapy in the two placebo-controlled studies just mentioned. In the meta-analysis literature, values of 0.8 are considered large for this type of effect size index (i.e., *d*) (Cohen, 1983). Some anecdotes from CI therapy patients whose outcomes ranged from average to exceptional help to flesh out what the improvements in more-impaired arm function mean for stroke survivors. A dentist returned to practicing his profession. A pilot returned to flying and met his true love between flights. A mother regained sufficient dexterity and confidence in using her more-impaired arm that she started picking up her child again. Second, treatment gains are independent of time since injury. Third, treatment gains are independent of age at time of treatment (Taub, Uswatte, & Pidikiti, 1999; Taub et al., 2006). Patients in our laboratory who are more than 20 years post-stroke and 80 years old have had gains equal to or better than the average outcome.

CI therapy was derived by Taub and coworkers from basic research using a deafferentated monkey model (reviewed in Taub, 1977, 1980). When a single forelimb is deafferentated in a monkey by surgically severing the sensory nerves that innervate that limb as they enter the spinal cord, the animal does not use the forelimb in the free situation (Knapp, Taub, & Berman, 1963; Mott & Sherrington, 1895). Several converging lines of evidence suggest that nonuse of a single deafferentated limb is a learning phenomenon involving a conditioned suppression of movement; the phenomenon is termed *learned nonuse*. (For a description of the experimental analysis leading to this conclusion, see Taub [1977, 1980].)

As a background for this explanation, one should note that substantial neurological injury usually leads to a depression in motor and/or perceptual function. Recovery processes then come into operation so that, after a period of time, movements can once again, at least potentially, be expressed. In monkeys, the initial period of depressed function lasts from 2 to 6 months following forelimb deafferentation (Taub, 1977; Taub & Berman, 1968). Thus, immediately after operation, the monkeys cannot use a deafferentated limb; recovery from the initial depression of function requires considerable time. An animal with one deafferentated limb tries to use that extremity in the immediate postoperative situation but cannot. It gets along quite well in the laboratory environment on three limbs and is therefore positively reinforced for this pattern of behavior, which, as a result, is strengthened. Moreover, continued attempts to use the impaired limb often lead to painful and otherwise aversive consequences, such as incoordination and falling, as well as to loss of food objects, and, in general, failure of any activity attempted with the deafferentated limb. These aversive consequences condition the animal to avoid using that limb. (Many learning experiments have demonstrated that punishment results in the suppression of behavior; Azrin & Holz, 1966; Catania, 1998; Estes, 1944.)

This response tendency persists, and, consequently, the monkey does not learn that several months after operation the limb has become potentially useful. In addition, following stroke (Liepert, Graef, Uhde, Leidner, & Weiller, 2000) and presumably after extremity deafferentation, there is a marked contraction in the size of the cortical representation of the affected limb; this phenomenon is probably related to the reports of persons with stroke that movement of that extremity is effortful. These three processes (i.e., punishment for use of the deafferentated limb, reinforcement for use of the intact limb only, and plastic brain reorganization) interact to produce a vicious downward spiral that results in a learned nonuse of the affected extremity that is normally permanent (Taub, Uswatte, & Elbert, 2002).

Learned nonuse of a deafferentated limb can be overcome by intensive training of that extremity, particularly by shaping (Catania, 1998; Skinner,

1968). Continuous restraint of the intact limb over a period of a week or more is also effective. Both procedures have the effect of changing the contingencies of reinforcement for the use of the affected extremity. For example, when the movements of the intact limb are restricted several months after unilateral deafferentation, the animal either uses the deafferentated limb or it cannot with any degree of efficiency feed itself, walk, or carry out a large portion of its normal activities of daily life. This dramatic change in motivation overcomes the learned nonuse of the deafferentated limb. If the movement restriction device is left on for several days or longer, use of the affected limb acquires strength and is then able to compete successfully with the very well-learned habit of learned nonuse of that limb in the free situation. The conditioned response and shaping techniques, just like the restriction of the intact limb, also involve major alterations in the contingencies of reinforcement; the animal must use its compromised limb or forego food or other reinforcers. Increased use of the more-impaired limb after CI therapy in stroke, and presumably also after forced used and shaping in deafferentated monkeys, stimulates an expansion in the cortical representation of the more-impaired limb (Liepert et al., 2000) and other changes in the brain (see next section). One might speculate that such CNS changes support movement that is less effortful and more skillful, in turn encouraging even greater use of the deafferentated limb and setting up a "virtuous" cycle.

Central Nervous System Changes in Stroke Survivors after Constraint-Induced Therapy

As noted, Liepert and coworkers showed a doubling in the cortical region from which electromyographic responses of a muscle in the more-impaired hand can be elicited by transcranial magnetic stimulation (TMS) after CI therapy (Liepert et al., 1998, 2000). A review of 20 studies on CI therapy effects on cerebral physiology revealed substantial evidence for brain reorganization based on a wide range of investigational modalities, including TMS, dipole source localization associated with magnetoencephalography (MEG) and electroencephalography (EEG), functional magnetic resonance imaging (fMRI), positron emission tomography (PET), and near-infrared spectroscopy (summarized in Mark, Taub, & Morris [2006]). However, findings overall were inconsistent with respect to the location of the changes in regional brain activation. Lack of control over therapy administration, evaluation methods, and participant recruitment are likely to account for these inconsistencies.

Structural MRI is free from some of the methodological challenges faced by fMRI and other functional neurophysiological measures, such as whether the behavior used to elicit brain activation during imaging changes from one testing occasion to another and how to interpret changes in activation. A computational analytic method termed *voxel-based morphometry* (VBM) was applied to structural MRI scans obtained before and after CI therapy from 16 chronic stroke survivors and showed widespread increases in gray matter in sensorimotor cortices both contralateral and ipsilateral to the more-impaired arm, as well as in the hippocampi bilaterally (Gauthier et al., 2008). The aforementioned sensorimotor clusters were bilaterally symmetrical and encompassed the hand/arm regions of primary sensory and motor cortices, as well as portions of Brodmann's area 6 and the anterior supplementary motor area. Scans from 20 stroke survivors who received a comparison therapy did not show such changes. Moreover, the gray matter changes, across all participants, were correlated with changes in use of the hemiparetic arm in daily life (r's >.45, p's <.05). The demonstration of these neuroanatomical changes supports a true remodeling of the brain after CI therapy. Furthermore, the size and location of stroke infarcts prior to treatment did not influence degree of recovery after CI therapy, suggesting that the neuroplastic processes harnessed by CI therapy can, to some degree, override the severity of the CNS injuries inflicted by stroke (Gauthier, Taub, Mark, Perkins, & Uswatte, 2009; Mark, Taub, Perkins, Gauthier, & Uswatte, 2008). The specific neuroplastic processes responsible for the increases in gray matter have yet to be identified. Three possibilities are (a) the formation of new blood vessels, (b) the growth of new connections (e.g., axonal sprouting), and (c) the growth of new neurons or supporting cells, such as glia (Taub et al., 2002).

In retrospect, the primacy of the view of the organization and structure of the adult CNS as static is curious given how common it is for spontaneous recovery of functions to take place even after substantial damage to CNS areas thought to represent them in adults or for adults to acquire new skills, such as playing the piano or speaking a new language, late in life (Uswatte & Taub, 2010). The coincidence of the overthrow of the static view of the CNS with a renewed emphasis on positive

psychology is a happy one. Research on neuroplasticity has shown that the organization of activity and structure of the CNS in adults is more malleable than ever imagined by most before 1980 and has thereby expanded our view of the capacity of adults both with and without CNS injury to undertake large shifts in patterns of thought and behavior. Positive psychology, among other aims, seeks to take advantage of this capacity for change to enhance human strengths and well-being. Without such a capacity, this aspect of positive psychology would be Sisyphean.

Equally importantly, this research provides guidelines for how researchers and practitioners can therapeutically harness neuroplastic processes. In particular, research on CI therapy suggests four general principles. They are (a) providing extended and concentrated practice in the desired behaviors by scheduling intensive training; (b) increasing use of the desired behavior in the treatment and home setting by providing reinforcement for its use, forcing its use by preventing the use of compensatory functions, or both; (c) emphasizing training on the behavior in context rather than small components of the behavior; and (d) implementing long-standing behavioral methods for transferring gains made in the treatment setting to daily life, such behavioral contracts and daily diaries (Uswatte & Taub, 2010).

Where Now? Future Directions

Clearly, a closer working relationship between theory and health care practice is needed to advance a positive psychology of physical disability. The promise of positive psychology's applicable constructs must be appropriately tempered by the reality of contemporary health care where delivery, cost, and policy are concerned. As noted earlier, consumer-oriented outcomes (e.g., Illness Impact Positive in PROMIS) offer new avenues for linking theory, empirical observations, and health care constraints in ways that may benefit consumers, practitioners, researchers, and policymakers. Such collaborative research should mindfully embrace the impact of various environments (and constraints found within them) on the experience of life with disability.

We urge researchers, practitioners, and policymakers to identify and apply principles linked to positive psychology (whether classic or contemporary in origin) judiciously in rehabilitation settings. Intrapersonal qualities, such as resilience, need to be understood in the context of interpersonal relationships (e.g., family, friends, coworkers) and key contexts (e.g., home, workplace, clinic). Researchers and practitioners both need to create effective interventions linking psychosocial factors to clinical states in constructive ways that are most likely to satisfy the goal of ameliorating disability while promoting psychological and physical well-being. What may seem like limitations imposed by resource constraints in the larger medical system would be better construed as a source of creative tension for improving disability services and the lives of clients and their families.

Acknowledgments

Portions of this article are adapted from G. Uswatte, E. Taub, V. W. Mark, C. Perkins, & L. Gauthier (2010), Central nervous system plasticity and rehabilitation, in R. G. Frank, B. Caplan, & M. Rosenthal, *Handbook of rehabilitation psychology* (2nd ed.), Washington, DC: American Psychological Association. Copyright 2010 by the American Psychological Association. Adapted with permission.

Writing of this chapter was partially supported by a Summer 2011 Moravian College SOAR grant and a Faculty Development and Research Committee Award to the first author. Work on this chapter was supported by National Institutes of Health Grants HD34273 and HD53750 to the second author. We thank Sarah Sacks Dunn for comments on an earlier draft of this chapter.

Address correspondence to Dana S. Dunn, Department of Psychology, Moravian College, 1200 Main Street, Bethlehem, PA 18018, dunn@moravian.edu

References

Aspinwall, L. G., & Staudinger, U. M. (Eds.). (2003). *A psychology of human strengths: Fundamental questions and future directions for a positive psychology.* Washington, DC: American Psychological Association.

Azrin, N. H., & Holz, W. C. (1966). Punishment. In W. K. Honig (Ed.), *Operant behavior: Areas of research and application* (pp. 380–447). New York : Appleton-Century-Crofts.

Barker, R. G. (1948). The social psychology of physical disability. *Journal of Social Issues*, 4(4), 28–38. Retrieved from EBSCO*host*. doi:10.1111/j.15404560.1948.tb01516.x

Barker, R. G., Wright, B. A., Meyerson, L., & Gonick, M. R. (1953). *Adjustment to physical handicap and illness: A survey of the social psychology of physique and disability* (2nd ed.). New York: Social Science Research Council.

Baumeister, R. F., Bratlavsky, E., Finkenauer, C., & Vohs, K. D. (2001). Bad is stronger than good. *Review of General Psychology*, 5, 323–370. doi: 10.1037/1089-2680.5.4.323

Bryant, F. B., & Veroff, J. (2007). *Savoring: A new model of positive experiences.* Mahwah, NJ: Erlbaum.

Buonomano, D., & Merzenich, M. M. (1998). Cortical plasticity: from synapses to maps.

Caplan, P. J. (2011). *When Johnny and Jane come marching home: How all of us can help veterans.* Cambridge, MA: MIT Press.

Catania, A. C. (1998). Learning (4th edition ed.). Upper Saddle River, NJ: Prentice Hall.

Charlton, J. I. (1998). *Nothing about us without us: Disability oppression and empowerment.* Berkeley: University of California Press.

Chou, C.-C., Lee, E.-J., Catalano, D. E., Ditchman, N., & Wilson, L. M. (2009). Positive psychology and psychosocial adjustment to chronic illness and disability. In F. Chan, E. da Silva Cardoso, & J. A. Chronister (Eds.), *Understanding psychosocial adjustment to chronic illness and disability: A handbook of evidence-based practitioners in rehabilitation* (pp. 207–241). New York: Springer.

Cohen, J. (1983). Statistical power analysis for the behavioral sciences (2nd ed.). Hillsdale, NJ: Lawrence Erlbaum Associates.

Compton, W. C. (2005). *An introduction to positive psychology.* Belmont, CA: Thompson-Wadsworth.

Csikszentmihályi, M. (1990). *Flow: The psychology of optimal experience.* New York: Harper & Row.

Davis, C. G., & Nolen-Hoeksema, S. (2009). Making sense of loss, perceiving benefits, and posttraumatic growth. In S. J. Lopez & C. R. Snyder (Eds.), *Oxford handbook of positive psychology* (2nd ed., pp. 641–649). New York: Oxford University Press.

Dembo, T. (1969). Rehabilitation psychology and its immediate future: A problem of utilization of psychological knowledge. *Rehabilitation Psychology*, 16, 63–72.

Dembo, T. (1982). Some problems in rehabilitation as seen by a Lewinian. *Journal of Social Issues*, 38, 131–139. doi:10.1111/j.1540-4560.1982.tb00848.x

Dembo, T., Leviton, G. L., & Wright, B. A. (1956). Adjustment to misfortune: A problem of social-psychological rehabilitation. *Artificial Limbs*, 3, 4–62.

Diener, E. (1984). Subjective well-being. *Psychological Bulletin*, 93, 542–575. 10.1037/0033-2909.95.3.542

Diener, E., & Biswas-Diener, R. (2008). *Happiness: Unlocking the mysteries of psychological wealth.* Malden, MA: Wiley-Blackwell.

Dunn, D. S. (1994). Positive meaning and illusions following disability: Reality negotiation, normative interpretation, and value change. *Journal of Social Behavior and Personality*, 9, 123–138.

Dunn, D. S. (1996). Well-being following amputation: Salutary effects of positive meaning, optimism, and control. *Rehabilitation Psychology*, 41(4), 285–302. doi:10.1037/0090-5550.41.4.285

Dunn, D. S. (2009). Teaching about disability: Cultures of experience, not expectation. In R. A. R. Gurung & L. Prieto (Eds.), *Got culture? Best practices for incorporating culture into the curriculum* (pp. 101–114). New York: Stylus.

Dunn, D. S. (2010). The social psychology of disability. In R. G. Frank, B. Caplan, & M. Rosenthal (Eds.), *Handbook of rehabilitation psychology* (2nd ed., pp. 379–390). Washington, DC: American Psychological Association.

Dunn, D. S. (2011). Situations matter: Teaching the Lewinian link between social psychology and rehabilitation psychology. *Journal of the History of Psychology*, 14(4), 405–411.

Dunn, D. S., & Brody, C. (2008). Defining the good life following acquired physical disability. *Rehabilitation Psychology*, 53(4), 413–425. doi:10.1037/a0013749

Dunn, D. S., & Dougherty, S. B. (2005). Prospects for a positive psychology of rehabilitation. *Rehabilitation Psychology*, *50*(3), 305–311. doi:10.1037/0090-5550.50.3.305

Dunn, D. S., & Elliott, T. R. (2005). Revisiting a constructive classic: Wright's *Physical disability: A psychosocial approach*. *Rehabilitation Psychology*, *50*, 183–189. doi:10.1037/0090-5550.50.2.183

Dunn, D., & Elliott, T. (2008). The place and promise of theory in rehabilitation psychology research. *Rehabilitation Psychology*, *53*, 254–267.

Dunn, D. S., Elliott, T. R., & Uswatte, G. (2009). Happiness, resilience and positive growth following disability: Issues for understanding, research, and therapeutic intervention. In S. J. Lopez & C. R. Snyder (Eds.), *Oxford handbook of positive psychology* (2nd ed., pp. 651–664). New York: Oxford University Press.

Dunn, D. S., Fisher, D., & Beard, B. (2012). Revisiting the mine-thine problem: A sensitizing exercise for clinic, classroom, and attributional research. *Rehabilitation Psychology*, *57*, 113–123.

Dunn, D. S., Fisher, D., & Beard, B. (2013). Disability as diversity rather than (in)difference: Understanding others' experiences through one's own. In D. S. Dunn, R. A. R. Gurung, K. Z. Naufel, & J. H. Wilson (Eds.), *Controversy in the classroom: Using hot topics to foster critical thinking* (pp. 209–223). Washington, DC: American Psychological Association.

Dunn, D. S., Uswatte, G., & Elliott, T.R. (2009). Happiness, resilience and positive growth following disability: Issues for understanding, research, and therapeutic intervention. In S. J. Lopez & C. R. Snyder (Eds.), *Oxford handbook of positive psychology* (2nd ed., pp. 651–664). New York: Oxford University Press.

Ehde, D. M. (2010). Application of positive psychology to rehabilitation psychology. In R. G. Frank, M. Rosenthal, & B. Caplan (Eds.), *Handbook of rehabilitation psychology* (2nd ed., pp. 417–424). Washington, DC: American Psychological Association.

Elbert, T., Sterr, A., Rockstroh, B., Pantev, C., Muller, M. M., & Taub, E. (2002). Expansion of the tonotopic area in the auditory cortex of the blind. *Journal of Neuroscience*, *22*(22), 9941–9944.

Elliott, T., & Frank, R. G. (2000). Drawing new horizons for rehabilitation psychology. In R. G. Frank & T. Elliott (Eds.), *Handbook of rehabilitation psychology* (pp. 645–653). Washington, DC: American Psychological Association Press.

Elliott, T. R., Kurylo, M., & Rivera, P. (2002). Positive growth following acquired physical disability. In C. R. Snyder & S. J. Lopez (Eds.), *Handbook of positive psychology* (pp. 687–699). New York: Oxford University Press.

Elliott, T. R., & Rath, J. F. (2012). Rehabilitation psychology. In E. M. Altmaier & J. C. Hansen (Eds.), *The Oxford handbook of counseling psychology* (pp. 679–702). New York: Oxford University Press.

Elliott, T. R., Witty, T. E., Herrick, S. E., & Hoffman, J. T. (1991). Negotiating reality after physical loss: Hope, depression, and physical disability. *Journal of Personality and Social Psychology*, *61*, 608–613. doi:10.1037/0022-3514.61.4.608

Estes, W. K. (1944). An experimental study of punishment. *Psychological Monographs*, *57*(3).

Emmons, R. A., & McCullough, M. E. (2003). Counting blessings versus burdens: An experimental investigation of gratitude and subjective well-being in daily life. *Journal of Personality and Social Psychology*, *84*, 377–389. doi:10.1037/0022-3514.84.2.377

Fine, M., & Asch, A. (1988). Disability beyond stigma: Social interaction, discrimination, and activism. *Journal of Social Issues*, *44*, 3–21. doi:10.1111/j.1540-4560.1988.tb02045.x

Folkman, S., & Moskowitz, J. T. (2000). Positive affect and the other side of coping. *American Psychologist*, *55*, 647–695. doi:10.1037/0003-066X.55.6.647

Fredrickson, B. L. (1998). What good are positive emotions? *Review of General Psychology*, *2*, 300–319. doi:10.1037/1089-2680.2.3.300

Gauthier, L. V., Taub, E., Mark, V. W., Perkins, C., & Uswatte, G. (2009). Improvement after Constraint-Induced Movement therapy is independent of infarct location in chronic stroke patients. *Stroke*, *40*, 2468–2472. doi: 10.1161/STROKEAHA.109.548347

Gauthier, L. V., Taub, E., Perkins, C., Ortmann, M., Mark, V. W., & Uswatte, G. (2008). Remodeling the brain: Plastic structural brain changes produced by different motor therapies after stroke. *Stroke*, *39*, 1520–1525. doi:10.1161/STROKEAHA.107.502229

Gilbert, D. T., & Malone, P. S. (1995). The correspondence bias. *Psychological Bulletin*, *117*, 21–38. doi:10.1037/0033-2909.117.1.21

Gillham, J. E., & Seligman, M. E. P. (1999). Footsteps on the road to positive psychology. *Behavior Research and Therapy*, *37*, S163–S173.

Gould, E. (2007). How widespread is adult neurogenesis in mammals? *Nature Reviews Neuroscience*, *8*, 481–488. doi: 10.1038/nrn2147

Isen, A. M. (2004). Some perspectives on positive feelings and emotions: Positive affect facilitates thinking and problem solving. In A. S. R. Manstead, N. Frijda, & A. Fischer (Eds.), *Feelings and emotions: The Amsterdam symposium* (pp. 263–281).

Johnson, C.L., Resch J. A., Villarreal, V., Elliott, T. R., Kwok, O.-M., Berry, J. W., & Underhill, A. T. (2010). Family satisfaction predicts life satisfaction trajectories over the first five years after traumatic brain injury. *Rehabilitation Psychology*, *55*, 180–187.

Kaas, J. H. (1995). Neurobiology. How cortex reorganizes [news; comment]. *Nature*, *375*, 735–736. doi: 10.1038/375735a0

Kahneman, D. (1999). Objective happiness. In D. Kahneman, E. Diener, & N. Schwartz (Eds.), *Well-being: The foundations of hedonic psychology* (pp. 3–25). New York: Russell Sage Foundation.

Kahneman, D. (2000). Expected utility and objective happiness: A moment-based approach. In D. Kahneman & A. Tversky (Eds.), *Choices, values, and frames* (pp. 673–692). New York: Russell Sage Foundation and Cambridge University Press.

Keany, K. M. H., & Glueckauf, R. L. (1993). Disability and value change: An overview and reanalysis of acceptance of loss theory. *Rehabilitation Psychology*, *38*, 199–210. doi:10.1037/h0080297

Keyes, C. L. M., & Haidt, J. (Eds.). (2003). *Flourishing: Positive psychology and the life well-lived*. Washington, DC: American Psychological Association.

King, L. A., Hicks, J. A., Krull, J. L., & Del Gaiso, A. K. (2006). Positive affect and the experience of meaning in life. *Journal of Personality and Social Psychology*, *90*, 179–196. doi:10.1037/0022-3514.90.1.179.

Knapp, H. D., Taub, E., & Berman, A. J. (1963). Movements in monkeys with deafferentated forelimbs. *Experimental*

Neurology, *7*, 305–315. doi: 10.1016/0014-4886(63)90 077-3

Lechner, S. C., Tennen, H., & Affleck, G. (2009). Benefit-finding and growth. In S. J. Lopez & C. R. Snyder (Eds.), *Oxford handbook of positive psychology* (2nd ed., pp. 633–640). New York: Oxford University Press.

Lewin, K. (1935). *A dynamic theory of personality.* New York: McGraw-Hill.

Lewin, K. (1951). *Field theory in social science.* New York: Harper.

Liepert, J., Miltner, W. H., Bauder, H., Sommer, M., Dettmers, C., Taub, E., et al. (1998). Motor cortex plasticity during constraint-induced movement therapy in stroke patients. *Neuroscience Letters*, *250*(1), 5–8. 10.1016/S0304-3940(98)00386-3

Liepert, J. J., Graef, S. S., Uhde, I. I., Leidner, O. O., & Weiller, C. C. (2000). Training-induced changes of motor cortex representations in stroke patients. *Acta Neurologica Scandinavica*, *101*(5), 321–326. doi:10.1034/j.1600-0404.2000.90337A.x

Linley, P. A., & Joseph, S. (2004). Positive change following trauma and adversity: A review. *Journal of Traumatic Stress*, *17*, 11–21. doi:10.1023/B:JOTS.0000014671.27856.7e

Linley, P. A., & Joseph, S. (2005). The human capacity for growth through adversity. *American Psychologist*, *60*, 262–264. doi:10.1037/0003-066X.60.3.262b.

Lollar, D. (2008). Rehabilitation psychology and public health: Commonalities, barriers, and bridges. *Rehabilitation Psychology*, *53*, 122–127.

Lopez, S. J., & Snyder, C. R. (Eds.). (2009). *Oxford handbook of positive psychology* (2nd ed.). New York: Oxford University Press.

Luthans, F., & Youssef, C. M. (2009). Positive workplaces. In S. J. Lopez & C. R. Snyder (Eds.), *Oxford handbook of positive psychology* (2nd ed., pp. 579–588). New York: Oxford University Press.

Lyubomirsky, S., King, L., & Diener, E. (2005). The benefits of frequent positive affect: Does happiness lead to success? *Psychological Bulletin*, *131*, 803–855. doi:10.1037/0033-2909.131.6.803

Mausbach, B. T., Chattillion, E. A., Moore, R. C., Roepke, S., Depp, C. A., & Roesch, S. (2011). Activity restriction and depression in medical patients and their caregivers: A meta-analysis. *Clinical Psychology Review*, *31*, 900–908.

Mark, V., Taub, E., & Morris, D. M. (2006). Neuroplasticity and constraint-induced movement therapy. *Europa Medicophysica*, *42*(2), 269–284.

Mark, V. W., Taub, E., Perkins, C., Gauthier, L., & Uswatte, G. (2008). MRI infarction load and CI therapy outcomes for chronic post-stroke hemiparesis. *Restorative Neurology and Neuroscience*, *26*(1), 13–33.

Marrow, A. J. (1977). *The practical theorist: The life and work of Kurt Lewin.* New York: Teachers College Press.

McMillen, J. C., & Cook, C. L. (2003). The positive by-products of spinal cord injury and their correlates. *Rehabilitation Psychology*, *48*, 77–85. doi:10.1037/0090-5550.48.2.77

Mott, F. W., & Sherrington, C. S. (1895). Experiments upon the influence of sensory nerves upon movement and nutrition of the limbs. *Proceedings of the Royal Society of London*, *57*, 481–488. doi: 10.1098/rspl.1894.0179

Nisbett, R. E. (1980). The trait construct in lay and professional psychology. In L. Festinger (Ed.), *Retrospections on social psychology* (pp. 109–130). New York: Oxford University Press.

Ottawa Panel, Khadilkar, A., Phillips, K., Jean, N., Milne, S., & Sarnecka, J. (2006). Ottawa Panel evidence-based clinical practice guidelines for post-stroke rehabilitation. *Topics in Stroke Rehabilitation*, 1–269.

Park, C. L., Cohen, L. H., & Murch, R. L. (1996). Assessment and prediction of stress-related growth. *Journal of Personality*, *64*, 71–105. 10.1111/j.1467-6494.1996.tb00815.x

Peterson, C. (2006). *A primer in positive psychology.* New York: Oxford University Press.

Peterson, C., & Seligman, M. E. P. (2004). *Character strengths and virtues: A handbook and classification.* New York: Oxford University Press.

Resch, J. A., Villarreal, V., Johnson, C., Elliott, T., Kwok, O., Berry, J., & Underhill, A. (2009). Trajectories of life satisfaction in the first five years following traumatic brain injury. *Rehabilitation Psychology*, *54*, 51–59.

Ross, L. (1977). The intuitive psychologist and his shortcomings: Distortions in the attribution process. In L. Berkowitz (Ed.), *Advances in experimental social psychology* (vol. *10*, pp. 174–221). New York: Academic Press.

Ross, L., & Nisbett, R. E. (1991). *The person in the situation.* New York: McGraw-Hill.

Scheier, M. F., & Carver, C. S. (1992). Effects of optimism on psychological and physical well-being: Theoretical overview and empirical update. *Cognitive Therapy and Research*, *16*, 201–228. doi:10.1007/BF01173489

Seligman, M. E. P. (2002). *Authentic happiness: Using the new positive psychology to realize your potential for lasting fulfillment.* New York: The Free Press.

Seligman, M. E. P. (2011). *Flourish: A visionary new understanding of happiness and well-being.* New York: The Free Press.

Seligman, M. E. P., & Csikszentmihályi, M. (2000). Positive psychology: An introduction. *American Psychologist*, *55*, 5–14. doi:10.1037/0003-066X.55.1.5

Seligman, M. E. P., Steen, T. A., Park, N., & Peterson, C. (2005). Positive psychology in progress: Empirical validation of interventions. *American Psychologist*, *60*(5), 410–421. doi:10.1037/0003-066X.60.5.410

Shontz, F. C. (1982). Adaptation to chronic illness and disability. In T. Millon, C. Green, & R. Meagher (Eds.), *Handbook of clinical health psychology* (pp. 153–172). New York: Plenum Press.

Skinner, B. F. (1968). The technology of teaching. New York : Appleton-Century-Crofts.

Smith, D. M., Lowenstein, G., Jankovic, A., & Ubel, P. A. (2009). Happily hopeless: Adaptation to a permanent, but not to a temporary, disability. *Health Psychology*, *28*, 787–791. doi:10.1037/a0016624

Snyder, C. R. (1989). Reality negotiation: From excuses to hope and beyond. *Journal of Social and Clinical Psychology*, *8*, 130–157. doi:10.1521/jscp.1989.8.2.130

Snyder, C. R. (1994). *The psychology of hope: You can get there from here.* New York: Free Press.

Snyder, C. R., & Lopez, S. J. (Eds.). (2002). *Handbook of positive psychology.* New York: Oxford University Press.

Taub, E. (1977). Movement in nonhuman primates deprived of somatosensory feedback. *Exercise and Sports Sciences Reviews*, *4*, 335–374.

Taub, E. (1980). Somatosensory deafferentation research with monkeys: implications for rehabilitation medicine. In L. P. Ince (Ed.), *Behavioral psychology in rehabilitation medicine: Clinical applications* (pp. 371–401). New York: Williams & Wilkins.

Taub, E., & Berman, A. J. (1968). Movement and learning in the absence of sensory feedback. In S. J. Freedman (Ed.), *The neuropsychology of spatially oriented behavior* (pp. 173–192). Homewood, IL: Dorsey Press.

Taub, E., Miller, N. E., Novack, T. A., Cook, E. W., 3rd, Fleming, W. C., Nepomuceno, C. S., et al. (1993). Technique to improve chronic motor deficit after stroke. *Archives of Physical Medicine and Rehabilitation*, 74(4), 347–354.

Taub, E., Uswatte, G., & Elbert, T. (2002). New treatments in neurorehabilitation founded on basic research. *Nature Reviews Neuroscience*, 3(3), 228–236. doi: 10.1038/nrn754

Taub, E., Uswatte, G., King, D. K., Morris, D., Crago, J., & Chatterjee, A. (2006). A placebo controlled trial of constraint-induced movement therapy for upper extremity after stroke. *Stroke*, 37, 1045–1049. doi: 10.1161/01.STR.0000206463.66461.97

Taub, E., Uswatte, G., Mark, V. W., & Morris, D. M. (2006). The learned nonuse phenomenon: implications for rehabilitation. *Europa Medicophysica*, 42, 241–255.

Taub, E., Uswatte, G., & Pidikiti, R. (1999). Constraint-Induced Movement Therapy: a new family of techniques with broad application to physical rehabilitation—a clinical review. *Journal of Rehabilitation Research and Development*, 36, 237–251.

Taylor, S. E. (1983). Adjustment to threatening events: A theory of cognitive adaptation. *American Psychologist*, 38, 1161–1173. doi:10.1037/0003-066X.38.11.1161

Tedeschi, R. G., & Calhoun, L. G. (2004). Posttraumatic growth: Conceptual foundations and empirical evidence. *Psychological Inquiry*, 15, 1–8. doi:10.1207/s15327965pli1501_01

Tugade, M. M., & Fredrickson, B. L. (2004). Resilient individuals use positive emotions to bounce back from negative emotional experiences. *Journal of Personality and Social Psychology*, 86, 320–333. doi:10.1037/0022-3514.86.2.320

Ubel, P. A., Loewenstein, G., Hershey, J., Baron, J., Mohr, T., Asch, D., & Jepson, C. (2001). Do nonpatients underestimate the quality of life associated with chronic health conditions because of a focusing illusion? *Medical Decision Making*, 21, 190–199. doi:10.1177/0272989X0102100304

Uswatte, G., & Taub, E. (2010). You can teach an old dog new tricks: harnessing neuroplasticity after brain injury in older adults. In P. S. Fry & C. L. M. Keyes (Eds.), *New frontiers in resilient aging* (pp. 104–129). Cambridge, UK: Cambridge University Press. doi: 10.1017/CBO9780511763151.006

Uswatte, G., Taub, E., Mark, V. W., Perkins, C., & Gauthier, L. V. (2010). CNS plasticity and rehabilitation. In R. G. Frank, M. Rosenthal, & B. Caplan (Eds.), *Handbook of*

rehabilitation psychology (2nd ed., pp. 391–406). Washington, DC: American Psychological Association.

van Praag, H., Kempermann, G., & Gage, F. H. (2000). Neural consequences of environmental enrichment. *Nature Reviews Neuroscience*, 1, 191–198. doi: 10.1038/35044558

Vash, C. L. (1981). *The psychology of disability.* New York: Springer.

Wang, K., & Dovidio, J. F. (2011). Disability and autonomy: Priming alternative identities. *Rehabilitation Psychology*, 56, 123–127. doi:10.1037/a0023039

Wolf, S. L., Winstein, C., Miller, J. P., Taub, E., Uswatte, G., Morris, D. M., et al. (2006). Effect of Constraint Induced Movement therapy on upper extremity function among patients 3-9 months following stroke: the EXCITE randomized clinical trial. *JAMA: The Journal of the American Medical Association*, 296(17), 2095–2104. doi: 10.1001/jama.296.17.2095

World Health Organization (2011). *World report on disability.* Geneva: World Health Organization.

Wright, B. A. (1972). Value-laden beliefs and principles for rehabilitation psychology. *Rehabilitation Psychology*, 19, 38–45. doi:10.1037/h0090869

Wright, B. A. (1975). Sensitizing outsiders to the position of the insider. *Rehabilitation Psychology*, 22, 129–135. doi: 10.1037/h0090837

Wright, B. A. (1983). *Physical disability: A psychosocial approach* (2nd ed.). New York: Harper Collins. doi:10.1037/10589-000

Wright, B. A. (1988). Attitudes and the fundamental negative bias: Conditions and corrections. In H. E. Yuker (Ed.), *Attitudes towards persons with disabilities* (pp. 3–21). New York: Springer.

Wright, B. A. (1991). Labeling: The need for greater person-environment individuation. In C. R. Snyder & D. R. Forsyth (Eds.), *Handbook of social and clinical psychology: The health perspective* (pp. 469–487). New York: Pergamon Press.

Wright, B. A., & Fletcher, B. L. (1982). Uncovering hidden resources: A challenge in assessment. *Professional Psychology*, 13, 229–235. doi:10.1037/07357028.13.2.229

Wright, B. A., & Lopez, S. J. (2002). Widening the diagnostic focus: A case for including human strengths and environmental resources. In C. R. Snyder & S. J. Lopez (Eds.), *Handbook of positive psychology* (pp. 26–44). New York: Oxford University Press.

Cognitive and Developmental Disabilities

Karrie A. Shogren

Abstract

Throughout history, deficits and limitations in functioning have been emphasized in the cognitive and developmental disability field. However, a shift has emerged in the field and greater attention has been directed to positive personal capacities and experiences. This chapter reviews historical factors that have contributed to deficit-based models of research, policy, and practice for individuals with cognitive and developmental disabilities and factors that are contributing to the emergence of a strengths-based perspective in the cognitive and developmental disability field. The influence of positive psychology in the field will be discussed and selected areas of positive psychology research in the cognitive and developmental disability field described. Directions for future research, policy, and practice are discussed.

Key Words: cognitive and developmental disability, positive psychology, self-determination, happiness, systems change

The intellectual and developmental disability field has been dominated throughout history by a focus on deficits and limitations. Diagnosing cognitive disabilities, such as intellectual disability, involves identifying significant limitations in intellectual functioning and adaptive behavior (Schalock et al., 2010). Developmental disabilities are defined by mental or physical impairments that lead to substantial functional limitations in major life activities. And, for much of modern history, the focus in the cognitive and developmental disability field has been on developing effective practices to identify these limitations and to develop treatments to eliminate, cure, or remediate them (Shogren, Wehmeyer, Pressgrove, & Lopez, 2006).

Although the field of intellectual and developmental disabilities has been dominated by a focus on deficits and limitations, each person with a cognitive and developmental disability—just as any person with or without a disability—has a unique profile of strengths, interests, abilities, and support

needs. Furthermore, as many people with disabilities assert, people with disabilities are people first—disability is not the only feature that defines them. Although historic conceptualizations of cognitive and developmental disabilities have focused on limitations, there is increasing recognition of the problems inherent to conceptualizing disability as a deficit that resides within a person. Alternative frameworks for research, policy, and practice in the cognitive and developmental disability field have emerged that draw on a social-ecological or person-environment fit model, which looks at the interaction between personal capacities and the demands of the environment in which individuals work, live, learn, and play (Wehmeyer et al., 2008).

Social-ecological models do not view disability as a deficit that resides within a person, but rather as an interaction between personal capacities and environmental demands. Such models facilitate the adoption of a strengths-based perspective to understanding disability, focusing on the capacities of people with disabilities and the supports needed to meet their environmental demands. This perspective emphasizes the importance of understanding the full range of the human condition, including positive traits and experiences, and building on strengths rather than exclusively focusing on identifying and remediating deficits.

The shift toward recognizing the importance of building on strengths and positive traits in the disability field mirrors in many ways the emergence of the field of positive psychology. The term "positive psychology" was coined to describe the movement away from a focus on deficits and damage and toward a psychology focused on human strengths and virtues. Seligman (1998) defined the mission of positive psychology as "to measure, understand and then build the human strengths and the civic virtues"(p. 2). Within the discipline, people are viewed "as decision makers, with choices, preferences, and the possibility of becoming masterful, efficacious, or in malignant circumstances, helpless and hopeless" (Seligman & Csikszentmihályi, 2000, p. 8). Seligman and Csikszentmihályi (2000) characterized positive psychology as focusing on three areas: (a) valued subjective experience, (b) positive individual traits, and (c) civic values and the institutions that support them.

Positive psychology has the potential to further expand the possibilities of a strengths-based approach to supporting people with cognitive and developmental disabilities so that they may, as positive psychologists say, "live the good life." This chapter reviews the historical factors that have contributed to deficit-based models of research, policy, and practice for individuals with cognitive and developmental disabilities and those factors that are contributing to the emergence of a strengths-based perspective in the cognitive and developmental disability field. Selected areas of positive psychology research in the cognitive and developmental disability field will be reviewed and directions for future research, policy, and practice identified.

Historical Trends in the Cognitive and Developmental Disability Field

Throughout history, disability has often been viewed through a medical lens, in which disability is characterized as a pathological condition that needs to be cured or remediated. This perspective has particularly dominated the cognitive and developmental disability field (Wehmeyer et al., 2008). Even the terminology used to refer to specific cognitive and developmental disabilities has reflected

this conceptualization. As Wehmeyer et al. wrote about the assumptions that undergirded the diagnostic term "mental retardation" and the terms that preceded it (e.g., mental deficiency, mental subnormality):

> The first such assumption was that the disability resided within the person. To have mental retardation was to be defective. The loci of that defect was the mind. The term *mental*, which is common to all of these terms, means of or pertaining to the mind. The nature of the defect of the mind (mental deficiency) was inferior mental performance (mental subnormality) characterized by mental slowness (mental retardation)....It is a disability determined by indicators of performance linked to limitations in human functioning. (p. 312)

This model of understanding cognitive and developmental disabilities, with its focus on curing or remediating deficits, has had negative consequences for people with disabilities, particularly when those perceived deficits could not be cured or remediated, but instead required ongoing supports. In the late 19th and early 20th centuries, institutions became the primary location for services for people with cognitive and developmental disabilities. Institutions initially emerged from the work of Edouard Seguin and focused on education and rehabilitation. Seguin asserted that individuals with cognitive and developmental disabilities could be educated and contribute to society. However, over time, the purpose and focus of these institutions changed. Political shifts and a growing emphasis on IQ testing, as well as a growing recognition that remediating cognitive and developmental disabilities was not, in many cases, a realistic goal led to institutions becoming less focused on education and rehabilitation and more focused on control and congregate care. Institutions grew in size and became more focused on their custodial mission and on eliminating the "menace" that people with cognitive and developmental disabilities were increasingly being viewed as posing to society (Trent, 1994).

However, in the latter part of the 20th century, shifts in the cognitive and developmental disability field began to emerge. The social-ecological model of disability was adopted by the World Health Organization (1980) in its *International Classification of Impairment, Disability and Handicap* (now *International Classification of Functioning, Disability, and Health* [2001]), and the same model was incorporated into the definition, classification, and systems of support Manual of mental retardation (now intellectual disability) put forward by the American Association on Intellectual and Developmental Disabilities (Luckasson et al., 1992). The social-ecological model recognized that disability was not just a deficit that resided within the person, but that disability results from an interaction of personal capacities and environmental demands. The disability rights movement capitalized on the person-environment fit model and built on the civil rights movements for women and African Americans that preceded it, directing attention to the need for environmental changes to make society more accessible to people with disabilities (Shapiro, 1993). It was increasingly recognized that changes in the environment could lead to changes in the experiences and outcomes of people with disabilities. The passage of Section 504 of the Rehabilitation Act, P.L. 94-142 (now the Individuals with Disabilities Education Act) and later the Americans with Disabilities Act acknowledged the need for environmental change and provided civil rights to people with disabilities.

For people with cognitive and developmental disabilities, the civil rights movement had a significant impact on access to both education and community environments. The normalization (Nirje, 1969) and deinsitutionalization (Bradley, 1994) movements also had a major impact, bringing increased attention to the inherent rights of people with cognitive and developmental disabilities to live in the community and participate in their local schools and neighborhoods. These movements led to a significant decrease in the numbers of people with cognitive and developmental disabilities living in large congregate settings and also served to increase access to neighborhood schools and classrooms (although there is still significant progress to be made). However, despite the increased focus on deinstitutionalization and community-based supports, the field has continued to struggle to move past its deficit-based history—a significant amount of research, policy, and practice still is driven by a deficit perspective despite an emerging focus on strengths-driven, individualized, personalized supports in the community.

Emerging Trends in the Cognitive and Developmental Disability Field

The civil rights movement for people with disabilities and the normalization and deinstitutionalization movements for people with cognitive and developmental disabilities have had substantial impact on the location and nature of the services and supports provided to people with cognitive and developmental disabilities. Although, historically, services and supports for people with cognitive disabilities

have been program-driven, as inclusive school and community-based services have become the preferred mode of service delivery, a key value of this framework for service delivery has been that supports must be individualized to the person's needs and preferences, rather than to program or facility needs, preferences, or conveniences. This recognition of the importance of an individual's needs and preferences has brought increased attention to (a) the assessment of support needs rather than the documentation of limitations as a key part of planning personalized services and supports; (b) the importance of understanding strengths, interests, and abilities and using this as the basis for person-centered planning; and (c) the importance of building on positive traits and subjective experiences to promote "the good life" for people with disabilities.

Schalock (2004) described the "emerging disability paradigm" (p. 204) that is driving supports and services in the disability field as encompassing four areas: (a) functional limitations that define disability; (b) individualized supports; (c) personal well-being, including positive psychological constructs and quality of life issues; and (d) personal competence and adaptation. In this framework, although functional limitations are still part of the model, there is also a strong emphasis placed on positive psychology constructs related to personal well-being and personal competence. Furthermore, functional limitations are viewed through a person-environment fit lens. Disability is recognized as the result of an interaction between personal capacities and environmental demands—not a deficit that resides within the person. This creates an emerging opportunity to shift the emphasis of research from deficits and limitations to strengths and positive traits and experiences.

The degree to which strengths-based research has infiltrated the cognitive and developmental disability field is growing, although such research still remains a minority, particularly in regards to research focused on positive internal traits and experiences (e.g., happiness, subjective well-being), which has received significant attention in the broader field of positive psychology. Shogren and colleagues (2006) reviewed research published in five prominent journals in the intellectual and developmental disability field published between 1975 and 2004. From these five journals, 144 issues were randomly selected and all articles in each journal coded to capture information about the strengths/positive psychological focus of each article. We found that 35% of articles adopted a strengths perspective; however, this focus changed significantly over time, from a low of 22% of articles in 1975–1984 to a high of 50% of articles in 1995–2004. Of these articles, 15% included a construct associated with positive psychology as a primary focus over time. However from 1975 to 1984, only 9% of articles focused on a positive psychology construct; this rose in 1985–1995 to 15% of articles, and from 1995 to 2004, to 24% of articles. Thus, although there is an emerging body of strengths-based research that places a growing emphasis on positive traits and experiences of people with cognitive and developmental disabilities, it still represent, overall, a minority of scholarship in the field. However, there is significant promise for this growing body of research to continue to push the focus in the disability field from deficits to strengths. In the following sections, we review selected areas of research that are contributing to this emerging emphasis on positive psychology research in the cognitive and developmental disability field.

Positive Psychology Research and Cognitive and Developmental Disabilities
Positive Experiences and Traits
Although the normalization and deinstitutionalization movements exerted significant influence on the cognitive and developmental disability field, these movements focused on conditions external to people with cognitive and developmental disabilities. However, the social-ecological model emphasizes that disability is an interaction of personal capacities and environmental demands. Although, historically, limitations in personal capacities have been the focus in the field, the social-ecological model introduces the possibility of a strengths-based approach to understanding and building on personal capacities while concurrently working to create accommodating, inclusive environments.

SELF-DETERMINATION
In the cognitive and developmental disability field, *self-determination* is one construct that fits within the parameters of positive psychology and has contributed to a growing emphasis on a strengths-based approach to building on the personal capacities of people with disabilities. The historical roots of self-determination for people with disabilities can be found in the normalization, deinstitutionalization, and disability rights movement (Ward, 1996). However, the self-determination movement pushed the field toward also focusing on understanding and supporting the development of positive internal traits.

The emphasis on self-determination emerged in the cognitive and developmental disability field as increased attention was directed toward the poor outcomes that students with disabilities were experiencing as they transitioned from school to adult life in the late 1980s and early 1990s (Blackorby & Wagner, 1996). Despite the environmental changes that had occurred in the 1970s and 1980s, including policy changes resulting in access to education and inclusive environments, students with cognitive and developmental disabilities were still experiencing negative outcomes (e.g., low rates of employment and independent living) as they transitioned from school to adult life. Promoting self-determination, or supporting students to develop skills and attitudes that would enable them to be causal agents over their lives, emerged as one way to promote better outcomes. Specifically, under deficit-based conceptualizations of disability, limited attention was directed to how individuals with cognitive and developmental disabilities could play an active role in making choices and decisions about their lives. In fact, many individuals questioned whether this was possible for people with significant cognitive disabilities. However, researchers began to document the negative effects of a lack of choice and control on people with disabilities (Shogren, Bovaird, Palmer, & Wehmeyer, 2010; Wehmeyer & Palmer, 1997), and increased attention was directed to creating innovative strategies to support people with cognitive and developmental disabilities to be self-determining. In the early 1990s, multiple projects were funded by the U.S. Department of Education that focused on developing frameworks for understanding and promoting self-determination (Ward, 2005).

Wehmeyer and colleagues (Wehmeyer, Abery, Mithaug, & Stancliffe, 2003; Wehmeyer et al., 2007) introduced a functional model of self-determination that characterized self-determination as a dispositional characteristic of individuals, based on the function of their behavior. They defined self-determined behavior as "volitional actions that enable one to act as the primary causal agent in one's life and to maintain or improve one's quality of life" (Wehmeyer, 2005, p. 117). Self-determined behavior thus refers to actions that are identified by four essential characteristics:

- The person acted autonomously.
- The behavior(s) are self-regulated.
- The person initiated and responded to the event(s) in a psychologically empowered manner.
- The person acted in a self-realizing manner.

These four essential characteristics describe the function of the behavior that makes it self-determined (or not). Thus, it is not specific behaviors that define self-determination; instead, it is the function of those behaviors. Thus, people with disabilities who may need supports to perform some behaviors can still be self-determining so long as they are the causal agent directing actions to achieve the quality of life outcomes they value. The concept of *causal agency* is central to the functional model of self-determination. Causal agency implies that it is the person who makes or causes things to happen in his or her life.

Self-determination emerges across the lifespan as children and adolescents learn skills and develop attitudes that enable them to be causal agents in their lives. The essential characteristics that define self-determined behavior emerge through the development and acquisition of multiple, interrelated component elements including choice making, problem solving, decision making, goal setting and attainment, self-advocacy, and self-management skills. The model has been empirically validated (Wehmeyer et al., 2000, 2012), has received significant attention in the cognitive and developmental disability field, and has contributed to the shift toward recognizing the importance of building on positive internal traits, or, as positive psychologists may characterize it, to understanding how people with disabilities become "decision makers, with choices, preferences, and the possibility of becoming masterful, efficacious" (Seligman & Csikszentmihályi, 2000, p. 8).

A growing body of research has established the impact of self-determination and self-determination instruction on children, youth, and adults with disabilities. Several meta-analyses have established the efficacy of instruction to promote self-determination and its component elements (Algozzine, Browder, Karvonen, Test, & Wood, 2001; Cobb, Lehmann, Newman-Gonchar, & Alwell, 2009). Also, self-determination status has been linked to the attainment of positive academic (Konrad, Fowler, Walker, Test, & Wood, 2007; Lee, Wehmeyer, Palmer, Soukup, & Little, 2008; Shogren, Palmer, Wehmeyer, Williams-Diehm, & Little, 2012) and adult outcomes (e.g., employment, independent living) (Wehmeyer & Palmer, 2003; Wehmeyer & Schwartz, 1997). Research has also linked enhanced self-determination with enhanced quality of life and life satisfaction (Lachapelle et al., 2005; Nota, Ferrari, Soresi, & Wehmeyer, 2007; Shogren, Lopez, Wehmeyer, Little, & Pressgrove, 2006; Wehmeyer & Schwartz, 1998).

HAPPINESS

Self-determination has emerged as one of the most frequently researched positive psychology constructs in the cognitive and developmental disability field (Shogren, Wehmeyer, Pressgrove, et al., 2006); however, a number of additional positive traits and experiences have received attention in the broader positive psychology field. An oft-cited construct in definitions of positive psychology is *happiness*, and happiness and subjective well-being are frequently studied in positive psychology research (Hart & Sasso, 2011). Happiness and subjective well-being in people with cognitive and developmental disabilities has been less frequently studied; the majority of research in this area has primarily examined happiness and subjective well-being in parents, siblings, and support providers of individuals with disabilities. In our review of positive psychology research in the disability field (Shogren, Wehmeyer, Pressgrove, et al., 2006) focused on research targeting individuals with disabilities (not family members or support staff), only 1% of articles included a focus on happiness. However, there has been a growing emphasis placed on the importance of assessing and supporting happiness in people with cognitive and developmental disabilities (Carr, 2007; Dillon & Carr, 2007). For example, Carr (2007), in discussing the "expanding vision of positive behavior support," identified happiness as a key outcome variable and stated that the field needs to use the broader research base on personal happiness and satisfaction needs to "organize, analyze, and utilize the concepts and strategies represented in this broad research base to maximize its relevance to the populations we serve. This job is both daunting and doable" (p. 4).

Other researchers (Dykens, 2006; Schalock, 2004) have also cited the need for more focus on happiness and subjective well-being in people with disabilities. However, developing ways to assess happiness and subjective well-being continues to be a major issue in the field. Some researchers have attempted to apply behavioral methods to the assessment of happiness, developing observational systems to attempt to quantify happiness through observations of engagement with preferred items (Dillon & Carr, 2007). Although such approaches can be useful, particularly for individuals with significant disabilities, there continues to be a need to develop strategies that assess the subjective experiences of people with cognitive and developmental disabilities and the complexity of the happiness construct. For example, Seligman (2002) identified three aspects of the happiness construct: positive emotion and pleasure, meaning, and engagement. Although strategies to assess engagement with items (i.e., preference) exist in the cognitive and developmental disability field, more work is needed to develop ways to assess positive emotions, pleasure, and meaning. Such work is needed, as Carr (2007) said, to capitalize on the growing knowledge base in the field of positive psychology on the benefits of happiness and well-being. Research has suggested that people who are happier are healthier and that happiness and optimism can impact learning and personal development (Seligman, 2003). Interventions have been developed that increase happiness and decrease depressive symptoms (Seligman, Park, & Peterson, 2005); however people with cognitive and developmental disabilities have not yet been included in this body of research. Work is needed to extend research on happiness and subjective well-being to people with cognitive and developmental disabilities, to continue to build on positive personal capacities to promote quality of life.

RESILIENCY

Another area of positive psychology that has received significant attention in recent years is resiliency (Hart & Sasso, 2011). Although not originally identified as a key dimension of positive psychology, positive psychology researchers have increasingly recognized that positive emotions and coping mechanisms, when applied to challenging circumstances, can have significant positive benefits. A primary mission of positive psychology, originally, was to restore balance in research and practice in psychology; researchers asserted that too much focus was directed to the negative, to deficit-based approaches, to disorder and distress. Thus, early on, positive psychology focused primarily on subjective well-being and fulfillment. However, researchers have increasingly begun to explore the buffering effects of positive psychological constructs on challenging environmental circumstances. For example, Dunn, Uswatte, and Elliott (2009) explored resiliency and positive growth following acquired physical disability, and Shogren and Broussard (2011) found that self-determination may affect resiliency and positive coping in people with intellectual disability facing employment discrimination.

Within positive psychology, there is a "broadening [of] the scope of the field to include the study of people who function in troubled human ecologies" (Hart & Sasso, 2011, p. 91). And, although efforts have been undertaken to change the environments in which people with disabilities live, learn, work,

and play within, there are clearly still significant barriers resulting from negative attitudes, stereotyping, and discrimination that can limit the opportunities available to people with cognitive and developmental disabilities. Thus, future research must work both to change these environments, but to also identify and build on research that suggests that positive, strengths-based approaches to challenging environmental contexts can have positive effects. For example, researchers have begun to study how individuals with autism have begun to use online communities to develop social relationships, creating their own accommodations to their social differences (Brownlow & O'Dell, 2006). Further research is needed that explores strengths-based approaches to supporting people with disabilities to cope with the human environments they experience.

Positive Systems

In addition to research on positive traits and experiences, another "pillar" of positive psychology is positive institutions or systems (Seligman & Csikszentmihályi, 2000). As Seligman and Csikszentmihályi write "people and experiences are embedded in a social context. Thus, a positive psychology needs to take positive communities and positive institutions into account" (p. 8). Research in the cognitive and developmental disability field has also emphasized the social context. As mentioned earlier, much of the focus in the latter portion of the 20th century was on changing the negative, restrictive environmental conditions experienced by individuals with cognitive and developmental disabilities. Thus, a wide array of research in the cognitive and developmental disability field has focused on creating positive systems and on recognizing the benefits that diversity, including disability, brings to families, communities, and society. In the following sections, we briefly highlight research on strengths-based systems approaches to the cognitive and developmental disability field.

FAMILY RESEARCH

Although limited research has focused on happiness and subjective well-being in individuals with disabilities, a growing body of research is focused on the positive experiences of families that include a child with a disability (Dykens, 2005). Although, historically, a common assumption was that a child with a cognitive or developmental disability created stress and promoted negative outcomes in the family system, increasingly, researchers are finding that negative, stress-based coping models do not capture the range of experiences of families with disabilities and the positive outcomes that can result from a child with a disability being part of the family system. Researchers have found that having or adopting a child with a disability can lead to positive adjustment within families, including increased positive coping strategies (Scorgie & Sobsey, 2000). Researchers have also found that siblings of youth with disabilities may experience many positive outcomes, including greater empathy and acceptance of differences (Stoneman, 2005). Researchers have also found positive psychological constructs, such as hope, can serve as a protective factor for parents of children with disabilities. For example, mothers of children with autism and Down syndrome tend to have less worry when they had higher levels of hope for the future (Ogston, Mackintosh, & Myers, 2011). This line of research clearly suggests that positive, strengths-based approaches to understanding disability and supporting families can have a positive impact on the family system. For example, Steiner (2011) found that a strengths-based approach to parent education was more effective than a deficits-based approach in increasing positive parent affect, affection, and statements.

Clearly, this line of research suggests the benefits of strengths-based approaches to disability for the family system. Although much of this work has focused on the impact on parents or siblings, further research examining the interactive effects of a strengths-based approach on the family system and on the child with a disability holds significant promise for promoting a comprehensive approach to understanding well-being and quality of life for all members of the family system.

SUPPORT ORGANIZATIONS

Significant change has also occurred in the frameworks that guide support organizations that serve people with cognitive and developmental disabilities. As inclusive, community-based services and supports have become the expectation in the disability field in recent years, this has led to a significant shift in the design and delivery of supports and services. Program needs or structure used to be the primary mechanism for determining the supports and services provided. For example, in education, rather than providing supports in the general education classroom that allowed all students to succeed—including students with disabilities—students were placed in programs for those with certain disability labels (e.g., segregated classrooms for students with specific IQ levels) that delivered

services organized around those labels rather than based on individual support needs. The same was true in adult services, where available residential options and employment options were determined by what programs had available. However, increasingly, a person-centered approach to service delivery has been promoted in the field. Although still not pervasive in practice, the goals of a person-centered approach are to start with an understanding of each person's goals, dreams, and desires for the future and to then use these as the basis for developing a personalized system of support that facilitates the achievement of these goals and dreams.

This model differs significantly from historical frameworks and promotes the development of positive, strengths-driven organizations. Further research is needed on the impact of strengths-based organizations on the outcomes experienced by people with disabilities. Although the evidence is still limited, researchers have suggested that using person-centered planning to organize supports for people with disabilities can lead to positive personal outcomes for these individuals (Claes, Van Hove, Vandevelde, van Loon, & Schalock, 2010).

POLICY INITIATIVES

In addition to family systems and organizations, the public policy context is another aspect of the environment that influences people with cognitive and developmental disabilities. Policies affording negative (e.g., freedom from discrimination) and positive (e.g., access to education and services) rights are a key aspect of the context within which people with disabilities live, learn, work, and play. Public policy is influenced (and influences) by a number of factors, including social factors, core principles of disability policy, and desired policy outcomes.

There is growing consensus on the key principles that guide national and international disability policy and their importance in defining desired outcomes of disability policy (Shogren et al., 2009; Shogren & Turnbull, 2010). The principles can be grouped into two broad categories: (a) *person-referenced*, encompassing such issues as self-determination, inclusion, empowerment, individual and appropriate services, productivity and contribution, and family integrity and unity; and (b) *system-referenced* (supports/service delivery), encompassing such issues as antidiscrimination, coordination and collaboration, and accountability (Montreal Declaration, 2004; Salamanca Statement, 1994; Stowe, Turnbull, & Sublet, 2006; Turnbull, Wilcox, Stowe, & Umbarger, 2001). These principles have been operationalized in the United Nations Convention on the Rights of Persons with Disabilities (United Nations, 2006), in articles that address the domains of rights (access and privacy); participation; autonomy, independence, and choice; physical well-being; material well-being (work/employment); inclusion, accessibility, and participation; emotional well-being (freedom from exploitation, violence, and abuse); and personal development (education and rehabilitation). These principles are congruent with positive psychology and work to create a framework for defining positive outcomes for individuals and systems (Shogren et al., 2009).

Directions for Future Research, Policy, and Practice

Although the cognitive and developmental disability field has a history dominated by a focus on deficits and limitations, there is clearly significant change emerging in the field. Congruent with positive psychology, there is a growing movement in the cognitive and developmental disability field to understand and build on the strengths inherent in individuals, families, and organizations. Future research, policy, and practice must continue to build on positive traits and experiences in the lives and environments of people with cognitive and developmental disabilities. At the individual level, research is needed to (a) examine ways to measure and build on positive traits and experiences in people with disabilities themselves, (b) explore the buffering effect that strengths-based approaches can have under challenging circumstances, and (c) integrate research that focuses on building personal capacities and changing environmental conditions. At the systems level, research is needed to (a) build on existing research to understand and promote positive family growth when a child with a disability joins the family, (b) explore the benefits of positive organizations for person- and system-referenced outcomes, and (c) integrate the key disability policy principles into research, policy, and practice.

At the broadest level, positive psychology provides a framework that can continue to move the cognitive and developmental disability field forward in recognizing and incorporating strengths-based approaches into research, policy, and practice. However, because the life experiences of all individuals includes a wide range of both positive and negative events, key issues in future research, policy, and practice will include:

1. *Integrating the positive and the negative.* Although positive psychology emphasizes positive traits and experiences, people with disabilities do experience functional limitations that, in certain environmental conditions, can create personal challenges. Understanding these functional limitations, the support needs they create, and ways to build on personal capacities will all be important to creating a comprehensive framework for understanding the entire range of experiences of people with cognitive and developmental disabilities. Historically, one aspect has been privileged, be it deficits or environmental conditions. Work is needed to build a comprehensive understanding of the range of experiences of people with disabilities and to use this comprehensive understanding of all experiences to promote the good life.

2. *Integrating the voices of people with disabilities.* A key factor in the growing emphasis on positive traits and experiences in the cognitive and developmental disability field was the introduction of the self-determination construct as a means of promoting positive outcomes for people with disabilities. Promoting self-determination is about supporting people with cognitive and developmental disabilities to be causal agents over their lives. As work on understanding and promoting positive traits, experiences, and systems proceeds in the field, people with disabilities must continue to be actively engaged in all aspects of research, policy, and practice.

3. *Integrating individual, family, and system change.* Although the social-ecological model and positive psychology have implications for change at the individual, family, and system change level, research has often only focused on one level of the system and not on the interactive effects that change in one system can exert on other systems. Building on the work of Bronfenbrenner (1979), work is needed to explore the effects across systems and over time. As we shift toward positive approaches to understanding and supporting individuals with cognitive and developmental disabilities, we must explore the impacts of changes in research, policy, and practice at the level of the individual, the family, and organizations.

References

Algozzine, B., Browder, D., Karvonen, M., Test, D. W., & Wood, W. M. (2001). Effects of interventions to promote self-determination for individuals with disabilities. *Review of Educational Research, 71,* 219–277.

Blackorby, J., & Wagner, M. (1996). Longitudinal post-school outcomes of youth with disabilities: Findings from the National Longitudinal Transition Study. *Exceptional Children, 62*(5), 399–413.

Bradley, V. J. (1994). Evolution of a new service paradigm. In V. J. Bradley, J. W. Ashbaugh, & B. C. Blaney (Eds.), *Creating individual supports for people with developmental disabilities: A mandate for change at many levels* (pp. 11–32). Baltimore, MD: Brookes

Bronfenbrenner, U. (1979). *The ecology of human development: Experiments by nature and design.* Cambridge: Harvard University Press.

Brownlow, C., & O'Dell, L. (2006). Constructing an autistic identity: AS voices online. *Mental Retardation, 44*, 315–321.

Carr, E. G. (2007). The expanding vision of positive behavior support: Research perspectives on happiness, helpfulness, hopefulness. *Journal of Positive Behavior Interventions, 9*(1), 3–14.

Claes, C., Van Hove, G., Vandevelde, S., van Loon, J., & Schalock, R. L. (2010). Person-centered planning: Analysis of research and effectiveness. *Intellectual and Developmental Disabilities, 48*, 432–453.

Cobb, R. B., Lehmann, J., Newman-Gonchar, R., & Alwell, M. (2009). Self-determination for students with disabilities: A narrative metasynthesis. *Career Development for Exceptional Individuals, 32*(2), 108–114.

Dillon, C. M., & Carr, J. E. (2007). Assessing indices of happiness and unhappiness in individuals with developmental disabilities: A review. *Behavioral Interventions, 22*, 229–244.

Dunn, D. S., Uswatte, G., & Elliott, T. R. (2009). Happiness, resilience, and positive growth following physical disability: Issues for understanding, research, and therapeutic research. In S. J. Lopez & C. R. Snyder (Eds.), *The Oxford handbook of positive psychology* (2nd ed., pp. 651–664). Oxford: Oxford University Press.

Dykens, E. M. (2005). Happiness, well-being, and character strengths: Outcomes for families and siblings of persons with mental retardation. *Mental Retardation, 43*(5), 360–364.

Dykens, E. M. (2006). Toward a positive psychology of mental retardation. *American Journal of Orthopsychiatry, 76*(2), 185–193.

Hart, K. E., & Sasso, T. (2011). Mapping the contours of contemporary positive psychology. *Canadian Psychology, 52*(2), 82–92.

Konrad, M., Fowler, C. H., Walker, A. R., Test, D. W., & Wood, W. M. (2007). Effects of self-determination interventions on the academic skills of students with learning disabilities. *Learning Disability Quarterly, 30*, 89–113.

Lachapelle, Y., Wehmeyer, M. L., Haelewyck, M. C., Courbois, Y., Keith, K. D., Schalock, R., et al. (2005). The relationship between quality of life and self-determination: An international study. *Journal of Intellectual Disability Research, 49*, 740–744.

Lee, S. H., Wehmeyer, M. L., Palmer, S. B., Soukup, J. H., & Little, T. D. (2008). Self-determination and access to the general education curriculum. *Journal of Special Education, 42*(2), 91–107.

Luckasson, R., Coulter, D. L., Polloway, E. A., Reiss, S., Schalock, R. L., Snell, M. E., et al. (1992). *Mental retardation: Definition, classification, and systems of supports* (9th ed.). Washington, DC: American Association on Mental Retardation.

Montreal Declaration. (2004). *Montreal declaration on intellectual disability.* Montreal, Canada: PAHO/WHO Conference.

Nirje, B. (1969). The normalization principle and its human management implications. In R. B. Kugel & W. Wolfensberger (Eds.), *Changing residential patterns for the mentally retarded.* Washington, DC: President's Committee on Mental Retardation.

Nirje, B. (1972). The right to self-determination. In W. Wolfensberger (Ed.), *Normalization: The principle of normalization in human services* (pp. 176–193). Toronto: National Institute on Mental Retardation.

Nota, L., Ferrari, L., Soresi, S., & Wehmeyer, M. (2007). Self-determination, social abilities and the quality of life of people with intellectual disability. *Journal of Intellectual Disability Research, 51*(11), 850–865.

Ogston, P. L., Mackintosh, V. H., & Myers, B. J. (2011). Hope and worry in mothers of children with an autism spectrum disorder or down syndrome. *Research in Autism Spectrum Disorders, 5*(4), 1378–1384. doi: 10.1016/j.rasd.2011.01.020

Salamanca Statement. (1994). *Salamanca statement and framework for action in special needs education.* Salamanca, Spain: University of Salamanca-Department of Psychology.

Schalock, R. L. (2004). The emerging disability paradigm and its implications for policy and practice. *Journal of Disability Policy Studies, 14*, 204–215.

Schalock, R. L., Borthwick-Duffy, S., Bradley, V., Buntix, W. H. E., Coulter, D. L., Craig, E. P. M., et al. (2010). *Intellectual disability: Definition, classification, and systems of support* (11th ed.). Washington, DC: American Association on Intellectual and Developmental Disabilities.

Scorgie, K., & Sobsey, D. (2000). Transformational outcomes associated with parenting children who have disabilities. *Mental Retardation, 38*, 195–206.

Seligman, M. E. P. (1998). What is the 'good life'? *APA Monitor, 29*(10), 2.

Seligman, M. E. P. (2002). *Authentic happiness: Using the new positive psychology to realize your potential for lasting fulfillment.* New York: Free Press.

Seligman, M. E. P. (2003). *Authentic happiness: Using the new positive psychology to realize your potential for lasting fulfillment.* New York: Free Press.

Seligman, M. E. P., & Csikszentmihályi, M. (2000). Positive psychology: An introduction. *American Psychologist, 55*(1), 5–14.

Seligman, M. E. P., Park, N., & Peterson, C. (2005). Positive psychology progress: Empirical validation of interventions. *American Psychologist, 60*(5), 410–421.

Shapiro, J. P. (1993). *No pity: People with disabilities forging a new civil rights movement.* New York: Three Rivers Press.

Shogren, K. A., Bovaird, J. A., Palmer, S. B., & Wehmeyer, M. L. (2010). Examining the development of locus of control orientations in students with intellectual disability, learning disabilities, and no disabilities: A latent growth curve analysis. *Research and Practice for Persons with Severe Disabilities, 35*, 80–92.

Shogren, K. A., Bradley, V., Gomez, S. C., Yeager, M. H., Schalock, R. L., with, . . . Wehmeyer, M. L. (2009). Public policy and the enhancement of desired outcomes for persons with intellectual disability. *Intellectual and Developmental Disabilities, 47*(4), 307–319.

Shogren, K. A., & Broussard, R. (2011). Exploring self-advocates' perceptions of self-determination. *Intellectual and Developmental Disabilities, 49*, 86–102.

Shogren, K. A., Lopez, S. J., Wehmeyer, M. L., Little, T. D., & Pressgrove, C. L. (2006). The role of positive psychology constructs in predicting life satisfaction in adolescents with and without cognitive disabilities: An exploratory study. *Journal of Positive Psychology*, 1, 37–52.

Shogren, K. A., Palmer, S. B., Wehmeyer, M. L., Williams-Diehm, K., & Little, T. D. (2012). Effect of intervention with the Self-Determined Learning Model of Instruction on access and goal attainment. *Remedial and Special Education, 33*, 320–330. doi: 10.1177/0741932511410072

Shogren, K. A., & Turnbull, H. R. (2010). Public policy and outcomes for persons with intellectual disability: Extending and expanding the public policy framework of the 11th edition of Intellectual Disability: Definition, Classification, and Systems of Support. *Intellectual and Developmental Disabilities*, 48, 387–382.

Shogren, K. A., Wehmeyer, M. L., Pressgrove, C. L., & Lopez, S. J. (2006). The application of positive psychology and self-determination to research in intellectual disability: A content analysis of 30 years of literature *Research and Practice for Persons with Severe Disabilities*, 31, 338–345.

Steiner, A. M. (2011). A strength-based approach to parent education for children with autism. *Journal of Positive Behavior Interventions*, *13*(3), 178–190. doi: 10.1177/1098300710384134

Stoneman, Z. (2005). Siblings of children with disabilities: Research themes. *Mental Retardation*, 43, 339–350.

Stowe, M. J., Turnbull, H. R., & Sublet, C. (2006). The Supreme Court, "our town," and disability policy: Boardrooms and bedrooms, courtrooms and cloakrooms. *Mental Retardation*, 44, 83–99.

Trent, J. W. (1994). *Inventing the feeble mind: A history of mental retardation in the United States*. Berkley: University of California Press.

Turnbull, H. R., Wilcox, B. L., Stowe, M. J., & Umbarger, G. T. (2001). Matrix of federal statutes and federal and state court decisions reflecting the core concepts of disability policy. *Journal of Disability Policy Studies*, 12, 144–176.

United Nations. (2006). Convention on the rights of persons with disability Retrieved March 28, 2008, from http://www.un.org/disabilities/convention.

Ward, M. J. (1996). Coming of age in the age of self-determination: A historical and personal perspective. In D. J. Sands & M. L. Wehmeyer (Eds.), *Self-determination across the life span: Independence and choice for people with disabilities.* (pp.1–16) Baltimore: Paul H. Brookes.

Ward, M. J. (2005). An historical perspective of self-determination in special education: Accomplishments and challenges. *Research and Practice for Persons with Severe Disabilities*, 30, 108–112.

Wehmeyer, M. L. (1996). Student self-report measure of self-determination for students with cognitive disabilities. *Education and Training in Mental Retardation and Developmental Disabilities*, 31, 282–293.

Wehmeyer, M. L. (2005). Self-determination and individuals with severe disabilities: Re-examining meanings and misinterpretations. *Research and Practice for Persons with Severe Disabilities*, 30, 113–120.

Wehmeyer, M. L., Abery, B., Mithaug, D. E., & Stancliffe, R. (2003). *Theory in self-determination: Foundations for educational practice.* Springfield, IL: Charles C. Thomas

Wehmeyer, M. L., Agran, M., Hughes, C., Martin, J. E., Mithaug, D., & Palmer, S. (2007). *Promoting self-determination in students with developmental disabilities.* New York: Guilford.

Wehmeyer, M. L., Buntix, W. H. E., Lachapelle, Y., Luckasson, R. A., Schalock, R. L., Verdugo, M. A., et al. (2008). The intellectual disability construct and its relation to human functioning. *Intellectual and Developmental Disabilities*, 46, 311–318.

Wehmeyer, M. L., & Palmer, S. B. (1997). Perceptions of control of students with and without cognitive disabilities. *Psychological Reports*, 81, 195–206.

Wehmeyer, M. L., & Palmer, S. B. (2003). Adult outcomes for students with cognitive disabilities three-years after high school: The impact of self-determination. *Education and Training in Developmental Disabilities*, 38, 131–144.

Wehmeyer, M. L., Palmer, S. B., Agran, M., Mithaug, D. E., & Martin, J. E. (2000). Promoting causal agency: The Self-Determined Learning Model of Instruction. *Exceptional Children, 66*, 439–453.

Wehmeyer, M. L., & Schwartz, M. (1997). Self-determination and positive adult outcomes: A follow-up study of youth with mental retardation or learning disabilities. *Exceptional Children*, 63, 245–255.

Wehmeyer, M. L., & Schwartz, M. (1998). The relationship between self-determination and quality of life for adults with mental retardation. *Education and Training in Mental Retardation and Developmental Disabilities*, 33, 3–12.

Wehmeyer, M. L., Shogren, K. A., Palmer, S. B., Williams-Diehm, K., Little, T. D., & Boulton, A. (2012). Impact of the Self-Determined Learning Model of Instruction on student self-determination: A randomized-trial placebo control group study. *Exceptional Children*, 78, 135–153.

World Health Organization. (1980). *The international classification of impairment, disability and handicap.* Geneva: Author.

World Health Organization. (2001). *International classification of functioning, disability, and health* Geneva: Author.

Severe Multiple Disabilities

Mats Granlund, Jenny Wilder, *and* Lena Almqvist

Abstract

Optimal human functioning is always relative to the characteristics of a person and the context in which that person lives. Thus, what constitutes optimal human functioning varies depending on subject characteristics and contexts. The optimal functioning of people with severe multiple disabilities (SMD) is challenged both by impairments in body functions and contextual barriers leading to participation restrictions. This chapter first situates people with SMD within a positive psychology framework. It then delimits the optimal human functioning outcome in this population and follows with a discussion of body function factors and contextual factors that may facilitate or hinder optimal functioning. Finally, assessment and interventions aimed at facilitating optimal functioning for people with SMD are discussed.

Key Words: severe disability, multiple disability, assessment, contextual factors

Optimal human functioning is always relative to the characteristics of a person and the context in which that person lives. Thus, what constitutes optimal human functioning varies depending on subject characteristics and contexts. The optimal functioning of people with severe multiple disabilities (SMD) is challenged both by impairments in body functions and contextual barriers leading to participation restrictions. What is actually leads to a good life for someone who depends on others in all life situations?

In this chapter, we first situate people with SMD within a positive psychology framework. We then delimit the optimal human functioning outcome in this population and follow that with a discussion of body function factors and contextual factors that may facilitate or hinder optimal functioning. In doing so, we use a positive psychology framework, suggested by Linley et al. (2006), that contains four levels of analysis. Finally, we discuss assessment and interventions aimed at facilitating optimal functioning for people with SMD.

Positive Psychology and People with Severe Multiple Disabilities

Basically, positive psychology is about functioning rather than not functioning, although its definition encompasses several closely related ideas. In a discussion article of the past, present, and future of positive psychology, Linley et al. (2006) provided a definition of positive psychology that was based on a review of previous definitions: "positive psychology is the scientific study of optimal human functioning" (p. 8). They further suggest four levels of analysis for positive psychology: outcomes, wellsprings, processes, and mechanisms. *Outcomes* are described as subjective/individual, social, and cultural states related to optimal human functioning. Examples of outcomes are happiness at an individual level, positive relations or communities on an interpersonal level, and policies that promote and sustain optimal functioning on a societal level. *Wellsprings* are precursors and facilitators of these processes and mechanisms and concern genetic mechanisms of well-being and early environmental experiences that promote strengths and virtues. *Processes* concern the psychological factors that lead to optimal functioning (e.g., happiness and engagement), whereas the *mechanisms* concern extrapsychological factors that facilitate or hinder optimal human functioning (e.g., social relationships and societal support systems). Starting from the standpoint that optimal human functioning is always situated, we then need to relate the four levels of positive psychology analysis to people with SMD and their living contexts. First, however, SMD and the group of people with SMD need to be defined.

Severe Multiple Disabilities

In this chapter, the definition provided by the Special Interest Research Group of the International Association for the Scientific Study of Intellectual and Developmental Disabilities (IASSIDD) (Nakken & Vlaskamp, 2002, 2007) is used to define SMD. The definition refers to individuals with profound cognitive impairments (measurable IQ of less than 25) and profound motor impairments (e.g., tetraplegia). Other aspects of disability for this group are sensory impairments (Nakken & Vlaskamp, 2002, 2007), medical problems, and challenging behavior. It is difficult to make a clear distinction between "severe" and "profound" motor and cognitive impairments of an individual with multiple disabilities due to the consequences of combinations of disabilities. A common functional characteristic of individuals with SMD is that they are dependent on others for all aspects of their daily needs.

People with SMD form a very heterogeneous group in terms of both origin of impairments and their functional and behavioral repertoires. Their communication is often characterized by pre- or protosymbolic communication (Olsson, 2006), and it is not always easy to know if people with SMD have intentional communication or not. Preintentional communication occurs when individuals do not deliberately or intentionally communicate, but their signals are interpreted by others to have significance as communication (Goldbart, 1994; Iacono, Bloomberg, & West, 2005). When it comes to cognitive functioning, people with SMD are often defined as being at an early cognitive stage in development and are sometimes described as having the mental age of infants. Such a comparison is not entirely duable as with chronological time experiences and events are stored in memory, which mean that older persons have a lot of experiences which they can recall some way or another, irrespective of their mental age. Most often memory functions are impaired in individuals

with SMD, especially semantic memory which is the long-term memory for facts, concepts, and meaning. Semantic memories are often stored as "words" in our minds; thus, people with SMD may "think without words." Episodic memory (memory of events or episodes) tends not to be as impaired in SMD. Memory can also be linked to sensations of smell and touch, and sensory memory may not be impaired in individuals with SMD.

Earlier studies have revealed few differences in optimal functioning between people with SMD related to maturation and chronological age Thus, maturation and development does not seem to have a large impact on functioning. (Granlund, 1993; Axelsson, Granlund, & Wilder, 2013). There are some indications that physical health may stabilize with age during the first years of life (Johnson et al., 2009; Wilder, 2008b). Based on the lack of empirical findings related to chronological age for optimal function for people with SMD, this chapter includes research articles focused on people with SMD independent of chronological age.

Outcomes in Positive Psychology and People with Severe Multiple Disabilities

Outcomes in positive psychology concern subjective, social, and cultural states related to optimal human functioning on individual, interpersonal, and societal levels. When people with SMD are considered, these positive outcomes must be framed within the functional limitations set by the physical impairments of people with SMD and the environmental conditions in which they live. On a societal level, positive outcomes for people with SMD are related to the enforcement of human rights in the form of support services and accessibility to a person's proximal and distal environment. At the societal level also lay the cultural openness and attitudes toward disability of the surrounding cultural majority. This chapter is primarily concerned with the individual and interpersonal levels.

On an individual level, a positive outcome can generally be described as encompassing those experiences and functioning that produce a "good life" (Ryan & Deci, 2001). These include, for example, subjective well-being (SWB), optimism, social well-being, self-determination, hope, and goal thinking, all topics covered in other chapters of this volume. Experiences of an optimal life have been related to two traditions in the study of well-being, the hedonic and eudaimonic views, as well as to a timeframe from past to future (Ryan & Deci, 2001). Those researchers who have adopted a hedonic view tend to focus on pleasures of the mind and body and operationalize the outcome in terms of subjective happiness and experiences of pleasure. Those who have adopted an eudaimonic view focus on doing what is worth doing and operationalize the outcome in terms of experiences like mastery and life purpose (Ryan & Deci, 2001). Concerning timeframe, some researchers focus on the past (e.g., well-being and contentment) some focus on the present (e.g., engagement, happiness, or flow), whereas others focus on the future (e.g., hope and self-determination) (Seligman & Csikszentmihalyi, 2000). These two traditional views and the chosen timeframes provide supplemental information about the multidimensional outcomes of optimal functioning.

On the interpersonal level, a positive outcome can generally be described as positive relations and communities. Thus, the links between the individual level and positive relations on an interpersonal level are the personal relationships that people experience. Positive relations and social networks are known to promote the well-being of individuals (Harty, Joseph, Wilder, & Rajaram, 2007). Tronto (as cited in Hostyn [2011]) suggests that this means that human beings can't be conceived as totally independent and autonomous but rather that they exist in a condition of interdependence. For people who have difficulty intentionally interacting explicitly with their environment, such as people with SMD, this interdependence become even more important and may become the most important level for positive psychology outcomes. As such, a person's appraisals of meaningful contexts are related to positive outcomes.

Outcomes for People with Severe Multiple Disabilities

Some outcomes described in positive psychology are not applicable to people with severe impairments in motor functioning, cognitive functioning, sensory functioning, and communication. Thus, we need to relate optimal life outcomes for people with SMD not only to traditional views and timeframes but also to impairments and their influence on experiences and actions.

Outcomes on the Individual Level

On an individual level, SMD will probably affect eudaimonic aspects of optimal functioning and expectations for the future to a larger degree than it will affect the hedonic aspects of functioning and experiences in the past and present. Hedonic outcomes, such as SWB, can at least momentarily be observed in people with SMD as expressions of happiness, pleasure, satisfaction, or contentment. These expressions are not always easily detected, often transitory, and may pass unnoticed, thus requiring a high degree of responsiveness in an interactive partner. Such expression requires a familiarity with how the person with SMD commonly expresses these states. Cognitive impairments in people with low intelligence and semantic memory problems affect their time processing ability and their ability to situate themselves mentally within a personal history. Thus, eudaimonic experiences and perceptions focusing on the future, such as life purpose and self-determination, probably will be more affected than hedonic experiences here and now, such as contentment and happiness. Although short-lived, such moments are probably important elements in these people's lives in their own right, but may be of even more importance if connected to episodic memories. The foundation for eudaimonic experiences focusing on the future, however, is anticipation regarding the near future and the person's awareness that his or her actions can affect others and/or the physical environment (Dunst et al., 2007). Since episodic and sensory memory in people with SMD are often intact, episodes of SWB, over time and with the help of responsive caregivers, can be elaborated into an understanding of a meaningful life that in the mind of a person with SMD is somewhat extended in time and includes engagement in the moment as well as anticipation of pleasure and happiness in the future (Fivush & Nelson, 2006; Young, Fenwick, Lambe, & Hogg, 2011). Thus, future-directed eudaimonic aspects of optimal functioning also have to be considered for people with SMD. The eudaimonic future perspective is especially important when stability in optimal functioning is considered.

Regarding hedonistic aspects of optimal functioning, SWB and happiness are two closely related concepts that have been applied to people with SMD. *Subjective well-being* is a broad concept that includes experiencing pleasant emotions, having low levels of negative moods, and experiencing high life satisfaction (Diener, Lucas, & Oishi, 2002). The most common ways of determining well-being in individuals with SMD are by observation or by asking proxies. Subjective well-being for individuals with SMD can be seen in their expressions of negative and positive emotions (Petry & Maes, 2006). The Mood, Interest, and Pleasure Questionnaire

(MIPQ) measures the SWB of individuals with profound multiple intellectual disabilities and draws on information from proxies (Ross & Oliver, 2003). *Happiness* can have both a multidimensional definition including well-being, pleasure, and contentment that is applicable to people without SMD and a more unidimensional definition based on behavioral expressions linked to pleasure and contentment for all people, such as smiling, laughing, and yelling (Lancioni, Singh, O'Reilly, Oliva, & Basili, 2005). This unidimensional definition is probably more applicable to people with SMD. Children and adolescents with SMD tend not to differ from other children in their expressions of basic feelings such as joy and expectation, but have more idiosyncratic expressions for more complex emotions such as curiosity and interest according to parent reports (Wilder, Axelsson, & Granlund, 2004).

From an eudaimonic perspective, experiencing happiness from time to time is not enough to produce a stable sense of well-being. One needs to add meaningfulness—that is, one must have an idea of self in relation to the social world and to the future (Ryan & Deci, 2001). But how could meaningfulness be operationalized in relation to a person with SMD? Eudaimonic views of optimal functioning that focus on "doing what is worth doing" and the future have been applied to people with SMD in terms of expressions of anticipation and engagement within a situation. *Expressions of anticipation* are closely related to contingency awareness and intentionality (Grove, Bunning, Porter, & Olsson, 1999). A majority of typically developing infants seem to be able to understand the relationship between their behavior and its environmental consequences somewhere between 3 and 6 months of age (Cavanagh & Davidson, 1977; Uzgiris & Hunt, 1975 in Dunst et al., 2007). Such an understanding requires a person with SMD to have a basic awareness that his or her behavior affects the future, as can be seen in the expressions of expectation/anticipation (Iacono, Carter, & Hook, 1998) but also in expressions of intentionality such as persistence (Bruce & Vargas, 2007), and that his or her behaviors are directed toward other people (Daelman, 2003).

Engagement can be seen as expressions of involvement or degree of involvement within a situation (Granlund et al., 2012; Bedell et al. (2011) asked parents of children with SMD about how they observed their child's engagement. Parents reported that they evaluated their child's level of involvement through their nonverbal behavior and focus of attention within different life situations. The Participation and Environment questionnaire (Coster et al., 2011), developed for use with parents of children with disabilities, can be used to rate the engagement of people with SMD in everyday life situations. Caregivers are provided with examples of typical everyday activities (e.g., listening to music) and asked how often the person in their care attends to this activity and how involved/engaged the person usually is. According to Hammel et al. (2008), engagement can be divided into *active engagement* or *meaningful engagement*. Whereas active engagement can be viewed as freedom of choice and the participation in activities or interactive processes that are enjoyable or satisfying, meaningful engagement frequently is described as including a social interaction component. As discussed by Felce and Emerson (2004), meaningful engagement is probably a significant aspect within most processes (e.g., in decision making and self-determination), as well as in social interaction. Furthermore, meaningful engagement probably occurs to a higher extent when an activity or interaction process is anticipated, self-determined, or in some way intended by the person with SMD. This suggests that engagement is present on different levels. As part of a process, for example, active engagement encourages the anticipation of higher levels of meaningful engagement that, over time and with opportunities, probably lead to outcomes such as more stable perceptions of SWB and meaningfulness.

Outcomes on the Interpersonal Level

The development of positive relations is founded in experiencing rewarding interactions (i.e., meaningful engagement). A basic assumption is that social interaction is especially rewarding for individuals with SMD because they have difficulties engaging in activities on their own and also because they have limited cognitive capacities. Thus, much of what can be observed of outcomes on the individual level occurs within social interaction. In social interaction, people with SMD are often dependent on interaction partners to identify their needs, preferences, and interests because their own interactive abilities are restricted (Grove et al., 1999). Nafstad and Rodbroe (1999) studied children who are deaf-blind and found that mutual interactions combined with feelings of joy make up the backbone in the development of further more complex interactions and experiences for these children. Research about parental perceptions of interaction with children with SMD found that dyadic interaction occurred throughout an ordinary day and that it constituted joint attention, mutual participation, and joy (Wilder & Granlund, 2003).

Moments of accord in these interactions were peak experiences in which parents and children paused in the ongoing activity and seemed to share a focus of attention (Wilder, 2008a).

Positive relations for people with SMD can be defined as a stable pattern of relatively frequently occurring moments of positive dyadic interaction over a longer time period, e.g., months or years, involving the person with SMD and a specific caregiver. The characteristics of positive interaction sequences that build positive relationships that have been suggested are *openness* (preparedness) to interact on the part of both parties, with the caregiver responsible for creating opportunities; *joint context,* in the form of sharing the same activity; and *negotiation,* as continuous turn-taking behavior that responds to the behaviors of the other partner (Hostyn & Maes, submitted). Individual appraisals of being part of meaningful contexts are built through such mutual experiences of positive interaction and relations. In this quest, another pivotal factor is to widen the number of skilled communication partners in a person's life and to broaden his or her social network so that he or she belongs to different categories of important others (e.g., grandparents, siblings, staff, and neighbors).

Wellsprings of Optimal Functioning for People with Severe Multiple Disabilities

Wellsprings of optimal functioning can be seen as the precursors of processes and mechanisms (Linley et al., 2006). These include facilitators of optimal functioning such as genetic foundations of optimal functioning (e.g., temperament and behavior style) and early experiences that promotes optimal functioning (e.g., contingent responses from caregivers on actions). Wellsprings also include personal characteristics that can act as barriers to an optimal life (e.g., various body impairments and their interactive effects).

Behavior Style

Concerning the genetic foundations for optimal functioning for people with SMD, probably the same factors are important as for nondisabled people. One important factor for facilitating optimal functioning related to temperament is *behavior style.* Most definitions of temperament contain four aspects of the quality of human behavior: emotionality (amount and intensity of positive and negative affect), activity (amount and intensity of motor activity), sociality (amount of and joy in being with others), and reactivity (level of approach

or withdrawal) (Wachs & Kohnstamm, 2001). Temperament is often difficult to deduce from the limited behavior repertoire that characterizes most people with SMD. However, in people with SMD, their characteristic display of affect and how they react to activities and people can be described as their behavior style (Goldbart, 1994). Measures of behavior style (e.g., the Carolina Record of Individual Behavior [CRIB]; Simeonsson et al., 1982) usually include dimensions such as activity, reactivity, goal directedness, frustration, attention span, and responsiveness. When compared to people without SMD, people with SMD seem to differ most from the average of behavior style when scales based on a hypo–average–hyperintense continuum are used (Simeonsson et al., 1982) than people without SMD. These differences may be related to the type and degree of body impairments. In a study including 48 children with SMD, Granlund and Björck-Åkesson (1998) studied individual differences in behavior style. The children were divided into three subgroups based on whether they had a predominant hypo, optimal/average, or hyper behavior style. The results revealed that those children who had a hypo behavior style more often had a combination of profound impairments in cognition, vision, and motor ability. Wilder (2008a) reported that parents of children with SMD who measured hypo on behavior style were perceived as more difficult to interpret and interact with, whereas children with a hyper style were considered as relatively easy to interpret and interact with.

Problems with Body Functioning

Concerning body factors that can create barriers to optimal functioning, both problems related to body functions and body impairments have been reported to negatively affect functioning. Vos et al. (2010) studied body functioning problems that contribute negatively to the SWB of individuals with SMD in a large Dutch sample. Factors associated with negative SWB were higher age, medical problems (constipation), medical treatments (sedatives), psychiatric problems (autism), and feeding problems. With respect to body impairments, both type and degree of body impairment, as well as the manner in which body impairments interact will affect optimal functioning.

Sensory Impairments

Sensory impairments primarily include visual and hearing impairments. Such impairments, taken singly, do not seem to have a strong relation to hedonic positive outcomes such as happiness or SWB in people with congenital impairments. People with acquired impairments do, however, report lower happiness and SWB (Nyman, Dibb, Rita Victor, & Gosney, 2011). Regarding eudaimonic outcomes such as self-determination and engagement, the level of self-determination may be affected in a negative direction by few opportunities for people with sensory impairments to act in a self-determined manner (Robinson & Lieberman, 2004). As well, for eudaimonic outcomes, the impact of impairments seems to be stronger for acquired impairments than for congenital impairments (Nyman et al., 2011). People who are deaf-blind have a combination of visual and hearing impairments and constitute a heterogeneous group containing both people with congenital impairments and people with acquired impairments. People with acquired deaf-blindness report participation restrictions and a lower quality of life (QOL) (Möller, 2008). People with congenital deaf-blindness are a very small and heterogeneous group (Preisler, 1998). People with severe congenital deaf-blindness are frequently a part of the population of people with SMD. The impact of sensory impairments on positive outcomes for people with SMD must always be related to the interaction effects occurring in combination with other impairments. Most people with SMD have combinations of visual impairment, motor impairment, and cognitive impairments, with hearing impairments having a much lower prevalence (Granlund & Olsson, 1986; van den Broek, Janssen, van Ramshorst, & Deen, 2006).

Cognitive Impairments

Assessment of cognitive impairments includes both overall measures of cognitive functioning, such as IQ or cognitive level, and measures of more specific cognitive functions, such as attention and memory. Different concepts concerning cognitive function have been applied to people with SMD to varying extents. Psychometric-based overall measures of cognitive functioning (such as IQ) have seldom been applied because of the difficulties of administering IQ tests in collaboration with people having profound intellectual disability who don't understand verbal language. Conversely, Piaget-based assessment instruments, such as the Uzgiris and Hunt scales of sensory motor intelligence (Uzgiris & Hunt, 1975), do not require an understanding of verbal language and have been used more frequently (Dunst, 1998; Granlund & Olsson, 1999). Overall, the results reveal that children with SMD seem to follow the same developmental stages as other children, independent

of diagnosis, and that people in higher sensory motor stages more frequently exhibit contingency awareness and use intentional communicative behaviors. Thus, the outcome on an interpersonal level might be related to level of sensory motor intelligence for people with SMD. Based on specific cognitive functions, Giuliani et al. (2009) propose a new way of evaluating memory and cognitive abilities in people with severe intellectual disabilities that is independent of language abilities. Rather, the subject's knowledge about his or her environment is assessed from movement decisions and displacement, whether encouraged by curiosity or by reinforcement expectation that indicates contingency awareness. The program they propose assumes that spatial memory is a precursor of episodic memory, and the program measures working memory, episodic memory and visuospatial capacities. The program takes into account the individual's motivation and known environment, which adds to the measurement's ecological validity. This measure requires that the person has relatively intact visual ability.

Another issue related to cognitive functioning in people with SMD is their level of arousal and alertness. Commonly, eight levels of alertness are described: inactive sleep, active sleep, drowse, daze, awake-inactive alert, awake-active alert, awake-active alert with stereotypy and crying/agitation (Guess, Roberts, Siegel-Causey, & Rues, 1995). The level of alertness in which people are most likely to interact is active awake-alert (Roberts, Arthur-Kelly, Foreman, & Pascoe, 2005). However, the occurrence of that state in people with SMD with low function is infrequent, and the level of alertness shifts frequently (Roberts et al., 2005). Findings from observational studies of alertness states and concomitant communicative behaviors and environmental stimuli (Arthur, 2003; Guess et al., 1995) indicate that people with SMD frequently spend time in solitude and/or without physical stimuli inviting activity when they are in an active awake-alert state.

Motor Impairments

The degree of motor impairments a person exhibits seems to be related to optimal functioning in terms of participation in everyday life situations. People with more profound motor impairments participate less often in leisure activities (Imms, Reilly, Carlin, & Dodd, 2008), and, if the motor impairment also affects the ability to speak, the frequency of interaction with peers is strongly impacted (Clarke et al., 2010; Raghavendra, Virgo, Olsson, Connell, & Lane, 2011). Most people with

SMD have severe to profound motor impairments (Nakken & Vlaskamp, 2007; Wilder & Granlund, 2011). Motor impairments restrict the possibilities for a person to act on his or her environment and increase his or her dependency on others to perform activities. For people with SMD, a further complication is that motor impairments interact with cognitive impairments and sensory impairments in complex patterns that strongly affect optimal functioning.

Interaction Between Impairments

A special aspect when considering the wellsprings of optimal functioning for people with SMD is the complex patterns of interaction between different types of impairments. Sensory, cognitive, and motor impairments reciprocally affect each other and optimal positive outcomes on the individual and interpersonal levels. Visual and motor impairments can have negative interactive effects on the development of intentionality and positive relations on an interpersonal level. For example, children with congenital blindness have delays in motor activities such as reaching and touching that affect the development of intentionality (Bigelow, 2003). Children who are deaf-blind use their whole body to explore their surroundings; if they also have a motor impairment, their opportunities to investigate their surroundings decrease dramatically (Nafstad & Rodbroe, 1999). Cognitive impairments reduce the knowledge and skills people with SMD can develop concerning how to compensate for other impairments (e.g., a person who has both visual impairment and intellectual disability may have difficulties choosing a seat with the proper degree and angle of incoming light from a window) (Wilder & Granlund, 2011).

Early Environmental Experiences and People with Severe Multiple Disabilities

Most people who have had their impairments since birth probably have early environmental experiences of barriers to the development of positive outcomes on the individual and interpersonal levels. The severe brain damage that these children have from birth, in combination with the fact that many are born extremely premature, means that a majority have spent much of their first years of life in a hospital (Petrou, Abangma, Johnson, Wolke, & Marlow, 2009), with its increased risks of less experiences of positive interaction with their parents. Over time, children who are extremely premature tend to become more stable in their physical

functioning, although they continue to spend more time in hospitals than do other children (Johnson et al., 2009). In addition, the complex interactions of impairments that infants with SMD experience may lead to a narrower repertoire of behaviors than in typically developing infants. Thus, parents may have to assign meaning to alternative expressions in infants with SMD. What is typically interpreted as a particular emotion consists of many behaviors organized into a particular configuration (Weinberg, Gianio, & Tronick, 1989). If a child with SMD lacks one or more of the characteristic expressions in a configuration, it may make it difficult to interpret the infant's behavior (Iacono et al., 1998).

Processes in Positive Psychology and People with Severe Multiple Disabilities

Those psychological factors that lead to optimal life experiences, as well as the psychological barriers to these experiences, constitute the processes of interest to positive psychology (Linley et al., 2006). Strengths and virtues that have been identified as increasing the probability of positive outcomes for people with typical functioning include self-efficacy (Bandura, 1989) and autonomy (Ryff & Keyes, 1995). The psychological ingredients leading to optimal life experiences are sometimes difficult to separate from the outcomes of positive life experiences. Granlund and Björck-Åkesson (2005) have suggested that positive functioning outcomes for children with mild to moderate impairments can be seen as lying along a continuum from person-based characteristics that are relatively stable over time, such as autonomy, to optimal experiences here and now, such as the experience of *flow*. People who are strong in those person-based characteristics (i.e., psychological factors such as autonomy) related to positive functioning will also more frequently experience optimal life experiences here and now. For people with SMD, important psychological factors are contingency awareness and pivotal behaviors, such as joint attention.

Processes and Severe Multiple Disabilities

Contingency awareness is a basic process that is highly specific to people with SMD. It is a prerequisite for other basic processes, such as pivotal behaviors. Contingency awareness has been defined by Dunst et al. (2008) as "a child's awareness and understanding of the relationship between environmental events and their consequences." A contingency is defined as a "temporal relationship between events A and B, where the presence or use of A increases the likelihood of the occurrence of B" (p. 5). Contingency awareness seems to be a basic process leading the person with SMD to understand that the setting he or she is in can be affected in a desired direction (.i.e., contingency detection). Problems with this understanding may lead to learned helplessness in people with SMD. Dunst et al. (2008) report that if early intervention practitioners work to elicit behaviors in children with SMD in a noncontingent manner, it results in lower rather than higher levels of responding. Three types of contingency detection have been delimited (Dunst et al., 2008): behavior-based contingencies, environmental-based contingencies, and caregiver-based contingencies. *Behavior-based contingencies* involve a person producing a behavior that results in a change in his or her environment (e.g., a person with SMD who realizes that when he hits a Big Mac microswitch, his electric wheelchair moves forward). *Environment-based contingencies* concern events external to the person that still provide the person with experiences that promotes the understanding of the consequences of an event (e.g., a person with SMD repeatedly experiences that he is placed in an activity setting where he usually listens to music, and he reacts with anticipation). *Caregiver-based contingencies* involve reciprocal interactions between a person and a caregiver (e.g., a person with SMD vocalizes and is imitated by a caregiver). Contingency awareness can be seen as a necessary but not sufficient mediator for facilitating functioning in everyday life activities for people with SMD. It can also be seen as a necessary prerequisite for pivotal behaviors.

Pivotal Behaviors

Pivotal behaviors have been defined as "behaviors that are central to wide areas of functioning such that a change in the pivotal behavior will produce improvement across a number of behaviors" (Mahoney, Kim, & Lin, 2007, p. 311). Adapted from Koegel, Koegel, Harrower, and Carter (1999) and Mahoney et al. (2007), those pivotal behaviors that seem to be important for interpersonal outcomes in individuals with SMD are *interest, reciprocity, initiation, affect,* and *joint attention.* These behaviors have been found to be related to communication and social emotional functioning. One prerequisite that seems especially important in attaining mutual interaction is the ability to achieve and maintain joint attention, which corresponds to *secondary intersubjectivity*, as described by Trevarthen (2004). Joint attention is defined as

"the ability of the infant to coordinate attention to an object or event and to another person within a single communicative act" (Watson, Baranek, & DiLavore, 2003, p. 205). Many individuals with SMD have difficulties achieving joint attention and maintaining it. Sharing a focus of attention with others allows the individual to acquire the types of skills that are socially learned, for example, language and play with peers. Positive changes in joint attention skills have been found to improve speech and language for children with autism (Kasari, Paparella, Freeman, & Jahromi, 2008).

For individuals with SMD, interaction partners must be sensitive in seeking proximity and using cues to encourage alternative sensory orientations (van den Broek et al., 2006) that promote joint attention as well as contingency awareness (Dunst et al., 2008). Thus, the quality of the natural environments in which people with SMD live is very important. Both the overall type and quality of their settings, as well as how caregivers act, will affect psychological processes important for optimal functioning in people with SMD.

Mechanisms in Positive Psychology and People with Severe Multiple Disabilities

Mechanisms to be considered in positive psychology concern extrapsychological factors on different ecological levels that facilitate or hinder optimal life experiences. Such extrapsychological factors become especially important for people who are very dependent on other people for functioning. Extrapsychological factors important for people with SMD can be identified on the societal level and on the level of the proximal environment in which the person with SMD lives. They are the person's support system within his or her society, and his or her form of living arrangements, relationships to others, and assistive technology.

Mechanisms on Societal Level

The support system. The support system within a society is a factor that affects the contextual frame within which people with SMD have to function. In an ongoing study (Ullenhag et al., 2012), participation in leisure activities for children and adolescents with motor disabilities, as well as for children and adolescents with typical functioning, was compared in Sweden, Norway, and the Netherlands. The countries are all European, but they have somewhat different social support systems for people with disabilities. Sweden and Norway have similar systems in which most children and youth with motor disabilities live at home with their biological families and attend mainstream schools, with the support of a personal assistant if necessary. In the Netherlands, most children live at home, attend special schools for children with motor disabilities, and are not provided with assistants. The comparison revealed that, for typically developing children, there were few differences in leisure activity patterns depending on country, although age and gender were related to leisure activity patterns. For children and adolescents with disabilities, the differences in leisure activity patterns were related to the country the children lived in, with few differences between those living in Sweden and Norway, whereas children living in the Netherlands perceived lower participation in leisure activities. The results indicate that a societal support system that promotes individualization of support and living arrangements also promotes optimal life experiences. Societal support systems, as well as the organization of care given to people with SMD, vary among countries, but few studies have investigated the relations among support systems, organization of care, and optimal outcomes for people with SMD. Based on research concerning people with moderate to mild intellectual disabilities, two important generic environmental factors that are partly molded by the support systems of a country seem to be living arrangements and personal assistance.

Form of living arrangements. In Northern Europe, children and youth with SMD primarily live at home with their biological parents. Society provides the health care and special services that are required to make it possible for parents to take care of their children at home. There are very few special institutions, and those that exist are situated close to hospitals for those children and youth living there who need constant medical supervision. In Sweden, a relatively high level of availability of services from the society is provided to children with SMD and their families (Björck-Åkesson & Granlund, 2003). In Sweden, according to Act LSS, which came into force in 1994, it is possible for the parent of a child with SMD to become employed as a personal assistant for his or her own child. In Sweden, young adults with SMD make the transition from living at home with their parents to other kinds of living arrangements rather smoothly with the help of the municipality. There are two primary options: either an independent living arrangement in the form of an apartment or housing of one's own supported by round-the-clock personal assistants or a living arrangement in the form of a group home with

support staff. The everyday life of young adults/adults with SMD is built around organized work at a day activity center.

There is a positive relation between self-determination and QOL for people with intellectual disability (Lachapelle et al., 2005) that is related to living arrangements. Stancliffe and Keane (2000) compared and discussed self-determination in relation to living arrangements and found that, in arrangements where people with intellectual disability were expected to be self-determined and the environment was arranged based on that expectation, they were also more involved in everyday activities. Similar arguments have been put forward by Duvdevany et al. (2002), in a study in which living arrangements were related to life satisfaction as perceived by people with intellectual disability. These researchers also stress the importance of having opportunities to make choices. People with SMD can't speak for themselves, but, with knowledgeable and engaged caregivers who speak for them and act to promote optimal life experiences, self-determination is possible. Personal assistance therefore becomes one means for facilitating self-determination for people with SMD.

The manner in which personal assistance is organized and financed differs between countries, but a common goal seems to be to support people with severe impairments to lead an independent life. Most of the existing research published in English concerns people who have severe motor impairments but no intellectual impairment (Clevnert & Johansson, 2007). If the perspective of the user is included, user satisfaction with the different means used to implement assistance in relation to organization form is frequently evaluated (O'Reilly, 2007; Roos & Hjelmqvist, 2009). Roos and his colleagues (2009), in a comparative study, evaluated users' satisfaction with personal assistance provided by primary communities, private enterprises, and user cooperatives. The results revealed that users who received assistance from private enterprises or user cooperatives were more satisfied. Regarding the manner in which the assistants acted toward the users, no differences were revealed. Qualitative studies indicate that when people receive personal assistance, both they and their relatives perceive increased independence and self-determination (Ahlström & Wadensten, 2011; Askeheim, 2005). When recruiting personal assistants, the services are rated as more positive by users when assistants are matched for gender and age. A frequently reported problem with personal assistance is that assistants lack the necessary knowledge and skills to promote self-determination and thus sometimes act in a manner that may prove detrimental to this goal (Ahlström & Wadensten, 20010). Two reviews (Mayo-Wilson, Montgomery, & Wilson, 2008, 2009) have evaluated the effects of personal assistance on people with SMD, finding that almost no studies have the methodological quality to provide evidence. However, a weak trend was seen in that people with SMD receiving personal assistance had better physical health than people with SMD receiving other forms of services. It seems that living arrangements organized to provide opportunities for choice making, initiation, and involvement can promote optimal life experiences in people with SMD. Such arrangements probably are facilitated by providing personal assistance from assistants knowledgeable in interacting with and relating to the person with SMD.

Mechanisms in the Living Environment

In the living environment, both social and physical aspects affect the probability that a person with SMD will have optimal life experiences. The more or less total dependency on others that people with SMD have means that their optimal functioning is strongly related to their relations with caregivers. Caregivers need the knowledge and skills necessary to adjust their communicative skills to meet the needs of the person with SMD and the knowledge and skills necessary to arrange both the social and physical environment in a manner that promotes optimal experiences.

Relationships to others. For dyadic interactions to be functionally instigative for individuals with SMD, these interactions need to be perceived as positive for both interaction partners, although the main responsibility for maintaining a good interaction climate lies with the caregiver. For those with SMD, moments spent in social interaction with caregivers and other important people provide satisfying and rewarding activities. Moments of social interaction can also be seen as contingency detection opportunities. Studies of children with profound multiple disabilities or developmental delay who were provided with contingency detection opportunities found these opportunities to be beneficial to both child and caregiver behavior (Dunst, Cushing, & Vance, 1985; Dunst et al., 2007). In addition to improvements in operant learning, the children responded to these activities with increased visual attention, enjoyment, and a general sense of excitement, as well as with increased competence in respondent-contingent learning in general. The children smiled, laughed, and vocalized during these activities, which made the caregivers increase their efforts to support and encourage child learning; caregivers enjoyed seeing their children display competent behavior and engagement. Furthermore, Dunst et al. (2007) showed that social contingency games were related to even more game trials, leading to improved child competence and a more positive child–caregiver interaction. Within a transactional regulation process, mechanisms of the person with disability influence responses from the social environment (Sameroff & MacKenzie, 2003). Thus, increased learning opportunities and outcomes, such as response-contingent learning, have a remedial effect, in that small improvements in the behavior of the person with SMD will increase the expectations of caregivers and others in the social environment. These expectations, in turn, will set the stage for a more positive transactional process involving increased anticipation, joint attention, persistence, and engagement.

To enhance positive relations between people with SMD over time, it is important to utilize their already existing behavior repertoires and promote experiences of interaction focused on feelings of mutual joy in being together. Research on parental perceptions of interaction with children with SMD found two concurrent processes to be working in the immediate interaction in the pursuit of well-functioning interaction: leading and monitoring (Wilder, 2008a; Wilder & Granlund, 2003). In leading and monitoring, a parent forms an overview and updates the immediate interaction with his or her child in relation to knowledge about the child's typical behavior repertoire, behavior style, mood, and the context.

Assistive technology. The rapidly growing development of and access to assistive technology is reflected in a growing body of research about assistive technology and aided communication in individuals with disabilities. Examples of such assistive technology are digital voice output (VOCA) devices, Daisy, and switches of different kinds. Research in this field using a focus group has explored the effect of introducing technological devices to people with SMD to enhance their ability to more clearly show their preferences. Lancioni and colleagues studied how microswitches and computer technology could enable students with SMD to request and choose among environmental stimuli (Lancioni et al., 2007). As an intervention, two students were provided with two microswitches that, when activated, made a computer system present a sample of a preferred or nonpreferred stimulus. During the intervention, the students learned to use the microswitches in a consistent manner and selected the preferred stimuli most of the time, largely rejecting the nonpreferred stimuli.

Chantry and Dunford (2010) have systematically reviewed the literature to identify evidence of computer assistive technologies enhancing participation in childhood activities for children with multiple and complex disabilities, a group that partially overlaps with children with SMD. The results indicate that computer assistive technologies enhance participation in several areas of functioning. For children with SMD, the review indicates that these technologies can facilitate assessing learning potential, social interaction, autonomous play, and family play activities that include several family members. A critical issue in using assistive technology to arrange activities that enhance engagement and optimal life experiences is the selection of stimuli for the activities, as well as of indicators of optimal experiences such as happiness. Lancioni et al. (2005), in a systematic review of the literature, suggest that the occasional failures reported may be related to difficulties with identifying highly favored stimuli, as well as difficulties with explicitly identifying the behavior indicators of happiness.

Optimal Functioning in People with Severe Multiple Disabilities—Some Conclusions

Before discussing assessment and intervention, some conclusions about optimal functioning in people with SMD are needed. Outcomes in positive psychology concern subjective, social, and cultural states related to optimal human functioning on the individual, interpersonal, and/or societal levels. In this chapter, we have discussed outcomes on the individual and interpersonal levels for people with SMD. Unique to people with SMD is their dependence on other people for all aspects of functioning. Thus, goals for intervention, as well as for assessment and intervention, will primarily be decided and implemented by others, not by the people with SMD themselves. This means that, to a large extent, the attitudes, knowledge, and skills of caregivers and service organizations about people with SMD and their living conditions will form the whole intervention process. This fact is especially important to keep in mind when desired outcomes for interventions are decided. On an individual level, optimal outcomes concern both hedonistic outcomes such

as SWB and feelings of happiness and joy and eudaimonic outcomes such as perceptions of anticipation and engagement. These individual outcomes primarily occur within contexts in which caregivers also participate. For this reason, outcomes on the interpersonal level that focus on mutually rewarding and positive interactions that, over time, form positive relationships between people with SMD and caregivers are a key issue when assessment and intervention is discussed. Identifying factors related to wellsprings, processes, and mechanism is necessary to assess and use information when designing methods for intervention. Of special interest are those mechanisms related to the social and physical living environments of people with SMD and, therefore, how caregivers are involved in assessment and intervention.

Assessment and Intervention

Intervention can be defined as "a superordinate construct for the different intentional steps taken to change people, interaction, events or environments in a desired direction" (Granlund & Björck-Åkesson, 2005, p.227). Interventions can be focused on individuals, groups, or society, and they can last for varying time periods, from weeks to several years. The intervention process encompasses the steps of defining the problem(s), explaining the problem(s), goal setting, designing method, implementing method, and evaluation (Björck-Åkesson, Granlund, & Olsson, 1999). Here, we first discuss key issues in assessment and intervention before discussing assessment and intervention for people with SMD. The primary focus is on outcomes and mechanisms.

Assessment is a key component of all steps in the intervention process. Assessment in intervention can have several sometimes parallel purposes, such as projection of goals for intervention (problem identification and goal setting), intervention planning (explaining problems and designing method), program monitoring (implementing methods), and evaluation of outcomes (Björck-Åkesson, Granlund, & Simeonsson, 2000). Assessment concerning people with SMD can also be an intervention in its own right if it is linked to goals such as learning about how to "read" or recognize communicative behaviors in a person with SMD or knowing what to look for in designing an environment that offers opportunities for engagement for people with SMD (Olsson & Granlund, 2003). Every phase in assessment needs to have a clear beginning and end (Simeonsson et al., 1996) if it is to function as an intervention. How explicit an assessment phase is perceived depends both on the phenomena to be studied and the formality of the assessment. Phenomena important for the outcome of interventions focused on optimal functioning in people with SMD are, by nature, relatively diffuse (e.g., idiosyncratic expressions of happiness or mutually rewarding interaction). To function as an intervention, caregivers need to be involved in the assessment, and the conditions to be assessed must be collaboratively defined. A formal assessment probably allows caregivers to have a more active learning experience and also allows them to compare the assessment results with their expectations (Björck-Åkesson et al., 2000). In informal assessment, it is difficult for caregivers to determine that assessment is taking place or when it is terminated. Thus, it is also more difficult for caregivers to learn from assessment. In interventions for people with SMD, few formal instruments are available to assess desired outcomes of interventions on the individual and interpersonal levels or of mechanisms. For the assessment of wellsprings and processes, more formal assessment instruments are available; however, a key issue here is to involve caregivers in the implementation of assessment so that it becomes a learning experience. In this chapter, the focus is on formal assessment of goals and mechanisms.

Because of their strong dependency on others, intervention methods for people with SMD always have to be implemented by caregivers. That is, the caregiver is a mechanism to promoting optimal functioning. The primary foci of the interventions may be, however, either on affecting the person with SMD (e.g., teaching contingency detection) or on caregivers (e.g., teaching responsiveness to expressions of happiness). Another possible focus is changing the physical environment; however, this kind of intervention must always be supplemented with supervision of caregivers. A final important issue in interventions for people with SMD is how goals and intervention methods on different levels and with different foci can be combined to achieve a good long-term outcome. Knapp (1995) has defined clinical intervention as "a menu of possibilities accompanied by a series of support that facilitate [the] consumer's interaction with these possibilities" (p. 7). Based on the need to evaluate a menu of clinical interventions for communication, Olsson and Granlund (2003) have formulated a set of questions that, in an adapted form, is applicable also for interventions aiming at optimal life experiences for people with SMD. In Table 28.1, questions to

Table 28.1 Questions To Be Asked About Interventions Aimed at Optimal Life Experiences for People with Severe Multiple Disabilities (SMD)

The level of the desired outcome	The timeframe for the effect
Individual level	
Expressions of subjective well-being (SWB) and happiness	Short-term effects
Expressions of SWB and happiness over several activities and caregivers	Long-term effects
Interpersonal level	
Do interactional patterns change following intervention?	Short-term effects
Are changes seen in social relationships?	Long-term effects

be asked when evaluating combinations of interventions over a longer time period are presented.

In the following sections, assessments and interventions concerning people with SMD are presented. In the presentation, we have tried to separate assessment and intervention. However, in reality, they are always occurring simultaneously because assessment can be seen as a continuously ongoing activity that is also an intervention method affecting the participants of assessment.

Assessment of Optimal Functioning and Mechanisms Related to Optimal Functioning in People with Severe Multiple Disabilities

Positive psychology emphasizes the desirability of leading a meaningful life and that a meaningful life should go beyond reducing suffering (Baumeister & Vohs, 2002). To understand if a person leads a meaningful life, we have to ask either him, her, or a close other. Another alternative is to directly observe the person in everyday contexts. In the case of individuals with SMD, most often researchers and practitioners use observations or ask people in the proximal environment (i.e., use proxy ratings). Because of usually severe cognitive disabilities, the individual with SMD is not considered by others to be able to understand questions related to meaningfulness.

Direct observations. Direct behavioral observations are used to identify the needs, preferences, interests, and competences of individuals with SMD. With this group, static assessment measures that either pinpoint specific behaviors or communication and/or compare these to a standardized measure do not apply (Snell, 2002). Individuals with SMD require more flexible, individualized assessment approaches that take into account behaviors over several situations and time points during several days. Such assessments also require knowledge about the person with SMD from people who are close caregivers. These types of direct observations are often time-consuming and should be performed in a flexible but systematic way. Important factors to be considered are the person's usual way of behaving over several situations, usual health status and divergences from it, usual states of alertness, and usual ways of communicating. Another common method is to ask people who are close to the individual with disabilities (proxies), using questionnaires or interviews.

Proxy reports. The aim with most proxy reports is to obtain information about the person with SMD, as well as about broader positive functioning within the specific context. Very little is known about the agreement between proxy ratings and the perceptions of people with SMD and how interrater agreement is related to the nature of the interview or assessment instrument or other situational factors. Clearly, this is not an easy issue to address since most people with SMD are not able to speak for themselves. In a review of proxy responding for assessments for SWB, Cummings (2002) reports several issues that might influence the proxy rating process. First, the rated variable has to be observable to obtain a significant correlation between proxy and subjective perceptions. Furthermore, it seems that the more the variables reflect a subjective state, the less cues of a certain behavior are observable to a proxy. This implies that, to use proxy respondents, one needs to determine to what degree the proxy has experience and knowledge of how the person with SMD usually exhibits different forms of states such as enjoyment or happiness. The more intimacy between the person and their proxy, the higher agreement between obtained ratings. Second, Cummings (2002) concludes that people tend to project their own expectations into the proxy process. With expectations of what people with disability are able to achieve, proxy raters tend, for example, to underestimate how important normalized life goals are to these people, particularly concerning people with SMD. When the proxy raters also are caregivers, there is an opposite tendency to overestimate. Since parental caregivers want their child to benefit from interventions, they tend to respond more optimistically concerning

their child's SWB than what is actually perceived, as was shown when it was possible to ask the children themselves. Some alternatives are available to improve person–proxy agreement, and it is possible to evaluate the agreement between proxy reports and self-reports from respondents who are able to speak for themselves (e.g., Wehmeyer & Metzler, 1995). By obtaining an average proxy correlation score, it is possible to correct statistically for proxy responses (e.g., Heal & Chadsey-Rusch, 1985; Schalock, Bonham, & Marchand, 2000). Hartley and MacLean (2006) have systematically surveyed the literature concerning interrater agreement between people with intellectual disability and caregivers. They report an average interrater agreement of 70–80% when the two groups were compared. Another alternative is to use less varied response alternatives in assessment instruments. Studies have shown that, when given fewer choices, the correlation between subjective perceptions of the person and proxy responses were more accurate (Cummings & Gallone, in Cummings, 2002). Of course, the use of more gross measures of proxy reports also diminishes the actual variation in perceptions of, for example, SWB, and thus is more suitable when using proxies who are less close to the person with SMD (e.g., professionals).

Shared life experiences are probably a more reliable source for proxy ratings of the ups and downs in everyday positive functioning of people with SMD. Two studies concerning participation in everyday activities and children with mild to moderate disabilities also indicate that it might be possible to obtain a rough estimate of the subjective experience of optimal functioning through proxy ratings or observations. In a study in which parents were interviewed about their children's participation in everyday activities, Coster et al. (submitted) report that parents evaluated child involvement based on estimates of their children's nonverbal behavior and focus of attention. Eriksson et al. (2007) compared observers' ratings of children's engagement in classroom activities, operationalized as focused on activity, with independent judges' ratings of children's verbal descriptions of their participation in the observed activities using the same rating scale. The results revealed a high interrater agreement between observations and ratings based on the verbal statements of the children. In all, previous research indicates that at least estimates of optimal life experiences of people with SMD can be deduced from behavioral indicators of happiness, engagement, or anticipation.

Assessing Expressions of Optimal Functioning in People with Severe Multiple Disabilities

To assess expressions of optimal functioning, both the behaviors patterns to be observed and the contingencies of these behavioral patterns must be defined. In an attempt to catch the whole behavior repertoire that individuals with SMD use to communicate, the Affective Communicative Assessment (ACA) instrument (Coupe O'Kane et al., 1985; Coupe O'Kane, & Goldbart, 1998) can be used. It facilitates detailed documentation of the individual's positive and negative affective responses to a variety of external stimuli. In interpreting the meaning of affective responses, the focus is on four crucial meanings: *like, dislike, want,* and *reject*. Divided into three stages, the instrument first documents the individual's behavior repertoire over a series of observations in which the child is exposed to several kinds of positive and negative stimuli, for example, specific foods or songs that the individual has shown clear affective responses to according to familiar people. In a second stage, identification of strong responses is documented, and more detailed information on these responses is gathered with further exposures to the stimuli and response in question. In a third stage, interventions can be formed following the previous identification of both stimuli and settings for the specific individual. By getting to know the individual's behavior repertoire like this, new ways to communicate can be formulated by using the typical reactions that the individual already performs in a new way (Coupe O'Kane & Goldbart, 1998).

Quality of life is a construct based on a hedonic perspective on well-being (Ryan & Deci, 2001) containing two types of indicators: (1) assessment of living standard and perceived environment and (2) subjective experiences of an optimal life, such as life satisfaction, SWB, and happiness. For people with SMD, the first type of indicator involves both objective measures, such as the societal support system and community regulations, and measures of availability and opportunities in the proximal environment. The availability and opportunity measures concern the availability of responsive interactive partners, opportunities for contingency learning, and the possibility for choice making. The subjective perspective of QOL is commonly synthesized with SWB. Individuals with SMD cannot judge the objective circumstances of their lives, and typical measures of these outcomes do not apply to this group. However, happiness is a subjective feeling and can be seen as a rough indicator of QOL For

individuals with SMD, happiness is felt in the immediate moment in which they exist. To assess happiness in individuals with SMD, direct behavioral observation or proxy ratings can be used. Indicators of happiness for the focus group are engagement in behavior such as smiling and laughing and positive facial expressions (Green & Reid, 1996; Wilder et al., 2004), that is, the same as for typically developing people.

Several instruments are solely designed to measure QOL in people with intellectual disability, through the use of proxies. One of the most widely used is the Quality of Life Questionnaire (QOL-Q; Schalock & Keith, 1993), with 40 criterion-referenced items reflecting four domains of QOL: satisfaction, competence/productivity, empowerment/independence, and social belonging/community integration. Another similar measure is the Comprehensive Quality of Life Scale (ComQoL; Cummins, 1994). This scale assesses QOL across seven domains and yields information on both importance and satisfaction of QOL. Although the instruments could be adapted to the use of people with SMD, many of the domains and items are not applicable to this population. Some attempts have been made to develop instruments aiming to assess QOL for people with SMD; one example is QOL-PMD (Petry, Maes, & Vlaskamp, 2009). The first results of the use of this instrument indicate that the medical condition of the person with SMD was most strongly related to QOL scores, followed by contextual characteristics such as setting location and the staff–client ratio (Petry et al., 2009). This points to the fact that there is both an objective and a subjective QOL domain. The subjective QOL domain, specifically measured as SWB, could be perceived as an optimal outcome of people with SMD, whereas the objective domain should be perceived as a mechanism in the transactional process influencing SWB. The two QOL domains are thus on different levels from the individual and should be treated as hierarchically dependent, not as a unified construct, when analyzing QOL data for people with SMD.

To design interventions focused on short-term eudaimonic outcomes such as expressions for anticipation, persistence, and engagement, the expressions of the person with SMD must be analyzed in a time sequence. Sequential analysis of, for example, social interaction could be used to keep track of brief moments of desirable behavior and the mechanisms that influence this behavior (Yoder, Short-Meyerson, & Tapp, 2004). In this kind of analysis, the association between a potential mechanism (e.g., a contingency learning game and the person's response-contingent behavior) could be specified. *Dynamic assessment* is one means for this kind of analysis. It uses a test-teach-retest model in which teaching may involve graduated prompts or mediated learning experiences (Snell, 2002; Snell, Chen, & Hoover, 2006). In dynamic assessment, the individual's own expressions are tested as a baseline, taught at the proximal zone of development, and finally retested to check if the individual has learned more advanced communication skills. For individuals with SMD, *communication temptations* signify interactions of a familiar joint attention in which the communication partner pauses and holds so that the child is tempted to take a turn to get the interaction going again (Snell, 2002). Dynamic assessment also considers what happens during communication breakdowns, the repair efforts, and the outcome. The repair of communication breakdowns entails finding keys to more knowledge about the individual's communication capacity and also highlights the behavior of the communication partner.

Sequential analyses or dynamic assessment is often implemented in specific situations for a shorter period of time. Situational mechanisms, such as learning opportunities provided in the environment, must, however, be taken into account if the assessor is to be able to identify possible relationships between processes (e.g., contingency learning) and long-term outcomes (e.g., contingency awareness). In addition, caregiver behaviors, knowledge, and skills in interacting with and developing relations with the person with SMD need to be assessed. Hostyn et al. (2010) has developed the Scale for Dialogical Meaning Making for use with caregivers to people with SMD. The caregiver is videotaped in dyadic interaction with a person with SMD and is afterward invited to analyze the dyadic interaction in collaboration with a supervisor. This can be repeated over time to enhance the learning effect for the caregiver. The scale has five subscales: (1) *mutual openness*, focusing on being aware of one's own and the communicative partner's behavior making up the dialogue; (2) *joint embedding context*, focusing on the joint creation of a context for dialogue; (3) *nonmanipulative negotiating*, focusing on how the dyadic partners negotiate possible meanings through acts such as pausing or being persistent; (4) *joint confirmation*, focusing on confirmation/responding to utterances, such as imitating; and (5) *nonevaluativeness*, focusing on the general attitude, such as being patient, sharing happiness, and the like. Sufficient, although not very high, interrater reliability between observers and

range of scores is reported for the scale. For interrater reliability between observers, a mean difference over observations of less than 0.5 scale steps was deemed as agreement.

Assessment is, as can be seen from these examples, also a learning opportunity for caregivers. It is also rather time-consuming and involves being in the everyday living contexts of those with SMD. Thus, assessment is best seen as, simultaneously, a means for planning intervention and as an intervention that needs to be supplemented by intervention methods with specific goals.

Interventions to Enhance Optimal Life Experiences in People with Severe Multiple Disabilities

Interventions for optimal life experiences for people with SMD can have one or all of the following foci: the person with SMD; the environment, including caregivers; caregiver–person with SMD interaction; and the physical environment. To have a good long-term outcome, interventions with different foci have to be related to each other. They also have to be implemented in a manner that increases the probability for sustainable outcomes. Because of their strong dependency on others in all aspects of life, this is especially important for people with SMD. Their everyday function will, by necessity, vary depending on how caregiver actions and the physical environment are adapted to their abilities, skills, and interests.

Interventions focused on the person with SMD. As previously stated, contingency awareness can be seen as the basic building block for most interventions focused on supporting people with SMD in having optimal life experiences over longer time periods. In addition to improvements in operant learning, children in contingency detection trials seem to respond to these activities with increased visual attention, enjoyment, and a general sense of excitement. Improvement in child operant learning and responses and sense of excitement seem to be stronger for social stimuli than for nonsocial stimuli. These child responses and their excitement make caregivers increase their efforts to support and encourage child learning, and caregivers seem to enjoy seeing their children display engagement (Dunst et al., 1985; Dunst et al., 2007). In the Dunst et al. study (2007) described earlier, 41 children with SMD participated with their teachers and mothers. The activities for learning contingency detection were developed by the children's caregivers (parents or teachers) and researchers in collaboration. In observations, the children's expressions were identified, as were the objects and people that the children seemed to enjoy. Activities that the caregivers used to engage the children in interactions with people or objects were also identified. From the identified behaviors, the most frequently occurring stimuli and activities were selected. All of the selected activities contained behavior-based contingencies in which the availability of a reinforcement or the production of an interesting consequence depended on the children's actions. The results revealed that the children improved their contingency detection skills, especially in activities containing social stimuli, and the caregivers exhibited a higher frequency of positive reactions to the children. The results are interesting in two ways. First, the fact that social stimuli generated stronger improvement than did nonsocial stimuli indicates that opportunities to interact are a key issue in interventions for people with SMD. This is despite the fact that most intervention studies are partially or solely focused on objects as stimuli. Second, the effects on the caregivers of receiving clear responses with positive valence from the children with SMD stimulated caregivers to exhibit more positive responses and provide more activities. Thus, assessment of possible activities for contingency learning should include surveying caregiver preferences, as well as the preferences of the people with SMD.

Lancioni et al. (2005) have systematically reviewed research on increasing indices of happiness in people with SMD. They report positive outcomes for six different procedures implemented in specific sessions: (1) structured stimulation; (2) microswitch-based stimulation; (3) leisure activities, favorite work tasks, or conditions; (4) positive behavior support programs; (5) mindful caregiving (*snoezelen*); and (6) favorite stimulation automatically delivered on exercise engagement. Some examples are provided for the first five procedures here.

Structured stimulation. Green and Reid (1996) conducted one of the first studies in this area and showed that staff could increase the happiness of the target group by presenting preferred items or activities. Further studies have showed that social interaction exclusively (Favell, Realon, & Sutton, 1996) and together with the presentation of preferred items can increase the happiness of individuals with profound multiple disabilities (Davis, Young, Cherry, Dahman, & Rehfeldt, 2004). Davis et al. (2004) compared happiness levels of three participants with profound multiple disabilities in three conditions: standard classroom condition, social interaction condition, and social interaction with preferred item condition. The combined condition produced higher indicators of happiness than did social interaction alone.

Microswitch-based stimulation. In two studies, one original study (2002) and one maintenance study (2003), Lancioni et al. presented people with SMD for microswitch-based stimulation sessions in which switch activation presented a favorite stimulus event for a short time period. The sessions continued for 5–6 months; to reduce the risk of satiation effects, new stimuli were presented during the maintenance period. For two people, the frequency of happiness indices increased during the sessions in the maintenance period, and for one person it decreased. However, all people continued to activate the switches and had high frequencies of in-session happiness indices.

Leisure activities. Yu et al. (2002) studied participants with SMD while attending leisure activities such as listening to music, watching TV, and work activities such as shredding papers. All participants, independent of whether they had severe or profound intellectual disabilities, exhibited higher frequencies of happiness indices in leisure activities compared to work activities. Overall, participants with severe intellectual disabilities had higher frequencies of happiness indices than did people with profound intellectual disabilities.

Positive environment. Realon et al. (2002) instructed caregivers on how to establish and maintain interactions with people with SMD using eye contact, providing positive comments and leisure materials, and responding to communication attempts. People with SMD were reported to improve in terms of alertness, engagement with materials, and indices of happiness.

Snoezelen. Special multisensory environments, known as *snoezelen*, are designed to provide people with SMD with stimulation, and these have been evaluated for effects (Lindsay, Black, Broxholme, Pitcaithly, & Hornsby, 2001). The evaluation revealed that people with SMD in the *snoezelen* environment had increased frequencies of friendly vocalizations and laughter. Vlaskamp, de Geeter, Huijsmans, and Smit (2003) studied the effects of multisensory environments on the level of alertness and interaction in 19 people with SMD. They found that stimuli offered by staff were more effective than stimuli offered by materials only in increasing alertness and interaction.

The primary goal of all these interventions has been to evaluate the reactions of people with SMD on being presented with situations having a positive value. Thus, the expected outcomes are primarily hedonic and short term. Other forms of intervention are likely necessary to promote increased control over the future (eudaimonic outcomes) for people with SMD.

Choice

Choice is the vehicle used to express preferences, which can remain constant or change over time (Canella, O'Reilly, & Lancioni, 2005). Choice-making involves selecting in one's own mind and communicating that selection to others (Brown & Brown, 2009). Because one requirement for choice-making is the ability to express a preference to others, the available opportunities for choice-making should be familiar to the person with SMD so that choices are made successfully (Wehmeyer, 2007). Concerning expressing preferences, individuals with SMD can most often display likes and dislikes. When it comes to understanding the communicative repertoire of likes and dislikes, interaction partners have a great responsibility to sensitively infer meaning (Grove et al., 1999). It is important to have some knowledge about an individual's preferences when providing him or her with choices because choices are based on these preferences (Canella et al., 2005). Historically, individuals with SMD have been given very limited opportunities to make choices. Making choices in everyday life for individuals with SMD can be simply choosing what food to eat at mealtimes or who one sits beside. It may also be showing preferences for things in one's environment, such as noise level (Brown & Brown, 2009). In a literature review of choice and preference assessment research in people with severe to profound developmental disabilities (Canella et al., 2005), 30 studies published between 1996 and 2002 were evaluated. The main findings of these studies were that choice interventions led to decreases in inappropriate behavior and increases in appropriate behavior, and that various preference assessments could be used to identify reinforcing stimuli. Twelve of the 15 studies on choice interventions reported clearly positive results, and nine of the remaining 10 studies reported mixed results. Overall, the studies also stressed the effectiveness of providing more choice opportunities throughout the day in different contexts (Canella et al., 2005).

Interventions Focused on Caregivers in the Proximal Environment

Because of their strong dependency on others, most intervention methods for people with SMD are focused on teaching caregivers the attitudes, knowledge, and skills necessary for arranging a context that invites active participation by people with SMD and/or for using methods to create dyadic interaction. That is, the intervention methods are planned to have an indirect effect on the people with SMD by changing caregivers and contexts. This indirect focus of intervention may decrease the probability of strong immediate effects on people with SMD from intervention, but it may also be a necessary prerequisite for sustainable effects of intervention. In the interventions reported earlier, with a focus on the individual only, the study by Lancioni et al. (2003) presents maintenance data and only the study by Dunst et al. (2007) presents data on the effects on caregivers of intervention. It seems as if studies focusing primarily on the effects of intervention implemented in sessions with single individuals have little information to provide concerning how a sustainable environment that promotes optimal life experiences for people with SMD should be designed. This is the niche in which intervention studies with a primary focus on caregivers are important.

Four types of interventions that have the primary aim of affecting the attitudes, knowledge, and skills of caregivers to people with SMD/presymbolic communicators have been suggested (Olsson & Granlund, 2003): (1) assigning a meaning, (2) how to "read the person with SMD," (3) interaction patterns and inference, and (4) changing the context. Concerning assigning a meaning, caregivers to people with SMD may need support in assigning a communicative meaning to idiosyncratic behavior patterns that may not be obviously directed toward the caregiver. Thus, the focus here is on helping caregivers to perceive and redefine behaviors and behavior sequences as interaction or intentional behavior. One example of an interventional method to be used for this purpose is the Scale for Dialogical Meaning Making (Hostyn et al., 2010) for use with caregivers to people with SMD. This scale is meant to be applied in collaboration with caregivers when analyzing videotaped sequences of actions or interaction.

Interventions focused on how to read the person with SMD are partially overlapping with the assigning a meaning interventions but are more focused on identifying configurations of behavior in which there is already a consensus that a person can interact and act on the environment in an intentional manner. One tool for this kind of intervention is the Affective Communicative Assessment (ACA) (Coupe O'Kane et al., 1985; Coupe O'Kane & Goldbart, 1998), to be applied in collaboration with caregivers.

Interaction pattern interventions are aimed at changing dialogue patterns, such as turn-taking patterns (Iacono et al., 1998). These intervention methods are also focused on providing feedback to caregivers and engaging in discussions with caregivers. Hostyn (2011) have investigated the applicability of scales from parent–infant research in assessing the interaction between adults with SMD and caregivers. The Maternal Behavior Rating Scale (MBRS) (Mahoney, 1992) and the Child Behavior Rating (CBR) scale (Mahoney, 1998) are designed to evaluate aspects of maternal and child interaction behaviors, such as mother's responsiveness, child orientation, and child's attention and initiations. These were used in combination with the Emotional Availability Scales (EAS) (Biringen, Robinson, & Emde, 1998), designed to evaluate the quality of attunement in dyadic interactions, to evaluate interactions between 18 people with SMD and their caregivers. They report high applicability validity and reliability but also stress the importance of being aware of the underlying philosophical and ethical assumptions on which these scales are based.

Interventions aimed at inferences and changing the context are focused on supporting caregivers in reflecting how they interpret the communicative meaning or intent of the behavior of a person with SMD in relation to activity and context. This type of intervention can be used to change contexts as a means to create more opportunities for optimal life experiences for people with SMD. Rowland and Schweigert (1993) describe how they involved caregivers in assessing the communicative environment of children with SMD. Their tool used was designed to be reactive by formulating the items as implicit instructions for how a functional environment should be designed. The result indicated that caregivers changed the environment after being involved in assessment.

The special benefit of interventions focusing on caregivers is that they can be designed to provide caregivers with the knowledge and skills necessary for sustaining positive relationships between people with SMD and their caregivers and for setting up a functionally comprehensible environment for people with SMD. Studies with this focus have, however, primarily evaluated short-term effects. Research focusing on factors that are important for sustainable effects are needed. Service system factors and staff environment factors are likely important to include in these studies. Sustainable effects on environments containing employed caregivers probably depend on knowledgeable staff and

low staff turnover (Butler, Simpson, Brennan, & Turner, 2010).

Conclusion

As stated in the introduction, optimal human functioning is always relative to the characteristics of a person and the context in which that person lives. The optimal functioning of people with SMD is challenged both by impairments in body functions and contextual barriers leading to participation restrictions. This population tends to be dependent on others for all aspects of life. Thus, what constitutes optimal functioning and optimal life experiences will depend on others. It also means that the relationship between outcomes on the individual subjective level and the interpersonal level is strong, almost to the degree that it becomes inseparable. Long-lasting positive relationships with caregivers are a necessary but insufficient requirement for optimal life experiences for people with SMD.

Concerning outcomes on the individual level, two supplemental types of outcomes can be defined. The first is short-term hedonic experiences of SWB, here and now (e.g., momentary happiness) occurring as a consequence of interactions with others and exposure to interesting stimuli and activities. The second is eudaimonic experiences of anticipation, engagement, and persistence following from repeated experiences that show the person with SMD that it is possible for him or her to affect the surrounding world (i.e., contingency awareness). Together, these constitute optimal life experiences for people with SMD. Both types of outcomes are dependent on, and almost exclusively occur in conjunction with interactions with caregivers. Repeated positive interactions with caregivers make up the basis for positive relations and an optimal life over time.

These outcomes depend on interventions focusing on wellsprings of optimal functioning and psychological processes important for optimal function, as well as on extrapsychological mechanisms. Important interventions in wellsprings of optimal functioning for people with SMD concern how, for example, severe visual and motor impairments can be compensated for through training and assistive technology. Especially important to consider is the interactive effect on functioning that multiple impairments have when they occur simultaneously. Currently, there is sparse knowledge in the literature about these interaction effects and about appropriate interventions.

Psychological processes important for optimal functioning concern factors such as contingency awareness and joint attention skills. These are person factors that are difficult to separate from the optimal life outcomes of those people with SMD who have a very limited behavior repertoire. In these cases, it may be better to see outcomes such as happiness, anticipation, and persistence for people with SMD as existing on a continuum of positive outcomes that range from traitlike decontextualized outcomes, such as contingency awareness and joint attention skills, to statelike highly contextualized outcomes, such as indices of happiness (Granlund & Björck-Åkesson, 2005). The traitlike outcomes are often rated without considering the context as psychological factors that describe a person's function over many contexts, whereas statelike outcomes are described as momentary expressions in the here and now. The probability that indices of happiness are observed is much higher in people exhibiting contingency awareness over several contexts (Dunst et al., 2007). This indicates that there is a two-way interaction between long- and short-term positive outcomes for people with SMD, and this needs to be supported by interventions linking experiences of positive interactions over time to a pattern of positive interactions—that is, positive relationships.

Because of their dependence on others for all aspects of life, extrapsychological mechanisms, such as the organization of service systems, living arrangements, and interactions within the proximal environment, are extremely important for optimal life outcomes in people with SMD. All interventions are implemented by caregivers in proximal environments that are partially shaped by living arrangements and social service systems.

Assessments and interventions for people with SMD exist in an integrated web within a larger intervention process implemented in dyadic interaction, in which formal assessment instruments and sessions also can be seen as interventions focusing on caregivers. Thus, it is important to involve caregivers in assessment as well as in implementing intervention methods. Intervention implementation and the effects of intervention focusing on optimal functioning and optimal life experiences are, at present, primarily evaluated over short time periods. Knowledge is scarce about how living environments that provide people with SMD with sustainable opportunities to experience happiness, anticipation, and long-lasting relationships should be designed. Today, we have knowledge about short-term optimal life outcomes for people with SMD in specific sessions. How optimal life experiences vary over time between these sessions are less well documented. To further enhance

optimal functioning in people with SMD, we need knowledge about the long-term optimal functioning of people with SMD in sustainable social and physical environments.

References

Ahlström, G., & Wadensten, B. (2010). Encounters in close care relations from the perspective of personal assistants working with people with severe disability. *Health & Social Care in Community Health 18* (2), 180–188.

Ahlström, G., & Wadensten, B. (2011). Family members' experiences of personal assistance. *Health and Social Care in the Community; In print.*

Arthur, M. (2003). Socio-communicative variables and behavior state in students with profound and multiple disabilities: Descriptive data from school settings. *Education and Training in Developmental Disabilities, 38*, 200–219.

Askeheim O. P. (2005). Personal assistance—direct payment or alternative public service. *Disability and Society, 20*, 247–260.

Axelsson, A-K., Granlund, M., & Wilder, J. (submitted). *Participation in family activities of children with profound multiple disabilities.*

Bandura, A. (1989). Regulation of cognitive processes through perceived self-efficacy. *Developmental Psychology, 25*, 729–735.

Bausmeister, R F., & Vohs, K D. (2002). The pursuit of meaningfulness in life. In C R. Snyder & S J. Lopez (Eds.), *Handbook of positive psychology* (pp. 608–618). New York: Oxford University Press.

Bedell, G., Khetani, M. A., Cousins, M., Coster, W., & Law, M. (2011). Parent perspectives to inform development of measures of children's participation and environment. *Archives of Physical Medicine and Rehabilitation, 92*, 765–773.

Bergsma, A., Veenhoven, R., ten Have, M., & de Graaf, R. (2010). Do they know how happy they are? On the value of self-related happiness of people with a mental disorder. *Journal of Happiness Studies, 12*, 793–806.

Bigelow, A. E. (2003). The development of joint attention in blind infants. *Development and Psychopathology, 15*, 259–275.

Biringen, Z., Robinson, J., & Emde, R. (1998). *The emotional availability scale* (3rd ed.). Fort Collins: Department of Human Development and Family Studies, Colorado State University.

Björck-Åkesson, E., & Grsanlund, M. (2003)

Björck-Åkesson, E., Granlund, M., & Olsson, C. (1999). Collaborative problem solving in communication intervention. In S. Von Tetzchner, & M. Hygum Jensen (Eds.), *Augmentative and alternative communication European perspectives.* London: Whurr.

Björck-Åkesson, E., Granlund, M., & Simeonsson, R. (2000). Assessment philosophies and practices in Sweden. In M. Guralnick (Ed.), *Interdisciplinary assessment of young children with developmental disabilities* (pp. 391–412). London: Paul H. Brookes.

Brown, I., & Brown, R. I. (2009). Choice as an aspect of quality of life for people with intellectual disabilities. *Journal of Policy and Practice in Intellectual Disabilities, 6*, 11–18.

Bruce, S. M., & Vargas, C. (2007). Intentional communication acts expressed by children with severe disabilities in high-rate contexts. *Augmentative and Alternative Communication, 23*, 300–311.

Butler, S., Simpson, N., Brennan, M., & Turner, W. (2010) Why do they leave? Factors associated with job termination among personal assistant workers in home care. *Journal of Gerontological Social Work, 53*, 665–681.

Cannella, H. I., O'Reilly, M. F., & Lanvioni, G. E. (2005). Choice and preference assessment research with people with severe or profound developmental disabilities: A review of literature. *Research in Developmental Disabilities, 26*, 1–15.

Cavanagh, P., & Davidson, M. (1977). The secondary circular reaction and response elicitation in the operant learning of 6-months old infants *Developmental Psychology, 13*(4), 371–376,

Chantry, J., & Dunford, C. (2010). How do computer assistive technologies enhance participation in childhood occupations for children with multiple and complex disabilities? A review of the current literature. *British Journal of Occupational Therapy, 73*, 351–365.

Clarke, M. T., Newton, C., Griffiths, T., Price, K., Lysley, A., & Petrides, K. V. (2010). Factors associated with the participation of children with complex communication needs. *Research in Developmental Disabilities, 32*, 774–780.

Clevnert, U., & Johansson, L. (2007). International view: Personal assistance in Sweden. *Journal of Aging & Social Policy, 19*, 65–80.

Coster, W., Law, M., Bedell, G., Khetani, M., Cousins, M., & Teplicky, R. (2011). Development of the participation and environment measure for children and youth: Conceptual basis. *Disability & Rehabilitation, Early Online*, 1–9.

Coupe O'Kane, J., Barton, L., Barber, M., Collins, L., Levy, D., & Murphy, D. (1985). *Affective communicative assessment.* Manchester: Melland School.

Coupe O'Kane, J., & Goldbart, J. (1998). *Communication before speech: Development and assessment.* London: David Fulton.

Cummins, R. A. (1994). The Comprehensive Quality of Life Scale: Instrument development and psychometric evaluation. *Educational and Psychological Measurement, 54*, 372–382.

Cummings, R. A. (2002). Proxy responding for subjective well-being: A review. *International Review of Research in Mental Retardation, 25*, 183–207.

Daelman M. (2003). Een analyse van de presymbolische communicatie bij blinde kinderen met een meervoudige handicap. Unpublished doctoral dissertation, Katholieke Universiteit Leuven, Afdeling Orthopedagogiek, Leuven.

Davis, P., Young, A., Cherry, H., Dahman, D., & Rehfeldt, R. A. (2004). Increasing the happiness of individuals with profound multiple disabilities: Replication and extension. *Journal of Applied Behavior Analysis, 37*, 531–534.

Diener, E., Lucas, R. E., & Oishi, S. (2002). Subjective well-being: The science of happiness and life satisfaction. In C R. Snyder & S J. Lopez (Eds.), *Handbook of positive psychology* (pp. 608–618). New York: Oxford University Press.

Dunst, C. J. (1998). Sensorimotor development and developmental disabilities. In J. A. Burack, R. M. Hodapp, & E. Zigler (Eds.), *Handbook of mental retardation and development* (pp. 135–182). New York: Cambridge University Press.

Dunst, C. J., Cushing, P. J., & Vance, S. D. (1985). Response–contingent learning in profoundly handicapped infants: A social systems perspective. *Analysis & Intervention in Developmental Disabilities, 5*, 33–47.

Dunst, C. J., Raab, M., Trivette, C. M., Wilson, L. L., Hamby, D. W., Parkey, C., et al. (2007). Characteristics of operant learning games associated with optimal child and adult social-emotional consequences. *International Journal of Special Education, 22*, 13–24.

Dunst, C. J., Trivette, C. M., Raab, M., & Masiello, T. L. (2008). Early child contingency learning and detection: research evidence and implications for practice. *Exceptionality, 16*, 4–17.

Duvdevany, I., Ben-Zur, H., & Ambar, A. (2002). Self-determination and mental retardation: Is there an association with living arrangement and lifestyle satisfaction? *Mental Retardation, 40*, 379–389.

Eriksson, L., Welander, J., & Granlund, M. (2007). Participation in everyday school activities—for children with and without disabilities. *Journal of Physical and Developmental Disabilities, 19*, 485–502

Favell, J. E., Realon, R. E., & Sutton, K. A. (1996). Measuring and increasing the happiness of people with profound mental retardation and physical handicaps. *Behavioral Interventions, 11*, 47–58.

Felce, D., & Emerson, E. (2004). Research on engagement in activity. In E. Emerson, C. Hatton, T. Thompson, & T. R. Parmenter (Eds.), *The international handbook of applied research in intellectual disabilities* (pp. 353–368). West Sussex: John Wiley & Sons Ltd.

Fivush, R., & Nelson, K. (2006). Parent-child reminiscing locates the self in the past. *British Journal of Developmental Psychology, 24*, 235–251.

Goldbart, J. (1994). Opening the communication curriculum to students with PMLDs. In J. Ware (Eds.), *Educating children with profound and multiple learning difficulties* (pp. 15–62). London: David Fulton.

Granlund, M. (1993). *Flerhandikapp (Multiple disabilities).* Stockholm: Stiftelsen ala.

Granlund, M., & Björck-Åkesson, E. (1998). Reagera och reglera-beteendestilar hos barn med grava funktionsnedsättningar [React and regulate—behavior style in children with profound disabilities]. In K. Sonnander, M. Söder, & K. Ericsson (Eds.), *Forskare om utvecklingsstörning [Research on intellectual disability].* Uppsala: Uppsala University Press.

Granlund, M., & Björck-Åkesson, E. (2005). Participation and general competence—do type and degree of disability really matter? In R. Traustadottir, A. Gustavsson, J. Tøssebro & J. T. Sandvin (Eds.), *Change, resistance and reflection: Current Nordic disability research* (pp. 277–294). Lund, Sweden: Studentlitteratur.

Granlund, M., & Olsson, C. (1986). *Talspråksalternativ kommunikation och begåvningshandikapp [Augmentative and alternative communication and intellectual disability].* Stockholm: Stiftelsen ala.

Granlund, M., & Olsson, C. (1999). Efficacy of communication intervention for presymbolic communicators. *Augmentative and Alternative Communication, 15*, 25–37.

Granlund, M., Arvidsson, P., Niia, A., Björck-Åkesson, E., Simeonsson, R., Maxwell, G., et al. (Accepted). Differentiating activity and participation of children and youth with disability in Sweden—A third qualifier in ICF-CY? *American Journal of Physical Medicine and Rehabilitation.*

Green, C. W., & Reid, D. H. (1996). Defining, validating, and increasing indices of happiness among people with profound multiple disabilities. *Journal of Applied Behavior Analysis, 29*, 67–78.

Grove, N., Bunning, K., Porter, J., & Olsson, C. (1999). See what I mean: Interpreting the meaning of communication by people with severe and profound intellectual disabilities. *Journal of Applied Research in Intellectual Disabilities, 12*, 190–203.

Guess, D., Roberts, S., Siegel-Causey, E., & Rues, J. (1995). Replication and extended analysis of behavior state, environmental events, and related variables among individuals with profound disabilities. *American Journal on Mental Retardation*, *100*, 36–50.

Hammel, J., Magasi, S., Heinemann, A., Whiteneck, G., Bogner, J., & Rodriguez, E. (2008). What does participation mean? An insider perspective from people with disabilities. *Disability and Rehabilitation*, *30*, 1445–1460.

Harty, M., Joseph, L., Wilder, J., & Rajaram, P. (2007). Social support and families of children with disabilities: Towards positive family functioning. *South African Journal of Occupational Therapy*, *37*, 18–21.

Heal, L. W., & Chadsey-Rusch, J. (1985). The Lifestyle Satisfaction Scale (LSS): assessing individuals' satisfaction with residence, community setting, and associated services. *Applied Research in Mental Retardation*, *6*, 475–490.

Hartley, S., & MacLean, W. (2006). A review of the reliability and validity of Likert-type scales for people with intellectual disability. *Journal of Intellectual Disability Research*, *50*(11), 813–827.

Hostyn, I (2011). *Interaction between people with profound intellectual and multiple disabilities and their direct support staff.* Leuven: Dissertation from Katholieke Universiteit Leuven, Fakulteit Psychologie en pedagogische wetenschappen.

Hostyn, I., Daelman, M., Janssen, M., & Maes, B. (2010). Describing dialogue between people with profound intellectual and multiple disabilities and direct care staff using the Scale for Dialogical meaning making. *Journal of Intellectual Disability Research*, *54*, 679–690.

Hostyn, I., & Maes, B. (submitted). Interaction with a person with profound intellectual and multiple disabilities: A case study in dialogue with an experienced staff member.

Iacono, T., Bloomberg, K., & West, D. (2005). A preliminary investigation into the internal consistency and construct validity of the triple C: Checklist of Communicative Competencies. *Journal of Intellectual & Developmental Disability*, *30*, 139–145.

Iacono, T., Carter, M., & Hook, J. (1998). Identification of intentional communication in students with severe and multiple disabilities. *Augmentative and Alternative Communication*, *14*, 102–114.

Imms, C., Reilly, S., Carlin, J., & Dodd, K. (2008). Diversity of participation in children with Cerebral Palsy. *Developmental Medicine & Child Neurology*, *50*, 363–369.

Johnson, S., Hennessy, E., Smith, R., Trikic, R., Wolke, D., & Marlow, N. (2009). Academic attainment and special education needs in extremely preterm children at 11 years of age: The EPICURE study. *Archive of Dis Child Fetal Neonatal Ed*, *94*, 283–289.

Knapp, M. (1995) How shall we study comprehensive collaborative services for children and families. *Educational Research*, *24*, 5–16.

Kasari, C., Paparella, T., Freeman, S., & Jahromi, L. B. (2008). Language outcome in autism: Randomized comparison of joint attention and play interventions. *Journal of Counseling and Clinical Psychology*, *76*, 125–137.

Koegel, L. K., Koegel, R. L., Harrower, J. K., & Carter, C. M. (1999). Pivotal response intervention I: Overview of approach. *Journal of the Association for People with Severe Handicaps*, *24*, 174–185.

Lachapelle, Y., Wehmeyer, M. L., Haelewyck, M-C., Courbois, Y., Keith, K. D., Schalock, R., & Walsh, P. N.

(2005). The relationship between Quality of Life and Self-Determination: an international study. *Journal of Intellectual Disability Research*, *49*, 740–744.

Lancioni, G. E., O'Reilly, M., Singh, N., Oliva, D., & Groenweg, J. (2002). Impact of stimulation versus micro-switch based programs on indices of happiness of people with profound multiple disabilities. *Research in Developmental Disabilities*, *23*, 149–160.

Lancioni, G. E., O'Reilly, M., Singh, N., Oliva, D., Campodonico, F., & Groeneweg, J. (2003). Stimulation and micro-switch program for enhancing indices of happiness: A maintenance assessment. *Behavioral Interventions*, *18*, 53–61.

Lancioni, G. E., Singh, N. N., O'Reilly, M. F., Oliva, D., & Basili, G. (2005). An overview of research on increasing indices of happiness of people with severe/profound intellectual and multiple disabilities. *Disability and Rehabilitation*, *27*, 83–93.

Lancioni, G. E., Singh, N. N., O'Reilly, M. F., Sigafoos, J., Oliva, D., & Baccani, S. (2007). Enabling students with multiple disabilities to request and choose among environmental stimuli through micro-switch and computer technology. *Research in Developmental Disabilities*, *28*, 50–58.

Lindsay, W., Black, E., Broxholme, S., Pitcaithly, D., & Hornsby, N. (2001). Effects of four therapy procedures on communication in people with profound intellectual disabilities. *Journal of Applied Research in Intellectual Disabilities*, *14*, 110–119.

Linley, P. A., Joseph, S., Harrington, S., & Wood, A. M. (2006). Positive psychology: Past, present, and (possible) future. *Journal of Positive Psychology*, *1*(1), 3–16.

Mahoney, G. (1992). *Maternal Behavior Rating Scale* (revised). Unpublished document. Cleveland, OH: Case Western Reserve University.

Mahoney, G. (1998). *Child Behavior Rating Scale* (revised). Unpublished document. Cleveland, OH: Case Western Reserve University.

Mahoney, G., Kim, J. M., & Lin, C. (2007). Pivotal behavior model of developmental learning. *Infants & Young Children*, *20*, 311–325.

Mayo-Wilson, E., Montgomery, P., & Dennis, J. (2008). Personal assistance for children and adolescents (0-18) with intellectual impairments. *Campbell Systematic Reviews*, 4.

Mayo-Wilson, E., Montgomery, P., & Dennis, J. A. (2009) Personal assistance for adults (19-64) with both physical and intellectual impairments (review). *Cochrane Library*, Issue 1.

Möller, K. (2008). *Impact on participation and service for people with deaf-blindness.* Örebro: Örebro University Dissertations.

Nafstad, A., & Rodbroe, I. (1999). *Att skapa kommunikation med dövblindfödda [Creating communication with children who are born deaf blind].* Finspång: Mo Gård Förlag.

Nakken, H., & Vlaskamp, C. (2002). Joining forces: Supporting individuals with profound multiple learning disabilities. *Tizard Learning Disability Review*, *7*, 10–15.

Nakken, H., & Vlaskamp, C. (2007). A need for a taxonomy for profound intellectual and multiple disabilities. *Journal of Policy and Practice in Intellectual Disabilities*, *4*, 83–87.

Nyman, S., Dibb, B., Rita Victor, C., & Gosney, M. A. (2012). Emotional well-being and adjustment to vision loss in later life: a meta-synthesis of qualitative studies. *Disability and rehabilitation, 34,* 971–981.

Olsson, C. (2006). *The kaleidoscope of Communication: Different perspectives on communication involving children with severe multiple disabilities.* Doctoral dissertation, Stockholm Institute of Education, Sweden.

Olsson, C., & Granlund, M. (2003). Presymbolic communication intervention for presymbolic communicators. In R. Schlosser (Eds.), *Efficacy research in augmentative and alternative communication* (pp. 299–322). New York: Academic Press.

O'Reilly, P. (2007). Involving service users in defining and evaluating the service quality of a disability service. *International Journal of Health care Quality Assurance, 20,* 116–129.

Park, C. L., & Folkman, S. (1997). Meaning in the context of stress and coping. *Review of General Psychology, 1,* 115–144.

Petrou, S., Abangma, G., Johnson, S., Wolke, D., & Marlow, N. (2009). Costs and health utilities associated with extremely preterm birth: Evidence from the EPICure study. *Value in Health, 12,* 1124–1134.

Petry, K., & Maes, B. (2006). Identifying expressions of pleasure and displeasure by people with profound and multiple disabilities. *Journal of Intellectual & Developmental Disability, 31,* 28–38.

Petry, K., Maes, B., & Vlaskamp, C. (2009) Measuring the quality of life of people with profound multiple disabilities using the QOL-PMD: First results. *Research in Developmental Disabilities, 30,* 1394–1405.

Preisler, G. (1998). *Att dela värld med dövblinda barn: En studie om samspel mellan dövblinda barn och deras föräldrar [Sharing the world with children who are deaf blind: A study of interaction between children who are deaf blind and their parents]* (vol. 98). Stockholm: Stockholm University, Department of Psychology.

Raghavendra, P., Virgo, R., Olsson, C., Connell, T., & Lane, A. (2011). Activity participation of children with complex communication needs, physical disabilities and typically-developing peers. *Developmental Neurorehabilitation, 14,* 145–155.

Realon, R., Bliegen, R., La Force, A., Helsel, W., & Goldman, V. (2002). The effects of the positive environment programme (PEP) on the behaviors of adults with profound cognitive and physical disabilities. *Behavioral Interventions, 17,* 1–13.

Roberts, S., Arthur-Kelly, M., Foreman, P., & Pascoe, S. (2005). Educational approaches for maximizing arousal in children with multiple and severe disability: New directions for research and practice in early childhood contexts. *Pediatric Rehabilitation, 8,* 88–91.

Robinson, B. L., & Lieberman, L. J. (2004). Effects of visual impairment, gender, and age on self-determination. *Journal of Visual Impairment and Blindness, 98,* 350–366.

Roos, J., & Hjelmqvist, E. (2009). *Arranging home-based personal assistance through private or public service providers: How satisfied are consumers?* Unpublished paper in thesis.

Ross, E., & Oliver, C. (2003). Preliminary analysis of the psychometric properties of the Mood, Interest & Pleasure Questionnaire (MIPQ) for adults with severe and profound learning disabilities. *British Journal of Clinical Psychology, 42,* 81–93.

Rowland, C., & Schweigert, P. (1993). Analyzing the communicative environment to increase functional communication. *Journal of the Association for People with Severe Handicaps, 18,* 161–176.

Ryan, R. M., & Deci, E. L. (2001). On happiness and human potentials: A review of research on hedonic and eudaimonic well-being. *Annual Review of Psychology, 52,* 141–166.

Ryff, C., & Keys, C. (1995). The structure of psychological well-being revisited. *Journal of Personality and Social Psychology, 69,* 719–727.

Sameroff, A. J., & MacKenzie, M. J. (2003). Research strategies for capturing transactional models of development: the limits of the possible. *Development and Psychopathology, 15,* 613–640.

Schalock, R. L., Bonham, G. S., & Marchand, C. B. (2000). Consumer based quality of life assessment: A path model of perceived satisfaction. *Evaluation and Program Planning, 23,* 77–87

Schalock R. L., & Keith K. D. (1993) *Quality of Life Questionnaire.* Worthington, OH: IDS Publishing.

Seligman, M. E. P., & Csikszentmihalyi, M. (2000). Positive psychology: An introduction. *American Psychologist, 55,* 5–14.

Simeonsson, R., Huntington, G., Short, R., & Ware, W. (1982). The Carolina Record of Individual behavior: Characteristics of handicapped infants and children. *Topics in Early Childhood Education, 2,* 43–55.

Simeonsson, R., Huntington, G., McMillen, J., Haugh-Dodds, A., Halperin, D., Zipper, I., & Leskinen, M. (1996). Services for young children and their families. Evaluating the intervention cycle. *Infants and Young Children, 9,* 31–42.

Snell, M. E. (2002). Using dynamic assessment with learners who communicate nonsymbolically. *Augmentative and Alternative Communication, 18,* 163–176.

Snell, M. E., Chen, L.-Y., & Hoover, K. (2006). Teaching augmentative and alternative communication to students with severe disabilities: A review of intervention research 1997–2003. *Research & Practice for People with Severe Disabilities, 31,* 203–214.

Stancliffe, R. J., & Keane, S. (2000). Outcomes and costs of community living: a matched comparison of group homes and semi-independent living. *Journal of Intellectual and Developmental Disability, 25,* 281–305.

Trevarthen, C. (2004). How infants learn how to mean. In M. Tokoro & L. Steels (Eds.), *A learning zone of one's own* (pp. 37–70). Amsterdam: IOS Press.

Ullenhag A., Bult M.K., Nyquist A., Ketelaar M., Jahnsen R., Krumlinde- Sundholm L., Almqvist L., & Granlund M. (2012). An international comparison of patterns of participation in leisure activities for children with and without disabilities in Sweden, Norway and the Netherlands. *Developmental Neurorehabilitation, 15*(5), 369–385.

Uzgiris, I. C., & Hunt, J. (1975). *Assessment in infancy: Ordinal scales of psychological development.* Champaign: University of Illinois Press.

Wachs, T. D., & Kohnstamm, G. A. (2001). The bidirectional nature of temperament–context links. In T. D. Wachs & G. A. Kohnstamm (Eds.), *Temperament in context* (pp. 201–222). Mahwah, NJ: Lawrence Erlbaum.

Watson, L. R., Baranek, G. T., & DiLavore, P. C. (2003). Toddlers with autism: Developmental perspectives. *Infants & Young Children, 16,* 201–214.

van den Broek, E. G. C., Janssen, C. G. C., van Ramshorst, T., & Deen, L. (2006). Visual impairments in people with severe and profound multiple disabilities: An inventory of visual functioning. *Journal of Intellectual Disability Research, 50,* 470–475.

Wehmeyer, M. J. (2007). *Promoting self-determination in students with developmental disabilities. What works for special-needs learners.* New York: Guilford Press.

Wehmeyer, M., & Metzler, C. A. (1995). How self-determined are people with mental retardation? The national consumer survey. *Mental Retardation, 33,* 111–119.

Weinberg, Gianio, & Tronick, 1989

Vlaskamp, C, de Geeter, K.I, Huijsmans, L. M., & Smit, I. H. (2003). Passive activities: The effectiveness of multi-sensory environments on the level of activity of individuals with profound multiple disabilities. *Journal of Applied Research in Intellectual Disabilities, 16*, 135–143.

Wilder, J. (2008a).Video observations of dyadic interaction: Behavior style of presymbolic children. *Scandinavian Journal of Disability Research, 10*, 104–124.

Wilder, J. (2008b). Proximal processes of children with profound multiple disabilities. Dissertation in psychology, Stockholm University, Sweden.

Wilder, J., Axelsson, C., & Granlund, M. (2004). Parent–child interaction: A comparison of parents' perceptions in three groups. *Disability and Rehabilitation, 26*, 1313–1322.

Wilder, J., & Granlund, M. (2003). Behaviour style and interaction between seven children with multiple disabilities and their caregivers. *Child: Care, Health and Development, 29*, 559–567.

Wilder, J., & Granlund, M. (2011). People with multiple disabilities. In L. Söderman, & S. Antonsson (Eds.), *Nya Omsorgsboken [The New Book of Care and Support].* Malmö, Sweden: Liber.

Vos, P., De Cock, P., Petry, K., Van Den Noortgate, W., & Maes, B. (2010). What makes them feel the way they do?

Investigating the subjective well-being in people with severe and profound disabilities. *Research in Developmental Disabilities, 31*, 1623–1632.

Yoder, P. J., Short-Meyerson, K., & Tapp, J. (2004). Measurement of behavior with a special emphasis on sequential analysis of behavior. In E. Emerson, C. Hatton, T. Thompson, & T. Parmenter (Eds.), *The international handbook of applied research in intellectual disabilities.* West Sussex, England: Wiley.

Young, H., Fenwick, M., Lambe, L., & Hogg, J. (2011). Multi-sensory storytelling as an aid to assisting people with profound intellectual disabilities to cope with sensitive issues: A multiple research methods analysis of engagement and outcomes. *European Journal of Special Needs Education, 26*, 127–142.

Yu, D., Spevack, S., Hiebert, R., Martin, T., Goodman, R., Martin, T. G., Harapiak, S., & Martin, G. L. (2002). Happiness indices among people with profound and severe disabilities during leisure and work activities: A comparison. *Education and Training in Mental Retardation and Developmental Disabilities, 37*, 421–426.

Positive Psychology and Children with Emotional and Behavioral Difficulties

Daniel E. Olympia, Lora Tuesday Heathfield, William R. Jenson, Holly Majszak,
Virginia Ramos-Matias, *and* Monique Thacker

Abstract

Although the work of positive psychology theory development and practice has accelerated over the past 10 years, limited conceptualization and application of this knowledge base has occurred for children and adolescents. Despite the high interest in various emerging areas of positive psychology and the promising results of adult studies, research has yet to establish a foundation of work within positive psychology for use in school- or clinic-based interventions with targeted groups such as children and adolescents with emotional and behavioral difficulties. This chapter provides a context for notable recent developments in the field, as well as for existing knowledge and practice with internalizing and externalizing students, and concludes with recommendations for future research.

Key Words: positive psychology, children, adolescents, emotional and behavioral disorders, internalizing, externalizing, interventions

The topical marriage of positive psychology and children/adolescents with emotional and behavioral difficulties at first appears somewhat paradoxical. The science of positive psychology typically focuses on the "scientific study of ordinary human strengths and virtues" (Sheldon & King, 2001, p. 216) and the experiences of average people, particularly to determine the nature and essential components of effective functioning. This includes an examination of the development and role of those qualities associated with the experience of subjective well-being (SWB) across both positive and negative life events (Seligman & Csikszentmihályi, 2000). The study of children who exhibit emotional and behavioral difficulties has typically focused on the associated psychopathology, behavioral excesses, and skill deficits, and the corresponding interventions to treat specific externalizing- or internalizing-type conditions (Jenson, Harward, & Bowen, 2011). Children with emotional and behavioral disabilities are very atypical in terms of their behaviors, symptoms, and treatments, and they often experience some of the

most segregated and restrictive settings in schools. Positive psychology runs contrary to the "disease" model of contemporary psychology, in which remediating deficits and treating disorders is of primary concern (Seligman, 2002). In fact, one might argue that children who exhibit symptoms of noncompliance, aggression, rule breaking, depression, or substance abuse would be the least likely to match any of the interest areas frequently cited in the positive psychology literature (Jenson, Olympia, Farley, & Clark, 2004). Although this may have been true early in the development of positive psychology theory, there has been a renewed interest in applying research findings in positive psychology to the treatment of these high-risk children.

For positive psychology, a central task has been to explain how, despite environmental, individual, and dispositional difficulties, many people are able to live full lives, replete with dignity and purpose. Central to the study of positive psychology are efforts to define the nature of happiness across various segments of the population. However, children with emotional and behavioral disabilities are often perceived as the antithesis or absence of happiness, particularly in settings where they experience high rates of failure.

Positive psychology also operates on a model of optimal functioning that relies on facilitating positive emotion, engagement, and participation in meaningful experiences. This has produced a body of work covering topics such as the identification and utilization of core character traits (courage, generosity, etc.) and factors such as SWB, gratitude, forgiveness, flow, optimism, and other "quality-of-life" outcomes (positive achievement, job performance, social relationships, etc.). Although current research has begun to establish important findings that relate positive psychology principles to children and schools in general (e.g., Miller & Nickerson, 2007; Seligman, 2011), it is still not entirely clear how children with emotional and behavioral difficulties can benefit on a practical, applied level from developments in positive psychology.

This chapter provides a context for the application of the principles of positive psychology to better understand the nature and treatment of children with emotional and behavioral disorders and how positive psychology can be interpreted or applied within this context. We highlight selected developments in positive psychology as they apply to children and provide a developmental perspective on contributing factors associated with emotional and behavioral development. Finally, we provide a review of internalizing and externalizing perspectives with respect to children and positive psychology, and we discuss areas for future research and study.

Positive Psychology, Subjective Well-Being, and Happiness

Positive psychology provides several important elements for the study of human behavior. These include the study of positive emotion, positive character traits, and the opportunities to become engaged in positive institutions. These elements align neatly with the presumed origins of SWB in adults and, presumably, in adolescents and children. *Subjective well-being* is defined in both quantitative and qualitative terms as how individuals evaluate their own lives in both thinking and feelings. It typically includes constructs such as positive life satisfaction (including one's feelings about work, school, and relationships) and the nature, source, and frequency of pleasant feelings. Positive psychology also addresses the implications of low levels of SWB or dissatisfaction in those areas (Diener, 2000). In one's

past, positive emotions are anchored in general life satisfaction and in the promotion of gratitude-like experiences. Present-day experiences reflect opportunities to experience happiness in different forms (i.e., flow experiences), whereas future-oriented emotions deal with levels of hope, optimism, and community engagement (Miller & Nickerson, 2007). Subjective well-being is also related to a number of circumstances, including temperament and personality, access to monetary resources, social comparison (how we look in comparison to others), the ability to meet universal needs, adaptive capacity, and person–environment match (Diener, 2000).

Psychology has historically concentrated on behaviors, emotions, and cognitions that deviate from the norm, and, subsequently, clinicians, therapists, and evaluators in psychology frequently focus on the dysfunctional or negative aspects of behavior. Psychopathology strives to understand, treat, and predict outcomes of abnormal or deviant behaviors. Positive psychology takes a broader view and aims to explain human behavior by considering not only individual deviance but overall strengths and abilities and other factors predisposing to happiness, including overall SWB.

Consolidating these two somewhat divergent directions to address the potential and current needs of children with emotional and behavioral disorders has not been an easy task. Some of the most impressive work to date has been that of Shannon Suldo and others to create a typology of mental health that incorporates the traditional conceptualization of psychopathology with positive psychology concepts of SWB. Suldo and Shaffer (2008) proposed a *dual-factor model* of mental health. This model posits that psychopathology and SWB are discrete constructs that contribute different information to the child's overall functioning (see Table 29.1).

Table 29.1 Dual-factor model of mental health. Adapted with permission from Suldo & Shaffer, 2008.

Psychopathology (Traditional)	Subjective Well-Being (Positive Psychology)	
	Low Subjective Well-Being	Average to High Subjective Well-Being
Low psychopathology	Vulnerable	Complete mental health
High psychopathology	Troubled	Symptomatic but content

Suldo et al. (2011) reported that 62.2% of the students in one sample could be classified as mentally healthy, whereas 15% exhibited "high psychopathology" but still viewed their life circumstances in a positive light. Another 11.4% of these students in Suldo's study were classified as vulnerable, and another 11.4% as troubled. Although vulnerable students reported low levels of psychopathology, they also expressed low levels of SWB, whereas troubled students had high levels in both domains. Nevertheless, although almost 80% of children were free from psychopathology using this dual-factor model approach, they may also have to anticipate situational/life events that, although not clinically significant or diagnosable, hinder their overall life satisfaction.

Professionals should strive for a complete and thorough view of their clients' current state. Having a good understanding of symptoms, strengths, and resources will provide clients with more complete mechanisms to facilitate change (Lopez et al., 2006). However, youths and adults may not have enough symptoms to warrant a diagnosis, even though they experience specific environmental, familial, and individual stressors that would influence their mental health.

For example, children go through school having to cope with academic challenges in addition to developmental stages and life events that are, in turn, mediated by individual characteristics. The U.S. Centers for Disease Control and Prevention indicate that, for 2009, 3.4 people per 1000 total population reported a marriage ending in divorce, affecting countless families and children (U.S. Centers for Disease Control and Prevention, 2010). For the same year, the Department of Health and Human Services reported that approximately 10% of children suffered either abuse or neglect (Department of Health and Human Services, 2010, p. 34). Furthermore, the National Institute of Mental Health reported that suicide was the third leading cause of death among 15- to 24-year-olds in 2007. For every completed suicide in this age group, 11 nonfatal attempts occurred (U.S. Department of Health and Human Services, National Institute of Health, National Institute of Mental Health, 2010). Reports of bullying continue to increase, and families with military obligations have added more stress to our youth's psychological, social, academic, and emotional well-being.

Subjective well-being and life satisfaction (or the lack thereof) have been associated with physical health (Diener & Chan, 2011) and suicide among youth (Valois, Zullig, Huebner, & Wanzwer Drane, 2004). Gilman and Huebner (2006) mention

that youth reporting high global satisfaction also reported more positive social interactions, less distress, and "higher levels of hope and a greater sense of personal control than youth reporting low global satisfaction" (p. 317). Moreover, children with low psychopathology and low SWB report lower levels of physical health than do mentally healthy youth, have lower self-concept, view school as less important for long-term goals, have reduced motivation to self-regulate behaviors necessary for learning, perform worse on reading achievement, and are absent from school more frequently (Gilman & Huebner, 2006; Suldo & Shaffer, 2008; Suldo et al. 2011).

As can be seen, the absence of psychological symptoms does not automatically indicate the presence of mental health. Children go through many changes during their school years, and their personal and developmental characteristics will strongly impact how they respond to stressors. Some may develop symptoms associated with more severe psychopathology and require prolonged and multifaceted treatments; others will need only brief and targeted interventions to function effectively. Miller and Nickerson (2007) point out that focusing only on how to resolve a child's current issues is not enough; intervention must help to enhance future expectations and harmonize and integrate the past. Subjective well-being provides a key indicator of positive development but also potentially provides a broad enabling factor that promotes and maintains optimal mental health (Park, 2004, p. 25).

It is also important to consider the influence of other factors on the experience of SWB, including temperament. Biological factors play an important role in the development of normal and atypical behavior in children and adolescents. Although many researchers believe there is an inherited biological risk for the development of externalizing and internalizing disorders (Dick, 2007; Hicks, Krueger, Iacono, McGue, & Patrick, 2004; Kendler, Jacobson, Myers, & Eaves, 2007), it is more commonly assumed that a reciprocal influence exists between one's genetic makeup and other factors, including temperament, the fit between temperament and the environment, parenting styles, the community, and other multiple related environmental factors (Carey, 1998; Smith, Barkley, & Shapiro, 2006; Gelfand, & Drew, 2003; McMahon, Wells, & Kotler, 2006; Patterson, 2002; Patterson, Reid, & Dishion, 1992).

Temperament, defined by Chess and Thomas (1984) as a repertoire of traits possessed by each child, determines how a child interacts with his or her environment. Nine dimensions of temperament lead to three temperament subtypes: children who are "easy," "slow-to-warm," and "difficult." The differing categories of temperament in children help us to understand one element of SWB as it pertains to children's relative level of adaptability in that, beginning in infancy, different styles of relating occur. Forty percent of infants and toddlers fall into the "easy" category. They adapt well, are friendly, have a pleasant mood, accept frustration, and maintain regular cycles (sleeping/eating/eliminating) of behavior. The "slow to warm" children comprise another 15% in the temperament typology. These children adapt over time to changes in their environment or to new persons, and they may have mildly fluctuating cycles. Another 10% are identified as "difficult," reacting poorly to change, crying more frequently, and appearing more irregular in their sleeping/eating/eliminating patterns. *Emotional reactivity* (a component of temperament) clearly emerges early in life and is believed to be stable over time (Diener, Lucas, & Scollon, 2006). Diener and others have referred to the existence of a "set point" for SWB that establishes a well-being "floor" or starting point. This set point is associated with individual temperament factors and accounts for a "predisposition" to factors associated with SWB and, ultimately, mental health. Related factors contributing to SWB include the presence of adaptive attribution styles and a more internal locus of control, which are directly affected by temperament. Temperament is a relatively stable quality with direct implications for how a child interacts with his or her environment. For example, children who have easy temperaments are more likely to process experiences throughout their life differently compared to children with difficult temperament features.

Since the early research of Chess and Thomas (1984) and the publication of their longitudinal study of temperament in children, there has been a great deal of research regarding the influence of temperament. Temperament also appears to be an important factor in the development of normal and atypical behaviors found in internalizing and externalizing disorders of childhood (Rettew, Copeland, Stanger, & Hudziak, 2004). Although temperament has a strong genetic link (Saudino, 2005; Torgerson & Kringlen, 1978), Chess and Thomas (1984) also found a number of children changed temperament categories as they grew older. It is most likely that the fit between a child's temperament and the demands of the environment significantly influence both normal and atypical development.

Life satisfaction also functions as a moderator for individuals in general and specifically for children with emotional and behaviors disorders (Suldo & Huebner, 2004). *Moderators* address "when" or "for whom" a variable most strongly predicts or causes an outcome variable. More specifically, a moderator is a variable that alters the direction or strength of the relation between a predictor and an outcome (Holmbeck, 1997). Positive levels of life satisfaction act as a protective asset, buffering psychopathology development during stressful life events. Encouraging human strengths such as optimism, emotional regulation, and effective coping style can be used to prevent mental illness, which is more effective than focusing on an individual's deficits during remedial methods (Seligman & Csikszentmihályi, 2000). Suldo and Huebner (2004) found that adolescents with low life satisfaction were at risk for developing problem behaviors. The authors report that life satisfaction interacted with stressful life events to predict consequent increases in externalizing but not internalizing problems.

Whereas moderators address "when" or "for whom" a predictor is more strongly related to an outcome, *mediators* establish "how" or "why" one variable predicts or causes an outcome variable. More specifically, a mediator is defined as a variable that explains the relation between a predictor and an outcome (Holmbeck, 1997). Life satisfaction can also function as a mediator for children with emotional and behavioral disorders, showing a concurrent relationship to coexisting psychopathology (Suldo & Huebner, 2004). For example, life satisfaction has been inversely correlated with internalizing behaviors such as anxiety, depression, and low self-esteem (Huebner, Gilman, & Suldo, 2007). These problem behaviors can easily go undetected until more obvious negative consequences result, such as poor academic functioning or social withdrawal. Assessment of SWB provides a more comprehensive view of the child, thus enhancing intervention planning and implementation (Huebner et al., 2007).

Although the positive psychology movement is not offered as a panacea for the treatment of psychological disorders, proponents encourage the incorporation of a strengths-based approach along with existing efficacious treatment methods. The goal of effective interventions would then shift from a sole focus on alleviating symptoms and addressing the behavioral excesses and deficits typically associated with children exhibiting emotional and behavioral difficulties to one that builds on strengths and promotes a sense of well-being and other healthy psychological qualities.

Elements such as gratitude, forgiveness, hope, and optimism have been shown to correlate with both mental health and happiness (Seligman, 2002). The relationship between stressful life events and adolescent risk behavior, such as suicide, substance use, and sexual risk taking, has been well documented (Suldo, Shaunessy, & Hardesty, 2008). Teaching children and adolescents to identify and implement the aforementioned elements of positive psychology can aid in buffering against the negative effects of stressful, impoverished, and adverse conditions eminent to some major life events. External stress has also been linked to negative pathology, such as anxiety, depression, and aggression, as well as to academic underachievement and decreased life satisfaction. External stress consists of normative stressors, such as school transitions and academic demands, along with non-normative stressful life events, such as divorce and deaths. Suldo et al. (2008) found that the negative effects of stress on life satisfaction were heightened for adolescents who experienced fewer positive appraisal behaviors.

Given the relatively recent interest in translating principles of positive psychology into clinical practice, specific applications with children and adolescents are somewhat limited. Research has focused on how SWB can be facilitated in normal and at-risk children with mixed results (Gillham, Brunwasser, & Frères, 2007; Gillham, Hamilton, Frères, Patton, & Gallop, 2006; Seligman, Ernst, Gillham, Reivich, & Linkins, 2009; Suldo, Savage, & Mercer, 2012). For example, the Penn Resiliency Program (PRP) attempts to increase student capacity to manage issues occurring during adolescence by teaching and practicing a variety of coping strategies (Seligman, 2011). Although results are generally quite positive and have established that teaching skills contained in the program reduce and prevent symptoms of depression, reviews using limited data (e.g., Brunwasser, Gillham, & Kim, 2009) from other aspects of the same project showed no evidence that PRP is superior to active control conditions. Preliminary analyses also suggested that PRP's effects on depressive disorders may be smaller than those reported in a larger meta-analysis of depression prevention programs for older adolescents and adults.

Suldo and Michalowski (2007) provided specific procedures to implement an SWB intervention program for general sixth-grade students that included an array of positive psychology interventions (gratitude visits, acts of kindness, use of signature strengths, optimistic thinking, etc.) as part of an overall focus on wellness and prevention. Evaluation of the program with a sample of middle school students with suboptimal levels of SWB indicates improvements in overall life satisfaction, whereas levels of SWB in a wait-list control group declined during the first semester of middle school (Suldo, Savage, & Mercer, 2012).

Although these studies are very promising, more specific and sustained applications for children with emotional and behavioral disorders have yet to be identified. In the next section, we review current and potentially promising developments across internalizing and externalizing disorders that support or address goals imbedded in positive psychology.

Internalizing and Externalizing Disorders and Positive Psychology

The current focus on positive psychology encourages a shift in how we view the psychological treatment of children from one that simply embraces the goal of an absence of pathology to one that embraces a wellness perspective. This applies to the treatment of children and adolescents with internalizing and externalizing disorders as well. Proponents of positive psychology argue that families of children with mental health issues, such as internalizing disorders, do not simply want their children to experience a reduction in symptoms (often used as the measure of an intervention's success), but yearn for the same outcomes of any family—that their children function adaptively as thriving and successful individuals (Beaver, 2008). Proponents of positive psychology encourage incorporating a strengths-based approach into existing evidence-based treatment methods. The goal of effective interventions would then expand from alleviating symptoms to identifying and capitalizing on children's strengths to promote enhanced well-being. For example, strengthening optimism and hope has been shown to serve as a protective factor against depression (Seligman, 2002).

Internalizing Disorders

Depression and anxiety are two of the most common psychological disorders seen among children and adolescents (Weisz, Jensen-Doss, & Hawley, 2005). Both depression and anxiety are broad diagnostic classifications that encompass diagnostic subcategories, all of which are subsumed in the broader category of *internalizing disorders*, meaning that the symptoms are primarily internal or within the individual rather than external or readily observable by others. Most children experience some sadness or worries in the course of their development, but those children who meet diagnostic criteria for one of the classifications of depression or anxiety experience numerous or severe symptoms over a prolonged period of time, and those symptoms have persisted to the point of interfering with expected functioning in the home, school, or community environments.

Internalizing disorders encompass a wide variety of anxiety and mood disorders. Diagnostic categories of depression among youth include major depressive disorder, bipolar disorder, dysthymic disorder, and adjustment disorder (Gueldner & Merrell, 2011). The symptoms of depression vary, but often include depressed mood, feelings of despair, low affect, lack of interest in previously enjoyable activities, sleep disturbance, loss of appetite, irritability, and difficulty concentrating (Merrell, 2008). There also are several diagnostic categories of anxiety for youth including generalized anxiety disorder, social anxiety disorder, separation anxiety disorder, social phobia, obsessive-compulsive disorder, and selective mutism. Feelings of fear, dread, or discomfort; heightened physiological arousal; somatic complaints; and social withdrawal are common symptoms of anxiety (Merrell, 2008). To complicate matters, anxiety symptoms frequently occur along with symptoms of depression (Angold, Costello, & Erkanli, 1999), and anxiety may be considered a risk factor for developing depression later in childhood or adulthood (Flannery-Schroeder, 2006). Furthermore, anxiety and depression can occur concurrently and sequentially, and both tend to cluster in families (Garber & Weersing, 2010).

Approximately 15–20% of children in the United States meet diagnostic criteria for anxiety disorder (Beesdo, Knappe, & Pine, 2009). Rates are somewhat lower for the prevalence of youth meeting diagnostic criteria for depressive disorders, with estimates of 2% of school-aged children and 8% of adolescents, and higher rates in female adolescents (Son & Kirchner, 2000). Rates of comorbidity have been estimated to be as high as 41% in clinical samples (Kovacs, Gatsonis, Paulauskas, & Richards, 1989).

The three most prevalent anxiety disorders in children and adolescents include separation anxiety disorder, generalized anxiety disorder, and social phobia (Kessler, Chui, Demler, & Walters, 2005). Children with anxiety often experience difficulties with social relationships (Verduin & Kendall, 2008) and functioning in school (Mychailyszyn, Mendez, & Kendall, 2010); as such, because of their heightened levels of anxiety in these kinds of situations, these children may tend to avoid social interactions

whenever possible, thus putting them at even greater risk for social development difficulties. Anxiety disorders may first become apparent in school settings since the ecology of school involves separating from one's parents, multiple social interaction opportunities with peers and adults, and ongoing academic evaluations (Mychailyszyn et al., 2011).

VIEWING INTERNALIZING DISORDERS THROUGH POSITIVE PSYCHOLOGY

Internalizing disorders such as anxiety and depression negatively impact a child's functioning at home, school, and with peers (Langley, Bergman, McCracken, & Piacentini, 2004), thus impairing interpersonal relationships and academic performance (Gould et al., 1998). Comorbid anxiety and depression result in even poorer prognostic outcomes. Internalizing disorders, particularly anxiety disorders, have been linked to substance use disorders, with comorbidity rates as high as 26% among a population of adolescents seeking substance abuse treatment (Deas-Nesmith, Brady, & Campbell, 1998). Children who experience anxiety or depression are also at significantly higher risk for anxiety or depressive disorders in adulthood (Pine, Cohen, Gurley, Brooks, & Ma, 1998). Additionally, youth who are depressed have an increased risk of suicide. Rates of suicide have been increasing since 2003, with suicide being the third leading cause of death for adolescents and young adults (U.S. Centers for Disease Control, 2007).

Approximately 26% of school-aged children have a diagnosable emotional or behavioral disorder that negatively impacts their school performance and requires mental health treatment (Costello, Egger, & Angold, 2005); however, it is estimated that up to 80% of these children do not receive the necessary services (U.S. Department of Health and Human Services, 1999). Unfortunately, youth with internalizing symptoms are often under-identified because of the internal nature of symptom expression, and they are underserved in terms of receiving mental health services, whether through school or community resources (e.g., Bird, Gould, & Staghezza, 1992). It is possible that a larger number of youth could access services if a more positive, preventive approach to treatment was utilized and implemented in a community or school environment to which all children have access.

Based on the principles of positive psychology, it is important to consider factors that contribute to the overall psychological well-being of children and adolescents who exhibit internalizing behaviors, rather than simply focusing on the behavioral deficits they exhibit. The construct of *resilience* can be viewed within a positive psychology framework in that resiliency or protective factors can serve to buffer a child from the potential negative effects of adversity that may place him or her at risk for poor outcomes (Esquivel, Doll, & Oades-Sese, 2011). For example, perceived life satisfaction was found to have a mediating effect between stressful events and internalizing behaviors, perhaps buffering the effects of stressful events for these individuals (McKnight, Huebner, & Suldo, 2002). A related assumption of the positive psychology model is that all individuals have strengths and assets that can be enhanced (Epstein et al., 2003), which applies to youth with internalizing disorders, as well as to youth at risk for anxiety and depressive symptoms. By including outcomes that enhance the well-being of children and adolescents as an expectation of service delivery, it is possible that youths with internalizing disorders could achieve higher functioning levels than they may attain with traditional intervention methods focusing on amelioration of already established behavioral symptoms.

Within the U.S. education system, the current focus on a tiered system of service delivery in schools inherent in the Response to Intervention (RTI) model could be adapted to incorporate some of the principles of positive psychology (Froh, Huebner, Yousef, & Conte, 2010) as they relate to preventing internalizing disorders. It is possible to utilize universal screening methods to assess for strengths among student populations in order to design and implement targeted interventions that could further enhance these strengths or serve to identify students who could benefit from specific skill training to acquire additional protective factors. Similar to academic interventions in which academic skills are specifically taught, social and emotional instructional programs have been developed that specifically teach social and emotional skills. Interventions that target social and emotional learning can serve to reduce problems of an emotional or behavioral nature and, ultimately, have a positive impact on academic performance (Greenberg et al., 2003). The experience of positive emotions "broaden people's momentary thought-action repertoires, which in turn serves to build their enduring personal resources, ranging from physical and intellectual resources to social and psychological resources" (Fredrickson, 2001, p. 218).

EVIDENCE-BASED TREATMENT OF INTERNALIZING DISORDERS

Cognitive-behavioral therapy (CBT) is one of the most common types of intervention used for the treatment of internalizing disorders in both school and clinical settings. Several meta-analyses have demonstrated the effectiveness of CBT in the treatment of anxiety (e.g., Silverman, Pina, & Viswesvaran, 2008) and depression (e.g., Klein, Jacobs, & Reinecke, 2007). Compton, Burns, Egger, and Robertson (2002) conducted a review of treatments for children with internalizing disorders with similar findings as these meta-analyses, although there was considerable more empirical support for effective treatments for anxiety disorders than for depressive disorders.

One well-researched, empirically validated intervention for the treatment of anxiety in children is the Coping Cat program (Kendall & Hedtke, 2006). Coping Cat is a cognitive-behavioral treatment for children aged 7–13 who have generalized anxiety disorder, separation anxiety disorder, or social phobia. Coping Cat includes 16–18 scripted 1-hour sessions focusing on skill training in awareness using the acronym FEAR to represent the strategies for feeling frightened (recognizing physical symptoms), expecting negative outcomes (recognition of cognitive distortions), attitudes and actions (coping self-talk), and results and rewards (self evaluation and reward). Clarke et al. summarized the empirical support for this intervention and classified it as "efficacious" using the system delineated by Chambless and Hollon (1998) to classify the relative efficacy of interventions. Similarly, the Coping with Depression Course for Adolescents (CWD-A; Clarke, Lewinsohn, & Hops, 1990) is an empirically validated intervention for the treatment of depression among youth. The CWD-A was rated as "probably efficacious" by Clarke et al. The CWD-A is a cognitive-behavioral intervention focusing on skill training in the areas of relaxation, reframing of thoughts, and social skills. The CWD-A course utilizes a cognitive-behavioral framework in a group format across sixteen 2-hour sessions. Although both of these intervention programs have strong research support, in their review, Compton et al. (2002) also highlighted the fact that most of the empirical investigations of treatments targeting depression and anxiety found evidence of symptom reduction, but with little or no attention paid to outcome variables designed to measure increases in adaptive functioning for participants.

INCORPORATING POSITIVE PSYCHOLOGY IN EVIDENCE-BASED INTERVENTIONS FOR INTERNALIZING DISORDERS

Several intervention programs for the treatment of internalizing disorders incorporate aspects of the positive psychology model. One program designed for children aged 9–13 with depression, the Taking ACTION Treatment Program (Stark & Kendall, 1996), includes a component to help these youth to develop a self-concept that is more positive and stay better focused on positive events occurring in their day-to-day lives (Stark et al., 2006). Similarly, the intervention program FRIENDS (Barrett, Lowry-Webster, & Turner, 2000) is designed to treat generalized anxiety disorder, separation anxiety disorder, and social phobia in children aged 6–16 (two parallel forms for 6–11 and 12–16) using a cognitive-behavioral approach in a group format similar to that of Coping Cat. The FRIENDS acronym is designed to help children remember useful strategies (F = feeling worried; R = relax and feel good; I = inner thoughts; E = explore plans; N = nice work, reward yourself; D = don't forget to practice; S = stay calm). A total of 10 weekly sessions and two booster sessions make up the program. FRIENDS differs from the Coping Cat intervention program in that it also includes a parent training component on skills of cognitive restructuring, providing support, and giving reinforcement that total 6 hours. FRIENDS also is applicable as a preventive intervention for children who are not demonstrating anxious behaviors. Several research studies have demonstrated the effectiveness of this intervention in lowering anxiety symptoms (e.g., Shortt, Barrett, & Fox, 2001).

Durlak and Wells (1997) conducted a meta-analysis demonstrating that preventive mental health interventions can successfully reduce both internalizing and externalizing behaviors, as well as improve competencies such as self-confidence. Greenberg et al. (2001) made similar conclusions in their meta-analysis, identifying 14 effective prevention programs that were school-based and met rigorous evaluative criteria. The series of Strong Kids programs is one such preventive curriculum for children with internalizing symptoms.

Strong Kids is a series of social and emotional learning programs designed to target internalizing problems through prevention and early intervention and to enhance social and emotional competence (Merrell, Juskelis, Tran, & Buchanan, 2008). The different programs target different age groups; Strong Start (Merrell, Parisi, & Whitcomb, 2007) is appropriate for children in kindergarten through second grade, Strong Kids (Merrell, Carrizales, Feuerborn, Gueldner, & Tran, 2007a,b) includes separate programs for third through fifth grade and sixth through eighth grade, and Strong Teens (Merrell, Carrizales, et al., 2007c) is for high school

students (ninth through twelfth grades). Each of the programs is comprised of 10 to 12 scripted lessons lasting less than 1-hour each. The Strong Kids programs are designed to be used class-wide or in small groups. Both cognitive-behavioral and affective education techniques are utilized (Merrell et al., 2008). Initial studies have demonstrated the effectiveness of the Strong Kids programs in reducing self-reported internalizing symptoms and increasing social-emotional competence (Harlacher & Merrell, 2010; Kramer, Caldarella, Christensen, & Shatzer, 2010; Marchant, Brown, Caldarella, & Young, 2010; Merrell et al., 2008).

Prevention programs that specifically target internalizing behaviors are limited and currently have a limited base of empirical support (Oswald & Mazefsky, 2006). However, some of these programs, like the Strong Kids series, show promise in effectively adopting a positive psychology approach to treatment to effect better outcomes for youth. The link between social-emotional competence and school success has been well documented (Payton et al., 2008). It is imperative that aspects of competence be incorporated into efficacious interventions to treat a wide array of issues impacting youth today, such as internalizing symptoms. Although it is difficult to predict which children will respond best to which intervention program, future research should be able to determine if some interventions with demonstrated effectiveness may have more powerful effects when positive psychology components are included. Similarly, the future of preventive mental health programs shows promise in potentially enhancing resiliency through the development of skills that can serve as protective factors when stressors are encountered, thereby minimizing the prevalence of internalizing disorders in youth.

Externalizing Disorders

The research literature is quite limited in delineating the relationship between positive psychology as it is currently practiced and youth with externalizing disorders. We have, in fact, described the relationship of positive psychology and externalizing youth as wallowing in a vast "sea of negativity" (Jenson et al., 2004; Olympia et al, 2004). Externalizing disorders describe those children and adolescents who exhibit behaviors that negatively affect other persons (i.e., peers, parents, and other adults) (as reviewed by Jenson et al., 2011). These externally directed behaviors commonly include behavior excesses such as noncompliance, arguing, aggression, rule breaking, and impulsive behaviors.

This is in contrast to children and adolescents referred to as *internalizers* (addressed in the previous section) or to those who inwardly direct their problematic behaviors to themselves, including those with somatic complaints, fears, anxieties, and phobic behaviors.

Common educational and clinical labels associated with externalizing disorders among children include severe emotional disturbance, behavior disorders, disruptive disorders, oppositional defiant disorder, conduct disorder, and attention-deficit hyperactivity disorder (ADHD). These children have also been referred to as *socially maladjusted* in federal legislation such as IDEA-2004 and denied special education services unless they can also be shown to be seriously emotionally disturbed (Jenson et al., 2004). Denying special education services to a child labeled as socially maladjusted is mistakenly based on an impression that these children are not truly disabled but rather act willfully and by choice to violate societal norms and rules (Jenson et al., 2006) . Although research (Costenbader & Buntaine, 1999) does not support this artificial distinction between seriously emotionally disturbed and social maladjustment, it is commonly used to deny special services to these students and thus shut one of the doors to society's most positive experiences, an education.

It is all too easy to focus on the disruptive behaviors exhibited by children with externalizing disorders because they are often annoying and sometimes frightening. Behaviors such as aggression, temper tantrums, arguing, and threats define these children and adolescents as "tough kids" (Rhode, Jenson, & Reavis, 2009). These behaviors can clearly interfere with children's happiness, resilience, and positive growth. Extreme behavioral excesses elicit punishing responses at home in the form of abuse, at school by being excluded, and in the community by often being rejected and sometimes incarcerated. The child-rearing practices of parents of externalizing children and adolescents often span the spectrum from being harsh and abusive to being neglectful and inconsistent (Burke, Loeber, & Birmaher, 2002; Patterson et al., 1992). Because of escalating "coercive" interactions between parents and children with externalizing disorders, these children are often at high risk for both emotional and physical abuse (Medley & Sachs-Ericsson, 2009). Rodriguez and Eden (2007) have shown that as a mother's parenting ability becomes more dysfunctional, her child with behavior problems shows substantial decreases in adaptive attributional style

and positive self-concept, with increasing feelings of hopelessness.

School experiences with adults and peers are also negative for students with externalizing disorders. In general, research has shown that high rates of negative interactions between teachers and students are common in public schools. Rates of disapproval far exceed rates of approval for student behavior (Beaman & Wheldall, 2000; White, 1975). This is especially true for students exhibiting externalizing disorders (Jenson et al., 2004). Shores, Gunter, and Jack (1993) reported that teachers are far more likely to attend and react to inappropriate behaviors than to positive behaviors. The general findings from the research show that general rates of positive to negative responses to students with externalizing disorders are surprisingly low (Sutherland, Wehby, & Copeland, 2000). Contrast these findings with the several studies (e.g., Fredrickson & Losada, 2005) concerning optimal ratios of positive to negative feedback in normal contexts, also described in this article.

It is interesting to note that one of the most commonly reported behaviors exhibited by externally disordered students—lack of compliance to adult requests (Nicholas, Olympia, & Jenson, 2001)—is rarely rewarded or acknowledged when compliance does occur. The common teacher–student interaction is one in which the teacher issues a command, the student complies or does not comply, and the teacher gives feedback (Shores et al., 1993). Gunter and Shores (1994) found that teacher praise following student compliance occurs infrequently, about 0.08 times per minute. Van Acker, Grant, and Henry (1996), in a study of 206 students at moderate risk for developing aggressive behavior patterns, found that teacher praise appeared to be a random event, whereas punishment was highly predictable. In this "curriculum of noninstruction" (Gunter, Denny, Jack, Shores, & Nelson 1993), the message sent to externalizing students is that when they behave appropriately, nothing happens. However, when they misbehave, they will surely be punished. With this message, any optimism about the future will surely suffer. To utilize a framework of positive psychology with students with externalizing disorders, the rate of positive responses from adults must be increased, and the punishing message from the "curriculum of noninstruction" must be decreased.

BEYOND BEHAVIORAL EXCESSES AND DEFICITS

First impressions can shape either positive or negative psychological experiences for children and adolescents. Unfortunately, the first impressions made by externalizing disordered youth to many adults and peers are not favorable, and focus is inordinately placed on their disruptive, externalizing behaviors. Clearly, externalizing disordered children and adolescents exhibit externally oriented behaviors that negatively impact others. However, there is another, more accurate and humane conceptualization of this disorder that can better serve both these children and the society in which they live. This conceptualization is that an externalizing disorder is a composite of both behavioral excess and deficits, and these behaviors are developmental in nature (Gelfand & Drew, 2003; Jenson et al., 2011; Rhode et al., 2009).

We have already reviewed many of the behavioral excesses associated with externalizing disorders including aggression, noncompliance, arguing, temper tantrums, rule breaking, being off-task in classroom settings, and being generally disruptive. It should be noted that none of these behaviors by itself is singularly abnormal or deviant. All children exhibit some of these behaviors to some extent during childhood. It is rather a function of intensity and excess that helps define these behaviors as deviant. If they are taken to excess and expressed with intensity, they can often lead to more deviant behaviors, such as bullying, revenge seeking, property vandalism, or cruelty to animals. There is also a developmentally based aspect to behavioral excess as the child ages. When a child is young, behavioral excess may be more overt and easily identified and observed, such as temper tantrums and severe noncompliance. As the child ages and enters adulthood, these behavioral excesses transform into more covert behaviors that are not as easily observed (Frick et al. 1993). These covert behaviors may take the form of substance abuse, running away, fire setting, animal cruelty, truancy, and theft. Both overt and covert forms of behavioral excesses are important to manage with evidence-based interventions because they disrupt positive interactions with others, preclude opportunities that lead to psychological growth, and stifle the development of adaptive academic and social skills. In addition, the research is clear that individuals who engage in these behaviors are often depressed and may be suicidal (Hills, Cox, McWilliams, & Sareen, 2005; Verona, Sach-Ericsson, & Joiner, 2004). Repeated negative interactions with others and failures because of behavioral excess can often lead to lack of optimism about the future and feelings of hopelessness.

Overt behavioral excesses may be the tip of the observable iceberg for externalizing disorders.

However, it is what is below the psychological waterline that may be most debilitating for the positive adjustment and happiness of externalizing children and adolescents. Here lie the behavioral deficits that are commonly associated with this disorder—a lack of rule-governed behavior or self-management skills, poor academic skills, and inadequate social skills (Rhode et al., 2009). These behavioral deficits close many doors to academic, social, and employment opportunities and can negatively impact overall SWB.

Externalizing youth who exhibit behavioral excess are more likely to be rejected and disliked by peers and develop negative social reputations as being noncooperative, aggressive, and often engaging in bullying (Coie & Kupersmidt, 1983; Dishion, 1990; Snyder, 2002). By exhibiting behavioral excess toward peers, externalizing youth often do not develop more sophisticated social skills in dealing with conflict, competition, and social problem solving. By being excluded, these children do not develop supportive friendships and adaptive social networking skills. Rejection by a normal peer group often leads externalizing children to seek other externalizing youth. They often form social affiliations with other externalizing children and adolescents, which adds to their social isolation and often leads to socially deviant peer relations. Simply hanging around in groups with other externalizing youth can foster antisocial behavior (Arnold & Hughes, 1999; Dishion, McCord, & Poulin, 1999). Research has shown that when externalizing youth associate with each other, they learn more antisocial behaviors. Associating with other externalizing youth is a sort of "deviancy training" in antisocial behavior. Externalizing youth need effective social skills training that allows them to form meaningful social relations with nondeviant peers.

Academic problems are commonly associated with externalizing youth with emotional problems (Hinshaw, 1992; Lane, Gresham, & O'Shaughnessy, 2002). These children exhibit academic deficits in several areas, such as poor reading ability; they are frequently off-task in the classroom; they have poor study and organizational skills; they have high drop-out rates; and they are commonly retained (Gelfand & Drew, 2003; Hinshaw, 1992; Walker, Ramsey, & Gresham, 2004). Patterson, DeBaryshe, and Ramsey (1989) have indicated that the externalizing student's behavior excesses, such as arguing and noncompliance, are major contributors to academic failure. Successful school adjustment is linked to academic ability and performance, especially reading ability. However, externalizing students are at particular risk when their reading ability is low and they receive the constant message—grade level to grade level—that they are academic failures (Morgan & Jenson, 1988; Walker et al., 2004). Academic deficits directly affect the immediate positive adjustment and life satisfaction of externalizing students in school. However, they also affect the long-term positive future prospects of externalizing students (Barbaresi, Katusic, Colligan, Weaver, & Jacobsen, 2007; Galera, Melchior, Chastang, Bouvard, & Fombonne, 2009). If an externalizing youth has academic deficits, especially in reading, his or her future prospects for positive adult adjustment and gainful employment are severely limited in our technologically oriented society.

Many existing interventions for children with externalizing disorders can be viewed as necessary precursors that can potentially set the stage for further implementation of specific positive psychology interventions. Given that externalizing youth have many adjustment difficulties within their families, school environments, and the community, the predominant conceptualizations of interventions have focused on symptom reduction and skill acquisition. Several evidence-based interventions have been demonstrated to make positive differences in the lives of externalizing children and youth. These interventions include working with families and training parents in effective techniques to reduce coercive interactions with their children. These are positive supervision interventions that can dramatically reduce the problems that externalizing youth have with school and community environments. There are also social skills programs that are designed to enhance the friendships and extend the appropriate social networks of externalizing youth. Although the interventions described in this section are effective, they have not been developed specifically to reflect components of positive psychology theory.

PARENT TRAINING FOR FAMILIES WITH EXTERNALIZING YOUTH

The prevention and positive management of early or sustained misbehaviors represent another potential intervention consistent with goals of positive psychology. Several behavioral parenting programs are also known as parent management training (Patterson, Reid, Jones, & Conger, 1975), behavioral family therapy (Griest & Wells, 1983), and parent-interaction therapy (Bell & Eyberg, 2002). The preventative strategies found in many of these programs are very consistent with principles of positive psychology. The basic approach used in these programs is to teach parents effective and positive behavior management techniques for their externalizing children. Some of these programs train parents without the child being present and utilize homework assignments to reach the child (Jenson, Rhode, & Hepworth-Neville, 2010); others train the parents under controlled conditions with the child being present (Forehand & McMahon, 2003). Both types of programs generally involve teaching parents to specifically define and pinpoint target behaviors to be modified, focus on positive reinforcement, increase praise statements, establish family rules, and implement motivation systems for appropriate behaviors. Parents are also taught to give effective commands and use reductive techniques, such as response cost and timeouts, to break the negative child–parent coercive cycle (Maughan, 2004).

These types of parent training programs have been shown to work in two extensive meta-analytic studies. Serketch and Dumas (1996) analyzed 26 behavioral parent training studies for externalizing youth with such behaviors as aggression, temper tantrums, and severe noncompliance. This study excluded children with ADHD. The overall effect sizes from this meta-analysis for reducing externalizing behaviors were large (i.e., parent report 0.84, independent observer of behaviors 0.85, and teacher report 0.74). These large effect sizes, when interpreted as the magnitude of treatment effectiveness, showed an 80% positive improvement in the child's behavior. In a second meta-analytic study, Maughan, Christensen, Jenson, Olympia, and Clark (2005) analyzed 79 parent training studies of externalizing youth that included children with ADHD; this study showed similarly large effective sizes in reducing behavior excesses, such as noncompliance, and improving positive family interactions, such as positive praise and reductions in stress (Kuhn, 2004; Maughan et al., 2005). Several evidence-based parent training programs are available and include Families: Applications of Social Learning to Family Life (Patterson, 1971), Helping the Noncompliant Child (Forehand & McMahon, 2003), the Incredible Years Parent Program (Webster-Stratton, 2000), Your Defiant Child: Eight Steps to Better Behavior (Barkley, 1998), the Kazdin Method for Parenting the Defiant Child: No Pills, No Therapy, No Contest of Wills (Kazdin, 2008), and the Tough Kid Parent Book: Practical Solutions to Tough Childhood Problems (Jenson et al., 2010).

POSITIVE SUPERVISION AND MONITORING INTERVENTIONS

The research is clear that when externalizing students are inadequately supervised and poorly monitored, they have difficulties in school and the community (as reviewed Jenson et al., 2011). One of the highest at-risk times is immediately after school (Pettit, Laird, Dodge, & Bates, 1997). Externalizing youth often lack the self-management skills and rule-governed capabilities to avoid at-risk opportunities and other antisocial youth. Several well-researched, structured supervision programs incorporate positive components and are effective in monitoring externalizing youth's high-risk school and community behaviors.

One such monitoring program, Check and Connect, has been developed at the University of Minnesota (Anderson, Christenson, Sinclair, & Lehr, 2004). It has two basic components. The Check component is a continuous assessment of a student's progress in school, such as attendance, grades, disciplinary problems, suspensions, and credits toward graduation. In essence, a designated adult (i.e., mentor) is continuously monitoring an externalizing student's school progress and is immediately made aware of problematic issues before they can manifest themselves into severe problems with crisis implications.

The Connect component of the program is a regular meeting with a supportive adult who provides advocacy, support, and training to the student. During the Connect meeting, the mentor provides academic support (homework assistance, tutoring, study skills instruction), social skills training, recreational activities, and community service opportunities. An important aspect of the Check and Connect program is that the mentor also acts as the externalizing student's advocate with other school personnel and community contacts. The Check and Connect program has been extensively researched and has been recognized by the U.S. Office of Education What Works Clearing House (2006) as improving student's behavior, reducing school dropouts, and helping students make meaningful academic progress.

A similar evidence-based supervision and monitoring program is the Behavior Education Program (BEP) developed at the University of Oregon (Crone, Horner, & Hawken, 2004). The BEP is a daily check-in and check-out program that uses an adult school staff member who monitors the at-risk student's progress. This program has been designed for students with externalizing problem behaviors such

as noncompliance, disruptive behavior, inappropriate language, and classroom talk-outs resulting in three to five discipline referrals in one academic year.

In the BEP program, a student checks in with a positive, supportive adult at the beginning of the school day and checks-out again at the end of the day. The program emphasizes that the supervising adult is supportive, positive, and someone the student trusts. The student develops a BEP contract with the supervising adult that lists a series of problem behaviors that will be tracked and monitored across the day. When developing the contract, the student negotiates a list of rewards that he or she can earn for making improvements with this list of behaviors. During the day, the student carries a Daily Progress Report (DPR) card with the list of behaviors (e.g., following directions, completing academic work, being prepared, classroom rule following, etc.); this card is filled out by teachers and other educational personnel. At the end of the day, the student's DPR card is reviewed by the supervising adult, and he or she is given feedback and his or her progress is graphed. Points are earned for appropriate behavior, and the supervising adult emphasizes the positive progress the student has made. The BEP program has been shown to be effective in reducing problem behaviors (50% reductions in discipline office referrals) while being viewed positively by the externalizing student (Fairbanks, Sugai, Guardino, & Lathrop, 2005; Hawken, MacLeod, & Rawlings, 2007).

SOCIAL SKILLS TRAINING FOR EXTERNALIZING YOUTH

Social skills deficits are a defining characteristic of externalizing youth that commonly lead to exclusion and being shunned by peers (Gresham, 1998; Patterson et al., 1992). Without age-appropriate social skills, externalizing children cannot develop suitable and supportive social networks with positive peers. These peers often see externalizing children as more socially inept, uncooperative, aggressive, and socially controlling. These social problems may be a function of externalizing children not knowing how to perform essential social skills (i.e., deficit) or performance problems (i.e., knowing how to perform the skills but not doing so) (Gresham, 1986; Gresham, Sugai, & Horner, 2001). The social skills deficits can result from inadequate modeling and instruction at an early age or from having the development of important social skills thwarted by the child's own behavioral excesses (Patterson et al., 1992). Performance problems can be a function of anxiety in performing the skill, negative reactions from peers, or the inability to generalize the skill from the social skills training environment to a more naturalistic social environment.

There are many different types of social skills training programs for externalizing children and adolescents. Most of these programs focus on foundation social skills (i.e., facing the other person, making eye contact, standing about 3 feet from the other person), starting conversations, making friends, handling difficult social interactions (i.e., teasing, bullying), and problem-solving skills. The general instruction model for social skills training includes a rationale for using the social skill, task analysis that teaches the steps involved in the skill, demonstration of the skill through modeling, role-playing the skill, and coaching the skill (Walker, Ramsey, & Gresham, 2004). Some programs include behavior management strategies for running social skills training groups, homework assignments, and generalization techniques to move the social skills from the training environment to natural social settings.

The general research results are mixed on the effectiveness of many social skills training programs for externalizing youth. A number of meta-analytic studies on the effectiveness of social skills training have shown limited support (Forness & Kavale, 1996; Quinn, Kavale, Mathur, Rutherford, & Forness, 1999). It seems that externalizing youth can learn the skills but often fail to use them in more naturalistic social environments. DuPaul and Eckert (1994) refer to this ability to learn the skill but not use it when needed as "now you see them and now you don't" (p. 13). Other meta-analytic studies on externalizing secondary school students have reported more promising but limited results (Cook et al, 2008). It appears that generalization techniques must be an integral part of the social skills program before these students will generalize learned skills to more naturalistic environments. One such program, the Superheroes Social Skills Program (Jenson et al., 2011), has shown that social skills training can be taught to externalizing children who then use these skills in nontraining environment, such as during recess (Hood, 2011). However, the generalization techniques must be part of the very fabric of the social skills training program and start with the first training session.

Several social skills program have been demonstrated to be effective with externalizing youth and also include active generalization components. The Incredible Years Program Parents, Teachers, and Children (http://www.incredibleyears.com) is one such effective program. This program has an extensive curriculum (Dino Dinosaurs) that includes video modeling tapes, behavior management, and dinosaur puppets for the instruction of toddlers through elementary school-aged externalizing students. Generalization by the students is enhanced by high-interest media (video models and puppets) and the training of other significant adults (i.e., teachers and parents). The Dino Dinosaurs program has been extensively researched and found effective in significantly reducing aggression in school and at home (Webster-Stratton & Reid, 2003).

Another program that has been found effective with externalizing youth is Problem-Solving Skills Training (PSST) (Kazdin, 2003). This program focuses on teaching social problem-solving skills for real-life situations. The model is based on an information-processing model that includes identifying a social problem, making a decision on how to solve it, and then evaluating its outcome. The PSST program also includes a parent training component that enhances generalization to the home and planned activities outside of the social skills training environment (called "super solvers") for practice and generalization of the skills. The PSST program has been compared to more traditional supportive therapy and client-centered therapy and has been shown to be more effective than both of these commonly used therapies (Kazdin Bass, Siegel, & Thomas, 1989; Kazdin, Esveldt-Dawson, French, & Unis, 1987). These studies have also found the social skills are generalized to nontreatment settings and maintained 1-year after treatment.

Life is not positive for many externalizing children and youth. The behavioral excesses of arguing, aggression, noncompliance, temper tantrums, and impulsive disruptive behavior often lead to negative life experiences. Because their behavioral excesses are so prominent, their behavior deficits in self-management, academic ability, and social skills are often ignored or overlooked. Positive interventions that cut across home, school, and community environments are needed for externalizing youth. Interventions such as behavioral parent training, supervision-monitoring programs, and social skills training can make the immediate and long-term adjustment of externalizing youth far more adaptive and positive. What is severely lacking is more definitive positive psychology research on those factors that contribute significantly to the adjustment and outcome for externalizing youth.

Conclusion

We have established some of the general components of positive psychology and also determined the evidence base for practices consistent with positive psychology in meeting the needs of children with internalizing and externalizing behavior disorders. However, it is not entirely clear if the field is merely engaging in more wishful thinking than substance without additional research, particularly as it applies to children. Recent work by McNulty and Fincham (2012) suggests that a more cautious and nuanced interpretation of the presumed benefits of practices or treatments associated with positive psychology is warranted. Indeed, they raise important questions about the relationship of various positive psychological traits, processes, and benefits flowing from interventions designed to enhance SWB and general psychological functioning. The impact of context or the "environmental receptivity" on both the expression and usefulness of particular subjective experiences or objective outcomes associated with gratitude, flow, and other components of SWB has not been completely addressed. Additionally, these researchers cite several examples in which the same traits may both threaten or promote improved psychological functioning. The experience of success for children with emotional and behavioral disorders, including positive emotional responses created by many of the evidence-based interventions cited here, can clearly be a primary source of SWB (Seligman & Csikszentmihályi, 2000). More research is needed to examine the impact of particular activities associated with positive psychology on psychologically healthy and unhealthy individuals, particularly children and adolescents with internalizing and externalizing behaviors.

Future Directions

Positive psychology is a quickly growing area of applied psychological knowledge that is beginning to impact work with at-risk children, including children with serious emotional disturbances. This chapter presented a brief review of several of the central tenets and theoretical bases for positive psychology, with a particular focus on temperament and other influences on individual behavior. The chapter also reviewed related issues and specific interventions intended to provide enhanced positive opportunities and outcomes for children with serious emotional disorders, including internalizing and externalizing disorders. We identified key problem areas for these distinct groups, summarizing research describing selected interventions with implications for positive psychology. Although the evidence base is substantial, research is needed in all the areas delineated, and important questions

regarding the value of specific practices with children remain: For example, which children/adolescents would receive the most benefit from the procedures, and where might opportunities occur to misuse or misapply the procedures? Are some procedures associated with positive psychology best used for prevention/tier 1 activities to promote resiliency (i.e., gratitude letters, identifying flow, etc.) or better suited to those with at-risk or more debilitating levels of psychopathology? Although results from initial studies conducted with adults have been promising (Seligman et al., 2005), there is a need to extend such work to child and adolescent populations (Seligman et al., 2009). In the meantime, school psychologists and others may find that the procedures alluded to in this chapter can be applied to children and youth in the context of school-based interventions, as long as the limitations of these approaches are clearly understood. As well, mental health professionals may find that they too can achieve benefits (i.e., improved perceptions of SWB) from engaging in these and other practices (Miller, Nickerson, & Osborne, 2006). Emerging research suggests that many individuals who engage in the procedures described herein can potentially exhibit a greater sense of gratitude for past joys and forgiveness for past slights, live more mindfully in the present while engaging in activities they find absorbing, and demonstrate an enhanced ability to be optimistic and hopeful about the future.

References

Anderson, A. R., Christenson, S. L., Sinclair, M. F., & Lehr, C. A. (2004). Check & Connect: The importance of relationships for promoting engagement with school. Journal of School Psychology, *42*, 95–113.

Angold, A., Costello, E., & Erkanli, A. (1999). Comorbidity. *Journal of Child Psychology and Psychiatry, 40*, 57–87.

Arnold, M. E., & Hughes, J. N. (1999). First do no harm— Adverse effects of grouping deviant youth for skills training, *Journal of School Psychology, 37*, 99–115.

Barkley, R. (1998). *Your defiant child: Eight steps to better behavior.* New York: Guilford Press.

Barrett, P., Lowry-Webster, H., & Turner, G. (2000). *FRIENDS program for children: Group leaders manual.* Brisbane: Australian Academic Press.

Barbaresi, W. J., Katusic, S. K., Colligan, R. C., Weaver, A. L., & Jacobsen, S. J. (2007). Long- term school outcomes for children with attention-deficit/hyperactivity disorder: A population-based perspective. *Journal of Developmental and Behavior Pediatrics, 28*, 265–273.

Beaman, R., & Wheldall, K. (2000). Teacher's use of approval and disapproval in the classroom, *Educational Psychology, 20*, 431–447.

Beaver, B. R. (2008). A positive approach to children's internalizing problems. *Professional Psychology: Research and Practice, 39*, 129–136.

Beesdo, K., Knappe, S., & Pine, D. S. (2009). Anxiety and anxiety disorders in children and adolescents: Developmental issues and implications for DSM-V. *Psychiatric Clinics of North America, 32*, 483–524.

Bell, S., & Eyberg, S.M. (2002). Parent-child interaction therapy. In L. VandeCreek, S. Knapp, & T.L. Jackson (Eds.), *Innovations in clinical practice: A source book* (vol. 20; pp. 57–74). Sarasota, FL: Professional Resource Press.

Bird, H. R., Gould, M. S., & Staghezza, B. (1992). Aggregating data from multiple informants in child psychiatry epidemiological research. *Journal of the American Academy of Child and Adolescent Psychiatry, 31*, 78–85.

Brunwasser, S. M., Gillham, J. E., & Kim, E. S. (2009). A meta-analytic review of the Penn Resiliency Program's effect on depressive symptoms, *Journal of Consulting and Clinical Psychology, 77*, 1042–1054.

Burke J. D., Loeber R., & Birmaher B. (2002). Oppositional defiant disorder and conduct disorder: A review of the past 10 years, part II. *Journal of American Academy of Child and Adolescent Psychiatry, 41*, 1275–1293.

Carey, W. B. (1998). Temperament and behavior problems in the classroom. *School Psychology Review, 27*, 551–563.

Chambless, D. L., & Hollon, S. D. (1998). Defining empirically supported therapies. *Journal of Consulting and Clinical Psychology, 66*, 7–18.

Chess, S., & Thomas, A. (1984). *Origins & evolution of behavior disorders.* New York: Brunner/Maze.

Clarke, G., Lewinsohn, P. M., & Hops, H. (1990). *Adolescent coping with depression course: Leader's manual for adolescent groups.* Portland, OR: Center for Health Research.

Coie, J.D., & Kupersmidt, J.B. (1983). A behavioral analysis of emerging social status in boys' groups. *Child Development, 54*, 1400–1416.

Cook, C. R., Gresham, F. M., Kern, L., Barreras, R. B., Thorton, S., & Crews, S. D. (2008). Social skills training for secondary students with emotional and/or behavioral disorders. *Journal of Emotional and Behavioral Disorders, 16*, 131–144.

Compton, S. N., Burns, B. J., Egger, H. L., & Robertson, E. (2002). Review of the evidence base for treatment of childhood psychopathology: Internalizing disorders. *Journal of Consulting and Clinical Psychology, 70*, 1240–1266.

Costello, E. J., Egger, H., & Angold, A. (2005). 10-year research update review: The epidemiology of child and adolescent psychiatric disorders: I. Methods and public health burden. *Journal of the American Academy of Child and Adolescent Psychiatry, 44*, 972–986.

Costenbader, V., & Buntaine, R. (1999). Diagnostic discrimination between social maladjustment and emotional disturbance. *Journal of Emotional and Behavioral Disorders, 7*, 2–10.

Crone, D. A., Horner, R. H., & Hawken, L. S. (2004). *Responding to problem behavior in schools: The behavior education program.* New York: Guilford Press.

Dick, D. M. (2007). Identification of genes influencing a spectrum of externalizing psychopathology, *Current Directions in Psychological Science, 16*, 331–335.

Deas-Nesmith, D., Brady, K. T., & Campbell, S. (1998). Comorbid substance use and anxiety disorders in adolescents. *Journal of Psychopathology and Behavioral Assessment, 20*, 139–148.

Diener, E. (2000). Subjective well-being: The science of happiness and a proposal for a national index. *American Psychologist, 55*, 34–43.

Diener, E., & Chan, M. (2011). Happy people live longer: Subjective well-being contributes to health and longevity. *Applied Psychology: Health and Well Being, 3*(1), 1–4.

Diener, E., Lucas, R.E., & Scollon, C. (2006). Beyond the hedonic treadmill: Revising the adaptation theory of well-being. *American Psychologist, 61*(4), 305–314.

Dishion, T. J. (1990). The peer context of troublesome child and adolescent behavior. In P. Leone (Ed.), *Understanding troubled and troublesome youth* (pp. 128–153). Beverly Hills, CA: Sage.

Dishion, T. J., McCord, J., & F Poulin, F. (1999). When interventions do harm: Peer groups and problem behaviors. *American Psychologist, 54*, 755–764.

DuPaul, G. J., & Eckert, T. L. (1994). The effects of social skills curricula: Now you see them, now you don't. *School Psychology Quarterly, 9*, 113–132.

Durlak, J. A., & Wells, A. M. (1997). Primary prevention mental health programs for children and adolescents: A meta-analytic review. *American Journal of Community Psychology, 25*, 115–152.

Epstein, M. H., Harniss, M. K., Robbins, W., Wheeler, L., Cyrulik, S., Kriz, M., et al. (2003). Strengths-based approaches to assessment in schools. In M. D., Weist, S. W. Evans, & N. A. Lever (Eds.), *Handbook of school mental health: Advancing practice and research* (pp. 285–299). New York: Klumer Academic.

Esquivel, G. B., Doll, B., & Oades-Sese, G. V. (2011). Introduction to the special issue: Resilience in schools. *Psychology in the Schools, 48*, 649–651.

Fairbanks, S., Sugai, G., Guardino, D., & Lathrop, M. (2005). An evaluation of a collaborative social behavior response to intervention system of behavior support for second grade students. *Exceptional Children, 73*, 288–310.

Flannery-Schroeder, E. C. (2006). Reducing anxiety to prevent depression. *American Journal of Preventive Medicine, 31*, 5136–5142.

Forehand, R., & McMahon, R. J. (2003). *Helping the noncompliant child: A clinician's guide to parent training.* New York: Guilford Press.

Forness, S. R., & Kavale, K. A. (1996). Treating social skills deficits in children with learning disabilities: A meta-analysis of the research. *Learning Disability Quarterly, 19*, 2–13.

Fredrickson, B. L. (2001). The role of positive emotions in positive psychology: The broaden- and-build theory of positive emotions. *American Psychologist, 56*, 218–226.

Fredrickson, B. L., & Losada, M. (2005). Positive affect and the complex dynamics of human flourishing. *American Psychologist, 60*(7), 678–686.

Frick, P. J., Lahey, B. B., Loeber, R., Tannenbaum, L. E., Van Horn, Y., & Christ, M. A. G. (1993). Oppositional defiant disorder and conduct disorders: A meta-analytic review of factors analyses and cross-validation in a clinic sample. *Clinical Psychology Review, 13*, 319–340.

Froh, J. J., Huebner, E. S., Youssef, A., & Conte, V. (2011). Acknowledging and appreciating the full spectrum of the human condition: School psychology's (limited) focus on positive psychological functioning. *Psychology in the Schools, 48*, 110–123.

Galera, C., Melchior, M., Chastang, J., Bouvard, M., & Fombonne, E. (2009). Childhood and adolescent hyperactivity-inattention symptoms and academic achievement 8 years later: the GAZEL youth study. *Psychological Medicine, 39*, 1895–1906.

Garber, J., & Weersing, V. R. (2010). Comorbidity of anxiety and depression in youth: Implications for treatment and prevention. *Clinical Psychology: Science and Practice, 17,* 293–306.

Gelfand, D. M., & Drew, J. C. (2003). *Understanding childhood behavior disorders.* Belmont, CA: Wadsworth/Thomson Learning.

Gilman, R., & Huebner, S. (2006). Characteristics of adolescents who report very high life satisfaction. *Journal of Youth and Adolescence, 35*(3), 311–319.

Gillham, J., Brunwasser, S. M., & Frères, D. R. (2007). Preventing depression early in adolescence: The Penn Resiliency Program. In J. R. Z. Abela & B. L. Hankin (Eds.), *Handbook of depression in children and adolescents* (pp. 309–332). New York: Guilford Press.

Gillham, J., Hamilton, J., Frères, D.R., Patton, K., & Gallop, R. (2006). Preventing depression among early adolescents in the primary care setting: A randomized controlled study of the Penn Resiliency Program, *Journal of Abnormal Child Psychology, 34,* 203–219.

Gould, M. S., King, R., Greenwald, S., Fisher, P., Schwab-Stone, M., Kramer, R., et al. (1998). Psychopathology associated with suicidal ideation and attempts among children and adolescents. *Journal of the American Academy of Child and Adolescent Psychiatry, 37,* 915–923.

Greenberg, M. T., Domitrovich, C., & Bumbarger, B. (2001). The prevention of mental disorders in school-aged children: Current state of the field. *Prevention and Treatment, 4,* 1–62.

Greenberg, M. T., Weissberg, R. P., O'Brien, M. U., Zins, J. E., Fredericks, L., Resnick, H., et al. (2003). Enhancing school-based prevention and youth development through coordinated social, emotional, and academic learning. *American Psychologist, 58,* 466–474.

Gresham, F. M. (1986). Conceptual issues in the assessment of social competence in children. In P. S. Strain, M. J. Guralnick, & H. M. Walker (Eds.), *Children's social behavior: Development, assessment, and modification* (pp. 143–179). New York: Academic.

Gresham, F. M. (1998). Assessment of social skills in students with emotional and behavioral disorders. *Assessment for Effective Intervention, 26,* 51–58.

Gresham, F. M., Sugai, G., & Horner, R. H. (2001). Interpreting outcomes of social skills training for students with high-incidence disabilities. *Exceptional Children, 67,* 331–344.

Griest, D. L., & Wells, K. C. (1983). Behavioral family therapy with conduct disorders in children. *Behavior Therapy, 14,* 37–53.

Gueldner, B. A., & Merrell, K. W. (2011). Interventions for students with internalizing problems. In M. A. Bray & T. J. Kehle (Eds.), *The Oxford handbook of school psychology* (pp. 411–427) New York: Oxford University Press.

Gunter, P. L., Denny, R. K., Jack, S. L., Shores, R. E., & Nelson, C. M. (1993). Aversive stimuli in academic interactions between students with serious emotional disturbance and their teachers. *Behavior Disorders, 19,* 265–274.

Gunter, P. L., & Shores, R. E. (1994). A case study of the effects of altering instructional interactions on the disruptive behavior of child identified with severe behavior disorders. *Education and Treatment of Children, 17,* 435–445.

Harlacher, J. E., & Merrell, K. W. (2010). Social and emotional learning as a universal level of student support: Evaluating the follow-up effect of Strong Kids on social and emotional outcomes. *Journal of Applied School Psychology, 26,* 212–229.

Hawken, L. A., MacLeod, K. S., & Rawlings, L. (2007). Effects of the behavior education program (BEP) on office discipline referrals of elementary school students, *Journal of Positive Behavior Interventions, 9,* 94–101.

Hicks, B. M., Krueger, R. F., Iacono, W. G., McGue, M., & Patrick, C. J. (2004). Family transmission and heritability of externalizing disorders: A twin-family study, *Archives of General Psychiatry, 61,* 922–928.

Hills, A. L., Cox, B. J., McWilliams, A. L., & Sareen, J. (2005). Suicide attempts and externalizing psychopathology in nationally representative sample. *Comprehensive Psychiatry, 46,* 334–339.

Hinshaw, S. P. (1992). Externalizing behavior problems and academic underachievement in childhood and adolescence: Causal relationships and underlying mechanisms. *Psychological Bulletin, 111,* 127–155.

Holmbeck, G. N. (1997). Toward terminological, conceptual, and statistical clarity in the study of mediators and moderators: Examples from the child-clinical and pediatric psychology literatures. *Journal of Consulting and Clinical Psychology, 65,* 599–610.

Hood, J. (2011). Validating the Superheroes Social Skills program with externalizing disordered children. Unpublished dissertation, University of Utah, Salt Lake City.

Huebner, E. S., Gilman, R., & Suldo, S. M. (2007). Assessing perceived quality of life in children and youth. In S. R. Smith & L. Handler (Eds.), *The clinical assessment of children and adolescents: A practitioner's handbook* (pp. 347–363). Mahwah, NJ: Lawrence Erlbaum.

Jenson, W. R., Bowen, J. A., Clark, E., Block, H., Gabrielsen, T., Radley, K., & Springer, B. (2011). *The superheroes social skills program.* Eugene, OR: Pacific Northwest Publishing.

Jenson, W. R., Harward, S., & Bowen, J. (2011). Externalizing disorders in children and adolescents: Behavioral excess and behavioral deficits (pp. 230–256). In M. Bray & T. Kehle (Eds.), *Handbook of school psychology.* New York: Oxford University Press.

Jenson, W. R., Olympia, D., Farley, M., & Clark, E. (2004). Positive psychology and externalizing students in a sea of negativity. *Psychology in the Schools, 41,* 51–66.

Jenson, W. R., Rhode, G., Evans, C., & Morgan, D. (2006). Tough kid principal's briefcase: A practical guide to school-wide behavior management and legal issues. Longmont, CO: Sopris West Publishing.

Jenson, W. R., Rhode, G., & Hepworth-Neville, M. (2010). *The tough kid parent book: Practical solutions to tough childhood problems* (2nd ed.). Eugene, OR: Pacific Northwest Publishing.

Kazdin, A. (2008). The Kazdin method for parenting the defiant child: No pills, no therapy, no contest of wills. New York: Houghton Mifflin.

Kazdin, A. E. (2003). Problem-solving skills training and parent management training for conduct disorder. In A. E. Kazdin & J. R. Weisz (Eds.), *Evidence-based psychotherapies for children and adolescents* (pp. 241–262). New York: Guilford Press.

Kazdin, A. E., Bass, D., Siegel, T. C., & Thomas, C. (1989). Cognitive behavior therapy and relationship therapy in the treatment of children referred for antisocial behaviors. *Journal of Consulting and Clinical Psychology, 57,* 522–536.

Kazdin, A. E., Esveldt-Dawson, K., French, N. H., & Unis, A. (1987). Problem-solving skills training and relationship therapy in the treatment of antisocial behavior. *Journal of Consulting and Clinical Psychology, 55*, 76–85.

Kendall, P. C., & Hedtke, K. A. (2006). *The Coping Cat workbook* (2nd ed.). Ardmore, PA: Workbook Publishing.

Kendler, K. S., Jacobson, K., Myers, J. M., & Eaves, L. J. (2007). A genetically informative developmental study of the relationship between conduct disorder and peer deviance in males. *Psychological Medicine, 38*, 1001–1011.

Kessler, R., Chui, W., Demler, O., & Walters, E. (2005). Prevalence, severity, and comorbidity of 12-month DSM-IV disorders in the national comorbidity survey replication. *Archives of General Psychiatry, 62*, 593–602.

Klein, J. B., Jacobs, R. H., & Reinecke, M. A. (2007). Cognitive-behavioral therapy for adolescent depression: A meta-analytic investigation of changes in effect size estimates. *Journal of the American Academy of Child and Adolescent Psychiatry, 46*, 1403–1413.

Kovacs, M., Gatsonis, C., Paulauskas, S. L., & Richards, C. (1989). Depressive disorders in childhood IV: A longitudinal study of comorbidity with and risk for anxiety disorders. *Archives of General Psychiatry, 46*, 776–782.

Kramer, T. J., Caldarella, P., Christensen, L., & Shatzer, R. H. (2010). Social-emotional learning in kindergarten classrooms: Evaluation of the Strong Start curriculum. *Early Childhood Education Journal, 37*, 303–398.

Kuhn, L. (2004). Validation of the effectiveness of a parent training program for parents of preschool-age children with attention deficit hyperactivity disorder. Unpublished master's thesis, University of Utah, Salt Lake City.

Lane, K. L., Gresham, F. M., & O'Shaughnessy, T. E. (Eds.). (2002). *Interventions for children with or at risk for emotional and behavioral disorders.* Needham, WA: Allyn & Bacon.

Langley, A. K., Bergman, L., McCracken, J., & Piacentini, J. C. (2004). Impairment in childhood anxiety disorders: Preliminary examination of the Child Anxiety Impact Scale—Parent Version. *Journal of Child and Adolescent Psychopharmacology, 14*, 105–114.

Lopez, S. J., Edwards, L. M., Teramoto Pedrotti, J., Prosser, E. C., LaRue, S., Vehige Spalitto, S. & Ulven, J. C. (2006). Beyond the DSM IV: Assumptions, alternatives, and alterations. *Journal of Counseling and Development, 84*, 259–267.

Marchant, M., Brown, M., Caldarella, P., & Young, E. (2010). Effects of Strong Kids curriculum on students with internalizing behaviors: A pilot study. *Journal of Evidence-Based Practices for Schools, 11*, 124–143.

Maughan, D. R. (2004). Behavioral parent training as a treatment for externalizing behaviors and disruptive behavior disorders: A meta-analysis. Unpublished dissertation, University of Utah, Salt Lake City.

Maughan, D. R. Christiansen, E. R., Jenson, W. R., Olympia, D., & Clark, E. (2005). Behavioral parent training as a treatment for externalizing behaviors and disruptive behavior disorders: A meta-analysis, *School Psychology Review, 34*, 267–286.

McKnight, C. G., Huebner, E. S., & Suldo, S. M. (2002). Relationships among stressful life events, temperament, problem behavior, and global life satisfaction in adolescents. *Psychology in the Schools, 39*, 677–687.

McMahon, R. J., Wells, K. C., & Kotler, J. S. (2006). Conduct problems. In E. J. Mash & R. A. Barkley (Eds.), *Treatment of childhood disorders* (pp. 137–270). New York: Guilford Press.

McNulty, J. K., & Fincham, F. D. (2012). Beyond positive psychology? Toward a contextual view of psychological processes and well-being. *American Psychologist, 67*, 101–110.

Medley, A., & Sachs-Ericsson, N. (2009). Predictors of parental physical abuse: The contribution of internalizing and externalizing disorders and childhood experiences of abuse. *Journal of Affective Disorders, 113*, 244–254.

Merrell, K. W. (2008). *Helping students overcome depression and anxiety: A practical guide.* New York: Guilford.

Merrell, K. W., Carrizales, D. C., Feuerborn, L., Gueldner, B. A., & Tran, O. K. (2007a). *Strong Kids for grades 3–5: A social-emotional learning curriculum.* Baltimore, MD: Brookes.

Merrell, K. W., Carrizales, D. C., Feuerborn, L., Gueldner, B. A., & Tran, O. K. (2007b). *Strong Kids for grades 6–8: A social-emotional learning curriculum.* Baltimore, MD: Brookes.

Merrell, K. W., Carrizales, D. C., Feuerborn, L., Gueldner, B. A., & Tran, O. K. (2007c). *Strong Teens for grades 9–12: A social-emotional learning curriculum.* Baltimore, MD: Brookes.

Merrell, K. W., Juskelis, M. P., Tran, O. K., & Buchanan, R. (2008). Social and emotional learning in the classroom: Evaluation of Strong Kids and Strong Teens on students' social-emotional knowledge and symptoms. *Journal of Applied School Psychology, 24*, 209–224.

Merrell, K. W., Parisi, D., & Whitcomb, S. A. (2007). *Strong Start for grades K–2: A social- emotional learning curriculum.* Baltimore, MD: Brookes.

Miller, D. N., & Nickerson, A B. (2007). Changing the past, present, and future: Potential applications of positive psychology in school –based psychotherapy with children and youth. *Journal of Applied School Psychology, 24*(1), 147–162.

Miller, D. N., Nickerson, A. B., & Osborne, K. (2006, March). Authentically happy school psychologists: Enhancing professional satisfaction and fulfillment. Paper presented at the annual meeting of the National Association of School Psychologists, Anaheim, California.

Morgan, D., & Jenson, W. R. (1988). *Teaching behaviorally disordered students: Preferred practices.* Columbus, OH: Merrill Publishing.

Mychailyszyn, M. P., Beidas, R. S., Benjamin, C. L., Edmunds, J. M., Podell, J. L., Cohen, J. S. et al. (2011). Assessing and treating child anxiety in schools. *Psychology in the Schools, 48*, 223–232.

Mychailyszyn, M. P., Mendez, J. L., & Kendall, P. C. (2010). Anxiety disorders and school functioning in youth: Comparison by diagnosis and comorbidity. *School Psychology Review, 39*, 106–121.

Nicholas, P., Olympia, D., & Jenson, W. R. (April, 2001). Saying and doing the right things: A comparison of teacher and school psychologist intervention and knowledge and competencies. Paper presented at the annual meeting of the National Association of School Psychologists, Washington, DC.

Olympia, D. E., Farley, M., Christiansen, E., Pettersson, H., Jenson, W. R., & Clark, E. (2004). Social maladjustment and students with behavioral and emotional disorders: School psychologists as facilitators or gatekeepers. *Psychology in the Schools, 41*, 835–847.

Oswald, D. P., & Mazefsky, C. A. (2006). Empirically supported psychotherapy interventions for internalizing disorders. *Psychology in the Schools, 43*, 439–449.

Park, N. (2004). The role of subjective well being in positive youth development. *Annals of the American Academy of Political and Social Science, 591*, 25–39.

Patterson, G. R. (1971). *Families: Applications of social learning to family life.* Champaign, IL: Research Press.

Patterson, G. R. (2002). The early development of coercive family process. In J. R. Reid, G. R. Patterson, & J. Snyder (Eds.), *Anti-social behavior in children and adolescents: A developmental analysis and model for intervention* (pp. 25–44). Washington, DC: American Psychological Association.

Patterson, G. R., DeBaryshe, B. D., & Ramsey, E. (1989). A developmental perspective on antisocial behavior. *American Psychologist, 44*, 329–335.

Patterson, G. R., Reid, J. R., & Dishion, T. J. (1992). *Antisocial boys.* Eugene, OR: Castalia Press.

Patterson, G. R., Reid, J. B., Jones, R. R., & Conger, R. E. (1975). *A social learning approach to family intervention: Families with aggressive children* (vol. 1). Eugene, OR: Castalia Publishing Co.

Payton, J., Weissberg, R. P., Durlak, J. A., Dymnicki, A. B., Taylor, R. D., Schellinger, K. B., et al. (2008). *The positive impact of social and emotional learning for kindergarten to eighth grade students: Findings from three scientific reviews.* Chicago, IL: Collaborative for Academic, Social, and Emotional Learning (CASEL).

Pettit, G. S., Laird, R. D., Dodge, K. A., & Bates, J. E. (1997). Patterns of after-school care in middle childhood: Risk factors and developmental outcomes. *Merrill-Palmer Quarterly, 43*, 515–538

Pine, D. S., Cohen, P., Gurley, D., Brooks, J., & Ma, Y. (1998). The risk for early-adulthood anxiety and depressive disorders in adolescents with anxiety and depressive disorders. *Archives of General Psychiatry, 55*, 56–64.

Quinn, M. M. Kavale, K. A., Mathur, S. R., Rutherford, R. B., & Forness, S. R. (1999). A meta- analysis of social skills interventions for students with emotional and behavioral disorders. *Journal of Emotional and Behavioral Disorders, 7*, 54–64.

Saudino, K. J. (2005). Behavioral genetics and child temperament. *Journal of Behavioral Pediatrics, 26*, 214–223.

Rettew, D. C., Copeland, W. E., Stanger, C., & Hudziak, J. J. (2004.) Associations between temperament and DSM-IV externalizing disorders in children and adolescents. *Journal of Developmental and Behavioral Pediatrics, 25*, 383–391.

Rhode, G., & Jenson, W. R., & Reavis, K. (2009). *The tough kid book: practical classroom management strategies.* Eugene, OR: Pacific Northwest Publishing Company.

Rodriguez, C. M., & Eden, A. (2008). Disciplinary style and child abuse potential: Association with indicators of positive functioning in children with behavior problems. *Child Psychiatry and Human Development, 39*, 123–136.

Seligman, M. (2002). *Authentic happiness: Using the new positive psychology to realize your potential for lasting fulfillments.* New York: Free Press.

Seligman, M. (2011). *Flourish: A visionary new understanding of happiness and well-being.* New York: Simon & Shuster.

Seligman, M., Ernst, R. M., Gillham, J., Reivich, K., & Linkins, M. (2009). Positive education, positive psychology and classroom interventions. *Oxford Review of Education, 35*, 293–311.

Seligman, M. E. P., Steen, T. A., Park, N., & Peterson, C. (2005). Positive psychology progress: Empirical validation of interventions. *American Psychologist, 60*(5), 410–421.

Seligman, M. E. P., & Csikszentmihályi, M. (2000). Positive psychology: An introduction. *American Psychologist, 55*(1), 5–14.

Serketch, W. J., & Dumas, J. E. (1996). The effectiveness of behavioral parent training to modify antisocial behavior in children: A meta-analysis. *Behavior Therapy, 27*, 171–186.

Sheldon, K., & King, L. (2001). Why positive psychology is necessary. *American Psychologist, 56*(3), 216–217.

Shores, R. E., Gunter, P. L., & Jack, S. (1993). Classroom management strategies: Are they setting events for coercion? *Behavior Disorders, 18*, 92–102.

Shortt, A. L., Barrett, P. M., & Fox, T. L. (2001). Evaluating the FRIENDS Program: A cognitive-behavioral group treatment for anxious children and their parents. *Journal of Clinical Child Psychology, 30*, 525–535.

Silverman, W. K., Pina, A. A., & Viswesvaran, C. (2008). Evidence-based psychosocial treatment for phobic and anxiety disorders in children and adolescents. *Journal of Clinical Child and Adolescent Psychology, 37*, 105–130.

Smith, B. H., Barkley, R. A., & Shapiro, C. J. (2006). Attention deficit/hyperactivity disorder. In E. J. Mash & R. A. Barkley (Eds.), *Treatment of childhood disorders* (pp. 65–136). New York: Guilford Press.

Snyder J. (2002). Reinforcement and coercive mechanisms in the development of antisocial behavior: Peer relationships. In J. R. Reid, G. R. Patterson, & J. Snyder (Eds.), *Anti-social behavior in children and adolescents: A developmental analysis and model for intervention* (pp. 101–123). Washington DC: American Psychological Association.

Son, S. E., & Kirchner, J. T. (2000). Depression in children and adolescents. *American Family Physician, 62*, 2297–2308.

Stark, K. D., Hargrave, J., Sander, J., Custer, G., Schnoebelen, S., & Simpson, J. (2006). Treatment of childhood depression: The ACTION treatment program. In P. C. Kendall (Ed.), *Child and adolescent therapy: Cognitive-behavioral procedures* (3rd ed., pp. 169–216). New York: Guilford.

Stark, K. D., & Kendall, P. C. (1996). *Treating depressed children: Therapist manual for "Taking ACTION."* Ardmore, PA: Workbook Publishing.

Suldo, S., & Michalowski, J. (2007). *Subjective well-being intervention program procedures manual wellness-promotion: Groups with 6th grade children.* Unpublished manuscript.

Suldo, S. M., & Huebner, E. S. (2004). Does life satisfaction moderate the effects of stressful life events on psychopathological behavior during adolescence? *School Psychology Quarterly, 19*, 93–105.

Suldo, S. M., Savage, J., & Mercer, S. (2012). *Increasing middle school students' subjective well-being: Efficacy of a positive psychology group intervention.* Manuscript submitted for publication.

Suldo, S. M., & Shaffer, E. J. (2008). Looking beyond psychopathology: The dual-factor model of mental health in youth. *School Psychology Review, 37*, 52–68.

Suldo, S. M., Shaunessy, E., & Hardesty, R. B. (2008). Relationships among stress, coping, and mental health in high-achieving high school students. *Psychology in the Schools, 45*(4), 273–290.

Suldo, S. M., Thalki, A., Frey, M., McMahan, M., Chappel, A. & Fefer, S. (2011, August). A first examination of the existence and utility of a Dual-Factor Model of mental health among high school students. Poster session presented at the 2011 Annual Convention of the American Psychological Association, Washington, DC.

Sutherland, K. S., Wehby, J. H., & Copeland, S. R. (2000). Effect of varying rates of behavior-specific praise on the on-task behavior of students with EBD. *Journal of Emotional and Behavior Disorders, 8*, 2–8.

Torgerson, A. M., & Kringlen, E. (1978). Genetic aspects of temperament differences in infants. *Journal of the American Academy of Child Psychiatry, 17,* 433–444.

U.S. Centers for Disease Control and Prevention. (2007). Suicide trends among youths and young adults aged 10–24 years, United States, 1990–2004. *Morbidity and Mortality Weekly Report, 56,* 905–908.

U. S. Centers for Disease Control and Prevention, National Center for Health Statistics. (2010). Marriage and Divorce. Retrieved from http://www.cdc.gov/nchs/fastats/divorce.htm.

U. S. Department of Health and Human Services, Administration for Children and Families, Administration on Children, Youth and Families, Children's Bureau. (2010). Child Maltreatment 2009. Retrieved from http://www.acf.hhs.gov/programs/cb/stats_research/index.htm#can.

U.S. Department of Health and Human Services (1999). *Mental health: A report from the Surgeon General.* Rockville, MD: Author.

U. S. Department of Health and Human Services, National Institute of Health, National Institute of Mental Health. (2010). *Suicide in the U. S.: Statistics and prevention* (NIH Publication No. 06-4594). Retrieved from the-us-statistics-and-prevention/index.shtml.

Valois, R. F., Zullig, K. J., Huebner, E. S., & Wanzwer Drane, J. (2004). Life satisfaction and suicide among high school adolescents. *Social Indicators Research, 66,* 81–105.

Van Acker, R., Grant, S. H., & Henery, D. (1996). Teacher and student behaviors as a function of risk for aggression. *Education and Treatment of Children, 19,* 316–334.

Verduin, T. L., & Kendall, P. C. (2008). Peer perceptions and liking of children with anxiety disorders. *Journal of Abnormal Child Psychology, 36,* 459–469.

Verona, E., Sach-Ericsson, N., & Joiner, T. (2004). Suicide attempts associated with externalizing psychopathology in an epidemiological sample. *American Journal of Psychiatry, 161,* 444–451.

Walker, H. M., Ramsey, E., & Gresham, F. M. (2004). *Antisocial behavior in school.* Belmont, CA: Wadsworth/Thomas Learning.

Webster-Stratton, C. (2000). The incredible years training series. *Juvenile Justice Bulletin* (June) 1–24.

Webster-Stratton, C., & Reid, M. J. (2003). Treating conduct problems and strengthening social and emotional competence in young children: The Dina Dinosaur treatment program. *Journal of Emotional and Behavioral Disorders, 11,* 130–143.

Weisz, J. R., Jensen-Doss, A., & Hawley, K. M. (2005). Youth psychotherapy outcome research: A review and critique of the evidence base. *Annual Review of Psychology, 56,* 337–363

White, M. A. (1975). Natural rates of teacher approval and disapproval in the classroom. *Journal of Applied Behavior Analysis, 8,* 367–372.

Positive Psychology and Autism Spectrum Disorders

Dianne Zager

Abstract

This chapter explores positive psychology as an adjunctive treatment for individuals on the autism spectrum. Positive psychology has the potential to enhance quality of life and emotional well-being by enabling individuals to focus on strengths and by providing hope for the future. An overview of autism characteristics, current practices in autism, and positive psychology in relation to autism interventions illuminates commonalities among treatments. Individuals with autism spectrum disorders (ASD) often present with comorbid conditions, such as executive dysfunction, anxiety, and depression, that contribute to states of emotional imbalance and negativity. Positive psychology may be useful in moving individuals with ASD away from negativity and immobility, thus yielding beneficial therapeutic results and increasing proactive behavior. Because positive psychology depends on an ability to deal cognitively with life situations, the chapter includes a review of literature pertinent to high-functioning young adults with autism, for whom this intervention may be especially beneficial.

Key Words: positive psychology, autism, autism spectrum disorders, Asperger syndrome

This chapter explores the usefulness of positive psychology as a means of promoting proactive behavior in people with high-functioning autism spectrum disorders (ASD). Relationships among current approaches in autism and positive psychology are explored to illustrate the connectedness of these two fields and to examine how these interventions can contribute to lifelong goals for people on the autism spectrum. The information presented draws on positive psychological techniques and educational interventions that empower individuals to improve executive functioning, circumvent negative disordered thinking associated with the anxiety and depression often associated with ASD, and foster self-determination. This chapter is intended to help bridge the gap between positive psychology and the field of autism through a discussion of the benefits of infusing positive psychology into interventions for students with ASD. In exploring the usefulness of positive psychology as a means of promoting

proactive behavior and a sense of well-being for persons on the autism spectrum, a strong case is made for the inclusion of positive psychology strategies in autism treatment.

Over the past decade, positive psychology has increasingly gained the acceptance of practicing psychologists (Diener, 2009). At the same time, the incidence of autism diagnoses has grown dramatically (Centers for Disease Control, 2011). Individuals with high-functioning autism often struggle with executive dysfunction (Oznoff, Pennington, & Rogers, 1991), along with anxiety and depression associated with their interpersonal challenges (Barnhill & Smith-Myles, 2001). These difficulties become especially pronounced as individuals mature into adolescence (Brissette, Scheier, & Carver, 2002) because adolescent youth confront an increasingly complex social milieu (White, Oswald, Ollendick, & Scahill, 2009; Zager & Alpern, 2010) as they become more aware of their differences and interpersonal difficulties. Although the adolescent years are difficult for all youth (Wehmeyer & Patton, 2012), for those on the autism spectrum, this already complex developmental stage is made even more difficult, especially affecting social and academic performance.

Most educators have not been exposed to the practice of positive psychology. Because the fields of education and psychology have not sufficiently cross-fertilized, positive psychology, although closely related to many autism interventions, is a relatively unfamiliar term among educators who build individualized programs for students with high-functioning ASDs. Nonetheless, many of the principles that underpin positive psychology also contribute to the foundation of autism interventions used in special education programs.

Applicability of Positive Psychology in Autism Treatment

In considering the current interpretation of positive psychology (Seligman & Csikszentmihályi, 2000), the relationship of positive psychology to autism intervention may not be readily apparent. However, on deeper investigation of the implicit mission of this intriguing field, there is a rich body of information that may bring a much needed further dimension to autism intervention. Positive psychology was developed to enhance quality of life. As opposed to providing treatment for disorders, it has been essentially a field of study focused on neurotypical people. Yet, despite (or perhaps because of) the field's emphatic attention to promoting health, as opposed to correcting pathology (Seligman, Steen, Park, & Peterson, 2005), it has the potential to yield favorable therapeutic outcomes for individuals with disabilities (Shogren, Lopez, Wehmeyer, Little, & Pressgrove, 2006).

Through examination of the applicability of positive psychology to autism, a field that often is defined by the presence of pathology and the absence of critical developmental skills, it is shown that the theme of positive psychology is well-aligned with existing autism interventions. Specifically, both fields focus on individual interests, strengths, and potential. The major area of overlap lies in the emphasis of both fields on maximizing strengths and utilizing interests to build healthy adaptive behavior. The goal of autism intervention is to develop needed skills and desired behaviors to enhance quality of life. Positive psychology focuses on strengths that enable individuals to progress toward meeting personal goals. Behavioral practitioners have long realized that, in order to ameliorate maladaptive behaviors, desired positive behaviors must be taught (Baer, Peterson, & Sherman, 1967). Each of these fields is directed toward the purpose of guiding people to increase satisfaction in their lives by focusing on their strongest abilities and interests and to enhance their fulfillment in relationships, career, and leisure activities.

There is a caveat in discussing positive psychology and autism intervention, which is that the power of positive psychology seems to be positively correlated with cognitive ability (Gillot & Standen, 2007). The autism spectrum encompasses a broad range of people with vast differences in intellectual ability, from persons with severe intellectual disabilities to those who are intellectually gifted. Because it would be impractical to apply the underlying theories of positive psychology in the same manner to individuals at all levels of autism (mild through severe), across the range of intellectual abilities (impaired through gifted), and for people of all developmental levels (infant through adult), this chapter addresses the applicability of positive psychology as a means of enhancing quality of life for young adults with high-functioning ASDs.

Diagnosis of Autism Spectrum Disorders

Autism is a neurodevelopmental disorder characterized by impairments in reciprocal social interaction and verbal and nonverbal communication, with a pattern of repetitive stereotypical activities, behaviors, and interests (Szatmari, 2000). In the United States, two widely used definitions of autism are those put forth by the American Psychological Association in its *Diagnostic and Statistical Manual of Mental Disorders* (DSM-IV-R, 2000) and by the Autism Society of America (ASA).

According to the DSM IV-TR (American Psychiatric Association [APA], 2000), individuals with autism exhibit qualitative impairment in social interaction and communication, and restricted repetitive and stereotyped patterns of behavior, interests, and activities. These impairments must have an onset prior to age 3 years and may impact social interaction, language and social communication, and/or symbolic or imaginative play.

The following definition of autism is used by the ASA:

> Autism is a complex developmental disability that typically appears during the first three years of life and affects a person's ability to communicate and interact with others. Autism is defined by a certain set of behaviors and is a spectrum disorder that affects individuals differently and to varying degrees. (Autism Society of America, 2011)

As one of the fastest growing developmental disorders, the unprecedented rise in autism has been referred to as an epidemic. It is estimated that 1% of the population of children in the United States aged 3–17 have an ASD. The prevalence of autism births is estimated at 1 in 110. Epidemiological studies have shed some light on the recent increase in incidence of this disorder (Fombonne, 2005). Speculation as to reasons for the rise in autism prevalence has focused on increased awareness, broadened diagnostic criteria, and environmental causes.

A separate classification under ASD is Asperger syndrome (AS). Asperger syndrome was first identified in 1944 by Viennese pediatrician Hans Asperger to describe a group of boys with difficulties in reciprocal social interaction. These children demonstrated fluent language but poor conversation skills, along with perseverative intense interests (Wing, 1981). Individuals with AS exhibit at least average intelligence (Autism Society, 2011). Although they may often desire to fit in socially and would like to interact with others, they simply do not know how to do so. They may be socially awkward and unable to understand conventional social rules. Eye contact may be limited, and they may lack awareness of body language and gestures.

One of the major differences between AS and autism is the absence of a significant speech delay in AS. Persons with AS tend to have good proficiency in their verbal language skills. Speech patterns and prosody, however, may be unusual, lack inflection, or have a rhythmic nature; the voice may be too loud or high pitched. Individuals with AS may not understand the subtleties of language, such as irony and humor, or they may not understand the give-and-take nature of a conversation (Alpern & Zager, 2007).

Autism is considered a distinct category from other behavior disorders, with a continuum of severity levels within the disorder; thus emerges the notion of *autism spectrum disorders*. Severity is usually measured using some cognitive measure, such as verbal or cognitive ability. Lower functioning individuals tend to have lower IQs with more severe autism-related symptoms, whereas those with AS or high-functioning autism tend to have fewer autism-related symptoms and be more intellectually capable (Szatmari, 2000). After the inclusion of AS in the DSM-IV in 1994, the percentage of individuals with high-functioning autism increased to approximately one-third of the autism population, with IQs in the average to above average range. There are no actual guidelines for diagnosing

high-functioning autism (Attwood, 2007). As such, it is a subjective, descriptive term that can be applied to individuals with both AS and ASD.

Comorbid Conditions in Autism

Conditions that occur comorbid with autism are varied and include (but are not limited to) anxiety, depression and mood disorders, obsessive-compulsive disorder, Tourette syndrome, and sensory problems. Matson and Nebel-Schwalm (2007) investigated mood disorders, phobias, and anxiety, showing that these conditions may be biologically based, as well as situation-induced. The DSM-IV-TR discourages co-diagnosis of attention-deficit/hyperactivity disorder (ADHD) and ASD. Recent studies indicate, however, that co-occurrence of clinically significant ADHD and autism-related symptoms is common; and, importantly, such comorbidity is likely to increase stress and anxiety, which can agitate individuals into states of depression and nonproductivity.

ANXIETY IN AUTISM

Individuals with autism were found to be more anxious than neurotypical children in a study by Gillot, Furniss, and Walter (2001). Factors receiving the highest anxiety scores were separation anxiety and obsessive-compulsive disorder. In another study by Gillot and Standen (2007), adults with autism were nearly three times more anxious than a comparison group of peers with intellectual disabilities. Areas of anxiety studies included panic, separation anxiety, obsessive-compulsive behavior, and generalized anxiety. Gillot and Standen noted that degree of stress correlated with high anxiety levels for the autism group, most dramatically pertaining to ability to cope with change, anticipation, and sensory stimuli. Not surprisingly, the higher the anxiety level, the less likely these persons were able to attend to tasks. These findings suggest a need to incorporate therapy designed to reduce stress and increase feelings of well-being for persons with ASD.

Youth with ASDs are at risk for developing anxiety disorders. Increased stress is clearly a feature of high-functioning autism and AS, despite the lack of mention of these conditions in the definition (Rudy, 2006). There is evidence to suggest that symptoms of anxiety develop as a result of environmental and biological factors (Reaven, 2009). Reaven reports that researchers now recognize that anxiety symptoms are directly related to specific fears and phobias.

For people with AS, stress can be particularly difficult to manage (Dubin & Gaus, 2009). According to Dubin, an author who is on the autism spectrum, being required to conform and "fit in" in social situations is a constant challenge because the neurotypical scene seems alien. Such pressure increases feelings of isolation and anxiety. Areas of particular stress often include difficulties establishing romantic relationships and uncertainty about employment. Dubin and Gaus (2009) recommends cognitive-behavioral therapy as a means of reducing stress and anxiety levels in people with AS.

DEPRESSION IN AUTISM

Several studies have reported comorbid symptoms of mood disorder and depression in individuals with AS (Barnhill & Smith-Myles, 2001; Ghaziuddin, Ghaziuddin, & Greden, 2002; Kim, Szatmari, Bryson, Streiner, & Wilson, 2000). From parent reports, Butzer and Konstantareas (2003) found that higher awareness of disability was related to higher levels of depression. Szatmari, Bartolucci, and Bremner (1989) also suggested that depression is more likely to occur in higher functioning individuals. Awareness of disability is more directly related to depression in individuals with AS than in the ASD population (DeLong & Dwyer, 1988). Another factor that influences temperament and depression in individuals with ASD is the lack of social skills, which has been found to act as a risk factor for depression (Bolton, Pickles, Murphy, & Rutter, 1998).

Higher levels of cognitive ability and social awareness have been shown to negatively affect children's self-concept (Butzer & Knostantareas, 2003). Similar to Dubin and Gaus (2009), these researchers recommend cognitive behavioral interventions to lessen negative feelings. Bauminger (2002) also reported evidence supporting the efficacy of cognitive therapy in individuals with AS.

Positive Psychology

The core of positive psychology incorporates (a) well-being, contentment, and satisfaction; (b) flow (i.e., mental state of operation in which a person is fully immersed in a feeling of energized focus, full involvement, and success in the process of the activity) and happiness; and (c) hope and optimism (Seligman & Csikszentmihalyi, 2000). Positive psychology focuses on those strengths that enable individuals to progress toward meeting personal goals, with the purpose of helping people lead fulfilling lives, cultivate what is best within them, and enhance their opportunities for satisfaction through love, work, and play. Emphasis is placed on ideals such as fulfillment through love, interpersonal empathy and caring, spirituality, consistent commitment (i.e., perseverance), ability to plan (future mindedness), and tolerance of others.

The field of positive psychology has been recognized by the American Psychological Association and has evolved over the past two decades, bringing together practitioners from varied disciplines and introducing practitioners to a different way of thinking about pathology and wellness. The change in focus from preoccupation with ameliorating deficits to developing positive qualities and hope represents a radical change in psychology. Positive psychology has three central concerns: positive emotions, positive individual traits, and positive institutions.

Fostering positive character traits, such as resilience and optimism, has the potential to significantly impact the way individuals with disabilities can perceive themselves. Through positive psychology, therapists guide people to promote feelings of well-being and satisfaction. Inherent in positive psychology are principles that foster a new perspective, and this focus may change how people with ASD can learn to cope with their unique characteristics, strengths, and weaknesses.

Positive psychology is not a new field. Its origins can be traced back to the works of Socrates, whose teachings note that the richest people are those who are content with their lot, for contentment is the greatest wealth. Aristotle, too, noted that happiness depends on personal perspective. Positive psychology aims to help people recognize and appreciate their strengths and accomplishments and to see these as bounty.

Seligman, Steen, Park, and Peterson (2005) define positive psychology as the study of positive emotions, positive character traits, and enabling institutions. Generally speaking, psychologists do not simply heal damage and treat specific disorders; most important, they guide people to help themselves by following fulfilling paths. Positive psychology is designed to help develop healthy, strengths-oriented people. It teaches people to cope more effectively and to grow even when faced with challenges. Positive psychology is founded on a strengths-based philosophy that leads to a positive emotional state.

Numerous researchers have explored mental health with regard to states of well-being, such as feeling good mentally and emotionally (e.g., Fredrickson, 2001; Jahoda, 1958). In exploring notions of happiness and well-being, Jahoda attempted to distinguish between an unhappy disposition and unhappiness from circumstance. Her work highlighted the importance of self-perception and self-actualization. Fredrickson investigated the effect of positive emotions on psychological resilience, suggesting that strategies to enhance resiliency can be developed through building and broadening positive emotions. Folkman and Moskowitz (2001) identified three kinds of coping that can generate positive affects during stressful circumstances: positive reappraisal, problem-focused coping, and infusion of positive meaning into events.

Strategies that incorporate positive psychology into autism intervention have the potential to improve the efficacy of professionals in both fields through a synergistic transdisciplinary approach. Autism is a disorder that transcends any particular discipline, being the focus of research in language and communication, social behavior, and academic learning. By bringing positive psychology into the autism interventional arena, anxiety and depression may be lessened in individuals with ASD. As students with autism learn to direct their energy into flow and positive thinking, improved learning and productivity may occur.

Positive Psychology for People on the Autism Spectrum

Few of the ideals on which positive psychology is based are found in special education textbooks related to teaching students with autism. Positive psychology emphasizes ideals, such as optimism, humor, well-being, and resilience, and one rarely finds terms such as optimism and hope in textbooks on autism. In autism treatment, there are those who would argue that these goals are unscientific, not sufficiently objective or quantifiable. When observing competent teachers of students with ASD, however, it is clear that they do, in fact, incorporate positive psychology goals into good education and treatment.

Widely Employed Autism Interventions

Autism intervention has been the focus of extensive study and controversial debate, and issues pertaining to treatment and education continue to intrigue professionals who work in this field. Over the past few decades, several approaches to autism intervention have been proposed, with minimal interfacing between the varied approaches. Three of the more widely employed autism interventions are applied behavior analysis (ABA); the developmental, individual-difference, relationship-based (DIR)

model; and the treatment and education of autistic and related communication handicapped children (TEACCH) model. In this section, a brief description of each of these major autism approaches is presented, followed by a consideration of the interventions, as a group, through the lens of a positive psychology perspective.

Applied Behavior Analysis

Practitioners of ABA are referred to as *behaviorists*. They postulate that by first learning basic skills, children will be able to make sense of their environment and will then be more likely to function successfully in their environment and to interact socially (Myles, Hubbard, Muellner, & Hider, 2008). In ABA, as children develop basic skills and become more able to deal with stimuli and events within the environment, increasingly positive behaviors emerge. This has been shown scientifically to be true, especially for young children with very limited skill repertoires.

In essence, behavioral theory and practice form a broad approach, not one specific intervention. In its broadest sense, ABA involves the arrangement of the environment to increase the likelihood of evoking a desired response. This science began with B. F. Skinner (Skinner, 1976). With regard to autism intervention, O. Ivar Lovaas is often considered the father of ABA. The Lovaas model is based on data that demonstrate that an intense comprehensive learning environment, in which appropriate responses to teacher-initiated actions are reinforced, will foster basic skill acquisition and enhance learning in young children with autism (Lovaas, 1987). The Lovaas approach to ABA is a highly structured, comprehensive program that relies heavily on discrete trial training (DTT) methods.

A discrete trial is a behaviorally based instruction routine in which the same task is repeated several times in succession, until skill mastery is accomplished. There are several steps in a discrete trial, including (a) presentation of the discriminative stimulus, (b) a request or cue to which the learner is supposed to respond, (c) a response emitted by the learner, and (d) a reward for correct response to motivate the learner to respond correctly in the future. Within Lovaas-type therapy, DTT is used to reduce stereotypical behaviors through individual instruction in discrete tasks, with reinforcement for correct responses. Intervention begins with young children and is often provided intensively throughout the child's routine.

Developmental, Individual-Difference, Relationship-Based Model

In the DIR model, interpersonal relationships are heavily emphasized as the key to skill acquisition (Greenspan & Wieder, 2006). Building on neuropsychological research (Greenspan & Wieder, 2006), Stanley Greenspan developed DIR as a means to foster relating, communication, and thinking skills in children with autism. The approach recognizes the need to form relationships and communicate interpersonally in order to grow (Greenspan & Wieder, 2006). Using a developmentally based perspective, DIR practitioners conduct learning situations to awaken and develop the learner's relatedness to his environment and to his teacher, rather than focusing on specific skill acquisition, as in classic DTT. In the application of the DIR (Floortime) approach, the teacher's consistent responsiveness to the child's initiations begins the journey to successful interpersonal interactions and the development of meaningful relationships.

The DIR model was designed to provide a developmental framework in which the learner's emotional interactions affect cognition and language abilities, as well as social and self-regulation skills. Greenspan and Weider (2006) based DIR practices on the hypothesis that by connecting sensation, affect, and motor action through pleasurable interactions that meet the unique needs of the child, engagement increases, as does reciprocal interaction and self-awareness. This theory is supported by recent neuroscience research (Dziuk et al., 2007).

Treatment and Education of Autistic and Related Communication Handicapped Children

The TEACCH model responds to the educational needs of students with autism by utilizing a highly structured approach with visual cues to foster skill mastery and independent functioning. TEACCH was established in the early 1970s by and colleagues at the University of North Carolina (Mesibov, Shea, & McCaskill, 2012). It emphasizes structure within the environment and the learning task.

In TEACCH, individualized classroom instruction is provided that is designed to accommodate the learning styles characteristic of students with ASDs. Students work at their own stations rather than with classmates, and also work in individual and group instructional sessions. Emphasis is placed on the use of visual cues and prompts that enable students to learn to complete tasks on their own. Transitions from activity to activity are fostered through structured routine, expectations, and schedules.

Using student strengths, structured teaching helps students learn new concepts and skills, which creates a state of comfort and increases motivation to continue to engage in learning activities. TEACCH strategies are designed to lead to successful task completion, increased confidence, and enhanced motivation.

Integration of ABA, DIR, TEACCH, and Positive Psychology

ABA, DIR, and TEACCH are generally considered to be basically distinct and unrelated approaches; however, this is not the case. For instance, in each model, students are rewarded for performing desired behaviors. These interventions are person-centered, and all strive to build a consistent trusting relationship among student, teacher/therapist, and environment. Fulfillment through trust, interpersonal caring, consistent commitment, and ability to plan are inherent in the underlying philosophies of ABA, DIR, and TEACCH. If any one of these approaches were to be utilized in synchrony with positive psychology, the resulting outcomes could potentially enhance quality of life for individuals with ASD by (a) raising awareness of personal strengths, (b) increasing trust in personal ability (i.e., empowerment), (c) helping them learn to engage in relationships, and (d) increasing self-satisfaction through success.

Although each of the approaches is evidence-based and has data to support its effectiveness, an innovative modified configuration of the combined approaches with the inclusion of positive psychology has not been empirically examined. The evidence base for each of the educational interventions, as well as that for positive psychology, holds promise for the future of autism intervention. Review of the extant research base illuminates the focus of each approach and leads to the hypothesis that combining ABA, DIR, and TEACCH could synergistically increase the power of these three related intervention models (Greenspan & Weider, 2006; Lovaas, 1987; Mesibov et al., 2012). In summary, although the approaches are presently viewed as distinct, they have substantial overlap. Further, combining these approaches with positive psychology could increase the arsenal of tools with which practitioners might build a sense of well-being and ameliorate anxiety, stress, and depression in persons with ASDs.

Feelings, behavioral repertoires, and abilities required in interpersonal relationships tend to be challenging for people on the autism spectrum, with the delay or absence of interpersonal relatedness emerging as a mainstay of the diagnosis. Positive psychology addresses the development of these abilities and characteristics. Combined with the scientific foundation of ABA, the critical relationship developmental focus of DIR, and the self-actualization fostered in TEACCH, positive psychology holds promise as an autism intervention. Whether viewed as an adjunctive or integral therapy, it can lead to enhanced quality of life for people with ASDs.

Goals of Positive Psychology as They Relate to Autism Characteristics and Interventions

As discussed earlier, the core goals of positive psychology concentrate on (a) well-being and contentment, (b) flow and happiness, and (c) hope and optimism (Seligman & Csikszentmihályi, 2000). These goals are well-aligned with desired outcomes in autism intervention, which include improved well-being, productivity, socialization, and satisfaction in life. Recently, strategies for integrating these core goals of positive psychology into autism treatment have begun to emerge (see, for example, Groden, Kantor, Woodward, and Lipsitt [2011]). To understand how the fields of positive psychology and autism intervention interface with regard to their theoretical underpinnings and core goals, the goals of positive psychology are examined in relation to autism characteristics and intervention practices, with attention paid to social interaction, executive functioning, self-determination, and self-regulation of individuals on the autism spectrum.

Social Interaction

Individuals with ASDs experience feelings of social isolation throughout their developmental years and into adulthood (Jobe & White, 2007). Freedman (2010) postulates that it may be inaccurate to think that people with ASD prefer to be alone. She explains that, after years of social confusion, rejection, and isolation, individuals with ASDs may fear taking chances socially. To be socially competent requires the ability to (a) maintain a comfortable level of anxiety in social situations, (b) be an active listener, (c) show interest in others, (d) develop rapport, (e) limit focus on oneself or one's interests, and (e) attend to the speaker (Martin, 2011). Impairment in social reciprocity is a central trait of persons on the autism spectrum, who often have difficulty mastering the give-and-take of social interaction. There is a marked difference between individuals with ASD and those with neurotypical development in their integration of verbal and nonverbal social conversational skills (Bregman & Higdon, 2012). Individuals with ASD often have difficulty comprehending and appreciating subtle emotional states within themselves and others and may be unable to predict the thoughts, feelings, and reactions of others (Bregman & Higdon, 2012). Naïveté and vulnerability are common concerns among parents and caregivers of adolescents with ASD, even when students are highly intelligent.

Often, these students lack guile and are extremely honest and blunt. They have had fewer opportunities to explore meaningful relationships with peers of either their own or the opposite gender, resulting in less reinforcement of appropriate behaviors (Zager, Alpern, McKeon, Mulvey, & Maxam, 2013). Personal relationships, etiquette rules, and boundaries are enigmatic, especially with regard to the opposite sex.

Executive Functioning

Executive functioning refers to those processes that permit individuals to manage themselves, their activities, and their resources in order to achieve goals (Chan, Shum, Toulopoulou, & Chen, 2008), and problems with executive function are a defining feature of autism. Executive functioning involves a set of neurologically based abilities, including self-regulation, cognitive flexibility, the organization of daily life and tasks, time management, and the ability to direct attention and focus (Perry, 2009). These abilities, enable a person to make decisions based on an awareness of possible outcomes, organize material and sequence steps to complete tasks, plan accordingly, and make modifications based on new information, may be impaired in individuals with ASDs (Attwood, 2007). Neurologically based skills involving emotional control and self-regulation fall under the umbrella of executive functioning.

Executive dysfunction can result in difficulty with focus and task completion (Azano & Tuckwiller, 2011). Individuals may be easily distracted; they may begin an unrelated task without realizing that their attention has drifted. Management of daily life activities, personal relationships, education, and employment may be negatively affected by executive dysfunction, and anxiety and depression significantly increase executive dysfunction. Persons with ASD have an especially difficult time with time management, structuring and organizing daily activities, and fulfilling obligations and responsibilities.

Executive functions are interrelated; thus, impairment tends to be spread among several areas of performance. The general path of treatment related to executive dysfunction is to build on strengths that help the individual to develop compensatory strategies for weaknesses.

SELF-REGULATION

Individuals who have an ASD may exhibit challenges in understanding others' mental states and also in self-regulation of social–emotional behavior. Information about other persons, their mental states, emotions, attitudes, and intentions, as well as the larger context of their actions, is necessary for regulating one's own behavior (Bachevalier & Loveland, 2006). Because of the continuously changing social environment, behavioral self-regulation in response to the social world is an essential adaptive process (Loveland, 2001). Developing an awareness of the precursors of inappropriate negative reactions, along with an understanding of the consequences of behavior, can be enhanced through positive psychology intervention.

THEORY OF MIND

Theory of mind involves inferring the full range of mental states (such as beliefs, intentions, and emotions) that cause people to act in particular ways (Baron-Cohen et al., 1994). Theory of mind allows people to reflect on the contents of their own and other's minds. Difficulty in understanding other minds is a core cognitive feature of autism spectrum conditions; related difficulties appear to be common among persons with ASD. Positive psychology treatment can help individuals with ASD to build a theory of mind, thus enabling them to predict and comprehend the actions of others. Being able to attribute mental states to others and understanding them as causes of behavior implies, in part, that one must be able to conceive of the purpose of thought (Cacioppo, 2002).

SELF-DETERMINATION

Self-determination encompasses concepts of free will, freedom of choice, independence, self-direction, and individual responsibility (National Research and Training Center, 2005). Wehmeyer, Kelchner, and Richards (1996) operationally defined self-determination as the creation of situations in which individuals are enabled to use knowledge and understanding of their personal characteristics, strengths, and limitations. Self-determination has been shown to increase the likelihood of successful adjustments and transitions as individuals mature throughout life (Wehmeyer & Schwartz, 1997). Systematic promotion of self-determination competence (Bremer, Kachal, & Schoeller, 2003) forms the foundation of interventions in autism, as well as in positive psychology (Deci & Ryan, 2000).

WELL-BEING AND CONTENTMENT

Well-being is a subjective ideal based on several factors. Basically, well-being has to do with people's affective and cognitive perception of their lives. People feel contentment when they are engaged in pleasurable activities, experience few pains or sorrows, and have satisfaction with their life (Diener, 2000). When learners' strongest qualities are nurtured and they are enabled to do what they do best, they are more likely to experience a state of contentment and well-being. Intervention that leads to wellness, and not merely to a reduction of pathology, enriches lives in a positive manner. When self-determined individuals are able to feel competent, have a sense of belonging, and enjoy autonomy, they are likely to feel satisfied and content. The autism interventions of ABA, DIR, and TEACCH are directed toward the goals of contentment and well-being by teaching skills that enable individuals to gain autonomy and a sense of accomplishment. When employed properly, these practices adhere to a philosophy of praise and reward for acquisition of positive behaviors.

Well-being and contentment are outgrowths of a meaningful life and a sense of belonging. Individuals derive a positive sense of well-being, belonging, and purpose from being part of a community. This may involve family, friends, social groups, organizations, religious affiliations, and the like. Feelings of belonging are foreign to many persons on the autism spectrum and are often cited, especially by young adults with AS, as their greatest desire, as well as their greatest disappointment.

Well-being is connected to socialization. Students with autism may exhibit asocial and antisocial characteristics. Successful socialization requires positive (or at least functional) interaction with others. These issues are of particular concern for high-functioning adolescents with autism (Brissette et al., 2002). Because this subgroup has sufficient intellectual ability to interact and communicate, expectations are that social skills will be at a typical developmental level. However, these individuals often remain socially challenged into adulthood. Although people with ASD may express a sense of loneliness, they often do not possess the skills required to approach their peers. Because they may fixate on narrowly focused interests, they may prefer to be alone than be with others who have dissimilar interests, and they may thus end up isolated and depressed.

Flow

First put forth by Mihály Csíkszentmihályi (1996), the positive psychology concept of *flow* relates to performing an activity with highly focused. It occurs when individuals immerse themselves with such single-minded focus that all else fades from consciousness (total concentration). Interestingly, flow occurs intensely for students with attention problems such as attention deficit disorder (ADD) and actually focuses their efforts to a task of great appeal. If special educators were to utilize the concept of flow to harness students' attention and increase time on task, learning and performance would be improved. During flow-laden activities, emotions are not simply contained and channeled, but are made positive, energized, and aligned with the task at hand.

Flow brings a feeling of joy while performing a task. Flow enables release from oneself and one's emotions. To be stuck in the ennui of or the agitation of anxiety is to be barred from flow (Csikszentmihályi, 1996). Individuals on the autism spectrum often exhibit particular interests and strengths. By utilizing activities that enable flow, people with ASDs can enjoy active engagement and may learn skills, build knowledge, and acquire appropriate social and communication behavior in favored activities, such as anime, computer games, animals, or other interests.

Flow is the epitome of an activity reinforcement that might be used in ABA programs. The purpose of reinforcement is to increase the likelihood and strength of a desired behavior, and flow can be used in various ways to accomplish this goal. For example, a favored activity can be promised as a reward for targeted behavior; or, when students learn the skills necessary to perform or excel at an activity, they may find that the activity is more gratifying, lasts longer, and produces more satisfaction. The *Premack principle*, a frequently employed ABA strategy, states that a high-frequency behavior can serve as an effective reinforcer for a low-frequency behavior (Domjan, 2010). In DIR, the teacher leads the student; this practice exemplifies how using interests and strengths can help develop skills in activities that are initially less favored. If a desired activity that provides flow for an individual is available, then that individual is more likely to initiate interaction.

The independent engagement in attainable tasks used in TEACCH settings can make good use of flow by embedding learning tasks in those activities that create flow for students. For instance, math can be taught to a baseball enthusiast through baseball statistics. The concept of flow effectively links ABA, DIR, and TEACCH practices.

Hope and Optimism

Optimism is the belief in the possibility of a desired outcome, a feeling that positive things will happen. Hope and optimism are based in confidence in personal ability and on trust in the support of others (Carver & Gaines, 1987). The development of optimism and the reduction of negative thinking are critical to success in all domains of functioning, including the academic and social arenas. When pessimism and negativity take hold, levels of agitation increase and individuals become stuck in their problem. By building a spirit of optimism, successful interaction and problem resolution are enhanced.

Individuals are better able to strive toward an objective when they have optimism and hope. If they are positively inclined, they are more likely to encounter and appreciate success. They are also better equipped to cope with disappointment when objectives are not attained. Hope energizes us, whereas fear immobilizes us. Courage and resiliency are born from hope and optimism. Individuals with ASDs, especially those with higher intellectual ability, are vulnerable to anxiety and depression. They require assistance to develop optimism, because moving forward from unsuccessful situations is extremely difficult for students with ASD (Zager et al., in press). Perceived failures build on each other and often lead to episodes of depression, and negative disordered thinking takes precedence over optimism.

To build hope, ABA utilizes prompts and cues embedded within stimuli to increase the likelihood of students performing correctly. Correct responses are consistently rewarded, thus building hope and trust. Students gain confidence as they are empowered to receive rewards. With confidence comes hope, fear is diminished, and anxiety lessens. In the DIR model, the student gains awareness of the trainer and learns to manipulate the trainer to interact in ways that are pleasing to the student. A consistently welcoming response to interactions builds trust and leads to optimism that the next approach will be met with a similar welcome. In TEACCH, a well-structured learning environment using organized tasks that are attainable for the student creates a feeling of satisfaction as tasks are completed and rewarded; this is followed by a willingness to engage in additional tasks because of optimism and hope that they too will be met with success. These scenarios are similar in that they strive to teach coping skills, adaptive behavior, self-determined learning, and resilience, as does positive psychology.

RESILIENCE

The concept of resilience has to do with the ability to bounce back from difficult situations and recover from setbacks. Resiliency involves springing back to shape; it is the opposite of rigidity and defeatism. Individuals who have hope and optimism naturally are more resilient. This must, of necessity, be implicit in any autism intervention, and each of the intervention approaches covered in this chapter addresses resiliency. By reinforcing targeted behaviors (ABA), engaging by following and validating the student's lead (DIR), and providing opportunities for successful mastery and accomplishment (TEACCH), the three major approaches to autism intervention fit seamlessly into positive psychology theory. Furthermore, when strategies grounded in these approaches are employed in combination with positive behavior supports (PBS), well-being and optimism levels are raised.

POSITIVE BEHAVIOR SUPPORTS

Positive behavior supports represent an effective evidence-based technology designed to address challenging behavior within living and learning environments (Kinkaid, 1996). Positive behavior support interventions are derived from a value base that reinforces the importance of quality of life (Anderson & Freeman, 2000) and can increase lifestyle options for persons with learning and behavior challenges. They are behavioral, evidence-based, and nonaversive. Positive behavior support intervention is based in person-centered values and reflects socially valid goals related to the individual's strengths and needs. The efficacy of PBS practices has been demonstrated across students of various ages, with different types of disabilities, and in multiple learning environments (Wheeler & Richey, 2010). According to Crone and Horner (2003), PBS can provide a means for increasing the capacity of schools, teachers, and families to engineer optimal learning environments that maximize behavioral outcomes for all students. In concert with positive psychology, PBS reflects the trend in the social sciences and education away from pathology-based models (Carr et al., 2002) and toward a new, positive model that stresses personal competence and environmental integrity.

ACCOMMODATING LEARNING DIFFERENCES

Individuals with autism often present with a myriad of learning differences and styles. Universal design for learning (UDL) is a framework for education that can foster access to learning for students with autism and help remove barriers from teaching methods and curriculum materials (Doyle & Giangreco, 2009). when applied to education, universal design can lead to flexible ways for representing and expressing information and for engaging in learning (Peck & Scarpati, 2009), thereby increasing access for diverse learners (Rose & Meyer, 2002). As a practice, UDL provides a framework to make it possible for students with autism and related learning differences to participate in all aspects of life. Similar to positive psychology, UDL fosters full participation in the learning community.

Conclusion

Positive psychology emphasizes the actualization of individuals through maximizing strengths, and it encourages participation and contributions to the community through activities that make use of personal interests and talents (Diener, 2009). The underpinnings of positive psychology are similar to the principles that form the foundation of autism intervention. In autism intervention and positive psychology, the focus is placed on building strengths and utilizing interests to teach new skills and behaviors. Clinicians and educators learn early in their training to draw attention away from maladaptive behavior and not to focus on what is wrong with students.

Positive psychology has been shown to be helpful in the development of optimism, humor, generosity, resilience, and tolerance (Groden et al., 2011). These traits, which lead to a state of well-being and contentment, are the antidote to anxiety and depression, two conditions that interfere with cognitive functioning in persons with ASD. Through feelings of well-being and faith, individuals with autism may be able to achieve increasing degrees of success; each success then contributes to the state of well-being, thereby lessening anxiety and depression. To reduce agitation and anxiety, which close down intellectual and social functioning, it is crucial to consider strengths and interests, with a goal of creating an environment in which individuals are able to engage in activities that yield productivity through flow. This is the essence of the three major autism interventions, which heretofore have been perceived as distinct from each other. Only through the lens of positive psychology does their relatedness become apparent.

Acknowledgments

Preparation of this manuscript was supported, in part, by the Michael C. Koffler endowment to Pace University and by MetSchools, New York.

References

Alpern, C., & Zager, D. (2007). Addressing communication needs of students with autism in a college-based inclusion program. *Education and Training in Developmental Disabilities*, *42*(4), 428–436.

American Psychiatric Association. (2000). *Diagnostic and statistical manual of mental disorders* (4th ed., text rev.). Arlington, VA:: American Psychiatric Association.

Anderson, C. M., & Freeman, K. A. (2000). Positive behavior support: Expanding the application of applied behavior analysis. *Behavior Analyst*, *23*, 85–94.

Attwood, T. (2007). *The complete guide to Asperger's syndrome.* London: Jessica Kingsley Publishers.

Autism Society of America (2011). About autism. Retrieved September 26, 2011, from .

Azano, A., & Tuckwiller, E. D. (2011). GPS for the English classroom: Understanding executive dysfunction in secondary students. *Teaching Exceptional Children*, *43*, 38–44.

Bachevalier, J., & Loveland, K. A. (2006). The orbitofrontal-amygdala circuit and self-regulation of social-emotional behavior in autism, *Neuroscience and Behavioral Reviews*, *30*, 97–117.

Baer, D. M., Peterson, R. F., & Sherman, J. A. (1967). The development of imitation by reinforcing behavioral similarity to a model. *Journal of the Experimental Analysis of Behavior*, *10*(5) 405–416.

Barnhill, G. P., & Smith-Myles, B. (2001). Attributional style and depression in adolescents with Asperger syndrome. *Journal of Positive Behavior Interventions*, *3*, 175–182.

Baron-Cohen, S., Ring, H., Moriarty, J., Shmitz, P., Costa, D., & Ell, P. (1994). Recognition of mental state terms: A clinical study of autism, and a functional neuroimaging study of normal adults. *British Journal of Psychiatry*, *165*, 640–649.

Bolton, P. F., Pickles, A., Murphy, M., & Rutter, M. (1998). Autism, affective and other psychiatric disorders: Patterns of familial aggregation. *Psychological Medicine*, *28*, 385–395.

Bauminger. N., & Kasari, C. (2000). Loneliness and friendship in high-functioning children with autism, *Child Development, 1*, 447–456.

Bregman, J. D., & Higdon, C. (2012). Definitions and clinical characteristics of autism spectrum disorders. In D. Zager, M. L. Wehmeyer, & R. L. Simpson (Eds.)., *Educating students with autism spectrum disorders: Research-based principles and practices.*(pp.13-44) New York: Routledge/Taylor & Francis Group.

Bremer, C. D., Kachgal, M., & Schoeller, K. (2003). Self-determination: Supporting successful transition, National Center on Secondary Education and Transition Research to Practice Brief, 2,(1), 1–6. Retrieved September 1, 2006, from http://www.ncset.org/publications/viewdesc.asp?id=962.

Brissette, I., Scheier, M. F., & Carver, C. S. (2002). The role of optimism in social network development, coping, and psychological adjustment during a life transition. *Journal of Personality and Social Psychology*, *82*(1), 102–111.

Butzer, B., & Konstantareas, M. M. (2003). Depression, temperament and their relationship to other characteristics in children with Asperger's disorder. *Journal of Developmental Disabilities*, *10*(1), 67–72.

Cacioppo, J. T. (2002). Social neuroscience: Understanding the pieces fosters understanding the whole and vice versa. *American Psychologist*, *57*, 819–831.

Carver, C. S., & Gaines, J. G. (1987). Optimism, pessimism, and postpartum depression. *Cognitive Therapy and Research*, *11*, 449–462.

Carr, E. G., Dunlap, G., Horner, R. H., Koegel, R. L., Turnbull, A. P., & Sailor, W. (2002). Positive behavior support: Evolution of an applied science. *Journal of Positive Behavior Intervention*, *4*(1), 4–16, 20.

Centers for Disease Control and Prevention. (2011). Autism spectrum disorders homepage. Retrieved September 25, 2011, from http://www.cdc.gov/ncbddd/autism/data.html.

Chan, R. C. K., Shum, D., Toulopoulou, T., & Chen, E. Y. H. (2008). Assessment of executive functions: Review of instruments and identification of critical issues. *Archives of Clinical Neuropsychology*. *23*(2), 201–216.

Crone, D. A., & Horner, R. H. (2003). *Building positive behavior support systems in schools.* New York: Guilford.

Csikszentmihályi, M. (1996). *Creativity: Flow and the psychology of discovery and invention*, New York: Harper.

Deci, E.L., & Ryan, R.M. (2000). The what and why of goal pursuits: Human need and the self-determination of behavior. *Psychological Inquiry, 11*, 227–268.

DeLong, R., & Dwyer, J. T. (1988). Correlation of family history with specific autistic subgroups: Asperger's syndrome and bipolar affective disease. *Journal of Autism and Developmental Disorders*, *18*, 593–600.

Diener, E. (2000). Subjective well-being: The science of happiness and a proposal for a national index. *American Psychologist*, *55*(1), 34–43.

Diener, E. (2009). Positive psychology: Past, present, and future. In C. R. Snyder & S. J. Lopez (Eds.), *Oxford handbook of positive psychology* (p. 7–11). Oxford: Oxford University Press.

Domjan, M. (2010). *Principles of learning and behavior*. Florence, KY: Cengage/Wadsorth.

Doyle, M. B., & Giangreco, M. F. (2009). Making presentation software accessible to high school students with intellectual disabilities. *Teaching Exceptional Children*, *41*(3), 24–31.

Dziuk, M., Gidley, L. J., Apostu, A., Mahone, E., Denckla, M., & Mostoofsky, S. (2007). Dyspraxia in autism: Association with motor, social, and communication deficits. *Developmental Medicine and Child Neurology*, *49*, 734–739.

Dubin, N., & Gaus, V. (2009). Asperger syndrome and anxiety: A guide to successful stress management. London: Jessica Kingsley Publishers.

Folkman, S., & Moskowitz, J.T. (2000). Positive affect and the other side of coping, *American Psychologist, 55*, 647–654.

Fombonne E. (2005). *Journal of Clinical Psychiatry*, *66*, 3–8.

Fredrikson, B.L. (2001). The role of positive emotions in positive psychology, *American Psychologist, 56*, 218–226.

Freedman, S. (2010). *Developing college skills in students with autism and Asperger's syndrome*, London: Jessica Kingsley Publishers.

Ghaziuddin, M., Ghaziuddin, N., & Greden, J. (2002). Depression in persons with Autism: Implications for research and clinical care. *Journal of Autism and Developmental Disorders*, *32*, 299–306.

Gillot, A., Furniss, F, & Walter, A. (2001). Anxiety in high-functioning children with autism, *Autism*, *5*(3), 272–286.

Gillot, A., & Standen, P. J. (2007). Levels of anxiety and sources of stress in adults with autism. *Journal of Intellectual Disabilities*, *11*(4), 359–370.

Greenspan, S. I., & Wieder, S. (2006). *Engaging autism.* Cambridge, MA: Da Capo Press.

Groden, J., Kantor, A., Woodward, C. R., & Lipsitt, L. P. (2011). How everyone on the autism spectrum can become resilient, be more optimistic, enjoy humor, be kind, and increase self-efficacy: A positive psychology approach. London: Jessica Kingsley Publications.

Jahoda, M. (1958). Current concepts of positive mental health. New York: Basic Books.

Jobe, L. E., & White, S. W. (2007). Loneliness, social relationships, and a broader autism phenotype in college students, *Personality and Individual Differences, 42*, 1479–1489.

Kim, J. A., Szatmari, P., Bryson, S. E., Streiner, D. L., & Wilson, F. J. (2000). The prevalence of anxiety and mood problems among children with autism and Asperger syndrome. *Autism, 4*, 117–132.

Kinkaid, D. (1996). Person-centered planning. In L. K. Koegel, R. L. Koegel, & G. Dunlap (Eds.), *Positive behavioral support: Including people with difficult behavior in the community.* Baltimore: Paul H. Brookes.

Lovaas, I. O. (1987). Behavioral treatment and normal educational and intellectual functioning in young autistic children. *Journal of Consulting and Clinical Psychology, 55*(1), 3–9.

Loveland, K. (2001). Toward an ecological theory of autism. In J. A. Burack, T. Charman, N. Yirmiya, & P. R. Zelazo (Eds.), *The development of autism: Perspectives from theory and research* (pp. 17–37). Mahwah, NJ: Erlbaum Press.

Martin, R. (2011). *Top tips for Asperger students.* London: Jessica Kingsley Publishers.

Matson J. L., & Nebel-Schwalm M. S. (2007). Comorbid psychopathology with autism spectrum disorder in children: an overview. *Research in Developmental Disabilities, 28*(4), 341–352.

Mesibov, G. B., Shea, V., & McCaskill, S. (2012). Structured teaching and the TEACCH program. In D. Zager, M. L. Wehmeyer, & R. L. Simpson (Eds.), *Educating students with autism spectrum disorders: Research-based principles and practices.* New York: Routledge/Taylor & Francis.

Myles, B. S., Hubbard, A., Muellner, K., & Hider, A. S. (2008). Autism spectrum disorders. In H. P. Parette & G. R. Peterson-Karlan (Eds.), *Research-based practices in developmental disabilities* (2nd ed.; pp.75–98). Austin TX: Pro-Ed.

National Research and Training Center. (2005). *Self-determination framework for people with psychiatric disabilities.* Chicago: National Research and Training Center. Retrieved July 18, 2002, from http://www.psych.uic.edu/UICNRTC/sdframework.pdf.

Oznoff, S., Pennington, B. F., & Rogers, S. J. (1991). Executive function deficits in high-functioning autistic individuals: Relationship to theory of mind. *Journal of Child Psychology and Psychiatry, 32*, 1081–1105.

Peck, A., & Scarpati, S. (2009). Special education by design. *Teaching Exceptional Children, 41*(3), 4.

Perry, N. (2009). *Adults on the autism spectrum leave the nest.* London: Jessica Kingsley Publishers.

Reaven, J. (2009). Children with high-functioning autism spectrum disorders and co-occurring anxiety symptoms: Implications for assessment and treatment. *Journal for Specialists in Pediatric Nursing, 14*, 192–199.

Rose, D. H., & Meyer, A. (2002). *Teaching every student in the digital age: Universal design for learning.* Alexandria, VA: Association for Supervision and Curriculum Development.

Rudy, L. J. (2006). *Mood disorders and Asperger's.* Retrieved October 1, 2011, from http://autism.about.com/od/aspergersyndrome/a/moodsasperger.htm.

Seligman, M., & Csikszentmihalyi, M. (2000). Positive psychology: An introduction. *American Psychologist, 55,* 5–14.

Seligman, M. E. P., Steen, T. A., Park, N., & Peterson, C. (2005). Positive psychology progress: Empirical validation of interventions. *American Psychologist, 60*(5), 410–421.

Shogren, K. A., Lopez, S. J., Wehmeyer, M. L., Little, T. D., & Pressgrove, C. L. (2006). The role of positive psychology constructs in predicting life satisfaction in adolescents with and without cognitive disabilities: An explanatory study. *Journal of Positive Psychology, 1*(1), 37–52.

Skinner, B. F. (1976). *About behaviorism.* New York: Random House.

Szatmari, P. (2000). The classification of autism, Asperger's syndrome, and pervasive developmental disabilities, *Journal of Psychiatry, 45*, 731–738.

Szatmari, P., Bartolucci, G., & Bremner, R. (1989). Asperger's syndrome and autism: Comparison of early history and outcome. *Developmental Medicine and Child Neurology, 31*, 709–720.

Wehmeyer, M., Kelchner, K., & Richards, S. (1996). Essential characteristics of self-determined behavior of individuals with mental retardation. *American Journal of Mental Retardation, 100*, 632–642.

Wehmeyer, M. L., & Patton, J. R. D. (2012). Transition to post-secondary education, employment, and adult living. In D. Zager, M. L. Wehmeyer, & R. L. Simpson (Eds.), *Educating students with autism spectrum disorders: Research-based principles and practices* (pp. 247–261). New York: Routledge/Taylor and Francis.

Wehmeyer, M., & Schwartz, M. (1997). Self-determination and positive adult outcomes: A follow-up study of adults with mental retardation or learning disabilities. *Exceptional Children, 63*, 245–255.

Wheeler, J. J., & Richey, D. D. (2010). *Behavior management: Principles and practices of positive behavior supports.* New York: Pearson.

White S. W., Oswald D., Ollendick, T., & Scahill, L. (2009). *Clinical Psychology Review, 29*(3), 216–229.

Wing, L. (1981). Asperger syndrome: A clinical account. *Psychological Medicine, 11*(1), 115–129.

Zager, D., & Alpern, C. (2010). College-based inclusion programming for students with autism. *Focus on Autism and Other Developmental Disabilities, 25*(3), 151–157.

Zager, D., Alpern, C., McKeon, B., Mulvey, J., & Maxam, S. (2013). Educating students with autism spectrum disorders in college: The OASIS model. New York: Routledge/Taylor & Francis.

PART 5

Considerations for the Field of Disability

Limitations to Positive Psychology Predicted by Subjective Well-Being Homeostasis

Robert A. Cummins

Abstract

The burgeoning literature on positive psychology has strongly impacted on the discipline and its application to disability, broadening the traditional psychological focus on pathology to include the benefits of enhancing subjective well-being (SWB) for both individual and societal functioning. However, as with all new fields of endeavor, the potential of this new approach has been sometimes exaggerated and periodic reviews are required. Crucial to such analysis is the topic of SWB malleability. That SWB can be easily chronically changed is challenged by the theory *subjective well-being homeostasis*, which proposes that levels of SWB are actively managed to remain within a set-point range for each individual and that efforts to shift SWB above or below this range are resisted. This chapter examines the theoretical and empirical basis for the claims of SWB homeostasis theory and positive psychology, concentrating on the areas of gratitude and forgiveness.

Key Words: limitations of positive psychology, subjective well-being, gratitude, forgiveness

The construct of positive psychology was introduced to the literature by Seligman and Csikszentmihályi in (2000), and the first major empirical study concerning the benefits of training in positive psychology techniques was published 3 years later (Emmons & McCullough, 2003). Many subsequent studies on this topic have been reported, so it is timely to consider the weight of their evidence. This chapter critically examines the empirical evidence provided from the positive psychology literature against theoretical predictions derived from homeostasis theory. The two special foci for empirical evidence come from intervention studies involving the induction of gratitude and forgiveness.

This chapter starts by considering definitions of positive psychology, followed by the conclusions of those reviewers who have fostered a positive regard for the area. This is followed by a description of

the theory of *subjective well-being homeostasis* and, in particular, the predictions made by this theory in relation to the limitations of positive psychology interventions. The empirical evidence arising from such interventions is then examined using a select group of influential studies. Finally, the views of other critics are presented, along with the overall balance of evidence and opinion. The chapter concludes, on the basis of the reviewed studies, that the specific benefits claimed for positive psychology interventions have been greatly exaggerated.

Definition

Issue 55 of *American Psychologist*, edited by Seligman and Csikszentmihályi (2000), contained the earliest journal articles to describe the idea of positive psychology. In the issue's introduction, Seligman and Csikszentmihályi's description of positive psychology (p. 5) encompassed the universe of positive psychological constructs, which Fredrickson (2001) later abbreviated to: "The mission of positive psychology is to understand and foster the factors that allow individuals, communities, and societies to flourish" (p. 218). However, Seligman (2007) remained more expansive, maintaining that "positive psychology is the study of positive emotion, of engagement, and of meaning, the three aspects that make sense out of the scientifically unwieldy notion of 'happiness.' Positive psychology attempts to measure, classify, and build these three aspects of life" (p. 266).

From the outset, these definitions wrong-foot positive psychology. The first confuses "flourishing" with a morally desirable life (see section Other critiques of positive psychology), whereas the second confuses the hedonic aspect of well-being (happiness) with the eudaemonic (see Kesebir & Diener, 2008). Despite this, the area has received much positive regard from the lay and research communities.

Positive Reviews of Positive Psychology

A number of scholars have offered highly positive and uncritical reviews of the positive psychology literature. In the most systematic, Sin and Lyubomirski (2009) performed a meta-analysis on 49 studies that had used positive psychology interventions to relieve depression. They report that the interventions significantly enhanced well-being and were effective for treating depressive symptoms. They found the magnitude of these effects to be medium-sized (mean r effect size = 0.29 for well-being and r = 0.31 for depression) and concluded that "not only do Positive Psychology interventions work, they work well" (p. 482). In the way of meta-analyses, the authors do not offer critical analysis of individual studies.

Several authors of conventional literature reviews also refrain from critiquing their material. For example, in reviewing gratitude interventions, Wood, Froh, and Geraghty (2010) state that "experimental interventions to increase gratitude...cause higher levels of well-being" (p. 896), whereas Lyubomirsky, Sheldon, and Schkade (2005) maintain that "[t]he potential of happiness-enhancing interventions is further reflected in emerging research in the positive psychology tradition demonstrating that practicing certain *virtues,* such as gratitude...can bring about enhanced well-being" (p. 114). In a similar vein, reviewing positive psychology interventions in adolescents, Norrish and Vella-Brodrick (2009) state that "there is steadily accumulating evidence for the effectiveness of positive psychology interventions"

(p. 276). Although these reviewers describe some studies in detail, they do not engage in methodological critiques; rather they simply accept authors' conclusions at face value and weave these into a positive story.

Finally, in this genre, there are reviews that serve to recommend the incorporation of positive psychology techniques into professional practice. It might be expected that they would project the worthiness of these techniques in the absence of deep analysis, and so it appears to be. For example, in relation to child education, Craig (2007) proposes teaching about optimism training and "flow," thereby "providing students with the research findings on what makes for fulfilling flourishing lives" (p. 96). Similarly, Seligman, Ernst, Gillham, Reivich, and Linkins (2009) state that "[t]here is substantial evidence from well controlled studies that skills that increase resilience, positive emotion, engagement and meaning can be taught to schoolchildren" (p. 293). In the area of professional counseling, Harris, Thoresen, and Lopez (2007) introduce positive psychology and claim that "intervention studies also have demonstrated notable reductions in chronic anger (trait-based), perceived stress, and depressive affect compared with randomized wait-list or assessment control groups" (p. 7). In the area of clinical supervision for psychologists, Howard (2008) states that "[r]esearch into concepts from the field of positive psychology...has begun to provide detailed understanding of workers' happiness, health and betterment" (p. 105).

An uncritical acceptance of what authors write in the abstracts to their papers does a disservice to both the advancement of understanding positive psychology and to science in general. The remainder of this chapter attempts to provide a more balanced view of the scientific worthiness of positive psychology techniques by looking closely at some of the key studies and also by relating this whole field of endeavor to several theoretical groundings. First is the *theory of homeostasis,* which sets predictive boundaries on what positive psychology techniques may be expected to achieve.

Subjective Well-Being Homeostasis

The theory of subjective well-being homeostasis (Cummins, 1995, 2010) proposes that, in a manner analogous to the homeostatic maintenance of body temperature, subjective well-being (SWB) is actively controlled and maintained by automatic neurological and psychological processes (see also Cummins & Nistico, 2002). The purpose of SWB homeostasis is to maintain a normally positive sense of well-being that is generalized and rather abstract. It can be measured by the classic question "How satisfied are you with your life as a whole?" Given the extraordinary generality of this question, the response that people give is not based on a cognitive evaluation of their lives. Rather it reflects the deep, stable, positive mood that is the essence of SWB. It is this general and abstract sense of positive mood that homeostasis seeks to defend. As a consequence of homeostatic maintenance, SWB has some interesting characteristics.

Subjective Well-Being Is Normally Stable and Positive

The stability of SWB at the level of population sample mean scores is remarkable. The Australian Unity Wellbeing Index has been used to monitor the SWB of the Australian population since 2001 using the Personal Wellbeing Index (International Wellbeing Group, 2006). A total of 26 surveys were conducted from 2001 to 2011, each involving a new sample of 2,000 people (Cummins et al., 2010). All results are standardized to a 0–100 scale and, using the survey mean scores as data, the average of these surveys is 75 points, with a standard deviation of 0.8 points.

To explain this positive stability in SWB, it is proposed that each person has a set-point for their SWB that constitutes a genetically determined, individual difference (see, e.g., Lykken & Tellegen, 1996). We propose, on the basis of empirical deduction (Cummins, 2010), that the range of set-points within large normative samples is from 60 to 90 points, with a mean of 75. We also calculate that each set-point has a normal operating range of about 6 percentage points on either side of its mean. Homeostatic processes seek to maintain SWB within this set-point range for each person.

The assumed normal distribution of set-points within large samples, together with the set-point ranges, explains why no population group chosen on the basis of demographic criteria has a reliable SWB higher than about 81–82 points (Cummins, Woerner, Tomyn, Gibson, & Knapp, 2007). That is, if all members of a demographically advantaged sample, such as people who are very wealthy, are operating at the top of their respective set-point ranges, then the sample SWB should be about 75 + 6 = 81 points.

How Is Subjective Well-Being Managed?

So, what kind of a system might be responsible for keeping SWB stable and positive? There is a substantial literature in which researchers describe the models they imagine responsible for quality of life. One of the earliest was proposed by Liu (1975), who created a composite model comprising nine "component indicators" and a formula for their combination. The components are all objective. Although he does include "psychological inputs" in his formula, he regards this "subjective component [as] qualitative in nature, [specific to] the individual and is not now measurable" (p. 12).

In the year following, two other models were published, each of which assumed the reliable measurement of SWB. The Lewinian lifespace model (Campbell, Converse, & Rodgers, 1976) and the two-dimensional conceptual model (Andrews & Withey, 1976) were both concerned with the deconstruction of quality of life into its objective and subjective components, but did not incorporate any of the psychometric characteristics described earlier. It took more than a decade for researchers to build models based on psychometric data.

The first of these pioneers were two Australian researchers, Headey and Wearing (1989). Using data from a panel study, they observed that people appeared to have a level of equilibrium for their SWB. That is, in the absence of significant life events, people tended to maintain a relatively steady level of SWB and if an event caused SWB to change, then, over time, it tended to regain its previous level. They called this their *dynamic equilibrium model* and considered the management of SWB to be vested in a genetically in-built psychological system, based in stable personality characteristics, which had the primary purpose of maintaining self-esteem. They characterized the positive sense of SWB as a "sense of relative superiority" because it had the consequence of making people feel that their subjective life experience is better than average for the population.

Four years later, Tesser (1988) and Beach and Tesser (2000) proposed the self-evaluation maintenance model. This also concerns the maintenance of positive feelings about the self, with the motivation provided by a preference for positive affective states and goal achievement. A balancing negative force was perceived as the need for accuracy, consistency, and control. However, the overall balance is weighted toward positivity due to the greater need to maintain positive feelings about the self than for accurate perceptions of self-performance. This model is limited to social interaction as the source of positive and negative feedback and does not build on the crucial insight provided by the idea of an equilibrium level.

The next researchers to use this insight were Stones and Kozma (1991) who proposed their *magical model of happiness*. Like Headey and Wearing, they depicted SWB as a self-correcting process that maintains stability around an equilibrium level that differs between individuals. They also regard SWB stability as a function of a dispositional system (Kozma, Stone, & Stones [2000] now referred to this as the *propensity model*). Importantly, they advanced understanding by noting that the stability in SWB could not be entirely explained through personality variables alone and that the best predictor of future SWB was the level of past SWB.

Other authors (Hanestad & Albrektsen, 1992; Nieboer, 1997; Ormel, 1983; Ormel & Schaufeli, 1991) have also developed models based around the assumption that SWB is neurologically maintained in a state of dynamic equilibrium. However, none of these incorporates the psychometric characteristics of SWB described in the previous section and the nature of the relationship between SWB and other demographic and psychological variables. The model that attempts such a grand synthesis is SWB homeostasis.

Subjective Well-Being Is Homeostatically Protected

Although SWB is normally held positive with remarkable tenacity, it is not immutable. A sufficiently adverse level of challenge can defeat the homeostatic system, and, when this occurs, the level of SWB falls below its homeostatic range; likely signaling depression (Cummins, 2010). However, under normal levels of challenge, homeostatic processes maintain SWB within its set-point-range for each person through three levels of defense we call "buffers."

The first line of defense is behavior. People are generally adept at avoiding strong challenges through established life routines that make daily experiences predictable and manageable. However, strong and unexpected events will inevitably occur from time to time. Such events will shift SWB out of its normal range, as attention shifts to the emotion generated by the event. Such deviations from the set-point-range will usually last for a brief period of time, until adaptation occurs. Adaptation to unusual positive challenges is very predictable and well understood (Helson, 1964). Adaptation to negative challenges is less certain but is assisted by the buffering capacity of the two "external buffers" of relationship intimacy and money.

Of these two external buffers, the most powerful is a relationship that involves mutual sharing of intimacies and support (Cummins, Walter, & Woerner, 2007). Almost universally, the research literature attests to the power of good relationships to moderate the influence of potential stressors on SWB (for reviews, see Henderson [1977] and Sarason, Sarason, & Pierce [1990]).

Money is also a powerful external buffer, but there are misconceptions as to what money can and cannot do in relation to SWB. It cannot, for example, shift the set-point to create a perpetually happier person. Set-points for SWB are proposed to be genetically determined (Lykken & Tellegen, 1996; Røysamb, Harris, Magnus, Vitterso, & Tambs, 2002; Stubbe, Posthuma, Boomsma, & de Geus, 2005) so, in this sense, money cannot buy happiness. No matter how rich someone is, their average level of SWB cannot be sustained higher than a level that lies toward the top of their set-point range. People adapt readily to luxurious living standards, so genetics trumps wealth after a certain level of income has been achieved.

The true power of wealth is to protect well-being through its use as a highly flexible resource (Cummins, 2000) that allows people to defend themselves against the negative potential inherent within their environment. Wealthy people pay others to perform tasks they do not wish to do themselves. Poor people, who lack such resources, must fend for themselves to a much greater extent. Poor people, therefore, have a level of SWB that is far more at the mercy of their environment. One consequence is that their mean SWB is lower than average.

Although external buffers assist with homeostatic management of SWB, they are not always successful. If these defenses fail, then the experience of SWB moves outside the set-point range and, when this occurs, it is proposed that internal buffers are activated.

The internal buffers comprise protective cognitive devices designed to minimize the impact of personal failure on positive feelings about the self. Such devices have been variously described as downward social comparisons (Wills, 1981), secondary control (Rothbaum, Weisz, & Snyder, 1982), benefit reminding (Affleck & Tennen, 1996), and positive reappraisal (Folkman & Moskowitz, 2002).

A detailed discussion of these internal buffers in relation to SWB is provided by Cummins and Nistico (2002) and Cummins, Gullone, and Lau (2002). Internal buffers protect SWB by altering the way we see ourselves in relation to homeostatic challenge, such that the negative potential in the challenge is deflected away from the core view of self. The ways of thinking that can achieve this are varied. For example, one can find meaning in the event ("God is testing me"), fail to take responsibility for the failure ("It was not my fault"), or regard the failure [dropping a fragile object] as unimportant ("I did not need that old vase anyway").

In summary, the combined external and internal buffers ensure that SWB is robustly defended. There is, therefore, considerable stability in the SWB of populations and, as has been stated, the mean for Western societies like Australia is consistently at about 75 points on a 0–100 scale. But what is the composition of SWB?

Homeostasis Is Defending Homeostatically Protected Mood

Most contemporary theorists regard the composition of SWB, obtained through a verbal or written response, as involving both affective and cognitive components. This was first recognized by Campbell et al. (1976) who suggested that this amalgam should be measured through questions of "satisfaction." This form of question has since become standard for SWB measurement. However, relatively little research has examined the relative contribution of affect and cognition. The conclusion by Diener, Napa-Scollon, and Lucas (2004), that SWB represents a dominantly cognitive evaluation, is moot. Indeed, to the contrary, more recent research (Blore, Stokes, Mellor, Firth, & Cummins, 2011; Davern, Cummins, & Stokes, 2007; Tomyn & Cummins, 2011) weighs the balance strongly in favor of affect, in the form of a deep and stable positive mood state we refer to as *homeostatically protected mood* (HPMood; Cummins, 2010).

We propose that HPMood comprises a blend of hedonic (pleasant) and arousal values (activation). The studies referenced show that SWB is highly saturated with HPMood. We therefore propose that a genetically generated level of HPMood provides each person with a unique level of felt positivity, which constitutes an individual difference between people. This level represents each person's set-point and is the level that SWB homeostasis seeks to defend.

Normal Ranges

A major implication of homeostasis is that it should be possible to create normal ranges for the variables that comprise, or are heavily saturated with, HPMood. The most closely defined of these is the normal range for SWB. Two kinds of normal range can be generated, one for individuals and one for normative groups.

The range for individuals is presented within Cummins et al. (2010). Section 2.12 in that publication describes the combined dataset derived from 24 independent national Australian surveys conducted between 2001 and 2010. Subjective well-being is measured through the Personal Wellbeing Index (International Wellbeing Group, 2006) administered to 48,225 respondents. Their mean is 75.19 points and the standard deviation is 12.40, so the normal range defined as two SDs around the mean is 50.39–99.99 points. Thus, the normal range for individuals fits the positive sector of the standardized 0–100 range.

The normal range for groups is derived using the survey mean scores as data. Thus, combining the 24 survey means yields a grand mean of 75.17 points, an SD of 0.76, and a normal range for groups of 73.65–76.69, which is a range of just 3.04 points. However, this range has been achieved through the use of constant methodology and a stable population. When the criteria for data collection are relaxed, the range naturally expands. Cummins (1995, 1998) determined that the normal SWB range for Western nations is 70–80 points, whereas the range for a broader set of countries was determined to be 60–80 points. This applied equally for single-item scales ("satisfaction with life as a whole") and multidomain scales.

The normal range for the Satisfaction with Life Scale (Diener, Emmons, Larsen, & Griffin, 1985) is about 5–10 points lower than the above estimates, caused by the extreme nature of the item wording and the consequential avoidance of the extreme upper end of the response scale. Numerous studies have shown that the normal range for this scale is about 65–75 points. For example, survey data collected by our team in 2004 from a general Australian population sample of 557 respondents produced a mean of 69.4 points. Other results from comparable cultural groups have been reported by Renn et al. (2009; Austrian Medical students, 72.0 points), Koo and Oishi (2009; European American college students, 67.3), Proctor, Maltby, and Linley (2011; English undergraduate students, 66.1), and Christopher and Gilbert (2010; U.S. college students: 62.7 points).

The final normal range to be estimated is for positive affect (PA) and negative affect (NA). PA tends to approximate the 70–80 point range for SWB measured through questions of satisfaction, whereas NA tends to be the reciprocal. However, choosing specific affects for the purpose of creating measurement scales is uncertain territory. The only commonly

Table 31.1 Levels of positive and negative affect

Authors	Scale	Sample	N	Mean	SD
Positive affect					
Culbertson et al. (2010)	PANAS	U.S. employed	102	67.50	11.68
Curhan et al. (2010)	Home-made	Elite grad students	387	71.50	12.41
Proctor et al. (2011)	PANAS	U.K. undergraduates	135	49.75	12.71
Negative affect					
Curhan et al. (2010)	Home-made	Elite grad students	387	27.25	11.73
Proctor et al. (2011)	PANAS	U.K. undergraduates	135	29.25	9.46

used list is that of the Positive and Negative Affect Scale (PANAS; Watson, Clark, & Tellegen, 1988). This is a 20-item self-report measure made up of two subscales, each comprising ten items: ten positive affects (PA: interested, excited, strong, enthusiastic, proud, alert, inspired, determined, attentive, and active) and ten negative affects (NA: distressed, upset, guilty, scared, hostile, irritable, ashamed, nervous, jittery, and afraid), each of which is normally rated 1–5. The problem with this scale is that it only samples affects from the activated half of the circumplex model (Yik, Russell, & Barrett, 1999) and thus excludes the deactivated affects, such as contented and sad. Some data are presented in Table 31.1.

The PA for the English undergraduates appears anomalous, but otherwise the means are much as predicted.

In summary, although these ranges are rough-and-ready, they do give ball-park views of the normal ranges as follows: SWB, Satisfaction with Life Scale, and PA 65–80 points; NA 20–30 points. It is a reasonable assumption that results lying outside these ranges are likely to be abnormal. This information is used in the evaluations of positive psychology interventions that follow.

The Implications of Homeostasis for Positive Psychology

The operation of homeostasis makes the following predictions in relation to positive psychology research:

1. No group comprising people selected at random will be able to sustain a level of SWB that exceeds 82 points.

Rationale: Assuming that (a) the sample contains a normal distribution of set-points between 60 and 90 points, (b) that the group is initially operating at the population average of 75 points, and (c) a 12-point range exists around each set-point. Then 75 + 6 = 81 points.

2. For a group of people operating normally within their set-point-range, it will not be possible to cause them to sustain an increased level of SWB exceeding about 6 points.

Rationale: See point 1.

3. For people suffering homeostatic defeat, a successful intervention will be able to raise their SWB to the point that they regain homeostatic control.

Implication: Groups with initially very low levels of SWB will show dramatic increases in SWB after a successful intervention.

4. Groups with initially low levels of SWB will be highly sensitive to the effects of interventions, as the provision of coping resources assists the return of homeostatic control.

Implication: For groups with a low initial level of SWB, almost any supportive intervention is likely to be effective in raising SWB. This is because the new resources provided by the intervention are working together with the homeostatic processes to restore SWB to its normal range. Importantly, this "low baseline sensitivity" means that many forms of intervention will be effective in raising SWB. This has been found in a "gratitude" intervention by Froh, Yurkewicz, and Kashdan (2009) and in the treatment of depression by Sin and Lyubomirski (2009) and Seligman et al. (2009). One implication is that little useful information is gained by studies using a single form of intervention. It is likely that most will be effective, and so comparisons between different intervention techniques are required to determine relative efficacy.

Evidence for the Claims of Positive Psychology

What follows in this section is not intended as a comprehensive coverage of evidence for the efficacy of positive psychology techniques. Rather, some influential articles related to key areas have been selected, based on citation ratings, and submitted to detailed analysis. The purpose of this examination is to establish whether the claims made by the authors in their abstracts and discussions can be reasonably supported from their results.

A further perspective on the selection of papers is the distinction between *common sense* and *surprise*. The former applies to interventions that have obvious substance, to a level such that most reasonable people would expect the generation of at least some positive outcome. For example, Kirschman, Roberts, Shadlow, and Pelley (2010) report that an intensive 6-week day camp, teaching dance and life skills to disadvantaged youth, resulted in enhanced levels of hope. This is a common sense result and such studies will not be further considered here.

Of more interest are the surprising reports, those in which the link between the intervention and the reported outcome is not intuitive. These are the studies where an intervention seems so insubstantial that most reasonable people would be surprised at the production of a reliable positive outcome.

Of course, there is a continuum of intervention intensity between common sense and surprise. From their meta-analysis, Sin and Lyubomirski (2009) describe such a continuum concerning the personalized nature of the intervention, with personalization being strongest with individual therapy and least with self-administered programs. They also found that longer interventions were more effective than shorter ones. So the concentration of this review is on the claims made by the use of the least intensive interventions and will be described for each study evaluated.

Just why the surprise studies are so surprising is informed by an excellent intervention study by Seligman et al. (2009). This provides an insight into just how difficult it is to make a long-term difference through positive psychology interventions. This ambitious project involved screening first-year undergraduate students, over three intake years, on the basis of being at risk for depression, as determined by low scores on the Attributional Style Questionnaire (Seligman, Abramson, Semmel, & von Baeyer, 1979). The 231 selected students were separated into intervention and control groups. Students in the intervention group were given intensive training and long-term follow-up. The training involved 2-hour sessions per week over 8 weeks, in small groups, learning positive psychological techniques such as secondary control, behavioral activation strategies, stress management, and interpersonal skills. In addition, individual trainer contact was made on six occasions, both during the training period and into their second year at university.

Students were assessed on a battery of measures at baseline and over the next 3 years. The major question of interest was whether the intervention would protect these vulnerable students from developing depression as measured both through self- assessment (Beck Depression Inventory [BDI]; Beck, Ward, Mendelson, Mock, & Erbaugh, 1961) and by clinical assessment (the 17-item clinician-rated Structured Interview Guide for the Hamilton Depression Rating Scale; Hamilton, 1960). The depression scores submitted to analysis were determined on the basis of a complex derived value, where 1–2 was normal and 3–6 was depressed. When the outcome was judged using BDI scores of 3–6, it was found that the groups did not statistically differ, with 40% of the intervention group and 48% of the control group developing depression sometime during the 3-year period. However, when the authors separated the scores to reflect only "moderate" depression, determined as a score of 3, they found a significantly lower proportion in the intervention group ($p < .03$). Curiously, the groups did not differ in the proportion of people who developed more severe depression (scores of 4–6). Moreover, these differences were not evident from the clinician-rated Hamilton scores of depression. Pretty clearly, despite the huge effort that had gone into the intervention, the result was, at best, a very marginal demonstration of advantage.

Assessments of the positive psychology literature, according to Seligman (2007), should follow conventional scientific criteria. He writes: "positive psychology is rooted in empirical research. It uses traditional methods of psychometrically established measurement, of experiments, of longitudinal research, and of random assignment, placebo-controlled outcome studies to evaluate whether interventions work. It discards those that do not pass these gold standards as ineffective and it hones those that do pass" (Seligman, Steen, Park, & Peterson, 2005: p. 266). So, the following section follows this lead to see how the surprising studies in positive psychology stand up to close scrutiny.

Gratitude

A detailed critique of gratitude within the context of positive psychology is presented by Cummins (Cummins, 2013). A summary of this analysis is as follows:

• To feel gratitude, the person must recognize that he or she is the recipient of good fortune attributable to the action to someone, or some entity, who has acted on their behalf. This usually means feeling indebted to that person, thereby acknowledging a debt to be repaid. Importantly for positive psychology, the state of indebtedness is commonly experienced as unpleasant and aversive (e.g., Greenberg & Westcott, 1983). Because of this, causing people to experience gratitude may be a negative experience. If it creates the recognition of unwanted obligations, then people will likely develop negative feelings relating to the causal agent (Elster, 1999).

• Consistent with this understanding, empirical data show that acknowledging gratitude has weak potential to induce positive mood (see, e.g., Watkins, Woodward, Stone, & Kolts [2003]). Not only is this likely due to the ambivalent nature of gratitude but also, as noted by Koo, Algoe, Wilson, and Gilbert (2008), recalling a positive happening in one's life yields a weak emotional attachment to the happening. This is because it has already been assimilated into the milieu of "self" and is therefore recalled as just part of normal life experience.

• In an attempt to circumvent the processes of assimilation, Koo et al. (2008) used induced counterfactual reasoning (Roese, 1997), in which people were asked to imagine how life would be without the positive happening, rather than with it. In a series of studies, they convincingly demonstrated that imagining the absence of the positive event, rather than inducing gratitude, was a stronger influence on mood induction. This result, and the reasoning behind it, is also consistent with adaptation theory.

• Given the uncertain personal advantage of generating gratitude and the weak mood induction capacity of gratitude, it would be surprising indeed if a few periods of "counting one's blessings" would have a lasting influence on well-being. This proposition, however, was first tested by Emmons and McCullough (2003) in a series of three studies. Their abstract states: "The gratitude-outlook groups exhibited heightened well-being across several, though not all, of the outcome measures across the 3 studies, relative to the comparison groups" (p. 377). Unfortunately, this statement does not accurately represent their results. Their first two studies reported the results of the nine ANOVAs that compared their gratitude intervention group to comparison conditions. Of these, only two comparisons showed a significant advantage for the gratitude group. Moreover, because of the lack of baseline measures, it is

not possible to deduce whether the difference was due to depressed scores in the comparison groups. Their third study involved people with neuromuscular diseases who rated their satisfaction with "life as a whole." An informed guess at how they scored this scale (see Cummins, 2013) yields 63.3 points for this measure at baseline, which is below the normal range of 65–80 points. During the 21 days of gratitude intervention, this mean rose to 75.7 points and, thus, back into its normal range. This result is consistent with a principle from homeostasis theory that, at least on a short-term basis, it is relatively easy to restore SWB from below normal back to its approximately normal level. It is also unlikely to be due to any specific effect of gratitude training.

• The abstract to another widely cited study involving school children (Froh, Sefick, & Emmons, 2008) states that "[r]esults indicated that counting blessings was associated with enhanced self-reported gratitude, optimism, life satisfaction, and decreased negative affect" (p. 213). This also misrepresents their results. First, although they measured life satisfaction using a composite 5-item scale, the only results to achieve significance were individual items within the scale. Second, they measured a total of eight variables, with no pre-test scores provided. A total of 16 ANOVAs compare these variables at post-test and follow-up. Of these, only two were significant at post-test and three at follow-up, all at $p < .05$. Thus, 69% of these comparisons failed to reach significance. Of those that did, only two ANOVAs, *both involving the same single item* from the Brief Multidimensional Students' Life Satisfaction Scale (BMSLSS), "satisfaction with school experience," showed the intervention group to have higher satisfaction than both the hassles and control groups. Notably, levels of life satisfaction did not distinguish between the groups. In terms of their other variables, measures of gratitude, optimism, and negative affect, analyzed as above, failed to show a clear advantage for the intervention group over the other two groups. In summary, the results within this paper failed to support the claims made in the abstract.

In the following year, Froh, Kashdanb, Ozimkowskia, and Millera (2009) published another study in which they claimed that a gratitude intervention raised PA. Although this study has serious methodological and statistical flaws (Cummins, 2013), it is interesting that the significant effect was confined to adolescents with low initial levels of

PA. Again, this is consistent with predictions from homeostasis theory.

In summary, these key studies provide results quite consistent with expectations based on the weak power of gratitude as a positive mood inducer and the predictions of homeostasis theory. Although gratitude induction may raise the well-being of people in homeostatic defeat, so may a wide variety of other forms of intervention. Moreover, there appears to be no reliable evidence that induced gratitude can raise the well-being of normally functioning people. In conclusion, this careful reading of relevant publications does not inspire confidence in the ability of gratitude interventions to yield robust positive effects.

Forgiveness

Although forgiveness is central to positive psychology (Seligman & Csikszentmihályi, 2000, p. 5), there is no agreed definition of the secular forgiveness construct. Indeed, the categorization of forgiveness within psychology is most uncertain. At the simplest level, it has been labeled an affect by Emmons and McCullough (2003), but this is surely incorrect. Forgiveness does not feature on the affective circumplex (see Yik et al., 1999) and has a very high cognitive content. Like so many positive psychology terms, it is a composite cognitive/affective variable with complex links to personality. Although "forgiveness" is assumed to be a simple personality dimension by some authors (e.g., McCullough & Witvliet, 2002), this would be surprising given its complex composition. In fact, it is only weakly predicted by personality (see Neto, 2007). Using the Forgivingness Scale (Mullet et al., 2003), Neto found that the combined power of agreeableness and neuroticism, plus belief in God and gratitude, could together only account for 18% of the variance. One reason for its complex composition is that forgiveness is not a unitary construct.

Forgiveness exists in two different forms, as positive and negative. *Positive forgiveness* describes the process of complete forgiveness, with a resumption of normal positive feelings to the offender (also called *emotional forgiveness*; Worthington, Witvliet, Pietrini, & Miller, 2007). *Negative forgiveness*, on the other hand, describes a situation in which public forgiveness is extended, even while continuing to regard the harmful actions of the offender as having been unjust (McCullough et al., 1998; McCullough, Worthington, & Rachal, 1997). Negative forgiveness (also called *decisional forgiveness*; Worthington et al., 2007) involves the inhibition of an overtly vengeful response, such as avoidance or revenge, most commonly in the spirit of social harmony (Tsang, McCullough, & Fincham, 2006), but also involves continued grudge-holding and mistrust.

Whereas the obverse of forgiveness is vengefulness, or the disposition to seek revenge following interpersonal offenses, the relationship between these constructs is not simply reciprocal. Someone can be either high or low on forgiveness and yet be low on vengefulness. The associated justificatory cognitions for vengeful thoughts may involve the right to "get even" derived from the reciprocity norm (see Gouldner, 1960) or to engage in moral education by "teaching the offender a lesson" (Baumeister, 1997; Heider, 1958).

This associated construct of vengefulness was studied by McCullough, Bellah, Kilpatrick, and Johnson (2001) and measured using the seven vengefulness items from Mauger et al.'s (1991) Forgiveness of Others Scale. They found it to be correlated with less forgiveness, greater rumination about the offense, higher negative affectivity, and lower life satisfaction. There is, thus, a personal cost to holding vengeful beliefs. However, this correlation may also come from disposition, with 30% of vengefulness variance accounted for by the NEO Personality Inventory (NEO-PI) being negatively associated with agreeableness and positively associated with neuroticism. Thus, overly vengeful people may have difficulty maintaining harmonious interpersonal relationships.

Other conceptions of forgiveness reflect its positive moral connotation. Thus, forgiveness has been considered part of "well-being" (e.g., Emmons & McCullough, 2003), "work-place well-being" (Ip, 2009), and "spiritual well-being" (e.g., Dobrikova, 2010); and as a component of social harmony (Ho & Chan, 2009) and even of health-related quality of life (Skevington, 2009). These authors assume that forgiving is necessarily a desirable human attribute, which is demonstrably false (see later discussion). Others go further, considering forgiveness to be a component of spirituality (MacKinlay & Trevitt, 2007), a "psychological virtue" (Lyubomirsky et al., 2005; Seligman et al., 2005), a component of temperance (Petersen & Seligman, 2004), and an "altruistic gift" (Seligman, 2002 p. 80).

It is evident that no simple definition is going to capture this complexity. Indeed, most definitions describe the surface structure of positive forgiveness. One such definition is offered by McCullough, Pargament, and Thoresen (2000) as "intra-individual, pro-social change toward a perceived transgressor that is situated within a specific interpersonal context"(p. 9). These authors further elaborate forgiveness as "a motivational transformation that inclines people to inhibit relationship-destructive responses and to behave constructively toward someone who has behaved destructively toward them" McCullough et al. (1997, p. 321). Other definitions also fail to acknowledge the dark side of forgiving. The absence of negative forgiveness in such definitions is notable and potentially misleading.

The Implications of Positive and Negative Forgiveness

The two different forms of forgiveness indicate two quite different psychological processes. Pure positive forgiveness is pure secondary control (Rothbaum et al., 1982) wherein cognitive restructuring is used to create the belief that any form of retribution for the hurt is unnecessary. This is a protective device, used as a form of coping when primary control (avoidance of the hurt) has failed. It would not be expected to enhance well-being but rather to restore well-being following the negative challenge. It is simply a return of the victim to status quo.

Negative forgiveness is quite different and, in its pure form, may involve primary control. That is, the victim has successfully managed the public face of the hurt, with the vengeful response being strategically delayed. This response yields a complex interplay of positive and negative. The victim feels good because he has successfully conveyed public forgiveness, thereby maintaining the relationship. His positive well-being may be further enhanced by the thought that he has lulled the perpetrator into a false sense of security, such that vengeance, when it is delivered, will be unexpected and brutal. When these positive influences on well-being are balanced against the hurt, the combined effect may approximate neutrality, which is highly adaptive. It is, however, a volatile and unstable state, involving the inhibition of overt action in the presence of continued activated negative affect (e.g., anger). This means the state of negative forgiveness will change over time.

The most dramatic change will become evident in the short term, before the anger has had time to diminish. If, during this period, either the inhibitory control is relaxed (e.g., through alcohol) or a further hurt is received, then an overt vengeful response may result.

However, if the act of retribution is delayed and no more immediate hurt is encountered, the activated negative affect will gradually subside. The reason for this is adaptation such that, over time, the hurt loses its immediate bite and softens as it becomes immersed in the caldron of remembered experiences. The prospect of retribution will also diminish as the motivation, powered by anger, also subsides. Thus, the whole incident will normally fade into barely remembered obscurity and the effect on well-being will be negligible.

However, this process of adaptation will occur to varying degrees, depending on such variables as the degree of hurt, recurrence of the hurt, and the victim's capacity for forgiveness. The victim may also be forced to confront the reality that, despite the continuation of her hurt, vengeance cannot be executed. For example, if the mother of dependent children has no reasonable prospect of her independent survival, she may feel forced to suffer the abuse of her husband. As such a victim faces the reality that vengeance is not possible, she loses any sense of primary control and is left with the negative thoughts of injustice and her own inadequacy. At its most severe, and especially if the hurt was repeated, this could lead to a condition of learned helplessness, which is very bad for well-being indeed (Callahan & Pincus, 1995; Seligman, 1975; Weisz, 1981).

The Link Between Forgiveness and Other Constructs

So, why do forgiveness scales correlate positively with positive self-constructs? The answer may be that such scales elicit responses that are loaded with HPMood. Take, for example, the Heartland Forgiveness Scale (Thompson et al., 2005). A sample item from the scale measuring forgiveness of other is "With time, I am understanding of others for the mistakes they've made." This is a leading question, which encourages a positive response, is quite abstract, and is therefore loaded with HPMood. The same can be seen within the Forgiveness of Others Scale (Mauger et al., 1991) with the item, "I am able to make up pretty easily with friends who have hurt me in some way."

It is, thus, not surprising to find that forgiveness as measured by such scales correlates weakly and positively with most other relevant constructs. These include beliefs in a just world for self (BJW-self; Strelan & Sutton, 2011), empathy (McCullough et al., 1997), gratitude (Neto, 2007), SWB, marital satisfaction (Miller & Worthington, 2010), pro-social motivation, and the like. It is also negatively associated with anxiety, depression, and stress (Miller & Worthington, 2010). These links have been established for many years (see McCullough [2000] for an early review), and these multiple weak links combined with weak predictive power confirm the compositional complexity of the construct.

Forgiveness has been made a part of scales that purport to measure many different constructs. It is part of the Tennessee Self-Concept Scale (Roid & Fitts, 1988), wherein a positive response to "I do not forgive others easily" rates as high self-esteem. It is interesting that this propensity for negative forgiveness factors with other items denoting high self-esteem. This also raises the issue of whether it is better for well-being to forgive others or to forgive oneself. Interestingly, among problem drinkers, the trait of "self-forgiveness" (a form of secondary control) but not "other forgiveness" was found to be positively associated with perceived and mental health (Webb & Brewer, 2010). Although it seems quite intuitive that self-forgiveness is more relevant to mental health than other forgiveness, this is not generally considered by the positive psychology literature. This omission may reflect an underlying moral dimension, such that forgiving others is more worthy.

Forgiveness as a Positive Psychology Technique

In the context of positive psychology, a basic assumption of the forgiveness procedure is that the hurt is continuing to damage well-being. Not only is this assumption rarely, if ever, tested but it is also unlikely. Although continued hurt that is powerful enough to damage well-being may be found as florid psychopathology, it is certainly uncommon. If people normally accumulated the negative influence of hurts, they would rapidly become dysfunctional.

Assuming, then, that the normal process of forgiveness is to create a neutral link between the hurt and wellness, as described in the preceding section, the wellness-enhancing technique of positive psychology becomes interesting. When the therapist asks someone to recall an old hurt in order to bestow forgiveness, the hurt is likely resurrected from a memory that is neutral in relation to well-being, but then becomes a contemporary, activated negative experience with the capacity to damage well-being. Then the act of forgiveness is intended to neutralize the resurgent anger and to restore neutrality, or even, as claimed, enhance positivity. As an example of this procedure, Hui and Chau (2009) conducted a forgiveness intervention with 11- to 12-year-old children, beginning the session with an "uncovering phase" that involved "activities to recall the offence, the hurt experienced, the reactions and feelings towards the offenders" (p. 145).

So how could this process result in enhanced feelings of well-being? The answer may lie in the nature of the task. The hurt that is recalled has lost most of its negative relevance through adaptation. The act of forgiveness is therefore easy to make. It also constitutes a determinedly positive act, for which encouragement and positive regard is given by the therapist. So, on balance, well-being is enhanced. There are two observations on this. First, the effect will be no more effective in raising well-being than any other therapist-prescribed, self-perceived positive act. Other examples could be expressing gratitude or performing an act of kindness. Second, the positive effect of expressing forgiveness will be transitory since the hurt was of little consequence anyway.

Other benefits can be envisaged by regarding positive forgiveness as a coping strategy (e.g., Folkman, 2008; Toussaint & Webb, 2005). In this conception, as has been mentioned, it is a form of secondary control (Rothbaum et al., 1982), whereby cognitive restructuring is used to create the belief that retribution is not required. Its use in such a manner would not be expected to enhance well-being as much as to protect well-being from challenge. However, this is more likely for positive than for negative forgiveness. There is a negative relationship between BJW-self and negative forgiveness (Strelan & Sutton, 2011), just as might be expected. This again emphasizes the importance of distinguishing between positive and negative forgiveness.

At a broader level, the benefit of forgiveness lies in benefits for interpersonal relationships. Positive forgiveness following a transgression allows the normal continuation of a relationship. It is also beneficial because it avoids both overt retaliation, which may likely terminate the relationship, and negative forgiveness, which may contribute to mental health problems (Worthington & Wade, 1999). As evidence, these authors cite its relationship with depression and anxiety (Toussaint & Webb, 2005). The logical conclusion, therefore, is that increased positive forgiveness will decrease such symptoms and also decrease perceived stress (Harris et al., 2006).

The Benefits of Forgiveness: Claims and Evidence

Seligman (2002) states that "rewriting history by forgiveness loosens the power of the bad events to embitter (and actually can transform bad memories into good ones)" (p. 70) and that "[p]hysical health, particularly in cardiovascular terms, is likely better in those who forgive than those who do not" (p. 77). He certainly points to the reasons to be vengeful (see section Other critiques of positive psychology) but then states "It is not my place to argue with you about what weights to assign to these pros and cons as you decide whether it is worth it to surrender a grudge. The weights reflect your values. My aim is merely to expose the inverse relationship between unforgiveness and life satisfaction" (p. 77).

This statement contains two distinct claims: (a) that positive forgiveness reduces the power of negative forgiveness to lower life satisfaction and (b) that positive forgiveness is associated with better cardiovascular health. Many other authors make the further claim (c) that positive forgiveness leads to higher life satisfaction (e.g., Martin, 2011). Each of these claims will now be examined, following an appraisal of the general links between positive psychological constructs.

REDUCING THE POWER OF NEGATIVE FORGIVENESS

The most obvious factor reducing the power of negative forgiveness is the passage of time. Confirmation that time since the hurt is associated with rising levels of positive psychological constructs has been provided by Bono, McCullough, and Root (2008). It also seems reasonable to expect that specific training in techniques to replace negative with positive forgiveness should be able to speed up this recovery process. Empirical confirmation comes from a meta-analysis by Wade, Worthington, and Meyer (2005) and a review of some dozen studies (Worthington, Sandage, & Berry, 2000) that found a positive relationship between the time spent in group counseling about forgiveness and the strength of forgiveness. Finally, and unsurprisingly, the meta-analysis of Wade et al. (2005) also revealed that specific forgiveness training was more effective in raising forgiveness than were indirect methods to promote forgiveness. In summary, changes in forgiveness reflect the passage of time and the intensity and specificity of training to negate negative forgiveness. All this seems rather obvious and unremarkable.

POSITIVE FORGIVENESS IS ASSOCIATED WITH CARDIOVASCULAR HEALTH

In a review of the general health benefits of forgiveness (for a review, see Worthington et al. [2007]), it is proposed that benefits may be generated either directly through the reduction of negative emotions (e.g., Webb & Brewer, 2010) or indirectly by strengthening relationships with health behavior, interpersonal functioning, and social support.

At the more specific level of cardiovascular health, benefit lies with the assumption of negative forgiveness (unforgiveness) as a stress response (see Harris & Thoresen, 2005). If it is then also assumed that stress contributes to cardiovascular pathology, it follows that high levels of positive psychological constructs should be protective. Support for this link comes from studies showing that high levels of positive attributes, such as trait coping, have been found to be associated with lower blood pressure and faster cardiovascular recovery from stress (e.g., Friedberg, Suchday, & Shelov, 2007). However, the validity of the assumed causal path is most uncertain, and this discussion concerns pathology rather than positive psychology. This topic will not be further pursued for this review.

FORGIVENESS INCREASES POSITIVE PSYCHOLOGICAL CONSTRUCTS

The topics covered so far seem rather uncontentious. But the claims that life satisfaction and related constructs can be raised through forgiveness would be surprising if they were true. The level of life satisfaction is dominated by the set-point of HPMood and the processes of homeostasis (see earlier discussion), so it would be surprising if positive forgiveness was able to chronically raise the SWB of normally functioning people. It would be less surprising if training in positive psychology techniques was able to raise the SWB of people in distress, taking levels back into their normal set-point range.

Thus, in assessing this claim, the crucial issue is the baseline. There are two distinct scenarios. First, if SWB is being lowered by the unfulfilled vengeful thoughts of negative forgiveness, then training in positive forgiveness will be expected to raise life satisfaction as it also reduces depression, stress, and anxiety. In other words, it is relieving the link with psychopathology. Second, if SWB is in the normal range, then training in positive forgiveness will not be expected to chronically increase SWB or related constructs to any substantial degree. Although evidence supporting the clinical effectiveness of forgiveness training has already been cited, evidence that forgiveness training can chronically raise positive psychological constructs for normally functioning people is much harder to find.

The first claim for enhanced optimism comes from Seligman (2002, p. 81), who states:

> [T]here are at least eight controlled-outcome studies measuring the consequences of procedures like REACH [positive psychology intervention]. In the

largest and best-done study to date, a consortium of Stanford researchers led by Carl Thoresen randomly assigned 259 adults to either a nine, 90-minute sessions, forgiveness workshop, or to an assessment-only control group. The components of the intervention were carefully scripted. . . with emphasis on taking less offense and revising the story of the grievance towards an objective perspective. Less anger, less stress, more optimism, better reported health, and more forgiveness ensued, and the effects were sizable.

The paper reporting this material was later published by Harris et al. (2006). The participants had responded to an advertisement for people who had experienced a hurtful interpersonal experience, from which they still felt negative emotional consequences. This is, thus, an extreme group that has suffered long-term damage as the result of a hurt. Compared with a nontreatment control group, a 6-week, 90-minute training program produced a significant increase in forgiveness self-efficacy, forgiveness that generalized to new situations, and lowered perceived stress and trait-anger. These effects generally persisted for 4 months after training. This paper does not mention either optimism or perceived health as outcomes. In conclusion, a substantial training program given to people self-selected for suffering long-term hurt succeeded in reducing stress and anger and in improving positive forgiveness, as measured by scales that were directly relevant to the content of the training program. It does not report results on optimism.

A second widely cited paper claiming enhanced positive constructs through forgiveness is that by Karremans, Van Lange, Ouwerkerk, and Kluwer (2003). In three similar experimental studies, these researchers employed the following procedures: (a) Participants recalled a situation of interpersonal hurt under two levels of commitment to the perpetrator; (b) they then engaged in various exercises designed to induce forgiveness; and (c) they subsequently rated themselves on life satisfaction, positive affect, negative affect, and state self-esteem. The authors state their results from the first study as "[t]ests of simple main effects revealed that when commitment was strong, participants in the forgiving condition (vs. those in no-forgiving condition) exhibited greater levels of life satisfaction—positive affect—and state self-esteem" (p. 1015). In fact, this statement is very misleading.

What their results actually show (their table 1) is that, of the four conditions (forgiveness/no

forgiveness, weak commitment/strong commitment), the condition causing the significance is strong commitment/no forgiveness. On all three positive variables, this is lower than the other three conditions, whereas on negative affect it is higher. This same result applied to the other two studies.

In other words, their results could not distinguish between the condition of forgiveness in the presence of strong or weak commitment, and the condition of no forgiveness in the presence of weak commitment. However, when participants recalled hurt from a strongly committed relationship with no forgiveness, then life satisfaction, positive affect, and self-esteem became lower, while negative affect became higher. So the significant effect was to decrease, not increase, well-being.

A third study (Hui & Chau, 2009), reported the results from a forgiveness intervention with 11- and 12-year-old children. Weekly 40-minute sessions were conducted for 2 months while a control group received a self-enhancement program, including topics such as self-discovery. Comparing pre-test and immediate post-test scores, no change was found for the control group, whereas the forgiveness group showed higher self-esteem and hope, with lower depression. At 3-month follow-up, only the lower depression score remained. However, the authors determined these differences using multiple t-tests, and all but the immediate post-test depression score difference achieved significance at .05. Thus, significance would disappear if type 1 error was controlled using a Bonferroni correction.

Most recently, a sophisticated proposition by Luchies, Finkel, McNulty, and Kumashiro (2010) states that forgiving someone close (the perpetrator) for a hurtful act bolsters the self-respect and self-concept clarity of the victim *as long as* the perpetrator has signaled the victim will be safe and valued in a continued relationship. In the absence of such signals, forgiving diminishes both self-respect and self-concept clarity. They tested this over four studies.

Their first study involved newly wed couples, followed-up over 6 months. They found weak support ($p = .05$) for *diminished* self-respect over time when a partner high on forgiveness was matched with one low on signals indicating safety and being valued (a partner low in agreeableness; e.g., "I feel little concern for others").

In their second study, participants recalled an unresolved hurt by a close perpetrator. The strength of their forgiveness was then experimentally manipulated, as was the extent to which the perpetrator had made amends. However, their manipulation was unsuccessful in that the level of felt forgiveness did not differ significantly between the high and low forgiveness manipulations. In comparing their four experimental conditions (high/low forgiveness/amends), they found nonsignificant results for self-respect. They found a single weak result ($p = .04$) for self-concept clarity ("I have a clear sense of who I am and what I am"). This showed that the combination of *high forgiveness and weak amends* yielded lower self-concept clarity than the combination *low forgiveness and weak amends* (the published paper is confusing in having reversed figure 2 and figure 3). In summary, this study involved four paired comparisons involving high/low forgiveness (self-respect/self-concept clarity; high/low amends), only one of which was marginally significant.

In their third study, participants were instructed to imagine themselves as the victim of a recent trust betrayal by their romantic partner. The hypothetical betrayal scenarios included manipulations of forgiveness (low vs. high), amends (weak vs. strong), and distress (low vs. high). They found the same result as in study 2, this time involving both self-respect and self-concept clarity. Interestingly, these results were not moderated by perceived levels of personal distress at the betrayal, which eliminates one possible explanation for the result. Again, the study involved four paired comparisons involving high/low forgiveness, two of which were significant.

Their final study was longitudinal, involving 14 periods of data collection (every other week) over a 6-month period. Participants reported on their self-respect and their self-concept clarity. The independent variables were (a) level of distress at betrayals committed by their romantic partner (high or low), (b) level to which they forgave their partner (high or low), and (c) level of amends made by their partner (high or low). Again, this involves two dependent variables each analyzed by a $2 \times 2 \times 2$ ANOVA. None of the results for self-respect was significant, and neither were they for low distress. The only significant result was that, in the presence of high distress and high partner amends, high forgiveness predicted higher self-concept clarity. In summary, of the eight paired comparisons involving high/low forgiveness, only one was significant. In summary, from this study it can be deduced:

• Being high on forgiveness appears to be risky business (Luchies et al. referred to this as the "door-mat effect"). If high forgiveness is paired with a partner low on agreeableness (study 1) or a sense that the perpetrator has made weak amends

(studies 2 and 3), then self-respect and self-concept clarity are at risk. Low levels of forgiveness are without such consequences.

• High levels of forgiveness had a positive outcome in study 4 in which, in the presence of high personal distress at the betrayal and perceived strong partner amends, it associated with higher concept clarity. However, this moderating effect of distress was not found in study 3, so it requires confirmation through further study.

• Overall, these effects are very weak. Either self-respect or self-concept clarity was significant in just four of the 16 paired comparisons involving high/low forgiveness.

In overall summary of the cited literature on gratitude or forgiveness, it is notable that the published positive and affirmative statements of outcome fail to withstand close scrutiny. This should give concern to those many authors who have uncritically accepted these studies as evidence for the special efficacy of positive psychology techniques.

Other Critiques of Positive Psychology

Other critiques of positive psychology come from several different viewpoints. Some concern a moral perspective (Fowers, 2008; Martin, 2007; Sundararajan, 2008), taking exception to the definitions of positive psychology offered in this chapter's first section as though they describe a good life. Sundararajan points out, as also has Seligman (2002), that all of the attributes of positive emotion, engagement, meaning, and flourishing can be achieved by evil people doing evil deeds willingly and well. In a similar vein, Fowers and Martin argue that positive psychologists present virtue incompletely, focusing on a few "signature strengths." Virtue ethicists, on the other hand, emphasize the unity of character and the development of a full range of virtues. Thus, all three reviewers decry positive psychology for representing the good life devoid of a moral map.

From a humanist perspective, Held (2004) lashes the "tyranny of the positive attitude" and notes the vital importance of negative affect in human functioning. In the field of education, Suissa (2008) points to obscurity in the meaning of happiness, as used in positive psychology, and notes the introduced confusion between education and therapy. For Miller (2008), concern lies with the exemplary characteristics championed by positive psychology and argues that: "The model of mental health depicted by positive psychology turns out to be little more than a caricature of an extravert" (p. 606). It is unfortunate that philosophers championing "positive ethics" (e.g., Handelsman, Knapp, & Gottlieb, 2005) fail to address these concerns.

Although it has taken longer for empirical critiques to emerge, Coyne, Tennen, and Ranchor (2010) present a heavy critique of conclusions reached by reviewers Aspinwall and Tedeschi (2010), who support for the idea that positive psychological states predict health. Coyne et al. take exception to these authors' "uncritical acceptance of the claims made in the literature, which we have shown to be biased in publication of positive findings, regardless of the quality of studies, biased in its portrayal of findings in subsequent publications, and exclusion of null and negative findings" (p. 39).

Conclusion

This chapter has matched the predictions and claims of two theoretical viewpoints. Proponents of positive psychology claim their techniques can raise SWB. Homeostasis theory, on the other hand, predicts that positive psychology techniques can only raise SWB for people who are in homeostatic defeat. The discovered evidence is consistent with the predictions from homeostasis. Moreover, although positive psychology techniques may raise the well-being of people in homeostatic defeat, at least on a short-term basis, a wide variety of other interventions are probably just as effective. The crucial demonstration, that positive psychology techniques are superior, has yet to be reported.

The substantial critiques of positive psychology included in this chapter have not been answered within the academic literature. In the spirit of informed debate and the passage of valid information to practitioners, it is surely time for the proponents of these techniques to do so.

References

Affleck, G., & Tennen, H. (1996). Construing benefits from adversity: Adaptational significance and dispositional underpinnings. *Journal of Personality and Social Psychology, 64,* 899–922.

Andrews, F. M., & Withey, S. B. (1976). *Social indicators of well-being: American's perceptions of life quality.* New York: Plenum Press.

Aspinwall, L. G., & Tedeschi, R. G. (2010). The value of positive psychology for health psychology: Progress and pitfalls in examining the relation of positive phenomena to health. *Annals of Behavioral Medicine, 39*(1), 4–15.

Baumeister, R. F. (1997). *Evil.* New York: Freeman.

Beach, S. R. H., & Tesser, A. (2000). Self-evaluation maintenance and evolution: Some speculative notes. In J. Suls & L. Wheeler (Eds.), *Handbook of social comparison: Theory and research* (pp. 123–141). New York: Kluwer Academic.

Beck, A. T., Ward, C. H., Mendelson, M., Mock, J. E., & Erbaugh, J. K. (1961). An inventory for measuring depression. *Archives of General Psychiatry, 4,* 561–571.

Blore, J. D., Stokes, M. A., Mellor, D., Firth, L., & Cummins, R. A. (2011). Comparing multiple discrepancies theory to affective models of subjective wellbeing. *Social Indicators Research, 100*(1), 1–16.

Bono, G., McCullough, M. E., & Root, L. M. (2008). Forgiveness, feeling connected to others, and well-being: Two longitudinal studies. *Personality and Social Psychology Bulletin, 34*(2), 182–195.

Callahan, L. F., & Pincus, T. (1995). The sense of coherence scale in patients with rheumatoid arthritis. *Arthritis Care and Research, 8,* 28–35.

Campbell, A., Converse, P. E., & Rodgers, W. L. (1976). *The quality of American life: Perceptions, evaluations, and satisfactions.* New York: Russell Sage Foundation.

Christopher, M. S., & Gilbert, B. D. (2010). Incremental validity of components of mindfulness in the prediction of satisfaction with life and depression. *Current Psychology, 29*(1), 10–23.

Coyne, J. C., Tennen, H., & Ranchor, A. V. (2010). Positive psychology in cancer care: A story line resistant to evidence. *Annals of Behavioral Medicine, 39*(1), 35–42.

Craig, C. (2007). The potential dangers of a systematic, explicit approach to teaching social and emotional skills (SEAL) Retrieved June 22, 2011, from http://www.centreforconfidence.co.uk/docs/EI-SEAL_September_2007.pdf

Culbertson, S. S., Fullagar, C. J., & Mills, M. J. (2010). Feeling good and doing great: the relationship between psychological capital and well-being. *Journal of Occupational Health Psychology, 15*(4), 421–433.

Cummins, R. A. (1995). On the trail of the gold standard for life satisfaction. *Social Indicators Research, 35,* 179–200.

Cummins, R. A. (1998). The second approximation to an international standard of life satisfaction. *Social Indicators Research, 43,* 307–334.

Cummins, R. A. (2000). Personal income and subjective well-being: a review. *Journal of Happiness Studies, 1,* 133–158.

Cummins, R. A. (2010). Subjective wellbeing, homeostatically protected mood and depression: a synthesis. *Journal of Happiness Studies, 11,* 1–17. doi: 10.1007/s10902-009-9167-0

Cummins, R. A. (2013). Positive psychology and subjective well-being homeostasis: A critical examination of congruence. In D. Moraitou & A. Efklides (Eds.), *Quality of life: A positive psychology perspective* (pp. 67–86). New York: Springer.

Cummins, R. A., Gullone, E., & Lau, A. L. D. (2002). A model of subjective well being homeostasis: the role of personality. In E. Gullone & R. A. Cummins (Eds.), *The universality of subjective wellbeing indicators: Social indicators research series* (pp. 7–46). Dordrecht: Kluwer.

Cummins, R. A., & Nistico, H. (2002). Maintaining life satisfaction: the role of positive cognitive bias. *Journal of Happiness Studies, 3,* 37–69.

Cummins, R. A., Walter, J., & Woerner, J. (2007). Australian Unity Wellbeing Index: Report 16.1 "The Wellbeing of Australians - Groups with the highest and lowest wellbeing in Australia." Retrieved June 22, 2011, from http://www.deakin.edu.au/research/acqol/index_wellbeing/index.htm

Cummins, R. A., Woerner, J. M. W., Perera, C., Gibson-Prosser, A., Collard, J., et al. (2010). Australian Unity Wellbeing Index: - Report 24.0 - "The Wellbeing of Australians - Trust,

Life Better/Worse and Climate Change." Retrieved June 22, 2011, from http://www.deakin.edu.au/research/acqol/index_wellbeing/index.htm

Cummins, R. A., Woerner, J., Tomyn, A., Gibson, A., & Knapp, T. (2007). Australian Unity Wellbeing Index: Report 17.0 - "The Wellbeing of Australians - Work, Wealth and Happiness." Retrieved June 22, 2011, from http://www.deakin.edu.au/research/acqol/index_wellbeing/index.htm

Curhan, J. R., Elfenbein, H. A., & Eisenkraft, N. (2010). The objective value of subjective value: a multi-round negotiation study. *Journal of Applied Social Psychology*, 40(3), 690–709.

Davern, M., Cummins, R. A., & Stokes, M. (2007). Subjective wellbeing as an affective/cognitive construct. *Journal of Happiness Studies*, 8(4), 429–449.

Diener, E. D., Emmons, R. A., Larsen, R. J., & Griffin, S. (1985). The satisfaction with life scale. *Journal of Personality Assessment*, 49, 71–75.

Diener, E. D., Napa-Scollon, C. K., & Lucas, R. E. (2004). The evolving concept of subjective well-being: the multifaceted nature of happiness. In P. T. Coista & I. C. Siegler (Eds.), *Recent advances in psychology and aging* (pp. 188–219). Amsterdam: Elsevier Science BV.

Dobrikova, P. (2010). Quality of life in incurable patients. *Studia Psychologica*, 52(2), 155–164.

Elster, J. (1999). *Alchemies of the mind: Rationality and the emotions.* New York: Cambridge University Press.

Emmons, R. A., & McCullough, M. E. (2003). Counting blessings versus burdens: an experimental investigation of gratitude and subjective well-being in daily life. *Journal of Personality and Social Psychology*, 84, 377–389.

Folkman, S. (2008). The case for positive emotions in the stress process. *Anxiety, Stress and Coping*, 21(1), 3–36.

Folkman, S., & Moskowitz, J. T. (2002). Positive affect and the other side of coping. *American Psychologist*, 55, 647–654.

Fowers, B. J. (2008). From continence to virtue - recovering goodness, character unity, and character types for positive psychology. *Theory & Psychology*, 18(5), 629–654.

Fredrickson, B. L. (2001). The role of positive emotions in positive psychology: the broaden-and-build theory of positive emotions. *American Psychologist*, 56, 218–226.

Friedberg, J. P., Suchday, S., & Shelov, D. V. (2007). The impact of forgiveness on cardiovascular reactivity and recovery. *International Journal of Psychophysiology*, 65(2), 87–94.

Froh, J. J., Kashdanb, T. B., Ozimkowskia, K. M., & Millera, N. (2009). Who benefits the most from a gratitude intervention in children and adolescents? Examining positive affect as a moderator. *Journal of Positive Psychology*, 4(5), 408–422.

Froh, J. J., Sefick, W. J., & Emmons, R. A. (2008). Counting blessings in early adolescents: an experimental study of gratitude and subjective well-being. *Journal of School Psychology*, 46, 213–233.

Froh, J. J., Yurkewicz, C., & Kashdan, T. B. (2009). Gratitude and subjective well-being in early adolescence: examining gender differences. *Journal of Adolescence*, 32(3), 633–650.

Gouldner, A. W. (1960). The norm of reciprocity: A preliminary statement. *American Sociological Review*, 25, 161–178.

Greenberg, M. S., & Westcott, D. R. (1983). Indebtedness as a mediator of reactions to aid. In J. D. Fisher, A. Nadler, & B. M. DePaulo (Eds.), *New directions in helping: recipient reactions to aid* (pp. 85–112). New York: Academic Press.

Hamilton, M. (1960). A rating scale for depression. *Journal of Neurology, Neurosurgery & Psychiatry*, 23, 56–62.

Handelsman, M. M., Knapp, S., & Gottlieb, M. C. (2005). Positive ethics. In E. L. Worthington (Ed.), *Handbook of forgiveness* (pp. 731–744). New York: Routledge.

Hanestad, B. R., & Albrektsen, G. (1992). The stability of quality of life experience in people with Type 1 diabetes over a period of a year. *Journal of Advanced Nursing*, 17, 777–784.

Harris, A. H. S., Luskin, F., Norman, S. B., Standard, S., Bruning, J., Evans, S., et al. (2006). Effects of a group forgiveness intervention on forgiveness, perceived stress, and trait-anger. *Journal of Clinical Psychology*, 62(6), 715–733.

Harris, A. H. S., & Thoresen, C. E. (2005). Forgiveness, unforgiveness, health, and disease. In E. L. Worthington Jr (Ed.), *Handbook of forgiveness* (pp. 321–333). New York: Brunner-Routledge.

Harris, A. H. S., Thoresen, C. E., & Lopez, S. J. (2007). Integrating positive psychology into counseling: why and (when appropriate) how. *Journal of Counseling and Development*, 85(1), 3–13.

Headey, B., & Wearing, A. (1989). Personality, life events, and subjective well-being: Toward a dynamic equilibrium model. *Journal of Personality and Social Psychology*, 57, 731–739.

Heider, F. (1958). *The psychology of interpersonal relations.* New York: John Wiley.

Held, B. S. (2004). The negative side of positive psychology. *Journal of Humanistic Psychology*, 44(1), 9–46.

Helson, H. (1964). *Adaptation-level theory.* New York: Harper & Row.

Henderson, S. (1977). The social network, support and neurosis. The function of attachment in adult life. *British Journal of Psychiatry*, 131, 185–191.

Ho, S. S. M., & Chan, R. S. Y. (2009). Social harmony in Hong Kong: Level, determinants and policy implications. *Social Indicators Research*, 91(1), 37–58.

Howard, F. (2008). Managing stress or enhancing wellbeing? Positive psychology's contributions to clinical supervision. *Australian Psychologist*, 43(2), 105–113.

Hui, E. K. P., & Chau, T. S. (2009). The impact of a forgiveness intervention with Hong Kong Chinese children hurt in interpersonal relationships. *British Journal of Guidance & Counselling*, 37(2), 141–156.

International Wellbeing Group. (2006). Personal Wellbeing Index Manual. *4th Edition* Retrieved June 22, 2011, from http://www.deakin.edu.au/research/acqol/instruments/wellbeing-index/pwi-a-english.pdf

Ip, P.-K. (2009). Developing a concept of workplace well-being for greater China. *Social Indicators Research*, 91(1), 59–77.

Karremans, J. C., Van Lange, P. A. M., Ouwerkerk, J. W., & Kluwer, E. S. (2003). When forgiving enhances psychological well-being: The role of interpersonal commitment. *Journal of Personality and Social Psychology*, 84, 1011–1026. doi: 10.1037/0022-3514.84.5.1011

Kesebir, P., & Diener, E. D. (2008). In pursuit of happiness empirical answers to philosophical questions. *Perspectives on Psychological Science*, 3, 117–125.

Kirschman, K. J. B., Roberts, M. C., Shadlow, J. O., & Pelley, T. J. (2010). An evaluation of hope following a summer camp for inner-city youth. *Child & Youth Care Forum*, 39(6), 385–396.

Koo, M., Algoe, S. B., Wilson, T. D., & Gilbert, D. T. (2008). It's a wonderful life: Mentally subtracting positive events improves people's affective states, contrary to their affective forecasts. *Journal of Personality and Social Psychology*, 95, 1217–1224.

Koo, M., & Oishi, S. (2009). False memory and the associative network of happiness. *Personality and Social Psychology Bulletin, 35*(2), 212–220.

Kozma, A., Stone, S., & Stones, M. J. (2000). Stability in components and predictors of subjective well-being (SWB): Implications for SWB structure. In E. Diener & D. R. Rahtz (Eds.), *Advances in quality of life: Theory and research* (pp. 13–30). London: Kluwer Academic Publishers.

Liu, B. (1975). Quality of life: Concept, measure and results. *American Journal of Economics and Sociology, 34*, 1–13.

Luchies, L. B., Finkel, E. J., McNulty, J. K., & Kumashiro, M. (2010). The doormat effect: When forgiving erodes self-respect and self-concept clarity. *Journal of Personality and Social Psychology, 98*(5), 734–749.

Lykken, D., & Tellegen, A. (1996). Happiness is a stochastic phenomenon. *Psychological Science, 7*, 186–189.

Lyubomirsky, S., Sheldon, K. M., & Schkade, D. (2005). Pursuing happiness: the architecture of sustainable change. *Review of General Psychology, 9*, 111–131.

MacKinlay, E. B., & Trevitt, C. (2007). Spiritual care and ageing in a secular society. *Medical Journal of Australia, 186*, S74–S76.

Martin, B. (2011). On being a happy academic. *Australian Universities' Review, 53*, 50–56.

Martin, M. W. (2007). Happiness and virtue in positive psychology. *Journal for the Theory of Social Behavior, 37*(1), 89–103.

Mauger, P. A., E., P. J., Freeman, T., Grove, D. C., McBride, A. G., & McKinney, K. E. (1991). The measurement of forgiveness: Preliminary research. *Journal of Psychology and Christianity, 11*, 170–180.

McCullough, M. E. (2000). Forgiveness as human strength: Theory, measurement, and links to well-being. *Journal of Social and Clinical Psychology, 19*, 43–55.

McCullough, M. E., Bellah, C. G., Kilpatrick, S. D., & Johnson, J. L. (2001). Vengefulness: Relationships with forgiveness, rumination, well-being and the big five. *Personality and Social Psychology Bulletin, 27*, 601–611.

McCullough, M. E., Pargament, K. I., & Thoresen, C. E. (2000). *Forgiveness: Theory, research, and practice*. New York: Guilford.

McCullough, M. E., Rachal, K. C., Sandage, S. J., Worthington Jr., E. L., Brown, S. W., & Hight, T. L. (1998). Interpersonal forgiving in close relationships II: Theoretical elaboration and measurement. *Journal of Personality and Social Psychology, 75*, 1586–1603.

McCullough, M. E., & Witvliet, C. V. (2002). The psychology of forgiveness. In C. R. Snyder & S. J. Lopez (Eds.), *Handbook of positive psychology* (pp. 446–458). Oxford: Oxford University Press.

McCullough, M. E., Worthington, E. L., & Rachal, K. C. (1997). Interpersonal forgiving in close relationships. *Journal of Personality and Social Psychology, 73*, 321–336.

Miller, A. (2008). A critique of positive psychology - or 'the new science of happiness.' *Journal of Philosophy of Education, 42*(3–4), 591–608.

Miller, A. J., & Worthington, E. L. (2010). Sex differences in forgiveness and mental health in recently married couples. *Journal of Positive Psychology, 5*(1), 12–23.

Mullet, E., Barros, J., Frongia, L., Usai, V., Neto, F., & Shafighi, S. (2003). Religious involvement and the forgiving personality. *Journal of Personality and Social Psychology, 71*, 1–19.

Neto, F. (2007). Forgiveness, personality and gratitude. *Personality and Individual Differences, 43*(8), 2313–2323. doi: 10.1016/j.paid.2007.07.010

Nieboer, A. P. (1997). *Life events and well-being: A prospective study on changes in well-being of elderly people due to a serious illness event or death of the spouse.* Amsterdam: Thesis Publishers.

Norrish, J. M., & Vella-Brodrick, D. A. (2009). Positive psychology and adolescents: Where are we now? Where to from here? *Australian Psychologist, 44*(4), 270–278.

Ormel, J. (1983). Neuroticism and well-being inventories. Measuring traits or states? *Psychological Medicine, 13*, 165–176.

Ormel, J., & Schaufeli, W. B. (1991). Stability and change in psychological distress and their relationship with self-esteem and locus of control: A dynamic equilibrium mode. *Journal of Personality and Social Psychology, 60*, 288–299.

Petersen, C., & Seligman, M. E. P. (2004). *Character strengths and virtues: A handbook and classification*. New York: Oxford University Press.

Proctor, C., Maltby, J., & Linley, P. A. (2011). Strengths use as a predictor of well-being and health-related quality of life. *Journal of Happiness Studies, 12*(1), 153–169.

Renn, D., Pfaffenberger, N., Platter, M., Mitmansgruber, H., Höfer, S., & Cummins, R. A. (2009). International Well-being Index: The Austrian version. *Social Indicators Research, 90*, 243–256.

Roese, N. J. (1997). Counterfactual thinking. *Psychological Bulletin, 121*, 133–148.

Roid, G. H., & Fitts, W. H. (1988). *Tennessee self-concept scale: Revised manual*. Los Angeles: Western Psychological Services.

Rothbaum, F., Weisz, J. R., & Snyder, S. S. (1982). Changing the world and changing the self: a two-process model of perceived control. *Journal of Personality and Social Psychology, 42*, 5–37.

Røysamb, E., Harris, J. R., Magnus, P., Vitterso, J., & Tambs, K. (2002). Subjective well-being. Sex-specific effects of genetic and environmental factors. *Personality and Individual Differences, 32*, 211–223.

Sarason, I. G., Sarason, B. R., & Pierce, G. R. (1990). Social support: the search for theory. *Journal of Social and Clinical Psychology, 9*, 137–147.

Seligman, M. E. P. (1975). *Helplessness; On depression, development and death*. San Francisco, CA: Freeman.

Seligman, M. E. P. (2002). *Authentic happiness: using the new positive psychology to realize your potential for lasting fulfillment*. New York: Free Press.

Seligman, M. E. P. (2007). Coaching and positive psychology. *Australian Psychologist, 42*(4), 266–267.

Seligman, M. E. P., Abramson, L. Y., Semmel, A., & von Baeyer, C. (1979). Depressive attributional style. *Journal of Abnormal Psychology, 88*, 242–247.

Seligman, M. E. P., & Csikszentmihályi, M. (2000). Positive psychology: an introduction. *American Psychologist, 55*, 5–15.

Seligman, M. E. P., Ernst, R. M., Gillham, J., Reivich, K., & Linkins, M. (2009). Positive education: positive psychology and classroom interventions. *Oxford Review of Education, 35*(3), 293–312.

Seligman, M. E. P., Steen, T. A., Park, N., & Peterson, C. (2005). Positive psychology progress: empirical validation of interventions. *American Psychologist, 60*, 410–421.

Sin, N. L., & Lyubomirsky, S. (2009). Enhancing well-being and alleviating depressive symptoms with positive psychology interventions: A practice-friendly meta-analysis. *Journal of Clinical Psychology, 65*(5), 467–487.

Skevington, S. M. (2009). Conceptualising dimensions of quality of life in poverty. *Journal of Community & Applied Social Psychology, 19*, 33–50. doi: 10.1002/casp.978

Stones, M. J., & Kozma, A. (1991). A magical model of happiness. *Social Indicators Research, 25*, 31–50.

Strelan, P., & Sutton, R. M. (2011). When just-world beliefs promote and when they inhibit forgiveness. *Personality and Individual Differences, 50*(2), 163–168.

Stubbe, J. H., Posthuma, D., Boomsma, D. I., & de Geus, E. J. (2005). Heritability of life satisfaction in adults: A twin-family study. *Psychological Medicine, 35*, 1581–1588.

Suissa, J. (2008). Lessons from a new science? On teaching happiness in schools. *Journal of Philosophy of Education, 42*(3–4), 575–590.

Sundararajan, L. (2008). Toward a reflexive positive psychology - insights from the Chinese Buddhist notion of emptiness. *Theory & Psychology, 18*(5), 655–674.

Tesser, A. (1988). Toward a self-evaluation maintenance model of social behavior. In L. Berkowitz (Ed.), *Advances in experimental social psychology* (pp. 181–227). New York: Academic Press.

Thompson, L. Y., Snyder, C. R., Hoffman, L., Michael, S. T., Rasmussen, H. N., Billings, L. S., et al. (2005). Dispositional forgiveness of self, others, and situations. *Journal of Personality, 73*, 313–360.

Tomyn, A. J., & Cummins, R. A. (2011). Subjective wellbeing and homeostatically protected mood: Theory validation with adolescents. *Journal of Happiness Studies, 12*(5), 897–914. doi: 10.1007/s10902-010-9235-5

Toussaint, L., & Webb, J. R. (2005). Theoretical and empirical connections between forgiveness, mental health, and well-being. In E. L. Worthington Jr. (Ed.), *Handbook of forgiveness* (pp. 349–362). New York: Routledge.

Tsang, J. A., McCullough, M. E., & Fincham, F. D. (2006). The longitudinal association between forgiveness and relationship closeness and commitment. *Journal of Social & Clinical Psychology, 25*, 448–472.

Wade, N. G., Worthington, E. L., & Meyer, J. E. (2005). But do they work? A meta-analysis of group interventions to promote forgiveness. In E. L. Worthington Jr. (Ed.), *Handbook of forgiveness* (pp. 423–439). New York: Routledge.

Watkins, P. C., Woodward, K., Stone, T., & Kolts, R. L. (2003). Gratitude and happiness: Development of a measure of gratitude, and relationships with subjective wellbeing. *Social Behavior and Personality, 31*, 431–451.

Watson, D., Clark, L., & Tellegen, A. (1988). Development and validation of brief measures of positive and negative affect: The PANAS scales. *Journal of Personality and Social Psychology, 54*, 1061–1070.

Webb, J. R., & Brewer, K. (2010). Forgiveness, health, and problematic drinking among college students in southern Appalachia. *Journal of Health Psychology, 15*(8), 1257–1266.

Weisz, J. (1981). Learned helplessness in black and white children identified by their schools as retarded and nonretarded: Performance deterioration in response to failure. *Developmental Psychology, 17*, 499–508.

Wills, T. A. (1981). Downward comparison principles in social psychology. *Psychological Bulletin, 90*, 245–271.

Wood, A. M., Froh, J. J., & Geraghty, A. W. A. (2010). Gratitude and well-being: A review and theoretical integration. *Clinical Psychology Review, 30*(7), 890–905.

Worthington, E. L., Sandage, S. J., & Berry, J. W. (2000). Group interventions to promote forgiveness: What researchers and clinicians ought to know. In M. E. McCullough, K. I. Pargament, & C. E. Thoresen (Eds.), *Forgiveness: Theory, research, and practice* (pp. 228–253). New York: Guilford.

Worthington, E. L., & Wade, N. G. (1999). The social psychology of unforgiveness and forgiveness and implications for clinical practice. *Journal of Social Clinical Psychology, 18*, 385–418.

Worthington, E. L., Witvliet, C. V. O., Pietrini, P., & Miller, A. J. (2007). Forgiveness, health, and well-being: A review of evidence for emotional versus decisional forgiveness, dispositional forgivingness, and reduced unforgiveness. *Journal of Behavioral Medicine, 30*(4), 291–302.

Yik, M. S. M., Russell, J. A., & Barrett, L. F. (1999). Structure of self-reported current affect: Integration and beyond. *Journal of Personality and Social Psychology, 77*, 600–619.

INDEX

A

AAIDD Model of Human Functioning, 10
Abbott, R. D., 190, 191
Abbott, S., 74
ABCX Model, 174
Abedi, M. R., 381, 382
Abery, B. H., 120, 324
abuse, and decision making, 216–18, 220
academic performance. *See* education
acceptance coping, 94
acceptance of disabilities, 433
acquired disabilities, 27
acronyms, 287
Active Support, 15
activities of daily living (ADL), 84, 86
activity limitations, 9
ADAPT (Americans Disabled for Accessible Public Transit), 280, 282
adaption after acquiring a disability, 432
adaptive behavior, 105–13; assessing, 109–12; complementary measures, 112–13; and family perspectives of disability, 170; history of, 107; intellectual versus adaptive functioning, 107–8; and IQ, 108; and problem behaviors, 108–9; skills of, 105–6
Adaptive Behavior Assessment System-2nd Edition (ABAS-II), 110–11
Adaptive Behavior Scale-Residential and Community, 2nd Edition (ABS-RC:2), 110
Adaptive Behavior Scale-School Edition (ABS-S:2), 110
adaptive outcomes, 183
adaptive systems, 183
adjustment after acquiring a disability, 432
adolescents and adolescence. *See* youths with disabilities
adults with disabilities, and friendships, 62–63, 64, 65–66, 67–69, 70, 71–72, 73–74, 76
Adults with Learning Difficulties in England 2003/4, 65

adversarial growth, 433
adversity, and optimism, 50, 51, 52–53, 56
aesthetics, 295–96
affect, and decision making, 209
affect (pivotal behavior), 459
Affective Communicative Assessment (ACA), 465, 468
African Americans, 444
age and aging, 320–21, 409–19; aging with/into disability, 411, 412–15; and cohorts, 410; and dementia, 413, 416; demographic context of, 412–15; desirable environments for, 411–12; and disability identity, 415–19; discourse on, 411–12; and disease prevalence and incidence, 413–14; and health and functioning of aging adults, 415; and inequalities, 411; life course approach to, 409–11; and life review, 416–17; and research challenges, 419; and social connectedness, 417–18
agency, 446; and self-regulated learning, 269. *See also* self-determination
agency thinking, 156, 157
agentic capability, 123
aggression, 479, 482, 483, 484, 485, 487
Agran, M., 129, 144, 405
AIR Self-Determination Scale, 120, 129, 131, 400
Ajzen, I., 204
Algoe, S. B., 516
Algozzine, B., 128
Alive Day Memories: Home from Iraq (2007), 292
Alriksson-Schmidt, A. I., 188
Alston, R. J., 258–59
Alwell, M., 128
Alzheimer's disease, 61
Amazon.com book reviews, 287
American Association for the Study of the Feebleminded, 5
American Association on Intellectual and Developmental Disabilities (AAIDD),

199, 242, 321, 327, 444; and adaptive behavior, 106, 107, 109, 110, 113; and adaptive behavior research, 106; and ecological model of disability, 40; and history of positive psychology, 23, 24, 27; *Model of Human Functioning*, 10; and strengths-based approach to disability, 7, 10; and supports system, 13–15
American Association on Mental Deficiency, 110
American Association on Mental Retardation (AAMR), 10, 166
American College of Sports Medicine, 87
American Deaf community, 280
American Journal on Intellectual and Developmental Disabilities (*AJIDD*; formerly the *American Journal on Mental Retardation*), 26, 242
American Psychiatric Association, 19, 106
American Psychological Association, 495
American Psychologist, 20, 22, 191, 509
American Sign Language, 291
Americans with Disabilities Act (1990), 281, 289, 342, 429
amputations, 52, 95–96, 433
amygdala, 211
Anderson, G., 216
Anglo families, 176–78
Angyal, A., 117–18
animal research, 155
anticipation, expressions of, 455
"anti-goals," 49
Antonak, R. F., 94
Antoni, M. H., 56
Antonovsky, A., 366
anxiety, 479–480, 482, 496–97, 518; and career development, 247; and risk taking tasks, 200
Applications of Social Learning to Family Life, 485
applied behavior analysis (ABA), 303, 305, 498, 499–500, 501, 502, 503; in

Brabner, Joyce, 293
Braddock, D., 322, 324
Bradley, V., 42
brain injury, 83–84
Brain Injury, 243
Breath & Shadow (journal), 282
Breeding, R. R., 253–54
Bremner, R., 497
Brenzel, A., 207–8
Breznitz, S., 155
Brief Multidimensional Students' Life
    Satisfaction Scale (BMSLSS), 516
Briggs, Ken, 228, 231, 232
Briney, J. S., 190
British Journal of Guidance and Counseling
    (*BJGC*), 242, 244
Brody, C., 241, 431
Brogli, B. R., 207–8
Brolin, D. E., 406
Bronfenbrenner, U., 8, 120, 183, 449
Broussard, R., 447
Browder, D., 128
Brown, A. A., 416
Brown, H. K., 328
Brown, R., 11, 369, 370, 372, 373, 375,
    376, 377, 385, 386
Brown, Steven, 280
Bruder, M. B., 380, 382
Brueggemann, Brenda Jo, 4, 290
Buckhead, J., 248
Buck v. Bell, 5
Buddhism, 228, 234
Buenning, M., 272
buffering hypothesis, 99
Buntinx, W. H. E., 3, 327, 328
Burch, Susan, 290, 292
burn injuries, 159
Burns, B. J., 481
Burns, M. K., 403
Butterworth, J., 318
Butzer, B., 497
Byrnes, J. P., 216
Byron, J., 404

C

Caitlin, G., 155
Caldwell, J., 417
Campbell, A., 513
Campeau, P. L., 141
Canada, 375, 383, 385, 386
Canadian Association for Community
    Living, 13
cancer diagnoses, 159
The Cancer Journals (Lorde), 293
Candide (Voltaire), 48
capacity, 120
capacity-challenge discrepancy analysis,
    123
Caraher, P. J., 141
Caran, D., 42
Carbone, P. S., 85
cardiovascular health, 520
Career Adapt-Abilities Inventory, 249

Career Adaptability International
    Collaborative Group, 249
Career Decision-Making Outcome
    Expectations (CDMOE), 246
Career Decision Self-Efficacy Scale
    (CDMSE), 253–54
Career Decision Self-Efficacy Scale-Short
    Form (CDSES-SF), 246
career development and career thoughts,
    127, 239–261; adaptability required
    in, 240; articles published on, 241–46;
    butterfly effect in, 240; research
    constructs and data on, 246–251;
    vocational guidance, 251–260
The Career Development Quarterly (*CDQ*),
    242, 244
Career Thoughts Inventory (CTI), 247
caregiver-based contingencies, 459
caregivers, 54–55, 159
carelessness, 201
Carey, Allison, 292
Carmeli, E., 87
Carr, E. G., 307, 309, 446, 447
Carrieri, L., 247
Carroll, 328
Carter, C. M., 459
Carter, E. W., 125, 126
Carver, C. S., 48, 49
Case, B. J., 210
Catalano, D. E., 427
Catalano, R. F., 190, 191
categorizing disability, 290–93
Cattaneo, L. B., 124, 125
Cattell, R. B., 328
Causal Affect, 123
causal agency, 119, 122–24
causal capacities, 123
causal perception, 123
causal view of disability, 9
Cea, C. D., 331
cellular aging, 170
Centre for Epidemiological Studies
    Depression Scale (CES-D), 83
cerebral palsy, 88, 353
Chambers, Robert, 238
Chambless, D. L., 481
Channon, S., 199
Chantry, J., 462
Chapman, A. R., 124, 125
Chapman, T. E., 328
Chappell, A. L., 76
character strength, 28
Character Strengths and Virtues: A
    Handbook and Classification, 20
Charles, Ray, 292
Charlton, James, 289
Charman, T., 199
Chavira, V., 177
Check, Connect and Expect, 313
Check and Connect, 313, 486
Check In/Check Out, 312
Chen, X., 86
Chess, S., 477–78

Cheyney, W. A., 353
children, 56, 62, 85–86, 157; and family
    quality of life (FQOL), 383; and
    positive behavior support, 310–11; and
    support needs, 321. *See also* emotional
    and behavioral difficulties
Children of a Lesser God (1986), 293
Children's Hope Scale (CHS), 157, 158,
    161, 162
Children's Mental Health Act, 370
child support, 100
China, 373, 383, 387
Chinese culture, 275–76
Choice for the Future: No Problem! 255
ChoiceMaker self-determination
    assessment, 130, 399–400, 401
choices: choice theory, 202; in disability
    culture, 280; and severe multiple
    disabilities, 468
Chon, K. K., 155
Chou, C.-C., 427
Christensen, E. R., 485
Christianity, 227, 228, 231, 232, 233–34
Christopher, M. S., 513
chronic hemiparesis, 84
chronic illness, 94
chronicity of support needs, 320
chronic stress, 170–72
Cicchetti, D. V., 112, 184, 192, 193
Cimera, R. E., 353–54
Cinamon, R. G., 250
Circle Stories (Lehrer), 286, 289
civil rights, 4, 124, 284, 285, 289, 304–5,
    444
Civil War, 4–5
Claes, C., 331, 332
claiming disability, 291
Claiming Disability (Linton), 286, 289
Clark, A. E., 210
Clark, E., 485
Clark, G. M., 398, 406
Clarke, G., 481
Clarke, S., 309
Classification of Leisure Participation
    (CLP), 88
coaching, 404–5
Cobb, B., 128
Cochran, L., 254
cognitive adaptation theory, 366
cognitive-behavioral therapy (CBT), 100,
    481
cognitive coping strategies, 101, 102
cognitive disability, 4, 292, 442–49;
    emerging trends in field, 444–45;
    future directions for, 449; and
    happiness, 446–47; individual-
    level outcomes for, 454; and policy
    initiatives, 448–49; and resiliency, 447;
    and self-determination, 445–46, 449;
    severe multiple disabilities (SMD), 457;
    and supported employment, 353–54
Cohen, D. B., 100

160, 162; and positive psychology research, 510
López, S. R., 177
Lorde, Audre, 293
Loughlin, G., 199
Lovaas, O. Ivar, 498
Love, P. F., 199
Lowe, K., 108
Lucas, R. E., 101, 513
Luchies, L. B., 521
Luckasson, R. A., 106
Luckmann, Thomas, 284
Luczak, Raymond, 289
Luecking, R. G., 357
Lunsky, Y., 328
Luskin, Frederic, 228
Lustig, D. C., 248
Lyons, 55
Lyubomirsky, S., 434, 510, 515

M

MacAdam-Crisp, J., 375
Macko, R. F., 84
MacLachlan, M., 96
MacLean, W., 464
magical model of happiness, 512
Magnificent Obsession (1954), 292
Mahoney, G., 459
mainstreaming, 61, 324–25. *See also* education
Mairs, Nancy, 289, 292
Making Action Plans (MAPS), 15
maladaptive outcomes, 185
Malesky, A., 248
malleable risk factors, 184
Maltby, J., 513
managerial decisions, 43
Manes, F., 210
Mank, David, 347
Mannan, H., 373
Marcel, G., 155
Marchand, C. B., 42
Margalit, M., 160
marriages and marital well-being, 54, 366, 518
Marshall, L. H., 130
Marshmallow Test, 139, 140
Martin, B., 522
Martin, C. A., 207–8
Martin, J. E., 144, 405
Martin, K. A., 82–83, 130
Martinez-Leal, R., 324
Martinez-Pons, M., 140
Martorell, A., 127
Maslow, A. H., 61, 317
Mason, C., 128
Masten, A. S., 93, 178, 182
mastery motivation, 121–22
material well-being, 13, 39, 42
Maternal and Child Health Services Block Grant, 370
Maternal and Title V of the Social Security Act, 370

Maternal Behavior Rating Scale (MBRS), 469
maternal optimism, 54–55
Matheson, C., 69, 71, 73, 77
Matlin, Marlee, 293
Matson, J. L., 496
Matuszewski, J., 122
Mauger, P. A., 517
Maughan, D. R., 485
Maxwell, L. E., 183
Maydeu-Olivares, A., 201
McConkey, R., 74
McCullers, Carson, 293
McCullough, M. E., 516, 517–18, 520
McDermott, D., 161
McGill Action Planning Strategy (MAPS), 330
McIntyre, L. L., 176, 177
McLaughlin, C. A., 327
McLean, L. A., 54
McNulty, J. K., 220, 488, 521
McParland, J. L., 96
McRuer, Robert, 281, 287, 290
McTell, Blind Willie, 292
McVilly, K. R., 64, 66, 69
McWhirter, E. H., 124–25
McWilliam, R. A., 379
MDA Telethon, 282
meaning-focused coping, 167
meaningfulness, 455
meaning-making, 95–96
Mean Little Deaf Queer (Galloway), 292
mediators, 478
Medicaid Home and Community-Based Services (HCBS), 341
medical model of disability, 22, 284–85, 286, 294, 318–19
meditation, 97–98
Meichenbaum, D., 405
memory, 519
Meneghetti, M. M., 204
Mengele, Josef, 281
mental health care, 161
mental illness, 25, 353, 354
mental retardation, 443
mentoring, 67, 404
metaphors, 287, 292
methodological practices, variety in, 304
Metzl, Jonathan, 290
Meyer, J. F., 520
Michalowski, J., 479
microswitch-based stimulation, 467
Middle Ages, 4
Midstream (Keller), 292
mild intellectual disability, 64
military, 191
Miller, A., 523
Miller, D. N., 477
Millera, N., 516
Miller Hope Scale, 155
Milsap, Ronnie, 292
mind, theory of, 501

The Miracle Worker (Keller), 292
Mischel, W., 139
Missing Pieces (Zola), 290
mission of positive psychology, 21
Mitchell, David, 281, 286, 291
Mithaug, D. E., 120, 122, 123, 141, 144, 146, 400, 405
Mithaug, D. K., 144, 146
modeling, 404
models of disability, 283–86
moderate intellectual disability, 64, 77
moderators, 478
Modified Fatigue Impact Scale (MFIS), 85
Modified Social Support Scale (MSSS), 85
Moffitt, T. E., 139, 209–10
Molleman, C., 328
Montgomery, Cal, 234–35
Mood, Interest, and Pleasure questionnaire (MIPQ), 454–55
Morgan, M. S., 95
Morris, P. A., 183
Moseley, C., 42
Moskowitz, J. T., 167, 433, 498
motivation and motivational states: and decision making, 203, 211, 213; and risk taking, 208–9; and self-regulated learning, 266, 268–276; and supported employment, 360
Motl, R. W., 85
motor impairments, severe multiple disabilities (SMD), 457–58
Motricity Index, 84
mourning period after acquiring a disability, 433
Moving Violations: War Zones, Wheelchairs, and Declarations of Independence (Hockenberry), 285, 290, 292
Mowrer, O. H., 155
Mr. Holland's Opus (1995), 293
Mullins, Aimee, 292
multiethnicity, 239
multifinality, 185
multipath approaches, 16
multiple chemical sensitivities (MCS), 53
multiple sclerosis, 84–85, 88
Multiple Sclerosis Quality of Life Inventory (MSQLI), 85
Multiple Sclerosis Self-Efficacy Scale (MSSE), 85
Muraki, S., 83
Murderball (2005), 281–82, 290
Murphy, N. A., 85
Murray, M. J., 200
musicians, 292
My Body Politic (Linton), 286, 290
Myers, T. G., 106
My Future Preferences, 247
My Later Life (Keller), 292
My Present and My Future interview, 249, 250
My Vocational Identity, 248

and education, 394; and exercise, 83–86; factors and domains of, 39; four principles of, 38; and friendships of disabled persons, 61, 64, 77; and history of positive psychology, 29; impact on disability field, 37–46; and individualized support, 41–42; measurement principles, 44; outcomes evaluation, 16; and paradigm shifts, 38, 45–46; and positive behavior support, 306, 307–10; and professional practice, 15–16; and public policy shifts, 38; and sensory disabilities, 457; and severe multiple disabilities, 460, 465; and social networks, 64; and social well-being, 61, 64, 77; and socio-ecological model, 24; and strengths-based approach to disability, 8, 11; and support systems, 13–15, 41–42; and UN Convention on the Rights of Persons with Disabilities, 12–13

Quality of Life Questionnaire (QOL-Q), 465

Quality of Life Research Questionnaire, 88

Quality of Life Research Unit, 11, 12

Quality of Life Scale-Brief (WHOQOL-BREF), 88

Quality of Well-Being Scale, 83

queer theory and activism, 282, 290, 297

Questionnaire on Resources and Stress (QRS), 173

Quinn, Marc, 289

R

racism, 4–5

Radio (2003), 292

Rafeeyan, Z., 84

The Ragged Edge, 280

Ramsey, E., 484

Ranchor, A. V., 523

"Ransom Notes" ad campaign, 282

Rao, P. A., 200

Raphael, S., 210

Rappaport, J., 119

rational action theory, 202

rational choice theory, 202–3, 206

Rayens, M. K., 207–8

reactive coping strategies, 92

reality negotiation, 433

Realon, R., 467

Reardon, R., 248, 255

Reauthorization of the Rehabilitation Act (1992), 348

Reaven, J., 496

reciprocity, 268–69; and forgiveness, 517; and pivotal behaviors, 459; and social well-being, 62–63, 64–65, 66, 67, 68, 70, 71, 72, 73, 76, 77, 78

Regular Education Initiative (REI), 325

rehabilitation, 160

Rehabilitation Act (1973), 283, 444

Rehabilitation Act Amendments (1986), 339, 340, 348

Rehabilitation Counseling Bulletin (RCB), 243

rehabilitation psychology, 27, 429–432

Rehabilitation Psychology, 243

Rehabilitation Services Administration (RSA), 343

Reid, D. H., 467

Reid, R., 267, 268, 271, 273

Reinders, Hans, 230, 233

Reiss, D., 119

Reivich, K., 510

The Rejected Body: Feminist Philosophical Reflections on Disability (Wendell), 279

relatedness, 118–19

religion, 177, 373, 374

The Renewal of Generosity (Frank), 234

Renn, D., 513

Reported Health Transition, 83

representations of disability, 286–87, 294–95

Required Behaviors (RB), 138

Required Outcomes (RO), 138

Reschly, D. J., 106

Research and Practice for Persons with Severe Disabilities (RPSD), 26

Research in Developmental Disabilities (RIDD), 26

residences, 373, 374, 378

resilience, 92–94; and autism, 503; and children with emotional and behavioral difficulties, 481; and cognitive and developmental disabilities, 447; and coping skills, 92–94; and ecological models, 183–84; and family perspectives of disability, 178; future directions of, 191–92; and history of positive psychology, 21; neurophysiological basis for, 434–37; and outcomes, 187–88; promoting, 188–191; promotive and protective factors, 186–87; and risk, 184–86; secondary and tertiary interventions, 192–93

resource allocation, 334

resource ownership, 345

Response to Intervention (RTI), 275, 400–401, 481

Revised Snyder Hope Scale (RHS), 157, 158, 162

Revised UCLA Loneliness Scale, 88

Reynolds, F., 28

rheumatoid arthritis, 53

RIASEC model, 247

Riby, D. M., 220

Rice, J. M., 268, 271–73

Richards, S., 127; and self-determination research, 501

Riches, V. C., 326, 328, 329

Riding the Bus with My Sister (2005), 292

The Right to Self-Determination, 124

Rimmer, J. H., 87

Rinne, S., 323

Rios, P., 199

risk, 184–86

risk-taking: developmental perspectives on, 207–11; and fuzzy-trace theory, 210; and human dignity, 321

risk-taking tasks, 199–200

Risley, R., 403

Rivermead Mobility Index, 84

"The Road to Myself" program, 162

Robb, C., 100

Roberts, Ed, 319

Roberts, M. C., 515

Robertson, E., 481

Roca, M., 210

Rodbroe, I., 455

Rodriguez, C. M., 483

Rodriguez, M. L., 139

Roehrs, T. G., 85

Roessler, R. T., 246

Rogan, P., 323

role models, 404

Rome, 4

Roos, J., 460

Roosevelt, Theodore, 5

Root, L. M., 520

Rose, L., 377, 378

Rosenberg, H., 353

Rousso, H., 127

Rouster-Stevens, K. A., 86

Rowland, C., 469

Rubin, Henry Alex, 290

Ruble, L. A., 206

Rumenap, J. M., 42

Rutter, M., 185

Ryan, Richard, 395

Ryan, R. M., 118, 403, 406

S

Sailor, A. P., 309

Saito, Y., 381, 382

Sale. P., 130

salutogenesis, 366

Sameroff, A. J., 182, 184, 186

Sample, P., 353

Sampson, J., 248, 255

Sandahl, Carrie, 291

Saramago, José, 292

Sartorius, J., 191

Sasso, T., 20, 26, 243, 244

satisfaction, 29

Satisfaction with Life Scale (SWLS), 85, 249, 513, 514

Savickas, M. L., 241, 248, 260

savoring, 97–98

scaffolding, 273, 274

Scale for Dialogical Meaning Making, 466, 468

Scales of Independent Behavior, 111

Scales of Independent Behavior-Revised (SIB-R), 111

Scent of a Woman (1992), 292

Sheldon, K. M., 118, 510

sheltered employment, 323–24, 338

Sheppard, Alice, 290

Shoda, 139

Shogren, K., 200, 444, 447; and history of positive psychology, 26; and hope theory, 160; and optimism research, 55; and positive psychology field, 3; and self-determination research, 125, 126, 128, 130, 131

Shores, R. E., 483

shortcuts, mental, 204

Short Form-36 Health Survey (SF-36), 83–84, 85, 88

Short-form McGill Pain Questionnaire (SF-MPQ), 85

Short Physical Performance Battery, 84

siblings of disabled children, 366, 375, 448

sickle cell disease, 159

Sigafoos, A. D., 119

Sigafoos, J., 324

Sight Unseen (Kleege), 285, 290, 291

significant disability (term), 339–340

Sikora, D. M., 200

Silfen, M., 141

similarity, 73, 75–76

Simon, Rachel, 292

Simon Birch (1998), 292

Sin, N. L., 510, 515

Sinclair, Jim, 282

Singer, Judy, 282

Singer, Peter, 230

Siperstein, G. N., 65, 66, 75, 199

Sitlington, P. L., 398, 406

situational assessments, 399

skill acquisition, 499

Skinner, B. F., 266, 498

Skinner, E. A., 117–18

Skinner, G. G., 177

Skinner, M, 177

Slovenia, 383, 385, 387

Small, B., 100

Smit, I. H., 467

Smith, A. C., 128

Smith, H. L., 101

Smith, R. S., 185, 187

Smith, Tyler, 283

Smith, W. J., 207–8

Smull, Michael, 330, 332

Snell, M. E., 325

snoezelen, 467

Snyder,, 281

Snyder, C. R., 117, 154–162

Snyder, Sharon, 286, 291, 297

Sobsey, D., 366

social acceptance, 62, 65, 66, 68, 76

social cognitive model, 246–47, 268

social comparison theory, 98

social competence, 106

social connectedness, 417–18, 431

social constructionism, 284

The Social Construction of Reality (Luckmann), 284

social contexts, 7, 8, 209–10

social development model (SDM), 189–190

social disconnection, 61

social-ecological model, 23–24, 25, 28, 29

social/environmental factors, 268–69

social exclusion and isolation, 63

social inclusion: and friendship, 61–63; indicators, 39; and individualized supports, 42; and QOL domains, 61; and quality of life domains, 13

social intelligence, 199

social interaction, 500

social limitation associated with intellectual disability and autism spectrum disorders, 199–200

social model of disability, 284–85, 286

social networks, 64

social participation, 24, 39

social phobia, 482

Social Provisions Scale, 85

social sciences, 8

Social Security Administration, 348

social skills, 67, 105–6, 125, 185, 486–87

social support, 98–101, 169

social validity of interventions, 303, 306

social well-being, **60–78**; and companionship, 70–75; described, 60–61; and friendship, 61–63, 65–70, 75–78; and intellectual disability, 63–75; and need to belong, 61; and social networks, 64–65

socioemotional system, 208

Socrates, 497

Solomonica-Levi, D., 200

Sontag, Susan, 293

Soresi, S., 125, 126, 241, 249, 251, 255, 259, 381, 382

Soukup, J. H., 128

South, M., 199

South Korea, 383, 385, 386

Sowers, J., 121, 122

Spain, 383, 386

Sparrow, S. S., 112

Sparta, 4

speaking in representation of disability, 295

Spear, P., 208

Specht, J., 88

"special benefits" view, 172–73

special education, 131, 140–41, 393–94; and externalizing disorders, 483; secondary and tertiary interventions, 193; and self-determination, 127, 140–43, 144–45, 151–52; and social well-being, 65

Special Education Elementary Longitudinal Study (SEELS), 141

Special Olympics, 290

spina bifida, 88

spinal cord injury (SCI): and exercise, 82–83; and hope theory, 159–160; and leisure activities, 88

spirituality, 226–238, 373, 374

Spooner, F,, 128

Staats, S. R., 155–56

staff direction, and individualized support, 41

stage-based decision making theories, 203

stakeholders, 303, 305

Stancliffe, R. J., 328, 460

Standard Rules on the Equalization of Opportunities for Persons with Disabilities, 12

Standen, P. J., 496

Stanovich, K. E., 205, 206, 221

Staring Back: The Disability Experience from the Inside Out (Fries), 280, 292

State Hope Scale (SHS), 157, 158, 162

State-Trait Anxiety Inventory (STAI), 83

Steel, R., 385, 387

Steen, T. A., and positive psychology, 497

Steinberg, L., 208, 210, 218

Steps to Self-Determination curriculum, 400, 406

stereotypes, 204, 411, 417

sterilization, 5

Stevens, N., 62

Stevens, S. L., 83

Stevenson, H. C., 145

Stigma: Notes on the Management of Spoiled Identity (Goffman), 293

stimulus-response, 116

Stock, S., 131

Stones, M. J., 512

The Story of My Life (Keller), 292

Stotland, E., 155–56

Stowe, M. S., 368, 369

Strauser, D. R., 248

strengths-based approaches: and AAIDD Model of Human Functioning, 10; and history of positive psychology, 21, 26; implications for professional practice, 15–16; and quality of life, 8, 11, 12–13; and research trends, 27; Seligman's call for, 20; and support systems, 10–11, 13–15; and UN Convention on the Rights of Persons with Disabilities, 11–13; and understanding disability, 8; and WHO models of disability, 9–10

stress: and autism, 497; and family perspectives of disability, 172; and forgiveness, 520; and parenting, 169–172; and physical health, 170; and resilience, 184–85, 188; and subjective well-being homeostasis, 518

stress reduction, 98

stretch goals, 159

striatum insula cortex, 211

Stroke Impact Scale (SIS), 84

strokes, 435–37

Strong Kids programs, 482

Work Locus of Control Scale (WLCS), 253–54

World Bank, 297

World Health Organization (WHO), 260, 297, 317, 326, 434, 443; and definitions of disability, 51; and ecological model of disability, 40; and history of positive psychology, 23; and quality of life, 11, 12; Quality of Life Scale, 88; Quality of Life Scale-Brief (WHOQOL-BREF), 88; and strengths-based approach to disability, 9–10

The World I Live In (Keller), 292

worldviews, restructuring, 287–89

World War II, 5, 19

Worthington, E. L., 520

The Wounded Storyteller (Frank), 293

wraparound care, 15

Wright, B. A., 427, 430–31

Wu, C.-L., 87

Y

Yanchak, K. V., 248, 255

"The Yellow Wallpaper" (Gilman), 293

Yirmiya, N., 200

Yorkston, K. M., 415

Young, L., 324

Your Defiant Child: Eight Steps to Better Behavior, 485

Youssef, A. -J., 26

youths with disabilities: and career development, 240–41; and friendship, 62–63, 65, 66, 68, 68–69, 69, 70, 70–71, 71–73, 73, 76, 77; parents of, 257–58; problem solving and decision making in, 207–11, 214, 215, 218–19; and vocational guidance, 254. *See* career development and career thoughts

Ysseldyke, J. E., 403

Yu, D., 467

Z

Zarb, G., 415

zero-tolerance policies, 314

Ziman, T., 160

Zimmerman, B. J., 268, 270, 272, 274

Zimmerman, M. A., 119, 125, 140

Ziv, O., 160

Zola, Irving Kenneth, 290

Zupan, Mark, 290